ALSO BY FRED ANDERSON

A People's Army:
Massachusetts Soldiers and Society in the Seven Years' War (1984)

Crucible of War

Crucible of War

THE SEVEN YEARS' WAR AND THE FATE OF EMPIRE IN BRITISH NORTH AMERICA, 1754–1766

FRED ANDERSON

With illustrations from the William L. Clements Library

ff
faber and faber

First published in the United States in 2000
by Alfred A. Knopf, a division of Random House, Inc.,
New York, and simultaneously in Canada by Random House
of Canada Limited, Toronto

First published in the United Kingdom in 2000
by Faber and Faber Limited
3 Queen Square London WC1N 3AU

Printed England by Clays Lts, St Ives plc

A CIP record for this book is available
from the British Library

ISBN 0–571–20535–6

2 4 6 8 10 9 7 5 3 1

To Virginia, at last

Contents

List of Illustrations xi
Introduction: The Seven Years' War and the Disruption of the Old British Empire xv
Maps xxv

Prologue: Jumonville's Glen, MAY 28, 1754 3

PART I.
THE ORIGINS OF THE SEVEN YEARS' WAR, 1450–1754

1. *Iroquoia and Empire* 11
2. *The Erosion of Iroquois Influence* 22
3. *London Moves to Counter a Threat* 33
4. *Washington Steps onto the Stage . . .* 42
5. *. . . And Stumbles* 50
6. *Escalation* 66

PART II. *DEFEAT,* 1754–1755

7. *The Albany Congress and Colonial Disunion* 77
8. *General Braddock Takes Command* 86
9. *Disaster on the Monongahela* 94
10. *After Braddock: William Shirley and the Northern Campaigns* 108
11. *British Politics, and a Revolution in European Diplomacy* 124

PART III. *NADIR,* 1756–1757

12. *Lord Loudoun Takes Command* 135
13. *Oswego* 150
14. *The State of the Central Colonies* 158
15. *The Strains of Empire: Causes of Anglo-American Friction* 166
16. *Britain Drifts into a European War* 169
17. *The Fortunes of War in Europe* 176
18. *Loudoun's Offensive* 179
19. *Fort William Henry* 185
20. *Other Disasters, and a Ray of Hope* 202
21. *Pitt Changes Course* 208

PART IV. *TURNING POINT,* 1758

22. *Deadlock, and a New Beginning* 219
23. *Old Strategies, New Men, and a Shift in the Balance* 232
24. *Montcalm Raises a Cross: The Battle of Ticonderoga* 240
25. *Amherst at Louisbourg* 250
26. *Supply Holds the Key* 257
27. *Bradstreet at Fort Frontenac* 259
28. *Indian Diplomacy and the Fall of Fort Duquesne* 267
29. *Educations in Arms* 286

PART V. *ANNUS MIRABILIS,* 1759

30. *Success, Anxiety, and Power: The Ascent of William Pitt* 297
31. *Ministerial Uncertainties* 312
32. *Surfeit of Enthusiasm, Shortage of Resources* 317
33. *Emblem of Empire: Fort Pitt and the Indians* 325
34. *The Six Nations Join the Fight: The Siege of Niagara* 330
35. *General Amherst Hesitates: Ticonderoga and Crown Point* 340
36. *Dubious Battle: Wolfe Meets Montcalm at Québec* 344
37. *Fall's Frustrations* 369

38. *Celebrations of Empire, Expectations of the Millennium* 373
39. *Day of Decision: Quiberon Bay* 377

PART VI. *CONQUEST COMPLETED*, 1760

40. *War in Full Career* 387
41. *The Insufficiency of Valor: Lévis and Vauquelin at Québec* 391
42. *Murray Ascends the St. Lawrence* 397
43. *Conquest Completed: Vaudreuil Surrenders at Montréal* 400
44. *The Causes of Victory and the Experience of Empire* 410
45. *Pitt Confronts an Unexpected Challenge* 415

VICTORY RECOLLECTED: *Scenographia Americana* 421

PART VII. *VEXED VICTORY*, 1761–1763

46. *The Fruits of Victory and the Seeds of Disintegration* 453
47. *The Cherokee War and Amherst's Reforms in Indian Policy* 457
48. *Amherst's Dilemma* 472
49. *Pitt's Problems* 476
50. *The End of an Alliance* 487
51. *The Intersections of Empire, Trade, and War: Havana* 497
52. *Peace* 503
53. *The Rise of Wilkes, the Fall of Bute, and the Unheeded Lesson of Manila* 507
54. *Anglo-America at War's End: The Fragility of Empire* 518
55. *Yankees Invade Wyoming—and Pay the Price* 529
56. *Amherst's Reforms and Pontiac's War* 535
57. *Amherst's Recall* 547

PART VIII. *CRISIS AND REFORM*, 1764

58. *Death Reshuffles a Ministry* 557
59. *An Urgent Search for Order: Grenville and Halifax Confront the Need for Revenue and Control* 560
60. *The American Duties Act (The Sugar Act)* 572
61. *The Currency Act* 581
62. *Postwar Conditions and the Context of Colonial Response* 588

63. *An Ambiguous Response to Imperial Initiatives* 604
64. *Pontiac's Progress* 617
65. *The Lessons of Pontiac's War* 633

PART IX. *CRISIS COMPOUNDED,* 1765–1766

66. *Stamp Act and Quartering Act* 641
67. *Grenville's End* 652
68. *The Assemblies Vacillate* 657
69. *Mobs Respond* 664
70. *Nullification by Violence, and an Elite Effort to Reassert Control* 677

PART X. *EMPIRE PRESERVED?* 1766

71. *The Repeal of the Stamp Act* 691
72. *The Hollowness of Empire* 709
73. *Acrimonious Postlude: The Colonies after Repeal* 714
74. *The Future of Empire* 729

Epilogue: Mount Vernon, JUNE 24, 1767 735

Notes 747
Acknowledgments 833
Index 837

Illustrations

MAPS

Following page xxv:

1. *Progress of the Seven Years' War*
2. *New France and the British Mainland Colonies in the Seven Years' War*
3. *Indian Groups, Regions, and Topography of the North American Interior*
4. *New England, New York, New France, and the Lake Champlain–Hudson Corridor*
5. *St. Lawrence River Valley and Québec,* JUNE–SEPTEMBER 1759
6. *Caribbean Operations,* 1759–62
7. *Central European Operations,* 1756–62
8. *Western Europe*
9. *Indian Subcontinent*

ILLUSTRATIONS

Popple map of North American empires, 1751 19
French chain of forts 31
The duke of Newcastle 34
Chief Hendrick of the Mohawk Nation 39
Fort Le Quesne 48
H.R.H. William, duke of Cumberland 69
Sir William Johnson 81
Benjamin Franklin 82

Thomas Hutchinson 83
Braddock's march to the Ohio 89
Disposition of Braddock's advanced party 98
Disposition of troops at the Battle of the Monongahela 101
William Shirley 111
Fort Edward 116
Fort St. Frédéric 117
The Battle of Lake George, 1755 120
Fort William Henry 122
William Pitt 126
The marquis de Montcalm 136
Fort Bull 138
Lord Loudoun 144
Louis-Antoine de Bougainville 155
Wood Creek and Oneida Lake 156
Robert Rogers 188
Siege of Fort William Henry, 1757 193
Jeffery Amherst 234
James Wolfe 235
The Battle of Ticonderoga, 1758 245
Assault landing at Louisbourg, 1758 251
Louisbourg 252
Capture of the Bienfaisant, 1758 255
Fort Frontenac 263
Fort Bedford 273
Prince Ferdinand of Brunswick 300
Negroland 307
Fort Pitt 328
A North View of Fort Johnson 332
The Siege of Niagara 334
New York: Fort Edward to Ticonderoga, 1759 341
Crown Point Fort 343
Robert Monckton 350
George Townshend 350
James Murray 350
The Battle of Québec, 1759 358
Mort du Marquis de Montcalm-Gozon 366
The Death of General Wolfe 367
The Battle of Minden 379
Île-aux-Noix 402
Fort Lévis, under siege 403

Montréal 405
Scenographia Americana 421
A New Map of the Cherokee Nation 459
Plan of a turret at Fort Loudoun 464
George III 478
The earl of Bute 480
George Grenville 489
The Siege of Havana, 1762 500
Montrésor map of Detroit 539
Fort Michilimackinac 540
The Niagara River from Lake Ontario to Lake Erie, showing portage road 551
The Proclamation of 1763 567
Cantonment of British forces in North America, 1766 697
Colonel George Washington 738

Introduction

THE SEVEN YEARS' WAR AND THE DISRUPTION OF THE OLD BRITISH EMPIRE

FEW REVERIES HAUNT history professors more insistently than the dream of writing a book accessible to general readers that will also satisfy their fellow historians' scholarly expectations. At least that dream has haunted me, and I must admit that I wrote this book because of it. What follows is a narrative intended to synthesize a sizable range of scholarship, which can (I hope) be read without specialized prior knowledge. Because my understanding of the period before the American Revolution differs from what I take to be the conventional one, however, it seems only fair to begin by sketching the broad outlines of the book's context, intent, design, and argument.

THE MOST IMPORTANT event to occur in eighteenth-century North America, the Seven Years' War (or as the colonists called it, the French and Indian War) figures in most Americans' consciousness of the past as a kind of hazy backdrop to the Revolution. As citizens of a nation created by an act of collective secession from the British empire, we Americans have always tended to take as our point of reference the thirteen rebelling colonies, not the empire as a whole—or the North American continent. This perspective has generally limited our ability to see the continuities between our pre-Revolutionary past and the rest of our history. Coming to grips with the Seven Years' War as an event that decisively shaped American history, as well as the histories of Europe and the Atlantic world in general, may therefore help us begin to understand the colonial period as something more than a quaint mezzotint prelude to our national history. For indeed, if viewed not from the perspective of Boston or Philadelphia, but from Montréal or Vincennes, St. Augustine or Havana, Paris or Madrid—or, for that matter, Calcutta or Berlin—the Seven Years' War was far more significant than the War of American Independence.

Unlike every prior eighteenth-century European conflict, the Seven Years' War ended in the decisive defeat of one belligerent and a dramatic rearrangement of the balance of power, in Europe and North America alike. In destroying the North American empire of France, the war created a desire for revenge that would drive French foreign policy, and thereby shape European affairs, for two decades. At the same time, the scope of Britain's victory enlarged its American domains to a size that would have been difficult for any European metropolis to control, even under the best of circumstances, and the war created circumstances of the least favorable sort for Whitehall. Without the Seven Years' War, American independence would surely have been long delayed, and achieved (if at all) without a war of national liberation. Given such an interruption in the chain of causation, it would be difficult to imagine the French Revolution occurring as it did, when it did—or, for that matter, the Wars of Napoléon, Latin America's first independence movements, the transcontinental juggernaut that Americans call "westward expansion," and the hegemony of English-derived institutions and the English language north of the Rio Grande. Why, then, have Americans seen the Seven Years' War as little more than a footnote?

In part it has been the intensity of our focus on the Revolution as a seminal event, one that even professional historians have assumed determined both the shape of our national institutions and all the significant outcomes of our national development before the Civil War. With so much riding on it, scholarly discussion of eighteenth-century American history has necessarily been dominated by concern over the fundamental character of the Revolution and perforce its origins. In the mid-1970s, when I was in graduate school, much of what early Americanists debated in one way or another related to the motivations of the Revolutionaries: Were they fundamentally driven by material interests or by ideological concerns? It was a Big Question then and remains a powerful one even now that it has achieved a scholastic—not to say sterile—maturity. By the late 1980s, when I undertook this project, the question had generated distinctive lines of interpretation that framed the ways historians explained eighteenth-century America almost as decisively as Vauban's magnificent fortifications framed eighteenth-century military campaigns.

On one hand (the left) ran the works of those scholars, descendants of the Progressive historians, who argued that the class interests of Americans stimulated both a movement for independence and an internal struggle over the forms of government to be imposed in the new United States. For Neo-Progressive scholars, the Revolution was an intensely human process rooted in the experience of social inequity and in a democratic striving against privilege. Concerned as they were with colonial social relations and economic conditions, the Neo-Progressives focused less frequently on the great men of the Revolution than on ordinary people—farmers, artisans, laborers, women—and such dispossessed or marginalized groups as blacks, Indians, and the poor. Looking to the opposite side of the field, one could see arrayed the intellectual fortifications of those numerous historians, sometimes called Neo-Whigs, who believed that republican political ideas determined the allegiance and the actions of the Revolutionary generation. Their Revolution, while not bloodless, was most importantly an ideological and ironic one: ideological because it followed from the shared belief that powerful men had always sought, and would always seek, to deprive their fellow citizens of liberty and property; ironic because in the conservative act of defending their liberties and estates, the decidedly elitist gentlemen who articulated the Revolution's ideals also liberated egalitarian impulses that would produce the most democratic, individualist, acquisitive society in the world.

Even in the late 1980s, of course, this military metaphor could hardly be said to depict with literal accuracy the range of scholarly opinion on the late colonial period and its relation to the Revolution. In fact, the positions of scholars fell along a spectrum that ranged from extreme materialism on one hand to an equally extreme idealism on the other. Few subscribed absolutely to a single kind of explanation, although most—if pressed hard enough—would have preferred one end of the spectrum over the other. No matter what their interpretative preferences, however, what most historians assumed without disagreement was a common starting point. And that was the problem I had in mind when I began this study.

Virtually all modern accounts of the Revolution begin in 1763 with the Peace of Paris, the great treaty that concluded the Seven Years' War. Opening the story there, however, makes the imperial events and conflicts that followed the war—the controversy over the Sugar Act and the Stamp Act crisis—into precursors of the Revolution. No matter how strenuous their other disagreements, most modern historians have looked at the years after 1763 not as contemporary Americans and Britons saw them—as a postwar era vexed by unanticipated problems in relations between colonies and metropolis—but as what we *in retrospect* know those years to have been, a pre-Revolutionary period. By sneaking glances, in effect, at what was coming next, historians robbed their accounts of contingency and suggested, less by design than inadvertence, that the independence and nationhood of the United States were somehow inevitable. With the assumption of inevitability came the desire to fix the original character of the Revolutionary controversies in radical or conservative impulses.

The more I thought about this problem, the more I became convinced that an alternative understanding might flow simply from beginning the story a decade earlier. Examining the period from a perspective fixed not in 1763 but in 1754 would necessarily give its events a different look and perhaps permit us to understand them without constant reference to the Revolution that no one knew lay ahead, and that no one wanted. To start in 1754 would be to begin in a world dominated by wars between the northern British colonies and New France: conflicts that had been frequent, costly, indecisive, and so central to the thinking of contemporaries that the colonists were all but incapable of imagining themselves apart from the empires to which they belonged. Such a story would begin when the greatest unity the British colonists knew came not from the relations of one colony with another, but from their common connection with what they thought of as the freest, most enlightened empire in history—and from the enemies they also shared, the papist French and their Indian allies.

Given these assumptions, and the requirements that they imposed on any narrative that would follow from them, other historical factors and agents would take on greater significance. To begin the story in the 1750s would require the inclusion of many more actors, for Indians would be anything but the incidental players they seem in accounts that look ahead to the Revolution. The Seven Years' War could not have begun unless a single desperate Iroquois chief had tried to keep the French from seizing control of the Ohio Valley; nor could the war have reached the conclusion it did, and created the consequences it did, without the participation of native peoples. This in turn cast subsequent events in a different light, suggesting that an equally interesting way to understand the last half of the eighteenth century was in imperial as well as Revolutionary terms. Perhaps we would be able to understand the founding of the United States differently, I thought, if we explained it not only in terms of political conflict within the Anglo-American community or the working out of Revolutionary ideals, but as a consequence of the forty-year-long effort to subject the Ohio Country, and with it the rest of the Transappalachian west, to imperial control.

As I wrote the chapters that follow, much exciting scholarship appeared in print: works that enriched my understanding of the events of the period and also (alas) helped to complicate my story. One strand of this new work proceeded from the efforts, largely of English historians, to describe the emergence of a British empire and national identity during the eighteenth century; the other, from the writings of American colonialists and ethnohistorians addressing the history of native peoples and their interactions with European settlers. Although they emerged from different concerns, and different scholarly communities, I found that these two strands braided together like plaits around a concept of empire best articulated by the historian Eric Hinderaker. The empires of eighteenth-century North America, he has written, can better be understood as "processes than structures," for they were not merely metropolitan creations imposed on a distant periphery of lands and peoples, but "negotiated systems," created by the interactions of peoples who "could shape, challenge, or resist colonialism in many ways." Empires, he observes, are "sites for intercultural relations."[1]

With this definition of empire in mind (or, to be honest, a less elegantly phrased understanding of my own that resembled it) I wrote what follows, a story of violent imperial competition that resulted first in a decisive victory and then in a troubled attempt by metropolitan authorities to construct a new British empire along lines that would permit them to exercise effective control over colonies and conquests alike. It is not, therefore, a story that has the birth of an American republic anywhere in view. Its centerpiece is a war that began when the diplomatic miscalculations of the Six Nations of the Iroquois allowed the French and British empires to confront each other over the control of the Ohio Valley. The ensuing conflict spread from North America to Europe, the Caribbean basin, West Africa, India, and the Philippine archipelago: in a real although more limited sense than we intend when we apply the words to twentieth-century conflicts, a world war. While the Seven Years' War resolved none of Europe's internecine conflicts, so far as North America and the British Empire were concerned, this immense conflict changed everything, and by no means only for the better. I argue that the war's progression, from its early years of French predominance to its climax in the Anglo-American conquest of Canada, and particularly in its protraction beyond 1760, set in motion the forces that created a hollow British empire. That outcome neither foretold nor necessitated the American Revolution; as any student of Spanish or Ottoman history can testify, empires can endure for centuries on end as mere shells of cultural affiliation and institutional form. Only the conflicted attempt to infuse meaning and efficacy into the imperial connection made the Revolution a possibility.

The story that follows depicts the Seven Years' War above all as a theater of intercultural interaction, an event by which the colonists of New France and British North America came into intimate contact both with metropolitan authorities—men who spoke their languages but who did not share their views of the war or the character of the imperial relationship—and with Indian peoples, whose participation as allies, enemies, negotiators, and neutrals so critically shaped the war's outcome. Its narrative logic suggests that the early experience of the war convinced British government officials (more mindful of colonial recalcitrance in the disastrous years of 1754–57 than of their enthusiasm in the years of victory, 1758–60) that the only rational way to deal with the American colonists was to exert control from Whitehall. Thus the war's lessons prompted a series of ministries to seek revenue from the colonies, even as they struggled to stabilize relations with the Indians and stem the outrush of settlers to regions that the war had made accessible. None of it worked.

The native peoples of the interior were the first to react negatively to changes imposed from above. They did it by launching the attacks that grew into the most successful pan-Indian resistance movement in American history, the war misleadingly called Pontiac's Rebellion. At almost precisely the same time, ministerial efforts to reform the administration of the colonies, raise modest revenues for their defense, and make the colonists more responsive to metropolitan authority precipitated violent civil disobedience in the Stamp Act crisis. Both Pontiac's Rebellion and the riotous resistance to the Stamp Act marked efforts of groups distant from the formal center of imperial power to "shape, challenge, [and] resist colonialism"—*not* with any intention to destroy the empire, but rather to define it in terms acceptable to themselves. Of course, no one in the British government saw the Indian insurrection or the Stamp Act riots in that way; nor did they appreciate the significance of the fact that both the Indians and the colonists, groups always more disposed to compete internally than to find common ground among themselves, had shown a sudden, unexpected capacity to achieve consensus.

This volume thus begins in a chaotic competition of two empires to control the Ohio Valley and ends with the losing empire in ruins and the victor seeking to control its fabulous gains—and seemingly being repaid for its pains with ingratitude and resistance. Taking 1766 as its stopping point allows us to understand the war as an event with direct consequences extending well beyond the conquest of Canada, detaches the Stamp Act crisis from its usual narrative function as the prologue to the

Revolution, and makes manifest the parallels between the Stamp Act riots and Pontiac's War as efforts to defend local autonomy within the empire. Britain resolved both crises by 1766 in ways that reassured Indians and colonists alike that the new empire would be a tolerable place to live. The British authorities, however, had no intention of letting either Indians or colonists define the character of empire. The future of Indian relations could, for the time being, be set aside; the question of the colonists' submission could not. Britain's subsequent efforts to specify the terms of the imperial relationship, and the reactions of the colonial populations to them, would begin a new chapter in the story of an Atlantic world transformed by war.

Thus, in the larger narrative of the period as I understand it, even the later crises precipitated by the Townshend Acts and the Tea Act did not reflect a movement toward revolution so much as an effort to define the nature of the imperial relationship. In this sense, the outbreak of fighting at Lexington and Concord, Massachusetts, on April 19, 1775, was less a moment in which the birth of a nation can be glimpsed than the traumatic dissolution of a once affectionate relationship between Britain and its colonies. Between 1766 and 1775 lay a decade-long effort to deal with the legacies of a great war and a prodigal victory—an effort that instead of solutions generated a constitutional stalemate. Until the shots rang out on that bright spring morning, the British empire had remained a transatlantic political community made up of subjects who, despite their differences, questioned neither their common allegiance to the Crown nor their common British identity. With April 19, however, began to dawn the kind of horrified realization that may come to a couple who, after years of bitter arguments and lengthening angry silences, suddenly find themselves hurling crockery at each other across a kitchen battlefield.

A full year stretched between the realization that the empire was falling to pieces and the Declaration of Independence—a year of war during which the American Revolution may finally be said to have begun. If I had to pick a moment from which to date that transformation, I would choose July 3, 1775, the day that the Virginian George Washington took command of a locally raised force of New England provincials who in the previous three months had killed or wounded fourteen hundred of His Majesty's troops. By taking command on behalf of all thirteen colonies, in the name of the Continental Congress, Washington turned a collection of New England regiments into a Continental Army—the physical embodiment of a political union. With that act, Washington and his men crossed at last from rebellion into revolution, and from there there was no turning back. It would still take a year to make the colonies' representatives at Philadelphia realize that the only reason for fighting was to establish the United States as an independent nation. War, and war alone, made possible the unanimity so painfully achieved in July 1776.

THIS BOOK, THEN, offers a closely focused narrative of events that did not imply or anticipate revolutionary change: events driven by military necessity, chance, miscalculation, desperation, hope, fear, patriotism, hatred, and all the other chaotic corollaries of war. It argues that, however else one might interpret the postwar era, one must never forget the power of war to shape relations between, and within, empires. Construed in such a context, the interpretations of materialist and idealist scholars who have sought to explain the coming of the Revolution may not in fact be irreconcilable, but rather different, and partial, views of efforts to define the limits of empire in a world suddenly reshaped by an epochal victory.

Throughout the story I do my best to describe the human dimensions as well as the systemic effects of military activity. In practice this has made for a large book, because while I have sought to give space to the traditional concerns of military history—operations, strategy, logistics, and so on—I have also tried to provide sufficient coverage of cultural, social, political, and economic matters to keep battles and campaigns from wholly absorbing the narrative. But there are two further reasons for the size of this book, and I might as well conclude by confessing them. I have tried to tell a story that is, in fact, epic in scope and consequence, and I believed that the only way to do its characters justice was by seeking to recapture their story's contingency without understating either the limitations of their understanding or the transcendence of their strivings. The colonists who shed their blood and gave their treasure in the 1750s on behalf of the British empire could think of themselves as nothing else but British subjects in 1763, when they fairly reveled in the name of Briton. By 1766 they had confronted, and in their own minds had surmounted, a challenge to the British rights and liberties they loved, on behalf of which they believed they had fought and paid and bled. Their commitment to empire structured their political ideas, identities, and hopes for the future. If in their view there was no problem without an imperial solution, it was because the victory that lay behind them had created their vision of the future, no less than their understanding of the past.

It is hardly surprising that the Britons of North America did not grasp how that war and its ending could impart a very different vision of the future, and a different understanding of the past, to the men who were trying to govern the empire from London. If it is also unsurprising, from the vantage point of two centuries, that those divergent views might lead to further conflict, we can best preserve our understanding of the contingency of the events that followed if we concentrate on how much their actions owed to the war, and the victory, that towered over their present. Thus the stories of blood spilled to create an empire and blood spilled to resist that empire's sway become the same story: one that can speak to us fully only if we resist the subtler tyranny of a hindsight that suggests the creation of the American republic was somehow foreordained.

Maps

Map 1
Progress of the Seven Years' War and Associated Conflicts

KEY

1. Virginia-Pennsylvania-Ohio Backcountry
Maps 2, 3
Washington's expedition, 1753
Fort Necessity, 1754
Braddock's expedition, 1755
Forbes's expedition, 1758
Bouquet's expeditions, 1763, 1764

2. Nova Scotia (Acadia)
Map 2
Expedition of 1754; Acadian expulsion

3. Hudson River–Lake Champlain–Richelieu River Corridor
Map 4
Battle of Lake George, 1755
Siege of Fort William Henry, 1757
Battle of Ticonderoga, 1758
Amherst's expedition, 1759
Haviland's expedition, 1760

4. Mohawk Valley–Lake Ontario–Upper St. Lawrence Valley
Maps 2, 4
Siege of Oswego, 1756
Bradstreet's expedition, 1758
Amherst's expedition, 1760

5. Battle and Siege of Minorca, 1756
Map 8

6. Central European Operations, 1756–62
Map 7

7. Operations in Bengal and Battle of Plassey, 1757
Map 9

8. Siege of Louisbourg, 1758
Map 2

9. West African Expeditions, 1758

10. Québec and the Upper St. Lawrence Valley
Maps 4, 5
Siege and Battle of Québec, 1759
Second Battle and Siege of Québec, 1760
Murray's expedition, 1760

11. The Eastern Caribbean
Map 6
Expedition to Martinique and Guadeloupe, 1759
Conquest of Martinique and the lesser islands, 1761–62

12. British Naval Operations from Gibraltar
Map 8
Interdiction of convoys from Toulon, 1758
Battle of Lagos, 1759

13. British Operations on the Coast of France
Map 8
Descents on French coast, 1757–58
Battle of Quiberon Bay, 1759
Belle-Île-en-Mer expedition, 1761

14. Upper Great Lakes
Maps 2, 3
Siege of Niagara, 1759
Bradstreet's expedition, 1764

15. The Cherokee War, 1759–61
Maps 2, 3

16. Operations on the Coromandel Coast, 1758–60
Map 9
Siege of Madras, 1758–59
Battle of Wandiwash, 1760
Siege of Pondicherry, 1760–61

17. Newfoundland Expeditions, 1762

18. Siege of Havana, 1762
Map 6

19. Conquest of Manila, 1762

20. Pontiac's Rebellion, 1763–65
Maps 2, 3

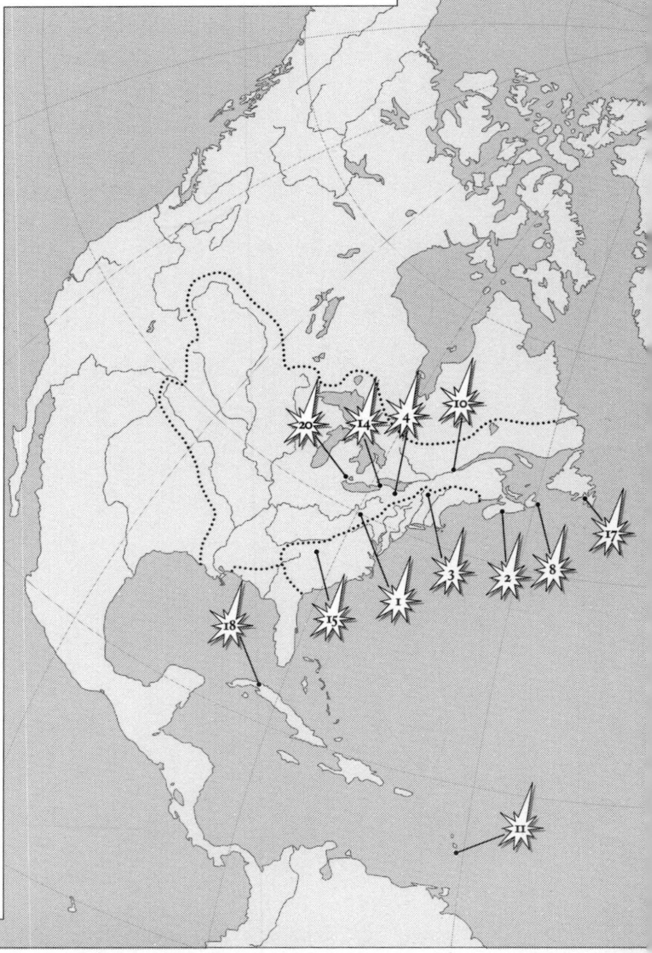

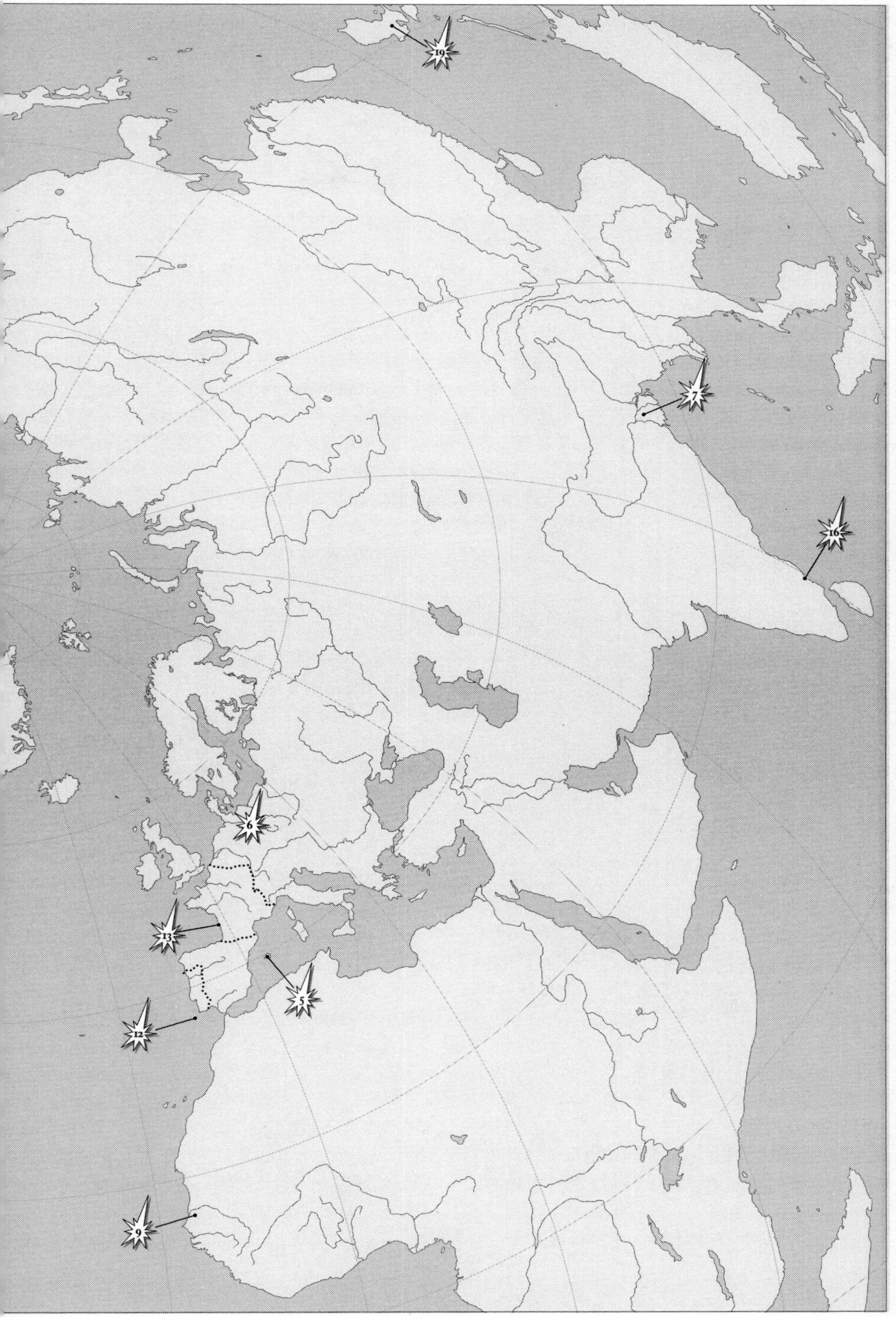
19
7
16
6
13
5
12
9

Lake Superior
Lake Michigan
Lake Huron
Lake Ontario
Lake Erie
NEW FR
Montréal
Ottawa R.
FT. LÉVIS
St. Lawrence R.
Lake Champlain
FT. FRONTENAC
CROWN POINT (FT. ST-FRÉDÉRIC)
TICONDEROGA (FT. CARILLON)
Lake George
FT. WILLIAM HENRY
FT. TORONTO
FT. NIAGARA
La Belle Famille
FT. OSWEGO
FT. BULL
FT. STANWIX
Mohawk R.
Albany
NEW YORK
Detroit
Sandusky Bay
FT. PRESQUE ISLE
FT. LE BOEUF
French Cr.
Allegheny R.
PENNSYLVANIA
Delaware R.
Hudson R.
FT. MACHAULT (VENANGO)
Beaver Cr.
Kuskuski
Kittanning
Logstown
Susquehanna R.
(W. Br.)
Wyoming Valley
SHAMOKIN (FT. AUGUSTA)
FT. ALLEN
Easton
New York
FT. LIGONIER
FT. DUQUESNE (PITTSBURGH)
Youghiogheny R.
FT. NECESSITY
FORBES ROAD
Aughwick
Carlisle
FT. BEDFORD
FT. LOUDOUN
Lancaster
Philadelphia
N.J.
Muskingum R.
Ohio R.
Great Miami R.
Scioto R.
Kentucky R.
Monongahela R.
FT. CUMBERLAND
FT. FREDERICK
BRADDOCK'S ROAD
Winchester
Baltimore
Annapolis
MARYLAND
Alexandria
DEL.
Kanawha R.
Greenbrier R.
Shenandoah R.
Rappahannock R.
Northern Neck
York R.
Louisa Court House
Chesapeake Bay
James R.
Williamsburg
VIRGINIA
BLUE RIDGE
ALLEGHENY MOUNTAINS
CHISWELL'S FORT
Cumberland R.
New R.
Great Dismal Swamp
Clinch R.
Holston R.
French Broad R.
(Overhill Cherokee Towns)
FT. LOUDOUN
Echota
Tennessee R.
Echoe
Estatoe
(Cherokee Middle Towns)
Keowee
Keowee R.
FT. PRINCE GEORGE
(Cherokee Lower Towns)
NORTH CAROLINA
Ninety Six (Long Canes)
SOUTH CAROLINA
Wilmington
Savannah R.
Santee R.
Orangeburg
GEORGIA
Charleston
Savannah

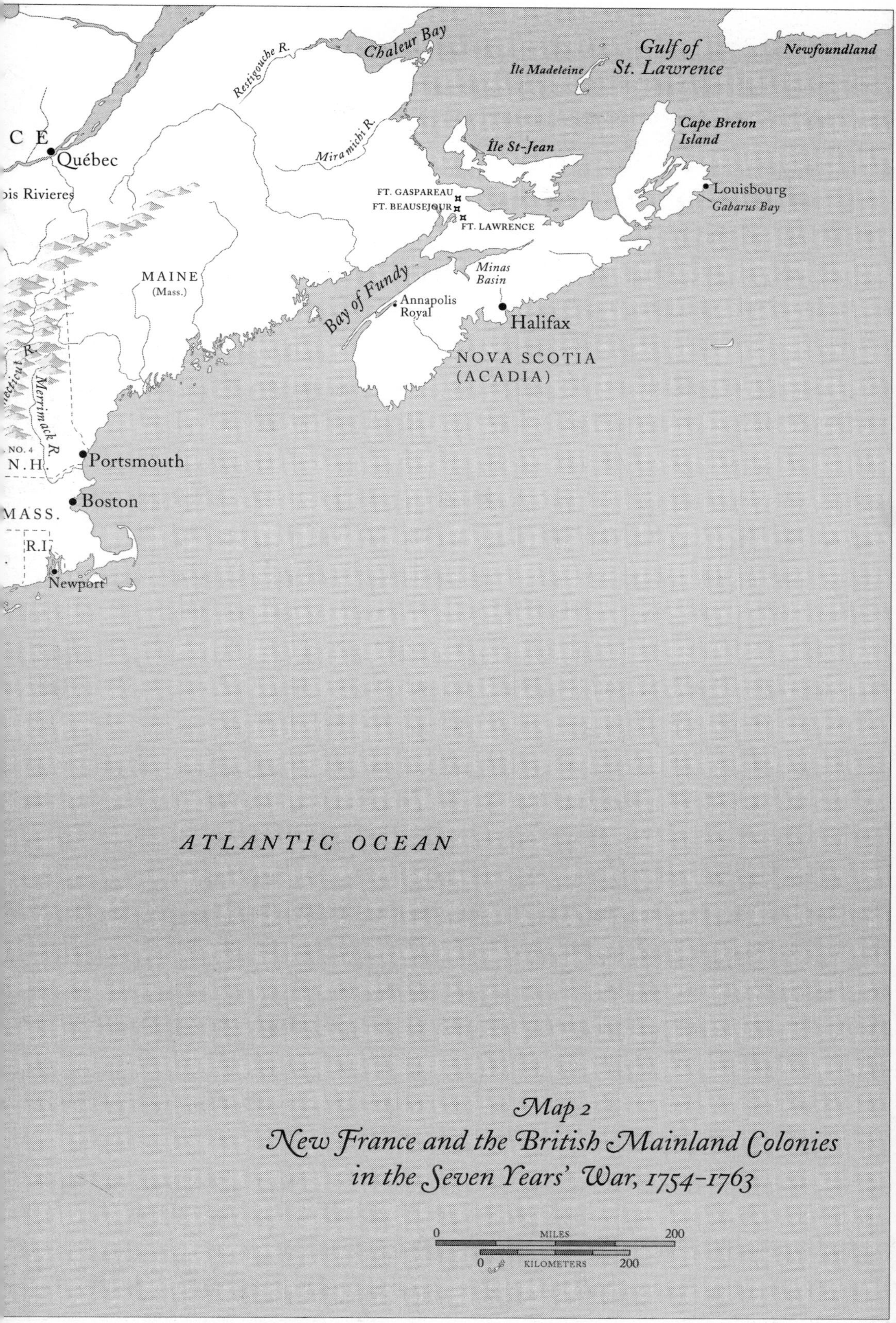

Map 2
New France and the British Mainland Colonies
in the Seven Years' War, 1754–1763

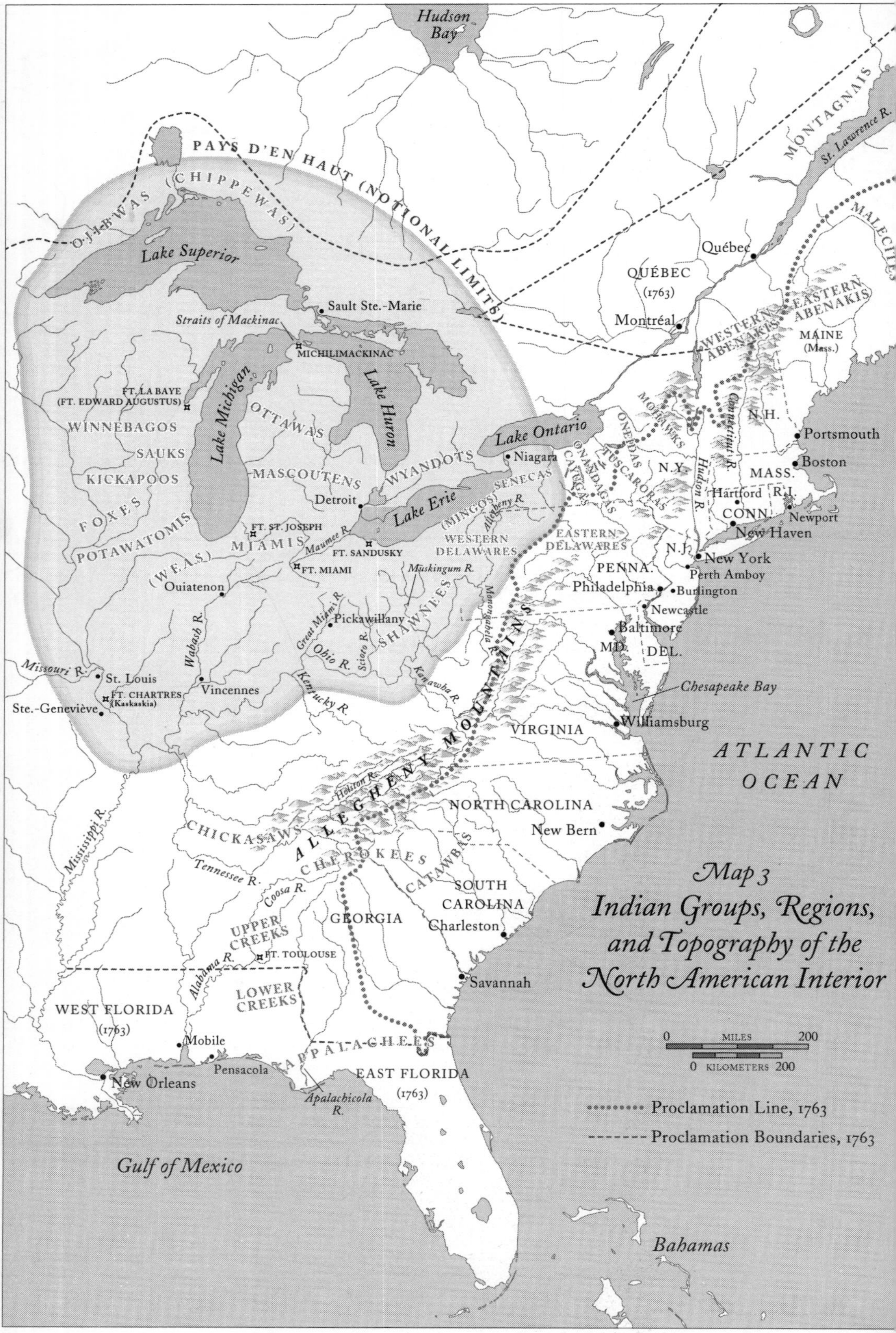

Map 3
Indian Groups, Regions, and Topography of the North American Interior

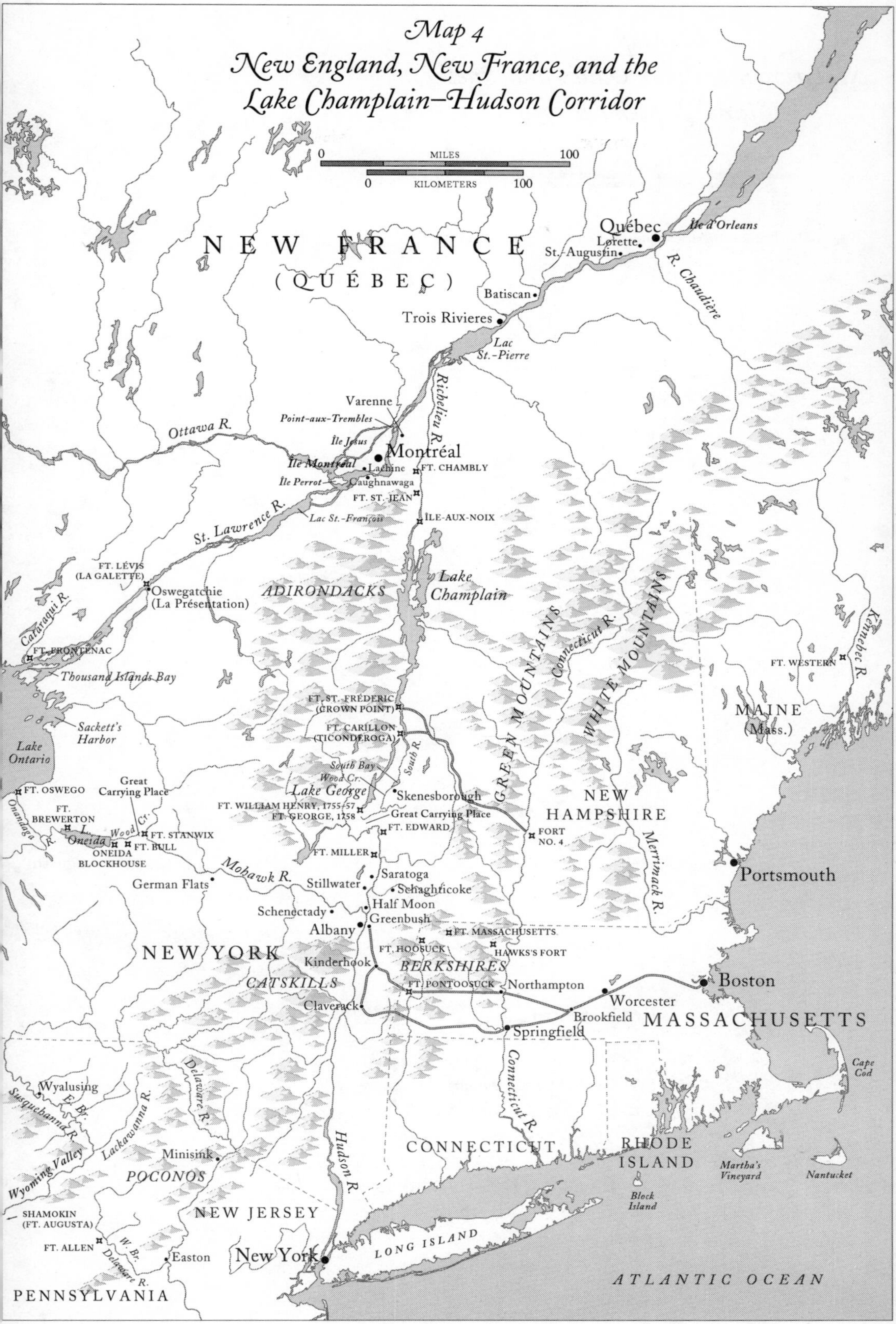
Map 4
New England, New France, and the Lake Champlain–Hudson Corridor
0 MILES 100
0 KILOMETERS 100
NEW FRANCE
(QUÉBEC)
Québec
Île d'Orleans
Lorette
St.-Augustin
R. Chaudière
Batiscan
Trois Rivieres
Lac St.-Pierre
Richelieu R.
Varenne
Point-aux-Trembles
Île Jesus
Montréal
Île Montréal
Lachine
FT. CHAMBLY
Île Perrot
Caughnawaga
FT. ST. JEAN
Ottawa R.
St. Lawrence R.
Lac St.-François
ÎLE-AUX-NOIX
FT. LÉVIS (LA GALETTE)
Oswegatchie (La Présentation)
ADIRONDACKS
Lake Champlain
Cataraqui R.
FT. FRONTENAC
Thousand Islands Bay
GREEN MOUNTAINS
Connecticut R.
WHITE MOUNTAINS
Kennebec R.
FT. WESTERN
MAINE (Mass.)
FT. ST. FRÉDERIC (CROWN POINT)
FT. CARILLON (TICONDEROGA)
Sackett's Harbor
Lake Ontario
South Bay
Wood Cr.
South R.
Lake George
Skenesborough
Great Carrying Place
FT. OSWEGO
Onandaga R.
FT. BREWERTON
L. Oneida
Wood Cr.
FT. STANWIX
FT. BULL
ONEIDA BLOCKHOUSE
FT. WILLIAM HENRY, 1755–57
FT. GEORGE, 1758
Great Carrying Place
FT. EDWARD
FORT NO. 4
NEW HAMPSHIRE
Merrimack R.
Portsmouth
FT. MILLER
Mohawk R.
German Flats
Saratoga
Stillwater
Schaghticoke
Schenectady
Half Moon
Albany
Greenbush
FT. MASSACHUSETTS
FT. HOOSUCK
HAWKS'S FORT
NEW YORK
Kinderhook
BERKSHIRES
CATSKILLS
FT. PONTOOSUCK
Northampton
Boston
Worcester
Claverack
Brookfield
MASSACHUSETTS
Springfield
Cape Cod
Wyalusing
Susquehanna R.
E. Br.
Lackawanna R.
Delaware R.
Connecticut R.
Hudson R.
CONNECTICUT
RHODE ISLAND
Martha's Vineyard
Nantucket
Wyoming Valley
Minisink
POCONOS
Block Island
SHAMOKIN (FT. AUGUSTA)
NEW JERSEY
FT. ALLEN
W. Br.
Delaware R.
Easton
New York
LONG ISLAND
ATLANTIC OCEAN
PENNSYLVANIA

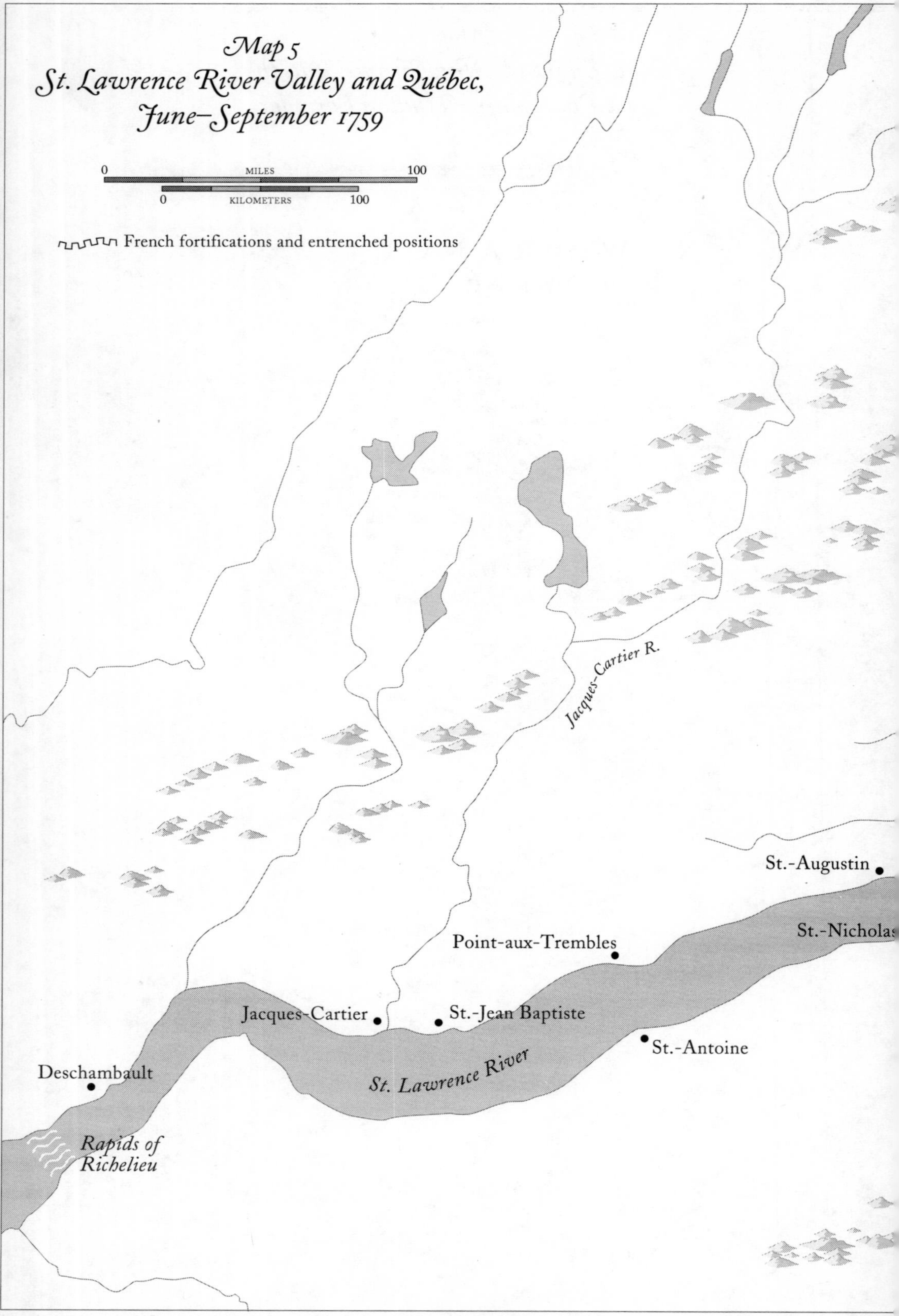
Map 5
St. Lawrence River Valley and Québec, June–September 1759
0 MILES 100
0 KILOMETERS 100
French fortifications and entrenched positions
Jacques-Cartier R.
St.-Augustin
St.-Nicholas
Point-aux-Trembles
Jacques-Cartier
St.-Jean Baptiste
St.-Antoine
Deschambault
St. Lawrence River
Rapids of Richelieu

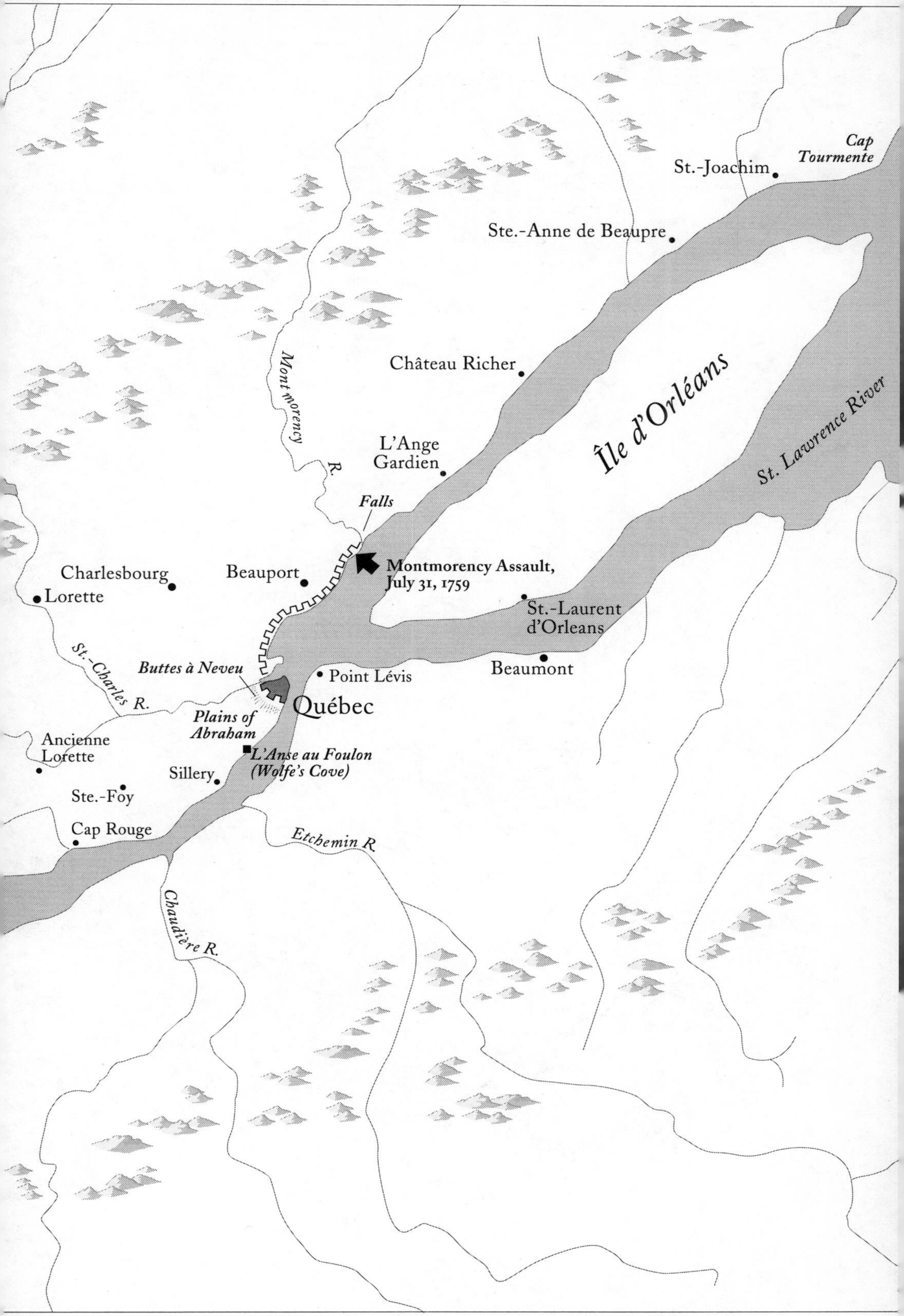
Cap
Tourmente
St.-Joachim
Ste.-Anne de Beaupre
Château Richer
Île d'Orléans
St. Lawrence River
Mont morency
R.
L'Ange
Gardien
Falls
Montmorency Assault,
July 31, 1759
Charlesbourg
Beauport
Lorette
St.-Laurent
d'Orleans
St.-Charles R.
Buttes à Neveu
Point Lévis
Beaumont
Québec
Plains of
Abraham
Ancienne
Lorette
L'Anse au Foulon
(Wolfe's Cove)
Sillery
Ste.-Foy
Cap Rouge
Etchemin R.
Chaudière R.

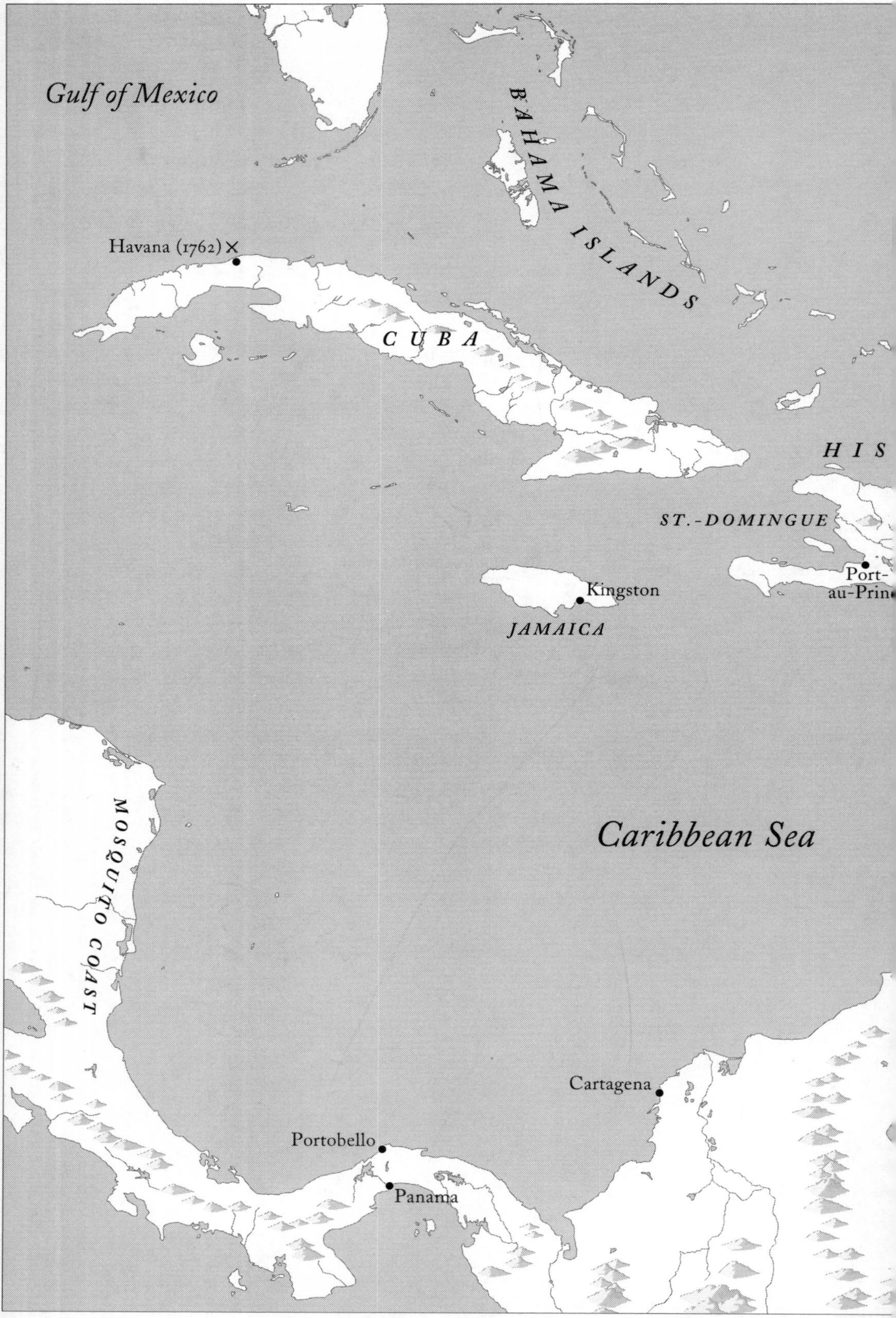

Gulf of Mexico
BAHAMA ISLANDS
Havana (1762)
CUBA
HIS
ST.-DOMINGUE
Port-
au-Prin
Kingston
JAMAICA
Caribbean Sea
MOSQUITO COAST
Cartagena
Portobello
Panama

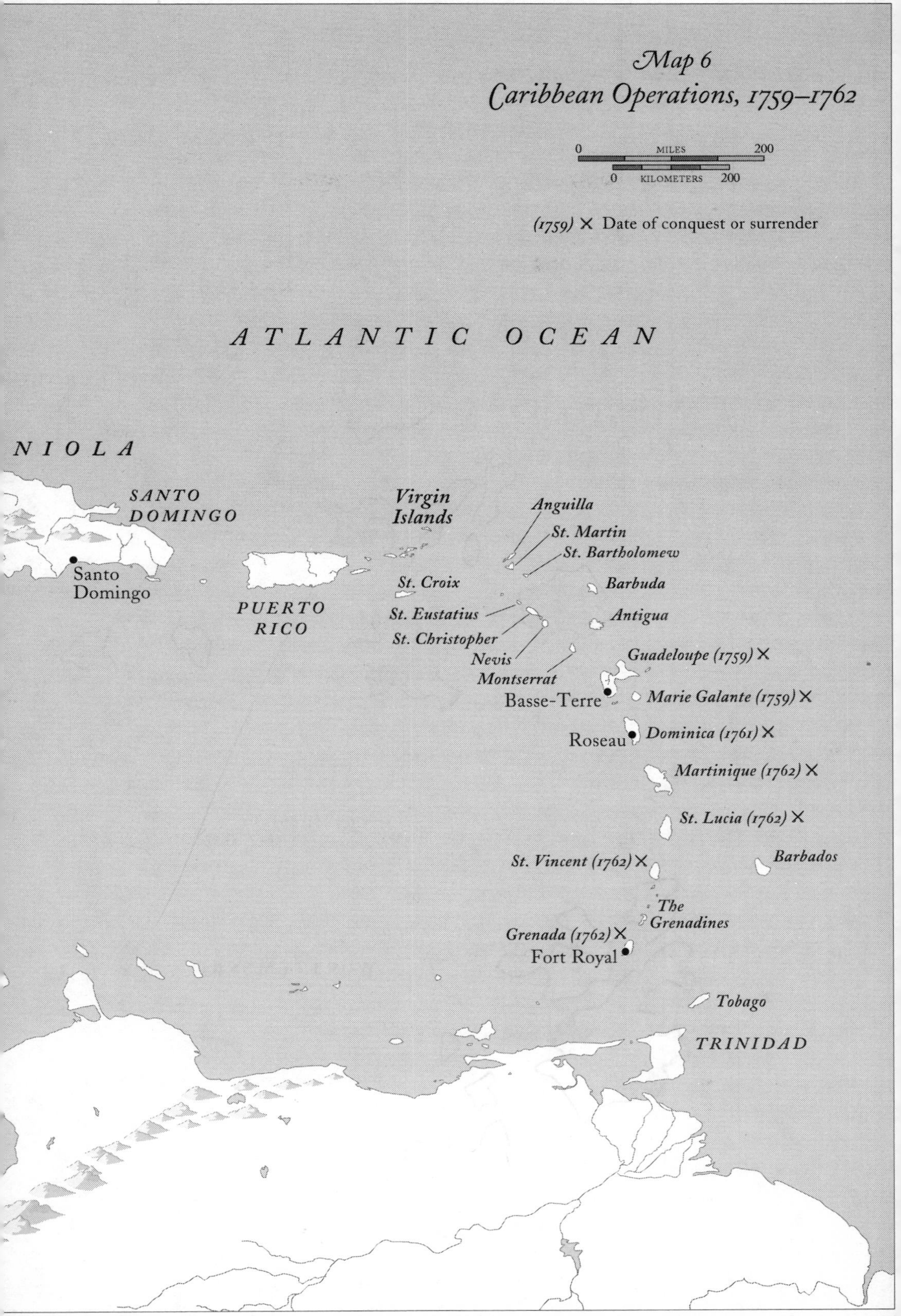
Map 6
Caribbean Operations, 1759–1762
0 MILES 200
0 KILOMETERS 200
(1759) ✕ Date of conquest or surrender
ATLANTIC OCEAN
NIOLA
SANTO DOMINGO
Santo Domingo
PUERTO RICO
Virgin Islands
St. Croix
St. Eustatius
St. Christopher
Nevis
Montserrat
Anguilla
St. Martin
St. Bartholomew
Barbuda
Antigua
Guadeloupe (1759) ✕
Basse-Terre
Marie Galante (1759) ✕
Roseau
Dominica (1761) ✕
Martinique (1762) ✕
St. Lucia (1762) ✕
St. Vincent (1762) ✕
Barbados
The Grenadines
Grenada (1762) ✕
Fort Royal
Tobago
TRINIDAD

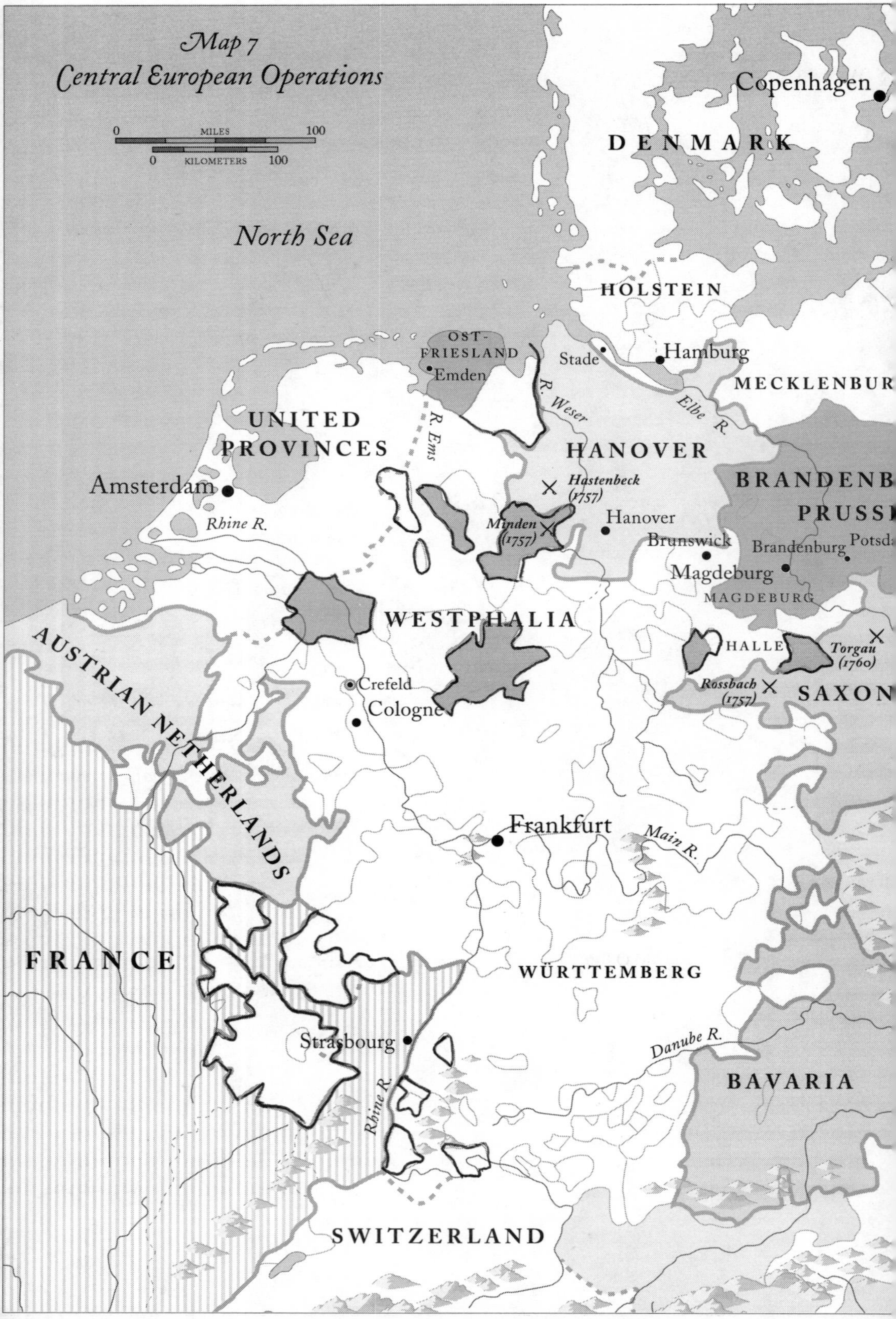
Map 7
Central European Operations
0 MILES 100
0 KILOMETERS 100
North Sea
Copenhagen
DENMARK
HOLSTEIN
OST-FRIESLAND
Emden
Stade
Hamburg
MECKLENBUR
R. Weser
Elbe R.
R. Ems
UNITED PROVINCES
HANOVER
Amsterdam
Hastenbeck (1757)
BRANDENB
PRUSS
Rhine R.
Minden (1757)
Hanover
Brunswick
Brandenburg
Potsda
Magdeburg
MAGDEBURG
WESTPHALIA
HALLE
Torgau (1760)
AUSTRIAN NETHERLANDS
Crefeld
Cologne
Rossbach (1757)
SAXON
Frankfurt
Main R.
FRANCE
WÜRTTEMBERG
Strasbourg
Danube R.
Rhine R.
BAVARIA
SWITZERLAND

SWEDEN
Baltic Sea
Königsberg
EAST PRUSSIA
Kolberg
WEDISH
OMERANIA
POMERANIA
Oder R.
Zorndorf (1758)
G-
Berlin
Frankurt
Kunersdorf (1759)
Vistula R.
Warsaw
POLAND
SILESIA
Oresden
Hochkirch (1758)
Liegnitz (1760)
Leuthen (1757)
Elbe R.
Lobositz (1756)
Glatz
Bunzewitz
Oder R.
Prague (1757)
Kolin (1757)
BOHEMIA
MORAVIA
Moldau R.
AUSTRIA
HUNGARY
Linz
Vienna
AUSTRIA
Danube R.
Pest
Buda

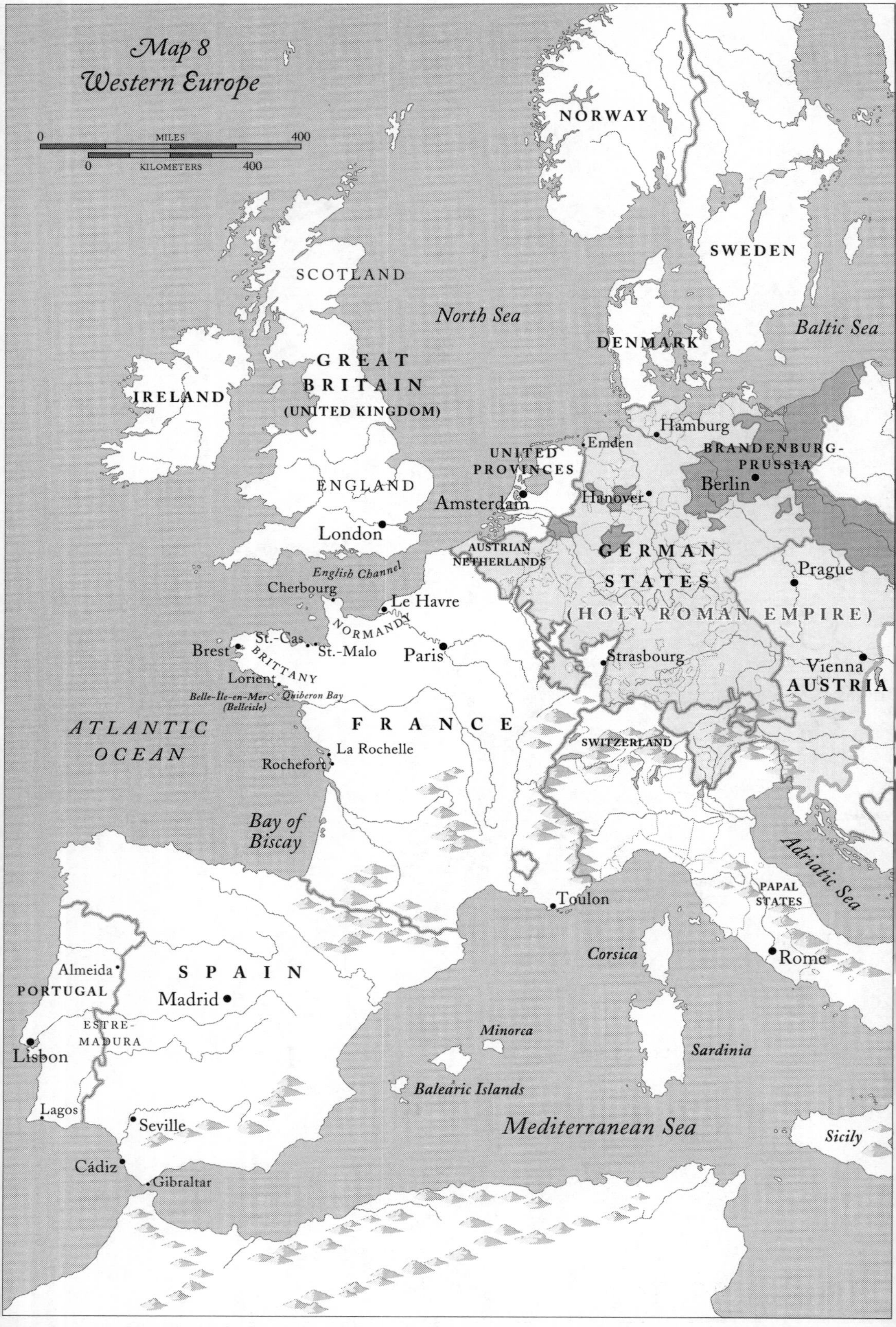
Map 8
Western Europe
0
MILES
400
0
KILOMETERS
400
NORWAY
SWEDEN
SCOTLAND
North Sea
Baltic Sea
DENMARK
GREAT
BRITAIN
(UNITED KINGDOM)
IRELAND
Hamburg
Emden
BRANDENBURG-
PRUSSIA
UNITED
PROVINCES
Berlin
Hanover
ENGLAND
Amsterdam
London
AUSTRIAN
NETHERLANDS
GERMAN
STATES
(HOLY ROMAN EMPIRE)
Prague
English Channel
Cherbourg
Le Havre
NORMANDY
St.-Cas
St.-Malo
Brest
BRITTANY
Paris
Strasbourg
Vienna
AUSTRIA
Lorient
Belle-Île-en-Mer
(Belleisle)
Quiberon Bay
ATLANTIC
OCEAN
FRANCE
SWITZERLAND
La Rochelle
Rochefort
Bay of
Biscay
Adriatic Sea
PAPAL
STATES
Toulon
Corsica
Rome
Almeida
SPAIN
PORTUGAL
Madrid
ESTRE-
MADURA
Minorca
Lisbon
Sardinia
Balearic Islands
Lagos
Seville
Mediterranean Sea
Sicily
Cádiz
Gibraltar

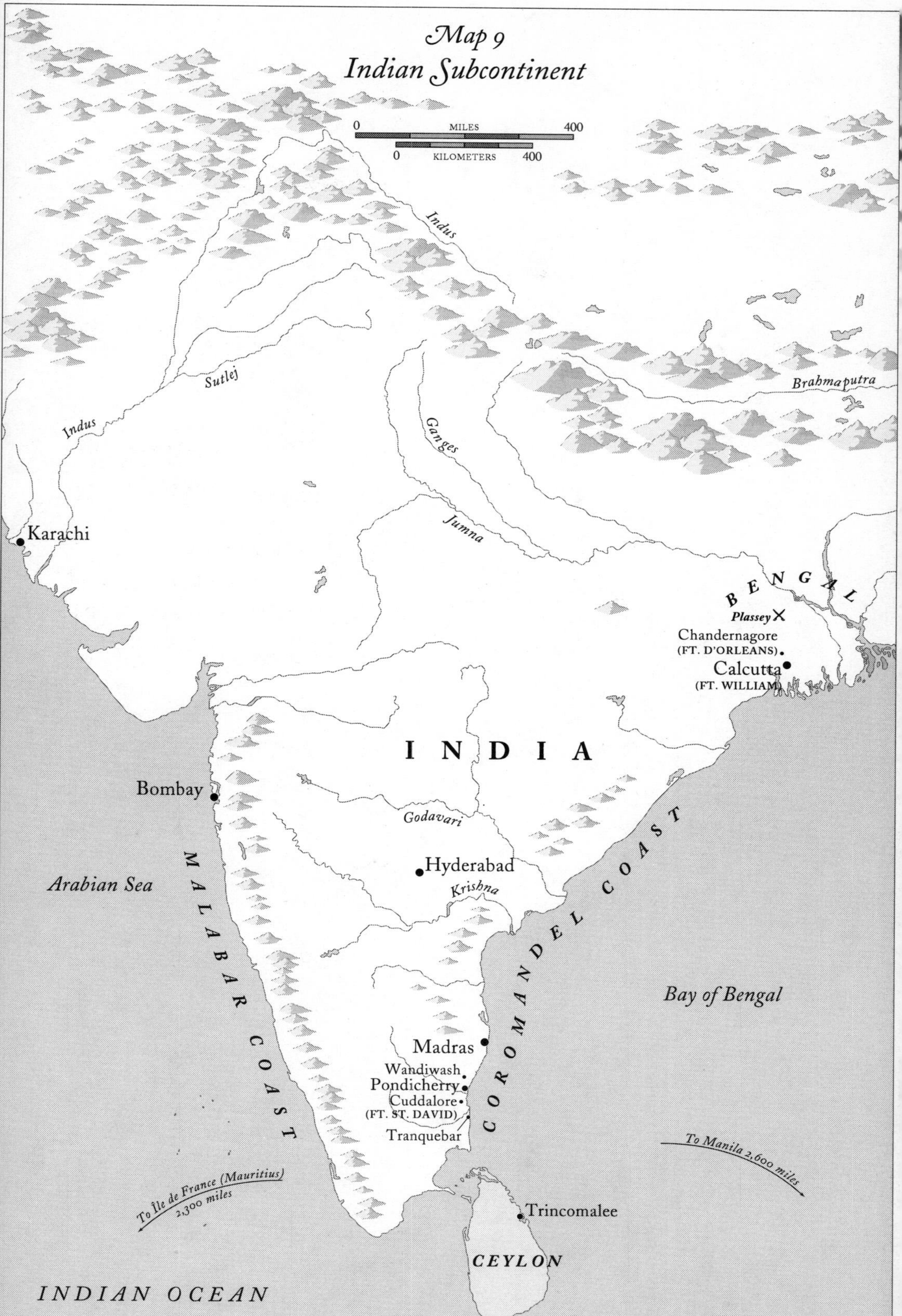
Map 9
Indian Subcontinent
0 MILES 400
0 KILOMETERS 400
Indus
Sutlej
Indus
Ganges
Brahmaputra
Jumna
Karachi
BENGAL
Plassey
Chandernagore
(FT. D'ORLEANS)
Calcutta
(FT. WILLIAM)
INDIA
Bombay
Godavari
Hyderabad
Krishna
Arabian Sea
MALABAR COAST
COROMANDEL COAST
Bay of Bengal
Madras
Wandiwash
Pondicherry
Cuddalore
(FT. ST. DAVID)
Tranquebar
To Manila 2,600 miles
To Île de France (Mauritius) 2,300 miles
Trincomalee
CEYLON
INDIAN OCEAN

Crucible of War

PROLOGUE

Jumonville's Glen

MAY 28, 1754

THE RAIN HAD fallen all night, a steady, miserable rain; and when at last the light grew to the point that he could see his troops, George Washington realized that seven of them were lost in the forest, God knew where. For hours he had blundered through the dripping dark, time and again leading the little column off the trail, sometimes taking a quarter hour just to grope his way back to the track. Confused, untrained, and wretched, the forty soldiers who had somehow held together through the night were hardly prepared to fight any enemy, let alone one experienced in forest warfare. Nonetheless the tall Virginian led them on, following the Indian warrior who had come to warn them of their peril.

Toward daybreak the rain stopped, and the remnants of Washington's patrol reached the Indian camp. There the soldiers dried and loaded their muskets while Washington conferred with the old chief who had summoned him. Tanaghrisson, called the "Half King" by the English who regarded him as an ally, described the tracks he had seen nearby. They led toward a sheltered place he knew; there, he suspected, the French had been bivouacked since the day before. Washington's soldiers could march to a spot nearby and wait while his own men reconnoitered. Once the warriors knew the enemy's strength and disposition, they and the Virginians could fall on the camp together. Washington agreed.

He had no choice. However little he cared for Indians, however little he trusted them, he could never have found the Frenchmen's camp without them. Surely he could not have found it in time to dispose his men in firing positions while the French, groggy with sleep, were just starting to cook breakfast at the foot of a tall rock face. Quietly his men and the

Indians stationed themselves above and around the narrow glen, while on its floor Frenchmen still crawled from their bark lean-tos and stretched themselves in the early light.

As always in such affairs, no one knows exactly what happened next. Perhaps, as the French later said, the English fired on them without warning. Or perhaps, as Washington maintained, a Frenchman shouted a warning that sent his comrades flying to their arms and firing up into the woods. All that is certain is that the English fired two volleys down into the hollow while the French returned a few ragged shots and tried to retreat into the shelter of the trees.

But there was no escape. The Half King's warriors had blocked the path, forcing the thirty-odd Frenchmen back into the clearing, where English fire pinned them down. An officer called for quarter, and Washington ordered his men to cease firing. Perhaps ten minutes had passed since the first shot.

It had been a lopsided skirmish. Around the rim of the hollow three of Washington's troops were wounded, and one lay dead; at its bottom the French had suffered fourteen casualties. One of the wounded, a thirty-five-year-old ensign named Joseph Coulon de Villiers de Jumonville, identified himself as the detachment's commander. Through a translator he tried to make it known that he had come in peace, as an emissary with a message summoning the English to withdraw from the possessions of His Most Christian Majesty, Louis XV. The letter he carried would make everything clear. His interpreter would read it.

As the combatants' adrenaline levels subsided and the wounded men moaned, the translation went badly. The letter had to be read a second time, and Washington turned to take it back to his own translator. As he withdrew, Tanaghrisson stepped up to where Jumonville lay. *"Tu n'es pas encore mort, mon père,"* he said; Thou art not yet dead, my father. He raised his hatchet and sank it in the ensign's head, striking until he had shattered the cranium. Then he reached into the skull, pulled out a handful of viscous tissue, and washed his hands in Jumonville's brain.

The tall Virginian who until that instant had thought himself in command did nothing while the Half King's warriors, as if on signal, set about killing the wounded. Within moments only one of the Frenchmen who had been hit in the firefight was left alive.

Recovering his composure, Washington now salvaged what he could by forming his men around the twenty-one surviving prisoners and hustling them to safety. Behind them, in the bloody hollow, the Half King's men scalped and stripped the thirteen corpses, decapitating one and impaling its head on a stake. Then they, too, abandoned the glen, and crows flapped noisily down from the trees to begin the feast. Soon wolves would lope in to do their part; eventually maggots and beetles and ants would finish the job in meticulous silence.

By afternoon Washington was back at his own camp, groping for explanations and trying to plan his next move. Since boyhood he had dreamed of battle's glory. Now he had seen combat but no heroism: only chaos and the slaughter of defenseless men. Why had it happened? What could he tell his superiors? What would happen next?

George Washington had none of the answers.[1]

THERE COULD HARDLY be a clearer example of a historical moment when events vastly incommensurate with human intention begin to follow from the efforts of an individual to cope with a situation run out of control than this otherwise ordinary Wednesday morning in May 1754. Nothing could have been further from Washington's mind, or more alien to the designs of the men who had entrusted him with troops and ordered him to the Ohio Valley, than beginning a war. Neither he nor his masters imagined that they were setting in train events that would destroy the American empire of France. Much less could they have foreseen that a stunning Anglo-American victory would lead to yet another war, one that would destroy Britain's empire and raise in its ruin the American republic that Washington himself would lead.

So extraordinary indeed were the events that followed from this callow officer's acts and hesitations that we must begin by shaking off the impression that some awesome destiny shaped occurrences in the Ohio Valley during the 1750s. For in fact the presence of French troops and forts in the region, the determination of Virginia's colonial governor to remove them, and the decisions of the French and British governments to use military force to back up the maneuverings of colonists deep in the American interior all resulted from the unusually powerful coincidence of some very ordinary human factors: ambition and avarice, fear and misunderstanding, miscalculation and mischance. How such a combination could produce a backwoods massacre is not, perhaps, hard to imagine. How that particular butchery gave rise to the greatest war of the eighteenth century, however, is less easy to explain. To understand it, we must first chart the paths by which the interests of the Iroquois Confederacy, the government of New France, the governor of Virginia, and a group of Anglo-American land speculators all converged, in the spring of 1754, at the spot where the Allegheny joins the Monongahela and the Ohio's waters begin their long descent through the heart of America to the Mississippi, and the sea.

PART I

The Origins of the Seven Years' War

1450–1754

The Iroquois League, the Ohio Valley, and the stability of the balance of power in eighteenth-century North America. The Anglo-French wars, the penetration of British traders and speculators into the Ohio Country, and the ominous convergence of British and French empires. George Washington steps inauspiciously onto the stage of history. European politics and the beginnings of the Diplomatic Revolution.

CHAPTER 1

Iroquoia and Empire

1450–1735

WARS BETWEEN France and England (or, after the Act of Union in 1707, Great Britain) dominated European politics between 1689 and 1815. The first three of these began in Europe and centered on dynastic issues: which member of what royal family would become the elector Palatine, or the king of Spain, or the emperor-king (or empress-queen) of Austria. Each had its North American counterpart—called by the Anglo-Americans King William's, Queen Anne's, and King George's Wars, respectively—and all of them were in one way or another important to the colonists of England and France. To European statesmen, however, the fighting in the New World was so much sideshow: Europe, its balance of power, and its monarchies were what mattered. Thus the first three wars were typical European conflicts of the eighteenth century, limited, bloody, expensive, indecisive affairs that ended not in great conquests but the belligerents' mutual exhaustion and a restoration of the balance of power. The fourth Anglo-French war, however, broke the mold. The Seven Years' War was about the control of territory, not thrones; it created a seismic shift in Europe's alliance system and balance of power; and its first shots were fired not on a European, but an American, frontier.[1]

That the greatest of Europe's eighteenth-century wars could have begun in the Pennsylvania backcountry reflected the growing importance of America in the diplomatic, military, and economic calculations of European governments. That it spread as it did from the New World to the Old resulted from the maneuverings of European diplomats who, seeking advantage, destroyed the fragile balance of power established by the Treaty of Aix-la-Chapelle (1748) at the end of the previous war. But what made the fighting begin where it did, and when it did, were circumstances specific to America, conditions at best imperfectly grasped by European statesmen. For 1754 marked the end of the prolonged collapse of a half-century-old strategic balance in eastern North America—a *tripartite* equilibrium in which the Iroquois Confederacy occupied a crucial position, both geographically and diplomatically, between the French and the English colonial empires. Through the first half of the century, the competition between empires in North America had been rendered inconclusive because the Iroquois maintained independence of action and thus a large measure of influence over affairs on the borderlands. The story of the last Anglo-French colonial war begins, therefore, not with Britain or France, nor even with their American colonies, but with the Six Nations of the Iroquois, and indeed with a single chief: Tanaghrisson.

WHY SHOULD a man born a Catawba, reared as a Seneca, acting as a spokesman for the Iroquois Confederacy in the Ohio Country, choose to smash open the skull of a Frenchman who was neither his enemy nor an enemy to his people? To unravel this riddle we must begin far from the place and time of Tanaghrisson's act, in the area that would one day become upstate New York, before the first Europeans arrived on the shores of North America. For it was there that the Iroquois nations made their home, and there that their unique religious and cultural system arose: one dedicated to ending warfare among themselves by directing aggression toward other peoples in the name of peace.

The Great League of Peace and Power, a ritual and cultural association that loosely united the original Five Nations of the Iroquois—the Mohawks, the Oneidas, the Onondagas, the Cayugas, and the Senecas—was perhaps three centuries old when Tanaghrisson washed his hands in Ensign Jumonville's brains. The cultural bonds fostered within the Great League had served as the basis for the much newer political union known as the Iroquois Confederacy, which emerged among the Five Nations in response to the European invasion of the seventeenth century. Although the ritual functions of the Great League and the diplomatic, political, and military functions of the Confederacy sometimes overlapped, they generally served separate and complementary ends: the Great League to perpetuate peace among its member nations, and the Confederacy to deal with European colonists and with Indian societies outside the league.[2]

The Great League of Peace and Power originated, according to Iroquoian tradition, in an ancient period when the Five Nations were locked in perpetual blood-feuding. Ethnographers have identified this mythological era with the larger aboriginal culture pattern of "mourning war," in which the families of people killed in raids can grieve properly for their loved ones only by replacing them—spiritually as well as physically—with captives taken from the enemy's community. These captives might be either permanently adopted into the bereaved family as a substitute for its lost member, or ritually slain to compensate for the family's loss. Mourning warfare could evolve into a closed system of raids, kidnapping, suffering, death, and grief. Such misery, the Iroquois believed, had been the lot of the Five Nations before the Good News of Peace and Power was revealed to them by a supernatural being, Deganawidah, who showed them ritual forms of condolence and gift-giving by which they could cope with bereavement without resort to war. To perpetuate Deganawidah's gospel and rituals—and, with them, peace among the nations—the heads of all the clans in the Five Nations formed a Grand Council beneath the Tree of the Great Peace at the settlement of Onondaga, which thereafter became the symbolic center of Iroquois life.[3]

Because all people might find shelter beneath the Tree of the Great Peace, the Five Nations took it as their duty to spread the gospel by allying themselves with other Indian groups and taking weaker nations under their protection as dependents. Peoples who refused to heed the Good News as allies or dependents, however, could only be dealt with as enemies. The Iroquois believed that war against such recalcitrant nations was not only just but necessary, because conquest and forcible subjection to the Great League offered the only remaining way that they, too, could find the path to peace. For perhaps two centuries before the Iroquois came into sustained contact with European colonists, their commitment to propagating the Good News of Peace and Power helped sustain almost continuous hostilities with peoples beyond the Great League and its growing penumbra of clients and allies.[4]

The appearance of European traders and settlers on the margins of Iroquoia in the seventeenth century confronted the Five Nations with grave, unprecedented threats in the form of desirable trade goods, devastating diseases, and ever-more-destructive warfare. The willingness of Dutch traders to exchange muskets for pelts made Iroquois warriors the most feared in eastern North America, while the losses Iroquois war parties suffered generated an increasing demand for captives. In a half-century-long exacerbation of mourning war, the Five Nations gained a legendary reputation for ferocity, conquering and dispersing Indian groups such as the Hurons, Eries, and Neutrals on either side of the Great Lakes, and emptying the Ohio Valley of its Monongahela, Shawnee, and other residents. But the fabulous military success of the Iroquois exacted a formidable price, for by the 1660s they found themselves so exhausted—

and their populations so heavily diluted by adoptees—that they were unable to continue the fight. When the English conquest of New Netherland ended the flow of Dutch arms and ammunition in 1664, the Iroquois could no longer continue. In 1665–67, each of the Five Nations made its peace with New France, the principal arms supplier and trading partner of their enemies, and the tide of conflict ebbed.

During these long, terrible years of bloodshed, the ancient ceremonial institution of the Grand Council had begun to take on new functions as the war chiefs of the Five Nations made it a forum for concerting policies to serve their peoples' mutual interests. Never before had the war leaders—a group of vigorous younger men, distinct from the older civil chiefs, or sachems, who still performed the Great League's necessary rituals—achieved so much cooperation. In the war chiefs' councils lay the origin of the Iroquois Confederacy as a diplomatic organization able to coordinate the policies of the various nations. The Confederacy's concentration on external relations complemented the internally unifying, peacekeeping role of the Great League. Eventually the Confederacy evolved a sophisticated diplomatic system based on the gift-giving practices and condolence ceremonies of the league.

Peace allowed the Iroquois to recover a measure of demographic stability but brought new challenges as French Jesuit missionaries began to evangelize among them, dividing each of the Five Nations internally. The Mohawks, in particular, suffered losses as the converts relocated along the St. Lawrence River. The secession of Catholic Caughnawagas (so called from the name of their biggest settlement) was the most dramatic instance of factionalization, but all five of the nations split internally into Francophile, neutralist, and Anglophile wings. Within the Confederacy council the Anglophiles gained the upper hand and in 1677 created a commercial and strategic alliance, the Covenant Chain, with the government of New York—and subsequently with colonies from Virginia to New England. English encouragement and weapons allowed the Confederacy, in the last quarter of the century, to inaugurate an aggressive policy aimed at penetrating "the French trading and alliance systems that spread over the Great Lakes and Mississippi valley regions."[5] The result, almost inevitably, was a renewal of the earlier pattern of warfare, which after 1689 merged into the first Anglo-French colonial conflict, King William's War.

Onondaga's alliance with the English now proved disastrous, for during the interval of peace the French had created a highly effective system of alliances with Algonquian-speaking refugee groups whom Iroquois warriors had driven far to the west, beyond Lake Michigan, in the first half of the century. The key to this French alliance system was the ability of missionaries, traders, and *officiers* to assume the cultural role of father, as understood among the Indians of the upper Great Lakes basin, or *pays d'en haut*. Because Algonquian fathers did not discipline their children but sought to create harmony, their real power stemmed from the ability to give gifts and mediate disputes; fathers might persuade but could not seek to exert direct control without forfeiting their moral authority. French mediators functioned in just this way among the fragmented, often mutually hostile refugee peoples of the *pays d'en haut*, groups that shared little but a common history of enmity with the Iroquois. Under the guiding influence of "Onontio," as the Algonquians called the French governor-general (and by extension, the king he represented, as well as the priests, traders, and military officers who represented him among the Indians), the refugee villages gradually cohered into an alliance system centering on French power. French diplomatic gifts, trade relationships emphasizing mutuality rather than competition, and French arms and military aid thus became the currency of power for the chiefs who led the refugee groups. Thus, as the Iroquois tightened their bonds with the English in the Covenant Chain, Onontio created a highly effective counterweight to their power.[6]

Whereas the comparatively united Five Nations had generally enjoyed the advantage over their disunited enemies earlier in the century, the renewal of hostilities brought defeat after defeat and carried the war to the very heart of Iroquoia. Faced with the realization that the English were incompetent military allies, war chiefs representing Anglophile, Francophile, and neutralist factions contended for control of policy until the Confederacy nearly fell to pieces. Finally the headmen of the various factions hammered out an internal truce that enabled Iroquois diplomats to conclude a peace treaty with the French at Montréal, and simultaneously to renew the Covenant Chain with the English at Albany. These agreements, known as the Grand Settlement of 1701, preserved the Five Nations' independence and inaugurated a new era of neutrality in Iroquois diplomacy.[7]

As factionalism gradually subsided in the Grand Council, the fragile agreement to stand aloof from Anglo-French disputes grew into a robust consensus that everything could be gained by playing off one European group against the other and preventing either from gaining preeminence. Iroquois neutrality thus became both the basis of stability within the league and the source of power to influence relations between the contending empires. Neutrality meant neither passivity nor pacifism to the Five Nations, but rather the pursuit of three complementary, activist policies: hostility toward Indian peoples far to the south, especially the Cherokees and the Catawbas of South Carolina; cooperation with the government of Pennsylvania to gain control over Indian peoples and lands on the southern flank of Iroquoia; and peace with the "Far Indians," or the French-allied Algonquians of the *pays d'en haut* and upper Mississippi Valley.[8]

The first of these three policies allowed young Iroquois men to fulfill their culturally sanctioned role as warriors and permitted population replacement to continue by the limited practice of mourning war. It was through a raid on the Catawbas, for example, that the boy Tanaghrisson and his mother were taken captive, eventually to be adopted as members of the Seneca nation. The second policy served two practical ends. By cooperating with the government of Pennsylvania, and later Virginia, the Iroquois lowered the risk of attacking the southern Indians; the settlements of two client peoples in Pennsylvania's Susquehanna Valley, the Shawnees and the Delawares, acted as a barrier against Catawba and Cherokee raiders from the south and served as way stations at which Iroquois warriors traversing their territory could be reprovisioned. Furthermore, once Pennsylvania and Virginia recognized Iroquois diplomats as spokesmen for the Delawares and the Shawnees, the Iroquois could dispose of those clients—and the lands on which they lived—as they pleased. The third policy, of maintaining peaceful relations with the Far Indians, also served a dual purpose, for it preserved the Iroquois heartland from the attacks of French-allied enemies even as it magnified the importance of the Iroquois to the English, both as diplomats and as trading middlemen. Only through Iroquois mediators could the English communicate with peoples deep in the interior; only through the Iroquois could the Far Indians acquire English trade goods. Thus all three policies obviously and directly benefited the Iroquois. But the central principle that actuated them all was Onondaga's ability to maneuver between the French and the British.[9]

The Iroquois chiefs' "aggressive neutrality" enabled them to manipulate both French and British imperial authorities. Representing themselves as the spokesmen for the Far Indians, acting on behalf of previously conquered dependent peoples such as the Delawares and Shawnees, and maintaining that they were the rightful overlords of vast western territories, the Iroquois seized and for a half century maintained the diplomatic initiative within North America, particularly in dealing with the British. Most significantly, they were able to use these tactics to claim suzerainty over the Ohio Country, a region that for a long time lay beyond the reach of either the French or the British, but which was nonetheless a zone of great strategic importance to both.[10]

France needed access to the Ohio River and its northern tributaries because this river complex offered the only efficient inland passage between their settlements in Canada and those in the mid-Mississippi Valley, in the region called the Illinois Country. The Illinois settlements had grown up along the Mississippi between the confluences of the Missouri and the Kaskaskia Rivers at the beginning of the eighteenth century, when the wide-ranging fur traders called *coureurs de bois* had founded villages without bothering first to obtain permission from New France. These villages prospered as centers of farming, fur trading, and eventually lead mining; by the 1710s, they were provisioning the new colony of Louisiana at the mouth of the Mississippi. French colonial administrators soon recognized the importance of the Illinois Country as the vertex of an arc of settlement and Indian alliances sweeping from the Gulf of St. Lawrence to the Mississippi Delta. Because this strategic system would restrict the demographically expansive British colonists to the area east of the Appalachians by denying them access to the rivers that permitted trade and travel through the interior of the continent, it held out the promise of rewards beyond America alone. Once the encirclement was complete, French diplomats reasoned, the British would have to divert so much naval and military strength to protect their colonies that they would be hobbled in Europe. It was thus vital to France that the British be excluded from the Ohio Country. So long as their traders, priests, and soldiers enjoyed unimpeded travel *through* it, the French did not need to control the Ohio Valley directly; indeed, because the expense of physical occupation might well prove insupportable, French policy makers preferred to see it remain under neutral Indian control—provided that the valley's Indians traded with France.[11]

The British feared a French cordon to the west as much as the French desired it. British imperial officials dreaded the prospect of a burgeoning colonial population indefinitely confined to the lands between the Appalachian barrier and the Atlantic, where demographic growth would inevitably drive down wages to the point that Americans would compete with British manufacturers, rather than consuming their wares; nor did His Majesty's government relish the stationing of expensive army and navy detachments in America as bulwarks against French aggression. British colonists themselves saw the Ohio Country mainly as a vast realm for future settlement—the more so since two vigorous provinces, Virginia and Pennsylvania, claimed that Ohio lands fell within their territorial limits. Until the middle of the eighteenth century, however, the impossibility of exercising direct control over so vast and remote a region mooted the prospect of Anglo-American colonization west of the Appalachians. The Ohio Country accordingly became an area within which the British sought to exercise indirect influence, against the day when they might finally colonize it. Until then it was imperative that the French be prevented from gaining control over the region and its waterways.

The Iroquois were only too happy to turn the geopolitical anxieties of Britain and France to their own advantage. This they did by insisting that the Ohio Country was theirs, by right of conquest: a claim for which the wars of the first half of the seventeenth century provided a plausible basis. Following the depopulation of the Ohio Country, the westernmost Iroquois nation, the Senecas, used the upper Ohio drainage as a vast hunting ground; eventually, westering Senecas known as Mingos set up permanent residence in the area between Lake Erie and the Allegheny River. Moreover, from the late 1720s onward, the Ohio Valley proper was being settled by Iroquois dependents, bands of Shawnees and Delawares moving west from Pennsylvania under growing pressure from European immigration into the Susquehanna Valley. Onondaga designated resident Iroquois village headmen as its representatives on the Ohio and authorized them to speak for the local dependent peoples as well as the Mingos. These representatives, known as "half-kings," had the power to negotiate and receive diplomatic gifts, but they could not make binding treaties without Onondaga's assent. Tanaghrisson, the adoptive Seneca who was living as village headman at Logstown (on the site of modern Ambridge, Pennsylvania) as early as 1747, was one such half-king; an Oneida chief named Scarouady was another, acting as regent over the Ohio Shawnees. In reality, Iroquois control over the Ohio Country rested entirely on the degree to which the Mingo, Shawnee, and Delaware residents were willing to cooperate with the half-kings, and thus on the willingness of Tanaghrisson and Scarouady—whose authority depended on their ability to retain local followings—to follow policies determined at distant Onondaga. Despite the tenuousness of their real influence, the Grand Council's chiefs were able to take the carefully constructed illusion of control and use it to play off the British and the French against one another in the great game of North American imperial politics.[12]

By controlling, or seeming to control, the Ohio Country, Onondaga made itself the fulcrum upon which relations between the French and British achieved the delicate balance that lasted for the first half of the eighteenth century. By shifting, or threatening to shift, its position to favor one side over the other, the Confederacy compelled the French

Cartographic imperialism. Henry Popple's *Map of the British Empire in America with the French, Spanish and Hollandish Settlements adjacent thereto* (1751) was, according to its explanatory note, undertaken "with y[e] Approbation of the R[t] Honourable LORDS COMMISSIONERS of TRADE and PLANTATIONS" and reflects the notions of imperial dominion current in London after King George's War. By depicting the boundaries of British colonies expansively—Virginia's southern border extends beyond the Mississippi and New York's northern boundary reaches the Saint Lawrence—and by demoting all other European colonies to mere "settlements," Popple anticipated expansion into the interior of the continent. Notwithstanding a commendation of the map's "*great Accuracy*" by "y[e] Learned D[r] EDM. HALLEY, Professor of *Astronomy* in ye University of *Oxford*," Popple was able to depict that interior in only approximate terms, derived from French reports. *Courtesy of the William L. Clements Library at the University of Michigan.*

and the British to bid for its friendship, or at least its continued non-alignment. The British, lacking effective connections with any northern Indians other than the Iroquois, were particularly susceptible to the Confederacy's claim to control vast numbers of warriors through its alliances with the Far Indians. At a time when all Iroquoia held only about 1,100 warriors, for example, and when the Shawnees and Delawares in the Ohio Valley counted perhaps 350 warriors between them, the most knowledgeable of Pennsylvania's Indian experts reported that the Iroquois could command the allegiance of 9,300 fighters among the Far Indians.[13]

To secure Onondaga's cooperation, both the French and the British strove to maintain friendly diplomatic relations on the Confederacy's terms, by the giving of gifts. Gift-giving in the form of ritual presentation of strings or belts of wampum beads had been a part of the ceremonies of the Great League since time immemorial; wampum, a sacred medium, was necessary to reinforce and ratify the words spoken in council. Beaded strings and belts also formed the ritual centerpiece of intercultural negotiations between the Iroquois and the Europeans, but as time passed trade goods greatly supplemented these ritual gifts. By the mid-eighteenth century, the conclusion of treaty negotiations could entail the delivery of a ton or more of European goods, including cloth, tools, firearms, ironware, ammunition, and liquor. Such gifts "brightened the chain" of friendship, providing manufactures and consumable commodities to peoples who would have found it hard to survive without them, and supplying the medium of trade by which Iroquois middlemen could obtain high-quality beaver pelts from groups north of the Great Lakes. The Confederacy therefore used its strategic value to make up for its lack of direct access to marketable furs, as well as to help preserve control over its own affairs and lands.[14]

For the eighteenth-century Iroquois, then, everything depended on the ability to maneuver between the two European colonial powers and to avoid becoming dependent on either. In Queen Anne's War (1701–13), this meant negotiating frequently with both Montréal and Albany, assuring both sides of their goodwill and cooperativeness but avoiding entanglement in the fighting whenever possible. When it became impossible, as it sometimes did, to deny the demands of the English for military aid, the Iroquois chose one of two prudent paths. In 1709, they cooperated minimally and delayed a planned invasion of Canada until it had to be aborted. In 1711 they showed ostensible enthusiasm for another expedition, while quietly sending word of what was afoot to the French; thus they thwarted the second invasion as effectively as the first. During the thirty years' peace that followed the end of Queen Anne's War, Onondaga's diplomats met regularly with both French and British officials, maintaining trading relations with both and allowing the Europeans to brighten the chain of friendship with gifts.[15]

Between 1713 and 1744, while peace endured between empires, the Iroquois gained strength by admitting the Tuscaroras to the Great League as a sixth nation, enhanced their formal claim to the Ohio Country by sanctioning the settlement of Mingos, Shawnees, and Delawares in the upper Valley, and extended the scope of their direct relations with British colonies beyond New York and Pennsylvania. Ironically, the very growth of Onondaga's self-assurance would cost the Confederacy its ability to maneuver between the rival empires and end the era of Iroquois neutrality. Although no one at the time saw it clearly, the events that seemingly marked the zenith of the Great League's influence would prove to have been the harbingers of its long decline—a change of fortune that owed as much to Iroquois hubris and greed as to the growth of European power.

CHAPTER 2

The Erosion of Iroquois Influence

1736–1754

In 1742 representatives of the Six Nations solemnly confirmed a prior land sale to the Penn family, by which the Delaware Indians were dispossessed of two-thirds of a million acres of eastern Pennsylvania territory. The Delawares had lived on that tract, in the valley that still bears their name, since pre-Columbian times, centuries before they had become clients of the Iroquois. Everyone involved knew that the original sale—the so-called Walking Purchase of 1737—had been a spectacular fraud. The spokesmen of the Six Nations nevertheless confirmed it at the Treaty of Easton in 1742 because to do so offered irresistible advantages to the Great League. Despite its tragic consequences for the Delawares, the transfer of their lands to the Penn family cemented an understanding between Pennsylvania and Onondaga: henceforth the Six Nations would act as sole agents for the sale of Indian land-rights within the province.

But the Walking Purchase would prove to be another kind of turning point, too. As white farmers began arriving in the late 1730s, the eastern Delaware bands relocated to the Susquehanna's north branch, settling in a remote region called the Wyoming Valley alongside Shawnees who had been there for several decades. At Wyoming, powerless to retaliate against their betrayers, they nursed a sense of grievance against both the Six Nations and the settlers who had taken their homeland. Meanwhile, the Iroquois sellout spurred the removal of other Shawnee and Delaware groups to the Ohio Country. Despite the continued pretense that they were Iroquois dependents, once they reached the valley the Shawnees and Delawares were beyond Onondaga's effective control. Iroquois influence in the Ohio Country would inevitably diminish as the numbers of refugees grew.[1]

But the single event of greatest consequence to the erosion of the Six Nations' neutrality was a great treaty negotiated at Lancaster, Pennsylvania, in 1744, when Iroquois diplomats met with representatives of Pennsylvania, Maryland, and Virginia. On its face, the Treaty of Lancaster marked the high point of Iroquois influence in dealing with the English colonies. In return for what at the time seemed minor concessions, the league received gifts that included eight hundred pounds in Pennsylvania currency and three hundred pounds in gold, as well as all three governments' acknowledgment of Onondaga's suzerainty over several southern Indian tribes, on whose behalf it could henceforth speak, as it spoke for the Delawares and the Shawnees. Perhaps most important to the league was Virginia's recognition of Iroquois warriors' right to pass through the province to attack the Cherokees and Catawbas, a concession that evidently included an agreement to provision war parties while in transit.[2]

If all these benefits seemed to expand Iroquois power, the Treaty of Lancaster in fact foretold its end, for the Confederacy's part in the bargain ceded all its remaining claims to land within the boundaries of Maryland and Virginia. Although it is quite clear that Canasatego, the Onondaga headman who negotiated on behalf of the league at both Easton and Lancaster, *thought* that he was giving up only a fictive Iroquois claim to the Shenandoah Valley, he was in fact trading away the whole of the Ohio Country. More than mere reticence made the Virginia commissioners refrain from mentioning that their colony's charter assigned the Old Dominion a western boundary on the Pacific Ocean (including "the 'island of California' and all other islands" within a hundred miles of the coast) and a northern limit that extended along a line roughly from the northern bank of the Potomac to the western shore of Hudson Bay.[3]

Canasatego's concession was no trivial oversight. By the spring of 1745, the Virginia House of Burgesses had granted nearly a third of a million acres on the Ohio to a syndicate of about twenty rich land speculators from the Northern Neck (the area between the Rappahannock and Potomac Rivers). Although the outbreak of King George's War temporarily delayed their activities, it would be only a couple of years more before the speculators, now calling themselves the Ohio Company of Virginia, would begin to press their western claims in earnest. They intended to sell lands at the confluence of the Allegheny and the Monongahela to settlers who, they believed, would soon cross the Appalachians.

Transappalachian white settlement—horrifying to Onondaga, whose neutrality policy rested on the illusion of control over the Ohio Country—would in fact be postponed. But the delay would have less to do with Iroquois maneuverings than with the developing competition of Virginians, Pennsylvanians, and Canadian French interests for control in the west. With the waning of the Confederacy's influence over the region and its supposedly dependent peoples, the Ohio Country would become the scene of intercolonial and international competition. The Great League, which had so recently acted as the diplomatic equal of the British and French empires, would over the course of the next decade become largely irrelevant to the imperial antagonists.

The fighting in King George's War—in Europe, the War of the Austrian Succession—lasted only until 1748, when the Treaty of Aix-la-Chapelle restored all conquests to their prewar owners. But the Iroquois would never regain the influential position they had occupied at Lancaster in 1744. The conflict had cracked open what had long been a fissure in the Confederacy's solidarity when the Mohawks, easternmost and most consistently Anglophile of the Six Nations, abandoned neutrality in favor of direct cooperation with New York. They chose a most inopportune time to do so.

Unlike the fervently anti-Catholic New Englanders, who quickly mounted an expedition against Louisbourg—the fortified town and naval base on Cape Breton Island that was the strategic key to the Gulf of the St. Lawrence—and actually conquered it in 1745, New Yorkers felt little enthusiasm for fighting the French. Their governor, George Clinton, very much a servant of the Crown, appealed to the Mohawks for help, and at his instigation they undertook raids on Canada in 1746, 1747, and 1748; but the merchants who dominated the assembly, led by the powerful, Albany-based De Lancey family, would consent to no military measures beyond the building of a few forts. Indeed throughout the war Albany's fur merchants traded enthusiastically with their counterparts in Montréal via Lake George, Lake Champlain, and the Richelieu River, even as the Mohawks' mounting losses made them ever more suspicious of New York's good faith. King George's War thus proved a disaster for the Mohawks specifically and gravely diminished the coherence of Confederacy policy-making. This in turn weakened Iroquois neutrality and accelerated the pace of Anglo-American trading and land speculation in the Ohio Valley.[4]

The war's effects on the Pennsylvanians and Virginians already active in the west had been predictable. As always in wartime, the insecurity of persons and property caused farmers and Indian traders to flee the frontier for the comparative safety of eastern settlements. As the war wound down, however, land speculation and trading ventures erupted into the Ohio Country as never before. The traders were mainly Pennsylvanians who had long lived among the Shawnees and Delawares on the Susquehanna, and who simply followed their customers to the Ohio Country in the 1730s. For these the fall of Louisbourg and the closure of the St. Lawrence to French shipping created a bonanza, as Indians from all over the interior began looking to English sources for the manufactures they needed. Offering English goods at prices no French trader could match, the aggressive Pennsylvanians expanded their trade to include commerce with tribes that lived far to the west, eventually reaching even the Miamis and Wyandots, who had never traded with any but French partners.[5]

As early as 1747 one particularly flamboyant Pennsylvania trader, an Irish immigrant named George Croghan, could be found on the site of modern Cleveland trading with the Mingos and luring "Northern Indians"—French allies—across Lake Erie by offering "goods on much better terms than the French." By 1749, Croghan and his associates had set up a big trading post on the upper Great Miami River, in what is now western Ohio, at a Miami Indian settlement called Pickawillany. This promising village stood near several important portages and trails, and—to Croghan, most importantly—had a chief, Memeskia, who was willing to send wampum belts to groups as far off as Michigan, inviting them to come to Pickawillany. Within a year or two, Memeskia's invitations and Croghan's emporium drew hundreds of families to the settlement, and the enterprising Irishman could see opportunities blossoming in every quarter. Soon he was trading with Shawnee bands as far down the Ohio River as the site of modern Louisville and sending boats up the Kentucky River. The French could hardly afford to be indifferent to such avid poaching on what had been their exclusive commerce; as they knew better than anyone, trade goods and gifts held their alliance system together. So, not forgetting that he had been a thorn in their side during the last war, the French put a price on George Croghan's head.[6]

Croghan treated the news that his scalp had acquired a market value as a joke, but in fact it offered a highly accurate gauge of the growing French fear that the English were about to seize control of the Ohio Valley. From the perspective of the increasingly jittery officials in Québec, Pennsylvania traders infesting the Ohio Country seemed to be a spearhead of aggression that had to be deflected—by force, if necessary. The imperious naval officer who was serving as governor-general of New France, the comte de La Galissonière, therefore dispatched a military detachment to make a circuit of the Ohio Country in 1749. La Galissonière gave the command to Captain Pierre-Joseph de Céloron de Blainville, an officer long experienced in Indian relations; he set off from Montréal in June with a party of more than two hundred Canadians and about thirty Indians. Céloron carried three instructions: to renew the ancient French claim (by right of La Salle's discovery) to the Ohio Country, to gather intelligence on the degree of English influence, and to awe the Indians by demonstrating France's ability to send soldiers into the heart of their country.

Céloron returned in November, having paddled and portaged a great circle of three thousand miles: up the St. Lawrence and across Lakes Ontario and Erie; along the Allegheny, Ohio, Great Miami, and Maumee Rivers to Detroit; and finally back down Lakes Erie and Ontario to the St. Lawrence and Québec. In a gesture of almost touching futility, he and his party buried small lead plates at intervals along the way—"as a monument," their inscriptions read, "of the renewal of possession that we have taken of the said River Ohio and of all those that fall therein and of all the lands on both sides, unto the sources of these said rivers." Céloron had treated with the Indian tribes he met, offered gifts to renew their devotion to their father Onontio, and warned them that as faithful children they must henceforth send home any Englishmen who appeared among them. In general, he noted, the Indians received this news coolly. On at least one occasion their reaction was so evidently "unsatisfactory" that he and his men were obliged to beat a hasty retreat.[7]

That much an old Indian hand like Céloron could hardly have found surprising. What unsettled him more was how many Pennsylvania traders he encountered, including parties leading pack trains of fifty horses, laden with pelts. He had warned them that they were trespassing on lands belonging to Louis XV, had written letters for them to take back to their governor, and had explained that their presence in the Ohio Country was unwelcome. But even the dutiful Céloron knew that such warnings would have no real effect. When he made his report to the new governor-general, the marquis de La Jonquière, he assessed the situation pessimistically. The Miamis had become estranged and were corrupting other groups, even the loyal Wyandots. Without permanent French trading stations in the Ohio Country, and without a subsidized flow of trade goods that could compete with the astonishingly cheap manufactures of Great Britain, the Indians of the region would inevitably gravitate to the British.[8]

Grave as the situation seemed in late 1749, however, the governor-general took no immediate action. A less decisive figure than his predecessor, La Jonquière overreacted, then dithered, contemplated half-measures, and died. The decision to oppose the growing English influence in the west would await the arrival from France of another governor-general, Ange Duquesne de Menneville, marquis de Duquesne, in 1752. Meanwhile English influence on the Ohio would continue to grow and further alarm the anxious Canadians by taking on an even more sinister aspect. For between 1749 and 1752 Virginia speculators began moving to create a permanent settlement at the Forks of the Ohio.

The Ohio Company launched its invasion of the western country in 1749 by building a fortified storehouse at the confluence of Wills Creek and the north branch of the Potomac—the spot high in the Alleghenies where Cumberland, Maryland, now stands. Not far from the storehouse lay the divide beyond which the Youghiogheny River begins its northwestward fall to the Monongahela and the Ohio. The company ultimately intended to sell Ohio land to farmers and then to supply them with manufactures, but in the meantime it planned to capitalize on its advantages in water transportation (via the Potomac, Youghiogheny, and Monongahela) to steal a march on the Pennsylvania Indian traders, who relied on slow and expensive transport by pack train. The Virginians therefore stocked the Wills Creek fort with four thousand pounds' sterling worth of trade goods and built a second fortified structure to house their employees. The following year, they hired an experienced Maryland surveyor, trader, and guide, Christopher Gist, to explore the valley as far west as the falls of the Ohio.[9]

Gist's surveys, conducted over the next two years, gave the Virginia investors a remarkable view of the Ohio Valley's potential. He reported broad flats covered with white oak forest, fertile river bottoms, wide grassy meadows unmarred by so much as a shrub, surface deposits of coal—even salt licks holding the fossil remains of mammoths whose four-pound molars he sent back to his astonished employers. Equal in importance to his surveys, however, were the diplomatic functions that Gist also performed for the company. With the help of the ubiquitous Croghan, Gist convened a treaty conference at the Delaware, Shawnee, and Mingo settlement of Logstown—the Half King Tanaghrisson's headquarters—in the spring of 1752. This conference, at which Croghan pretended to be the representative of Pennsylvania's government and acted as a mediator, would prove to be a critical gathering, for it secured an important concession from Tanaghrisson, whom Gist and Croghan acknowledged as spokesman for Iroquois interests in the region.[10]

The ostensible purpose of the council at Logstown—a substantial village about fifteen miles downstream from the Forks—was to secure the consent of the local Indians to the construction of an Ohio Company "strong house" at the confluence of the Allegheny and Monongahela Rivers. This installation, like the Wills Creek storehouse and barracks, was to be a fortified trading post at which, Gist stressed, trade goods would be made available at highly favorable rates. But it would also serve two other purposes, about which Gist had less to say. First, its location at the Forks would make it the strategic key to the valley of the Ohio; second, it would become the focus for a settlement of two hundred pioneer families that the company intended soon to establish at the Forks. These matters were of concern to every Indian leader at the conference, since they knew full well that a permanent Anglo-American settlement would gravely threaten their peoples' ability to control their lands, and hence their destinies. But Tanaghrisson, as sole spokesman of the Iroquois League, was the only figure with whom Gist and Croghan would deal, and his overwhelming desire, in the aftermath of Céloron's expedition, was to obtain enough material support from the British to shore up his shaky standing with the peoples he was supposed to lead.

Thus Tanaghrisson—persuaded no less by the thousand pounds' worth of gifts that Gist had heaped on the ground before him than by the assurances of goodwill he and Croghan were piling even higher—agreed to the construction of the strong house and remained silent about the settlement it implied. But in order to gain the acquiescence of the Delawares (after the Mingos, the most numerous of the Ohio Indians) the Half King was also compelled formally to recognize one of their headmen, Shingas, as their "king," a status that would entitle him to speak on behalf of his people, and thus to negotiate in his own right. Tanaghrisson tried to hedge his bets by maintaining that everything done at Logstown would have to be ratified by the Grand Council at Onondaga, but his actions testified to the tenuousness of Iroquois influence in the Ohio Country. With or without Onondaga's approval, the Delawares would soon have begun to act for themselves under Shingas's leadership anyway. They had grown too numerous and had moved too far west to remain indefinitely under the Confederacy's tutelage. From this point onward, the Delawares and other Ohio Indian peoples would begin to steer their own course.[11]

Of more immediate consequence for the governments of Pennsylvania and Virginia was an event that occurred not long after the conference ended, two hundred miles farther west, at Pickawillany—the Miami town where George Croghan and his associates maintained their trading post. At about nine o'clock on the morning of June 21, 1752, a party of about 180 Chippewa and 30 Ottawa warriors, accompanied by 30 French soldiers from Detroit under the command of a French-Ottawa officer named Charles-Michel Mouet de Langlade, attacked the settlement. Most of Pickawillany's men were away hunting; most of its women, who had been working in the cornfields, were made captive. After a six-hour attack, Langlade called a cease-fire. He would, he said, return the women and spare the defenders (who numbered only about twenty) if they agreed to surrender the traders. Lacking any alternative, the defenders agreed, then looked on while the raiders demonstrated what the consequences of trading with the English could be. First they dispatched a wounded trader "and took out his heart and eat it"; then they turned their attention to the settlement's headman, Memeskia. This chief, known to the French as La Demoiselle, had lately acquired a new sobriquet, Old-Briton, from Croghan and his colleagues. Now, to repay "his attachment to the English" and to acquire his power for themselves, the raiders "boiled [him] and eat him all up." Then, with five profoundly apprehensive traders and a vast quantity of booty in hand, they returned to Detroit. Behind them lay the smoking ruin that, twenty-four hours earlier, had been one of the largest settlements and the richest trading post west of the Appalachians.[12]

Unlike Céloron's little lead plates and letters of warning, Langlade's raid quickly disinfested the west of Pennsylvanians. The Miami chiefs sent urgent requests to the governments of Pennsylvania and Virginia for arms and aid, but the Quakers who dominated the Pennsylvania Assembly refused to become entangled in a developing war, and the Virginians found that they had no compelling reason to support so distant a people. When no help came, the Miamis quietly returned to the protection of their French father. Langlade's bold stroke thus drove the most irritating English traders from the Ohio Country, even as it restored an important Indian alliance. Yet all English activity in the region did not immediately cease. The Ohio Company of Virginia continued with its plans to found a settlement at the Forks, now taking the precaution of building a second fortified storehouse at the mouth of Red Stone Creek on the Monongahela River—a spot just thirty-seven miles upstream from the river's confluence with the Allegheny.[13] Red Stone Fort gave the company its first permanent foothold in the Ohio watershed. It also suggested forcibly to the French that Langlade's coup had been only a half victory over the English invaders.

This was not, as it happened, an accurate inference. The French had always understood English activities in the Ohio as being far more cooperative and highly organized than they really were. Pennsylvania traders and Virginia speculators had in fact never constituted two prongs of a single invasion, but rather had been determined rivals. The interests of Pennsylvanians who made their living by trading with the Indians for deerskins, bearskins, and beaver pelts were in two ways incompatible with those of the Virginians. In the short run, the Ohio Company was a dangerous competitor in the Indian trade. Ultimately, however, if the company's plans to promote the migration of farm families to the Forks succeeded, the new settlers and their livestock would inevitably displace both Indians and wildlife. Thus the Pennsylvanians had done their best to set the Indians against the Virginians, and the Virginians had done their best to return the compliment. Even the close cooperation between the Ohio Company's man, Christopher Gist, and George Croghan, the "king of the Pennsylvania traders," at the Logstown council had nothing to do with solidarity between the groups. In fact, the Philadelphia assets of Croghan's trading partnership had lately been seized in bankruptcy proceedings, and he had fled to avoid arrest. Acting on his own account, Croghan had acquired a highly dubious claim to 200,000 acres of land adjacent to the Ohio Company's patent. Because that claim would have been invalid under Pennsylvania law, Croghan promoted Virginia's interests at the treaty conference as a means of securing his own.[14]

The governments of Pennsylvania and Virginia had also weighed into the competition for the west, pressing claims based on their respective charter rights to the lands near the Forks of the Ohio. Colony agents in London wrangled with one another before the Board of Trade—the British government body that supervised colonial affairs—as vigorously as their counterparts conspired against one another in the depths of the backcountry. Moreover, deep internal divisions within Virginia itself, between gentlemen belonging to different speculative companies, had also retarded the invasion of the west. The members of the Loyal Company—a syndicate interested in securing the rights to territory south of the Ohio River, in what would become Kentucky—had done their best to thwart the Ohio Company's plans and indeed succeeded in doing so until 1749. Only when the head of the Ohio Company became acting governor of Virginia did the company begin to make headway in the west. With his death, the stockholders prudently offered a share to the newly appointed lieutenant governor of the province, Robert Dinwiddie.[15]

French policy makers in Paris and imperial officials in New France saw none of this. They recognized neither the real nature of the British incursions nor the fact that once Langlade had dealt with the Pennsylvanians, the Virginia menace could have been handled more effectively by

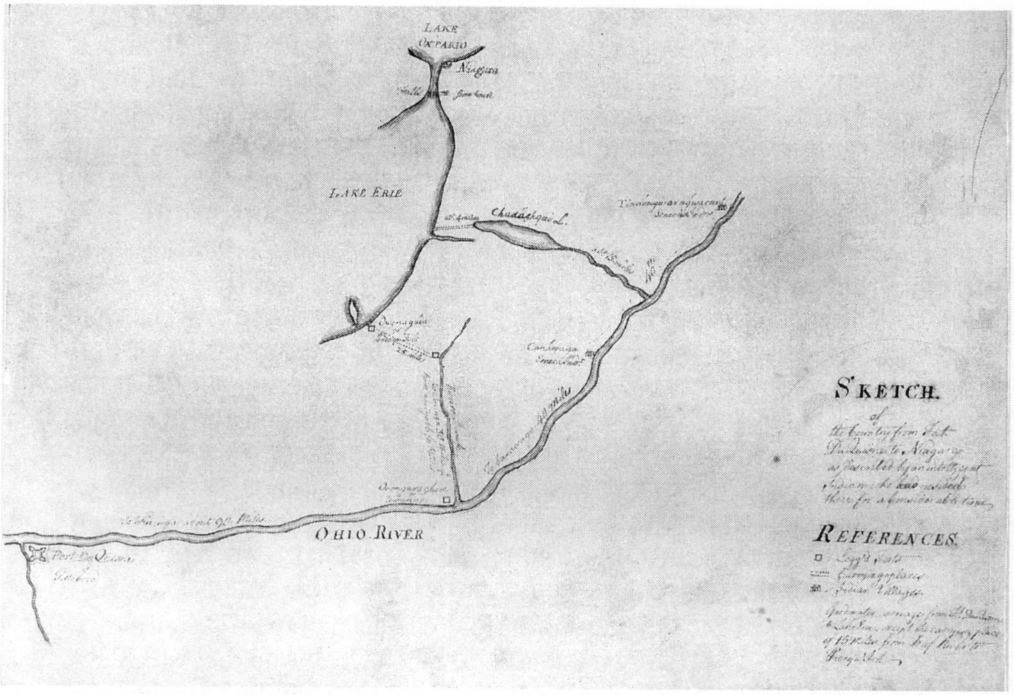

The French chain of forts. This sketch map, made sometime after 1758 from the description of "an intelligent Indian who had resided there for a Considerable time," uses small square symbols to depict the French "Logg'd Forts" constructed by order of the marquis Duquesne in 1753–54; broken lines indicate portage roads. A note accompanying the legend describes "Good water carriage from Ft. DuQuesne to Lake Erie, except the carrying place of 15 Miles from Beef River to Presqu'Isle." *Courtesy of the William L. Clements Library at the University of Michigan.*

diplomacy than force. Tanaghrisson, after all, had been willing to give the Virginians permission to build a trading post at the Forks only because he understood this as a gesture of alliance, and hence a measure of defense against French military domination. Had the French offered the Delawares, Shawnees, and Mingos cheap trade goods and reassurances instead of seeking to enforce a new hegemony over the Ohio Country, the outcome might have been different. Both the personality and the instructions of the new governor-general, however, precluded moderation.

The marquis de Duquesne, like his predecessor and patron the comte de La Galissonière, was a blunt naval officer who preferred action to talk.

A man utterly unafflicted by self-doubt, Duquesne arrived at Québec in July 1752 carrying orders that were deeply consistent with his natural bent. His superior, the minister of marine, had stressed the critical importance of preserving communication between the Canadian and the Illinois settlements via the Ohio and directed him "to make every possible effort to drive the English from our lands . . . and to prevent their coming there to trade." Duquesne was to "make our Indians understand . . . that we have nothing against them, [and] that they will be at liberty to go and trade with the English in the latter's country, but that we will not allow them to receive [the English] on our lands." Accordingly the new governor required the Canadian militia (165 companies including over 11,000 men) to begin drilling every week and ordered a series of four forts built to establish a permanent military presence in the Ohio Country.

By the spring of 1753, two of the forts were already under construction. The first stood on the south shore of Lake Erie, at Presque Isle. A portage road connected it to the second, on the Rivière aux Boeufs (French Creek), a tributary of the Allegheny River. By autumn, the French had established a third post, Fort Machault, at the Delaware village of Venango, near the confluence of French Creek and the Allegheny; it incorporated a convenient complex of buildings, including a storehouse and forge, lately abandoned by a Pennsylvania trader, John Fraser. The last fort of the chain, which would stand at the Forks of the Ohio and furnish the strategic key to the Ohio Country, was scheduled for construction in 1754.[16]

Whether reckoned in *livres* or lives, this fortified system cost the French a prodigious amount. More than four hundred men perished and at least four million *livres* were spent in the feverish building. Duquesne believed that the English threat was so severe that the haste, cost, and lives lost were no more than the necessary price for securing French interests in the Ohio Country. But the ground on which the crucial fourth fort of the chain would rise—the post that would bear Duquesne's own name—happened to be the spot that the Ohio Company had chosen as the site of its fortified trading post. That single fact would do more to create cooperation among the British colonies than any measures that the fragmented, competitive colonists could have devised on their own initiative.

CHAPTER 3

London Moves to Counter a Threat

1753

In London, the activities of the French in the Ohio Country had long been the focus of concern among the members of the Privy Council, that body of thirty or so courtiers and ministers who advised the king and acted as the heads of the principal executive, judicial, and ecclesiastical offices. Since 1748 the three privy councillors collectively responsible for the conduct of foreign and colonial affairs had gotten on badly enough among themselves, but they had always agreed that the greatest threat to Britain was, and always would be, France. First among these was Thomas Pelham-Holles, duke of Newcastle, who held the office of secretary of state for the Northern Department, a post that gave him responsibility for conducting foreign relations with Protestant Europe and Russia. He was one of the most experienced men in Britain's government, and nothing in his past reassured him when it came to the French. Newcastle—a man no less remarkable for his eccentricities than for his accomplishments as a politician and diplomatist—understood French policies in Europe and the New World as complementary and aimed in no uncertain way at the aggrandizement of power. He believed that Louis XV and his ministers would not hesitate to start another war with Great Britain if they thought they could gain by it. Yet he also hoped that Britain could avert, or at least delay, that war by steadfastly resisting French influence on both sides of the Atlantic.[1]

Newcastle's counterpart minister, responsible for conducting foreign relations with Catholic Europe and the Ottoman Empire, was the secretary of state for the Southern Department. The right honorable gentle-

Thomas Pelham-Holles, duke of Newcastle (1693–1768). This engraving depicts a youthful duke, perhaps from the 1720s, following his installation as a Knight of the Garter. *Courtesy of the William L. Clements Library at the University of Michigan.*

man who had held that post since 1748—John Russell, the fourth duke of Bedford—had little use for Newcastle but shared his Francophobia. Finally, the first commissioner of the Lords Commissioners of Trade and Plantations (more commonly called the president of the Board of Trade) headed the sixteen-member panel that supervised the administration of the American colonies, as well as the trade of the empire as a whole. Although the incumbent, George Montagu Dunk, second earl of Halifax, was a person of less eminence than Newcastle or Bedford, he did his best to steer an independent course and avoid being dominated by either duke. In his distrust for France, however, he yielded to neither. From the moment of his appointment, Halifax accumulated evidence of French "encroachments" on the frontiers of the American colonies and plotted ways to increase the efficiency of imperial administration, the better to resist French aggression.[2]

Newcastle, Bedford, and Halifax had good reason to fear France, which seemed at the point of gaining dominance over Europe as a whole. The War of the Austrian Succession had gone badly for Great Britain and its allies. Britain's only important conquest of the war, Louisbourg, had been returned to France at the Treaty of Aix-la-Chapelle as the price to be paid for sparing the British army in Europe. To gain a peace it desperately needed, England had forced its chief ally, Austria, to recognize Prussian control over Silesia, an Austrian province that Prussia had conquered in the First Silesian War (1740–42). Because Austria had gone to war in 1744 intent on recovering Silesia, this concession left the Austrians deeply disaffected. Thus despite formal provisions that restored relations between France and England to the status quo ante bellum, the Treaty of Aix-la-Chapelle left France stronger than before and weakened the half-century-old partnership by which Britain and Austria had counteracted French power. In North America there seemed equal cause for alarm, and not only because the New Englanders openly denounced the return of Louisbourg to France as a betrayal. Céloron's expedition through the Ohio Country had been anxiously noted during the first year of peace, and French agents had been reported within Nova Scotia—a particularly disturbing development, since the overwhelming majority of Nova Scotians were French-speaking Catholic Acadians. This population, a part of the British empire since 1713, was officially held to be neutral in all Anglo-French disputes; but their loyalty to the Crown seemed, at best, dubious.

Newcastle believed that the only reasonable response to this unpromising state of affairs was to treat French actions in Europe and America as two aspects of a single policy. On the Continent he therefore proposed to strengthen what he called his "System," a set of alliances intended to maintain the balance of power and thus to thwart French designs to impose a "universal monarchy" on Europe. Britain's commitment to perpetuating a multilateral balance dated from the beginning of the century and had always centered on keeping France out of the Low Countries, where it could disrupt English trade and whence it could easily threaten an invasion from the superb harbors of the Netherlands. To minimize French influence in the Low Countries, Britain subsidized a variety of northern European Protestant states, especially in western Germany, allowing them to maintain armies that could be called into the field against France; it had also relied on maintaining a firm alliance with Austria, a Catholic power with strategically valuable territories in the

Netherlands, and with dynastic interests opposed to France. Newcastle thus believed that Britain must offer new subsidies to strengthen the Low Countries, enabling them to refortify and rearm against a French invasion; rebuild friendly ties with Austria; and try to create alliances with Spain and Denmark, countries not yet firmly within the French orbit. These European strategies had their indispensable counterpart in Newcastle's determination to resist all French efforts at expanding territorial holdings or influence in North America.[3]

To make Europe and North America the two sides of Britain's foreign policy coin applied what Newcastle saw as the most significant lesson of the Treaty of Aix-la-Chapelle, where France's desire to regain Louisbourg had induced it to negotiate a status quo peace, despite the current preeminence of French armies in Europe. Moreover Lord Halifax, the government official most knowledgeable in American affairs, was adamant on the necessity of stopping French expansionism in the New World. As the man responsible for supervising (and hence corresponding with) all of the colonial governors, Halifax also was the first to be convinced that the French were pursuing a dual plan of aggression in America, seeking to wall in the British provinces both in the northeast, along the Nova Scotia frontier, and in the west, by extending direct control over the Ohio Country.

Newcastle supported Halifax's views on America in part because Halifax had once been Bedford's political ally, and Newcastle was determined to weaken Bedford sufficiently that he would resign: a plan that proved successful in mid-1751. Equally as significant in Newcastle's attention to winning over Halifax, however, was Newcastle's concern with American affairs. The duke supported Halifax's attempts to turn Nova Scotia into a bulwark against New France and the French settlements on Cape Breton Island. Newcastle's backing made it possible to overcome Parliament's reluctance to undertake expensive measures that included creating a new naval base (called, unsurprisingly, Halifax), augmenting its garrison, and fortifying the isthmus that connected Nova Scotia to the mainland—a course that committed Great Britain to ever-stronger measures in America. In 1750 the cabinet had authorized the use of force to resist French incursions in Nova Scotia. It thus marked no abrupt departure from a policy of responding militarily to French challenges in America when, in the summer of 1753, Halifax asked Newcastle to authorize measures that would counter the construction of French forts in the Ohio Country.

Since late 1750 Halifax had been receiving anxious reports from the governors of New York, Pennsylvania, Virginia, and South Carolina, suggesting that France was determined to seize the Ohio Country. The most insistent warnings, and the most forcible arguments for armed intervention, had come in a series of letters from Lieutenant Governor Robert Dinwiddie of Virginia—a man who happened to be not only the chief executive officer of the colony but a stockholder in the Ohio Company. We will probably never know whether his private interest in protecting the company's claims or his sense that French control over the Ohio Country posed a threat to settlers in the Virginia backcountry (or for that matter some mixture of the two) motivated Dinwiddie to sound the call for intervention. What *is* clear, however, is that Dinwiddie's warnings fell on ears already disposed to hear them. On August 21, 1753, the cabinet agreed that conditions in America were grave enough to warrant instructing all colonial governors "to prevent, by Force, These and any such attempts [to encroach on the frontiers of the British colonies] that may be made by the French, or by the Indians in the French interest." A week later, Robert D'Arcy, fourth earl of Holdernesse (Bedford's successor as Southern secretary) sent a circular letter to the governors instructing them to "repel Force by Force [within] the undoubted limits of His Majesty's Dominions."[4] On that same day Lord Holdernesse also dispatched a special set of instructions to Governor Dinwiddie.

It had been His Majesty's pleasure, the Southern secretary wrote, to order thirty pieces of artillery sent to Virginia to improve its defenses. To make it clear under what conditions these could be used, Holdernesse elaborated upon "the spirit, and meaning" of "the royal orders." "You are warranted by the king's instructions," he wrote,

> to repell any hostile attempt by force of arms; and you will easily understand, that it is his majesty's determination, that you should defend to the utmost of your power, all his possessions within your government, against any invader. But at the same time, as it is the king's resolution, not to be the aggressor, I am, in his majesty's name, most strictly to enjoin you, not to make use of the force under your command, excepting within the undoubted limits of his majesty's province. . . .
>
> . . . You have now his majesty's orders, for erecting forts within the king's own territory. —If you are interrupted therein, those who presume to prevent you from putting into execution, an order, which his majesty has an undoubted, (nay hitherto an undisputed) right to give, are the aggressors, and commit an hostile act. —And this is one case, in which you are authorized to repell force by force. Another is if you shall find persons not subjects to his majesty, not acting under his royal commission, presuming to erect fortresses upon the king's

> land, and shall not upon your requiring them to desist from such proceedings, immediately forbear the continuance of them, the persevering in such unlawfull act, in disobedience of the requisition made by the king's authority, is an hostility; and you are required by your instructions to inforce by arms, (if necessary) a compliance with your summons.[5]

Given the state of knowledge of the American interior current within the British government, it seems unlikely that either Holdernesse or George II could have known whether or not the Ohio Valley fell within the undoubted limits of Virginia. Dinwiddie had his own opinion, however, and that would come to matter most.

Within a year, these issues would prove to be of more than cartographic interest. Yet as summer turned to autumn in 1753, they were only one aspect of a matured policy by which Newcastle hoped to stop French adventuring short of war. At that moment other colonial matters required attention, too, and none more urgently than the deterioration of Indian relations on the northern frontier. The Board of Trade had recently learned that on June 16, a meeting between Mohawk representatives and the provincial council of New York had exploded in discord when an angry Hendrick, the Mohawks' chief spokesman, informed Governor Clinton that "the Covenant Chain is broken between you and us." Discontentment over the terms of trade that merchants were offering at Albany and the all-too-evident lack of interest on the part of the province in supporting the Mohawks in the previous war's raids against Canada had already strained relations to the breaking point. Now the attempt by a speculative syndicate, the Kayaderosseras partners, to defraud the Mohawks of more than three-quarters of a million acres of their land had finally snapped Hendrick's patience: "So brother you are not to expect to hear of me any more, and Brother we desire to hear no more of you."[6]

Halifax did not need to be reminded that the Mohawks had long been the most reliably Anglophile of the Six Nations and indeed the only one that had offered its aid in the previous war. Accordingly the Board of Trade ordered the governor of New York to convene an Indian conference to repair relations with the Indians and simultaneously dispatched a circular letter to the governors of the provinces from Virginia to New Hampshire inviting them to attend and take part in the negotiations. Availing himself, as he always did, of an opportunity to promote uniformity within the colonies, Halifax required "that all the Provinces be (if practicable) comprized in one general Treaty to be made in his Majesty's

Chief Hendrick (Theyanoguin, 1680?–1755). This engraving, sold in London in 1755, is the last of several English images of Hendrick and depicts him as an aged, scarred warrior holding a tomahawk in his right hand and a wampum belt in his left. The laced coat and ruffled shirt accurately represent his dress, at least on formal occasions such as the Albany Congress. *Courtesy of the John Carter Brown Library at Brown University.*

name, it appearing to us that the practice of each Province making a separate Treaty for itself in its own name is very improper and may be attended with great inconveniency to His Majesty's Service."[7]

When the Board of Trade's instructions arrived in New York, the acting governor, James De Lancey, set about organizing a conference for the following June, at Albany. Although the board had never before taken such a direct role or ordered the negotiation of "one general Treaty," such meetings were far from unfamiliar in the colonies. Over the previous century there had been at least a dozen intercolonial congresses, in which the provinces had tried (and usually failed) to coordinate Indian policy and promote their collective security.[8] Thus it might seem curious that, as a province facing an increasingly ominous French and Indian threat on its frontiers, Virginia would decline the invitation to send delegates to the Albany Congress. But the governor of the Old Dominion would choose not to ask the Burgesses to send delegates for reasons that were, in his view, eminently sound. Just before the board's circular letter arrived, Dinwiddie had received Holdernesse's directive of late August, assuring him that enough cannon, shot, and powder were being shipped to arm the fort that he and his partners in the Ohio Company planned to build at the Forks of the Ohio. Armed with instructions that he could interpret as authorizing him to proceed militarily against the French, Dinwiddie was prepared to shape his own frontier policy. Holdernesse's promise of support had spared him the trouble of cooperating with Pennsylvania, and for that matter the vexation of consulting his own House of Burgesses, where members involved in other western speculative schemes would cast a cold eye on any action that might favor Ohio Company interests at the expense of their own.

Even so, Dinwiddie did not move precipitately against the French in the Ohio Country for two reasons. First, he was a prudent Scot, inexperienced in military matters and more fussy than aggressive in temperament. Second, and more significantly, his political position within Virginia was too precarious to risk provoking any crisis that might require him to ask the House of Burgesses for money. Since the summer of 1752 Dinwiddie had been embroiled in a nasty dispute with the Burgesses over the fee of one pistole (a Spanish coin worth about sixteen shillings, or five-eighths of a pound sterling) to which he was legally entitled in return for setting his seal and signature on patents for lands granted from the king's domain. It was not so much the size of "the pistole fee" as the principle of it that infuriated Virginia's legislators. No previous governor had ever succeeded in collecting such a fee, and Dinwiddie was trying to do it on the mere basis of his executive authority, without so much as consulting the Burgesses—much less asking them to pass a law granting him the power to collect the money.[9]

Trivial as it might seem, the pistole fee had ignited a political firestorm in Virginia. To allow the governor to collect it, the Burgesses argued, would be to authorize him to collect a tax—a levy to which they, as representatives of the freeholders of the colony, had not consented. Once the Burgesses invoked the Englishman's right to freedom from arbitrary taxation, the dispute escalated into a constitutional confrontation between the powers of the prerogative and the rights of the subject. The pistole fee controversy would drag on until mid-1754, when it would be settled at last, in the governor's favor, by a special Privy Council decision. In the meantime, and in the half-year or more after the decision that it took to sort out the political consequences of the controversy within Virginia, the governor and the Burgesses remained locked in a bitter, immobile embrace.[10]

Thus in the fall of 1753 Dinwiddie could not have acted forcibly to remove French "encroachments" from the Ohio Country even if he had wanted to. Instead he decided to send an emissary to the region to acquaint the French with George II's desire that they "desist" from constructing more forts and withdraw from the installations they had already built.[11] The man Dinwiddie chose for this mission, Major George Washington, was an unlikely candidate in that he had no more experience as a diplomat than he had command of French; and he was, moreover, just twenty-one years old. Yet Washington, young as he was, had three important qualifications: a close connection with the Ohio Company, the hardihood to undertake the journey, and an obvious eagerness to go. His longing to see the west and to prove himself worthy of public trust was sufficient to overcome whatever doubts he may have felt when Dinwiddie offered him the mission. Like so many of his better qualities, Washington's capacity for misgiving was something that would only develop with time.

CHAPTER 4

Washington Steps onto the Stage . . .

1753–1754

THROUGH THE untimely deaths of his father and older half brother, George Washington had recently become the master of substantial plantation holdings in the Northern Neck and gained a somewhat firmer social footing. His father, Augustine, had stood solidly enough within the ranks of the Virginia gentry but made no pretext of equality with the province's grandees. Washington's own connections with the greatest of the Northern Neck families, the Fairfaxes, had been strong enough to get him invited, five years before, to help survey Fairfax holdings in the Shenandoah Valley, and thus to begin acquiring the knowledge that had launched him on the complementary careers of surveyor and land speculator. Fairfax connections had also secured two modest public offices, as adjutant general of militia and as surveyor of Culpeper County, which conferred a modest income and, more important, a degree of public status. Yet however highly Thomas, Lord Fairfax, may have regarded the young neighbor with whom he rode to the hounds, Washington never really amounted to more than a protégé.

His schooling had been haphazard, and much of what he knew beyond the basics that his tutors could provide—for example, his knowledge of surveying, of military tactics and strategy, of English literature, of polite manners—he had taught himself by reading. He had always been, and would remain, an eager self-improver; but he lacked polish, and he would lose his sense of social unease with agonizing slowness. Certainly he had not lost it at age twenty-one, when he was still recognizably related to the adolescent who practiced his penmanship by copying out dozens of maxims from a comportment manual. "When in Company," one admonished, "put not your Hands to any Part of the Body, not usualy Discovered"; "Spit not in the Fire," warned another, "especially if there be meat before it." By 1753, the boy who had once found it necessary to remind himself to "Kill no Vermin as Fleas, lice ticks &c in the Sight of Others, [and] if you See any filth or thick Spittle put your foot Dexteriously upon it," had grown to a towering height (six feet, two inches) and become a superb horseman. But he had yet to develop self-assurance to match his stature. Perhaps in compensation for the awkwardness he felt socially, and perhaps also in an attempt to govern a dangerous temper, Washington had already begun to cultivate a reserved, even aloof manner. He had few close friends and evidently wanted no more. Rather than companionship he yearned for public recognition, "reputation," fame. Surely this ambition was what overrode whatever doubts he may have had when Dinwiddie asked him to carry the letter to the French, for to decline such a mission would have jeopardized his reputation as a public-spirited gentleman. Moreover, the opportunity to see for himself a region in which he had lately acquired a speculative interest was too good to pass up.[1]

Thus as soon as his instructions and the letter he was to carry to the French commandant at Fort LeBoeuf were complete, Washington left Williamsburg for the Ohio Country. At Fredericksburg he picked up Jacob Van Braam, a Dutch friend of the family who had once taught him fencing and who spoke French more or less reliably. At Wills Creek he hired the Ohio Company's agent, Christopher Gist, to guide him into the valley, and retained four other backwoodsmen to accompany them as hunters, horse-wranglers, and bodyguards.[2] As the party descended the Youghiogheny to the Monongahela and the Ohio, Washington examined the country with a surveyor's eye. He found that the Forks of the Ohio would indeed furnish an ideal site for a fort with "the entire Command of the Monongahela," which would also be "extremely well designed for Water Carriage, as [the river there] is of a deep Still Nature." Gathering intelligence as they went—from the refugee trader John Fraser at his new post on the Monongahela, from a group of French deserters at Logstown—the party learned that the French were in earnest about securing control of the valley. Perhaps even more disturbingly, they also learned that the Ohio Indians were anything but eager to help the English resist France's designs. After considerable parleying with Shawnee, Delaware, and Mingo chiefs at Logstown, Washington and Gist failed to secure a sizable escort to accompany them to their meeting with the French. When they left for Fort LeBoeuf on

November 30, only Tanaghrisson and three other Mingos went along: hardly a large or diverse enough group to impress the French with the solidarity of Anglo-Indian interests in the west.

And indeed the French at Fort LeBoeuf, although they were impeccably polite and hospitable to the bedraggled party that arrived in the midst of a snowstorm on December 11, were anything but impressed. The rugged fifty-two-year-old commandant, Captain Jacques Legardeur de Saint-Pierre ("an elderly gentleman with much the air of a soldier," Washington thought, missing the measure of a man who had served his king at posts from Beaubassin in Acadia to Fort Assumption on the site of today's Memphis, Tennessee, to Fort La Jonquière, 350 miles northwest of modern Winnipeg), looked upon Dinwiddie's letter and the solemn young man who presented it with equal parts amusement and concern. "The lands upon the River Ohio," he read in the governor's letter,

> are so notoriously known to be the property of the Crown of Great Britain that it is a matter of equal concern and surprise to me, to hear that a body of French forces are erecting fortresses and making settlements upon that river, within his Majesty's dominions.
>
> The many and repeated complaints I have received of these acts of hostility lay me under the necessity of sending . . . to complain to you of the encroachments thus made, and of the injuries done to the subjects of Great Britain. . . . I must desire you to acquaint me by whose authority and instructions you have lately marched from Canada with an armed force, and invaded the King of Great Britain's territories, in the manner complained of; that according to the purport and resolution of your answer I may act agreeable to the commission I am honored with from the King, my master.
>
> However, sir, in obedience with my instructions, it becomes my duty to require your peaceable departure; and that you would forbear prosecuting a purpose so interruptive of the harmony and good understanding, which his Majesty is desirous to continue and cultivate with the most Christian King.

While Legardeur and his officers retired to compose a reply, Washington made notes on the dimensions and defenses of the small square palisade and the barracks that lay outside its walls and sent his men to count the large numbers of canoes (some 220, "besides many others which were blocked-out") being readied "to convey their forces down in the Spring." The French clearly meant business; and the reply that Legardeur gave

Washington to carry back to Dinwiddie made it clear that they were in no mood to abandon their enterprise.[3]

The "rights of the King, my master," Legardeur had written, "to the lands situated along the Ohio," were "incontestable," but it was not his job to argue the point. He would forward Dinwiddie's letter to the marquis Duquesne, so that the proper authorities could decide what to make of "the pretensions of the King of Great Britain." In the meantime, "as to the summons you send me to retire, I do not think myself obliged to obey it. Whatever may be your instructions, mine bring me here by my general's order; and I entreat you, Sir, to be assured that I shall attempt to follow them with all the exactness and determination which can be expected from a good officer." To Washington's chagrin, Tanaghrisson and his Mingos decided to stay and confer further with the French, but the Virginians had seen and heard enough. They left on December 16. A month later, after risking—and twice nearly losing—his life in a headlong return, Washington rode into Williamsburg, reported directly to the governor, and handed him the French reply.[4]

Convinced by Washington's report that Virginia was now facing a crisis in the west, Dinwiddie asked the weary major to produce an account of his journey for publication and immediately summoned the provincial council. The members of the upper house, more tractable than the Burgesses, listened to Washington's account, read Legardeur de Saint-Pierre's letter, and agreed with Dinwiddie. The French, by refusing to "desist" from building forts and by declining to evacuate the Ohio Country, had committed "an hostility" within the explicit meaning of Holdernesse's instructions; thus it had become Dinwiddie's duty to drive them out, or at least to prevent them from proceeding further, by force of arms. With the council's consent, Dinwiddie therefore ordered the raising of two hundred men, who would proceed under Washington (now promoted to lieutenant colonel) to the Forks of the Ohio and defend Virginia's interests against further French encroachments. At the same time, the governor sent military commissions to the Indian traders and Ohio Company agents already in the region, thus giving the construction of the company's strong house at the Forks the color of an official act. To William Trent—the brother-in-law and former business partner of George Croghan, now an Ohio Company factor in charge of fort and storehouse building—Dinwiddie sent a commission as a captain of Virginia militia, with orders to raise a company of men "to keep Possession of His Majesty's Lands on the Ohio; & the Waters thereof."[5] John Fraser, whose storehouse and smithy the French had taken over as the nucleus of their fort at Venango, became his lieutenant; while Edward Ward, a third refugee from Pennsylvania and George Croghan's half brother, was commissioned as the company's ensign. Construction of the fort at the Forks, which would otherwise have started in the spring, was pushed ahead to begin immediately, in the hope of forestalling the French from seizing the site once the rivers became navigable. Finally, Dinwiddie notified the governors of provinces from Massachusetts Bay to South Carolina of an impending crisis in the backcountry and asked them to stand ready to come to Virginia's assistance.

Only then, after all these preparations were well under way, did the governor call the House of Burgesses into special session and ask for the money necessary to pay for everything. Faced when they convened on February 14 with the fait accompli of war measures already undertaken, the Burgesses did their patriotic duty and appropriated ten thousand pounds, but only after attaching provisions that guaranteed them strict oversight of all expenditures. A war may have been in the offing, but the legislators were not such fools as to forget that the threat to their own authority (and even perhaps to their rights as Englishmen) came not from the French but from the rotund Scot who demanded that they outfit an expedition to the Ohio Country. The last thing they intended to do was to give an unpopular governor carte blanche to start a war that, for all they knew, would be no more than a pretext to expand the scope of the prerogative in Virginia government while enriching himself and his Ohio Company cronies at public expense.[6]

As Dinwiddie and the wary Burgesses circled one another at Williamsburg, fort-building proceeded apace at the Forks. Captain Trent's company of volunteers arrived to begin construction on February 17—much to the relief of Tanaghrisson, who at last could point to evidence that the English intended to do more than just talk about resisting French incursions in the valley. Indians from up the Allegheny had already brought word that the spring floods would bring a strong French force to take possession of the Forks. The arrival of Trent, who brought a large present from the governor of Virginia as well as men, arms, and tools, meant that the Half King now had some hope of rebuilding his eroded influence over the Ohio Indians. Tanaghrisson himself laid the fort's first log in place, declaring (through the translation of George Croghan, lately arrived to investigate whatever commercial opportunities the situation might afford) that the fort would belong to the Indians as well as to the English. Together they would make war on the French, he said, should the French try to intervene. These brave words had little to do with a current state of affairs in which the Shawnees, the Delawares, and most of the Mingos were already ignoring him. In the midst of a hard winter, with uncertain prospects for the future and with no reason to trust the English, they had no intention of doing more than biding their time and then pursuing their own interests in whatever Anglo-French confrontations might ensue.[7]

The depth and consequences of the Ohio Indians' indifference became clear in March when the fort-builders began to run low on supplies, for the Delawares who lived in the vicinity of the Forks refused to hunt to feed the Virginians. Despite Trent's willingness to pay well ("even Seven Shill[ing]s & six pence for a Turkey"), the construction party soon found itself living on Indian corn and flour. Thus even though everyone knew that the French would soon arrive, the shortages forced Captain Trent to return east of the mountains for provisions. Ensign Ward stayed on to direct construction, which was nearing completion on April 13 when word reached the Forks that a large French force was descending the Allegheny. Ward rushed the news to Lieutenant Fraser, who had been staying at his trading post, about eight miles up the Monongahela. Would Fraser come down immediately and assume command, until Trent could return and organize defenses? Fraser's reply—that "he had a shilling to loose for a penny he should gain by his Commission at that time. And that he had Business which he could not settle in under Six Days"—was not exactly what Ward had hoped to hear. Still the plucky ensign declared that he "would hold out to the last Extremity before it should be said that the English retreated like Cowards" and urged his men on to finish the stockade. They had just hung the gate on April 17 when at least five hundred French troops appeared on the river in canoes and pirogues, carrying with them eighteen cannon. Beaching their boats near the fort, the troops arrayed themselves in ranks, marched to within musket shot of the walls, and demanded a conference with the English commander.[8]

The commanding officer of the French force, Captain Claude-Pierre Pécaudy, seigneur de Contrecoeur, was Legardeur de Saint-Pierre's successor as commandant of the Ohio Country. Like Legardeur, Contrecoeur was a tough old veteran of frontier service. Governor-General Duquesne had ordered him to take advantage of the spring freshets and move his command from Fort LeBoeuf down to the Forks, where he was to lose no time in establishing the final fort in the chain that would secure the valley to New France. When Contrecoeur's spies in the region reported that the English had begun building a fort on the site, he had moved quickly, and now he was undisposed to negotiate. He bluntly informed Ensign Ward that he could choose between immediate surren-

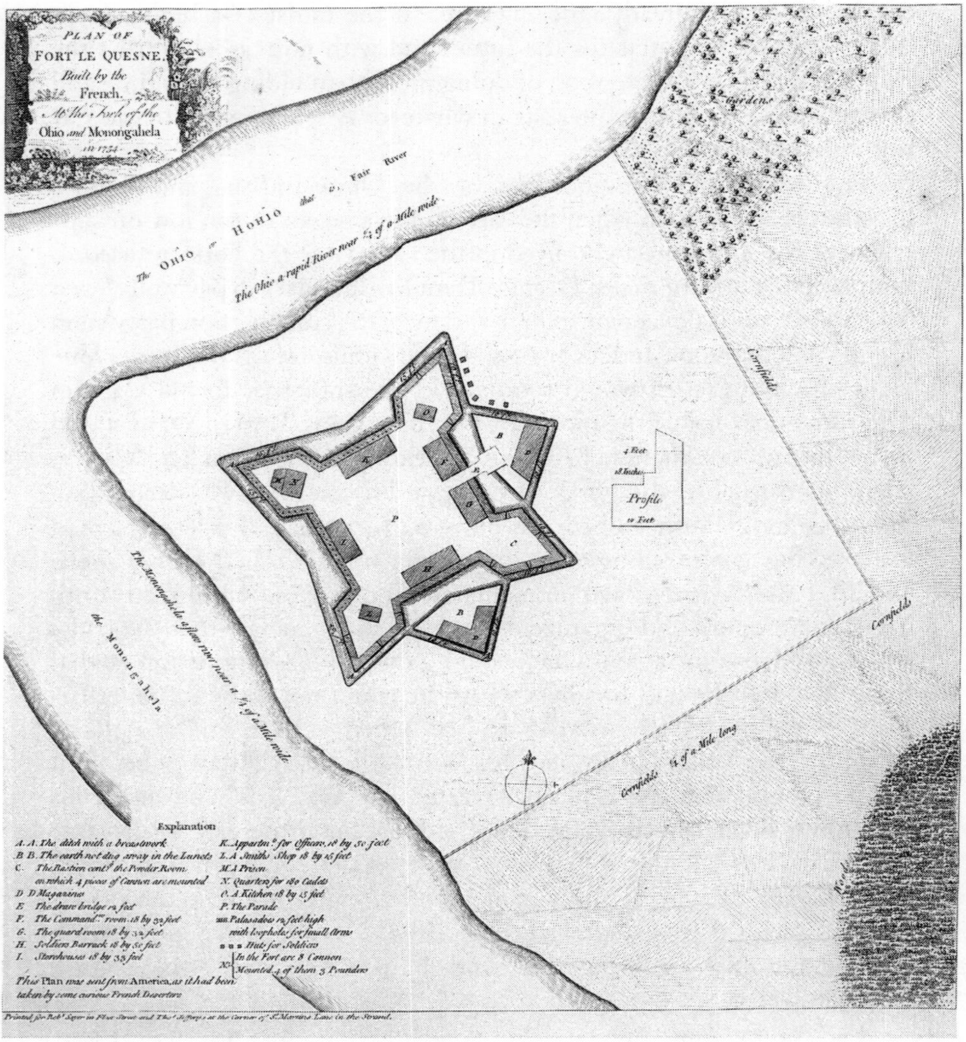

This *Plan of Fort Le Quesne,* the first accurate depiction of the French fort to be published in Britain, was based on a diagram drawn in 1754 by a Virginian prisoner, Captain Robert Stobo, and smuggled out of the fort by the Delaware chief Shingas. The cross-section to the right of the diagram depicts southeast and northeast walls, which were ten to twelve feet thick at the base and made of horizontal logs infilled with earth and rubble. The walls facing the rivers, less likely to be cannonaded, consisted only of a log palisade. The two ravelins—the arrowhead-shaped structures in front of the land-side walls—were designed as defensive outworks but, because of the small size of the fort, eventually came to house a hospital, living quarters, and a storage magazine. The stockaded barracks (hornwork) in which most of the troops lived, is not shown here. It lay northeast of the fort, a one-hundred-by-four-hundred-foot rectangle in line with the right-hand ravelin. *Courtesy of the William L. Clements Library at the University of Michigan.*

der and having his post seized by force. Ward weighed the odds—forty English volunteers and carpenters with next to no food in a hastily completed palisade, against a force of professional soldiers that looked to him at least a thousand strong, wielding enough firepower to blow his fort to matchsticks—and chose the better part of valor. Once it became clear that Contrecoeur would allow him and his men to leave the post with their honor and possessions intact, Ward made no further protest. That evening, as if to show there were no hard feelings, Contrecoeur treated Ward and his men to a handsome, and welcome, dinner.

At noon on the following day the Virginians quietly took their leave while Tanaghrisson "stormed greatly against the French . . . and told them that he order'd that Fort, and laid the first log of it himself." His rage, fueled by the knowledge that French control at the Forks spelled the end of his regency over the Ohio Indians, was of interest mainly to himself. Contrecoeur ignored his complaints, surveyed the pitiable stockade that the Virginians had just finished, and decided to build in its place a fort worthy to bear the name of the governor-general of New France. The post that Contrecoeur's men would erect at the confluence of the Monongahela and the Allegheny would be no mere palisade but a compact square measuring 160 feet between the points of its four bastions. Flanked by two ravelins and surrounded by a dry moat, the log-and-earth walls of Fort Duquesne eventually enclosed a small central parade ground, a guardhouse, officers' quarters, supply and powder magazines, a hospital, a blacksmith's shop, and a bakery. At first its bastions mounted eight cannon; more would be added later. The better to withstand a siege, the fort was outfitted with an interior well and a pair of latrine aqueducts to convey the defenders' sewage impartially to both rivers. Although Fort Duquesne was never large enough to house its entire garrison—a stockaded barracks, or hornwork, had to be built nearby for that purpose—it could accommodate two hundred men in case of attack.[9]

Apart from Detroit and Niagara, it would be the most impressive military installation in the interior of the continent. One look could tell the story: the French had come to stay.

CHAPTER 5

. . . *And Stumbles*

1754

ON THE DAY that Ensign Ward and his men abandoned the Forks to Contrecoeur, Lieutenant Colonel Washington was still toiling up the eastern slope of the Alleghenies, marching his troops toward the Wills Creek storehouse. He had not been able to leave Alexandria until April 2, after failing to enlist the 200 men he had been commissioned to raise and conduct to the Ohio Country. When the news of Ward's surrender reached Washington on April 20, the Virginia Regiment consisted of fewer than 160 untrained, poorly equipped, inadequately supplied, badly clothed soldiers. The only reason that most of the men had enlisted was Washington's promise that, upon completion of their service, they would receive land grants near the fort they were going to defend. The pay they had been promised—eightpence per day, or only a bit more than one-third of a laborer's wage—was certainly no inducement. Nor were the leaders of the expedition pleased with their own salaries. Washington himself complained to Dinwiddie of the paltriness of the pay and indeed only kept his company commanders from resigning over the issue by appealing to their sense of honor. Dinwiddie, who had no background as a military leader but who knew a contract when he saw one, remained unmoved by these "ill timed Complaints." "The Gent[lemen] very well knew the Terms on w[hi]ch they were to serve & were satisfied," he reminded Washington. If they had intended to object, their objections "sh[ould] have been made before engaging in the Service."[1]

The governor underestimated the significance of the officers' complaints, for pay was only one dimension of a larger, deeply disquieting picture that was coming into focus by the time the expedition reached Wills Creek. Dinwiddie had pressed forward on the operation with inadequate funds—the ten thousand pounds the Burgesses had appropriated was soon exhausted—and with little understanding of what it meant to launch even a small campaign in the backcountry. Given the governor's background as a merchant and civil servant, this is perhaps not surprising; moreover, because Virginia had not raised a military expedition on its own since the end of the seventeenth century, there was no one to whom he could turn for advice. Thus an operation had been set in motion when no one, least of all Washington, knew what it would cost or require; nor did Dinwiddie and the Burgesses, obsessed with their own disagreements and determined to run the expedition on the cheap, care to find out. The consequences of inattention and amateurishness only became clear once Washington's little force had left Wills Creek and had begun trying to accomplish its mission. The governor's orders were clear enough: "You are to act on the Difensive, but in Case any Attempts are made to obstruct the Works or interrupt our Settlem[en]ts by any Persons whatsoever, You are to restrain all such Offenders, & in Case of resistance to make Prisoners of or kill & destroy them." As Washington would learn, however, it was one thing to take orders, and another to carry them out.[2]

For Contrecoeur had obstructed the works about as thoroughly as Washington could have imagined, even before the Virginians reached Wills Creek. Too few in number to intimidate the French, too poorly supplied with wagons and horses and clothes and provisions and ammunition to sustain a campaign, the Virginia Regiment had little hope even of harassing, much less killing and destroying, the French. Meanwhile the provinces, from South Carolina to Massachusetts, to which Dinwiddie had appealed for support, proved slow and grudging in their response. Despite Dinwiddie's appeals for their help, no Cherokee or Catawba allies had appeared to join the expedition. On top of everything else, the empires of Great Britain and France were at peace, while Dinwiddie's orders—issued on his own authority, without explicit direction from London—amounted to an invitation to start a war. Taking stock of this unpromising situation, a mature and self-confident commander might well have bided his time, awaited reinforcements, sought better intelligence, advised the governor of the state of affairs. Washington decided to advance.

He planned to push ahead to the Ohio Company's fortified storehouse on Red Stone Creek, a spot less than forty miles from the Forks but more than twice that distance, over a narrow forest track, from his supply base at Wills Creek. Widening the road as they went to permit the passage of their wagons, Washington's men made only two or three miles' progress a day, a pace that at least allowed some hope that reinforcements would catch up to them before they reached Red Stone Fort. The Virginians, chopping and sawing their way noisily through the woods, could hardly have failed to attract the attention of Indian observers.

And indeed Captain Contrecoeur, at the Forks, was following reports of their progress closely as he pondered his options. It was clearly unwise to allow an armed and presumably hostile force to approach his unfinished fort. Yet he dared not strike preemptively, for his orders forbade him to attack without provocation. Eventually he decided to send an emissary to the English force and learn its intentions. Choosing as his representative the scion of a distinguished military family, Ensign Joseph Coulon de Villiers de Jumonville, Contrecoeur instructed him to determine whether the party had reached French territory. If it had, he was to send word back to Fort Duquesne, then seek a conference with the commander and instruct him to withdraw immediately from the domains of Louis XV. Jumonville left on May 23 with an escort of thirty-five men. Since Contrecoeur's Indian informants had described a force several hundred strong, he clearly intended Jumonville's small party to do no more than gather reliable intelligence and deliver his message.[3]

Washington, of course, knew nothing of Contrecoeur's intentions or of Jumonville's orders when he learned, four days later, that a party of French soldiers was scouting his position. Since May 24 his men had been encamped in Great Meadows, a marshy clearing perhaps a mile long by a quarter mile wide, tucked between the hills that flanked two imposing mountains, Laurel Ridge and Chestnut Ridge. Because Great Meadows halved the distance between Wills Creek and Red Stone Fort, because a constant stream ran through it, and because its grasses could feed the expedition's draft animals, Washington planned to erect a fortified post there. The Virginians were accordingly entrenching, clearing brush, and preparing to build a stockade on the morning of May 27 when Washington's old guide Christopher Gist rode into camp. At noon on the previous day, Gist said, a party of French troops had passed his trading post, a way station twelve miles to the north. He had seen signs of their march while riding to Great Meadows. The tracks were less than five miles away.[4]

Washington, concerned about a surprise attack, ordered Captain Peter Hogg to take seventy-five men and intercept the French between the meadows and the Monongahela, where they presumably had left their canoes. His concern changed to alarm after sunset, however, when a warrior arrived with a message from Tanaghrisson, who had encamped with a small group of Mingos a few miles away: the Half King himself had located the French camp just beyond Laurel Ridge, about seven miles northwest of Washington's position. Washington, realizing that he had sent half his troops off in the wrong direction, decided that he had to take action. Setting off before ten o'clock "in a heavy Rain and a Night as dark as Pitch" with forty-seven men (half of the number left at Great Meadows), Washington made for Tanaghrisson's camp. When the Virginians arrived at "about Sun-rise," Washington and Tanaghrisson conferred, then "concluded that we should fall on them together." Washington's men, together with the Half King and several warriors, set off toward the hollow where the French had camped, then paused a short way off while two Indians went ahead "to discover where they were, as also their Posture, and what Sort of Ground was thereabout." Then, as Washington described it in his diary,

> we formed ourselves for an Engagement, marching one after the other, in the *Indian* Manner: We were advanced pretty near to them, as we thought, when they discovered us; whereupon I ordered my company to fire; mine was supported by that of Mr. *Wag[gonn]er's,* and my Company and his received the whole Fire of the *French,* during the greatest Part of the Action, which only lasted a Quarter of an Hour, before the Enemy was routed.
>
> We killed Mr. *de Jumonville,* the commander of that Party, as also nine others; we wounded one, and made Twenty-one Prisoners, among whom were M. *la Force,* M. *Drouillon,* and two Cadets. The *Indians* scalped the Dead, and took away the most Part of their Arms. . . .[5]

This was hardly a detailed account of the action, but it was the one that Washington was prepared to stand behind. He so nearly replicated it on May 29 in his official reports to Dinwiddie, and again (with flourishes appropriate for a kid brother's consumption) in a letter to Jack Washington on May 31, that one might reasonably assume that he made his diary entry as a memorandum of record. His account was not, however, the only version of the skirmish.[6]

In the confusion of the firing, one of Jumonville's soldiers managed to hide in the woods, where he watched the fight and part of its aftermath before slipping away to make his report. Contrecoeur described it in a letter to Duquesne on June 2:

> One of that Party, *Monceau* by Name, a *Canadian,* made his Escape and tells us that they had built themselves Cabbins, in a low Bottom, where they sheltered themselves, as it rained hard. About seven

> o'Clock the next Morning, they saw themselves surrounded by the *English* on one Side and the *Indians* on the Other. The *English* gave them two Volleys, but the *Indians* did not fire. Mr. *de Jumonville,* by his Interpreter, told them to desist, that he had something to tell them. Upon which they ceased firing. Then Mr. *de Jumonville* ordered the Summons which I had sent them to retire, to be read. . . . The aforesaid *Monceau,* saw all our *Frenchmen* coming up close to Mr. *de Jumonville,* whilst they were reading the Summons, so that they were all in Platoons, between the *English* and the *Indians,* during which Time, said *Monceau* made the best of his Way to us, partly by Land through the Woods, and partly along the River *Monaungahela,* in a small Canoe. This is all, Sir, I could learn from said *Monceau.*

Contrecoeur, however, had a conclusion for the story, provided by another witness. An Indian from Tanaghrisson's camp had come to Fort Duquesne and informed him "that Mr. *de Jumonville* was killed by a Musket-Shot in the Head, whilst they were reading the Summons; and the *English* would afterwards have killed all our Men, had not the Indians who were present, by rushing between them and the *English,* prevented their Design."[7]

Here, then, is a different event from the one in Washington's diary. In Washington's narrative the action occurs cataclysmically: the Virginians, in self-defense, unleash a deadly fire that leaves ten men dead and one wounded. The Indians take no active part until the skirmish is over, then scalp and despoil the enemy dead. Monceau's version agrees with Washington's only insofar as Indians are present but take no direct role in the combat. It differs in that the English fire first, in two volleys, after which the action breaks off: Jumonville calls for a cease-fire to allow the "summons" to be translated, and the French gather around him, flanked by Indians on one side and English on the other. Monceau slips away with Jumonville still alive and the summons being translated, sees no more, and hears no more shots. The denouement, provided by a witness from the Half King's camp, describes Jumonville as the victim of an English coup de grâce administered before he can finish explaining his mission. Only the timely interposition of Tanaghrisson and his warriors save the French from being slaughtered by the English barbarians. As Contrecoeur understood it, then, what happened was not a battle, but an ambush followed by a massacre.

The disparity between these accounts, unsurprising insofar as the French and English governments both insisted that their troops were innocent of aggression, leaves everything significant in dispute. Was it a fair fight or a massacre? If only Washington's and Contrecoeur's narratives existed, we could never know. But two other accounts also survive, and between them it becomes possible not only to understand what happened, but why.

The most plausible, relatively complete version of the encounter in English was rendered by an illiterate twenty-year-old Irishman from Washington's regiment who was not in fact a member of his detachment on the morning of May 28. Private John Shaw, however, heard detailed accounts of the engagement from soldiers who had been present, and he recounted them in a sworn statement before South Carolina's governor on August 21:

> That an Indian and a White Man haveing brought Col. Washington Information that a Party of French consisting of five and thirty Men were out [scouting] and lay about six miles off upon which Col. Washington with about forty Men and Capt. Hogg with a Party of forty more and the Half King with his Indians consisting of thirteen imediately set out in search of them, but haveing taken different Roads Col. Washington with his Men and the Indians first came up with them and found them encamped between two Hills[. It] being early in the morning some of them were asleep and some eating, but haveing heard a Noise they were imediately in great Confusion and betook themselves to their Arms and as this Deponent has heard, one of [the French] fired a Gun upon which Col. Washington gave the Word for all his Men to fire. Several of them being killed, the Rest betook themselves to flight, but our Indians haveing gone round the French when they saw them imediately fled back to the English and delivered up their Arms desireing Quarter which was accordingly promised them.
>
> Some Time after the Indians came up the Half King took his Tomahawk and split the Head of the French Captain haveing first asked if he was an Englishman and haveing been told he was a French Man. He then took out his Brains and washed his Hands with them and then scalped him. All this he [Shaw] has heard and never heard it contradicted but knows nothing of it from his own Knowledge only he has seen the Bones of the Frenchmen who were killed in Number about 13 or 14 and the Head of one stuck upon a Stick for none of them were buried, and he has also heard that one of our Men was killed at that Time.[8]

As in Washington's account, the French fire first, the English shoot back, and the Indians take no part in the battle except to block the retreat of the French and drive them back to the glen. As in Monceau's narrative, a pause follows the firing; and, as in the conclusion furnished by Contrecoeur's Indian informant, a massacre ensues, in which Jumonville dies of a head wound. But this time his assassin is not a savage Virginian but the Half King himself.

Several features commend this version, despite the fact that Shaw was not an eyewitness. Much of what can be verified in Shaw's account is in fact more accurate than Washington's elliptical, compressed narrative. He states the size of Jumonville's command correctly: Contrecoeur's official report noted that the party consisted of Jumonville, another ensign, three cadets, a volunteer, an interpreter, and twenty-eight men—a total of thirty-five. Shaw correctly describes the division of the English command into parties commanded by Hogg and Washington; he gets the size of Washington's party and its Indian escort exactly right and the distance from Great Meadows to the glen approximately so. As in Monceau's version, the French are eating breakfast when they discover that they have been encircled; and as in the anonymous Indian witness's account, Jumonville is murdered in cold blood. Shaw gives a more accurate tally of the French dead than Washington—"thirteen or fourteen," he says, as opposed to ten—a particularly significant detail since he takes care to note that he himself saw the remains. Even his comment that Tanaghrisson "took out [Jumonville's] Brains and washed his Hands with them" makes good, if gruesome, sense. Once the tough meningeal membrane that enclosed the brain had been breached, as it would have been by the edge of a hatchet and the many sharp shards of bone driven into the wound, Tanaghrisson could easily have scooped out the exposed brain with his bare hands. Because the gray matter would have been the consistency of thick, wet plaster, the Half King could in fact have squeezed it between his fingers, seeming, as Shaw said, to wash his hands in the tissue. Most of all, however, Shaw's version makes the best sense of Tanaghrisson's role in the encounter.[9]

The Half King had compelling reasons to kill Jumonville in a public, spectacular way. After Ensign Ward surrendered the fort, Tanaghrisson had "stormed greatly against the French," but the Delawares and Shawnees had paid him no heed. Soon thereafter he left the Forks as a refugee. His party, encamped near Great Meadows, consisted of about eighty people, mostly women and children, virtually all of them Mingos. Only about a dozen warriors had followed him. Everything about the group suggested the flight of a man, his family, and his immediate supporters. If he cherished any hope of reestablishing his (or the Six Nations') authority on the Ohio, Tanaghrisson would have known that he could do it only with British support. The colonies with which he had previously dealt, Virginia and Pennsylvania, had proven so vacillating that he had good reason to believe that only severe provocation to the French—enough to cause them to retaliate militarily—would galvanize them into action.[10]

Tanaghrisson, then, had ample motive to murder Jumonville—and good reason, thereafter, to send word to the French that the English had killed him, then attempted to massacre his men. But what can we make of Shaw's puzzling comment that the Half King split Jumonville's skull only after first "haveing asked if he was an Englishman and haveing been told he was a French Man"? The final account of the battle, which Contrecoeur obtained more than three weeks after his initial report to Duquesne, holds the key to that riddle.

Contrecoeur's informant was one Denis Kaninguen, a deserter "from the English army camp" whose name suggests that he was a Catholic Iroquois and thus most likely a member of Tanaghrisson's party. Lieutenant Joseph-Gaspard Chaussegros de Léry, commandant at Fort Presque Isle, transcribed Contrecoeur's summary of Kaninguen's statement before he forwarded it to Montréal.

> [July] The 7th, Sunday, at midday, a courier arrived from the Ohio [la Belle Rivière]. Monsieur de Contrecoeur . . . sends the attached deposition of an English deserter.
>
> Denis Kaninguen, who deserted from the English army camp yesterday morning, arrived at the camp of Fort Duquesne today, 30 June.
>
> He reports that the English army is composed of 430 men, in addition to whom there are about 30 savages. . . .
>
> That Monsieur de Jumonville had been killed by an English detachment which surprised him[. T]hat that officer had gone out to communicate his orders to the English commander[. N]otwithstanding the discharge of musket fire that the latter [Washington] had made upon him, he [Washington] intended to read it [the summons Jumonville carried] and had withdrawn himself to his people, whom he had [previously] ordered to fire upon the French[. T]hat Monsieur de Jumonville having been wounded and having fallen[,] Thaninhison [Tanaghrisson], a savage, came up to him and had said, Thou art not yet dead, my father, and struck several hatchet blows with which he killed him.
>
> That Monsieur Druillon, ensign and second in command to Monsieur de Jumonville, had been taken [captive] with all of the

> detachment, which was of thirty men[.] Messieurs de Boucherville and DuSablé, cadets, and Laforce, commissary, were among the number of prisoners[. T]hat there were between ten and twelve Canadians killed and that the prisoners had been carried to the city of Virginia [Williamsburg].
>
> That the English had little food with them.
>
> That if the French do not come into the territory of the English, the latter will no longer want [to] come into the land of the former.
>
> That the said Denis Kaninguen had been pursued in leaving the English camp by a horseman, whose thigh he broke with a gun shot, [and that he] had taken his horse, and had ridden at full speed to the French camp.[11]

Here again is an exchange of shots followed by a cease-fire during which Jumonville tries to convey his message to Washington; and again violence cuts short the effort to communicate. But unlike John Shaw's informant, who evidently inferred that the French words Tanaghrisson spoke to Jumonville were a question—Are you English?—Denis Kaninguen understood exactly what Tanaghrisson had said, and why he said it. The last words Jumonville heard on earth were spoken in the language of ritual and diplomacy, which cast the French father (Onontio) as the mediator, gift-giver, and alliance-maker among Indian peoples. Tanaghrisson's metaphorical words, followed by his literal killing of the father, explicitly denied French authority and testified to the premeditation of his act.

All of this enables us, at last, to understand Washington's behavior and attempt to conceal the truth of what happened in Jumonville's Glen. Despite his rank as a field officer, Washington had never before led troops in battle. Commanding a body of men about the size of a modern infantry platoon, he seems to have behaved like any ordinary second lieutenant in his first firefight. Excited and disoriented by combat—he later described the hiss of passing bullets as "charming"—and in the midst of more confusion, smoke, and noise than he would ever have experienced before, he could hardly have been in full control of himself and his men, let alone of the Half King and his warriors. The effect upon Washington of seeing Jumonville's cranium shattered is impossible to calculate, but it seems likely that the sight would have unmanned him long enough to allow the Indians to kill most of the wounded prisoners.[12]

That a massacre followed Jumonville's murder, moreover, is the only explanation consistent with the casualty figures that Washington himself gave. Shots fired in battle almost invariably produce two to four times as many wounds as deaths, as the three-to-one ratio among the Virginia casualties attests. The scanty training of Washington's men, no less than the inaccuracy of their Brown Bess muskets and the fact that men firing downhill will always overshoot their targets unless they have been instructed to aim low, makes it impossible to believe the Virginians killed thirteen men (or even, as Washington maintained, ten) while wounding only one. That a massacre followed the surrender of the French also makes sense of Washington's abbreviated account, which collapsed events to make it seem as if all of the French soldiers had been killed in battle. It also explains Washington's insistence that the French were spies and his repeated urgings to Dinwiddie to believe nothing of what the prisoners said.[13]

Finally, such covering-up of the truth would have been consistent with Washington's concern to protect a fragile reputation for military competence. The anxious undertones of the letters he wrote following the skirmish belied their veneer of bravado. On one hand Washington boasted that he had the physical stamina and courage to face whatever challenges lay ahead: "I have a Constitution hardy enough to encounter and undergo the most severe tryals," he wrote to Dinwiddie on the day after the encounter, "and I flatter myself [that I have] resolution to Face what any Man durst, as shall be prov'd when it comes to the Test, which I believe we are upon the Border's off." On the other hand, the future left him worried about his capacities as a commander. Two weeks after the murders of Jumonville and his men, Washington would write that he "most ardently wish'd" to be "under the Command off an experienced Officer."[14]

Thus on the day of the massacre Washington returned to Great Meadows and carefully composed his diary account. The next day, May 29, he wrote his official letters to describe the incident in ways just technically shy of falsehood and sent the prisoners (or, as he said, spies) under guard to Dinwiddie, along with an urgent request for more supplies and reinforcements. Concerned that a French and Indian attack would ensue, he also began pushing his men to finish the fortifications. By June 2 their small circular palisade, aptly named Fort Necessity, was complete, and Washington had prayers read within its walls.[15]

Prayer was certainly in order. Consisting only of a seven-foot-high circular stockade of split logs enclosing a shelter for storing ammunition and supplies, Fort Necessity was about fifty feet in diameter and thus big enough to hold only sixty or seventy men. Trenches had to be dug around its perimeter to shelter the rest of its defenders in case of an attack. Moreover, the situation of the fort and its entrenchments on the valley floor, overlooked by hills, made the position dangerously vulnerable to enfilading fire. So poorly sited and so dubiously constructed was this fort that only an amateur or a fool would have thought it defensible; the Half King, who was neither, tried to explain the ways in which "that little thing upon the Meadow" could prove a death trap. Washington, unfazed, brushed off the criticism in full confidence that the fort could withstand "the attack of 500 men." The facts that he had never before built a fort or come under attack by any number of men at all did not shake his opinion.[16]

Washington's behavior over the next month suggests that it was not merely foolish self-confidence that made him unwilling to invest more than minimal effort and time in the construction of Fort Necessity. Rather, it would seem, he neglected to take adequate defensive measures because he had no intention of making a stand at Great Meadows. He intended instead to advance and carry the campaign to the gates of Fort Duquesne itself.

Given what Washington knew about the French strength at the Forks—next to nothing—and what he thought was happening back beyond the mountains—that an intercolonial effort to supply and reinforce him was under way—his intention to take the offensive may not have been quite as deranged as it looks in retrospect. During the second week of June two hundred more troops arrived from Virginia, bringing with them nine swivel guns (small cannon capable of firing a two-pound projectile). Three days later one of the South Carolina independent companies marched in, adding about a hundred British regulars and forty beef cattle to the expedition's effective strength. Washington had also been getting assurances from George Croghan, whom Dinwiddie had appointed as a supply contractor and who was with the army at Fort Necessity, that a great pack train would deliver fifty thousand pounds of flour by the middle of June. He had hopes of using Tanaghrisson and Croghan as intermediaries to attract Delawares, Shawnees, and Mingos to the cause of expelling the French. How could he know, in the middle of June when he had four hundred men on hand and when things looked as if they would continue improving, that he had already received his last reinforcements, that no further supplies would ever arrive, and that the Ohio Indians had no intention of acting against the French?

A more cautious commander might have expected the worst and planned for it, but Washington was too inexperienced to see prudence as a virtue. On June 16, leaving the independent company to garrison Fort Necessity (Captain James Mackay, commissioned by the king, refused to place himself under command of a lieutenant colonel commissioned by the governor of Virginia), Washington marched his three hundred Virginians down the trail toward Gist's settlement, Red Stone Fort—and Fort Duquesne.[17]

Over the next two weeks, as his men and horses struggled to move their baggage, supply wagons, and the nine heavy swivel guns over unimaginably bad trails, Washington began to learn the value of planning for the worst. Wagons broke down constantly, and horses died at an appalling rate. Every wagon abandoned and every horse destroyed meant that more of the army's baggage and artillery had to be hauled by the men themselves. Each mile the column traveled became a slower, more exhausting mile than the last. When the expedition reached Gist's settlement, Washington, Croghan, and Tanaghrisson met for three days with Delaware, Shawnee, and Mingo representatives and tried to convince them to join the expedition against the French. They would have nothing to do with the plan.[18]

Tanaghrisson now knew that the situation was hopeless, for the refusal of the Indians who remained on the Ohio to follow his lead was clearly hardening into something much more like a willingness to take up the hatchet on behalf of the French. He could easily understand why. For the Ohio Indians to join the English would require them to abandon the valley and move their families, for safety's sake, to the white settlements of Pennsylvania or Virginia, where they would live as refugees as long as the war lasted. Meanwhile their young men would risk their lives as warriors in the service of a government that had never yet shown itself to be a reliable ally, cooperating with a force commanded by a man who had yet to show himself to be competent; and for what? To enable the English to secure control of the Ohio Country, into which their settlers and their animals would move, like so many locusts, as soon as the French had been expelled. It was clear to Tanaghrisson that his position was now hopeless, and nothing could be gained by remaining with Washington's force. When the conference broke up he quietly returned to Great Meadows, gathered his family and all but a few of his followers, and left for Aughwick (now Shirleysburg, Pennsylvania), George Croghan's frontier trading post. There he would die, on October 4, the victim of a disease that his followers suspected was witchcraft. Before he died he would be heard to say that Washington was "a good-natured man, but had no Experience," and that despite his utter lack of familiarity with woodland warfare and with Indians, he was "always driving them on to fight by his Directions."[19] Who in his right mind would fight for such a man?

Washington regretted Tanaghrisson's departure and sent a messenger to try to persuade him to return; but he had never been convinced that Indians could make a decisive difference in European-style military operations and therefore did not depart from his earlier plans to press on toward the French. If he would not be able to count on the Indians to help him attack Fort Duquesne, he could still advance to Red Stone Creek, build fortifications around the Ohio Company blockhouse, and await the reinforcements that he knew were on the way. Thus, despite dwindling food supplies and the steady loss of horses and wagons, he drove his men on, by sheer force of will, to improve the road from Gist's settlement to Red Stone. His resolve held until June 28, when Indian informants brought word that a powerful French force had left Fort Duquesne with the intention of driving the Virginians back beyond the mountains. After pausing for a day to consider making a stand at Gist's settlement, Washington and his officers decided to retreat.[20]

It was a wiser decision than Washington knew, for he and his men were in no condition to meet the force that was advancing from the Forks. Soon after word of Jumonville's defeat and death reached Contrecoeur, his garrison had received a great reinforcement of more than a thousand men from Canada. Captain Louis Coulon de Villiers, Ensign Jumonville's older brother, commanded this detachment and begged Contrecoeur to allow him to lead an expedition to punish Washington and his men. Contrecoeur had already begun to outfit a force of six hundred French regulars and Canadian militiamen, together with about a hundred Indian allies, and he readily agreed. Thus when Coulon de Villiers set out from Fort Duquesne in late June, he was at the head of the most formidable military force for a thousand miles in any direction. Traveling light, they quickly ascended the Monongahela Valley toward the Virginians.

Meanwhile Washington's retreat had become a nightmare. So many draft animals died that the men themselves were forced to drag or push wagon loads of supplies and cannon a distance of about twenty miles in two days' time. When the force reached Fort Necessity on Tuesday, July 1, further retreat would have been out of the question, even if anyone had proposed it. The men were too exhausted to continue, and reports from Indian scouts suggested that the French were not far behind them. Washington's Virginians and the independent company therefore did what they could to improve their defenses and waited for the attack.[21]

On Wednesday night it began to rain. The luckiest of the men slept, if they slept at all, in leaky tents. Most lacked shelter of any sort. Long before dawn the valley floor had become a bog and pools of water lay deepening in the trenches that flanked the fort. At roll call on Thursday morning, only three hundred of the four hundred men at Fort Necessity were fit for duty.[22]

The French attack came at about eleven o'clock. Washington seems initially to have thought that his adversary would fight in the open, and he marched his men out to give battle on the meadow. Coulon de Villiers, a veteran of the previous war and able to spot the terrain that would give him the greatest tactical advantage, preferred to disperse his men along the forested hillsides that overlooked the fort. Realizing his mistake as the French force began to rake his formations with musketry, Washington ordered his men back to the stockade and its outworks. There they stayed, for eight hellish hours, while their enemies fired down into shallow trenches that offered little cover from musket balls and none at all from the rain. Sheltered under trees, at ranges as close to the British lines as sixty yards, the attackers had every advantage, including the ability to keep their muskets dry enough to fire. Since their firing mechanisms were not watertight, the English muskets exposed to the rain rapidly became useless; they could be restored to service only by the tedious process of extracting their balls and powder charges, then cleaning and drying their barrels and locks before reloading. Since the Virginians and the independents between them had "only a Couple of Screws"—the implements needed to extract the useless charges—by midafternoon almost none of their muskets still functioned. Trapped in trenches only two or three feet deep and half-full of water, exposed to relentless musket fire and unable to shoot back at the enemy even when they could see them clearly, the defenders of Fort Necessity made a compact, helpless target. By the time darkness fell, a third of them were either dead or wounded.

As the light faded, discipline disintegrated—unsurprisingly, since the troops, who had already endured enormous stress, now had every reason to think that the French and Indians would soon be slaughtering them like hogs—and men broke into the fort's rum supply. "It was no sooner dark," wrote one of Washington's company commanders, Captain Adam Stephen, "than one-half of our Men got drunk."[23] Washington must have known that even if the rain stopped, his men would be unable to defend themselves against another attack. His first battle had ended in massacre when he had been unable to protect the French from Tanaghrisson and his warriors. Now, with his own men out of control, it looked as if his second battle would end in a massacre of another sort.

Then, at eight o'clock, as the firing from the French lines tapered off in the gloom of dusk and rain, relief came from an unexpected quarter. A voice called out from the tree line inviting the English to negotiate; Captain de Villiers was offering safe conduct to any officer who wished to discuss terms. Washington hesitated—was it a ruse?—then sent his old companion and interpreter Jacob Van Braam off to meet with the French. Captain Van Braam, who had been commanding a Virginia company, realized how very poor the chances of extricating the English troops were. He was therefore probably even more surprised than relieved to learn that Coulon de Villiers was offering a chance to withdraw from the field of battle with honor. He had come, the French commander explained, to avenge the death of his brother and his brother's men. That he had done. If the English were now prepared to sign articles of capitulation, to withdraw from the Ohio Country and pledge not to return within the space of a year, to repatriate the prisoners they had taken, and to leave two officers as hostages at Fort Duquesne to guarantee the fulfillment of the surrender terms, he would allow them to march off the next day carrying their personal possessions, their arms, and their colors. But if the English did not agree to these terms, Coulon assured the Dutchman, he would destroy them.

Van Braam returned to the stockade with an account of the French offer and a rain-soaked copy of the capitulation terms for Washington to sign. He evidently did not understand, or at least did not say, that the nearly illegible document fixed responsibility on Washington for the "assassination" of Ensign Jumonville. No one within the stockade realized what Washington was admitting when he signed the terms, or understood how great the value of the admission could be to the French if a war should ensue. Nor did Washington, or anyone within his command, have any idea why the French were prepared to offer the terms they did. No one knew that the attackers were low on provisions and almost out of ammunition; no one could have guessed that Coulon de Villiers both feared that the fort would soon be reinforced and doubted that he had any right to take prisoners of war in a time of peace.

Inside the fort's leaking storehouse, puzzling over a document they could not read by the light of a guttering candle, Washington and his officers knew only that they were being offered a way out, and they took it. Van Braam and another company commander, Robert Stobo, volunteered to remain with the French as hostages, and a few minutes before midnight Washington signed the instrument of surrender. At ten o'clock the next morning—July 4—the demoralized, exhausted, hungover survivors of the battle straggled out of Fort Necessity and prepared to drag themselves back to Wills Creek. Only then did they realize that the Indians who had taken part in the attack were not Ottawas or Wyandots, traditional allies of the French. With a shock, as one witness wrote, "what is most severe upon us" suddenly became clear: "they were all *our own Indians,* Shawnesses, Delawares and Mingos."[24]

The Anglo-American forces had lost thirty killed and seventy wounded (many severely) out of about three hundred combatants on July 3. The members of the French and Indian party had suffered only three deaths in addition to an indeterminate number of wounds, most of which were minor.[25]

It was July 9 before Washington's force had limped the fifty miles back to Wills Creek, carrying the worst of the wounded on makeshift litters. Washington made his first report of the defeat to Dinwiddie and requested that an additional surgeon be sent to help his regimental doctor perform amputations on the wounded men who could still be saved. His soldiers began deserting immediately and continued to do so, in groups as large as sixteen at a time, through the next two months. Those who remained, whether due to loyalty or mere lack of the physical capacity to desert, did not cease to suffer. "The chief part" of his men, Washington wrote on August 11, "are almost naked, and scarcely a man has either Shoes, Stockings or Hat." It was no wonder that "they will desert whenever they have an opportunity. There is not a man that has a Blanket to secure him from cold or wet."[26]

Defeated in spirit no less than in the flesh, Washington's Virginians were incapable of further action. The triumphant French, in contrast, paused only long enough to destroy Fort Necessity, then marched for the Forks. By July 6 they had burned down the last vestiges of English occupation in the Ohio Country, Christopher Gist's trading post and Red Stone Fort. Coulon de Villiers and his men entered Fort Duquesne to volleys of musketry and cannon salutes, welcomed as heroes who had completed the task Céloron had begun five years before.

The marquis de Duquesne, delighted to receive Contrecoeur's report that the Ohio Valley was secure at last, ordered the garrisons of the Ohio forts to assume a strictly defensive posture, reduced their strength to a total of five hundred men, and directed that a subsidized trade be begun to insure that the Ohio Indians would not be drawn back into Britain's commercial orbit. Confident that he had accomplished his mission, he wrote to the minister of marine, resigning his post as governor-general and asking that he be posted once again to the navy. In October, while he awaited the opportunity to return to France, he performed one of his final diplomatic duties, a task in which he probably took more than usual satisfaction. An Iroquois delegation had come from Onondaga to mend relations with the French. Far from being dead, as Tanaghrisson had wished, Onontio had become the overlord of the Ohio Country.[27]

CHAPTER 6

Escalation

1754

In Williamsburg, the news of Washington's defeat fell on Robert Dinwiddie like a thunderclap. Within a few days he had reported to the Southern secretary, the secretary at war, the president of the Board of Trade, and practically everyone else in authority at home; had written urgently to the governors of the neighboring provinces for aid; had ordered more troops to be raised and marched to Wills Creek; had begun urging Washington to reassume the offensive before the end of the summer; and had started laying plans for a campaign of his own to extract a twenty-thousand-pound military grant from the Burgesses in their August session. With a single exception, all these endeavors failed to produce results. The Burgesses dug in their heels and refused to appropriate funds without first receiving what was tantamount to an admission of defeat from Dinwiddie in the pistole fee dispute. Washington, of course, could do no more at Wills Creek than struggle to keep the remnants of his command from falling apart entirely. Without further money from the Burgesses no further troops could be raised. Substantive help was forthcoming from none of the neighboring provinces except North Carolina, which stipulated that the monies it appropriated could only be expended within the province (a proviso that suggests the legislature was less concerned with supporting Virginia than with enlarging North Carolina's meager supply of paper money). By early September, Dinwiddie was so depressed by his failure to elicit any response to the French threat that he was contemplating resignation. He did not yet know that the reports he had sent to his masters in London were creating the galvanizing effect that all his other efforts failed to generate.[1]

The duke of Newcastle first heard the alarming news of Washington's defeat two weeks before Dinwiddie's official account arrived on September 16. As early as September 5 he had written that the British government did not dare

> suspend, or delay, taking the proper measures, to defend ourselves, or recover our lost Possessions. . . . All North America will be lost if These Practices are tolerated; And no War can be worse to This Country than the Suffering of Such Insults as these. The Truth is, the French claim almost all North America, and from whence they may drive us whenever They Please, or as soon as There shall be a Declar'd War. But that is What We must not, We will not suffer: And I hope We shall forthwith take such Measures . . . as will, for the future, put the labouring Oar, and the Complaint, upon Them.[2]

Newcastle still hoped that decisive action in America could restore balance there without renewing a general war between France and Britain. Such initiatives would need to be more carefully managed than ever to avoid provoking the French to further hostilities, but he believed that his continental "System" (aid to the Low Countries, subsidy agreements with strategic western German states, friendly overtures to Denmark and Spain, a defensive alliance with Austria) had made it difficult for France to respond militarily in Europe. The key to success short of war thus lay in moving swiftly, secretly, to strike a blow in America before the French could ward it off. Caught unprepared for an American war and on the defensive diplomatically in Europe, the French would be so weakened (or, as Newcastle put it, would find themselves pulling so hard on "the labouring Oar") that they would negotiate a peaceful conclusion to the American dispute. By the time Dinwiddie's detailed reports arrived, Newcastle had already begun thinking of sending a commander in chief and one or more regiments of infantry to the colonies, where they could be used to assert control over the Ohio lands. Indeed he had even gone so far as to approach the captain-general of the army, His Royal Highness William Augustus, duke of Cumberland, for support.

Nothing revealed the depth of Newcastle's concern better than his willingness to enlist Cumberland's aid, for in the ordinary course of events he regarded the duke as a dangerous man. In addition to his high station in the army, Cumberland was the favorite son of George II and notable for favoring military action over diplomacy. He had earned his reputation as a general who preferred sledgehammer tactics to restraint when he had commanded the English army in the suppression of the Highland uprising of 1745: it was not finesse that had earned him his nickname, the "Butcher of Culloden." Allowing him too great an influence in formulating a response to the French victory on the Ohio, Newcastle knew, might be the greatest threat of all to peace. Yet because in the absence of his cooperation there was no prospect of removing the French from the Ohio Country at all, Newcastle made the necessary approaches.

Within a week after Dinwiddie's official dispatches arrived, Newcastle and Cumberland had secured the king's approval for a plan to send two regiments of Irish infantry to America under the command of Major General Edward Braddock. The plan of operations on which the dukes initially agreed was a comparatively moderate one, providing for the removal of French "encroachments" in three stages. First, in the spring of 1755, Braddock was supposed to dislodge the French from the Ohio Country; then he was to move northward to the New York frontier and destroy Fort St. Frédéric, which the French had maintained for the previous two decades at Crown Point on Lake Champlain; and finally he was to drive the French from the forts they had recently constructed on the isthmus connecting the Nova Scotia peninsula to the Canadian mainland. Provincial troops could be raised in the colonies to provide whatever support Braddock might need. His office as commander in chief would be expansively defined to give him authority over the colonial governors and allow him to organize the defense of the colonies as a whole. It was a plan that Newcastle approved because it progressed by stages, between which negotiations with France could be undertaken as needed. When the earl of Halifax learned of it, he was "extremely pleased," and not only because it adopted the vigorous measures against New France that he had always believed were necessary. What Halifax liked about the plan was that it created a virtual viceroy in the person of the commander in chief: a royal official who could rationalize colonial defense and centralize colonial administration in the ways Halifax had long advocated.[3]

Unfortunately for Newcastle, Cumberland soon proved uncontrollable. He and his allies—especially Henry Fox, the secretary at war and one of Newcastle's more important enemies—soon began tinkering with the original plan, making it more overtly aggressive. Fox's public announcement in early October that "officers appointed to command regiments in America [were] to repair forthwith to their posts" destroyed the secrecy essential to Newcastle's plans, alerted the French to English intentions, and gave Cumberland a virtual free hand in proposing further measures.

William Augustus, duke of Cumberland (1721–65). Depicted here at age twenty-six not long after the Battle of Culloden and the suppression of Scottish resistance in the Rising of '45, the second (and favorite) son of George II was already captain-general of the British army and the most powerful military figure in Britain. By 1754 he had grown to truly formidable dimensions in both girth and political influence. *Courtesy of the William L. Clements Library at the University of Michigan.*

By the end of October the Newcastle-Cumberland plan for the staged removal of French forts from the backcountry had transmogrified into a distinctly Cumberland plan, calling for simultaneous assaults on four fronts. One expedition was to proceed against the Ohio forts, another to destroy Fort Niagara on Lake Ontario, a third to demolish Fort St. Frédéric, and the fourth to eradicate the French fortifications on the Nova Scotia isthmus. When Braddock's instructions were formally completed in late November, his orders encompassed much more than the use of the two regiments that would accompany him. Braddock would assume command over all existing regular forces in America (the three regiments of the Nova Scotia garrison and the seven independent companies stationed in New York and South Carolina); two regiments that had been deactivated in the colonies at the end of the last war were to be revived and recruited up to strength. A common defense fund was to be established from all the colonies to support the operations of these forces, and Braddock was to be its sole administrator. He had, in addition, authority to draw on the paymaster general for expenses too great or emergencies too pressing to be met from the common fund. The colonial governors were to provide all necessary quarters, supplies, and transport, and to make available up to three thousand men—to be drafted from the militia if too few volunteers enlisted to man the regiments that were to be raised or filled out under Braddock's command.[4]

As the drift of policy became clear, Halifax cast his lot with Cumberland, Fox, and the rest of the militants in the cabinet. Halifax was no diplomatist, but a man whose views on foreign policy had been shaped entirely by his interest in the colonies. Once it seemed as if America was about to take center stage, he willingly ignored Newcastle's insistence that the real issue at stake was how best to stop French adventuring without also sacrificing the peace in Europe. Measures Halifax had proposed as long ago as 1749, such as the creation by the colonial assemblies of a common defense fund, were already being implemented. How could he not have been delighted by the Southern secretary's directive to the governors in late October, requiring them to collect monies from their assemblies and to place it at the disposal of the commander in chief?[5]

When Halifax threw his support entirely to Cumberland's faction and began giving advice on military measures to be undertaken in America—good advice, because he knew more about American conditions and geography than anyone else in the government—his abandonment of Newcastle signaled the end of the duke's ability to influence the formulation of American policy. Quite abruptly, between the middle of September and the end of October 1754, Newcastle found himself transformed from the architect of British foreign policy into an anxious onlooker. He could only wring his hands and hope that Braddock would move so quickly and succeed so brilliantly in America that the French would be unable to defend their positions there; and he could pray that the continental "System" he had worked so assiduously to maintain would forestall French action in Europe. Unfortunately for Newcastle, events in Europe were moving in a direction that made it almost certain that when Braddock sailed, all hopes for a peaceful resolution to the disputes in America would sail with him.[6]

As soon as the French ministry understood the aggressive bent of the British cabinet in the fall of 1754, its leaders began planning to shore up Canada's defenses with a massive reinforcement of troops from France. Time was of the essence, for whereas the British could dispatch their troops to Virginia during the coming winter, the French had no hope of organizing an expedition in time to reach Canada before the St. Lawrence River would freeze over. It was therefore imperative to have troop transports ready to sail from Brest at the earliest moment in the spring, so as to arrive as soon as the St. Lawrence became navigable. Ultimately the French decided to send seventy-eight companies of regular infantry to Canada (nearly equivalent to the number of men in eight British regiments), and to give the command to an experienced general, Jean-Armand, baron de Dieskau. In the meantime, the French government intensified diplomatic activities on two fronts. On one hand, in an attempt to buy time and perhaps even to stave off open conflict in America, they opened direct negotiations with the British cabinet to create a neutral zone in America between the Alleghenies and the Wabash River. On the other, they continued to pursue secret negotiations with Austria that were aimed at destroying the British "System" of alliances on the Continent.[7]

The empress-queen of Austria, Maria Theresa, had grown increasingly unhappy with her alliance with Great Britain since the end of the War of the Austrian Succession, when the Treaty of Aix-la-Chapelle had left the province of Silesia under Prussian control. By about 1751 she had begun to encourage her greatest diplomat, Count (later Prince) Wenzel von Kaunitz, to make efforts to reach a new understanding with France. Although no formal agreement would be signed until May 1756, when Austria and France concluded the Treaty of Versailles, Kaunitz and the French court had made considerable progress toward rapprochement by the end of 1754. What Kaunitz aimed at was nothing less than upending the existing balance of power by reversing Austria's half-century-old alliance with Britain in opposition to France and Prussia, and replacing it with an alliance with France and Russia against Prussia. Thus Kaunitz hoped to give the empress-queen the means to regain her lost province of Silesia.[8]

As of late 1754, Kaunitz's maneuvering and the French responses were still profoundly secret, but Newcastle was already beginning to suspect something was amiss. In mid-December he wrote that "the conduct of

Vienna is astonishing. They act as if they had no occasion for Us." He feared that "the great System is on the point of being dissolved."[9] In fact Newcastle's anxieties were running ahead of his information, since it would not be until the middle of 1755 that diplomatic dispatches from the Austrian court would clearly indicate the shift in policy. Nonetheless, with his position deteriorating steadily and with the aggressive Cumberland riding high in the cabinet, Newcastle knew better than anyone else how much peace between England and France depended upon the actions of Maria Theresa and her diplomats. And if a war were to break out in Europe, no one knew better than Newcastle how weak Great Britain's position would be.

The departure of two understrength Irish regiments from Cork to Virginia on January 16 thus carried an importance that could hardly be overstated. Everything would depend, as Newcastle knew only too well, on Braddock's success in ejecting the French from their positions on the Ohio. All that Newcastle could do was wait, and hope.

IN FACT, events had reached a stage at the beginning of 1755 that made war between Britain and France all but inevitable. The origins of that war lay in a skein of developments so tangled that neither Newcastle nor any other diplomatist in Europe could fully have unraveled, let alone controlled, them. The decay of the Iroquois Confederacy's neutrality policy and the rising independence of the Indians of the upper Ohio Valley; the surge of Anglo-American traders and land speculators into the region; the fears of the French for the loss of contact by way of the Ohio between New France and the Illinois Country; the anxiety of British ministers at the growth of French influence both in the interior of America and on the European Continent; the personalities of Dinwiddie, Duquesne, Newcastle, Cumberland, and even such obscure figures as Washington, Croghan, and Tanaghrisson: in the interaction of all these lay the beginnings of a conflagration that in fact already smoldered on the eastern fringe of the Ohio Valley. The realignment of the European alliance system, the posting of British and French troops to America, and the dominance of aggressive British politicians would take such comparatively minor episodes as Jumonville's death and the Battle of Fort Necessity and make of them something much larger, much more dangerous, than even Newcastle at his most pessimistic could have foreseen. How the clash of tiny numbers of men in a frontier conflict would grow into a world war, how that war would redraw the map of Europe's empires, and how it would transform the relationship between England and her American colonies—such a chain of events would have defied the most exuberant imagining. But in a very real sense, as Braddock's force sailed for Virginia in the first days of 1755, everything had already come to depend upon what it would accomplish, or fail to accomplish, in the depths of the American wilderness.

PART II

DEFEAT

1754–1755

On the eve of war, the British colonies prove less interested in uniting than in jockeying for advantage. The British impose cooperation by assigning a commander in chief to the colonies. Edward Braddock arrives, assumes command, and awakens—too late—to the nature of colonial warfare. William Shirley succeeds him, with equivocal results: the deportation of the Acadians, the Battle of Lake George, and the fortification of the New York frontier. Political paralysis in Britain accompanies a Diplomatic Revolution in Europe. William Shirley falls, the victim of an adversary's ambition and a patron's weakness.

CHAPTER 7

The Albany Congress and Colonial Disunion

1754

THE MASSACRE at Jumonville's Glen and the Battle of Fort Necessity precipitated a stronger reaction at Whitehall than in any government in the colonies, whose legislatures showed a marked indifference toward matters of mutual defense. Even though French and English soldiers had spilled each other's blood in May, June, and July, and even though a French garrison had occupied the Forks of the Ohio, colonial politicians showed little sense of urgency in complying with the Board of Trade's order to send representatives to Albany for a conference intended to improve Indian relations and promote frontier defense. The Albany Congress's limited and ultimately ineffectual efforts to repair relations with the Iroquois and failure to create a colonial union seemed to prove that Halifax and the militants in the cabinet were right: the colonies could be made to cooperate only by the appointment of a commander in chief who would act as the Crown's direct representative. But the colonial response to Edward Braddock's efforts to coordinate colonial defense, and the even more vexed relations of the colony legislatures with his successor, the earl of Loudoun, would more nearly paralyze than promote colonial defense. The first phase of the conflict that became the Seven Years' War would thus prove a period of such consistent defeat for British arms and such strain in the relations between the colonies and the mother country that Britons on both sides of the Atlantic had cause to tremble for the empire's future.

THE DELEGATES who met in congress at Albany between June 19 and July 11, 1754, knew of Washington's encounter with Jumonville; before they adjourned, they even knew of his defeat at Fort Necessity. Such news was obviously of the greatest consequence to their deliberations, since it was anxiety at the prospect of war that had moved the Board of Trade to order the conference in the first place. But to judge from the actions of the colonial commissioners and hangers-on at Albany, the concerns that drove events there had more to do with the usual business of colonial self-aggrandizement than with the creation of the Plan of Union for which the congress is usually remembered.[1]

Despite the outward decorum of its proceedings, the congress fairly seethed with intrigue, and the most important developments took place outside the formal sessions altogether. Out "in the bushes" (as the saying went), a fierce contest raged between representatives of a Connecticut land-speculating syndicate and the agent of Pennsylvania's proprietary family, who were vying for a huge Iroquois cession of land in Pennsylvania. A Congregationalist Indian missionary, the Reverend Timothy Woodbridge, worked hand in glove with a shadowy one-eyed New Yorker named John Henry Lydius—an Indian trader as short on scruples as he was long in experience as a smuggler between Albany and Montréal—in a scheme to buy five million acres in the Wyoming Valley on the upper Susquehanna River. Woodbridge provided the respectability while Lydius did the dirty work, waylaying chiefs at every turn and plying them with liquor until they sold whatever title they said they had to the valley. In addition to a considerable amount for rum, the Susquehannah Company laid out two thousand pounds in New York currency for their signatures. Because all three of the Connecticut commissioners were stockholders in the company, it seems likely that they were not averse to Lydius's methods; indeed, they evidently regarded the deal for the Wyoming lands as their one real achievement at Albany.[2]

The Pennsylvania authorities, meanwhile, had no intention of letting Connecticut speculators acquire title to millions of acres of proprietary lands and dispatched their own Indian diplomat, Conrad Weiser, to negotiate a cession of all remaining Iroquois claims within Pennsylvania. Like Lydius and Woodbridge, Weiser also succeeded in obtaining a deed to hitherto unceded Iroquois lands—in this case everything west of the Susquehanna between 41°31' north latitude and the Maryland boundary—in return for a nominal sum (four hundred pounds New York currency) and the promise of further payments to follow. Unlike the indiscriminate Lydius, Weiser took care to deal only with Onondaga's official spokesman at the congress, Chief Hendrick, and thus acquired a deed that reeked somewhat less strongly of fraud. Yet it was really only in the degree of dishonesty that the two land deals differed, and the conflict between these tainted claims would poison relations between Connecticut, Pennsylvania, the Iroquois Confederacy, and the Delaware Indian inhabitants of the Wyoming Valley for years to come. Much more than its visionary, fizzled Plan of Union, the most enduring legacy of the Albany Congress would be a deadly struggle between Yankees, Pennsylvanians, and Indians over the lands of the Wyoming Valley.[3]

The competition for political power and economic leverage was more subdued but no less rife among the delegates themselves. The New York delegation, for example, wanted the delegates of other colonies to commit their governments to help New York build forts along its exposed northern frontier. The New England delegates, fearful of exposing their provinces to expense in constructing forts that would do nothing to protect their own people, blocked the suggestion. In the meantime New Yorkers and Pennsylvanians competed for trade advantages with the Iroquois while positioning themselves to take advantage of Onondaga's waning influence over the Mohawks and the Ohio tribes.

Yet it was not all, or even mostly, economic and provincial interests that were at stake in the jockeying that went on at Albany: private ambitions and factional plotting were everywhere rife. The leading members of the New York delegation, for example, availed themselves of every opportunity to steal a march on those other New Yorkers who happened to be their political opponents. The Congress's presiding officer, Acting Governor James De Lancey, was not only New York's preeminent politician but one of New York City's leading merchants. Through his alliance with another of the colony's delegates, the powerful Mohawk Valley Indian trader William Johnson, De Lancey hoped to expand his own business relations with the Mohawks and thus to weaken the hold on the Indian trade that the Albany merchants had enjoyed for more than a century. In keeping with their general disposition to expand their political and economic interests, De Lancey and Johnson took great care to cultivate friendly relations with Thomas Pownall, an ambitious and exceptionally well connected young Englishman who had lately come to New York to seek his fortune. Pownall was not a delegate but an informal observer whom De Lancey had invited along as a member of his entourage; he merited more than the usual consideration because he happened to be the younger brother of the secretary of the Board of Trade, a relationship that gave him access to the earl of Halifax's highly significant ear. Not surprisingly, when Pownall sent his account of the congress to Halifax, he stressed the contributions of De Lancey and Johnson and suggested that the board would be well served by placing the conduct of Indian affairs in the hands of a single, experienced individual—William Johnson, perhaps.[4]

De Lancey and Johnson were not the only delegates to the congress to recognize Pownall as a man worth cultivating: Benjamin Franklin did, too. Franklin, arguably the smartest man in colonial America and beyond any doubt the most ambitious, represented Pennsylvania and advocated intercolonial cooperation—his "Short Hints toward a Scheme for Uniting the Northern Colonies" became the basis for the Plan of Union that the congress ultimately approved. But Franklin the representative of Pennsylvania at Albany occupied a position inferior to Franklin as representative of the interests of Benjamin Franklin. The runaway apprentice who had risen to become Philadelphia's leading printer and one of its richest men had retired from business in 1748, intending to devote his energies to public service and the gentlemanly pursuit of science. Within six years he had become deputy postmaster general for the colonies, an inventor and scientist of international repute, and one of the most influential private men in America. By 1754 he foresaw a vastly expansive empire for Great Britain in America—and not coincidentally envisioned a prominent role in it for himself. He was particularly interested in the strategic (and speculative) potential of the Ohio Valley, where he believed the Crown should create two new colonies as a bulwark against French domination of the interior. For these reasons Franklin procured himself a position on the Pennsylvania delegation, and once in place at Albany he indefatigably promoted his plan of colonial union, both with the other delegates and with Thomas Pownall, who was much taken by the energetic Philadelphian and his views.[5]

Of all those present at the congress, perhaps the least self-interested delegate was the leading commissioner from Massachusetts, Thomas Hutchinson. Hutchinson was, in his way, as remarkable as Franklin: a gifted historian, Hutchinson was also rich, talented, and as clearly marked for advancement in the administration of the empire as any American provincial could be. He had been only slightly less precocious in politics than in trade, a calling at which he had made a small fortune even before he graduated from Harvard at age sixteen. He had first been elected one of Boston's representatives in the general court in 1737, when he was only twenty-six; had arranged the financing of the Louisbourg expedition in 1745; had engineered his province's transition from its depreciated fiat currency to hard money in 1749; and had become Massachusetts's most trusted diplomat in intercolonial gatherings like

William Johnson (1715–74). Shown here much as he would have looked in 1754, Johnson was already well on his way to transmuting excellent English political connections and influential positions on the New York frontier (Mohawk Valley merchant, colonel of militia, army contractor, great land speculator, and diplomat representing New York's interests to the Six Nations) into one of the largest fortunes in colonial America. From 1755 through the end of his life he would represent British interests generally as the Superintendent of Northern Indian affairs—the most powerful man in North American Indian diplomacy. *Courtesy of the Albany Institute of History and Art.*

the Albany Congress. These qualifications partly explained his presence, but most of all Hutchinson's close relationship as an advisor to his province's governor, William Shirley, brought him to Albany. Shirley, the most consistently successful royal governor in America, deeply believed in bringing the colonies more closely under London's control, and to that end favored the idea of colonial union. Moreover he, like Franklin, was hardly indifferent to the prospect of taking a leading role in such a union himself. Thus Hutchinson worked closely with Franklin in

Benjamin Franklin (1706–90). This engraving of Franklin in his mid-fifties is perhaps the best visual representation we have of the man as he looked around the time of the Albany Congress: mature, self-confident, and vigorous. He appears here in his public persona as the famed electrical experimenter who had been named a Fellow of the Royal Society in 1756 and a Doctor of Laws at the University of St. Andrews in 1759. *Courtesy of the William L. Clements Library at the University of Michigan.*

creating the Albany Plan, but less to promote his own immediate interests than to forward those of his governor and his province. For Hutchinson also knew that the Bay Colony had borne the brunt of the fighting and the expense of King George's War, and he wished to see the obligations of any future conflict shared more equitably among the provinces.

Only Hutchinson, among all the major actors at the congress, made no effort to ingratiate himself with Thomas Pownall. Temperamental factors helped account for his indifference to Pownall's connections—Hutchinson hated playing the courtier and was a notably cold fish in personal relations—for although he and Pownall respected one another's abilities, they simply never liked each other very much. Principally, however, it was Hutchinson's keen sense of the politic that kept him at arm's

Thomas Hutchinson (1711–80). Shown here in an American copy of a portrait painted in England in 1741, Hutchinson appeared at the Albany Congress as both an older and a sadder man, having been a widower for about a year. He was still, however, one of the most successful merchants in Boston, and Governor William Shirley's right-hand man in the Massachusetts Council: an indispensable member of the Massachusetts delegation and his province's most capable representative in intercolonial relations. *Courtesy of the Massachusetts Historical Society, Boston.*

length. Hutchinson well understood that his patron Governor Shirley and Pownall's friend Lieutenant Governor De Lancey were allied with rival factions within the British government—Shirley owed his job to the duke of Newcastle, while De Lancey was a political dependent of the duke of Bedford. He also knew, as most of the men at Albany did, that Shirley and De Lancey had developed a deep mutual antipathy during the previous war.[6]

As all this suggests, the proceedings of the congress were anything but straightforward. Wheels turned within wheels at Albany: colonies, business interests, political factions, and individuals sought to realize some advantage in trade or land or influence or power. At one level, such activities as these were so commonplace that one might almost dismiss them as the background noise of colonial politics. But the clash of Britain and France in America and the crises that lay beyond the war's conclusion would in large measure be shaped by the enmities and ambitions of De Lancey, Johnson, Franklin, Hutchinson, Shirley, and others like them. All of these men would ordinarily have been too small and too far removed from the center of power to figure in the determination of policy and grand strategy; but now their positions on the periphery of an empire tipping into a great war gave their actions uncommon weight and consequence. The congress's adoption of a Plan of Union unprecedented in its potential for creating colonial cooperation suggests that, for all their reflexive self-interest, the delegates may have sensed the uniqueness of their position, or at least that they understood how extreme the risk of war had grown. No matter what they thought or glimpsed, however, the reception that awaited the plan in the colonial assemblies would remove any doubts about the ability of Americans to make common cause, whether for the empire, their mutual defense, or any other purpose.

Most of the legislatures to which the plan was submitted rejected it with little or no discussion. In Pennsylvania and Virginia, the two colonies most at risk in case of war and therefore presumably the ones with the most to gain from the proposed confederation, nothing happened. The Pennsylvania Assembly, dominated by Quakers, had no use for a union whose main purpose was military defense; the Friends in the legislature took care to schedule debate on the plan when Franklin could not attend and summarily buried it.

The Virginia House of Burgesses never even considered the plan. The feature that doomed it in the Old Dominion was its provision for curtailing the western land claims of provinces with sea-to-sea grants; Governor Dinwiddie, who was as interested as anyone in protecting Virginia's rights to western lands, did not bother to submit it to the Burgesses for debate. The legislatures of North and South Carolina, Maryland, New Jersey, and New York all gave the plan short shrift, while Connecticut emphatically rejected it as inimical both to its privileges as a charter colony and to its ability to take advantage of the Susquehannah Company's newly acquired claim to the Wyoming Valley. Rhode Island's legislature was hostile to the plan but with typical disorganization neglected to take the definitive step of voting a rejection. New Hampshire ignored it; Delaware and Georgia probably never heard of it.

Only in Massachusetts, where William Shirley urged serious consideration and where the memories of the province's nearly solitary stand in the previous war remained strong, did the idea of union receive much support. Yet even there the House of Representatives rejected the Albany

Plan as a measure too corrosive of local autonomy. In its place, a legislative committee suggested a weaker confederation that would be limited to six years' duration. Such ferocious opposition to this weakened plan arose in the Boston town meeting, however, that the legislature refused even to consider it in formal session. Thus by the beginning of 1755 not only the Albany Plan, but the very idea of union, was a dead letter everywhere—even in the colony most disposed to favor intercolonial cooperation and imperial designs. Franklin, losing hope that the colonies would ever unite voluntarily, wrote to an English correspondent that confederation would never occur unless Parliament imposed one—and he hoped it would.[7]

Even had the Plan of Union received a warmer welcome in the provincial legislatures, of course, it would have been doomed in England, for by the time it arrived Newcastle had already decided to appoint a commander in chief as the most direct means of promoting colonial unity in matters of defense. From the perspective of the empire, the only significant result of the Albany Congress's deliberations was that Pownall's reports to Halifax prompted the creation of two new posts, the Indian superintendents for the northern and the southern colonies, as a component of the larger plan to unify and rationalize military operations in North America. Thus when General Braddock received his instructions as commander in chief, they included the order to appoint Colonel William Johnson as the Crown's direct representative to the Iroquois and other northern Indians, an office that conferred sole authority to negotiate military alliances—and, for that matter, land cessions—everywhere north of Virginia.

As usual, then, the colonies had shown themselves incapable of taking common action on their own initiative and unwilling to take any step toward cooperation without direction from London. Whatever union they would know and whatever coherence their efforts at defense would have, would rest in the hands of the bluff, profane major general whose ship entered Hampton Roads, Virginia, on February 19, 1755.

CHAPTER 8

General Braddock Takes Command

1755

Edward braddock's two regiments, the 44th and the 48th Foot, would not arrive until March 10, three weeks after he disembarked in Virginia, but Braddock was not a man to wait around. By February 23, he was already at Williamsburg conferring with Governor Dinwiddie about the coming campaign. Braddock had been the duke of Cumberland's choice to assume the supreme command in North America not because he was an able tactician or even a particularly experienced battlefield leader, but because he was a noted administrator and disciplinarian who was also politically reliable. As Dinwiddie brought him up to date on developments in Virginia and the neighboring colonies, Braddock began demonstrating the qualities that Cumberland so valued in him, in a blunt, imperious way that would endear him to few colonists. The Quakers in the Pennsylvania Assembly had refused to appropriate money to support the army's operations, had they? Braddock fired off a letter to Governor Robert Hunter Morris deploring "such pusillanimous and improper Behaviour in your Assembly," and threatening to quarter his troops on the province, should the Pennsylvanians fail to provide the support he required, without delay. The merchants of Albany, Boston, New York, and Philadelphia were still trading with the French at Montréal and Louisbourg, were they? He sent dispatches ordering the governors of New York, Massachusetts, and Pennsylvania to attend him at a conference he would convene with the governors of Virginia and Maryland at Annapolis in early April: then he would instruct them on how properly to conduct a war. And so it went through all of March, as Braddock issued a stream of commands and directives for quartering, provisioning, enlistments, and dozens of other organizational matters, imparting direction and energy to a war effort unlike any ever seen in North America.[1]

When Braddock finally convened his conference with the colonial governors, it was at Alexandria, Virginia, not at Annapolis, and in the middle of April, not the beginning, but his energy was as undiminished as his sense of how to prosecute the war was uninformed. Braddock never understood that the virtually viceregal powers granted in his commission and his instructions gave him great formal authority but little real influence; never appreciated the extent to which persuasion rather than command would be needed to mold a colonial war coalition. At Alexandria he treated the governors as if they were his battalion commanders instead of men who would have to cajole stubborn, suspicious, locally minded assemblies into supporting the common cause. Rather than seeking their advice, he simply read his commission and then laid out as much of his plan of the year's campaigns as he thought they needed to know. First, he informed them, there was the matter of money: the colonies were to contribute to the common fund that would pay for military operations, and each governor would be responsible for the fulfillment of his province's obligations.

As for the military operations themselves, Braddock revealed that Admiral Edward Boscawen was being sent with a fleet to the Gulf of St. Lawrence with orders to prevent reinforcements from reaching Canada, thus inhibiting the ability of the French to resist the land campaigns that would proceed under his own direction. Braddock's two regiments, the 44th and the 48th, were already on their way to Wills Creek, from which they would depart as soon as possible on an expedition against Fort Duquesne. The 50th and 51st Regiments, deactivated at the end of King George's War and lately resuscitated, were to march under the command of William Shirley from Albany to seize the French fort of Niagara, at the head of Lake Ontario. After driving the French from the Forks of the Ohio, Braddock's force would move north along the Allegheny, rolling up the remaining western forts; then he and Shirley would join forces at Niagara in the autumn. Braddock surprised Shirley with the news that he had been named as major general and second-in-command of all British forces in America—a position for which the governor had more than enough talent but no training whatsoever. William Johnson, summoned to the conference from his home and trading post in the Mohawk Valley, was equally surprised to receive not one but two commissions. Braddock told him that he had been named both superintendent of the Iroquois and other northern Indians and commander of an expedition composed of Mohawk warriors and provincial soldiers from New England and New York, which would proceed to Lake Champlain and seize Fort St. Frédéric at Crown Point. Finally, Braddock confirmed that a fourth expedition, which he had already ordered to be outfitted in Boston, would eradicate two French forts from the Chignecto isthmus in Nova Scotia.[2]

It was a madly ambitious plan approved by men studying maps in London unaware that their ignorance of American geography, politics, and military capacities had foredoomed it to failure. Indeed it was less one plan than two, each of which contradicted the other. Its projected expeditions against Crown Point and the Nova Scotia forts had simply been appropriated from a scheme that Shirley had concocted the previous fall. He intended them as cooperative intercolonial campaigns that, like Louisbourg in 1745, would yield both military victory and a rich harvest of political patronage. When he had proposed these ventures to the ministers, he did not know what plans they were making for Braddock; when the ministers approved his plans in December, they had not fully worked out the implications of what they had set afoot.

Seeing that the Crown Point and Nova Scotia expeditions would primarily use provincial soldiers—troops paid by their own colonies, who enlisted for specific campaigns and terms of service not exceeding one year—the ministers evidently understood Shirley's plans as complements to the expeditions that would employ regular regiments to seize Forts Duquesne and Niagara. But the two provincial expeditions would consume men and matériel, making it much more difficult to recruit enough colonists to fill the ranks of both the understrength 44th and 48th and the reactivated 50th and 51st Regiments; the sheer number of simultaneous campaigns would strain the ability of the provinces to provision them all. It was inevitable that recruiters, quartermasters, and commissaries from the various armies would compete for men, arms, shelter, clothing, and supplies; that expenses would therefore be driven up, preparations would be retarded, and the prospects that any expedition could succeed would be proportionally diminished.[3]

The men who had studied the maps in London, moreover, had seen rivers and lakes and roads as open corridors for the advance of the expeditions. According to their plans, Braddock would follow Washington's road toward the Forks, then ascend the Allegheny to French Creek and Lake Erie, in order to meet Shirley at Niagara. Shirley could make his way from Albany to Lake Ontario via the Mohawk and Onondaga Rivers, then paddle on to Niagara. Except for a couple of short portages, Johnson's provincials and Indians would be waterborne on the Hudson, Wood Creek, Lac St. Sacrement (Lake George), and Lake Champlain,

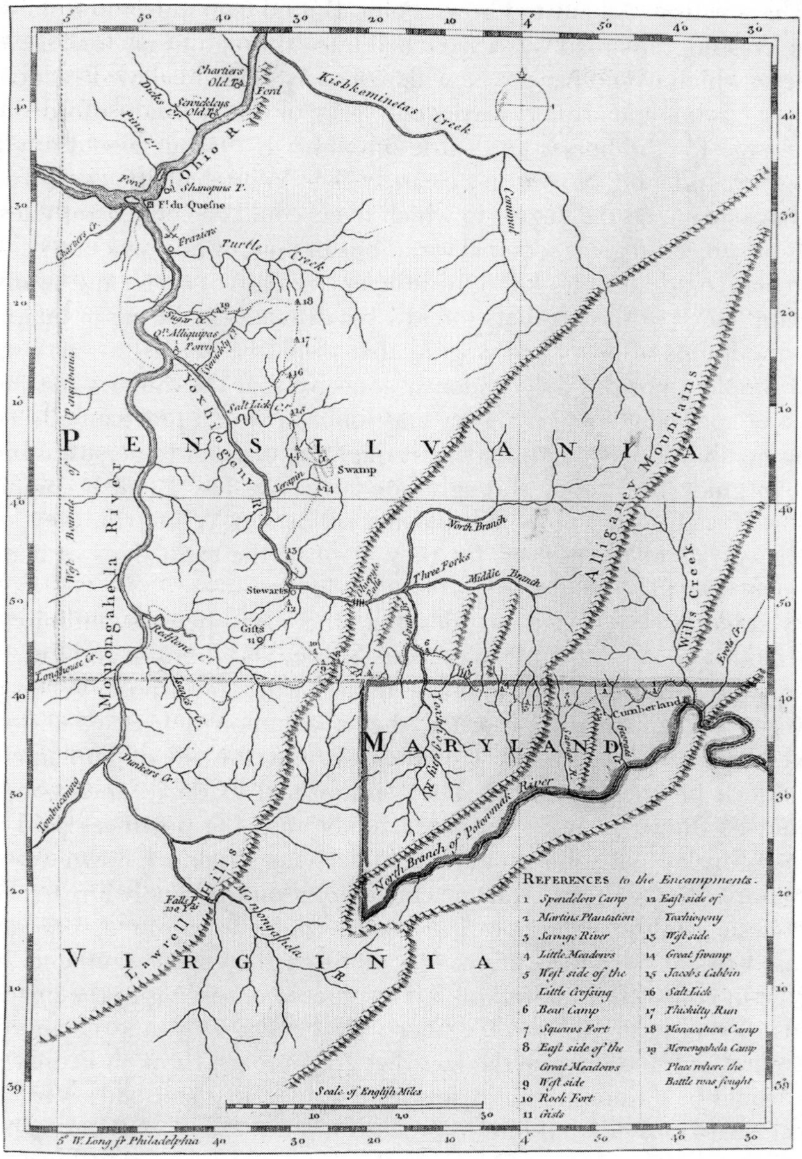

Braddock marches to the Ohio, 1755. This detailed campaign map was part of a set of six plans and maps published in 1768, along with a pamphlet by Captain Robert Orme, one of General Edward Braddock's aides. It shows the route of march from Fort Cumberland, on the north branch of the Potomac, across the Allegheny divide into the Youghiogheny ("Yoxhiogeny") drainage, the Monongahela Valley—and disaster. *Courtesy of the William L. Clements Library at the University of Michigan.*

all the way from Albany to Crown Point. But no map in London showed that Washington's road was a wretched track through heavy forest, every mile of which would have to be widened and graded to allow Braddock's supply wagons and artillery carriages to pass; or that its route afforded little forage for the horses and cattle on which his troops would rely for transport and food. No one in a clean, well-lit Whitehall office could easily have imagined the degree to which rivers could be choked with deadfalls or subject to great seasonal variations in flow, or how evidently short portages could turn into killingly difficult stretches of rough and swampy terrain. None of the planners foresaw the difficulty of hiring or building the thousands of boats and wagons that would be needed to carry men and supplies; nor did they evidently conceive that the military inexperience of commanders like Shirley and Johnson would prove an obstacle. Nor, finally, did anyone think that it might be difficult to persuade Indians to guide the troops through woods that so few English colonials knew. If such things troubled the staff officers at Whitehall, they kept their worries to themselves, for they planned the campaigns as if they were reviews to be conducted in Hyde Park.

Braddock clearly had no idea that the plans he was outlining at Alexandria were impossible to execute. Shirley and Johnson and the governors did and tried to tell him so—to no particular purpose. When the governors unanimously protested that a common defense "Fund can never be established in the Colonies without the aid of Parliament," Braddock brushed them off. They simply had to do it, and soon; he would be drawing on discretionary funds until the provinces paid up. When Shirley and Johnson advocated delaying Braddock's own expedition until Niagara—the strategic choke point on the supply line for Fort Duquesne and all its supporting posts—could be captured, Braddock refused to consider the option. He admitted that their arguments had force but considered himself bound to proceed according to the instructions he had received from Cumberland's hand. Nor would he alter his route to the Ohio, despite the fact that an approach through Pennsylvania would be a hundred miles shorter than one that started in Virginia. His instructions ordered him to proceed "up the *Potomach* River, as high as *Will's Creek,*" and he would do so. Braddock was by no means a stupid man, but he was not a particularly flexible one either, and he was above all loyal. He had risen high in the service of his king not by virtue of his creativity, but his ability to follow orders. Nothing he had heard at Alexandria inclined him to forsake lifelong habits of obedience.[4]

But nothing the other participants in the conference had heard at Alexandria enabled them to forgo their own preexisting habits of belief and behavior, either, much less their old alliances and attachments. Shirley and Governor Morris of Pennsylvania left Alexandria together, traveling to New York to begin preparing Shirley's campaign against Niagara by contracting for the expedition's supplies. Their arrangements made excellent sense. Morris had superb business contacts in Philadelphia, the provisions capital of North America; Shirley had equally good relations with Bostonian merchants like Thomas Hutchinson; both had connections to powerful English merchant houses. Now, at New York, they joined forces with a firm headed by Morris's nephew, Lewis Morris III, and Peter Van Burgh Livingston. The connections thus forged gave Governor (and now General) Shirley the ability to contract for the supplies he needed in all of the major North American markets as well as in London. Even more important, Shirley's ability to award supply contracts gave him patronage to strengthen his political allies in all three of the major northern provinces.

It was a magnificent arrangement, and one that could not have been better calculated to enrage the lieutenant governor of New York, James De Lancey—for bad as it was that the De Lancey family's firm was being cut out of the contracting bonanza that the Niagara expedition would bring, it was worse that all the contracts to be let in New York would benefit De Lancey's mortal enemies, the Livingston-Morris faction. Shirley, typically, had used a military expedition to create commercial advantages for his friends and patronage resources for himself, while at the same time dealing a blow to a political rival. For the moment De Lancey and his kinsman William Johnson were powerless to respond. Both, however, were men who knew how to nurse a grudge, and they would do what they could to show William Shirley that he had been too clever by half.[5]

For his part, Johnson had urgent business to transact in the Mohawk Valley, and after conferring with Lieutenant Governor De Lancey hastened back to his estate, Mount Johnson. From there he directed preparations for the Crown Point expedition and opened negotiations with the Iroquois, on whose cooperation much would depend in the summer's campaigns. As usual, great delays attended the arrival of Onondaga's representatives; indeed it was not until June 21 that Johnson kindled the fire for a great conference, attended by over a thousand Iroquois chiefs, warriors, and dependents. The superintendent had three goals. First, he hoped to obtain Onondaga's commitment to send warriors to aid Braddock in his expedition against Fort Duquesne. Second, he needed to secure Mohawk support for his own expedition against Fort St. Frédéric. Finally, he intended to do everything he could to insure that Shirley's expedition against Niagara would have no Iroquois aid whatever.

By brilliant diplomacy Johnson secured his every objective at the conference. The Iroquois for their part wanted two concessions from the new superintendent—London's repudiation of the fraudulent land cession Lydius and Woodbridge had negotiated for the Susquehannah Company at the Albany Congress, and a reduction in the size of the grant that Conrad Weiser had simultaneously secured from Chief Hendrick. Johnson readily agreed, and on July 4 the conference adjourned. As usual in diplomatic encounters between the Iroquois and the English, more had been said than accomplished. The Iroquois promised to go to Braddock's aid and accepted the arms and presents that would have enabled them to do it—had not the lateness of the season and the great distance to be traveled prohibited their warriors' departure. Johnson himself, thanks to his long personal connection with the Mohawks, fared better: two hundred warriors would accompany his provincial army against Crown Point.[6]

Braddock lingered briefly at Alexandria to attend to a few organizational details after the conference broke up, then rode off to catch up with his army. He found it on April 22 near Frederick Town, Maryland, in the midst of "a fine Cuntry, Plenty of Corn and Milk," mainly "inhabited by the Germans." There he also met two ambitious colonials, George Washington and Benjamin Franklin. Washington had declined the opportunity to serve as a commander of Virginia provincials in order to join Braddock's expedition as a "volunteer"—a gentleman serving without pay in a junior officer's capacity, in the hope of either being commissioned in the field or obtaining his commander's patronage. Because Washington came with Dinwiddie's endorsement and because he knew the Ohio Country better than any other gentleman in Virginia, Braddock invited him to join his official family and serve as his aide-de-camp.[7]

Benjamin Franklin was another story. He had ostensibly come to Frederick Town in his capacity as deputy postmaster general for the colonies, to arrange for the efficient exchange of dispatches between the army and the coastal cities. In fact, the real purpose of his trip was that the Pennsylvania Assembly—concerned that Braddock "had conceived violent prejudices against them"—had chosen him as the man likeliest to smooth out relations between their province and the general. Luckily, Braddock's deputy quartermaster general, Sir John St. Clair, had been unsuccessful in hiring wagons and horses in the Virginia and Maryland countryside. Franklin seized the opportunity to ingratiate himself and his province by offering to procure 150 wagons with teams from southern Pennsylvania.

Braddock, whose expedition could not move without draft animals, teamsters, and wagons, was relieved to meet at least one cooperative American and advanced the Philadelphian several hundred pounds. Franklin quickly composed two broadsides and appealed to his acquaintances throughout the Pennsylvania backcountry to call together meetings and read the announcements. One broadside specified generous terms of payment for animals, wagons, and service as a teamster; the other announced that "Sir John St. Clair, the hussar, with a body of soldiers, will immediately enter the province" to seize whatever horses and wagons the army needed, if they were not promptly subscribed. The latter was not even a half-truth, but it worked a gospel wonder: within three weeks 150 wagons and teams, along with perhaps 500 packhorses, had arrived in Braddock's camp at Wills Creek. At the same time a train of 20 packhorses arrived from Philadelphia, each animal staggering under a load that included a half-dozen cured tongues, two smoked hams, two gallons of Jamaica rum, two dozen bottles of good Madeira, sugar, butter, rice, raisins, tea, coffee, and other items. They were gifts to the junior officers of the 44th and the 48th Regiments, forwarded by a grateful Pennsylvania Assembly, at Franklin's suggestion. Braddock continued to entertain his doubts about American legislatures in general. Benjamin Franklin, however, had removed from his mind all reservations about Pennsylvania's.[8]

CHAPTER 9

Disaster on the Monongahela

1755

THE TEAMS AND WAGONS that converged throughout May on Wills Creek and Fort Cumberland—the new fort-and-barracks complex that rose on the Maryland bank of the Potomac, opposite the old Ohio Company storehouse—gave Braddock what he needed to begin his expedition against Fort Duquesne. For three weeks after Braddock's arrival, the fort buzzed with activity. Companies of provincial troops from Virginia, Maryland, and North Carolina marched in to join the force, artillery and stores arrived, recruits drilled, and Braddock attended to every detail of preparation, down to ordering medical examinations for the camp women (sixty to a regiment) "to see who was Clean and proper" to accompany the expedition. Indeed, the only detail that Braddock neglected during these weeks of preparation was the one that mattered most: Indian affairs.[1]

Soon after his appointment as superintendent, William Johnson had made George Croghan his deputy and ordered him to bring what support he could to Braddock. Accordingly, Croghan had organized forty or fifty refugee Mingos—remnants of Tanaghrisson's band, who had been living near his trading post at Aughwick—and brought them to Wills Creek. He had also sent a messenger to the Ohio Country with wampum belts to invite the Delawares, Shawnees, and Mingos to meet with the commander in chief at Fort Cumberland. Eventually six chiefs appeared: a group that included Scarouady, the Oneida who had succeeded Tanaghrisson as half-king, and Shingas, the leading war chief of the Ohio Delawares. It was a delegation of great weight, but Braddock failed to grasp its importance. In a few days' time he managed to alienate them permanently, as well as most of the Mingos whom Croghan brought from Aughwick.

Braddock could understand Indians only as exotics, and troublesome ones at that. His dismissive remark to Franklin—"it is impossible that [savages] should make any impression [on disciplined troops]"—made it clear that he did not fear Indians as enemies; his actions now demonstrated how little he valued them as allies. First, believing that the women who had accompanied Croghan's Mingos would prove a disruptive influence on his troops, Braddock summarily ordered them back to Aughwick. When they left, most of their husbands, sons, and brothers went with them, never to return. In treating with the Ohio chiefs, however, Braddock blundered even more seriously. Despite the lack of enthusiasm they had previously shown for the British, the Ohio Indians still hesitated to ally themselves fully and finally with the French. In fact they would have liked nothing more than to see the French out of the valley. If the British were willing to cooperate in removing them, the Ohioans would have welcomed their aid, and their trade—provided only that the British refrain from trying to assert direct control over the region. Shingas indicated his own willingness to help the British in the most direct possible way by presenting Braddock with a detailed plan of Fort Duquesne. Captain Robert Stobo, held hostage there since the previous July, had drawn the diagram in secret; Shingas himself, at considerable personal risk, had smuggled it out of the fort.

Braddock either did not understand what this gesture of goodwill meant or did not care. When the Delaware chief stood before him and asked the only question that mattered to the Ohio Indians—"what he intended to do with the land if he Could drive the French and their Indians away"—Braddock summoned all his considerable reserves of arrogance, and replied, "that the English Shou[l]d Inhabit and Inherit the Land[. Up]on which Shingas ask[e]d Genl Braddock whether the Indians that were Friends to the English might not be Permitted to Live and Trade Among the English and have Hunting Ground sufficient To Support themselves and Familys as they had no where to Flee Too But into the Hands of the French and their Indians who were their Enemies (that is Shingas' Enemies). On which Genl Braddock said that No Savage Should Inherit the Land."

The next day, hoping for a change of heart, the chiefs approached Braddock again and asked him to reconsider. "And Genl Braddock made the same reply as Formerly, On which Shingas and the other Chiefs answered That if they might not have Liberty To Live on the Land they would not Fight for it, To which Genl Braddock answered that he did not need their Help and had no doubt of driveing the French and their Indians away." That ended the conference. Shingas and the other Ohio chiefs returned to the valley with news that so "much Enraged" the tribes there that "a Party of them went Immediately upon [hearing] it and Join'd the French." Almost no Indians remained with Braddock. When on May 29 the first elements of his army marched from Fort Cumberland, his force was more than 2,200 strong but included only the Half King Scarouady and 7 other Mingo warriors.[2]

The general, of course, did not know that Johnson had not even begun to treat with the Iroquois for support, and he still expected to receive the reinforcement of about four hundred Cherokee and Catawba warriors that Governor Dinwiddie had promised to procure. Why Dinwiddie should have thought he could produce them remains a mystery, since he knew well enough that the Catawbas and Cherokees were inveterate enemies of the Iroquois whom Johnson was supposed to recruit. Braddock, in his blunt, self-assured way, was too naive to understand the tensions of Indian-white relations in North America, let alone the character of relations between the various Indian nations. His naïveté would cost him dearly. But when his army marched out of Fort Cumberland—"the Knight [Sir John St. Clair] swearing in the van, the Genl cursing & bullying in the center & their whores bringing up the rear"—Braddock had no doubt that he had prepared for this expedition as fully as any man could.[3]

What lay beyond his control, as much as anything else, was the mountainous, heavily wooded terrain through which his army would have to march, building a road as it went to permit the passage of its baggage column and train of artillery. Only a man with supreme confidence in his own abilities and his men's stamina would have dreamed of trying to haul siege guns, including monstrously heavy eight-inch howitzers and twelve-pound cannon, through "an hundred and ten Miles [of] . . . uninhabited Wilderness[,] over steep rocky Mountains and almost impassable Morasses," but Braddock never doubted he could do it. The terrain, of course, took its toll: at the end of the first week, only thirty-five miles from Fort Cumberland, Braddock decided to divide his army into a "flying column" of picked men that would press forward as rapidly as possible and a support column that would follow with the bulk of the baggage, improving the road as it went. Thereafter the lead element moved comparatively fast—at least three, and sometimes as much as eight miles a day—while the second division, hauling most of the army's food, ammunition, and about half of its artillery, fell farther and farther behind. Men sickened with dysentery, wagons shook themselves to kindling, horses dropped dead at an appalling rate: eventually sixty miles separated the two divisions. Still Braddock pressed on, emboldened by the lack of opposition that the flying column encountered and by the ease with which his men dispersed the few Indians who appeared to scout his force.[4]

By the morning of July 9, Braddock's force had advanced to within ten miles of Fort Duquesne. As the army forded the Monongahela River near the ruins of John Fraser's trading post, the troops were short on food but high in morale. They expected to invest the fort on the following day, or even to hear the roar of its works being blown up and abandoned by the French. By now the march was proceeding in what had become its usual order, with its 7 Mingo guides and George Croghan in front preceding an advance guard of about 300 light infantry and grenadiers under an earnest young lieutenant colonel named Thomas Gage. Next came a New York independent company led by Captain Horatio Gates, guarding the 250 or so pioneers who widened the road under the direction of Sir John St. Clair and two engineers. A half-dozen wagons bearing tools and supplies accompanied the fatigue party. The main body followed, perhaps a hundred yards behind, with more guards, more axmen and laborers, Braddock and his staff (including Washington, "very weak & low" from dysentery and suffering such pain from hemorrhoids that he could ride a horse only by tying cushions over the saddle), and 500 infantry in parallel columns that flanked a long line of wagons, artillery pieces, camp women, and cattle. At the end trailed a rear guard of 100 or so men, mostly Virginia provincials under Captain Adam Stephen, a veteran of Fort Necessity. Sweating and swearing their way through the woods on either side of this mile-long column were small parties of flankers, alert for enemy scouts. Three days earlier the flanking parties had repelled Indian raiders, and now they were especially alert. Everyone knew that Fort Duquesne lay just ahead, and the force proceeded with great caution, skirting likely spots for ambush.[5]

Braddock's opposite number at Fort Duquesne, Contrecoeur, had followed the reports his scouts had brought of the approaching army with mounting concern. Fort Duquesne was now complete and in good repair but too small to hold more than about 200 of the 1,600 French regulars, Canadian militiamen, and Indian warriors who were presently under his command. Moreover, Contrecoeur was experienced enough to realize that his Indians would not fight to defend ground but only to destroy enemies or take captives and trophies. They would, he knew, disperse if the English successfully invested Fort Duquesne. His best hope was to disrupt the English advance, and so on the morning of July 9 he gave

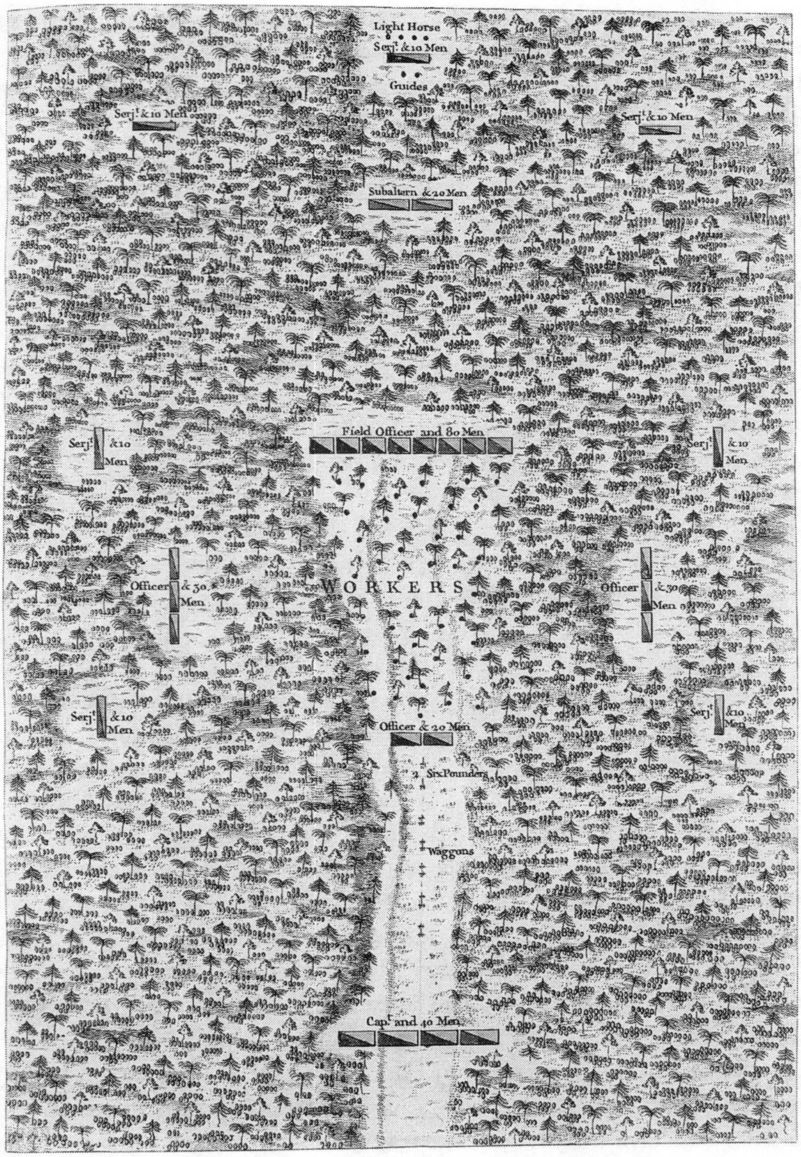

Braddock's advanced party. Another of Orme's set, this plan shows the disposition of troops and pioneers at the head of the column, more or less as they would have been arrayed on the morning of July 9, 1755. Far from a column blundering blindly through the woods, Braddock's advanced party had secured its flanks with the equivalent of a company on both the left and the right. The main body—including Braddock and his staff, the baggage train, most of the artillery, and five hundred troops—followed the advance guard, a hundred or so yards to the rear. *Courtesy of the William L. Clements Library at the University of Michigan.*

Captain Daniel Liénard de Beaujeu command of half the men at the fort—36 officers, 72 colonial regulars (*troupes de la marine*), 146 Canadian militiamen, and 637 Indians—and ordered a sortie against Braddock's column. The Indian group included a few Mingos and Delawares and a somewhat larger contingent of Shawnees but was mostly composed of French allies from the north and west—Ottawas, Mississaugas, Wyandots, Potawatomis—lured by the prospect of captives and booty. Among the leaders of the Far Indians was Charles Langlade, that tough and experienced officer who had destroyed Pickawillany in 1752. The party, well armed but otherwise unburdened with supplies and equipment, set out from the fort at about nine in the morning, intending to ambush Braddock's column.[6]

It was about one o'clock when Scarouady and Croghan spotted the French and Indians through open woods, no more than two hundred yards to their front. The French party, surprised, halted to organize itself. Gage's men hurried forward and fired three quick volleys; despite the great range, one of the balls killed Captain Beaujeu as he stood in front of his men, waving his hat to direct their disposition. The sudden loss of their commander threw the regulars and militiamen into confusion, but the Indians needed no one to tell them what to do. Streaming into the forest along either flank of the British force, they took up positions wherever they found cover: behind trees, in a defile, on a hill to the column's right. Then they began to pour fire into the British advance guard, which responded with a few ineffectual volleys and began to fall back.[7]

According to St. Clair, the woods for most of the march had been so dense and choked with vegetation that "one may go twenty Miles without seeing before him ten yards." Once across the Monongahela, however, the forest had opened out and was now so clear of underbrush "that Carridges Could have been drove through any part." The openness of the forest meant that Braddock's column had entered an Indian hunting ground, a region from which the undergrowth was annually burned to improve the fodder qualities of its vegetation, to reduce the cover available to game animals, and to allow the easy movement of hunters. Conditions that ordinarily favored Indian huntsmen now favored Indian marksmen, who dispersed, took cover, and fired at will into the British column.[8]

The Indians fought in the ways they knew, and the redcoats did their best to do the same, trying repeatedly to form themselves into companies and return fire, a process that drew them ever more tightly together in the road. As the pressure of Indian fire drove Gage's men back and the unarmed laborers fled pell-mell to the rear, Braddock ordered the troops from the main body forward. As the retreating and advancing parties collided, units mixed together in confusion. Officers tried to control and reorganize their men; but the officers themselves, mounted on horses, waving swords, and wearing glittering silver gorgets at their throats, made the best targets of all. Within the first ten minutes of the battle, fifteen of the eighteen officers in Gage's advance party had been killed or wounded. Discipline and control disintegrated as more and more officers fell.

Braddock, who had ridden to the front at the sound of the first shots, tried to restore order by directing that the colors of the two regiments be "advanced," or posted as rallying points for their units, but he never succeeded in reorganizing his men. Within minutes, nothing larger than a platoon retained its integrity. The regulars, "with little or no order, but endeavouring to make Fronts towards the Enemys Fire," huddled together in a confused and hopeless mass, crammed into an area less than 250 yards from end to end and perhaps no more than 100 feet wide. The rear guard was left to defend itself and the twelve-pound fieldpiece it had been pulling, while the civilian teamsters unhitched their horses from the wagons and rode away. The women who had been traveling with the wagon train and driving the cattle fared less well. Of the fifty or so with the column in the morning, almost all would be lost—fewer than half of them, apparently, taken captive.[9]

We cannot easily imagine how the battlefield looked on that day; hardest of all would be to imagine how it looked to the British soldiers trapped in the road. Circumstances favored the French and Indians to an almost incredible degree. They were well fed and well rested, accustomed to the woods, and could easily see their enemies, who "were always in column, unfortunately for them, for that made them easy to kill." The British, on the other hand, had endured days of hard marching, hunger, thirst, and heat; weeks of anxiety, compounded by tales of Indian barbarity; and now they found themselves in the midst of a battle that nothing in their training had prepared them to fight.[10]

The forest itself was entirely outside the experience of most of them, for the bulk of the troops whom Braddock had chosen for the flying column were hardy, thoroughly disciplined "Old Standers" who had come with the 44th and the 48th from Ireland. The woods hid their enemies almost completely. "The French and Indians crept about in small Parties so that the Fire was quite round us, and in all the Time I never saw one, nor could I on Enquiry find any one who saw ten together," one survivor recalled. "If we saw of them five or six at one time [it] was a great sight," another remembered; "and they Either on their Bellies or Behind trees or

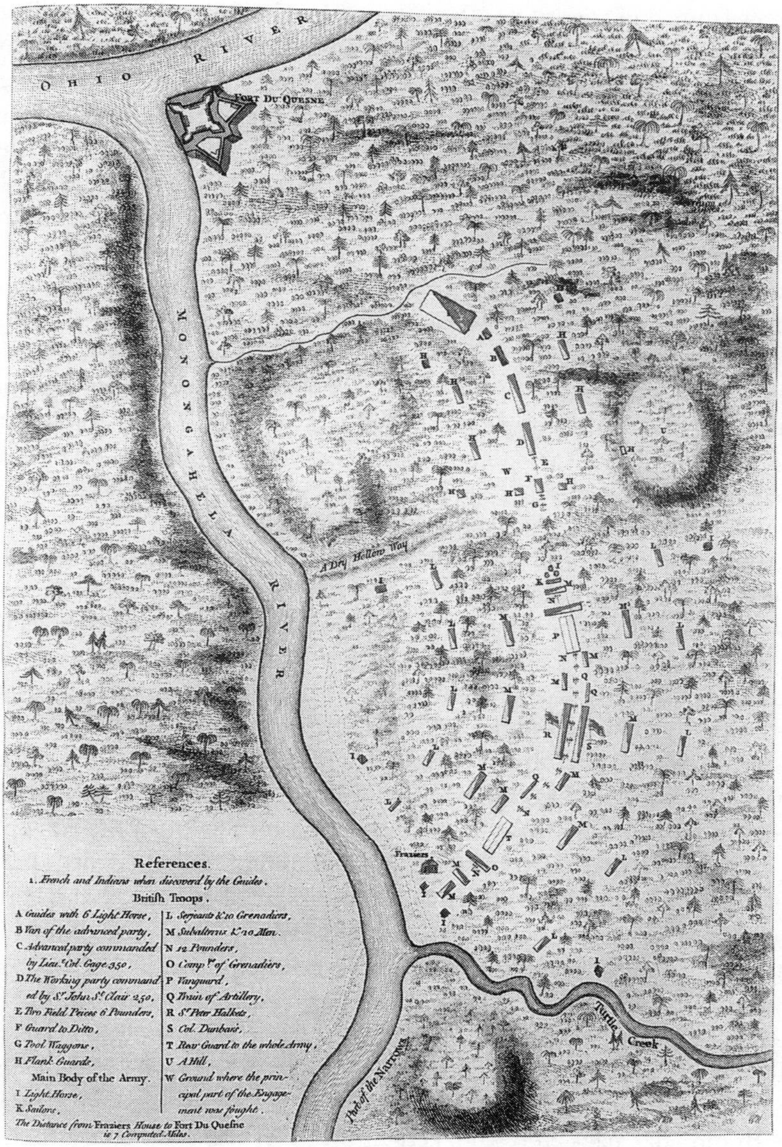

Disposition of Braddock's column at the Battle of the Monongahela, July 9, 1755. Although this map radically understates the distance from the field of battle to Fort Duquesne, it gives a good idea of the organization of the British column at the moment of encounter with Beaujeu's Franco-Indian force. The main body, drawn forward by the firing, collided with the advanced party as it fell back; the battle took place between the hill, at the right center of the map, and the ravine, or "Dry Hollow Way," leading down to the Monongahela, on the left. From Captain Robert Orme's set of plans and maps, 1768. *Courtesy of the William L. Clements Library at the University of Michigan.*

Runing from one tree to another almost by the ground." The redcoats' training had prepared them to confront adversaries they could see, to fire their muskets upon order and in volleys, to stand shoulder-to-shoulder in orderly ranks, and to follow the commands of their officers and sergeants precisely, no matter how great the confusion and slaughter around them. But trapped as they were on the road, virtually all the sensory cues they had been trained to look for were missing. There were no massed enemies in sight; no drums beat them to order; few officers were visible in the tangle of men, and no one was giving coherent orders. Instead, all around them were trees, smoke, the screams of wounded men and horses, incessant gunfire. The war cries of the Indians—"ravenous Hell-hounds . . . yelping and screaming like so many Devils"—came from every direction, terrifying men whose imaginations had fed on tales of how Indians tortured and mutilated their prisoners. Weeks after the battle one witness would write that "the yell of the Indians is fresh on my ear, and the terrific sound will haunt me until the hour of my dissolution."[11]

Amid chaos and disorientation the regulars clutched at what shards of discipline they could. Even in the absence of their officers they maintained platoon formations, and indeed continued to fire together, as they had been trained to do. This was worse than useless under the circumstances, for "if any got a shott at one [of the enemy] the fire imediately ran through ye whole line though they saw nothing but trees." So strong was the instinct to perform as they had been trained that, to their officers' horror, platoons fired volleys directly into one another. "Capt. Mercer marching with his company to take possession of an advantageous post, was fired upon by our men from behind, and ten of his men dropt at once. Capt. Polson lost many of his men by irregular platooning behind him, on which he faced about, and intreated the Soldiers not to fire and destroy his men. They replied they could not help it. . . ." The only sign of order in the British ranks was Braddock himself, riding through the shambles with astonishing composure as horse after horse was shot from under him. Clinging madly to the patterns that had ordered their lives, the troops did not begin to break and retreat until a musket ball slammed into Braddock's back and knocked him out of the saddle. By then his men had stood their ground for more than three hours.[12]

Not everyone in Braddock's command behaved as his redcoats did. The Americans with the army, lacking years of training, fled or took cover as soon as the attack began; many of those crouching behind trees were mistaken for the enemy and killed by British volleys. In the rear guard, Captain Adam Stephen's Virginia provincials even managed to fight effectively from behind the trees, because after his previous year's experiences as a company commander under Washington, Stephen had taught his men how to load and fire from cover. Following the battle, recovering from his wounds, Stephen heaped scorn on Braddock, who he believed had allowed the enemy to "come against Us, creeping near and hunting Us as they would do a Herd of Buffaloes or Deer; whereas you might as well send a Cow in pursuit of a Hare as an English Soldier loaded . . . with a Coat, Jacket, &c. &c. &c. after Canadeans in their Shirts, who can shoot and run well, or Naked Indians accustomed to the Woods."[13]

Yet it was not, as Stephen charged, Braddock's absurd adherence to European tactics of "formal attacks & Platoon-firing" that destroyed his force, but rather the redcoats' training and Braddock's own courage. No matter how horrifying their losses or how terrifying their situation, the regulars had been conditioned to stand their ground and fight; and fight they did, even if they did it in suicidally dysfunctional ways. Braddock, brave and stubborn, sat calmly on his mount and waited for the enemy to give way, as he assumed all irregulars must, before the regulars' superior discipline.

Instead it was his own men who gave way, without any formal order being given, once word spread that he had been shot. Yet even then the redcoats maintained a semblance of order until they reached the river, where the Indians charged them with hatchets and scalping knives and their retreat disintegrated into a rout. Men fled screaming in terror, sometimes running for miles before they collapsed, exhausted. Only when the panic had finally spent itself could the surviving sergeants and officers reassert control and organize the men into units once more.

The British broke and ran, of course, because they believed that they were about to be massacred. In fact they were in less danger at that moment than at any time since the attack began—not because the Indians lacked the capacity to pursue and destroy them, but because they no longer had a reason to try. Unlike European soldiers, Indians did not fight to destroy their enemies so much as to take the captives, plunder, and trophies by which they could gain spiritual power and prove their merit as warriors. What they valued most therefore lay behind them: the captives they had left tied to trees, the wounded and dead who lay on the field of battle, and the abandoned equipment strewn everywhere about.

The killing of the wounded and the taking of scalps from corpses went on for some time after the battle; so, too, did the consumption of the expedition's stock of rum, two hundred gallons of which was soon discovered in the supply train. For Private Duncan Cameron of the 44th Foot (who had been wounded at the start of the fight and left behind in the retreat, but who managed to hide himself in a tree, from which he observed the battle's aftermath), the Indians seemed "ravenous Hell-hounds" and their behavior mere savagery. Like most Europeans, he did not understand that in fact the warriors did not kill and mutilate indiscriminately. Captives were symbolically valuable because warriors demonstrated greater valor by taking men alive than killing them. Among groups that had not converted to Catholicism, prisoners had great cultural value as replacements for dead kin, whether as adoptees or as the objects of ritual sacrifice. Canada's converted Indians saw another kind of value in them, as slaves who could be sold or ransomed. Unharmed or lightly wounded captives therefore stood a good chance of being spared, as children and female captives almost always were, provided that they were fit enough to make a forced march back to the villages of their captors. The deaths that came speedily to the more gravely wounded at least spared them further suffering, did not hinder the retreat of the war party, and provided the victor with a scalp, which, while less desirable than a captive, still offered evidence of prowess in battle.[14]

None of this was evident to the terrified refugees; nor, for that matter, did Braddock's young aide, Washington, understand much more than the grisly horror of the experience. Unwounded though he had ridden beside the general all afternoon and had two horses shot from under him, he rode all night to bring aid from the army's rear element. Years later he would recall "the shocking Scenes which presented themselves in this Nights march" vividly: "The dead—the dying—the groans—lamentation—and crys along the Road of the wounded for help . . . were enough to pierce a heart of adamant. The gloom & horror . . . was not a little encreased by the impervious darkness occasioned by the close shade of thick woods. . . ."[15]

Two days of flight brought the survivors of Braddock's command at last into contact with the army's second division, where they rested briefly and ate their first full meal in days. The only wounded who now remained with them were those who could walk or the few who (like Braddock) had been carried by their comrades; the rest had been abandoned to die in the woods. Now the troops destroyed mortars, ammunition, baggage, and supplies, and loaded the remaining wounded in the empty wagons. Covering the remaining seventy-five miles to Fort Cumberland took five more agonizing days. Braddock, with a musket ball lodged in his chest, did not live to see the fort. On July 14 his men buried him without ceremony in the middle of the road, then the entire army marched over his unmarked grave to keep it from being discovered by the enemy troops, who everyone believed were still in pursuit. The spot was within five miles of Jumonville's Glen and perhaps a mile from the site of Fort Necessity.[16]

The British had suffered a devastating casualty rate, with fully two-thirds of the men and officers of the flying column killed or wounded. The French and their Indian allies in comparison had lost only twenty-three dead and sixteen seriously wounded, or about one in every twenty-five of those who had taken part in the battle.[17] Yet victory, ironically, left Fort Duquesne more vulnerable than ever. Within two days most of the Indians had gathered their plunder, trophies, and prisoners and gone home, leaving Contrecoeur with only a few hundred men to defend the Forks. The English forces, despite the magnitude of their defeat, still numbered nearly two thousand when a muster was finally held at Fort Cumberland on July 25. More than 1,350 of them were fit for duty. Until the officers in the rear guard had ordered the destruction of the train's supplies and mortars during the retreat, in other words, it would have been possible, in theory at least, to return to Fort Duquesne and destroy it.

But whatever the numbers of men and arms and barrels of beef at Fort Cumberland might be read to say, psychologically it was impossible for Thomas Dunbar, the sole surviving colonel of Braddock's command, to do more than order the retreat to continue. After reorganizing the men who remained unhurt and giving the surgeons a chance to care for those among the wounded who could still be helped ("the wether being very hot [having] Ca[u]sed a great many magets in the mens wounds," one witness observed), Dunbar headed for Philadelphia. There he compounded defeat with humiliation by demanding winter quarters for his troops, in July.[18]

The extent to which the debacle at the Monongahela could be blamed on Braddock himself was a matter of intense concern to contemporary Americans, who searched the event for its meanings and generally concluded that a mindless adherence to European tactics had caused his downfall. In their conclusion lay the origins of the myth that Americans were uniquely fitted for fighting in the wilderness, and by extension the belief in the superiority of American irregular troops (no matter how poorly trained) over European regulars. Fixing the degree of Braddock's responsibility for the disaster is of less compelling interest today, however, than is the character of contemporary criticism. His civilian detractors were, of course, mainly armchair generals; but the reactions of two participants in the action merit attention.[19]

The man who remained closest to Braddock throughout the battle and who had a better chance to observe him than anyone else never criticized him at all. Rather he blamed the "dastardly behaviour of the Regular Troops." "How little does the World consider the Circumstances," George Washington exclaimed, "and how apt are mankind to level their vindictive Censures against the unfortunate Chief, who perhaps merited least of the blame[!]" Indeed, even after more than a quarter century had passed and Braddock had become one of the most vilified figures in American popular memory, Washington barely criticized the general's behavior. Far from concluding that Braddock's professionalism lay at the root of his defeat, the Virginian emerged from the battle determined to impose a more stringent discipline on his men when he resumed command of the Virginia Regiment. Scarouady had severer strictures for a man he thought proud and foolish. Braddock, he told the governor and council of Pennsylvania, "was a bad man when he was alive; he looked upon us as dogs, and would never hear anything what was said to him. We often endeavored to advise him of the danger he was in with his Soldiers; but he never appeared pleased with us. . . ."[20]

Taken together, the opinions of Washington and Scarouady reveal much about the character of the war that was developing in America. Braddock, a confident and highly professional European soldier, had had little time for anyone who did not see the campaign as he did: that is, as a contest between French and British forces, distinguishable from any similar clash in Europe only by the smallness of the forces involved, the remoteness of the setting, and the uncommon difficulty of operations. For Braddock, war was war, an activity to be conducted according to the norms of civilized European powers, and those dictated preeminently that one fought for the control of territory. George Washington, a young and eagerly Anglophile provincial gentleman, affirmed Braddock's system of values and his approach to warfare without question. That was why he believed that the fault lay not with Braddock but his men, and why he concluded that a combination of better discipline and training adapted to American conditions would have saved the day. Given such views, it is hardly surprising that Washington should have shared Braddock's disdain for Indians, but he also shunned them as allies for powerful reasons of his own. In the first place, he was a speculator who knew that a continuing Indian presence in the Ohio Valley would only delay the day that settlers would begin buying Ohio Company lands. Moreover, because his military disappointments had all in one way or another resulted from the actions of Indians, he had strong emotional reasons to want them, no less than the French, driven from the Ohio Valley.

Scarouady, loyal to the old and now nearly defunct idea that the valley belonged to the Iroquois, had no choice but to make common cause with Braddock if he hoped to see the French expelled. But his hope that the war would be a fight of Indians in alliance with the English to restore Indian autonomy in the west was a vision shared by almost no one else. To Braddock he had not been an ally but a partisan auxiliary. To Washington he was more hindrance than help, a probable obstacle to civilized settlement. To his own people, living with the fact of French dominion in the valley, he was irrelevant. And so, although Scarouady would continue to seek English aid for the Ohio Indians until his death in 1757, the potential for Anglo-Indian alliance that he represented diminished almost to the vanishing point after Braddock's defeat. Only the Mohawks in the north, swayed by an Anglophile tradition, the loyalty of Chief Hendrick, and the blandishments of William Johnson, would be actively allied with the English—and only for a little longer.

Braddock had been taught a valuable lesson about wilderness war at the Monongahela, but he did not live long enough to understand it: there could be no success without the cooperation, or at least the acquiescence, of the Indians. It was a lesson lost on Washington and other provincials like him, whose cultural preferences were entirely English and whose practical concerns for realizing the speculative potential of western lands made them even more averse to cooperating with Indians. By contrast, the French understood the importance of Indian alliances very well and used them to foil virtually every Anglo-American military initiative for the next three years. Thus on a strategic level the collapse of the British force at the Monongahela foretold much of the shape of the war that was to come. But the conflicting views and the underlying attitudes of Braddock, Washington, and Scarouady also hinted at what neither they nor any contemporary fully understood, the cultural dimensions of the conflict. Before it would end, the Seven Years' War in America would become the stage on which the members of very different cultures—French, Canadian, British, Anglo-American, and Amerindian—would meet and interact in ways that were by turns violent and accommodating, shrewd and fraught with misunderstanding: encounters and actions that would define the character of American history for decades to come.

CHAPTER 10

After Braddock

WILLIAM SHIRLEY AND THE NORTHERN CAMPAIGNS

1755

BRADDOCK'S DEFEAT shocked all of British America, but the backwoods settlements of Pennsylvania, Maryland, and Virginia felt it like a blow to the solar plexus. Dunbar's flight to Philadelphia left Braddock's road as an undefended avenue of approach for raiders from Fort Duquesne. Only a small garrison of Virginia provincials and an independent company from South Carolina remained at Fort Cumberland—a force barely adequate to defend the fort itself, let alone 250 miles of discontinuous valley settlements stretching from the Susquehanna to the Shenandoah Valley. Pennsylvania had no militia to mobilize; the Quakers who dominated the assembly agreed to appropriate a thousand pounds that frontier settlers could use to buy weapons but otherwise left the westerners to shift for themselves. Maryland had a single company of soldiers under arms. Virginia had raised about eight hundred men to accompany Braddock; approximately a quarter of them, three companies of infantry and one of light horse, were with him on the Monongahela. Of these troops, who numbered twelve officers and more than two hundred men, perhaps thirty survived the battle. Among those who had not been in combat, desertion picked up sharply.[1]

With so few soldiers to protect it, the frontier simply collapsed. Before the end of July, reports had already reached Williamsburg that Indian war parties had killed thirty-five Virginia backwoods settlers. In August, frontier inhabitants who could afford to abandon their homesteads were streaming back to more heavily settled regions in the east. By autumn over a hundred Virginians were known to have been slain or lost to captivity, and the flood of refugees had grown so heavy at Winchester that one could hardly cross the Blue Ridge to the west "for the Crowds of People who were flying, as if every moment was death."[2]

Governor Dinwiddie shipped muskets to the frontier, called out the militia of three northwestern counties, and summoned the House of Burgesses into emergency session. Before the end of August, the Burgesses had voted to raise a thousand-man provincial regiment and appropriated forty thousand pounds to equip and pay it. Dinwiddie offered Washington the command, and—following negotiations to make sure he would have more control and better support than in 1754—Washington accepted. By the end of their session, the Burgesses had stiffened the penalties that backed the militia laws, authorized the payment of bounties on Indian scalps, and provided for the construction of forts as refuges for settlers and bases from which Washington's troops could patrol the frontier. This arrangement would offer essentially all the security backwoods Virginians would know for the next three years. The redcoats would never return to the Old Dominion during the war.[3]

For the Ohio Indians as much as the white inhabitants of the Virginia-Pennsylvania backcountry, Braddock's defeat marked a point of no return. The Shawnees in the valley had already accepted French control, but the Delawares and Mingos had held back. By the middle of July, however, they had little room left for maneuver. The French had demonstrated their ability to call large numbers of Wyandot, Ottawa, and other allies down to the valley, and the risk was steadily growing that they would punish the Delawares and Mingos for any further reluctance to take up the hatchet against the English. Still, the Delaware chiefs decided to make one last attempt to obtain English aid and sent emissaries (including Captain Jacobs, their greatest warrior) to Philadelphia. From August 16 through 22, the delegation met with Governor Morris and the Pennsylvania Council to ask for arms. Still conforming to the protocols of Iroquois diplomacy, Scarouady the half-king spoke on their behalf: "One word of Yours will bring the Delawares to join You; . . . any Message you have to send, or answer you have to give to them, I will deliver to them." But Morris and the council had no message to send and answered only that the Ohio Indians should await further instructions from the League Council at Onondaga. No word would ever come from Onondaga, the ambassadors of which would soon be making their way to the mission of La Présentation to reassure the new French governor-general, Pierre de Rigaud de Vaudreuil de Cavagnial, marquis de Vaudreuil, that the Iroquois intended to remain neutral in the fighting between the French and the English. Leaving Philadelphia "without meeting with the necessary Encouragement," Captain Jacobs and his fellow delegates returned to Fort Duquesne and "agreed To Come out with the French and their Indians in Parties to Destroy the English Settlements." That fall, Shingas and Captain Jacobs helped lead combined French and Indian war parties that took captives, plunder, and scalps throughout the Virginia-Pennsylvania backcountry.[4]

Word of Braddock's defeat reached William Shirley in early August at his headquarters in New York. There, at a portage between the upper Mohawk River and Wood Creek, he was supervising the transit of troops and provisions to Fort Oswego, the trading post on Lake Ontario that was to be the jumping-off point for his planned attack on Fort Niagara. Shirley was frustrated, his campaign weeks behind schedule. Both the Niagara and the Crown Point expeditions had been staged from Albany, which—predictably—had become the scene of fruitless, time-consuming competition between the supply officers of the two armies. A bitter dispute had erupted between Shirley and the De Lanceys, who had "thrown all imaginable obstructions in [his] way," even denying him, on the flimsiest of pretexts, the use of New York cannon that were lying unused at Albany. His relations with William Johnson and the Indians had deteriorated into open hostility. Shirley had infuriated Johnson by shifting men from the Crown Point expedition to his own forces, and in retaliation Johnson had refused to provide him with any Mohawk scouts. Shirley had tried to obtain them on his own by employing the odious John Henry Lydius as a recruiter—a serious error, which had served only to offend the Mohawks and thus to render his situation even more difficult. Already the strain had begun to tell on the sixty-one-year-old governor: now the news of the disaster in Pennsylvania came as a stunning double blow. Shirley's son William Jr., Braddock's personal secretary, had been shot through the head and killed in the battle. This shock, coming in tandem with the realization that he was now commander in chief of His Majesty's forces in North America, was almost more than Shirley could bear. The responsibilities he now assumed were ones for which his training as a lawyer and politician had done little to prepare him.[5]

Taking stock of the situation over the next weeks, Shirley saw little to hearten him. Reports arrived that Admiral Edward Boscawen, dispatched in April to patrol the Gulf of St. Lawrence and prevent French reinforcements from reaching Canada, had failed in his mission. Of a large convoy carrying six battalions of regular troops, Boscawen had intercepted only two ships and ten companies, or fewer than four hundred of the three thousand regular reinforcements; the remainder had

William Shirley (1694–1771). This nineteenth-century lithograph shows Shirley as a fashionable London portraitist, Thomas Hudson, depicted him, c. 1750. He appears as the self-confident royal governor of Massachusetts, a post he occupied from 1741 to 1756. The architect of the Louisbourg expedition of 1745 and of the successful operations in Nova Scotia during 1755, Shirley's broad strategic vision served him best before he became commander in chief; thereafter his lack of administrative and organizational skills would prove to be his downfall. *Courtesy of the Massachusetts Historical Society, Boston.*

reached safe harbor at Louisbourg and Québec. Their commander, Baron Jean-Armand de Dieskau, *maréchal de camp,* sent to assume overall direction of Canada's defense, by now had had more than enough time to deploy them against the British. Colonel Dunbar, meanwhile, cringed at Philadelphia, awaiting orders and holding immobile the remnants of Braddock's force. Johnson's campaign against Crown Point was proceeding at a snail's pace.[6]

Shirley's own force, short on provisions, was looking less able to mount an assault on Niagara with every passing day. A lack of ready money hindered everything, for in the confusion that followed Braddock's defeat, the deputy paymaster general was refusing to honor drafts that various military contractors were presenting for payment. Shirley still pressed forward with his men to Lake Ontario, but once he arrived at the shore it quickly became evident that he could proceed no further with the campaign. The old trading post, Fort Oswego, was virtually indefensible, and therefore unsuitable to serve as a supply base for the army's advance by boat against Niagara. Shirley therefore ordered the decrepit structure repaired and fortified, arranged for supplies to be brought up, and sent his two regular regiments into winter quarters there. The next spring, he thought, they could attack Niagara. In the meantime they would have to make Oswego a suitable base of operations while he returned to New York City to sort out the muddle into which everything had fallen and lay plans to recover the initiative the next year.[7]

The only bright spot visible in the campaigns of 1755, from Shirley's perspective, was the New England expedition against French military posts in Nova Scotia. He had promoted this campaign as a means of resolving longstanding difficulties in British control over the region, which had remained unstable since the end of King George's War. One of the earl of Halifax's pet projects had been to Anglicize Nova Scotia and make it a bastion of defense against New France. To that end he had ordered Halifax built in 1749, as a counterweight to Louisbourg, and he had promoted immigration by New Englanders and other Protestants. This worried the French—in part because the French-speaking Acadian majority in the region would be swallowed up in a tide of Anglophone newcomers, and in part because the Acadians would be unable to continue, as they had for years, to sell provisions covertly to the fortress of Louisbourg. The English worried, in turn, that the French were intriguing among the Acadians and the local Abenaki and Micmac Indians, seeking to stir up rebellion. And, in fact, they were: a French missionary priest among the Micmacs, Abbé Jean Louis de Le Loutre, openly agitated for an insurrection to return Acadia to French control and ultimately offered to buy the scalps of English settlers for a hundred *livres* each. Early in 1750, affairs had reached a crisis when the French erected a substantial pentagonal fort, Beauséjour, on the narrow isthmus of Chignecto, which connected the peninsula of Nova Scotia to the Canadian mainland. This had moved the British to construct a countervailing post, Fort Lawrence, on the opposite side of the Missaguash River. Between these two forts, bristling with cannon, an uneasy balance of power had rested until the beginning of 1755. Then the ministry had adopted Shirley's plan to send two New England battalions and a detachment of regulars from the Halifax garrison against Beauséjour.[8]

Shirley, as usual, had had practical reasons for promoting this expedition—it promised a harvest of patronage that would increase his influence over Massachusetts politics—but he had also realized that it would be popular among New England colonists interested in finding lands to colonize outside their own increasingly crowded region. Recruitment had gone well. Since the Crown had agreed to pay the wages of the troops, no political objections had been raised in the New England assemblies, and as Shirley had guessed, popular enthusiasm for the expedition quickly filled the ranks. And for once, at least, everything went according to schedule. While Braddock was still fuming at Fort Cumberland and waiting for his horses to arrive, the New England regiment was sailing for the Bay of Fundy. On June 2, when Braddock's engineers were blasting rocks out of the road less than twenty-five miles from Wills Creek, the New Englanders were off-loading cannon and provisions at Fort Lawrence, a half-day's march from Fort Beauséjour. Ten days later they were digging trenches before the French fort; in two more they were bombarding it. On June 16—after "one of our Large Shell[s] had Fell threw what they Called thare Bum Proof & Brok in one of thare Cazments whare a Number of thare officers ware Seting [and] Killed 6 of them Dead"—the French garrison capitulated. While the New Englanders were gawking at the guns in the fort that their commander had just renamed Fort Cumberland, Braddock had moved less than fifty miles and in frustration was preparing to detach a flying column to speed the march toward his objective.[9]

With the conquest so easily completed, the New England regiment had only one task remaining: to disarm, detain, and deport the indigenous Acadians to the mainland colonies. This extraordinary move—perhaps the first time in modern history a civilian population was forcibly removed as a security risk—ostensibly came as a consequence of the Acadians' unwillingness to declare unqualified allegiance to George II. For the previous forty years the Acadians, under the terms of the Treaty of Utrecht, had practiced their Catholic faith and retained possession of their lands in return for swearing only a highly limited loyalty oath that promised neutrality in all disputes between the Crowns of England and France. Now, worried about their potential for rebellion, Nova Scotia's governor and provincial council tried to force the Acadians to take an oath of submission that would revoke their religious privileges and make them ordinary subjects of the British Crown. Thinking that this was just one more attempt to deprive them of their treaty rights by trickery—a tactic the English had tried before—the Acadians refused.

They had no way of knowing that the governor and council intended to use any resistance as an excuse to get rid of them, and they were dumbfounded when the governor and council responded to their recalcitrance by imprisoning householders, declaring all their lands and cattle forfeit, and ordering them and their families deported from the province. In October the "Grand Dérangement" began. Most of the Acadians from the settlements along the Bay of Fundy were caught in the British trap and shipped out to England and the mainland colonies, where their families were scattered among the colonial population. Perhaps 5,400 were herded aboard ships and sent off with what few possessions they could carry. Those who could escape—perhaps seven to ten thousand—fled to the mainland or to the Île-St.-Jean (now Prince Edward Island), allied themselves with the Abenakis and Micmacs, and fought back as best they could, in the hope of regaining their homeland.[10]

By the close of the campaign, the combination of deportations and flight had effectively depopulated Acadian Nova Scotia. The entire scheme, so chillingly reminiscent of modern "ethnic cleansing" operations, was executed with a coldness and calculation—and indeed an efficiency—rarely seen in other wartime operations. There are strong indications that William Shirley himself was the architect of deportation, and that his real intention was less to take Beauséjour and neutralize any Acadian military threat than to make the farms of the Acadians available to recolonization by New Englanders and other Protestant immigrants. There can at any rate be no doubt that New Englanders were the principal beneficiaries of the deportation. Even before the New England troops returned home, some had begun to contemplate returning to settle; beginning in 1760, they did. Before the end of 1763, no fewer than five thousand Yankee farmers and fishermen would move to Nova Scotia, taking over Acadian farmsteads and rechristening Acadian towns with English names.[11]

If by the middle of August 1755 the Nova Scotia campaign seemed to the new commander in chief to be well on the way to unqualified success, Johnson's expedition against Crown Point looked unlikely to get under way at all. By then Shirley knew that Braddock's papers, which contained the complete plan of the campaigns, had been abandoned on the Monongahela battlefield. Thus there was at least a strong likelihood that the French knew all about Johnson's intended attack on Fort St. Frédéric, and that Dieskau would send reinforcements to aid in its defense. Shirley had warned Johnson that, should strong French opposition appear, he was to be prepared to go on the defensive and protect Albany from possible attack. A quick strike toward Crown Point might still forestall French countermeasures, but it would not be until the beginning of September that Johnson's forces would be encamped at the south end of Lac St. Sacrement, from which they were to embark by boat for Crown Point.[12]

There had been many causes for delay, beginning with the competition for supplies that had hindered Shirley's own departure from Albany. Hundreds of shallow-draft boats, or bateaux, had to be constructed to carry men and supplies from Albany northward to the Great Carrying Place beyond Saratoga (the site of Lydius's old smuggling post); a new fort, called Fort Edward in honor of the duke of York, had to be built there as a base for supply; a portage road had to be cut from Fort Edward to Lac St. Sacrement, a distance of about sixteen miles; the boats and cannon and gear of the expedition had to be dragged from Fort Edward to the lake; and the troops themselves—about 3,500 men from the New England provinces and New York—had to receive at least some degree of training. Finally, although Shirley did not yet know it, Johnson was also distracted from preparing his army for movement by his demanding duties as a conspirator, for he was busy scheming with De Lancey and Pownall to have Shirley removed from command. On September 3, for example, shortly after joining his forces at the lake, Johnson spent a good deal of his day writing one letter to the earl of Halifax denouncing Shirley as a bad influence on Indian affairs, and another to Pownall denouncing him as "a bad Man abandoned to Passion & enslaved by resentment"—sentiments that he knew Pownall would pass along discreetly to his English contacts.[13]

As September began, then, Johnson's provincials were still hauling bateaux, supplies, and munitions to the lake. Johnson's Mohawk allies, led by Chief Hendrick, were just arriving in camp. Johnson himself had decided that it would be necessary to build an armed galley and erect one or perhaps two more forts before he could proceed safely against Crown Point. The weather was already turning cold and the campaigning season was fast slipping away, but his only lasting achievement to date had been the gesture—not unlike Céloron's burials of the lead plates—of giving Lac St. Sacrement the new name of Lake George, as a means of claiming it for the English king. Never eager to seek combat and doubting his skills as a general, Johnson expected to go into winter quarters without facing the disagreeable prospect of battle.[14]

The baron de Dieskau, however, had other plans. He had arrived at Québec on June 23 along with his troops and the marquis de Vaudreuil, the new governor-general of New France. Dieskau and Vaudreuil took stock of the situation that confronted them at the beginning of July—Braddock marching on Fort Duquesne, New Englanders driving the defenders from Fort Beauséjour, Shirley advancing toward Niagara, and Johnson preparing to proceed against Fort St. Frédéric—and saw that the greatest threat was the Niagara campaign, which if successful would

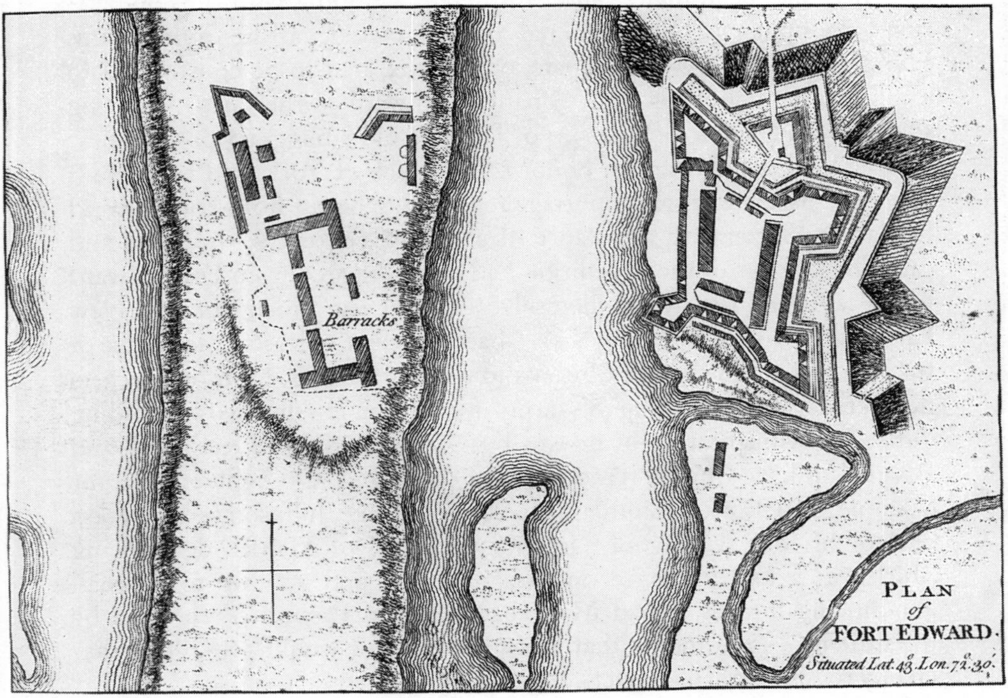

Fort Edward, New York. Shown here as it appeared in a collection of plans of North American forts published in London after the end of the war, Fort Edward evolved from a trading post on the upper Hudson into a substantial (if awkwardly sited) fort defended by nearly thirty cannon. Here it appears as what it became, the main supply base for staging operations on the Lake George–Lake Champlain corridor. From Mary Ann Rocque, *A Set of Plans and Forts in America, Reduced from Actual Surveys* (London, 1765). *Courtesy of the William L. Clements Library at the University of Michigan.*

destroy Canada's ability to maintain its links to the western forts. Dieskau therefore assembled about four thousand French regulars, Canadians, and domiciled Indians at Montréal and by early August was ready to ascend the St. Lawrence and reinforce Fort Niagara.[15] At that point, however, Vaudreuil began receiving urgent, exaggerated reports of Johnson's strength and movements and decided that he would have to divert Dieskau and about three thousand of his men to defend Fort St. Frédéric—the walls of which were in such bad repair that they would be unable to withstand even a brief cannonade. Thus just as the heartening news of Braddock's defeat arrived at Montréal, Dieskau and his men set

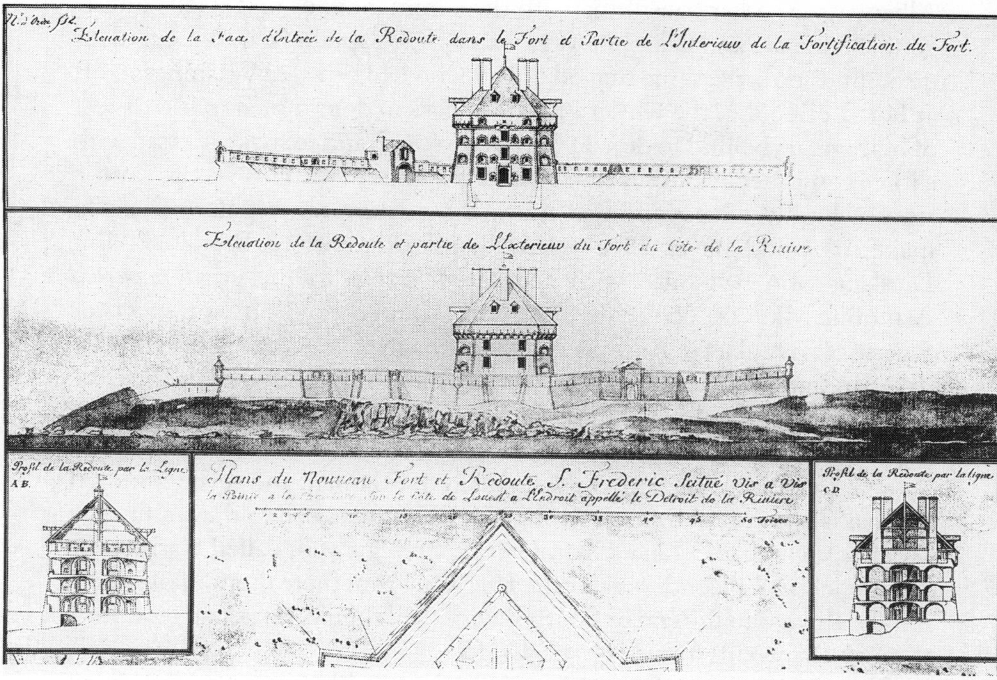

Fort St. Frédéric, 1737–59. A formidable fort used as a base for raids by the French and their Indian allies against the New York and New England frontiers, this post at Crown Point was one of the most imposing elements in the defensive network of New France. The bombproof tower, or redoubt, shown here both from within the fort and from the lake, dominated the narrows of Lake Champlain, while the fort as a whole mounted forty cannon. By 1755, however, the structure was in such bad repair that the French knew it would have to be abandoned in the event of siege; hence the urgent construction of Fort Carillon on the Ticonderoga peninsula, at the head of the lake. *Courtesy of the William L. Clements Library at the University of Michigan.*

out for Lake Champlain and Crown Point, to mount a similar spoiling campaign against Johnson's expedition.

Arriving at Fort St. Frédéric, Dieskau sent out scouts to assess the situation of Johnson's unsuspecting provincials. Their reports made him decide to mount a raid on the partially completed and lightly defended Fort Edward, destroying the boats, cannon, and supplies stored there before they could be used to stage an advance down the lake. Such a blow would be even more disabling than the one that Contrecoeur had recently dealt Braddock, for it would not only forestall any further threat to Crown Point, but would roll back New York's and New England's defenses to

Albany itself. After consulting with the commander of his mixed contingent of Abenaki and Caughnawaga warriors—Captain Jacques Legardeur de Saint-Pierre, the same rugged officer who had brushed Washington off at Fort LeBoeuf in the winter of 1753—Dieskau determined to leave most of his regulars behind to defend Fort St. Frédéric and to make his raid with a force composed primarily of Canadians and Indians. This was, to say the least, a highly unconventional move for a European regular officer to make; it would never have occurred, for example, to Braddock. But Dieskau, who had once been an aide-de-camp to the great *maréchal* Arminius Maurice, comte de Saxe, had acquired from him a respect for the use of irregulars in Europe, and he seems to have accepted the similarity of Indians and Canadians to the partisans Saxe had used against the British army in Flanders during the War of the Austrian Succession.[16] By September 4, he and fifteen hundred picked men—about two hundred regular grenadiers, six hundred Canadian militiamen, and seven hundred Abenakis and Caughnawaga Mohawks—had advanced to the confluence of Lake George and Lake Champlain, a strategic spot called Carillon by the French and Ticonderoga by the English. From there they paddled quietly southward to the end of South Bay, cached their canoes, and struck off through the woods toward Fort Edward.

Late in the day on September 7, Dieskau and his men emerged from the forest on the portage road, three miles north of Fort Edward. There the Indians informed him that they would not attack a fort, no matter how poorly defended, but that they were willing to proceed against Johnson's men at Lake George, who had not yet begun to fortify their camp. Dieskau, a flexible officer who had little choice in the matter anyway, changed his plans. The next morning, with his two companies of grenadiers marching up the road and Canadians and Indians flanking them in the woods, Dieskau turned north, toward Johnson's camp.

That same evening Mohawk scouts brought Johnson the news that a substantial body of the enemy was lurking near Fort Edward. Men were set to improving the camp's defenses—a breastwork reinforced with trees that had been felled to clear a field of fire around the lines—and the next morning Johnson, on the recommendation of his regimental commanders, sent a thousand provincials under Colonel Ephraim Williams of Massachusetts, along with a covering force of about two hundred Mohawk warriors, to reinforce Fort Edward. At about nine o'clock the column, with Chief Hendrick in the lead on horseback, marched out of the camp—toward Dieskau and his fifteen hundred raiders.[17]

Dieskau knew they were coming, for a deserter whom his men had captured on the road earlier that morning had told them of the column's advance. Now he blocked the road with his grenadier companies and positioned his Canadians and Indians in ambush ahead of them, choosing a spot about four miles south of the lake where the road dipped to pass along the floor of a ravine. Moving hurriedly, without flanking parties deployed because they did not expect to meet enemies until they neared Fort Edward, Hendrick's Mohawks and Williams's provincials blundered into the trap a few minutes after ten. Old Hendrick, at seventy-five the veteran of more than a half century of warfare and diplomacy, stopped when someone called out from the trees. Since the Canadian Mohawks and their New York kin generally refused to shed one another's blood, it seems likely that a Caughnawaga warrior was trying to warn him of his peril. But Hendrick's reply was cut short when from another quarter a shot rang out, triggering a general exchange of fire in which he and about thirty other Mohawks were killed. Within the jaws of the ambush and exposed to musketry on both flanks, Colonel Williams tried to lead an assault up a bank of the ravine; he too was killed together with about fifty of his men. Thus began the first skirmish of the Battle of Lake George, an episode New Englanders would come to call the "Bloody Morning Scout."[18]

In size and position, the forces engaged were similar to those at the Battle of the Monongahela, but the outcome was quite different. The Mohawks who had survived the first exchange of shots quickly began a measured retreat, fighting their way to the rear along with perhaps a hundred of Williams's provincials. The rest of the column, provincials unencumbered by the discipline that had doomed Braddock's regulars to stand their ground, ran for their lives. While there was nothing heroic about it, theirs was an eminently rational response and indeed one that saved the day. The sound of gunshots alerted the camp, and by the time the survivors came streaming back from the ambush, their compatriots had hastily reinforced the breastwork with bateaux and overturned supply wagons. The sole regular officer with the expedition, a captain of engineers named William Eyre, whom Braddock had assigned to supervise siege operations, quickly positioned four fieldpieces to cover the road. Dieskau's men came on in hot pursuit, then pulled up short at the edge of the clearing. To one observer in Johnson's camp, it seemed as if "the Enemy had been obliged to halt upon some Disputes among their Indians."[19]

That was more or less accurate. The Caughnawagas had lost their leader, for Legardeur de Saint-Pierre had been killed at the ambush; now they did not wish to attack an entrenched camp, the defenders of which included hundreds of their Mohawk kinsmen. The Abenakis would not go forward without the Caughnawagas, and neither would the Canadi-

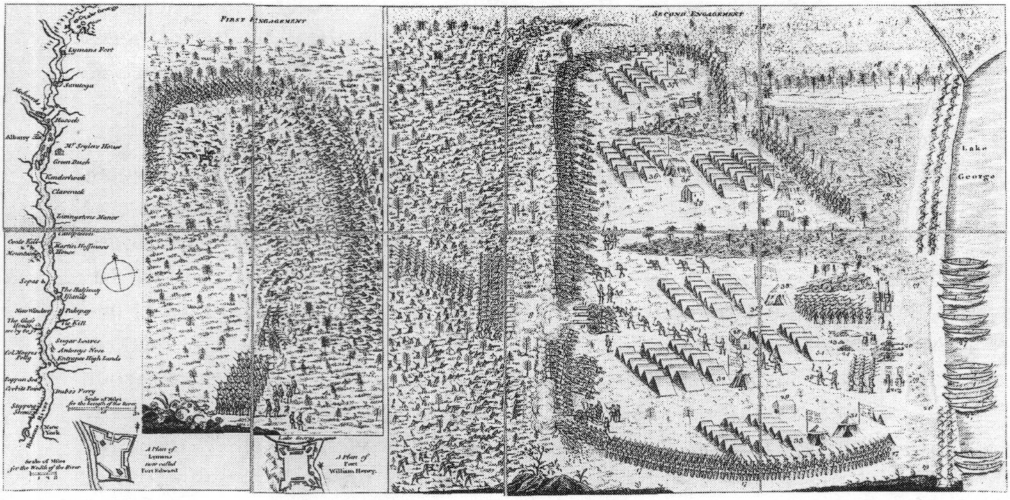

The Battle of Lake George, 1755. The three panels of this engraving, published at Boston by Samuel Blodget in 1756, depict (from left to right) the location of the battle by a map of the Hudson Valley and the head of Lake George; the horseshoe ambush of the "Bloody Morning Scout"; and Dieskau's attack on the fortified camp. Although obviously schematic, Blodget's view was based on eyewitness accounts and shows the battle, and even individual behavior, with surprising accuracy. Chief Hendrick appears mounted on a horse in the center panel, while the other Mohawks are shown kneeling and firing individually, from cover; the provincials either stand in ranks or fire by platoons. On the right, provincial troops under attack fire prone from behind the breastwork or stand upright within the camp; the Indians crouch in postures that grow lower to the ground the nearer they approach the firing line. *Courtesy of the William L. Clements Library at the University of Michigan.*

ans, who "in general regulated themselves by the Conduct of the Ind[ia]ns when upon War parties with them." Dieskau seized control of this shaky situation by ordering his two grenadier companies to form a close-order column and charge the guns at the entrance of the camp. He intended to shame the wavering Indians and Canadians into attack; directing them to disperse around the perimeter of the camp and fire from the cover of logs and stumps, he gave orders to swarm over the breastwork whenever the opportunity presented itself.[20]

From the edge of the clearing to the mouth of Captain Eyre's battery was perhaps 150 yards. Dieskau's grenadiers—the biggest, most imposing men of the Languedoc and La Reine Regiments, among the best soldiers in the French army—charged along the road across the clearing with bayonets fixed, six abreast, in a column 100 yards long. Magnificent in white uniforms and disciplined as only the cream of Europe's proudest army could be, they were not halfway to their goal when the grapeshot charges of the English guns cut "Lanes, Streets, and Alleys" through them, annihilating their order and forcing them back. From cover at the edge of the woods, the Indians and Canadians fired steadily at the defenders through much of the afternoon, but with little real effect. Dieskau, who sustained a crippling wound, remained on the field, but the failure of the charge and the loss of Legardeur had doomed the attack. After four or five hours of increasingly uncoordinated firing his men began to retreat without order.[21]

The provincials from the camp made little effort to pursue them beyond the clearing. As one witness explained, "The Day was declining—The Rout of the Enemy not certain,—The Country all a Wood,—our Men greatly fatigued, provided neither with Bayonets or Swords, undisciplined, & not very high spirited." A sortie onto the battlefield, however, recovered the disconsolate Dieskau, "wounded in his Bladder," along with about twenty other wounded men. The remainder of the attackers vanished into the forest's lengthening shadows, making off for Fort St. Frédéric or returning to the site of the ambush to recover the captives they had left tied to trees.[22]

It was there, in the ravine, that perhaps four hundred Indians, Canadians, and Frenchmen were resting and trying to regroup under their surviving officers when they were surprised by a column of New Hampshire provincials. About two hundred men under Captain William McGinnis had begun to march to the aid of Johnson's camp from Fort Edward when the sounds of the battle had first been heard. Now, in deep dusk, they attacked the disorganized enemy "& made a great Slaughter amongst them." Most of the French and Indian casualties of the day occurred in this final phase of the disjointed battle, which also occasioned more English casualties: not only were Captain McGinnis and two of his men killed, but so were all the prisoners the Caughnawagas and Abenakis had come back to collect. Several would later be found dead and scalped, still bound hand and foot. Unable to retreat with the prisoners in hand and unwilling to abandon them, the Indians had taken trophies that, while less valuable than captives, still offered evidence of their participation in the battle.[23]

The fall of night ended both the Battle of Lake George and the Crown Point expedition of 1755. Johnson had taken a musket ball in one buttock and was in no shape to continue; nor were his men, who spent the next three days searching out and burying the dead, a gruesome and "most meloncoly Peace of busaness," for the weather had turned fair and hot. Despite the fact that the battle could be regarded as a provincial vic-

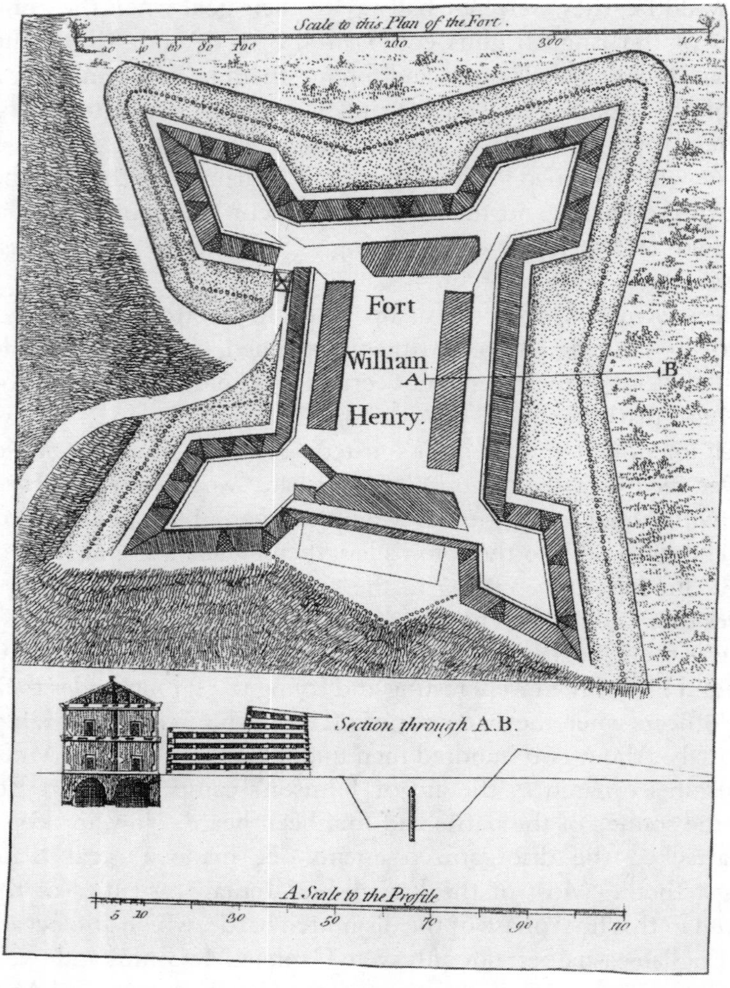

Fort William Henry, New York. This view, from Rocque's *Set of Plans and Forts* (1765), shows Captain Eyre's design of a stout fort with four bastions, situated on a rise that falls steeply away, at the bottom (north) of the picture, to the lakeshore. A ditch, or dry moat, surrounds the fort on its other three sides. The cross-section view depicts, from the left, a two-story barracks with subterranean "bomb-proofs," or casemates; the "curtain," or wall, thirty feet thick and fifteen feet high, made of horizontally laid logs, infilled with earth and rubble; the "terre-plein," or cannon platform, shielded by the parapet at the top of the wall; the "fraising," a line of sharpened logs projecting horizontally from the parapet to discourage scaling parties; the ten-foot-deep ditch, along the bottom of which runs a palisade of sharpened logs eight or more feet in height; and, beyond the ditch, the fifty-yard-long, gently sloping "glacis," an open field of fire that attackers would have to traverse before reaching the interior obstacles of ditch, stockade, and fraised wall. Cannon, sited along the wall in embrasures, were positioned both to fire at distant besiegers and to "enfilade," or fire along the face of, the curtain. *Courtesy of the William L. Clements Library at the University of Michigan.*

tory—the French had been driven from the field, and the casualties on both sides were evenly balanced—demoralization beset the camp, and men began to sicken in large numbers. Although reinforcements soon arrived from Fort Edward, provisions remained short enough to forestall a new offensive; moreover, as soon as the plundering was done the Mohawks went home to conduct their condolence rituals, taking along prisoners to adopt—or torture and kill—as replacements for the dead.[24]

By late September, scouts sent down Lake George on reconnaissance missions were returning with reports that the French had begun to fortify Ticonderoga. At that point, even if Johnson and his officers had been eager to resume the expedition against Crown Point, they could not prudently have done so. As it happened, they were not eager. At a council of war on September 29, Johnson's principal officers opted to build a fort sufficient to hold five hundred men in order to protect their position on the lake and prevent future attackers from gaining access to the road that now pointed like a gun barrel at Fort Edward, Saratoga, and Albany. The indispensable Captain Eyre accordingly began to lay out a substantial earth fort of four bastions, and the garrison undertook the huge tasks of excavation, woodcutting, and interior construction necessary to complete it. Fort William Henry—which Johnson named after the duke of Cumberland (William) and the duke of Gloucester (Henry), so as to honor as many princes of the blood royal as possible before the end of the campaign—would mark the limit of the Anglo-American advance for longer than anyone in England or its colonies could have expected.[25]

All that fall, the French and the English matched ax blow for ax blow and shovelful for shovelful as they raced winter and each other to build their forts. By the next spring, the French defensive position would be anchored by Fort Carillon at the north end of Lake George and the English position would be similarly held at the south by Fort William Henry. The beautiful, island-studded lake and the steep, forested hills along its shores would become avenues for raiders and invading armies as the two sides contended for the advantage that, for a long time to come, neither would be able to retain.

CHAPTER 11

British Politics, and a Revolution in European Diplomacy

1755

THREE THOUSAND miles away, the duke of Newcastle shuddered at the news from America. In the middle of July, word reached London that Boscawen had failed to intercept the whole of the French reinforcement, while the action in which he had succeeded—the seizure of several hundred soldiers and two ships belonging to a crown with which England was still technically at peace—seemed certain to provoke hostilities with France. On July 18, Charles de Levis, duc de Mirepoix, French ambassador to the court of St. James, left London in a fury. Not long afterward, in August, word arrived of Braddock's defeat. Without realizing any substantial gain, the British had muddled their way into the posture of an international aggressor, while the French had landed sufficient men and arms to defend Canada and enable Onontio's allies to threaten the frontier of every American colony from New Hampshire to North Carolina. British policies had, in short, handed both the casus belli and the strategic advantage to France, giving the French court occasion and motive to declare war. Newcastle's relations with the man he blamed for these disasters—the duke of Cumberland—had deteriorated so far that they had become the subject of common gossip. At home, the British government was paralyzed; abroad, Britain's diplomatic position was in disarray.[1]

Newcastle faced two difficulties, both intractable: a constitutional-political problem that immobilized the government and threatened his position as prime minister; and a diplomatic problem that prevented him from strengthening himself politically. Newcastle was hamstrung as prime minister because as a peer of the realm he could not sit in the House of Commons. The duke desperately needed someone he could trust to build a reliable majority among the M.P.s, but there were only two possible candidates for the job, and in different ways they both spelled trouble. One was Henry Fox, secretary at war and the protégé of the hated duke of Cumberland. Fox was a superb parliamentary manipulator but also a libertine and opportunist—a man whose deficiencies of character and excesses of ambition, no less than his ties to Cumberland, made him an unattractive partner. Moreover, Fox was no orator: an immense handicap for a war leader, who needed not only to be able to manage the votes of the placemen in the Commons but also to inspire loyalty to government policies among the independent backbenchers—the rustic squires without whose support no war effort could long be sustained.

The other possible leader in the Commons was William Pitt, a man of astonishing oratorical power and equally astonishing, almost megalomaniacal, ambition. Newcastle detested Pitt personally, for Pitt loved nothing more than to ridicule Newcastle's policies in the Commons; but what made him even less attractive was Pitt's close connection to the heir apparent, the teenaged boy who would one day become George III. It was a trait almost as genetically fixed in the Hanoverian kings as their protuberant eyes, prominent noses, and petulant expressions to loathe those princes in line to succeed them. Pitt was closely associated with the Leicester House faction (as politicians allied with the dowager princess of Wales and her household were called, after her residence) and thus was offensive to the king, who would never admit those whom he regarded as enemies to his inner circle. And there was, finally, Pitt's celebrated disdain for the day-to-day management of political affairs in the Commons. Brilliant orator that he was, he had no patience for the mundane concerns of patronage and voting discipline that insured the stability of all eighteenth-century British governments. Neither Fox nor Pitt offered an easy alternative for Newcastle, and his basic timidity kept him from making a firm commitment to either. So long as he could not forge a lasting alliance with one or the other, however, he could not control the Commons, and thus could not govern. This problem would go unresolved for a dangerously long time.[2]

Because Newcastle had little influence over American military initiatives that originated with Cumberland, he hoped to avert war in Europe by the one means still under his control, diplomacy. In this effort the problems and complexities he faced were staggering, but in the end they

The Great Commoner. William Pitt (1708–78); an engraving after a portrait painted in the studio of William Hoare, published in London c. 1757. *Courtesy of the William L. Clements Library at the University of Michigan.*

could be reduced to a single cause: the electorate of Hanover. Ever since 1714, when the British throne had passed into the reliably Protestant hands of the Hanoverian kings, the fortunes of Great Britain had been tied to those of the small north German state that had been their home. The first two Georges were adamant that Britain protect Hanover militarily in time of war. This insistence had led to the construction of a durable alliance system on the Continent, by which Britain aligned itself with Holland and Austria in order to preserve Hanover against seizure by France and France's ally, Prussia.[3]

Newcastle's "System" had survived the Wars of the Spanish and the Austrian Successions, and its preservation virtually obsessed him; yet it had been slowly, inexorably disintegrating since the Peace of Aix-la-Chapelle. The Dutch were too ground down by misfortune and military losses to welcome the renewal of hostilities between France and Britain and were unable in 1755 to recognize any compelling interest in joining a dispute over who should control the wilds and savages of North America. The Austrians, as we have seen, regarded the recovery of Silesia from Prussian control as an object of such importance that they had already begun to explore a possible rapprochement with France.

Desperate to maintain the Austrian alliance and to keep Prussian attentions turned away from Hanover, Newcastle had proposed a treaty with Austria's ally, Russia, early in 1755. In return for a great subsidy (£100,000 annually in peacetime, £500,000 annually in the event of war), Russia was to keep an army ready to invade East Prussia. Newcastle hoped that the threat of war on his eastern frontiers would keep Frederick II, king of Prussia, from attacking Hanover. Newcastle knew, of course, that neither Russia nor Austria could keep France from overrunning the electorate if it chose to do so. Thus he undertook to shore up Hanover's defenses by concluding subsidy treaties with the rulers of various German states, in effect negotiating contracts to retain their armies as mercenary forces in the event of war. To Hanover itself went a subsidy of £50,000 annually to increase its army by 8,000 troops; to the landgrave of Hesse-Cassel, £60,000 to provide 8,000 men if war broke out; to the margrave of Ansbach and the bishop of Würzburg, more money for more mercenaries.

All this diplomatic activity may have helped increase the security of Hanover, but it did nothing to calm the French, who at this point were refraining from a formal declaration of war solely to build up their navy to the point that it could oppose Britain's on the high seas. Finally, because in the House of Commons Pitt and his followers denounced the subsidy treaties as prostitutions of English interests and treasure to the maintenance of a petty German state, the only purpose Newcastle's diplomacy served in parliamentary politics was to make him perpetually vulnerable to the loss of his majority.[4]

Throughout the summer of 1755, as disaster followed disaster and Pitt heaped scorn on the ministry and its measures, subsidies grew so unpopular in the Commons that eventually Newcastle's own Chancellor of the Exchequer refused to release money to Hesse without a special act of Parliament. Such crippling opposition finally drove Newcastle into alliance with Henry Fox, who joined the government in November as secretary of state for the Southern Department and manager of the ministry's interests in the Commons. Once formed, the Fox-Newcastle partnership seemed to work wonders. In a rancorous debate on the subsidy policy begun on November 13, Pitt lashed the ministry mercilessly, ridiculing the partnership of Newcastle and Fox as "the conflux of the Rhône and Saône; this a gentle, feeble, languid stream, and though languid, of no depth—the other, an impetuous torrent." Such brilliant vituperation would have earned him the acclamation of the House in the previous session, but now that Fox was protecting the duke's interests in the Commons, Pitt's speech was only the noisy prelude to a vote by which the M.P.s affirmed their support for subsidies by a two-to-one margin. With barely a pause to relish this crushing defeat of a man he hated, Newcastle unceremoniously turned him and his supporters out of their offices. If the new alliance with Fox could not permanently silence Pitt, Fox's deft parliamentary management had at least shown that Pitt's disruptive potential could be contained.[5]

And yet Newcastle's policies, secure at last, were even then in the process of bringing down the whole alliance system on which the duke had lavished such attention and energy. In Berlin, King Frederick brooded on the likely effects of the Anglo-Russian treaty and the possible consequences of the entente that was rumored to be developing between his old enemy, Austria, and his old ally, France. Frederick—who, it was said, feared Russia more than God—accordingly directed his diplomats to find a means of coming to terms with Great Britain. By the beginning of the new year, what would six months earlier have been unfathomable was quickly coming to pass: a treaty of friendship between Prussia and Britain. Under the Convention of Westminster, signed January 16, 1756, the Crowns of Britain and Prussia mutually pledged that neither would invade or distress the other. Should any aggressor disturb the tranquillity of "Germany"—a term vague enough to cover both Hanover and Prussia—they would unite to oppose the invader. The Convention of Westminster was not a formal defensive alliance, nor was it intended to do more than secure Hanover from attack. Prussia was to remain neutral in the present disputes between France and Britain. Unlike all the ministry's previous treaties, this one required no peacetime subsidies: here, at last, was a means of protecting Hanover that would cost the Exchequer not a farthing.[6]

What the convention did cost England, of course, was its alliance with Austria. Or, more properly, it removed all obstacles to the final dissolution of the alliance and permitted the formal reversal of alignments known as the Diplomatic Revolution. Now the negotiations between the courts of Maria Theresa and Louis XV, previously conducted with such discretion and secrecy, moved rapidly and openly toward completion. When word of the convention arrived at Versailles in early February, the French Council of State repudiated the alliance with Prussia, clearing the way for formal rapprochement with Austria. On May 1, 1756, Austrian and French diplomats signed the Convention of Versailles, a mutual defense pact that mirrored the Convention of Westminster. By this agreement, the French agreed to come to Austria's aid, should it come under attack; while by a special article the Austrians were freed from any reciprocal responsibility to support the French in their present dispute with Great Britain.

The combination of the two conventions should, reasonably, have immunized Europe against a war spreading from North America. Hanover had been made as secure as any flat and virtually indefensible country could be; Austria's anxieties at the prospect of a Prussian attack had been allayed as fully as a defensive alliance with the greatest land power in Europe could allay them. France and Britain might now attack one another's colonies and shipping at will, but only a truly bizarre—indeed almost unthinkable—act could disturb the peace of Europe. The only thing that could shatter the new equilibrium would be for the king of Prussia to attack Austria, and that would be the act of a madman. Frederick had a large and capable army, it was true, but it was no match for the army of France, let alone for those of France and Austria together. Moreover, Frederick's country was poor and had a population of less than four million; the combined populations of France and Austria were ten times as large.[7] No one doubted Frederick's boldness, but everyone knew that he was not fool enough to launch an attack that would give Maria Theresa all the excuse she would need to recover her beloved Silesia, at last.

Thus in the first month or two of 1756, the duke of Newcastle could look around him at affairs that seemed to be stabilizing; indeed, the future looked almost rosy. Although it had not been a result he had intended when he undertook his diplomatic offensive, and although George II had been unhappy to witness the demise of an Austrian alliance to which his family had been devoted, the new alignment of Britain with Prussia seemed to promise both security for Hanover and a limitation of hostilities with France. Pitt, neutralized in Parliament, had been driven with his remaining few supporters into noisy, ineffectual opposition. The disarray in America remained to be attended to, and the alliance that he had been compelled to forge with Fox and Cumberland promised to make the resolution of those problems personally unpleasant. Nonetheless, Newcastle had more reason to feel secure, and even optimistic, than at any time in the previous year.[8]

The reckoning on America came in January. On the seventh a meeting of the cabinet considered the pleas from the colonies for further military aid and examined a plan Halifax had drawn up to centralize, coordinate, and expand the war effort. Having received reports from William Johnson and Thomas Pownall denouncing Shirley as a meddler in Indian affairs and a poor commander, Halifax recommended that a new commander in chief be sent from England with expanded powers, and that Johnson receive a new commission, directly from the king, appointing him as colonel of the Six Nations. The ministers generally agreed with these suggestions, although they dismissed as excessively expensive the remainder of Halifax's program, which called for the creation of a royally funded central storehouse for provisions, the reinforcement of the regulars in the colonies, and the raising of large numbers of provincial troops.[9]

Two weeks later, in a gathering of the ministers at Newcastle House, Cumberland and Fox proposed their own program, adopting Halifax's suggestions concerning the replacement of Shirley and a new commission for Johnson, but otherwise reaffirming the plan under which Braddock had been dispatched the previous year. Cumberland disliked Halifax's idea for using provincial troops—he thought them too expensive, inefficient, and undisciplined—and therefore called for sending two new regiments of redcoats from Britain and raising four new, thousand-man battalions of regulars in the colonies. In addition to Johnson, Cumberland and Fox proposed the appointment of an Indian superintendent for the southern colonies as well, the South Carolina trader Edmund Atkin. Finally, as Shirley's replacement they proposed sending John Campbell, the fourth earl of Loudoun, an experienced military administrator. The other ministers present, including Newcastle, accepted it all.

Although Newcastle had for many years been Shirley's patron, the decision to abandon him probably did not come hard. Over the years the two men had become estranged, and Fox and Cumberland, on whom Newcastle now depended for his political life, were united against him. Moreover, Thomas Pownall, after orchestrating a great letter-writing campaign against Shirley, had returned to London to manage the final phases of the offensive in person. He was fortunate in that four deeply troubling letters written in America and addressed to the duc de Mirepoix were intercepted at about the time of his arrival: letters that seemed to promise treason in return for French money. The letters, the work of an anonymous author calling himself Filius Gallicae, contained enough accurate information on North American military affairs to make Halifax, Cumberland, Fox, and others fear that a high army officer was about to turn his coat. Pownall suggested that, since Shirley had spent several years in Paris and had a French wife, Filius Gallicae might well be the commander in chief himself. In fact, the letters were probably a hoax intended to discredit George Croghan or even John Henry Lydius, but that hardly mattered. In Pownall's opportunistic hands their effect was to discredit Shirley and insure his immediate recall. Whereas once it had been contemplated to relieve him of his military command but to compensate him for his long and faithful service by giving him the governorship of Jamaica, now Cumberland clamored to have him sent home in chains. Cooler heads prevailed, but Shirley's career was effectively finished. On March 31, Fox wrote him a brusque letter confirming that he had been superseded in command of His Majesty's forces, and that upon receipt of the letter he was to "repair to England with all possible Expedition."[10]

With Shirley taken care of, Pownall swept all before him. First he saw to it that Shirley's leading political ally, Robert Hunter Morris, was removed from the governorship of Pennsylvania. The supply contracts for the army in New York, which Shirley had awarded to the partnership of Livingston and Morris, were diverted to the powerful, politically wired London firm of Baker and Kilby—the New York correspondent of which happened to be Oliver De Lancey, the younger brother of Lieutenant Governor James De Lancey. The records of Livingston and Morris in their dealings with Shirley were seized and submitted to a Treasury audit, a process that would take years to complete.

William Johnson, now known as Sir William because the king had conferred a baronetcy on him in November, hardly needed Pownall's help; he was secure politically and his positions as northern Indian superintendent and colonel of the Six Nations brought him an annual stipend of six hundred pounds sterling. Nevertheless, Pownall continued energetically to publicize him as a man who (in contrast to Shirley) had sacrificed his own estate in the defense of the colonies and had proven himself a hero at the Battle of Lake George. In February, Parliament showed its gratitude by voting Sir William a reward of five thousand pounds for his services to the nation.

Only one piece of business remained. With Shirley dismissed from his governorship, the Crown needed a man of judgment and political acumen to head the crucial province of Massachusetts Bay. Modestly, and only after a decent interval, Thomas Pownall consented to accept that burden himself.[11]

WILLIAM SHIRLEY's career lay in ruins long before he knew it. In itself that would hardly have surprised him, for the tactics Pownall used to destroy him were the classic ones that men who wished to become royal governors employed. They were, for that matter, not dissimilar to those Shirley himself had employed to bring down his predecessor in the Massachusetts governorship, fourteen years before.[12] Rather than his almost predictable destruction, what was most important about Shirley's brief, thwarted tenure as commander in chief was the fact that six months passed between the time the ministers decided to replace him and the date his successor arrived. During that period, as government officials dawdled and the cumbersome machinery of army bureaucracy ground slowly forward in preparation for the change of command, Shirley had already set the campaign of 1756 in motion.

More ominously for Britain, at that same time the French ministry was more efficiently setting afoot its own military operations for 1756. Even before Lord Loudoun's commission as lieutenant general and commander in chief for America had been issued, a new French commander, Dieskau's replacement, had already sailed for Canada with reinforcements.[13] Within six weeks after Loudoun took command of his army, two great French victories—one in America, the other in the Mediterranean—would call into question the whole British war effort and throw the British government into chaos.

And that would be only the beginning.

PART III

NADIR

1756–1757

Shirley undertakes operations in 1756, then turns over command to Lord Loudoun and suffers public disgrace. A thwarted campaign and a French victory suggest the importance of intercultural relations in deciding the war's outcome. Colonial politics and the war effort; resistance to the commander in chief. War erupts in Europe. Britain fails to achieve political stability and sustains two notable military defeats. As 1757 begins, Lord Loudoun proves more adept at fighting the colonists than the French. The Anglo-Americans lose an important fort in New York and see hope glimmer, faintly, in Pennsylvania. As colonial opposition to Lord Loudoun edges toward deadlock and Britain faces a European shambles, William Pitt takes over direction of the war.

CHAPTER 12

Lord Loudoun Takes Command

1756

THE SIX FRENCH warships that sailed up the St. Lawrence in May 1756 carried several hundred troops and the man who would lead Canada's defending forces for the next three years, Louis-Joseph, marquis de Montcalm-Gozon de Saint-Véran. At the age of forty-four, Montcalm was not one of France's leading generals, but an experienced professional officer—a small, bright-eyed, quick-witted man whose courage and presence of mind in battle had earned him the rank of *maréchal de camp,* or brigadier general, during the previous war. The reflective cast of his mind has made Montcalm an attractive figure to many American historians, who have tended to portray him as the brilliant opposite number of the prickly, pompous British commander in chief, Lord Loudoun. His disdain for Canadians, his reluctance to use Indian allies to advantage, and his pessimism about achieving victory over the vast numbers of his enemy have made him a far more problematic figure for Canadian scholars.[1]

In fact Montcalm did fritter away advantages, particularly in the use of Indians, that had long preserved New France from conquest; and he did it quite consciously—indeed, almost conscientiously, for he saw his actions as matters of principle, undertaken in defense of civilization itself. Yet Montcalm's alienation of his allies, and eventually of the Canadians themselves, was a gradual process that did not immediately result in Anglo-American victories; indeed, for more than two years the redcoats and their provincial auxiliaries suffered a virtually uninterrupted series of defeats at his hands. The downward spiral of Anglo-American military fortunes in 1756 and 1757 cannot be understood apart from the increas-

The marquis de Montcalm (1712–59). A soldier's soldier in the European mode, Montcalm was horrified by the style of warfare he encountered in America and did everything in his power to make his operations conform to civilized standards as he understood them. He may have lived long enough to regret it. *Courtesy of the McCord Museum of Canadian History, Montreal / Musée McCord d'histoire canadienne, Montréal.*

ingly bitter disputes between the colonial assemblies and Lord Loudoun, which finally led to the bottoming-out of Britain's war effort in America. To understand how and why the Anglo-Americans failed to take advantage of their vastly superior numbers and resources, and to see the reasons behind Montcalm's abandonment of strategies of proven merit, is to begin to grasp the decisive influence of cultural factors in shaping the last and greatest of America's colonial wars.

As THE SHIPS bearing Montcalm and his men fought their way westward against the Atlantic's March gales, the men William Shirley had left behind at Oswego battled the deadlier enemies of scurvy and starvation. The 50th and 51st Regiments had been on short rations ever since their long river-and-lake supply line from Albany had frozen shut. With his men so weak that they could barely mount guard, Lieutenant Colonel James Mercer in the late winter found himself with no choice but to evacuate the fort. He had already set March 25 as the day he would order his men to march for Schenectady when, on March 24, fourteen bateau-loads of supplies arrived and staved off disaster.

Still there was no immediate relief. For the next month and more, provisions trickled in at a rate just sufficient to sustain the garrison, for with the coming of spring, travel between the advance supply base at Schenectady and Oswego became mortally dangerous. On March 27 French and Indian raiders appeared, as if from nowhere, outside the palisade of Fort Bull at the west end of the Great Carrying Place—the portage road across the divide between the east-flowing Mohawk River and west-running Wood Creek. The raiders annihilated Fort Bull's small garrison, razed its buildings and palisade, destroyed supplies and boats, and vanished back into the woods. Thereafter from the headwaters of the Mohawk to the walls of Oswego there was no security for the bateaumen who carried the post its lifeblood. Weak and sick, dying at an appalling rate, the men of Mercer's garrison held on, but only barely. Their sufferings and the loss of Fort Bull seemed grim omens for the year that had barely begun.[2]

Smoke may still have drifted from the wreck of the fort when, thousands of miles away, Henry Fox began to draft the letter ordering Major General Shirley to turn over command to his successor and "repair to England with all possible Expedition." Weeks would pass before Shirley would realize how bad circumstances were, either at Oswego or at Whitehall; at the moment he was back in Boston, catching up on his duties as governor and drumming up political support for the campaigns he had planned for the coming summer. He hoped to convince the Bay Colony's legislators to join the other New England provinces and New York in raising thousands of provincials for an assault on Crown Point, and he had reason to anticipate success. Massachusetts had always been zealous to prosecute wars against the French and Indians; although its population was still less than a quarter million, for example, nearly eight thousand of its men (one in five of those in the prime military ages) had enlisted in provincial and regular units during the previous year.[3]

As Shirley well knew, the problem was less enthusiasm than money, for the General Court had levied heavy taxes to support the previous campaigns, and the legislators wanted assurances that sufficient subsidies or reimbursements would be forthcoming from England to allow them to

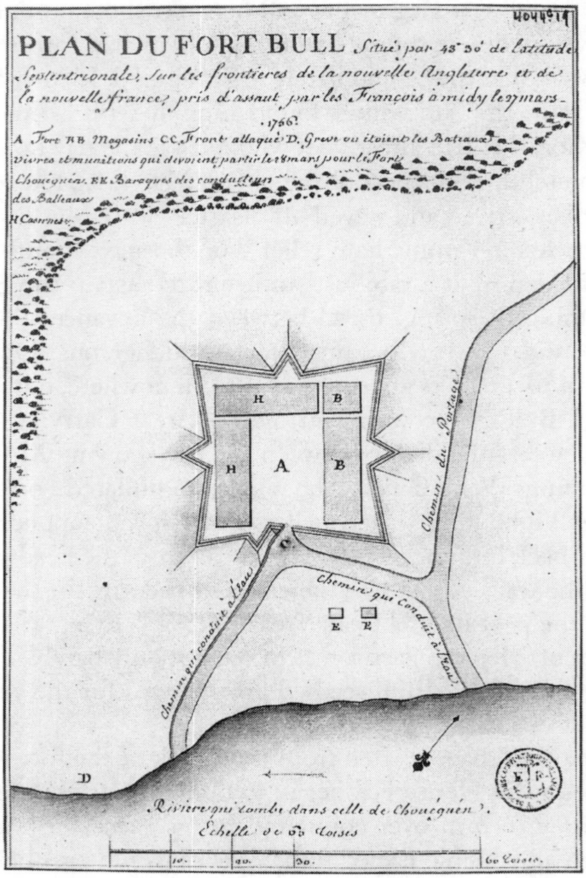

Plan of Fort Bull . . . on the frontiers of New England and New France, taken by assault by the French at mid-day, 27 March 1756. Joseph-Gaspard Chaussegros de Léry, lieutenant of the *troupes de la marine* and commander of the Franco-Indian raiding party, recorded the outlines of Fort Bull before he ordered it blown up and put to the torch. As this engraving, made from his sketch, suggests, the post was not so much a fort as a way station: a collection of storehouses and barracks, enclosed in a single palisade. *Courtesy of the William L. Clements Library at the University of Michigan.*

meet the empire's demands without bankrupting their province. Shirley did his best to reassure them, promising to press their claims with the authorities at home and in the meantime lending the province thirty thousand pounds from his war chest to help meet current expenses. Conscious that many of them were discontented with the way William Johnson had managed the previous year's expedition, he also promised to appoint a popular, thoroughly experienced Massachusetts officer, John

Winslow, as major general in command of the combined provincial forces on the Crown Point expedition. Pleased with his attention to their concerns, the legislators agreed to raise 3,000 men for the coming year, as Massachusetts's contribution to the total of 7,500 provincials to be recruited from the northern colonies.[4]

The enthusiasm of Massachusetts together with that of Connecticut ensured that a large provincial expedition would proceed against Crown Point in 1756. The remainder of Shirley's plans for the year called for the regulars under his command in New York—now including four infantry battalions and a substantial train of artillery—to attack the French forts of the upper St. Lawrence basin. Since New France's western posts were all supplied from Montréal, the seizure of the Fort La Galette (Oswegatchie) on the upper St. Lawrence and Fort Frontenac (Cataraqui) at the foot of Lake Ontario would render the rest of the western forts untenable—and that included everything from Niagara and Detroit on the Great Lakes to Duquesne in the Ohio Country. Shirley had also been encouraging the colonies of Pennsylvania, Maryland, and Virginia to send a provincial army over Braddock's road to attack Fort Duquesne, but this was not a prerequisite for victory. Even if these provinces did not, or could not, cooperate—and given the chaos on their frontiers, he could not realistically hope for much from them—the elimination of Fort Frontenac alone would destroy France's ability to control the west.[5]

These expeditions by no means added up to a war of conquest, but if successful they would cripple New France militarily, and they would do so in a way that was both more economical and more strategically elegant than Braddock's plan. Most of all, however, Shirley's proposals for 1756 utilized the complementary strengths of the provinces and the regular army without asking for unrealistic exertions from any of them.

William Shirley was nothing if not a consummate judge of what could and could not be expected of colonial societies at war. He knew that he could rely only on the militant New England provinces (in practice, Massachusetts and Connecticut) for heavy commitments of men and money. He also understood the limits within which he had to operate in dealing with them. Thus, his allocation of provincial and regular forces to separate expeditions, which to any professional military officer or British government minister would have seemed bizarre, in fact reflected an astute appraisal of those limits.

Shirley wanted to keep provincials apart from regulars because fourteen years of experience as Massachusetts's governor told him that two British military policies would wreck any campaign in which the two kinds of forces had to operate together. First was the Royal Proclamation of November 12, 1754, which stipulated that all provincial officers (that is, all officers commissioned by the governors of colonies) would be deemed junior to all regular officers (those holding commissions issued by the king or his commander in chief). This order reduced the most experienced colonial military leaders, colonels and generals not excepted, to a level below that of the newest pimpled ensign in the regular army. No self-respecting colonial officer would willingly serve under such conditions; Shirley knew that only too well. He also understood that the second British policy might prove even more devastating to colonial participation in the war effort.[6]

In December 1754, the solicitor general had ruled that "all Officers and Soldiers . . . raised in any of the *British* Provinces in *America,* by Authority of the respective Governors or Governments thereof, shall, . . . when they happen to join, or act in Conjunction with, his Majesty's *British* forces, be liable to [the same] martial Law and Discipline, . . . as the *British* Forces are; and shall be subject to the same Trial, Penalties, and Punishments." The extension of regular discipline to provincial armies would discourage if not put a stop to enlistment, for no matter how patriotic or eager for the pay potential recruits might be, they knew very well that regular courts-martial routinely sentenced soldiers to severe whippings, and not infrequently to death, for infractions of discipline.[7]

Realizing all this, Shirley planned operations for 1756 that would require no contact between the all-provincial campaign against Crown Point and the all-regular expedition against Fort Frontenac. Although he understood that provincial troops were amateurish, hard to discipline, and deficient in the technical expertise needed to conduct siege warfare, Shirley clearly believed that the risks of employing them against the nearest target, Crown Point, were worth running. In order to lay to rest all doubts in the colonial assemblies, he gave explicit assurances that any provincials raised for the expedition would serve only under their own officers, that they would be subject to provincial and not regular discipline, and that they would be employed only in an area east of Schenectady and north of Albany.[8]

The New England assemblies responded warmly to Shirley's plans and promises, and thousands of New England men would eventually volunteer for the Crown Point expedition. In the meantime, Shirley was trying to solve the problem of supplying Oswego in an equally inventive, equally irregular way. An American-born officer in the 51st Regiment, Captain John Bradstreet, had shown exceptional talent during the previous war, when Shirley had taken the unusual step of making him lieutenant colonel of a Massachusetts provincial regiment, and he had gone on to serve with distinction at the Louisbourg siege. In 1755 Shirley had once again sought to exploit his genius by placing him in charge of the bateaumen who supplied Fort Oswego. In January, Shirley promoted Bradstreet to the rank of lieutenant colonel in the regular army—an unauthorized, utterly illegal promotion for which Shirley would later pay—and ordered him to organize a corps of two thousand bateaumen and boatbuilders to handle all transportation between Schenectady and Lake Ontario.

Bradstreet, an unorthodox regular officer with rare talent for dealing with provincials, quickly enlisted hundreds of rivermen, then armed and trained them to fight in the woods. In May, despite Indian attacks along the route, Bradstreet's men pushed large quantities of supplies through to Oswego. By June the garrison was sufficiently recovered from its winter ordeal to begin improving the post's fortifications. The persistent lack of skilled workers and money sharply limited attempts to strengthen Oswego's defenses, and soldiers and carpenters remained subject to harassing Indian raids from the surrounding woods, but Bradstreet's bateaumen had saved the fort.[9]

By early summer, notwithstanding the concerns of Lieutenant Colonel Mercer and his fellow officers about the security of their position, things seemed at last to be looking up. While it was clear that the depleted regiments (the effective strength of which had dwindled by May to half what it had been eight months earlier) would not be strong enough to attack Fort Frontenac without reinforcements, the supply crisis was over, and three newly raised companies of rangers were patrolling the supply route to keep off Indian raiders. With new recruits arriving to fill the ranks of the 50th and 51st, and with the addition of a battalion of New Jersey provincials, the garrison seemed at least strong enough to hold the fort and thus able to sustain Britain's strategic foothold on the Great Lakes. The most pressing task was to strengthen the fortifications, which remained in poor condition but were at last coming under repair.[10]

On June 25, Major General James Abercromby, Lord Loudoun's second-in-command, arrived in Albany and relieved Shirley of all further responsibility for His Majesty's forces in North America. Shirley, who had heard through informal channels more than two months earlier that he would be superseded, accepted it calmly and proceeded to New York to await the new commander in chief. For his part, Abercromby was determined to do as little as possible. A corpulent man and an indifferent officer, he wanted to undertake nothing for which he might later be blamed; thus he contented himself with taking stock of the situation. What he saw gave him pause.[11]

At this point, the campaigns were well under way. A provincial force made up of nearly seven thousand men from New England and New York was assembling at Forts Edward and William Henry, preparing to move against Fort Carillon (at Ticonderoga) and Fort St. Frédéric (at Crown Point). Like virtually all other regular officers, Abercromby did not approve of using badly trained and imperfectly disciplined provincials as combat troops, but theirs seemed likely to be the only campaign that would actually proceed before the campaigning season ended—unless, of course, Loudoun should decide to send the new troops he was bringing from England to strengthen Oswego's depleted regiments and attack Fort Frontenac. Not knowing his lordship's preferences, Abercromby could not decide what to do with the regulars he now commanded in the Albany region. In all there were about three thousand of them, including four understrength regiments, several independent infantry companies, assorted artillerists, and a few engineers. Lacking any better idea, he deployed them as guards along the supply line between Albany and Fort Edward and waited for Loudoun to arrive and solve his problems for him. But Loudoun was slow in coming.[12]

At length, dogged by doubts about letting a pack of half-disciplined provincials undertake what seemed likely to be the sole expedition of the year while His Majesty's troops stood guard over the pork barrels and bateaux of Albany, Abercromby asked Major General Winslow for advice. What would happen if Abercromby ordered regulars up to Lake George, to join the campaign against Crown Point? Because Winslow had served in a regular regiment during King George's War and still ranked as a captain in the British army, his personal alternatives were limited to two: he could obey Abercromby's commands or he could expose himself to arrest and court-martial for insubordination. He therefore assured Abercromby that he personally would gladly follow any orders he received but warned him that most provincial field officers would resign their commissions rather than take orders from regular officers far junior to them in rank. Even more ominously, Winslow predicted that the common soldiers of the expedition would desert en masse before submitting themselves to the lash and noose of regular discipline.[13]

Abercromby found this a most worrisome response and so convened his senior officers as a council of war to advise him on what to do—they urged him not to press the issue—while Winslow promised to take up the question with his own officers at Lake George. There the matter hung, with the provincials entering upon a "grand debate" in a three-day council of war and Abercromby squirming in indecision, when H.M.S. *Nightingale* dropped anchor off Sandy Hook on July 22. Early the next morning Lieutenant General John Campbell, earl of Loudoun—fiftyish, "short, strong made &. . . fit for Action"—stepped off a pilot boat onto the quay at New York City. Abercromby's problems were solved, those of Winslow and his officers about to begin; but the first to feel the force of Lord Loudoun's will would be William Shirley.[14]

Loudoun brought with him all the accoutrements of his rank and office. Six thousand more troops had been authorized to support him, including two regiments (the 35th Foot and the 42nd Foot, the Black Watch) sent from Britain. A new, unique regiment of four battalions, the 62nd Foot (or Royal Americans, soon to be redesignated the 60th), was to be raised in the colonies, largely among the Germans of Pennsylvania. Loudoun's commissions and instructions granted him the most extensive civil and military powers in the history of British imperial governance—powers as nearly viceregal as it was constitutionally possible to make them—and he carried a commission as governor of Virginia as well. His entourage numbered no fewer than twenty-four, including his mistress and her maid, seventeen personal servants, and one "secretary extraordinary"—Thomas Pownall.[15]

Loudoun and Pownall had conferred throughout the two-month crossing about how best to handle American affairs, and Loudoun arrived convinced that the first order of business would have to be settling with his predecessor. That he did straightaway, calling Shirley in on July 24 for consultations on the state of the campaigns. Their first meeting was restrained and correct, but relations between the two men deteriorated sharply thereafter. Almost from the moment of his arrival, Loudoun heard accusations of impropriety from the concourse of Shirley's enemies who had been on hand to welcome him to New York. As Loudoun's first days in America passed, he heard, among other allegations, that Oswego was in a dangerously exposed state; that Shirley had violated every conceivable point of army procedure in recruitment, promotions, and the allocation of supply contracts; that he had drained the military chest by unauthorized and unaccounted expenditures; that his contractors had been behindhand in procuring supplies and profligate in spending money for them; that he had allowed the provincial officers of the Crown Point expedition to operate as if they were an autonomous force, permitting them to recruit their troops on conditions that in effect insulated them from the control of the commander in chief.[16]

As Loudoun confronted Shirley with these accusations, Shirley came for the first time to understand that prosecution might well lie in his future, and began peppering the commander in chief with self-justifying letters (nine within the first week alone). His lordship received each with

John Campbell, fourth earl of Loudoun (1705–82). Shown here as painted by Allan Ramsay perhaps fifteen years before he was appointed commander in chief, Lord Loudoun was an energetic man, a thoroughly professional military administrator, and a keen critic of American foibles. Notwithstanding formal powers that made him little less than a viceroy for America, his inability to work with provincial troops and colonial legislative leaders alike kept him from realizing the advantages of manpower and matériel he built up while supreme commander. *Courtesy of the National Galleries of Scotland.*

more displeasure than the last, annotated them with critical comments, and dispatched them to England, where they became part of the dossier that Cumberland and Fox were compiling for use against the unfortunate governor. Soon Loudoun and Shirley were no longer on speaking terms.

What troubled Loudoun most about Shirley's misrule was the position in which he had left the provincials on the Crown Point expedition. Loudoun, a supremely orderly man who amused himself on his Ayrshire estate by planting a wood along the avenue to the house "in the form of [an infantry] regiment drawn up in review, a tree to a man," could not tolerate so carnivalesque a campaign. For such a general as he, a dedicated administrator and a stickler for discipline, it was almost intolerable that the un-uniformed, untrained, mobbish provincials of Winslow's army should be bumbling about on the most direct route to Canada, separating the king's regulars from the enemy. What made it worst of all was the result of the provincial officers' council of war at Lake George, which had been meeting to discuss the consequences of joint operations with the regulars when Loudoun arrived in New York. As Winslow reported the proceedings of the council, the majority of his colonels had agreed that any effort to put them and their men under joint command with the redcoats would end in "a dissolution of the army." The reason they gave for this remarkable conclusion was that the conditions under which they had accepted their commissions and the understandings of the troops at the time of their enlistment had been contractual in character, and those contracts would be violated if the provincials were placed under direct regular command. Once the agreement that created it was broken, the army would cease to exist.[17]

Such reasoning was nonsense to Loudoun, who immediately identified Shirley as "the *first contriver* and *fomenter* of all the Opposition, the *New England* Men make, to being Join'd to the Kings Troops." In fact Loudoun, to a degree unappreciated among Winslow's subordinates, had done his best to improve the status of provincial officers serving jointly with regulars; before he left Britain he had seen to it that the regulation on precedence was modified so that provincial field officers and generals would rank as "eldest captains" when in joint service with regulars. This so-called Rule of 1755 meant that twenty-year-old subalterns could no longer issue orders to senior colonial officers, although the most junior redcoat majors were still free to do so.[18]

In Loudoun's mind, this was a great concession. The provincials thought otherwise. Their intransigence so irked the commander in chief that when he went to Albany at the end of July he made it his first priority to set Winslow straight. When the New Englander (mistaking an order for an invitation) proved slow to respond to Loudoun's summons, Loudoun ordered him to Albany in peremptory terms, on August 5. Winslow did not make the same mistake a second time. Within two days of receiving Loudoun's letter, he and all his principal subordinates were waiting on his lordship at Albany.

And yet—concerned as they were at the sight and sound of the squat, irate Scot who was demanding that they explain, in writing, why they did not wish to place themselves under his command—Winslow and his officers stood fast. As for himself, Winslow replied, "your lordship may be assured I shall ever be ready to obey your commands." His fellow officers, he continued, were "ready and willing to act in conjunction with his majesty's troops and put themselves under the command of your lordship, who is commander in chief; so that the terms and conditions, agreed upon and established by the several governments to whom they belong and upon which they were raised, be not altered. . . ." So there would be no mistake, the next day one of Winslow's subordinates provided Loudoun with a list of the "terms and conditions on which the provincial troops, now on their march towards Crown Point, were raised."[19]

Since the provincials had made it clear that they would resign before they would submit, and since Loudoun had no means to defend the Lake George frontier without them, all that the commander in chief could do was look for some face-saving compromise. It did not make him happy to have to do so. In the end, he settled for having each of the officers sign a formal written submission to the king's authority, in return for which he promised that he would allow their expedition to proceed without the injection of regular troops or direct regular command. By August 19, the provincials were back at Fort William Henry, preparing once more to embark for Ticonderoga and Crown Point.[20]

Loudoun now wrote furious reports to Whitehall and to the duke of Cumberland, detailing the outrages that Shirley and his henchmen, the Massachusetts officers, had perpetrated. Yet even as he wrote the commander in chief was beginning to see that it was not just Shirley who was causing these problems. On the basis of his monthlong acquaintanceship with Americans, it was already clear to Loudoun that they lacked a proper sense of subordination to constituted authority. The New Englanders, prattling about contracts, were the worst; even their legislatures so distrusted his authority when he attempted to rationalize the provincial supply system that they refused to cooperate until they could be sure he was not trying to use provisioning as a pretext for claiming direct control over the provincial forces. Something larger was indeed afoot in America, but he did not know what to call it.[21]

Loudoun did not—because a man of his background, class, and position could not—understand that the New Englanders clung so obstinately to contractual principles and seemed to care so little for efficiency and professionalism because they understood military obligations and ideals differently from him. If they saw their undertaking of a campaign against the French and Indians as a function of agreements openly entered into between soldiers and the province that employed them, it was because much in the culture of New Englanders, the descendants of seventeenth-century Puritans, was premised upon covenantal relationships, and therefore upon the strict observation of contractual obligations. Moreover, if New Englanders were loath to allow their soldiers to be subjected to the strict discipline of His Majesty's forces, it was because New England's comparatively unstratified society, when required to create armies as large as those of 1755 and 1756, could not produce the kind of armies that contemporary European states did.

Given the social configuration of their provinces, New England governments simply could not field forces made up of economically marginal men led by their social superiors, on the model of the British army. Instead, the provinces had to commission as officers those ordinary farmers and tradesmen who could most effectively convince the young men of their towns to follow them for a year of campaigning. As often as not, this meant that recruits served in companies commanded by older neighbors or relatives; in most cases there was some personal bond, or at least prior acquaintanceship, between officers and the men they enlisted. Among the provincials the relationships of civil society thus carried over directly as the basis for military life, narrowing what was in professional European forces a vast social gulf between officers and enlisted men to a barely perceptible gap. To expect the officers of such an army to subject their men to the strict discipline required by His Majesty's regulations was to expect the impossible. Neither the contractual understanding of military service nor the close social connections between officers and men would allow it.

Because such circumstances as these were so utterly outside Loudoun's experience as an aristocrat and professional officer, and because the army they produced was so anomalous when judged by the standard of professionalism the British army set, it is scarcely surprising that the commander in chief should have railed against the New Englanders. It was not much longer, however, before Loudoun came to realize that the New Englanders were only the worst of a bad lot. All over the colonies during the summer of 1756, local officials and provincial assemblies were refusing to provide adequate housing for His Majesty's troops. Shirley had avoided the problem of quartering by paying what amounted to the market rent for room and board: his warrants for "slap-gelt" (as the victualing and billeting allowance was called) helped drain the military chest to the bone-dry state in which it stood at the end of his tenure as supreme commander. Loudoun would have none of such outrageous expedients, and he insisted that the colonists contribute quarters on his terms or face the consequences. To his astonishment and vexation, such resistance arose that even in Albany, his very headquarters, he had to use armed force to secure quarters for his men and officers.[22]

Loudoun could not comprehend the unwillingness of colonial civilians to provide accommodations for the soldiers who had been sent so far, at enormous expense, to protect them. All he heard from the people who opposed him, like the mayor of Albany and the sheriff of Albany County, were sermons on how the English Bill of Rights guaranteed freedom from the arbitrary quartering of troops as one of the most cherished of all the rights of Englishmen. No American he met seemed to understand the concept of self-sacrifice, of service to the common cause; there was, by contrast, no shortage of Americans willing to plunder the royal purse. The result for Lord Loudoun was continual frustration and rising anger. "The delays we meet with," he wrote in exasperation to Cumberland, "in carrying on the Service, from every parts of this Country, are immense; they have assumed to themselves, what they call Rights and Priviledges, totaly unknown in the Mother Country, and [these] are made use of, for no purpose, but to screen them, from giving any Aid, of any sort, for carrying on, the Service, and refusing us Quarters."[23]

America was a topsy-turvy place where "opposition [to royal authority] seems not to come from the *lower* People, but from the *leading* People, who raise the dispute, in order to have a merit with the others, by defending their Liberties, as they call them." Magistrates could not enforce the law against the popular will; "from whence there is no Law prevailing at present here, that I have met with, but the Rule every man pleases to lay down to himself." Governors themselves were mere "*Cyphers*" because the provincial assemblies were their paymasters; they had

> sold the whole of the King's *Prerogative,* to get their Sallaries; and till you find a Fund, independent of the Province[s], to Pay the Governors, and new model the Government, you can do nothing with the Provinces. I know it has been said in *London,* that this is not the time; if You delay it till a Peace, You will not have a force to Exert any Brittish Acts of Parliament here, for tho' they will not venture to go so far with me, I am assured by the Officers, that it is *not uncommon,* for the People of this Country to say, *they would be glad to see any Man, that dare exert a Brittish Act of Parliament here.*[24]

Although it could hardly be called dispassionate, Loudoun's analysis was astute, even prescient. It was based on what was for him the almost inevitable assumption that departures from British standards and practices were evidence of retrograde development, if not outright degeneracy, and therefore signified problems that required correction. Cumberland, Fox, Halifax, and the rest of the men who supported him in England could hardly have agreed more; nor could any of them have been expected to credit more highly than Loudoun himself did the objections Americans made to the authority of the Crown.

That the ministers did not take Loudoun's advice and "new model" the colonial governments when the troops were on hand to enforce Parliament's will proceeded less from any reservation they might have had about the rightness or the necessity of such reforms than from the sheer impossibility of undertaking them. For indeed, Loudoun's quarrels with the Americans who refused to cooperate in quartering his troops and his inability to get the New England provincials to submit to joint operations with the regulars were only the quietest harbingers of the whirlwind of defeat and political disorder that was about to engulf the British war effort. In western New York, the marquis de Montcalm was preparing to unleash the storm even as Winslow was groping for the words that could make Loudoun understand why his provincial army would self-destruct if the commander in chief tried to give it a direct order.

CHAPTER 13

Oswego

1756

On the afternoon of August 10, more than two hundred miles to the west of Loudoun's Albany headquarters, soldiers at Fort Ontario (one of Fort Oswego's defensive outworks) spotted the recently scalped corpse of a comrade not far from the palisade. It had been a coup of extraordinary boldness, for the raiders had killed their victim in broad daylight. No other soldiers recently had been lost from the garrison, and since the local Oneidas had refused to act as scouts or communicate any useful intelligence to the garrison, this was the first solid evidence in more than a month that enemy Indians were in the vicinity. The next morning Lieutenant Colonel Mercer ordered one of his post's vessels, a small armed schooner, to scout the lakeshore for evidence of the enemy. Before she had sailed a mile and a half, her crew spotted a great encampment on the shore. The captain put about and scuttled back to the fort. His report was the first intelligence to reach Oswego of the three-thousand-man expeditionary force with which the marquis de Montcalm was preparing to besiege the British outpost. By late that afternoon, Indian snipers had scaled trees at the edge of the forest and begun firing down into the interior of Fort Ontario.[1]

Montcalm had left Montréal on July 21, after having rather reluctantly agreed with Governor-General Vaudreuil that his first order of business would be to destroy Britain's military and commercial outpost on the Great Lakes. Since coming to New France, Montcalm had found that he and Vaudreuil agreed about very little, and he was far from pleased with the situation in which he found himself. Both the Canadian-born governor and his brother, François-Pierre de Rigaud de Vaudreuil (known as Rigaud)—a tough and experienced officer in the colonial regulars, *les troupes de la marine*—firmly believed that the war should be fought by making maximum use of Indian allies and raids. Indians and Canadian troops had been crucial to the defense of New France in the previous colonial wars, for their ability to devastate the frontier had always forced the northern provinces to concentrate on defense and lessened their ability to mount an invasion. "Nothing," Vaudreuil had said, "is more calculated to disgust the people of those Colonies and to make them desire the return of peace" than frontier raiding. Similarly, nothing was more likely to win and retain the favor of Indian nations eager to make war against the British than to let them do it in their own ways, and on their own terms. The affection of Vaudreuil, Rigaud, and the other Canadian veterans for Indian warfare and their commitment to cultivating friendly relations with Indian tribes, however, did nothing to win the affection or the respect of the new commander in chief.[2]

As almost any conventionally minded European regular officer would have, Montcalm disliked departures from what he understood to be civilized standards of military conduct. He distrusted Indians, who operated according to their own understandings of warfare and could not be subjected to military discipline. Because Indians fought to gain prisoners, trophies, and booty, they could be ungovernable in the aftermath of a battle and were particularly prone to what Montcalm could only understand as acts of savagery—scalping, torture, even cannibalism. But most important, to use Indians seemed futile to Montcalm because no matter how many small victories they might win, they could inflict no lasting defeat on the British: once a battle had been won, they would simply take their captives and loot and return home. So far as Montcalm could see, the Canadian militia and even the *troupes de la marine* were only marginally preferable to the Indians, since whatever their skills in woodcraft, neither could compare with properly disciplined European troops in reliability under fire or staying power.

For these reasons Montcalm was unwilling to assign the Canadians, Indians, and *troupes de la marine* and their style of fighting the preeminent role that Vaudreuil and Rigaud advocated. Yet the severe shortage of available manpower left Montcalm little choice; if he was to defend New France, he could hardly dispense with Indian and Canadian help. Thus the force that he led against Oswego included not only 1,300 highly trained French infantrymen and artillerists of the regiments of Béarn, La Sarre, and Guyenne, but about 1,500 *troupes de la marine* and militiamen under Rigaud, and at least 250 Indians from a half-dozen nations, from the Abenakis of upper New England to the Menominees from the western shore of Lake Michigan. Montcalm intended to use Canadians and

Indians to harry Oswego's defenders out of the woods, but his regulars and gunners would conduct a siege in the European style. Only such a decisive engagement, he believed, could eliminate Britain's strategic presence on the Great Lakes.[3]

On the afternoon of August 11, the defenders of Fort Ontario could hear Canadian axmen felling trees in the woods, opening a cannon road from their camp to the entrenchments that the militiamen were already starting to dig just east of the fort. Unfortunately for the garrison, Oswego's fortifications were not yet complete. Even after the weakened 50th and 51st Regiments had regained their health, the improvement of their defenses had been hampered by the uncertainties that attended the transfer of command from Shirley to Abercromby to Loudoun. Moreover, thanks in part to Shirley's amateurism and in part to the difficult geography of the site, Oswego's defenses had been poorly laid out. The original trading post, a stone blockhouse that dated from 1727, stood on a low rise beside the bay where the Oswego River emptied into Lake Ontario. Hardly more than a quarter of a mile to the east, across the river, a hill rose fifty feet above the lake; while a quarter mile west of the blockhouse, a second hill stood even higher. Attackers on either hill with even light cannon could so easily batter down the old trading post and its outbuildings that a prudent commander might have decided to abandon the complex and construct a defensible fort on stronger ground. But Shirley had decided instead to build a hornwork, or rampart, on the landward side of old Oswego and to emplace small outlying forts on the two hilltops that overlooked it.[4]

Thus on the day Montcalm opened his siege, Oswego consisted of three separate posts: in the center lay Oswego proper, a decrepit blockhouse defended on its land side by a hornwork, but open to the river and lake; east of the river stood Fort Ontario, a square palisade with four bastions; and to the west crouched new Fort Oswego, a fort so "poor [and] Pittyful" that the soldiers of the garrison had nicknamed it Fort Rascal. Even had all its parts been complete and properly laid out, Oswego would have been a hard spot to defend. As it was, not one of its forts had been planned correctly or built well, and Lieutenant Colonel Mercer had only 1,135 soldiers to hold off Montcalm's 3,000 men and eighty cannon.[5]

The defense of Oswego would not prove a long one. Once he had surveyed the site, Montcalm decided first to invest Fort Ontario. Under cover of a small ridge less than a hundred yards from the fort, Montcalm's men began on the afternoon of the eleventh to dig a trench parallel to the fort's eastern wall. That night and all the following day they dug, throwing up a parapet and constructing platforms from which their cannon could fire, at virtually point-blank range, into the wooden palisade. Seeing no purpose in subjecting the garrison to a murderous cannonade, Mercer gave the order to abandon Fort Ontario on the thirteenth. At dawn the next morning, he looked across the river and saw that the French had not only occupied Fort Ontario but had emplaced a dozen cannon next to it, on high ground. It was a horrifying sight, because the cannon in Fort Oswego's own batteries were all mounted on the hornwork, and therefore pointing away from the enemy.

Mercer, a courageous officer, ordered the guns reversed on their platforms. This left his gunners without a parapet to cover them and aiming their cannon over the heads of the garrison, but Mercer gave the order to open fire anyway. According to Stephen Cross, a civilian carpenter who had come to Oswego to build ships, what followed was "as Severe A Cannonade on Both Sides, as Perhaps Ever was, until about 10 o'clock." Then, Cross continued, "about this time we Discovered the Enemy, in Great Numbers, Crossing the River [upstream from Oswego, out of range]; and we not in force Sufficient to go up and oppose them, and being Judged not safe, any longer, to Keep the Men, in Fort Raskel, that was Evacuated; and [while] we all were Huddled together, in and about the Main Fort, the Comandent . . . was killed by a Cannon Ball. . . ."[6]

In fact, the shot had beheaded him. The command passed to Lieutenant Colonel John Littlehales, a man so unnerved by Mercer's grisly death and so disheartened by his hopeless position that within an hour he ordered a cease-fire and dispatched a representative under flag of truce to ask for terms. Montcalm, as a professional officer exquisitely sensitive to the etiquette of surrender, judged that the brief British defense had been insufficient to merit magnanimity. He therefore refused to offer Littlehales the honors of war—to have granted them would have allowed the British to depart with their colors, personal possessions, and a symbolic cannon, in return for the promise that they would not return to active service for a specified period—and instead insisted on taking the entire garrison prisoner. Prudently, ingloriously, Littlehales acquiesced.

> Thus, this Place fell into the hands of the French; with a Great Quantity of Stores [, which] we suppose [amount to] about 9000 Barrells of Provisions, A Considerable Number of Brass, and Iron Cannon, and Morters; one Vessell just Launched, two Sloops Peirced for 10 Guns each, one Schooner Peirced for 10 Guns, and one Row Gally, with Swivels, and one Small vessell on the Stock about Half Built, A great Number of Whailboats, and as Near as I can Judge between 14 & 16 hundred Prisoners; Including Soldiers,

> Sailers, Carpenters, and other artifisers, Settlers, Indians, traders, Women, and Children.[7]

The only promise Montcalm made was that he would protect the British from the attacks of his Indian allies and would guarantee their safe conduct to Montréal. But it soon became clear that he had promised too much.

The Indian warriors who had accompanied the expedition were under French leadership only in the attenuated sense that each group had a Canadian *officier* assigned who spoke its language. The warriors received no payment beyond provisions and presents. Unlike French and Canadian troops who (at least in theory) served for the greater glory of church and king, the Indians fought in order to demonstrate personal courage and to gain plunder, trophies, and captives. Now, in the aftermath of the surrender, they helped themselves to what they regarded—and what previous French commanders had always accorded them—as the proper reward for their services.[8] In a long afternoon of disorder, Indians killed and scalped the sick and wounded in the British hospital, appropriated supplies from the stocks of the trading post and the forts, seized personal property, and took captives from among the soldiers' and traders' families. To the colonials and the defenseless British, it seemed an orgy of violence. As Stephen Cross told the story, once

> the Indians had got into our fort [old Oswego], they went searching for Rum; which they found, and began to Drink, when they Soon became like so Many hel Hounds; and after Murdering, and Scalping, all they Could find on that Side, Come over the River [to Fort Ontario, where Cross and most of the defeated soldiers were being held] with A Design, to do the Same to all the Rest; and on their Coming Near the Fort where we was, and hearing the Confused noyes of those within [the walls, they] United their Hideous Yells and Rushed the [French] Guards Exceeding hard, to git in among us, with their Tomehawks; and it was with Great difficulty the French, Could Prevent them.[9]

All in all, the Indians killed between thirty and a hundred Anglo-American soldiers and civilians and made captives of an indeterminate number before Montcalm could restore order. He was intensely embarrassed by this "massacre," which he believed dishonored him as an officer pledged to protect prisoners of war. The incident left him so abashed that he omitted all mention of it from his report to the minister of war except

Louis-Antoine de Bougainville (1729–1811). Appointed as an army captain and aide-de-camp to the marquis de Montcalm in 1756, Bougainville was already the author of a celebrated treatise on integral calculus when he made his way to America. Although he was not particularly gifted as an infantry leader, his splendidly observed journals still provide the best account of the American war from the perspective of a French regular officer. After the war Bougainville embarked on a second career as a naval officer—in which uniform he appears in this late-eighteenth-century stipple engraving. From 1766 to 1769 he became the first Frenchman to circumnavigate the globe, exploring Tahiti and other South Pacific islands. During the American Revolutionary War he served as a frigate captain and was eventually promoted to the rank of rear admiral. *Courtesy of the McCord Museum of Canadian History, Montreal / Musée McCord d'histoire canadienne, Montréal.*

for a single, cryptic notation: "It will cost the King from eight to ten thousand livres, which will preserve to us the affection of the Indian Nationals." It was his only mention of the funds he had laid out to ransom what prisoners the Indians were willing to give up.[10]

Oswego had been Montcalm's first victory, and it was one in which Vaudreuil and Rigaud and other Canadians could take a certain satisfaction, because they had played a crucial role in winning it. Yet victory had come at what for the marquis de Montcalm was entirely too high a price. Like Loudoun in his encounters with the provincials of the British colonies, Montcalm too was learning his first unwelcome lessons about the cultural dynamics of war in the wilderness, and he was beginning to draw exactly the same conclusions. To Montcalm, as to Loudoun, it

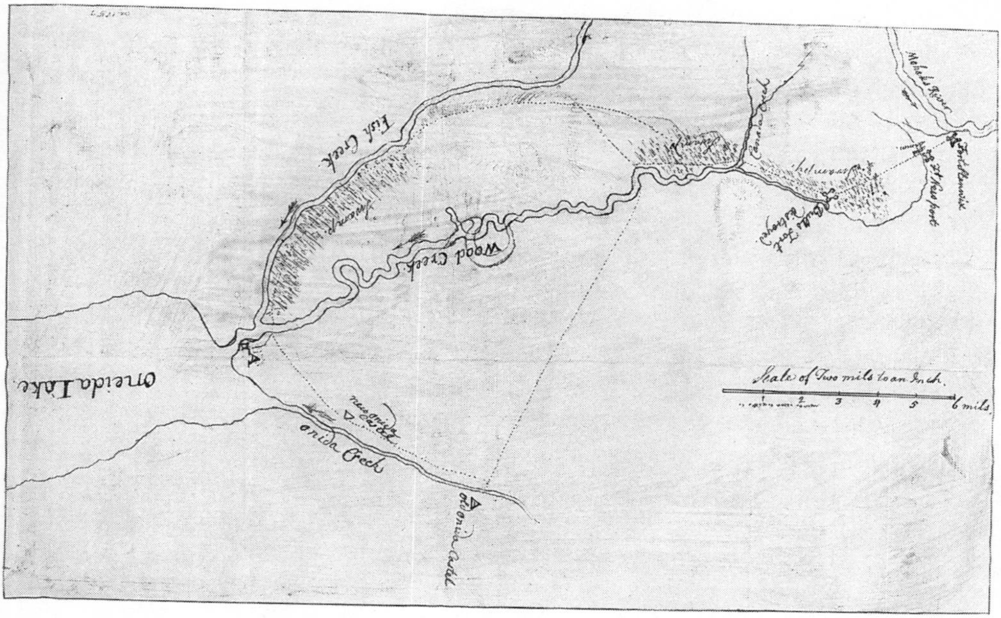

Wood Creek and Oneida Lake. This sketch map, with much of the lettering inverted, shows the course of Wood Creek from Fort Bull to Oneida Lake—most of which General Daniel Webb ordered filled with felled trees in anticipation of a French invasion that existed only in his panicked imagination. *Courtesy of the William L. Clements Library at the University of Michigan.*

seemed that a strange degeneracy afflicted everything and everyone who lived in North America; that war there would be better fought by men who knew the right and honorable way to conduct themselves, the regulars; that the less one had to rely on colonials or Indians, the better. Eventually Montcalm's aide-de-camp, Louis-Antoine de Bougainville, would crystallize the attitude that most European officers who served in America instinctively shared: "The air one breathes here is contagious, and I fear lest a long sojourn here makes us acquire the vices of a people to whom we communicate no virtues."[11]

By the time word of Montcalm's attack reached the nearest substantial British force, it was already August 17 and too late to relieve a garrison that was already under guard and on its way to Montréal. Major General Daniel Webb, third in the command hierarchy after Loudoun and Abercromby, had earlier been dispatched with the 44th Regiment to reinforce Oswego. He heard the news at German Flats, a small Mohawk Valley settlement seventy miles west of Albany. Webb advanced cautiously to the Great Carrying Place, where, on August 20, the rumors circulating in the nervous garrison convinced him that Montcalm was preparing to march for the Mohawk. Without pausing to send scouts west to see if the French were indeed headed his way, Webb ordered the recently rebuilt Fort Bull to be burned, directed that axmen fell trees to obstruct Wood Creek, and then without losing a moment beat a hasty retreat to German Flats, which now became Britain's westernmost outpost in New York.[12]

Lord Loudoun seldom criticized other regular officers, and especially not other protégés of the duke of Cumberland, but even he thought Webb had gone too far. Nonetheless, Webb had so efficiently destroyed the advanced posts on the Mohawk that there was little Loudoun could do to reverse the situation. Fearful that the stroke against Oswego would be followed by another against the provincials at Fort William Henry, Loudoun had already ordered Winslow, on August 20, to abandon all further preparation for the expedition against Crown Point and concentrate on improving his post's fortifications. By the end of August the collapse of the British offensive capability on the northern frontier was complete. Loudoun had been in New York less than a month. While the provincials longed to be disbanded and the regulars waited for the order to go into winter quarters, the commander in chief applied himself to the organizational duties at which he excelled, sparred with civilian authorities over quarters for his troops, and surveyed the state of the British war effort in America. He could do little to repay the French and not a great deal to reform the Americans, but at least he was beginning to understand what he was up against.[13]

CHAPTER 14

The State of the Central Colonies

1756

BAD AS CONDITIONS were in New York, when Lord Loudoun stopped to consider reports from the rest of the colonies he found more cause for concern on western frontiers in Pennsylvania, Maryland, and Virginia. These provinces had all begun building forts in the backcountry during the winter and spring of 1755–56, staffing each with a small garrison of provincials or with local militiamen. Some of them—Fort Augusta at the forks of the Susquehanna in Pennsylvania, Forts Cumberland and Frederick in Maryland, Fort Loudoun at Winchester, Virginia—were true forts, commanding strategic passes, designed and constructed according to accepted principles of fortification, and capable of storing the provisions necessary to stage offensive operations against the enemy. But most were simple blockhouses, and some were mere stockades enclosing settlers' cabins. By the end of 1756 more than a score had been built in Pennsylvania, and seventeen in Virginia. In principle they comprised a "chain of forts" linked by frequent patrols of soldiers scouting for enemies. In reality, most were so undermanned that patrols seldom ventured far from their walls. Even when the whole "chain" had been completed the forts remained eighteen to twenty miles apart, making them better targets for French and Indian war parties than barriers against raiders. At most they furnished refuges to which the remaining backwoods settlers might flee in case of attack. Montcalm accurately described them as "pretended forts," and most of them quickly proved themselves (in the judgment of George Washington) to be of "no Singular Service to our Country."[1]

None of the three colonies exposed to raids from the Ohio Country had made significant military progress against the French and Indians during 1756. Maryland, with the shortest frontier and the smallest backwoods population, had shown the least disposition to act. Its assembly had raised only 250 provincials in the spring and, by autumn, had concluded that even Fort Cumberland was not worth defending. Usurping the governor's authority to control the disposition of the province's troops, the legislature ordered Maryland's troops to withdraw more than seventy miles eastward to Fort Frederick, which it officially designated as the westernmost position the province would defend. The only offensive action any Maryland soldier had undertaken all year was Captain John Dagworthy's hard-fought campaign to assert his right, as an officer who in the previous war had held a royal commission, to issue orders to Colonel George Washington of Virginia, whose provincial commission bore only Robert Dinwiddie's signature.[2]

The Old Dominion had shown much greater official interest, and marginally greater success, in defending its western settlements. In the spring the House of Burgesses had appropriated £55,000 for defense, authorized Colonel Washington to enlist fifteen hundred men in the Virginia Regiment, enacted a draft law to fill the ranks if an insufficient number of men volunteered, and stiffened the disciplinary regime of the militia. Yet despite the best efforts of Washington and his second-in-command, Lieutenant Colonel Adam Stephen, Virginia's provincial regiment never reached even half of its authorized strength. Unlike the New England provinces, which raised substantial armies by paying wages and bounties that compared favorably with what laborers and journeyman artisans could earn, Virginia's assembly offered such miserable compensation that few men would enlist voluntarily, while it drew up a conscription law that mainly applied to vagrants and men too poor (or too lacking in initiative) to flee the colony. Nor did the Burgesses manifest much concern for the health and welfare of the officers and men who had already joined the regiment, a fact so painful to Washington that he repeatedly threatened to resign. Through the whole of 1756, Virginia made no effort to supply clothing or shoes to replace the ones that had worn out, and it paid its provincials so irregularly that, their colonel complained, "the Soldiers . . . suspect finesse."[3]

Yet the root reason for such neglect was not, as Washington believed, the "ill judg'd OEconomy" and lack of honor prevailing among the "Chimney Corner Politicians" at Williamsburg. The fact was that the great planters who comprised the assembly feared French and Indians on the frontier less than the possibility that the war would encourage a slave rebellion in the tidewater. Their priorities could hardly be mistaken in the Burgesses' decision to allocate 55 percent of the 1756 military appropriation to the militia, which bore the responsibility for internal security and control of the slaves, and 45 percent to the Virginia Regiment, charged with defending the frontier. As was the pattern in all the colonies from Pennsylvania to Georgia, the coastal representatives who dominated the legislatures attended more closely to their own interests than to the remoter concerns of a few thousand backwoods families.[4]

Despite Washington's discouragement and almost continual complaints, he and his men did as creditable a job, under the circumstances, as could be expected. Virginia's ragged and not infrequently shoeless provincials fought at least a score of small actions against French and Indian raiders in 1756, and in doing so suffered nearly a hundred casualties. Gradually, despite low morale, high rates of desertion, and the difficulty of stimulating reenlistment, Washington and his officers would succeed in instilling both discipline and a sense of common purpose in the Virginia Regiment; but by the end of 1756 that long process was just beginning. Although he could note with pride "that notwithstanding we are more contiguous to the French and their Indian allies, and more expos'd to their frequent Incursions than any of the Neighboring Colony's, we have not lost half the Inhabitants which they have done," because of the efforts of the Virginia Regiment, Washington knew better than anyone else how tenuous his unit's hold on the frontier really was. Particularly in the absence of an effective alliance with any of the southern Indian nations—despite Governor Dinwiddie's frequent offerings of diplomatic gifts, neither the Catawbas nor the Cherokees showed any lasting disposition to fight alongside Virginia—Washington realized that his troops would never be able to do more than parry, at great disadvantage and great cost, the raids that the French and Indians could direct wherever they chose.[5]

Of all the colonies reeling under the lash of raids from the west, Pennsylvania had come the furthest in improving its ability to defend itself by the end of 1756. That was true, however, only because the colony had started from a position of virtually complete defenselessness. Pennsylvania had never had a formally constituted militia, and through most of 1755 its assembly had made no effort to protect exposed backcountry settlements from attack. It was the settlers who paid the price: the annihilation of the Moravian pacifist community of Gnadenhutten late in November was only the most striking episode in the wholesale collapse of the province's frontiers. This did not happen, as many contemporaries charged, because the Quaker oligarchs in the assembly preferred watching defenseless backwoodsmen die to troubling their own consciences by making military appropriations. Although the Friends' pacifism and their history of amicable relations with the Indians cannot be minimized as influences in slowing the assembly's movement toward military measures, the relationship was not a direct one. The most significant cause of Pennsylvania's inaction lay instead in the character of provincial politics, which had been deadlocked since 1740 over the question of taxing proprietary lands.[6]

As proprietors of the province, the Penn family owned all Pennsylvania's unallocated lands and enjoyed the sole right to acquire title to tracts held by Indian nations. Together with rents from the Penns' manorial estates, the sale of lands from these reserves generated most of the family's enormous annual income. Pennsylvania's governors, who represented the interests of the family as well as those of the Crown, had steadfastly resisted the assembly's efforts to tax proprietary lands. The assembly, however, would not agree to levy any tax on the population, even for the immediate defense of the colony, unless the proprietary lands could also be rated. So firmly did each side adhere to its accustomed position that neither would budge until Germans from the backcountry were actually carrying the mangled corpses of their relatives down High Street and Scotch-Irish backwoodsmen were threatening to take up arms against the assembly itself. Only then, in the midst of the greatest crisis in the province's history, did two creative political outsiders—Benjamin Franklin and an ex-Quaker ally in the assembly, Joseph Galloway—manage to break the impasse by working out a compromise between the governor and the antiproprietary Quaker legislative majority. In return for a gift of £5,000, offered by the proprietors to the province in lieu of taxes, the assembly agreed to appropriate £55,000 "for the King's use"—a circumlocution that allowed the Quaker legislators to avoid mentioning the military uses to which the king's servants would undoubtedly put the money. Neither side gave ground on its constitutional claims concerning taxation, but at last Governor Morris could begin organizing the defense of the colony by raising a thousand provincial volunteers and starting to build forts along the frontier.[7]

Once the process of militarization had begun, the governor undertook more aggressive measures and the province's old political alignments disintegrated. Governor Morris's formal proclamation of war in April 1756, together with the actions of the seven commissioners he appointed to administer the province's defenses, horrified the Quaker grandees who had for so long dominated the assembly. While most of the commissioners, like Benjamin Franklin and John Hughes, were not Quakers, two of them, John Mifflin and Joseph Fox, were members in good standing of the Philadelphia Meeting. Their concurrence in the commissioners' decision to offer bounties for Indian prisoners and for the scalps of Indians over ten years of age hit the Quaker community like a bombshell. The Philadelphia Meeting reproached Mifflin and Fox, and when they would not disavow their action, disowned—excommunicated—them. This profoundly unsettling incident intensified a movement among Quakers to withdraw themselves from political life. By the October elections, what had so recently been an oligarchy of antiproprietary Quaker legislators had simply vanished from the assembly.

The onset of war thus forced Pennsylvania's Friends to decide whether they would remain faithful to their political stance or to their peace testimony, and with virtual unanimity they chose pacifism. This act of collective conscience accelerated the Quakers' abandonment of public life, renewed their commitment to benevolent activity, and summarily redrew the map of Pennsylvania politics. Henceforth the province's Friends would focus their attention on informal diplomacy, opening their own negotiations with the eastern Delaware Indians in the hope of discovering the cause of the Indians' alienation and promoting a peaceful resolution of the conflict. And henceforth Benjamin Franklin and his allies in the assembly—Joseph Galloway, John Hughes, Isaac Norris—would become the arbiters of Pennsylvania politics, filling the vacuum created by the departure of the Quakers and taking over leadership of the province's antiproprietary faction.[8]

These stunning, unanticipated developments finally broke the logjam that had for so long prevented Pennsylvania's government from undertaking defense measures. But the backcountry settlers experienced little immediate relief from the attacks of French and Indian war parties. Throughout 1756 the raiders struck within seventy miles of Philadelphia, killing, looting, burning, and taking captives; most of the five hundred scalps that the commandant of Fort Duquesne counted and most of the two hundred prisoners who were still present at his post at the end of the year had come from Pennsylvania. Despite the best efforts of Governor Morris and his commissioners to establish discipline among the newly raised provincial troops and to encourage freelance Indian hunting by offering scalp bounties (including a special reward of seven hundred dollars for the heads of the western Delaware chiefs Shingas and Captain Jacobs), the security of the province's frontiers increased not at all during a summer of bloodshed. On July 30, in a bold stroke, a party of French and Delawares led by Captain Jacobs attacked and burned Fort Granville on the Juniata River, a post that a shocked Loudoun knew was "one of our best Forts upon the frontier." Once Fort Granville had been destroyed, the province's westernmost post, Fort Shirley (located at Croghan's old trading house of Aughwick), could no longer be defended and had to be abandoned. This effectively rolled the Pennsylvania frontier all the way back to Carlisle, a settlement not much more than a hundred miles from Philadelphia. When Governor Morris's replacement, Lieutenant Colonel William Denny, arrived to stiffen Pennsylvania's defenses, he "found the Frontier in a deplorable situation." As if to confirm his judgment, within a few days raiders struck the settlement at Lebanon, east of the Susquehanna and barely seventy-five miles from the capital, killing settlers and burning everything up to the walls of the local fort.[9]

It must be noted that the only successful Anglo-American offensive to be mounted in America in 1756 did occur in Pennsylvania, but even that victory cost the Pennsylvanians more lives than it took from their enemies and probably aggravated the situation on the province's frontier. The raid was a daring attempt to attack Shingas's and Captain Jacobs's base, the Delaware settlement of Upper Kittanning, a town of thirty houses on the Allegheny River perhaps twenty-five miles above Fort Duquesne. Colonel John Armstrong, a surveyor from Carlisle, led a party of three hundred provincials overland from Aughwick and succeeded in surprising the town at dawn on August 8. Resistance proved stiff, however, and Armstrong's men suffered at least forty casualties before setting fire to the town and retiring, having recovered eleven English captives and taken perhaps a dozen scalps. Among the Indian dead was Captain Jacobs, the chief who almost exactly a year earlier had stood before the Pennsylvania Council and asked for aid against the French, only to be sent away "without meeting with the necessary Encouragement." Throughout the fight, Jacobs had kept firing from the window of his house while his wife reloaded his muskets; and, Armstrong noted, he "seldom mist of Wounding or killing some of our People." When, late in the battle, the attackers called upon him to surrender or have the house put to the torch, the wounded chief "replied that 'they might if they would; he could eat fire.' " When the Pennsylvanians finally succeeded in setting fire to the house, the gunpowder stored within detonated with such force that "the Leg and Thigh of an Indian with a Child of three or four years old" were thrown to "such a height that they appeared as nothing and [then] fell in the adjacent Corn Field."[10]

Had the French and Indians inflicted the same blow on a Pennsylvania settlement, it would inevitably have been called a massacre, but Armstrong and his men were greeted as heroes upon their return to Philadelphia, where they collected the reward the commissioners had placed on Captain Jacobs's head. Of course, in the Ohio Indians' view Armstrong's victory *was* a massacre, and to avenge it they redoubled their efforts against the Pennsylvania frontier. Because the Kittanning raid came on the heels of Oswego's fall, the western Delawares who renewed their attacks on the backcountry were liberally supplied with captured arms, shot, and powder. Their raids that autumn were the fiercest of the year, and with every success their hopes rose that they might not only defeat the English, but eventually drive the French themselves from the Ohio Country. So chaotic did the Pennsylvania frontiers become that only the timely completion of Fort Augusta—at the confluence of the west and north branches of the Susquehanna, near the eastern Delaware settlement of Shamokin—kept the eastern Delawares from joining their western cousins on the warpath. As the Pennsylvania authorities understood more fully than the Delawares, however, Fort Augusta was too isolated and weak to withstand a determined attack. Thus it was with some relief in the summer of 1756 that the governor and council of the province received the first tentative response to the peace feelers they had been sending through Quaker emissaries to Teedyuscung, the chief of the eastern branch of the Delaware nation.[11]

What moved Teedyuscung to open negotiations with the English was hardly Anglophilia—neither he nor any of the three factions in his tribe could reasonably be called pro-English—but a growing sense of desperation. Warfare had disrupted the lives of his people no less than those of the English. Because Indian agriculture did not produce large surpluses, even a single missed harvest could cause severe privation, and in the summer of 1756 the eastern Delawares were on the verge of losing their second harvest in a row. Moreover, the interruption of the normal patterns of hunting, as young men went off on raiding expeditions, meant the loss of both the group's main source of animal protein and the skins and furs that provided its only trading commodities. In this respect the war had hit the eastern Delawares particularly hard, for while they depended upon European manufactures as heavily as any other Indian nation in eastern North America, the resident traders on whom they relied had all evacuated the Susquehanna Valley in 1755. The only other possible suppliers—French traders in the Ohio Country—were too distant to provide the volume of goods the eastern Delawares needed. Teedyuscung agreed to meet with representatives of the Pennsylvania government at Easton, a Delaware Valley town about fifty miles north of Philadelphia, because he hoped to gain concessions from the Pennsylvanians as the price for peace with his people and as a reward for his good offices in arranging negotiations with the western Delawares.[12]

Despite the specter of famine that drove him to negotiate, the price Teedyuscung intended to ask was a steep one: a formal admission from the Penns that the Walking Purchase of 1737 had been a fraud, and compensation to his people in the form of a grant, of 2,500,000 acres of the Wyoming Valley and adjoining lands, as a perpetual reservation for the eastern Delawares. These were audacious demands, for Teedyuscung was not only asking that the Penns surrender a vast proportion of the best land in the province, but risking the wrath of the Iroquois, who would be officially recognized as having been complicit in the Walking Purchase fraud. Yet while the first substantive meeting between Teedyuscung and Governor Denny, in November 1756, must have been a tense one—four Iroquois chiefs had come from Onondaga to observe Teedyuscung's actions and report back to the Grand Council—it was also remarkably promising. Supported in the negotiations by Quaker advisors who had promoted and financed the negotiations from the beginning, Teedyuscung managed to wring three important concessions from Pennsylvania. Denny distributed a gift of trade goods worth four hundred pounds, promised to open a trade at Fort Augusta and to provide "a large uninhabited country to Hunt in," and agreed to consider the charges of fraud impartially at a meeting to be held in the coming year. In return Teedyuscung promised only to bring whatever white captives he could obtain to the next conference.[13]

Although the results of the Easton conference were inconclusive, the mutual desperation of the Delawares and the government of Pennsylvania had led to the opening of real dialogue. The Quakers, having withdrawn from politics, had become able to act as honest brokers and could begin to hope that a peaceful solution to the conflict might be reached if both the governor and Teedyuscung behaved in good faith. For the first time since the beginning of the war in Pennsylvania, hope flickered in the gloom. Yet it was only a glimmer, and the raids and the killings along the frontier meanwhile continued unabated.

CHAPTER 15

The Strains of Empire

CAUSES OF ANGLO-AMERICAN FRICTION

1756

LORD LOUDOUN, taking stock of the year's developments, put little hope in the Easton negotiations, which after all depended on the good faith of a savage. Convinced that the Pennsylvanians were incapable of protecting themselves, he saw the killings on the frontier more clearly than the hope of peace and merely dispatched a battalion of the Royal American Regiment to stiffen Pennsylvania's defenses. The troops arrived at Philadelphia in December, however, to face something like a reprise of the quartering crisis that Loudoun had experienced at Albany in August: there were too few rooms in taverns and other public houses to accommodate five hundred men, and the assembly refused to billet them in private homes. The legislators had prudential as well as constitutional concerns, for smallpox had just broken out in the regiment. Loudoun, however, found any resistance to housing the troops he had sent to defend the province deeply offensive. As in the case of Albany, he threatened to use force to obtain quarters, this time with the concurrence of Governor Denny, who as a regular field officer could hardly have agreed more with Loudoun's judgments.

Faced with the prospect of having not only soldiers but an epidemic imposed on Philadelphians at bayonet-point, the assembly followed the suggestion of Benjamin Franklin and handed over the new province hospital as a temporary barracks for the troops. As in Albany, only force or the threat of force had moved the assembly to comply with Loudoun's directives; also as in Albany, it would be nearly another year before the province would finally build adequate barracks for the regulars. Lord

Loudoun might well have wondered what madness afflicted Americans, who seemed to regard the king's troops as if they, not the French and Indians, were the enemy. Denny simply concluded that such "open neglect of Humanity was the highest Instance I have ever met with of the Depravity of human nature."[1]

The collapse of Britain's war effort in the colonies during 1756 had resulted from a variety of factors, including the confusion that resulted from the change in command from Shirley to Loudoun, the general weakness of the position in which Shirley had left the campaigns, the stunning loss of Oswego, and the deftness of the French in using Indian allies against the British settlements. These were all the reasons Loudoun and his masters at Whitehall recognized, and each was in its way valid as an explanation. Yet there were two other factors, neither of which they could fully have grasped, that contributed even more dramatically to the failures of British arms in America.

The first of these was Lord Loudoun himself. As his repeated wrangles with colonial legislatures over quartering showed—and before his tenure as commander in chief ended, such disputes would have occurred in five colonies, or practically everywhere he had stationed large elements of the army—both his personality and his understanding of Americans inhibited cooperation between the provinces and the Crown.[2] As a professional officer who had been granted extraordinary powers and as an aristocrat with scant sympathy for the cultural norms of the provinces, Loudoun interpreted any resistance to his authority as evidence of colonial inferiority, corruption, and rebelliousness. His virtually automatic response to opposition was to threaten to use force to compel submission. That tactic, while effective in the short term, tended over time to convince the colonists that Loudoun himself posed at least as grave a threat to their liberties as the French and Indians—and one much closer at hand. In this way the actions of His Majesty's own commander in chief, because he enjoyed the support of the most influential men in English government as well as the obedience of thousands of regular troops, became the most convincing arguments many Americans had yet seen for the lack of identity between their own and the empire's interests. Resistance to Loudoun's edicts, haphazard and sporadic at first, grew more general and more consistently sullen as his tenure lengthened.

The second factor contributing to the failure of the war effort was the lack of willingness, either on the part of the Crown or the colonies, to expend the vast sums of money necessary to make the war a success. Although Loudoun's powers were virtually viceregal in character, his purse was notably short, for the ministry had sent him to America on the assumption that the provinces could be made to create a common fund to pay for the war. When the various provincial assemblies refused to comply with his requisitions without exercising the kind of oversight that their previous experience had led them to believe was their prerogative, Loudoun saw more evidence of colonial recalcitrance and degeneracy. But particularly in the colonies from Pennsylvania to North Carolina, which had known no serious external threat for years, assemblies regarded military expenditures as undesirable at best, and as an absolute threat to their rights if dictated by Lord Loudoun. The parsimony of the House of Burgesses in funding its own provincial regiment offers the best case in point. By refusing to offer wages and bounties to compete with what civilian laborers and artisans could earn, and relying instead on the conscription of socially marginal men, Virginia's government virtually insured that its provincial forces would be both chronically undermanned and next to impossible to discipline. In the end, Virginia got exactly as much defense for its frontiers as the Burgesses were willing to pay for, and despite Washington's best efforts by the close of 1756 the bloody results were only too clear.

Friction between the colonists and their commander in chief over issues of finance and local control incapacitated British arms in North America during 1756. Although the next year would see substantial gains in organizational stability and a new efficiency in supply and transport services among the British and colonial forces, these underlying problems would go unresolved for a very long time. Before the remedy could be found would fall the darkest hours of the war for Great Britain and its colonies.

CHAPTER 16

Britain Drifts into a European War

1756

THE NEWS OF OSWEGO's loss arrived in London on September 30, in time to contribute to a governmental crisis that had been brewing since May. With the reorientation of European alliances, Hanover had ceased to be a target that France could threaten as a means of influencing British policy. The first unanticipated result of the Diplomatic Revolution was thus to convince the French foreign ministry that it might most effectively encourage Britain to suspend hostilities at sea and in the New World by threatening to invade England itself. France accordingly built up its army strength in the Channel ports to a hundred thousand men, forcing the British ministry to take stock of its ability to defend the home isles. Newcastle, concluding that the army and navy were stretched too thin to prevent the French from devastating the coast with raids or even launching an invasion, decided that he had no choice but to summon Hessian and Hanoverian troops to bolster England's defenses—and thereby handed Pitt the occasion to question both his competency and his patriotism. Although Fox continued to manage the ministry's business in the House of Commons deftly enough, he was growing more and more alienated from Newcastle, whom he regarded as a man of little real capacity; at the same time Newcastle was making no secret of his distaste for the ambitious, grasping Fox. As the rift between the two men widened and became common knowledge, the cabinet began to split apart internally. Meanwhile Pitt could not be silenced, and the more he railed, the more the ministers blamed one another for the disarray in Britain's defenses. How could this travesty, Pitt cried, be called "an

Administration? They shift and shuffle the charge from one to another: says one, I am not General; the Treasury says, I am not Admiral; the Admiralty says, I am not Minister. From such an unaccording assemblage of separate and distinct powers with no system, a nullity results."[1]

Pitt's jabs told all the more heavily for their accuracy, for the military situation grew more critical by the day. In addition to the forces gathering across the Channel, the French were assembling a fleet at Toulon, from which they could threaten Britain's strategic naval base on the Mediterranean island of Minorca. No one knew whether the French were trying to distract British attention from Minorca by building up their forces in the Channel ports, or preparing to send a massive reinforcement to their army in Canada. Newcastle, whose temperament virtually prohibited decisive action, could bring himself to detach only a small squadron from the defense of the home waters. At the end of March, he ordered ten warships to proceed to Gibraltar, where their commander, Admiral John Byng, was to respond to whatever the French might attempt. If French ships had already passed the Straits, he was to pursue them to America; otherwise, he was to proceed to Minorca and help the garrison resist attack.

Byng, alas, was no fighting admiral, but rather a senior officer notable for administrative skills and strong family political influence. Moreover, the ships in his task force had only recently returned from raiding French commerce on the Atlantic. It was, therefore, with depleted crews, unmade repairs (two vessels were taking on water fast enough to need frequent pumping), and fouled hulls that Byng's ships sailed from Portsmouth on April 7. When he reached Gibraltar nearly a month later, news was waiting that the French had landed on Minorca and besieged the island's fortress, St. Philip's Castle. Without waiting to refit, Byng sailed off to meet his enemy.[2]

By the time Byng found the French fleet off Minorca on May 20, the British government had been at war with France for two days. Newcastle had long hesitated to issue a formal declaration of war, for domestic no less than diplomatic reasons. Given the gravity of the news from Minorca, however, where a small garrison under the command of an octogenarian colonel was being attacked by a much stronger force, the ministry had had little choice. Byng's mission thus assumed enormous significance for the government, for as Newcastle knew only too well, a failure to relieve St. Philip's Castle would bring down the ministry. The duke was frantic to avoid taking the blame himself, and long before the first news had arrived from the Mediterranean, at least one old political hand was advising Henry Fox to consider if there was "anybody to make a scape-goat" in the event Minorca should be lost.[3]

When the news finally arrived from the Mediterranean, all of it was bad. Byng's leaky, barnacle-fouled, undermanned squadron had engaged a better-equipped force under the marquis de La Galissonière—the same man who as governor of Canada in 1749 had ordered Céloron de Blainville to make his celebrated reconnaissance of the Ohio Valley. In a four-hour action, half of Byng's ships had been heavily damaged without inflicting any appreciable loss on La Galissonière's force. That was humiliating enough, but not in itself disastrous, for following the exchange of fire La Galissonière had declined to press his advantage and sailed off to support the troops on Minorca. What turned this indecisive battle into a catastrophe was Byng's decision, four days after it was over, to return to Gibraltar for repairs rather than to stand off Minorca and await the reinforcements that were on their way from the Rock. Byng's retreat to Gibraltar doomed the Minorca garrison. Even so, the defenders held out until June 28 before capitulating, with full honors of war, to the French.

As the reports of these disasters filtered back to England, Newcastle's divided ministry began to fall apart. Fox, fearing that the "scape-goat" would be him, blamed Newcastle for giving Byng too few ships, having concluded that "those who had direction of [the country] could no more carry on this war, than his three children," and decided to resign when the right moment came. Newcastle, desperate to escape responsibility for the disaster, determined to blame Byng and set in motion the court-martial proceedings that would end with Byng's execution by firing squad on March 14, 1757.[4]

Voltaire would later explain that in England it was thought a good thing to shoot an admiral, from time to time, in order to encourage the others, but in the aftermath of the Minorca debacle many English politicians thought that Newcastle's obsessive pursuit of Byng signaled only his lack of fitness to lead the government. Thus opposition M.P.s were already in full cry against a disintegrating ministry when news arrived that the king of Prussia had precipitated a crisis certain to result in a continental war. On August 30, 1756, Frederick, without consulting and indeed almost without bothering to inform the British, invaded Saxony and launched military operations against the Austrian empire. The Convention of Versailles now operated inexorably to bring France to the defense of Maria Theresa, Austria's empress-queen. The Russians, unprepared for war and knowing that they could expect no support from the English, abrogated the subsidy treaty and sought an accommodation with France and Austria. Once again Hanover stood exposed to invasion, and—Newcastle's hopes and diplomatic efforts to the contrary notwithstanding—Great Britain found itself slipping over the brink into a general European war.[5]

Stories of Oswego's fall, spreading from newspaper to newspaper across England in early October, therefore seemed to be the final calamity in a string of misfortunes that made it hard to imagine how Newcastle could face a new session of Parliament. Choosing his moment to wound the duke most gravely, Fox resigned on October 13. With no one to manage the Commons, and with Pitt, the only M.P. with sufficient stature to lead, trumpeting his refusal to serve in any administration that included Newcastle, the duke had no choice but to resign. By October 20 he knew the end had come and prepared for it by paying off his supporters with honors and pensions. On November 11, Newcastle formally surrendered the seals of office as first lord of the Treasury, and, for the first time in nearly four decades, retired from public life.[6]

Yet while Newcastle was formally out of power at the end of 1756, he was not yet shorn of political influence. Formed under the leadership of William Pitt as Southern secretary (Pitt disdained the Treasury along with all issues of public finance, so the new first lord was a figurehead, the duke of Devonshire), the new ministry was destined to be a weak one for reasons that contemporary observers found self-evident. In the first place, Pitt's base of support in the House of Commons was anything but secure. After years in opposition, his greatest constituency was external—the merchants and financiers of London and that vaguer body he called "the People" or "the Nation," by which he meant the urban middle class and lesser gentry. Among active politicians in Parliament, Pitt could count on the votes of three groups only: "the faction of cousins," as his in-laws the Grenvilles and their supporters were known; the Leicester House faction, or those politicians attached to the interest of the teenaged prince of Wales, his tutor the earl of Bute, and his mother the dowager princess; and the so-called independents, mostly Tory backbenchers who could be swayed by Pitt's oratory and reputation as an incorruptible statesman.

What weakened Pitt even more, however, was the fact that George II detested him and his Grenville kin for the warmth of their connections with the heir apparent and the Leicester House faction generally. Nothing could budge the old king from keeping faith with his favorite son, the duke of Cumberland, and Cumberland's protégé, Henry Fox. The enmity of the king was no mere inconvenience, for British monarchs remained powerful enough in the mid-eighteenth century that no ministry could long endure without royal cooperation. Finally, Pitt's prospects were sharply limited by the fact that many members of the House of Commons remained under the influence of the duke of Newcastle, whose decades of assiduous attention to patronage had made him a man, in or out of power, whose opinion few M.P.s could afford to ignore. From the start Pitt was, therefore, a minister on a very short leash, capable of governing only at the sufferance of the king and Newcastle—and he knew it.[7]

Thus Pitt's policies marked no great departure from the substance of those that Newcastle and Fox had pursued, although the Great Commoner did succeed in placing his distinctive rhetorical stamp on them by declaring the American war to be his first priority. Both the army and the navy were to be built up to new levels of strength and proficiency, he promised, and principally committed to American and West Indian operations. Lord Loudoun was to have no fewer than 17,000 regulars at his disposal by the beginning of the campaigning season, and use them first to seize Louisbourg, then Québec. Because the Hessians and Hanoverians who had been summoned to defend against French invasion had returned home at the outbreak of hostilities in the Germanies, Pitt also proposed to supplement the regular army by creating a militia for home defense—a 32,000-man territorial force raised in the counties under the leadership of local squires (eventually including the pudgy, bookish Edward Gibbon, whose service as a captain in the south battalion of the Hampshire militia would prove invaluable to history, if not necessarily indispensable to the defense of the realm).[8] As for the Continent, Pitt had no intention of committing British soldiers there at all, preferring to let Germans spill German blood. The man who had so roundly reviled Newcastle for his policy of foreign subsidies accordingly advocated pouring vast sums into the coffers of Hanover, Hesse, and Prussia. These three together, he maintained, could raise 50,000 or 60,000 men to defend Hanover, and Britain should pay them to do it. Since Prussia was strong enough to carry the main burden of the land war against France and Austria, it deserved a subsidy of £200,000 annually.

Pitt intended this vigorous trimming of sail—and especially the attention to defending Hanover—to win the king's trust and to secure Newcastle's neutrality, if not necessarily his support. He achieved the latter only. George II could scarcely bear Pitt's presence and absolutely loathed Pitt's brother-in-law Richard Grenville, Lord Temple, who was serving as first lord of the Admiralty. Thus at the first flicker of independence on the part of Pitt—it came when he made a plea for clemency on behalf of Admiral Byng, then under sentence of death for neglect of duty—George sacked the lot. In early April 1757, after a little more than four months in office, Pitt was once again without a job, and the country, in the midst of a war going worse with every passing day, was without a government.[9]

Fox and Cumberland had forced this turn of events. Fox hoped to replace Pitt as first minister, and Cumberland gave him the support he needed by bluntly refusing to go to Hanover and assume command of the army there, so long as Pitt remained in office. Given the king's unconcealed distaste for Pitt, this gambit had every prospect for success and doubtless would have worked brilliantly—had Newcastle agreed to cooperate. The duke, however, had never cared for Cumberland and refused to forgive Fox for his recent treachery. Without Newcastle's support no progress could be made in any direction. Thus what followed the dismissal of Pitt in April was a bizarre three-month interlude of maneuvering and intrigue during which no one seemed to be in control of the government. Horace Walpole, half-amused and half-appalled, called it "the *inter-ministerium.*"[10]

None of what happened during this period, while the duke of Devonshire stayed on to head a ghostly caretaker cabinet, had anything to do with policy, for no one suggested that any change should be made in the way the war was to be waged. The only real issues at stake had to do with personalities. The king wished to revive the coalition of Fox and Newcastle, but Newcastle refused to have anything to do with Fox. The duke would undertake no ministry without first being assured that the king and the Leicester House faction could be reconciled, for he had no wish to find himself caught between feuding halves of the royal family. Yet Pitt, high in influence at Leicester House, would cooperate only if he could name his own terms, and they were too steep for either the king or Newcastle to tolerate. Fox wished to return to power, or—failing that—to be appointed to a position of profit; nothing would be possible unless some way could be found to satisfy his ambitions. To reconcile these competing desires and contradictory demands within the rigid frame of parliamentary politics demanded that equations of Einsteinian intricacy be solved. But until all the necessary calculations had been worked out, nothing—not even the war—could take precedence.[11]

The *interministerium* did not end until June was nearly over, when Newcastle and Pitt finally resolved, to their own and to the king's grudging satisfactions, the all-important question of who should occupy what offices. In the end it was agreed that Newcastle would return to office as first lord of the Treasury and would exercise control over all patronage and financial affairs; the formulation of policy would be left to Pitt, who would reassume the Southern secretaryship. Thus Pitt would become "minister of measures" and the duke, "minister of money." Newcastle's old friend Robert D'Arcy, earl of Holdernesse, would return to the Northern secretaryship, balancing Pitt in the other of the two chief administrative posts in the Privy Council. Fox, whose patron Cumberland had gone off to defend Hanover, found himself cut off from power but amply rewarded by the paymaster generalship of the forces, a position that paid handsomely (above £4,000 per annum) and provided its incumbent with the choicest opportunities for profiteering that eighteenth-century English government afforded. Fox knew full well when he accepted the post that so long as he held it he would be putting himself on the shelf politically, for the paymastership communicated no influence whatever; but in the end he was happy enough to trade power for profit. Before his tenure ended in 1774, Fox would harvest more than £400,000 from the office. As for the rest of the interested parties, the king saw to it that no single interest triumphed. The detested Grenvilles received offices that conferred (at most) prestige, not power, and that kept them out of his closet. The Townshend brothers, important allies of Pitt among the independents, got nothing at all. Even Newcastle, who had tried to have a ministerial post created for Lord Halifax—a secretaryship of state for America and the West Indies—found himself brought up short.[12]

What would come to be known as the Pitt-Newcastle ministry was a coalition created by strenuous bargaining, and it was obviously one that could function only so long as its major parties remained willing to compromise. Relieved that the long weeks of drift were at an end, politicians and others outside the new ministry greeted its formation with expressions of hope for the future. Given the lack of goodwill and trust between the ministers at the outset, however, optimism was hardly the order of the day within the government itself. The king had been deeply offended during the *interministerium* by Newcastle's unwillingness to do his bidding; Newcastle was still speaking of Pitt as "my enemy"; Pitt was calling his role in the new ministry a "bitter but necessary cup," which he approached with a "foreboding mind."[13] As if all that were not enough, on the very day that Newcastle and Pitt kissed the king's hand for their seals of office, news of the most forbidding sort arrived from the Continent.

CHAPTER 17

The Fortunes of War in Europe

1757

STRIKING SOUTH out of Saxony into the Austrian province of Bohemia, Frederick of Prussia won a smashing victory over the Austrian army outside Prague, then trapped more than forty thousand Austrian soldiers in the city and laid it under siege in early May 1757. While waiting for them to submit or starve, however, he found his own supply lines cut by a second Austrian force, commanded by Field Marshal Leopold, Count von Daun. With his options suddenly limited to attack or withdrawal, Frederick again took the offensive and marched an army of more than thirty thousand Prussians against Daun's fortified camp near Kolín. He lost nearly half of them in a great battle during which fully two-thirds of the infantrymen in his army were killed, wounded, or captured: as Frederick would explain to George II, he was compelled to break off his attacks "for lack of combatants." Defeat left him with no choice but to raise the siege of Prague and withdraw his army from Bohemia. This crisis in the continental war furnished "dreadful auspices . . . [to] begin with," but Pitt and Newcastle would soon hear worse. Even as Frederick was retreating from Bohemia, the French were moving against his territories in East Friesland, their allies the Swedes were sending thousands of troops against Pomerania, and the Russians were poised to invade East Prussia.[1]

By the middle of July, the Prussian king was bombarding Pitt with pleas to do something, anything, to relieve his distress: at the very least, he might dispatch British troops to Hanover, to replace the Prussian contingents in the Hanoverian army and free them to defend their own country. Yet that, for reasons soon to become apparent, was the least possible of all solutions to Frederick's problems.[2]

Although Britain had sent no troops to defend Hanover, the king had dispatched his son, William Augustus, the duke of Cumberland, to lead the electorate's armies. Cumberland had not been a bad choice. At age thirty-six, he had already gained considerable experience as an army administrator, had seen battle during the previous war, and had the physical courage to lead men in combat—but the terms of his appointment were ambiguous, and he had come to the Continent with "orders that read more like the minutes of a cabinet meeting than an operational document." In mid-July, as Frederick pelted Pitt with demands for help, a large French force crossed the Weser. Frederick helpfully suggested that Cumberland attack immediately, despite the fact that the French outnumbered his army by approximately two to one. Cumberland, declining the king's advice, took up defensive positions at a village called Hastenbeck, not far from the Weser, and waited. The French attacked on July 25, dislodged Cumberland's army, and forced it to retreat northward, toward the mouth of the Elbe. Cumberland hoped that the British navy could bring him the reinforcements and supplies he needed to counterattack; but the French outflanked him and cut him off from the river, then sat back and waited for him to make the next move.[3]

Cornered and impotent, the duke now came under intense pressure from Hanover's ministers of state to make a peace that would save their country from being overrun. In early August it only remained unclear when, not if, Cumberland would negotiate. His father privately instructed him if necessary to make a separate peace for Hanover, and there was no doubt that his commission, muddled as it was, empowered him to negotiate any settlement he thought prudent. The longer he delayed in negotiating, however, the less credible his defeated army grew as a threat, and the less likely he would be to obtain favorable terms from the French. As August wore on, the ministry's hopes for retrieving the military situation on the Continent waned, the king's anxieties for preserving Hanover's sovereignty mounted, and Frederick's concerns for the defense of Prussia grew more desperate. Everything now focused on Cumberland's ability to extricate himself from a situation that grew more dismal by the day.[4]

Only a few hopeful developments relieved the grimness of the Pitt-Newcastle ministry's first days. On July 8 news arrived from India that military affairs in that distant quarter, at least, were improving. Fragmentary reports had been coming in since Christmas that the army of the nawab of Bengal had attacked the British East India Company post of

Fort William at Calcutta the previous June, with disastrous results for its garrison. Now word arrived that at New Year's, Lieutenant Colonel Robert Clive—deputy governor of Fort St. David, the East India Company factory at Madras—had retaken Calcutta from the nawab's army. With the receipt of dispatches informing him that Britain and France had declared war, Clive had gone on to attack Fort d'Orléans, the French Compagnie des Indes factory at Chandernagore, and had forced its surrender on March 23.[5]

Because months of travel were necessary to relay information from India, no one in England yet knew that on June 23 the indefatigable Clive had gained a decisive victory over the nawab at the Battle of Plassey and seized control of all Bengal. That knowledge would surely have cheered Pitt, but in early July he remained wary. "This cordial," he wrote to a political ally of the news that Calcutta had been regained and Chandernagore taken, "such as it is, has not the power to quiet my mind one minute till we hear Lord Loudoun is safe at Halifax" and ready to launch an assault on Louisbourg. To his great relief, the dispatches that arrived from America on August 6 brought the news he longed to hear. Loudoun had arrived in Nova Scotia at the beginning of July and his preparations for the amphibious attack on the great Cape Breton fortress were proceeding apace. "I am infinitely happy to think of the joy this news will give [in the household of the Prince of Wales]," Pitt wrote to the prince's tutor, the earl of Bute. Unfortunately for Pitt's peace of mind, this would prove the last piece of encouraging news from America for a long, long time.[6]

CHAPTER 18

Loudoun's Offensive

1757

LORD LOUDOUN had been pleased to learn that Pitt supported an all-out war in the colonies, though he doubtless found it disquieting that the minister showed so much eagerness to intervene in the planning of his campaign for 1757. Loudoun had initially intended to send regulars to Pennsylvania and South Carolina to strengthen their defenses, but otherwise to defend the colonial frontier with provincials. His redcoats he would use in a single daring offensive against Québec. When word of Pitt's plans for the campaign of 1757 arrived at Loudoun's headquarters, however, he discovered that the minister wanted him first to attack Louisbourg and only then to proceed against the Canadian heartland via the St. Lawrence—a plan with strategic merit, but one that inevitably left the New York–New England frontier exposed to raids, or even invasion, from Canada. Good soldier that he was, Loudoun proceeded according to orders, swallowing his reservations along with whatever resentment he felt at Pitt's intrusion into his operational planning. Since Pitt had promised a reinforcement of eight thousand regulars for the coming campaign, and since he was making it a point for Loudoun "to be refused nothing," the commander in chief may not have thought the bargain an especially bad one. Moreover, he believed that his efforts in reforming colonial affairs would contribute to the success of the 1757 campaign, no matter whether its immediate goal was Louisbourg or Québec.[1]

Loudoun had spent the whole fall of 1756 and much of the ensuing winter trying to impose order on the American war effort. In September and October he concentrated on rationalizing the supply system, introducing efficiency and economy into what had been a notoriously complex and (he believed) corrupt operation. With centralized storehouses at

New York, Albany, and Halifax, and with a vigilant commissary of stores working to inspect the victuals for wholesomeness, Loudoun's new system guaranteed that adequate stocks of equipment, clothing, and provisions would be available to regulars and provincials alike, for the first time in the war.[2]

Significant as they were, however, Loudoun knew that improvements in procurement, storage, and inventory control would be meaningless without a reliable means of moving the supplies to the forts and troops that needed them. Thus he decided to retain the services of John Bradstreet and his corps of armed bateaumen, despite Bradstreet's close ties to the detested Shirley. In consultation with Bradstreet, Loudoun undertook the measures without which no successful campaign could ever be mounted against the French, widening roads and improving portages, creating an army wagon train to supplement the services of the expensive and often unreliable civilian wagoners, building standardized supply bateaux and scows, and constructing way stations to shelter supplies and men in transit from station to station. The fall in the cost of moving supplies offers the best index of Loudoun's success in improving the efficiency of the transport system. In 1756 it had cost nearly sixpence a mile to move a two-hundredweight barrel of beef from Albany to Lake George, which meant that the army was spending more than half the value of the beef itself to carry it sixty miles. By the end of 1757, the same barrel could be transported over the same route for less than twopence a mile.[3]

Loudoun undertook these reforms to lessen his reliance on Americans, whom he found untrustworthy as well as ungrateful. He followed the same course in dealing with provincial troops, requesting for the campaigns of 1757 less than half the number that had served in 1756. Loudoun also hoped to establish control over the contract-minded soldiers of New England and their rank-conscious officers by changing the method of recruitment. Whereas in the past each province had supplied what amounted to a small complete army, now Loudoun asked the colonies to provide troops in standardized, hundred-man companies, with only one field officer per province ranking above the company commanders. These provincial companies were to be integrated into campaign forces and garrisons under redcoat command.

In this way Loudoun expected to solve the two most intractable problems of 1756. No man could now maintain that his enlistment contract exempted him from joint service with the redcoats, and thus from redcoat discipline; and the commissioning of a single colonel from each province would minimize disputes between provincial and regular field officers over rank and precedence. Although he could not escape using Americans altogether, Loudoun's clear preference was to use them on his own terms. Even the colonial backwoodsmen who made up the the army's ranger companies were, in Loudoun's eyes, temporary substitutes for regulars. Although the unwillingness of most Indians to serve as scouts for the British left him with no choice but to use Americans, Loudoun encouraged junior officers to accompany the rangers on their patrols to learn woodcraft and bush-fighting techniques. Within a year or so, he hoped to be able to form ranging companies under the command of these officers, within regular regiments. Then he would be free to dissolve the troublesome, expensive, undisciplinable American ranger units.[4]

Loudoun's reforms and his plan for 1757 reflected his disappointments in 1756 and seemed likely to solve the problems that had hobbled that year's misbegotten campaigns. Quartering remained a difficult issue—Loudoun's legal position was as weak as his men's need for housing was desperate—but progress seemed likely to result from Pitt's willingness to introduce a bill authorizing the billeting of troops in American private homes. Until such a measure could be secured, Loudoun contented himself with his usual tactic of threatening to take quarters by force, a system that effectively produced colonial cooperation, if not goodwill. After a trial of strength between the commander in chief and the mayor and town council of New York late in 1756, the provincial assembly agreed to build a barracks on Manhattan to house the first battalion of the Royal American Regiment. At about that same time, Philadelphia's city government and the Pennsylvania war commissioners were knuckling under to Loudoun's threats and making the new provincial hospital available as a barracks for the regiment's second battalion; in 1758 the Pennsylvania assembly would follow New York's example and build permanent accommodations.[5]

So developed what Loudoun came to recognize as a common pattern of requisition, refusal, threat, and (finally) submission: informal ways of dealing with the colonists, perhaps, and not altogether legal ones, but methods that nonetheless produced the effect he desired. "I have taken these measures," he had explained to Fox, "because they appear to me right, and . . . I hope they will appear to You in the same light[.] If they do not, I shall alter them whenever I receive directions to do so; but I do expect to get through, for the People in this Country, tho' they are very obstinate, will generally submit when they see You [are] determined."[6] If Loudoun realized that his tactics of force and the casualness of his concern for the law were alienating the colonists, he did not show it. Winning the war, not coddling Americans, was his concern. Besides that, he harbored no particular animus toward colonists per se: he coerced anyone who differed with him, with complete impartiality. Governors who, hoping to preserve amiable relations with their assemblies, hesitated to comply with his requisitions were the first to feel the lash.

Loudoun's conviction that the colonists were incapable of self-sacrifice and his determination to bring the colonies into line by whatever means necessary manifested itself in another initiative that, like quartering, produced short-run results at the cost of eroding colonial affections. This was the instruction that Loudoun issued to the governors in early March 1757, to lay an embargo on all trade from their provinces, in effect prohibiting all ships, other than those engaged in official military business, from leaving port. As early as the previous October, Loudoun had received reliable evidence that at least one prominent Boston merchant was "carrying on a Correspondence with, and supplying the People in Canada." Even before that, he had suspected that "there are many more in this Situation, Particularly among the dutch in Albany," and he could hardly have missed hearing the perennial reports of illicit trading between the northern provision merchants and the sugar planters of the French West Indies.[7]

At first Loudoun had not known what to do. Governors, under the influence of their assemblies, were unlikely to arrest those guilty of trading with the enemy when the offenders included some of the most prominent merchants—and assemblymen—in the colonies. He himself could not prevent flagrant smuggling at New York, literally in his headquarters' backyard, and he was too distant from the other port cities to do anything more on his own; the home government was too distant and preoccupied to do more than raise a meaningless hue and cry against the practice. The embargo was Loudoun's answer. By prohibiting *all* ship clearances except those that he or his subordinates ordered for military purposes, he would effectually cut off illegal commerce along with the rest. At the same time, he would also keep word from leaking out about the intended expedition against Louisbourg, insure that he would have enough shipping on hand to undertake it when the time came, and guarantee that adequate supplies of food would be available in the ports to provision it at reasonable rates.[8]

To order such a measure lay well within Loudoun's authority as commander in chief, and the governors of all the colonies from Virginia to the north complied without hesitation. Temporary embargoes in time of war were nothing new—several provinces acting on instruction from the Board of Trade had imposed them in 1755 and 1756—and the merchants in the various ports did not protest. Indeed, the very universality of the measure may have prevented them from doing so, for it guaranteed that no one port would gain at the expense of any other. The merchants did not immediately understand that Loudoun intended his embargo to remain in effect indefinitely. But as the weeks passed, the price of flour and corn in Philadelphia plummeted in markets glutted by unshippable stocks of provisions; the Virginia and Maryland tobacco crops remained locked in warehouses or stowed in the holds of ships riding at anchor; the price of bread skyrocketed in Boston while the departure of cod fishermen on the spring fare was indefinitely delayed.

Everywhere except New York—insulated from the misfortunes of the other colonies by the presence of the army with its large supply demands—Loudoun's embargo caused painful economic dislocation. He either did not grasp or did not care that it convinced colonial merchants and tobacco planters of his indifference to their welfare. Despite their increasingly urgent pleas, Loudoun refused to lift the ban. Why should he, since the protests of the various assemblies were motivated (he thought) by mean self-interest and the pressures of smugglers to resume their trade? Ultimately it was the Burgesses of Virginia who forced the issue in early May by refusing to grant a supply of money to the army unless the embargo was lifted. Lieutenant Governor Dinwiddie acquiesced—thereby convincing Loudoun that he was trying to enrich himself at the expense of the war effort—and soon thereafter Maryland's governor agreed to lift the embargo on his colony's trade, so as not to forfeit Maryland's share in the London tobacco market to the earlier arrival of Virginia's leaf. Loudoun, furious but powerless to arrest the governors and legislators of two colonies, had no choice but to allow the reopening of trade, which began on June 27, seven days after the departure of his fleet for Louisbourg. He made no effort to hide his disgust at what he saw as the pusillanimous conduct of the governors and the virtual treason of the colonial assemblies.[9]

As all these measures illustrated, Loudoun was moving steadily toward the creation of a de facto military union of the colonies, of a sort not greatly different in its effect from the plan that the Albany Congress had proposed and the colonial assemblies had uniformly rejected. That the colonists would resist and resent his measures seems not to have bothered a man whose conceptions of responsibility derived from his experiences as a courtier and military officer, and who cared as little for the niceties of law or the expedients of politics as for the technicalities of trade. When he sailed from New York harbor with the Louisbourg fleet, Lord Loudoun was disappointed by the lateness of his departure—he blamed the backwardness of the colonies in making preparations, the tardiness of the Royal Navy in providing an escort, and the unfavorability of the winds—but had no reason to doubt that he had increased the likelihood of the expedition's success. He had systematized the war effort in America, corrected the abuses that Shirley had fostered, and struck a blow against trade with the enemy. For the first time, an American campaign would go forward with efficiency, economy, and real prospects for success.

Loudoun's great invasion fleet, numbering more than a hundred sail and carrying six thousand troops, cleared Sandy Hook on June 20—nervously, for the promised escort of Royal Navy warships had not arrived and the transports were for all practical purposes defenseless; but the commander in chief was convinced that he could wait no longer. He had done everything in his power to prepare for the campaign. In February he had met with the commissioners representing the New England provinces at Boston to organize the northern war effort for the year. In March he had convened a meeting of the governors from Pennsylvania to North Carolina at Philadelphia and delivered his instructions for the defense of their frontiers. From Philadelphia he had gone on to meet with both the Pennsylvania and New Jersey assemblies, to compose differences between themselves and their governors and to assure (insofar as possible) that intragovernmental conflicts would not hobble the war effort. He had provided for the defense of the lake frontier in New York with two regular regiments and 5,500 provincials and had performed the unprecedented feat of getting the provincials into the field on schedule. Not least of all, he had mounted the largest seaborne expeditionary force ever to sail from an American port, under conditions of tighter security than anyone had ever managed before. All these accomplishments paid tribute to Loudoun's vigor, administrative skill, and attention to detail. All of them augured well for the success of this, the best-planned, -manned, -equipped, and -coordinated campaign in the history of British North America. But other developments were already looming when Loudoun's fleet weighed anchor, against which no amount of planning could have prevailed.[10]

CHAPTER 19

Fort William Henry

1757

THE MOST OMINOUS problems were taking shape in New York, where Loudoun had left the defense of the lake frontier in the palsied hands of General Daniel Webb, the man who in 1756 had responded to rumors of a French advance down the Mohawk Valley by destroying Fort Bull, blocking Wood Creek with trees, and ordering a retreat to German Flats. Webb's continued position as Loudoun's third-ranking officer owed principally to the undiminished confidence of Webb's patron, the duke of Cumberland, which left Loudoun little choice but to entrust the command to him. Although in one of the last letters he wrote from New York before departing for Louisbourg, Loudoun had urged Webb to establish an advanced post at the north end of Lake George and if possible to besiege Fort Carillon, Loudoun probably realized that he could be expected to do no more than defend New York against invasion. This was only in part because the commander in chief lacked confidence in the "timid, melancholic, and 'diffident' " Webb, with his regrettable tendencies to panic and overreact. Loudoun's desire to make the Louisbourg expedition an all-redcoat show had made him willing to allot Webb only two regular regiments to augment the questionable fighting capacities of 5,500 untrained provincials. Most of all, however, offensive action was realistically out of the question because Fort William Henry, the British post guarding the main approach to the upper Hudson Valley at the south end (or head) of Lake George, had already been damaged by a surprise attack.[1]

In mid-March a force of fifteen hundred Canadians, French, and Indians under the command of the governor-general's wiry, sawed-off younger brother, François-Pierre Rigaud, had approached the fort over the frozen lake and harassed its small winter garrison for four days. The raiders had come equipped only with scaling ladders, not cannon, and therefore stood little chance of actually seizing the fort unless they could surprise or stampede its commander. As it happened, Fort William Henry that winter was under the highly competent command of the man who had designed it, Major William Eyre; and Eyre made no mistakes in directing its defense. Before the raiders withdrew to Ticonderoga, however, they burned all of the fort's outbuildings (including a palisaded barracks, several storehouses, a sawmill, and a hospital), its exposed bateaux, and the half-built sloop that stood on stocks near the lake.[2]

Although its defenders had suffered only a handful of minor casualties and its wood-and-earth walls had been untouched by anything heavier than musket balls, the damage to Fort William Henry as a strategic outpost had been grave. The valuable supplies that would have to be replaced from Albany and the external buildings that would take weeks to rebuild were the least consequential losses. More serious by far was the loss of the fort's bateaux, without which troops could not be moved down the lake against Fort Carillon; but most damaging of all was the loss of the sloop, which left the fort with only one serviceable gunboat to launch in the spring. As the winter's experience showed, Fort William Henry was safe from attackers who lacked artillery. Unless the British could dominate Lake George with armed vessels, however, they could not prevent an invading French army from bringing siege cannon from Fort Carillon. It would take weeks of labor, once shipwrights had been brought in from New England, to construct a replacement for the lost sloop. In the meantime, Fort William Henry would be vulnerable to any siege the marquis de Montcalm cared to mount.

There was one other critical way in which Rigaud's raid had put the British in New York at a disadvantage: the loss of intelligence. At the beginning of the winter Eyre's garrison at Fort William Henry had included about a hundred rangers under Captain Robert Rogers. But Rogers had led them on a disastrous scout against Fort Carillon in January that had cost nearly a quarter of that number, and he had sustained a wound of his own that required treatment at Albany. He would not recover and return to the fort until the middle of April. Given these circumstances the rangers could not have ventured far from the fort even if conditions had favored them. But following Rigaud's raid, the woods around Lake George grew thick with French-allied Indians. Word of Rogers's defeat and of Rigaud's adventure brought hundreds of Ottawa, Potawatomi, Abenaki, and Caughnawaga warriors to Fort St. Frédéric and Fort Carillon in the spring of 1757. From April through June, under the leadership of their own chiefs and of Canadian officers like Charles Langlade (who had directed the destruction of Pickawillany in 1752 and helped defeat Braddock in 1755), they raided English outposts and ambushed supply trains in the woods between Fort Edward and Fort William Henry. So effectively did the Indians and Canadian irregulars confine the rangers to the vicinity of the British forts that General Webb and his senior officers were deprived of virtually all intelligence concerning French preparations for the coming campaigns. If they had known what was coming Webb and his subordinates might conceivably have prepared more vigorously for the summer, but as late as the beginning of June the garrison at Fort William Henry had not undertaken repairs.[3]

What Webb and his officers did not know was that since late in the summer of 1756 the most successful recruiting drive in the history of New France had been under way among the Indians of the *pays d'en haut,* the upper Great Lakes basin. The combination of Governor-General Vaudreuil's enthusiasm for using Indian allies and the widespread reports of French victories at the Monongahela and Oswego attracted warriors from a vast area to serve in the principal campaign planned for 1757: a thrust against Fort William Henry. Montcalm, still unhappy with the uncontrollable behavior of his Abenaki, Caughnawaga, Nipissing, Menominee, and Ojibwa warriors after the surrender of Oswego, entertained more reservations than ever about relying on Indians, but these were overborne by the sheer numbers who presented themselves at Montréal and the Lake Champlain forts between the fall of 1756 and the early summer of 1757. Stories that the Ojibwas and Menominees carried back home to the Great Lakes after the fall of Oswego had "made a great impression," Montcalm's aide-de-camp noted; "especially what they have heard tell of everyone there swimming in brandy." Of equal importance, perhaps, was the news that Montcalm had been willing to ransom English prisoners from their Indian captors after the battle. At any rate, the Indians came in numbers that exceeded even Vaudreuil's fondest hopes and included warriors who had traveled as far as fifteen hundred miles to join the expedition.[4]

By the end of July nearly 2,000 Indians were assembled at Fort Carillon in aid of the army of 6,000 French regulars, *troupes de la marine,* and Canadian militiamen that Montcalm was preparing to lead against Fort William Henry. More than 300 Ottawas had come from the upper Lake Michigan country; nearly as many Ojibwas (Chippewas and Mississaugas) from the shores of Lake Superior; more than 100 Menominees and almost as many Potawatamis from lower Michigan; about 50 Winnebagos from Wisconsin; Sauk and Fox warriors from even farther west;

Robert Rogers, of the rangers (1731–95). Shown here in a Revolutionary-era engraving as the Loyalist "Commander in Chief of the Indians in the Back Settlements of America," Rogers spent most of the Seven Years' War leading ranger units that were supposed to replace the Indian allies that the British lacked. He tried indefatigably to perfect the rangers' skills in woodlands warfare, yet never entirely succeeded in doing so; twice he and his men suffered terribly (and he himself nearly died) at the hands of French *marines* and Indians whose expertise was of a markedly higher order. What Rogers lacked as an irregular, however, he made up as a self-publicist. His *Journals,* published in London in 1765, secured his reputation as the very model of the frontier guerrilla leader. *Courtesy of the William L. Clements Library at the University of Michigan.*

a few Miamis and Delawares from the Ohio Country; and even 10 Iowa warriors, representing a nation that had never been seen in Canada before. In all, 979 Indians from the *pays d'en haut* and the middle west joined the 820 Catholic Indians recruited from missions that extended from the Atlantic to the Great Lakes—Nipissings, Ottawas, Abenakis,

Caughnawagas, Huron-Petuns, Malecites, and Micmacs. With no fewer than thirty-three nations, as many languages, and widely varying levels of familiarity with European culture represented, problems of control were magnified even beyond their usual scope. Since Montcalm realized that "in the midst of the woods of America one can no more do without them than without cavalry in open country," he did what he could to accommodate, appease, and flatter his allies. But as he knew better than anyone else, he could not command them. Montcalm could only rely on the persuasive abilities of the missionary fathers, interpreter-traders, and warrior-officers like Langlade whom he "attached" to each group in the hope of gaining its cooperation.[5]

In the spring Lieutenant Colonel George Monro had brought five companies of his regiment, the 35th Foot, to Fort William Henry to relieve Major Eyre's winter garrison. Together with two New York independent companies and nearly eight hundred provincials from New Jersey and New Hampshire, Monro's command numbered more than fifteen hundred men in late June when two escaped English prisoners brought the first reliable intelligence of the eight-thousand-man force that Montcalm was gathering at Fort Carillon. Monro—"an old Officer but [one] who never ha[d] served" in the field—dispatched several ranger patrols over the next several weeks to observe the French and Indian buildup at the foot of the lake. None succeeded, and the lack of serviceable boats prevented Monro from mounting a reconnaissance-in-force until late July. It was only on the twenty-third that he finally hazarded five companies of New Jersey provincials under Colonel John Parker in a raid intended to burn the French sawmills at the foot of the lake and to take as many prisoners as possible. Traveling in two bay boats under sail and twenty whaleboats—virtually all of the vessels available at Fort William Henry—Parker's command made its way north down the lake toward Sabbath-Day Point. They did not know until the next morning that more than five hundred Ottawas, Ojibwas, Potawatomis, Menominees, and Canadians were waiting for them. According to Louis Antoine de Bougainville, Moncalm's aide-de-camp,

> At daybreak three of [the English] barges fell into our ambush without a shot fired. Three others that followed at a little distance met the same fate. The [remaining] sixteen advanced in order. The Indians who were on shore fired at them and made them fall back. When they saw them do this they jumped into their canoes, pursued the enemy, hit them, and sank or captured all but two which escaped. They brought back nearly two hundred prisoners. The rest were

> drowned. The Indians jumped into the water and speared them like fish. . . . We had only one man slightly wounded. The English, terrified by the shooting, the sight, the cries, and the agility of these monsters, surrendered almost without firing a shot. The rum which was in the barges and which the Indians immediately drank caused them to commit great cruelties. They put in the pot and ate three prisoners, and perhaps others were so treated. All have become slaves unless they are ransomed. A horrible spectacle to European eyes.[6]

In fact, four of the boats escaped the trap, but three-quarters of the Jersey Blues on the expedition were killed or captured. The arrival of the panic-stricken survivors offered the first tangible evidence of a large enemy presence at Fort Carillon, and it thoroughly rattled General Webb, who was making his first visit to Fort William Henry when the remnants of Parker's command appeared. Webb ordered Monro to quarter the garrison's regulars within the fort and directed him to have the provincials construct an entrenched camp on Titcomb's Mount, a rocky rise about 750 yards southeast of the fort, to prevent the enemy from siting cannon on its summit. Then, promising to send reinforcements, he beat a hasty retreat to Fort Edward.

Monro needed the promised men badly. When Webb left on July 29, Fort William Henry's garrison consisted of only about eleven hundred soldiers fit for duty, together with sixty carpenters and sailors, about eighty women and children, and a handful of sutlers. Since its total complement of vessels on the lake now consisted of five whaleboats and two armed sloops (one in need of repair), Monro knew that he could not prevent the French from investing the place with artillery. The larger the number of men in place at the fort on the day the siege began, therefore, the better the chances would be that they could resist the attackers.[7]

And yet Webb, fearful of stripping the defenses of his own post, Fort Edward, persuaded himself to dispatch only about two hundred regulars of the Royal American (60th) Regiment and eight hundred Massachusetts provincials under Lieutenant Colonel Joseph Frye. They arrived on the evening of August 2—the same night that lookouts spotted three large fires on the western shore of the lake at about seven miles' distance. Two scouting boats were dispatched to investigate. Neither returned.

At dawn the next morning, observers on the ramparts of William Henry could begin to make out shapes on the dark surface of the lake: there, beyond cannon range, bobbed nearly 250 French bateaux and at least 150 Indian war canoes. To officers surveying the scene through field telescopes, the growing light revealed that more than sixty of the bateaux had been joined together catamaran-style by platforms of planks; these rode low in the water, borne down by the weight of the siege guns they carried. "We know that they have Cannon," Monro wrote to Webb, in one of three pleas for help he sent that day. If anyone had entertained any lingering doubts, it was now unmistakable that the second siege of Fort William Henry would be conducted in the European style.[8]

The three bonfires that sentries at the fort had seen the night before had been kindled by an advance party of six hundred regulars, a hundred *troupes de la marine,* thirteen hundred Canadians, and five hundred Indians under Brigadier François-Gaston, chevalier de Lévis, Montcalm's second-in-command. They had been toiling south through the woods "in heat . . . as great as in Italy," since July 29. Montcalm's main army, numbering more than four thousand men, needed only a day to traverse the same distance by boat. Unlike the overburdened advance party, they had made the trip in a festive mood. Perhaps the beauty of the lake—a drowned valley between mountain ranges, its waters studded with "a very great quantity of islands"—animated those who rowed and rode in the dark, stolid ranks of bateaux; or perhaps it was the sight of scores of birch-bark canoes in the vanguard, gliding like a cloud over the lake's blue surface, that lifted their spirits—for, as Bougainville wondered, "who could imagine the spectacle of fifteen hundred naked Indians in their canoes?" Whatever the cause, not even Montcalm's strict orders for silence could restrain the gaiety his soldiers felt, and they fired musket salutes, beat rolls on the drum, and sounded hunting horns as their flotilla made its way up the lake. Disapproving of the breach of discipline and yet stirred by the fanfares that echoed between the mountains, Bougainville believed that these must have been "the first horns that have yet resounded through the forests of America."[9]

Lévis's advance party fired the first shots at the fort's defenders on August 3. Even before the main body had landed its artillery and supplies, Montcalm ordered Lévis to circle through the woods behind the fort and cut the road leading southward to Fort Edward. This task his Indians and Canadians quickly accomplished, driving a guard of Massachusetts provincials back to their camp on Titcomb's Mount and seizing virtually all of their livestock—about 50 horses and 150 oxen, most of which the Indians slaughtered to supplement the scanty rations they had been receiving from the army. Meanwhile, as Indian sharpshooters began sniping at the defenders of William Henry from the main garrison garden—a seven-acre plot lying just fifty or sixty yards from the western wall of the fort—Montcalm brought the main body up from the landing place and surveyed the shoreline for a position from which to begin his entrenchments.

At three in the afternoon Montcalm formally opened the siege by sending in a messenger under flag of truce, in accord with European custom, bearing a demand for the garrison's surrender. "Humanity," he wrote, "obliged him to warn [Monro] that once [the French] batteries were in place and the cannon fired, perhaps there would not be time, nor would it be in [his] power to restrain the cruelties of a mob of Indians of so many different nations." With equal gravity Monro replied that he and his troops would resist "to the last extremity." While the commanders exchanged their ceremonial courtesies, the Indians stood "in a great crowd in the space around the fort," obeying the norms of their own cultures by hurling taunts at the defenders. "Take care to defend yourself," shouted one Abenaki warrior in clear (though "very bad") French to the soldiers on the ramparts, "for if I capture you, you will get no quarter."[10]

Although Fort William Henry was clearly in trouble on August 3, its position was far from desperate. The fort's magazines held adequate if not ample stocks of ammunition and provisions; its batteries mounted eighteen heavy cannon (including a pair of thirty-two–pounders), thirteen light swivels capable of raking the wall faces and glacis with grapeshot, two mortars, and a howitzer. A stout stone-and-log breastwork enclosed the provincial camp atop Titcomb's Mount, which had six brass fieldpieces and four swivels, as well as the small arms of its men, to defend it. The most immediate threat to the fort's garrison was fire, and Monro soon minimized that danger by ordering the flammable roof shingles removed from the interior buildings and having all stocks of firewood dumped into the lake. The greater dangers were those of the longer term: that a portion of the fort's wall would collapse under sustained cannonading, allowing attackers to rush through the breach and overwhelm the defenders, or (if the walls held up) that the garrison would be starved into submission.[11]

Since time inevitably favored the besiegers, such eventualities could be prevented only if Webb dispatched a relief expedition to attack Montcalm before he had a chance to organize his own camp's defenses. Hence the urgency of Monro's three attempts to notify Webb that Montcalm was about to besiege (or, as he said, using the technical term, "invest") the fort; for without reinforcement from below, Fort William Henry would be no more immune to prolonged cannon siege than Oswego or St. Philip's Castle had been. Thus on August 4, as Montcalm's engineers laid out the first line of entrenchments less than half a mile from William Henry's north bastion and as his Canadian militiamen began to construct

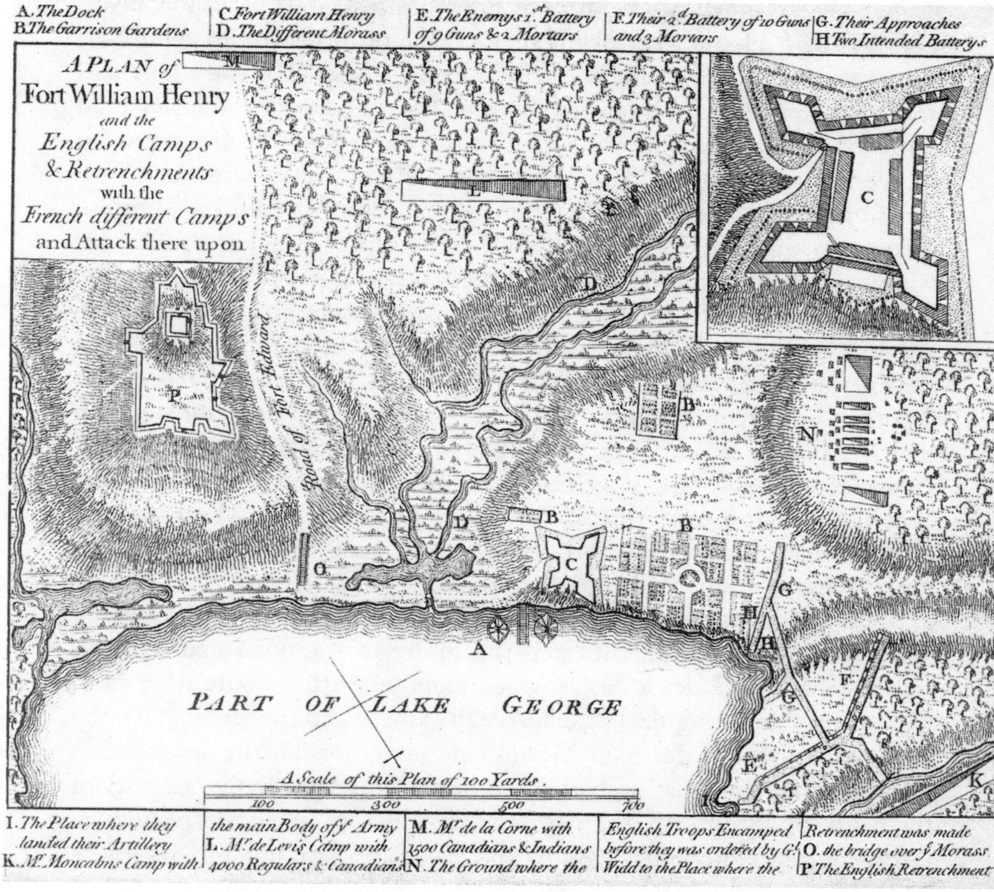

The Siege of Fort William Henry, August 3–9, 1757. On the left, atop Titcomb's Mount, is the "retrenched camp" of the New England provincials; at the center, across a marshy creek, the fort and its gardens stand on a plateau above the lake. Beyond the large garden on the right are the French siege works. The initial parallel trench is at the far right, with Montcalm's first two batteries (marked E and F), from which the French gunners began to shell the fort on August 6. An approach trench, or "sap," (marked G) connects the first parallel to a second parallel, at the edge of the garden. This entrenchment's breaching batteries (marked H) were never actually used; the British surrendered on August 9, before Montcalm could give the order to open fire. From Rocque, *A Set of Plans and Forts. Courtesy of the William L. Clements Library at the University of Michigan.*

artillery emplacements opposite the fort's western wall, Monro knew better than anyone that—barring a great mistake on his adversary's part, the arrival of a relief column from Fort Edward, or a miracle—his garrison's days were numbered.

Yet Webb, as Monro would not know until August 7, responded to Fort William Henry's predicament by deciding not to send reinforcements until he himself had been reinforced by militia from New England and New York. As Webb saw it, to weaken Fort Edward's garrison would expose Albany and the rest of upper New York to invasion. If Montcalm succeeded in seizing William Henry, after all, he would have not only a fort from which to launch further operations, but a splendid road to use in transporting siege guns against Fort Edward. In a letter of noon, August 4, Webb's aide-de-camp therefore advised Monro that the general "does not think it prudent (as you know his strength at this place) to attempt a Junction or to assist you" at present. Indeed, in view of the eleven-thousand-man strength of the French force that Monro had reported, and the possibility that Webb "should be so unfortunate from the delay of the Militia not to have it in his power to give you timely Assistance," Monro might well consider how (if worse came to worst) he "might make the best Terms" of capitulation possible. Monro would receive this message only on August 7 because one of Montcalm's Caughnawaga scouts stalked the courier into the woods after he left Fort Edward and killed him, long before he could reach Fort William Henry. The bloodstained letter, cut from the lining of the dead man's jacket, came to Monro under a flag of truce together with a polite note from Montcalm suggesting that he take Webb's advice and surrender.[12]

Colonel Monro declined Montcalm's invitation on the seventh but knew how far his situation had deteriorated from the relative security of the third. In the intervening days, the chevalier de Lévis had posted his force opposite Titcomb's Mount, and his Canadian and Indian scouts had made it all but impossible for the provincials to leave the entrenched camp. Indian war parties operating in the woods had cut all communication with Fort Edward. Despite harassing fire from Fort William Henry's artillery, Montcalm's sappers had quickly completed the first siege parallel and emplaced a battery from which his gunners had opened fire on August 6. On the morning of the seventh the French had brought a second battery into action and had driven an approach trench to within three hundred yards of the fort's western wall. From this point, Monro knew, they would dig another parallel trench along which they would site one or more "breaching batteries"; and these guns, firing at point-blank range, would blast passageways through the wall.[13]

When Monro received Montcalm's message on the morning of August 7, Fort William Henry's walls and bastions were still intact, which according to the elaborate etiquette of siege warfare meant that Monro could not—yet—honorably contemplate capitulation. But he also could not ignore the effect of the indirect, or high-trajectory, fire of the French mortars and howitzers, which had been raining shrapnel on his men and those in the entrenched camp for two days. Monro had been disturbed to learn that some of the solid shot recovered within the fort bore royal ordnance markings: proof that they, like the guns firing them, had been captured at the Monongahela or Oswego. Meanwhile the guns of his own batteries had been bursting at a fearful rate. Since the first shots had been fired at the French on August 4, more than half of William Henry's heavy cannon had split from prolonged firing, often injuring their crews as they exploded.[14]

By sunset on August 8, the relentless French bombardment had shattered the morale of Monro's garrison, most of whom had not slept for five nights running. Already on the seventh Monro had felt compelled to threaten to hang cowards, or indeed anyone who advocated surrender, over the walls of the fort; now his men seemed "almost Stupified" with stress and fatigue, and there was no telling how they would react to an assault if the western wall, weak from sustained shelling, were to collapse.[15]

Knowing now that Webb would send no reinforcements, Monro ordered one of his engineers to survey the damage and report the state of the fort's defenses. What he heard was that the top three feet of the bastions most exposed to French fire had been shot entirely away; that the casements, or bunkers within them, had been heavily damaged; that all but five of the fort's cannon were inoperable; and that stocks of ammunition had dwindled to near exhaustion. Nor were the reports he received from the entrenched camp any more encouraging. The Massachusetts troops stationed there had suffered even heavier losses from indirect fire than the fort. As their commander, Colonel Frye, reported, they "were quite worn out, & wou'd stay no longer, And [say] that they wou'd rather be knock'd in the Head by the Enemy, than stay to Perish behind the Breastworks." That same night the French completed a breaching battery of eighteen-pound guns within three hundred yards of the fort's west wall. With so much discouraging information in hand, Monro summoned a council of war from among his officers for the next morning. They unanimously advised him to send a flag of truce to Montcalm and negotiate a surrender on the best terms possible.[16]

By one o'clock on the afternoon of August 9 the articles of capitulation had been worked out. Montcalm offered terms identical to those allowed the British garrison on Minorca in 1756—an intentional compliment to Monro, acknowledging that he had conducted his defense according to the highest professional standards. In return for a pledge that they would remain noncombatants "on parole" for eighteen months, the entire garrison of Fort William Henry would be granted safe passage to Fort Edward under French escort, and—in recognition of their valor—would be permitted to retain their personal effects, small arms, unit colors, and a symbolic brass fieldpiece. All English and provincial soldiers too sick or badly wounded to make the trip to Fort Edward would be cared for by the French and repatriated when they had recovered. In return, Montcalm demanded only that all French military and civilian prisoners in Anglo-American custody be returned to Fort Carillon by November; that the cannon, ammunition, stores of war, and provisions within the fort would be surrendered to the French; and that one British officer would remain as hostage until the escort of troops accompanying the garrison to Fort Edward had safely returned.[17]

These terms, so honorable by European conventions of war and military professionalism, were not only alien to the cultures of Montcalm's Indian allies but had been negotiated entirely without consulting them, with notable disregard for what they regarded as their legitimate expectations. Only after the capitulation had been concluded, immediately before it was signed, had Montcalm summoned the war chiefs to explain the surrender terms. They could not harm the defeated soldiers, he said, nor take their personal effects or arms from them; while all food stocks, arms, and matériel left behind were to be respected as the property of His Most Christian Majesty. Although the chiefs listened politely to Montcalm's explanation, they could not have doubted that their warriors would never obey such outrageous prohibitions. The warriors had fought bravely and indeed more selflessly than the French, who served for wages; they had asked only for their rations, ammunition, and what few gifts Montcalm had bestowed. The only rewards that the Indians—whether Christian or heathen—had expected were plunder, trophies to prove their prowess in battle, and captives to adopt or sacrifice as replacements for dead warriors or perhaps hold for ransom. When it became clear that the man whom they had called "Father" intended to do what no real father would and deprive them of the reward they had earned, most of the warriors decided merely to take what they had come for, and then to leave. And that was exactly what they did.[18]

The episode that the colonists and the English would come to know as "the massacre of Fort William Henry" began on the afternoon of August 9, immediately after the last British detachment handed over the fort to the French and made its way to the entrenched camp, where the soldiers and civilians of the garrison were to remain until they would march for Fort Edward on the following day. As they left, Indians entered the fort in search of booty and, finding little, set upon the seventy or so sick and severely wounded men who had been left to be cared for by the French. The prompt intervention of French soldiers and missionaries saved at least some of them, but many lost their lives when the Indians made trophies of their scalps. Through the rest of the afternoon and well into the terrifying night that followed, Indians roamed the entrenched camp and plundered its inhabitants. When French guards finally cleared them out of the camp around nine o'clock they hung about its perimeter, menacing the Yankees with "more than usual malice in their looks which made us suspect they intended us mischief."[19]

Dawn brought all the mischief the Anglo-Americans had feared. As the regulars prepared to lead the column down the road to Fort Edward, hundreds of warriors armed with knives, tomahawks, and other weapons swarmed around them, demanding that they surrender arms, equipment, and clothing. Other Indians entered the entrenched camp, where the provincial troops and camp followers anxiously awaited the order to march, and began carrying off not only property but all the blacks, women, and children they could find among the camp followers. When at last the column began to move out, at around 5:00 a.m., the regulars in the lead marched alongside the column's French escort and thus were spared the worst of the violence that followed. The provincials at the rear of the column, however, lacked all protection and found themselves beset on every side. Within minutes, Indians had seized, killed, and scalped the wounded from the provincial companies and stripped others of clothes, money, and possessions. As noise and confusion mounted, discipline disintegrated. Terrified men and women huddled together, trying as best they could to defend themselves. Then, with a whoop that witnesses took to be a signal, dozens of warriors began to tomahawk the most exposed groups, at the rear of the column.

The killing lasted only a few minutes, but more lives would be lost in the panic that followed. Frye's regiment dissolved in chaos as men bolted screaming in every direction: some into the woods, others toward the French camp, others back to the fort, with Indians in hot pursuit. Since prisoners were more valuable than trophies, most of those whom the Indians caught were in less immediate danger than they thought. When Montcalm and other senior French officers ran up to stem the disorder, however, they first tried to intervene and free the captives, only to find that the result was often fatal: many warriors preferred to kill their captives and take trophies rather than be deprived of them altogether.

By the time order could be restored, as many as 185 soldiers and camp followers had been killed and a much larger number—between 300 and 500—had been taken captive. Another 300 to 500 provincials and regulars had found refuge with the French. The rest either fled down the road or escaped into the woods and eventually made their way toward Fort Edward. As for the Indians, virtually all of them left without delay once they had secured the prisoners, scalps, and plunder they had earned in battle. By sunset on August 10, only about 300 domesticated Abenakis and Nipissings remained with Montcalm's army. The other 1,300 warriors and their captives were already paddling north on the first leg of the long journey home.[20]

Also by sunset on August 10, substantial numbers of men had begun to reach Fort Edward, where they brought the first, exaggerated reports of the massacre to General Webb and a garrison that was now beginning to swell with the arrival of thousands of New England and New York militiamen. Refugees continued to straggle in from the woods—scared, starving, and sometimes stark naked—for more than a week. On August 15 the largest single group arrived, a contingent of perhaps five hundred survivors including Colonel Monro, dragging with them the brass six-pounder that was supposed to symbolize their honor in defeat. They had been brought under French escort to Half-way Brook and handed over to a British guard along with Montcalm's assurances that the rest of the garrison would be returned as soon as its members could be recovered from the Indians.

Indeed, Montcalm, his officers, and the missionary fathers who had accompanied the expedition's Indians had gone to great lengths to retrieve prisoners ever since the tenth, and Governor-General Vaudreuil was doing his best to intercept warriors returning to the *pays d'en haut* at Montréal in order to ransom their captives. Thanks to all these strenuous efforts at least two hundred prisoners were recovered by the end of August, at an average cost to the crown of 130 *livres* and thirty bottles of brandy each. Further redemptions followed, piecemeal, along with a few escapes. Including those who died before they could be recovered and as many as forty who were adopted into Indian families and refused to return, only about two hundred captives would fail to return to the British colonies by 1763.[21]

Both humanitarian and practical concerns made Montcalm and Vaudreuil eager to retrieve the prisoners. Montcalm desperately wanted to preserve the integrity of the capitulation proceedings, for as the officer who had guaranteed the safety of the surrendered garrison he would be personally dishonored by any violation of the surrender terms. Moreover, as he clearly understood, the British would be disinclined to behave generously toward any French garrison in the future, should they ever gain the upper hand; and he could ill afford to antagonize an enemy so potentially powerful by seeming to sanction uncivilized warfare. As for the governor-general, Vaudreuil hoped to minimize the damage to Franco-Indian relations by an episode that the Indians regarded as a betrayal of trust, and that Montcalm saw (with equal conviction) as evidence of an ineradicable savagery. Vaudreuil, convinced that Indian alliances were the key to the successful defense of Canada, understood that the appalling aftermath of victory at Fort William Henry threatened two possibilities, equally dire: that the Indians would not volunteer their services again, or if they did that Montcalm would decline to use them. Thus he did his best to appease both the commander in chief, by ransoming as many prisoners as possible, and the Indians, by offering the most generous terms he could afford. He also did his best to overlook such distasteful incidents as the ritual eating of a prisoner outside Montréal on August 15.[22]

In the end the violent sequel to Montcalm's victory would both defeat Vaudreuil's best efforts to salvage Indian relations and realize Montcalm's worst fears of British vengeance. Never again would Indian allies flock to the French colors as they had in 1757. The western Indians would discover too late that the English and provincials at William Henry had been suffering from smallpox, and thus that the captives, scalps, and clothing they brought back carried the seeds of a great epidemic, which would devastate their homelands. No warriors from the *pays d'en haut* would help Montcalm again, and even the converts from the St. Lawrence missions would become reluctant to take up the hatchet. In coming campaigns Montcalm would rely on regulars and Canadians to oppose the regulars and provincials of the British, fighting increasingly in the European mode that he preferred. But although the conflict would in this sense be Europeanized after 1757, British officers would never be inclined to offer the honors of war to any French force. At the same time, provincial outrage over "the massacre of Fort William Henry" would feed an already ferocious anti-Catholic tradition in New England and intensify an undiscriminating Anglo-American hatred of Indians.[23]

But while the fall of Fort William Henry thus marked a critical juncture in the war, its long-term significance remained latent in 1757. American colonists and British ministers alike saw it as one more humiliation, one more instance of military incapacity, in the long, dismal litany of defeat that the war had become. Yet two events that followed the capitulation, the full implications of which no one in British North America understood, foretold important dimensions of what was to come. The first was Montcalm's decision not to attack Fort Edward.

After Montcalm's victory, nothing seemingly prevented him from following the road that pointed toward the next logical objective; yet he opted instead to destroy Fort William Henry and return to Fort Carillon. Webb was greatly relieved without understanding why. Montcalm had in fact had no choice but to withdraw, for he was hobbled both by the loss of his Indian supporters—which was to say, his main source of intelligence—and by an acute shortage of provisions. New France had suffered a disastrous crop failure in 1756; Montcalm indeed had had to delay his departure from Fort Carillon until the necessary foodstuffs arrived from France. Unable to open his campaign before the very end of July, now he could not delay in releasing the Canadian militiamen who made up more than half of the non-Indian troops at the siege, for they urgently needed to return home to the harvest. Yet even dismissing them at the earliest possible moment did not prevent further disaster, for the harvest of 1757 would be one of the worst in Canadian history. Conditions were especially bad in the vicinity of Montréal, ordinarily "the granary of Canada" and also the home of many of the militiamen who served on the expedition. By late September the inhabitants of Montréal were each subsisting on a half-pound of bread a day, and those of Québec on half that. No one contemplating New France's military prospects could escape the conclusion that, without provisions from Europe, the colony would soon become indefensible.[24]

The second event that accompanied the fall of Fort William Henry was the equally significant, but equally unremarked, mobilization of thousands of militiamen from the New England provinces. In response to Webb's frantic summons for help, between August 7 and 10 Connecticut drafted five thousand men from its militia regiments—about one-quarter of all the militiamen in the colony—formed them into temporary companies, and marched them off to defend Fort Edward. Massachusetts's response was equally impressive. Upon receiving the first appeals for help, Governor Pownall ordered the four westernmost regiments of militia to march for New York and warned all twenty-six of the province's battalions "to hold themselves in readiness to march at a minutes warning." On August 8 he "ordered up all the Troops of Horse and a fourth part of the Militia of the province," and began assembling a train of artillery, as well as provision magazines, to support them. Between August 9 and 12 more than seven thousand Massachusetts militiamen left their homes and began to march for Fort Edward. Because of the distances to be covered, none actually arrived before Fort William Henry surrendered, but soon thereafter they came streaming in in numbers that overwhelmed Webb's ability to feed and control them. As soon as it had become clear that the French were not advancing on his post, Webb dismissed the militiamen at the fort and dispatched couriers to turn back those still on the road. Even so, by August 12 no fewer than 4,239 New England men were encamped outside the walls of Fort Edward.[25]

This response cost the northern provinces a vast sum of money, for militia privates on active service earned more than twice as much per day as provincial soldiers of the same rank. The total charges for maintaining the Connecticut militia in the field for the eighteen days of the alarm equaled one-third of the expense of all its operations in 1757. Yet notwithstanding the expense and the logistical difficulty of mobilizing large proportions of their male populations on short notice, the northern provinces had demonstrated a capacity to respond to a military emergency without parallel in the English-speaking world.[26]

Even though in the aftermath of this great mobilization colonial governments remained chiefly aware of its futility and expense, and even though regular officers tended to ignore or to dismiss it as having made no difference to the outcome of the campaign, the response of the New England provinces provided unmistakable evidence of the willingness of the colonists to fight. The alarm proved that no lack of popular motivation or military resources could account for the growing uncooperativeness of the New England assemblies. If only the means could be found to tap them, and some way discovered effectively to direct them, the energies and the manpower of the northern colonies alone could tip the strategic balance in North America. But how they could be tapped, and how they might be directed, remained problems that were still very far from being solved.

CHAPTER 20

Other Disasters, and a Ray of Hope

1757

IN THE REGION that Lord Loudoun had designated as the Southern Department of operations—the colonies from Pennsylvania to Georgia—the picture at the time of Fort William Henry's fall was hardly an encouraging one. Only in the lower south, a region still spared much military activity, did things seem to be progressing satisfactorily. The completion of Fort Loudoun in what would later become southeastern Tennessee established a strategic foothold for the Crown and the colony of South Carolina in the Overhill Cherokee country. French agents ranging northward from Fort Toulouse (a post at the forks of the Alabama River on the approximate site of modern Montgomery) and Shawnees operating to the south from the Ohio Valley had been in the area since 1754, seeking to forge an alliance with the Cherokees. Fort Loudoun and its supporting post of Fort Prince George, located about a hundred miles to the southeast amid the Cherokee Lower Towns, seemed ready to foster stable relations with the Cherokees by furnishing foci for trade and fortified bases for the operations of provincial and redcoat troops. North of the Carolinas, however, in the backwoods of the middle and southern colonies, relations with the Indians were anything but stable. There the war in 1757 proceeded very much as it had in the previous year, as raiders from Fort Duquesne lengthened to seeming endlessness the melancholy list of kidnappings, scalpings, and settlement-burnings.[1]

In the Chesapeake colonies, Maryland continued to spend as little as possible on defense. The backwoods settlements to the east of Fort Cumberland in the Conococheague Valley had all but emptied themselves of people in 1756 after the assembly announced that it would defend nothing to the west of Fort Frederick. Although Loudoun in his March conference with the governors had ordered Governor Horatio Sharpe to garrison Fort Cumberland with 150 men, the Maryland Assembly had flatly refused to support them so long as they remained there. They stayed in place but ultimately had to be provisioned by the regular army. Although Maryland did raise 500 men in 1757, relations were so strained between the upper house of the assembly, controlled by a faction friendly to the interests of the proprietary family, the Calverts, and the lower house, dominated by the antiproprietary (or popular) party, that these two halves of the legislature never agreed on a supply bill, and the soldiers were never paid.[2]

Virginia, with an increasingly disciplined regiment attempting to defend its frontier, seemed to offer a better example of coordination between colony and empire. On closer inspection, however, the situation could be seen to have improved only slightly, if at all, over the previous year. By early 1757 the Virginia provincial officers had grown so discouraged by the unwillingness of the House of Burgesses to supply and pay their regiment that Washington himself had approached Lord Loudoun at his Philadelphia conference and pleaded for the Virginia Regiment to be taken into the regular establishment. The Virginia officers, he maintained, "want nothing but Commissions from His Majesty to make us as regular a Corps as any upon the Continent." His men had "been regularly Regimented and trained, and have done as regular Duty for upwards of 3 Years as any regiment in His Majesty's Service," and, he concluded hopefully, "we are very certain, that no Body of regular Troops ever before Servd 3 Bloody Campaigns without attracting Royal Notice." Loudoun had not been impressed enough by the towering young colonel's arguments to agree to absorb his regiment into the regular army, but he evidently thought enough of its proficiency to leave the defense of the Virginia backcountry entirely in its hands. Instead of issuing Washington the regular commission he coveted, Loudoun decided to station a battalion of the Royal American (60th) Regiment in Pennsylvania for 1757 and to give its commander, Colonel John Stanwix, authority over Washington and the Virginia provincials. Since Stanwix's first communication to Washington was an order to deliver a hundred barrels of gunpowder, twelve thousand flints, and three tons of lead from his regimental stores to wagoners that Stanwix was sending down from Pennsylvania, Washington had reason to think that his new, closer connection to the regular army would only make a hard job worse.[3]

And indeed it did. Although Washington would eventually find his way to a cordial relationship with the competent, long-experienced Stanwix, nothing about the defense of Virginia's backcountry came easily in 1757. Plagued by desertions and distressed by the behindhand way in which the province sent him replacements, Washington found himself no more able than before to defend 350 miles of frontier against raiders from the Ohio Country. As if this were not difficult enough, Loudoun had detached two hundred of Washington's men and sent them to South Carolina under the regiment's second-in-command, Lieutenant Colonel Adam Stephen. There they helped to garrison Charleston—in effect, to deter slave insurrection—while regulars from the province's independent companies, the Royal Americans, and the Highland (63rd) Regiment defended the frontier against an invasion that never materialized. Left with as few as four hundred (and never more than seven hundred) men to hold Virginia's chain of eighteen forts, Washington abandoned all but seven, a move that enabled French and Indian raiding parties to enter the province virtually at will. Although Lieutenant Governor Dinwiddie made efforts to supplement Washington's forces with Catawba and Cherokee warriors imported from the Carolinas, Washington never found them to be more than burdensome: they consumed inordinate amounts of supplies, came and went as they pleased, and generally "behaved very insolently" when he tried to employ them as scouts.[4]

In October, beset not only by enemies he could not stave off but by his own quartermaster's embezzlement of supplies and desertion, Washington was near despair. "Another campaign, such as was the last," he wrote to Dinwiddie, "will depopulate the country." Purely defensive strategies had failed, and unless an expedition could be sent to destroy Fort Duquesne, "there will not . . . be one soul living on this side the Blue-Ridge [by] the ensuing autumn." He was not exaggerating. When Governor-General Vaudreuil reported to his superior, the minister of marine, on the raids conducted from Fort Duquesne in 1757, he could describe "nothing very important"—just twenty-seven scalps and twenty-seven prisoners taken since his previous account. It had not been for want of activity, but rather because there were so few English settlers left on the frontier; one group had been in the field for two months and taken only two scalps. Indeed, Vaudreuil wrote, "all our parties have carried terror among our enemies to a point that the settlements of the English in Pinsilvanie, Mariland, and Virginia are abandoned. All the settlers have retreated to the city or into the forest."[5]

Only in Pennsylvania did there seem to be any cause for hope in 1757, and the improvement in that quarter came not from military factors—

Stanwix's Royal Americans based at Carlisle and the provincial companies posted at forts along the frontier could do little to deter enemy raiders—but rather from the diplomatic negotiations between private intermediaries and the eastern Delaware leader, Teedyuscung, which had begun at Easton in 1756. These talks had continued, despite Sir William Johnson's insistence that only he was authorized to conduct diplomacy with the northern Indians, because of two compelling, complementary needs. On one hand, Governor Denny realized that, given the failure of provincials and redcoats alike to defend the frontier, diplomacy offered his best (and perhaps only) hope for ending the devastation of his province. On the other, the flight of traders from Shamokin and the Susquehanna generally had left Teedyuscung's people in desperate need of the manufactures—blankets, ironware, weapons, ammunition—that they needed to survive.

Pennsylvania's informal representatives were Quakers, now formally out of politics. They had begun by making individual efforts to negotiate an end to hostilities; then, in December 1756, several "weighty" Friends had founded an organization called the Friendly Association for Regaining and Preserving Peace with the Indians by Pacific Measures. This organization and the remarkable man who headed it, the merchant Israel Pemberton, had maintained contacts with Teedyuscung, raised large sums of money to support the negotiations, and purchased the diplomatic gifts necessary to keep the talks alive. Apart from the eastern Delawares' precarious situation, the goodwill and impartiality of Pemberton and the Friendly Association were probably the biggest factors inducing Teedyuscung to negotiate. The presence of the Quakers at the renewed Easton negotiations of July and August 1757, as the financial supporters and informal monitors of the proceedings, added an element of integrity uncommon in Pennsylvania's treaty-making after the passing of William Penn.[6]

And, it must be said, the presence of Pemberton and the Quakers also added an element of complexity unusual even in the ordinarily complicated setting of intercultural diplomacy. As we have seen, Teedyuscung's intentions in opening the talks at Easton in the previous year had included two goals: first, to nullify the Walking Purchase of 1737, by which Iroquois chiefs had connived with the representatives of the Penn family to deprive the Delawares of their lands in eastern Pennsylvania; second, to gain a perpetual grant of approximately 2,500,000 acres in the Wyoming Valley region as a territorial reserve within which the eastern Delawares could be forever safe from white encroachments. As a result, the Easton talks of 1757 had a distinctively multilateral character.

Governor Denny was there to represent the province of Pennsylvania and of course the interests of the Penn family. But William Denny was also his own man and shrewdly capable of seeming "in the morning [to be] for the proprietaries, at noon of no party, and at night, plump for the Assembly." At Easton, he was acting most of all as the direct subordinate of the earl of Loudoun and as a career officer in the British army. He aimed therefore at obtaining a strategic peace with the eastern Delawares. If in so doing it was necessary to expose and renounce a twenty-year-old land fraud, that was merely unfortunate for the proprietors. His oath was to the king, not the Penns, and the interest of the king in restoring peace with the Indians and gaining them as allies against the French far superseded any obligation he had to protect the pecuniary interests of the proprietors. Denny was not, however, the only delegate from Pennsylvania at the conference. Four commissioners representing the assembly attended, vigilant to protect their constituents' interests against the power of the proprietors; agents of the Penn family were there too, intending to preserve the Walking Purchase, thwart the massive cession of Wyoming lands to the Delawares, and make sure that Denny did not respond too eagerly to the advice of the assembly's commissioners. Observers from the Iroquois Confederacy were also on hand—chiefs who were as reluctant as the Penns to see the Walking Purchase renounced and by no means pleased to see Teedyuscung, who was supposed to be taking orders from them, negotiating his own people's settlement with the government of Pennsylvania. To complicate matters further, George Croghan was at Easton as the deputy of Sir William Johnson, charged with preserving Johnson's status as the sole Crown authority authorized to negotiate with the northern Indians; yet Croghan was also on the lookout—as always—for opportunities to promote his own interests as a private trader and land speculator. And of course, Pemberton and his colleagues from the Friendly Association were also in attendance, acting as ostensibly neutral observers but—insofar as they advised the Indians and kept an independent record of the proceedings—as de facto allies of Teedyuscung and the Delawares. Yet even the Quakers' presence was complicated, and perhaps compromised, by the fact that Pemberton had been cultivating close relations with Colonel Stanwix, who supported a peace settlement in order to gain eastern Delaware allies for a campaign into the Ohio Valley, not to realize the Quakers' hope of bringing a prompt, diplomatic end to the bloodshed.[7]

Ultimately these complex affiliations among the participants and observers at Easton resolved themselves into the pragmatic alignment of interests that determined the conference's outcome. Denny, the commissioners from the assembly, the Quakers, and Teedyuscung all wanted peace and had no objection to having the Walking Purchase reviewed by higher authorities in order to determine its legitimacy. The agents of the Penns, the representatives of the Iroquois, and George Croghan sought to defend the Walking Purchase but were willing to have it examined—*if* the higher authority who would examine it was Sir William Johnson. Denny and Croghan wanted peace to be accompanied by an alliance between the eastern Delawares and the British; Croghan and the Iroquois wanted the alliance to be understood as coming under the Confederacy's sanction. Teedyuscung was willing to defer the grant of land to his people in return for immediate aid in the form of a permanent settlement, to be built at Pennsylvania's expense in the Wyoming Valley—with houses, a trading post, and teachers to instruct his people in reading and writing. In return for this, he was prepared to offer a military alliance between his people and the British, under the formal aegis of the Iroquois. The commissioners from the Pennsylvania Assembly were willing (once the representatives of the Friendly Association had assured them of financial support) to subsidize the construction of Teedyuscung's Wyoming town in return for an alliance.[8]

Thus between July 21 and August 8 at Easton, the representatives of several cultural communities and a vast range of competing interests were able to negotiate something that even six weeks earlier would have seemed impossible: the beginnings of a peace. It was far from a comprehensive settlement, of course, and given its indeterminate character, it was at best a fragile one. Understood in strategic terms, the Treaty of Easton merely neutralized the eastern Delawares as a first step toward opening contacts with the western Delawares—a group still allied with the French. Nothing could dislodge the French from the Ohio Country, and nothing could make the raids along the frontier cease, unless the alliance between the French and the Delawares, as well as the other Ohio Indians, could be broken. In August 1757—as French and Indian raiders continued to pillage backcountry settlements from New York to North Carolina, and as Fort William Henry's broken masonry and shattered timbers littered the headland above Lake George—any well-informed observer of the war would surely have found the likelihood remote that the Easton conference would prove a pivotal moment. Least of all would it have seemed a likely turning point to the best-informed observer of them all, the earl of Loudoun, who even then was sitting in Halifax watching his prospects for capturing Louisbourg fade into the blank face of a Nova Scotia fog.

CHAPTER 21

Pitt Changes Course

DECEMBER 1757

LOUDOUN AND HIS transports arrived at Halifax on June 30. Admiral Francis Holburne's Royal Navy squadron dropped anchor there on July 9. By that time no fewer than three French squadrons, including eighteen heavily armed ships of the line and five frigates, had made it safely into Louisbourg harbor—a force that clearly overmatched Holburne's. Loudoun had been unable to launch his expedition until Holburne had arrived, and Holburne would only proceed once he had determined the strength of the enemy fleet at Louisbourg; but weeks of fog and foul weather kept his reconnaissance vessels from returning with a report. When the fog lifted and the wind finally turned fair on August 4, the first reliable intelligence came in with the arrival of the frigate *Gosport*, which had taken a French prize carrying a complete list of the ships at Louisbourg.[1]

Loudoun now asked Holburne the critical question. Could they "attempt the reduction of Louisbourg with any probability of success?" "Considering the strength of the enemy and other circumstances," the admiral replied, "it is my opinion that there is no probability of succeeding in any attempt upon Louisbourg at this advanced season of the year." On the same day that Monro watched Montcalm's men open their siege entrenchments outside Fort William Henry, Loudoun ordered preparations to begin for the return to New York.[2]

It was a prudent decision; indeed, in view of the recent firing-squad execution of Admiral Byng for failing to do his utmost against the enemy, even a courageous one. To hazard almost the entire regular army in North America by landing it on Cape Breton—late in the year, in uncertain weather, under threat of a superior naval force—would have daunted any but a foolhardy officer, and rashness was never one of Loudoun's shortcomings. Admiral Holburne's later experience, moreover, proved that he had decided wisely. After escorting Loudoun's transports back to New York, Holburne returned to the Gulf of St. Lawrence where, reinforced by four new ships from home, he waited to waylay the enemy fleet when it emerged from Louisbourg. Instead of ambushing the French, however, Holburne found his squadron trapped against the shore of Cape Breton by a hurricane that blew in suddenly from the southeast on September 24. The fleet was within an hour or two of being dashed to pieces on the rocks when the wind finally came round the following day and began to blow from the southwest; but even so, six ships of the line were dismasted and one was completely destroyed. Only three vessels could be sailed back to England. The rest, stricken and unseaworthy, limped to Halifax for repairs. The French, having ridden out the storm in the shelter of Louisbourg harbor, sailed for Brest in October.[3]

By then Lord Loudoun was back in New York, trying with customary energy and application to restart a stalled war effort in the midst of newly heightened colonial discontents. His first concern was to regain the military initiative from the French, who had conducted the only successful offensive operations in America since 1755. Loudoun fell to the task immediately and on October 17 was able to inform the duke of Cumberland of his plans for a winter campaign against Ticonderoga. As he explained, there had been no time to rebuild Fort William Henry after his return, and to do that and build a fleet of boats would take most of the coming summer. He therefore intended only to wait for the first sustained frost before marching four thousand regulars and rangers from Fort Edward to Lake George, and then over the ice with light cannon and mortars to attack Fort Carillon's small winter garrison.[4]

This plan, inspired by Rigaud's attempt on Fort William Henry, might actually have succeeded if the frost had not come late (in February) and with so much snow (three feet) that the expedition could not proceed. In the meantime Loudoun had more than enough to keep him busy. He had to correspond with the governments of the northern colonies, ordering them to recruit rangers for the winter campaign (they were unenthusiastic); with the new governor of Massachusetts, Thomas Pownall, who had lately fallen out with him over the issue of quartering and who seemed bent on outdoing even William Shirley as a subverter of Loudoun's authority; and with Governor Sharpe of Maryland, who had failed to discipline his assembly after its outrageous defiance of Loudoun's orders to garrison Fort Cumberland. Moreover, problems with enlistment for the regular regiments required his constant attention, for colonists in every province from Maryland to New Hampshire were not only refusing to volunteer, but actually harassing recruiters. The military humiliations of Oswego and Fort William Henry may have focused popular resentment on the redcoats, or perhaps the forceful and abusive techniques of the recruiters themselves did the trick. At any rate, resistance appeared everywhere and antirecruitment riots erupted in Delaware, Connecticut, Massachusetts, and New Hampshire in the fall and early winter of 1757. (Indeed the violence grew so severe in New Hampshire, where a mob waving axes chased one officer and his party for four miles, that Loudoun put a permanent stop to recruiting in the province.)[5]

On top of all this came the necessity of planning four new expeditions for the coming year, a grinding process that required hundreds of hours of information gathering, analysis, writing—virtually all of which Loudoun performed himself—and wrangling with the provincials. As the winter of 1758 wore on, Loudoun found it increasingly difficult to gain the acquiescence of the governors and assemblies of the various colonies. In February commissioners representing the New England colonial assemblies met at Boston, in Loudoun's absence and without his permission, to determine the numbers of men they would supply for the coming year. He was compelled in response to summon all the New England governors to a meeting at Hartford and lay down the law: their assemblies would provide men according to quotas he would dictate, not numbers to be determined by the legislators' whim. To his amazement, the governors proved recalcitrant and in the end cooperated only on a minimal level.[6]

For all his energy, Loudoun now found his job more and more frustrating, more and more taxing. "My Sittuation," he wrote to his kinsman the duke of Argyll, in February,

> is that, I am more a Slave to Business than any man alive by having not only the affairs of the Army as a Soldier to manage and that being divided in three or four places and each to provide for without one man to assist me but M[ajor] G[eneral] Abercromby or to consult with but him and he very often at a Distance from me in the time when I want his Advice most.
>
> Besides which I have an Eternal Negotiation to carry on with Governments 1500 miles in length where every Day Produces not only New Plans, which effect the carrying on the Service but likewise meet with all sorts of opposition in it. So that my Business Begines every Day the moment I am out of Bed and lasts from that time to Dinner and from then till nine at night and this from day to

> day without Intermission or even allowing myself an hower for any Amusements and this for want of propper Assistance under me.

In only one respect were these complaints exaggerated, for the tireless Scot did in fact manage to take an occasional hour for amusement: his personal accounts showed that during the Christmas week just past he and his guests had somehow found the time to consume "nineteen dozen bottles of claret, thirty-one dozen of Madeira, a dozen of Burgundy, four bottles of port and eight of Rhenish."[7]

What Loudoun did not know, as he drank health to the king and confusion to the French, would have encouraged him to drink even deeper than he did. Ten days before Christmas, William Pitt had decided to relieve Loudoun of his duties and indeed to change the policies by which he had done his best to fight the war. The content of Pitt's new measures and the extent to which they departed from what had come before would remain unclear for months to come, since official notice of them would arrive in the colonies only in March. Pitt had in fact been contemplating a new approach to the war for more than a year. Only since the fall of 1757, however, when news of calamities in North America had come raining down on Whitehall along with accounts of even worse developments in Europe, had his position strengthened enough to put them into effect.[8]

Pitt could change course in the last days of 1757 because recent events had altered the balance of power within the British government, strengthening his position by destroying the influence of his adversary, the duke of Cumberland. The critical development in what was by any measure the worst string of disasters in the war was Cumberland's capitulation on September 8 to the French, who had trapped him and the Hanoverian army he commanded between the Rivers Aller and Elbe. Nearly encircled and with no prospect of reaching the sea where the British navy would resupply him, Cumberland had tried to make the best of a hopeless position by negotiating a surrender on terms that saved his army. The French commander—Louis-François-Armand de Plessis, duc de Richelieu, victor of Minorca—agreed to hold a parley at the village of Kloster-Zeven.

Richelieu named only two conditions: Cumberland must send home the troops in his army that came from Hesse, Brunswick, and Gotha; and he must withdraw half of his Hanoverian battalions beyond the Elbe, leaving the remainder in internment camps near the port of Stade. These seemed to Cumberland honorable—his troops did not even have to surrender their arms—but back in Britain the Convention of Kloster-Zeven seemed only to heap diplomatic humiliation upon military defeat. The

French were left to occupy all of Hanover except for a neutralized zone along the Elbe. Richelieu would be free to turn his attention to his real target, Prussia, where England's only significant ally, Frederick the Great, was in the direst of straits, facing a Russian invasion in East Prussia, a Swedish invasion in Pomerania, and an Austrian invasion of Silesia that threatened to break through to Brandenburg, and thus Berlin itself.[9]

In England the old king wept for shame. George had empowered his son to treat with the French and even if necessary to make a separate peace for Hanover; but this was "a convention shameful and pernicious." To Newcastle he complained that "his honour and interest were sacrificed by it, that he had been by it given up, tied hand and foot, to the French. That he did not know how to look anybody in the face: that he had lost his honour and was absolutely undone." He ordered his son back to England immediately. When Cumberland returned in October to defend his behavior, the king treated him with a cruelty notable even by the generous standards of the Hanoverian kings. "Here," he remarked to his guests on the night that Cumberland reappeared at court, "is my son, who has ruined me and disgraced himself"; then he refused to speak to him at all. That same night the duke sent word that he intended to resign all his military offices. The king accepted his offer with no expression of regret on October 15.[10]

Cumberland's resignation, the previous relegation of Henry Fox to the profitable oblivion of the paymaster generalship of the forces, and the king's willingness in the aftermath of Kloster-Zeven to listen to Pitt's advice with a new respect left Pitt better able than ever before to shape and implement policy. Cumberland's disgrace deprived his supporters of influence to such an extent that all responsibility for financing and supplying the war effort now fell into the hands of the duke of Newcastle, while control of the navy, army, and diplomatic corps fell more or less exclusively to Pitt. Without real restraint from any quarter in Parliament or at court, Pitt could direct the war in accordance with his "system," as he would come to call the pragmatic, fluid mixture of strategies that he was now free to apply. Although it marked a less radical departure than he was apt to claim in later years, Pitt's system would finally reverse the balance that had hung so heavily against Britain.[11]

The heart of Pitt's system was his intention to hold the line against France where it was strongest, in Europe, while striking at its weakest point, North America. To do so, Pitt planned to take advantage of Britain's greatest strength, its navy, to achieve naval superiority on the Atlantic and thus to prevent France from resupplying its troops overseas; this would in turn enable Britain's relatively small army to cooperate with its much more numerous American colonists to overwhelm Canada's defenders. Pitt's ultimate goal, the elimination of France as an imperial presence in North America, was by far the most original and distinctive aspect of his plan, for no one before him had conceived of any Anglo-French war as an opportunity to strike at the sources of French wealth. Indeed, Pitt intended to attack French colonies not only in North America, but anywhere—in the West Indies, West Africa, India—that opportunities to profit from French weaknesses might present themselves.

To be free to concentrate British force on France's empire, Pitt had to insure that the British army would not be drawn into the fighting on the Continent, where French and Austrian armies inevitably had the advantage. To sustain his resolve not to send "a drop of our blood . . . to be lost in that sea of gore" which was Germany, Pitt's system required that Britain subsidize its German allies—most of all Prussia—virtually without limit, so as to keep France preoccupied while British forces conquered its empire. There was, of course, nothing new in British subsidies to European allies. What made Pitt's approach unusual was the scale on which he proposed to subsidize, for he would soon ask Parliament to approve payments to Frederick and other German princes that vastly outstripped any Britain had ever made.[12]

Pitt also proposed, as he had argued was necessary since 1755, to defend the home isles not with the army, but rather to rely upon a reformed militia or territorial force based in the counties. This measure conformed nicely to the preferences of many backbench M.P.s, country squires who disliked the standing army both because it was expensive and because it could be used to exert direct control over their localities. Their support for a militia defense, then, was critical to sustaining Pitt's program in the Commons. The militia was crucial for another reason, too: it would free up army units stationed in England to cooperate with the home fleet in making "descents," or raids, on the French coast. If the French wished to protect their Atlantic ports, he reasoned, they would have to divert troops from their operations against Germany. Pitt had gotten this idea from Frederick, who as early as 1756 had pointed out that "if France strips her Channel coasts to form her army [for Germany], the English fleet can profit by it and . . . spread an alarm the whole length of Brittany and Normandy." The descents would employ only a few thousand men and sailors, Pitt thought, and by lessening French pressure on the Prussians might indefinitely forestall the need to send troops to Frederick's support.[13]

Pitt's approach to the war in the colonies essentially inverted every policy Braddock and Loudoun had pursued. Because everything in his plans depended upon the conquest of New France, Pitt needed to tap America's strengths as never before, and particularly its manpower. He knew that Halifax had long before advocated raising large numbers of provincials to use against Canada, only to have the idea discarded by Cumberland, who preferred to use regular troops. Moreover, he had talked to experts on the colonies—notably Sir Charles Hardy, governor of New York, whose opinion of Loudoun had taken a turn for the worse after the Louisbourg expedition, and Thomas Pownall, who never hesitated to serve his own interest at the expense of former patrons—and from these had concluded that Loudoun's efforts to unify the colonies had served only to antagonize the colonists and frustrate the war effort.[14]

By mid-December 1757, Pitt knew that if the American assemblies were to be transformed from centers of resistance into sources of men and money, he would have to reverse entirely the course of colonial policy. Instead of treating the colonies like subordinate jurisdictions and requiring them to finance the war effort by forced contributions to a common fund, Pitt resolved to treat them like allies, offering subsidies to encourage their assemblies to aid in the conquest of New France. Rather than continuing to demand that civil authority, in the persons of the colonial governors and legislatures, submit to military power in the person of His Majesty's commander in chief, Pitt resolved to withhold from Loudoun's successor direct authority over the provinces. In the future, as always in the past, the governors would receive their instructions directly from the secretary of state for the Southern Department. By this new grant (or more properly, restoration) of autonomy to the provinces, by offering inducements to cooperation rather than by seeking to compel union among them, Pitt hoped to create a patriotic enthusiasm that had not been much in evidence since 1756.[15]

Finally, because not only provinces but provincials would need to demonstrate this enthusiasm, Pitt also decided to reverse the policy that had made all provincial field officers rank only as eldest captains while on joint service with regular units. In the campaigns of 1758, he decreed, provincial majors, colonels, and generals would enjoy a status equivalent to their counterpart ranks in the regular army, ranking as juniors only to the regular officers of comparable grades.

In order to implement these policies, Pitt needed supporters not only in the Commons and at court, but in the armed forces, and these he also found in the fall and winter of 1757. He had already nominated George, Lord Anson, to the post of first lord of the Admiralty. This was a politic choice in that Anson was an important ally of Newcastle; but it was also a prudent one, for Anson was a capable administrator who fully supported

Pitt's navalist approach to the war. As a replacement for Cumberland at the head of the army, Pitt secured the appointment of another Newcastle supporter, General Sir John Ligonier—at an astonishingly vigorous seventy-seven not only an immensely experienced officer, but probably the ablest general to wear a red coat between Marlborough's time and Wellington's. Together Anson and Ligonier would serve as chiefs of staff to Pitt and, in an unprecedented example of cooperation between army and navy, implement the strategic system by which Pitt proposed to win the greatest victory in English history.[16]

WHEN WILLIAM PITT gained control of strategy and policy late in 1757, the war entered a new phase. Thereafter the army and navy would conduct descents on the French coast—a series of militarily indecisive operations that would indeed diminish the proportion of its army that France could commit to Germany. At Pitt's urging, the king would renounce (probably illegally, on a technicality) the Convention of Kloster-Zeven. Thereafter George II, acting as elector of Hanover, would appoint one of Frederick's most capable military protégés, Prince Ferdinand of Brunswick-Wolfenbüttel, as commander of the Hanoverian army; and Parliament, at Pitt's insistence, would take the Hanoverian army into British pay as a continental proxy for British troops. Great Britain would begin to pour vast quantities of subsidy money into Hanover's and Prussia's treasuries. Despite predictions to the contrary, Parliament would meekly submit to every request for funds—in part because Newcastle controlled patronage distribution and could ensure support for the ministry's money bills in the Commons, and in part because the financiers in the City of London were usually delighted to float the loans that Newcastle required. The members of the ministry would begin to work together well, largely because Pitt's energy and willingness to accept responsibility for the war earned him Newcastle's admiring support. Although relations between the two were never free of strain, their complementary activities would impart a momentum to the war effort that it had never before seen.[17]

On the Continent, the fortunes of war would favor Frederick once more. At the Battle of Rossbach, on November 5, Frederick overwhelmed a French army under the prince de Soubise, inflicting casualties at the unheard-of rate of ten to one. Rossbach literally turned the tide against France, which now evacuated Saxony. With barely a pause, Frederick marched his army nearly two hundred miles westward into Silesia, where he engaged the forces of Count von Daun at Leuthen on December 5.

This battle, the tactical masterpiece of Frederick's career, left one-third of Daun's army dead, wounded, or captured, and forced the Austrians to withdraw from Silesia. Meanwhile, in Hanover, Prince Ferdinand had given Richelieu formal notice of the renunciation of Kloster-Zeven and moved his army into the field. Before the end of the year the French withdrew to the Aller River and dug in at the town of Celle, abandoning half the territory they had conquered during the summer.[18]

Thus stood politics in Britain, and the war in Europe, at the end of 1757 when William Pitt informed North America's colonial governors of the new course he intended to pursue in North America. He had had Ligonier canvass the army for the most capable young field officers available, to be sent to America in the spring; he had approved elaborate plans for the coming year's campaigns. Everything would now depend upon the war in America. Surely Pitt realized more acutely than anyone else that his whole system rested upon the supposition that British arms could succeed there, where British arms had as yet achieved nothing. But would new measures and new men mobilize the latent strength of the colonies and redeem the losses of Braddock, Shirley, and Loudoun? To the man who in an unguarded moment had said that he knew that only he could save his country, no question could be more important; no answer awaited with more dreadful anticipation.

PART IV

TURNING POINT

1758

Pitt's new direction breaks a deadlock between the colonial governments and Lord Loudoun. New commanders and approaches revitalize the British war effort. Crises in Canada and changes in French strategy. Montcalm defeats the British yet again at Ticonderoga, but this time they reply with victories at Louisbourg and Fort Frontenac. Indian diplomacy and the success of the Forbes expedition against Fort Duquesne. The war as a formative experience.

CHAPTER 22

Deadlock, and a New Beginning

JANUARY–MAY 1758

TO THE MASSACHUSETTS provincial soldiers huddled against the cold in huts near Stillwater, New York, the year 1758 dawned bleakly, and not only because they remembered the previous summer's defeats. The eighty men of Captain Ebenezer Learned's company had come to think of their enemies not so much as the Indians and French as cold weather, short rations, and their own British superiors. Learned's provincials—farmers, laborers, and artisans from central and western Massachusetts—had enlisted in the spring of 1757 to serve for a campaign that they understood would last only until November 30. Because their notions of military obligation were no less contractual than those of New Englanders generally, it had come as "a greate & unexpected disappointment" to learn, as their tour of duty was about to end, that Lord Loudoun had ordered them to remain in service until Candlemas (February 2, 1758).[1]

Loudoun had extended the enlistments of Learned's and three other Massachusetts companies because he needed men to garrison the blockhouses and forts north of Albany. The fall of Fort William Henry had laid the region open to enemy raids, and in September he had asked the assemblies of New York, New Jersey, and the New England colonies to recruit rangers to defend it over the winter. Nobody questioned the need—had anyone done so, the French and Indian destruction of German Flats in early November, a raid that resulted in the deaths of 50 settlers and the seizure of 150 more, would have made it undeniable—and despite their lack of enthusiasm for the additional expenditure, most of the assemblies acceded to Loudoun's demand. But Massachusetts, unlike the other colonies, garrisoned a chain of forts and blockhouses along its own frontier, and its general court refused to raise the men Loudoun asked because the province was already carrying more than its share of the burden. With the German Flats incident on his mind, Lord Loudoun found this even more exasperating than the usual colonial obstinacy and so dealt with it directly. On November 18, as the provincials were disbanding, he detained 360 Massachusetts soldiers, advanced them two months' pay from his own funds, and ordered them to remain in service—or suffer the consequences.[2]

Captain Learned's men had acquiesced but among themselves agreed not to serve beyond the time for which they had been paid. Learned had returned to Massachusetts on sick leave, and when he returned in early January his men told him that they planned to march for home on February 3. Rather than upbraiding them for their lack of loyalty or warning them of the consequences of desertion, Learned offered to represent their case to Captain Philip Skene, the regular who commanded at Stillwater. If Skene refused to make some reasonable accommodation, Learned said, he would lead the "retreat" himself. In the meantime his men continued to save food out of their rations to provision the journey home and improved their leisure hours by making snowshoes. According to a nineteen-year-old private in the company, Rufus Putnam, when Candlemas ("the day . . . that we wished for") arrived,

> we were all ordered into the Fort whe[re] Capt. Skean read a part of a letter to us, that Major General Abercrombie sent to him, the contents of which was this. You are hereby required to persuade the Massachusetts [men] that are under your care to tarry a few days longer, till I shall hear from their government, to know what the government intends to do with them. To these orders, there was answer made by some of our Company, that they looked upon him to be a good soldier, that tarried till his time was out; and that the Province had no business to detain us any longer; neither would we be detained any longer by any power that they could raise. He told us that if any man had been duly enlisted into His Majesty's service and should leave the same, without a Regular Discharge, he should Suffer Death. We told him we did not value that, for according to our Enlistment, neither they not the Province could hold us any longer, and that we did not break the Court Act by going off.[3]

At three o'clock the next morning, leaving behind only a second lieutenant to care for ten men who were too sick to walk, Ebenezer Learned's company—with its captain and first lieutenant in the lead—marched for home. Seven days later, half-starved, frostbitten, and minus their mascot ("a large dog" they had eaten two days earlier) they staggered into Hawks's Fort in Charlemont, Massachusetts. The garrison received them "very Kindly," offering the deserters food and a place to rest before sending them on their way. No one at the fort seems to have thought that Learned's men had done anything wrong. Indeed, the hospitality they offered gives us every reason to believe that the provincials at Charlemont admired the deserters' willingness to brave the winter woods rather than remain at Stillwater without enlistment contracts to protect them from enslavement.[4]

"He is a good Soldier that Serves his time out" was a maxim as transparently true to the soldiers of the Bay Colony as it was unmeaning and pernicious to Captain Philip Skene and his fellow regular officers in America, adherents of a military system based on the gospel of subordination and discipline, men with neither time nor sympathy for contractualist sophistry. That whole companies of soldiers, together with their officers, would defy the king's officers in the name of a supposed principle, was a fact significant in ways Lord Loudoun never quite grasped. Soon, however, he would discover that soldiers who defied his authority to preserve what they called their rights were the least of his problems.[5]

THE SMALL SAGA of Ebenezer Learned's company bears retelling because it illuminates the larger pattern of resistance to imperial authority that was emerging in New England at the beginning of 1758. Even as Learned's men floundered through the snowdrifts of the Green Mountains, politicians in the Massachusetts Assembly were gathering their resolve to challenge Lord Loudoun on issues that went to the very heart of his power as commander in chief. Already they had refused to recruit rangers for winter duty in New York. Now they were actually attempting to revive the form of intercolonial military union that had prevailed in previous wars, a system in which each assembly had appointed military commissioners to meet with the commissioners of the other colonies to determine by negotiation the level of support their respective provinces would provide for each campaign.

Lord Loudoun looked on this development with horror. If the assemblies could decide for themselves what they would contribute to the common cause, even if the numbers of men and pounds sterling exactly matched what he would have asked of them anyway, the legislators would in effect nullify his authority as the representative of the king in Parliament. Loudoun knew that if he surrendered to such pretensions as these, he would be allowing the colonists to determine the nature of the empire itself, and that would be a loss to the Crown far more grave than any military defeat. Thus as the year 1758 opened, the question was not whether but when the confrontation would come between a man unsuited by temperament to compromise and a colonial assembly unwilling to go on complying with demands that took no account of local conditions and laws.

Before the loss of Fort William Henry and the abandonment of the Louisbourg expedition it would have been unthinkable that the New England assemblies would mount a direct challenge, but on December 24 the Massachusetts House of Representatives invited its counterparts in Rhode Island, Connecticut, and New Hampshire to appoint commissioners to meet and "concert measures for our mutual defence in this time of war and great danger." Such defiance, of course, infuriated Lord Loudoun, but what stoked his wrath to white heat was the knowledge that the Massachusetts legislators had dared to act so flagrantly because the province's new governor had encouraged them to do it. And that official was none other than his own former secretary and protégé, Thomas Pownall.[6]

Loudoun's policies and attitudes had always reflected both his professional soldier's understanding that his authority flowed from the royal prerogative and a royal commission that made his authority over the colonial governors virtually indistinguishable from his authority over his colonels. He knew well enough that governors needed the cooperation of their legislatures to carry out his commands, but he either failed to understand the difficulties they faced when their assemblies proved recalcitrant or he simply refused to regard such problems as anything more than evidence of the governors' timidity. All of Loudoun's experience in America had led him to believe that the only effective way to gain the cooperation of colonists, whether assemblymen or ordinary civilians, was to threaten them with force whenever they did not promptly submit to his demands. But Pownall, who had taken up his office only in August, immediately after Fort William Henry's fall, was in no position to command. Whatever Lord Loudoun expected of him, Pownall knew that he could do nothing unless a majority of the representatives in the General Court decided to cooperate; and he set out to gain their support by adopting the techniques that successful governors had always used.[7]

One of the quickest ways for a new governor to acquire support in any colonial assembly was to align himself with his predecessor's enemies, a tactic that suggested itself to Pownall with particular force since he had been instrumental in orchestrating the downfall of William Shirley. In the Massachusetts legislature, however, it was not only Shirley's former opponents who had appropriated the republican stance of a country party: virtually every legislator who took exception to Loudoun and his policies had simultaneously taken up the banner of rights, liberty, and property. Pownall's early adoption of country rhetoric—in his initial speech he promised to protect civil liberty and promote civic virtue and appreciatively acknowledged the province's heavy contributions to the war effort—clearly appealed to these politicians. Yet Pownall did not spout republican principles merely to gain popularity, for he sincerely believed that the colonists had constitutional rights equivalent to those of Englishmen at home, that colonial civil governments should be no more subject to military authority than English counties, and that the best way to gain the colonists' cooperation in the war effort was to invite, not compel, it. In November he showed that he was as good as his principles by siding with the General Court in a dispute with Loudoun over quartering in Boston: a move that gained him credit with the legislators at the cost of creating a permanent breach with the commander in chief.[8]

Pownall understood that, important as it was to show his sympathy for popular principles, his long-term success depended on building a patronage network through which he could exert effective leverage in the assembly. This practical goal, as much his conviction that "there is a Spirit in the People of New England on which to build such a Scheme," underlay the plans he placed before the General Court during the winter of 1757–58. Pownall proposed measures to reform Massachusetts's militia, to launch an all-provincial expedition to secure the Penobscot region at the mouth of the Bay of Fundy and attack the French settlements along the St. John River, and—most significantly—to mobilize the latent strength of the New England colonies by reviving the independent military union of the previous wars.[9]

What made each of these proposals distinctive, apart from their almost uncanny resemblance to William Shirley's programs, was that each would have given the governor exclusive control of military commissions and supply contracts, and hence the currency of patronage with which to reward political allies. All that Loudoun could see in Pownall's measures was an ambitious man's attempt to undermine the legitimate authority of the commander in chief, betraying not only a former patron but the king's own trust. In fact, what Pownall wanted most was to govern his province effectively, and the only way he could do that was by making common cause with the legislators who opposed Lord Loudoun's viceregal claims and detested his imperious behavior. Pownall's political needs would catalyze an explosive reaction between the determination of the commander in chief to protect his authority and the intention of a majority of the Bay Colony's assemblymen to protect their constituents' rights and reassert control over Massachusetts's manpower and money.

It was therefore with Pownall's blessing that the House of Representatives invited the other New England legislatures to send commissioners to Boston to discuss the common defense independently of Lord Loudoun. The restraint those commissioners showed when they actually met, in February, owed much to the caution of Massachusetts's leading delegate, Thomas Hutchinson, whose reservations about Pownall reinforced his disinclination to defy the commander in chief. Pownall regretted that the commissioners proved willing only to discuss general issues, and not only because they had failed to allocate the military resources of the colonies on their own authority. He knew that their tentativeness had weakened his position against Loudoun, who was bound to be displeased when he heard of the commissioners' meeting.

Displeasure, however, hardly described his lordship's response. Loudoun was apoplectic and still virtually incoherent with anger when he informed Pitt on February 14 that this attempt to override his authority

> Appears to me to be an Affair of great Consequence, which if not prevented, is likely to create disputes and Animosities among the Provinces, and will probably prevent, in a great Measure, the Harmony that ought to be cultivated amongst them at this time, and deprive the Public, in a great Measure, of that Aid they have a right to expect from them at this time; And as to their Applying the combined Force, I take that to be entirely in the King, who sends his Orders on that Subject, to whomever he thinks proper to appoint to the Command of his Troops, to whom what Men the Provinces Raise are intended as an Aid, and not at all under the Command of the Governor, after they are raised, as to the Services they are to be Employed in.
>
> In order, as far as I can, to prevent the bad consequences I apprehend from this Measure, I have Invited [*read:* summoned] the Governors of the four New England Colonies; New York and the Jerseys, to meet me at Hartford . . . on the 20th of this Month, in order to prevent, if I can, any Measure being taken by a part, that may affect the whole, or . . . to, at least So[l]der up matters so, that we may be able to go on with the Publick Service: I shall lose the less time by this, as the Boston Assembly has been adjourned to the 2d of March, before I was informed of it.[10]

Loudoun had decided to exert his authority directly over the governors at Hartford, and on February 23 and 24 he did just that. Explaining his plans for the coming year—a new expedition against Louisbourg, an advance against Fort Carillon on Lake Champlain, a bateau-borne attempt to seize Fort Frontenac at the mouth of Lake Ontario, and an overland expedition against Fort Duquesne—he informed them that he would require the services of precisely 6,992 provincial soldiers. The governors of Rhode Island and New Hampshire were to see to it that their assemblies voted to raise 608 men each; New Jersey was to procure 912; New York would provide 1,216; Connecticut, 1,520; and Massachusetts, 2,128. Pownall, as Loudoun had anticipated, objected to the quotas: the Massachusetts House would no longer be dictated to, he said, and would resist or perhaps balk altogether. Loudoun replied that if Pownall could not explain their duty to the members of the Massachusetts Assembly, he would. Then, trailing a worried Pownall, he left for Boston, where the General Court was about to resume its session.[11]

Lord Loudoun knew that he had supporters, including Thomas Hutchinson, in the Massachusetts legislature, but after a few days in Boston he must have wondered if he had overestimated their influence. For more than a week the House of Representatives debated his proposals for the coming campaign, refusing to take action until the commander in chief had responded to their queries. "The matter labour'd greatly," Pownall reported to Pitt, while "the House seemed to advance in nothing but Difficulties and Objections, Diffidence in the Plan, Objections against the Number [of provincials to be raised] as a Quota." Meanwhile, "dissatisfaction against a Junction [of the provincials] with the Regulars as the Matter of Rank . . . stood," built yet another barrier to agreement. On the morning of March 10 the issue remained deadlocked, with the House stubbornly refusing to vote the men Loudoun demanded and Loudoun steadfast in his insistence that the legislators had no right to refuse demands he placed on them in the name and by the authority of their king. For the first time it seemed possible that Massachusetts, heretofore the chief contributor of men and money among the North American colonies, would vote no more troops and no further financial support for the war.[12]

But on the morning of the tenth, a courier delivered a pair of letters to Pownall that changed everything. "*Sir,*" William Pitt had written in the first, "The King having judged proper, that the Earl of Loudoun should return to England; And His Majesty having been pleased to appoint Major General Abercromby to succeed his Lordship, . . . I am commanded to signify to you His Majesty's Pleasure, that you do apply to, and correspond with, Major General Abercromby, on all Matters relating to the King's Service. . . ."[13] Pownall surely smiled at that. If so, he must have beamed with delight when he turned to the second letter and read:

> His Majesty having nothing more at Heart than to repair the Losses and Disappointments, of the last inactive, and unhappy Campaign; . . . And His Majesty not judging it expedient to limit the zeal and Ardor of any of His Provinces, by making a Repartition of the Force to be raised by Each respectively, for this most important Service; I am commanded to signify the King's Pleasure, that you do forthwith use your utmost Endeavours, and Influence with the Council and Assembly of your Province, to induce them to raise, with all possible Dispatch, as large a Body of Men within your Government, as the Number of Its Inhabitants may allow; and, forming the same into Regiments, . . . That you do direct them to hold Themselves in Readiness, . . . to make an Irruption into Canada. . . .[14]

But what followed must have seemed the answer to Pownall's prayers.

> All Officers of the Provincial Forces, as high as Colonels inclusive, are to have Rank, according to their several respective Commissions, in like Manner, as is already Given, by His Majesty's Regulations, to the Captains of Provincial Troops in America.
>
> The King is further pleased to furnish all the Men, so raised as above, with Arms, Ammunition, and Tents, as well as to order Provisions to be issued to the same, . . . in the same Proportion and Manner as is done to the rest of the King's Forces. . . .
>
> The Whole, therefore, that His Majesty expects and requires from the several Provinces, is, the Levying, Cloathing, and Pay of the Men; And, on these Heads also, that no Encouragement may be wanting to this great and salutary Attempt, The King is farther most Graciously pleased to permit me to acquaint You, that strong Recommendations will be made to Parliament in their Session next Year, to grant a proper Compensation for such Expences as above, according to the active Vigour and strenuous Efforts of the respective Provinces shall justly appear to merit.[15]

Pownall sent a messenger to inform the assembly that he had important information to lay before it and to request the members' attendance at a special session.

That evening the governor laid Pitt's letters before the assembly and told them he did not doubt Massachusetts would do its duty. Only the briefest of debates followed. The next morning the same legislators who had refused to raise 2,128 men voted unanimously to raise 7,000 and gave Thomas Pownall a formal cheer. Lord Loudoun's reaction, although nowhere recorded, can easily be imagined. He rode immediately for New York, turned his official papers over to Abercromby, and at the first opportunity sailed home.[16]

Enthusiasm like that of the Bay Colony's legislators blossomed throughout the colonies as their assemblies learned of Pitt's new policies. Connecticut voted to raise 5,000 men, Rhode Island 1,000, and New Hampshire 800. New York increased its levy to 2,680 and Pennsylvania to 2,700; even Delaware voted to raise 300 provincials for the coming campaign. Virginia doubled its military establishment, calling up militiamen to garrison the frontier forts and offering two regiments for expeditionary service against Fort Duquesne. All in all, within a month of receiving word of Pitt's offers of aid and support, the continental colonies resolved to put more than 23,000 provincials under arms, in addition to the thousands more who were to be employed as bateaumen, wagoners, artificers, privateers, and sailors. Of all the North American provinces, only Maryland, locked in an internal dispute that pitted its lower house against the upper, failed to increase its level of involvement in the war effort.[17]

This stunning reversal cannot be explained merely by the colonials' dislike of Loudoun, although their glee at the news of his removal cannot be denied. Rather the abandonment of the policies that Loudoun had represented made the greatest difference, and for reasons that Pitt himself could have understood only in part. The colonists embraced his new plans with such ardor because they seemed likely to solve the problems that the old approach had created. But even among the Americans, few could have appreciated how strongly Pitt's policies resonated with the circumstances of colonial life.

Loudoun's desire to recruit thousands of colonists into regular regiments and to fill a large common fund with contributions from the colonial assemblies had been at odds with American social and economic conditions. Colonial societies—particularly in New England, where most of the support was to come from—simply did not harbor enough poor white men to satisfy the manpower appetite of a regular army at war. Most of the service-age males that the northern colonies could supply, moreover, were unwilling to submit themselves to long enlistments and rigorous discipline in the regular army. Unlike recruits from the lower strata of British society, most potential soldiers in the northern colonies were not permanently poor men, marginalized to such a degree that enlistment offered an attractive alternative to indentured servitude, emigration, or destitution. Rather they were for the most part merely ordinary young men who had not yet become independent of their fathers or masters, but who expected one day to own farms or shops and to head households of their own. Instinctively or consciously, such men understood what Loudoun never did: that the colonies had few workers with respect to their supply of available land, and for that reason (and not the crass opportunism that Loudoun blamed) soldiers' wages had to be as high as the wages civilian workers could command.[18]

Nor had Loudoun appreciated how starved for cash the colonial economies were, and therefore how unable they were to generate the revenues necessary to make the war in America self-funding. Accustomed to the sight of rural impoverishment in England and Scotland, he looked at New England's evidently prosperous countryside and believed that the representatives these yeomen elected to their assemblies were reluctant to tax their constituents because they lacked the patriotic spirit of self-sacrifice. He did not realize—or at least did not see as clearly as the colonies' legislators did—that so little money circulated in the countryside and so much indebtedness prevailed among farmers that heavy taxation could reduce even substantial yeomen to penury.

In such a setting, the exquisite sensitivity of legislators to the interests of the localities they represented was no more than fidelity to the trust that their constituents had reposed in them. To an aristocrat like Loudoun, such behavior seemed merely to indicate a self-interested willingness to sacrifice the good of the whole to the parochial needs of whatever town or county claimed the assemblymen's first allegiance. Lord Loudoun enjoyed the confidence of the king, counted the king's son a friend, understood the complexities of British politics, knew the ways of the world, had a French mistress; how could such a man fail to condescend to the rustics of North America? And how could they fail to resent his condescension?

To a truly remarkable degree, Pitt's new policies took advantage of the strengths of the colonists and compensated for their deficiencies, tolerated their parochialism and capitalized on their hatred of Loudoun. The colonies had men who were willing to serve, not as long-service, highly disciplined regulars but as short-term provincials; Pitt would take as many of these as the colonies could raise. If the provincials were expensive, untrained, and hard to discipline, they could still build roads, garrison forts, haul supplies, and thereby free effective soldiers—redcoats who had the discipline and training that seemed all but impossible to instill in Americans—to win battles. If the colonial economies were short on capital, credit, and cash, Pitt would make up for these with subsidies and reimbursements offered in the same proportion to their efforts as the subsidies that sustained the exertions of Hanover and Prussia.

And so it would run, through the whole range of problems that had so far hobbled the war effort in North America. Were colonial majors and colonels touchy about their rank and status, offended at being reduced to the status of senior captains when they served jointly with the regulars? Pitt would make them junior only to redcoats who held the same rank as they, so that no provincial field officer needed to suffer the humiliation of taking orders from an English officer of lesser rank. Were the assemblies protective of some supposed right to initiate taxation? Then let them consent to requisitions, if they preferred to hear the Crown's needs communicated in that form. Did the colonial assemblymen fear the imposition of military control over their governments? Pitt's instructions made Loudoun's successor a mere military commander with no claims to control over the civil administration of the colonies, because Pitt intended to exercise the full authority over the governors that belonged to him as secretary of state for the Southern Department. Were colonial governors hobbled in their ability to manage politics in the provincial assemblies by lack of patronage? Pitt's new approach promised supply contracts by the score and military commissions by the hundred, and all of them could be distributed in return for political support.

In all of these measures Pitt did not hesitate to overthrow the reforms of Halifax and his colleagues at the Board of Trade, who had worked so diligently before the war to impose some measure of administrative control on America. Pitt could do what he did with so little apparent concern for their efforts because he cared nothing for administration or reform or the depressing history of colonial intrusions on the prerogative. He only wanted to win the war, and no centralizing reform measure would help him do that. Pitt's action in reversing the thrust of a decade-long policy toward the colonies can only be properly understood if we see him as a man to whom caution was no longer a constraint, a gambler either so desperate or so sure of his luck that he could stake everything on the next roll of the dice.

The effects of the new policies were immediately evident in the response of the assemblies, but it was another three months before it became clear that the enthusiasm of the legislators could be translated into enough enlistments to fill the newly created provincial regiments. In New England, it was perhaps unsurprising that recruitment proceeded vigorously, and it cannot have failed to gratify Pitt to learn that by late April, Massachusetts had enlisted nearly five thousand volunteers and was willing to draft another two thousand from its militia if the remainder did not volunteer in time to begin the summer's campaign. But the colony that offered the most striking evidence of the new policies' effect was Virginia, where enthusiasm for provincial service had never been high. From 1754 through 1757, the Old Dominion had paid its soldiers poorly and attracted few volunteers. Although the Burgesses had tried to make up the chronic deficit in enlistments by authorizing the impressment of men who had "no visible Way of getting an honest Livelihood," it also allowed draftees to escape service by paying a ten-pound fine, without even requiring them to hire substitutes to serve in their stead. As a result, the ranks of the Virginia Regiment were rarely more than half-full, and Washington had never succeeded in inducing many veterans to reenlist. With the news that Parliament stood willing to reimburse its expenses, however, the Burgesses resolved to raise a second regiment and—"thinking by that means to compleat with greater dispatch and better men"—to offer a ten-pound bounty to every volunteer.[19]

Recruitment went so well that before the end of May the 1st Virginia Regiment had enrolled 950 of the 1,000 men it had been authorized and the 2nd Regiment had enlisted 900. Every one of them was a volunteer. Even Sir John St. Clair, the crusty regular quartermaster who had lost no opportunity to denigrate the Virginia provincials since Braddock's defeat, admitted that they seemed "a fine body of men." Even more surprising than the caliber of the men and their enthusiasm for enlistment, however, was the social quality of their officers. Washington had been one of the few planters of stature willing to lead the provincials before 1758, and he was both young and descended from a family of the second rank. Like many of his company commanders, Washington's second-in-command, Lieutenant Colonel Adam Stephen, was a Scot and therefore, in the reckoning of Virginia's Anglophile gentry, barely a gentleman. But the policy change that gave provincial field officers rank equivalent to that of their counterparts in the regular army had swept away the biggest deterrent to service by members of the colony's first families. In 1758 the man who volunteered to head the new 2nd Virginia Regiment was no less than William Byrd III, a member of the Governor's Council and the master of Westover, the Chesapeake's archetypal estate. Byrd's second-in-command, Lieutenant Colonel George Mercer, came from a family by no means inferior to the Washingtons; his company commanders were on balance much more socially acceptable than those of the 1st Regiment.[20]

Thus Loudoun had thought the colonists poor raw material, had bent every effort to improving them, and had failed—not through want of effort, but because the raw material had been unwilling to improve. Pitt took the same men and conditions that had thwarted the imperious laird and adapted his policies to suit them, asking not for perfection or submission but only for help, making clear his willingness to take it on the colonists' own terms. Not surprisingly, the new generals Pitt appointed to command in America would experience frustrations so like Loudoun's that their complaints about unsoldierly provincials and self-interested assemblies would look as if they plagiarized his letter books. But the complaints and the disdain of Loudoun's successors would not vex Anglo-American relations after 1758 because Pitt had deprived them of the authority to act on their opinions. Pitt himself would direct policies and, insofar as possible, plan campaigns. The result would prove to be a series of victories unparalleled in British history. Pitt's policies would gain him not just the colonists' help but their adulation. Never before had the energies of so many colonists been engaged on behalf of the empire as they would be in the three remarkable years that began in 1758; never before had their affection for Great Britain been so heartfelt, or their passion for the empire burned with so bright a flame.

CHAPTER 23

Old Strategies, New Men, and a Shift in the Balance

EARLY 1758

PITT'S PLANS for 1758 were not in fact much different from Loudoun's. In a sense they could not be, for the geography of eastern North America gave only a few options to anyone contemplating "an Irruption into Canada" or the removal of the French forts from the Ohio Country. There were only two promising invasion routes into New France. One was up the St. Lawrence, which meant first taking or neutralizing Louisbourg. The other was along the Lake Champlain corridor, which meant fighting one's way past Fort Carillon, Fort St. Frédéric, and the forts that guarded the Richelieu River. The third approach, up the Mohawk Valley to Lake Ontario and then down the St. Lawrence to Montréal, remained impracticable so long as the French maintained naval command of Lake Ontario and continued to occupy the forts that dominated either end: Frontenac at its outlet and Niagara at its head. Fort Frontenac held the key to communication between Québec and the interior of the continent. To destroy it would be to render insecure all the posts that lay farther west—Niagara, Detroit, Michilimackinac, and the Ohio Country forts—and to deprive the French of their trade with the *pays d'en haut.* Because Fort Duquesne's strategic importance depended upon its ability to serve as a base for Indian raids, it needed a steady supply of arms, ammunition, and other trade goods. Duquesne would become vulnerable if Fort Frontenac were destroyed, and the drying up of trade would doubtless diminish the local Indians' affection for the French; yet because much of its food came from the Illinois Country, the garrison itself could potentially survive even in the absence of support from Canada. The only way to be sure of establishing control over the Ohio Country and its Indians was therefore to destroy Fort Duquesne, and that meant building a road across the Alleghenies—either from the upper Potomac, as Braddock had tried to do, or across Pennsylvania.

As he had informed the governors at Hartford, Loudoun intended to attempt campaigns on all these fronts in 1758. By the time he was recalled, Loudoun had planned and begun preparations for a campaign by twelve regiments against Fort Carillon; for a bateau-borne provincial expedition under Lieutenant Colonel John Bradstreet against Fort Frontenac; for an overland march through Pennsylvania by two battalions under Colonel John Stanwix; and for an amphibious attack on Louisbourg by the six regiments that had wintered in Nova Scotia together with provincials to be sent from New England. Pitt, too, envisioned expeditions against Fort Carillon, Fort Duquesne, and Louisbourg, and later approved of Bradstreet's expedition against Fort Frontenac; his plans differed, however, in the allocation of forces, for he intended to send many more regulars to America than were already in place and (as we have seen) to augment them with enormous numbers of provincials. But the most significant difference between Pitt's and Loudoun's plans lay in the men who would command the expeditions.[1]

Although Pitt had named Loudoun's fat, fussy, indolent subordinate, Major General James Abercromby, commander in chief for North America, he had authorized Lord Ligonier to nominate four new men to take charge of the expeditions of 1758. These were in every way surprising choices, for they had nothing to do with seniority in the service and very little to do with experience in command. To lead the all-important Louisbourg expedition Ligonier had promoted Jeffery Amherst, a forty-year-old colonel who had never commanded anything larger than a regiment, to the temporary rank of "Major General in America." As acting brigadier under Amherst, Ligonier suggested an even younger man, a lieutenant colonel known mostly for emotional volatility and readiness to criticize his superiors, James Wolfe. Ligonier and Pitt decided to entrust the campaign against Fort Duquesne to Acting Brigadier John Forbes, previously a colonel under Lord Loudoun: a fifty-year-old Scot, originally educated as a physician, who had distinguished himself as an officer of great experience and capacity but who was now so tormented by an inflammatory disease of the skin that he could at times barely move. To aid Abercromby in leading the expedition against Fort Carillon, they agreed upon the promotion to the rank of acting brigadier of George Augustus, Viscount Howe. At age thirty-three, Howe was one of the most promising field officers in the British army and had already gained

Jeffery Amherst (1717–97). Shown here in a postwar engraving based on Joshua Reynolds's portrait-in-armor as the victor of Montréal, Amherst seems very much a formal and aloof figure. He was; even in 1758, as the newly appointed commander of the Louisbourg expedition, he inspired respect, but not affection, in his subordinates. His most important brigadier, James Wolfe, found him maddeningly uncommunicative and "slow." *Courtesy of the William L. Clements Library at the University of Michigan.*

experience with American conditions by commanding the 55th Regiment in New York.[2]

Except for Abercromby, all of these officers held only temporary ranks because all of them had been promoted ahead of more senior and experienced colleagues. In part that was because Pitt preferred to appoint as his commanders men without independent standing who would ultimately need to rely on him personally; but principally it was because he valued talent. What Amherst, Wolfe, Forbes, and Howe had in common was

James Wolfe (1727–59). In every sense Amherst's temperamental opposite, Wolfe was bold to the point of rashness, and only good luck (and a timely death) can account for his reputation for tactical brilliance. This watercolor by George Townshend, a subordinate who came to detest him, ironically shows him in a more appealing light than any other contemporary portrait; his sharp nose and weak chin almost inevitably invited caricature. *Courtesy of the McCord Museum of Canadian History, Montreal / Musée McCord d'histoire canadienne, Montréal.*

either a strong reputation for competence or past service under Lord Ligonier in which they had convinced the old campaigner of their capacity. Significantly, since they were being entrusted with commands in a setting where everything depended on maintaining adequate supply services, three of the four (Amherst, Wolfe, and Forbes) had previously demonstrated superior skill as quartermasters or commissaries. Indeed, in view of their uniform lack of experience in command above the battalion level, their administrative aptitude may have been uppermost in Ligonier's mind when he commended them to Pitt.

These officers were to head the largest forces that had ever operated in North America. The command Amherst was to lead against Louisbourg consisted of 14 regular battalions, 5 companies of American rangers, a company of carpenters, and a train of siege artillery: nearly 14,000 men in all. Abercromby was given 9 regiments of regulars and the provincial troops of the colonies north of Pennsylvania—about 25,000 men—to hold New York, attack Ticonderoga, and "irrupt" into Canada. Forbes was to lead 2,000 regulars and about 5,000 Pennsylvania, Delaware, Maryland, Virginia, and North Carolina provincials against Fort Duquesne. Even without including sailors, marines, and the enormous miscellany of artificers, bateaumen, wagoners, sutlers, and other camp followers who supported the armies, the campaigns of 1758 would go forward with nearly 50,000 Anglo-American troops under arms: a number equivalent to two-thirds of the whole population of Canada.[3]

Against these evidently overwhelming forces New France could muster 6,800 regular troops, about 2,700 *troupes de la marine,* and the Canadian militia, which included all able-bodied habitant males between fifteen and sixty years of age and numbered perhaps 16,000 men. At most the marquis de Montcalm would be able to field half as many men as the British could throw against him; but his problems in defending Canada only began with the imbalance in manpower. The Indian auxiliaries that had formerly been more than adequate to offset the British advantage in numbers were nowhere to be seen in the spring of 1758. In large part this was because a smallpox epidemic had ravaged the villages of the *pays d'en haut* following the previous campaign, convincing many nations that the French had sent bad medicine among them. The Ottawas were said to be entertaining "evil designs" and the Potawatomis seemed "indisposed" to offer any aid; in Wisconsin the Menominees had grown so far alienated that they actually attacked a French fort and killed a trader's family.[4]

Of even more pressing concern than the absence of the Indians was the extreme shortage of food supplies. The harvest failed in 1757 for the second year in a row. In normal times Canadian wheat had commanded four to five *livres* per *minot;* by January of 1758, a *minot* cost fifteen *livres*—supposing one could find a person willing to sell. In order to stretch out the scarce grain resources of Canada, peas had been mixed with flour in the making of bread since 1756. By the winter of 1757–58 even that expedient no longer sufficed, and the ration of bread and of other staples had to be reduced for civilians and soldiers alike. In December 1757, the colony government cut the beef ration, which was supposed to be a pound a day but had long stood at half that, to a pound and a half a week. In place of beef the butchers supplied horse meat and, when available, codfish. At first the women of Montréal had pelted Governor-General Vaudreuil's door with their substitute rations, but the protests subsided when it became clear that Canadians could eat horse meat or no meat at all. As the winter wore on, food supplies dwindled to the vanishing point. By early April, Québec's daily bread ration was down to two ounces. A month later, with unstable weather holding up the spring planting, the weekly meat ration had dropped to a half-pound of beef or horse, a half-pound of salt pork, and four ounces of salt cod. Only the arrival of a convoy of ships from France on May 22 averted actual starvation in Québec, where "some of the inhabitants [had been] reduced to living on grass," but the necessity of diverting food supplies to the campaigns meant that the suffering of the civilian population did not cease. By the beginning of June, the daily bread ration had yet to rise above four ounces a day.[5]

The famine winter of 1757–58 can be blamed only in part on the failed harvests of 1756 and 1757. In normal times Canada produced enough grain to sustain its own population with enough left over to feed an additional twelve thousand people. During any average war year rations had to be found for at least fifteen thousand regulars, *troupes de la marine,* Indian warriors, and militia on permanent assignment, which meant that even bumper crops would have had to be supplemented with shipments of food from France. By the fall of 1757, however, the British navy had established effective blockades at Gibraltar, along the Channel coast, and in the Gulf of St. Lawrence. Thus to arrive safely in Canada, any French merchantman had to run a gauntlet of Royal Navy vessels twice as well as avoid Anglo-American privateers on the high seas. The only reliable blockade-runners were French warships sailing *en flûte,* or stripped of most of their cannon: a configuration in which they could outsail virtually any ship in the British navy. But most flutes carried official dispatches and reinforcements; their typical cargoes of powder, shot, and Indian trade goods contributed little food to the colony's meager supply.[6]

Moreover, a pervasive corruption exacerbated the problems that overwhelming demand, poor harvests, and blockades had created. King George's War and the current conflict had so distorted Canadian economic life that the leading sector of trade was no longer in fish, furs, and skins, but rather in military supplies and provisions. Contracting was the responsibility of the colony's chief civil administrator, or intendant; and François Bigot, the man who occupied that post from 1744 through 1760, had no compunctions about using his position to create a monopoly for himself and his partners, a group called *la grande société.* Bigot's business correspondent in Bordeaux would ship cargoes of provisions and luxury goods, at government expense, to Bigot, who in turn remitted government bills of exchange to pay the correspondent. In peacetime Bigot's partners sold these cargoes on the open market and divided the profits with the intendant. In time of war, Bigot could sell the cargoes to the Crown (which is to say, to himself, as the officer responsible for provisioning the king's forces in Canada) at a tremendous markup. Meanwhile

Bigot's agents bought Canadian grain at prices fixed by law at from five to seven *livres* per *minot;* milled it, at government expense, into flour; and sold the flour to the Crown—that is, to Bigot—at the market price, which eventually reached twenty-six *livres.* When famine ensued, it was Bigot, who as intendant was responsible for civil welfare, who sold rations of publicly owned flour to the populace at a government-subsidized price. What this system lacked in ethical purity it more than made up for in profits. By the winter of 1757–58 Bigot had grown so rich that he was able to sustain gambling losses in excess of 200,000 *livres* without visibly suffering in his style of life.[7]

Bigot never failed to keep the army supplied but he did it at a staggering expense to Crown and colony. Together with the skyrocketing costs of provisions, military expenditures sent the domestic economy of New France into an inflationary spiral that was entirely out of control by the beginning of 1758. At the end of King George's War, the French treasury was annually spending 2,000,000 *livres* on Canada; by 1755, 6,000,000; and by the end of 1757, 12,000,000. Imperial administrators tried to stem the tide of Canadian paper money they believed was fueling this grotesque inflation by sending specie to pay the regulars and buy their provisions, but the appearance of gold and silver merely accelerated the rate of depreciation. Merchants speculating in grain sold only to the army, which could pay in gold, and refused to sell to fellow Canadians trying to pay in depreciated paper. This intensified food shortages and drove up prices on the open market; farmers began refusing to sell their produce for any price, hiding it from Bigot's agents; and Gresham's law operated inexorably to drive gold and silver out of circulation. When Bigot tried to salvage the situation by making it a crime to refuse payment in paper money, he only succeeded in aggravating the problem. The tons of coin shipped to New France simply vanished, melted down into plate by the bourgeois and buried by the peasants in hoards that would not be dug up again until peace had returned to their ravaged, hungry land.[8]

None of this made the army easier to provision, and all of it helped convince Montcalm and his officers that they had been sent to defend a people so abandoned to self-interest that they were barely worth saving. Relations between Montcalm and the governor-general, never cordial, deteriorated. By the beginning of the campaign season in 1758 they were barely on speaking terms, communicating in letters that breathed an icy mutual contempt. Montcalm believed that Vaudreuil, technically his superior, was so committed to a strategy of using Indian allies and guerrilla warfare to defend Canada that he would do anything to undermine Montcalm's more "civilized" strategies, which was mostly true; that Vaudreuil expected him to fail and intended to make him the scapegoat for the loss of New France when it occurred, which was not altogether untrue; and that Vaudreuil was in league with Bigot, which was false. Vaudreuil believed that Montcalm disdained him as a member of the Canadian aristocracy, which was true; that Montcalm did not appreciate the value of the Indians as allies, which was also true; and that Montcalm was militarily incompetent, which was not. Each complained copiously about the other in official dispatches. Eventually Montcalm felt it necessary to send two personal emissaries back to France—ostensibly to plead for more support, but in reality to make his case against Vaudreuil and Bigot. Vaudreuil rushed his own representative to Paris, in order to arrive ahead of Montcalm's men.

The wrangling between Vaudreuil and Montcalm arose from an antagonism between Canadian provincials and representatives of the imperial metropole quite similar to the tension that produced such bitter disputes in the British colonies during Lord Loudoun's regime. In the case of New France, however, there was no Pitt to decide the issue by recalling one of the contending parties. Despite all their mutual complaint and maneuvering, Louis XV decided to leave both in place, honoring Montcalm with promotion to lieutenant general, placating Vaudreuil with the Grand Cross of the Order of Saint-Louis, and urging the governor-general to consult closely with the commander in chief on all matters civil and military. Thus the weakness at the center that was already evident at the beginning of 1758 would only grow worse, while the shortages of men and supplies that so desperately straitened the defenders of New France would remain unrelieved.[9]

What neither Vaudreuil nor Montcalm realized was that the king and his ministers regarded their disputes as trivial because they were quietly writing North America out of France's grand strategy. In the late winter and spring of 1758, the attention of Versailles and the military resources of France were both coming to center on the army in Hanover, the defense of the Channel coast against British raids, and the potential of mounting an invasion of England. No flood of foodstuffs, no tide of troops, would relieve the shortages that crippled New France. Insofar as warships would be employed in American waters in numbers large enough to be decisive, they would defend the valuable sugar islands of Guadeloupe and Martinique, not succor the hungry, unprofitable colony against which the English were about to fling such overwhelming force.

CHAPTER 24

Montcalm Raises a Cross

THE BATTLE OF TICONDEROGA

JULY 1758

FROM 1758 ONWARD, the French would fight to maintain their influence in continental Europe while the British would fight to conquer an empire, a difference in goals that would eventually prove decisive. Canada would only continue to grow weaker, more impossible to defend against the Anglo-American onslaught. Yet when the British opened the campaigns of 1758 not much seemed to have changed, for the first blow to be struck in Pitt's monumental American offensive produced only the familiar result of defeat. With the possible exception of Braddock's defeat, Montcalm's encounter with General Abercromby at Fort Carillon on July 8 would result in Britain's greatest humiliation of the war.

By the last week of June, Abercromby had established his headquarters beside the wreck of Fort William Henry, where he would preside over the assembly of the most formidable army yet seen in America. Over twelve thousand regulars and provincials were already on hand along with the eight hundred bateaux and ninety whaleboats they would need to transport them to a promontory called Ticonderoga, where Fort Carillon stood waiting. Among the privates in the camp was Rufus Putnam, who had no more than recovered from the ordeal of his winter's desertion before reenlisting in the Massachusetts regiment of Timothy Ruggles. "Every thing here seems to carry the face of war on it," he observed on June 28: "Ammunitions, Provisions and Artillery &c loading continually into the bateaux in order for Ticonderoga." The loading took a week to complete, and while it was in progress another four thousand provincials arrived in camp, bringing more supplies and bateaux with them. At dawn on July 5 the expeditionary force, now sixteen thousand strong, boarded its boats and rowed north. Arrayed in four columns, the thousand small craft "covered the Lake from side to side," in lines that "extended from Front to Rear full seven Miles." By the next daybreak they were within sight of the French advance guard, a camp at the foot of Lake George just four miles from Fort Carillon. The French troops fled, abandoning "a considerable [amount] of valuable Baggage, which our men plundered," wrote Rufus Putnam. Lord Howe, who had charge of the advance element, quickly rallied a party to pursue the retreating enemy. Before anyone quite knew what had happened he was dead, killed by a French musket ball in a confused skirmish in the woods.[1]

Lord Howe had been Pitt's choice as the expedition's second-in-command because he had all the vigor, youth, and dash that Abercromby lacked. Now "his death struck a great damp on the army," for the soldiers had little faith in a commander in chief they commonly called "Granny." Indeed, Howe's death struck a considerable damp on Granny himself: "I felt it most heavily," he reported, without exaggeration, to Pitt. Although the skirmish had taken place in the morning, Abercromby allowed his units to blunder aimlessly about in the forest for the rest of the day before ordering them back to the landing place to re-form. That night his soldiers lay on their arms less than two hours' march from the fort, but the next day he marched them no more than halfway there, pausing at a French sawmill site two miles from Ticonderoga to establish an entrenched camp as a base for further operations. Although Abercromby ordered his men to make ready for an attack, neither he nor any of his senior officers had yet reconnoitered the fort and its defenses. "I can't but observe since Lord How's Death Business seams a little Stagnant," a provincial surgeon named Caleb Rea observed in his diary that night, wondering, like the rest of the army, what would happen next. Only on the following morning, July 8, did Abercromby send forward an engineer to examine the French position; by then two full days had passed since the landings.[2]

Abercromby's delay gave Montcalm the gift of time, and he employed it well to prepare for the assault he knew could overwhelm Carillon's defenses. He had arrived on June 30 to find the fort manned by "eight battalions of French regulars very weak . . . , forty men of La Marine, thirty-six Canadians ready to go to war, and fourteen Indians." Their depleted food stock consisted of "provisions only for nine days, and for an emergency, 3600 rations of biscuits." Over the next few days more men and rations arrived, but too few of each to make Carillon able to withstand a siege. On the morning of July 8 Montcalm had only 3,526 men, including just 15 Indian auxiliaries, to defend the post and less than a week's supply of food. "Our situation is critical," wrote Montcalm's chief aide, Bougainville. "Action and audacity are our sole resources." On the evening of the sixth, as Abercromby and his men remained inert at their landing place, Montcalm had ordered fieldworks to be laid out across the Ticonderoga promontory on high ground, about three-quarters of a mile north of the fort. Throughout the next day "the army was all busy working on the abatis outlined the previous evening." "The officers, ax in hand, set the example" for their men, who "worked with such ardor that the line was in a defendable state the same evening."[3]

The "abatis" that the French built was a defensive barrier, so called both because it was made of felled trees, *arbes abattus,* and because it was intended to become the attackers' abattoir. Above shallow entrenchments rose a log breastwork topped with sandbags, to shelter the defenders from enemy fire. Extending perhaps a hundred yards down a slope in front of it lay a tangle of felled trees with branches sharpened and interlaced to ensnare advancing infantrymen and make them easy targets for grapeshot and musket fire. Like a modern concertina-wire entanglement, the abatis made a highly effective barrier against frontal attack. Formidable as it was against infantry, however, it could not protect the fort from artillery fire.

Artillery was always the key to siege warfare, and there—in his train of sixteen cannon, eleven mortars, and thirteen howitzers, supplied with eight thousand rounds of ammunition—lay Abercromby's greatest advantage. Because of the shortage of men and time, Montcalm had not secured Rattlesnake Hill (later renamed Mount Defiance), which rose about seven hundred feet above the lake, a little over a mile to the southwest of Carillon. If Abercromby chose to have a road cut up the side of the hill, and then to have two or three twelve-pounders hauled to its summit, Montcalm would be forced to withdraw—at least from the breastwork, the open rear of which would have been exposed to cannon fire, and perhaps from the fort itself. Even if he chose not to make use of the hill, Abercromby could still advance his howitzers to the edge of the clearing and smash the breastwork to splinters before launching an assault on the French lines. Montcalm's decision to stake the defense of Ticonderoga on these hasty fortifications therefore represented a gamble of the most extreme sort.[4]

As it happened, the engineer whom Abercromby dispatched to survey the French lines on the morning of July 8 was a very junior lieutenant, and he made only a hasty inspection before returning to advise his chief that the works could be carried by storm.[5] Abercromby did not bother to take a look himself, or to trouble Major William Eyre—the vastly experienced engineer who was acting commander of the 44th Regiment—for a second opinion. Nor did he evidently consult his new second-in-command, Colonel Thomas Gage, a physically brave if undynamic officer; or if he did, Gage did not manage to dissuade him from doing what indecisive eighteenth-century generals often did, convening his senior officers as a council of war to choose the method of attack. Traditionally in such councils, the commander set the limits of discussion by asking his assembled commanders to choose from a range of alternatives; depending on his temperament and eagerness to diffuse responsibility for the decision's outcome, he might or might not regard himself as bound by their majority vote. In this case, Abercromby only asked his assembled subordinates whether they preferred to have the infantry attack the French lines in three ranks or four. The majority favored three. Abercromby thanked them for their counsel, then dismissed them to prepare for the assault. He did not order his field artillery forward from the landing place, where it remained. Infantry alone would bear the burden of battle.

Immediately thereafter British skirmishers—Gage's light infantry regiment (the 80th Foot), Major Robert Rogers's ranger companies, and a battalion of Massachusetts light infantry—moved up to the edge of the abatis, driving in the French pickets and taking up sniping positions. This vanguard of light infantry and rangers, men trained to aim and fire individually and practiced in fighting from cover, testified to the tactical adaptations that had taken place in the British service since Braddock's defeat. But the plan of attack suggested that for Abercromby not much had changed after all. He intended to use his most thoroughly disciplined troops in the most thoroughly conventional way: by arraying them in three long, parallel lines and sending them straight up against the French barricade. They were, his orders said, "to march up briskly, rush upon the Enemy's fire, and not to give theirs, untill they were within the Enemie's Breastwork." By noon the eight regular battalions designated to make the assault were moving into position backed by the six provincial regiments that were to act as reserves.[6]

The attack began half an hour later with a signal that sent more than a thousand light troops rushing forward into the abatis, taking cover among the trees and firing at the enemy's position. Behind them, as sunlight flashed from the barrels and bayonets of their muskets, seven thousand men in brilliant scarlet formed ranks along battalion fronts and dressed right to straighten their lines. Moving at the quick step to the beat of the drum and (because the Inniskillings were on the right wing and the first battalion of the Black Watch was in the center) the wail of bagpipes, the regulars marched uphill toward the French breastwork. Despite its intended precision, the attack began raggedly: the battalions on the British right entered the abatis before the units in the center and on the left had finished dressing their ranks. It was a bad start. As the redcoats came within range, the French at the breastwork opened fire, and the abatis began to earn its name.

"Trees were fell down in Such Manner that it Broke our Batallions before we got near the Breastwork," wrote Major Eyre. "All [that] was left for each Commanding Officer of A Reg[imen]t to do, was to support & march up as quick as they could get Upon their Ground And so on to the Intrenchm[en]t." But the fragmented battalions, with their men struggling forward through a nightmare of branches and stumps and musketry, never reached the breastwork. In attack after attack, the magnificently disciplined redcoats advanced into the barrier, only to be "Cut . . . Down Like Grass," according to a Massachusetts private, Joseph Nichols, who watched from the ranks of Colonel Jonathan Bagley's regiment, at the edge of the field. "Our Forces Fell Exceeding Fast," he wrote. "It was Surprizing to me to think [that] more of ye Regiments Should be Drawn up to the Breast work for Such Slaughter." An ensign in another company of the same regiment agreed. "The fier began very hot," he wrote: "the Regalors hove down thair pak and fixed their bayarnits came up in order stod and fit very corage[ous]ly. . . . [T]he fi[gh]t came on very smart it held about eaght [h]ours a soreful Si[gh]t to behold the Ded men and wounded Lay on the ground having Som of them legs thir arms and other Lims broken others shot threw the body and very mortly wounded to hear thar cris and se thair bodis lay in blod and the earth trembel with the fier of the smal arms was a mornfull [h]our as ever I saw."[7]

If to look on this shambles was mournful, to march into it must have been hell. "Our orders were to [run] to the breast work and get in if we could,' " a survivor later remembered.

> But their lines were full, and they killed our men so fast, that we could not gain it. We got behind trees, logs and stumps, and covered ourselves as we could from the enemy's fire. The ground was strewed with the dead and dying. It happened that I got behind a white-oak stump, which was so small that I had to lay on my side, and stretch myself; the balls striking the ground within a hand's breadth of me every moment, and I could hear the men screaming, and see them dying all around me. I lay there some time. A man could not stand

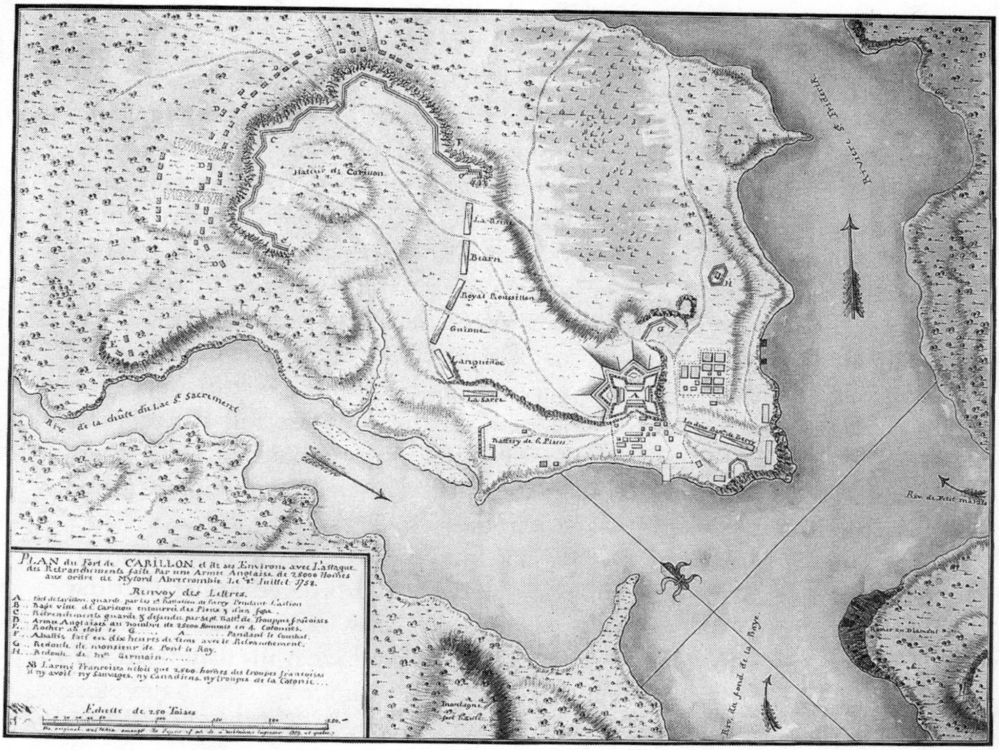

The Battle of Ticonderoga, July 8, 1758. This superb topographical rendering by a French engineer shows Fort Carillon's commanding position on the Ticonderoga peninsula, at the head of Lake Champlain. The Anglo-American positions are sketched in a semicircle outside the log breastwork and abatis ("made in ten hours," according to the legend) that surround the heights of Carillon, three-quarters of a mile north of the fort. The battalions of *troupes de terre* that took part in the defense are shown in order of battle between the fort and the breastwork. *Courtesy of the William L. Clements Library at the University of Michigan.*

erect without being hit, any more than he could stand out in a shower, without having drops of rain fall upon him; for the balls came by handsfull. It was a clear day—a little air stirring. Once in a while the enemy would cease firing a minute or two, to have the smoke clear away, so that they might take better aim. In one of these intervals I sprang from my perilous situation, and gained a stand which I thought would be more secure, behind a large pine log, where several of my comrades had already taken shelter but the balls came here as thick as ever. One of the men raised his head a little above the log, and a ball struck him in the centre of the forehead. . . . We lay there till near sunset and, not receiving orders from any officer, the men crept off, leaving all the dead, and most of the wounded.[8]

Meanwhile, outside Abercromby's headquarters at the sawmill camp, a mile from the battle, Rufus Putnam worked alongside the other soldiers of his regiment, digging entrenchments, listening to the "constant peele of Cannon and Musquetry," and worrying that he would be thought a coward for having occupied so safe a post during the battle. As evening came on, he decided to prove his courage by volunteering to carry ammunition forward to the troops; but "When I came to the Army they were Retreated into a Breast-work that Col. Williams' men had builded [at the rear of the battlefield]. I was very much amazed to see so many of our men killed and wounded. The path all the way was full of wounded men. . . . [Then I returned to my] Regiment where I found them employed as before. [Soon thereafter,] the most of the Troops retreated into the Breast[work] which we had builded."[9]

General Abercromby, who had known of the battle only from the dispatches sent back by his commanders, had ordered attacks all day without seeing any of the consequences. Now, at nightfall, fearing a French counterattack, he began to comprehend what his army had suffered, with nearly two thousand dead and wounded. "It was therefore judged necessary," he later reported to Pitt (prudently choosing the passive voice), "for the Preservation of the Remainder of so many brave Men, & not to run the risk of the Enemy's penetrating into His Majesty's Dominions, which might have been the Case if a Total Defeat had ensued, that we should make the best retreat possible." Late that night he ordered his officers to muster their men and march them back to the bateaux. Unfortunately no one told the soldiers why they were retreating; haste compounded confusion, and fear and rumor fed on one another as men stumbled through the darkness. As the troops neared the landing place, anxiety exploded in panic and a stampede for the boats. "News came that the Enemy was Coming to fall upon us—Oh the Confusion we was in at that Time for we was in a poor Cituation for an Enemy to Attack us, Being Joyn'd to a Point of Land & the Battoos Lay Joyning to one another 15 deep from Land—The Cry of Enemy made our People Cry out & make Sad Lamentations [, but] We made the Best of our way off & Rec[eive]d not Hurt." By dawn on July 9, the largest English army ever assembled in America was rowing for its life up Lake George, fleeing an enemy not a quarter its size—and not in pursuit. By sunset the ruin of Abercromby's army collapsed, exhausted, beside the hulk of Fort William Henry.[10]

That Abercromby had crowned defeat with humiliation was apparent to everyone. "Shamefully retreated," noted Artemas Ward, a Massachusetts lieutenant colonel, in a diary otherwise almost devoid of adverbs. "This Day," the Reverend John Cleaveland of the Massachusetts provincials wrote on the tenth, "where ever I went I found people, officers and soldiers astonished that we left the French Ground and lamenting the strange conduct in coming off." Private Joseph Nichols, too, thought it an "Astonishing Disappointment" but concluded that "we must Submitt for Twas Gods Holy will & Pleasure." Like many other provincials, Nichols believed that the Lord had deprived them of the victory because he wanted to teach them humility and because he was chastising the regulars for their inveterate profanity and Sabbath-breaking. Private Nichols's chaplain, John Cleaveland, did not disagree with such providentialist reasoning, but in looking for the proximate cause did not hesitate to blame "the General [and] his Rehoboam-Counsellors." "We now begin to think Strongly," he wrote on July 12, "that the Grand Expedition against Canada is laid aside and a Foundation is going to be made totally to impoverish our Country."[11]

Eventually the muddle of defeat and disorientation resolved itself when Abercromby ordered his troops to build a fortified camp next to Fort William Henry, but Rufus Putnam and his fellow soldiers saw only confusion in the weeks after the battle. "After our return from Fort Ticonderoga, we were employed in almost everything," he wrote after nearly two weeks when he had been too busy to write at all: "in the building of Breast-works—and moving of our encampment from one place to another—had hardly time to pitch in one place before we were ordered to remove and pitch in another; and no body, to see us, would be able to tell what we were about."[12]

Provincials were by no means the only ones to find fault. Experienced regular officers were also sending home scathing accounts of the battle and its aftermath, and none was more violent in his censure than a cerebral and intemperate captain of the 44th Foot, Charles Lee:

> These proceedings must undoubtedly appear most astonishingly absurd to people who were at a distance, but they are still more glaringly so to us who were upon the spot. . . . There was one hill in particular which seem'd to offer itself as an ally to us, it immediately Commanded the lines from hence two small pieces of cannon well planted must have drove the French in a very short time from their breast work . . . but notwithstanding some of our Cannon was brought up & in readiness, this was never thought of, which (one

wou'd imagine) must have occur'd to any blockhead who was not absolutely so far sunk in Idiotism as to be oblig'd to wear a bib and bells.[13]

The French, not least of all their commander, saw the Anglo-American retreat as a providential deliverance from evidently certain defeat and the loss of Canada itself. Montcalm at first believed the retreat was a ruse, and waited for two days after the battle before he sent out a battalion "to find what had become of the enemy army." What the troops found—"wounded, provisions, abandoned equipment, shoes left in miry places, remains of barges and burned pontoons"—convinced Montcalm that his adversaries had indeed suffered a general collapse, even though at the close of the battle they had still had more than enough troops, cannon, ammunition, and supplies to besiege and destroy Fort Carillon. On the twelfth, while Cleaveland bitterly marked the parallels between Abercromby and Rehoboam, the worst of Israel's kings, Montcalm and his men sang a Te Deum of thanksgiving. Even so hardheaded a rationalist as Montcalm's chief aide, Bougainville, believed that "never ha[d] a victory been more especially due to the finger of Providence." The marquis himself was moved to compose a Latin couplet and have it inscribed on a great cross, which he ordered erected at the breastwork:

> Quid dux? Quid miles? Quid strata ingentia ligna?
> En signum! En victor! Deus hic, Deus ipse triumphat.

> *To whom belongs this victory?*
> *Commander? Soldier? Abatis?*
> *Behold God's sign! For only He*
> *Himself hath triumphed here.*[14]

By the time Montcalm raised his cross, August was drawing to a close and he had dismissed his militiamen to harvest the grain in the Montréal district. Too strapped for men and provisions to take the offensive, Montcalm had spent the rest of the summer improving Carillon's fortifications. Reconnaissance patrols sent to the head of Lake George brought back prisoners and intelligence that indicated that Abercromby, too, had gone on the defensive. Yet Montcalm knew that unless the war ended first, some other British officer would return to try again.[15]

It would be some weeks before Montcalm, lingering at Carillon, heard tell of providences more ominous than the one he had seen on July 8: the loss of Louisbourg and the destruction of Fort Frontenac. On the evening of September 6, the same day that couriers brought word of these defeats, Montcalm left for Montréal to confer with the man he now regarded as his enemy, Vaudreuil. The season was so far advanced that there was little chance that Canada itself would come under attack before the next spring. But the news of these defeats and the suspicion that Vaudreuil was conspiring against him filled Montcalm with dreadful forebodings. Perhaps his defeat of Abercromby had bought some time; but with the loss of Louisbourg, the destruction of Frontenac, and the prospect of yet another failed harvest, time now seemed to have become Britain's most formidable ally.[16]

CHAPTER 25

Amherst at Louisbourg

JUNE–JULY 1758

ALTHOUGH MONTCALM heard nothing of it until September, Louisbourg had been in British hands since July 26. Jeffery Amherst had begun operations against Cape Breton Island immediately upon his arrival, landing troops at Gabarus Bay about four miles southwest of the fortress on June 8. As they came ashore in heavy surf and under fire from entrenched French defenders, only luck prevented the British from suffering a defeat as devastating as Abercromby's. Wolfe, who commanded the operation, thought it "a rash and ill-advised attempt to land," and believed that it succeeded "by the greatest of good fortune imaginable." Because the French fell back to the safety of the city once the landings were well under way, the British suffered only about a hundred casualties, and by the evening of that same day they had taken up positions in a long arc just outside the reach of Louisbourg's guns. From that point onward, bad weather, rough terrain, and the determined opposition of the city's defenders slowed the progress of the siege to a crawl.[1]

Louisbourg was a typical eighteenth-century fortress and no more than middle-sized by European standards, but so formidable in its New World setting that it had been called "the American Dunkirk" and "the Gibraltar of the North." The fortress and two outlying artillery batteries guarded the entrance to a large, sheltered harbor within which eleven French warships (including five ships of the line) rode at anchor, displaying hundreds of cannon to discourage Admiral Boscawen's Royal Navy fleet from trying to force an entrance. Two bastions (King and Queen) and two half-bastions (Dauphin and Princess) defended Louisbourg's landward wall, mounting cannon that could sweep the outer defenses, glacis, and ditch clear of assaulting infantrymen. Manning the bastions

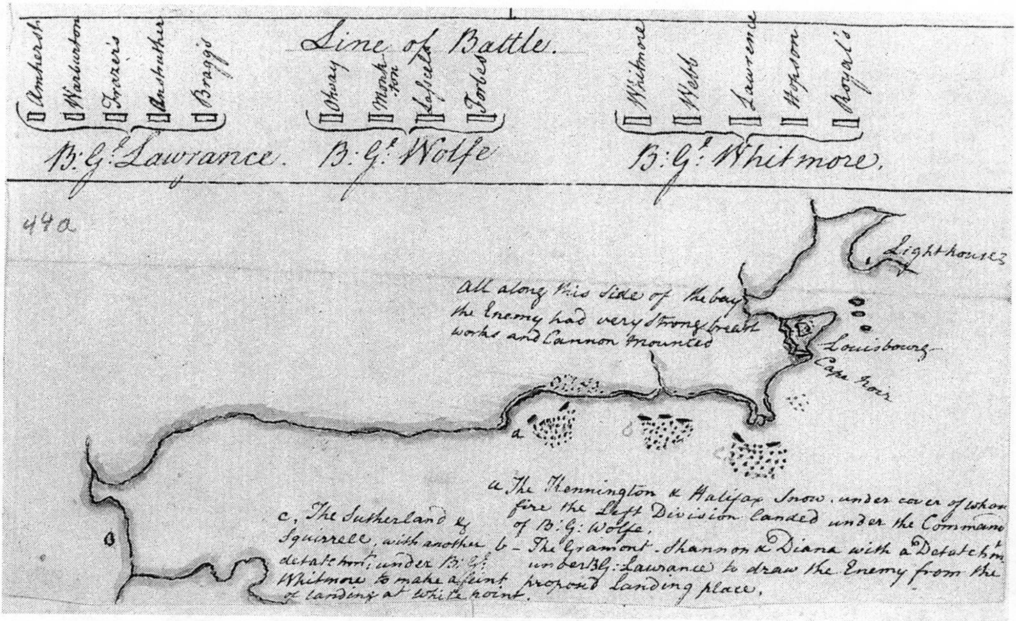

The assault landing at Louisbourg, June 8, 1758. This sketch depicts the three divisions of the invading force just before troops under Wolfe's command landed at the cove on the left. The French had, as an annotation says, "very Strong breast works and Cannon Mounted" along the shore. In heavy surf and under fire, Wolfe tried to call off the landing, but a boat commander misinterpreted the signal and ran his craft ashore anyway; seeing this accidental success, Wolfe reversed himself and led the remaining boats in, to land at the same point. That night the invaders established their siege camp in the vicinity of the creek (Fresh Water Brook) at the center, two miles from the city. *Courtesy of the William L. Clements Library at the University of Michigan.*

and walls were eight battalions of regular infantry, twenty-four companies of *troupes de la marine,* and two companies of artillerists, plus the town militia and the sailors and marines from the ships in the harbor: in all nearly six thousand men.[2]

Louisbourg was an impressive adversary, but like all Vauban-style fortresses, it was vulnerable to an attack conducted according to the principles of siege craft that Vauban himself had perfected. Every professional European officer knew the rules and rituals of that epitome of eighteenth-century civilized warfare, the *siège en forme.* Once the commander of the attacking force had formally notified the defending commander that he intended to invest his position, and after the defenders had responded with defiance (as honor demanded), the attackers would withdraw beyond cannon range to begin digging the network of trenches

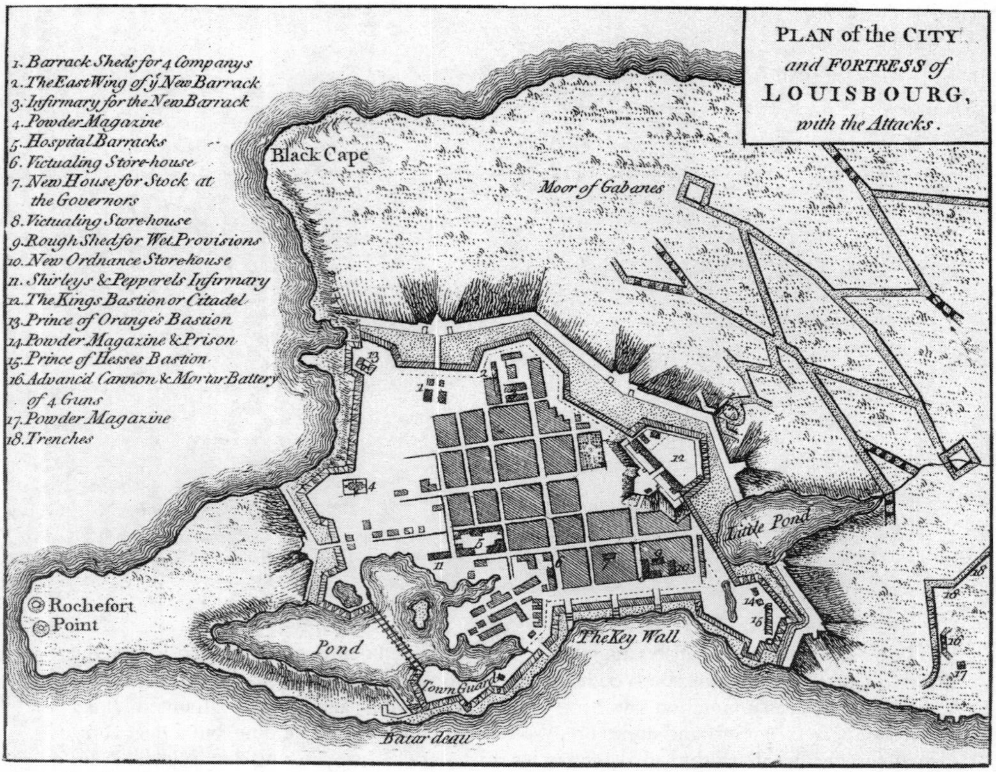

The Siege of Louisbourg, June 8–July 26, 1758. This map, from Rocque's *Set of Plans and Forts,* accurately depicts both the formidable land-side defenses of Louisbourg and the three parallels of the British siege lines, at the upper right. (The illustration is oriented with north at the bottom.) *Courtesy of the William L. Clements Library at the University of Michigan.*

that would seal the fate of any fortress, unless relief came from outside. First a parallel trench, opposite one of the fortress walls; then a sap, or approach trench, running toward the wall; then a second parallel; another sap; a third parallel; and so on, until cannon, hauled forward through the trenches, could be brought close enough to form breaching batteries that would pound the walls and bastions of the fort to rubble.

As the besieging forces inched closer, protected by their trenches—or by gabions, huge earth-filled wicker baskets thrown up where the ground refused to yield to picks and shovels—the defenders would rain artillery and musket fire on them; launch spoiling raids, or sorties, from the fortress; and work day and night to repair the damage to the walls. Everything the defenders could do, however, only served to delay the inevitable, for no unrelieved fortress could indefinitely withstand a well-supplied siege. Vauban had calculated that a properly invested fortress should be able to hold out no longer than forty days if cut off from external aid.[3] By the middle of the eighteenth century the virtual certainty of a siege's outcome was so well known that these ponderous minuets almost never ended with the attackers storming through broken walls and slaughtering fortresses' last starved defenders. Instead, garrison commanders who believed that they had satisfied the demands of honor generally asked to be granted terms of surrender that comported with the stout-heartedness of their defense. If the siege had been a long one, the victor would respond with terms like those Montcalm had offered at Fort William Henry in 1757: the defenders would be allowed to keep their colors, personal property, small arms, and perhaps even a symbolic cannon, and would be allowed to withdraw on parole—that is, having given their word that they would not appear in arms for a stated period—without being made prisoners of war.

More than any other siege of the war in America, Louisbourg in 1758 offered the opportunity to operate in strict accordance with these rules. The city held out steadfastly for more than six weeks against besiegers whose techniques conformed exactly to the precepts Vauban had set down in his essay *On the Attack and Defense of Fortified Places.* Immediately after landing on June 8, the British began to dig their first parallel trenches. By the twelfth Wolfe had driven the last of the defenders back to the city from the outlying works and batteries around the harbor. On the nineteenth the first British cannon opened fire, from extreme range, on the city's bastions and the ships in the harbor. The digging of parallels and saps went forward relentlessly until, on July 3, batteries had been erected within six hundred yards of the city's landward wall. By the sixth British shells—mortar bombs and incendiaries—were falling within the walls of the city. In growing desperation, and without much effect, the French tried launching night sorties against the enemy batteries. Day after day the shelling continued; night after night the digging went on. On July 21, a red-hot cannonball struck one of the French ships of the line at anchor in the harbor and detonated the powder in its magazine. The vessel and its two nearest neighbors burned to the water line.[4]

By this time fire was taking as inexorable a toll on the city as on the ships. On July 22 the King's Bastion, key to the landward defenses of the city, burned; under a rain of red-hot shot from the British guns, buildings within the walls were going up in flames faster than fire crews could put them out. On the night of the twenty-fifth, concealed by a heavy fog, sailors from Boscawen's fleet entered the harbor in boats and boarded the two remaining ships of the line, burning one and towing the other to safety across the harbor. The capture of this second vessel—the sixty-four–gun *Bienfaisant,* which was not only the last surviving line-of-battle ship but also the squadron's flagship—struck a heavy blow to the morale of Louisbourg's defenders. But it was the next twelve hours, during which at least a thousand rounds of British shot and shell landed within the city, that convinced Louisbourg's governor, the chevalier de Drucour, that further resistance was folly. Already nearly a third of the defending garrison was out of action, since four hundred soldiers had been killed under the bombardment and more than thirteen hundred had been incapacitated by wounds or disease. Thus on the morning of the twenty-sixth, with only four serviceable cannon left in the last working battery of the last bastion, with six British ships of the line making sail to enter the harbor and shell the town from its undefended water side, and with a breaching battery preparing to open fire on the landward wall at close range, Drucour hoisted a flag of truce and asked for terms. He had done all that he could to satisfy the conventions of honor and military professionalism. The well-learned etiquette of siege craft gave him confidence that the British would grant his garrison the honors of war.[5]

And yet, in ways Drucour had not yet grasped, the siege of Louisbourg had only superficially conformed to civilized European practice. At least one Englishman realized with shock on the very day of the landings that this was no ordinary encounter between professionals. Surveying the French lines after the defenders had fled back to the city, a naval officer had found "the Bodies of one hundred & odd French Regulars & two Indians, which our Rangers Scalped"—a gruesome token of the intention to repay the massacre of Fort William Henry in kind.[6] The rangers who accompanied the expedition were mainly men from Massachusetts, and some were veterans of the 1757 campaign, but this episode in fact demonstrated more than a few New Englanders' desire to settle scores. In a letter to his uncle, Wolfe himself casually and approvingly mentioned the English policy of massacring whatever Indians they encountered. As for the savages, he wrote, "I take them to be the most contemptible *canaille* upon earth. Those to the southward are much braver and better men; these are a dastardly set of bloody rascals. We cut them to pieces whenever we found them, in return for a thousand acts of cruelty and barbarity."[7]

But the legacy of Fort William Henry in fact extended beyond the hunting down and slaughter of the Micmacs and Abenakis in alliance with the French, for in the end the heroism of the defenders and the civilians who had endured weeks of bombardment counted for nothing.

The capture of the *Bienfaisant*. Admiral Boscawen ordered two detachments of sailors to enter the harbor in boats on the night of July 25 to capture the only two surviving French men-of-war. In this splendid 1771 mezzotint the *Prudent*, aground at left, has been set ablaze; meanwhile, the *Bienfaisant*, already wearing the Union Jack, is being towed out of cannon range as the harborside batteries open an ineffectual fire. *Courtesy of the William L. Clements Library at the University of Michigan.*

Amherst replied to Drucour's request for terms by denying him and his garrison all honors. The town would not be opened to plunder and the civilians within it would be allowed to retain their personal effects, but all those who had resisted in arms would be made prisoners of war and transported to England. Louisbourg's civilian population, along with the rest of the inhabitants of Cape Breton and the neighboring island of St.-Jean (today's Prince Edward Island), would be deported to France: in all, more than eight thousand men, women, and children. No longer would Britain count only the soldiers of the French king their enemies; at least in New France, civilians would also be subject to military action.[8]

Such harsh measures had been in a sense foretold by the expulsion of the Acadians in 1755; yet that was arguably the act not of professional soldiers but of politicians interested in land speculation. No officer in the British army was a more thoroughgoing regular than Jeffery Amherst, however, and his refusal to play the magnanimous victor imparted a kind of totality to this war in the New World that was alien to the presumptions and standards of the old. Amherst's policy henceforth would be the one that Montcalm, in the aftermath of the Fort William Henry debacle, had feared most. No matter how gallant the conduct of a defending force, Amherst would never again accord any defeated enemy the honors of war.

CHAPTER 26

Supply Holds the Key

1758

Like eighteenth-century sieges in general, the reduction of Louisbourg had been a spectacular affair; yet in a purely strategic sense the fortress's fate was sealed weeks before the first redcoat wallowed ashore through the surf of Gabarus Bay. Neither Amherst's meticulous siege craft nor Wolfe's flashier acts of daring but British control of the sea had denied the defenders the hope of withstanding the siege. Indeed, the decisive factor had not even been the twenty-three ships of the line and numerous frigates with which Boscawen patrolled the waters off Cape Breton during the siege, but the growing ability of the Royal Navy to dominate the French in European waters. Two engagements fought there had been critical. First, at the end of February, Admiral Henry Osborne's Gibraltar-based fleet had prevented a strong French squadron from leaving the Mediterranean with reinforcements and supplies for Louisbourg. Then, at the beginning of April in the Bay of Biscay, Vice Admiral Edward Hawke had interdicted a second Louisbourg convoy off La Rochelle, forcing it to abandon its cargo and armament. The only French vessels to slip through the British net and aid in Louisbourg's defense were those that rode at anchor under the city's guns when Amherst and Boscawen arrived. They had escaped from Brest while Hawke had been busy breaking up the much larger convoy of store ships and escort vessels in the Basque Roads. Thus before Amherst had gotten halfway to Nova Scotia, the British navy had tipped the balance in his favor by preventing at least eighteen ships of the line, seven frigates, and more than forty store ships and troop transports from crossing the Atlantic to reinforce the Cape Breton garrison.[1]

In a more complex way, the ability to control the enemy's lines of communication would also decide the outcome of the third major Anglo-American offensive of 1758, the long march against Fort Duquesne. Brigadier John Forbes, a man whose spirit toughened even as his body decayed, had begun organizing this expedition in early spring with a plan that was precisely the opposite of Braddock's. Whereas Braddock had hoped to expel the French quickly and therefore carried a minimum of provisions with his column, Forbes knew that he would need to hold the Forks once he had driven out the French, and that meant transporting vast quantities of food, clothing, ammunition, arms, and trade goods overland from the coast. He moved, consequently, with an almost maddening deliberation, planning the construction of intermediate forts and supply depots, appealing to the governors of colonies in the region for support, and seeking scouts from the Cherokees and other nations. He progressed so slowly that it was the end of June before his troops began to construct the first advanced base of supply (Fort Bedford, at Raystown) in preparation for opening the road toward Fort Duquesne. Moreover, the route that Forbes chose was by no means calculated for speed. Instead of making use of Braddock's road from the upper reaches of the Potomac watershed on the Maryland-Virginia border, he decided to proceed more or less straight west across Pennsylvania from Carlisle. Preexisting roads traversed less than half this distance, which meant that Forbes's men had to cut a new wagon trail through a hundred miles of forest and cross two substantial mountain ranges, the Alleghenies and Laurel Ridge, in order to reach the Forks.

Forbes's slowness allowed not only time for his force to proceed with substantial security but also for two critical developments to take place, both of which severed Fort Duquesne from the support it needed to survive. The first of these was a dramatic military victory, the destruction of Fort Frontenac on Lake Ontario in late August. The second was the most important diplomatic breakthough of the war: at about the time Fort Frontenac fell, the Ohio Indians abandoned their alliance with France and made peace with Britain, as the result of contacts established with the help of the eastern Delaware chief, Teedyuscung.[2] Although the fall of Fort Frontenac and the neutralization of the Ohio Indians were in no sense coordinated developments, together they determined the outcome of Forbes's expedition as decisively as Osborne's and Hawke's naval actions had enabled Amherst to capture Louisbourg.

CHAPTER 27

Bradstreet at Fort Frontenac

JULY–AUGUST 1758

THE STORY OF Fort Frontenac's fall is largely the story of Lieutenant Colonel John Bradstreet's strategic insight, persistence, and ingenuity. Born Jean-Baptiste Bradstreet in Nova Scotia in 1714, this son of a British army lieutenant and an Acadian mother had literally grown up in the army, serving from the age of fourteen as a volunteer attached to the 40th Regiment of Foot, the unit in which he finally received his ensign's commission in 1735. Ten years later he distinguished himself at the siege of Louisbourg while serving as a temporary lieutenant colonel in a Massachusetts provincial regiment. This was an extraordinary assignment for a man who, at the age of thirty, had not yet passed the rank of ensign in the 40th Foot; but Bradstreet was no ordinary officer. He was in fact a massively ambitious if comparatively poor man who had taken advantage of a casual meeting with William Shirley in 1744 to plant in the governor's mind the idea of an expedition against Louisbourg—and then had promoted himself as its leader. Although Bradstreet played a major role in the capture of the fortress, his achievements failed to bring him the preferment he longed for, and at the outbreak of the Seven Years' War he was still a captain, the rank he held in the revived 51st Regiment of Foot. Once again William Shirley stepped in, eager to use Bradstreet's special gifts as a regular who could deal effectively with irregular troops by putting him in charge of bateau transport service in the Mohawk-Oswego corridor and promoting him—illegally—to the rank of lieutenant colonel. It is a testimony to Bradstreet's sheer ability that despite his close ties with Shirley, the earl of Loudoun also concluded that he was worth using—even if Bradstreet was a man who had to "be rode with a bridel."[1] In December 1757 Loudoun repromoted Bradstreet to the rank of lieutenant colonel and made him his deputy quartermaster general.

Whatever satisfaction Bradstreet may have derived from Loudoun's recognition of his logistical talents, however, his real desire was to lead a raid against Fort Frontenac. The idea of such an expedition had come to him in 1755, when in the course of supervising the supply of Fort Oswego he realized the key position that Frontenac occupied in Canada's western Indian trade. By the summer of 1757, a raid to destroy Fort Frontenac had become something like his idée fixe—a plan he promoted in letters to his English patron and about which he ceaselessly pestered the commander in chief. Early in 1758 he finally convinced Loudoun to let him undertake it by offering to pay all expenses from his own pocket, to be reimbursed only in event of success.[2]

Loudoun's dismissal thwarted Bradstreet's design, for Pitt's instructions made no mention of Fort Frontenac, and the cautious Abercromby would no more have added a jot or tittle to those than he would have weakened the force he intended to send against Ticonderoga. Defeat gave Bradstreet the opportunity he needed, and in the hugger-mugger that followed the retreat he bludgeoned the commander in chief with requests for permission to undertake the expedition. On July 13, just three days after Abercromby's beaten army had reestablished itself at the head of Lake George, Bradstreet induced the general to detach 5,600 men and to send them, under the command of Brigadier John Stanwix (and himself, as Stanwix's second), "to distress the enemy" on Lake Ontario and—"if found practicable"—to attack Fort Frontenac.[3] Abercromby may or may not have appreciated the plan's strategic elegance, but he could not have missed the fact that a successful outcome might help offset the disgrace of defeat at Ticonderoga.

Bradstreet's force would proceed with the announced intention of rebuilding the fort at the Great Carrying Place that General Webb in his panic had destroyed in 1756, and to provide it with a permanent garrison. The reestablishment of an advanced post in the upper Mohawk Valley would serve two useful purposes. In the first place, it would secure the river route against invasion and reopen trade in the heart of Iroquoia—a trade that the Six Nations now needed desperately, since European manufactures had grown steadily scarcer and dearer as the war progressed. In the second, the Iroquois could be counted on to let the French know that the expedition was limited in intent, and thus (Bradstreet hoped) lull them into thinking that it posed no immediate threat. Only at the Carrying Place were Stanwix and Bradstreet authorized to reveal the secret orders to attack Fort Frontenac; then Bradstreet would take a force of picked men by bateaux and whaleboats along a route he knew so well—down Wood Creek to Oneida Lake, thence to the Onondaga River to Lake Ontario—to carry out the raid. Surprise was of the essence, for the raiding party could carry only a few cannon to use in the attack (four twelve-pounders and four eight-inch howitzers, each with seventy rounds of ammunition). As soon as he had Abercromby's blessing, Bradstreet left the Lake George camp for Schenectady, where with his customary energy he made ready for the expedition. By the end of July the task force was on its way up the Mohawk.[4]

Two weeks later Stanwix, Bradstreet, and their provincials—for only 157 regulars and 27 artillerists along with 70 Onondaga and Oneida warriors accompanied a force made up overwhelmingly of troops from New York, New Jersey, and New England—arrived at the Great Carrying Place. There, according to plan, Stanwix and Bradstreet revealed their true mission. With that, the Onondagas (about half of the Indians) left; only by promising the Oneidas first claim to any plunder did Bradstreet persuade the remainder to continue with the expedition. Secrecy, so scrupulously preserved up to this point, now served Bradstreet well. Word had already passed to the French through Iroquois channels that the Anglo-American force intended to rebuild Fort Bull. Even if Francophile or neutralist Iroquois factions got word of the impending attack to Montréal, there would be too little time to reinforce Fort Frontenac.

From the Carrying Place, Bradstreet and about 3,100 men proceeded to Lake Ontario, which they reached on August 21. Resting only one night at Oswego (where "there was scarce the appearance, of there ever having been a fort, or any place of defence") they pressed on for Sackets Harbor at the east end of the lake. There they organized themselves for the attack, worrying that they might be discovered by one of the armed sloops that they knew patrolled the waters of Ontario.[5]

The lake fleet posed the greatest threat to the expedition, for the French sloops carried cannon enough to sink every boat in Bradstreet's command. If they appeared before the provincials made the twenty-mile run from Sackets Harbor to their objective, all would surely be lost; but no sail broke the horizon for the next three days. Late in the afternoon of August 25 Bradstreet's men pulled to within sight of the promontory where the Cataraqui River enters the lake and the lake in turn empties into the St. Lawrence: the spot where Fort Frontenac and its warehouses stood bursting with military supplies destined for the Ohio Country and trade goods and peltry from the whole *pays d'en haut.* Less than a mile from the fort they beached their bateaux and threw up hasty defenses for the night. The next morning they landed the guns, assembled their dismantled carriages, and began hauling them toward the fort. Apart from random, ineffectual cannon shots, the French offered no resistance.[6]

Bradstreet had no time to dig the elaborate parallels and saps of a *siège en forme.* Taking advantage of what seemed the extraordinary timidity of the garrison, he ordered his men to seize an old breastwork the French had dug about 250 yards from the fort; then, after nightfall, he led a party to emplace guns on a rise still nearer Frontenac's west wall—perhaps 150 yards, or virtually point-blank range. From these vantage points at dawn on the twenty-seventh the British gun crews opened fire on the fort, the stone walls of which had been constructed to defend against musket shot, not twelve-pound cannonballs. Before eight o'clock the sixty-three-year-old commandant of the garrison, Major Pierre-Jacques Payen de Noyan, ran up a red flag of truce. Bradstreet briskly dictated his terms—the members of the garrison could keep their money and their clothes but would proceed as prisoners of war to Albany, from which they would be exchanged for an equal number of British prisoners—and gave Noyan ten minutes to make up his mind. The old soldier hardly needed so much time. Within the hour Bradstreet's men took possession of the fort. What they found within its walls revealed both why the French defense had been so lackluster and why Bradstreet had found this post so mesmerizing an objective.[7]

The seigneur de Noyan's garrison consisted of only 110 soldiers, along with a great many women and children; the remainder of the fort's ordinary complement had been withdrawn to defend Fort Carillon. The defenders could man fewer than a dozen of the fort's sixty artillery pieces, a number already reduced by the casualties inflicted in Bradstreet's brief cannonade. Although Noyan's Indian allies had reported Bradstreet's force three days before it landed, and Noyan had immediately sent to Montréal for help, he knew that his messenger could not have arrived at the city in less than four days and that a relief expedition would take even longer to make its way the two hundred miles upriver. (In fact, Vaudreuil received Noyan's message on the twenty-sixth and immediately organized a militia force from harvesters in the fields around Montréal; they left on the morning of the twenty-seventh and despite every exertion did not arrive until after the first of September.) Noyan, a veteran of forty-six years' service in the *troupes de la marine* and a man familiar with every weakness of his fort's ancient walls, harbored no illusions about heroic resistance; yet surely surrender pained him beyond words, for he knew what treasures lay in the fort's magazines, in the storehouses at the waterside, and in the holds of the sloops in the river.

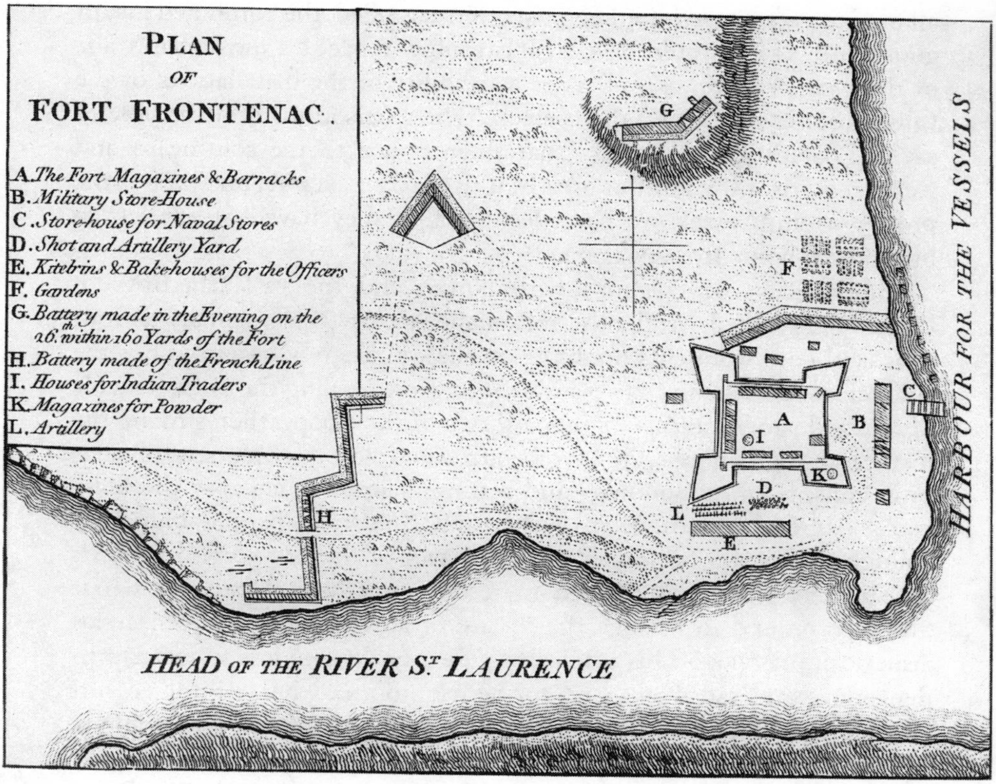

Bradstreet's attack on Fort Frontenac, August 26–27, 1758. Rocque's engraving, from *A Set of Plans and Forts,* vividly suggests the smash-and-grab quality of Bradstreet's attack, which improvised a siege trench from an old French breastwork, at left. *Courtesy of the William L. Clements Library at the University of Michigan.*

To the Anglo-Americans, the sight of the booty they had gained was "uncrediable." "The stores of the fort wer Exceeding many," observed one Massachusetts lieutenant: "warlike Stores of all Sorts for the Endions and there was Sixtey Piecs of Cannon which was Distroyed[.] The Chief [plunder] that we Brought off was Bailes of Cloth[,] Laist [laced] and plain Coats and Shirts of all sizes[,] a great Number of Dear skins and fur of all sorts[,] and Several othe[r] things." When Bradstreet made his report from Oswego on August 31, he estimated the value of goods seized at £35,000, or 800,000 *livres.* The nine sloops that lay in the Cataraqui anchorage comprised the whole of French shipping and naval strength on Lake Ontario. Because Fort Frontenac served as the base from which all of Canada's western trading posts were supplied, the combined loss of goods and vessels would have a catastrophic impact on the Indian trade of the *pays d'en haut* as well as on the ability of the installations of the Ohio Country to defend themselves. "The garrison made no scruple of saying," Bradstreet reported, "that their troops to the southward and western garrisons will suffer greatly, if not entirely starve, for want of the provisions and vessels we have destroyed, as they have not any left to bring them home from Niagara."[8]

Bradstreet's conversations with Noyan and the vast quantities of bread being baked within the fort made it clear that as many as four thousand reinforcements might be on the way from Montréal. Thus the colonel lost no time in setting his men to work, loading the most valuable of the trade goods and peltry aboard two of the sloops, then sinking the rest; disabling cannons, destroying arms and accoutrements, spoliating provisions; burning buildings and setting charges to collapse the fort's walls. Amid this carnival of destruction Bradstreet paused only long enough to alter the surrender terms in favor of the tiny garrison and its dependents, whom he allowed to return directly to Montréal, where Noyan promised to arrange the release of an equal number of Anglo-American prisoners. This ostensibly generous gesture was in fact a prudent move on Bradstreet's part, for he had no idea when reinforcements might arrive and dreaded having his retreat slowed by women, children, and wounded prisoners.

By the afternoon of August 28, with nothing left to demolish, Bradstreet ordered his troops to their boats. By the thirty-first they were back at Oswego, where they paused only long enough to transfer the booty from the ships to the bateaux and destroy the vessels. On September 8, back at the Great Carrying Place, the victors at last divided the spoils equally among themselves. Only Bradstreet—evidently content in the glory that came from winning so important a victory without the loss of a single life—took no share. The irrepressible Nova Scotian had, at any rate, more important things on his mind than the skins of deer and beaver.[9]

Bradstreet had no sooner reached Albany than he began to press Abercromby for permission to return to Lake Ontario with a new and larger force, one with which he could take Fort Niagara and perhaps conquer other western posts as well. Fort Frontenac's condition suggested that the garrisons on the lakes had been stripped bare and would fall easily before vigorous attacks. With the lake fleet destroyed, even the slightest pressure in the west would oblige the French "to abandon their settlements, forts, and possessions on lake Erie, the streights of lake

Huron, and the lake Superior; their trade and interest with the Indians inhabiting those countries, must consequently decay, and if a proper use is made of these advantages, may be utterly taken from them." What he envisioned was nothing less than the conquest of an empire stretching eight hundred miles into the North American interior, from the Thousand Islands to Thunder Bay: a scheme that Abercromby thought grandiose. Made cautious once more by Bradstreet's success, he dispatched the colonel to Lake George, where he could supervise the fulfillment of the conditions of prisoner exchange he had worked out with the seigneur de Noyan.[10]

Bradstreet, incredulous that Abercromby could let so great an opportunity slip away, obeyed his orders but also wrote furiously to his English patrons to urge the commander in chief's recall and composed an anonymous pamphlet to publicize his own role in the taking of Fort Frontenac. *An Impartial Account of Lieut. Colonel Bradstreet's Expedition to Fort Frontenac, to which are added a few reflections on the conduct of that Enterprize . . . by a volunteer on the Expedition,* however, was not only an exercise in self-aggrandizement, for the principal argument it made to its intended (British) audience was that the time was ripe for seizing "the dominion of the lakes" from the French. "Had any one measure been taken by [Abercromby]," Bradstreet wrote, "our advantages might have been multiplied almost beyond imagination"; a change in command was obviously in order. Nor was Bradstreet the only officer to complain of Abercromby's timidity in following up the raid on Cataraqui. Captain Charles Lee was recuperating from a wound he had suffered in the attack at Fort Carillon but still capable of working himself into a rage at the "blunders of this damn'd beastly poltroon (who to the scourge and dishonour of the Nation is unhappily at the head of our Army, as an instrument of divine vengeance to bring about national losses and national dishonour)." Taking care to instruct his sister to give the letter and its enclosures to the parliamentary agent of the 44th Regiment, Lee described Bradstreet's victory and its likely consequences. "If our Booby in Chief had only acted with the spirit and prudence of an old Woman," he wrote, "their whole Country must inevitably have this year been reduc'd."[11]

Letters like Lee's, passing reliably along the lines of family, clientage, and influence that tied writers on the colonial periphery to recipients with access to ministers at the core of British politics, destroyed the hapless general's chances of retaining his command. And yet, lethargic as he was, to judge him solely by the condemnations of his critics would be to miss his real significance in shaping the campaigns of 1758. For Abercromby did, after all, decide on July 13 to permit Bradstreet to undertake his mission to Cataraqui, despite the fact that nothing in Pitt's instructions authorized him to do so. And ten days thereafter he made a second unauthorized decision that would prove equally consequential in destroying France's hold on the Ohio Valley.

CHAPTER 28

Indian Diplomacy and the Fall of Fort Duquesne

AUTUMN 1758

WHAT JAMES ABERCROMBY did on July 23 took a kind of courage that was none the less real for being expressed in the form of an administrative mandate. On that day he authorized Brigadier General Forbes to negotiate directly with the Ohio Indians, even though such negotiations violated the protocols of Indian diplomacy. Forbes and Governor William Denny of Pennsylvania had been making overtures to the western Indians through Teedyuscung since the spring, and these efforts had set them at odds with the Crown's Indian superintendent, Sir William Johnson; Johnson's connections to the Iroquois had made him deeply averse to approaching the Ohio Indians directly. By giving Forbes permission to act independently of Johnson, Abercromby opened a diplomatic channel that would otherwise have remained blocked. Doing so, however, required him to undercut a man with formidable access to the centers of power in Britain. Abercromby's decision thus gave Forbes the opportunity to neutralize the Ohio Indians, but only at the price of adding Sir William Johnson's name to the lengthening list of his enemies.

Perhaps no British commander in North America had ever needed Indian allies more than John Forbes; probably no officer ever tried harder to obtain them; and certainly none had a worse time getting and retaining them. Charged with succeeding where Braddock had failed, Forbes knew very well that the lack of Indian allies had doomed the expedition of 1755. Sir William Johnson had seemed either unwilling or unable to deliver Iroquois warriors to his army, so Forbes had turned southward in the hope of recruiting Cherokee auxiliaries. But the Cherokees came so early and in such large numbers—as many as seven hundred had arrived by mid-May—that Forbes had difficulty arming, equipping, feeding, and finding functions for them all. Moreover, he had no experience of his own in managing Indian affairs and neither Johnson nor Edmund Atkin, the Southern superintendent, sent anyone to help him. Within a month Forbes was complaining that "the Cherokees are most certainly a very great plague," and that while he had done everything he could "to please them, . . . nothing will keep them." The Indians understood him no better than he did them. Impatient with Forbes's slow progress and offended by what he interpreted as Forbes's efforts to reduce his warriors from allies to subordinates, the Cherokee leader Attakullakulla, or Little Carpenter, tried to withdraw from the expedition, only to find himself under arrest as a deserter. Forbes eventually understood his mistake and released the chief, but the Cherokees had taken permanent offense. Before the summer was out virtually all of them had gone home, taking along the expensive arms and presents with which Forbes had tried to induce them to stay.[1]

If Forbes was no more culturally sensitive than any of the other British commanders, he was virtually unique among them in that he grasped the strategic importance of the Indians and—notwithstanding his missteps and frustrations—never ceased to seek accommodation with them. Thus even as he was having such trouble in dealing with the Cherokees, he also entreated Governor Denny to fulfill the promises Pennsylvania had made to Teedyuscung at the Easton Treaty of 1757. Houses for the Delawares must at all events be built in the Wyoming Valley, Forbes wrote, in part because "he [Teedyuscung] has the Publick Faith for the making of such a Settlement," and in part because Forbes wanted to use Teedyuscung's eastern Delawares to guard the "Back Settlements this Summer." But most of all Forbes needed to keep communications open with Teedyuscung because the eastern Delaware chief controlled the only channel through which he could send messages to the western Delawares and hence the other Ohio Indians. As early as the beginning of May he was trying to set "a Treaty on foot . . . between the Shawanes, the Delawares, and the people of this province [Pennsylvania]" in order to deprive the French of allies before his army arrived at Fort Duquesne. Arranging this treaty was a task to which Forbes applied himself with no less determination than to building the road itself. In the end it would prove an almost equally herculean undertaking.[2]

In June, while Forbes's commander in the field, Colonel Henry Bouquet, was leading the expeditionary force westward from Carlisle to begin building the road and its supporting forts, Forbes himself was seeking by all possible means to employ Teedyuscung as a conduit to the Ohio Indians. He relied on allies of a most unconventional sort to promote these contacts, for he had established a close working relationship with Teedyuscung's friend and patron, the pacifist merchant Israel Pemberton, founder and leading light of the Friendly Association for Regaining and Preserving Peace with the Indians by Pacific Measures. It was Pemberton who advised him that Teedyuscung had sent wampum belts and messengers to the western Indians following the 1757 Easton conference, but that the Iroquois had done everything to thwart these contacts and to prevent direct negotiations that might lead to peace. Pemberton, likewise, explained the urgent need of the Ohio tribes to hear directly from the Pennsylvania authorities before they would agree to any change in their allegiance. As always in Pennsylvania, however, the very need for governmental action created formidable barriers to obtaining it.[3]

Pemberton and his colleagues in the Friendly Association, as promoters of peace initiatives based on concessions to Indian interests, had never found much favor with Pennsylvania's proprietor and his appointees. Proprietary authorities (including, of course, the governor) generally opposed any measures likely to reduce income from the sale of lands, or, worst of all, anything that would call into question the validity of previous purchases from the Iroquois—especially that most flagrant of frauds, the Walking Purchase, which both the Quakers and the Delawares wanted to see invalidated. The previous year's treaty at Easton, establishing peace between the province and the eastern Delawares, had been possible only because Governor Denny, in a most ungovernorly way, agreed to set aside the Penn family's interests and accede to Teedyuscung's demands for aid, trade, land, and an inquiry into the Walking Purchase. But Denny could go only so far without jeopardizing his job, and everyone—the Quakers of the Friendly Association, the antiproprietary leaders in the Pennsylvania Assembly, Forbes, and particularly Denny—knew it. They also realized that the interlocking interests of the proprietor, the Iroquois, and Sir William Johnson, none of whom wished to promote the independent standing of the Delawares or any other Iroquois client group, would inevitably delay and frustrate efforts to negotiate with the Ohio Indians.

In view of all this, and of his anxiety over the desertion of the Cherokees, Forbes asked Abercromby for the authority to conduct Indian diplomacy without waiting for Sir William to take action. By the time Abercromby's reply of July 23 arrived the negotiations were already under way, for Forbes had already taken Pemberton's advice and asked Denny to pursue contacts, through Teedyuscung, with the Ohio nations. These efforts had borne fruit early in July, when Teedyuscung had conducted two western Delaware chiefs to Philadelphia, where Denny assured them that Pennsylvania was indeed eager to end hostilities. The emissaries from the Ohio Country were both sachems of great stature; one of them, Pisquetomen, was the elder brother both of Shingas and of Tamaqua, the former the preeminent Delaware war leader, and the latter a civil chief inclined to seek accommodation with the English. Because there could be no doubt that the appearance of such representatives offered real hope of peace, Denny appointed a personal envoy to return with them to the Ohio Country carrying his invitation to attend a treaty conference in the fall.[4]

The man whom the governor asked to undertake the perilous journey to the west was a brave and shrewd Moravian proselytizer, Christian Frederick Post. This Prussian-born cabinetmaker had come to Pennsylvania in 1742 as a disciple of the religious visionary Count Nikolaus Ludwig von Zinzendorf; soon thereafter he began to act as a lay missionary, a calling for which his genius for learning Indian languages and his ability to understand Indian cultures made him uniquely suited. By 1748 he had taken up residence among the eastern Delawares in the Wyoming Valley, learned their language, and married into the community. All this made him the perfect ambassador to send to the western Delawares, but even so his life would have been worthless in the Ohio Country without Pisquetomen's guarantee of safe conduct. As it was, the French learned of his presence and his mission as soon as he entered the region but could do nothing to stop him.[5]

By the middle of August, Post and Pisquetomen had reached Tamaqua's town of Kuskuski on upper Beaver Creek, a tributary of the Ohio that joins the river about twenty-five miles below the Forks. There, on August 18 and 19, Post addressed the assembled chiefs and warriors of the Delaware, assuring them that the English wished to make peace. Thereafter, in towns down Beaver Creek and on the Ohio practically to the walls of Fort Duquesne, Post repeated his message to Shawnee, Delaware, and Mingo leaders while the Indians protected him from French attempts to capture or assassinate him. Everywhere he went, his hosts expressed real interest in ending hostilities but seemed convinced that if they abandoned the French, the English would repay them by entering the Ohio Country and seizing their lands. Post tried to reassure them by pointing out that the English had undertaken military operations in the west only after the French had established forts there, and by reading to them the provisions of the 1757 Easton agreement that offered aid, and presumably guaranteed land, to Teedyuscung's people in the

Wyoming Valley. These facts, he argued, could be taken as proof that the English did not intend to colonize beyond the Alleghenies, but only to expel the French and then revive the trade that the Ohio tribes desperately needed.[6]

The Ohioans remained skeptical. "It is plain," they insisted, "that you white people are the cause of this war; why do not you and the *French* fight in the old country, and on the sea? Why do you come to fight on our land? This makes every body believe, you want to take the land from us by force, and settle it." Yet no matter how skeptical of British intentions, the Indians could hardly mistake the rapid weakening of the French hold on the Ohio or ignore the fact that Forbes was advancing with a kind of deliberateness and power that Braddock had never shown. Thus despite their misgivings, the western Delaware chiefs decided to send Post back with a message for Denny, Forbes, and their "brethren" in Pennsylvania:

> [W]e long for that peace and friendship we had formerly. . . . As you are of one nation and colour, in all the *English* governments, so let the peace be the same with all. Brethren, when you have finished this peace, which you have begun; when it is known every where amongst your brethren, and you have every where agreed together on this peace and friendship, then you will be pleased to send the great peace belt to us at *Allegheny*. . . . Now, brethren, let the king of *England* know what our mind is as soon as possibly you can.[7]

On September 8, Post, Pisquetomen, and a bodyguard of warriors set off for the English settlements. After two perilous weeks spent dodging scouts sent out from Fort Duquesne to intercept them, they arrived at Teedyuscung's town of Shamokin, on the Susquehanna. There they parted company, as Pisquetomen traveled on to Easton where he would represent his people in the coming peace talks while Post headed for Forbes's headquarters to report what he knew of French strength in the Ohio Country.[8]

Post finally found the general at Raystown, within Fort Bedford's palisade. Forbes was delighted to meet a man of such "ability and Fidelity" and so gratified to have reliable information on the enemy that he made him a personal reward of fifteen pounds sterling. But it was clear to Post that he had found a man sick and staggering under the duties of command. In addition to suffering from his painful skin condition, Forbes was in the midst of "a long and severe attack of a bloody flux"—dysentery—that left him so debilitated he could travel only "in a Hurdle carried betwixt two Horses." Forbes was, in his own words, "quite as feeble as a child" and forced to spend much of his time "in bed wearied like a dog." Yet to a remarkable degree he managed to keep up with his duties, issuing orders to Bouquet, sending weekly reports to Abercromby, pelting governors with demands for aid, and hurrying supplies forward to the expeditionary force.[9]

Post found the general burdened by cares and worries enough to dishearten a healthy man. The two Virginia colonels, Washington and Byrd, had been insisting throughout the campaign that Forbes would never reach Fort Duquesne before the end of the year if he held to the plan of building his road across Pennsylvania; he must shift his forces southward and use the Braddock road if he hoped for success. Forbes, convinced that their preference for the Braddock route grew from land-speculating interests in the Ohio Country, had lately found it necessary to reprimand them for having "showed their weakness in their attachment to the province they belong to" above "the good of the service." Because Forbes did not value such "provincial interest, jealousys, or suspicions, one single twopence" he had been feeling anxious ever since word had come back from the roadhead that the last mountainous stretch, Laurel Ridge, would prove extremely difficult to cross. He feared in his heart that Washington and Byrd might have been right, and that the expedition might not reach the Forks before winter after all.[10]

Nor was the difficulty of building the road by any means the worst news to have found its way back to Forbes's headquarters. He had also recently learned that on September 11 Bouquet, acting on his own authority, had detached a large force to reconnoiter toward Fort Duquesne from Loyalhanna, where the bulk of the army was busy constructing Fort Ligonier. Bouquet and Major James Grant, the officer to whom he gave command of the eight-hundred-man detachment, had hoped to end the campaign with a quick coup de main, despite Forbes's orders that they avoid all such risky ventures. The result of their boldness had been a coup of another sort, for early on the morning of September 14 a large party of French and Indians surrounded Grant's force near the Forks. In what nearly became a small-scale reprise of Braddock's defeat, a third of the British and American troops under Grant's command were killed, wounded, or captured. The remainder saved themselves as best they could: some by fighting their way out in an orderly retreat, others by throwing down their equipment and running away. Grant himself—after Bouquet, Forbes's most experienced field officer—had been taken prisoner and sent to Canada.[11]

The news of Grant's defeat depressed Forbes all the more since it substantiated Post's report that the French and Indians at Fort Duquesne

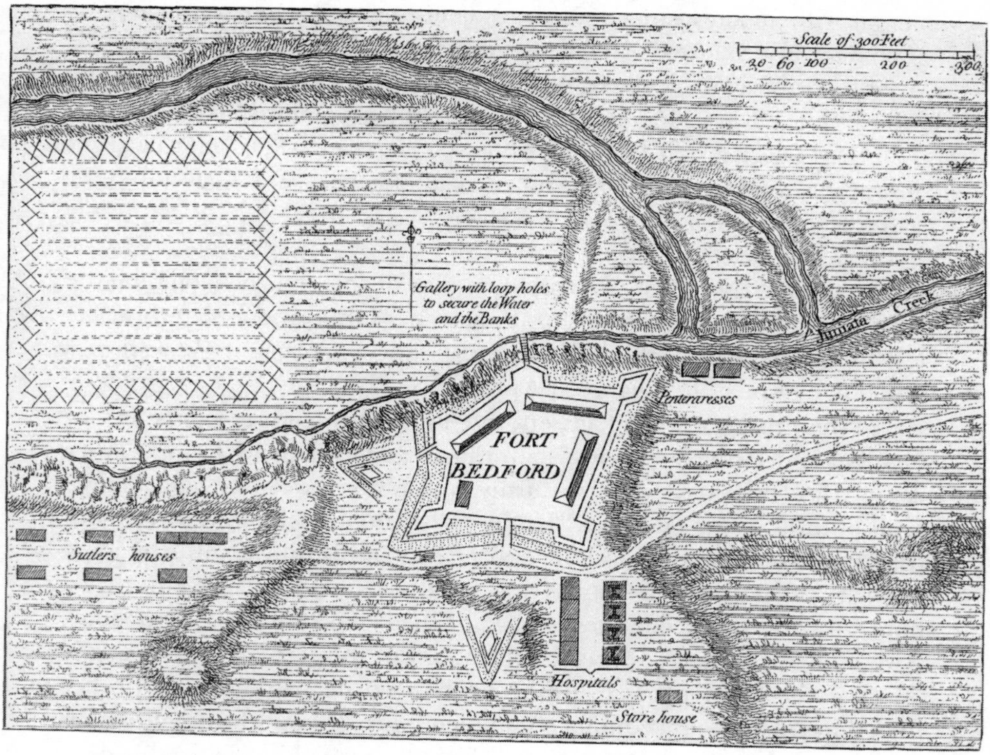

Fort Bedford, Pennsylvania. The meeting place of Christian Frederick Post and John Forbes, this small pentagonal fort was Forbes's supply base in the construction of the road to Fort Duquesne. Fort Ligonier, a similarly sized post on Loyalhanna Creek about forty-five miles to the west of Bedford, was the jumping-off point for the assault on Fort Duquesne. Between them, and along the length of Forbes Road generally, smaller blockhouse forts lay about a day's march apart. From Rocque, *A Set of Plans and Forts. Courtesy of the William L. Clements Library at the University of Michigan.*

were still strong enough to defend the Forks; but most of all it aggravated him, because Bouquet and Grant had gotten into the predicament by ignoring his orders. It was bad enough to be saddled with provincials who lacked discipline and devotion to the common cause, but holders of the king's commission should not need to be taught their duty. In a stinging rebuke to Bouquet, Forbes wrote that he had

> rested secure, and plumed myself in our good fortune, in having the head of the army advanced, as it were, to the beard of the enemy, and secured a good post well guarded and cautioned against surprise. Our road almost completed; our provisions all upon wheels, and all

> this without any loss on our side, and our small army all ready to join and act in a collected body whenever we pleased to attack the enemy, or that any favorable opportunity presented itself to us.
>
> Thus the breaking in upon—not to say disappointments of—our hitherto so fair and flattering hopes of success touches [me] most sensibly. How far we shall find the bad effects of it, I shall not at present say.

What worried him most was that the result of this setback would be the "alienating and altering the disposition of the [Ohio] Indians, at this critical time, who (tho' fickle and wavering), yet were seemingly well disposed to embrace our alliance and protection."[12]

To this crushing load of anxiety, the "unusual and unexpected rains" of October added one last straw. "I am ruined and undone by Rain," Forbes complained on a day when the army could "not move one yard." "Pray God send us a few fair days." Under these gloomy circumstances, with the campaigning season and the enlistments of his provincials (the great majority of his army) both drawing rapidly to a close, Forbes fixed his hopes on the peace conference that opened at Easton on October 11. Although he no longer expected direct aid in the form of Indian auxiliaries, if the Ohio tribes could be neutralized he might yet—all other impediments notwithstanding—complete his mission. Thus on October 16 although Forbes was "quite tyred" he still dragged himself to his desk to write a long letter to Pennsylvania's provincial secretary at the Easton Congress, urging him and his fellow delegates in the proprietary interest to do everything in their power to make it a success.[13]

"I am this moment flattering myself," he wrote, "that from the joint endeavours of all with you, the dropping of foolish trifles, some measure will be taken with those originale Inhabitants[, the Indians, so] as to strengthen ourselves and diminish our Ennemys Influence with them [on the Ohio]. . . . As I see things giving up sometimes a little in the beginning will procure you a great deal in the end." Although on the twelfth the enemy had made a strong raid against "our advanced post at Loyal Hannon," Forbes reported, Bouquet's men had repelled them, inflicting "Considerable" casualties without sustaining comparable losses of their own. The repulse of the raiders had actually raised morale, making "all the Waggoners, horse drivers &ca . . . on the road as brave as Lyons." Therefore, he wrote, because "I have everything in readyness at Loyal Hannon, [and] I only want a few dry days to carry me to the Ohio Banks," he had dispatched Christian Frederick Post to Easton, so that the moment peace had been concluded Post could return to the valley "with proper Messages (as the Governor shall direct) to the Ohio Indians to retire directly." No one knew better than Forbes that everything now depended upon the success of the peace conference: "Pray heartily," he concluded, "for fair weather and dispatch of Business."[14]

Post brought Forbes's letter to Easton on October 20, the day that the congress reached its climax. From its beginning the gathering had been a large and confused one, fraught with tension and conflict.[15] Although this conference had been convened under the joint aegis of the governors of Pennsylvania and New Jersey, the parties present and the interests they represented closely paralleled those at the previous year's Easton treaty. As in 1757, the divided interests of Pennsylvania were represented by its governor, a delegation of antiproprietary commissioners from its assembly, a variety of officeholders attached to the proprietary interest, and the proprietor's veteran Indian diplomat, Conrad Weiser. As in 1757, George Croghan attended as the deputy of Sir William Johnson; and as before Croghan was being shadowed by Johnson's (and the proprietor's) Quaker antagonist, Israel Pemberton. As in 1757, Indians of several nations were on hand: a few to speak and a few to counsel with the speakers, and many more to lend support to their nations' spokesmen with choruses of assent or murmurings of disapproval. But despite these resemblances, the 1758 conference also differed significantly from its predecessor.

In the first place, there were more Indians present, from many more tribes, and their larger numbers and greater diversity made the internal dynamics of this gathering more complex than those of its predecessor. In 1757 there had been only one principal Indian negotiator, Teedyuscung, who had brought with him a sizable group of Delawares; a considerable number of Senecas had also attended, but they had come as observers from the Iroquois Confederacy, not as independent negotiators. By contrast, more than five hundred Indians from thirteen nations attended the great congress of 1758. The western Delaware delegation was the most important one, but it was also one of the smallest, consisting only of Pisquetomen and his counselors. The eastern Delawares far outnumbered them, for Teedyuscung brought along approximately sixty supporters; but even that group was dwarfed by the numbers of Indians from the Iroquois League. Each of the Six Nations had sent official representatives, and the Onondaga Council had encouraged many of the small nations that lived under its protection—Nanticokes, Tuteloes, Chugnuts, Minisinks, Mahicans, and Wappingers—to send observers. The large number of Iroquois gave the first indication that this congress would differ from its predecessor, for the Grand Council had decided that the time had come to reassert its claim to preeminence over its tributary peoples.

Onondaga had therefore sent no fewer than three powerful chiefs—the great Oneida orator Thomas King, the Seneca sachem Tagashata, and the Mohawk chief Nichas (Croghan's father-in-law)—with the express intent of silencing Teedyuscung and quelling the tendency he represented toward independent action.

Teedyuscung saw this from the start and realized that the gains he had made at the 1757 conference—the promise of an inquiry into the validity of the Walking Purchase and the promise of a permanent Delaware reservation in the Wyoming Valley—could all be lost if the Iroquois successfully reasserted their claim to power over himself and his people. But he also knew that, having already concluded a peace between his own eastern band and the English, and having helped to bring the western Delawares to this peace table, he had become dispensable. With nothing left to offer as a mediator, he had lost his power to make demands. Teedyuscung's impotence helps to explain his behavior at Easton, for before the sessions began and frequently thereafter, he was loudly, belligerently, disruptively drunk. Whatever emotional reasons he may have had to drink, he gained nothing by it and made such a nuisance of himself that the Iroquois spokesmen scarcely even needed to argue that he was unfit to speak for his people. Once again, by virtue of adroit diplomacy if not the reality of control, the Iroquois reasserted their claims to hegemony over the eastern Delawares.

This was possible because both Denny and his cosponsor, Governor Francis Bernard of New Jersey, were coming to see Teedyuscung more as a liability than an asset. If the promises previously made to inquire into the Walking Purchase could be permanently deflected, and if the Wyoming Valley could be left under the control of the pliant Iroquois rather than being deeded to Teedyuscung's upstart Delaware band, they reasoned, so much the better. Such a solution suited the proprietor's men, who wished neither to see the Walking Purchase invalidated nor to have two and a half million acres of superb land removed from their master's control. Once it was clear that the Iroquois delegates at the conference would be speaking, as it were, in a chorus of agreement—and that the chorus was being harmonized by George Croghan and his father-in-law, Nichas—Teedyuscung was, for all practical purposes, isolated. Since the welfare of this man and his people was of no driving concern to the commissioners who represented the assembly, his sole remaining support came from Israel Pemberton. But Pemberton was present only as an unofficial observer and, saddest of all for Teedyuscung, he was not about to squander the chance for regaining peace by defending the claims of a drunk and frequently abusive chief. Thus between the rum that robbed him of his wits and the dynamics of power and peace that robbed him of his influence, Teedyuscung found himself abandoned at Easton; and before the conference ended, he sobered up and made the best accommodation he could with his, and his people's, plight.

It was on October 20 that Teedyuscung formally submitted to Iroquois control in a moving plea for a Wyoming Valley homeland. "*Uncles,*" he said, addressing the Iroquois chiefs,

> You may remember that you have placed us [Delawares] at *Wyomink,* and *Shamokin,* Places where *Indians* have lived before. Now I hear since, that you have sold that Land to our Brethren the *English;* let the matter now be cleared up, in the Presence of our Brethren the English.
>
> I sit there as a Bird on a Bough; I look about, and do not know where to go; let me therefore come down upon the Ground, and make that my own by a good Deed, and I shall then have a Home for ever; for if you, my Uncles, or I die, our Brethren the English will say, they have bought it from you, and so wrong my Posterity out of it.[16]

The Oneida spokesman Thomas King replied loftily that, for the time being, Teedyuscung could "make use of those Lands in Conjunction with our People, and all the rest of our Relations." As for the "good Deed" that Teedyuscung wanted, that was the concern of the sachems of the Iroquois at Onondaga; King would not presume to speak for them, but he would pass along the request. The proprietor's men rejoiced. Now they were prepared to make two carefully rehearsed concessions, the net effect of which would be simultaneously to hamstring Teedyuscung, seal the peace with the western Delawares, and reestablish the Iroquois hegemony that was invaluable to the Penn family.[17]

When Teedyuscung said in his speech that he had heard the Iroquois had "sold that Land [at Wyoming] to our Brethren the *English*" he alluded to the cession at the Albany Congress in which Conrad Weiser, acting as agent for the Penn family, had secured from the Iroquois title to all the land in Pennsylvania that lay west of the Susquehanna River, between 41°31' north latitude and the Maryland border. Weiser had intended to preempt the Wyoming Valley land purchase that his competitor, John Henry Lydius, was attempting to negotiate for the Susquehannah Company of Connecticut: hence Teedyuscung's anxiety to obtain a "good Deed" to Wyoming. But Weiser's enormous purchase had also included all Iroquois claims to the region around the Forks of the Ohio, and thus the Albany purchase also went to the heart of Pisquetomen's concerns. Everyone at Easton realized that the Ohio Indians would never make peace with the English unless they were satisfied that the Ohio Country would remain theirs once the war was over. Thus as soon as Teedyuscung had acknowledged his submission to Iroquois authority, Conrad Weiser, acting as the agent of the Penn family, formally returned to the Iroquois all the land from the Albany purchase that lay *west* of the Allegheny mountains.[18]

This masterstroke allayed the immediate fears of the Ohio Indians for their land even as it reaffirmed the Iroquois's status as lords of the valley, but it also raised a second issue that needed to be resolved. Pisquetomen had no less reason to worry about the long-run consequences of Iroquois control than that of the English, since he knew as well as Teedyuscung did that the Iroquois had never hesitated to sell land out from under their tributary nations. Thus Governor Denny stepped forward to make the second of the two planned concessions, by promising to "kindle up again" the "first Old Council Fire" at Philadelphia—that is, making a pledge on behalf of the proprietor to negotiate directly with representatives of the Delawares (and through them, the Ohio Indians generally) in the future, as William Penn had negotiated with their ancestors in 1682. Thus the form of Iroquois predominance over the Ohio Country was revived but the substance of Iroquois control over the Ohio Indians was not, for the Ohioans would be free to act for themselves in future dealings with the Penns. With these concessions secured, Pisquetomen agreed to peace on behalf of the western Delawares and the other Ohio bands for whom he spoke.[19]

The formal conclusion of the Treaty of Easton came on October 25 and 26, 1758, with feasting and the distribution of gifts. It had been the most important Indian congress in Pennsylvania's history, and its significance was by no means limited to the restoration of peace with the Ohio tribes. By subtle and compliant diplomacy, the Iroquois had regained predominance over the eastern Delawares and had reestablished their claim to the Ohio Country, an asset of far greater importance to the Confederacy than the one they ostensibly surrendered—the ability to speak for the western Delawares. The Penn family's representatives had staved off a considerable threat to the proprietary interest and had cemented anew the proprietor's ties to the Six Nations. If the Penns' enemies in the Pennsylvania Assembly and the Friendly Association were compelled to concede those gains to the proprietary interest, they could at least look forward to an end of bloodshed in the backcountry. Forbes could now strike at Fort Duquesne, supposing that the weather permitted and that word of the peace could be gotten to the western Indians before the enlistments of his provincial troops expired. And Pisquetomen had gained for his people the cessation of hostilities they could no longer afford to sustain, Onondaga's recognition of their autonomy, and an English promise that the whites would not establish permanent settlements in the Ohio Country after the war.

Of all the parties present at Easton, only the two men most responsible for regaining the peace had sustained irreversible losses. Israel Pemberton and the Friendly Association would never again play so prominent a role in Indian diplomacy; Teedyuscung would forfeit the freedom of action he had striven to achieve. In the end, however, Teedyuscung's people would lose much more. After a brief hearing in 1759, the Privy Council referred the promised investigation of the Walking Purchase to the Board of Trade, which in turn assigned it to Sir William Johnson. Teedyuscung's request for a reservation in the Wyoming Valley was referred to the Iroquois Council, which of course took no action. The lack of satisfactory resolution in the issues of the Walking Purchase and the Wyoming question would prove, over the long run, to be among the most painful legacies of the Easton Congress—and not only for the eastern Delawares. On October 25, however, only Teedyuscung, weeping and promising to look to God for guidance as he bade Israel Pemberton farewell, sensed what the failures, as well as the achievements, of the Easton treaty might mean.[20]

Meanwhile, Christian Frederick Post, Pisquetomen, and their escorts were already hurrying back to the Ohio Country with news of the peace. Following the new road (which Post thought "one of the worst roads that ever was travelled") they caught up with Forbes and the rest of his army at the Loyalhanna advanced post, Fort Ligonier, on November 7. Forbes welcomed them, feted them, toasted their healths, and hustled them on their way with wampum belts and letters to Shingas, Tamaqua, and the other Ohio chiefs. "Brethren," Forbes had written,

> I embrace this opportunity . . . of giving you Joy of the happy Conclusion of that great Council [at Easton], w[hi]ch is perfectly agreable to me; as it is for the mutual advantage of Y[ou]r Brothers, the Indians, as well as the English nation.
>
> . . . As I am now advancing, at the Head of a large Army, against his Majesty's Enemies, the French, on the Ohio, I must strongly recommend to you to send immediate Notice to any of your People, who may be at the French fort, to return forthwith to your Towns; where you may sit by y[ou]r Fires, w[i]th y[ou]r Wives and Children, quiet and undisturbed, and smoke your Pipes in safety. Let the

> French fight their own Battles, as they were the first Cause of the War, and [the] occasion of the long difference, w[hi]ch hath subsisted between you & your Brethren, the English; but I must entreat you to restrain y[ou]r young Men . . . , as it will be impossible for me to distinguish them from our Enemies; . . . lest . . . I should be the innocent Cause of your Brethren's Death. This Advice take and keep in your own Breasts, and suffer it not to reach the Ears of the French.[21]

By the sixteenth Pisquetomen and Post were delivering Forbes's message to the Indian settlements along Beaver Creek. The task was far from easy, for they arrived at a "precarious" time, just as many warriors were returning from a raid against the Anglo-Americans near Loyalhanna. For three days Post and his companions found themselves confined in a house in Kuskuski from which they dared not venture. In part their peril proceeded from the French officers present, who urged the town's young men "to knock every one of us messengers on the head." But most of all their lives were at risk, Post thought, "because the people who came from the slaughter . . . were possessed with a murdering spirit; which led them as in a halter, in which they were catched, and with bloody vengeance were thirsty and drunk." Anxiously the emissaries waited first for calm, then for a decision to emerge from the Indians' private debates over whether to accept the peace belts and messages from Easton. Everything depended upon their interpretation of English intentions. As Post well understood, "the *Indians* concern themselves very much about the affair of land; and are continually jealous, and afraid the *English* will take their land."[22]

After what seemed an eternity, Tamaqua and Shingas formally agreed to accept the messages and peace belts on November 25. Several days of speeches in public council followed, but these only served to ratify the decision, already made, to accept the Easton settlement. At the conclusion of the council on November 29, Tamaqua told Post that he and Shingas would take the word personally to the other Ohio villages and asked the missionary to carry the news of their acceptance to the English. Then, as "we made ready for our journey," another sachem approached with a final request.

> *Ketiushund,* a noted *Indian,* one of the chief counsellors, told us in secret, "That all the nations had jointly agreed to defend their hunting place at *Alleghenny,* and suffer nobody to settle there; and as these *Indians* are very much inclined to the *English* interest, so he begged

> us very much to tell the Governor, General, and all other people not to settle there. And if the *English* would draw back over the mountain, they would get all the other nations into their interest; but if they staid and settled there, all the nations would be against them; and he was afraid it would be a great war, and never come to a peace again."[23]

The missionary agreed to carry this news, too. Somberly: for he could not guarantee that anyone would listen.

When Christian Frederick Post rejoined the army on December 4, he found that the Ohio world had changed forever. Forbes's campaign was finished: the British controlled the Forks; a new fort was under construction a few hundred yards upstream from the blasted ruin of Fort Duquesne; the area was being called by a new name, Pittsburgh; Forbes himself was already being carried back to Philadelphia in a desperate attempt to save his life.[24] This is how it had all come to pass:

The Delaware raiders whose return to Kuskuski had caused such trouble for Post and his companions had set out on November 9 to carry off or destroy horses and cattle near Loyalhanna. They had undertaken this raid without much enthusiasm, at the insistence of François-Marie Le Marchand de Lignery, the captain of *la marine* in command at Fort Duquesne, who hoped to create such havoc in the British transport service that Forbes would be unable to continue the campaign. It was a raid conceived in desperation. Lignery, a tenacious fifty-five-year-old officer who had been active on the Ohio since Braddock's defeat, was a past master of hit-and-run warfare, but following Fort Frontenac's fall he had begun to despair of his position. As his supplies dwindled and his scouts told him of the road-builders' steady progress toward the Forks, he had launched raid after raid, hoping to keep the British off balance until the onset of winter forced them to abandon their expedition. But with each successful raid more and more of his Far Indian auxiliaries had taken their captives and trophies and returned home. Ironically, his greatest victory, the defeat of Grant's reconnaissance party on September 14, had resulted in the departure of so many Ottawa, Wyandot, and other warriors from the *pays d'en haut* that soon thereafter he found himself with few Indians beside the local Delawares, Shawnees, and Mingos left to rely upon. Meanwhile the straitened state of his supplies compelled him to reduce the numbers of French and Canadian troops at Duquesne to a minimum. At the beginning of November he commanded a skeletal garrison of three hundred regulars and militiamen. Only a third of them were fit for duty.[25]

The raid on Forbes's horses and cattle at the "grass guard" near Loyalhanna on November 12 was in fact a success, despite what seemed to Lignery the halfhearted participation of the Ohio Indians, for the raiders killed and seized more than two hundred animals before withdrawing. Warned that an attack was under way, Forbes ordered out two parties of five hundred men: one under Colonel Washington "to give them chace," the other under Lieutenant Colonel George Mercer of the 2nd Virginia Regiment "to Surround them." Night was coming on when Washington's men finally ran three of the raiders to ground. Shortly thereafter, in the deepening dusk, Washington's force collided with Mercer's and the two formations opened fire on each other. Before anyone understood what was happening, two officers and thirty-eight men had been killed or wounded, a heavier toll by far than the raiders had exacted. Luckily the prisoners remained unharmed, and one of them, a Pennsylvania backwoodsman named Johnson whom the Delawares had adopted and who had joined the raid as a warrior, revealed the weakness of Lignery's garrison. Forbes had been ready to abandon the campaign for the winter, but Johnson's report convinced him to seize the chance that now presented itself. He ordered immediate preparations for an advance on the Forks.[26]

With Washington's 1st Virginia Regiment and detachments of Delaware, Maryland, and North Carolina provincials in the lead, the army marched from its Loyalhanna camp on the morning of November 15. The troops left their camp women and even their tents behind at Fort Ligonier and advanced as rapidly as they could toward the Forks, cutting between three and five miles of road a day as they went. Each day a special detail built a hut with a chimney for Forbes, who though weaker than ever had himself carried forward in his litter, spending each night as close as possible to the head of the column. By November 21, the advance guard was encamped at Turtle Creek, twelve miles from Fort Duquesne.[27]

That was also the day that Lignery finally admitted that the game was up. Knowing that the Delawares were still debating whether to accept the peace belt from Pennsylvania, on the twentieth he had sent a war belt to Kuskuski along with a message asking them to join him in a new attack on the English. To his chagrin, the Delawares refused to accept the belt and instead kicked it about as if it were a snake. "Give it [back] to the *French* captain," they told Lignery's messenger, "and let him go with his young men; he boasted much of his fighting; now let us see his fighting. We have often ventured our lives for him; and had hardly a loaf of bread [in return] . . . ; now he thinks we should jump to serve him." The French emissary, "pale as death," endured their ridicule until midnight, then sent word back warning Lignery not to expect help from his erstwhile allies.[28]

When the unwelcome news arrived at the Forks, the commandant took the only option left to him and ordered the fort evacuated and destroyed. Sending what provisions were left to the nearest Wyandot band ("to induce them always to take our side and attack the English," he explained), he had the fort's cannon and munitions loaded on bateaux and ordered the militiamen from Louisiana and Illinois to convey them, along with the remaining prisoners, to the Illinois Country. Finally, on November 23, while the remaining two hundred men of his garrison waited in their canoes, he ordered the fort to be set afire and a mine of fifty or sixty barrels of powder to be detonated under its walls. Pausing only long enough to make sure "that the fort was entirely reduced to ashes and that the enemy would fall heir to nothing but the ironwork of the community buildings," Lignery and his men paddled up the Allegheny for Fort Machault, the supply station that stood at the mouth of French Creek. There he and a hundred of his healthiest men would hold the line for the winter, awaiting the return of spring and the reinforcements needed to reconquer the Forks before the English, too, could reinforce their winter garrison.[29]

Although the Anglo-Americans at ten miles' distance heard the explosion that blasted Fort Duquesne into oblivion, they advanced with caution and did not occupy the site until the following day, November 24. By then, Forbes's little army was within a week of dissolution, for the enlistments of the provincials who comprised two-thirds of its strength were due to expire on the thirtieth. Thus Forbes made haste to consolidate his gains, ordering a stockaded fort to be constructed just up the Monongahela from the rubble of the French post. Its purpose was to shelter a winter garrison of just two hundred Pennsylvania provincials under another Scottish physician-turned-soldier, Lieutenant Colonel Hugh Mercer. This was a tiny number, indeed a perilously small one; but not a man more could be provisioned from Fort Ligonier, forty miles to the east. Even more important than this fort, Forbes knew, was settling the minds of the local Indians, who would easily be able to overwhelm its garrison. He therefore dispatched George Croghan, who had joined him after Easton, to invite the local village chiefs to meet with him at the fort.

But Forbes himself could not remain, and when the conference opened on December 4 it was Colonel Bouquet who was there to distribute gifts and assure the assembled chiefs that the English had come not to settle, but only to reopen trade and guard against the return of the

French. On November 26, Forbes's health had finally, irrevocably collapsed: "being seized with an inflammation in [his] stomach, Midriff and Liver, the sharpest and most severe of all distempers," he realized that if he was to survive he would have to return to Philadelphia, where he could receive proper medical care before going home to England.[30]

Although he had doubted that he would survive the journey, Forbes lived to reach Philadelphia about six weeks later. There he recovered only enough strength to set his affairs in order and to write a few letters: the administrative and strategic testament of a man who could feel his life ebbing away. The most important of Forbes's last letters were addressed to Jeffery Amherst, recently named as Abercromby's successor. Indian affairs continued to concern Forbes, for he worried that Amherst (still inexperienced in wilderness warfare) would assume that the Indians were primitives who would merely side with the likeliest winner and that relations with the Indians could therefore be reduced to a simple calculus of force. Forbes begged Amherst "not [to] think trifflingly of the Indians or their friendship." If he hoped to preserve Britain's foothold on the Ohio, Amherst would need to "have [Indian affairs] settled on some solid footing, as the preservation of the Indians, and that country, Depends upon it." Relations with the tribes had generally been misunderstood, Forbes wrote, "or if understood, perverted to purposes serving particular ends." In this regard the greatest problems had arisen from two sources: "the Jealousy subsisting betwixt the Virginians & Pensilvanians . . . as both are aiming at engrossing the commerce and Barter with the Indians, and of settling and appropriating the immense tract of fine country" around the Forks; and "the private interested views of Sir William Johnstone [Johnson] and his Myrmidons." Unless Amherst exerted a strong hand, Forbes feared, the result would be chaos in the west and the loss of a country that he had literally given his life to win.[31]

His last act was a sentimental gesture. Ordering "a Gold medal to be struck . . . [for] the officers of his Army to wear as an honorary reward for their faithful services," he gave detailed instructions for the inscription. "The Medal has on one side the representation of a Road cut thro an immense Forrest, over Rocks, and mountains. The motto Per tot Discrimina—on the other side are represented the confluence of the Ohio and Monongahela rivers, a Fort in Flames in the forks of the Rivers at the approach of General Forbes carried in a Litter, followed with the army marching in Columns with Cannon. The motto Ohio Britannica Consilio manuque. This to be worn round the neck with a dark blew ribbon. . . ."[32] John Forbes succumbed to his "tedious illness" on March 11, 1759, three weeks after he ordered the medal struck, and a little less than five months short of his fifty-second birthday. Pennsylvania gave him an extravagant state funeral and buried him at public expense in the chancel of Philadelphia's Christ Church.[33]

It was the least that Penn's province could do, and not only because the general had secured its frontiers after three years of horrific bloodshed. What was already being called Forbes Road had opened a direct line of communication, with way stations no more than a day's travel apart, from Philadelphia to the Ohio Valley. And that, from the various perspectives of Pennsylvania's proprietary family, merchants, land speculators, Indian traders, and farmers, would prove to be the most important achievement of all.

CHAPTER 29

Educations in Arms

1754–1758

BY THE END of November, when the weary, freezing, ragged provincials of Forbes's army received their discharge at Pittsburgh, most of their counterparts in the northern theater of operations had already made their way home. Abercromby had closed down the New York campaigns in late October and thus avoided the usual mass desertions of provincials disinclined to serve past the expiration of their enlistment contracts. The mere absence of desertions, however, did not indicate contentment among the thousands of New England, New Jersey, and New York provincials any more than it bespoke admiration for the regular officers under whom they had served the past six months.[1] Something nearer the opposite was the case. For the six thousand or so provincials who witnessed the debacle of Abercromby's defeat at Ticonderoga the principal lesson was clear enough: it had been an almost incredibly "injuditious and wanton Sacrefise of men," a tragic demonstration of how an arrogant or incompetent commander could destroy hundreds of lives in a few hours.[2] The provincials at the edge of the battle could not have doubted the discipline or the courage of the regulars who had met their deaths in Montcalm's abatis, but nothing about the sight could have made them eager to emulate the redcoats' example, either.

Or, more properly, none of them wished to be compelled to emulate that example. Service alongside the king's troops made nothing more obvious to the provincials than that a coercive disciplinary system was the engine that drove the British army, and that the blood of common soldiers was its lubricant. Provincials who had volunteered to serve for a single campaign under their neighbors or older kinsmen were simply stunned to witness the operation of a system of military justice in which officers routinely sentenced enlisted men to corporal punishments that stopped just short of death, and not infrequently inflicted the death penalty itself.

In previous wars when New Englanders had served only under provincial, not regular, officers, they had behaved more or less like civilians in arms. A soldier who insulted his captain could expect to bear the consequences, which—depending upon the officer—might range from being knocked down on the spot to being placed under arrest, being court-martialed, and receiving ten or twenty lashes with a cat-o'-nine-tails. But under regular military discipline, insolence to an officer was a crime that carried a penalty of five hundred lashes; the theft of a shirt could earn a man a thousand; and desertion (no uncommon act among New England troops) was punishable by hanging or a firing-squad execution. An average provincial soldier serving with Abercromby's army could witness a flogging of fifty or a hundred lashes every day or two, a flogging of three hundred to a thousand lashes once or twice a week, an execution at least once a month. Men could be seen enduring less formal "company punishments," such as being compelled to walk the gauntlet or ride the wooden horse, almost any time. A provincial surgeon with Abercromby's army noted that one had to make a special effort *not* to see punishments inflicted. "I saw not ye men whiped," Dr. Caleb Rea wrote after a punishment parade at which one man was hanged and two others were flogged a thousand lashes each; "for altho' there is almost every Day more or less [men] whiped or Piqueted or some other ways punished I've never had ye curiosity to see'm, the Shrieks and Crys being Satisfactory to me without ye Sight of ye Strokes."[3]

The experience of service with the regulars left enduring marks on the provincials, and not only on those who left the army with scars on their backs. Most private soldiers in the New England regiments that made up most of the northern army's manpower were young native-born men between seventeen and twenty-four years old, not yet married and still living in or near their hometowns. Most of them had grown up assuming that they were Englishmen of a particularly virtuous sort, for they were not only the sons of freeholders and men who could expect to become independent landholders in their own right, but the descendants of religious dissenters who had come to America to establish a *New* England, one more pleasing to God than the old. Their army service gave most of these young Yankees the opportunity to meet sizable numbers of real Englishmen—and Scots, and Welsh, and Irishmen—for the first time. What they saw and heard and experienced in this, their first extended experience away from home, was all the more striking because it challenged so many of their inherited preconceptions: notions about everything from the character of relations between men—which they had assumed were contractual and fundamentally voluntary but that British officers regarded as being founded on status and coercion—to the nature of Englishness itself. While the war demonstrated the manifest differences between themselves and their British comrades-in-arms, it by no means convinced them that they were inferior to the redcoats, who, as one provincial wrote, "are but little better than slaves to their Officers."[4] Nor did contact with regular officers do anything to convince them that these representatives of the metropolitan ruling class were their moral superiors. The treatment they received from the likes of Abercromby and Loudoun nonetheless made it emphatically clear that the army's leaders regarded them at best as "an Obstinate and Ungovernable People, Uterly Unaquainted with the Nature of Subordination," and at worst as "the dirtiest most contemptible cowardly dogs that you can conceive."[5]

From 1756 onward, the Anglo-American armies became arenas of intercultural contact in which tens of thousands of American colonists encountered the British cultural and class system as refracted through the prism of the regular army. Because the war did not affect all the colonies equally, its impact varied from region to region; New England in particular contributed vastly more men in proportion to its population than the Chesapeake or the Middle Colonies. Yet especially after Pitt's policies took effect in 1758 and the total numbers of colonists engaged in fighting the war rose to unprecedented levels, provincial soldiers came from everywhere in North America, and the experience of military service became correspondingly widespread. Wherever provincials served alongside regulars they could no more escape noticing the differences between themselves and their redcoated superiors than they could avoid hearing the "Shrieks and Crys" of the men being "whiped or Piqueted or some other ways punished" in their camps. Moreover, because the great majority of provincial common soldiers were young men, men whose influence on their society would grow more palpable as they acquired property and household-headship in later years, the impact of their wartime experiences might be felt for years after their discharge from service. By sheer weight of numbers the war's greatest long-term impact would be felt in New England, where between 40 and 60 percent of the men in the prime military age range would pass through the provincial forces before peace finally returned. At least in Massachusetts and Connecticut, the war's ultimate effect would be to create a generation of men from people who had been mere contemporaries. But everywhere in the colonies that men had served as provincial soldiers, the war would have its influence, even if it was less encompassing than in New England. The intense, shared experiences of fatigue and discipline, of boredom and fear, of physical hardship and battle, would for years inform the perceptions and help shape the actions of the men who had served.[6]

Indeed, even at the end of 1758 the effects of the great campaigns were evident throughout the colonies, as men like Rufus Putnam and John Cleaveland returned home with stories to tell and pay to collect; as less fortunate men returned with the wounds and injuries that would blight their lives; as still other men never came back at all. In no case, however, were the effects of the war and military service more important than they had been in the life of the tall, grave Virginian who rode into Williamsburg on Christmas to resign his commission as colonel of the 1st Virginia Regiment.[7]

George Washington had been at war more or less continuously for five years. Now, with the expulsion of the French from the Forks and presumably the restoration of peace to the Virginia frontier, he believed that he had done enough. Although he had told almost no one that he intended to resign if the campaign reached a successful conclusion, he had prepared carefully for his reentry into civilian life. The previous spring he had proposed marriage to the richest and most eligible widow in the Northern Neck, Martha Dandridge Custis, and she had accepted; they were to be married on January 6. By joining their lands, slaves, and wealth they would position the family (for Martha was already the mother of two small children) well up in the ranks of northern Virginia's planter elite. Shortly after Martha agreed to marry him, Washington had decided to confirm his new standing by seeking election to the House of Burgesses as a representative of Frederick County. The freeholders had elected him to the seat, by a wide margin, in late July, and he would take his place in the House when the winter session began in February. Any interested observer might reasonably have concluded that Washington's military career—inauspiciously begun with defeat in 1754 and marked thereafter by increasing competence, if not glory—had been no more than a preliminary and perhaps calculated stage in the rise of an unusually ambitious man. But Washington's career as commander of the 1st Virginia Regiment had in fact been much more.[8]

Most of all the war had been a kind of education, in many aspects of life, for a man who had undergone very little formal instruction. Most obviously, his military experience had taught him a variety of technical and practical lessons. In defending the Virginia frontier from 1754 through 1757, he had learned how to make the most of manpower that was never adequate to the task, how to lay out and build forts and blockhouses, organize supply and transport services, dispense military justice, drill and train soldiers, manage the manifold tasks of administration and paperwork that the service required. He had learned less palpable but equally important skills of command as well: how to earn the respect and maintain the loyalty of his subordinate officers, how to issue clear and concise orders, how to keep his distance, how to control his temper. He had acquired these skills in part by study—he had been an indefatigable reader of military manuals and treatises, devouring everything from Caesar's *Commentaries* to Colonel Humphrey Bland's *Treatise of Military Discipline*—and in part by observing experienced officers in action. He had transcribed the orders issued by the regular officers, Braddock and Forbes and Bouquet, under whom he served, and studied them carefully. Unlike the New Englanders, who had generally recoiled from redcoat discipline and clung the more strongly to their region's contractualist military traditions, Washington had observed how the regulars conducted themselves in order to emulate them. Thus he acquired their attitudes, copied their habits of command, and absorbed their prejudices to the point that he became one of them in virtually every respect but the color of his coat and the provenance of his commission. As fully and as self-consciously as possible, Washington made himself a professional military officer between 1754 and 1758 and learned to handle regimental affairs with a proficiency not inferior to that of many colonels in the British army.[9]

To say that Washington became a capable military administrator, of course, is not to say that he also became a brilliant tactician. Beyond the quality—indispensable in an infantry commander—of unshakable physical courage, he had shown little obvious skill on the battlefield. His first encounter with an enemy force had ended in a massacre; his second in crushing defeat. He had ridden beside Braddock through one of the worst disasters in Anglo-American military history and kept his nerve, but that was about all. The experience did not translate into mastery of woodland warfare. Throughout 1756 and 1757 his regiment had skirmished with Indians along the Virginia frontier, but there is no evidence that it inhibited the raids or lessened their deadly effect. On the Forbes expedition he had shown himself capable of controlling a thousand or more men on the march through difficult country—no mean feat—but in his only encounter with an enemy force he had been unable to identify a friendly detachment in time to stop his men from opening fire on it. Yet even these experiences had, in their way, served him well, for Washington at the end of 1758 was a man much more fully aware of the hazards of combat and of the limitations of command than was the inexperienced, hasty, and seemingly much younger officer who in the summer of 1754 had professed to be charmed by the sound of bullets whistling past his ears.

The best single indication of his growth as a military leader can be found in a memorandum he wrote to Henry Bouquet on the night of November 6, 1758, following a conference over plans for the remainder of the campaign. November 6 was, of course, the day before Post arrived at Loyalhanna with the news of the Easton treaty, so neither Bouquet nor Washington had any reason to think that the Ohio Indians would abandon their allies. The best recent intelligence of enemy strength dated from Grant's defeat, and that gave no one cause for optimism. Even so, Bouquet had told Washington that he intended to advise Forbes to cut the army loose from its supply base at Fort Ligonier and march without delay to Fort Duquesne. Washington had tried to demur, but Bouquet had been unconvinced. Hours after their meeting, Washington found himself haunted by the thought that Bouquet would convince Forbes, so eager to bring the campaign to a successful close, to take the risk. His memorandum was a final effort to dissuade Bouquet from advocating an immediate attack.

With the history of Braddock's expedition obviously in mind, Washington first urged Bouquet to consider what the consequences would be of meeting the enemy on his own ground, with only the supplies they could carry and no system capable of replenishing stocks of food and ammunition when they were exhausted. Under such circumstances, a defeat might mean being forced back to Fort Ligonier, which they would then be compelled to evacuate for lack of provisions, "ab[and]oning our Artillery either to the Enemy or a general destruction." But then, he went on, "suppose the Enemy gives us a meeting in the Field and we put them to the Rout[. W]hat do we gain by it? perhaps triple their loss of Men in the first place, thô our numbers may be greatly superior (and If I may be allowd to judge from what I have seen of late, we shall not highten much that *good* opinion they seem to have of our skill in woods fighting)—therefore to risk an Engagement when so much depends upon it, without having the accomplishment of the main point in view, appears in my Eye, to be a little Imprudent."[10]

This remarkable document suggests several things about Washington, not least of which is that he had sufficient confidence in his own judgment to press his views home to a regular officer who disagreed with them: an officer who was not only his superior, but a man who had seen his first military service before Washington was five years old. Most of all, however, the memorandum shows that Washington had grasped the most significant lessons that the wilderness war had to offer: that to win campaigns, or presumably even the war itself, one need not necessarily win battles; that, indeed, to win a battle at the wrong time or in the wrong way could lead to failure in the larger realm of conflict. Any number of tactical defeats could be compensated for by merely retaining discipline and maintaining one's force in the field longer than one's enemy.

Braddock's experience had suggested as much, and Forbes's campaign was on the verge of proving it. Braddock's army had forfeited the advantage to the French in 1755 not because it suffered a grievous defeat in which Braddock himself had been killed, but because Dunbar had succumbed to the momentum of demoralization and flight. By ordering the army's supplies and cannon destroyed, he had destroyed the army's chance to return and fight again. Forbes fully understood this lesson and thus spent enormous amounts of time and money securing his lines of communication and studding them with fortified supply depots. As a result, individual defeats—even ones as substantial as Grant's—might slow his advance, but they could not stop it. In the end Forbes's army would not win a single engagement with its enemy, but it would gain its ultimate goal. The absence of a strict relation between victory on the battlefield and achieving one's strategic purpose was by no means obvious, even to officers as experienced and sophisticated as Henry Bouquet. But it was a lesson that Washington understood as fully, as decisively, as Forbes himself.

It would be merely silly, if it were not morally repugnant, to maintain that war builds character. And yet it ought not to be denied that, for better or for worse, military service and combat mold the views and the character of those who experience them. The Washington who advised Bouquet not to act rashly was a man who no longer entertained the illusions of his youth. He was, instead, a man for whom the strains of command and the experience of seeing men killed and wounded as a result of his orders had burned away the delusion that courage and valor—or even victory—will necessarily make the decisive difference that commanders long to achieve. He had acquired the professionalism of a British officer, even as he had been denied the commission that would have made him one. He had met many regular leaders and had modeled himself on those whom he took to be the best among them. He had learned how to give commands and how to take them. He had gained self-confidence and self-control, and if he could not honestly number humility among his virtues, he had at least begun to understand his limitations. George

Washington, at age twenty-seven, was not yet the man he would be at age forty or fifty, but he had come an immense distance in five years' time. And the hard road he had traveled from Jumonville's Glen, in ways he would not comprehend for years to come, had done much to prepare him for the harder road that lay ahead.

PART V

Annus Mirabilis

1759

Military successes at Louisbourg and elsewhere consolidate Pitt's power and increase his determination to strip France of its empire. American anxieties and commitment to the war effort grow as the invasion of Canada nears. British successes at Niagara, Ticonderoga, and Crown Point. Wolfe meets Montcalm—and both meet their Maker—at the Battle of Québec. Amherst reacts unenthusiastically to provincial behavior; the colonists react ecstatically to British victories. The state of the European powers and the increasingly perilous circumstances of Frederick the Great. The year's decisive battle: Quiberon Bay.

CHAPTER 30

Success, Anxiety, and Power

THE ASCENT OF WILLIAM PITT

LATE 1758

AT SEVEN O'CLOCK on Friday morning, August 18, 1758, a weary young infantry officer knocked at William Pitt's door. Captain William Amherst had landed at Portsmouth the previous day with dispatches from America, then posted more than sixty miles to London by an overnight coach. The secretary was out but expected back; the captain was welcome to wait. Amherst cooled his heels for three hours more before Pitt returned. Then, at last, he could speak the words that he had come three thousand miles to say: Louisbourg had surrendered four weeks before, and he had the honor of being sent to inform His Majesty of the event. Unable to restrain himself, Pitt hugged the startled captain and cried, "This is the greatest news!" Amherst, he exclaimed, was "the most welcome messenger that had arrived in this kingdom for years!"

As they hurried from dignitary to dignitary that morning, Pitt found "many handsome things to say" about Amherst's brother Jeffery, who "would make nothing of Quebec after this." Lord Ligonier was so delighted that he gave the young captain five hundred pounds and then added another hundred so Amherst could buy himself a suitable sword. The king, characteristically, asked many questions and offered no reward. The prince of Wales—himself a young man who longed for distinction—said that "he had expected great things" of General Amherst, but "what he had done exceeded his expectation and added that it was a very fine thing for so young a man to distinguish himself in so particular a manner." And Newcastle's enthusiasm, of course, overflowed. "His

Grace," Captain Amherst noted, "in great joy often repeated that he had sent 'orders for two Corporations to be made drunk.' "[1]

More than two corporations, of course, honored the duke's desire. Britain's beer barrels gurgled dry in their thousands to honor Amherst, Pitt, and the sovereign. On every hill, it seemed, bonfires blazed; from every battery cannons boomed. Amid pealing bells a procession of eminences bore Louisbourg's colors to Saint Paul's, there to deposit them among the cathedral's sacred symbols and to hear a sermon on the victory's providential significance. It was incomparably the greatest news to come from America since the war's beginning, and the nation spared nothing in its jubilation.[2]

BRITAIN WOULD HAVE so many more occasions to celebrate before the year was out that Horace Walpole could facetiously complain that "our bells are worn threadbare with ringing for victories." Yet for many months after Amherst delivered his news, it was far from apparent that the victory at Louisbourg would set the pattern for events yet to come. Indeed, just two days after Pitt had hugged Amherst in delight, news arrived of disaster at Ticonderoga and the death of Lord Howe, plunging the secretary into a gloom that would remain unrelieved for days. Not until October would he know that Bradstreet had destroyed Fort Frontenac, nor until the New Year that Forbes had taken Fort Duquesne. Thus in the last days of August, as Pitt considered what to do next, he was less prone to contemplate the glories of victory at Louisbourg than the problems that clouded his horizon. The darkest of them all loomed up from Europe.[3]

Although Pitt's strategic vision still focused on attacking France's imperial periphery rather than her armies in Europe, during 1758 the fighting on the Continent had forced itself to the center of his attention and had commanded an increasingly large share of his government's resources. There was no way to avoid this, for since the middle of 1757 Britain's ally Frederick of Prussia had been beset from every quarter by French, Austrian, Russian, and Swedish enemies. While Frederick had won impressive victories—he had beaten the French, brilliantly, at Rossbach in November 1757 and just a month later had stunned the Austrians with even greater tactical mastery at Leuthen—his armies had paid a heavy price in casualties. Encouraged by his successes, the British had tried to compensate for his losses by dramatically increasing their subsidies. In April 1758, as part of a formal treaty of alliance in which both powers promised not to conclude a separate peace, Pitt's government agreed to provide Frederick with £670,000 sterling per year. Money could not relieve the pressure on Prussia's armies, however, and the treaty accordingly stipulated that Britain would take the Hanoverian army into its pay (an obligation that would cost £1,200,000 a year) and would garrison the North Sea port of Emden—the first redcoats to be committed on the Continent.[4]

Heretofore Pitt had resisted direct involvement, worrying that to commit so much as a battalion to the fighting in Germany would open the door to endless escalations in the demand for troops. Events soon showed how prescient that fear had been, for even before the Emden garrison had taken ship, the calls for thousands more redcoats to be sent to the Continent were becoming steadily more urgent. What ultimately made them irresistible was not the necessity of plugging up the drain of manpower in Prussia, but rather the hope of inflicting a decisive defeat on the French army in Western Europe; and Pitt, ironically, would reverse the policy himself.

After the renunciation of the Convention of Kloster-Zeven, Prince Ferdinand of Brunswick had taken command of Cumberland's army of observation in Hanover and with remarkable speed rebuilt it into a force capable of taking the offensive. He waited only for Frederick's victory at Rossbach before opening a winter campaign against the French in Hanover and the Prussian territory of East Friesland. Ferdinand's deft maneuvering, together with the timely arrival of a few British warships, had compelled the French and Austrians to evacuate Emden in March 1758. Their withdrawal had made it necessary to send a British garrison to hold the city; but it was the subsequent retreat of the French from the River Ems across the Rhine that had created the demand for a large number of redcoats.[5]

To this point Pitt had preferred to make "descents"—amphibious raids—on the coast of France. These had proven less successful than he hoped, for although they tied down thousands of French soldiers in shore defenses, they were risky, difficult to execute, inherently indecisive, and unpopular among the officers assigned to lead them. The most recent descent, a raid in June on the Breton shipbuilding port of St.-Malo, had destroyed a great deal of French shipping but gained little else; its commander, fearing a French counterattack, had withdrawn without even attacking the town. This inglorious result became known in Whitehall shortly after word arrived that Prince Ferdinand had moved his army across the Rhine in pursuit of the French, who were withdrawing toward the Austrian Netherlands. On June 23 Ferdinand finally goaded his opposite number, Prince Louis de Bourbon Condé, comte de Clermont,

Prince Ferdinand of Brunswick (1721–92). Brother-in-law of Frederick the Great and the duke of Cumberland's successor in command of the army of observation, Ferdinand was a master of the art of maneuver and an exemplar of eighteenth-century military professionalism. His success in reanimating the army in early 1758 made him a hero in England, and the most ambitious officers in the British army clamored to serve under him on the Continent. *Courtesy of the William L. Clements Library at the University of Michigan.*

to give battle at the town of Crefeld, near Düsseldorf. The result, a sharp defeat for the French, caused Clermont to retire up the Rhine all the way to Cologne.[6]

With such dramatic developments afoot in Westphalia and the Austrian Netherlands, and with his coastal raids showing so few tangible results, Pitt reversed his policy against direct engagement on the Continent and agreed to send six regiments of cavalry and five of infantry (in all, about seven thousand men) to Ferdinand's aid. As it happened, this reinforcement came too late to make a difference. After a year of maneuvering, many minor engagements, and one major battle, Ferdinand had taken his army as far as it could go. In November he went into winter quarters, making his Hanoverian, Hessian, Prussian—and now British—force once more into an army of observation. Spring would come before he would again take them into action against the French.[7]

Thus the principal result of Pitt's decision to send troops to the Continent was to increase the expense of the war—between three and four million pounds sterling a year would now be required to maintain British commitments in Europe—while diminishing the number of men available to defend the home islands. Sending British troops to serve with Ferdinand's army undeniably rendered Hanover more secure and lessened the ability of the French to launch an invasion of England from the Low Countries. It did nothing, however, to alter the strategic balance in Europe—an equation that depended on the relative strength of Prussia. And, to Pitt's consternation no less than Frederick's, Prussia seemed to be growing steadily weaker.[8]

Frederick had followed up his spectacular victories at Rossbach and Leuthen by reconquering those parts of Silesia that had fallen to Austria and then by pressing south into Austrian Moravia. As he was pursuing this enterprise, however, a great Russian army struck into the Prussian heartland, threatening Frankfurt an der Oder and Berlin. Dashing back from Moravia, Frederick met his adversaries on August 25, about twenty miles east of Frankfurt near the village of Zorndorf. In what was technically a Prussian victory, he forced the Russians to withdraw, but only at a horrendous price: his army of 36,000 men had suffered losses of 13,500 killed, wounded, and missing—a casualty rate of nearly 40 percent. Worse followed. No sooner had the Russians assumed the defensive than Frederick learned that a huge Austrian army was threatening Dresden. Dividing his battered troops in two, he left half to watch the Russians and took the remainder south into Saxony, by a series of rapid marches, to seek battle with the Austrians. On October 14, Field Marshal von Daun gave him one near Hochkirch, where Frederick saw a quarter of his army destroyed before he broke off contact and withdrew to Dresden—which the Austrians promptly besieged.[9]

Winter now gave the grim little monarch breathing space enough to concentrate on rebuilding his forces. Even though he had won three major victories and suffered only one defeat in 1758, even though he had retained his hold on Saxony and Silesia and forced the invaders to back out of East Prussia, Frederick was anything but the master of the European war. His position was in fact becoming critical, for his victories had cost him as dearly as any defeat. The matchless discipline of the Prussian army had given Frederick an edge early in the war, but that discipline was an asset less easy to replace than the dead and broken bodies of the men who had once possessed it. Whereas Prussia had boasted the best-trained troops in Europe at the outset of the war—so much so that virtually any company could fire four or even five volleys a minute, a phenomenal rate for the day—by the time of Hochkirch, Frederick had lost more than a hundred thousand soldiers to death, wounds, capture, disease, and desertion. These he could only replace with untrained men, many of whom were foreigners, and prisoners of war. By the autumn of 1758 many of his regiments were barely half-disciplined, and Frederick's early advantage had all but vanished. Without British money to recruit, pay, and supply his troops, he knew, the army itself would vanish in short order.

Pitt understood Frederick's position and thus had continued throughout the summer to harass the coast of France in the hope of tying down French forces there. Unfortunately for his hopes, the one unqualified success in the history of these operations—a raid on Cherbourg in August—was followed, in early September, by the disaster that would bring them to a halt. Part of the reason for this stemmed from the fact that as soon as Pitt had decided to send troops to the aid of Prince Ferdinand, the most capable officers in the army had rushed to claim commands on the Continent, and the leadership of the coastal raiding force had fallen, as if by default, to a seventy-three-year-old lieutenant general named Thomas Bligh.

General Bligh's qualifications for command included enviably strong connections to the prince of Wales's political establishment, Leicester House, but not, unfortunately, military competence. His descent on Cherbourg in August had succeeded by virtue of good fortune, lack of French preparedness, and the sensible advice he received from the descent's naval commander, Captain Richard Howe (younger brother of Viscount Howe, recently killed near Ticonderoga). Bligh's September descent on St.-Malo possessed none of those fortunate qualities. The French had so strengthened defenses in the months following the June raid that the town could no longer be taken without a prolonged siege. Moreover, foul weather so interfered with the landing that only about 7,000 men and very few supplies came ashore before the attempt had to be abandoned. This put the whole expedition in jeopardy, for in order to reembark his men safely, Bligh had to march them overland about nine miles to the Bay of St.-Cas, a sheltered anchorage where Howe could meet him. Bligh managed the march badly, moving so slowly that the

French had time to gather at least 10,000 men and attack as the British tried to embark. Notwithstanding the courageous efforts of Howe and his sailors to cover the infantry's retreat, Bligh lost between 750 and 1,000 men killed, wounded, and captured. It was an episode more humiliating than militarily significant, but the fiasco of St.-Cas helped convince Pitt to send troops to the direct aid of Frederick and Ferdinand, a policy he had ridiculed not six months before.[10]

Historians have taken Pitt's ability to reverse himself in questions of policy as evidence of intellectual flexibility, and indeed it was. But it was also much more, for Pitt's abrupt abandonment of his previous course reveals three distinctive features of his situation in the aftermath of Louisbourg: elements that together enabled him to exercise almost sole control over British strategy and policy from 1758 through 1760. The first derived from the temporarily abnormal configuration of British politics, in which no effective opposition existed to constrain his actions. The duke of Newcastle was nervous—justifiably so—about Pitt's indifference to the costs of the war, worrying that the financiers in the City of London would become unwilling to satisfy the government's bottomless appetite for credit. But while his money-anxiety would make the duke yearn for the peace that Pitt spurned, that alone would not make him withdraw from what by 1758 had become a solid partnership. Newcastle, admiring Pitt's willingness to accept responsibility, conceived a dogged loyalty to him, while Pitt came to trust Newcastle's judgment in matters of patronage and finance. Since Newcastle was the only politician in England capable of bringing the secretary down, his support in effect guaranteed Pitt's political survival. Newcastle's refusal to grant offices to Pitt's would-be critics shielded him from effective opposition in the House of Commons. Pitt so much appreciated this that his tilt toward engagement in Germany in part reflected his growing regard for Newcastle, who continually pressed him to concentrate on the European war instead of the expensive empire-building that Pitt preferred.[11]

Of course Newcastle's support could not prevent a disorderly opposition from arising among the independent backbenchers in Parliament, men who habitually opposed any measure likely to raise their taxes, diminish their local authority, or expand the power of the state. Pitt, however, was fully capable of protecting himself on that front. In part his reputation as a politician above party and his previous eminence as an opposition figure preserved his standing with the country M.P.s, but he also preserved their affections by refusing to increase taxes on land and corn and by proposing to rely upon militia instead of regulars to defend against invasion. The establishment of a national militia in 1757 had indeed proven especially useful in maintaining good relations with the backbenchers for, as Walpole observed, "by the silent *douceurs* of commissions in the Militia" the conservative squires "were weaned from their opposition, without a sudden transition to ministerial employment."[12]

Pitt's power over policy, like Newcastle's command of patronage, ultimately derived from the king's confidence, without which—as the duke of Cumberland himself had learned the hard way—no one could survive in office. Royal support, then, was the critical second element in Pitt's algorithm of power, and that was growing ever more secure. Pitt quite deliberately cultivated the king by committing substantial subsidies, and eventually troops, to the defense of Hanover; meanwhile, the conquest of Louisbourg fired George's imagination to such a degree that he endorsed Pitt's plan to expel France from North America for good and all. From the fall of Louisbourg onward, in the frail old king's one good eye Pitt could do no wrong, while he reserved the deafest of the royal ears for any complaints—even Newcastle's—about the expense of the war.[13]

So firm indeed was the king's support that Pitt remained unconcerned when his relations with Leicester House, once so ardent, cooled in the fall of 1758. The dowager princess, the prince of Wales, and the prince's tutor, Lord Bute, still opposed the Crown's heavy commitment to defending Hanover, and Pitt's newfound willingness to send troops to reinforce Prince Ferdinand had put a great strain on his relations with them. The final break came when the king refused to receive the Leicester House favorite General Bligh after the disaster of St.-Cas. The prince and Bute complained to Pitt of the king's callousness, but Pitt refused to curry favor on Bligh's behalf and, irritated by Lord Bute's insistent letters, finally broke off correspondence with him. The prince fumed at Pitt's refusal "to communicate what is intended to be done." "Indeed my Dearest Friend," the prince wrote to Bute, "he treats both you and me with no more regard than he would do a parcel of children[. H]e seems to forget that the day will come, when he must expect to be treated according to his deserts."[14] And indeed, Pitt *did* forget. The staunchness of the king's support had given him more freedom of action than any first minister since Robert Walpole and enabled him to indulge the megalomaniacal streak that he had never fully repressed. From Louisbourg onward, George II's approbation meant that Pitt would feel little personal constraint in making his decisions, even as Newcastle's loyalty freed him from those limits that were merely political.

The third factor that allowed Pitt to control policy was the institutional character of the British war effort—or, more properly, the lack of strong institutions to stabilize and give continuity to it. Although the army and navy had both produced substantial bureaucracies to deal with supply, finance, and other technical functions, neither had developed anything approaching a general staff. The armed forces and the government lacked organizations to gather intelligence or to present Pitt with reasoned estimates of enemy—or allied—strengths and capabilities. No minister, no agency, had the authority to supervise defense policy; the Crown's nominal chief military officer, the secretary at war, was not ordinarily even a member of the cabinet, and his duties consisted almost exclusively of presenting financial estimates to Parliament and dealing with legal issues affecting the services.[15]

The absence of bureaucratic machinery gave Pitt the ability to control strategy and policy personally, but it also imposed upon him a workload that not even he, at his most manic, could sustain. He had turned for help not to the secretary at war, Viscount Barrington—a man he despised as a hack—but to the first lord of the Admiralty, Lord Anson, and to the commander in chief of the army, Lord Ligonier. By late summer 1758, Anson and Ligonier had learned to cooperate better than any two service chiefs in British history and in effect were functioning as Pitt's rudimentary general staff. Ingenious, vigorous, experienced, and loyal, they offered the advice he needed to make sound policy and the administrative expertise necessary to keep the armed forces capable of performing the missions he might assign. Capable as they were, however, Anson and Ligonier could not provide sound intelligence estimates on which Pitt might base his decisions.[16]

In fact no one could, and throughout the war Pitt relied largely on instinct and private advice to decide where he should concentrate his forces to take maximum advantage of the weaknesses of the enemy. This meant that he made decisions about where to send military expeditions with a casualness that would have been unthinkable had any trustworthy intelligence service existed to offer him advice. In the absence of accurate information about enemy and allied forces alike, success did not always crown his decisions: had he known more about Prince Ferdinand's army, for example, he might well have declined to send thousands of men to reinforce a general who had already decided to assume the defensive.[17] Yet Pitt's willingness to respond to suggestions, together with his generally reliable ability to distinguish sensible from crackpot schemes, led to some of the most important breakthroughs of the war. Finally, when something happened to work, Pitt was opportunistic enough to capitalize on his success. Thus in 1757 he had taken the advice of Thomas Pownall in replacing Lord Loudoun and encouraging the colonies to cooperate voluntarily in return for reimbursements, and once the fruits of those changes were clear to see, he was prepared to pursue them to the end, regardless of expense. In the same way, in 1758 Pitt had listened to an even less likely figure than Pownall and parlayed a visionary scheme into one of the war's more spectacular coups.

In this case, the man with a plan had been Thomas Cumming, a Quaker merchant from New York who had approached Pitt with information about France's trading stations on the west coast of Africa—weakly defended posts rich with slaves, gold dust, ivory, and gum senega (the sap of the acacia tree, also known as gum arabic—a product critical to the sizing and dyeing of silk, and always in short supply in Britain). In return for a trade monopoly in Senegal, Cumming offered to guide an expedition to the region and to negotiate with the native rulers for aid. At the beginning of 1758, Pitt had appointed the enterprising Quaker as his political agent and had sent him to West Africa with a small naval squadron (two ships of the line and four auxiliary vessels carrying a couple hundred marines). When this minute force appeared before the unformidable walls of Fort Louis on the Senegal River at the end of April, the French commandant promptly surrendered, the resident factors swore allegiance to George II, and the British took control without losing a man.

The return to England of Cumming's ships, deep-laden with slaves, gold, silver, and four hundred tons of valuable gum, prompted Pitt to dispatch a second expedition to seize France's remaining African posts, Fort St. Michaels on the island of Goree and a slave-trading factory on the River Gambia. By the end of the year, all of it was in British hands. French silk manufacturers had been deprived of the gum senega they needed; sugar planters in the French West Indies had been deprived of the supply of slaves without whom they could not survive; the French privateers who had previously preyed on the Anglo-American slave trade had lost their only secure base of operations on the African coast. By the same token, British textile makers no longer had to buy their gum from the neutral Dutch at high prices, and British sugar planters found their profits growing as a new supply of slaves lowered labor costs. Uncharacteristically for wartime, the pace and the profitability of trade between the mother country and the sugar islands were on the upswing. And all of this had been possible because William Pitt, who would once have had trouble finding Senegal on a map, had been willing to listen to a buccaneering Quaker who had had the persistence to seek him out.[18]

Pitt's virtually unassailable political position, his robust combination of flexibility and opportunism, his suggestibility, and his ability to exploit whatever measures seemed to work all furnish the backdrop to the

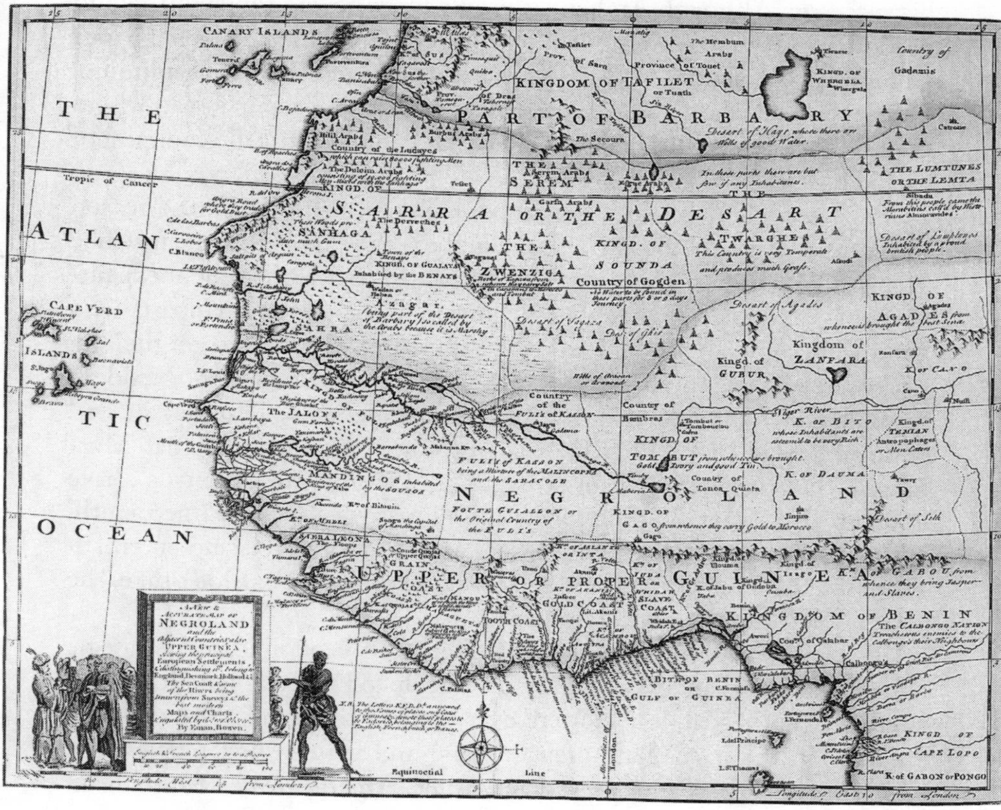

Negroland. Emmanuel Bowen's *New and Accurate Map of Negroland and the Adjacent Countries* (1760) shows the location of Fort Louis, at the mouth of the "Sanaga" (Senegal), the longest river depicted. Goree lies to the south, just below Cape Verde and fifteen degrees north latitude; the next river to the south is the Gambia, site of the slave factory seized in early 1759. Bowen responded to English interest in the commercial potential of the region by carefully portraying the location of the gum forests on either side of the Senegal River, as well as the region's other resources: gold, ivory, "good Tin," and slaves. *Courtesy of the William L. Clements Library at the University of Michigan.*

important moves he made in September 1758. The news from Louisbourg and Senegal, together with his fading hopes that a decision would soon be gained on the battlefields of Europe, only increased his determination to strip France of her empire while Frederick and Ferdinand held the line in Europe. Thus even before Pitt had finished formulating plans for 1759 he took two steps that would be of great consequence for the coming year's campaigns. The first came on September 18 when he issued orders relieving Abercromby from command and appointing Jeffery Amherst as his successor. Although Amherst was only forty, he had shown himself to be both competent and successful, qualities combined in no previous American commander in chief. In him Pitt recognized an able administrator who knew how to follow orders as well as give them: a man whom the colonials could trust, and to whom Pitt could entrust the conquest of Canada.

Pitt's second step was to organize—and once the hurricane season was safely over, to dispatch—an amphibious expedition against the French West Indian island of Martinique. Like the Senegalese expedition, this venture originated in a suggestion from an interested party who knew something about the local scene and who happened to get the secretary's attention. In this case it was William Beckford, a nonresident sugar baron of Jamaica, alderman of London, member of Parliament, and political confidant of Pitt. He had informed the secretary that Martinique "has but one town of strength . . . ; all the inhabitants . . . have not victuals to support themselves and numerous slaves for one month, without a foreign supply. The Negroes and stock of that island are worth above four million sterling, and the conquest easy. . . . For God's sake," he concluded, "attempt it without delay."[19]

To capture Martinique would confer both economic and strategic advantages: the island was roughly as valuable to France as Jamaica was to England (both islands exported over twenty thousand tons of sugar annually in the immediate prewar years) and it furnished a base from which French privateers preyed on Anglo-American merchantmen in the West Indies. But Martinique was worth more to Pitt than either commerce or strategy alone would indicate, for it represented a diplomatic counter valuable enough to be exchanged for Minorca. As Newcastle never failed to remind him, the nation could sustain Pitt's monstrously expensive war only so long as the financiers in the City of London went on lending the government money. An irresolvable credit crisis—and one had threatened to become irresolvable as recently as August—would force the government to ask France for terms. Martinique would be Pitt's ace in the hole.[20]

Pitt began planning the expedition in September. On November 12, six thousand troops, aboard sixty-four transports, together with eight ships of the line, a frigate, four bomb-ketches, and a hospital ship, sailed from Plymouth. To commit so many men and ships to the West Indies made Anson fret that England might be unable to stave off a French invasion, but Pitt was well past caution. When the House of Commons reconvened in November it proved as cooperative as he could have wished. Without objection the M.P.s approved the largest budget in

British history, nearly thirteen million pounds sterling, for the coming year. Over half of this staggering sum was to be borrowed, and nearly half of the expected tax revenues were to be assigned to pay interest on the skyrocketing public debt. Nevertheless, Horace Walpole quipped, "you would as soon hear *No* from an old maid as from the House of Commons"; Pitt had become its "absolute master." And Pitt's plans for 1759, declared in general terms to the Commons at the beginning of their session and then dispatched in the form of orders to military officers and colonial governors, left no doubt that he intended to become the absolute master of more than just 558 compliant M.P.s.[21]

In Europe, Pitt proposed to stand by Prussia financially and to honor the commitment, now firmly in place, to support the army of Prince Ferdinand with troops as well as money. The subsidy treaty with Hesse, currently under negotiation, was to be renewed with increased payments that would continue for two years after the conclusion of the war. The navy, lately so successful in restraining the French fleet, would maintain its operations in the English Channel, the Bay of Biscay, the North Sea, and the Mediterranean; would put pressure on the shipping of neutrals like the Dutch and the Danes, who sustained what was left of France's foreign trade; and would support the operations of the East India Company's troops on the subcontinent by opposing France's Indian Ocean squadron. These were all strategically defensive missions; there were of course also offensive operations under way against Goree on the West African coast and Martinique in the Caribbean. To sustain such massive maritime commitments, Anson's shipbuilding program would continue to receive the highest priority. Already the Admiralty was pressing the very limits of British capacity for ship construction; various improvements were being introduced into the design of both frigates and line-of-battle ships; and every effort was being made to raise the number of seamen above the 71,000 currently in service—the largest number in the history of the Royal Navy. The army, with a current strength of 91,000 men, was to be increased by another 10,000 if it was possible to do so without taking the politically difficult step of impressment. At present the army was so heavily committed in America—and now in the West Indies and Germany, to boot—that barely 10,000 men would be available in early 1759 for the defense of the home isles. This in turn meant that the militia, which had been authorized in 1757 and funded in 1758 but never yet embodied, would have to take up the slack. Preparations for raising the territorial regiments were therefore to be stepped up in the spring. Pitt hoped the full force of 32,000 men that had been authorized would be raised and put into service by summer.[22]

These measures added up to the most extensive, expensive, and well-thought-out military preparations in British history. Yet all of them were subordinate to what was to be the year's principal effort: the conquest of Canada. On December 9, Pitt wrote to the governors of the northern colonies requesting twenty thousand provincial troops for the coming campaign: "at least as large a Body of Men as . . . for the last Campaign, and even as many more, as the Number of . . . Inhabitants may allow." As in the previous year, the king would provide the provincials with arms, ammunition, tents, and supplies, and Parliament would "grant a proper Compensation" for the colonies' expenses, "according as the Active Vigour and strenuous Efforts of the respective Provinces shall justly appear to merit." These troops were to be used "for invading Canada by the way of Crown Point, and carrying the War into the Heart of the Enemy's Possessions." To the governors of Pennsylvania and the southern provinces went a similar request for "several Thousand Men to join the King's Forces in those Parts, for some Offensive Operations against the Enemy."[23]

To Amherst, Pitt sent a series of more detailed orders directing him to invade Canada either by way of Lakes George and Champlain or by way of Lake Ontario and the upper St. Lawrence River; to refortify the south end of Lake George and the Forks of the Ohio; to reestablish an advanced post at the site of Fort Oswego, to mount an expedition against Fort Niagara, and (if possible) to proceed against French posts farther to the west. Pitt also informed Amherst that he had assigned James Wolfe to an independent command that would invade Canada from Louisbourg by way of the lower St. Lawrence. Amherst was to detach troops from his present command to rendezvous with Wolfe at Louisbourg so that the expedition would be able to depart "as early in the Year, as on or about, the 7th of May, if the season shall happen to permit."[24]

There was nothing in all of these instructions that Amherst would have found surprising, except perhaps that last provision, for he had seen nothing and heard little of Wolfe in more than half a year. Yet this feature of Pitt's plans for 1759 would have been instantly recognizable to anyone familiar with the secretary's habits as a decision maker. Wolfe had excused himself from his duties on Cape Breton in September and had taken ship for England, where he hoped both to recover his health (which was, in truth, atrocious) and to campaign for an independent command in America. Even while in America, Wolfe had maintained steady contact with his family and influential friends, writing vivid letters that magnified his personal role in the winning of Louisbourg and cast Amherst as an excessively cautious fuddy-duddy. Thanks to such thoughtful preparation, when Wolfe arrived in England he was already being lionized, in influential circles at least, as Louisbourg's real conqueror.[25]

As soon as he was well settled at his London club Wolfe wrote to inform Pitt that he had come back to repair his constitution, but that he had "no objection to serving in America, and particularly in the river St. Lawrence, if any operations are to be carried on there." Suggestible as ever—and seemingly drawn to this strange young officer, whose personality was as streaked by manic egotism as his own—Pitt altered his plans in late December, giving Wolfe command of the expedition against Québec, and even (with some difficulty) convincing the king to promote him to the temporary rank of major general.[26]

Wolfe's appointment to the Québec expedition completed Britain's strategic program for 1759. How it would play out remained to be decided by forces and fortunes uncontrollable by the will, and even the furious energy, of William Pitt.

CHAPTER 31

Ministerial Uncertainties

1759

THE RESULTS OF the campaigns of 1759 are now so well known that it requires deliberate imaginative effort to recapture the uncertainties of the year's first nine months. In London the whole period from February through April was taken up with a budgetary crisis of the direst sort, as the ministers failed to find ways to finance the massive deficits that the Commons had so obligingly approved in December. At the root of the problem lay two related factors: a severe shortage of specie (the result of large shipments of gold and silver coin abroad to support the war efforts in America and Germany), and an intractable disagreement among the ministers over what new taxes could be laid to finance the debt. This combination made the directors of the Bank of England and indeed the whole British financial community so jittery that government bonds began selling at the steepest discounts of the war, even though trade was booming and public optimism about the outcome of the conflict had never been higher. At the same time, reports of French preparations for launching an invasion across the Channel worried every minister except perhaps Pitt. The slowness with which militia regiments could be raised—less than half their projected strength had been embodied by June—only compounded the anxieties of those who, like Newcastle, expected the worst.[1]

Nor were the early developments in the West Indies campaign particularly promising. The British expeditionary fleet had reached Barbados after an uneventful voyage on January 3 and there had joined the West Indies squadron for the attempt on Martinique. Two weeks later the British naval commander, Commodore John Moore, and his army counterpart, Major General Peregrine Thomas Hopson, launched their invasion. On the sixteenth they landed six thousand troops near Fort Royale, one of the two principal towns on the island's west coast, and its naval base. Although the landing itself went off easily, the terrain proved extremely difficult and resistance rapidly stiffened on the following day—even as it became clear that it would be as impractical to besiege the French fortifications by land as it would be to bombard them from the harbor. Hopson withdrew his troops to the ships on the evening of the seventeenth. When a trial attack on the defenses of St.-Pierre, the island's main town, met with heavy opposition two days later, Hopson and Moore agreed to abandon the attempt and look northward to what they hoped would be easier pickings, the island of Guadeloupe.[2]

But Guadeloupe, too, proved a tough nut to crack. On January 23, Moore's ships shelled and burned the island's main town, Basse-Terre. The French defenders withdrew to take positions in the mountains near the town; thus on the following day when Hopson's troops took possession of the ruined settlement and its fort they met no opposition but gained only a slender foothold. Hopson, a cautious, aged officer who had been on active service since Marlborough's day, was already in failing health. He lacked both the energy and the inclination to do more than construct field fortifications to make Basse-Terre secure. He may have hoped that that would be enough to make the French surrender. Soon he realized that they had no intention of giving up, and a few unsuccessful probes into the countryside showed that they could neither be driven from their highland defenses nor forced to give battle. Meanwhile tropical diseases were destroying his army with an efficiency that no mortal enemy could match. Within a week after the landing, a quarter of the British troops were too ill to stand; by late February at least 2,100 of them had to be evacuated, and no more than 3,000 men remained who were still capable of fighting. On February 27, with his army in possession of not one more square mile of territory than it had held a month earlier, a fever finished off old Hopson himself.[3]

The new commander, Major General John Barrington, was the younger brother of the secretary at war, but it had not been political connections that had earned him his position. Like Amherst and Wolfe, he had been only a vigorous young colonel at the time Lord Ligonier had given him a temporary rank for service in the New World and made him second-in-command for the expedition. Immediately after Hopson's death Barrington showed his mettle by proposing to launch amphibious raids on the periphery of the island; but before he could escape the static misery of Basse-Terre, word arrived that a French fleet had been sighted, heading for Martinique. On March 13, Commodore Moore therefore ordered his squadron to Prince Rupert Bay on the neighboring island of Dominica, from which they could block any attempt that the French admiral, Maximin de Bompar, might make to relieve Guadeloupe. This was a prudent and necessary move, since Bompar had with him eight ships of the line and three frigates; but it indefinitely postponed Barrington's chances of conquering the island from the sea.[4]

News of these discouragements reached London in May, when other reports advised that the militia units had not yet been raised and French shipwrights were filling Le Havre with shallow-draft barges to be used in an invasion. In western Germany all auguries looked grim. Prince Ferdinand had left winter quarters in April and moved against the French base at Frankfurt am Main, only to encounter a superior enemy at the crossroads village of Bergen. There, on April 13, one of France's ablest generals, Victor-François, duc de Broglie, inflicted a defeat on the prince that cost 2,500 casualties and sent his army reeling northward across Hesse. Over the next month, the French put Ferdinand and his increasingly dispirited troops at greater and greater disadvantage; in another six weeks' time they would succeed in cutting him off from his base of operations at Minden on the Weser River, thus regaining command not only of Hesse but of the southern approaches to Hanover.[5]

As to the fate of the Canadian campaigns, Pitt knew next to nothing. Wolfe had left Portsmouth on February 14, but it would be June before word would arrive in England that he and his men had made a safe crossing. Amherst's letters, by contrast, arrived regularly, filled with discouraging reports of how provincial politics, obstinacy, and inefficiency hindered his operations. At the beginning of June, all that Pitt knew about operations on the far side of the Atlantic was that neither of the Canadian invasions could yet have gotten under way; that the invasion of Guadeloupe had stalled; and that a French squadron—one easily capable of foiling Barrington's operations—had reached the West Indies. Those who saw the secretary during these weeks thought him discouraged, defensive, tense.[6] What news might come next, only God knew; but Pitt knew only too well that unless it was word of some substantial progress, Newcastle might be tempted to force negotiations and forestall the victory that, Pitt believed, lay almost within his grasp.

Although Pitt would not know it until the middle of June, the fate of the West Indies expedition had been decided before the end of April. Bompar did not immediately sail from Martinique to threaten Barrington, enabling him to leave a small force to hold Basse-Terre and launch amphibious attacks on the settlements that rimmed the island. The plantations near the coast had already suffered badly from the raids of Anglo-

American privateers; now they proved virtually defenseless against even the fifteen hundred troops that Barrington could spare for his raids. With most of the French regulars tied up in the mountains outside Basse-Terre, the task of defense fell mostly to the planters, who quickly lost both the will and the means to resist. On April 24 the island's leading men, ignoring their governor's pleas to fight on, asked Barrington for terms of surrender. He replied with notably liberal conditions, which in effect would allow Guadeloupe's planters to continue as neutrals for the remainder of the war, enjoying the same trading privileges as British colonists while being guaranteed security in their persons, properties, and the practice of the Catholic faith. On May 1 the island's governor, facing the inescapable reality that the planters had abandoned him, signed the capitulation.[7]

And not, from Barrington's perspective, a moment too soon. Even as the ink was drying on the surrender documents Bompar's fleet—lately reinforced by eight line-of-battle ships and three frigates from France—put in at the desolated settlement of Ste.-Anne, landing arms, supplies, and 2,600 troops to reinforce the island's defenses. The planters on the scene, however, knew how much they stood to lose by repudiating the surrender and refused to cooperate. Bompar, fearful of being trapped by Moore's squadron, slipped back out to sea.[8]

Bompar's withdrawal put the outcome of the invasion beyond question. Britain had acquired a prize of greater value than anyone at Whitehall realized. Only later did it become clear that Guadeloupe and its neighboring island of Marie-Galante (which the British seized before the end of May) were as rich as or richer than Martinique. Between them Guadeloupe and Marie-Galante had a population well in excess of fifty thousand (over 80 percent of whom were slaves) and more than 350 plantations producing sugar, cocoa, coffee, cotton, and other tropical goods. These planters, starving for the trade that the war had stifled, immediately began shipping their produce to Britain and its colonies in return for the goods and slaves that they desperately needed.[9]

Within a year after the conquest, Guadeloupe sent more than ten thousand tons of sugar, valued at £425,000, to Great Britain. In return the islanders imported great quantities of wrought iron, manufactures of all sorts, and four or five thousand slaves a year. To the North American colonies the planters exported huge volumes of molasses, in exchange for provisions, barrel staves, and other wood products. By 1760 Guadeloupe would provide Massachusetts rum distillers with nearly half of the molasses they used—fully three times as much as from the leading British West Indian source, Jamaica.[10] Even Pitt could hardly have anticipated how quickly the alchemy of trade would transmute the humiliation of conquest into profits for the conquered. Largely by luck, the British had hit on the surest formula by which their empire could grow large and rich, while securing its conquests at the least expense in blood and treasure. Whether they would also have the good fortune to understand the secret of their success, of course, remained to be seen.

CHAPTER 32

Surfeit of Enthusiasm, Shortage of Resources

1759

THE HEARTENING NEWS of Guadeloupe's capitulation came to Pitt's hand on June 13, just as the North American campaigns upon which his greatest hopes rested were about to begin. Bad weather had delayed the Québec expedition—the ice was not out of the river until the end of April, and heavy fogs kept Wolfe from meeting his naval escort at the Isle of Bic until June 18. The slowness of launching the year's other campaigns, however, resulted from the equivocal outcomes of 1758. The problem was not that provincial morale had collapsed—although Abercromby's defeat had in fact made enlistment much more difficult in New England—but rather that the previous year's exertions had nearly exhausted the northern colonies. Particularly in New England it initially seemed impossible to comply with Pitt's wish that the provinces field "at least as large a Body of Men as . . . for the last Campaign."[1]

Massachusetts, like the rest of New England, had supported the previous campaign to the utmost of its ability. Even before its great effort of 1758 the Bay Colony had spent £250,000 on the war, most of which it had had to borrow. Adding the expenses of 1758, Massachusetts by the outset of 1759 carried a public debt of over £350,000 lawful money, the repayment of which, with interest, would cost the province nearly £500,000 by the end of 1761. Since the annual revenue that the province could generate from taxes on polls, land, and trade seldom exceeded £100,000, it did not take a financial genius to see that the province had long passed the point of technical insolvency when the 1758 campaign ended. Without Parliament's reimbursement for part of the province's expenses in 1756, which arrived in the form of seven great chests of gold and silver in January 1759, Massachusetts would almost certainly have defaulted. Moreover, the numbers of men the Bay Colony had enlisted in its provincial forces in 1758, some seven thousand in all, comprised only a part of the total that had served in the campaigns. Including artificers, bateaumen, rangers, men serving in regular regiments and aboard Royal Navy ships, as well as privateers and the sailors aboard the province's own frigate, the whole number in service during 1758 far surpassed ten thousand men—more than a quarter of the whole service-eligible male population of the colony. The extraction of so many workers from the rural economy had greatly concerned the province's legislators even before the 1758 campaigns had begun; the prospect of duplicating the effort in 1759 offered cause for real alarm.[2]

On March 10, 1759, the assemblymen of Massachusetts had therefore informed Governor Pownall that "the House find it necessary to take into Consideration the Distresses brought upon the Inhabitants of the Province by Means of the great Levies which have been made from Year to Year since the War [began], and particularly by Means of the disproportion'd Number of Men that were in the Service the last Year[.] The House likewise consider, that . . . the Government is now burdened with a very heavy Load of Debt, and the Charges arising from the Services of the last Year are unpaid; and that it will be extremely difficult to procure such a Sum of Money as will be necessary to be immediately advanced in Case of engaging in any further Service." They therefore agreed to make only five thousand men available for provincial service in 1759.[3]

Pownall responded with characteristic vigor, appealing to their patriotism and sense of duty, alternately wheedling and threatening (the Bay Colony had led in the war effort so far—and besides, Parliament would see any falling-off as cause for cutting reimbursements), offering what concessions he could (several hundred of the men would be used in an all-provincial expedition to fortify the Penobscot River region, a popular idea among legislators eager to secure new lands for the colony's farmers), and even allowing them a recess to consult their constituents. Finally, on April 17, the General Court caved in and agreed to increase the number of enlistments. Nevertheless, the representatives warned Pownall,

> The Distress brought upon the Inhabitants is . . . extremely great. The Number of Men raised this Year, we are sensible, [cannot be] equal to that of the last. The Assembly then made the greatest Effort that has ever been known in the Province. They looked upon it to be the last Effort; they had no Expectations that it could be repeated,

> and it was really so great as to render it impracticable for us to make the like a second Time. The Number of our Inhabitants is since then much lessened: Some were killed in Battle; many died by Sickness while they were in Service, or soon after their return Home; great Numbers have inlisted as Rangers, Artificers, Recruits in his Majesty's Regular Forces, and for other Branches of the Service.

The war had diminished the province's capacity, if not necessarily its will, to carry on the fight:

> We are told, that we are the leading Province; We have been so for many Years past, and we have been as long unequally burdened. We have borne it patiently, although we have seen our Inhabitants leaving us, and removing to other Governments to live more free from Taxes; and a few Years ago, for this Reason alone, four of our principal Towns refused any longer to submit to our Jurisdiction, and another Government [Connecticut] found a Pretence for receiving them, and they are not yet returned to us.
>
> Under these Difficulties we are still willing to afford every reasonable Aid in our Power. A further Impress would distress and discourage the People to such a Degree, that . . . we are bound to decline it. But great as our Burthens are, we have now engaged a Bounty more than double what has ever yet been given by the Province, in order to procure a voluntary enlistment of Fifteen Hundred Men, over and above the Five Thousand already raised; and we have Reason to hope that this Bounty will be sufficient, and have the Effect your Excellency desires.[4]

And indeed the new bounty—of fourteen pounds in provincial treasury notes, payable in installments with interest accrued over the next two years—did prove sufficient to raise the number of volunteers required. No smaller inducement could have done it, for the demand for men in the armies was also driving up the wages that civilian laborers could command, whether in ordinary work or in war-related occupations. Any attempt to draft militiamen and pay them only the standard provincial wage of one pound sixteen shillings per month would have triggered resistance more massive than the province's minuscule coercive capacity could have overcome: this was why the representatives had felt "bound to decline" the option of impressment. The assemblymen of the Bay Colony had reason to believe that their province had no more left to give the cause of empire. Such exertions as they agreed to make would have been impossible if they had not been sure that Parliament would make good the expense of mounting this supreme effort to conquer Canada.[5]

Indeed it was only the promise of reimbursement that enabled the northern colonies to raise men for the 1759 campaigns in numbers comparable to those of the previous year. The Connecticut Assembly cited the same reasons as its Massachusetts counterpart in initially agreeing to enlist 3,600 men. After a certain amount of prodding, it raised the number to 4,000 but it was only Amherst's thinly veiled threat to advise Parliament against making further reimbursements that finally induced the assembly to offer "some Considerable additional Encouragements" and secure the enlistment of the final 1,000. Like Massachusetts, the announcement of a large additional bounty alone enabled Connecticut to meet its goals. "The Colony before this was greatly dreined of Men and seemed almost impracticable to raise many more yet as the Assembly took all imaginable Methods to rouse & revive the Spirit of the People, these additional Levies were made with uncommon Dispatch and beyond the Expectation of Many."[6]

As Connecticut went, so went New Jersey, New York, New Hampshire—and even Rhode Island. In each colony the numbers raised finally approximated those of 1758; in each, virtually all the troops were raised without resorting to impressment; and in all, the regiments were finally filled after the assemblies agreed to pay extremely high bounties for enlistment. New Jersey once more raised a 1,000-man regiment, notwithstanding the loss of 500 men in each of the campaigns of 1756 and 1757 and the heavy participation of Jerseymen in privateering ventures; but it managed this feat only by offering a twelve-pound bounty—high enough to attract recruits from outside the province. New York enlisted 2,680 men but had to offer a fifteen-pound bonus to keep pace with the competition from Connecticut and New Jersey. New Hampshire, a sparsely populated colony with a long frontier to defend and little commercial wealth, recruited 800 provincials for the campaign, also by paying an enlistment bonus. Rhode Island's assembly tried to meet its obligations without offering a bounty, by retaining its soldiers from 1758 in pay over the winter. Disease and desertion, however, required new enlistments, which in the end could only be had at a considerable expense. To raise the final 115 men for the colony's 1,000-man regiment it was necessary to offer over twenty pounds in province bills of credit, plus a knapsack, a blanket, two months' advance pay, and the promise of a ten-pound gratuity to be paid when Canada finally capitulated.[7]

Thus in 1759 it was possible for New Jersey, New York, and the New England colonies to field nearly seventeen thousand provincials to support the invasion of Canada: a phenomenal number given the exertions of the colonies in the previous year, and in every sense a number that would have been inconceivable without parliamentary reimbursements. But it was not only Parliament's money that induced the northern colonies to cooperate at this level, for they now routinely showed themselves willing to resolve, with perfect amicability, issues that had crippled the war effort when Loudoun was commander in chief. Nothing had been more disruptive than quartering controversies, but there were no more of these after 1758. Every colony in which British troops were stationed built barracks at public expense and funded the incidental charges for firewood, salt, and small beer by voluntary acts of their legislatures. Massachusetts went so far as to billet regular recruiting parties in designated private houses, reimbursing the householders from province funds when their expenses exceeded the fourpence per day per man that the army paid for accommodations. Recruiters went about their business with little opposition, even in Boston, where justices of the peace now dealt summarily with anyone who tried to obstruct enlistment, instead of harassing the redcoats themselves.[8]

Similarly, issues of short-term finance, always a problem when Braddock, Loudoun, or Abercromby needed money, no longer troubled relations between the commander in chief and the colonies. Amherst was as short on operating funds as any previous commanding general had ever been, indeed shorter: the military chest he had taken over from Abercromby was almost empty, and his expected funds from England were slow to arrive. By mid-March 1759, he had no money on hand at all and found himself compelled in effect to kite checks in order to prepare for the coming campaign: when he issued warrants he did so with the request that recipients not present them to the paymaster general until money came from England. Faced with the prospect of having to suspend operations for lack of funds, he appealed to the New York Assembly for a loan of £150,000 against future payments from the Treasury. No colonial legislature had ever agreed to loan money on such terms to a commander in chief. When short on cash, Loudoun and Abercromby had always had to borrow from individual merchants, at very high interest; thus Lieutenant Governor De Lancey, himself a merchant, fully expected the New York Assembly to refuse the loan. To his surprise, they did not, and the delighted Amherst accepted the money with expressions of gratitude for the legislators' "loyalty to the king and their Zeal for this service." Since this loan could in no sense have been coerced, and since the assembly's merchants must have known that they would lose an opportunity to line their own pockets by making it, Amherst's praise was not just flattery.

Loyalty and zeal must in fact have motivated the assemblymen in ways unknown to their notably self-interested predecessors.[9]

The most plausible explanation for such evident changes of heart is simple enough. The colonists, so long antagonized by British policies and behavior, by 1759 had become convinced that they were full partners in Pitt's imperial adventure. Previously, no matter how much the colonies' legislators may have approved individually of the effort to expel France from North America, collectively they had never been willing to reach for that goal by surrendering local control and local prerogatives to a distant authority. But now they were being asked to help, not ordered to participate in a war that almost everyone wished to see carried to a successful conclusion—and that shift from the imperative to the subjunctive mood removed the last misgivings of legislatures even so wary as those of New York and Massachusetts. Reimbursements were crucial because they removed the practical fear of public bankruptcy, but the enthusiasm for the common cause that Amherst called "Zeal" was the only engine that could drive the campaigns against Canada to their completion. So long as they thought the British were treating them as tools, the colonists had been suspicious, surly, uncooperative; once they thought that Pitt and Parliament were appealing to them as equals, they could indeed become zealots.

But if that was the lesson that 1759 offered, it was not the only one. A different and in some degree contradictory message could also be read in the replies of the provinces to the south of New York to Pitt's appeal for renewed efforts against the enemy. Neither Georgia nor South Carolina had faced serious external threats and neither had participated heavily in the war to date; nor did either offer more than token support now. Georgia was so poor, sparsely populated, and exposed that it had to be defended by regulars, while South Carolina raised only five provincial companies for garrison duty. North Carolina did nothing at all. Maryland, its assemblymen locked in an endless, irresolvable dispute with the proprietary family, had long done nothing, and continued to do it.[10] Only the two colonies that had been most directly threatened by French and Indians on their frontiers, Virginia and Pennsylvania, chose to participate actively in the campaigns of 1759. Both did so in ways that were less than satisfactory to Amherst and Pitt but that reveal something of their legislators' views on the war and its consequences.

The return of peace to the backcountry was the single most important fact so far as either Virginia's or Pennsylvania's legislators were concerned, and insofar as it was necessary to maintain a military presence at the Forks in order to keep the French from returning, both agreed to raise provincials for yet another year. Thus Virginia's House of Burgesses moved with unaccustomed dispatch to authorize the enlistment of men to be employed under Amherst's general direction, outside the province. Yet the Burgesses saw no reason to duplicate the effort of 1758 and voted to raise only a single regiment of a thousand men, to be commanded, now that Washington had resigned, by Colonel William Byrd III and seconded by Washington's old subordinate, Lieutenant Colonel Adam Stephen. The Burgesses intended that the regiment should be used only to secure the Forks, not that it would be marched north to participate in the invasion of Canada. Another five hundred men, to be drawn from the militia, would garrison the colony's chain of forts and defend the settlers who had already begun to move back beyond the Blue Ridge. Eventually two hundred of these militiamen would be sent to Pittsburgh as artificers, to help build Fort Pitt.[11]

Although Pennsylvania's assembly eventually authorized 3,060 provincials to be raised for service—a small increase over the previous year's number—it moved slowly because its members once more found themselves absorbed in the old dispute with the proprietors over the taxation of Penn family lands. The return of peace to the frontier had allowed politics to resume its habitual course, as antiproprietary assemblymen sought to establish their right to raise revenue by taxing the proprietors' estates; but whereas Governor Denny had found it prudent to cooperate with the antiproprietary majority in the previous year, he now resumed the defense of his employers' interests and refused to assent to the tax bill that the assembly sent him. In April, with no troops yet raised and Amherst worried that none would ever be, the commander in chief finally pressured Denny into signing the tax bill, despite the fact that doing so would cost the Penn family about forty thousand pounds. Their victory won, the legislators quickly agreed to raise the number of provincials Pitt had requested and even offered a fifty thousand–pound loan to Brigadier General John Stanwix (Forbes's successor as regional commander), so that he could undertake the year's operations without delay.[12]

Indeed at this point the legislators were positively eager for Stanwix to begin refortifying the Forks and improving Forbes Road, for everyone realized that Pittsburgh was too important a position to risk losing once more to the French. Equally salient for the Pennsylvanians, however, was the knowledge that the western posts were largely being held by Virginia provincials, and that Byrd's regiment was already nearly completed. If Pittsburgh was too important to lose to the French, it was *far* too valuable to be surrendered to the Virginians.[13]

Thus even the temporary removal of the enemy threat to the frontiers of Virginia and Pennsylvania—and no one doubted that the French would try to recapture the Forks—was enough to permit the rival colonies to resume their competition for control over the Ohio Country, even as it also allowed the endemic internal factionalism of Pennsylvanian politics to reemerge. The colonies had shown themselves to be capable of cooperation, and even enthusiasm, in support of the war. But their underlying disunity—their localism and inveterate competition—had by no means been extinguished. While the previous year had shown that Virginians and Pennsylvanians could act together under a British commander, it could hardly have been clearer that such cooperation was only possible under limited, and limiting, conditions.

The war had lately taken a promising turn because of Pitt's change of policy and because Amherst was capable of behaving with more tact and restraint that any previous commander in chief. The prospect of winning a great victory over the French had thus made the Americans into British patriots—of a sort. As Amherst and his superiors saw it, however, all their enthusiasm for the empire, all their protestations of loyalty, were superficial appearances beneath which the colonists remained unchanged. Although it was by no means an entirely just inference, British observers in 1759 tended to conclude that Parliament's subsidies had bought the provincials' enthusiasm. No matter how much zeal he might profess for the common cause, you could still scratch a colonist and, beneath his patriotic veneer, find only—an American.

CHAPTER 33

Emblem of Empire

FORT PITT AND THE INDIANS

1759

IF INTERNAL POLITICAL frictions and intramural distrust delayed the opening of the campaign to consolidate British control over the Forks, problems stemming from the previous year's operations hindered it even more severely once it began. Building Forbes Road and supplying the troops along it had destroyed thousands of wagons and perhaps tens of thousands of horses that the army had leased for the expedition; Forbes's death had slowed the settlement of the owners' claims against the army. These conditions hardly encouraged civilians to come forward when Stanwix began to appeal for wagoners and teams, and through most of the spring his army suffered an acute shortage of transport. Meanwhile the state of the troops holding Pittsburgh and Fort Ligonier was becoming perilous. Provisions could be brought in only in heavily guarded pack trains until the woods cleared of snow and enough grass grew in the meadows to feed the herds of cattle that would have to be driven westward to sustain the big summer garrisons. It was the middle of June by the time drovers brought the first cows to Pittsburgh, where the soldiers had been eating horses and dogs. When the first cattle arrived, the troops butchered forty of them on the spot and, barely pausing to cook them, devoured the beasts without pausing to distinguish entrails from meat.[1]

The shortage of supplies at the western posts was more than a matter of discomfort for the garrisons. When the French had withdrawn, they had taken with them, destroyed, or dispersed to friendly villages all the provisions and trade goods that they had stored at Fort Duquesne. The Shawnees, Delawares, and Mingos of the valley therefore found themselves facing a winter subsistence crisis: the first and most tangible effect of their decision to make peace with the Anglo-Americans. To retain their cooperation, the trade that Forbes and the Pennsylvania authorities had promised had to be opened as soon as possible; as long as it was not, the possibility remained that the Indians would revert to their old French suppliers. Fort Duquesne's commandant, Captain François-Marie Le Marchand de Lignery, had withdrawn only as far as the Allegheny River post of Fort Machault, or Venango. During the winter he sent out appeals for aid not only to such traditional French allies in the *pays d'en haut* as the Potawatomis, Ottawas, and Ojibwas, but to the defecting Shawnees and Delawares themselves. All winter long Lignery was able, even with a skeleton force, to keep up his raids on the pack trains that were barely sustaining Pittsburgh and Fort Ligonier. There was no doubt that when the rivers cleared of ice in the spring and he once more built up his troops at Fort Machault, he would return. As winter slowly waned in 1759, the only real question seemed to be whether the Ohio tribes would stand by the Anglo-Americans or change sides once again.[2]

A vigorous trade at the Forks was therefore critically important if the British hoped to maintain control in the west, but disorganization and competition among those who wished to dominate it perilously delayed its revival. As part of its obligations under the Easton agreements, the Pennsylvania Assembly in 1758 had passed a law creating a provincial monopoly over the Indian trade. Stores were to be established in each of the province's three great valleys: at Fort Allen on the Delaware, Fort Augusta (Shamokin) on the Susquehanna, and Pittsburgh on the Ohio. There "honest, prudent, and Sober Men" would sell goods to Indians at fixed prices as a means of countering the abuses and correcting the destabilizing effects of unregulated trade; there missionaries, schoolmasters, and "other sober and Virtuous Men" were to take up residence to "civilize and instruct" the Indians. It was an ambitious and philanthropic scheme, endorsed by the Friendly Society, but conditions in wartime Pennsylvania made it supremely unrealistic. Shortages of capital and poor planning prevented the colony from establishing its store at Pittsburgh before September 1759, and in the interim Israel Pemberton—at the urgent request first of Forbes, then of Stanwix—did his best to fill the need with a private establishment. With great difficulty and expense Pemberton's employees managed to get a pack-train load of goods to Pittsburgh before the end of April 1759. These items and the shipments that followed helped to preserve the goodwill of the Ohio tribes, but they came too late to relieve the pressure on Pittsburgh's slender supplies of trade goods and food during the winter. Thus the garrison's commandant, Lieutenant

Colonel Hugh Mercer, allowed many small traders (primarily farmers from Virginia with produce and whiskey to sell) to operate an all-but-unrestricted trade at the Forks.[3]

The final element in this rapidly developing muddle of Indian commerce—all of it technically illegal, since it contravened Pennsylvania law—was heralded by the arrival of George Croghan in June, at the head of a long pack train bearing the official gift from the Crown to the Ohio tribes. Croghan, as Sir William Johnson's deputy agent in the Ohio Country, came to Pittsburgh no less as a diplomat than as a trader in his own right. In both capacities he intended to prevent the establishment of a Pennsylvania monopoly trade at the Forks. As official representative of the superintendent of Indian affairs he was eager to rebuild a lively trade in the valley as a means of tying the Indians closely to the British interest; therefore he granted licenses to several Philadelphia mercantile houses, enabling their representatives to carry on commerce in the Indian villages themselves—the setting in which, he knew, the Ohioans preferred to do business.[4]

Croghan was also eager to establish himself at Pittsburgh because he had land-speculating interests there to protect. Back in 1749, the wily Irishman had purchased from the Iroquois Council the rights to 200,000 acres near the Forks. Because he thus had a plausible claim to owning the land on which the British army intended to build Fort Pitt, Croghan had every reason not only to be present in the vicinity but to seek to dominate it commercially. If the British retained control of the Forks, he knew, both Indians and whites would gravitate to the fort. What better position could any businessman be in than to trade goods to the Indians for deerskins while selling land to the arriving whites? Who was better qualified than he to supply them with the provisions and tools they would need to turn their wilderness freeholds into working farms?[5]

The Ohio Indians, of course, needed the goods that the traders sold and to that degree welcomed even the chaotic commerce that grew up at Pittsburgh in 1759. They did not welcome dishonest treatment, a permanent British military presence, and the potential of thousands of white settlers swarming into the Ohio Country; as the year wore on, however, it grew steadily clearer that those were what they were actually getting. Tamaqua, Pisquetomen, Shingas, and the other chiefs had agreed to terms of peace that, they believed, promised the British would open a trading post at the Forks and then withdraw their soldiers across the mountains as soon as the French threat had been eliminated. By the middle of July the French had not reappeared, but the English were coming in ever-larger numbers and obviously preparing to build something more

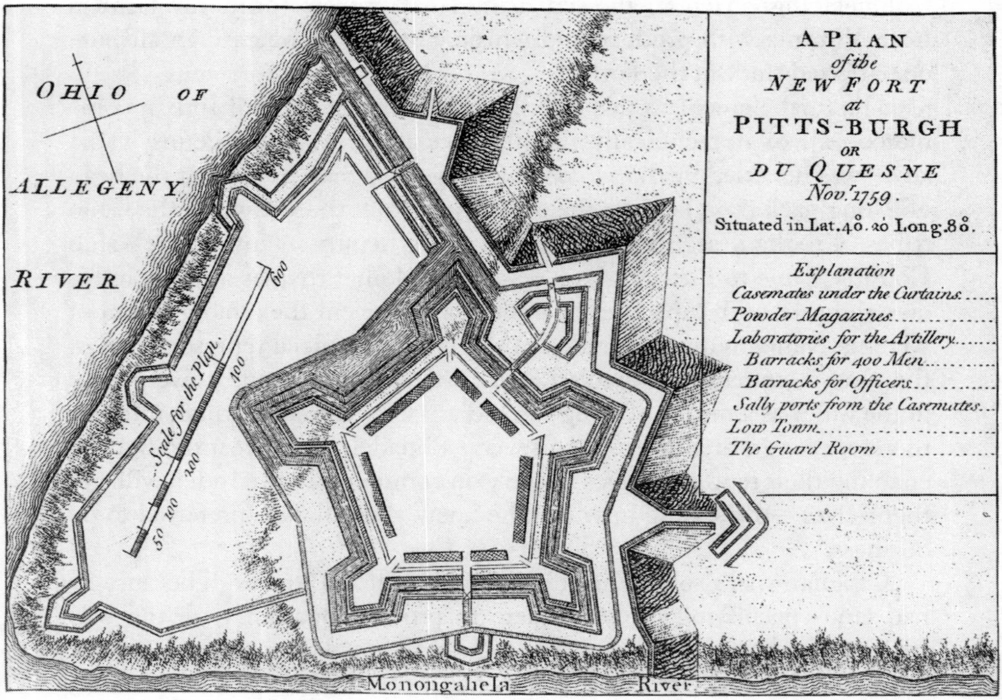

Fort Pitt. Unlike the cramped Fort Duquesne it replaced, Fort Pitt was a powerful pentagonal fort with walls nearly sixty feet thick at the base, substantial outworks along the riverfront, and a ditch, covered way, and glacis that extended across the width of the peninsula. It was, however, poorly defended against other enemies: in the floods of 1762 and 1763 water stood from five to seven feet deep within the walls. The fort, never fully repaired, decayed until it was finally abandoned in 1772. From Rocque, *A Set of Plans and Forts. Courtesy of the William L. Clements Library at the University of Michigan.*

formidable than a trading post, or even Fort Duquesne. A British army engineer was laying out a huge pentagonal fort at the junction of the Monongahela and the Allegheny: a fort that would measure more than four hundred feet from bastion tip to bastion tip, with outworks that would enclose more than seventeen acres, interior barracks to shelter a thousand men, and embrasures that could mount more than a score of cannon. By mid-August soldiers and artisans were busily constructing a sawmill, felling and hauling trees, quarrying sandstone, mining coal, burning lime, making bricks, and shoveling and hauling the tens of thousands of cubic yards of dirt necessary to build the fort. On September 10, its inner walls began to rise within a wide glacis and moat.[6]

As early as July 9, Pisquetomen had "put it closely to" James Kenny, the man who ran Israel Pemberton's store, "to tell what . . . ye General [Stanwix] meant by coming here with a great army." All the honest storekeeper could say was that, so far as he knew, the soldiers were there merely to prevent the French from returning, and that "when they were subdued, ye army would be called away home." Pisquetomen also wished to think that this was so, for although he reminded Kenny that "Quakers always should speak truth & not lie," he "commended" the answer and went on his way. By the time Kenny left Pittsburgh two months later, neither he nor Pisquetomen would have thought this answer plausible. No one could have mistaken Fort Pitt, ten times the size of Fort Duquesne, for a trading post.[7] It was a symbol of dominion, an emblem of empire; and by autumn the Ohio Indians were beginning to discern its meanings only too well.

CHAPTER 34

The Six Nations Join the Fight

THE SIEGE OF NIAGARA

JULY 1759

THE POSITION of the British at Pittsburgh, so precarious at the beginning of summer, had become one of mastery by summer's end—not because anything decisive had occurred at the Forks of the Ohio, but because in July, two hundred miles to the north, an Anglo-American army had seized Fort Niagara. The Niagara expedition, under the command of Brigadier General John Prideaux, had been the first to take the field, beginning its trek up the Mohawk River from Schenectady before the end of May. There could be no better indication of the dramatic shift in the North American balance of power than the fact that when Prideaux's Anglo-American troops reached Oswego on June 27, a thousand Iroquois warriors and Sir William Johnson were waiting to join them.[1]

Onondaga's new willingness to support the British proceeded from the well-founded fear that the Shawnees and Delawares were about to create an independent Indian confederacy in the west: a new regional power that might potentially include French allies like the Miamis and the Munsees, who shared an interest in excluding Iroquois influence from the area south of the Great Lakes. At the Treaty of Easton the Six Nations had reasserted their claims to suzerainty over the Ohio Country, but the leaders of the Confederacy knew only too well that that same agreement had recognized the Delawares' right to negotiate directly with the government of Pennsylvania, and neither the Delawares nor any other people on the Ohio would gladly resubmit to Iroquois dominion.

Sometime during the fall or early winter of 1758, the League Council seems to have concluded that the only means of restoring substantial influence over the Ohioans was by cooperating directly with the British, and they therefore began to send the necessary signals. At the beginning of January an Iroquois delegation at Pittsburgh took aside the commandant, Hugh Mercer, to warn him privately that "the Shawanese and Delawares [intended to] Join in the Confederacy against [the Iroquois, and that] their ruin would soon be compleated, unless a very powerfull aid is afforded them by the English." The Six Nations' spokesmen were obliged to maintain strict secrecy, Mercer reported, because "they observe too great an intimacy Still Subsist[s]" between the Ohio nations and the French. Yet, he continued, "at the Same time they appear to be convinced that the French may be easily drove from this Country; that one or two Defeats will make their Indians drop their Alliance, and universally join the English."[2]

Soon thereafter, emissaries from Onondaga evidently also approached Sir William Johnson and offered what they knew he could not refuse—military aid in an expedition against Fort Niagara. The northern superintendent hurried to his desk on February 16, writing to inform Amherst that he would require "a large Augmentation" of Indian gifts for a meeting in the spring. If he had the support he needed, he wrote, he would "be able to engage a large Body of Indians" for a campaign against the last French stronghold on Lake Ontario. "I flatter myself," he wrote, "and have some Reason to expect that (as Affairs are now Circumstanced) if an Expedition was designed against Niagara . . . thro' the Country of the Six Nations, I shou'd be able to prevail upon the greater Part if not the whole of them, to join His Majesty's Arms."[3]

This was indeed a remarkable change, particularly in Johnson's suggestion that perhaps even "the whole of" the Iroquois would "join His Majesty's Arms." With the exception of thirty or forty Oneidas who had accompanied Bradstreet to Cataraqui the previous year, only the Mohawks (to whom Johnson was related by marriage) had shown any willingness to aid the British, and even they had done little since the death of Chief Hendrick in 1755. Throughout the war Iroquois warriors, and particularly the Senecas, had aided the French as participants in frontier raids if not as formal allies. Yet when Prideaux's field force reached Oswego, warriors from all of the Six Nations were there to greet them, including even substantial numbers of Senecas.

This reversal was so abrupt that no British officer—not even Johnson—was sure of its meaning, and no one thought to look beyond the

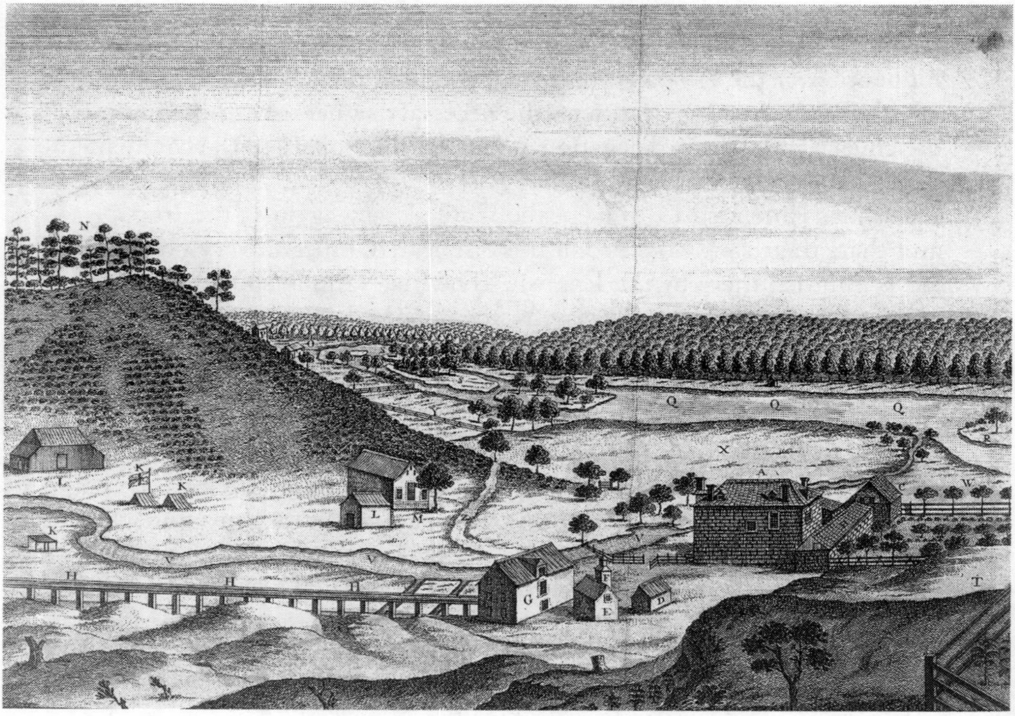

Fort Johnson, c. 1759. Unlike its successor, Johnson Hall (1763), an elegant Georgian mansion, Sir William Johnson's base of operations during the Seven Years' War was a thoroughly utilitarian complex, including a campground for visiting Indian delegations, several storage structures, a mill, and stout, defensible living quarters. The lack of outward-facing windows in the main house, center right, suggests that Johnson's highest priority was security. His modest original house is partially visible at the bend of the Mohawk, just beyond the flank of the hill at left. *Courtesy of the William L. Clements Library at the University of Michigan.*

Iroquois themselves to understand its origins. The "nativist" impulse among the western Indians was so recent, so much a product of the war and its upheavals, that the Anglo-Americans could scarcely have been expected to see what was going on in the Ohio villages. But resistance in the valley was already developing a powerful religious dimension, and the leaders of the Six Nations were not as slow as the whites to grasp its significance. Because Iroquois influence in the west had always depended upon Onondaga's ability to manipulate the Europeans diplomatically, any exclusionary resistance movement among the Ohio nations would gradually wear away the Iroquois position. Insofar as the roots of resistance were religious, however—insofar as the Ohio Indians became convinced that contact with the Europeans had spiritually contaminated the Iroquois, making them in effect indistinguishable from whites—the influence of the Six Nations would vanish like smoke in the wind.[4]

Thus during the winter of 1758–59 the chiefs at Onondaga concluded that the only way to restore their ascendancy over the interior tribes was to harness British military power to serve Iroquois ends. If Fort Niagara were to fall to the Anglo-Americans, the French would lose control of the critical portage to Lake Erie and their power in the west would shrivel. Yet merely to exclude the French from the Ohio Country would not enable the Iroquois to control the region. The Anglo-Americans somehow had to be encouraged to remain at the Forks in force, for only British hegemony could guarantee Onondaga's influence over the western Indians. The virtually simultaneous approaches of Iroquois emissaries to Johnson, urging an expedition against Niagara, and to Mercer, informing him of the dangers posed by an incipient western confederacy, had formed complementary halves of a single Six Nations strategy. In the end, therefore, it was not pressure from the Europeans but the Confederacy council's well-founded fear that the Iroquois would be unable to reestablish influence over their former client peoples that made the Six Nations abandon neutrality for an open military alliance with the British. No doubt the chiefs at Onondaga thought of this move as a temporary, tactical accommodation—only one of many pragmatic policy shifts in the long history of relations between the Confederacy and the British Crown. But this time the tilt toward the British would prove irrevocable, and its consequences would exceed any that the Iroquois could have intended. For the commitment to an active alliance, in fact if not in name, meant the acceptance of dependency. Once French power in the west had been broken, Britain's economic and military might would serve the needs not of the Iroquois, but of the empire.

Once begun, the Niagara campaign was no prolonged affair. General Prideaux—yet another junior colonel serving as a temporary brigadier—did not tarry at Oswego. He detached a thousand men to begin rebuilding the fort there, then hurried on toward Niagara on June 30 with the remainder of his troops and Johnson's warriors. For four days they rowed westward along the wild south shore of Lake Ontario, then put in about three miles from their goal, a handsome gray granite "castle" overlooking the lake from a bluff at the mouth of the Niagara River. Fort Niagara was by no means as easy a target as Fort Frontenac had been in the previous year, for its commandant, a forty-seven-year-old regular captain named Pierre Pouchot, was also an experienced military engineer, and he had greatly improved the post's defenses. When the British arrived on July 6, they faced the only fort in the North American interior that was pro-

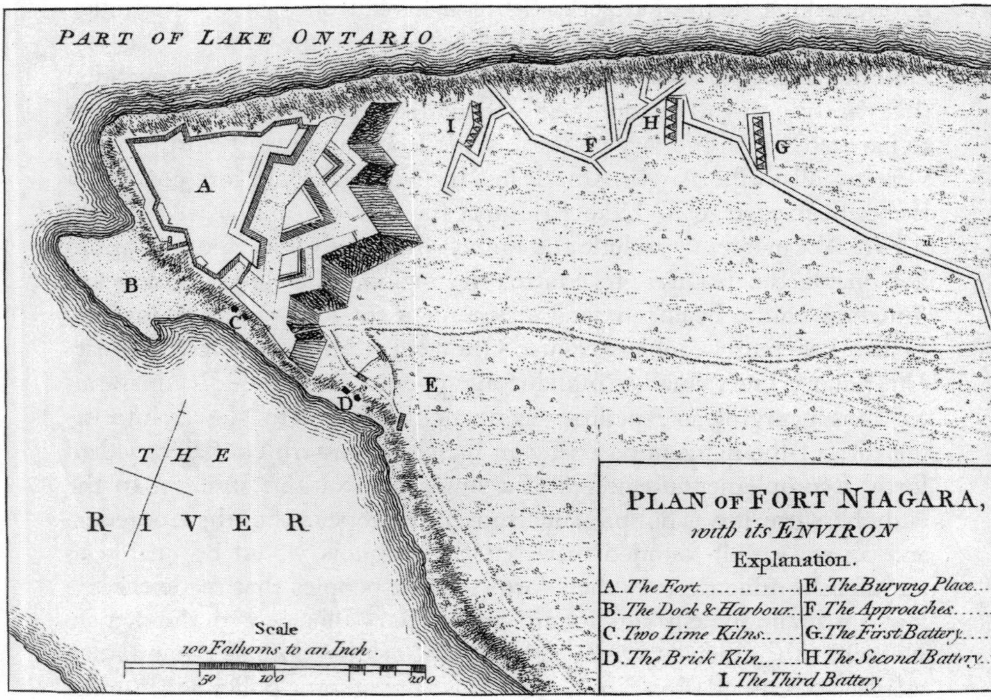

The Siege of Niagara, July 10–25, 1759. This map of Fort Niagara and its outworks, from Rocque's *Set of Plans and Forts,* shows the state of the siege as of about July 20, when the third battery was in place. *Courtesy of the William L. Clements Library at the University of Michigan.*

tected by extensive, European-style earthen outworks: a glacis, ditch, and covered way stretching across the peninsula and screening the castle and other buildings within the ramparts.[5]

Captain Pouchot was one of the most capable regular officers in America, and under ordinary conditions he would have been able to defend the fort and its crucial portage against any feasible assault. This was so for reasons that went beyond the impressive fortifications he had built. First of all, he had taken great care to cultivate relations with the Iroquois. The local band of Senecas had for so many years held a monopoly as carriers on the Niagara portage that he had had no reason to doubt their continued loyalty. They in turn had assured him he would have ample warning should any British force pass through Iroquoia to attack his post, and—since the timely communication of such intelligence had been the cornerstone of the Iroquois-French entente in the west for more than a half century—he had believed them.

Secondly, Pouchot knew that the best time for a British attack had already passed. Niagara had been most vulnerable in the spring, before he had returned from Montréal with men to reinforce its winter garrison. When no British force appeared in May, and when his Seneca informants had brought him no word of any British movement in the Mohawk-Oswego corridor by the beginning of June, Pouchot had felt confident enough to send 2,500 of his 3,000 men off to reinforce Lignery at Fort Machault, in preparation for the planned summer's campaign in the Ohio Valley. Vaudreuil had instructed him to detach this force, but Pouchot would doubtless have done it on his own authority, for he shared Vaudreuil's strategic vision. If Lignery and his troops could descend the Allegheny before the British had a chance to build up their strength at the Forks, the French would regain command of the Ohio passage to Louisiana, Indian raids on the Virginia and Pennsylvania backcountry would resume, and the British would have to divert substantial numbers of men to frontier defense. New France would be saved from invasion, once again.[6]

Therefore no one could have been more surprised than Captain Pouchot on July 6, when Iroquois warriors attacked a working party outside the walls of the fort: it was his first indication that anything out of the ordinary was afoot. Quickly ascertaining that thousands of British and American troops were landing nearby, he recalled his fatigue details, buttoned up the fort, and sent urgent word to Fort Machault for Lignery to return with the force intended for the Ohio Country. He had on hand fewer than five hundred men to defend his post, along with perhaps a hundred Indians—principally Senecas as bewildered as he was at seeing so many of their kinsmen in the company of an Anglo-American army. Now Pouchot needed time, a commodity that seemed all the more precious as the British opened their first siege trenches a half mile from the fort on July 10. Thus on the next day, although the etiquette of sieges scarcely sanctioned it, he called a truce to allow Kaendaé, the chief of the Niagara Senecas, to approach Johnson and his Iroquois supporters and see if he could dissuade them from participating in the attack.

Kaendaé was astonished by what had taken place, and he berated Johnson—who merely smiled in response—for "having plunged his Nation into bad business." Over the next three days, the Iroquois war chiefs endeavored to convince Kaendaé that continued support for the French was no longer tenable, while he in turn tried to persuade them that the wisest course was to let the Europeans fight their own battles and withdraw, along with his band, up the Niagara River as far as La Belle Famille. He almost succeeded. In the end Johnson managed to keep "his"

Iroquois from taking Kaendaé's advice by promising them the first chance to plunder the fort after it fell; even so, they took no active part in the siege after the conference ended on July 14. At this point Pouchot—reluctant to have within his walls warriors of dubious loyalty, who would at best be unenthusiastic fighters—permitted Kaendaé's people to withdraw under a flag of truce. This episode, which nearly ended with the British-allied warriors joining the Niagara Senecas at La Belle Famille, puzzled Prideaux and Johnson, who worried that the Iroquois were about to resume their old preferences for neutrality. In fact the negotiations had served every purpose the Six Nations could have wished, for they had avoided the unacceptable prospect of fratricidal bloodshed at the same time that they had done nothing to improve the ability of the French to resist.[7]

Pouchot had bought a little time, but his adversaries had not ceased to drive their trenches forward during the cease-fire. After Kaendaé's Senecas passed through the lines to safety on the fourteenth, British cannoneers opened fire from an advanced battery less than 250 yards from Fort Niagara's glacis. Now the garrison's only hope lay in the arrival of Lignery's relief force from Fort Machault. On the seventeenth, British howitzers began shelling the fort from across the Niagara River, enfilading the works from the rear and dominating the river- and lakefront approaches. By day and night the digging continued, until on the afternoon of the twentieth heavy guns opened fire from a breaching battery sited murderously close (80 yards) to the fort's covered way. At that point even the sudden death of General Prideaux—the back of his head blown off when he stepped in front of a mortar, while visiting a battery at dusk—could not slow the progress of the siege. Sir William Johnson assumed command, but his limited capacities as a field commander could not slow operations that continued as if by their own momentum.[8]

By the twenty-third the Anglo-American trenches had crawled almost the whole length of the peninsula; the nearest lay within musket range of the fort's outer defenses. Inside the walls, red-hot shot and mortar bombs fell in a lethal hail. Shell-shocked men, sleepless for days, were refusing to mount the walls. All the guns in the battery of the main bastion had been blown off their carriages and a great hole had been shot through the parapet; unable to make proper repairs under fire, the defenders were reduced to cramming bales of furs and skins into the breach.[9]

At this point, when all seemed lost, Lignery's relief force appeared in the Niagara River above the falls. In all there may have been as many as sixteen hundred French, Canadians, and Indians; they seemed to one observer like "a floating island, so black was the river with bateaux and canoes." Pouchot's hopes soared; but Johnson, whose Indian observers had also kept him well informed, had time to order out a force to block the road from the portage to the fort. By the following morning Johnson had sent Iroquois emissaries to warn Lignery's Indian allies of what was waiting for them. Meanwhile, Lieutenant Colonel Eyre Massey of the 46th Regiment had had time to construct a log breastwork and abatis across the road near La Belle Famille and to position approximately 350 regulars and a hundred New York provincials behind it. An approximately equal number of Iroquois warriors, acting on their own initiative, quietly took up positions in the surrounding woods.[10]

When Lignery's force came marching down the road toward the British at about eight o'clock, his Indian allies had heeded the Iroquois messengers' warning and decided not to participate in the battle. It was, therefore, perhaps six hundred French regulars, *troupes de la marine,* and Canadian militiamen who charged the British abatis and, at a range of about thirty yards, ran headlong into volley after volley of British musket fire. Only about a hundred men, mostly wounded, survived long enough to be taken prisoner; among them were nineteen officers and cadets, including one of the most experienced of New France's Indian diplomats, Joseph Marin de La Malgue. The remainder, who broke and ran for their lives, were pursued by Iroquois warriors who, it would seem, either killed or captured most of them; the French would report that at least 344 men were killed or captured, but the number may have been much higher. Lignery himself—veteran of more than a dozen campaigns, hero of the Battle of the Monongahela, and the last commander of Fort Duquesne—was found among the French wounded in the abatis. He lived long enough to realize that no French expedition would ever take back the Ohio Country.[11]

Captain Pouchot's field telescope revealed that a battle had taken place at La Belle Famille, but it could not disclose the totality of Lignery's defeat. He learned of that only when the British ceased shelling the fort late in the afternoon and sent an emissary to invite him to surrender with guarantees of personal safety for his men but without the honors of war. Pouchot, his last hope gone, accepted Johnson's terms on July 25. Over the next two days he and his garrison were loaded aboard British bateaux for transportation to New York, and imprisonment. Many would be repatriated to France; Pouchot himself would be exchanged in December and return to help defend Canada once again.

The massacre that Pouchot had feared would follow the surrender never came. The Iroquois contented themselves with the plunder of

Niagara and its outlying storehouses, which contained furs, skins, and trade goods of vast value. Having lost few or no warriors in the siege, they had no pressing need to adopt more captives than those they had taken after the engagement on the portage road. Most of all, however, their docility reflected the Six Nations' need to maintain the goodwill of the British, on whom they necessarily had to depend if they hoped to regain influence on the Ohio.[12]

With the French safely gone, Johnson moved quickly to consolidate control over the west end of Lake Ontario before his Indians too took their leave. Dispatching whaleboats to reconnoiter Fort Toronto, he learned that the garrison had burned it and retreated. Immediately therefore he set about establishing friendly relations with the local Chippewas, in the hope (he informed Amherst) of "Settling an Alliance between Us & them distant Nations" of the *pays d'en haut*. With this accomplished, and with little interest in hanging about to superintend the repair of Fort Niagara, Johnson handed command over to a regular lieutenant colonel and returned to Oswego. Amherst, anxious to have in charge a commander who knew something about running an army, dispatched his best administrator, Brigadier General Thomas Gage, to take command of the western posts. Sir William would linger yet a while at Oswego, where he could more efficiently attend to the activities at which he excelled: the management of Indian affairs, the pursuit of his business interests, and the cultivation of his laurels. He had held his last military command of the war.[13]

Although the French would post a small detachment at Cataraqui to observe the Anglo-Americans, the loss of Niagara effectively rolled back their western frontier to Oswegatchie, about 115 miles upriver from Montréal. Montcalm, realizing the danger of invasion by way of the upper St. Lawrence, sent his second-in-command, the chevalier de Lévis, along with as many troops as he could spare from Québec, to defend Montréal. But the British had already delivered their greatest blow in the west, for Gage was too cautious to risk sending troops from Oswego down the St. Lawrence.

The effects of Niagara's loss thus would be felt not at Montréal but in the posts that remained on the Great Lakes and the Ohio. The French now had no choice but to abandon Forts Presque Isle, LeBoeuf, and Machault. The settlements in the Illinois Country would remain under French control but would have to shift for themselves; they would have no further communication with New France during the war. Similarly, the forts and trading posts on the upper Great Lakes, from Detroit to Michilimackinac and beyond, would also remain awhile in French hands, but the British occupation of the Niagara portage meant that they would only wither for lack of supplies. No western commandant would persuade any of the Indians of the *pays d'en haut* to send warriors to Canada's aid. For the first time in its history, New France would face its enemies alone.

CHAPTER 35

General Amherst Hesitates

TICONDEROGA AND CROWN POINT

JULY–AUGUST 1759

JEFFERY AMHERST learned of Prideaux's death and Niagara's fall on Saturday night, August 4, when he was busy taking possession of Fort St. Frédéric at Crown Point, the spot a dozen or so miles from Ticonderoga where Lake Champlain narrows to a dramatic strait, then widens to dominate the broad Champlain Valley to the north. This was the second post the French had blown up and abandoned at his approach, a circumstance for which he was grateful but one that left him puzzled and ill at ease. Amherst, never inclined to show his emotions anyway, responded to this uncertainty as he typically did, by clamming up—and slowing down.

For a variety of reasons Amherst had been late in taking the field. The Niagara expedition and his own had shared a common base of supply, in Albany, and despite John Bradstreet's expertise as quartermaster general, even that gifted officer could only attend to one major task at a time. The New England provincials, on whose axes, picks, and shovels Amherst would have to rely in the sieges he expected to direct, had as usual arrived slowly. Finally, Amherst habitually preferred security to speed. Before he felt ready to venture even as far as the head of Lake George, he had improved the road from Fort Edward and built a fortified way station at Half-way Brook. Once he established his base camp at the lake, he had spent a month assembling matériel and beginning construction on the new post, Fort George, that was to replace Fort William Henry. As a consequence of so much deliberation and attention to detail, it had been July 21 before Amherst's men boarded their bateaux and pulled oars for

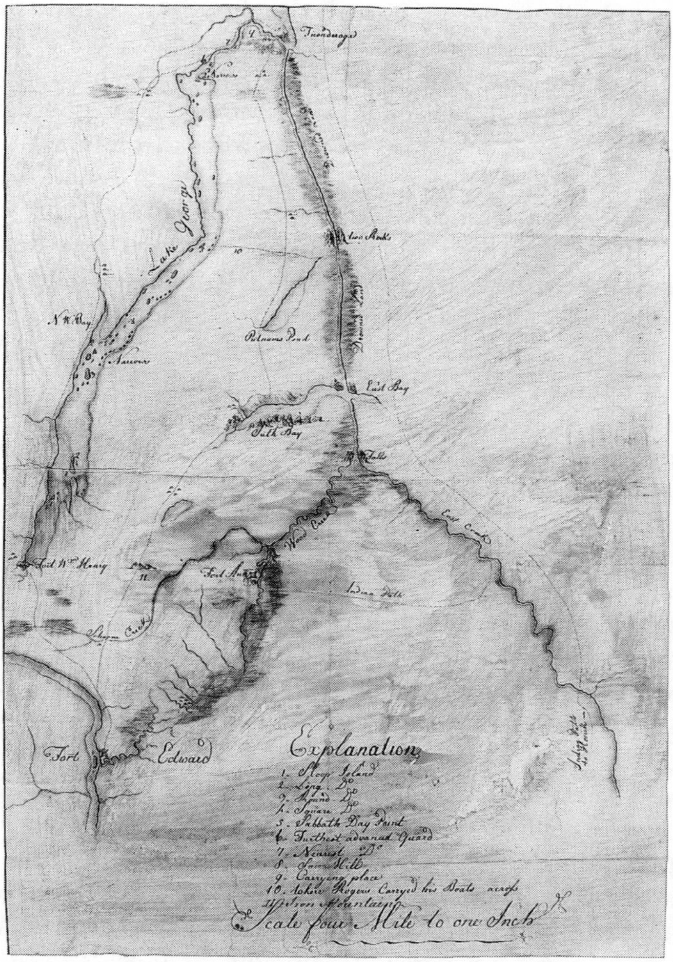

Fort Edward to Ticonderoga, 1759. This manuscript map, from the papers of Thomas Gage, shows what had become by 1759 a thoroughly familiar geography of lake, stream, and marsh. The preferred route to Ticonderoga and Lake Champlain remained via Fort William Henry, despite its destruction. As the shading on this map makes clear, the alternative route, along Wood Creek, South Bay, and South River, ran through swampy, difficult ground. *Courtesy of the William L. Clements Library at the University of Michigan.*

Ticonderoga. The seven battalions of regulars and nine of New England provincials in his command, plus nine companies of rangers and a train of artillery, amounted to about ten thousand men: many fewer than Abercromby had taken down the lake the previous year, and, in the mind of the commander in chief, another reason to proceed with caution.[1]

But Fort Carillon, the site of such slaughter in 1758, had fallen just four days after Amherst's arrival on the twenty-second, at a total cost to the attackers of five dead and thirty-one wounded. Amherst's men had barely emplaced their siege cannon when the token force of defenders had spiked their guns, lit a fuse to the powder in the magazine, and retired to Crown Point. There they joined the three-thousand-man army of Brigadier General François-Charles de Bourlamaque, the capable, asthmatic officer to whom Montcalm had entrusted the defense of Montréal's southern approaches. Methodical to a fault, Amherst paused to survey the ruins of Fort Carillon before sending a detachment of rangers ahead to observe Bourlamaque's activity at Fort St. Frédéric. When they returned on August 1 with news that the French had already blown up the post and withdrawn, Amherst ordered his army ahead to take control—and stopped once more to take stock of his position.[2]

By the time the commander in chief learned of Niagara's fall, then, he had gained command of Lake Champlain as far north as Crown Point, a "great Post" which "secures entirely the country behind it." He had also begun to acquire intelligence on the enemy from rangers and deserters and thus knew that the French had withdrawn all the way to Île-aux-Noix, a fortified island at the foot of the lake. But the lack of determined resistance only served to make Amherst more circumspect, and less willing to make a headlong thrust toward Montréal, for two reasons. In the first place, the French had a small fleet of warships on the lake, and he had none. The enemy's schooner and three xebecs mounted thirty-two cannon between them and could easily make hash of his bateaux. Amherst accordingly resolved to wait for his own shipwrights, back at Ticonderoga, to build a brigantine and a large armed raft, or radeau, to protect the army's advance down the lake.[3] The second factor that weighed on his mind was perhaps even more disabling than the lack of naval protection, for he could do nothing about it: he had heard nothing of Wolfe since the beginning of July.

Without some knowledge of the progress of the campaign against Québec, Amherst had no reliable way to interpret the lack of resistance to his army's advance. If operations on the St. Lawrence were tying down large numbers of men, he could proceed against Bourlamaque in relative safety. But Amherst was anything but an optimist by nature and almost certainly expected Wolfe to fail. If this had happened—if Wolfe had fallen back to Louisbourg—Montcalm would be free to shift his forces to Île-aux-Noix and achieve local superiority over Amherst and the five thousand or so men he would be able to bring northward after garrisoning Fort George, Ticonderoga, and Crown Point. For all Amherst knew,

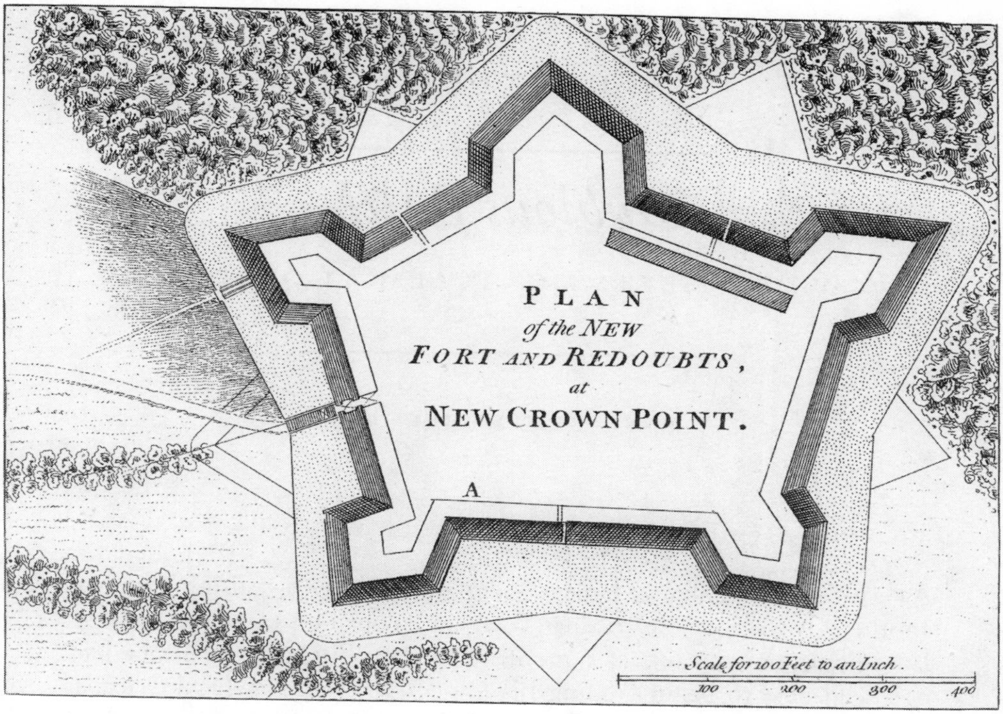

Crown Point Fort, 1759. At least a third larger than its predecessor, Fort St. Frédéric, Amherst's new post was fully as large and expensive as Fort Pitt. And as ill-fated: a chimney fire in 1773 ignited a general conflagration that blew up the magazines and leveled the fort, which was never rebuilt. From Rocque, *A Set of Plans and Forts. Courtesy of the William L. Clements Library at the University of Michigan.*

the withdrawals of the French had been no more than bait to a cunning trap. Île-aux-Noix was eighty miles (three days) down the lake from Crown Point, and he knew next to nothing about its situation. To venture so far from his base of supply, so far from reinforcements, would be to place his whole army and all his gains at risk. Thus in August, Amherst set his men to repairing Ticonderoga and to constructing a new pentagonal fort at Crown Point; to planting gardens; to scouting northward through the woods; and to building roads—one to connect Ticonderoga to Crown Point, another to run seventy-seven miles overland from Crown Point to Fort Number 4 in the Connecticut Valley—the better to secure the supplies he needed to retain his conquests.[4]

Until he had his ships or knew whether Wolfe had triumphed or failed, Jeffery Amherst would be content to build. And wait.

CHAPTER 36

Dubious Battle

WOLFE MEETS MONTCALM AT QUÉBEC

JUNE–SEPTEMBER 1759

AT QUÉBEC in August, James Wolfe was playing a waiting game of another, savage, sort. He, too, had been late to open his campaign, leaving Louisbourg only on June 4, a month later than Pitt had wished; he had not been able to begin landing his 8,500 troops on the Île d'Orléans, below Québec, until June 28. Throughout July he had been unable to dent the city's defenses, either by the relentless shelling of the town that he began on July 12 or by the frontal assault on the French lines six miles below it, which he ordered on the last day of the month: a foolhardy attack that had cost his army 443 casualties, including 210 killed. By the beginning of August, Wolfe was out of ideas and at odds with his brigadiers, three talented, aristocratic officers who had come to distrust his judgment. With no more promising target offering itself, and lacking the strength to drive the French from their defenses, Wolfe therefore "reduced [his] Operations to . . . Skirmishing Cruelty & Devastation," launching a "War of the worst Shape" in the hope of goading his enemy to give battle. By the end of August Wolfe's terrorism had reduced the "agreeable prospect of a delightful country" that had delighted the eye in June—"windmills, water-mills, churches, chapels and compact farm-houses, all built with stone and covered, some with wood and others with straw"—to a smoldering wasteland. A conservative contemporary estimate held that fourteen hundred farms had been destroyed. No one ever reckoned the numbers of rapes, scalpings, thefts, and casual murders perpetrated during this month of bloody horror.[1]

But the defenders of Québec could no more be drawn out of their trenches by British terrorism than they could be driven out by bombardment and frontal attack. In the midst of his brutal enterprise, Wolfe's health broke down. From August nineteenth until the twenty-second he was too sick to leave his bed: by turns wracked by fever and convulsed with pain from "the gravel," or kidney stones, Wolfe despaired of ever forcing a decision, or even of living to see the end of the campaign. Gradually he improved, but by the beginning of September he was sick again and verging on mental collapse. More than a third of his army was unfit for duty, eaten alive by the same fevers that threatened his life; healthy men were deserting to the enemy in alarming numbers.[2] The French had proven themselves more resourceful, and much more difficult to defeat, than he had imagined. But why? And what—supposing his health even permitted him to remain in command—could he do to lure them out of their fortifications, to fight the battle that haunted his feverish dreams?

The French were able to put up so successful a resistance in part because their situation was so desperate—who in Québec could have doubted that New France was fighting for its life?—and in part because, at literally the last possible minute, a small relief convoy had arrived from France. In late April, before Wolfe's transports and their powerful escort could begin to ascend the St. Lawrence, a couple of French frigates and fourteen supply ships had picked their way through the ice in the Gulf of St. Lawrence and slipped up the river, carrying food, reinforcements, and Montcalm's returning aide, Bougainville. These, and ten or so unescorted merchantmen that crept in after them, reached Québec between May 9 and 23. In all, they numbered just two dozen vessels, but few as they were, they had come in time to make Wolfe's task a nightmare. For these ships not only carried five hundred badly needed reinforcements but two commodities that the defenders of New France needed even more desperately than men: food and instructions.[3]

The harvest of 1758 had been the worst of the whole war in Canada, and the winter of 1758–59 the coldest in memory. Without provisions from France, no defense at all would have been possible. Even with sufficient supplies, Canada had too few men left to mount a full defense along every possible invasion route; but Bougainville (who returned bearing the rank of colonel and a knighthood in the order of Saint-Louis) had brought intelligence concerning Wolfe's expedition and its target, and he arrived early enough to alert Québec's defenders of their peril. At the same time, and equally important, he carried detailed instructions from the French court, which were intended to settle the festering dispute between Vaudreuil and Montcalm—a feud that had nearly destroyed the ability of Canada to defend itself. The cultural divide between Canadian and Frenchman, as well as the personal animosity that set the provincial aristocrat against the professional soldier, had aggravated relations between the two men to the point that neither could see the sense in the other's plans. In fact, both had strategic merit; but they were in effect mutually exclusive, and the letters that Bougainville carried determined that Montcalm's conception would prevail.[4]

Vaudreuil saw the problem of defense in light of the proven Canadian strategies of Indian alliance and wilderness warfare. His was essentially a guerrilla's conception of defense, for it rested upon his confidence that although the British might conquer territory, they could never hold it so long as Canada's French and Indian peoples remained united and capable of resisting in the interior. The true security of New France therefore lay in keeping open communication with the tribes of the *pays d'en haut,* for if properly led these warriors could visit such havoc on the enemy's frontiers that the British would eventually be forced to sue for peace. Québec itself might be abandoned to the enemy without disabling the colony's defenses; if the west held the key to Canada's survival, then Montréal was the critical post to defend, and that meant giving priority to manning both the forts that flanked its southern approaches and those like Niagara that protected its links with the *pays d'en haut.* Thus while Vaudreuil's plan envisioned the defense of Québec, its overriding concern was not with improving the city's fortifications, but with evacuating the region's civilian population upriver to Trois-Rivières, halfway to Montréal. The governor-general's strategy thus called for a staged withdrawal rather than a supreme effort to stop the invaders outside the walls of the capital.[5]

Montcalm had seen matters in almost exactly the opposite way. As a conventionally minded European professional officer, he thought it suicidal to dissipate the forces available for defense by holding western posts. In his view the only key to Canada was the city of Québec; the only way to hold it was to concentrate as much force as possible there and oppose to the last extremity the coming invasion. Montcalm did not entirely discount the value of Indian allies, but he distrusted them as uncontrollable, unreliable, and barbarous. The specters of Oswego and Fort William Henry had convinced him that Vaudreuil's preferred approach was no better than a surrender to savagery. Nor did he wish to rely upon Canadians. The rapacity of Bigot and the imperfect discipline of the militiamen, like Vaudreuil's parochial "prejudices" and preference for irregular warfare, had led Montcalm to disdain the military capacities of the people he had been sent to defend. He therefore intended to contract the perimeter of defense to a core region centering on the St. Lawrence Valley from Québec to Montréal. Unlike Vaudreuil's plan, which required dispersion of force, his would maximize the number of disciplined men—regulars and *troupes de la marine*—available to stave off the British attack. If the invaders could be repulsed, Canada might be preserved until a general peace could be concluded in Europe, and the prewar frontiers might be restored diplomatically. But if, on the other hand, the colony should fall to an overwhelmingly strong enemy, at least Montcalm would have conducted an honorable defense. For the diminutive marquis held as an article of faith what so few Canadians seemed able to grasp: that there were more important things in war than winning.

Until Bougainville arrived with the clarifying directives from Versailles, Vaudreuil had directed Canada's defenses. He had decided to reinforce Niagara and to support Lignery's efforts to regain the Forks of the Ohio; by the same token, he had placed little emphasis on repairing Québec's fortifications. After May 10, however, once it was known that the king had given Montcalm the principal military authority in New France, Montcalm's strategic vision prevailed. Hence the order for Bourlamaque to withdraw by stages from the advanced posts on Lake Champlain; thus the sudden emphasis given, in the days before Wolfe's arrival, to constructing entrenchments and emplacing artillery around Québec. By pulling every available soldier into the vicinity of the capital, by mobilizing the region's militia, and by accepting as volunteers both graybeards and boys whose ages ordinarily would have excluded them from serving, Montcalm managed to meet Wolfe's invaders with between twelve and fifteen thousand men. All the regulars in Canada except Bourlamaque's three battalions were there: the *Régiments* Béarn, Guyenne, Languedoc, La Sarre, Royal-Roussillon. So were the militia companies of Québec as well as those from settlements as far up the valley as Trois-Rivières; so too were companies made up of the sailors from the ships that had arrived in May, of refugee Acadians, of three hundred or so Indians (about half of whom were Indian converts from the local missions and the remainder Crees from the remote north, who had heretofore taken no role in the fighting), and even of thirty-five scholars from Québec's Jesuit seminary—a unit so improbable that some wit labeled it the *Royal-Syntaxe.* After years of fighting and few replacements, the regulars were too thin on the ground to do all the fighting, so Montcalm integrated the fittest of the militiamen into their ranks. The rest of the militia he set to work on the prodigious task of fortifying the countryside around the city, turning what was already difficult terrain into a network of obstacles to defy the most ingenious attacker.[6]

Québec stood on the northern shore of the St. Lawrence at the point where the river flowed into a broad basin, its channel widening from three-quarters of a mile to nearly two miles across. Atop a headland, 200 to 350 feet above the water, the Upper Town nestled snugly within walls, looking out across the basin and down upon the houses and docks of the Lower Town as well as the suburbs of St.-Roch and Palais. Immediately below, the St. Charles River flowed into the St. Lawrence, defining the northern boundary of the city's promontory with a steep escarpment. From the confluence downriver for the next three miles or so the northern shore lay low along the basin; then, near the village of Beauport, the land began to rise. From that point onward, bluffs and increasingly steep slopes lined the shore for another three miles, until they climaxed at the spot where the Montmorency River hurled itself off a three-hundred-foot cliff in a fall so spectacular that a contemporary observer could only describe it as "a stupendous natural curiosity." Thus below the town the St. Charles and the Montmorency presented substantial obstacles to the movement of attackers overland, while the shoreline offered few promising footholds for assaults from the St. Lawrence itself. Above Québec, steep wooded slopes, naked cliffs, and bluffs lined the river's northern shore for miles. Behind them lay farmland that, west of the city, flattened into a narrow plateau between the St. Lawrence and the St. Charles, where Abraham Martin, one of Champlain's pilots, had settled to farm in the early seventeenth century. There, on what has ever since been called the Plains of Abraham, the level ground swept gently upward through farms and woodlots to a broken ridge, and then on to the walls of Québec.[7]

Viewed from the river, the least forbidding approach to the city lay on the eastern (downstream) side, and it was there that Wolfe had first probed the French defenses. But Montcalm had strongly fortified the riverbank and the hillsides from the St. Charles all the way to the Montmorency Falls, and Wolfe's inability to crack this defensive barrier had frustrated him into launching his campaign of "Skirmishing Cruelty & Devastation" in August. Montcalm had stationed most of his regular troops along these so-called Beauport lines, where he expected Wolfe to concentrate his attacks. The French commander had, however, also fortified the heights west (upriver) of the city as insurance against the possibility that the British fleet would be able to ride the tides past Québec's batteries. Because the threat seemed less severe upriver, Montcalm had posted militia units to defend those lines, reinforcing them with a thousand picked men under Bougainville—a mobile force poised to repel any effort to land above the city. Montcalm's final measure had been to send his supply ships about fifty miles upriver, to the settlement of Batiscan near Trois-Rivières. This made defenders dependent on a long supply line, which could be cut if the British managed to land above the city. But by refusing to concentrate his provisions and munitions in the city, Montcalm intended to leave himself an out: should Québec have to be abandoned, his army could retreat upriver without losing its supplies.[8]

Montcalm's efficient, conventional disposition of his forces baffled the equally conventional Wolfe. Military operations in America so far had consisted either of sieges or raids, and thus far no full *siège en forme* had failed to bring an attacker victory. But the defenses of Québec were so nearly seamless that Wolfe could not gain a foothold on the north shore of the St. Lawrence from which he could open a formal siege. So long as the French remained able to resupply themselves, and so long as Montcalm could shift his forces freely from one part of the lines to another, Wolfe had little hope of even beginning a successful siege. To decide the issue he needed something that had never yet taken place in America, an open-field battle. Until Montcalm consented to give him one, he could do no more than shell the town, ravage the countryside, and issue bombastic proclamations calling upon the French to surrender. As he explained in a letter to his mother, "My antagonist has wisely shut himself up in inaccessible entrenchments, so that I can't get at him without spilling a torrent of blood, and that perhaps to little purpose. The Marquis de Montcalm is at the head of a great number of bad soldiers, and I am at the head of a small number of good ones, that wish for nothing so much as to fight him—but the wary old fellow avoids an action doubtful of the behaviour of his army." In recognition of this predicament, hoping that perhaps they would approve of an all-out assault on the Beauport lines, Wolfe at the end of August convened his three brigadiers—Robert Monckton, George Townshend, and James Murray—as a council of war, and asked their advice. He did so not because he particularly valued their opinions (indeed, he had come to such bad terms with them that he would have preferred not to deal with them at all), but because the etiquette of eighteenth-century command demanded that he consult his chief officers before ordering a major attack. Their response was categorically to deny the wisdom of making another assault on Montcalm's stoutest defenses. Instead they advised Wolfe to look for an opening upriver from Québec and sever the defenders' line of supply.[9]

Three brigadiers. All three of Wolfe's chief subordinates came from social origins superior to their commander, and by late summer 1759 all of them had come to despise him. The feeling was entirely reciprocated. Clockwise from top left, in order of seniority: Robert Monckton (1726–82); Lord George Townshend (1724–1807); and James Murray (1722–94). Monckton and Townshend appear more or less as they looked in 1759; Murray as he looked at about age sixty. *Monckton and Townshend portraits are courtesy of the William L. Clements Library at the University of Michigan; Murray, courtesy of the McCord Museum of Canadian History, Montreal / Musée McCord d'histoire canadienne, Montréal.*

By the ordinary expectations of professional military leadership, the brigadiers' opinion was binding upon Wolfe only if he wished it to be, but he was too sick, and in too precarious a mental state, to ignore their advice. He had only recently recovered from his fever enough to leave his bed; his consumptive cough was worsening; he was weak from the blood-letting to which he had been subjected; and except for the opiates his physician prescribed, he was unable even to urinate without excruciating pain. His weakness was so apparent that when he collapsed once more on September 4, the rumor spread throughout the army that he was dying. He himself believed that he had little time left and begged his doctor only to patch him up sufficiently to do duty for a few days more. Even if he lived, Wolfe realized, he would have to abandon the campaign unless he could bring Montcalm to battle before the end of September. Thereafter the change of season meant that his naval support would have to withdraw, for although the army had supplies sufficient to survive the winter, the crews of the ships, numbering more than thirteen thousand sailors, did not.

Wolfe also knew that if he did not succeed, he alone would bear the blame for failure. His brigadiers, who had come to loathe him—especially George Townshend, a member of Parliament, heir to a viscountcy, and political ally of Pitt—would see to that. Convinced that he had not long to live and fearing that inaction would bring disgrace upon his memory, with his judgment clouded by opiates and his body weakened by therapeutic bleedings no less than disease, Wolfe threw himself into planning a final desperate attack on the French lines above Québec. No one knew what he hoped to accomplish or how or where he intended to act. He consulted neither Monckton, Townshend, Murray, nor his senior naval commanders, Rear Admirals Charles Saunders and Charles Holmes, who had previously run ships past Québec and from whose vessels he surveyed the shoreline for a place to land troops.[10] Wolfe sought the advice of only one officer, a man who knew Québec better than anyone else on the expedition, Captain Robert Stobo.

Stobo, one of the most vivid characters in a story that has no shortage of them, had lived in the city from 1755 through the spring of 1759 as a prisoner of war. He was, in fact, one of two British prisoners of longest standing, for he and Jacob Van Braam had been the officers whom Washington had given up as hostages at the surrender of Fort Necessity. Thereafter he and Van Braam had been moved from Fort Duquesne to Québec for safekeeping, but not before Stobo had drawn—and, in folly or bravado, signed—a sketch of the fort's defenses and arranged for Shingas to smuggle it out to the Pennsylvania authorities. The letter in which he described the fort turned up in Braddock's captured baggage after the Battle of the Monongahela. Before this damning document came to light, Stobo had had the run of Québec, mingling in its high society and even forming a business partnership with one of its biggest merchants. Once his role in revealing Duquesne's defenses became known, however, both he and Van Braam were arrested and tried as spies. The court acquitted Van Braam but found Stobo guilty and sentenced him to death—a punishment he escaped only when the sentence was sent to Versailles for confirmation, and ordered suspended. Thereafter he enjoyed less freedom but eventually managed to move around the city and its immediate vicinity, carefully noting (as was his habit) the disposition of its defenses. Twice in 1757 he tried to escape; twice he was caught. Finally, on May 1, 1759, he led eight other prisoners, including a woman and three children, in the attempt that finally succeeded. Descending the St. Lawrence—first in a stolen canoe, later in a schooner that he and his companions hijacked, complete with captain and crew—he had reached Louisbourg shortly after the Québec expedition had sailed. With barely a pause, he turned around and ascended the river, joining Wolfe's army in July.[11]

Although no independent evidence survives to corroborate Stobo's own account, there is good reason to believe that it was he who told Wolfe of the footpath at L'Anse au Foulon (Fuller's Cove)—a track that angled steeply up the bluff from the riverside to the Plains of Abraham, a couple of miles west of the city. On September 5, Wolfe ordered preparations for the move upriver, and on that or the following day met with Stobo. Then, evidently feeling that he had critical secret information to communicate to Amherst, he sent Stobo off with a packet of dispatches on the seventh. The next day he reconnoitered with his brigadiers above the city. He spent a good deal of time looking through a field telescope at L'Anse au Foulon but said nothing to Murray, Townshend, and Monckton about any plan to land there. They believed that the assault would be made higher up the river, at Cap Rouge, which they had recommended, or perhaps at Pointe aux Trembles. As the reconnaissance progressed, more than a score of transports and warships, bearing approximately 3,600 men, rode the flood tides upriver past Québec, anchored off Cap Rouge, and awaited Wolfe's command.[12]

But his command did not come on the tenth—a heavy storm did, forestalling all amphibious operations. Nor did it come on the eleventh, when Wolfe ordered another thousand men upriver, stripping bare the defenses of his base camp on Île d'Orléans. At last on the twelfth he issued an order warning the army to make ready for an attack that would take place that night. Even then he did not inform his brigadiers of where he intended their forces to land; nor of when, exactly, they were to do so; nor of what objectives they were to seize. On the evening of the twelfth, nervously, they sent him a letter requesting further instructions. It was not until 8:30 that night—a half hour before the troops were to begin boarding their boats—that Wolfe wrote to inform them that the goal was "the *Foulon* distant upon 2 miles, or 2½ from Quebec, where you remember [from the reconnaissance] an encampment of 12 or 13 Tents and an abbatis, below it."[13] They and their men would wait until the signal that had been announced was given—two lanterns hoisted on the main topmast of Holmes's flagship, H.M.S. *Sutherland*—and then would ride the ebbing tide downriver, under the direction of naval officers who knew the spot at which they were to disembark.

Wolfe's partisans have interpreted his delay in informing his brigadiers of their objective as a sign of his genius. More likely than any concern for secrecy, however, it would seem that a combination of disdain for his subordinates and a highly precarious state of mind explain Wolfe's silence. When the brigadiers' letter arrived at his cabin on the *Sutherland,* he was busy making what can only be interpreted as careful preparations for his death. He had summoned a friend, Lieutenant John Jervis of the Royal Navy, in order to hand over a copy of his will, all his personal papers, and a miniature portrait of his fiancée, along with instructions on how to dispose of them. Jervis had found him dressed in a bright new uniform. The two men were talking over Wolfe's presentiments of death when a messenger brought in the brigadiers' letter, impelling him to pen his irritated reply. There is no evidence that he would otherwise have troubled to tell them where they and the army were bound. Wolfe would be in one of the first boats. Somehow, that was supposed to be enough.[14]

Although Wolfe was more eager to court his grim muse than to anticipate what might happen when the boats reached the cove, his troops embarked without a hitch. Quietly the river's current and the ebbing tide began to carry the first wave of boats downriver, close to the north shore, at about 2:00 a.m. The night was calm. The moon, in its last quarter, gave little light. Sentries ashore could dimly make out the silent passing column, and they challenged it, but when French-speaking officers in the boats responded that they were convoying supplies down from Batiscan, the guards let them continue unimpeded. About a half hour before first light, the lead boats scraped ashore a little below the cove. Without waiting for further instructions, a detachment of light infantrymen scrambled up the 175-foot-tall bluff face, following the 58th Regiment's big, nimble lieutenant colonel, William Howe. He had just turned thirty and had served in the siege of Louisbourg. Wolfe respected him for his physical courage no less than for his distinguished family connections—he was the youngest brother of Lord Howe, killed at Ticonderoga—and had given him command of a light-infantry battalion formed from the most agile men of several regiments. Now, as the boats carrying Wolfe and the rest of the advance party ground onto the shingle in the cove, Howe proved himself worthy of Wolfe's confidence. In the last minutes of darkness he and his men mounted to the top of the cliff, fixed bayonets, and charged into the little French camp. When the brief flurry of musket fire was over, the British found among the wounded the detachment's commander, Captain Louis Du Pont Du Chambon de Vergor—an officer whose only previous distinction was that in 1755 he had surrendered Fort Beauséjour to Robert Monckton. Vergor had barely had time to dispatch a runner to warn Montcalm that the British had begun to land at L'Anse au Foulon.[15]

It was about four o'clock when Wolfe struggled up the path from the cove to the top of the bluff. Together with Howe's party, there were perhaps two hundred men with him. The remaining troops of the first wave were disembarking from their boats in the cove and starting to labor upward under the weight of their arms and packs; a French artillery battery several hundred yards upriver had just opened fire on the transports and armed sloops of the second wave, which were now approaching the cove. Things were not going as he had expected.

Wolfe had assumed that he would come ashore with the advance guard, that there would be resistance, and (if his meticulous preparations are evidence of his expectations) that he would be killed leading his men against the French outpost. If his wish were granted, he would have risked only the advance guard, the survivors of which would be free to reembark; Monckton, the second-in-command, would be free to call off an operation of which he clearly disapproved. In the event that he escaped death, Wolfe would at least have led one last heroic attempt to land troops before Québec and could order a withdrawal from the St. Lawrence with a certain degree of honor. His maladies were sure to kill him before he reached home—and disgrace; he would merely exchange a wretched lingering death for the quick glorious one he coveted.[16]

But now on the heights Vergor's men had fled, there was no resistance except the ineffectual fire from the battery up the river, and Howe had already led his light infantry off to silence the guns. The three brigadiers were still below, and Wolfe, alone in the gray light before dawn, had no idea what to do next. In confusion he sent word down to the officer supervising operations at the cove, Major Isaac Barré, to halt the landings. Fortunately for Wolfe's historical reputation, Barré ignored the order and rushed more men up the path. Howe's light infantry meanwhile drove off the French gunners; the landings proceeded with dispatch; and Wolfe, at length collecting himself, went off to find a position for his men. Shortly after sunrise, in weather that had turned "showery," Wolfe returned and gave the order to march for Québec.

By the full light of day, seven British battalions could be seen drawn up in battle order across the Plains of Abraham, blocking the Grande Allée—the main road into town—a little less than a mile from Québec's western wall. Behind them, five more battalions were busy improving the path, guarding the landing, and harrying Canadian and Indian skirmishers out of the woods and cornfields. At the cove a detachment of sailors manhandled a pair of brass six-pounders up the trail. More than twenty sail of ships rode at anchor in the river. Wolfe's luck, always uncommonly good, had held once more.

Indeed, it had outlasted his judgment. Wolfe might have ordered his men six hundred yards farther on, to entrench along the highest ground in front of Québec, the Buttes à Neveu, as a first step toward opening a *siège en forme.* To do so would have given them both protection from an enemy assault and a clear view of the walls of the city, which would have lain within the range of siege guns brought up from the ships. But he did not. Instead he continued to extend the line of battle across the thousand-yard breadth of the plains, and to wait. What happened next would rest entirely in the hands of the French.[17]

THE REDCOATS HAD already formed a preliminary line across the plains between 6:30 and 7:00 when the disbelieving marquis de Montcalm rode in from Beauport. He had been up all night, supervising defenses on the Beauport shore, where he had expected the British to make an assault landing. As part of an elaborate ruse, Admiral Saunders's sailors had begun placing buoys off Beauport on the eleventh, as if to mark obstacles for assault craft to avoid. At eleven o'clock on the night of the twelfth Saunders had ordered sailors into the ships' boats and instructed them to row noisily back and forth between Beauport and the mouth of the St. Charles, to convince the French that an attack was imminent. Montcalm had taken the bait and bent every effort to improving the defenses east of the city; he was convinced that the ships that had passed up the river were intended merely to distract him from fully manning the Beauport lines. He knew, of course, that the ships above the city represented a real threat, and as a result he had also detached enough men to bring Bougainville's flying column up to a strength of about two thousand; but he himself remained in command of the eastern defenses, where he expected Wolfe to strike.

Montcalm and his officers at Beauport had spent so tense a night waiting for the attack that they had missed the first warning signal from the city, which indicated that something was amiss west of town. The general had sent his haggard men to their tents as soon as it was light enough to see that the British had withdrawn their boats and were not in fact preparing to land. Even the arrival at daybreak of a panting, panicked refugee from Vergor's camp did not immediately set the army in motion. An aide, listening to the man, concluded that he was a lunatic; rather than further disturb his commander (or himself) the aide had gone off to bed. But not for long: a flurry of urgent messages suddenly arrived, verifying the initial report without clarifying the size of the threat. Only then had Montcalm been summoned from his bed and the general alarm sounded. Finally, after some hesitation—for he could not believe that any substantial number of men had been able to mount the cliffs above town—Montcalm had ordered his four regular battalions to post themselves before the walls of the city. Then, leaving fifteen hundred men behind to hold the Beauport lines in the event that the British landing was only an elaborate diversion, he had mounted his horse and ridden off to see what could be done.[18]

Nothing had prepared Montcalm for what he saw when he finally arrived on the Buttes à Neveu, overlooking the plains. To the aide who rode beside him, even the sight of the redcoats was less striking than their effect on Montcalm, who sat in the saddle as if thunderstruck, wordlessly surveying the long scarlet line: for a long moment, "it seemed as though he felt his fate upon him." Then, somberly, he set about arranging his battalions in a line of battle facing the British. Elsewhere on the field, sporadic firing was already under way, as Canadian militiamen and Indians who had moved out from the city on Vaudreuil's orders sniped from cover at the double rank of redcoats, who seemed unperturbed by the harassment. More than anything else it was the impassiveness of the British that unnerved Montcalm, for their very lack of response to the snipers bespoke a kind of discipline that he knew his own forces, so heavy with militia, lacked. With increasing anxiety he waited—for it was several miles from the east end of the Beauport defenses to the Plains of Abraham—while his men marched up and assumed the positions he indicated before the walls.[19]

As they arrived, and as he rode up and down the line positioning them for action, Montcalm's thoughts surely eddied around the perils of his situation. Québec was almost out of provisions; Wolfe's army was standing astride the road to Batiscan; and the British ships in the river were blocking access to the supply depot by water. The walls of the city offered little protection in comparison to the trench network at Beauport and Montmorency; indeed the section of wall behind his men, around the Bastion of St. Louis, was particularly weak. At most he could position about 4,500 men on the field, a number perhaps equivalent to the force of redcoats arrayed a half mile or so ahead of him. No more reinforcements were available unless Bougainville and his flying column should appear; but although a messenger had been dispatched to Bougainville's camp at Cap Rouge at 6:45, Montcalm knew that to put two thousand men in motion and to march them in good order over the eight miles to Québec would take three hours.[20] But did he have that much time to spare?

It was about half-past nine when Montcalm concluded that he had no choice but to attack. To his chief of artillery he distractedly announced, " 'We cannot avoid action; the enemy is entrenching, he already has two pieces of cannon. If we give him time to establish himself, we shall never be able to attack him with the sort of troops we have.' He added with a sort of shiver, 'Is it possible that Bougainville doesn't hear all that noise?' " Without waiting for a reply, he cantered off down the line to warn his officers to prepare their men to advance.[21]

In fact his enemy was not entrenching, even though from a distance of six hundred yards it looked to Montcalm like they were. What had actually happened was that, once the last units had joined his line at about eight o'clock, Wolfe had ordered his men to lie down, and so they remained until after nine. The Indian and Canadian snipers in the woods on the British left and in the cornfields that lay between the British right and the cliff edge had been gallingly effective since early in the day. By eight o'clock Howe's light-infantrymen had done a fair job of clearing them out, but then Montcalm's gunners had opened fire with four or five fieldpieces, and the cannonballs, bounding over the turf with enough force to cut a man in two, had begun to tell on the redcoat battalions. Notwithstanding the legend of a thin red line standing calmly under fire, to order one's men to lie on their arms was far from unknown under such circumstances. Although Wolfe himself continued to walk the line and tempt the enemy gunners to try their skill on his brilliantly clad, scarecrow figure, he knew perfectly well that if he hoped to have an army fit to do battle he would have to preserve it until the moment came for his men to receive the French charge.[22]

While it is clear that by this point Wolfe had long since recovered from his cliff-top bout with indecision, it is by no means obvious that he had any plan other than to wait for Montcalm to make the next move. He

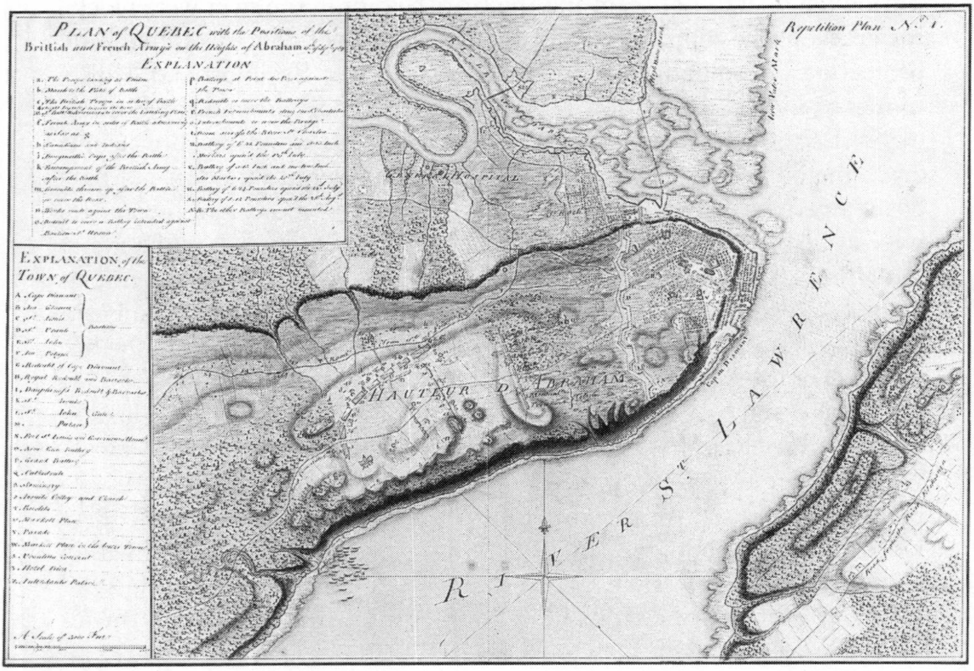

The Battle of Québec, September 13, 1759. This shaded topographical rendering of the locale shows the city, within its six-bastioned wall; the rise, called the Buttes à Neveu, where Montcalm ordered his men into line; and the open, gradually sloping fields to the west, where Wolfe took his stand. The westward arm of the compass rose points almost directly to Wolfe's landing place, L'Anse au Foulon. Note the steepness of the escarpment (indicated by darkness of shading) along the north side of the river, above the city. Downstream, north of the entry point of the St. Charles River, the flatness of the terrain presented a different kind of obstacle. As the sketched-in featureless expanse at the top of the map suggests, at low tide mud flats extended a half mile or more between high- and low-water marks. *Courtesy of the William L. Clements Library at the University of Michigan.*

knew that he had the better, more disciplined troops, and that in any open-field encounter they should be able to prevail against the imperfectly trained levies Montcalm had at his disposal. But he also knew, or should have known, that his chances of winning such a battle were diminishing by the minute. For not only were his men exposed to fire from the French cannon to their front; they were intensely vulnerable to attack from the west, their rear, and when Bougainville's flying column came, it would approach from that direction. Because he had not formed a plan that went beyond taking a position in front of Québec, Wolfe had succeeded in placing his entire army between the hammer of

Bougainville and the anvil of Montcalm. He had not given an order to entrench, as Montcalm feared: he had not even thought to order entrenching tools to be brought from the ships.[23]

Indeed Wolfe had denied his men not only the protection of a ditch but even the chance for escape, since there were now nearly 4,500 of them on the field and the only route of retreat lay back the way they had come, down a path so narrow that men could descend it only by twos. If he had hoped to sacrifice his own life heroically and then to leave the inglorious business of retreat to the brigadiers he despised, his hopes had been dashed. Instead—because he had enjoyed such extraordinary good fortune in landing his men, and because they had shown such professionalism in taking their position before Québec—James Wolfe now stood a fair chance of sacrificing twelve superb battalions to no larger purpose than gratifying his desire for a heroic death. We cannot know whether he worried, in the last moments of his life, over the consequences of his actions, or whether he even fully understood them. But his men, lying facedown in the mud while cannon shot ricocheted through their ranks and musket balls whistled overhead, could hardly have relished the position into which their commander, ardent for any desperate glory and maudlin in his attachment to Gray's *Elegy,* had thrust them.[24]

What Montcalm really needed to do was wait for Bougainville, whose force of picked men included some of the best regulars in Canada; but he did not. He had long been pessimistic about his chances of preserving the colony and had even joked about the prospects of defeat. Yet self-deprecating and even defeatist as he had been, until this moment he had either acted on the offensive or had been able to exploit defensive advantages in such a way as to deprive his adversaries of the initiative. Now, for the first time in the war, Montcalm found himself out-generaled, and it rattled him out of his wits. Despite the fact that he knew Wolfe's soldiers were, man for man, far superior to his own, at ten o'clock Montcalm ordered his troops to advance, head-on, against the British line. Now that he had decided to attack, the topography of the plains gave him no alternative to a frontal assault: with the British line extending virtually from the St. Charles escarpment on Montcalm's right to the St. Lawrence cliffs on his left, he had no room to maneuver, no opportunity to outflank his adversary. The battle would be a firefight, pure and simple.[25]

In the French center were the regular battalions of Béarn and Guyenne, in wide shallow columns; on the left stood the men of Royal-Roussillon and the Montréal and Trois-Rivières militia, in line; on the right, also in line, were the battalions of Languedoc, La Sarre, and the militia of Québec. All told they numbered about 4,500 men, and they were keen for a fight. When the order came to advance, they responded with a tremendous cheer. It was almost the last thing they would do in unison that day.

In the eighteenth-century infantryman's world, everything depended upon deliberation, precision, order: the better the army, the more machinelike its maneuvers on the battlefield would be. Cohesion was all, and in order to maintain it the best soldiers of the day had been trained to march at a parade-ground pace to within hailing distance of an enemy line, halt, and fire a final volley on order before they could charge headlong, bayonets fixed, at their opponents. The fate of every infantry battle ultimately rested on the ability of soldiers to withstand the physical and psychological shock of that climactic volley. But while the white-coated regulars of Montcalm's army had the discipline to perform as their general needed them to do, the un-uniformed militiamen mixed throughout their ranks had no appreciation of the necessity of making a deliberate, dress-right-dress approach to their enemy. Accordingly, almost as soon as they heard the order to advance, the militiamen broke into a run, despite the fact that the British line was at least five hundred yards away. The loss of coherence was instantaneous. "We had not gone twenty paces," wrote one witness, before "the left was too far in [the] rear and the centre too far in front." As his efforts to restore order failed, all Montcalm could do was ride along with the adrenalized tide that surged toward the still, scarlet line of British troops.[26]

Seven redcoat battalions stood facing the French in a double rank that stretched a half mile from end to end. Wolfe had ordered the men to load their muskets with an extra ball and had instructed their officers to fire the first volley only when the French were within forty yards. The redcoats stood quietly, more intent on the orders that were to come than on the enemy soldiers they could see haring wildly toward them. Every battalion, and most of the men in them, had seen combat before. The 58th and 78th Regiments, on the left, like the 43rd, the 28th, and the Louisbourg Grenadiers on the right, had all been at Louisbourg in 1758. Wolfe had put the units with the longest service in America in the center and the second line: the 47th had fought at Fort Beauséjour, and the 48th had accompanied Braddock to the Monongahela.[27] There was remarkably little movement within the British formation. Apart from Wolfe's aides, sprinting with orders to various commanders, the British ranks stood stock-still as they awaited the onslaught.

Montcalm's men, shouting as they ran, finally halted at about "half-musket-shot" range, between 125 and 150 yards, from the British front; dropped "down on one knee," and fired, probably in platoon volleys among the regulars, followed by "wild scattering" shots from the rest. Wolfe, standing on a rise near the Louisbourg Grenadiers, was one of the first to be hit. His wound, a shattered wrist, would have been agonizing, but he responded almost casually, wrapping it in a handkerchief without leaving his post. Other men, wounded more seriously, dropped from the ranks, which closed up as they fell. The range, however, was extreme; the effects of the French fire were virtually random and not (except to the individual victims) severe. No one in the British line shot back.[28]

At this point, when they were still at a considerable distance from the British line, Montcalm's men had their last chance to regroup, but did not. Instead their cohesion dissolved altogether as the regulars paused to load in conventional style, standing upright in ranks, while the militiamen reloaded as they had been trained to do in forest fighting, by taking cover or throwing themselves onto the ground. "This false movement," wrote a participant, "broke all the battalions"; and with that, the attack disintegrated. Men continued to advance and to fire, by companies and platoons and as individuals, but their piecemeal movement toward the British line exposed them to grave danger and guaranteed that their shots would be without collective effect. The redcoats stood impassive until the first attackers were within sixty yards; then they opened fire by platoons, especially on the left and the right wings. In the center, however, the 43rd and 47th Regiments stood fast until the enemy was within forty yards. Then, according to a captain of the 43rd, they delivered as

> close and heavy [a] discharge, as I ever saw performed at a private field of exercise, insomuch that better troops than we encountered could not possibly withstand it: and, indeed, well might the French Officers say, that they never opposed such a shock as they received from the center of our line, for that they believed every ball took place, and such regularity and discipline they had not experienced before; our troops in general, and particularly the central corps, having levelled and fired—*comme une coup de canon.* [H]ereupon they gave way, and fled with precipitation, so that, by the time the cloud of smoke was vanished, our men were again loaded, and, profiting by the advantage we had over them, pursued them almost to the gates of the town[,] . . . redoubling our fire with great eagerness, making many Officers and men prisoners.[29]

As the pursuit began, the British stood in danger of losing their discipline for the first time in the day. With hair-raising cries, the Highlanders of the 78th Foot slung their muskets, unsheathed their claymores—theirs was one of the few regiments left in which privates as well as officers carried swords—and set off at a run after the enemy. Along the rest of the line, huzzahing and shouting, the men of the English regiments charged forward with bayonets fixed. At the extreme right, Wolfe himself led the 28th Foot and the Louisbourg Grenadiers in the advance.

After a morning of intermittent rain, the sun broke through the clouds and now shone warmly over a field where blood lust had banished caution. As the British began to chase the scattering mob helter-skelter toward the city and the St. Charles River, Canadian and Indian skirmishers opened fire from their positions on the margins of the battlefield. They took the heaviest toll of the day. On the left it was the Scots of the 78th, charging along the woods that lined the northern edge of the field, who suffered the most heavily. On the right the 28th and the Louisbourg Grenadiers fell victim to marksmen concealed in a cornfield. It was there, as he urged the Grenadiers on, that one bullet tore through Wolfe's intestines and another punctured his chest. In shock and hemorrhaging uncontrollably, he clung to consciousness long enough to learn that the French had fallen into a general rout. He gurgled a few words in reply. Then James Wolfe achieved the consummation he had so long sought, and so devoutly wished.[30]

As WOLFE BLED to death, his second-in-command, Monckton, also lay severely wounded with a musket ball through the lungs. Meanwhile, Murray, a Scot, had led his countrymen of the 78th in their wild charge, only to be tied down along with them in a vicious firefight near the St. Charles River. Barré, who as adjutant general had been acting as Wolfe's chief of staff, had been hit in the face with a musket ball and was unable to give any direction at all. Everywhere on the Plains of Abraham battalions were disintegrating; men who had stood fast all morning responded to their sudden release by trying to skewer every Frenchman in sight. At last someone found Townshend, the only available brigadier; he assumed command with an intense awareness that the British force was falling to bits around him. Immediately he sent runners to the battalion commanders with orders to halt the pursuit and re-form their units on the battlefield. Discipline slowly reemerged, and none too soon. Within minutes Bougainville and his flying column appeared on the road from Cap Rouge, hoping to reinforce Montcalm, and not yet aware of his defeat. Townshend scraped together every available man and gun—two battalions and two fieldpieces—to oppose them. Even though his men outnumbered the redcoats blocking his path by more than two to one, Bougainville was taken aback. He drew off to assess his situation from the safety of the nearby Sillery Woods.

In calling off the pursuit Townshend saved the day for the British. Even though later critics would denounce him for betraying Wolfe's boldness and success, Townshend's prudence and presence of mind enabled him to face down a comparatively well-rested force with the capacity to wreak havoc on his still scattered, disorganized command. By about noon, with security reestablished, his soldiers could tend to the wounded, eat their first meal of the day, and count the dead. The British army had lost fifty-eight killed and six hundred wounded, almost exactly the same number as the French. At last Townshend sent to the ships for the picks and shovels that his men now needed more than the muskets and bayonets that had been the tools of a bloody morning's work. Although somewhat fewer than four thousand weary redcoats remained on the field and fit for service on the afternoon of September 13, Townshend set them to digging the first trenches for a *siège en forme.*[31]

So small a number of effective troops should not have been able to invest the city successfully, for they had no hope of isolating it from reinforcement and resupply. Within the walls of Québec and in the Beauport camp, however, the comparative weakness of the British went unremarked as the shock of defeat bred disorganization and despair. Montcalm had had his belly and one leg ripped open by grapeshot during the retreat but tried to retain command, sending advice to Vaudreuil and even dictating a letter to the British commander, despite shock and pain that steadily loosened his grip on reality. He died at four o'clock the next morning. Other than Montcalm, there was no senior commander within the walls of Québec. The two lieutenant colonels who had acted as his brigadiers in the battle, Fontbonne and Sénezergues, had both received mortal wounds; Bougainville was somewhere west of the city, out of contact. Nobody had reliable information on the state of the French forces, let alone that of their enemy. No one was sure of how many soldiers had been killed and wounded on the field, how many had deserted, how many had made it back to Beauport.

In the Beauport camp Vaudreuil was nominally in charge. He had witnessed only the end of the battle, lacked a clear sense of the overall situation, and could form no idea of what could be done until late afternoon, when he finally managed to convene a council of war. At about six in the evening, on the council's advice, he ordered the army to evacuate the Beauport lines. Giving the British a wide berth, the troops were to march to the north and then west as far as the settlement of Jacques-

Cartier, about twenty-five miles up the St. Lawrence. Neither Vaudreuil nor the officers he consulted believed there was any alternative. The retreat would preserve whatever remained of the army and protect whatever was left of the supplies at Batiscan; Bougainville's force could cover their rear and then consolidate with them at Jacques-Cartier; and the chevalier de Lévis, who had been summoned from Montréal, could assume command of the whole. Québec, of course, would have to be left to the British. Vaudreuil hoped against hope that the city would be able to hold out until the army could be reorganized but nonetheless left behind draft terms of surrender along with his other instructions for the city's garrison when he rode off with the army at nine o'clock.[32]

It is a measure of the confusion in the French command that they abandoned artillery, ammunition, and large stores of provisions in the Beauport camp without making any effort to move them into Québec proper. The force left behind to defend the city numbered about 2,200 men, mainly militia and sailors. None of them could have been happy to be charged with protecting the four thousand or so civilian, sick, and wounded noncombatants who had taken refuge within the walls—especially when it became known that the city had less than three days' supply of food on hand, and when anyone with eyes could stand on the ramparts and see the British constructing batteries and redoubts within a thousand yards of the fragile western wall. Thus when the formal siege opened on September 14, the demoralization of Québec's defenders posed at least as great a threat to the city's survival as the guns of the besiegers. The British, in fact, did not fire a shot that day—or the next, or the next, or the next—but instead concentrated on digging siege works and hauling cannon and howitzers up from the Foulon cove. Meanwhile Québec's garrison noisily shelled its enemy and quietly collapsed from within. On the afternoon of the seventeenth, with a heavy British battery making ready to fire on the St. Ursule Bastion and with Admiral Saunders preparing to open a bombardment of his own from a line of ships in the basin, the French commandant ordered his gunners to cease fire. At four o'clock an envoy preceded by a flag of truce approached the British lines bearing the terms of capitulation that Vaudreuil had left behind.[33]

The town major of Québec, Jean-Baptiste-Nicholas-Roch de Ramezay, hoped to spin out the negotiations long enough to allow the army to return from Jacques-Cartier and attack the British. Delay was the only defense he had left, for his troops were out of food and the city's civilian population lacked protection from the coming bombardment. But no relief was imminent, the terms to which Townshend and Saunders were willing to agree turned out to be surprisingly generous ones, and to judge by the rate at which they jumped the walls and deserted to the enemy, Québec's militiamen seemed prepared to make peace regardless of what the town major intended. At eleven o'clock that night Ramezay accepted the British terms, and at eight o'clock the next morning, Tuesday, September 18, 1759, signed the formal capitulation of Québec. That afternoon a detachment of the Royal Artillery marched into the city to raise the Union Jack over the citadel while the Louisbourg Grenadiers mounted guard on the walls. After nearly three months of trying, a British army had conquered Québec. But now they had to keep it.[34]

For in fact the action of September 13, despite the haze of romance that has come to envelop it, was no more a decisive battle than a brilliant one. Few battles, perhaps none, are ever as decisive as generals hope that they will be; and nowhere was it truer than in eighteenth-century North America that victories on the battlefield win wars only when the victors can retain their conquests. Therefore Townshend, Murray, Saunders, and Holmes immediately set about consolidating control over Québec and the surrounding countryside, preparing to defend it against the return of the French army. Here their most effective weapon was clemency, for they were far too weak to impose order on the city and its people and therefore offered terms infinitely more generous than those Amherst had allowed at Louisbourg. For the only time after Fort William Henry, the British permitted a defeated Franco-Canadian garrison to surrender with the honors of war. The regulars were not to be made prisoners of war but rather transported under flag of truce to France, where they would be free to rejoin the French army. Militiamen who had borne arms in the siege would not be required to accompany the army, but could remain with their families, providing that they surrendered their weapons and swore an oath of fidelity to the British Crown. No one from the civil population would be subject to exile. Citizens would be guaranteed the security of their property and assured of their right to continue practicing their religion under the care of the bishop of Québec. Anyone willing to take the oath of fidelity would enjoy all the protections normally afforded to British subjects.[35]

Thus from the occupation's beginning, the British sought to secure the voluntary cooperation of a civil population they knew they could not control by force. And from the beginning it could hardly have been clearer that at the very least the neutrality of this population would be necessary, for a reorganized French army was marching back toward the city even as the terms of capitulation were being negotiated. François-Gaston, chevalier de Lévis, the tough Gascon brigadier who had served Montcalm as second-in-command, was in every sense equal to the

Mort du Marquis de Montcalm-Gozon. This engraving, after a painting by Louis-Joseph Watteau, attempts to cast Montcalm's demise in the same heroic mold as Benjamin West's more famous *Death of General Wolfe*. Montcalm was in fact buried within the city on the evening of the day after the battle; his grave was a shell hole inside the chapel of the Ursuline convent. Here the shell hole alone remains true to the facts. Watteau's decision to show the two Indian warriors lifting a spent mortar shell from the crater at left reflects sheer fancy, or perhaps an homage to the Mohawk warrior whom West gave a central position in *The Death of General Wolfe. Courtesy of the William L. Clements Library at the University of Michigan.*

responsibilities he had inherited. He had taken over at Jacques-Cartier on the seventeenth, and at once had stiffened the spines of the refugees he found there. Showing nothing but scorn for their flight, he had ordered the troops back downriver—so rapidly that by the time the Union Jack first fluttered over Québec, his advance guard had reached St. Augustin, less than a day's march from the city. Had Ramezay held out for two more days, Lévis could have invested the lightly entrenched British camp. Since he lacked cannon and the supplies sufficient to besiege the city, however, he had had no choice but to order his men back to Jacques-Cartier, once he learned of the surrender. There he ordered a fort to be built and watched for an opportunity to run a ship past the British fleet at

The Death of General Wolfe. Benjamin West's 1771 history painting caused an immense stir when first exhibited in London; William Woollett made this engraving in 1776 and grew rich on the sales of thousands of copies. At least in part, West's success depended on his ability to depict so much in a single scene. Here, simultaneously, is a classically ordered tableau with historical figures (Robert Monckton stands at the apex of the left-hand grouping, clutching his wounded chest, while Colonel Isaac Barré cradles his dying commander at the center); a mythically climactic moment (the figure running in from the left brings news of victory while Wolfe gasps thanksgiving to God and gives up the ghost); and an allegory of empire that unites all ranks and nationalities in symbolic witness to a martyr's death. The central figures are a general, a colonel, a major, and two captains, but on the right a grenadier private clasps his hands in prayer, and in the background a detachment of sailors drags a cannon up from the river, where the Royal Navy's ships ride at anchor. Most significant of all, however, was West's decision to place in the left foreground a Mohawk warrior, who views the drama from a pose of classic contemplation while an American ranger and a Scottish soldier point back to the running messenger and relay the news of victory to the dying Wolfe. That none of this happened in the way West shows it did not matter. His enterprise was not to create a historically accurate painting, but to apotheosize both Wolfe and the empire, and at that he succeeded brilliantly. *Courtesy of the William L. Clements Library at the University of Michigan.*

Québec. With reinforcements and supplies from France, Lévis knew, he could regain the city for his king.[36]

The rugged chevalier did not doubt that he could make it through the coming winter, and indeed that the winter might actually serve his interests better than those of the British. For once his army had adequate, if not copious, provisions on hand: Montréal had at last enjoyed a bountiful harvest, and even an early one. Most of the Québec district, of course, had had no harvest at all, but that was a British problem. As the redcoat officers prepared their men to enter winter quarters in the city they were acutely aware of what Wolfe's August campaign of terror had actually accomplished. Together with the large numbers of Canadian civilians who were coming to Québec to swear fealty to King George, the British garrison would face great hardships during the winter, for all they had to live on was what they had brought from England. No British provision fleet could possibly reach Québec before the St. Lawrence froze.

In the meantime the British prepared for the ordeal that lay ahead. Virtually every soldier—including those sick and wounded men deemed likely to recover—would have to remain at Québec to make the garrison strong enough to stand off an attack. This amounted to more than seven thousand troops, a number that would stretch the food supply to its uttermost limit. Moreover, they all had to be sheltered, along with the returned civilians, in a city that ordinarily housed about seven thousand souls. Few structures in Québec and its suburbs had come through the ordeal of the summer undamaged; thus the month between the capitulation and the departure of the fleet was consumed with feverish efforts not only to strengthen the city's walls, bastions, and batteries, but to repair enough shell-shattered houses to preserve the garrison against a Canadian winter.

Since no sane person who was free to leave would have stayed at Québec under such circumstances, Monckton—who had made enough of a recovery from his wounds to assume command but was still far from fit—elected to return to New York to convalesce. Townshend, who had his political health to nurse, opted to return to England. On October 18, therefore, when Admiral Saunders's fleet weighed anchor and slipped downriver on the ebbing tide, it was the junior brigadier, James Murray, who remained as commandant of His Majesty's garrison and governor of Québec. He could hardly have been delighted with his prospects. Unpleasant as his future looked, however, Murray's men must surely have known that theirs was bound to be worse.[37]

CHAPTER 37

Fall's Frustrations

OCTOBER–NOVEMBER 1759

OCTOBER 18 WAS also the day that a fretful Jeffery Amherst finally learned that Québec had fallen. Word reached him on Lake Champlain, where he was shepherding his troops cautiously north to attack Bourlamaque at Île-aux-Noix. Captain Stobo, whom Wolfe had sent with letters back on September 7, had arrived at Crown Point on October 9. Unfortunately for Amherst, he arrived without the dispatches; a French privateer had overtaken his ship near Halifax and he had thrown Wolfe's letters overboard lest they be discovered among his possessions. He had therefore been able to give Amherst general information only, leaving the commander in chief intensely frustrated. "I am not a whit the wiser," he complained, "except that [Stobo] says Gen Wolfe had got with allmost his whole Army above the Town & [Wolfe] thinks he will not take it."[1]

Inconclusive as it was, the captain's report nonetheless convinced Amherst that he dared not delay launching his attack on Île-aux-Noix, for if Wolfe had indeed failed, Montcalm's whole force at Québec would soon be available to reinforce Bourlamaque. The arrival over the next couple of days of the three long-awaited vessels from the shipyard at Ticonderoga—the brigantine *Duke of Cumberland*, the radeau *Ligonier*, and the sloop *Boscawen*—gave Amherst the naval protection he craved, and on the afternoon of October 11 he had at last ordered his men into their bateaux and set them rowing north. But from the thirteenth through the seventeenth storms, cold, and "northerly & contrary" winds had held up the boats and forced the army to take shelter on the lakeshore. Thus the letter from New York that arrived on October 18, carrying news of Québec's fall, came to Amherst as a great relief. On the following day, with the "appearance of winter" everywhere in evidence, he called off the expedition. Two days later he was back at Crown Point; within two weeks he dismissed his provincials and ordered his regulars into winter quarters.[2]

The Anglo-American forces officially welcomed the news of Québec's fall with *feux-de-joie* and thanksgiving sermons, but for the provincials the northern campaigns generally ended with all the usual irritations, for all the usual reasons. As in every previous year, their camps had grown sicklier as the summer waned; their provisions had proven scantier and less wholesome than promised; and they had worried that they would be kept in service after their enlistment contracts had expired. On the road from Crown Point to Fort Number 4 in New Hampshire, for example, where a ranger captain named John Stark was supervising about 250 New England provincials in the last phases of construction, the men complained of short rations, hard work, and bad weather more and more bitterly until they finally mutinied on November 13. Even though Stark was a popular commander, nothing he said could dissuade them from throwing down their tools and refusing to work. Only the timely arrival of provisions, the nearness of the builders to the end of the road, and Stark's promise that he would release them at Number 4 prevented a mass desertion.[3]

While Stark scrambled to keep his men from vanishing into the woods, back at the Fort Ticonderoga sawmill Sergeant Rufus Putnam of the Massachusetts provincials also chafed at what he understood to be a violation of his enlistment contract. As the workman who had supervised the building of the mill (which in turn had sawn the planks of the *Boscawen,* the *Ligonier,* and the *Duke of Cumberland*), Putnam was too valuable to be released with his fellow provincials and had been kept on as foreman of the sawyers at the site. Only the promise that he would be paid an extra dollar a day for his services had kept him from leaving when his enlistment expired. At the end of November, however, the regular officer in charge at Ticonderoga refused to pay Putnam off at the agreed rate and instead allowed him only his sergeant's wages. Making his way home in bitter weather, Putnam brooded on how often he had "ben disappointed of the rewards promised for extra Service." Once back in Brookfield, he "came to a ditermnation never to engage again as a Solder."[4]

Seven hundred miles away, Private Gibson Clough of Salem was coming to the same conclusion at about the same time. He had enlisted to serve on the Crown Point expedition only to find that his unit was sent to garrison Louisbourg and release regulars to accompany Wolfe to Québec. This had been disappointing enough, but life in the fortress had begun to look even gloomier as September turned to October. It seemed increasingly likely "we shall stay all winter here within stone walls," he grumbled in his diary, without even the prospect of having "good Liquors for to keep up our Spirits on cold Winter's days." To be kept beyond the term of his contract was nearly unbearable for Clough, who complained that "although we be Englishmen Born yet we are debarred Englishmens Liberty" and noted grimly that "we now see what it is to be under Martial Law and to be with ye regulars who are but little better than slaves to their Officers." The soldiers in Clough's regiment agreed, and on November 1 they mutinied, refusing to do further service. Even the arrival of a letter from the governor of Massachusetts bearing news that the General Court had agreed to pay a bonus for service over the winter did nothing to pacify them. Only the threat of force, the impossibility of escape from Cape Breton, and their colonel's promise that he would return to Boston and seek their release convinced the soldiers to resume their duties.[5]

Such episodes of disappointment and outright mutiny among the provincials—and many more could be added—suggest the extent to which their experience of military service shaped their views of the regulars alongside whom, and under whose command, they served. Even in so successful a year as 1759, the dominant memory that a New England provincial might take home from the armies was unlikely to be a pleasant one. For thousands of ordinary men like Rufus Putnam (who "made up [his] mind not to engage any more in the Military Service") and Gibson Clough (who resolved that "when I get out of their pen [i.e., Louisbourg, but more generally, the power of the regulars] I shall take care how I get in again") the net effect of provincial military service was disillusionment. No matter how much colonists in general rejoiced in the British victories, for the provincials themselves, the war was nothing so much as a protracted, often painful lesson in the differences between themselves and the regulars: differences more profound than almost any of them, believing that they were neither more nor less than "Englishmen Born," had had any reason to expect.[6]

At the same time, the provincials' seemingly incorrigible casualness about discipline and their readiness to desert or mutiny when they suspected that their enlistment contracts were being violated had convinced Jeffery Amherst, like Braddock and Loudoun and Abercromby before him, that Americans had much less in the way of character and toughness than real Englishmen. When the New Englanders began to desert from Crown Point at the beginning of November, Amherst found that he had no alternative but to dismiss them, since there was no way to force them into line. "The provincials," he wrote, "have got home in their heads &

will now do very little good. I hear they are deserting from every Post where I have been obliged to leave some & several ran away who had a good deal of money due to them. 'Twill be so much saved to the Publick." Already he had gone far toward forming what would become his summary opinion: "The Disregard of Orders, and Studying of their own Ease, rather than the good of the Service, has been too often Just Grounds for Complaint Against Some of the Provincial Officers, and all their Men." They were no more than a necessary evil, settled upon him by the need for laborers and garrison troops in a frustrating wilderness war. Whatever else Amherst might say of the Americans, he would never think of them as soldiers, and he could hardly wait to put them, and their wretched country, behind him.[7]

CHAPTER 38

Celebrations of Empire, Expectations of the Millennium

OCTOBER 1759

PERHAPS PREDICTABLY, the reactions of civilians and government officials to the news of Québec's fall were more ecstatic—because they were unmingled with the irritations and anxieties of military service—than those of the soldiers themselves. Everywhere local and province governments staged elaborate public ceremonies, while people in general demonstrated their joy in less structured ways. In Pennsylvania, where the war-driven market for agricultural produce was helping to counter the memory of a devastated frontier, Philadelphians—except for Quakers, who refused to observe holidays set aside to recognize military victories—celebrated by illuminating their windows and building so many bonfires that they were said to dim the moon. In New York, where merchants and artisans were feasting on military contracts, an evening celebration "was ushered in with a large Bonfire and Illuminations," continued with "an elegant Entertainment" for "all the principal Persons of the Place," and concluded with "every . . . Toast that Loyalty and Gratitude could dictate . . . ; each being accompanied with the Discharge of a Round of Cannon, amounting in the Whole to above a Hundred."[1]

Boston observed the occasion with an intensity suited to the colony most enthusiastically engaged in the war. "The Morning [of October 16] was ushered in by the ringing of the Bells of the Town, which continued the whole Day"; an "excellent sermon was preached" to the governor, both houses of the legislature, and "a vast Auditory"; militia units performed "Rejoicing Fires," and all the artillery pieces of the town and the ships in the harbor joined in a massive salute. That evening there was a

"Concert of Musick" at the Concert Hall and then a procession to Faneuil Hall, where Thomas Pownall threw a formal dinner for the legislators, "a great Number of Civil and Military Officers, and other Persons of Distinction." Into the shank of the night the governor and guests toasted their monarch and his generals before reeling outdoors to observe the "beautifuly illuminated" windows of the town, the "large Bonfires formed in a pyramidical Manner . . . on several Eminences" around about, and the "Abundance of extraordinary Fire-Works [that] were play'd off in almost every Street; more especially the greatest Quantity of Sky-Rockets ever seen on any Occasion."[2]

Indeed, New Englanders everywhere joined in "great Rejoicings." Yet as one would expect of this region where people remained eager to discern providential meanings in events, when the smoke finally cleared, sermons had probably outnumbered bonfires; and the preachers, both Old Light and New, had achieved virtual unanimity in their interpretation of the fall of Québec. Since the end of the seventeenth century, they agreed, God had chastised his people with defeat and discouragements in order to make them mindful of their sins and to bring them back to the paths of righteousness. Through the previous three wars and the first years of the present one, the enemy "gain'd ground, fortified and secur'd every pass into their own country, grew more and more animated," the Reverend Samuel Langdon told his New Hampshire auditory. "But when God had thus prov'd and humbled and convinc'd us that *the race is not to the swift* . . . His Providence bro't about a change" of truly miraculous nature.[3]

This pattern recapitulated the ways in which the Lord had always dealt with his chosen ones. He had sent afflictions on the people of Israel in exactly the same way he had recently sent them on New England, and for exactly the same purpose: to call forth moral regeneration, humility, renewal of faith. The return of divine favor, unmistakable in such a great military event as the taking of Québec, spoke directly to the hearts of a people conscious of their special relationship with the Almighty. "I know not how to express the importance of that success and *yet I feel it,*" the Reverend Samuel Cooper told Governor Pownall and the members of the General Court in his thanksgiving sermon on October 16. "We have received a Salvation from Heaven, greater perhaps than any since the Foundation of the Country."[4]

As he had in Israel of old, God had found within New England a saving remnant of saints whose righteousness he imputed to the whole of the English nation—and for that matter to all the Protestants fighting to destroy the popish powers. The Catholic and heathen enemies of God's people, once so mighty, had been brought low not merely by the exertions of the British and American soldiers but by God's own doing. No case in all of salvation history had made clearer God's willingness to fight his people's battles than the encounter on the Plains of Abraham, where every circumstance manifested divine intervention. Many preachers found even more in the events of 1759 than a reconfirmation of God's mercy to his people, for the cumulative impact of so many victories suggested that God was preparing to drive the minions of Antichrist out of America altogether, as the opening stroke of the millennium.[5]

As often happens in times of war and cultural stress, apocalyptic meanings were plain to those who, like the Reverend Jonathan Mayhew of Boston, saw parallels between the prophecies in the Book of Revelation and current events. Mayhew encouraged his audience to look forward to the day when the defeat of the Whore of Babylon (France) would lead the peoples of Spain and Portugal to reject Catholicism and join in a great Protestant revival; to the day when the Indians, delivered from the delusions of popery and priest-craft, might accept the true religion and adopt peaceful ways; to the day indeed when North America would be home to "a mighty empire (I do not mean an independent one) in numbers little inferior to the greatest in Europe, and in felicity to none." Fairly transported by a vision of peace and harmony, Mayhew invited his auditors to imagine with him the glories of that millennial America:

> Methinks I see mighty cities rising on every hill, and by the side of every commodious port; mighty fleets alternately sailing out and returning, laden with the produce of this, and every other country under heaven; happy fields and villages wherever I turn my eyes, thro' a vastly extended territory; there the pastures cloathed with flocks, and here the vallies cover'd with corn, while the little hills rejoice on every side! And do I not there behold the savage nations, no longer our enemies, bowing the knee to Jesus Christ, and with joy confessing him to be "Lord, to the glory of God the Father!" Methinks I see religion professed and practiced in this spacious kingdom, in far greater purity and perfection, than since the times of the apostles; the Lord being still as a wall of fire round about, and the glory in the midst of her! O happy country! happy kingdom![6]

Even preachers less willing to speculate into God's plans for the future believed that something momentous was coming to pass. Wolfe's victory and sacrificial death, crowning so many recent Anglo-American triumphs, had confirmed the special place of the Protestant British—and particularly the saving remnant of New Englanders within the empire—within the Lord's design. With such evidence of divine favor spread on every hand, who could doubt the reality of God's covenant? And who could doubt that it was New England's duty to hold fast until God gave them the final victory?[7]

CHAPTER 39

Day of Decision

QUIBERON BAY

NOVEMBER 20, 1759

IF ENGLAND HAD blazed with a thousand bonfires when the news of Louisbourg arrived, ten thousand lit the skies in late October, when word spread that Québec, too, had fallen. The news arrived in London at almost exactly the same time it reached Amherst on Lake Champlain. By then Pitt had almost given up hope; on October 15 the duke of Newcastle had observed that "with reason" Pitt "gives it all over, and declares so publicly." In his last gloomy dispatches Wolfe had brooded on all the failures of the summer and confessed that he was "at a loss how to determine" his next move. "I am so far recovered [in health] as to do business," his final letter had read, "but my constitution is entirely ruined, without the consolation of having done any considerable service to the State, or without any prospect of it." Now, as he read the letter in which Townshend described the battle and the surrender of the city, Pitt's mood swung abruptly from despair to exaltation, and he ordered the letter published in a *Gazette Extraordinary.* Quickly thereafter, to the accompaniment of bells and bonfires, cannon salutes and toasts, the news spread throughout the realm.[1]

The fact that Wolfe had died in the battle only made the victory somehow richer, more meaningful to the self-consciously sentimental members of the English ruling and middle classes. "The incidents of dramatic fiction could not be conducted with more address to lead an audience from despondency to sudden exultation" than the circumstances of the conquest, wrote that accomplished fictioneer, Horace Walpole. The "whole people" of Britain "despaired—they triumphed—and they wept—for Wolfe had fallen in the hour of victory! Joy, grief, curiosity, astonishment, were painted in every countenance: the more they inquired, the higher their admiration rose. Not an incident but was heroic and affecting!" In the end, Walpole thought, not even Pitt's oratory could encompass so sublime an event. When on October 21 the secretary "pronounced a kind of funeral oration" in the Commons, his attempts to find "parallels . . . from Greek and Roman [hi]story did but flatten the pathetic of the topic. . . . The horror of the night, the precipice scaled by Wolfe, the empire he with a handful of men added to England, and the glorious catastrophe of contentedly terminating life where his fame began—ancient [hi]story may be ransacked, and ostentatious philosophy thrown into the account, before an episode can be found to rank with Wolfe's."[2]

As befit the leading figure of his class in this latitudinarian age, William Pitt paid his respects to the superintending hand of providence without any of the embarrassing apocalyptic zeal of the New England divines. Indeed Pitt had barely finished embalming Wolfe rhetorically with a proposition that Parliament erect a monument in his memory before he was thinking ahead to the campaigns that would, he hoped, end the war. He wanted as much as ever to reduce France from an imperial power to a merely European one. But could he induce the French to make peace without also offering them their empire back?

The situation of France in the autumn of 1759 was bad but by no means perilous. At the beginning of August, Prince Ferdinand had finally countered the big territorial gains that the duc de Broglie had made on the southern approaches to Hanover by recapturing the town of Minden and its strategic bridges over the Weser. Following his famous victory, in which the French lost nearly five thousand killed and wounded and several thousand captured, Ferdinand regained control over most of Hesse, pushing Marshal Contades's army slowly back nearly seventy miles to the River Lahn, a tributary of the Rhine. There in September the two armies had dug in, ending what had been a frustrating and expensive campaign for the French.[3]

Of even greater expense and frustration had been the delays that France had suffered in staging its projected invasion of England. Shortly after the Battle of Minden, the French admiralty had tried to sneak its Toulon fleet past Gibraltar and up to Brest, where it was to join in the invasion attempt. The British fleet commander at Gibraltar, Admiral Edward Boscawen, gave chase and caught up with the French squadron near the Portuguese coast. Off the Bay of Lagos, in a running fight on August 18–19, Boscawen's squadron captured three French battleships

The Battle of Minden, August 1, 1759. This popular, schematized view of the battle shows Prince Ferdinand and his staff looking on from conventionally rearing horses, at the climax of the battle. In the center British and Hanoverian infantry rout the French cavalry, then advance against the French line, forcing a general retreat. The massing and maneuver of armies was a characteristic of the Seven Years' War in Europe, where (as at Minden) more than a hundred thousand men might clash in open-field encounters. The greatest battles in North America involved fewer than fifteen thousand combatants. *Courtesy of the William L. Clements Library at the University of Michigan.*

and forced two more onto the rocks; the rest of the fleet ran for Cádiz, where the British promptly blockaded them in. Thereafter the French continued to plan an invasion from their Channel ports, but they did so under increasing financial difficulties. In October a shortage of funds compelled the treasury to suspend "for a year the payment of orders upon the general receipts of the finances, . . . the bills of the general farms[,] . . . [and] the reimbursement of capitals"—a virtual admission of bankruptcy.[4]

But despite this unhappy state of affairs the French had not sued for peace, and remained unlikely soon to do so, for two reasons. First, they could still do England great damage if they could only launch their invasion fleet. The British had retained only a few thousand regulars to support the untested and still understrength militia; and, amazingly, they had done little to strengthen the home island's coastal defenses. Second, the army of Prince Ferdinand could no longer threaten the French forces in western Germany, in part because the British could spare no men to reinforce him, and in part because after the Battle of Minden, Ferdinand had had to detach troops to reinforce his brother-in-law, Frederick II. And in Prussia, where the strategic balance of Europe remained delicately poised, the situation was fast becoming critical.

Although Frederick had preserved Dresden against the besieging Austrians through the winter and had done what he could to rebuild his armies, with the return of marching weather in the spring, the Austrians and Russians had joined forces to reinvade the Prussian heartland. Frederick tried to stop them on August 12 at Kunersdorf, just east of Frankfurt an der Oder. The result had been sheer disaster. Attacking an enemy force of about seventy thousand with just fifty thousand men, Frederick lost more than nineteen thousand dead and wounded before his army collapsed under an Austrian counterattack and ran for its life. Incapable of re-forming his forces and also of reinforcing Dresden, Frederick gave up the city on September 12, and with it most of Saxony. Only the fortunate end of Austro-Russian cooperation—the Austrians set off to invade Silesia while the Russians remained in place to threaten Berlin—and the arrival of reinforcements from Ferdinand's army allowed Frederick to hang on until the campaigning season ended.[5]

Desperate for any means to preserve his kingdom against the combined forces of two empresses who wanted nothing more than to efface it—and him—from the map of Europe, Frederick had begged Pitt to convene a peace conference. On October 30, with news of Québec still fresh, the British government had asked Prince Louis of Brunswick, the Dutch regent (a neutral, but also the brother of Prince Ferdinand), to invite the belligerent states to send emissaries to a general congress at Augsburg. There was, realistically, no reason to assume that the conference would even convene. The Austrians and Russians had the maddening Prussian exactly where they wanted him, and his position could only deteriorate with time. The issue was less clear for the French. Their finances were in disarray; they had lost Guadeloupe and their West African slaving stations; they seemed likely to lose Canada; and the war had gone badly in western Germany. But their armies were still intact, and still the largest in western Europe. England could do nothing to threaten France itself; and there remained the invasion card to play.

Two weeks after Prince Louis had issued his invitation to the Augsburg peace conference, the French made their move. All summer long the Royal Navy had kept up a close watch on the Brittany coast, as Admiral Sir Edward Hawke had found a way to maintain what had never before been possible, a continuous blockade. But not even the ingenious system that he and Anson had devised, of continuously refitting and resupplying the fleet by rotating ships home a few at a time, could keep the Channel squadron on station in the teeth of the Atlantic's late-autumn gales. One of these, on November 7, drove Hawke back to seek shelter on England's southwest coast and gave his counterpart, Admiral Herbert de Brienne, comte de Conflans, a chance to run southwestward from Brest to Quiberon Bay, where the French had lately reconcentrated the invasion army and its transports. Because the same storm had also blown the returning West Indies fleet of Admiral Bompar into Brest, on November 15 Conflans was able to put to sea with full crews and no fewer than twenty-one ships of the line. If he could collect the transports and troops and get back to sea before the British could reestablish their presence in the Channel, he would have at his disposal a force powerful enough to strike anywhere he chose along the coasts of Ireland or Scotland, where not even militia detachments stood guard.[6]

But Hawke was already heading back down the Channel with twenty-three ships of the line by the time Conflans made sail, and erratic winds kept the French fleet from making a direct approach to its destination; so that at dawn on November 20 both squadrons were closing in—the British from the northwest, the French from the south—on Quiberon Bay. Between eight and nine, with a new gale blowing up from the northwest, they sighted one another. Conflans headed for the shelter of the bay. Despite the heavy weather, the bay's treacherous waters and narrow mouth, and the lack of pilots to guide his ships in, Hawke signaled his captains to attack.[7]

Rigid tactics, codified in standing instructions to which captains were expected to adhere without fail, ordinarily governed eighteenth-century naval engagements. The Fighting Instructions of the Royal Navy called for ships to form a line of battle parallel to (and if at all possible to the windward of) the enemy fleet, then to sail slowly ahead, with each ship in the line blazing away broadside at its enemy counterpart. Since the ability of naval officers to advance in the service depended more on conformity than on imagination, a slavish adherence to the Fighting Instructions was commonplace, and—because similar instructions governed the tactics of every European navy—naval battles tended to be inconclusive affairs in which roughly comparable forces, engaging in relatively calm weather, inflicted approximately equal damage on one another until one or the other of the admirals in charge signaled his ships to withdraw. For squadrons to attack squadrons (much less fleets to attack fleets) and fight until one had destroyed the other was virtually unknown.[8]

At Quiberon Bay, however, only Conflans tried to form a conventional line of battle. Hawke—one of the most imaginative, and certainly one of the boldest, officers in the Royal Navy—had ordered an attack under weather conditions so severe as to be all but unthinkable, in winds that would have made line-ahead battle tactics impossible. Trusting in the superior seamanship of his crews, Hawke therefore hoisted flags signaling "general chase"—in effect ordering his captains to attack at will—and then, despite high and rising winds, crowded on all the sail his ships could bear and bore down on the French without regard to the hazards of the bay or the ferocity of the gale.

If judged by the conservative standards of the day, Hawke's order to initiate a general melee represented a decision of incredible audacity—or foolhardiness. Its effect on Conflans and his captains was almost stupefying. The British, swarming around them like wolves around sheep, kept the French from forming a defensive line; then, through a short and sanguinary afternoon, fought in no discernible order. Ships collided, crashed onto rocks, ran aground, and bombarded one another with convulsive fury in a virtually indescribable action. Throughout the battle, no British crew fought more fiercely than that of the ninety-gun *Magnanime,* which led the chase into the bay; nor was any captain more aggressive in the attack than her commander, Richard, Viscount Howe. Perhaps there was an element of vengeance in his conduct, an intention to pay the French back for his brother's death at Ticonderoga. At any rate, before the day was out, the *Magnanime* alone had sunk one eighty-gun ship, the *Thésée,* and made a wreck of another, the *Formidable.*

At evening, in the midst of the storm, darkness came on so suddenly that the combatants broke off contact and anchored without attempting to regroup. Only when the light gathered the next morning, as the storm still howled, did the result of Hawke's attack become clear. Only two French ships had made it back to sea and run before the gale for shelter farther down the coast. Two had been sunk; one had been taken; a fourth had run aground; a fifth had limped off to sink while trying to escape. The tempestuous dawn also disclosed to Admiral Conflans that in the darkness he had anchored his flagship, the *Soleil Royale,* in the midst of several British ships. After running aground in a vain attempt to escape he refused to surrender and ordered her abandoned and burned. Seven

French vessels, aided by the high storm tide, had made it into the mouth of the Vilaine River.

Because the storm had not abated, Hawke hesitated to renew his attack: and wisely so, for although his fleet had somehow made it through the battle of the previous day without losing a ship, two vessels ran aground after the action was over and had to be abandoned. Hawke's restraint on the twenty-first allowed the remaining five French ships to straggle into the Vilaine estuary before the day was out—but only after their crews had lightened them by heaving guns and tackle overboard. Hawke tried for the next few days to get at the refugees, but in the end contented himself with ravaging the nearby coasts and withdrawing to resume the blockade. For all practical purposes, however, the French vessels that escaped destruction at the Battle of Quiberon Bay might as well have been sunk, for the shallow Vilaine would become their prison. Of the twelve ships that crossed its bar and took shelter under the shore batteries, only three would ever make it out. The rest would remain trapped in the mud, never to serve again. All in all, the Royal Navy had lost two ships and about 300 men in the battle and its aftermath; the French had seen their last effective squadron on the Atlantic destroyed, along with the lives of perhaps 2,500 sailors.

Hawke had delivered a smashing blow to French sea power and forestalled all hope of invading the British Isles. Even though he professed disappointment at the outcome—he felt cheated by the short and stormy day of the battle, believing that "had we had but two hours more daylight, the whole [enemy fleet] had been destroyed or taken"—Hawke had won the only truly decisive battle of the year. The Royal Navy could now destroy French seaborne commerce at will, prevent all attempts to reinforce France's overseas garrisons, and fear not the slightest harassment along Britain's coasts. Although few contemporaries realized it, the Battle of Quiberon Bay, and not the more celebrated Battle of Québec, was the decisive military event of 1759.[9]

HAWKE'S VICTORY was decisive in another sense as well, for it clarified Pitt's understanding of how he should proceed. The prospective conference at Augsburg could go ahead, and if the French were inclined to make peace, so much the better. If they were not, Britain could continue the war against what was left of the French empire on its own terms. With the specter of invasion laid to rest, more British troops could be sent to reinforce Ferdinand or employed in colonial ventures. The public credit, which had been under threat on two notable occasions during

1759, now seemed likely to remain secure. The economy was booming as it had in no previous war, while so many victories rendered open political opposition unthinkable. Even though the estimates that Newcastle submitted to the Commons for 1760 called for the largest budget yet—fourteen million pounds, half of which would have to be borrowed—the M.P.s acquiesced with barely a wince, equably agreeing even to levy a new tax on malt, something unimaginable in ordinary times.[10] With such security on all fronts, it only remained to sustain Frederick and Ferdinand while stripping the bones of the French empire bare. Another campaign like the last one, surely, would bring the Most Christian King's ministers to the table, irrespective of what the Austrians and Russians wished.

Accordingly, the instructions that Pitt sent to Amherst and the governors in North America on January 7, 1760, were the simplest yet. He ordered the governors to ask their assemblies to approve at least the same level of exertion as in the previous year and promised the same subsidies and support, under the same conditions, as before. To Amherst he gave almost complete discretion in designing operations for the conquest of Canada. The commander in chief could use the forces at his disposal to mount a single campaign or several, as he wished; he could build or repair what forts he pleased to secure the conquests already obtained.[11] Pitt's directions were simple, for once, because there was only one objective left for Amherst to conquer: Montréal.

PART VI

Conquest Completed

1760

Amherst plans a climactic, three-pronged invasion of Canada in the midst of a colonial world transformed by Pitt's military policies and expenditures. Outside the walls of Québec, the chevalier de Lévis wins one last battle but finds that he cannot change the course of the war. Murray, Haviland, and Amherst converge on Montréal. An accounting for Britain's victory, and an assessment of its costs. Pitt, at the zenith of his power, confronts a crucial challenge: the sudden death of George II.

CHAPTER 40

War in Full Career

1760

AMHERST RECEIVED Pitt's directions on February 20, when he was already deep in preparations for the coming campaigns. Upon his arrival at New York in December he had settled arrangements with the contractors for supplying the expeditions. In January he had written to the governors, asking for the same numbers of troops their provinces had furnished in 1759, and he had applied to the New York Assembly for another loan to cover his operating expenses until money arrived from Britain. In February he had arranged with Sir William Johnson to procure as many warriors from the Six Nations as possible for the coming year. Throughout the winter, artisans working under contract with the army busily repaired arms and tents and boats, readying them for the next summer's use; ranger and regular officers recruited men to replace those lost in the previous campaign; sergeants drilled their troops in both the conventional tactics of the line and the newer techniques of aimed fire and bush fighting. By the beginning of March, Amherst was looking forward with considerable confidence to completing the conquest of Canada.[1]

Since the capture of Niagara and the withdrawal of the French from their Allegheny forts had reduced activity in the west from an operational to an administrative level, Amherst gave over command of the provinces south of New York to Robert Monckton. With 400 Royal Americans and about 4,000 provincials (300 from North Carolina, 761 from Virginia, and 2,800 from Pennsylvania), he was to consolidate control at Fort Pitt, Niagara, and the old French posts on the Allegheny. Otherwise—apart from the 1,300 regulars he had had to send to South Carolina to help put down a Cherokee uprising—Amherst intended to use practically every redcoat in America, together with thousands of provincials from New England, New Jersey, and New York, in a great three-pronged attack on Canada. He would personally lead the main army of 12,000 men from Albany to Oswego, and then down the St. Lawrence to Montréal; if the Canadians and French were to try to escape westward, they would find their route blocked by overwhelming force. A second army, numbering about 3,500 redcoats and provincials, would advance under the command of Acting Brigadier General William Haviland along the Champlain corridor from Crown Point, taking Île-aux-Noix and the Richelieu River forts on its way to Montréal. The third force, under Brigadier General James Murray, would be made up of as many men as could be spared from the garrison of Québec, plus regular reinforcements sent up from Louisbourg; these would ascend the St. Lawrence by ship. All three forces were to converge, if possible simultaneously, on Montréal, where they would trap the last defenders of New France.[2]

AMHERST'S BOLD PLAN not only called for a degree of strategic coordination never before seen in America, but also for provincial troops essentially equal in number to those that had been raised in the two previous years. That in turn would require greater outlays, man for man, than ever before. Despite problems in enlistment that stemmed both from the extreme exertions of the previous years and from the effects of rumors that peace was at hand in Europe, the governments of the northern provinces did their best to meet the demand for recruits.

As usual, Massachusetts led the way. In January the General Court agreed to raise 5,000 volunteers for the campaign, notwithstanding the heroic expenditures that would be needed to accomplish it. The legislators had already voted to retain, over the winter of 1759–60, the 2,500 men who had been sent to garrison Louisbourg—the decision that had so distressed Gibson Clough.[3] This unprecedented step had occasioned unanticipated expenses, for the province not only had to continue paying the troops' wages so long as they remained in service, but also had to promise support for every "necessitous" soldier's family and pledge an additional four-pound bonus upon completion of duty. In response to Amherst's request for troops, the legislators agreed to pay a nine-pound bounty to any soldier at Louisbourg who would reenlist for the coming campaign and the same amount to as many more volunteers as would be needed to bring the province's forces up to its 5,000-man quota. In the end, it proved necessary to add yet another three pounds to the bounty to raise the last 500 men. All in all, to reimburse a private soldier at Louisbourg—

for example, Gibson Clough—for serving past the expiration of his previous enlistment and then reenlisting for 1760, the province had to lay out twenty-two pounds; and that did not include his wages for the coming campaign, which would cost nearly thirteen pounds more. This was an extraordinary sum to procure the services of a single common soldier, but nothing less would suffice.[4]

As in the previous years, a high bounty offered in one province drove up the bounties in the neighboring ones, so overall costs were greater than in 1758 and 1759; yet the northern colonies responded without complaint, as if they had become accustomed to mobilizing men and resources for the war. Although recruiting went as slowly as usual, by the end of June they had placed nearly 14,500 provincials at Amherst's disposal: 5,000 from Connecticut, 4,000 from Massachusetts, 2,680 from New York, 1,000 each from New Jersey and Rhode Island, and 800 from New Hampshire.[5]

The enthusiasm that lay behind these efforts was real enough, for if anything the prospect of ending the war had enhanced the patriotic spirit of the assemblies. But there was also great practicality in their cooperation. By now the provinces most heavily engaged in the fighting had contracted such massive public debts in proportion to their tax resources that they had become dependent upon Parliament's reimbursements, even to meet current expenses. They were, therefore, no longer in a position to balk at the demands of Amherst and Pitt and risk bringing an end to transfer payments that totaled about £200,000 sterling per year.

Furthermore, throughout the northern colonies military service and such related civilian jobs as those for artificers, wagoners, and crewmen on privateering vessels were generating steady employment for tens of thousands of young men and pumping specie into circulation at a rate unparalleled in colonial history. Agriculture was becoming a steadily more commercialized activity, even in New England, where the purchases of military provision contractors drove commodity prices to extraordinary heights. Beef and pork, bellwethers for the effects of military demand because of their importance in soldiers' rations, commanded prices that were on average half again higher at the beginning of 1760 than they had been at the outset of the war.[6] What Thomas Hutchinson observed of Massachusetts at the beginning of 1760 might be said with equal force about any northern colony: "The generous compensations which had been every year made by parliament, not only alleviated the burden of taxes, which otherwise would have been heavy, but, by the importation of such large sums of specie, increased commerce; and it was the opinion of some, that the war added to the wealth of the province, though the compensation did not amount to one half the charges of government."[7]

Thus in British America the seventh and climactic year of the war began in an atmosphere of confidence, prosperity, and cooperation between colonies and metropole that no one could have predicted on the evidence of the conflict's first years. The scale of the war itself had become almost inconceivably large: a conflict that had begun in an Allegheny glen with the massacre of thirteen Frenchmen had spread over two oceans and three continents—half a world—and had claimed hundreds of thousands of lives. There had been nothing direct about the path, and certainly nothing inevitable about the events, that connected Washington's wretched fort in the Great Meadows to the huge encampments of Anglo-American troops preparing for the war's climactic campaign. And yet, even in the spring of 1760—as officers were beating up for recruits across the northern countryside and ships laden with munitions butted their way across the Atlantic, as John Stanwix was supervising the completion of Fort Pitt and Jeffrey Amherst put the finishing touches on his plans for the summer's expeditions—even then, nothing was foreordained. At Montréal, the chevalier de Lévis had been making plans of his own. He needed only a few ships carrying men and munitions and Indian trade goods from France to make those plans succeed, and if he did, Canada might yet hold out until peace could be made in Europe. In that case, all Amherst's meticulous preparations, all the manpower of the colonies, and all the military strength and logistical weight of Great Britain, would add up to nothing more than one more chapter of frustration to the long, fruitless history of Anglo-American attempts to conquer New France.

CHAPTER 41

The Insufficiency of Valor

LÉVIS AND VAUQUELIN AT QUÉBEC

APRIL–MAY 1760

LÉVIS'S ONE OBJECTIVE was to retake Québec, and with only a little help from home he had it within his power to accomplish this. Wolfe's devastation of the countryside around the city had forced most of the Québecois to seek refuge in the Trois-Rivières and Montréal districts during the winter. The flood of refugees had strained the available food supply, but it had also placed at his disposal several thousand men eager to help expel the enemy from their city. The grain harvest in the Montréal district had been sufficient to provision a siege; once the streams thawed and wheat could be milled into flour, full-scale operations could begin.[1]

The trick would be in timing the start of the campaign, for although he had the troops and the bread, Lévis lacked siege guns and ammunition sufficient to hammer the city into submission if Murray chose to shut himself up within its walls. Lévis had sent a messenger to France after the British fleet had departed in October, urgently requesting reinforcements, heavy cannon, and supplies: all of which had to arrive as soon as the St. Lawrence became navigable and ahead of the British supply fleet. He therefore intended to open his siege in April. If the supply ships came promptly with the men and matériel he needed to finish the job, he would have recaptured the city before the British could relieve it; at which point his enemy would have to perform, once more, the feat that Wolfe had taken all summer to accomplish in 1759.

Since Lévis did not propose to repeat Montcalm's mistakes, he did not assume that the British would succeed—or indeed, that they would even try to besiege the city again. If, as seemed likely, they chose to withdraw from Québec and to concentrate their efforts on seizing Montréal by way of the upper St. Lawrence or the Richelieu River, he was reasonably confident that he could fight them to a standstill. Captain Pouchot, the talented former commandant of Niagara, had lately returned in a prisoner exchange, and Lévis had placed him in charge of Montréal's upriver defenses. Île-aux-Noix still stood unchallenged at the head of the Richelieu, supported by newly built gunboats. The British would have to take the Montréal district inch by inch, by sieges and in woodland combat against Canadian militiamen and Indians: no easy prospect. If by winter the Anglo-Americans had not captured their prize, they would have no choice but to withdraw once more to their base of supply, in New York.[2]

Thus on April 20, having made what preparations he could, the chevalier de Lévis led a surprisingly large army (over seven thousand men) with a tiny train of artillery ("twelve miserable old cannon") out of Montréal, for Québec. The spring thaw was well along, and in the middle of the river enough water lay open for two of the four frigates in Canada, the *Atalante* and the *Pomone,* to escort the barges and bateaux that carried the troops. Lévis was staking everything he had on the venture. On board the boats rode all eight of his regular battalions, their ranks brought to full strength by militiamen; two battalions of *troupes de la marine;* a battalion of Montréal militia; a variety of Indians from the St. Lawrence missions; and even a kind of scratch cavalry squadron, its horses still bony from the winter's privations. Other than a few hundred men left behind at Montréal, the garrison of Île-aux-Noix, and the detachments that had accompanied Pouchot upriver, practically every able-bodied soldier and militiaman in Canada was rowing down the great river, hoping against hope that a supply fleet was also making its way toward them. On April 24, at Pointe aux Trembles, they stopped, unloaded supplies, and readied themselves to march overland toward the city. By dawn on the twenty-seventh, the advance guard had almost reached the little village of Ste. Foy, less than six miles from Québec. That was where they saw the British, entrenched across the road in front of them.[3]

A lucky accident had given Murray advance warning that a French force was advancing on Québec, for it was not until early that same day he had had any inkling of the size of the threat he faced.[4] For many reasons, the appearance of so formidable a force made him almost desperate with worry. Murray's men had suffered dreadfully during the winter. The troops had lacked clothing adequate for the climate—the Highlanders in the 78th, in fact, had had only their kilts, along with whatever Scotsmen wear underneath, to fend off the cold—but disease and inadequate nutrition had taken the gravest toll. By late April, the Québec garrison, which had originally included seven thousand men, could count fewer than four thousand "effectives." The diseases and mishaps of a cruel winter—typhus, typhoid, dysentery, scurvy, frostbite, hypothermia—had killed a thousand men and rendered "above two thousand of what remained, totally unfit for any Service."[5]

Even those men who remained capable of mounting guard and performing the tasks of garrison duty suffered from scurvy and overwork. In particular the necessity of fetching firewood—a task that required long daily treks through snow to the city's woodlots—had grown steadily more fatiguing for the fit as the numbers of sick men mounted. Finally, Murray knew no better than Lévis whether the first ships to arrive with supplies and reinforcements would be English or French. By taking the field at Ste. Foy on the twenty-seventh, therefore, he was not trying to entice Lévis to battle, but only to cover the retreat of his light infantry, which had been manning outposts as far upriver as Cap Rouge. Unlike Lévis, Murray had no plan. Although he had expected the French to move against Québec, when faced with the reality, he could only play for time.[6]

Lévis was too canny a commander to attack the British abatis at Ste. Foy, and so waited for nightfall and the chance to flank the redcoats through the woods that lay to their left. Murray, realizing this danger, ordered a retreat as evening drew on, pulling his men back to a position not far from where Montcalm had arrayed his troops seven months before. He worried that he had too few men to construct advanced lines with which to hold the French outside cannon range from the city's weak western wall. He knew, moreover, that his effective strength was dwindling by the day, and that if the French (whose numbers he had estimated at "ten thousand men, and five hundred Barbarians") laid siege, his garrison might not be able to sustain a defense. But he also knew that his men, weakened as they were, were all regulars, while Lévis's army had to be composed principally of militia. Therefore, mindful "that our little Army was in the habit of beating that Enemy," Murray "resolved to give them Battle" on the Plains of Abraham. Early on the morning of April 28 he mustered about 3,800 troops—every man healthy enough to carry a musket—along with twenty field guns, and ordered them into position on the broken ridge where Montcalm's line had stood before the attack on September 13. Having effectively recapitulated Montcalm's reasoning, Murray was about to reenact the Battle of Québec.[7]

Lévis had expected to lay siege, not to fight an open-field engagement, but he was willing to take advantage of the opportunity that Murray seemed intent on offering. Even though he had so far brought up about half of his force, when between six and seven o'clock he saw that the British had assumed a position outside the city, he ordered his available men (also numbering about 3,800) forward, to take up an opposing position. Murray, who was at this same time reconnoitering ahead of his lines, realized that the French were still on the march and impulsively decided to abandon the high ground. If he could deliver an attack on the enemy's left flank while they were still in column, he reasoned, he might hope to drive them back against the cliffs of the St. Lawrence and annihilate them once and for all.

But eager as they were to fight, Murray's men could not deliver the quick blow he wanted. On the lower ground the melting snow still lay half a leg deep, and underneath it was a mire of mud; what he had intended as a decisive maneuver bogged down near the village of Sillery in ferocious combat. Eventually, after more than an hour of fighting, often at hand to hand, the French began to push back both flanks of the British line, forcing Murray to order a withdrawal. Since their field guns had become hopelessly trapped in the muck and slush, the redcoats spiked and abandoned them on the battlefield. By midday they were back where Montcalm had been seven months earlier, within the walls of Québec, and Lévis was exactly where Townshend had been, opening siege lines before the city. Back at Sillery, French artillerymen were busy drilling the touchholes of the cannon that Murray had obligingly supplied.[8]

The Second Battle of Québec had been a much bloodier affair than the first. Out of approximately equal numbers engaged on each side, the French lost 193 killed and 640 wounded (22 percent of the men on the field) while the British sustained losses of 259 killed and 829 wounded (28 percent). Since Murray not only had sustained heavier casualties, abandoned his artillery, and retreated, but had also lost a much higher proportion of his effective men than the French (28 percent as opposed to less than 12), it is no exaggeration to say that he had taken a spectacular gamble and sustained a spectacular loss. The sight of French engineers laying out siege lines opposite the walls of Québec could hardly have made it clearer that Murray's "passion for glory" would in all likelihood cost him the city, unless help soon arrived from below. By May 11, with his lines complete and his guns securely in place, Lévis was ready to begin bombarding Québec. Although the British could respond with twenty rounds to every one the Gascon brigadier could afford to fire from his meager stock of ammunition, Murray knew that the outcome of the siege would depend not on guns and gunners but on whatever ships and sailors the northeast winds were carrying up the river.[9]

And so, in the end, it was Lagos and Quiberon Bay that proved decisive at Québec, and control of the Atlantic that settled the ownership of Canada. Although the French ministry had ordered up a convoy of five big store ships carrying four hundred regulars and a large quantity of supplies, it had been able to send only a single frigate, the thirty-gun *Machault,* as an escort. Boscawen's blockaders picked off three of the transports when they sailed from Bordeaux early in April; when the rest reached the mouth of the St. Lawrence on May 14, they found that warships from Louisbourg had sailed up the river six days earlier. Rather than risk certain disaster they had then put in at Chaleur Bay, a deep inlet on the south shore of the gulf, and anchored in the Restigouche River, where Acadian refugees still kept up an armed resistance. Making the best they could of their situation, the surviving two hundred regulars and the sailors of the *Machault* used the ship's cannon to erect shore defenses and strung a chain boom across the river's mouth; meanwhile, their commander sent a messenger overland to communicate with Lévis and Vaudreuil. Long before any word came back from Québec, however, the Restigouche had become the expedition's grave. On July 8 two squadrons of British warships converged on Chaleur Bay. Hopelessly outmatched, the defenders sank the forlorn *Machault,* burned all but one of the other vessels to the waterline, and fled into the woods. When the first warships appeared at Québec on the evening of May 12, therefore, the blunt fact that they wore not the Lilies of France but the Union Jack compelled Lévis to raise his siege and retreat to Jacques-Cartier.[10]

"Ah!" Jean-Nicholas Desandrouins, Lévis's engineer, exclaimed: "A single ship of the line and the place would have been ours!" That was very likely true; but the only ship of the line in the river was H.M.S. *Vanguard,* which sailed past Québec to the cheers of Murray's men and opened fire on the French lines. On the morning of the thirteenth, carrying what they could on their backs and leaving everything else behind, Lévis's men scrambled on board their boats and rowed for their lives. The frigate *Pomone* ran aground while trying to maneuver into position to cover the retreat, leaving the sturdy *Atalante* alone to stand off two British warships until the bateaux had made good their escape. Captain Jean Vauquelin, who had been master of the only frigate to escape Louisbourg in 1758, sailed his little man-of-war upriver to Pointe aux Trembles and ordered his men to drop anchor. There he nailed his colors to the mast and shot it out with his pursuers, refusing to give up until his gunners ran out of powder. In the end, wounded but still defiant, he ordered his crew to abandon ship, threw his sword into the river, and waited on his quarterdeck for the British to take him prisoner.[11]

Jean Vauquelin's defiance was, in the classic sense, heroic: as audacious, and as futile, as the eleventh-hour attack on Québec. And in miniature Vauquelin's fate, and that of his ship, foretold what lay in store for the chevalier de Lévis and French Canada. Henceforth Lévis's operations would be limited to retreat and defense; henceforth his hopes would be limited to finding some last gesture by which he could temper defeat with honor. As with Vauquelin and the crew of the *Atalante,* neither Lévis's audacity nor his soldiers' courage, nor any possible act of collective valor, could stop the impending juggernaut.

CHAPTER 42

Murray Ascends the St. Lawrence

JULY–AUGUST 1760

SUPPLY SHIPS and their escorts began arriving at Québec soon after the French retreated upriver. Within a few days six ships of the line and seven frigates lay anchored in the basin; by July 13, when Murray was ready to order the advance toward Montréal, he had at his disposal thirty-two armed vessels, nine floating batteries, and scores of barges and bateaux. Although the dispatches that arrived with the ships explained that Amherst intended to meet him and Haviland at Montréal, he expected that he would be the only one to reach the city before the end of the summer; therefore he was relieved to learn that two regiments from Louisbourg were ascending the river to join him. Murray had scraped 2,200 serviceable men out of the wreckage of the Québec garrison—not a reassuringly large force, even though it was in fact far superior to the 1,500 that Lévis had given the chevalier de Bourlamaque to guard the river below the rapids of Richelieu. This tricky stretch of water, with its narrow navigable channel defended by shore batteries, offered the best opportunity of stopping the British before Montréal, but by July 26 Murray's force had passed the rapids without significant loss.[1]

Thereafter, French cannon on shore occasionally lobbed rounds at the passing flotilla, but only the current, contrary winds, and the weakening force of the tides slowed its progress. Frustrated, the defenders followed the ships, hoping to prevent them from landing forces on shore. In the event, they could not even do that; Murray stopped at most of the settlements he passed to proclaim their conquest and to receive the submission of their populations. The habitants proved tractable, for they were relieved to be spared further punishment and eager to trade poultry, garden crops, and other perishables for the salt that they desperately needed to preserve eels and fish against the coming winter.[2]

In the absence of effective opposition Murray's advance became less an expedition into the heart of enemy territory than a kind of triumphal progress. When Captain John Knox of the 43rd Foot chronicled the army's passage by the "garrison town" of Trois-Rivières on August 8, he might almost have been describing an unusually elaborate *tableau vivant* rather than the largest concentration of French soldiers below Montréal. "The [enemy] troops," he wrote,

> apparently about two thousand, lined their different works, and were in general cloathed as regulars, except a very few Canadians and about fifty naked . . . savages, their bodies being painted of a reddish colour, their faces of different colours, which I plainly discerned with my glass; and otherwise whimsically disfigured, to strike terror into their enemies: their light cavalry, who paraded along the shore, seemed to be well appointed, cloathed in blue, faced with scarlet; but their officers had white uniforms; in fine, their troops, batteries, fair-looking houses, their situation on the banks of a delightful river, our fleet sailing triumphantly before them, with our float[ing batterie]s drawn up in line of battle, the country on both sides interspersed with neat settlements, together with the verdure of the fields and trees, afforded, with the addition of clear pleasant weather, as agreeable a prospect as the most lively imagination can conceive.[3]

Simply by bypassing enemy opposition in this way, Murray was able to sustain a steady progress toward Montréal and to avoid almost all loss of life in doing so. August 23 found the British fleet in the basin called Lac St.-Pierre, where the Richelieu River emptied into the St. Lawrence; at this point they were less than forty miles below Montréal. There, at last, the two Louisbourg regiments that had all the while been trailing them up the river finally joined Murray's battalions, bringing the expedition's fighting strength up to about four thousand men.

On August 27, with French and Canadian troops watching impotently from either shore of the river, the fleet dropped anchor just below the island of Montréal. Against slight resistance, Murray landed troops on the south shore and on September 1 took possession of the parish of Varenne, just downriver from the town. Still he met no significant opposition; indeed, the most difficult task he faced was administering the oath of loyalty to the habitants and the deserting French and Canadian troops who flocked to his camp. Even so—perhaps because he remembered his last encounter with the chevalier de Lévis—he made no move to engage the enemy. Instead he contented himself with digging in and anticipating the arrival of Haviland and Amherst. James Murray was not a particularly patient man, but he would not have long to wait.[4]

CHAPTER 43

Conquest Completed

VAUDREUIL SURRENDERS AT MONTRÉAL

AUGUST 1760

WILLIAM HAVILAND, the imperious forty-two-year-old brigadier who commanded the regulars and provincials who were to approach Montréal via Lake Champlain and the Richelieu River, had launched his expedition only on August 11, when Murray was already past the halfway point. For once it was not the provincials who were at fault, for most of them had arrived at Crown Point by mid-June. Instead, the huge task of carrying provisions and stores forward from Albany had held up the campaign, as had the necessity of giving Amherst time to reach Oswego, from which his western expedition would descend the St. Lawrence. Amherst, guessing that Haviland's small army would take about as long to besiege and take Île-aux-Noix as his larger force would require to make the passage from Oswego down the river, had ordered the two armies to jump off, as nearly as possible, simultaneously. Surprisingly, that almost happened: although it had been delayed by low water in the Mohawk, Amherst's force managed to leave Oswego on August 10. Thus on the sixteenth, when Amherst's bateaux and their escorts, the armed sloops *Onondaga* and *Mohawk,* were approaching the first obstacle in their path—Fort Lévis, Captain Pouchot's island post at La Galette—Haviland's men were disembarking opposite Fort Île-aux-Noix and preparing to open their siege.[1]

Although Amherst and Haviland (the former with almost 11,000 men at his disposal after leaving behind garrisons for the Mohawk River posts and Fort Oswego, and the latter with 3,500 effectives) commanded forces much larger than either of their adversaries, their tasks were formidable ones. At Île-aux-Noix, the chevalier de Bougainville blocked Haviland's advance with 1,450 men in an island fort that dominated the Richelieu River. The French had prepared to receive the invaders by building temporary dams and flooding the land on either shore to a depth of two or three feet, while a schooner and a radeau lay moored just below the island to prevent the British from attempting to run their floating battery, the *Ligonier*, past the fort. Similarly, on the St. Lawrence, the ingenious Captain Pouchot had had enough time to fortify an island at the head of an imposing stretch of rapids. Although he had only about three hundred men under his command, the situation of this stout little fort and Pouchot's thoroughness in preparing its defenses meant that Amherst could not simply pass it by. Like Haviland, he would have to carry out one last complicated siege before he could pass on toward Montréal.[2]

In the end, although the two sieges were conducted under dissimilar circumstances, they lasted about equally long. Haviland opened his batteries against Île-aux-Noix on the nineteenth, and shelled the fort relentlessly until Bougainville evacuated it on the night of August 27–28. Punishing as it had been, it was not Haviland's bombardment that had made him abandon the post, but a raid on the twenty-fifth in which the British seized the schooner and radeau moored below the island. Without these, and lacking any other way to deny the British passage down the Richelieu, Bougainville could only withdraw overland toward Montréal and join forces with Bourlamaque on the south shore of the St. Lawrence.

Haviland, like Amherst a systematic commander, took his time in following Bougainville, securing his conquests as he went; but it was only caution that slowed his advance. Rather than defend the two remaining forts on the Richelieu, St.-Jean and Chambly, Bougainville ordered them burned. Thus, impeded less by force of arms than by the necessity of taking oaths of allegiance from the habitants and deserters who poured into his camps to surrender, Haviland marched overland for the St. Lawrence. On September 3 his messengers reached Murray at Varenne, advising him to expect the southern army in two or at most three days.

Meanwhile Amherst had forced the surrender of Fort Lévis, but only after Pouchot's tiny garrison had held up his huge army for a week. Then, with typical care, Amherst repaired the battered fort (which he renamed William Augustus in Cumberland's honor) and refitted his gunboats before pressing on to face the deadliest obstacles to his progress: the rapids of the upper St. Lawrence. Twenty-one redcoats and provincials had been killed in the siege of Fort Lévis; four times that number drowned before Amherst's boats had shot the last of the white water that

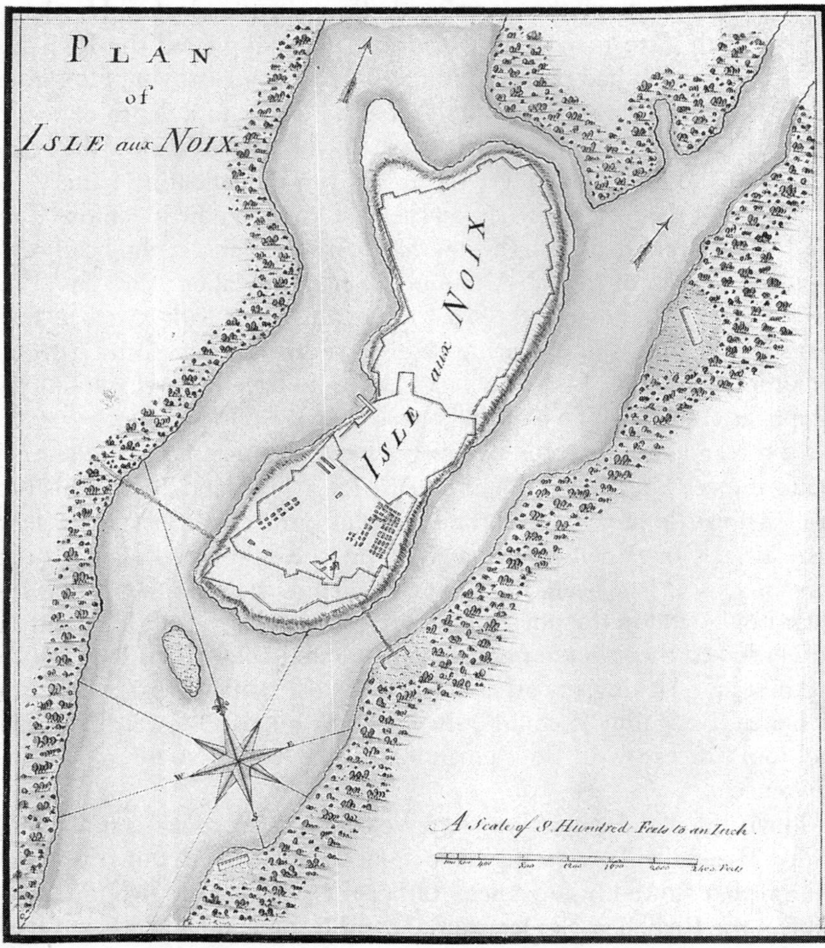

Île-aux-Noix. This island, its fortifications, and its obstacles—chains stretched across the channels and flooded woods on either shore—posed the only serious tactical problem that Haviland had to face between Lake Champlain and Montréal. *Courtesy of the William L. Clements Library at the University of Michigan.*

lay between the fort and Montréal. Although irregulars would have found the army extremely vulnerable as it tried to negotiate the rapids, neither Canadian militiamen nor Indian warriors appeared to harass the British force. Thus even with time taken to repair damaged boats and to raise cannon that had fallen into the river, the western army encamped on Île Perrot near the mouth of the Ottawa River, virtually within sight of Montréal, on September 5. Like Murray and Haviland, Amherst found

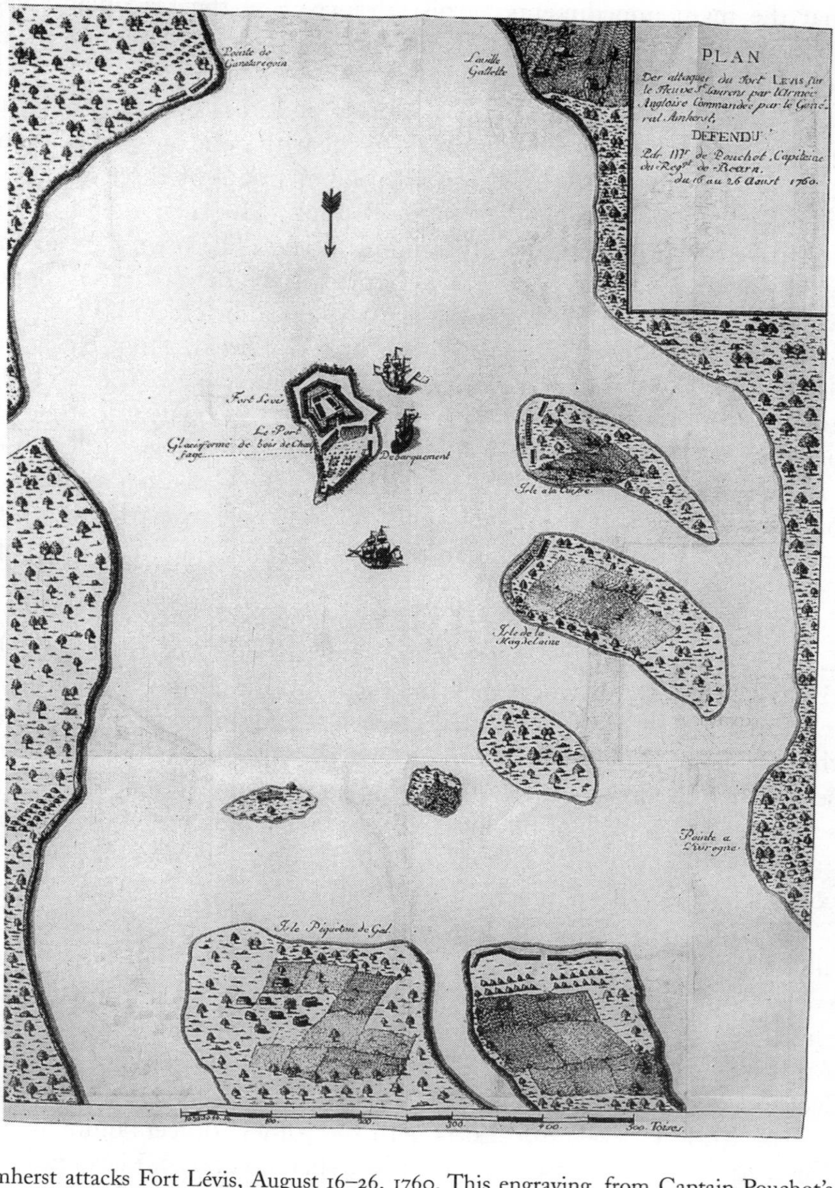

Amherst attacks Fort Lévis, August 16–26, 1760. This engraving, from Captain Pouchot's *Mémoires sur la dernière guerre de l'Amérique septentrionale entre la France et l'Angleterre* (1781), shows the English shelling the fort from three vessels on the river, and batteries located on nearby islands and Pointe de Ganataragoin, upstream. The French battered two of the ships to hulks and held out until they had exhausted their ammunition. When Pouchot surrendered on August 26 his fort had been reduced to a heap of earth and splintered logs. He and his officers were sent to France as prisoners on parole in 1761. *Courtesy of the William L. Clements Library at the University of Michigan.*

that the main impediments to his advance were the Canadians who flooded into his camps, begging his men to trade and his officers to administer the oath of allegiance.[3]

Within the jaws of the vise now closing on him, Lévis had pulled all his regulars back to defend Montréal—a site with none of Québec's geographical advantages. As an island with enemy troops on three of its four sides, lacking any independent base of supply, Montréal would in any case have had little hope of withstanding a siege. The town's "mean and inconsiderable" fortifications, however, made the task of defense a hopeless one even before the first enemy battery could be erected. Lying low to the river, the town was surrounded by a dry ditch, about eight feet deep, and a "slight wall of masonry, solely calculated to awe the . . . Indians." At the northeast end, near the arsenal and boatyard, stood its pathetic excuse for a citadel—"only a Cavalier [an artificial hill, ten or twelve feet high] without a Parapet." Most of the Canadian militiamen had already vanished; the regulars and *troupes de la marine* who were left, including the wounded and men too sick to stand, numbered perhaps four thousand.[4]

And yet, as recently as the day before Amherst landed at Île Perrot, Lévis had continued to maintain substantial bodies of troops on the river's southern bank, where they and the forces of Murray and Haviland eyed each other with the mutual respect of old adversaries. Lévis had thought he could still strike out against the invaders, if only he could secure the support of a few hundred Indian warriors. To that end he had summoned the chiefs of the local villages to a conference on September 4, at the settlement of La Prairie. Warriors from the *pays d'en haut,* of course, had not been much in evidence since 1757, but thus far the Catholic Indians of the St. Lawrence missions had remained steadfast allies. As Lévis was in the very midst of his appeal for help, however, an envoy from one of the upriver villages arrived, stepped into the council circle, and announced that his people had concluded peace with Amherst's army, which would be arriving as soon as the next day. Nothing more needed to be said. "In a moment [the chiefs] dispersed leaving M. le Chevalier de Lévis with the [other] officers quite alone." Thereafter the grim Gascon could only prepare to make his last stand. By the morning of the fifth, he had withdrawn all his remaining forces to the island of Montréal, where they made ready to defend what little was left of New France against an enemy they knew they could not stop.[5]

The outcome of Lévis's last Indian conference demonstrated that, man for man, the most valuable component of Amherst's army was the one that Amherst most despised and distrusted: the seven hundred Iro-

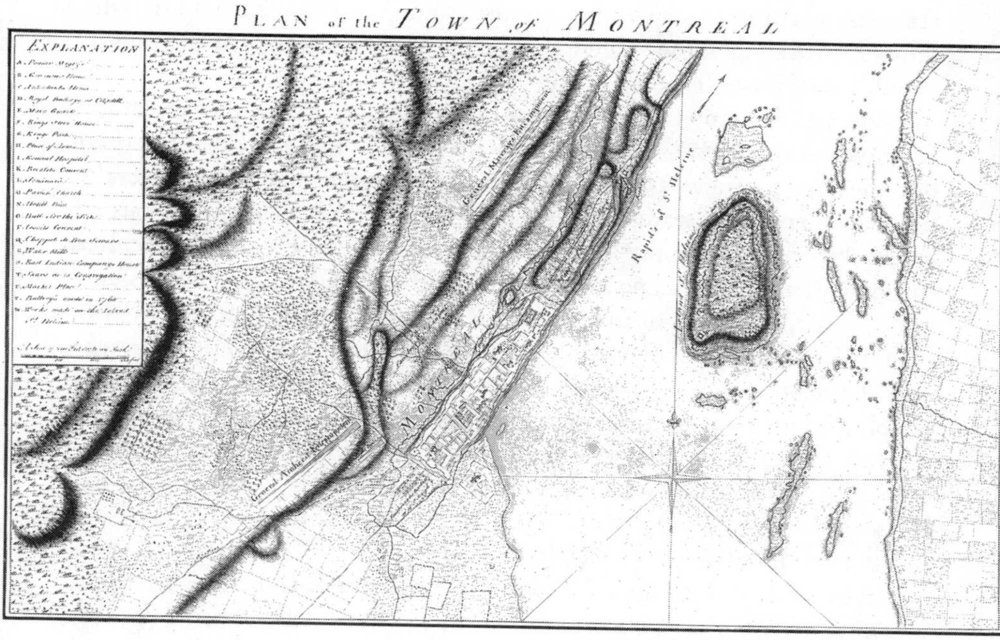

Montréal, c. September 8, 1760. This topographical map suggests exactly how hopeless the position of the French had become in the last hours of the North American conflict. The city, dominated by the heights on which Amherst and Murray had encamped, was defenseless against shelling. If Amherst had chosen to fire red-hot shot, as he did at the sieges of Louisbourg and Fort Lévis, he could easily have reduced the city to ashes. *Courtesy of the William L. Clements Library at the University of Michigan.*

quois warriors who had accompanied him from Oswego. Amherst had been outraged at the size of the present Sir William Johnson had thought necessary to secure their cooperation—£17,000 worth of goods and cash—and had never believed they were anything but an expensive, savage nuisance. Thus he, like every British general who served in America except John Forbes, failed to grasp the Indians' real significance. Wherever his army appeared at a mission village—as, for example, at the mission of La Présentation near Fort Lévis—the mere presence of the Iroquois, and their testimony to the benefits of alliance with the British, gave enough weight to Sir William's offers of amnesty and trade to procure not only peace but active support for the invaders. Through the whole of Amherst's expedition, therefore, the very Indian villages that had always furnished New France with its most loyal auxiliaries actually expedited the British advance. Caughnawaga Mohawks guided

Amherst's army through the rapids from La Présentation onward. Amherst barely acknowledged their help, but this service undoubtedly saved scores, if not hundreds, of his soldiers' lives.[6]

Among the many things that Amherst failed to understand about the Indians was that they were not crass opportunists, eager to abandon their old masters for new and richer ones, but rather that they—like the Shawnees and Delawares of the Ohio Country—had always regarded themselves as free agents: allies, not servants, of the French. In the late summer of 1760 the Canadian mission Indians—like the Ohioans two years before, and most of the nations of the *pays d'en haut* after the battle of Fort William Henry—had decided that the time had come to terminate the relationship. Without the services of the Iroquois diplomats and of Johnson, who made the case for forging a new alliance with the British in every village and mission along the way, and without the seven hundred Iroquois warriors whose presence with the army testified to Great Britain's power and largesse, Amherst's campaign could never have been as quick, and as comparatively bloodless, as it was.[7]

The commander in chief's inability to understand Indians as anything but expensive, barbaric encumbrances would have serious consequences for his later career in America, but for the present he would be spared anything more unpleasant than organizing the surrender of the last effective enemy force in Canada. On Saturday, September 6, his army rowed the short distance from Île Perrot to the west end of the island of Montréal, landing at the settlement of Lachine. His messengers had already established contact with the armies of Murray and Haviland, which in turn were moving to join forces on the south shore, opposite the city—a process facilitated by hundreds of habitants who offered their wagons, their horses, and their services as teamsters, eagerly hauling Haviland's supplies and cannon overland from Chambly. On the night of the sixth while his army made camp near Lachine, Amherst reconnoitered a route to Montréal.[8]

At eight o'clock on Sunday morning, as the great force of regulars and provincials prepared to march, the chevalier de Bougainville rode up to Amherst's headquarters under a flag of truce. He told Amherst that he had come as an emissary from Governor-General Vaudreuil, with instructions to propose an armistice until it could be ascertained whether peace had already been concluded in Europe. Amherst replied, in fluent disdainful French, that "[he] was come to take Canada and [he] did not intend to take anything less." If Bougainville's master wished to propose terms of capitulation, he could have a cease-fire until noon. In the meantime British forces would continue to land on the island and prepare to lay siege.[9]

Within Montréal's fragile walls remained about 2,100 effective soldiers together with a nearly equal number of men too sick or badly wounded to fight. The militiamen had long since deserted along with many of the regulars who had married Canadian women: they had all gone home to protect their families. There were no Indians; almost no provisions; a few pathetic cannon; scarcely any cannonballs; little powder. The wooden buildings would burn like so much kindling if the British gunners threw incendiary shells over the walls. Worst of all, the place was thronged with civilian refugees and its hospitals were crowded with sick and wounded soldiers. These circumstances enabled Vaudreuil to convince Lévis that further resistance, while undeniably glorious to the arms of France, would only serve to immolate thousands of His Most Christian Majesty's subjects in an otherwise meaningless holocaust.

Therefore, promptly at noon, Vaudreuil sent back a long, elaborate list of articles for the surrender of the colony. Nearly half of these dealt with the disposition of French and colony troops, all of whom—in Montréal and everywhere else, from Michilimackinac to Restigouche—would surrender in return for being granted the honors of war, and thus the privilege of returning on parole to France, where they could continue to serve their king. The remainder of the proposals specified protections for those colonists who might choose to remain in Canada, especially concerning their ability to continue unmolested in the practice of their faith and the ownership of their property. One article hopefully proposed that those who remained would be regarded, like the Acadians under the Treaty of Utrecht, as "neutrals," and forever exempted from bearing arms against France. Another proposed with equal improbability that His Most Christian Majesty and his successors on the throne of France would continue to name the colony's bishop.[10]

Amherst agreed to a surprising number of the conditions that Vaudreuil had proposed. With respect to the future of the civil population of Canada, in fact, he agreed to every provision that did not (as in the case of the neutrality of the Canadians and the appointment of the bishop of Québec) obviously impair British sovereignty. Indeed Amherst intended to be a magnanimous victor in every respect except the one that was, to Lévis, the most important of all. For Amherst had replied to the proposals dealing with the French forces by denying that they deserved the honors of war and insisting that instead they "must lay down their arms, and shall not serve during the present war." The regulars would be transported to France with their personal effects intact, but without the emblems of honor that professional officers held sacred: their colors and a symbolic artillery piece. On this point Amherst would not compromise, for he was determined to punish "the infamous part the troops of France had acted in exciting the savages to perpetrate the most horrid and unheard of barbarities in the whole progress of the war."[11]

Lévis and his officers, furious at this deliberate insult, demanded that Vaudreuil break off negotiations. If the governor-general would not permit them to defend Montréal to the last man, he should at least allow them to withdraw with their troops to the nearby Île Ste.-Hélène, where they could die without dishonor. Fortunately for the enlisted men, whose opinion the officers had not solicited before making this offer, Vaudreuil would have none of it. His charge was to protect the welfare of all the colonists of New France, not to sustain the reputation of French arms. Because he had no intention of letting a generous peace slip through his fingers, he agreed only to give Lévis and his officers time to burn their regimental standards before he accepted Amherst's terms.

Before sunset on Monday, Amherst and Vaudreuil exchanged signed copies of the surrender and Amherst dispatched Major Barré to carry the news to Pitt. A quiet night passed; then, "On the 9th, the ten French Battalions layed down their Arms, and delivered up two Colours, which had been taken from Pepprels and Shirley's Regts. at Oswego[. T]he Marquis de Vaudreuil, Generals, and the Commanding Officers of the Regts., [all gave] their words of honour, that the Battalions had not any Colours; they had brought them six years ago with them, they were torn to Pieces, and finding them troublesome in this Country, they had destroyed them."[12]

So ended the dominion of France in North America, not with a bang but with a lie calculated to save face for the officers of an army that could no longer preserve it. Vaudreuil's unwillingness to countenance further sacrifices of life denied Lévis the kind of heroic exit that Vauquelin and Montcalm had made; and yet, in the end, the conventions of military professionalism and honor remained powerful enough to make Amherst accept Lévis's improbable explanation of why he had no colors to surrender.

But then to be a regular officer was everything to Jeffery Amherst. As to Montcalm, who died rather than compromise his values, and to Lévis, who snapped the blade of his sword rather than surrender it, Amherst esteemed military professionalism above all else. The conqueror of Canada allowed himself only a single sentence of self-congratulation on the occasion of the conquest: a passage that ascribed the victory not to

God nor to valor nor to good fortune, but to the necessary effects of military efficiency, properly applied. "I believe," he wrote, that "never three Armys setting out from different & very distant Parts from each other, Joyned in the Center, as was intended, better than we did, and it could not fail of having the effect of which [we] have just now seen the consequence."[13]

CHAPTER 44

The Causes of Victory and the Experience of Empire

1758–1760

OF COURSE AMHERST was right; the convergence of the three armies *was* a remarkable event, and it had had an undeniably stunning effect on the French. But there had been much more to the conquest of Canada than the superbly timed convergence of armies. The very composition of the armies now ceremonially united under Amherst's command testified to the fact that professionalism alone could not explain what had happened. Of the approximately 18,000 men who witnessed the French surrender at Montréal, only about 60 percent (fewer than 11,000) were regulars; the remainder included more than 6,500 provincial soldiers, drawn from every colony north of Pennsylvania, and more than 700 Iroquois warriors. The soldiers' physical appearance bore witness that this was no conventional army: most of the provincials wore ordinary civilian clothes, while the regulars wore uniforms that would have made them a laughingstock in Europe. Since 1758 they had routinely cut the tails of their coats back almost to the waist; had trimmed the brims of their hats to within a couple of inches of the crown, and had worn them slouched, not cocked; had had their hair cut to a length of just an inch or two. At least one Highland regiment had given up the kilt in favor of breeches. Officers now seldom wore the gorgets and sashes that invited the attention of enemy marksmen; some had taken to wearing ordinary privates' coats; a few had even begun to carry tomahawks. Except for the color of their coats, regulars had come to look more like provincials than many of their officers liked to admit. When one of them tried to describe "the droll figure we cut" in a letter home, the best he could do was to tell his correspondent that "you would not distinguish us from common plough men."[1]

Changes in the uniform reflected more profound alterations in the army. Its tactics had undergone a transformation in America and now included "bush fighting" as well as conventional drill; a new command, for example, had been invented to deal with ambushes—"Tree all!" For at least three years the redcoats had been firing at marks and were now accustomed to aiming, rather than merely leveling, their muskets at the enemy. Rifles had been issued to the best marksmen in at least a few regular battalions, in tacit abandonment of the unwritten rule that no gentleman would countenance the intentional killing of enemy officers. The army employed specialized units on a scale that would have been extraordinary in Europe. In proportion to the total number of men under arms, for example, the American forces included fewer grenadiers, but many more light infantry: and not just companies of them, but whole battalions of little wiry men able to move quickly through the woods and secure the flanks of heavy columns traveling by road. And there were more exotic units, too, some of which would have seemed bizarre to European soldiers: ranger companies to make the raids and reconnaissance patrols that, in the absence of Indian auxiliaries, the regulars could not otherwise perform; a corps of armed bateaumen, raised specifically to fight and ferry supplies between Albany and Oswego; a unit of armed wagoners, formed to transport provisions from Albany to Lake George; crews for the armed schooners, sloops, and radeaux that had sailed the inland lakes to protect troops who could only "march" against the enemy in whaleboats and bateaux.[2]

The measures necessary to overcome the distances and difficulties of overland communication were both heroic and alien to the standards by which professional officers ordinarily judged themselves and their adversaries. By 1760 there were forts everywhere in America, in locations that would have seemed impossibly remote to anyone who had not yet become acquainted with American warfare. From Fort Loudoun on the South Carolina frontier to the soon-to-be-leveled fortress of Louisbourg on the windswept tip of Cape Breton Island, these posts defended strategic points that, if overlaid on a map of Europe, would have stretched from London to Constantinople. To build such forts required phenomenal expense and exertion; to sustain them demanded the building of hundreds of miles of roads where none had ever been, as well as the construction of fortified way stations to protect the huge supply trains on which the whole system depended. To create and maintain this network required millions of pounds sterling and millions of man-hours of labor, the mobilization of tens of thousands of provincial soldiers and scores of thousands of civilians. These civilians were not just the wagoners, artificers, sutlers, and contractors directly involved in meeting the needs of the armies, but farmers and farm wives, laundresses, seamstresses, cordwainers, tanners, tailors, sail-makers, gunsmiths, laborers, mariners, farriers, boat-wrights, shipwrights, wheelwrights, rope-makers, coopers, carpenters, chandlers, butchers, bakers, and other ordinary colonists without whose skills and products—and without whose loyalty, taxes, and enthusiasm for the cause—the armies could never have remained in the field.[3]

Warfare on the fantastic geographical scale of the Seven Years' War in America had been conceivable because Parliament was willing to grant the sums necessary to fund far-flung campaigns; because the British people were able to shoulder the taxes required by a war vaster than any their nation had ever fought; because the colonists cooperated in the imperial enterprise with an enthusiasm and a vigor unprecedented in their history. Amherst, the beneficiary of these vast financial, military, and emotional resources, could complete the conquest of Canada not just because his three northern armies converged in such remarkable synchrony on Montréal, but because the Royal Navy had cut off the French shipping without which Canada could not survive, and because the northern Indian nations had at length decided to cast their lot with the British. Most of all the conquest of Canada had become a reality because Pitt, the northern governors and legislatures, and Amherst himself had been able to mobilize the resources of entire colonial societies in support of the campaigns of 1758, 1759, and 1760. As a result, to a degree virtually unknown in the eighteenth century, every colony north of Virginia had experienced the conflict as a people's war.

Much more than military professionalism, then, enabled three armies to converge on Montréal: a combination of factors so complex that no one present at the surrender ceremony on September 9, 1760, could fully have understood them. Certainly not Amherst and his generals, who believed that British discipline and efficiency had won the victory, and who accordingly discounted the contributions of amateurish Americans and savage Indians. Nor indeed could the provincials, who were as quick to dismiss the Indians as the British were, but who keenly appreciated how much their own labors had contributed to the outcome, and who had come to believe that the redcoats wished only to deprive them of their share of the glory. When, immediately after the surrender, Amherst ordered all of his provincials back to work on the rear-line forts while sending his regulars into early winter quarters, his action spoke clearly of what he understood to be the value, if not the worth, of the provincial troops. It was an opinion that the provincials did not share, and which they—predictably—resented.[4]

The alienating consequences of this disparity between the viewpoints of regular officers and their provincial counterparts can be glimpsed in the journal of Captain Samuel Jenks, a thoughtful blacksmith from Point Shirley (Chelsea), Massachusetts, who served in the Bay Colony regiment that had accompanied Haviland's expedition down Lake Champlain. Jenks and his fellow officers had already been offended when, after the surrender of Île-aux-Noix, Haviland would not allow them onto the island to take a look at the fort. It was, Jenks had written on August 28, "lookd upon as a very high affair, when we have done most part of the fatigue dureing the siege, & our men have been more exposed than [the regulars, that we] must now be denyd the liberty to go & see what [we] have fought for." Following the surrender of Montréal, he and his comrades were intensely curious about the capital of Canada, but they had to content themselves with what sights they could see from two miles off. "This city," he wrote, "makes a very beautiful appearance & [has] very fine buildings & beautiful improvements." Or so "they look," he added ruefully, "at a distance." That very afternoon his regiment received its orders to march for Crown Point, where, he wrote, "I fear we shall be kept until ye last of November, for ye command is left to Haverland, & I know he delights to fatigue ye provincials." And there in fact they stayed until November 18, working on the fort and its barracks despite a terrifying outbreak of smallpox, severe weather, and the utter lack of an enemy threat. In the end there was no love left to be lost between the provincials and regulars who together had added Canada to the British empire. "To day," Jenks had commented on October 31, "the commanding officer [Haviland] keeps all the [provincial] troops on fatigue, so eager are they to git all they possibly can out of us before they dismis us. I think this parallell with ye devils rage, when he knew his time was short to plague mankind in; so I know their time is short like their masters." A couple of weeks later, hearing that Haviland had fallen in the snow and broken his leg, Jenks could only comment, "I am sorry it was his leg."[5]

Thus for many of the homesick—and more seriously ill—provincials, even the triumphant final campaign of the American war ended bitterly. Others no doubt felt mainly weariness, and gratitude at having survived their service. But not one of them who kept a record of his service thought to comment on the great imperial victory as a vindication of British military professionalism. Instead, they thanked God that the war had ended with so little shedding of blood. Gibson Clough, returning from Louisbourg after an absence of nearly two years, merely wrote, on

New Year's Day, 1761, "I arrive at Salem my native place, to my great Joy and content, and thus I conclude my Journal, with my best wishes and good will to all brother soldiers."[6]

Ensign Rufus Putnam, back in New Braintree, found more to say. He had overcome his scruples against further service when offered a commission, but then had found himself assigned once more to the Ticonderoga sawmills he detested. In this way he had been "deprived of the honour, and of Shearing in the feteague of twelve days Seage at the Isle de nanx,—which opened the way for the junction of the three British armies before Montreal." At home once more on December 1, Putnam congratulated himself that, for the first time since 1757, he had not been cheated by regular officers. Then, in a final entry, he tried to sum up his reactions to the four campaigns he had served in. "And now, soon after my return home, I [have] concluded not to go into the service any more, not from any dislike to the service of my King and Country, or any misfortunes in the service, for, through the goodness of Divine Providence, I was always prospered in some measure, and had my health entirely the whole 4 years that I have been out. And, although I underwent many hardships and difficulties; yet, by the good hand of my God upon me, I was enabled to bear up under them all."[7] Then, without ceremony, ex-Ensign Putnam got on with his life. In the spring he married and, using money saved from his pay, set himself up as a farmer and millwright. Ex-Private Clough went back to his bricklaying; ex-Captain Jenks returned to his smithy.

Although Samuel Jenks, Gibson Clough, and Rufus Putnam never met to discuss the significance of what they had seen and learned during their service with the British armies, their experiences as provincials had given them strong, and fundamentally similar, opinions about the regular officers under, and the redcoat soldiers alongside, whom they had served; about the contributions that they, and other provincials like them, had made to the victory; about the importance of honoring the enlistment contracts they had entered into, in order to serve their king; about the mercy of a God who had ordained both a successful conclusion to the war and the preservation of their own lives through the perils of disease, accident, fatigue, and battle. More than they—and like them, thousands upon thousands of other provincial veterans—knew, the war had transformed their world. Moreover, the war had changed them, too, by laying the groundwork for something unprecedented in the history of the colonies: a generation capable, on the basis of shared experience, of forming a common view of the world, of the empire, and of the men who had once been their masters.

CHAPTER 45

Pitt Confronts an Unexpected Challenge

OCTOBER 1760

On the fifth of October, Isaac Barré, face disfigured and sight partially destroyed by the wound he had received at the Battle of Québec, brought word to Pitt of Canada's capitulation. While most welcome, the news was hardly unexpected and did not occasion the kind of outburst that William Amherst's visit had evoked a little more than two years earlier. Instead Pitt responded in a manner that had become almost routine, presenting the dispatches to the king, issuing a *Gazette Extraordinary* to make the news public, allowing himself to bask awhile in the adulation of the people, and then sending Amherst a letter full of congratulation, instruction, and advice.[1]

The king, the man now known as the Great Commoner wrote, was delighted, but would of course expect a full account of the territories and posts that had been added to his dominions. Naturally Amherst would also want to suppress the rebellion of the Cherokee Indians in Carolina, news of which had been troubling His Majesty of late. With so little left to conquer in America, the commander in chief could take his choice between seizing the remainder of the French West Indian islands or launching an expedition against those forts that remained in enemy hands in the Mississippi Valley and at Mobile. At any rate Amherst did not need to wait for detailed instructions, "the King reposing the most entire Reliance on [his] Experienced Judgement, and Ability." Finally, Pitt concluded, he should *not* expect to come home until the war was over or until the king saw fit to summon him back, and so might as well stop asking to be relieved of his command.[2]

Pitt finished this letter on October 24, a Friday on which—had he chosen to do so—he could have taken considerable pleasure in the current state of affairs. If he did not allow himself to feel self-satisfied, it was because in Europe there had been no breakthrough and he was growing impatient both with Prince Ferdinand and with Frederick II. Ferdinand in particular seemed unwilling or unable to take the offensive against the French army on the Rhine. Still, if Pitt had been willing to give him his due, he would have had to admit that the prince, although always outnumbered and sometimes outmaneuvered, had fenced all summer with France's best general without losing any significant territory and had made Hanover safe once more. The end of the invasion threat after the Battle of Quiberon Bay had freed ten battalions of British horse and twelve of foot for service in Germany: these formed a "Glorious Reinforcement" sent to the prince in September and brought the number of redcoats on the Continent up to about 22,000. Although they had arrived too late to make any difference in 1760, if properly employed in the coming year they might conceivably tip the balance enough to make the French willing to sue for peace. The early indications at least were favorable. At the recent victory of Kloster Kamp, British units—especially Sir John Granby's cavalry—had done excellent service and helped insure that the French would be on the defensive when they went into winter quarters.[3]

As for the war in the east, Prussia seemed more than ever to be a sewer down which German blood and British money flowed in approximately equal volumes. Impatient as Pitt was, however, he could not have failed to see that Frederick was holding his own, and indeed even retaining the initiative. Despite (or because of) the impossibility of regaining Saxony, he had reinvaded Silesia in August, and there, at Liegnitz, had brilliantly defeated a larger Austrian army; then, with even greater brilliance, he had hoaxed the commander of the main Russian army into withdrawing his forces from Prussia for the remainder of the campaigning season. Although a small combined force of Austro-Russian raiders managed to seize and partially burn Berlin on October 9, they had retreated as soon as Frederick marched to the city's relief. Now, Pitt knew, the doughty little king was moving to engage the main Austrian army, which had withdrawn to the Elbe and encamped near Torgau. Frederick had always won more battles than he lost. Perhaps this one would be decisive.[4]

In short, had Pitt taken stock of the war on that late autumn Friday, he would have realized that if European operations had not moved beyond stalemate, at least they had not deteriorated. He might well have hoped to force the French (if not necessarily the Austrians and Russians) to make peace, supposing he could put more pressure on them in the coming year. In this respect the West Indies, the Mississippi River forts, and the Alabama posts to which he directed Amherst's attention were particularly important. And then, of course, there was that other theater of war, even more distant from Europe than America, in which the last years' developments also looked promising—events that could only discomfit the French court, further weaken France's overseas commerce, damage the monarchy's credit, and thus erode the country's ability to continue the war. For in India, the forces of the United East India Company, the company's Indian allies, and a handful of regular troops seemed to be on the verge of erasing French power and influence altogether.

Anglo-Indian arms were succeeding on the subcontinent late in 1760 largely because the Royal Navy had come to dominate the Indian Ocean almost to the same extent it controlled the North Atlantic. Early in 1757, a remarkable clerk-turned-conqueror, Robert Clive of the East India Company, had learned of the declaration of war against France and seized the opportunity to attack the Compagnie des Indies, France's counterpart to his own employer. In March of that year, Clive's troops had captured one of the leading French factories, Chandernagore. In June he defeated the nawab of Bengal and the French units that supported him at the Battle of Plassey, thus gaining direct control over Bengal. In northern India, then, everything had gone splendidly; in the southeast, where the Compagnie des Indies competed more directly with British interests, the situation had initially looked less promising but had improved as time and the Royal Navy asserted their influence.

The arrival at Pondicherry, early in 1758, of a strong force from France under Thomas-Arthur, comte de Lally, had gravely threatened British interests on the Coromandel Coast. By the beginning of June, Lally had seized the rich and important company post of Fort St. David, near Cuddalore, south of Pondicherry. Before the year was out he had besieged the very seat of British power in southeast India, Fort St. George, at Madras. This had been particularly dangerous, since Clive had the majority of the company's troops with him in far-off Bengal; and indeed Lally and his men came extremely close to taking Fort St. George during the winter. Only the arrival at Madras in mid-February of British store ships, convoyed by armed East Indiamen and a Royal Navy squadron, shifted the balance against the French commander. Not a moment too soon: Lally's sappers had actually breached the fort's outer wall when he found himself forced to raise the siege and retire to his base of supply at Pondicherry.[5]

Lally could not sustain his army without money and adequate supplies, and he could obtain neither by sea. Throughout 1759 his troops became more and more demoralized, mutinying over their lack of pay, ragged clothing, and miserable rations; and those shortages in turn could be traced to the inability of the regional naval commander, Admiral Anne Antoine, comte d'Aché, to bring them in from Île de France (Mauritius), the principal naval base in the Indian Ocean. Lally's situation deteriorated as the year progressed, but it was not until September 10 that his fate was sealed. On that day Admiral d'Aché—who at long last had acquired food, supplies, and reinforcements, and who was sailing for Pondicherry at the head of a powerful eleven-ship squadron—encountered the smaller nine-ship fleet of Rear Admiral Sir George Pocock off Tranquebar. In an engagement rendered indecisive because both commanders adhered scrupulously to the line-ahead tactics specified in their Fighting Instructions, Pocock's gunners inflicted considerable damage on their adversaries. Admiral d'Aché limped on to Pondicherry, but his squadron had been so badly battered that he could not remain. To save his ships, he retired to Île de France on October 1, never to return.[6]

In saving his fleet, d'Aché doomed Lally and the French trading stations on the Coromandel Coast. The turning point actually came at the beginning of 1760 when the British military commander in the region, Lieutenant Colonel Eyre Coote of the 84th Regiment, lured Lally out to do battle at Wandiwash, some forty miles northwest of Pondicherry. On January 22, Coote defeated his opponent in an open-field engagement; thereafter, Lally broke down psychologically and proved incapable of defending the outposts that protected Pondicherry. By the middle of April only the city and its immediate surroundings remained under French control. Meanwhile, a powerful British naval squadron had blockaded it, allowing Coote to besiege the city in August. On January 16, 1761, he would accept the sword of Pondicherry's neurasthenic commandant and extinguish, four months after the capitulation of Canada, the influence of France in India.[7]

Because it took six months for news from India to reach England, Pitt knew only of the Battle of Wandiwash and the skirmishes prior to the siege of Pondicherry when he finished his letter to Amherst on October 24. Yet there is no reason to doubt that he anticipated that Coote's and the company's operations in India would conclude as successfully as Amherst's campaigns in America. More than any other British minister except Anson, Pitt understood that the Royal Navy's mastery of the seas could decide the fate of France's empire.

Pitt was, indeed, so enamored of seaborne operations that he was willing to believe they could be decisive even in Europe, where experience actually suggested the opposite. His newest scheme was in fact to renew raiding on the French coast as a means of moving the European war off dead center. Specifically he intended to seize Belle-Île-en-Mer, the island off the Breton coast that British sailors called Belleisle. Thirty miles south of Lorient and a hundred twenty miles northwest of La Rochelle, commanding the approaches to Quiberon Bay, Belleisle dominated the Bay of Biscay. A British naval base and army garrison there, Pitt thought, could divert thousands of French troops from Germany to coastal defense. Lord Anson believed it a mad scheme and opposed it; so did Sir Edward Hawke, who arguably knew the region better than anyone else in Britain. Typically, the disapproval of the nation's two greatest admirals deterred Pitt not in the least, and in the hope of enlisting the king's approval for the venture, he had requested an audience for the same day on which he sent off Amherst's instructions, the twenty-fourth. The results, however, were not what he had anticipated. George II disapproved. Pleased as he was with the recent victories overseas, he worried that seizing Belleisle would lead to the recall of British army forces supporting Ferdinand, and might thereby endanger his beloved Hanover.

Pitt, angry that Anson had gotten in ahead of him and primed the king with arguments against the plan, knew that now he would have to campaign long and hard to gain the stubborn old man's acquiescence.[8] Yet he surely did not doubt that he could do it. Since the fall of Louisbourg the king had denied him nothing. How likely was he permanently to refuse his approval to the minister who had lately delivered to him half of North America and would at any moment be able to announce the conquest of France's last stronghold in India? How likely was the king to decline the counsel of a minister who was on the threshold of making him master of an empire greater than Alexander's?

BUT PITT WOULD never convince the king of the strategic benefits of seizing Belleisle because, before the palace clocks had struck eight the next morning, George II was dead. He had gone to bed on Friday night feeling as well as most men of seventy-seven are permitted to feel. According to Horace Walpole, who mined the gossip of the court for every detail of the next morning's events, he "rose at six . . . as usual, looked, I suppose, [to see] if all his money was in his purse, and called for his chocolate. A little after seven, he went into the water-closet—the German *valet de chambre* heard a noise louder than the royal wind, listened, heard something like a groan, ran in, and found the hero of

Oudenarde and Dettingen on the floor, with a gash in his right temple, by falling against the corner of a bureau—he tried to speak, could not, and expired."[9] The autopsy showed that he had suffered a massive heart attack—brought on, it was supposed, "from his exertions."[10]

For three years, everything William Pitt touched had turned to gold. But when the old king died, the world of British politics changed forever. In a twinkling, Leicester House ceased to be a country faction and became the court. The earl of Bute ceased to be the prince's tutor and became instead his monarch's most trusted counselor. And the prince of Wales, thickheaded adolescent that still he was, became George III, by the grace of God king of England, Scotland, Wales, Ireland, and America. Pitt had proven himself to be many things, but he had not been pliable, and nothing he had done in the last two years (ever since his abandonment of Bligh after the fiasco of St.-Cas) had endeared him to George and Bute, the oddly assorted pair who had suddenly become the most important men in Britain. Pitt must have sensed that he had become vulnerable; and yet no one believed more fervently than he did that he was indispensable to the Crown and its gigantically expanded empire. So he did not panic or even make extraordinary efforts to patch up relations with Bute and the new king, but rather assumed that he would carry on as he had for the last three years.

Pitt had no real conception of how unlikely it was that he would succeed in that endeavor. Since 1758 the Great Commoner had only had to reckon with his nation's enemies and its sometimes equally bellicose allies. But the new king offered challenges of a different—and sterner—sort than any that belligerent states had posed. No one but Bute and George's mother had ever succeeded in mastering the turbulent emotions and the passionate convictions of the man whom time and chance had made king. They had been able to do it because George loved them without question. But Pitt, who knew his worth very well, failed to understand, at the most critical moment of his career, that there was nothing about him that George III could love.

VICTORY RECOLLECTED

Scenographia Americana

The Seven Years' War brought many artistically talented officers to America. Engineers like Archibald Campbell rendered landscapes with topographical precision; amateur artists like General Wolfe's aide-de-camp Hervey Smyth (shown supporting his chief's right arm in *The Death of General Wolfe*) practiced the genteel art of the sketch. After the war, several London printsellers engaged engravers to turn these eyewitness records into twenty-eight superb, folio-sized mezzotints. The set went on sale in 1768 for the considerable sum of four guineas (four pounds, four shillings).

Scenographia Americana: Or, a Collection of Views in North America and the West Indies . . . From Drawings taken on the Spot, by several Officers of the British Navy and Army appealed to affluent print buyers, although Britons of modest means could buy individual views for three shillings, sixpence each. French and Spanish translations of the print titles suggested that the *Scenographia* was also intended for export. Yet it is hard to believe that many copies sold in France or Spain, for the set as a whole illustrated a narrative of British imperial glory.

The story began with the capitals of the old British colonies. Boston (plate 1), Charleston (2), and New York (3) appeared as prosperous port towns, while a second view of New York (4) from inland depicted its setting in conventional pastoral terms. The first glimpses of the colonies thus emphasized civility, but, moving inland, a less constrained nature soon emerged. Dramatic cliffs and mountains dominate views of the Tappan Zee (5) and the Catskills (6), while eighty-foot-high cataracts dwarf human figures in *Great Cohoes Falls* (7) and *Falls on the Passaick* (8).

Yet the engravings also showed that despite nature's power, civilization advanced with the plow. *A Design to represent the beginning and completion of an American Settlement or Farm* (9) directed the eye from the gloomy forest and rude cabin at the left to a Georgian house, sunlit fields, and coppiced woods on the right. A similar message appeared in *A View of Bethlem* (10), which testified to the industry of Count Zinzendorf's Moravian followers, who had prospered under Britain's beneficent rule.

War and conquest shaped the narrative's second half. Neither Indians nor colonists played any role in this story, which began in 1758 with Britain's first notable victory. *A View of Louisburg* (11) showed an artillery crew manhandling a gun into place while sailors bring fascines to shield it. The French fleet lies captive in the harbor while the British fleet rides at anchor in Gabarus Bay (left); the fortress awaits its doom.

Louisbourg's fall opened Canada to invasion, as depicted in images from Hervey Smyth's sketchbook. The dense forest surrounding a fishing settlement on Gaspé Bay (12) and a farming village at Miramichi (13) suggested how little the French improved their possessions, yet a note that 4,500 quintals—half a million pounds—of fish had been captured at the Gaspé settlement indicated how the conquests would improve British trade. The fleet passes *Pierced Island* (14) on its way to Québec, where several dramatic scenes ensue. Montmorency Falls' natural sublimity frames the courage and self-sacrifice of Wolfe's abortive July 31 attack (15). Plate 16 shows Cap Rouge, the departure point for the British boats on September 13, while plate 17 depicts Québec itself. The *East View of Montreal* (18) shows a scene from 1760, when Canada's last defenders lay trapped within the indefensible city.

From Canada, the scene shifted to the conquest of the West Indies. This series begins outside Havana, where exotic plants (like the weirdly bent mountain aloe in plate 19) and exotic people (like the creoles and slaves in plates 20 and 21) inhabit an alien landscape. Two urban views strike a similar chord. Tropical light drenches the Franciscan Church and Convent (22) and the Market Place (23); yet both scenes remind viewers of British conquest. Men-of-war ride at anchor near the church; an infantry company forms up in the marketplace, while sailors in short, baggy trousers look on from the left foreground. Plate 24 shows boat crews towing a man-of-war seaward, past sunken wrecks. At the harbor's mouth the Punta (left of the ship) and Morro Castle fly the Union Jack, testifying to British power.

The war returned in scenes from the conquests of Dominique (25) and Guadeloupe (26)—views that illustrate the heroism of amphibious assaults. The final plates, however, turned from battle to its serene aftermath. *A North View of Fort Royal* (plate 27) depicts soldiers at ease in camp. British social order and British services frame the scene: at left, an officer shows a lady the camp, while at center a soldier kisses an unresisting wench; on the right, a soldier and a sailor shake hands, symbolizing the cooperation that had made victory possible. *An East View of Fort Royal* (28) similarly shows officers, soldiers, and sailors contemplating a glorious sunset. Inshore a sloop skims the water, while along the horizon ships sail eastward at cable's length intervals.

Viewers could decide for themselves whether those distant ships were merchantmen, deep-laden with the fruits of conquest, or men-of-war sailing off to new triumphs. Whatever they were, Britons of 1768 could read the same message in that tranquil scene. The sun had set on France's empire. Britain reigned supreme over its dominions, safe by land and by sea. The future of empire stretched ahead toward vistas of prosperity and power as majestic as the American landscape, as boundless as the sea.

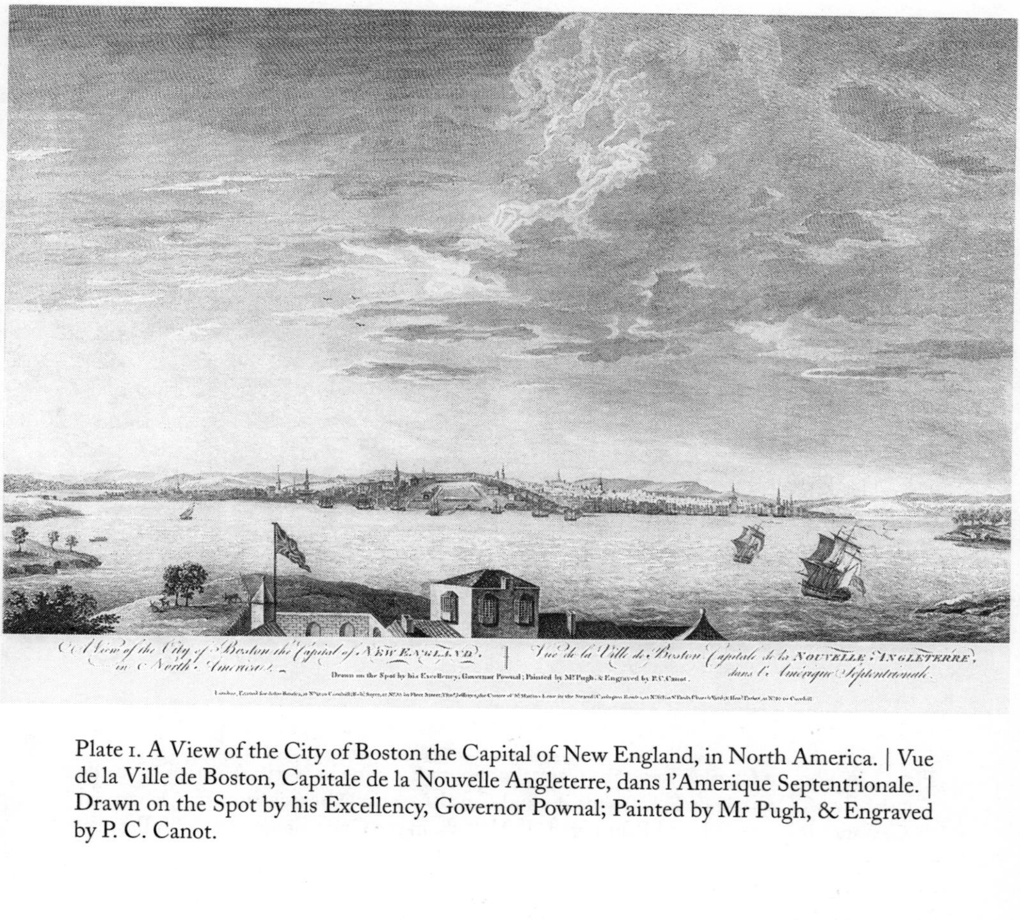

Plate 1. A View of the City of Boston the Capital of New England, in North America. | Vue de la Ville de Boston, Capitale de la Nouvelle Angleterre, dans l'Amerique Septentrionale. | Drawn on the Spot by his Excellency, Governor Pownal; Painted by Mr Pugh, & Engraved by P. C. Canot.

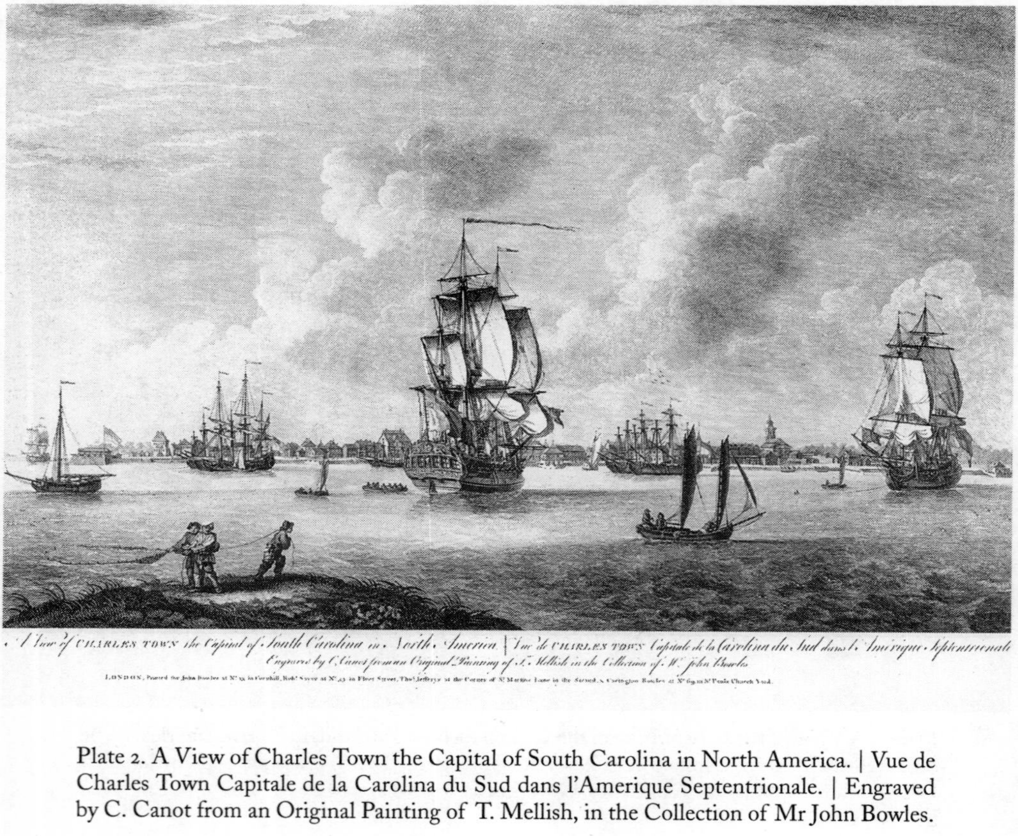
A View of CHARLES TOWN the Capital of South Carolina in North America. | Vue de CHARLES TOWN Capitale de la Carolina du Sud dans l'Amerique Septentrionale
Engraved by C. Canot from an Original Painting of T. Mellish in the Collection of Mr. John Bowles

Plate 2. A View of Charles Town the Capital of South Carolina in North America. | Vue de Charles Town Capitale de la Carolina du Sud dans l'Amerique Septentrionale. | Engraved by C. Canot from an Original Painting of T. Mellish, in the Collection of Mr John Bowles.

Plate 3. A South West View of the City of New York, in North America. | Vue de Sud Ouest de la Ville de New York, dans L'Amerique Septentrionale. | Drawn on the Spot by Capt Thomas Howdell, of the Royal Artillery. Engraved by P. Canot.

Plate 4. A South East View of the City of New York, in North America. | Vue de Sud Est de la Ville de New York, dans L'Amerique Septentrionale. | Drawn on the Spot by Capt Thomas Howdell, of the Royal Artillery. Engraved by P. Canot.

A View in Hudson's River of the Entrance of what is called the Topan Sea.
Vue sur la Riviere d'Hudson, de l'entree counue sous le nom de Mer de Topan.
Sketch'd on the Spot by his Excellency Governor Pownal. Painted by Paul Sandby. Engraved by Peter Benazech.

Plate 5. A View in Hudson's River of the Entrance of what is called the Topan Sea. | Vue sur la Riviere d'Hudson, de l'entree counue sous le nom de Mer de Topan. | Sketch'd on the Spot by his Excellency Governor Pownal. Painted by Paul Sandby, Engraved by Peter Benazech.

Plate 6. A View in Hudson's River of Pakepsey & the Catts-Kill Mountains, From Sopos Island in Hudson's River. | Vue sur la Riviere d'Hudson dans Pakepsey et des Montagnes de Catts-Kill, Prise de l'Isle de Sopos, situee dans cette Riviere. | Sketch'd on the Spot by his Excellency Governor Pownal. Painted & Engraved by Paul Sandby.

Plate 7. A View of the Great Cohoes Falls, on the Mohawk's River; The Fall about Seventy feet; the River near a Quarter of a Mile broad. | Vue de la Grande Cataracte de Cohoes, sur la Riviere des Mohawks; La Hateur est l'environ 70 pieds; l sa Riviere a pres l'un quart de Mille de large. | Sketch'd on the Spot by his Excellency Governor Pownal. Painted by Paul Sandby, & Engraved by Wm Elliott.

Plate 8. A View of the Falls on the Passaick, or second River, in the Province of New Jersey. The height of the Fall between Eighty and Ninety feet; the River about Eighty Yards broad. | Vue de l'Cataracte du Passaick, ou seconde Riviere, dans la province du Nouveau Jersey. La Hauteur de cette Chute est de 80 à 90 pieds, et la Largeur de la Riviere d'environ 40 Toises. | Sketch'd on the Spot by his Excellency Governor Pownal. Painted and Engraved by Paul Sandby.

Plate 9. A Design to represent the beginning and completion of an American Settlement or Farm. | Dessein qui represente la maniere d'etablir et de parachever une Habitation ou Ferme Americaine. | Painted by Paul Sandby, from a Design made by his Excellency Governor Pownal. Engraved by James Peake.

Plate 10. A View of Bethlem, the Great Moravian Settlement in the Province of Pennsylvania. | Vue de Bethlem, principal Etablissement des Freres Moraves dans la Province de Pennsylvania. | Sketch'd on the Spot by his Excellency Governor Pownal. Painted and Engraved by Paul Sandby.

A View of Louisburg in North America, taken near the Light House when that City was besieged in 1758.
Vue de Louisburg, dans L'Amerique Septentrionale, prise du fanal durant le dernier Siege en 1758.
Drawn on the Spot by Capt. Ince of the 35t Regt. Engraved by P. Canot.

Plate 11. A View of Louisburg in North America, taken near the Light House when that City was besieged in 1758. | Vue de Louisburg, dans L'Amerique Septentrionale, prise du fanal durant le dernier Siege en 1758. | Drawn on the Spot by Capt Ince of the 35t Regt. Engraved by P. Canot.

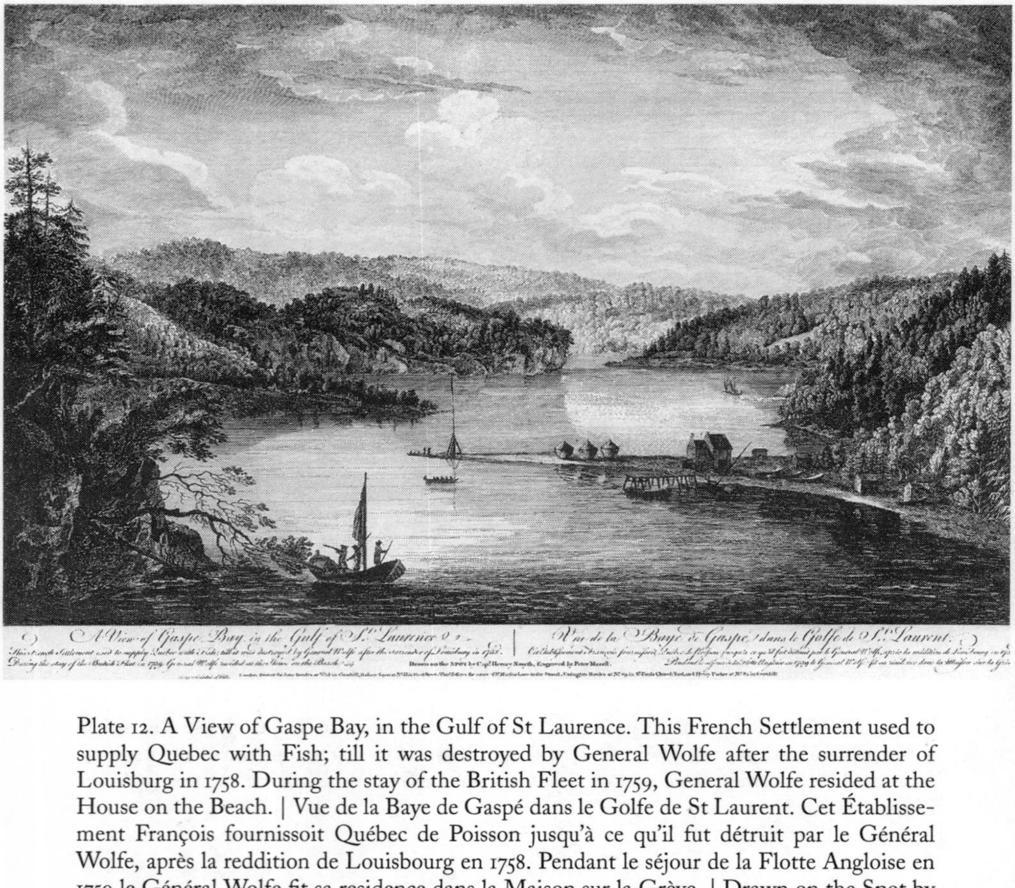
A View of Gaspe Bay in the Gulf of St. Laurence
Vue de la Baye de Gaspe dans le Golfe de St. Laurent.

Plate 12. A View of Gaspe Bay, in the Gulf of St Laurence. This French Settlement used to supply Quebec with Fish; till it was destroyed by General Wolfe after the surrender of Louisburg in 1758. During the stay of the British Fleet in 1759, General Wolfe resided at the House on the Beach. | Vue de la Baye de Gaspé dans le Golfe de St Laurent. Cet Établissement François fournissoit Québec de Poisson jusqu'à ce qu'il fut détruit par le Général Wolfe, après la reddition de Louisbourg en 1758. Pendant le séjour de la Flotte Angloise en 1759 le Général Wolfe fit sa residence dans la Maison sur la Grève. | Drawn on the Spot by Capt Hervey Smyth. Engraved by Peter Mazell.

Plate 13. A View of Miramichi, a French Settlement in the Gulf of St Laurence, destroyed by Brigadier Murray detached by General Wolfe for that Purpose from the Bay of Gaspe. | Vue de Miramichi Établissement François dans le Golfe de St Laurent, détruit par le Brigadier Murray, détaché à cet effet de la Baye de Gaspé, par le Général Wolfe. | Drawn on the Spot by Capt Hervey Smyth. Etch'd by Paul Sandby. Retouch'd by P. Benazech.

Plate 14. A View of the Pierced Island, a remarkable Rock in the Gulf of St Laurence. Two Leagues to the Southward of Gaspée Bay. | Vue de l'Isle Percée, Rocher remarquable dans le Golfe St Laurent a 2 Lieues de la Baye de Gaspe. | Drawn on the Spot by Capt Hery Smyth. Engraved by P. Canot.

Plate 15. A View of the Fall of Montmorenci and the Attack made by General Wolfe on the French Intrenchments near Beauport, with the Grenadiers of the Army, July 31, 1759. | Vue de la Chute ou Saut de Montmorenci et de l'Attaque des Retrenchments François près de Beauport, par le Général Wolfe avec le Grenadiers de l'Armée le 31 Juillet 1759. | Drawn on the Spot by Capt Hervey Smyth. Engraved by Wm Elliott.

Plate 16. A View of Cape Rouge or Carouge, Nine Miles above the City of Quebec on the North Shore of the River St Laurence. From this place 1500 chosen Troops at the break of Day fell down the River on the Ebb of Tide to the place of Landing 13 Sept. 1759. | Vue de Cap Rouge vulgairement Carouge, à 9 Miles au dessus de la Ville de Québec, sur le bord septentrional de la Riviere de St Laurent. C'est de Carouge que 1500 Hommes de Troupes choisies descendirent ave La Marée, au Lieu du debarquement 13 Sept. 1759. | Drawn on the Spot by Capt Hervey Smyth. Engraved by Peter Mazell.

Plate 17. A View of the City of Quebec, the Capital of Canada, Taken partly from Pointe des Peres, and partly on Board the Vanguard, Man of War, by Captain Hervey Smyth. | Vue de la Ville de Québec, Capitale du Canada, Prise in partie de la Pointe des Peres, et en partie abord de l'Avantgarde Vaisseau de Guerre par le Capt Hervey Smyth. | To the Right Honourable William Pitt, One of his Majestie's most Honourable Privy Council & Principal Secretary of State, These Six Views of the most remarkable Places in the Gulf and River of St Laurence are most humbly Inscribed, by his most Obedient humble servant Hervey Smyth, Aid du Camp to the late Genl Wolfe.

An East View of MONTREAL, in Canada.
Vue Orientale de MONTRÉAL, en Canada.
Drawn on the SPOT by Thomas Patten
Engraved by P. Canot.
4. The Nunnery 5. The Jesuits Church. 6. The Fort.

Plate 18. An East View of Montreal, in Canada. | Vue Orientale de Montréal, en Canada. | Drawn on the Spot by Thomas Patten. Engraved by P. Canot.

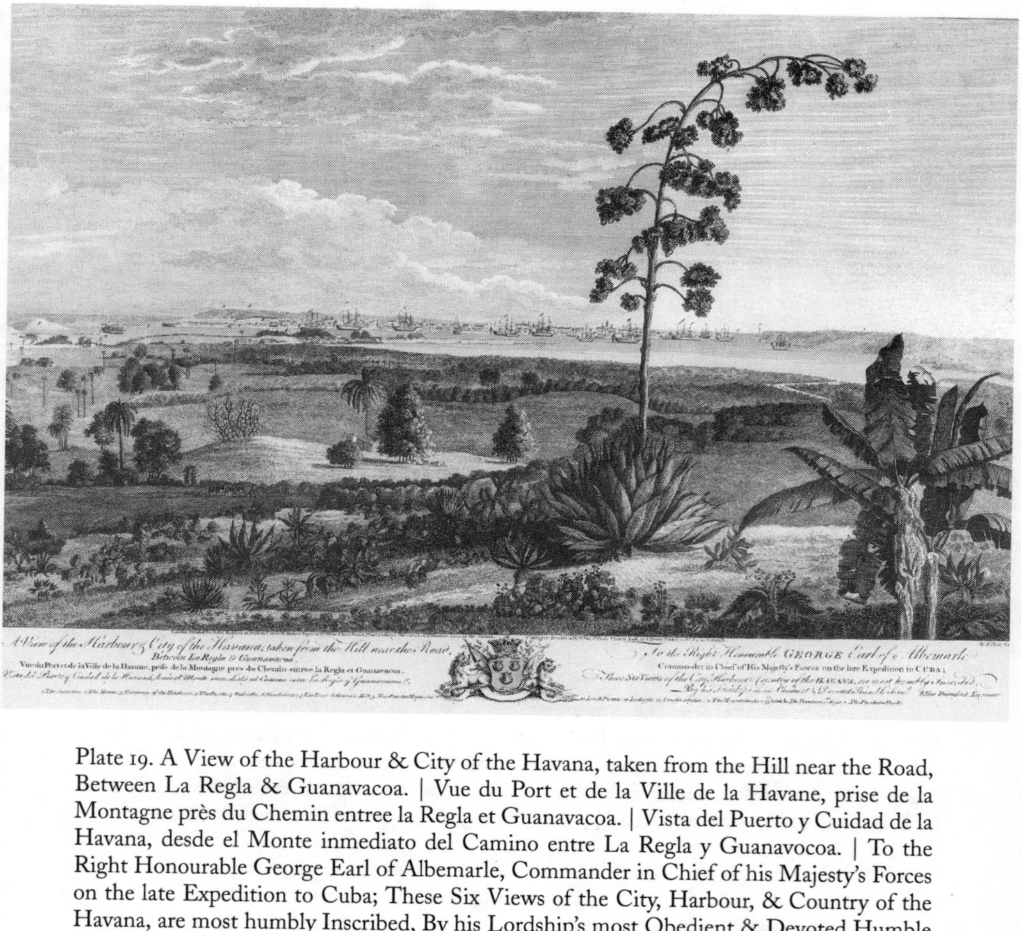

Plate 19. A View of the Harbour & City of the Havana, taken from the Hill near the Road, Between La Regla & Guanavacoa. | Vue du Port et de la Ville de la Havane, prise de la Montagne près du Chemin entree la Regla et Guanavacoa. | Vista del Puerto y Cuidad de la Havana, desde el Monte inmediato del Camino entre La Regla y Guanavocoa. | To the Right Honourable George Earl of Albemarle, Commander in Chief of his Majesty's Forces on the late Expedition to Cuba; These Six Views of the City, Harbour, & Country of the Havana, are most humbly Inscribed, By his Lordship's most Obedient & Devoted Humble Servt Elias Durnford, Engineer.

Plate 20. A View of the City of the Havana, taken from the Road near Colonel Howe's Battery. | Vue de La ville de La Havane prise du chemin pres de La batterie du Colonel Howe. | Vista de la Ciudad de la Havana desde el camino de la bateria del Coronel Howe. | Drawn by Elias Durnford Engineer. Etch'd by Paul Sandby, & Engraved by Edwd Rooker.

Plate 21. A View of the Harbour and City of the Havana, taken from Jesu Del Monte. | Vue du Port et ville de La Havane prise de Jesu del Monte. | Vista del Puerto y Ciudad de la Havana desde Jesus del Monte. | Drawn by Elias Durnford, Engineer. Engraved by T. Morris.

Plate 22. A View of the Franciscan Church & Convent in the City of Havana, taken from the Alcalde's House in Granby Square. | Vue de l'Eglise et du Convent des Franciscains, dans la Ville de la Havane, prise de la Maison de l'Alcalde das la Place de Granby. | Vista de la Iglesia y Convento de San Francisco en la Ciudad de la Havana, desde la Casa de los Alcaldes en la Plaza de Granby. | Drawn by Elias Durnford, Engineer. Engraved by Edward Rooker.

A View of the Market-Place in the City of the Havana.
Drawn by Elias Durnford Engineer.
Engraved by C. Canot and T. Morris.

Plate 23. A View of the Market Place in the City of the Havana. | Vue de La Place du Marché dans La ville de La Havane. | Vista de la Plaza del Mercado en la Ciudad de la Havana. | Drawn by Elias Durnford Engineer. Engraved by C. Canot and T. Morris.

Plate 24. A View of the Entrance of the Harbour of the Havana, taken from within the Wrecks. | Vue de L'entrée du Port de la Havane prise en dedans des Bâtiments echoues. | Vista de La entrada del Puerto de la Havana desde los Naufragios. | Drawn by Elias Durnford, Engineer. Engraved by Peter Canot.

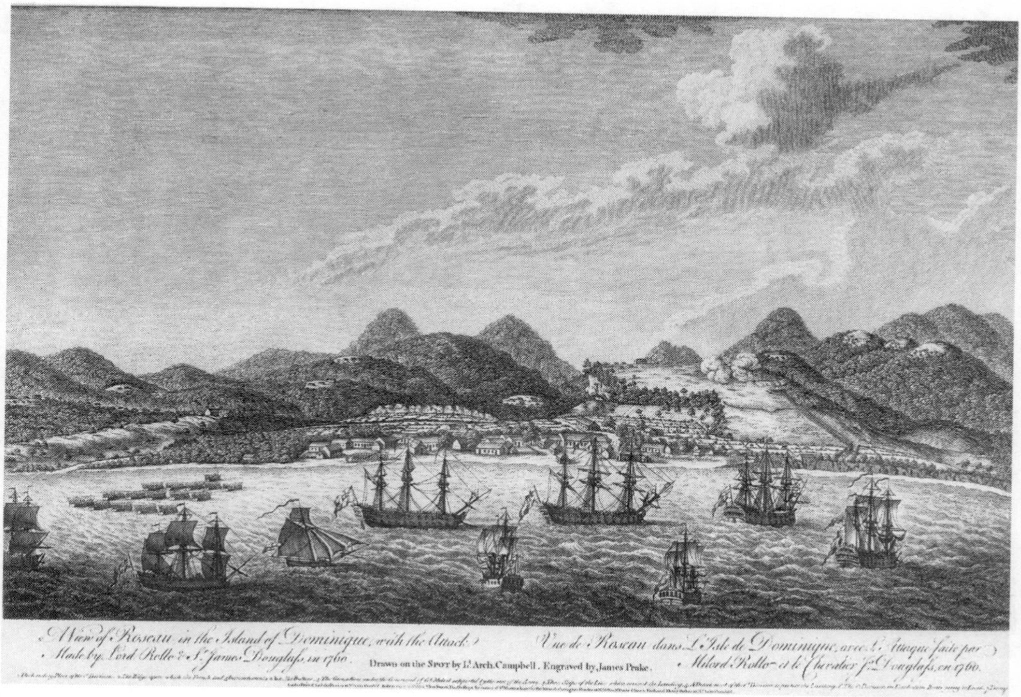

Plate 25. A View of Roseau in the Island of Dominique, with the Attack Made by Lord Rollo & Sr James Douglass, in 1760. | Vue de Roseau dans L'Isle de Dominique, avec L'Attaque faite par Milord Rollo et le Chevalier Js Douglass, en 1760. | Drawn on the Spot by Lt Arch. Campbell. Engraved by James Peake.

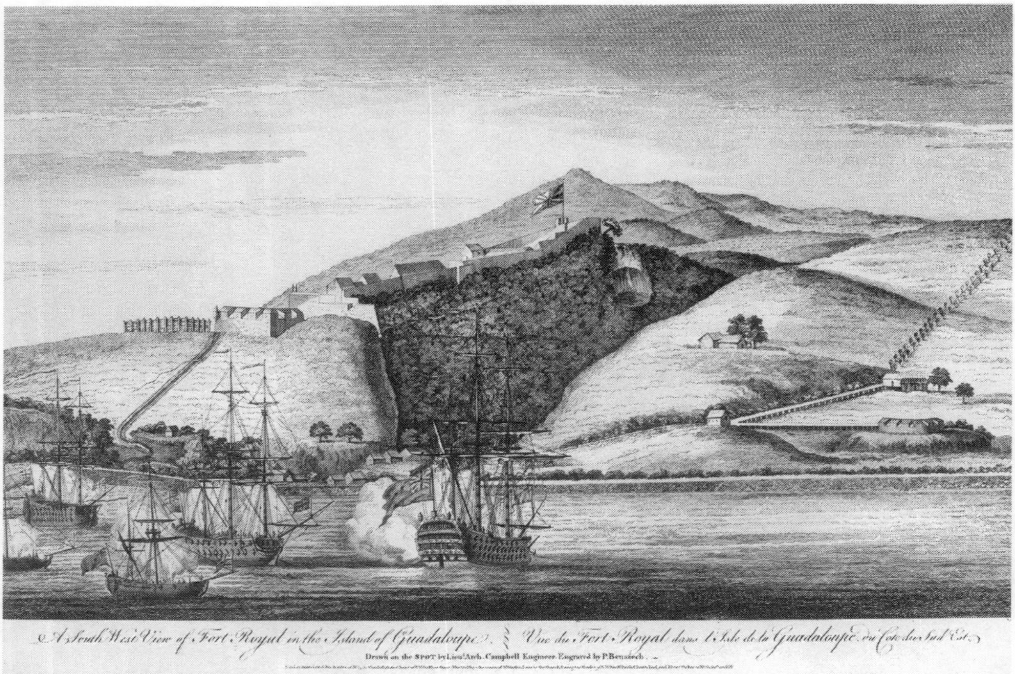

Plate 26. A South West View of Fort Royal in the Island of Guadaloupe. | Vue du Fort Royal dans l'Isle de la Guadaloupe, du Cote du Sud Est. | Drawn on the Spot by Lieut Arch. Campbell Engineer. Engraved by P. Benazech.

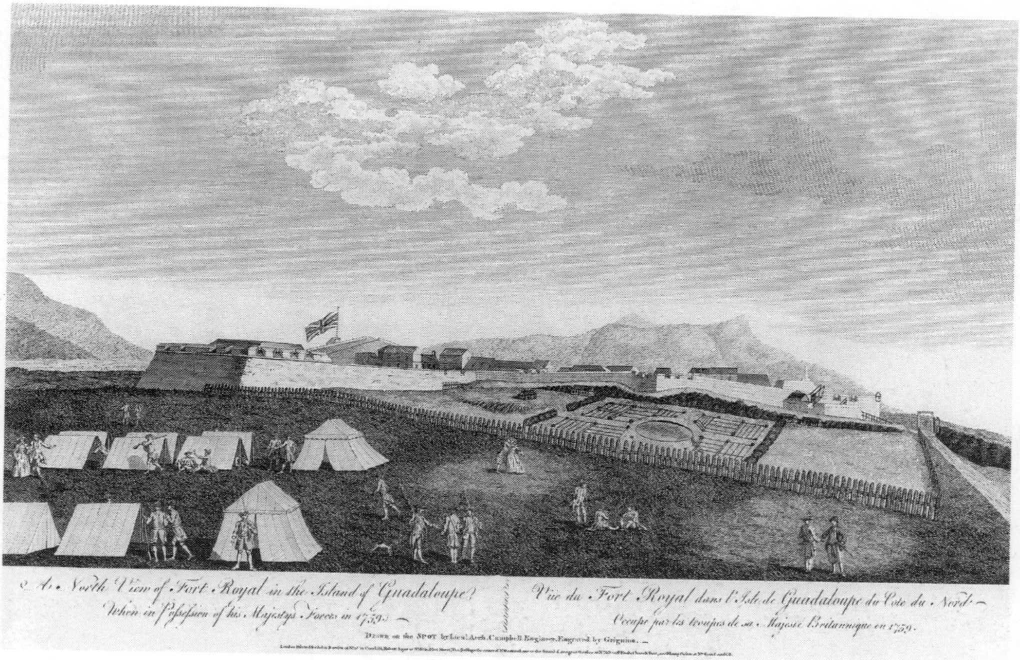

Plate 27. A North View of Fort Royal in the Island of Guadaloupe, When in Possession of his Majestys Forces in 1759. | Vue du Fort Royal dans l'Isle de Guadaloupe du Cote du Nord, Occupé par les troupes de sa Majesté Britannique en 1759. | Drawn on the Spot by Lieut Arch. Campbell Engineer. Engraved by Grignion.

An East View of Fort Royal in the Island of Guadaloupe.
Vue du Fort Royal dans l'Isle de Guadaloupe du Cote de l'Est
Drawn on the SPOT by Lieut Arch. Campbell Engineer. Engraved by Peter Mazell.

Plate 28. An East View of Fort Royal in the Island of Guadaloupe. | Vue du Fort Royal dans l'Isle de Guadaloupe, du Cote de l'Est. | Drawn on the Spot by Lieut Arch. Campbell Engineer. Engraved by Peter Mazell.

PART VII

VEXED VICTORY

1761–1763

The British fail to realize that the fruits of imperial victory can carry the seeds of an empire's disintegration. The Cherokee War and its effects on Amherst's Indian policy. Amherst and Pitt confront very different but equally severe challenges in 1761. Pitt's resignation, war with Spain, and the disintegration of the Anglo-Prussian alliance. The conquest of Havana, 1762, illustrates the complex intersections of empire, trade, and war. The Peace of Paris, the reorientation of British politics, and the unlearned lessons of Manila, 1763. The effects of war's prolongation in North America: migration, instability, and the rising potential for violence. Pontiac's Rebellion, Britain's humiliation, and the recall of Jeffery Amherst.

CHAPTER 46

The Fruits of Victory and the Seeds of Disintegration

1761–1763

A FEW MONTHS more than six years separated the nightmare dawn when Washington witnessed the massacre of Jumonville and his men from the ceremonious morning when Amherst accepted Vaudreuil's surrender at Montréal. During those years thousands of men, women, and children lost their lives from causes directly or indirectly related to the war; thousands more lost their homes; tens of thousands of men bore arms; millions of pounds and scores of millions of *livres* were spent to support them; Britain's empire, engorged by a prolonged feast on the colonial possessions of France, swelled to prodigious size. But victory in North America did not determine the outcome of the conflict as a whole. In Europe, Ferdinand and Frederick fought against lengthening odds, while English ministers discovered that they could not agree on how and when, or even whether, to conclude a war that had seemingly acquired a life of its own. Two more long years of bloodshed would pass before the European powers would cease hostilities in the midst of financial collapse and military exhaustion. During those years the British ministers would largely ignore North America and its problems, leaving the colonists to deal as best they could with a prolonged and troubled transition from war to peace.

GREAT BRITAIN TRIUMPHED in North America for two related reasons. One was military and well understood at the time; the other was in the broadest sense cultural, and understood not at all. The military factor, as we have seen, centered on supplies and supply lines. Once the British navy had swept the French fleet from the seas, as it had by the end of 1759, there was no safe passage for men or munitions or provisions from France to its colonies. In the absence of these, the soldiers and militiamen charged with defending New France soon lost the ability to resist the well-supplied, vastly more numerous Anglo-American invaders. If Occam's Razor could shave historians' arguments as handsomely as it does those of logicians, this factor might fully account for the fall of Canada; but it does not. Only an understanding of the cultural interactions that the war had shaped, and that in turn had shaped the war, can explain the Anglo-American victory in such a way as to make sense of the problems that arose between the British and various North American groups after the conquest of Canada. It may, therefore, be worthwhile to review the course of the war in terms of those broadly influential cultural factors.

France maintained its empire in America for more than a century despite the steady increase of British power and population because the governors of Canada had generally sponsored cordial relations with the Indian peoples of the interior. Trade was the sinew of these intercultural relationships, which in time of war became the military alliances that made the frontiers of the British colonies uninhabitable and rendered a successful invasion of the Canadian heartland impossible. The tide had turned against the French only when their alliances with the nations of the *pays d'en haut* began to fail after the fall of Fort William Henry in 1757; it rose inexorably thereafter, as trade goods became more difficult to transport from France to North America. But the marquis de Montcalm had aggravated the situation, and accelerated the failure of the alliances, by seeking to command the Indians as auxiliaries, rather than to negotiate for their cooperation as allies. Eventually the combined effects of poor supply and Montcalm's Europeanized command alienated even the converted Indians and the habitants, so that in 1760 the chevalier de Lévis and his regulars stood alone, abandoned by the peoples they had crossed the Atlantic to defend.

The progression had been almost precisely the opposite for the British. From 1755 through early 1758, British attempts to subject the colonists to what amounted to the viceregal command of Braddock and Loudoun had virtually destroyed the willingness of the colonists to cooperate. Only Pitt's reversal of policy—his disposition to treat the colonists in effect as allies rather than subordinates, to ask for their help rather than to compel it, and to reimburse them in proportion to their exertions in the war effort—had arrested the decline of British military fortunes in

America. Just as the French were forfeiting allies among the Indians of the *pays d'en haut,* then, the British were forging effective alliances between the metropolis and most of its colonies. As the French in Canada were losing access to the supplies and trade goods they needed to survive militarily, British military contracts, reimbursements, and shipments of specie in the form of soldiers' pay were fueling an expansion in the economies of the mainland colonies and offering an alternative trading partnership, in return for a change in allegiance, to the Indians of the interior. Thus at the same time that the redcoats, supported by vast provincial levies, were winning their first victories, the strategically crucial Ohio Indians moved to realign themselves through the peace negotiations at Easton, Pennsylvania. When the Iroquois shifted from a posture of neutrality to active support of the British in 1759, the tide surged against the French, who never won another battle, and who watched their Indian allies slip away until none remained.

It was in early 1761, at the zenith of British military fortunes in America, that Amherst—soon to become Sir Jeffery, knight of the Bath—began in the name of rationality and economy to reverse the openhanded policies that had produced such remarkable cooperation between the colonists and the empire and the Indians. Perhaps nothing in the postwar period was more predictable than the effect that Amherst's shift in policy produced among the Indians, who reacted as adversely to the restriction of trade and the end of gift-giving that he decreed in 1761 as they had to the strangulation of French commerce during the latter years of the war. Amherst's action, however, was no more an act of caprice than it was an expression of arrogance. Rather it arose from his intention, as a conscientious European professional soldier, to impose order on a frontier that seemed, at the very moment of victory, to be slipping out of control. For reasons perfectly understandable in terms of his own culture, Amherst sought to reform Indian relations without fully understanding why they functioned as they did. He hoped to improve the character of Indians without comprehending how different from Englishmen Indians were, much less appreciating how they would understand his efforts. Despite his intentions, Amherst's postwar efforts at reform produced not a new coherence on the frontier but a new wave of violence: the sporadic extension of the war in the west, long after the defeat of the French.

The Indians who rebelled against British control after the Seven Years' War were trying, in the only way they knew, to maintain local autonomy and customary rights against an imperial authority heedless of local conditions. In that sense the catastrophic breakdown of Anglo-Indian relations following Britain's great victory was both a mirror of the past and an eerily accurate predictor of the future. Like the failure of Montcalm to transform the Indians into reliable auxiliaries and the failure of Loudoun to compel the colonists to participate in the war on his terms rather than their own, the uprisings in the American interior would demonstrate the limited potential of coercion as a basis for imperial control. But this was not a lesson that the victor was prepared to learn.

CHAPTER 47

The Cherokee War and Amherst's Reforms in Indian Policy

1760–1761

THE FIRST INDICATION that something was amiss in Anglo-Indian relations came in the form of a bloody, unexpected uprising in what had been the quietest sector in eastern North America, the far southern frontier, during the last year of the war. There, for three decades, the largest single Indian nation in contact with the British colonies, the Cherokees, had been the peaceable trading partner of South Carolina. With a population of perhaps ten thousand living in three groups of villages near what is now the eastern border of Tennessee—the Lower Towns east of the Great Smoky Mountains, the Middle Towns in their hollows, and the Overhills in the valley of the Little Tennessee River beyond—the Cherokees dominated the South Carolina frontier and served as important allies of the low-country–dominated government. For years they had sold deerskins and slaves (war captives taken from nations of the interior) to the licensed Carolina traders based in their towns. They had functioned as slave catchers, too, handing runaways back to their masters in return for rewards. Most recently they had participated, after a fashion, in the defense of the Virginia frontier. At the high point of the alliance, in 1758, as many as seven hundred warriors had briefly offered their services to John Forbes. Broadly speaking, the Cherokees' rebellion stemmed both from the Seven Years' War, which destabilized what had been a durable relationship between the nation and South Carolina, and from the disorderly settlement of white farmers and hunters in the backcountry, beyond the control of the colony government. But in a narrow, immediate sense, Forbes's expedition was where the trouble started.[1]

The Forbes campaign did nothing to endear the British military command to the Cherokees, who streamed northward in the summer of 1758 to offer themselves as British allies. Warriors who had traveled hundreds of miles for trophies, captives, and plunder found only frustration in Forbes's stolid advance and insult in his commanding manner. Virtually all of them left before the end of summer, taking home the muskets and ammunition he had provided. On the way south through the Virginia and North Carolina backcountry, the combination of these arms and the fighters' warlike appearance unsettled the frontier farmers, who suspected them of stealing horses and killing livestock. Acting on rumor and fear, unable or unwilling to distinguish between Indian allies and Indian enemies, local militiamen treated the returning Cherokees with offhanded savagery. In one episode, a militia patrol hunted down, murdered, and mutilated three Overhill chiefs, then claimed the reward Virginia offered for enemy scalps. In another, a group of whites surrounded a party of Lower Town warriors whom they suspected of theft, forced them to lay down their arms, and then opened fire—killing three and wounding a fourth before the survivors could make their escape. No fewer than thirty warriors lost their lives while trying to return to their villages.[2]

These murders alone would have impaired the Cherokee alliance, but what the warriors discovered when they finally reached their villages made hostilities virtually inescapable. White hunters from the Long Canes settlement in South Carolina had taken advantage of the warriors' absence to cross over into Indian country and poach Cherokee game. This invasion of the Lower Towns' hunting grounds disrupted the Indians' winter hunt, threatened their food supply, diminished the number of deerskins available for trade, and added weight to the nativists' arguments that the time had come to teach the backwoodsmen a lesson. Civil chiefs—mainly older men who had had some role in establishing the alliance and maintaining peace with the colony government—still urged caution. The spring of 1759 was therefore a time of division and confusion: even as parties of Overhill and Lower Town warriors set out to avenge the deaths of the previous summer, moderate emissaries were trying to reach some agreement with Governor William Henry Lyttelton in Charleston.[3]

If anything could hold the rapidly disintegrating alliance together, it was some material improvement in the terms of trade, for the Cherokees were no less dependent than any other native people on European manufactures, and licensed traders monopolized all of South Carolina's Indian

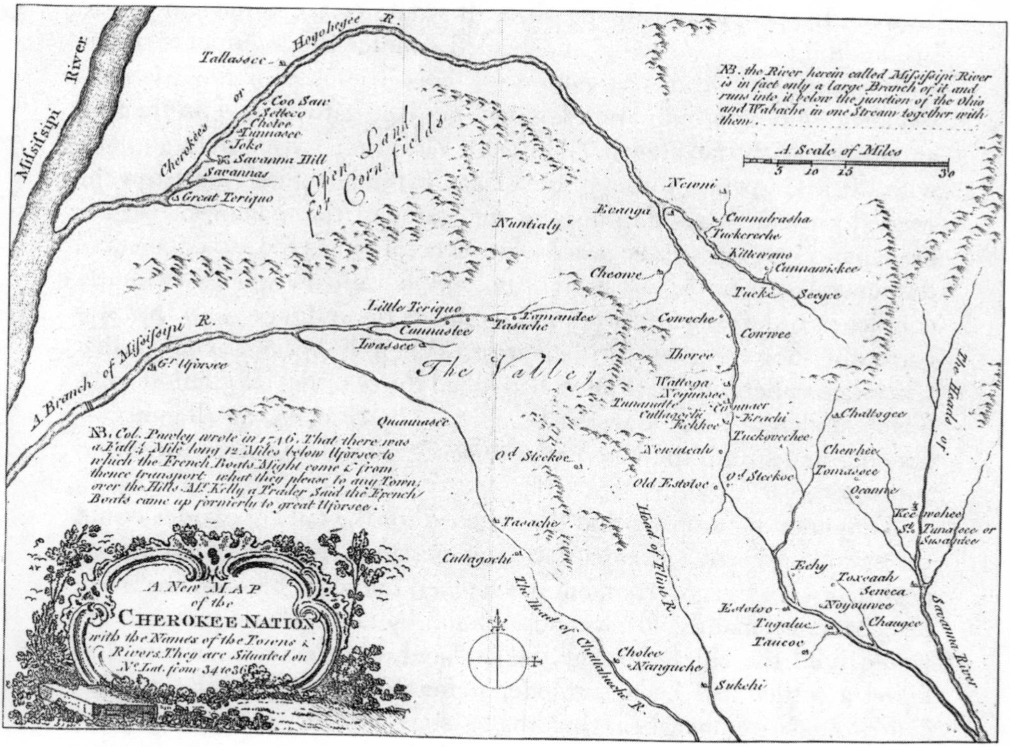

A New Map of the Cherokee Nation, 1760. Published in the *London Magazine* from "an Indian Draught," this view of the Cherokee settlements responded to public curiosity about what had been until recently almost entirely unknown territory. Although the engraver was far from literally accurate in his depiction, he does actually represent something like the number and distribution of Cherokee towns. Here the Lower Towns appear along the river systems that flow southeast to the Atlantic; the Middle and Overhill Towns on the tributaries of the Coosa (here labeled, with wild inaccuracy, "a branch of Mississipi R."), the Hiwassee (shown as a tributary of the Coosa rather than the Tennessee), and the Tennessee (here called the "Cherokees or Hogohegee R." and shown as a tributary of "Mississipi River"). Fort Prince George is not shown among the Lower Towns, but would appear opposite Keewohee (Keowee), lower right; Fort Loudoun appears as "Savanna Hill" at upper left. *Courtesy of the William L. Clements Library at the University of Michigan.*

commerce. Because exchange principally occurred at two remote and exposed posts—Fort Prince George in the Lower Towns, and Fort Loudoun in the Overhill country—the colony had excellent reason to seek common ground with moderates. The nation's leading accommodationist, Attakullakulla (Little Carpenter), had tried to lessen tensions by seeking concessions and demanding a substantial gift from the Carolina government. This tactic, if successful, might have strengthened the bonds between his people and the province. It would certainly have increased his credibility as a mediator and helped counter the arguments of the Creek emissaries from the vicinity of Fort Toulouse in the Alabama Country, who reportedly were urging Cherokee nativists to join them in an alliance with the French.[4] Although Governor Lyttelton negotiated with Little Carpenter through the spring of 1759, he refused to bestow the needed present—thus diminishing the status of the man who had the best chance to preserve the peace—either because he failed to understand the tenuousness of the situation or because he actually wished to force a conflict in order to gain for himself some of the military glory that was currently showering on British arms. When it became known that Cherokee raiders on the frontier had killed thirty settlers, Lyttelton completely undercut Little Carpenter's position by embargoing all gunpowder shipments until the Cherokees surrendered the murderers to colony authorities.

Desperate for ammunition they needed for the fall and winter hunts, the nation now sent a new delegation of moderate chiefs to Charleston to negotiate with the governor, but in October, Lyttelton blasted what slender chances remained for accommodation by taking them prisoner. He would hold the chiefs hostage, he declared, until every man who had killed a settler had been surrendered for punishment in the colony's courts. In November, believing that a show of force would bring the Cherokees to their senses, he carried his hostages up-country to Fort Prince George at the head of thirteen hundred provincial soldiers. In anticipation of a restoration of normal relations he also brought a great gift, including three tons of gunpowder, to bestow once the Cherokees had turned over the guilty warriors.[5]

The governor had made peace all but impossible to preserve. By imprisoning the chiefs who had been most inclined to negotiate, Lyttelton strengthened the hand of militant nativist leaders and rendered suspect any arguments that the last remaining moderate chief, Little Carpenter, could make. Eventually he persuaded his fellow chiefs to surrender two suspected murderers to the Carolinians, and Lyttelton responded by releasing a handful of his captives; but this hopeful turn of events was lost when the governor announced that he would hold the remaining twenty-two hostages at Fort Prince George until twenty-two more murderers had been turned over. Since by now most of the participants in the spring's war parties had taken to the woods, and since according to Cherokee law and custom they had acted legitimately to avenge deaths inflicted on their families or clans, the surrender of twenty-two warriors was beyond the power of any Cherokee leader. Lyttelton blustered on and issued ultimatums regardless: a tactic that would have been counterproductive enough even had smallpox not broken out in the vicinity of the fort and made his provincials, whose enlistments were set to expire on January 1, eager to return home. The combination of an epidemic and the prospect of mass desertions left him no choice but to withdraw. Lyttelton accordingly marched for Charleston with the two accused murderers on December 31, escorted by his officers and the few troops who had not already deserted or been discharged. Behind him he left both the hostages and the gift, instructing Fort Prince George's commandant to complete the exchange of malefactors for prisoners—then distribute the gunpowder. He might as well have lit a fuse to it.[6]

On January 19, 1760, a party of Cherokee warriors tried to free the hostages by force. Failing, they laid siege to the fort, cut communications between it and its distant satellite in the Overhill country, Fort Loudoun, and launched a series of sanguinary raids on backwoods settlements from southwest Virginia to Georgia. Within a month, following a surprise attack that killed their commanding officer, the garrison of Fort Prince George massacred the twenty-two hostage chiefs. Meanwhile, Cherokee raiders struck all along the southwestern borderlands; by the end of March they had killed or captured more than a hundred settlers and traders. With the exception of those families "forted up" in isolated stockades like Ninety-six, the warriors had rolled the frontier back a hundred miles, from Long Canes to Orangeburg—and Orangeburg lay just seventy-five miles from Charleston.[7]

Lyttelton, who had done so much to bring about this state of affairs, seems to have been genuinely surprised by it, and found himself almost completely helpless to restore order. Since disbanding the previous year's provincial regiment, he had only militiamen—unembodied, untrained, and unwilling to leave their homes—and a couple hundred regulars to defend the province. Early in February, Lyttelton accordingly demanded that the legislature appropriate emergency funds to raise a new regiment and seven mounted ranger companies, asked Governor Fauquier to send Virginia troops down to relieve Fort Loudoun, and appealed to Amherst for two or three regiments of regulars. All this would take time, three or four months at the least, to produce any result; and in the meantime smallpox, carried back in January by the returning provincials, broke out in Charleston, along with rumors that the slaves were planning to rebel. Fortunately for Lyttelton, the British government had already seen fit to reward his political and military skill by making him governor of Jamaica, the richest post in the colonies. He sailed for Kingston in March, presumably without regret.[8]

Meanwhile all that restrained the Cherokees was the growing awareness that they stood alone. The Creeks, who had so insistently pressed for hostilities, now showed no disposition to attack settlers on the Georgia frontier, but bided their time, to see if they might reap advantage by offering themselves to the English as mediators or even allies. The commandant of Fort Toulouse, the French outpost on the Alabama River 250 miles to the southwest, gave his best wishes to the Cherokee emissaries who approached him, but he had no powder to spare. The Indians of the Ohio Country, who had lately made their peace with the English, were equally unwilling to offer aid.[9]

Thus despite their success in emptying the frontiers of whites, and despite the military impotence of the South Carolinians, the Cherokees hesitated to attack Forts Loudoun and Prince George in the spring of 1760—not because they feared the tiny mixed garrisons of redcoats and provincials, but because they understood the consequences of diplomatic isolation. Had the Carolinians been willing to make peace on the basis of the status quo ante bellum, the war could undoubtedly have been ended at this point. The arrival in April of more than thirteen hundred regulars from the 1st and 77th Regiments of Foot under Colonel Archibald Montgomery, however, forestalled the option of negotiation. By May 24, with support from about three hundred mounted Carolina rangers, a handful of provincial infantry, and forty or fifty Catawba warriors, the redcoats reached the stockade at Ninety-six. On the first of June they marched into the Lower Towns, skirmished with their defenders, killed or captured over a hundred warriors, and burned five villages. Only then did Montgomery halt and invite negotiation and find that the Cherokees were not disposed to parley. As the population of the Lower Towns retreated to the Middle Towns, the war chiefs refused even to respond to Montgomery's summons. The British would have to dig them out of the mountains.[10]

When the ten days he had allotted as time for the Cherokees to answer had passed, Montgomery ordered his men to prepare to march against the Middle Towns, sixty miles to the northwest, in the midst of some of the most rugged terrain in eastern North America. The redcoats, virtually all of whom were Scots, therefore set about improvising panniers and packsaddles for the horses of the baggage train, cutting up tents for packs and provision bags, cooking rations for the march, and taking what other measures they could to enable them to operate without wagons, which could not pass beyond the Lower Towns. In the country they were about to enter, operations would be infinitely more taxing than before and strictly limited in duration by the supplies that men and horses could carry on their backs. On June 23, Montgomery's men began their sixty-mile trek up the traders' path to the Middle Towns.

By July 1 they were back, bone-weary and deeply shaken by the resistance they had encountered. They had met the Cherokees near the first of the Middle Towns, Echoe, on June 27, sustaining a hundred casualties to the Indians' fifty and losing so many pack animals that it was impossible to proceed further. The next day, after ordering excess provisions jettisoned and the wounded to be loaded onto the remaining horses, Montgomery had led his men in a hasty retreat to Fort Prince George. They remained at the fort only long enough to turn over supplies to the garrison and to leave off men who were too sick or badly wounded to travel. On July 3, Montgomery marched for Charleston; by the middle of August he and his men were sailing for New York. Amherst called Montgomery's expedition "the greatest stroke the Indians have felt," but to Charlestonians it looked very much as if the Cherokees had sent the British packing.[11]

Although Montgomery's expedition accomplished little of military significance, it had unquestionably written Fort Loudoun's death warrant. The garrison had been under a kind of open siege since March, cut off from communication with the outside world and surviving largely on what food Cherokee women (mainly the soldiers' wives) brought in from the surrounding towns. Little Carpenter, still a voice for peace, had also done his best to protect the garrison, at one point discouraging a rumored attack by moving his own family into the fort. Once word of Montgomery's devastation of the Lower Towns arrived in the Overhill country, however, nothing could stay the hand of the nativists. On June 3 they began a close siege, with the intent of starving the defenders out. In a week's time the commander, Captain Paul Demeré (or Demere), was forced to cut the daily corn ration to two-thirds of a pint per man; by the time another week passed, the men had eaten the last of their horses. At the end of July, "miserable beyond belief" and living on a few kernels of parched corn a day, the civilian traders and packhorse drivers who had sought shelter in the fort began stealing away under cover of darkness, preferring captivity to starvation. Soon thereafter individual soldiers (most likely those with Cherokee wives) began to desert. On August 5 the garrison's remaining troops declared their intention to depart en masse if their officers did not capitulate. Two days later Captain Demeré, his options gone along with his food, surrendered the fort and its contents to the Cherokees in return for safe passage to Fort Prince George.[12]

On the morning of August 9 the troops, carrying their muskets and colors and leading a small column of wives and children, marched off

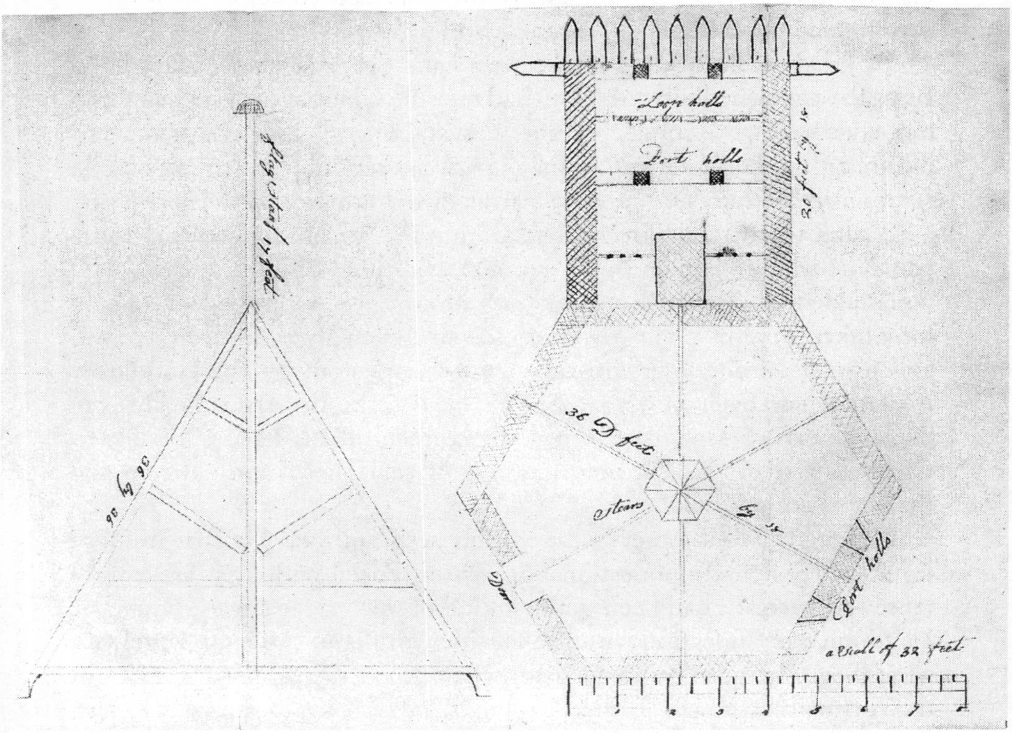

Plan of a turret at Fort Loudoun, 1759. Captain Paul Demeré enclosed these sketches of features of Fort Loudoun in a letter to William Henry Lyttelton of February 27, 1759. At left is the flagstaff, some fifty feet tall and supported by a pyramidal base. On the right is the plan of a three-story hexagonal turret, or tower, of the sort sometimes erected at the points of bastions, to give a better view of the surrounding area. A sturdy structure constructed of logs, it was capable of mounting swivels (light cannon) to fire through the portholes on the second floor, and had loopholes for muskets on the first and third levels. The footprint of the tower, with eighteen-foot exterior faces, a thirty-six-foot diameter, and a circular center stair, appears at bottom right. The sketch immediately above it shows the appearance of one face, some twenty feet tall, with a palisade and fraising to protect the rooftop firing platform. *Courtesy of the William L. Clements Library at the University of Michigan.*

under a Cherokee escort. The garrison, relieved to be freed from the wretched prison of Fort Loudoun, marched a few miles down the trail and encamped by Ball Play Creek. The night passed peacefully. But the following morning, as the soldiers were forming up to march, suddenly "two guns were fired at Captain Demere who was wounded by one of the shots. . . . [T]he war whoop was . . . sent up and vollies of small arms with showers of arrows poured in . . . [from] 700 Indians, who, as they advanced surrounded the whole garrison and put them into the greatest confusion. . . . [The soldiers] called out to one another not to fire and surrendered."

A good deal of quite deliberate killing followed the surrender. Between casualties sustained in the initial firing and the butchery that ensued, a total of twenty-five people lost their lives—three women plus a number of soldiers equal to the hostages massacred at Fort Prince George six months before. All the officers save one—a South Carolina provincial and former Scots merchant, Captain John Stuart, who had become a friend of Little Carpenter—were killed, but only Captain Demeré, who was scalped while alive and then forced to dance until he died, seems to have been ritually tortured. The common soldiers were stripped, beaten, and driven off into captivity; their wives and children were evidently treated gently. Captain Stuart was allowed to accompany Little Carpenter on a peace mission to Virginia. The remainder of the captives, about two hundred in all, remained in the Overhill Towns until the end of the war.[13]

Following Montgomery's flight and Fort Loudoun's fall, Cherokee leaders and the South Carolina authorities warily observed a six-month truce. Although Fort Prince George was nearly as vulnerable as Fort Loudoun had been, the Indians did not subject it to close siege, and as a goodwill gesture even allowed a limited amount of supplies to be brought in. Meanwhile, the Cherokees talked: to the French, who sent small symbolic gifts from Fort Toulouse, but no ammunition; to the Creeks, who continued to refuse a direct alliance while they explored ways to increase their standing at Cherokee expense; to the Virginians, who threatened invasion and sent gifts to support Little Carpenter; to Lyttelton's successor, Lieutenant Governor William Bull, who advocated peace and tried desperately to persuade men to enlist in the South Carolina provincial regiment. Everyone but the Cherokees played for time. And time—as the nativist leaders, whose prestige and morale were at the zenith, were too slow to realize—was the one element that favored the Cherokees least.

The winter of 1761 weakened the Indians, who suffered by the great depth of snow, scarcity of ammunition, shortages of food brought on by the loss of the Lower Towns' harvest, and disease. Yet the warriors' morale remained high, bolstered by the surrender of Fort Loudoun, their success in driving Montgomery's troops out of the Middle Towns, and the appearance of a present of trade goods from the French—goods, as it happened, that were English in origin, having been brought to the Gulf Coast by clandestine Anglo-American traders and then transported up the Alabama River to Fort Toulouse. The war chiefs did not yet know that on January 6 a new complement of regulars had arrived from New York under Lieutenant Colonel James Grant, a man whose experiences as Montgomery's second-in-command and as a field commander under Forbes and Bouquet had made him a systematic, and therefore dangerous, opponent. He had orders from Amherst "to chastise the Cherokees [and] reduce them to the absolute necessity of suing for pardon," and he had brought with him a body of Mohawk and Stockbridge Indian scouts. The South Carolina government, moreover, had finally raised a substantial number of provincials and rangers and had recruited Catawba and Chickasaw warriors as well.[14]

The threat that all this posed to the Cherokees would not in fact be clear until late spring, because the severe weather, the lack of forage, and the necessity of training Lieutenant Colonel Henry Laurens's provincials all kept Grant from reaching the frontier settlement of Ninety-six until May 18. But by then his force numbered more than 2,800 men, half of whom were well-seasoned regulars of the 1st, 17th, and 22nd Regiments; and this time, unlike the last, they were prepared to operate for an extended period in the mountains. When Grant's men marched from Fort Prince George toward the Middle Towns on June 7, they were followed by a pack train a mile long—six hundred horses carrying a month's worth of food and ammunition—and a herd of beef cattle so big that scores of slaves were needed to manage it.[15]

A great Cherokee force of a thousand warriors met Grant's invading army on June 10 near Echoe, where the previous year's battle had taken place. Once again the Indians attacked the British column from ambush and concentrated on destroying the British pack animals, but this time they failed to repeat their earlier success. Six hours of long-range firing from "amazingly advantageous" positions on "the Tops & Brows of Hills upon our right [and] across the River Cowhih on our left" cost Grant's army an officer and eleven men killed and fifty-two soldiers and wagoners wounded, along with perhaps sixty horses and an indeterminate number of cattle killed or stampeded. The Cherokees may have lost twice as many men, but more important, they exhausted most of their ammunition and thus lost the ability to prevent Grant from carrying through his chastising mission. During the remainder of the month and the first days of July, the warriors could only pick off unwary sentries and watch helplessly from the woods as Grant's men burned all fifteen of the Middle Towns and laid waste to fifteen hundred acres of corn- and bean-fields. Any Indian man, woman, or child luckless enough to be caught was summarily executed, by Grant's express order.[16]

When Grant returned to Fort Prince George on July 9, he had

marched his men nearly to exhaustion—three hundred were too sick or lame to walk, and another thousand had worn their shoes to shreds—but he had made at least four thousand inhabitants of the Middle Towns homeless and destroyed the crops they needed to survive the coming winter. Perhaps three Cherokees out of every five now lived as refugees in the Overhill settlements, overwhelming the available food stocks, and effectively incapable of carrying on the war. The Cherokee economy had spiraled down to a virtually neolithic level: the last resistance against Grant's men had been made by warriors armed only with bows and arrows. Meanwhile, the Creeks had been playing off Cherokee, French, and British interests in a classic neutrality strategy and battening on trade with the English. Well-armed Chickasaw, Catawba, and Iroquois war parties were beginning to raid Overhill settlements whose warriors could no longer defend them. Disease had risen to epidemic levels, and a winter's famine had become a certainty. On top of it all, over the last year's time, Colonel William Byrd's Virginia Regiment had succeeded in building more than eighty miles of road from Chiswell's Fort on the southwestern frontier of the Old Dominion to the upper reaches of the Holston River in North Carolina. While Grant's men were laying the Middle Towns in ashes, Byrd's Virginia provincials and a large accompanying contingent of Tuscarora warriors were advancing to the Long Island of the Holston, little more than a hundred miles from the Overhill Towns. If the Virginians and their allies chose to descend the Holston Valley, they could reach the Overhill Towns in a month's time without ever overstretching their supply lines. Then they could wreak a kind of havoc that even Grant had been unable to contemplate.[17]

So the council of the Cherokee nation sued for peace in August, sending a delegation under Little Carpenter to meet with Grant at Fort Prince George. There, and later in Charleston, the chief showed how much he deserved his reputation as a negotiator. Under the treaty's remarkably mild terms all white prisoners, slaves, and captured livestock were to be returned, and the line of demarcation between white settlement and the Cherokee lands was to be moved to within twenty-six miles of the Keowee River—a forfeiture of about half of the Lower Towns' hunting grounds. Lyttelton's old insistence that the twenty-two braves who had killed settlers in the spring of 1759 be surrendered was quietly forgotten, along with Grant's demand that the chiefs choose four from among their number to be executed. It was close to a status quo ante bellum peace, and it came even closer in the next few months, when subsequent negotiations moved the line of demarcation back to forty miles east of the Keowee. Moreover, the resumption of peace brought at least one considerable advantage to the Cherokees, for the war had broken the old Carolina trade monopoly. Overhills, having lost the mart at Fort Loudoun, had begun to deal with the Virginia and North Carolina traders who accompanied the Virginia Regiment to the Holston, while Georgia traders operating out of Augusta had responded to a Lower Town invitation to set up camps in the woods southwest of Fort Prince George.

Finally, the previous Indian superintendent for the southern department, the comparatively ineffectual Charleston trader Edmund Atkin, died in the fall of 1761. Atkin had been content to leave management of Cherokee affairs largely in the hands of South Carolina's governor, where control had rested since 1730. But the man whom Pitt chose to take Atkin's place was John Stuart, the friend of Little Carpenter, a committed imperialist, and an activist administrator. Although he would face problems enough during his tenure as superintendent, Stuart would never permit another South Carolina governor to exert the kind of baleful influence William Henry Lyttelton had had on relations with the Cherokee nation.[18]

At least three paradoxical lessons could be extracted from the war. In the first place, the conflict had severely damaged the Cherokees, who had seen half their settlements destroyed and lost a great deal of population—we do not know how much, but the proportion was high—to disease and famine. At the same time, however, the strategic position of the nation actually improved insofar as the war had destroyed the Carolina trade monopoly, the peace settlement ultimately required a negligible cession of lands to the province, and the legislature had left Cherokee sovereignty effectively undiminished.

Second, the events leading up to the outbreak of hostilities had shown that moderate or neutralist leaders like Little Carpenter could easily lose control of policy to more aggressive nativist chiefs whenever the Anglo-Americans tried to direct Indian relations by coercion, intimidation, the manipulation of trade, or the suspension of such necessary diplomatic gifts as ammunition. At the same time, the collapse of Cherokee resistance in the face of Grant's expedition also demonstrated that the Indians depended so heavily on European supplies that even skilled warriors protected by distance and difficult terrain could be brought to terms once their stocks of lead, powder, and other strategic goods were spent.

Third, nativist leaders had proven strong enough to override the counsel of experienced mediators like Little Carpenter, and capable of retaining control of policy until all possibility for resistance had been destroyed. Nevertheless, the war gave no indication that nativists in *dif-*

ferent nations could cooperate against the British. Indeed, virtually every native group that the British had approached for help, from the Creeks, Chickasaws, and Catawbas of the south to the Iroquois and Ohio peoples of the north, had been only too willing to profit from the defeat of a powerful rival.

The outcome of the Cherokee War therefore lent itself equally well to contradictory interpretations. Militarily, the conflict made it plain that Indian populations could be incapacitated by the denial of European manufactures, and that Indian nations lacked the capacity to cooperate when French leadership was weak or absent. The cultural messages of the war, however, were both more ambiguous and more powerful: first, that any attempt to control the behavior of Indian nations by manipulating the supply of trade goods could tip the balance of tribal policy from accommodation to hostility; second, that while British soldiers might be capable of inflicting great direct damage on an Indian enemy, even a failed attempt at resistance could result in gains for nativist leaders.

Unsurprisingly, Jeffery Amherst construed the meaning of the conflict in a purely military way and ignored the war's cultural implications. As early as February 22, 1761, he had begun to think about how Indian relations might best be conducted now that the French could no longer organize opposition to English power. Writing to Sir William Johnson concerning the establishment of trade at the recently acquired post of Detroit, and clearly conscious as well of the state of affairs in South Carolina, Amherst explained that while trade was clearly necessary and desirable, the lavish giving of gifts was not:

> So long as I am honored with the Command, these Officers [commanding the posts in the interior of the continent] Shall be Instructed to keep up a Steady, Uniform, and friendly Conduct & behavior towards the Indians; with regard to furnishing the latter, with a little Cloathing, some arms & ammunition to hunt with, that is all very well in Cases of Necessity; but as, when the Intended Trade is once Established they will be able to supply themselves with these, from the Traders, for their furrs, I do not see why the Crown should be put to that Expence.—I am not neither for giving them any Provisions; when they find they can get it on Asking for, they will grow remiss in their hunting, which Should Industriously be avoided; for so long as their minds are Intent on business they will not have leisure to hatch mischief. . . .
>
> . . . Services must be rewarded; it has ever been a maxim with me; but as to purchasing the good behavior either of Indians, or any

> Others, [that] is what I do not understand; when men of what race soever behave ill, they must be punished but not bribed. . . .[19]

By August the commander in chief had ceased propounding maxims and had begun issuing orders. Instructing Johnson on how to proceed at the Indian Congress to be held at Detroit that would confirm Canada's capitulation and create amicable ties with the nations of the *pays d'en haut,* Amherst thought it worthwhile to call to his attention "the Chastizement the Cherokees have met with from the King's Troops, . . . in Carolina." The superintendent had previously warned the commander in chief, from Niagara, that the Geneseo Senecas—a Francophile band traditionally engaged to portage goods and supplies around the falls—had been trying to raise a western confederacy to oppose English interests. He had taken every occasion to denounce the Geneseo scheme, Johnson wrote, and because of it advised Amherst of the "absolute necessity for . . . allowing [the commanding officer at Niagara] to give the dist[ant] Nations & others who resort here Ammunition & a little prov[isio]ns on their return if we want to continue their friendship." This had made no sense to Amherst, who believed that self-interest alone would ensure the Indians' cooperation. Grant's campaign had recently furnished an "Example [by which] the Indians may be Convinced that We have it in our power to Reduce them to Reason, and You will accordingly make use of this . . . piece of Intelligence, among those You are to Treat with, in such a manner as You Shall see most for His Majesty's Interest." As for the gifts Johnson wished to bestow, Amherst wrote,

> You are sensible how averse I am, to purchasing the good behavior of Indians . . . ; wherefore as a Trade is now opened for them, and that you will put it under such Regulations as to prevent their being imposed upon, I think it much better to avoid all presents in future, since that will oblige them to Supply themselves by barter, & of course keep them more Constantly Employed by means of which they will have less time to concert, or Carry in to Execution any Schemes prejudicial to His Majestys Interests; and to abolish entirely every kind of apprehension on that account, the keeping them scarce of Ammunition, is not less to be Recommended; since nothing can be so impolitick as to furnish them with the means of accomplishing the Evil which is so much Dreaded.[20]

In practice this meant that, starting in the fall of 1761, traders at the interior forts would have to operate under rules so stringent that commerce actually diminished instead of growing, as the British had promised it would, in diplomatic conferences from 1758 onward. Real suffering ensued in Indian villages throughout the west. The better to supervise the traders, and prevent them from charging excessive prices for their goods, Amherst forbade them to carry on commerce in Indian villages. This compelled the Indians, who frequently lacked the horses to transport large packs of peltry, to haul skins and furs to the forts in small quantities. Once there, they discovered that the traders had been forbidden to sell them any rum or other liquor, and that they could buy only five pounds of lead and five pounds of powder in any single transaction.[21]

Amherst wanted these measures to reduce the disorders of a trade in alcohol that he rightly believed had gotten out of hand, to economize on presents that he knew had become too expensive, and to minimize Indian military capabilities that he feared had become too great. What he did, however, was disable Indian men from carrying on their fall and winter hunts, inhibit their ability to provide for their families and villages, and deprive them of a drug that had become an important part of their social life. Rather than improving their character by forcing them to become soberly attentive to the business of hunting, Amherst had begun to turn the Indians of the interior into sober (and vastly more dangerous) enemies.[22] Far from keeping the Indians so busy that they had no time to hatch mischief among themselves, he had given them what they had never had before: a common grievance, and tangible evidence that the English would not hesitate to threaten their way of life.

CHAPTER 48

Amherst's Dilemma

1761

INDIAN POLICY WAS only one of many matters on Jeffery Amherst's mind in 1761, and it was by no means the most pressing. For a variety of reasons—notably the willingness of post commanders and traders on the frontier to disregard the new regulations—rebellions did not immediately erupt in response to the changes he had decreed. Thus Amherst paid comparatively little attention to reports from Detroit of a rumored Indian conspiracy and news of unrest among the Indians around Fort Pitt; he merely assumed, notwithstanding the dire warnings of Sir William Johnson, that his reforms in the Indian trade were having the beneficial, economizing effect he intended. In the meantime Amherst addressed himself to the many problems of winding up the war in North America while fighting dragged on in Europe and elsewhere, with no clear end in sight. These difficulties all derived in one way or another from the need to control a conquered population and secure vast, newly won territories; and to do so with less money and fewer men than ever before.[1]

Amherst had established a military government for Canada in September 1760, immediately after Vaudreuil's capitulation. This improvised system of administration, which divided what had been New France into the three districts of Québec, Trois-Rivières, and Montréal, would last until civil government could be instituted in August 1764. Until then, despite the fact that the governors of the three districts—Brigadier James Murray, Colonel Ralph Burton, and Brigadier Thomas Gage, respectively—ruled with comparative lenity, the government of Canada rested on essentially coercive foundations. At the beginning of 1761, seventeen battalions were stationed in the three districts, and another four battalions controlled the communications corridors that linked Canada to the British colonies and to the interior. Smaller units, of from one to eight companies, garrisoned the remote posts of the west, from Fort Pitt in the Ohio Valley, to Detroit at the head of Lake Erie, to Fort Michilimackinac at the confluence of Lakes Michigan and Huron. Eventually the absence of rebelliousness among the French allowed the garrisons of the Canadian heartland to be reduced, but there would always be at least five and a half battalions in the St. Lawrence Valley, and many more small units would be dispatched to take over French posts as they surrendered on the remote shores of the Great Lakes, in the Illinois Country, on the lower Mississippi, along the Gulf Coast, and in the southern interior. Finally, the British still had to man posts along the Atlantic coast, at St. John's, Newfoundland, at Halifax and other Nova Scotia sites, and at army headquarters in New York. These together required a steady commitment of approximately four battalions.

Amherst at the beginning of 1761 had about sixteen thousand regular troops under his command, barely enough to perform the tasks of administration and control that confronted him—particularly since, as he well knew, desertion, death, and discharge would inexorably erode that number. In the best of times, Amherst's battalions had been about 30 percent understrength; now, owing to the chronic difficulty of replenishing their ranks by enlistment in the colonies and the heavy demand for troops in Europe, which kept large numbers of replacements from being shipped across the Atlantic, he faced a situation that he knew would deteriorate, even as his responsibilities grew. To make matters worse, Pitt had recently ordered him to detach two thousand men for immediate service in the West Indies, and to prepare another six or seven thousand to depart in the fall for the invasion of the French island of Martinique. As much as he had come to despise American provincials—whom he thought barely worth their rations, much less their princely pay—Amherst had no choice but to request more than ten thousand troops from New England, New York, and New Jersey to help garrison his far-flung forts. This in turn meant more expense, and Amherst's superiors were pressing him to economize with an urgency that would only intensify as the costs of the European war continued to mount. Always eager to please, Amherst constantly searched for ingenious ways to cut expenses while fulfilling his administrative responsibilities and securing the conquests. In the end, his solutions mainly succeeded in rendering his job more difficult.[2]

One of Amherst's initiatives involved the early promotion of settlement. As early as 1759 he had agreed to requests from enterprising officers, provincial and regular alike, for grants of land in the vicinity of various posts. On November 10 that year, the colonels of the Massachusetts and Connecticut regiments had asked for permission to promote settlement along the road that had recently been completed from Fort Number 4 on the Connecticut River to Crown Point. That same day Major Philip Skene of the 27th Regiment had approached him with a request to ratify a venture he had already begun by settling a "number of poor families and some servants" at the head of Lake Champlain. Amherst tentatively agreed to both ventures and asked Pitt to have the Privy Council confirm his grants. Later he encouraged regular officers to begin settling civilians on a ten thousand–acre grant near Fort Niagara, and on a similar tract in the neighborhood of Fort Stanwix, at the Great Carrying Place between the Mohawk and Wood Creek. He also sanctioned settlements along the Forbes Road around Forts Bedford, Ligonier, and Pitt and was at least aware of settlements near other backwoods posts. The promoters of these schemes intended to make a speculative profit on the sale of lands to farmers, to promote trade, or even (in the case of Skene) to create manors on which they could settle tenants whom they would import from Europe. To Amherst, however, the new settlements offered a practical, economical solution to two problems. Most important, these settlements would insure the local availability of food, at a reasonable price, to garrisons that would otherwise have to continue hauling in provisions over vast distances. Second, they seemed to provide the only possible way to contain and control the migration of farm families to the now presumably safe frontier.[3]

By the fall of 1761 the valleys of the Youghiogheny, Monongahela, Loyalhanna, and Allegheny Rivers upstream from Pittsburgh were attracting backwoods settlers and hunters in such numbers that the commandant of Fort Pitt found it necessary to issue a proclamation forbidding settlement except where specifically authorized. Eventually he ordered the houses of squatters burned. Under such pressure, the officially sanctioned community at the Forks of the Ohio grew rapidly, as its inhabitants felled tracts of forest for fuel and building materials; planted fields of corn and beans; began a school for their children; constructed houses and barns, stores and warehouses, mills, brick kilns, and tanyards; excavated quarries for stone and lime, and opened a coal mine on a hill overlooking the Monongahela.[4]

Pittsburgh, and even the smaller settlements that grew up at Niagara, Fort Stanwix, on Lake Champlain, and elsewhere near frontier forts, were larger and more intrusive than any French trading post had ever been. Indian leaders understood only too well that the settlers had not necessarily come to trade with and live peaceably among them. While many had indeed come as traders whose presence was at least in general desirable, many more were coming to farm and to hunt, activities that competed directly with Indian subsistence. Those farmers and hunters, moreover, harbored attitudes shaped by seven years of bloody backwoods war, by no means favorable to Indians. Yet disruptive—and menacing—as their presence might be, no nativist leader could hope to expel them by force without first reckoning with the soldiers of the forts themselves: troops who were at once more alien, more numerous, and more heavily armed than the French had ever been.

Thus what seemed to Amherst to be sensible, economical solutions to the problems of supplying his garrisons and controlling the immigration of frontier families onto Indian lands looked to the Indians who traded at the forts like something else: colonization in the wake of conquest. In persuading them to abandon the French alliance, the British had pledged themselves to open a plentiful trade on favorable terms, and when the war was done to withdraw their soldiers. But more and more, in 1761 and after, the Indians came to understand these promises as lies. How else could they reasonably interpret the failure of the British to pull troops out of the west? How else could they explain the growth of civilian communities around the forts, or Amherst's abrupt refusal to bestow presents, or new trade regulations that would render them both defenseless and dependent? At the end of 1761, however, Sir Jeffery Amherst saw none of the Indians' concerns, for he had problems enough of his own.

CHAPTER 49

Pitt's Problems

1761

BACK IN LONDON, William Pitt had problems too—political ones that dwarfed anything that Amherst faced in America. These would shape the remainder of the war and its conclusion and deeply influence the politics of a critical decade in British and American history. To understand them, we need first to realize that while in late 1760 William Pitt was the most powerful figure in British politics, his power depended on two factors beyond his control. More than even Pitt knew, his fortunes were hostage to the character of the new king and to the course of a stalemated European war.

George III was twenty-two years old when he ascended the throne, a limited, immature man, and all too easy to underestimate. His father, Frederick Lewis, prince of Wales, had died when George was only thirteen. Frederick had rejected his father's and grandfather's devotion to Hanover along with their embrace of the Whig party. Had he lived, he would doubtless have striven to make the monarchy symbolically central to the British national identity that was still taking form. George was old enough at Frederick's death to have absorbed his ambitions, but he was fated to pass his teenage years at Leicester House, the focus of the "reversionary interest" and the very heart of opposition to the court and its policies. Because of his youth, George as heir apparent was more observer than actor in the schemes of his mother, the dowager princess Augusta, and his tutor, Lord Bute. Because of this, he imbibed their views on politics and politicians wholeheartedly, leavening them with his own powerful conviction that people and issues must be divided into morally absolute categories of right and wrong. George had been a reluctant student—he evidently did not read until he was eight years old and wrote like a child through his teens—but like many late bloomers he made great strides at the end of adolescence. At the time of his accession no informed observer could have missed his marked intelligence, nor failed to see the odd skew his emotions had given it.[1]

It was not limitations of mind but certain characteristics of personality that made the new king a problematic figure for Pitt and the rest of Britain's ruling oligarchy. George was unswervingly loyal to people he trusted and ideas he believed to be true; and he behaved in ways that a modern psychologist might interpret as obsessive. As a young man he developed remarkably regular habits. As he aged these would grow rigid: he would, for example, eat virtually the same dinner every day of his adult life (bread, soup, beets or turnips, and mutton—varying only on Sundays, when he allowed himself roast beef). The regularity of his tastes bespoke a deeper hunger for order. It was no accident that he would become a great collector of Canaletto paintings and of ingenious orreries and chronometers, for both Canaletto and clockwork offered the reassuring precision he looked for in the universe and longed for in human relationships.[2]

Mercurial, brilliant, and charismatic, William Pitt at the zenith of his power seemed to George to be precisely the kind of man who was most dangerous in politics. Once Pitt had been Leicester House's darling and had seemed to the prince to exemplify the principles that would be Britain's salvation: incorruptibility in politics, aversion to factionalism and self-interest, and a refusal to compromise British interests by allowing foreign policy to be driven by concern for Hanover. Everything George had loathed in his grandfather, especially his partisanship and his fixation on "that horrid Electorate," Pitt had opposed before he had become chief minister. But Pitt's alliance with Newcastle, his volte-face on engagement in the continental war, his willingness to ingratiate himself with the old king without regard to prior expressions of principle: these had helped convince George that Pitt was a man of no moral character, no trustworthiness, at all. Pitt's refusal to intervene with the king and preserve the reputation of General Bligh after the disaster of St.-Cas, his rejection of the advice that George's beloved Bute offered, and his readiness to jettison his Leicester House connections once they became inconvenient: these had proven to the prince that Pitt was "the most dishonorable of men . . . the blackest of hearts."[3]

George wanted most of all to be a king who stood as truly above party as Pitt had once seemed to stand: a king of all the people of Great Britain, as his father had intended to be, and not just the servant—as his grandfather had been—of the Whig oligarchs who controlled the House

The young king: George III (1738–1820). This Woollett engraving of a portrait by Allan Ramsay shows the king as he would have appeared at court in his early thirties. *Courtesy of the William L. Clements Library at the University of Michigan.*

of Commons. In his first address to Parliament, he took pains to announce that he gloried "in the name Briton," and he meant it with all his callow soul. He intended to serve the interest of all Britons, Scots and Welsh and English alike, and above all he understood that to do so would require ending what in his inaugural statement to the Privy Council he attempted to call "a bloody war." *Attempted,* because Pitt had caught his tone beforehand and insisted that he change the words to "an expensive but just and necessary war," which he would would pursue "in concert with our allies" until it was possible to obtain "an honourable and lasting peace."[4] The new king acquiesced. But he had not been persuaded that the war was either just or necessary, and from the beginning of his reign he made it his goal not only to end it, but to terminate the political ascendancy of the man he identified with its continuance. The interests of the whole people, George III believed, were no longer being served by William Pitt; they would be better protected by a Briton as truehearted and impartial as he was himself, the earl of Bute.

But while Lord Bute coveted the office of first lord of the Treasury, he also feared Pitt, who had declared on the first day of the new reign that "he must act as an independent minister or not at all, that his politics were like his religion, which would admit of no accommodation," and that "if the system of the war was to undergo the least change or shadow of a change," he would resign. That statement required no decoding: Newcastle and all the rest of the ministers would stay on, or Pitt would go. And thus although the former prince's tutor was beyond doubt the man whom the king trusted most in all the world, his ambitions were for the moment blocked by Pitt's popularity as the most successful war leader in British history. Sophisticated and handsome, and yet also an outsider, and temperamentally aloof—as Walpole put it, "unknown, ungracious, and a Scot"—Bute would for the time being hold only the ceremonial office of Groom of the Stole. George stipulated that Bute be admitted to meetings of the cabinet, but he would have to wait more than five months before he assumed an official role in government. In the meantime, Pitt would continue to operate as before and assume that his control was as complete as it had ever been. In the realm of strategy, this meant the execution of his plan to seize Belle-Île-en-Mer, the fortified island just outside Quiberon Bay, and the continuation of plans to conquer Martinique. Both expeditions went forward in 1761, and both succeeded in obtaining yet more territory for Britain, more leverage to be exerted in the peace negotiations. As a matter of practical fact, however, the entry of Bute into active politics changed more than Pitt realized, for it put a direct contender for power into the cabinet and gave Newcastle—ironically Newcastle, for his was the job Bute wanted—an ally in his search for a way to end the war.[5]

Because Newcastle acted as the government's chief fund-raiser among the "money'd men" of the City, the war's expense never ceased to torment him. Better than most politicians—and much more acutely than Pitt, who naively believed that the government's credit was bottomless—Newcastle understood that the financial resources of the nation had been stretched taut by taxation and borrowing. Yet the war on the Continent dragged on, seemingly without any prospect of ending, while its costs mounted to ever more terrifying heights. Decisive victories were nowhere

The "Dearest Friend": John Stuart, third earl of Bute (1713–92). Allan Ramsay's 1760 portrait, engraved by William Wynne Ryland in 1763, shows the "unknown, ungracious" Scot at the height of his influence, wearing the ceremonial robes of a member of the House of Lords, as well as the chain that symbolized his recent appointment as first lord of the Treasury. *Courtesy of the William L. Clements Library at the University of Michigan.*

to be seen. Frederick had finished the campaign of 1760 with a victory over Daun at Torgau, a strategic crossing on the River Elbe. This victory, however, cost the Prussian army seventeen thousand men against sixteen thousand Austrians, and it settled nothing. Daun merely withdrew across the river, while Frederick's forces were so depleted that he could only send them into winter quarters. He had staved off the Austrian threat to Berlin but remained powerless to remove the enemy from Silesia, or even from Saxony.[6]

In the west, Prince Ferdinand's army had gone into winter quarters following the indecisive Battle of Kloster Kamp, in October. Thereafter much complaint had been made (privately by Ferdinand, publicly by British officers serving under him) that the army had been hobbled by lack of adequate supplies. Since the British Treasury was solely responsible for supplying Ferdinand's force, these allegations greatly concerned Newcastle. He was relieved to find, upon inquiry, that the commissariat's problems had been exaggerated. But that there were problems on the western front was confirmed in March when Ferdinand, who had attacked the French in a winter campaign, was forced by shortages of men and supplies to scuttle back from the Rhine to the River Diemel—a retreat that cost him all of Hesse. Neither Ferdinand nor Frederick seemed likely to force the French, Austrians, and Russians to make peace. Every gain seemed to be compensated for by a loss sustained elsewhere, every victory dampened by its cost and lack of decisiveness.[7]

Increasingly, all Newcastle could see was how expensive the war had become. The virtually continuous reconstruction of the Prussian army from the ruin that Frederick's campaigns made of it, year after year, had already cost the British Treasury millions of pounds. The commissariat of Ferdinand's army alone was consuming more than ten thousand pounds a day and producing little but complaints. Even though, to the duke's great relief, the House of Commons had approved the year's budget estimates for the German war on a voice vote, he still had to find the money somewhere. This was no trivial task. The war was eating up twenty million pounds annually. Tax receipts to the Treasury could supply only about a third of that sum, and nearly half of those revenues were previously obligated to pay the interest on the existing debt.[8] Incessantly Newcastle worried that any disruption in the securities market would lead to financial panic and bring the whole house of cards slithering down. And what was Pitt's response? To blame him for extravagance, and to propose more expeditions!

The duke had served George II faithfully through practically his whole reign and had always drawn strength from his relationship with the monarch. Deprived of that emotional anchor, he responded in a not altogether rational way to his fears and to Pitt's bullying refusal to consider peace. In February, when Pitt was immobilized by gout, Newcastle set out to curry favor with the new king by suggesting that the earl of Holdernesse be dismissed from his position as secretary of state for the

Northern Department, and that Lord Bute be named as his replacement. Superficially this made sense—Bute as the king's confidant deserved a formal place in the cabinet, and Holdernesse had been little more than a nonentity—and George jumped at the chance to serve the interests of his favorite. In the most important ways, however, Newcastle's gambit made no sense at all. He proposed the change to the king without consulting Pitt, who was furious at what he saw as both a personal betrayal and an attack on his authority. Holdernesse, it was true, had been a cipher; but he had been Pitt's cipher, and Pitt knew that he would never be able to dictate to the man whom the king called his "Dearest Friend" as he had to Holdernesse. Newcastle had perhaps forgotten his colleague's capacity for pettiness. If so, he would soon have cause to remember it, for Pitt would henceforth make it his purpose to humiliate and thwart the duke at every turn. Moreover, Newcastle would soon discover that he had made an even more significant oversight, for he had not attended to the differences between Bute's ideas about the *kind* of treaty that was desirable and his own.

The duke wanted peace as soon as possible, but not at the expense of Britain's allies. He therefore favored economizing by scaling back operations against France but sustaining the German war as long as necessary to obtain an honorable peace. Given his driving fear of bankruptcy, this was at best an inconsistent policy; it was certainly at odds with Pitt's evident determination to strip France of her empire, humble her diplomatically, and in effect dictate the peace terms. Bute, on the other hand, wanted a prompt settlement and was willing to accept the status quo as its basis, which meant that he wanted to cut the German subsidies and leave Frederick and Ferdinand to shift for themselves. So Newcastle in fact compounded his woes by suggesting that Bute be made a minister, yet realized it too late to stop the appointment. On March 10, before the duke had a chance for second thoughts, before Pitt even knew what was happening, Bute kissed his former pupil's hand for the seals of office. With that ritual act began Pitt's descent from power and the somewhat more protracted decline of Newcastle himself.[9]

Shortly thereafter, at the end of March, Louis XV made a formal appeal for a peace to be concluded, on the basis of the current status quo, at a general conference of all the belligerent powers. Simultaneously Pitt received a letter from the French war minister, Étienne-François de Stainville, duc de Choiseul, proposing that Britain and France exchange envoys to discuss the issues—implicitly, an offer to begin negotiations for a separate peace. Although neither Pitt nor Newcastle was as willing to make peace without reference to the interests of Prussia, they agreed to send a diplomat to Paris and to receive a French representative in return. In the meantime, Pitt's long-planned expedition against Belle-Île-en-Mer went ahead. By the time the envoys were beginning to state their governments' respective positions in Paris and London, the island was in British hands, following a campaign that afforded yet another example of the cooperation between army and naval forces that had come to characterize the war effort under Ligonier and Anson.[10]

Belleisle was more than just a diplomatic counter to be bargained back in return for Minorca or those parts of the Prussian Rhineland that France had conquered. Reviving his old navalist strategy, Pitt intended Belleisle to be a stage from which coastal raids could be launched to take pressure off Ferdinand by forcing the French to concentrate on coastal defense. Thus while the seizure of an island that lay less than twenty miles off the Brittany coast shook the French court, it also frightened Newcastle, Bute, and others in the British ministry who were inclined to negotiate for peace. They feared both any addition to Pitt's popularity and the prospect that more defeats would drive France, in desperation, to seek an alliance with Spain—and there were plenty of indications that Madrid would favor such an agreement. Yet Pitt, far from fearing the prolongation of the war, seemed actually to welcome it. As his colleagues in the cabinet knew only too well, his war aims had grown with every victory; they worried that he would refuse to make peace so long as he could go on expanding British military and commercial power. They had good reason to fear that he would think the Spanish colonies, too, were ripe for the picking, and that he would find only a kind of perverse benediction in Spain's belligerency.[11]

The Southern secretary's haughty reception of France's peace envoy seemed only to prove the substance of Bute's and Newcastle's fears. Despite the announced willingness of the French to deliver up most of their American empire, Pitt insisted that he would not make peace until they also surrendered their rights to the Newfoundland fishery, and that demand was strictly nonnegotiable. This was not solely, or even principally, because the French market for cod sustained a £500,000 annual trade, a sum larger than the whole fur production of Canada. It was rather because every eighteenth-century strategist held it as an axiom that a great fishery was a "nursery of seamen," and thus crucial to maintaining a significant navy. Pitt was demanding, in effect, not only that the French surrender the bulk of their colonies, but that they prostrate themselves before a British commercial monopoly and foreswear rebuilding their naval power—thus placing their international trade permanently at Great Britain's mercy.[12]

Virtually everyone in the cabinet except Pitt saw this as madness, an invitation to make Britain into an international pariah in the postwar era. As the duke of Bedford (lately lord lieutenant of Ireland, but now a cabinet member without portfolio) observed to Newcastle, Pitt's gambit for supremacy "would be as dangerous for us to grasp at as it was for Louis XIV, when he aspired to be the arbiter of Europe, and might be likely to produce a grand alliance against us." More immediately it produced deep divisions within the cabinet, stopped the negotiations cold, and finally aligned every important minister against a sublimely unconcerned Pitt.[13]

Meanwhile, the Spanish court had grown concerned that France was at the point of selling out Spain's interests, and promised Choiseul a formal alliance if he would refrain from making a separate peace. In fact Choiseul, deeply committed to rebuilding French power, had no intention of agreeing to peace on Pitt's terms and eagerly took advantage of Spain's offer. The alliance, concluded at Paris on August 15, was called the Family Compact because its signatories represented the two branches of the Bourbon dynasty. It took the form of a defensive mutual pledge that Spain and France would settle their differences with Great Britain in concert. The signatories made no special effort to conceal its provisions, but they took care not to publicize the existence of the secret convention that accompanied it. This instrument promised that if the war had not ended by May 1, 1762, Spain would enter hostilities as France's ally.[14]

The Spanish hoped that the Family Compact would make Great Britain reasonable and that the convention would make France resolute. Only the latter hope had any prospect of fulfillment. The conclusion of the Franco-Spanish alliance inaugurated the last futile phase of the peace negotiations, in which the stakes were higher than ever and the fishing-rights issue—now that Spanish demands for consideration had to be included as well—was even less susceptible to resolution. By mid-September Pitt was pressing hard for a preemptive declaration of war against Spain. An intercepted letter from the Spanish ambassador to Paris to his counterpart in London had suggested that a secret protocol of the Family Compact provided for a military alliance to take effect after the treasure fleet arrived from the New World. This, Pitt argued, could only mean that the Spanish intended to enter the war. If war with Spain was inevitable, what was to be gained by waiting? But Pitt's fellow ministers were not about to be swept into an expanded conflict by torrents of eloquence. Some, like Bute and Bedford, opposed declaring war on Spain for diplomatic reasons, since victory in such a conflict would threaten the balance of power. Others, including Anson and Ligonier, doubted the ability of the navy and army to take on a new enemy and demurred for strategic reasons. Newcastle, worrying that tremors in the securities markets in May and June portended worse problems to come, dissented on financial grounds.[15]

When the cabinet met on September 15 and 18, only Richard, Earl Temple, the lord privy seal and Pitt's brother-in-law, supported the Great Commoner's demand for an immediate declaration of war. The other ministers agreed to reinforce the Caribbean and Mediterranean fleets but wanted to try to buy Spain out of the alliance by offering to withdraw Britain's logwood cutters from the Honduras coast—a significant concession in a long-standing dispute between London and Madrid. It was clear in the meeting of September 15 that the cabinet would not be bullied. In desperation, therefore, at the next meeting, Pitt and Temple produced a minority report they had drawn up for presentation to the king. This was a maneuver for which there was no precedent, and George, treating it as "Mr. Pitts black scheme," refused to accept the report.

"Were any of the other Ministers as spirited as you are my Dearest Friend," he wrote to Bute, "I would say let that mad Pitt be dismissed, but as matters are very different from that we must get rid of him in a happier moment than the present one." Cannily, the king insisted on waiting for the expected return from Paris of the British peace envoy before hearing arguments for and against a declaration of war. While they waited, the ministers convinced themselves that they could not afford to follow the Southern secretary's line, and George braced himself for the political hurricane that would inevitably accompany Pitt's offer to resign.[16]

When the critical meeting of the cabinet came on October 2, Pitt once more made his case for a declaration of war. When all of his fellow ministers except Temple declined to support him, however, he gave up. In better grace than anyone who knew him expected, he thanked "the old ministers for their civility to him" and took his leave. Three days later he tendered his resignation to the king; Temple followed suit on the ninth. Astonishingly, there was no crisis. The king, with ceremonial expressions of regret, accepted the seals from the secretary and immediately "made him a most gracious and unlimited offer of any rewards in the power of the crown to bestow." Pitt, who had been under extraordinary psychological strain, broke down and wept. That evening, he and Bute worked out the terms of his reward: a pension (for his, his wife's, and their son's lifetimes) of three thousand pounds per year and a peerage, as Baroness Chatham, for his wife.[17]

It was a generous reward, although not an extravagant one. It secured Pitt's family from possible financial embarrassment and it allowed him—since it was his wife who had received the title—to remain in the House of Commons. But it served another purpose, too, and one Pitt could hardly have expected when he tearfully accepted the king's offer. The terms of pensions granted by the Crown were customarily kept secret, but Bute ordered the details of this one to be reported in the government's next *Gazette.* That alone would have been sufficient to harm the Great Commoner's reputation for disinterestedness, but Bute also had pamphleteers engaged to write tracts with titles like *The Patriot Unmasked* and *The Right Honourable Annuitant Unmasked,* lest anyone miss the point. Insofar as possible, the ungracious Scot had insured that if Pitt went into opposition, he could not easily stake his customary claim to the moral high ground. And for that, three thousand pounds a year must have seemed a bargain indeed.

CHAPTER 50

The End of an Alliance

1762

THE KING AND BUTE were now free to replace Pitt and Temple, but not to reshuffle the rest of the cabinet's ministries according to their liking. Newcastle, without whose complicity Pitt could never have been unseated, would remain in the post Bute coveted, while the aging architects of military operations, Anson and Ligonier, would continue to direct the navy and the army. Thus while Pitt's departure averted an immediate declaration of war on Spain, it generated only marginal changes in long-established patterns. The duke of Bedford, Newcastle's old enemy and an ally of Bute, was named to replace Temple as lord privy seal, while Charles Wyndham, the second earl of Egremont—an aristocrat qualified by irreproachable pedigree, if no other qualities, for the office—took over Pitt's old position as Southern secretary.[1]

Since no commoners now held ministerial posts, someone had to be designated to manage the government's interests in the House of Commons, and for that role Bute and the king settled on George Grenville. This was in some ways a clever choice, for Grenville was Temple's brother and Pitt's brother-in-law, and an important figure in "the faction of cousins" that had been the Great Commoner's base in Parliament during his long career in opposition. Although he put himself on bad terms with the other members of his party by accepting the position as the ministry's leader in the Commons, Grenville was still bound by familial and political ties to Pitt, and thus at least potentially offered another means of keeping Pitt out of opposition. Grenville was a deeply unimaginative man but a legendarily hard worker and an able fiscal technician—all qualities that commended him to Bute. A rarer quality commended him to the king: a reputation for incorruptibility equal to Pitt's, before Pitt accepted the pension. This made him a figure capable of retaining the loyalty of the independent M.P.s on the backbenches and thus limiting the damage Pitt could inflict as an opposition leader. At the top of his form Grenville was no better than a lackluster orator, but his talents as a parliamentary operative seemed adequate to offset that deficiency.[2]

In policy, as in personnel, the changes that followed Pitt's resignation all came at the margins. The circumstances of the Great Commoner's departure and the necessity of avoiding a crisis that would compel the king to recall him to office dictated that George and his ministers take a hard line on the war, particularly on questions relating to Spain. Thus the negotiations with France, long fettered by a fisheries issue that might now have been resolved, were allowed to lapse. The British ambassador in Madrid was instructed to demand assurances that Spain's intentions in concluding the Family Compact were peaceable and was authorized to open negotiations on the logwood question. In the meantime, however, Ligonier and Anson set to work preparing for a widened war.[3]

In the event of hostilities, Spain's likeliest first move would be to invade Portugal, a country bound to Britain by a defensive treaty and so tightly tied to the British empire economically as to be a virtual dependency. To defend Portugal would take perhaps 10,000 soldiers more than the approximately 110,000 currently on active service. This posed a major problem because since 1760 the number of volunteers enlisting had been no more than adequate to replace losses. Ligonier and Charles Townshend—the brilliant young opportunist who had been appointed secretary at war in March—therefore grasped the nettle of necessity and sanctioned "raising for rank," or offering commissions as field officers to gentlemen who could raise new battalions from among their tenantry. To revive this antique practice was a desperate measure, since the personal loyalties that produced such units weakened the professionalism of the army; yet the only alternative, conscription (declaring a "land impress"), would have produced worse effects and probably riots. Lord Anson, meanwhile, faced even more inflexible limits in ships and manpower as he began trying to identify potential targets in the Spanish empire. So fully was the navy committed that any expeditions would have to rely heavily on troops already based outside the home isles—an expedient, it was true, but one that had the advantage of speed. If plans could be laid before the declaration of war, orders might be sent overseas soon enough to enable the expeditions' commanders to surprise their opponents. Or so, at least, Anson hoped.[4]

Pitt's departure, then, created paradoxical effects. A king who had

George Grenville (1712–70). Shown here in an engraved version of a Hoare portrait, issued after his appointment as treasurer of the navy in 1754, Grenville appears as a fortyish, but still youthful, figure. He holds an Act of Parliament, "establishing a regular method for the punctual, frequent & certain payment" of seamen's wages—appropriately enough, a law dealing with the kind of technically complex financial issues that Grenville understood better than any other politician of his day. *Courtesy of the William L. Clements Library at the University of Michigan.*

hoped to effect great changes in the cabinet found its composition barely altered; ministers who had plotted Pitt's downfall because they hoped to sidestep a war with Spain found that hostilities were all but inevitable. On November 19, Egremont instructed the British ambassador to deliver an ultimatum: if Spain did not immediately declare that it had no intention of acting as an ally to Britain's enemies, Britain would regard its silence as "an aggression" equivalent to "an absolute Declaration of War." Madrid made no reply. Thus on January 4, 1762, Great Britain declared war; Spain responded in kind on the eighteenth. By then, Anson and Ligonier had already dispatched orders for British forces in America to initiate operations against Havana, and those in India to prepare for an assault on Manila.[5]

Thus the strategy and policy of Pitt's "System" survived its architect's political eclipse. Britain would continue to concentrate on imperial, not continental warfare. The Martinique expedition, which Pitt ordered Amherst to organize at the beginning of the year, had proceeded irrespective of the political changes in London and now produced the kind of result to which Britons had become accustomed. On November 19, with the hurricane season over, Robert Monckton (once more fit for duty, and a major general) led a task force of seven thousand men from New York, heading for a rendezvous with another seven thousand redcoats and a large naval task force in the West Indies. Although British command of the sea in effect decided the outcome of the Martinique venture in advance, the island's terrain made the campaign difficult: a month and nearly five hundred British casualties separated the landings of mid-January and the surrender of the last defenders on February 16, 1762.[6]

Once Martinique capitulated, the rest of the French West Indies islands fell like dominoes: St. Lucia on February 26, Grenada on March 5, and St. Vincent soon thereafter. In each case, the planters—starved for manufactures and foodstuffs, glutted with unshippable produce, nervous about their slaves—welcomed the chance to begin trading legitimately within the world's most prosperous empire. What British arms had begun, therefore, British commerce completed with admirable thoroughness. A correspondent reported to the *Pennsylvania Gazette* from Martinique that "the Inhabitants" seemed "never so happy before." Perhaps he exaggerated, but some kind of relief was unmistakable in the "elegant service of Plate" that the merchants of the island gave Monckton as a going-away present.[7]

So in a sense Pitt's war went on without him: partially because Bute and the other ministers feared the consequences of an abrupt change in policy, and partially because no one dared propose an alternative to the military strategies perfected during his ministry. But these continuities implied a similar persistence in the war's greatest problems, too, for in Europe nothing the British could do had yet enabled Ferdinand or Frederick to gain a permanent advantage over their vastly more numerous adversaries. Indeed, it may be that Britain's renewed concentration on colonial war grew most of all from the sense that military progress could be made nowhere else.

The year 1761 saw an alarming deterioration on both the eastern and western fronts in Germany. After his winter campaign had foundered on shortages of men and supplies, forcing him to withdraw from the Rhineland, Ferdinand had regrouped, invaded Hesse, and won a victory at Vellinghausen on July 15 and 16—only to be forced to retreat before a powerful French counteroffensive. By the end of the campaign the French had pushed him back east of the Weser: further east, in fact, than he had been in March. There, despite the exhaustion of his men, he resupplied his army and in early November counterattacked to halt a French invasion of Hanover. He was therefore able to enter winter quarters without having lost what was still (to Newcastle, if not to Bute or the king) the most important territory in western Europe. But as tactically brilliant as his campaigning had been, Ferdinand could only be judged a success if his record was measured against his brother-in-law's. In the east, Frederick II had narrowly escaped disaster in 1761 only to face the prospect of certain destruction in the following year.[8]

Frederick's problem lay in the erosion of manpower. Although briefly buoyed by the costly victory of Torgau, late in 1760, Prussia began the campaigns of 1761 with only a hundred thousand men under arms, as against three times that number of Austrian and Russian troops. The Austrians had refused to exchange prisoners at the close of the 1760 campaigns in order to deny Frederick access to the last significant reservoir of trained Prussian infantry; at the beginning of 1761, therefore, new recruits and foreigners comprised at least half of his forces. The Prussian army now had nothing in common with the force Frederick had wielded like a rapier at the war's beginning. Once he had sought battle, hoping to gain a decisive victory; now he knew that a single defeat could destroy his army and desperately tried to avoid combat. The strain told on him so heavily, he wrote to an old friend, that "the hairs on the right side of my head have gone quite grey; my teeth are rotting and falling out; my face is wrinkled like the folds of a lady's dress, my back [is] as bent as a fiddlestick and my mind as melancholy as a Trappist's."[9]

Austrian troops now occupied most of Silesia, Frederick's most prized conquest. His efforts to save what was left of it very nearly cost him the main force of his army: on August 20, after failing to prevent the junction of Austrian and Russian armies in northern Silesia, he found himself cut off from Prussia and forced to retreat to high ground near the village of Bunzelwitz, about twenty miles east of Glatz on the present Czech-German border. There, for ten days in late August and early September, his men feverishly improvised fortifications while the Austrian and Russian commanders debated whether to attack. Only their inability to decide saved him. On September 9 the Russians withdrew, leaving the Austrians no choice but to enter winter quarters. But Frederick's luck held only briefly. In December a Russian army seized Kolberg, depriving him of his last port on the Baltic, and for that matter control of the province of Pomerania. For the first time in the war, a Russian army could winter on the doorstep of Brandenburg and within easy striking distance of Berlin, in a position to deny Frederick access to the grain harvest of Poland, on which he had come to rely for provisions.[10]

As Frederick's year of disasters ended, he controlled only Prussia's heartland provinces of Brandenburg and Magdeburg, a fragment of northern Silesia, and parts of Saxony. The Austrians occupied the rest of his conquests, the Russians held East Prussia and Pomerania, and the French controlled his Rhineland provinces. His remaining subjects were prostrate under the burdens of taxation and conscription. Britain's annual subsidy of £670,000 no longer compensated for the resources he had lost. He knew that he would be able to field fewer than seventy thousand men in the coming year, against four times as many enemies. Desperately, Prussian diplomats beseeched the Ottomans to attack Russia, implored the Crimean Tatars to invade Hungary. But Frederick knew that unless the Turks attacked Russia by February 20 his game would be up. Since a severe bout with depression in 1758 he had carried a small box containing a lethal dose of opium pills. Now he wrote to his brother, Prince Henry, that he would "not die a coward's death[.] When I see on 20th February that [the Ottomans have not declared war on Russia], I shall cling to my Stoics and the little box." Then Prussia's diplomats could make peace on any terms they pleased on behalf of Frederick William, the nephew and heir whom Frederick despised. The house of Brandenburg, he believed, was done for.[11]

Frederick was not a religious man, but what happened next he would ever after regard as God's miraculous intervention on Prussia's behalf. On January 6, 1762, the tsarina Elizabeth, daughter of Peter the Great and Frederick's most determined enemy, died suddenly of a stroke. Her Germanized nephew, the duke of Holstein-Gottorp, ascended the throne as Tsar Peter III: a man whose greatest contribution to Russian history would be his wife, Catherine, and whose only strong personal trait was an abject adoration of the king of Prussia. Peter's first diplomatic venture as tsar was to ask Frederick to grant him a Prussian title, the Order of the Black Eagle. Frederick's spirits revived: he had barely finished composing a nasty epitaph for

the Russian Messalina, the Cossacks' whore
Gone to service lovers on the Stygian shore,

before he began drafting terms of peace for consideration at St. Petersburg. He would offer East Prussia in return for peace; would the tsar accept? Peter protested in reply that he would rather be one of Frederick's generals than tsar of all the Russias, and all that remained to be worked out were technicalities. In May, Russia and Prussia ratified the peace, Peter handed East Prussia back to his hero and asked if Frederick would care to have the use of a Russian army corps for the rest of the war. Sweden did not fail to discern its future prospects in these developments and made a hasty peace. By the end of May 1762, a king who would otherwise have taken his own life months before found himself very much alive, militarily reinvigorated, and facing only Austria. He was prepared to deal with them, whether the British continued their subsidy or not.[12]

All these improbable events, so fortunate for the house of Brandenburg, could hardly have been better timed, for the British alliance had in fact fallen apart. The first signal had come on January 6, the day of the tsarina's death and two days after the declaration of war on Spain, when Bute, now preeminent in the cabinet, posed "the Great Question, *for Consideration only,* of withdrawing all our troops from Germany and giving up the German war." Newcastle was aghast. To abandon the Germans, and with them the diplomatic and military "System" that he and Pitt had devised, would allow France to seize Hanover, and—because Elizabeth's death would not be known in England for some days, and its consequences would remain uncertain for months—would permit Russia and Austria to dismember Prussia. More than economy was at stake: honor, too, must have some place in Britain's foreign policy.[13]

And yet Newcastle knew only too well that Britain could not go on expending heroic sums on the Continent and fight the Spanish as well. He well remembered how hard it had been to negotiate the loans to pay for 1762's campaigns, when the "money'd men" had agreed to lend only at a heavy discount—eighty pounds currency to buy a hundred pounds' worth of securities—and at the steep effective interest rate of 5 percent. Even so, Newcastle had been able to secure only twelve of the fourteen million pounds the budget estimates required and was facing the unpleasant prospect of covering the difference by issuing Exchequer bills without the cooperation of the Bank of England. The Spanish war would inevitably reduce revenues generated from the customs on Mediterranean trade, pressing the government even harder in meeting its obligations. To the nervous duke, this looked ominous indeed. Yet he passionately insisted that to abandon the German war would be to surrender everything in Europe to France, at the very moment France was staggering on the verge of financial disaster. Bute, having gauged the old man's will to resist, retreated from his proposal. Once the "Great Question" had been broached, however, time would only make it more insistent.[14]

As Pitt had earlier, the duke now found himself looking for allies that no longer existed in the cabinet. With the tacit approval of the king and Bute, the duke of Bedford actually made a motion in favor of abandoning the German war in the House of Lords on February 5—an extraordinary act for the lord privy seal, and one that Newcastle recognized as a slap in the face. News of Peter III's reversal of Russian policy so thoroughly undermined Newcastle's position that all Bute and his allies needed was a pretext to force him out of office. That excuse came soon enough, in the form of a minor crisis in finance. Sending troops to Portugal to oppose the expected Spanish invasion required an emergency appropriation of a million pounds. In order to ask the House of Commons for authority to borrow this sum, Newcastle in early April asked for cabinet approval. Bute, Grenville, and Bedford refused to agree. The money would have to come from somewhere. The German budget was the only possible source.

The ministers had given Newcastle the opportunity to resign on an issue of principle. Newcastle, unlike Pitt, missed his cue. In a futile effort to retain office, he trimmed his opinions to match those of the majority and agreed to suspend the subsidy to Prussia. Frustrated, Bute and his allies adopted more direct measures, ones that would be unmistakable even to the duke. In mid-April, Grenville began intervening directly in Treasury operations, issuing orders to the secretaries who ran its day-to-day operations. Newcastle informed the king that if such meddling did not cease, he would resign. His Majesty chose to construe this ultimatum as an offer and promptly accepted it. As Newcastle described it on May 15, "without one word of concern on my leaving him, nor even . . . a polite compliment—after near fifty years service and devotion to the interest of his Royal Family," George III turned him out. On the twenty-sixth he delivered up the seals of his office, declined the pension the king offered, and retired from public life.[15]

It was a sad, graceless exit for a minister who had been central to the creation of the modern British state and indispensable to the most prodigious military triumphs in British history. Yet Newcastle's departure, bitter as it was for him, cleared the way for the king and Bute to end the war on their own terms. None of the men who had been instrumental in winning the war's victories would be able to play a role in making the peace.

Perhaps George felt that he could afford to be surly in dismissing Newcastle, for the duke could no longer block Bute's advancement to the post of first lord of the Treasury. The manner in which the "Dearest Friend" responded to the chance to seize the office he had so long schemed to get, however, has left posterity almost no alternative to judging him a ninny. His whining expressions of self-doubt, his worry over possible lack of support in the Commons, his protestations and hesitations and neurotic twitches surprised even George, who sent encouraging little notes to brace him up. "The thought of [your] not accepting the Treasury, or . . . retiring chill my blood," the king wrote. "Is this a moment for despondency? No for vigour and the day is ours; . . . to be short take the Treasury and the numbers [of supporters in Parliament] will be with you." Reassured of his monarch's love if unconvinced of a secure majority in the Commons, Bute at length accepted the office. And that, at last, put paid to the Prussian alliance.[16]

Bute hated Frederick with a fervor exceeded only by Frederick's detestation of him. The new first minister wanted to end the war without delay, and Prussia's newly strengthened position against Austria threatened only to prolong the war. Frederick was anything but cooperative. When Bute advised him to make peace with Austria by giving back Silesia, the king replied with scorn: "Learn your duty better, and take note that it is not your place to proffer me such foolish and impertinent advice." When Bute subsequently asked the tsar to keep armies in the field against Prussia—a note that Peter forwarded to his idol—Frederick's contempt overflowed. "To break faith with an ally, to hatch plots against him, to work zealously for his downfall, such enormities . . . [are] abominable." In the end the Anglo-Prussian alliance dissolved less because Britain could no longer afford to continue its subsidy than because Bute and Frederick, two accomplished haters, regarded one another with unalloyed mutual loathing.[17]

In 1762, therefore, the war of Prussia against Austria proceeded to its conclusion on a course parallel to, but independent of, Britain's war against France and Spain. This placed Prince Ferdinand in an anomalous position, but Bute and his allies feared Pitt's power in Parliament too much to terminate aid to Hanover. Ferdinand thus continued to fight the French with no more than his accustomed handicaps of understrength regiments and underfed horses. Frederick himself was almost relieved by the end of the relationship, for it gave him the opportunity to repair his fortunes without British interference. Ironically, the subsidy money from 1761 had been shipped late in the year, and he embarked on his 1762 campaign in a relatively sound financial state. That, and the timely arrival of twenty thousand Russian soldiers, enabled him to reinvade Silesia. Making the most of his opportunities, he engaged Daun's Austrians at Burkersdorf on July 24 and won the battle that positioned him to recapture the province.

It was well that Frederick acted quickly, for his victory at Burkersdorf in fact came at the last possible moment. The nobles of the Russian court, acting with the encouragement of the tsarina, had deposed Tsar Peter on July 9. Tsarina Catherine, who despised Frederick as much as her husband had worshiped him, immediately recalled the Russian forces, but Frederick persuaded (or perhaps bribed) the Russian commander into remaining with him just long enough to tie down a large component of the Austrian army while he came to grips with Daun. Because Austria had been in financial trouble since 1760, and had come to rely so much on Russia for military support, Burkersdorf proved a blow disproportionate to its actual size.[18]

Daun's refusal or inability to resume offensive operations allowed Frederick to invest the last Austrian stronghold in Silesia, the fortress of Schweidnitz. They gave it up, and with it the province, in October—not long before Prince Henry's army routed a superior Austrian force at the Battle of Freiberg and reasserted Prussian control over Saxony. Meanwhile, in the west, Prince Ferdinand prevented France from making a last-ditch attempt to regain Hanover when he defeated a French army at Wilhelmsthal on June 24. Then, moving southward, he broke up the French forces in Hesse during July and besieged Cassel, which capitulated on November 2. At that point armistices were at hand both in the east, where Austria despaired of regaining Silesia, and in the west, where the intervention of Spain had produced nothing but further humiliations for the house of Bourbon.[19]

CHAPTER 51

The Intersections of Empire, Trade, and War

HAVANA

AUGUST 1762

As LORD LIGONIER had expected, Spain invaded Britain's vulnerable ally Portugal, but not until May 9. This gave him time enough to dispatch officers to Portugal to organize a kind of peasant militia, which hindered the advance of the Spanish army in the northern part of the kingdom while he raised men and shifted regiments to form an expeditionary force. In early July six thousand redcoats under Lord Loudoun arrived from Belleisle and joined with perhaps two thousand more from Ireland to block a Spanish attempt on Lisbon. The Spaniards tried again in August, sending a second army westward toward the capital through the central province of Estremadura. This force, together with thousands of French reinforcements, seized the important city of Almeida on July 25, but that would prove to be the limit of their advance. A flamboyant young British brigadier, John Burgoyne, counterattacked by striking deep in the enemy rear to destroy a major supply depot on the twenty-seventh. In October, Burgoyne staged another raid, wiping out a second critical magazine: an operation led by a subordinate who exceeded even Burgoyne in intemperance and daring—Charles Lee, lately arrived from America and newly promoted to lieutenant colonel. Immobilized by supply shortages, unable to secure their lines of communication, and suffering disastrously high rates of desertion, the Bourbon armies withdrew, in early November, to bases across the Spanish border.[1] With that, all active military operations in Europe ceased and the diplomats of the belligerent powers were left to work out the formalities of peace.

Financial exhaustion was not, in the end, what made the Bourbon courts willing to negotiate an end to the war. Rather it was financial exhaustion compounded by news from America of two more British victories. The smaller of these was most significant for the French, because it frustrated their last hope of gaining a strategic asset to bargain back in return for some major British concession. In the single exception to the Royal Navy's success in bottling up the French Atlantic fleet after the Battle of Quiberon Bay, a small squadron had slipped out of Brest in May under cover of fog and carried eight hundred troops to Newfoundland. Since Amherst had assigned only about three hundred infantry and artillerymen to defend the island, the French had no trouble taking it in late June. Embarrassed, Amherst patched together an expedition from about a thousand regulars from New York, Halifax, and Louisbourg, added another five hundred Massachusetts provincials from Nova Scotia, put his brother William in charge, and sent them off to recapture the place. This they did, with light casualties and little evident difficulty, between September 12 and 18.[2]

The news that the British had reconquered Newfoundland, coming in October as Spain was pulling its troops out of Portugal, completed the despair of French and Spanish diplomats, for it arrived on the heels of the other report from the New World—one that heaped military disgrace on the political disaster that the Spanish intervention had already become. On August 13, after a siege of two months, the British army had seized Havana, the crown jewel of the Spanish Caribbean.

As we have seen, Ligonier and Anson had set their sights on Havana even before the formal declaration of war. Beyond its considerable significance as the point of departure for Cuba's exports of tobacco, sugar, and hides, this city of 35,000 was the entrepôt of the Spanish Caribbean, the major port for ship repair, and the chief magazine of naval supplies and provisions for Spain's transatlantic trade. As this would suggest, Havana had enormous strategic importance; so much so that the imperial administration had stationed a permanent regular garrison there and fortified it more strongly than any other American port. A bastioned wall surrounded the city proper, and two stout forts, the Punta on the west and Morro Castle on the east, guarded its seaward approaches. Secure on a promontory overlooking the best deepwater harbor in the Caribbean, Havana—the "key to the New World"—had stood as the symbol of Spanish maritime power for more than a century.[3]

Havana's location had made the city a target irresistible to Anson and

Ligonier. Britain had thousands of troops in the West Indies, and thousands more in North America, in addition to the provincials who could be raised for an expedition that promised to yield mountains of plunder. Even though Havana would have to be invested during the summer months, when disease would exact a heavy toll from the invaders, there was every reason to believe that a quick expedition could arrive before the garrison could prepare for a siege. And to a degree remarkable for the eighteenth century, the British did move rapidly against Havana. The expedition's commander, George Keppel, earl of Albemarle, received his preliminary orders only three days after the declaration of war and was able to sail from Portsmouth on March 6 with four regular regiments, a train of siege artillery, and a corps of French Protestant prisoners of war who had enlisted in British service.[4]

Despite adverse winds, Albemarle's force reached the West Indies on April 20. Within a month General Monckton had brought his command from Martinique to rendezvous with them off Hispaniola's Cap Nicolas. At this point, although the troops from North America had not yet arrived, Albemarle had about twelve thousand soldiers on hand and felt sufficiently confident to proceed. On June 7 the British landed about six miles east of Havana. By the next evening they had scattered a screen of Spanish defenders and secured a position on high ground from which they could invest Morro Castle. Under the direction of such veterans of American operations as Colonel Guy Carleton and Colonel William Howe, the redcoats efficiently isolated city from hinterland and on the tenth opened a *siège en forme*. With the Royal Navy in possession of the sea approaches and the eighteen warships in Havana's squadron trapped within the harbor, it should have been just a matter of time, and backbreaking work, to bludgeon the city into submission.[5]

But overexertion, heat, disease, scarcity of drinkable water, and the evident impregnability of Morro Castle's walls took such a toll on the besiegers that it soon became clear they would succeed only if they could win a race with death. A month after the siege had begun, Albemarle had lost a third of his force: a thousand men were dead from wounds, yellow fever, malaria, and gastrointestinal disorders, and three thousand more were too sick or badly wounded to serve. Albemarle could see that the guns of his siege train and the fleet were steadily reducing the number of Spanish guns able to reply; but would he have men enough left to storm the fort, once they had breached the Morro's defenses? He ordered sappers to tunnel beneath the castle's walls, in order to detonate a mine and hasten the day of battle; but the miners soon hit solid rock, and their work proceeded by inches. Meanwhile the redcoats sickened and died at

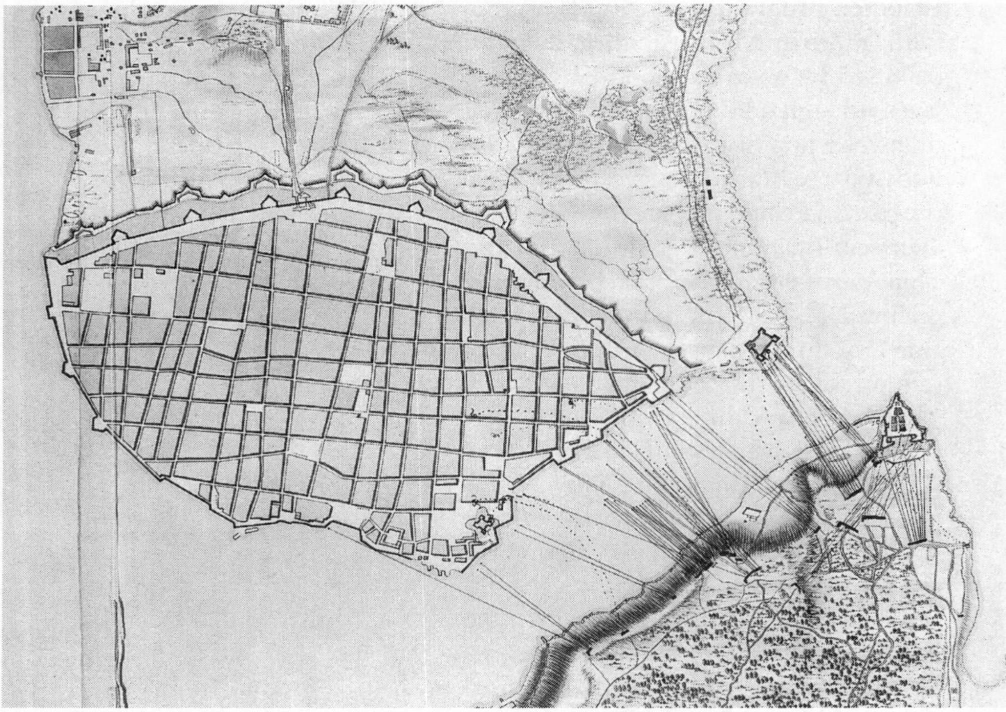

The Siege of Havana, June 8–August 13, 1762. This fine engineer's rendering shows British siege lines and battery positions on the lower right. Morro Castle appears to the east (right) side of the channel into the harbor; the Punta on the west. The straight lines projecting from the batteries indicate trajectories of individual cannon; dotted, curved lines depict mortar ("bomb") trajectories. Unlike Québec, the interior buildings of which suffered badly from British bombardment, the city of Havana itself remained comparatively undamaged by shellfire. *Courtesy of the William L. Clements Library at the University of Michigan.*

an appalling rate, and the survivors had to work harder than ever to keep up the siege. When there were no longer enough men to sustain three eight-hour shifts in the lines and underground, the troops worked twelve hours on and twelve off, with disastrous effects. "The fatigues on shore were excessive," wrote Ensign Miller, who had endured other horrors in the Québec winter of 1759–60. "The bad water brought on disorders that were mortal. You could see the men's tongues hanging out like a mad dog's; a dollar was frequently given for a quart of water[.] In short, by dead, wounded or sick the army was reduced to two reliefs and it was supposed that we should be obliged to re-embark without taking the place."[6]

Only the arrival, between July 28 and August 2, of about four thousand troops from North America—half of them regulars of the 46th and 58th Regiments and the New York independent companies, the other half provincials from New York, New Jersey, Rhode Island, and Connecticut—enabled Albemarle to bring his siege to a successful end. Using the fresh units to replace four battalions wholly wasted by disease, he ordered the mine under Morro Castle to be blown on July 30, then stormed the fort. Once that great obstacle had been taken all fires could be concentrated on the Punta and the walls of the city proper, across the ship channel. By nightfall on August 11 the Punta's guns had been silenced, and the commandant of Havana requested a truce to work out terms of capitulation. He formally surrendered the city, with all the honors of war and with guarantees that rights of property and religious observance would be secure, on August 14. With the "Key to the New World" in hand, the British also laid hold of three million pounds in gold and silver and most of Spain's Caribbean fleet: twelve ships of the line and several frigates—a quarter of the Spanish navy. The whole of the Floridas and eastern Mexico now lay exposed to British assault.[7]

Or would have, had not the land forces suffered so badly during the siege and afterward that there was no realistic hope for the British to do anything but cling to their conquest. A total of 1,800 men had been killed or had died of disease during the siege, and another 4,000 had fallen ill. Within six weeks after the surrender, 560 more soldiers and sailors had succumbed to their wounds, and 4,700 were dead of yellow fever and other maladies. Taken together with the four battalions of regulars who had been evacuated to New York (where most of those who survived the passage died in the hospital), it seems likely that at least half of the regulars who shipped out on the expedition died. The provincials seem to have fared as badly, or perhaps even worse.[8]

The British could retain Cuba not because they had the military strength to control its population but because the merchants and planters of the island, like those of the French West Indies, quickly discovered the advantages of trading within the British empire. Cuba had always traded more freely within the Caribbean than with Spain itself, for commerce with the metropolis was variously restricted by monopolies, taxation, and the flota system, by which transatlantic cargoes traveled in huge annual convoys. Now British and colonial merchants offered a more profitable market and more flexible marketing for Cuban tobacco, sugar, and cattle hides than any that the *habaneros* had ever known. During the eleven months of occupation as many as seven hundred British and colonial ships would swarm into Havana harbor, bringing in thousands of tons of English manufactures and at least seventeen hundred Africans to satisfy the planters' twin hungers for consumer goods and slaves. When they sailed away, they carried to British markets twenty thousand cattle hides and warehousefuls of sugar and tobacco that had been awaiting transportation to Cádiz, the monopoly destination of Spain's American trade.[9]

Thus the last great British conquest of the Seven Years' War demonstrated, with the greatest clarity of them all, the paradoxical relations between empire, trade, and military power. In proportion to the losses sustained by the conquerors, the occupation brought prosperity to Cuba; and the prosperity of the British empire, not the power of its army and navy, secured the cooperation of vanquished peoples as surely as it had gained the goodwill of Anglo-American colonists. Where British arms reaped costly laurels, the merchants, the colonies, and the conquered harvested profits. The war's prolongation had delayed the day when the costs of victory would have to be reckoned, but the return of peace would require those who had seemingly profited from the war to shoulder some of the burdens of glory.

CHAPTER 52

Peace

SEPTEMBER 1762–APRIL 1763

NEITHER THE ARMY'S sufferings nor Havana's postconquest boom would be known in London until long after news of the victory ignited popular celebrations on September 29. What must have been clearest to Lord Bute as he listened to crowds huzzah their approval was how much this particular conquest had complicated the process of making peace. With the king's knowledge, but without consulting the rest of the cabinet, Bute had continued negotiating secretly with Choiseul after the suspension of formal talks. By June they had sketched the terms of a settlement. What Bute promised France—to return Martinique, Guadeloupe, and St. Lucia; to allow French fishermen to continue taking cod on the Grand Banks; and to grant them two small islands off Newfoundland's south shore as places to erect drying stages—had prompted the French court to agree to exchange ambassadors plenipotentiary in September.

The rumor that preliminary understandings had been reached and the appointment of the outspokenly pacific duke of Bedford as emissary aroused a furor in imperialist circles. These, Pitt's idolators, believed that Britain should dictate, not negotiate, a treaty, and that whatever peace was finally made must leave France incapable of rebuilding its naval strength. Bute understood only too well that once the terms to which he had assented became known in Parliament, there would be fierce opposition. The ministry itself was divided: Grenville (since May the secretary of state for the Northern Department) and even Egremont, once Bute's tool, strongly disapproved of the terms and of the underhand way he had negotiated them. Now Bute worried that he would have to return Havana in order to induce Spain to make peace, for the French had been negotiating without consulting their ally and Spanish antagonism was therefore assured. Yet to return Havana without extracting some major concession, an "equivalent," in exchange, would give Pitt all the fuel he needed to create a political firestorm.[1]

Bute and the king therefore tried to improvise a solution to the divisions within the cabinet. Grenville, who had announced his opposition to Bute's peace overtures in no uncertain terms, would be deprived of the Northern secretaryship; that in turn would be bestowed upon Bedford's ally, Lord Halifax, who believed in the necessity of making peace. Grenville's alienation, of course, left no one to shepherd the proposed treaty through the House of Commons. Bute thought to solve that problem by offering the job of government leader in the Commons to Henry Fox, an acknowledged mastermind of parliamentary management. Yet Fox's ambition, unscrupulousness, and greed were all so notorious that the solution threatened only to exacerbate the problem. In the end it was not these ham-fisted efforts, but French diplomatic ingenuity, that would save the day for Bute and George and deliver the peace treaty they desperately desired.[2]

Restoring peace required a diplomatic calculus complex enough to challenge even the duc de Choiseul's subtle intelligence. The positive aspects of his position all derived from the draft treaty's provisions, which he and Bedford had worked out along the guidelines suggested by Bute's earlier, secret negotiations. Given France's military impotence, these terms were almost incredibly favorable to the postwar recovery of French power. They would cost the Most Christian King most of his overseas possessions, it was true, but only the least profitable parts of the empire would in fact be surrendered: a Canada that had never been anything but a sinkhole of money and a set of East Indian and African trading posts that had never fully paid their way. The negative aspect of the equation was more complicated. Half of the problem there was Spain. King Charles III would never abandon Havana, nor would he sacrifice valuable New World territory in order to regain it; and he resented the high-handed way in which Choiseul had worked out the draft peace terms without consultation. The problem's other half was the British Parliament, which would never accede to Bute's generous peace unless Spain surrendered Havana or some comparable asset. If opposition in the House of Commons proved strong enough to drive Bute from power, only the recall of Pitt would calm the crisis—and everyone knew what kind of peace Pitt would demand.

Choiseul's ingenious answer to this puzzle had three parts. France would give Spain its last remaining territory in North America,

Louisiana; Spain would surrender Florida (that is, the territory from the Mississippi to Georgia) to Britain; Britain would return Havana to Spain. In this way Spain would lose its claim to a sparsely inhabited, commercially unprofitable coastal plain and recover the Key to the New World and its trade. As a reward for its cooperation Spain would gain title to the western half of North America, access to the continent's interior via the Mississippi River, and possession of the valuable port of New Orleans. True, France would bid adieu to the rest of its North American holdings; but, as Choiseul understood, the colony of Louisiana had little population and no conceivable value to France if its destiny were to become a buffer between the demographically vital British colonies and the North American holdings of a disgruntled Spain. And Britain would gain undisputed control of the eastern half of North America—a prize glittering enough to satisfy even the most rabid imperialists in the House of Commons.

Thus ingenuity and guile restored peace, at last, to Europe. On November 3, 1762, the emissaries of Britain, France, and Spain signed the preliminary articles of the Treaty of Paris. Simultaneously, by the Treaty of San Ildefonso, France ceded Louisiana to Spain. In London, given the public furor that accompanied the submission of the treaty to Parliament for approval, one might almost have thought the treaty's provisions confirmed Britain's defeat rather than the most far-reaching conquests in its history. On December 9, at the conclusion of the Commons debates, William Pitt ordered his servants to carry him from his sickbed to the House, where for three and a half hours he denounced the articles as a betrayal of Britain's faithful German allies, a wanton sacrifice of the national interest, and a travesty of his own glorious achievements. At the division, however, it was clear that neither the London mob nor the disapproval of the Great Commoner would be sufficient to deter approval of the treaty. In the end only sixty-four M.P.s voted to reject the preliminary articles, against an approving majority of 319. In the House of Lords, Newcastle failed so miserably to organize an opposition that the treaty passed on a voice vote.[3]

The contents of the Definitive Treaty of Peace, as implemented on February 10, 1763, convinced everyone except William Pitt and his die-hard followers that France had indeed been humbled in the dust. France surrendered to Great Britain all territories and claims in North America east of the Mississippi River except New Orleans and guaranteed the unrestrained navigation of the river to all British subjects. The West Indian islands of St. Vincent, Dominica, Tobago, Grenada, and the Grenadines were all secured to Great Britain, along with Senegal in West

Africa. France returned Minorca as well as two East India Company posts in Sumatra captured during the war. France also surrendered all fortifications built and all territories occupied in India since 1749; renounced all claims to compensation for shipping seized by British privateers and naval vessels since 1754; agreed to level its fortifications at Dunkirk; restored all territories still under its army's control in Hanover, Hesse, and Brunswick; and evacuated the Rhineland possessions of the king of Prussia. Spain turned over Florida to Great Britain, renounced its claims to participation in the Newfoundland fishery, sanctioned the continued cutting of logwood by British subjects along the coast of Honduras, and agreed to allow British admiralty courts to adjudicate all disputes concerning Spanish vessels seized by Britain during the war. In return for all these concessions, Great Britain restored the islands of Belle-Île-en-Mer, Goree, Martinique, and Guadeloupe to France, along with the flyspeck islands of St. Lucia in the West Indies and St.-Pierre and Miquelon in the Gulf of St. Lawrence; permitted the French to resume fishing in the waters off Newfoundland and to trade in India at the posts it had acquired before 1749; returned Havana to Spanish control; and promised Spain that British logwood cutters would not erect fortifications in Honduras.[4]

That the Peace of Paris was a phenomenal diplomatic coup for Britain can best be seen in light of the contrasting provisions of the Treaty of Hubertusburg, which Prussia and Austria concluded on February 15 at a hunting lodge in Saxony. Despite the vigorous maneuverings of Frederick the Great and of Maria Theresa's representative, Count von Kaunitz, Hubertusburg concluded the Austro-German war on the basis of the status quo ante bellum. This meant, in effect, that Frederick kept Silesia and renounced his desire to retain Saxony while Maria Theresa kept Saxony and gave up her wish to regain Silesia. Both king and empress-queen pledged an undying friendship and agreed to promote trade between their realms; Frederick promised to vote, as elector of Brandenburg, for Maria Theresa's son, Archduke Joseph, in the next election for Holy Roman Emperor. Otherwise—apart from the fact that Saxony received no compensation for the taxes and soldiers that Frederick had drained out of her since 1756—no strategic or financial assets changed hands. Beyond the inevitable adjustments in the way diplomats would think of Prussia as a player in European politics, six years of heroic expenditure and savage bloodshed had accomplished precisely nothing.[5]

CHAPTER 53

The Rise of Wilkes, the Fall of Bute, and the Unheeded Lesson of Manila

SPRING 1763

IF HUBERTUSBURG was a conventional diplomatic settlement of the eighteenth century—and it was, in every way, typical—then there is no mystery in George III's desire to detach Great Britain from the quarrels of Europe, no puzzle in his wish to end the long entanglement between the foreign policies of Hanover and Great Britain. To disengage from European alliances and European wars was, so far as he understood it, the absolute precondition for the regeneration of British political life—the building of a new patriotic spirit centered on the monarchy, Protestantism, and the union of British peoples. Bute's efforts to end the war, awkward as they were, had fully reflected the will of his master. Indeed, insofar as such views stressed detachment from Hanover and embodied a chauvinist nationalism, they were shared by an overwhelming majority of the political nation. But that alone could not save Bute's political career, nor make the king a popular figure. Within two months of the signing of the most favorable peace treaty in European history, Bute had been driven from office and a London mob had bombarded the royal coach with stones and horse manure. Such striking developments might almost make one wonder if winning a great empire had somehow made the British people lose their wits.

The explanation can be found at the interface of two strata in British society and politics, where sometimes violent interactions occurred between the nation's political elite and a politically aware but generally unenfranchised populace (especially that of London). On both sides of this class boundary, within as well as outside the closed world of parliamentary politics, imperialists had convinced themselves that Britain was invincible and therefore entitled to retain every conquest. They saw the Peace of Paris as a sellout and a sham, and they despised the Scottish interloper (and secretly, the king) who had sacrificed valuable possessions to obtain a craven peace. The imperialists included Pitt and other brilliant figures but, as the Commons vote on the treaty had shown, they were not numerous in proportion to the rest of the political elite. Unfortunately for Bute, the imperialist illuminati were not the only people who detested him.

Within the ruling class, where ideology generally took a backseat to the politics of personal connection and advantage, Bute had made himself a large number of enemies late in 1762 when he and his new lieutenant in the Commons, Henry Fox, purged Newcastle's old supporters from office. So ruthless was this ouster of placeholders—in effect, the dismantling of the patronage infrastructure that had sustained the previous administration—that even politicians who approved of the peace treaty came to hate and fear Bute for what he had done. As Horace Walpole described it, "A more severe political persecution never raged. Whoever, holding a place, had voted against the preliminaries [of peace], was instantly dismissed. The friends and dependents of the Duke of Newcastle were particularly cashiered; and this cruelty extended so far that old servants, who had retired and been preferred to very small places, were rigorously hunted out and deprived of their livelihood."[1]

The patronage system that Newcastle had perfected, of course, could not have worked without the threat of dismissal to ensure discipline; but political housecleanings had generally been restricted to leading figures. This "massacre of Pelhamite innocents" seemed in this context a supremely ungentlemanly act, heralding a new, savage era in British politics. Because Bute was thin-skinned and socially vulnerable he would have been an inviting target for abuse, anyhow; because the normal rules of political discourse did not permit attacks on the king, however, his position as royal favorite made him the ideal candidate for vilification as the "Northern Machiavel."[2]

The nature of opposition politics had shifted in response to the circumstances of the new reign, and this helped promote a disturbingly violent tone in public life. This change reflected the fact that George III was a young, recently married king with no heir apparent living outside the palace. Throughout the previous two reigns, the household of the prince of Wales had been the natural focus of opposition to the policies of the court. In part this was because of the almost chemical disaffinity between the Hanoverian kings and their eldest sons; in part it was because the heir apparent, as prince of Wales, could dispose of a large number of patronage posts, while as duke of Cornwall he could influence elections to the forty-four Commons seats that represented the county and its boroughs. The prince's household therefore attracted, as honey does ants, ambitious politicians who found themselves out of office. But when there was no independent prince of Wales, political opposition lacked an alternative court around which to coalesce and fragmented into the personal followings of magnates. This made the opponents of the ministry and its policies infinitely noisier than they otherwise would have been.[3]

Without a prince to follow into power upon his accession, the most reliable way for an ambitious opposition leader and his followers to gain office was to make such a hullabaloo that the prime minister or the king would shut them up in the only way possible, by inviting them to join the existing administration and giving them offices. To a point, this was well understood in the highest circles of the British ruling class. What made the noisy opposition of the 1760s unusual and worrisome was that it erupted suddenly, after a long period in which support for the government and the war had been essentially unanimous; and it seemed to be getting out of hand. This too represented a shift in the character of British politics.

Traditionally, opponents of sitting ministries had presented themselves as friends of English liberties, defenders of the Ancient Constitution against its would-be corrupters. Ironically, this "patriot" (or "country," or "real whig," or "commonwealthman") rhetoric had been the political mother's milk of George III at Leicester House, when it had been the center of opposition to George II's ministries; patriot ideals nourished his desire to rule as a monarch who stood above party. That the men who opposed Bute's ministry adopted libertarian language, therefore, was not in itself surprising. What made it alarming was the context in which this message could now be heard, for social conditions had changed since the last period of highly charged public opposition (an acute phase that had lasted from about 1727 through 1737–38, tapering off after George's father had established himself at Leicester House). The most important change had been the rapid growth—especially in London, Middlesex County, and the booming provincial cities—of middle-class groups engaged in commerce and the professions. These aspiring merchants, retailers, lawyers, and other professionals were generally not landed and therefore lacked a political voice in proportion to their wealth and ambition. Yet their exclusion from the franchise only made them readier consumers of political literature, more eager advocates of reforms that would enable men like themselves to participate in the political life of the nation. Thus in 1762 and 1763 the writings of opposition politicians found a larger and more avid readership than ever before, and the press responded to the demand by pumping out torrents of ballads, broadsides, pamphlets, cheap ephemeral periodicals, magazines, and newspapers.[4]

It was from this striving English middle class, fervently nationalist and deeply supportive of the wars against France, that John Wilkes emerged as the most remarkable publicist of the day. Wilkes's ability to speak both to unenfranchised middle-class groups and to the plebeians of London made him the most outrageous—and to Bute and the king, the most dangerous—penman of the opposition. Wilkes came from a prosperous distilling family that had given him a genteel education and sufficient means to marry into the Buckinghamshire gentry. There in the mid-1750s he had affiliated himself with the party of Pitt and Grenville, the so-called faction of cousins. Wilkes entered the House of Commons in 1757 and avidly supported Pitt and the war, but he had lacked the social standing and the oratorical skill (not to mention the self-restraint and common sense) to make himself a significant figure in Parliament. His cutthroat wit and skill as a writer of invective, however, opened career opportunities of another sort.

After resigning as lord privy seal in 1761, the earl Temple set Wilkes up to publish a newspaper called the *North Briton,* the sole purpose of which was to make Lord Bute look ridiculous, or worse. In successive and ever more outrageous issues, the *North Briton* identified Bute as (among other things) the man who betrayed the nation's military glory with an ignoble peace, the author of an unpopular excise tax on cider, a schemer against the liberties and property of freeborn Englishmen, a corrupter of Parliament, the illicit lover of the king's mother, and, worst of all, a Scot whose family name was—Stuart! Ludicrous as it may seem, the identification of Bute with this absolutist, papist dynasty was by no means the least damaging of Wilkes's libels, for it played to strands of anti-Scottish prejudice and anti-Jacobite fears common to most middle-class and virtually all plebeian Englishmen.[5]

Wilkes's influence would be hard to overestimate, if only because he aroused such fear and hatred in the ministry and such ardent support in both the middle classes and the London mob. Reveling in his growing celebrity, Wilkes hounded his quarry through the pages of the *North Briton* until Bute, at best a neurotically hypersensitive man, lost his will to continue in politics. Long before the Peace of Paris it had become obvious that war-created problems would be extraordinarily difficult to solve. Bute's first, tentative effort to address the issue—a tax of four shillings on each hogshead of cider produced in Britain, to be paid by the maker—proved to be such a disaster that, by the beginning of March, he was begging the king to allow him to resign as first lord of the Treasury.

It was not so much the strength of the opposition to the new tax itself that posed a problem. Despite the instantaneous protests of the M.P.s from the cider-manufacturing counties, and Pitt's efforts to portray the measure as an invasion of Englishmen's liberties, the opposition in the end could never muster more than 120 votes against the excise in the House of Commons, or more than 38 against it in the House of Lords. Rather than an unmanageable political situation, it was the relentless vilification in the *North Briton* and the rituals of public execration enacted by mobs in the cider counties and London that destroyed Bute's desire to lead Britain through its difficult transition to peace. At the beginning of April, weary of reading opposition libels and sick of seeing makeshift gallows festooned with top boots and petticoats—the symbols that mobs used to depict him and his supposed lover, the king's mother—the earl of Bute surrendered the seals of his office to the king.

He would have quit earlier if he could have, but the king had been unwilling to put the Treasury in the hands of Henry Fox, a man devoid of every conviction except the unshakable belief that he deserved to be rich. For a variety of reasons other candidates for first lord (especially Pitt and Newcastle) were equally unacceptable. Finally the king, unable to hold off Bute's flight from office another day, broke down and offered the Treasury to George Grenville, a move he dreaded. In part it was personal dislike: Grenville not only bored the king, but seemed responsible for dividing the cabinet and forcing him and his "Dearest Friend" into Fox's odious embrace. Beyond that, however, the king realized that Grenville made a poor choice for prime minister because he was not a politician of the first rank.

Before November 1761, when Grenville had become the government's leader in the House, he had never been more than a secondary figure in a small but significant parliamentary faction. Thereafter he occupied high office only briefly, but even so had managed to put himself at odds with practically everyone more powerful than he—with Bute and the king no less than with his own older brother (Temple), Pitt, Newcastle, and everyone else who had gone into opposition. Finally, the king knew that Grenville's political skills were more technical than managerial. Even with Henry Fox bought off with a profitable post and exiled from the Commons by a peerage, Grenville was unlikely to be more than a weak political leader. Had he been blessed with personal charm or oratorical genius, his inexperience in distributing patronage alone would have hobbled him. Unluckily for Grenville, his reputation as a self-righteous, condescending windbag had long preceded him when, on April 13, 1763, he assumed the offices of first lord of the Treasury and Chancellor of the Exchequer.[6]

And yet, unpropitious as it was, Grenville's advent as prime minister was not without promise. Above all, he was prepared to apply what Bute had not possessed—a seat in the House of Commons, a real grasp of legislation, and the willingness to work hard—to the resolution of those problems that Bute had lacked the nerve to face: the issues of finance and order that were the legacy of the Seven Years' War. Despite his deficiencies as a manager, Grenville understood and should have been able to address these pressing affairs. Two important factors favored him. First, he possessed an unexcelled knowledge of public finance. Second, because he, Egremont, and Halifax together formed the "Triumvirate" that helped bring an end to Bute's administration, all three men entered office as a kind of team. Thus Grenville had access not only to Egremont's connections but to Halifax's vast experience in dealing with the colonies. For the first time, a man with a genuine grasp of taxation headed the Treasury at the same moment that a man knowledgeable in American affairs was in a position to formulate colonial policy. Had opposition slackened and the Triumvirate been able to attend to the great issues of postwar reconstruction in an interval of relative calm, the next years should have stabilized both British public finance and relations between the metropolis and its colonies.

But there was no calm, nor would there be, for a very long time to come. In May the biggest Indian uprising in the history of North America threatened to erase British control over the Transappalachian west: a rebellion that would take Whitehall as much by surprise as the riotous defiance of British authority that would erupt everywhere from New Hampshire to Georgia in the summer of 1765. Two occurrences during April would frame and limit the ways in which the ministers could perceive and respond to these perplexing events. Neither, ironically, had anything to do with America. The first was the refusal of John Wilkes to shut up after Bute slunk off the political stage. The second was news of Britain's final victory of the war, the conquest of Manila.

Had Wilkes only known when to stop thumbing his nose, he might have found himself offered some sinecure as a reward for silence. Grenville, no lover of Bute, would surely have preferred it that way. He must therefore have been one of the unhappiest readers of the forty-fifth number of the *North Briton,* published on April 23. Always before,

Wilkes had carefully affirmed his loyalty to the king and attacked only Bute. In number 45, however, he took as his subject the king's address to Parliament of April 19, and particularly its celebration of the return of peace. Strictly speaking Wilkes attacked only the speech, which, he maintained, Bute had written. His language was so intemperate, however, that the attack seemed an assault on the king himself. By contemporary standards the *North Briton* number 45 constituted an enormity that no responsible minister of state could ignore. Grenville and Halifax therefore proceeded against Wilkes legally, requesting the issuance of a general warrant, under which he and forty-eight others were arrested and had their households searched for incriminating materials.

While this was in fact a perfectly legal way of proceeding in cases of seditious libel, the use of a general warrant (rather than an ordinary court order that identified suspects by name and authorized searches for specified kinds of evidence) aroused an immediate outcry. Surely, Wilkes's supporters said, there could be no clearer indication of the government's willingness to abridge subjects' rights at wholesale, as a means of crushing dissent. Wilkes did his masterful publicist's best to turn the uproar to his advantage in the press, but his greatest aid came from the government itself. Unfortunately for the Crown they wanted to serve, Grenville and Halifax had failed to foresee how Wilkes's status as an M.P. would cloud the legality of the prosecution. Members of the House of Commons were ordinarily immune from arrest for all crimes but treason, felony, and breach of the peace, and it was altogether unclear that to write slightingly of a royal speech constituted anything more than a libel that *tended* to breach of the peace. Within days the lord chief justice of the Court of Common Pleas had released Wilkes and—to the delight of crowds shouting "Wilkes and liberty!"—dismissed the charges against him as inconsistent with the principle of parliamentary privilege.[7]

This outcome might only have embarrassed His Majesty's government, but Wilkes chose to sustain the whirlwind. Capitalizing on his new status as the symbol of liberties threatened by the shadowy crypto-Scottish designs of the king's ministers, he commenced lawsuits against Halifax and other royal officials, reprinted the entire run of the *North Briton* in volume form, made public appearances to accept the plaudits of his admirers, and generally cultivated his notoriety like a garden. The government, goaded beyond good sense, fought back, pursuing him in the courts for blasphemy (law officers had discovered an obscene, irreligious poem, *An Essay on Woman,* in Wilkes's papers when they searched his house for evidence of seditious libel). At the same time, the ministry opened an assault on him in the Commons, where a substantial majority of M.P.s resolved that the *North Briton* number 45 was "a false, scandalous, and seditious libel."

Through the rest of 1763 the London political scene became a vast political carnival over which Wilkes, a prince of disorder if ever there was one, seemed born to preside. Because no legal action against him could be assured of success so long as he sat as a member in good standing of the House of Commons, the government's hands were tied. In frustration, the ministers and their allies in the House of Lords tried to silence Wilkes by impeaching his moral character as a blasphemer and pornographer. This immediately backfired, since the peer who took the lead as spokesman against Wilkes was the earl of Sandwich, a former friend of Wilkes's and himself a notorious libertine; as it happened, the opening lines of *An Essay on Woman* had originally begun

> *Awake, my Sandwich, leave all meaner things;*
> *This morn shall prove what rapture swiving brings!*[8]

Thus Wilkes's antagonists found themselves more than ever the butt of satire and popular ridicule. So great was government—and royal—irritation, in fact, that there is reason to suspect that when Samuel Martin, an M.P. with ties to Grenville, challenged Wilkes to a duel in November, he was acting as the ministry's agent in a plot to silence the gadfly once and for all. But Martin succeeded only in wounding Wilkes (significantly, perhaps, with a pistol ball in the groin), and Wilkes fled to Paris once he had recovered sufficiently to travel. Early in 1764, his fellow members voted to expel him from the House of Commons. With the issue of parliamentary immunity thus resolved, the Court of King's Bench issued writs for his arrest as a publisher of blasphemy and seditious libel. When he prudently decided to remain abroad, the court pronounced him an outlaw. Yet all of these measures to discredit and silence Wilkes only tended to make "that squinting rascal" more a folk hero than ever: a man who, when he finally returned from exile in 1768, would become the preeminent symbol of a radicalism new to Britain, and uniquely worrisome to its rulers.[9]

The controversies that swirled about Wilkes from April 1763 onward preoccupied the government and escalated the intensity of opposition politics. While Grenville tried to chart the wisest course to deal with the problems of postwar finance, he could scarcely forget the storm that the *North Briton* number 43 had helped stir up in response to the cider tax. When Halifax pondered how best to impose order on the empire in

North America and elsewhere around the world, he could scarcely ignore the disorders of radical opposition evident in the streets of London—much less the presence, a few doors down Great George Street from his own house, of a neighbor who was harassing him with lawsuits and reviling him as a tool of despotism, John Wilkes. To perform the difficult tasks that faced them in the aftermath of the war would have been challenge enough, regardless of the circumstances, for the ministers of any government as politically weak as Grenville's. To undertake them in an atmosphere of disorientation and uncertainty like that of 1763, and then to be confronted with the crisis of an Indian rebellion in the heart of the North American continent, posed challenges to which no conceivable government could have responded adequately.

But even as British domestic politics seemed to be pratfalling into chaos, the arrival of news concerning the outcome of Britain's last military operation of the war carried a heartening message to Grenville and his colleagues. The conquest of Manila had taken place six months earlier, while Bedford was in Paris trying to negotiate an end to the war and Choiseul was devising the settlement with Spain that would make peace possible. From the perspective of the ambassadors this was just as well: if Manila had had to be factored into the settlement, Choiseul's tricky equations might well have proven impossible to balance. Despite its diplomatic irrelevance, however, this final victory carried great significance, for on its face the taking of Manila seemed to confirm the overwhelming power of British arms. Once the full story of the expedition made it clear that the Spanish had not been pushovers, the conquest acquired even greater resonance. Then it became possible to see how with pluck, audacity, and hardihood Britons could win through in the face of great adversity, in a setting as far from Europe as anyone could imagine.[10]

Lieutenant Colonel William Draper, an officer of the 79th Foot (one of the regular regiments that had fought at the Battle of Wandiwash), had been on leave in England in the winter of 1761–62 when he suggested an expedition against the Philippines to Anson and Ligonier. Reasons similar to those that had made them choose Havana as a target disposed them to listen to Draper's proposal. Manila was the center of trade and administration for the Spanish Philippines and perhaps even more important in the Pacific than Havana in the Atlantic. Nor was conquest an impossible goal, for although the Spanish had built the fort of Cavite to protect the harbor and had enclosed the city's core within a bastioned wall, they had clearly believed that Manila's best source of security was its remoteness. That the Philippines took six to eight months to reach from Europe, in fact, only made the expedition more attractive to Ligonier and

Anson, for Draper assured them that all the troops he would need were already in India, just six or eight weeks' sail from the archipelago. Since Spain communicated with the colony via Mexico on the Manila galleon, there was good reason to hope that the invaders might arrive before the garrison even knew that Spain and Great Britain were at war.

Soon after the declaration of war, therefore, the ministers decided in favor of the venture. In February, Draper left Britain with a temporary commission as brigadier general and authority to raise an expeditionary force of two regular battalions and five hundred East India Company troops. By the end of June he had reached Madras. Once there, however, nothing went as planned, and the would-be conqueror of Manila found that the local authorities were willing to release only one redcoat regiment (his own 79th Foot), and a company of Royal Artillery. Draper therefore recruited what men he could—two companies of French deserters and several hundred Asian recruits ("such a Banditti," he grumbled, as had "never assembled since the time of Spartacus")—and sailed from Madras at the end of July.

When Draper's little flotilla of warships and transports entered Manila Bay on September 22, the Manila galleon had yet to arrive. Thus the British sailed unchallenged past the guns of Cavite, landed near Manila, and attacked the city on the twenty-sixth, before the Spanish commander had heard that a state of war existed between their monarch and his own. Despite the tiny number of troops Draper had at his disposal (only about two thousand, including a battalion of sailors pressed into service), and despite the onset of the monsoon, which repeatedly held up siege operations, the British managed to breach the wall and storm the city on October 5. Manila surrendered later that day. Five days later the fort of Cavite capitulated, and on October 30 Spanish authorities throughout the archipelago made their formal submission. The booty captured exceeded $4,000,000—more than £1,300,000 sterling—in value.[11]

There could have been no more conclusive demonstration of the global reach that the army and navy had acquired during the Seven Years' War. In the whole military history of Europe nothing quite compared to it. Even as the government faced unprecedented postwar challenges—as Wilkes railed against the ministers and the London crowds roared back their approval—the conquest seemed to affirm Britain's essential invincibility. Even more than Havana, Draper's feat was the crowning accomplishment of Britain's most glorious war, and in it the British people for one last shining moment saw reflected all their nation's glory. What they did not see (and perhaps would not have understood if they had) was the significance of what happened once the conquerors ran the Union Jack up Manila's flagstaff.

Unlike Canada, Guadeloupe, Martinique, and Havana, the people of the Philippines did not turn out en masse to trade with the British. Instead the East India Company, to which Draper turned over the task of governing in November 1762, never did establish control over the archipelago, or indeed over any territory outside the immediate vicinity of Manila itself. Don Simón de Anda, a junior judge of the royal Audencia (supreme court), managed to slip out of the city during the siege and escape to the province of Pampanga, on the north shore of Manila Bay. There, in the town of Bacolor, thirty-five miles from Manila, he established a provisional government and began to organize an army. The highest officers of the Spanish colonial administration hesitated to join him, but thousands of Filipinos did not. Soon Anda's guerrilla army mustered ten thousand men, and even though more than seven thousand of them lacked arms more formidable than bows and arrows, they still denied the British control over anything outside of Manila and Cavite. Despite news that a treaty had been signed, Anda refused to agree to a truce until orders arrived from London in March 1764, restoring the archipelago to Spanish control. Even then he would not order his men to lay down their arms until the new Spanish governor arrived. On the last day of May 1764, Anda led a column of native soldiers into Manila to receive the city from its British rulers. Any casual bystander would have concluded that he was witnessing a British surrender.[12]

Administering Manila from November 2, 1762, to May 31, 1764, cost the East India Company over £200,000 sterling above its (modest) share of the booty and its (negligible) profits on trade. The conquest of Manila differed from other British overseas victories, therefore, insofar as the occupants of the colony refused to be subdued either by force or by commerce. Anyone paying attention to the history of Great Britain's occupation of the Philippines at the moment it ended might well have pondered its implied lessons in the relationship between arms and trade, loyalty and empire. In the Philippine episode more than any other of the Seven Years' War, the principles of imperial dominion stood out with unmistakable clarity. Military power—particularly naval power—could gain an empire, but force alone could never control colonial dependencies. Only the voluntary allegiance, or at least the acquiescence, of the colonists could do that. Flags and governors and even garrisons were, in the end, only the empire's symbols. Trade and loyalty were its integuments, and when colonial populations that refused their allegiance also declined to trade, the empire's dominion extended not a yard beyond the range of its cannons.

CHAPTER 54

Anglo-America at War's End

THE FRAGILITY OF EMPIRE

1761–1763

BY THE SPRING of 1763 it had been two years since Great Britain's leaders had paid more than occasional attention to North America. Ministers concerned with ending the war and plagued by unstable domestic politics had few reasons to worry about a sector in which the fighting was finished. The Cherokee rebellion had caused concern, of course. Yet Grant had evidently restored order on the Carolina frontier; Amherst had initiated reforms in the Indian trade and begun to regulate backwoods settlement; and Johnson had induced the formerly French-allied nations of the interior to accept King George as their new father at a Detroit conference in September 1761. In some ways the colonists were more troublesome than the Indians, but they did nothing so outrageous as to require action. Thus Whitehall could afford to ignore America, and did.

To ministers and commander in chief alike, the main significance of the mainland colonies after the conquest of Canada had been their ability to continue providing provincial troops, and that they had done adequately. True, the colonies' legislatures had not found it intuitively obvious why they should go on raising and paying for soldiers once Canada had fallen and the threat of Indian raids had subsided. But governors like Massachusetts's new chief executive, Francis Bernard, hastened to remind their assemblymen that they "must not think that if the War does not rage at your own Doors, you many therefore be unconcerned spectators in it," and the representatives had for the most part responded well.[1]

The continuation of parliamentary subsidies helps explain the willingness of representatives in various colonies to heed the empire's calls for men. But the fact remains that most assemblies showed a degree of enthusiasm nearly comparable to what they had manifested in 1759 and 1760. Only two colonies, both proprietaries split by chronic disputes, refused to raise provincials in 1761 and 1762: Maryland, which kept to its well-worn path of nonparticipation, and Pennsylvania, where the assembly returned to fighting the Penn family once the Indians ceased to be active enemies. Other provinces did their best to comply with the Crown's request for two-thirds the number of men they had raised in 1760. In all, the four New England colonies plus New York, New Jersey, Virginia, and the Carolinas raised 9,296 men in 1761. In 1762, with the Cherokee War over and no troops needed from the lower south, the same colonies, less the Carolinas, supplied 9,204 troops. These figures represented, respectively, 80 and 90 percent of the total numbers requested—levels that in retrospect would seem to indicate high enthusiasm for the empire. Perhaps equally remarkable was the willingness of the New England provinces to enlist men for full-year terms. Both in 1761–62 and in 1762–63, more than 1,000 New Englanders wintered, without compulsion or mutiny, in garrisons from Halifax to Oswego.[2]

And yet, ready as most colony governments were to offer their inhabitants' military services, colonists and their legislatures made no better impression than ever on the men who administered the empire. Amherst, committed to supplying troops for the West Indies expeditions but unable to dispatch redcoat battalions until provincials had relieved them at their posts, despised the Americans who always arrived late and seemed to show initiative best when it came to embezzling rations and pay. To him every case of malfeasance and every shortfall in meeting enlistment quotas demonstrated the poor character of the colonists and the self-interest of their governments, features of American life he had come to expect—and detest. But the commander in chief characteristically kept his own counsel, complaining to his superiors more bitterly than to the provincial legislatures. Amherst's reports therefore accumulated along with Loudoun's and Braddock's older complaints in London, where they formed the consistent pattern on the basis of which ministers understood the character and patriotism of Americans. Yet disturbing as they were, such evidences precipitated no official action. Even the outrage that the Southern secretary, Lord Egremont, felt at what he believed was the Pennsylvanians' "premeditated Resolution not to afford any Assistance" once "the immediate danger is removed from their own Doors" produced only a peevish letter to the province's acting governor.[3]

Of more immediate concern to Whitehall was the colonies' commerce with the enemy, which had caused problems from the beginning of the war. In August 1760, Pitt had ordered the colonial governors to crack down on the "illegal and most pernicious Trade, carried on by the King's Subjects, . . . whereby [the French colonies] are, principally, if not alone, enabled to sustain, and protract, this long and expensive War." Despite this ringing denunciation, however, smuggling was so extensive, and so many colonial customsmen were on the take, that most governors could do little more than echo Pitt's condemnation of practices they could not hope to stop. Only a handful of royal officials made any attempt to enforce Pitt's order. The most significant case occurred in the Bay Colony, where the unusually conscientious Governor Bernard and the equally punctilious chief justice of the colony's superior court, Lieutenant Governor Thomas Hutchinson, tried to help an honest customs surveyor act against Boston's smuggling merchants and their ally, the port's corrupt collector of customs. The results were far from encouraging.[4]

Early in 1761, Massachusetts's surveyor general of customs applied to the colony's superior court for a renewal of what were called writs of assistance—general warrants enabling customs officers to enter warehouses and private residences where they suspected smuggled goods had been stored. The merchants of the town petitioned against the issuance of the writs. In mesmerizing arguments before Hutchinson and the other justices, the merchants' counsel, James Otis Jr., contended that by authorizing general searches the court would unleash a "monster of oppression," endangering both the common-law rights of the subject against unreasonable searches and the natural rights of man. Otis's arguments created a local sensation, prompted popular demonstrations against "tyranny," and launched his career as a leader of the opposition in the General Court. Moreover, they redefined politics in Massachusetts by simultaneously giving opposition politicians a cause (the protection of rights), a hero (Otis), and a set of enemies (the customs officers, Bernard, and Hutchinson) as targets for their rhetorical barbs. Yet for all that, they could do no more than delay the issuance of the writs. Hutchinson deferred his decision until he could consult authorities in London and then, satisfied that the warrants were indeed legal, granted them in November 1761.

The result—not surprisingly, given the intensity of merchant anxieties, the popularity of Otis's oratory, the political capital to be made by appeals to liberty, and the willingness of the smugglers to protect their investments by extralegal means—was that merchant-inspired mobs intimidated the customs officers and in effect nullified the writs. This placed Bernard in a difficult, embarrassing position at the outset of his administration, and many of the political problems that would blight both his and Thomas Hutchinson's future years would descend directly from the episode. But the most significant short-run result of Bernard's frustrations was to ensure that the secretary of state for the Southern Department, the Board of Trade, and the rest of his British correspondents would receive ample accounts of how the smugglers, their pet lawyer, and their toadies in the General Court had formed a "confederacy" to thwart the Crown's legitimate power. Like Amherst's complaints about the ways colonies provided troops, Bernard's reports gave British officials evidence that smuggling was a problem that would require the attention of responsible imperial authorities.

There could hardly be a more vivid example than this case of the way in which public disputes can create political alignments that persist long after the original issues of the controversy have vanished. In fact, the Bostonians' resistance to writ-wielding customs officers lasted a very short time, because the surrender of Martinique in February 1762 opened that island and the rest of the French West Indies to legitimate trade within the British empire. French molasses, the main smuggled commodity in Massachusetts, suddenly became a perfectly legal commodity. Boston's merchants, no longer worried that customs officers would break into their warehouses and discover contraband, lost interest in protesting the constitutional dangers of general warrants. Down to the late 1760s the writs of assistance remained in force, and others would be issued without arousing political furor, mob violence, or indeed much notice. By the end of 1762 opposition in the General Court had more or less fizzled out, primarily because its animating issue had fallen in abeyance. In 1763, tranquillity, or what passed for it locally, reigned in Massachusetts politics. Although the alignments of blocs in the assembly would reappear in subsequent controversies, the uproar over the writs of assistance had blown itself out as quickly as any other tempest in Boston's teapot.

Taken together, the writs of assistance case and Amherst's discontentment with the way the colonies levied provincial troops suggest that while the ties between the metropolis and the colonies remained fundamentally strong during the long transition to peace, the gulf that had always yawned between American conditions and British perceptions was gaping wider than ever. The war had propelled the colonies, for five long years, to the center of Britain's political stage, and had sent powerful administrators to the periphery of empire, increasing manyfold both the numbers of reports on American conditions and the attention that ministers were willing to pay them. The shift in the war's focus after 1760 had diminished the willingness of Britain's political leaders to think about the colonies without lessening the status or destroying the connections of those men, like Amherst, who remained in place—men whose jobs grew more frustrating in the aftermath of victory. Both in raising troops and in seeking to suppress smuggling, harassed officers of the Crown encountered less than perfect responsiveness, and indeed resistance, from the colonists. When they complained, their superiors took their reports as accurate representations of the deficient character and lawless disposition of Americans.

And yet, at least for the time being, the ministers took no action. The war, in effect, prevented them from trying. In the first place, they were simply too busy with European affairs to concern themselves with a theater of operations where the war was effectively over. In the last critical years of the conflict, therefore, the ministers of Great Britain accepted less than perfect compliance, and even tolerated what seemed to them radically imperfect behavior, rather than add complications to their already complex lives. But they understood how well Amherst's complaints about recruitment squared with those of his predecessors; they saw how the ingrained self-interest of the colonial merchants threatened the welfare of the empire in 1762 as much as it had in 1755 or 1756. And they knew that when peace finally returned, responsible officers of the Crown would need to take the colonies in hand, to promote the order and the due subordination without which the empire could not survive.

If the prolongation of the war kept British officials from addressing colonial issues, it also focused their attention on strategic concerns (manpower and trade with the enemy) and delayed the formulation of policies to deal with the single most striking, and potentially disruptive, trend in North America—the rapid movement of colonists and European emigrants into backwoods and newly conquered regions. As a result, during the last years of the war some of this migration would be officially encouraged, and some would enjoy at least a degree of official sanction, but most would simply be uncontrolled. All of it would tend to destabilize localities, muddle politics and business enterprise, and, at least indirectly, render the periphery of the empire less manageable than ever.

Nova Scotia exemplified the equivocal effects of even officially sponsored migration. The expulsion of the Acadian population had created what amounted to a depopulated colony, and that in turn created huge problems of finance and security for the province government. As early as the fall of 1758, Governor Charles Lawrence and the Nova Scotia Assembly tried to address these issues by inviting New Englanders and other colonists to take over the farms of the dispossessed Acadians. So many groups and individuals responded to the inducements they offered—large land grants (hundred-thousand-acre townships), low quitrents (and none due until ten years after settlement), liberty of conscience (to Protestants only), and guarantees that taxes would be imposed only by act of a colony legislature—that in less than two years Nova Scotia's civilian population doubled, to about 8,500 settlers. During that period the legislature granted fourteen new townships to migrants from eastern Connecticut and Rhode Island.

Meanwhile, Governor Lawrence entered into negotiations with a high-flying Ulsterman named Alexander McNutt, whose promises climbed to stratospheric heights as it became clear that there was no limit to what Governor Lawrence was prepared to offer. Eventually McNutt failed spectacularly to fulfill his promises, but not before he had agreed to bring in more than eight thousand settlers from northern Ireland and the American colonies, in return for well over a million and a half acres of land. The effect of Nova Scotia's policy thus was to inaugurate a decade of feverish speculation—"a veritable carnival of land grabbing"—and to encourage the wild schemes, conflicting claims, and unfulfillable promises that actually hindered the colony's recovery from the devastations of war and depopulation.[5]

Legitimate and quasi-legitimate settlement projects proliferated everywhere in the colonies as the threat of Indian attack subsided. We have already seen how Amherst's provisional land grants stimulated settlement in the neighborhood of his forts. In the spring of 1761, more than thirty families were already living on the enthusiastic Major Skene's manor in the Champlain Valley, and something like a miniature land rush was beginning on military grants in the Mohawk Valley.[6] Elsewhere in the northern colonies settlement processes interrupted by the war resumed, following courses marked out by the recently constructed forts and the roads that served them. The most spectacular case was that of the so-called New Hampshire Grants.

In the four years before the war began, Governor Benning Wentworth of New Hampshire had made 16 township grants in lands west of the Connecticut River and north of the Massachusetts border. The onset of hostilities stifled settlement on these grants, which at any rate were remote from established towns, difficult to reach in the absence of wagon roads, and—since the province with the best claim to jurisdiction over the land they occupied was not New Hampshire, but New York—of the most dubious legitimacy. But during the war the Bay Colony garrisoned a line of outposts along its northwestern border, and when the fighting ended Forts Massachusetts, Pelham, and Shirley all offered the springboards from which provincial veterans plunged northward to settle on the grants. Ease of access now erased worries about technicalities of title, and Governor Wentworth, short on scruples wherever profits beckoned, responded to the demand for more grants in a truly heroic way. In 1760 and 1761 he renewed 9 lapsed prewar patents and made 64 new ones. Before he finished, in mid-1764, the enterprising governor had erected 128 townships, encompassing three million of the region's most farmable acres. These included most of the west side of the Connecticut Valley and all of the flat and fertile land east of Lake Champlain; they lined the Massachusetts border 2 or 3 deep and flanked the military road that Amherst had built from Fort Number 4 to Crown Point. In a little over three years, Benning Wentworth handed out more than half the land in what would become Vermont. In so doing he set the stage for a protracted, eventually violent conflict between the New Englanders who settled on his grants and the government of New York, which—in law if not in fact—possessed the better right to distribute the land.[7]

At the same time, the return of peace to the Pennsylvania and Virginia backcountry allowed movement to the southwestern frontier to resume, both along its old paths and on new ones that the war had carved. Already in 1759, Scotch-Irish and German migrants were following their accustomed routes from Lancaster and York, across Maryland and down the Shenandoah Valley of Virginia, toward the Carolina backcountry. Although the Cherokee War briefly deterred settlers and hunters from moving southwestward, settlement proceeded briskly across western North Carolina except in periods of active hostility. Even the remote settlements near Long Canes Creek, South Carolina, which as the district nearest the Cherokees remained tense for the longest period after the war, began to attract white farmers and hunters as soon as peace returned.[8]

Meanwhile the Forbes Road and Braddock Road provided farmers with routes to the Ohio Country and places to settle near the military posts that the roads connected. The area around Fort Pitt throve with settlements of all sorts: licensed, at Pittsburgh itself; unlicensed but tolerated, on the Allegheny Valley lands that George Croghan owned and began to develop as early as 1760; and illegal in hollows and valleys everywhere. The Monongahela Valley, Colonel Bouquet complained to Virginia's governor in early 1760, was being "over run by . . . Vagabonds, who under pretense of hunting, were making settlements." Seeing how much these squatters and hunters were aggravating relations with the Indians, Bouquet issued a proclamation in the fall of 1761 requiring them to leave. When they ignored him, he sent out detachments the following April to burn down their cabins. But the squatters only came back or moved on and had their places taken by others.[9]

Those were only the settlers who lived near enough to Pittsburgh to enter Bouquet's field of vision. Many more lived along the roads and rivers leading to Fort Pitt, and many of these were simply too useful to be driven off. The hundred families who settled near Fort Bedford, east of the Alleghenies at the beginning of Forbes Road, grew more than enough corn, fodder, and cattle to feed the garrison there, and even smaller numbers living at considerable distances from the forts could hardly be dispensed with lightly. Only fourteen families were reported to be living in the vicinity of Red Stone Old Fort in 1761, forty or so miles from Pittsburgh; but that fall they floated a thousand bushels of corn down the Monongahela to the Forks. The comparable number of families living near Fort Ligonier would have been able to supply most of that small garrison's needs. Thus the forts furnished markets that helped stimulate the movement of population to the west, and an ironic symbiosis emerged between the forts and settlers that placed contradictory pressures on commanders like Bouquet, who sought to discourage the squatters on whom their garrisons were coming to rely.[10]

Given the eagerness of settlers to cross the Alleghenies, it is hardly surprising that the Ohio Company of Virginia, dormant during the years of fighting, should have tried to revive itself as hostilities tapered off. The difficulties it encountered in doing so reveal yet another dimension of the war's effects, for even as military roads furnished new conduits for migration and forts became magnets for settlement, competition between speculating groups intensified and complicated the renewal of prewar claims. As early as 1759 members of the Ohio Company, fearful that Pennsylvanians would take over the Pittsburgh area, had sought to persuade Virginia's new lieutenant governor, Francis Fauquier, to support their claims to the Forks. At the same time, however, the Ohio Company's old competitor, the Loyal Company, was pressing Fauquier to recognize its overlapping claim to the southern (Kentucky) half of the Ohio Valley. Finally, besieged by both groups, Fauquier consulted the Board of Trade for instructions. They ordered him to promote neither claim, but rather to discourage any settlement that would interfere with Indian hunting rights.

Finding no help at Williamsburg, the Ohio Company looked westward to Fort Pitt. In July 1760, its agents offered Colonel Bouquet a share of company stock in return for allowing them to sell titles to the squatters already occupying company lands in the valleys of the Youghiogheny, Monongahela, Loyalhanna, and Allegheny Rivers. Bouquet, who had earlier expressed an interest, declined to be bought out. His duty, he explained, required him to enforce the provisions of the Easton treaty restricting white settlement west of the Alleghenies. He declined to elaborate on how his own acquisition of speculative rights to land in western Maryland had contributed to his lack of interest in diverting settlers to the Ohio Valley. In December representatives of the company tried to bribe him again, only to be rebuffed once more. Finally, frustrated, the company turned its efforts to London, where its shareholder the duke of Bedford promised to present its case to the Privy Council. But Bedford, preoccupied with the war's political endgame, moved so slowly that the company's steering committee decided to send an agent, Colonel George Mercer, to present its memorials. Despite these efforts, the company sold no land at all until 1763—and then only in the vicinity of Fort Cumberland, not on the Ohio, where so many settlers had already located.[11]

The intertwined histories of land speculation and frontier settlement in the postwar colonies often seem no more than a snarled skein of ambition, self-interest, greed, and deceit. But these instances, from Nova Scotia to the Carolina frontier, in fact reveal patterns that help clarify the essential processes of change in the 1760s. The fundamental force at work in them all, the power that animated the whole system of settlement and speculation, was the dynamism of a farming population seeking opportunity. In the aftermath of the Seven Years' War, American farmers moved to take up new lands regardless of virtually every factor but the safety of their families. Only violent resistance by native peoples, as in the case of the Cherokee War, could effectively restrain the movements of a population that paid little heed to any contravening laws, boundaries, or policies of the colonial governments. With the defeat of the French accomplished and the Indians unlikely to mount effective military resistance, therefore, both governments and private enterprises tried to position themselves to take advantage of population movements that no one could control.

In Nova Scotia and New Hampshire, the war decisively altered the circumstances of settlement—in one case by forcibly ejecting the Acadians from their homes, in the other by suppressing a French and Indian threat and providing new access to lands previously too remote and hazardous to colonize. Weak provincial governments and ambitious governors moved quickly to take advantage of these opportunities and enrich themselves. In the case of the Ohio Company, the pattern was somewhat more complicated. There, too, the settlers were following roads that had been built to fight a distant enemy; but there it was a private business partnership, not a government or a governor, that sought to profit from the surge of farm-seeking migrants. Unlike Lawrence and Wentworth, who responded to the lure of profit by inviting farmers and speculators to colonize newly opened lands, Virginia's governor understood his duty as requiring him to discourage new settlement. When Fauquier declined to support the Ohio Company's claims, therefore, he was trying to do what Colonel Bouquet attempted by burning cabins: halt the further invasion of Indian lands. The net effect of such official discouragement, however, was not to prevent the settlement from taking place—nothing but overt Indian hostility could accomplish that—but rather to displace the company's energies from the frontier to London, where by means fair and foul it lobbied Fauquier's and Bouquet's masters to alter policy in its favor.

These patterns foreshadowed developments in settlement and land speculation that would emerge in full force during the later 1760s. Whenever imperial officials and colonial governors tried to block settlement, groups of speculators like the Ohio Company focused their activities and competition in London. There, where the need for access to the inner circles of power inevitably encouraged them to offer shares to political insiders and influence-peddlers, the result would be the growth of ever larger and more powerful speculative syndicates, maneuvering to gain access to ever larger grants of land. As time passed and the potential for profit escalated, the activities of such groups would assume a kaleidoscopic complexity. Yet always their motives and tactics would remain the same: to gain control of policy at the highest levels by the manipulation of powerful men. Insofar as their maneuvers and countermaneuvers, plots and counterplots, would cancel one another out or inhibit the making of policy, these speculative syndicates would tend to slow the actual processes of settlement in America. They could not, however, *prevent* settlement from occurring. In the absence of a policy to legitimate it, the settlement that did take place would be unsanctioned, secretive, and chaotic.

Of course, not all of the new postwar colonization would take place on trans-Allegheny lands, any more than all speculative activity would occur in London. Wherever colonial governments or speculative groups directly tied to those governments sought to promote settlements where territorial jurisdiction was fuzzy or contested, conflicts would tend to arise between competing groups of settlers. Rather than the maneuverings of powerful groups in the metropolis, these competitions to define the future of American settlement would manifest themselves on the frontiers of empire—as boundary disputes between provinces, violent confrontations between bands of white settlers with titles based on colonies' conflicting claims, or as open warfare between invading whites and the Indian groups that already occupied the land. In this final permutation, the most violent and in terms of human life the most costly conflicts could arise; and among them all the most tragic instance would be the Susquehannah Company's attempts to settle the Wyoming Valley of Pennsylvania.

CHAPTER 55

Yankees Invade Wyoming—and Pay the Price

SPRING 1763

SINCE 1754, when John Henry Lydius and Timothy Woodbridge had tried to acquire the Iroquois Confederacy's claim to five million acres in Pennsylvania, the Susquehannah Company's membership had greatly expanded, particularly among the farmers of eastern Connecticut. In part this resulted from the sheer land-hunger of families in this, the poorest part of a populous colony; in part it came from the relatively low cost of stock (as little as eight pounds Connecticut currency per share, with half-shares available). But in large part, too, the company prospered because Connecticut's government made no effort to discourage it, and indeed gave all but formal blessing to its operations. Because the Charter of 1662 had fixed Connecticut's western boundary at the Pacific, and because that patent preceded the establishment of the Pennsylvania proprietary by nearly twenty years, Connecticut's government could in fact maintain it had the right to erect townships within Pennsylvania, and that claim (however zany on its face) was better grounded in law than that any Benning Wentworth could make for his New Hampshire grants. But if low entry costs made the enterprise popular and legal technicalities made it plausible, wartime developments rendered it frankly bizarre. The Susquehannah Company's supposed purchase included the 2,500,000-acre tract that Governor Denny had promised Teedyuscung as a reserve for the eastern Delawares at the 1757 Treaty of Easton. Promised, but not guaranteed: the following year's Easton conference, at which the western Delawares had made their peace with the British, had blurred Teedyuscung's right to the Wyoming Valley by making it subject to the approval of the Iroquois Confederacy—and presumably to the assent of the Penn family as well.

The war, of course, had rendered the occupation of the Wyoming Valley theoretical for all but Teedyuscung's people, but it was not long after hostilities had ceased in middle Pennsylvania that the first Connecticut Yankees made their appearance. In the autumn of 1760, three justices of the peace and the sheriff of Northampton County, acting on a complaint from Teedyuscung, found that twenty settlers associated with the Susquehannah Company had established a village on the west bank of the Delaware, at Cushitunk. The New Englanders made no effort to conceal that they were the vanguard of a much larger number of migrants who were to follow in the spring. They were unconcerned with Pennsylvanian opposition because, as they assured the investigators, majorities in both houses of the Connecticut Assembly warmly supported their enterprise. This invasion—there was no other adequate term for it—triggered a quick proclamation from Governor James Hamilton, forbidding unauthorized settlement on Pennsylvania lands and warning of Indian retaliation; occasioned an exchange of official correspondence between Hamilton and Governor Thomas Fitch, who claimed that Connecticut had no official connection to a company with more than a thousand shareholders, including many of the colony's most influential political figures; and scared the Penn family into asking the Board of Trade and the Privy Council to block further Susquehannah Company activity.[1]

None of this activity blunted the spearhead of Yankee colonization. By the end of 1760, Connecticut surveyors had laid off three townships along the Delaware, millwrights had built a sawmill and a gristmill, and settlers had settled into cabins to wait out the winter. The following year, while in Britain the attorney general and the solicitor general assured the Penns that Connecticut's charter gave "no Colour of Right to Claim the Tract of Land in Question," at Cushitunk the settlers—by this time, scores of them—built houses, constructed and armed a stout blockhouse, and began work on the road that would cross the mountains to the broad Wyoming plain.[2]

It took the Yankee axmen until the fall of 1762 to cut their way through the sixty miles of hills, forest, and swamp that separated the valleys of the Delaware and the Susquehanna. When in mid-September the advance party of about 120 armed pioneers finally reached their destination on Lechawanock (Lackawanna) Creek, seven or eight miles up the valley from Teedyuscung's town, they found only a few Delawares on hand—by no means enough to keep them from cutting tons of hay, raising three blockhouses, building three miles of road along the river, and making other preparations for the larger numbers of settlers who, they said, would follow. Significantly, Teedyuscung was not among the half-dozen warriors who turned out to warn the Connecticut men off. Indeed, at the time they arrived he had no idea that invaders had even entered Wyoming, because he was off trying to deal with threats that seemed more immediate—and those proceeded from Philadelphia and Onondaga.[3]

Except for a short time in July and early August, the Delaware king was absent from his settlement from late May through September, trying by diplomacy to preserve his people's claim to the promised reservation. Nothing that summer had favored him or his people. Even before he left the valley, an epidemic of dysentery carried off his wife, Elisabeth, her sister, and her sister's husband, an important counselor. Teedyuscung suspected that they had been poisoned, by witchcraft; and both fear and grief probably contributed to the drunkenness that made him such a poor advocate for his people at the summer's two conferences. At the first of these, at Easton in June, Sir William Johnson presided over a quasi-judicial inquiry into the validity of the Walking Purchase. This investigation fulfilled the promise, made at the Easton negotiations of 1757 and 1758, that a representative of the Crown would determine whether the Penn family and the Iroquois had conspired to defraud the Delawares of their lands in eastern Pennsylvania at the time of the Walking Purchase. If Johnson found fraud, he could recommend that the eastern Delawares receive compensation in the form of the permanent title to the Wyoming Valley. Unfortunately for the Delawares, Johnson not only habitually favored Iroquois claims to overlordship, but saw great political utility in strengthening his connections with the Penn family. Teedyuscung made these formidable obstacles insurmountable by drinking heavily throughout the conference.[4]

The chief's erratic behavior in presenting his case made it relatively easy for the lawyers who represented the Penn family to discredit him before Johnson, whose basic hostility to the Delawares was obvious from the start. Eventually Israel Pemberton of the Friendly Association—present, as at every Easton conference since 1756, to support the Indians—found the proceedings so blatantly unfair that he lost his temper and tried to intervene on Teedyuscung's behalf. Accusations flew and anger flared; Johnson drew his sword and threatened to run the Quaker through; and in the end, Pemberton succeeded only in adding the humiliation of the Friendly Association to the defeat of the Delawares' hopes. On June 27, Teedyuscung settled for what he could get, agreeing to "bury under Ground all Controversies about Land . . . and to Sign a Release for all the Lands in Dispute," in return for a gift of two hundred pounds in goods and four hundred pounds in cash.[5]

The route back to Wyoming was a *via dolorosa* to a man who understood that he had little chance of gaining a clear title to the valley at the summer's second conference, a peace congress between representatives of the Pennsylvania government and the Ohio Indians. Nonetheless he assembled his warriors into an entourage that would support him in his last effort to plead for a reservation and left the valley in early August. By the twelfth his delegation had reached Lancaster, where they met Governor Hamilton, Tamaqua and other leaders from the Ohio Country, and representatives of the Six Nations who had come to confirm the treaty as the "uncles" of the Delawares and Shawnees. Predictably enough, neither the Iroquois nor Hamilton felt inclined to give the Delaware king what he asked. Nothing compelled them to do so. Teedyuscung's uncles and Governor Hamilton instead urged him to stand fast against all intruders from Connecticut, while offering nothing concrete—least of all an inalienable title—to help him. The Iroquois chiefs seemed most interested in ceding tracts of land on the lower Susquehanna, which did nothing to reassure Teedyuscung that the upper reaches of the valley would not be next. Bitterly accusing the whites of trying to poison his delegation, as he believed his wife and others had been poisoned in the spring, Teedyuscung left Lancaster with presents—a hundred pounds in cash and four hundred pounds in trade goods—but without satisfaction. His dream of a secure homeland, born in the war that had briefly given him leverage against both the Iroquois and the Penns, lay dead in the ashes of the Lancaster council fire.[6]

Bitter as his disappointment was, what awaited Teedyuscung at home was worse. He could hardly have been pleased to find the entire Iroquois delegation from Lancaster encamped at Wyoming when he returned at the end of September, but when they told him why they had come, it must have seemed as if the events of the summer had only been the prelude to something far worse. Thomas King, the Oneida chief who headed the Iroquois group, explained that a week earlier, on their way back to New York, they had encountered settlers from the Susquehannah Company. He and his men had ordered them out of the valley on pain of death, and the Yankees had left. But everywhere Teedyuscung looked along Lechawanock Creek, he found evidence that they intended to return.[7]

King told Teedyuscung to wait for instructions from the Six Nations and then made his way home, leaving the situation in considerable doubt. When 150 or so of the Connecticut men returned to the valley a few days later, bringing "all sorts of Tools as well for Building as Husbandry" and announcing that they intended to start erecting houses, Teedyuscung threatened to carry them before the governor of Pennsylvania for punishment. But the Yankees only laughed at him, cached their tools in the woods, and left vowing to bring back 3,000 settlers in the spring. Other parties followed, carrying more implements, including a great blade and the tools necessary to build a sawmill—which, they told Teedyuscung, they intended to locate on the Susquehanna about a mile from his house. As before, each group hid its supplies and left, its members saying "the very same things to [Teedyuscung] that the others had Said," assuring him that there was no way to stop them. Finally, in November, Teedyuscung traveled to Philadelphia to ask the governor for help. Hamilton encouraged him to stand fast, warned him not to shed the "Blood of the White People," and suggested that he consult the Six Nations. In the meantime, the governor said, he would ask the proper British authorities to intervene and stop the Connecticut scheme.[8]

None of this helped Teedyuscung, who needed more than advice if he hoped to stand off hordes of heavily armed New Englanders in the spring. When he returned to Wyoming, therefore, he sent a war belt and a message to the Ohio Country. If the government of Pennsylvania would not defend his people, and the Iroquois could not be trusted to refrain from selling the ground out from under him, perhaps his kinsmen the western Delawares would offer the support he needed. He had cause for hope in this, for at Lancaster the Ohio delegates had been so offended by the Pennsylvanians' behavior that they actually discarded the presents they had been given on their way home. Tamaqua, who for four years had been the leading advocate of accommodation among the western Delawares, had lost status as a result of the conference, his place taken by a more militant chief called Newcomer. Although no record survives of the reply Newcomer and the other Ohio chiefs made to Teedyuscung's pleas for support, they evidently gave the Delaware king enough assurances that he was able to withstand strong pressures from within his group to abandon Wyoming. He and his warriors settled in to await the Yankees' return.[9]

But when Connecticut men and their families came back in the spring of 1763, they met no resistance, for by the time they arrived, the Delaware king was dead and his people had scattered to the winds. On the night of April 19, while Teedyuscung lay drunk and asleep, arsonists set fire to his cabin and the others in his settlement. Mingo Senecas were visiting the town when the fires broke out and supplied the liquor that insured Teedyuscung's sleep would be his last. Whether they acted on behalf of the Susquehannah Company or the Six Nations, or even whether they started the fires, can never be known. What cannot be denied, however, is that the Susquehannah Company realized an immediate benefit from the tragedy. No warriors were there to keep the Yankee intruders from planting in Delaware cornfields, turning livestock out into the meadowlands along the river, building houses in the deserted and burned-out Indian towns, and constructing fortifications to preserve their hold on the valley.

Yet they would not hold it long. When during the summer news reached the valley that a great Indian uprising had broken out in the west, most of the New Englanders withdrew, and the expected influx of settlers—the more than seven hundred men and families who had made ready to migrate from Connecticut—never materialized. By the fall only thirty or forty stubborn farmers remained at Wyoming, confident that the blockhouse would protect them until they could bring in the year's corn harvest. Their confidence was misplaced. On October 15, Teedyuscung's son, Captain Bull, appeared at the head of a Delaware war party. They made short work of the settlers' defenses, killing ten of the Yankees and driving the rest upriver into captivity, at Wyalusing. When a company of Pennsylvania provincials arrived a couple of days later, they could read the story in the ruins. "Nine men and a woman," they reported, "had been most cruelly butchered[.] The woman was roasted, and had two Hinges in her Hands, supposed to be put in red hot, and several of the men had Awls thrust into their Eyes, and Spears, arrows, Pitchforks, &c sticking in their Bodies." All the victims had been scalped, but an "immense quantity" of corn stood unharmed in the fields nearby. Hastily burying the dead, the Pennsylvania soldiers burned the undamaged buildings, torched the corn crop to keep the Indians from returning to harvest it, and retreated to safer territory.[10] Five years would pass before Susquehannah Company settlers would return to the bloodstained plains of Wyoming.

CHAPTER 56

Amherst's Reforms and Pontiac's War

1763

CAPTAIN BULL attacked the New Englanders at Wyoming in October to avenge his father's death. In that sense his was a local and personal act, a response to Yankee aggression against Delaware lives and lands. In a larger sense, however, Captain Bull and his fellow warriors were being drawn into the backdraft of "Pontiac's War," which had ignited more than 350 miles west of Wyoming at almost exactly the same time that Teedyuscung's assassins set fire to his cabin. The fuel for that larger conflagration lay in the incursions of backcountry settlers onto Indian lands and in Amherst's postconquest reforms in Indian diplomacy and trade, and the spark that set it off was struck when an obscure Ottawa chief organized an assault on the British garrison at Detroit. But what made this conflict unique among Indian wars of the colonial period—what ultimately combined a number of local attacks into an uprising that stretched from the Susquehanna to the Mississippi and from northern Michigan to the Ohio Valley—was a religious vision, which for the first time in American history enabled many Indian groups to act together. That spiritual message, interestingly enough, had emerged in the Susquehanna Valley as a series of Delaware prophets responded to the crisis that followed their people's dispossession by the Iroquois and the heirs of William Penn.

The earliest Delaware prophecies were purely nativist denunciations of alcohol as the substance by which Indians had been made dependent upon Europeans. Once the Delawares had been deprived of their lands by the Walking Purchase, however, the message of the prophets began to take on a potentially political and implicitly anti–Six Nations character. In the last years before the Seven Years' War, a female prophet at Wyoming and two male preachers who lived farther up the Susquehanna's east branch began to elaborate on the earliest prophecies. They preached that Indians had been created separately from whites and blacks and had displeased the Master of Life by departing from the separate way he had ordained for them. As a result of their sins, which included alcohol abuse and greed for trade goods, the Master of Life had sent epidemics and hard winters, thinning out the game and causing crop failures, in order to turn them back to their earlier ways of life. The teachings of these three prophets were new, and significant, because they carried potentially pan-Indian, as well as nativist, overtones. The even more dramatic afflictions of the Seven Years' War would amplify these messages, which assumed a particularly potent form in 1759–60 when a fourth prophet, Neolin, emerged among the western Delawares of the upper Ohio Valley.

Like his Susquehanna Valley predecessors, Neolin emphasized the separate creation of whites and Indians and enjoined abstinence from alcohol as a means to regain sacred power and reconcile the Delawares with the Master of Life. But in important ways he went beyond the earlier prophets. If the Indians were to avoid dependence on whites, they would ultimately have to abstain from trade as well as from alcohol, relearn the ancient ways of hunting and manufacture they had forgotten, and abandon all intercourse with Europeans. As a means to this end, Neolin encouraged his followers to practice ritual purgations and to undertake a seven-year process of training young men in the making and use of traditional weapons, so that they could defend their people without having to depend upon European arms. In 1761 Neolin began predicting a new war in the west. The signs he identified with that impending conflict—declining game populations, large numbers of whites encroaching on Indian lands, and Amherst's prohibition against gifts and supplying gunpowder in quantity—helped persuade the western Delawares of the truth in his message. The resulting religious revival had important political implications. As Neolin's following grew, accommodationist chiefs like Tamaqua and Shingas, who had led their people in the abandonment of the French and who still counseled patience with the British, lost standing in Delaware councils.[1]

Although Neolin may have intended his teachings to promote regeneration among his own people, in 1761 and 1762 they spread far beyond the upper Ohio and began to figure strongly in the spiritual lives of Indians from western New York to Minnesota, from the Great Lakes basin to the Kentucky and Illinois Countries. In part the religious awakening of these years stemmed from the dual afflictions of disease and famine that beset the western Indians generally in 1761 and 1762. Epidemics and want, of course, were messages that the Master of Life sent to prompt his children's renewal. In addition, however, British commanders forbidden by Amherst's policies from distributing gifts did little to alleviate the suffering and much to fulfill prophecies that relations between whites and Indians would continue to deteriorate until war broke out. Under such stresses, revivals based on Neolin's purification rituals and nativist message appeared among the Chippewas, Miamis, Ottawas, Potawatomis, Shawnees, and Wyandots, and even occurred within Iroquoia among the Senecas and Onondagas. As they did, the pan-Indian elements implicit in Neolin's prophecies began to furnish common ground for nativist resistance to the British.[2]

War belts had in fact never ceased to circulate among the western Indians after the conquest of Canada. Some remained from Vaudreuil's efforts to reanimate the failed alliances of the *pays d'en haut*. Others originated in the Geneseo Senecas' efforts to organize rebellions against the British at Niagara in 1761 and 1762. Some probably came from French traders and others unwilling to accept the surrender of Canada; still others had been issued by French officers who still commanded posts in Louisiana. At least one of them represented Teedyuscung's eleventh-hour call for help against the Susquehannah Company invaders. But if the wampum symbols were nothing new, Neolin's revelations gave them a common context of meaning and interpretation. As they did, accommodationist chiefs everywhere began to forfeit control over relations with the British. Among the Delawares, for example, by early 1762 all the chiefs who had made peace with the British in 1758 either withdrew from public life or lost standing. Pisquetomen and Delaware George both vanished, perhaps dying; Tamaqua and Shingas ceased to influence western Delaware policy.[3]

In the winter of 1762–63 the question was no longer whether, but when and where, the fighting would begin. The western Indians made no secret of their discontentment with Amherst's trade and settlement policies and could not conceal the ascendancy of nativist leaders. Croghan and the other western traders were deeply apprehensive; the commanders of isolated forts looked nervously to their stocks of food and ammunition. Only the highest-ranking British officers, secure in their headquarters, remained unconcerned. At Philadelphia late in 1762, Colonel Bouquet casually referred to reports of a "pretended new conspiracy" among the western Indians, and in New York the following April,

Amherst dismissed warnings of impending war as "Meer Bugbears." As late as June 6, 1763, the commander in chief could still persuade himself, as he read the first reports of the uprising, that "this alarm will end in nothing."[4]

The great Indian rebellion began about ten miles from Detroit on April 27, 1763, when the Ottawa war leader Pontiac invoked Neolin's teachings at a "council of the three nations, Ottawas, Potawatomies, and the bad Huron [Wyandot] band," and persuaded them to join him in attacking the local British garrison—although not the French settlement that lay outside its walls. Among the local villagers Pontiac could raise about 460 warriors, more than enough to attack the 125 redcoats and 40 traders whom Major Henry Gladwin commanded at Fort Detroit. Pontiac and his allies resolved to surprise the garrison on May 7. They failed in the attempt because a Wyandot woman—perhaps Gladwin's mistress—warned the British of the plot. Pontiac and his allies, joined by a Chippewa band, therefore laid siege to the fort on May 9. Within the first week they killed or wounded 20 British soldiers and refugees and took 15 more captive. A week thereafter they captured a convoy of supply bateaux approaching the fort from Niagara, killing or making prisoners of more than 50 soldiers and bateaumen; a few days later they intercepted another party on its way to the fort and made prisoners of 19 more redcoats and civilians. Except for a single sloop carrying provisions that arrived on June 30, no relief convoy would make it safely to the fort's anchorage until the end of July. By then Pontiac's besieging force had grown to more than 900 warriors from a half-dozen nations.[5]

Throughout May, messengers raced from village to village across the *pays d'en haut,* carrying the news that war had begun at Detroit. As if by prearrangement other Indian groups took up the hatchet against remote, thinly manned British outposts. On May 16, Wyandot warriors surprised and seized Fort Sandusky near the west end of Lake Erie, 50 miles south of Detroit. Nine days later, Potawatomies captured Fort St. Joseph (modern Niles, Michigan), southeast of Lake Michigan and about 170 miles west of Detroit. A hundred miles up the Maumee River from Lake Erie and 140 miles to Detroit's southwest, Fort Miami (now Fort Wayne, Indiana) fell to the local Miami Indians on the twenty-seventh. Flushed with victory, the Miamis made a quick portage to the Wabash drainage, persuaded Kickapoo, Mascouten, and Wea warriors to join them, and seized Fort Ouiatenon (near Lafayette, Indiana) on June 1. The next day, 275 miles to the north, Chippewas pretending to play a game of lacrosse gained entry to Fort Michilimackinac, on the strait between Lake Huron and Lake Michigan. Within minutes they killed or captured its entire

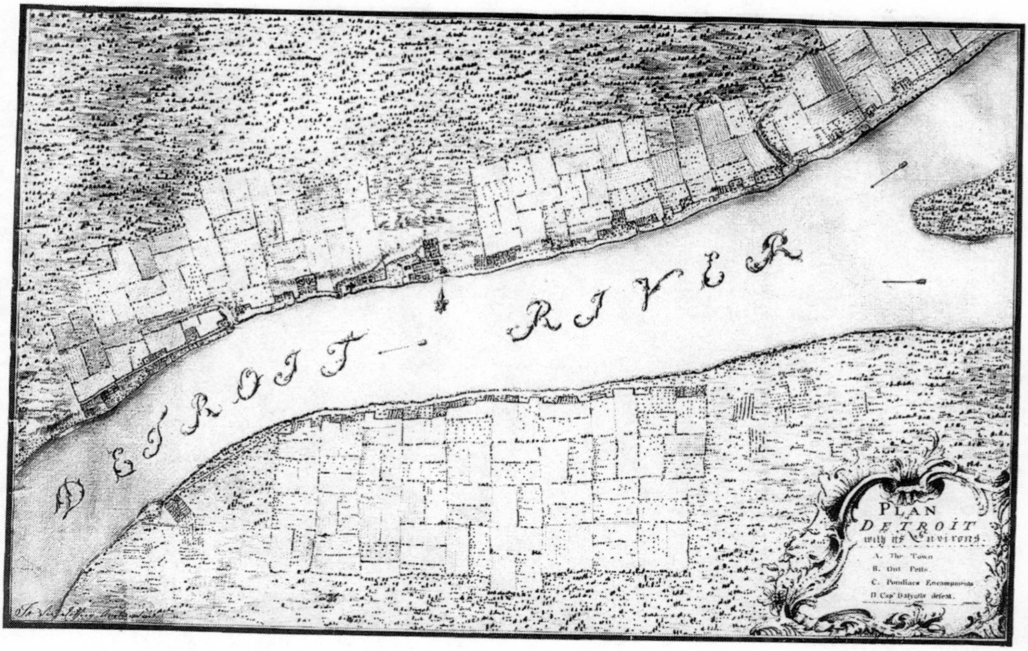

Detroit under attack, 1763. Lieutenant John Montrésor, an engineering officer sent with a small detachment in August, remained at Detroit until November; on his return to Niagara he sent the original of this map of Detroit and the surrounding countryside to Jeffery Amherst. The "fort" of Detroit—a small walled town intended for trade, rather than a Vauban-style fortification—appears on the north shore of the river, immediately above the compass rose. The farms of the local French habitants, indicated by their rectangular fields, lie on either side of the fort, and opposite it across the river. The settlements of the besieging Indians bracket the farmed areas. At the west end of the fields above the river is the Potawatomi village; on the opposite shore the Huron (Wyandot) village; and at the east end of the south-shore fields, the Ottawa village. Pontiac's own camp is on the north shore of the river, above the arrow indicating the direction of the current. It lay a little over two miles east of the fort, not far beyond a creek known to the French as Rivière Parent. In memory of Captain James Dalyell's defeat there on July 31, the British called it Bloody Run. *Courtesy of the William L. Clements Library at the University of Michigan.*

complement of soldiers and traders. The commander of the most isolated garrison on Lake Michigan, Fort Edward Augustus (Green Bay, Wisconsin), turned his post over to the local Indians, Anglophile eastern Sioux who remained aloof from the rebellion, on June 21. When he and his men tried to make their way over the lake to safety, however, Ottawa and Chippewa warriors intercepted them near the Straits of Mackinac and eventually carried them to Montréal for ransom, along with the survivors of the Michilimackinac garrison.[6]

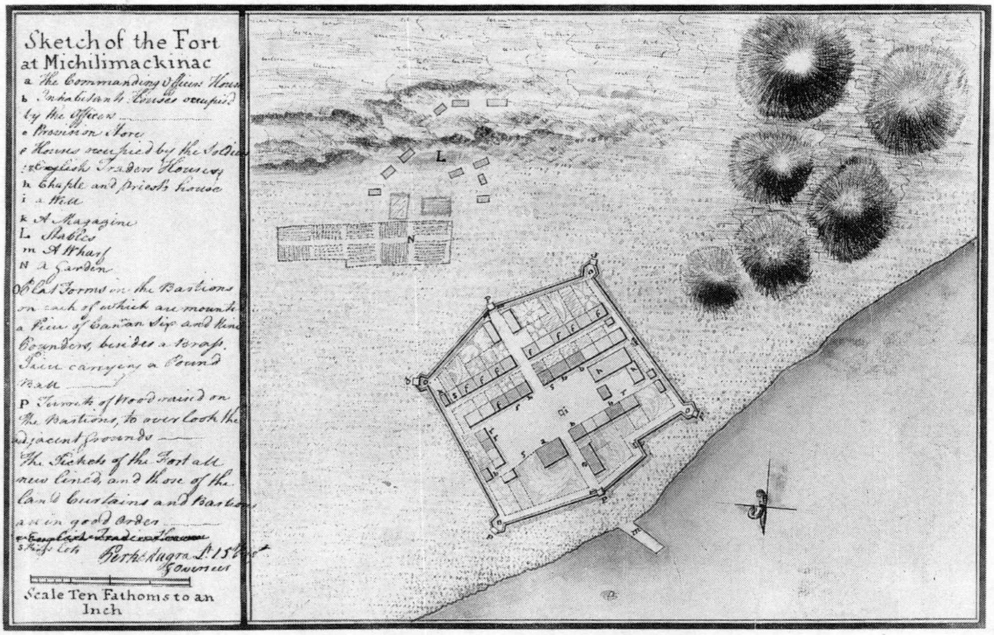

Fort Michilimackinac. Although it was only about one-seventh the size of Detroit, Michilimackinac was similarly situated on a strait between two of the Great Lakes and similarly constructed as a stockaded trading settlement. This finely detailed sketch gives an excellent idea of the interior layout of both posts, where short streets were lined by traders' houses, each with its own small garden plot. *Courtesy of the William L. Clements Library at the University of Michigan.*

During the last half of June, Seneca war parties, in some cases cooperating with bands of Ottawas and Chippewas, attacked and seized all the blockhouse way stations between Fort Niagara and Fort Pitt. Fort Venango fell, its garrison annihilated, on about June 16. Fort LeBoeuf followed on the eighteenth and Fort Presque Isle on the twenty-first. With the loss of these posts, Fort Pitt could no longer communicate with its supply bases on the Great Lakes and in Canada. At the same time, Delaware and Shawnee warriors severed communications between Pittsburgh and eastern Pennsylvania by destroying the settlements along Forbes Road and attacking Forts Ligonier and Bedford. Fort Pitt's commandant, Captain Simeon Ecuyer of the Royal American Regiment, had first understood his peril a month earlier, when Tamaqua began warning traders to leave Delaware villages. On May 28, Delaware and Mingo warriors shed the first blood in the upper Ohio Country when they wiped out Colonel William Clapham's small settlement, twenty-five miles up the Monongahela from the Forks; the next day they killed two redcoats at Fort Pitt's sawmill. Although Ecuyer remained confident of his strength—with 250 regulars, traders, and settler militiamen on hand, Fort Pitt was not only the most stoutly constructed, but the most strongly manned of all the western posts—he could not disguise his apprehensiveness in the letter he sent to Bouquet, at Philadelphia, describing recent events and transmitting reports that Detroit was besieged and Fort Sandusky had been "cut off."[7]

The Indians, however, would not threaten Fort Pitt itself until late June. On the twenty-fourth, two Delaware leaders approached and asked for a parley. They informed Ecuyer of the destruction of the posts between Fort Niagara and Fort Pitt and advised him to evacuate Pittsburgh or face destruction. Ecuyer, who by the addition of refugees from the surrounding settlements now had 338 men under his command, refused to surrender. Although at least 500 soldiers and refugees crowded his fort and smallpox had lately broken out among them, he had enough provisions on hand to make him confident that he could hold out until Bouquet organized a relief expedition. He therefore thanked the chiefs, warned them that attacks would be severely punished, and advised them to dissuade their young men from violence. Then he concluded the parley by making the emissaries a gift of provisions, liquor, and other small items to ease their journey homeward. Two of the blankets and a handkerchief in the bundle had come directly from the fort's smallpox hospital.[8]

By the beginning of July every British post west of Detroit had fallen to the Indians. Detroit, with three months' provisions, lay under close siege. Fort Pitt waited tensely for a general attack—an assault delayed only by the fact that Delaware, Shawnee, and Mingo war parties were raiding Pennsylvania settlements as far east as Carlisle and ranging the Virginia backcountry from the Potomac to North Carolina. Everywhere in this recently reoccupied region confusion reigned. Colonel Bouquet, struggling at Carlisle to organize a relief column for Pittsburgh, reported "a general Panick" in the vicinity, despite the presence of his regulars. At New York, Sir Jeffery Amherst, resisting the notion that anything could have gone so far wrong, was only beginning to understand what was happening.[9]

The commander in chief first learned of Indian trouble when dispatches that Ecuyer and Bouquet had sent in late May reached New York on June 6. In response he ordered light infantry companies from the 17th, 42nd, and 77th Regiments—units stationed near his headquarters and still recuperating from the malarial devastation of Havana—to make ready to march for Pennsylvania. For reasons both psychological and practical he could do little more. Preoccupied by the wish to return to England (where, he had lately learned, his wife's sanity was ebbing away), Amherst did not wish to think that anything could detain him in America; moreover, his forces had been so badly depleted by the Cuban campaign that he simply had no reserves to commit. When in mid-June Amherst received the first verified account of the siege of Detroit, he directed his aide-de-camp, Captain James Dalyell, to travel from Albany to Niagara, collect whatever reinforcements he could along the way, and, if the situation merited, proceed with them as far as Detroit. But no report truly convinced Amherst that his commanders had lost control of the interior until June 21, when a letter arrived that Major Gladwin had written nearly six weeks earlier. Even so, it took the commander in chief another week to inform the Southern secretary of recent developments, probably because he found it so "difficult . . . to account [for] any causes that can have induced these barbarians to this perfidious attempt." Whether it was the denial of alcohol under his reform policies ("they have pretended to be very dissatisfied at not getting rum") or some more substantial cause, Amherst could only conclude that the rebellion resulted from a conspiracy—doubtless one the French had started.[10]

Bewilderment at the Indians' success in capturing forts and defeating redcoat detachments, delay in understanding what was going on, inability to restore order once the rebellion's scope became clear—all these factors now helped promote a singular bloody-mindedness among the British commanders. Bouquet, still trying to organize a relief column to lead to Pittsburgh, wrote to Amherst from Lancaster that he hoped "to extirpate that Vermine from a Country they have forfeited, and with it all Claim to the Rights of Humanity." Amherst, not yet knowing that Ecuyer had already put the theory into practice, replied that when Bouquet reached the valley he should try to spread disease among the Indians by passing smallpox-infected blankets among them. "We must," he wrote, "Use Every Stratagem in our Power to Reduce them." To Gladwin and other officers he issued orders that all Indians taken prisoner should "immediately be put to death, their extirpation being the only security for our future safety, and their late treacherous proceedings deserving no better treatment at our hands."[11]

This was not, of course, the first time British officers had ordered extreme measures to be taken against Indian enemies: Amherst had permitted the killing of Indian prisoners at Louisbourg in 1758 and Wolfe extended the policy to include Canadians dressed as Indians during the Québec expedition in 1759. Even thoroughly professional European officers could rationalize such policies as no breach of civilized behavior because Indians routinely killed their captives. Sanctioning the "extirpation" of enemy populations by spreading smallpox among them, however, had no precedent. Amherst's and his fellow officers' sense that Indians were less than fully human helps account for their willingness to contemplate such measures; but only the regulars' overwhelming sense of impotence can fully explain them.

Appalling as they were, Amherst's orders did not occasion genocide so much as reflect his and his colleagues' genocidal fantasies; for in fact there was nothing that he or any British officer in America could do to reverse the tide of Indian military success. As Amherst well knew, the measures he could take—appealing to the provinces for militiamen or drafting invalids from the Havana regiments to replace soldiers in garrisons, freeing what healthy men he could find to aid in the relief of Fort Pitt or Detroit—were only stopgaps, and at most they could buy time. Since he knew better than to expect reinforcements from Britain, Amherst realized that he could restore order in the west only with the help of provincial troops. That meant waiting until governors could summon their assemblies, and (worse) waiting for the representatives to slake their thirst for debate; it meant, realistically, that no expeditions could be mounted until the summer of 1764. Thus while Amherst awaited reports from Detroit and Pittsburgh, and even before he wrote to notify the governors of his troop requirements, he began planning the coming year's campaign. In the process he put the hysteria of June and July behind him. But his recovery of composure did not enable him to comprehend, much less correct, the conditions that had created the war. Indeed, insofar as his plan relied on military means to restore stable Anglo-Indian relations, it would tend only to delay the return of peace.[12]

Amherst thought it essential that peace be restored by force of arms rather than by negotiation. As he explained to Sir William Johnson, he was

> determined to go through with [the suppression of the rebellion] in such a manner that the whole race of Indians who have any connection with the English may see the folly and madness, as well as the ingratitude of setting themselves in opposition to a people from whom they have received so many benefits, and whose power is such as can in a very short time, make the Savages feel the utmost extremity of want, and render their pretended importance of very little effect. . . .
>
> . . . Their punishment must [therefore] be previous to the treating with them, and when that shall happen, all they can expect is for-

> giveness, and a Trade, under proper regulations, opened to them. But as to *presents,* it would certainly be the highest presumption in them to expect any. Justice they shall have, but no more; for they can never be considered by us as a people to whom we owe *rewards;* and it would be madness, to the highest degree, ever to bestow favors on a race who have so treacherously, and without any provocation on our side, attacked our Posts, and butchered our Garrisons. Presents should be given only to those who remain our firm friends.[13]

Amherst believed that, regardless of their losses, his redcoats would inevitably defeat the Indians. From the Cherokee War he had learned that Indian uprisings would peter out once trade goods and gunpowder ran short and warriors lost the ability to protect their families and crops from destruction. While it was true that the Indians had seized the stores of eight forts, the great posts that functioned as central distribution points (Forts Detroit, Pitt, and Niagara) all remained in British hands, and these held the largest supply magazines. Because the Indians had only canoes for transport, they could scarcely move heavy barrels of provisions, powder, and shot from the posts where they had been captured to the forts still under siege. Since the present summer's warfare and the coming winter's hunts were sure to deplete the Indians' stocks of ammunition, the summer of 1764 would offer Amherst his first realistic opportunity to subjugate the Indian rebels militarily.

Amherst's plan therefore presupposed that the three critical western forts—Niagara, Detroit, and Pittsburgh—could be held until the coming summer, when they would become the bases from which punitive expeditions could be launched. This was an easy enough assumption to make, for Amherst had no doubt that Bouquet would soon relieve Fort Pitt, and that Dalyell's reinforcement would enable Gladwin to maintain control at Detroit. (In fact Amherst's instructions to the commanders of the two expeditions assumed that they would be able to undertake limited offensive actions against the Indians even before the end of the summer; Bouquet, for example, was supposed to ascend the Allegheny and French Creek, retaking Forts Venango and LeBoeuf, and if possible Fort Presque Isle as well!) Building on control of these strategic points, Amherst's plan had three parts. First, as soon as possible, Sir William Johnson would use his influence with the Six Nations to insure that those Senecas who had joined the rebellion would be isolated from the rest of the Confederacy. Thereafter, at the earliest possible moment in 1764, one expedition of regulars and provincials from New York and New Jersey would move westward from Niagara to Detroit, bringing the Great Lakes Indians to heel.

At the same time, a second expedition, made up of regulars and provincials from Pennsylvania and Virginia, would strike westward from Fort Pitt and reduce the Ohio Indians to submission. Only Indians who had first been chastised and made to return their captives would be allowed to treat for peace.[14]

Amherst's strategic plan made sense in light of lessons he had extracted from the Cherokee War, but its principal *policy* aim—the forcible imposition of British sovereignty over the Indians—reflected his stubbornness more clearly than any appreciation of the war's origins or cultural dynamics. As Johnson, Croghan, and others who had had direct experience with Indian affairs could have explained to him, British sovereignty was the root, not the solution, of the Indian problems. The French, to whom the Indians were accustomed, had acted as trading partners and as paternalist mediators of disputes among Indian groups, but they had rarely tried to intervene forcibly in Indian life. Their comparatively generous attitude toward the giving of gifts, their tolerance of Indian cultures and willingness to adopt Indian social mores, their preference for trade over farming and their accompanying lack of insistence that Indians cede large tracts of land to them: these had sustained stable relations between the Indians of the interior and their French "father," Onontio. Britain's conquest of Canada and Amherst's economizing reforms threatened every one of these elements of stability. Indeed, to an extent that even Johnson and Croghan only dimly understood, the precipitating cause of the Indian attacks on British posts throughout the west had been the arrival of news that Britain and France had, at long last, made peace.

Neither Pontiac nor any other important Indian leader of the *pays d'en haut* had believed it was possible that Onontio would hand over eastern North America to British control. The Indians knew that they had never been defeated, and to be deprived of their land by white men signing papers across the sea made no sense. Their uprising therefore represented an attempt to "awaken" Onontio, who had somehow fallen asleep: an effort to revive New France, both by ritual means—through ceremonies that employed uniforms, flags, and other symbols of French power—and by military action, to defeat the British and enable the French to return from over the sea.

When British officers heard reports that Pontiac and other Indian leaders referred to the return of the French, they assumed that such talk proved French provocateurs had instigated the conspiracy against British control. How else, Amherst and his colleagues wondered, could so many diverse Indian groups have acted in concert against them? The British, trapped within their understanding of the Indians as childlike, violent creatures, could not explain what had happened to them in the west unless they could stipulate a French conspiracy behind it all. They never understood that the evidently synchronized attacks were loosely coordinated local revolts, all responding to the common stimuli of conquest, white encroachment, and Amherst's Indian policies, all animated by a religious revival with pan-Indian overtones, and all motivated by the desire to restore to North America a sympathetic European power to act as a counterpoise to the British and their numerous, aggressive colonists.[15]

CHAPTER 57

Amherst's Recall

AUTUMN 1763

Amherst's assumption that Detroit, Pittsburgh, and Niagara would hold out until the campaigns of 1764 could begin was one that seemed reasonable enough to a man sitting at a desk in New York City. The prospects seemed less certain at each of the three critical forts. The garrisons' survival depended most of all on their supplies of food, a factor far more significant than their stocks of weapons and ammunition. Because they were also heavily outnumbered by their besiegers, the garrisons needed reinforcements as well. Every skirmish took a toll beyond the direct loss of life: with each man wounded or killed, a heavier burden fell on the survivors, who still had to mount round-the-clock guard details and conduct local security patrols outside the walls. And yet if the needed reinforcements arrived without provisions adequate to sustain both themselves and the soldiers and refugees already in the forts, they were worse than no help at all, for they would inevitably deplete the existing food more rapidly than ever. Before the end of the summer, the tricky calculus of manpower and provisions would give the defenders at all three forts cause for gravest concern.

Captain James Dalyell's relief convoy reached Fort Detroit on July 28. Arriving with twenty bateaux and 260 men—including a variety of companies he had assembled en route from the 55th, 60th, and 80th Regiments, and a detachment of rangers under Major Robert Rogers—Dalyell brought few provisions but a massive desire to earn glory in battle. Because his position as the son of a baronet and as Amherst's aide-de-camp gave him clout disproportionate to his modest rank, Gladwin could not stop him from ordering the detachment he had brought to attack the Indians. At 2:30 in the morning on July 31 he led a sortie of 247 men out of the fort to attack Pontiac's camp. Less than an hour later, at a creek soon to be called Bloody Run, he marched them directly into Pontiac's ambush. When the survivors finally made it back to the fort at eight o'clock, 20 men had been killed, 35 wounded (3 of them seriously enough to die of their injuries soon thereafter), and about 100 had been captured. Dalyell, shot dead in the battle, had his heart cut out and his head impaled on a stake at the Indian camp.[1]

With the arrival of Dalyell's expedition, therefore, Gladwin found himself with twice as many mouths to feed as before and twice as badly off as ever. Had not the sloop *Michigan* brought a cargo of provisions from Niagara in June and the schooner *Huron* continued to land supplies in September and October, Gladwin would have had to abandon Detroit or see his men starve. As it was, his troops remained on short rations and so heavily outnumbered that, apart from patrols near the fort, they never again sought contact with the enemy. It was not British pressure that compelled Pontiac to raise the siege on October 15, but rather a combination of circumstances Pontiac could not control: the refusal of the French commandant in the Illinois Country to support the revolt, growing internal divisions among the Indians, and the necessity of beginning the winter hunt. No one in the Indian camp knew it, but on the day Pontiac finally offered a truce, Detroit had less than two weeks' supply of flour remaining and no prospect of replenishment.[2]

Although different in that it yielded a kind of qualified victory rather than an unequivocal defeat, the "relief" of Fort Pitt resembled that of Detroit. It was not until July 18 that Colonel Henry Bouquet succeeded in assembling 460 troops from the remnants of the 42nd, 60th, and 77th Regiments, plus a detachment of rangers. Finding troops fit to march was hard enough, but in the panicked Pennsylvania countryside it proved even more difficult for Bouquet to assemble provisions, cattle, horses, wagons, and teamsters for his troops to escort to Pittsburgh. Having begun late, the expedition proceeded slowly. Pennsylvania's assembly voted to raise 700 provincials to defend the backcountry only on July 6 and had not yet recruited enough men to garrison the forts along Forbes Road. To his great irritation ("I feel myself uterly abandoned by the very People I am ordered to protect") Bouquet therefore found it necessary to drop off redcoats, food, and ammunition at undermanned and inadequately supplied posts along the way. When the column reached Fort Ligonier, west of Laurel Ridge, on August 2, Bouquet probably had less than 400 men left to march the last forty miles to Pittsburgh. At Ligonier he paused long enough to abandon the wagons and convert 340 horses into a pack train to haul flour, then ordered his men to march for the

Forks on the fourth. Just after noon the next day, moving through hilly, forested country near Bushy Run Creek twenty-five miles from Fort Pitt, they walked into a trap. Within minutes they were fighting for their lives.[3]

The Shawnees, Delawares, Mingos, Wyandots, Ottawas, and Miamis who beset Bouquet's force had until lately been subjecting Ecuyer's garrison to a severe attack, at the height of which they fired on the defenders from the ditch immediately outside the walls of the fort. They had broken off that assault only to destroy the supply train that their scouts had informed them was heading for the Forks. They very nearly succeeded. Halted near the top of a rise called Edge Hill, dominated by higher ground nearby, Bouquet's men formed a perimeter around the packhorses and cattle and did their best to defend themselves. Without water in blistering heat, under fire by marksmen they could not see from one o'clock until dark, men and livestock alike suffered terribly. That night, knowing that his men could not long survive such torment, Bouquet made a desperate plan. In the center of the perimeter his men had constructed a breastwork from provision bags to shelter the wounded. After the Indian firing resumed the next day, acting on his order, two companies of light infantry abruptly withdrew from their positions on the west side of the perimeter as if to retreat within the breastwork. The Indians, seeing what looked like the beginnings of disintegration, broke from cover and charged the British line—only to find that the light infantry companies had not taken shelter within the breastwork, but instead had assumed firing positions on a ridge flanking the hillside. From there they delivered a volley at the warriors—exposed for the first time since the battle had begun—and then charged toward them with bayonets fixed. As the Indians turned to face their assailants, Bouquet quickly advanced two more companies from the perimeter. When they opened fire, the outmaneuvered and disorganized Indians dispersed into the woods.

When the battle ended, Bouquet's men were able to move to Bushy Run for water, but that was all. They had lost fifty men killed and sixty wounded, a quarter of their strength. The Indians had destroyed so many horses that Bouquet ordered the entire stock of flour destroyed in order to use the surviving animals to carry the wounded to Fort Pitt. The exhausted, battered column took three more days to limp the last twenty-five miles to Pittsburgh. There Bouquet quietly suspended his plan to "extirpate" the "vermin" that had so nearly exterminated him. Limited not only by the extreme insecurity of his position and the continuing illnesses of the Havana veterans in the ranks, but also by the demands of men in the 60th Regiment for the discharges that were due them, Bouquet never found it possible to patrol more than a mile from the fort. At length he did assemble a detachment to return to Fort Ligonier for supplies, and another convoy to escort Pittsburgh's women and children back east of the Alleghenies and return with more provisions. But that was all. The pack trains that brought the food Pittsburgh needed to survive the winter succeeded in making the trip only because the Indians abandoned operations against the fort and the road, left the area around the Forks, and reestablished their villages downriver in the Scioto River drainage. Like Detroit, Pittsburgh survived the winter of 1763–64 not because the British had broken the Indians' siege but because the Indians, no longer able to delay the winter's hunting, had lifted it.[4]

While Gladwin watched his supplies dwindle at Detroit and Bouquet tried to recuperate from his costly victory at Pittsburgh, the Senecas struck severe blows at the most important western post of all, Niagara. There geography was the critical factor, and the Senecas made masterful use of it. No supplies could pass from Canada or New York to Detroit, or indeed to any western location, without first being off-loaded at Fort Niagara, portaged around the falls over a twisting nine-mile road, and reembarked at a small fort on Lake Erie, near the mouth of Buffalo Creek. On September 14, where this trail skirted the edge of the ravine near a whirlpool called Devil's Hole, at least three hundred Geneseo Senecas, Ottawas, and Chippewas attacked a supply train and annihilated both the wagoners and their escort. When two companies of the 80th Regiment nearby tried to come to the rescue, half were killed or wounded. In all, seventy-two men died and eight survivors suffered wounds. Worse, if anything, than the casualties was the fact that the Indians now controlled the portage road, ending all efforts to resupply Detroit.

Weeks passed before the Niagara garrison achieved even a tenuous command of the portage, and even then the Senecas were able to attack a six hundred–man expeditionary force headed for Detroit on October 20, killing eight and wounding eleven. By this time the weather had grown so bad that communication over the lake was virtually impossible. The expedition intended for Detroit, its departure delayed by the attack, foundered in a storm on November 7; seventy men drowned. Thereafter efforts to resupply Detroit from Niagara had to be suspended, and only Pontiac's truce saved the fort. Major Gladwin held on, in the end, not because he received adequate supplies from his own army, but because the raising of the siege allowed him to send half his men back to Niagara and to buy enough food from the local habitants for those who stayed to survive the winter.[5]

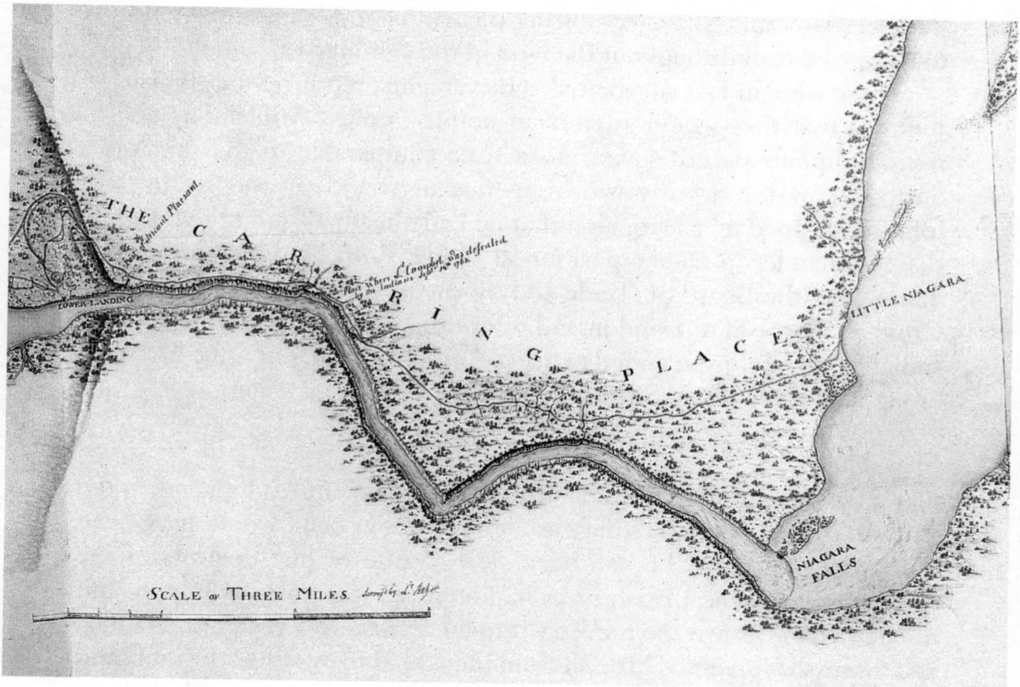

The Niagara portage. A British engineer's depiction shows the route along which cargoes had to be carried between Little Niagara, a port two miles above the Falls, to the Lower Landing at the foot of the last rapids, where water carriage could resume. Fort Niagara lies seven miles downstream to the north (left on this map). An inscription near the center of the image indicates the "Place where Lt Campbell was defeated by the Indians, Sept[r] 14th 1763"—the point at which the road ran closest to the edge of the cliff above the river. *Courtesy of the William L. Clements Library at the University of Michigan.*

Amid so much failure, the most promising prospect for the British in the fall of 1763 was the one diplomatic initiative Amherst had been willing to countenance—the conference Sir William Johnson held with delegates from the Six Nations (less the Geneseo Senecas) and the Caughnawaga Mohawks during September. There, at his new mansion, Johnson Hall, the northern superintendent appealed to Onondaga's self-interest to nudge the Confederacy from its posture of hostility-tinged neutrality into one of tentative cooperation. Alliance with the British would, Johnson argued, enable the Six Nations to reassert dominion over the Ohio Country and their breakaway dependents, the Delawares, Shawnees, and Mingos. It was an argument calculated to appeal to the assembled Iroquois chiefs, who agreed to negotiate with the belligerent Senecas and to cooperate militarily with the British by raiding against the Delawares and Shawnees during the winter and helping the redcoats to restore control throughout the west in the coming year.

These were in fact substantial achievements, but it remained clear to Johnson that they would amount to nothing unless Amherst agreed to resume diplomatic gift-giving on a scale comparable to that practiced during the war. Since it was obvious that he would never agree to that, Johnson stepped up a campaign that he had already begun to undermine the commander in chief's position at home. Both by direct correspondence with the Board of Trade and by encouraging his deputy, George Croghan, to travel to London and offer expert testimony on the crisis in Indian affairs, Johnson aimed to bring Amherst down, just as he had once brought down William Shirley.[6]

EVEN WITHOUT THE formidable enmity of Sir William Johnson, in the autumn of 1763 Amherst's days as commander in chief would have been numbered. Although he had been slow to inform his superiors of the Indian uprising, the British press had reported it as early as July 16, and the news had thrown the ministry into an uproar. To Egremont, Halifax, and Grenville it seemed little short of incredible that with eight thousand men under his command, Amherst had failed to keep a collection of naked savages from driving the British out of virtually every stronghold in the American interior. Indeed, by the end of the summer, with more than four hundred redcoats killed and an indeterminate number in captivity, with perhaps two thousand civilians dead and chaos engulfing every frontier from New York to North Carolina, it remained unclear that Amherst had even diminished the Indians' momentum. And that was not all that had gone wrong in America. Everywhere from Newfoundland to Fort Pitt, troops—and not the contemptible provincials of the late war, but His Majesty's troops, *regulars*—were mutinying or threatening to mutiny over reductions in pay and delays in the granting of discharges. Nowhere in America—not even in Pennsylvania and Virginia, the frontiers of which were actually under Indian attack—were colonial legislatures rallying to help the empire by raising troops. Nowhere was any legislature appropriating the money that Amherst desperately needed to suppress the insurrection.[7]

Meanwhile, the supreme commander scarcely had a friend, let alone a patron, left in the British government. Pitt was in opposition, Ligonier had been deprived of his most lucrative offices and all effective control over the army in March, and the duke of Cumberland had been incapacitated by a stroke that left him partially paralyzed and half-blind. When in August the earl of Egremont gave Amherst his long-sought permission to return home, however, he spared him the embarrassment of a formal dismissal by indicating only that His Majesty required advice on military affairs in America. Overjoyed, Amherst summoned Major General Thomas Gage down from Montréal, where he had marooned him as military governor in October 1760. Gage, equally happy to be spared a fourth Canadian winter, arrived at New York on the evening of Wednesday, November 16. Without ceremony Amherst handed over his papers, sketched the plans he had set in motion for the coming year's campaigns, and formally invested Gage with the supreme command of His Majesty's forces in North America. The next day, aboard the packet *Weasel* bound for Plymouth, we may suppose that Amherst heaved a sigh of relief as the coastline sank below the horizon. A man not prone to reflection, he probably wasted little time musing on his successor's prospects. Leaving a set of colonies he despised in the care of an officer he distrusted, in the midst of an rebellion he had not foreseen, Amherst was undoubtedly preoccupied with his own immediate future. He would have to minister to a mad wife and salvage a languishing estate; but at last he would receive his hero's reward. Only after he arrived in London would Sir Jeffery Amherst realize that he had been summoned, not to be feted as the conqueror of Canada, but to be blamed for a rebellion that—in his own mind, at least—had come out of thin air.[8]

PART VIII

Crisis and Reform

1764

Pontiac's War brings a new sense of urgency to George Grenville's efforts to deal with American affairs. The future of the army and the demand for revenue. The need for a coherent Indian policy and the Proclamation of 1763. The American Duties Act of 1764 and the dual necessity of taxation and control. The significance of the Currency Act. The colonists, confronting depression and political unrest, react ambiguously to Britain's reforms, while Gage prolongs Pontiac's War into 1765. The lessons of a pan-Indian rebellion.

CHAPTER 58

Death Reshuffles a Ministry

1763

THE LONDON PRESS broadcast the first news of Indian rebellion in July 1763, further clouding a political atmosphere heavy with the smoke of Wilkes's fires. The Triumvirate of Grenville, Halifax, and Egremont groped through the murk, recalling Amherst in the hope of averting more military calamities and accelerating plans for imperial reform in order to preserve order once the Indians had been pacified. As the news from the colonies worsened during the first three weeks of August and the London mob grew steadily more obstreperous, the ministry weakened and wavered. The king made no secret of his readiness to hand the government over to another leader, should a suitable candidate present himself. It was not until the morning of Sunday the twenty-first that George's fears of aggravating the crisis overrode his desire to give Grenville the sack. Summoning the prime minister to the palace at nine, the king announced that he had chosen not to alter existing arrangements. Whatever relief Grenville felt, however, lasted only until he reached Egremont's door and discovered that the earl had just suffered a heart attack. By nine that night he was dead.[1]

The secretary of state for the Southern Department could hardly have found a less opportune time to die, and not only because he was responsible for formulating colonial policy. The necessity of replacing him raised questions of patronage requiring royal assent, and that gave George III a fresh chance to eject Grenville from office in favor of a patriot minister capable of rising above party. The king's unsteady compass now swung toward Pitt, and he spent another week making overtures to the Great Commoner while consulting Bute for advice. He had every right to do these things, of course, and given the ordinary pace of eighteenth-century British politics, a week was not a long time to take. But a week was long enough to destroy the last vestiges of confidence between monarch and prime minister. When George at last understood that Pitt's terms for accepting office included giving the Treasury to Grenville's odious brother, the earl Temple—the man who had paid for John Wilkes's press—he decided once more that he would have to trust the incumbent. Grenville, for his part, decided that he could never trust the king again.

Two more weeks passed before the shuffling of offices finally ended. The earl of Halifax moved into the position for which his experience and preferences suited him, secretary of state for the South. John Montagu, fourth earl of Sandwich, took over as secretary for the North. The earl of Shelburne, president of the Board of Trade, had been so embarrassingly implicated in a plot to supplant Grenville with the duke of Bedford that he was forced to resign. This allowed Halifax to hand the presidency over to a protégé with an interest in American affairs, Wills Hill, earl of Hillsborough. Shelburne, with nowhere to go but the opposition, gravitated into an alliance with Pitt; Bedford, too powerful to be ignored, became lord president of the Privy Council. By mid-September sufficient equilibrium returned to the high politics of place and honor that the ministers could turn again to questions of imperial policy and order. That was none too soon. While the ministry sorted itself out, America had been turning into an issue no one could ignore.[2]

The previous ministry neglected the colonies until an Indian uprising had practically destroyed Britain's hold on the interior of North America, but from the fall of 1763 through the following spring Grenville and Halifax attended to reforming imperial relations with an intensity rarely seen before. They set out to create a secure and financially stable empire: to institute political order within the conquests, restore peace in the west, and use the prosperity of the older colonies to strengthen the empire as a whole. These were innovations, but Grenville and company were not making up a program out of whole cloth. The king himself had set the priorities according to which they acted. The pivot on which the new imperial relationship would turn, the army, was already in place. Since the beginning of the year the Board of Trade had been drafting plans for colonial reorganization. Every measure that Grenville and Halifax would propose reflected a consensus, broadly shared in Whitehall and Westminster, on the nature of the empire and Britain's power to control it. Halifax, who had been thinking about the colonies for fifteen years, was arguably the best man in Britain to direct reforms in the imperial relationship, and nobody knew more about taxation than Grenville.

And yet, for all that, the program that Halifax and Grenville proposed, which Parliament would pass into law and which the king would approve, would prove more energetic than coherent, setting the stage for disasters beside which the Indian insurrection would seem trivial. The reason why was simple. Down to virtually their last detail, the reforms reflected the legacies and the lessons of the Seven Years' War as construed at the highest levels of metropolitan power. Grenville and Halifax, in that regard, responded to current problems not on an ad hoc basis, but with a firm sense of historical context. Unfortunately for the empire's future, they had no equally well considered sense of how their reforms would interact with postwar conditions, nor—given those—any clear idea of how their initiative might appear to colonists whose understandings of the war and its lessons differed significantly from their own.

CHAPTER 59

An Urgent Search for Order

GRENVILLE AND HALIFAX CONFRONT THE NEED FOR REVENUE AND CONTROL

SUMMER–AUTUMN 1763

LIKE AN ELEVATION benchmark from which a surveyor begins his loop and to which he must return at its end, the ministers' planning for America started, and in time would conclude, with the British army. By the end of the summer few Americans and no Englishmen doubted that the redcoats were the colonies' best bulwark against Indian attacks. This in turn seemed to validate a decision taken at Whitehall near the end of 1762, seven months before anyone in Britain had heard of Pontiac, to maintain a large peacetime garrison in America. But Bute's ministry had decided to keep troops in the colonies for reasons that had less to do with the empire than with other—and at the time, seemingly more pressing—concerns. In late 1762 the prospect of demobilization posed devastating problems in parliamentary politics, and a permanent American army seemed to offer the only reasonable solution.

The army had expanded enormously during the war, ending with approximately 100,000 men under arms in 115 regiments.[1] To maintain such a force permanently was inconceivable financially, ideologically, and politically. With peace in the offing, virtually everyone from the duke of Newcastle to otherwise mute Tory squires on the Commons backbenches demanded severe reductions in the army and navy and rigid economy in government spending. A government that chose not to reduce the armed forces would be handing the opposition a club with which to beat it senseless. Yet to return the army to its prewar level of 49 regiments and 35,000 men was impossible, for two reasons.

First came the strategic necessity of securing the new empire. Peace was clearly going to leave Britain in possession of overseas territories, and alien populations, that would need to be policed internally and defended against foreign aggression. No one thought that seventy or eighty thousand former French subjects in Canada would long remain docile unless a substantial armed force remained to remind them of Britain's power. Nor did any minister seriously propose leaving the west to the Indians. In December 1762, no one knew what hell French traders and former officers might try to raise among their old clients and friends. The sensibleness of those fears seemed only to be confirmed in the following fall when it became clear how nearly simultaneous the attacks on the western posts had been, suggesting the obvious conclusion that French agents coordinated them all, in a great conspiracy to retain Louisiana and Illinois and regain control of the *pays d'en haut*. Immediate withdrawal from either Canada or the west was so unthinkable that, in formulating policy, no one even asked whether British forces should remain in America. The only real questions concerned how many battalions should be left, where they should be stationed, and how long they should stay. Factors other than imperial policy, however, would decree that the American garrison should be a permanent one.

The second, more significant, reason that the ministers decided in favor of a large peacetime force for the colonies was a matter of practicality and parliamentary management—which made it, of course, the most pressing concern of all. To demobilize the army to prewar levels would force hundreds of colonels, lieutenant colonels, and majors (not to mention hordes of captains and subalterns) into retirement on half pay. If the welfare of fifty thousand suddenly unemployed enlisted men caused the government little concern, the fate of fifteen hundred officers had the opposite effect, for the excellent reason that many of them either sat in Parliament or were the sons and brothers and nephews and cousins of men who did. No prudent minister, and certainly no patriot king, could let so many deserving gentlemen go unrewarded. But how could they be provided for in a financially responsible way? America held the answer, and the king himself found it.[2]

Like his grandfather and great-grandfather before him, George III took a keen interest in the army. He was determined to preserve it at levels of strength and readiness higher than those at which it had entered the Seven Years' War, and he dedicated considerable ingenuity to finding a way to do so while holding costs down to a politically manageable level. After careful thought and much labored calculation (sums never having been his strong suit), the king concluded that it would in fact be possible to maintain more than eighty regiments on active duty and still make "the expence . . . some hundred pounds cheaper than the establishment [had been] . . . in 1749."[3]

Two conditions had to be met in order to perform this improbable feat. First, every regiment would have to be reduced to a single battalion of five hundred men. The political advantages of more than halving the number of enlisted men on active service while maintaining nearly three-quarters of the army's current regiments—and therefore almost three-quarters of its officers—could hardly be missed. The king of course understood that perfectly, but his real interest in keeping so many under-strength battalions on active service was to render Britain more secure in the event of war. British patriotism could be relied upon to fill the ranks with recruits, as it had since 1756; but only his new-modeled army would insure enough trained officers and sergeants to lead them.

Second, a double obstacle had to be surmounted: finance, since keeping up eighty permanent regiments would necessarily cost more than the forty-nine regiments of 1749; and ideology, for Tories and opposition Whigs alike were sure to raise the traditional objections against enlarging the peacetime establishment. George's solution showed his genius in full flower, for it leveled both barriers with one deft stroke. It was simply this: there would be no expansion of the number of troops stationed *in Britain.* Twenty of the new battalions would be stationed in the American colonies (including the West Indies) and twelve would be added to the Irish establishment. Parliament would pay for these new garrisons only in 1763. Thereafter taxes on the colonies would support the troops stationed there, and the Irish Parliament would bear the expense of that island's new defenders.[4]

It was imperative that the colonies, not Parliament, pay for the American regiments. The furor over the cider excise, which contributed to Bute's departure from political life in April 1763, left no doubt about British ratepayers' enthusiasm for tax increases. Grenville knew that one of the biggest fights that awaited his government when the Commons reconvened in mid-November would come when the opposition moved to revise or repeal the cider tax. Faced with the responsibility for servicing a national debt that had practically doubled during the war and now approximated £146,000,000 sterling, the government literally could not afford to surrender any source of revenue. Grenville thought he might be able to modify the operation of the cider tax, but if the opposition wanted more than symbolic concessions and could assemble a majority in favor of repeal, the government would be overthrown on what amounted to a no-confidence vote. Given the drained state of the Treasury and the government's tenuous hold on its majority in the Commons, the minimum of £225,000 a year it would cost to keep twenty battalions in the colonies could not be added to the budget. But virtually everyone agreed that the Americans could comfortably bear such an expense, which worked out to substantially less than two shillings per capita, per annum.[5]

No British politician who had been awake for the past six years would have denied that the colonies benefited handsomely from the war. Army and navy expenditures in the colonies from 1756 through 1762 amounted to over six million pounds sterling, in addition to parliamentary reimbursements in excess of a million pounds paid directly to the colonial governments. This influx of credit and specie had enabled the Americans to double the volume of their imports from Britain during the conflict. Everybody knew, of course, that the colonists paid for their own governments and militia establishments. Yet they also knew that the colonists contributed to the support of the empire only by paying customs revenues on their trade, and the customs receipts barely covered the costs of collection. Moreover, the regiments were being stationed in America to protect Americans. Justice, no less than economic realism, decreed that the colonies should contribute modestly from their prosperity to relieve the burdens under which the metropolis now groaned.[6]

In fact Parliament had already taken a step toward enhancing collections from the colonial customs in the Revenue Act of 1762. This measure aimed at reducing the volume of smuggling by authorizing naval officers to assist customs officials, and by offering them incentives to do so energetically. In a way more or less typical of Bute's ministry, this measure had been passed only to be forgotten. In May 1763, however, Grenville revived it when he committed the Treasury to improving customs collections in the colonies and asked that the Privy Council direct the implementation of the act. The resulting Order in Council of June 1 foretold Grenville's determination to implant teeth in a system that colonial smugglers and corrupt, absentee customs officers had effectively defanged. In early July the Southern secretary put the colonial governors on notice that His Majesty expected the customs to be collected according to law and assigned forty-four Royal Navy vessels to aid in enforcement. Late that month, Grenville ordered all absentee customsmen to resume their posts in the colonies. Anyone who had not left Britain by August 31 would be dismissed from the service.[7]

Thus the push to collect revenues from colonial sources began, in a general way, during the summer of 1763. In September, however, when the ministers turned their full attention to reform, raising revenues in the colonies became a matter of first priority. If they understood nothing else about America, the ministers knew that an army engaged in suppressing an Indian rebellion would cost the Treasury more than an army tucked up in forts and barracks. They also knew that there were two ways to raise a colonial revenue. George Grenville decided to try both.

The most obvious, least troublesome means was merely to make the colonists pay what they already owed. That this would be Grenville's first priority was evident in his disposition to end the lackadaisical, corrupt collection of customs duties. It became unmistakable in an order he signed on October 4, directing that enforcement measures in American ports be carried out as strictly as in Britain, and recommending that the Admiralty establish a uniform system of vice-admiralty courts in the colonies, in order to make the seizure and sale of smuggled cargoes as efficient there as at home.[8]

The second way to raise a colonial revenue was to impose new taxes. This would be trickier to manage than the suppression of smuggling: whereas tightening up on customs enforcement could be accomplished by executive action, to create a new tax, or to adjust an old one, required the House of Commons to pass the necessary legislation—and Grenville was by no means certain of his majority. Moreover, he knew that American colonists would react at least as unfavorably to new taxes as British cider producers. Any political issue as potentially explosive as taxation had to be approached cautiously, and only after thorough study. Accordingly, late in August, Grenville ordered a subordinate to investigate how revenues might be enhanced by adjusting the rate of an existing tax on molasses imported to the mainland from the West Indies. In early September he asked two other assistants to draft a bill for Parliament's consideration, by which the colonists could be taxed directly through revenue stamps—a small levy of the sort that Englishmen paid, almost unwittingly, whenever they undertook legal processes or bought newspapers, playing cards, and other mundane items.[9]

Grenville had no intention of immediately introducing his revenue measures when the House of Commons began its winter session on November 15. He knew very well what challenges lay ahead, and he understood that two impending struggles—the opposition's efforts to modify or repeal the cider tax, and the inevitable brouhaha over John Wilkes—would make it clear whether his ministry had the parliamentary majority and the royal support needed to enact colonial reforms. By spring either his ministry would have gone down to defeat, or the dust would have settled enough to allow him and his colleagues to proceed with vigor. In the meantime Grenville would be content to defer action on the revenue measures and allow his subordinates to refine proposals and draft the necessary legislation. More immediate concerns growing out of the war and the Indian rebellion, however, would not wait, and could at any rate be handled by executive action. To those urgent matters the new secretary of state for the South, Lord Halifax, turned his attention.

In a cabinet meeting on September 16, Halifax presented his plan for organizing the American conquests into four new colonies and a vast interior Indian preserve. The scheme he proposed, to be implemented by royal proclamation, incorporated suggestions from two drafts that dated from early 1763: one prepared at Egremont's request by a former governor of Georgia named Henry Ellis, and the other written mainly by John Pownall on behalf of the Board of Trade. The cabinet had discussed both plans back in July, suggested modifications, and directed the board to combine them into a single document. The board proceeded in a characteristically leisurely way until August, when news of Pontiac's Rebellion moved Pownall to urge the cabinet to issue the proclamation immediately and reassure the Indians that Britain had no designs on their lands. At that moment, of course, the intricate tasks of ministerial reorganization had to be addressed; but once Halifax presented the scheme on September 16, things moved quickly. By October 4 the earl of Hillsborough, the board's new president, had touched up the draft, run the document by the attorney general for legal amendments, and returned it to Halifax. Three days later, after the Privy Council gave its pro forma approval, the king officially promulgated it. The Royal Proclamation of 1763 marked Britain's first effort to impose institutional form on the conquests, and the Grenville ministry's first attempt to outline a policy for the empire. Under the circumstances it was probably better than nothing. But that did not make it a good start for the organization of the postwar empire.[10]

Essentially the ministry attacked the problem of organizing the conquests at the margins, deferring the central issues for later consideration. The map of the proclamation's new civil governments made this peripheral approach clear. North of New England and New York the French settlements along the St. Lawrence, as high as the Montréal district, became the new province of Québec. To the south and west of Georgia the proclamation erected two new provinces: East Florida, consisting of the peninsula from the Atlantic to the Apalachicola River; and West Florida, from the Apalachicola to the Mississippi between 31° north latitude and the Gulf of Mexico. All three colonies were to operate under English law and to be organized as soon as possible according to the familiar model of royal provinces elsewhere, with appointed governors and elected assemblies.[11]

Everything else—from the Great Lakes basin to Florida, and from the Mississippi to the western slope of the Appalachians—was reserved for the use of the Indians. No colonial governments were to grant lands in this zone, no surveyors were to operate there, and no negotiations were to be undertaken for purchase of Indian titles within it except by the Crown's designated representatives. Whites were forbidden to settle beyond the Appalachian ridge, and all those presently living there were "forthwith to remove themselves." Although the proclamation decreed that "the trade with the said [western] Indians shall be free and open to all our subjects whatever," it would not be unregulated. Traders could pass beyond the mountains only with "a license for carrying on such trade, from the Governor or commander in chief of any of our colonies respectively where such person shall reside." The proclamation established no civil government for this vast inland realm. The only Crown representatives within it would be the commanders of whatever interior forts the king might choose to maintain and whatever representatives the two Indian superintendents would station there. Since British military officers could enforce the law over civilians only at the direction of civil magistrates, the proclamation required the commanders to arrest all fugitives from justice who fled to the Indian country, "and to send them under a proper guard to the colony where the crime was committed of which they shall stand accused, in order to take their trial for the same."

Halifax wanted to impose order on the chaotic interior of North America and intended the proclamation only as the start of a lengthy process. Yet the document's improvised, impermanent character promised anything but a satisfactory beginning. The proclamation remained vague on too many critical points. It did not make it clear, for example, how the commandant of a fort in (say) the Illinois Country was supposed to know that a white man who appeared among the local Indians was a fugitive from justice in Pennsylvania—or how he would transport the suspect to Philadelphia to stand trial. Nor was it evident how the commanders of western posts were supposed to deal with the local French and métis inhabitants, whom the diplomats at Paris had rendered British subjects with a few deft strokes of the quill. Were they to remove themselves forthwith to Québec, which their ancestors had left two or three generations earlier? Suppose one of them murdered an Indian: how, where, and by whom would he or she be tried?

If these were not headaches enough, there was the difficulty of the French already living in Québec. The Treaty of Paris had guaranteed them security in their property and the right to practice their Catholic faith unmolested. But the proclamation stipulated that the new colonies

By the KING,

A PROCLAMATION.

GEORGE R.

WHEREAS We have taken into Our Royal Conſideration the extenſive and valuable Acquiſitions in *America*, ſecured to Our Crown by the late Definitive Treaty of Peace, concluded at *Paris* the Tenth Day of *February* laſt; and being deſirous, that all Our loving Subjects, as well of Our Kingdoms as of Our Colonies in *America*, may avail themſelves, with all convenient Speed, of the great Benefits and Advantages which muſt accrue therefrom to their Commerce, Manufactures, and Navigation; We have thought fit, with the Advice of Our Privy Council, to iſſue this Our Royal Proclamation, hereby to publiſh and declare to all Our loving Subjects, that We have, with the Advice of Our ſaid Privy Council, granted Our Letters Patent under Our Great Seal of *Great Britain*, to erect within the Countries and Iſlands ceded and confirmed to Us by the ſaid Treaty, Four diſtinct and ſeparate Governments, ſtiled and called by the Names of *Quebec*, *Eaſt Florida*, *Weſt Florida*, and *Grenada*, and limited and bounded as follows; *viz.*

Firſt. The Government of *Quebec*, bounded on the *Labrador* Coaſt by the River *St. John*, and from thence by a Line drawn from the Head of that River through the Lake *St. John* to the South End of the Lake nigh *Piſſin*; from whence the ſaid Line croſſing the River *St. Lawrence* and the Lake *Champlain* in Forty five Degrees of North Latitude, paſſes along the High Lands which divide the Rivers that empty themſelves into the ſaid River *St. Lawrence*, from thoſe which fall into the Sea; and alſo along the North Coaſt of the *Baye des Chaleurs*, and the Coaſt of the Gulph of *St. Lawrence* to Cape *Roſieres*, and from thence croſſing the Mouth of the River *St. Lawrence* by the Weſt End of the Iſland of *Anticoſti*, terminates at the aforeſaid River of *St. John*.

Secondly. The Government of *Eaſt Florida*, bounded to the Weſtward by the Gulph of *Mexico*, and the *Apalachicola* River; to the Northward, by a Line drawn from that Part of the ſaid River where the *Chatahouchee* and *Flint* Rivers meet, to the Source of *St. Mary's* River, and by the Courſe of the ſaid River to the *Atlantick* Ocean; and to the Eaſtward and Southward, by the *Atlantick* Ocean, and the Gulph of *Florida*, including all Iſlands within Six Leagues of the Sea Coaſt.

Thirdly. The Government of *Weſt Florida*, bounded to the Southward by the Gulph of *Mexico*, including all Iſlands within Six Leagues of the Coaſt from the River *Apalachicola* to Lake *Pontchartrain*; to the Weſtward by the ſaid Lake, the Lake *Maurepas*, and the River *Miſſiſſippi*; to the Northward, by a Line drawn due Eaſt from that Part of the River *Miſſiſſippi* which lies in Thirty one Degrees North Latitude, to the River *Apalachicola* or *Chatahouchee*; and to the Eaſtward by the ſaid River.

Fourthly. The Government of *Grenada*, comprehending the Iſland of that Name, together with the *Grenadines*, and the Iſlands of *Dominico*, *St. Vincents*, and *Tobago*.

And, to the End that the open and free Fiſhery of Our Subjects may be extended to and carried on upon the Coaſt of *Labrador* and the adjacent Iſlands, We have thought fit, with the Advice of Our ſaid Privy Council, to put all that Coaſt, from the River *St. John's* to *Hudſon's Streights*, together with the Iſlands of *Anticoſti* and *Madelaine*, and all other ſmaller Iſlands lying upon the ſaid Coaſt, under the Care and Inſpection of Our Governor of *Newfoundland*.

We have alſo, with the Advice of Our Privy Council, thought fit to annex the Iſlands of *St. John's*, and *Cape Breton* or *Iſle Royale*, with the leſſer Iſlands adjacent thereto, to Our Government of *Nova Scotia*.

We have alſo, with the Advice of Our Privy Council aforeſaid, annexed to Our Province of *Georgia* all the Lands lying between the Rivers *Attamaha* and *St. Mary's*.

And whereas it will greatly contribute to the ſpeedy ſettling Our ſaid new Governments, that Our loving Subjects ſhould be informed of Our Paternal Care for the Security of the Liberties and Properties of thoſe who are and ſhall become Inhabitants thereof; We have thought fit to publiſh and declare, by this Our Proclamation, that We have, in the Letters Patent under Our Great Seal of *Great Britain*, by which the ſaid Governments are conſtituted, given expreſs Power and Direction to Our Governors of Our ſaid Colonies reſpectively, that ſo ſoon as the State and Circumſtances of the ſaid Colonies will admit thereof, they ſhall, with the Advice and Conſent of the Members of Our Council, ſummon and call General Aſſemblies within the ſaid Governments reſpectively, in ſuch Manner and Form as is uſed and directed in thoſe Colonies and Provinces in *America*, which are under Our immediate Government; and We have alſo given Power to the ſaid Governors, with the Conſent of Our ſaid Councils, and the Repreſentatives of the People, ſo to be ſummoned as aforeſaid, to make, conſtitute, and ordain Laws, Statutes, and Ordinances for the Publick Peace, Welfare, and Good Government of Our ſaid Colonies, and of the People and Inhabitants thereof, as near as may be agreeable to the Laws of *England*, and under ſuch Regulations and Reſtrictions as are uſed in other Colonies: And in the mean Time, and until ſuch Aſſemblies can be called as aforeſaid, all Perſons inhabiting in, or reſorting to Our ſaid Colonies, may confide in Our Royal Protection for the Enjoyment of the Benefit of the Laws of Our Realm of *England*; for which Purpoſe, We have given Power under Our Great Seal to the Governors of Our ſaid Colonies reſpectively, to erect and conſtitute, with the Advice of Our ſaid Councils reſpectively, Courts of Judicature and Publick Juſtice, within Our ſaid Colonies, for the hearing and determining all Cauſes, as well Criminal as Civil, according to Law and Equity, and as near as may be agreeable to the Laws of *England*, with Liberty to all Perſons who may think themſelves aggrieved by the Sentences of ſuch Courts, in all Civil Caſes, to appeal, under the uſual Limitations and Reſtrictions, to Us in Our Privy Council.

We have alſo thought fit, with the Advice of Our Privy Council as aforeſaid, to give unto the Governors and Councils of Our ſaid Three New Colonies upon the Continent, full Power and Authority to ſettle and agree with the Inhabitants of Our ſaid New Colonies, or with any other Perſons who ſhall reſort thereto, for ſuch Lands, Tenements, and Hereditaments, as are now, or hereafter ſhall be in Our Power to diſpoſe of, and them to grant to any ſuch Perſon or Perſons, upon ſuch Terms, and under ſuch moderate Quit-Rents, Services, and Acknowledgements as have been appointed and ſettled in Our other Colonies, and under ſuch other Conditions as ſhall appear to Us to be neceſſary and expedient for the Advantage of the Grantees, and the Improvement and Settlement of Our ſaid Colonies.

And whereas We are deſirous, upon all Occaſions, to teſtify Our Royal Senſe and Approbation of the Conduct and Bravery of the Officers and Soldiers of Our Armies, and to reward the ſame, We do hereby command and impower Our Governors of Our ſaid Three New Colonies, and all other Our Governors of Our ſeveral Provinces on the Continent of *North America*, to grant, without Fee or Reward, to ſuch Reduced Officers as have ſerved in *North America* during the late War, and to ſuch Private Soldiers as have been or ſhall be diſbanded in *America*, and are actually reſiding there, and ſhall perſonally apply for the ſame, the following Quantities of Lands, ſubject at the Expiration of Ten Years to the ſame Quit-Rents as other Lands are ſubject to in the Province within which they are granted, as alſo ſubject to the ſame Conditions of Cultivation and Improvement; *viz.*

To every Perſon having the Rank of a Field Officer, Five thouſand Acres.—To every Captain, Three thouſand Acres.—To every Subaltern or Staff Officer, Two thouſand Acres.—To every Non-Commiſſion Officer, Two hundred Acres.—To every Private Man, Fifty Acres.

We do likewiſe authorize and require the Governors and Commanders in Chief of all Our ſaid Colonies upon the Continent of *North America*, to grant the like Quantities of Land, and upon the ſame Conditions, to ſuch Reduced Officers of Our Navy, of like Rank, as ſerved on Board Our Ships of War in *North America* at the Times of the Reduction of *Louiſbourg* and *Quebec* in the late War, and who ſhall perſonally apply to Our reſpective Governors for ſuch Grants.

And whereas it is juſt and reaſonable, and eſſential to Our Intereſt and the Security of Our Colonies, that the ſeveral Nations or Tribes of *Indians*, with whom We are connected, and who live under Our Protection, ſhould not be moleſted or diſturbed in the Poſſeſſion of ſuch Parts of Our Dominions and Territories as, not having been ceded to, or purchaſed by Us, are reſerved to them, or any of them, as their Hunting Grounds; We do therefore, with the Advice of Our Privy Council, declare it to be Our Royal Will and Pleaſure, that no Governor or Commander in Chief in any of Our Colonies of *Quebec*, *Eaſt Florida*, or *Weſt Florida*, do preſume, upon any Pretence whatever, to grant Warrants of Survey, or paſs any Patents for Lands beyond the Bounds of their reſpective Governments, as deſcribed in their Commiſſions; as alſo, that no Governor or Commander in Chief in any of Our other Colonies or Plantations in *America*, do preſume, for the preſent, and until Our further Pleaſure be known, to grant Warrants of Survey, or paſs Patents for any Lands beyond the Heads or Sources of any of the Rivers which fall into the *Atlantick* Ocean from the Weſt and North Weſt, or upon any Lands whatever, which, not having been ceded to, or purchaſed by Us as aforeſaid, are reſerved to the ſaid *Indians*, or any of them.

And We do further declare it to be Our Royal Will and Pleaſure, for the preſent as aforeſaid, to reſerve under Our Sovereignty, Protection, and Dominion, for the Uſe of the ſaid *Indians*, all the Lands and Territories not included within the Limits of Our ſaid Three New Governments, or within the Limits of the Territory granted to the *Hudſon's Bay* Company, as alſo all the Lands and Territories lying to the Weſtward of the Sources of the Rivers which fall into the Sea from the Weſt and North Weſt, as aforeſaid; and We do hereby ſtrictly forbid, on Pain of Our Diſpleaſure, all Our loving Subjects from making any Purchaſes or Settlements whatever, or taking Poſſeſſion of any of the Lands above reſerved, without Our eſpecial Leave and Licence for that Purpoſe firſt obtained.

And We do further ſtrictly enjoin and require all Perſons whatever, who have either wilfully or inadvertently ſeated themſelves upon any Lands within the Countries above deſcribed, or upon any other Lands, which, not having been ceded to, or purchaſed by Us, are ſtill reſerved to the ſaid *Indians* as aforeſaid, forthwith to remove themſelves from ſuch Settlements.

And whereas great Frauds and Abuſes have been committed in the purchaſing Lands of the *Indians*, to the great Prejudice of Our Intereſts, and to the great Diſſatiſfaction of the ſaid *Indians*; in order therefore to prevent ſuch Irregularities for the future, and to the End that the *Indians* may be convinced of Our Juſtice, and determined Reſolution to remove all reaſonable Cauſe of Diſcontent, We do, with the Advice of Our Privy Council, ſtrictly enjoin and require, that no private Perſon do preſume to make any Purchaſe from the ſaid *Indians* of any Lands reſerved to the ſaid *Indians*, within thoſe Parts of Our Colonies where We have thought proper to allow Settlement; but that if, at any Time, any of the ſaid *Indians* ſhould be inclined to diſpoſe of the ſaid Lands, the ſame ſhall be purchaſed only for Us, in Our Name, at ſome Publick Meeting or Aſſembly of the ſaid *Indians* to be held for that Purpoſe by the Governor or Commander in Chief of Our Colonies reſpectively, within which they ſhall lie; and in caſe they ſhall lie within the Limits of any Proprietary Government, they ſhall be purchaſed only for the Uſe and in the Name of ſuch Proprietaries, conformable to ſuch Directions and Inſtructions as We or they ſhall think proper to give for that Purpoſe: And We do, by the Advice of Our Privy Council, declare and enjoin, that the Trade with the ſaid *Indians* ſhall be free and open to all Our Subjects whatever; provided that every Perſon, who may incline to trade with the ſaid *Indians*, do take out a Licence for carrying on ſuch Trade from the Governor or Commander in Chief of any of Our Colonies reſpectively, where ſuch Perſon ſhall reſide; and alſo give Security to obſerve ſuch Regulations as We ſhall at any Time think fit, by Ourſelves or by Our Commiſſaries to be appointed for this Purpoſe, to direct and appoint for the Benefit of the ſaid Trade; and We do hereby authorize, enjoin, and require the Governors and Commanders in Chief of all Our Colonies reſpectively, as well Thoſe under Our immediate Government as Thoſe under the Government and Direction of Proprietaries, to grant ſuch Licences without Fee or Reward, taking eſpecial Care to inſert therein a Condition, that ſuch Licence ſhall be void, and the Security forfeited, in caſe the Perſon, to whom the ſame is granted, ſhall refuſe or neglect to obſerve ſuch Regulations as We ſhall think proper to preſcribe as aforeſaid.

And We do further expreſly enjoin and require all Officers whatever, as well Military as Thoſe employed in the Management and Direction of *Indian* Affairs within the Territories reſerved as aforeſaid for the Uſe of the ſaid *Indians*, to ſeize and apprehend all Perſons whatever, who, ſtanding charged with Treaſons, Miſpriſons of Treaſon, Murders, or other Felonies or Miſdemeanors, ſhall fly from Juſtice, and take Refuge in the ſaid Territory, and to ſend them under a proper Guard to the Colony where the Crime was committed of which they ſtand accuſed, in order to take their Tryal for the ſame.

Given at Our Court at *Saint James's*, the Seventh Day of *October*, One thouſand ſeven hundred and ſixty three, in the Third Year of Our Reign.

GOD ſave the KING.

LONDON:
Printed by *Mark Baskett*, Printer to the King's moſt Excellent Majeſty; and by the Aſſigns of *Robert Baskett*. 1763.

The Proclamation of 1763. This broadside, issued in London on October 7, 1763, officially announced the government's plans for dealing with the conquests. It also—in light of reports from America detailing the Indian uprising—made public a high degree of official desperation in the face of spreading chaos. Very few of its long, detailed provisions would serve the purposes intended. *Courtesy of the William L. Clements Library at the University of Michigan.*

were to be organized "agreeable to the laws of England," and those laws forbade Catholics from voting and holding civil office. Halifax and his colleagues wanted the new colonies to attract English-speaking Protestant colonists, who preferred to settle where they enjoyed the protections of the common law and the right to tax themselves according to British tradition. But in 1763 Québec had only a handful of Anglophone inhabitants. Did His Majesty's government actually intend to constitute a few hundred carpetbagging Anglo-Americans as the body politic of Québec and permanently disfranchise eighty thousand Québecois? Those Québecois had long experience with, and implicit faith in, a legal system based on Roman law traditions; did His Majesty's ministers really intend to substitute wholesale a common law that the French neither understood nor trusted?

The problems of dealing with Anglo-American colonists beyond the Appalachians would be no easier to solve than any of those affecting the French. A boundary inscribed along the Appalachian crest did nothing to divide existing enclaves of white settlement—some of which were completely legitimate—from Indian hunting grounds. How was the army supposed to deal with settlers who refused to leave? Or with the white hunters who ranged across the mountains in search of game, but who were uninterested in settlement? If white interlopers refused to leave voluntarily, were the Indians entitled to deal with them according to Indian notions of justice? In what amounted to a state of nature, the Indians had as good a theoretical claim to jurisdiction as anyone else, and more real ability to exercise it. But even supposing that all trans-Appalachian whites could somehow be peaceably expelled, no proclamation could contravene the social forces that had propelled them westward in the first place. And that raised the related issue of land speculation. The proclamation forbade colonial governments to make land grants beyond the Appalachian crest, but it could not extinguish the claims of those colonies like Virginia and Connecticut, whose patents extended to the Pacific. Indeed, in a typically contradictory way, it opened a loophole that would allow them to apply for exemptions.

For among its several provisions, the proclamation also announced the king's generous intention to grant lands to "such reduced officers as have served in North America during the late war, and to such private soldiers as have been or shall be disbanded in America, and are actually residing there and shall personally apply for the same" to any colonial governor. The amounts of land stipulated—five thousand acres for field officers, three thousand for captains, two thousand for subalterns and staff officers, two hundred for sergeants and corporals, and fifty for privates—added up to substantial amounts, more than enough to whet the appetite of speculators willing to buy up the warrants of men who wanted the rewards of their service but did not intend personally to take up land in the wilderness. Halifax intended that these grants should be made only within the bounds of the three new provinces or, in the case of the preexisting ones, within the limits of the Proclamation Line; and that they should go to veterans of the regular army. But the language of the passage was vague enough to admit the possibility that grants would be possible anywhere within the limits of the colonies and open to provincials as well as regulars. Given the enormous numbers of men who had served as provincials and the expansive patents of colonies like Virginia and Connecticut, provinces full of enthusiastic speculators, these provisions promised to create vast complications for a king whose stated wish was only "to testify our royal sense and approbation of the conduct and bravery of the officers and soldiers of our armies, and to reward the same."[12]

Thus the issue of western land speculation lay like a trip wire ahead, waiting to trigger an explosion that could injure not grubby squatters and half-savage hunters, but elite figures: gentlemen whose political connections extended into the Privy Council itself. Partnerships of investors like the Ohio Company could hardly be expected to abandon their plans to profit from the west, and it was absolutely predictable that their shareholders in Britain (including, for example, the duke of Bedford) would seek to have the limits on western settlement lifted. The proclamation's own provisions, in short, guaranteed that the line prohibiting settlement in the American west would be politicized—in Britain. If there was no way to predict the outcome of the struggles that would ensue, it did not take a prophet to foresee that so long as the line remained in place the stakes resting on its removal would rise; and that ministers committed to limiting white settlement would sooner or later be called to account.

These problems, while unforeseen, were hardly unforeseeable. Halifax, who proposed the document that would create so many difficulties for himself and his successors, was not only intelligent, conscientious, and politically sophisticated, but thoroughly versed in American affairs. Why the proclamation reads as it does cannot, therefore, be explained by the usual factors of ignorance, unconcern, and sloth. Rather the proclamation's problematic elements arose from the earnest, urgent desire of Halifax and his colleagues to restore peace and create order in America, especially in relations with the Indians. Because Halifax, particularly, understood the proclamation as a first step toward placing Indian relations on a firm foundation, immediately after its promulgation he began to concentrate on reforming the Indian trade. The provisions of this plan reveal more of how he intended to restructure relations between the colonies, the Indians, and the metropolis.

By October 19, Halifax had sketched the outlines of an Indian program, which he turned over to the Board of Trade to elaborate and refine. Although the board would work on a draft all winter and the ministry would approve it only in early July, the outlines were clear enough from the beginning. The essence of the plan was to exclude both the colonial governments and the commander in chief from participating in Indian affairs, and to turn their management over entirely to the northern and southern superintendents. Trade would be carried on at specified locations, either in forts (in the northern department) or in designated Indian towns (in the southern department), where representatives of the superintendents would insure fair treatment for the Indians, provide necessary services, and adjudicate disputes. The expense of operating this system would be covered entirely by taxes on the Indian trade. Like the revenue measures Grenville was preparing, these reforms would have to be enacted by Parliament, so planning proceeded on the assumption that they would be introduced after the ministry was sure of its majority, and of the king's support.[13]

Halifax's organizational measures and Grenville's plans for raising revenue had evolved into a definable colonial policy in the fall of 1763. But no theory, no vision of empire, dictated that policy's shape. Rather its pattern arose from the Seven Years' War, which had created the problems the ministers were trying to solve and taught them the lessons that directed their attentions and limited their choices. The war had left behind in North America a large, dispersed army, no longer particularly effective, but voracious of funds nonetheless; a powerful (although no longer viceregal) commander in chief, whose misguided intervention in Indian affairs had precipitated a costly, embarrassing insurrection; and a set of troublesome commitments in the Easton Treaty of 1758, by which the British had promised to withdraw from the west and promote a vigorous trade among the region's tribes. In light of these legacies, Halifax's prohibition of western settlement under the Proclamation of 1763, the recall of Amherst as commander in chief, and the approval of a plan to give the Indian superintendents untrammeled authority over the Indian trade made perfect sense.[14]

The lessons of the war, similarly, directed Grenville's attention to revenue measures that would leave as little as possible to the discretion of American assemblies—legislatures that had demonstrated the quality of their commitment to the empire when they eagerly opened their hands to Parliament's subsidies in 1758, after years of tightfisted refusal to contribute to the common cause. The lessons of the war encouraged Grenville to concentrate on the elimination of smuggling, which he (like Pitt) believed had prolonged the conflict and which now denied income to his Treasury, even as the smugglers remained openly contemptuous of British authority. And the lessons of the war, finally, encouraged both Grenville and Halifax to conceive of the great new empire in strategic terms, as an entity to be directed from Whitehall according to British policy aims. To allow the colonies to return to their old, slovenly, parochial ways would in effect permit the colonists to define the relationship of the Indians to the empire, allowing Americans to benefit from Britain's protection without contributing anything in return. All that, inevitably, would invite disasters like the current insurrection to recur, give the designing French carte blanche to stir up more revolts, and hamstring imperial officers when they tried to restore order and security. And those, surely, were outcomes that no responsible minister could tolerate.

CHAPTER 60

The American Duties Act

(THE SUGAR ACT)

1764

AS EXPERIENCE rather than theory engendered its plans for reform, so the ministry implemented its program less systematically than opportunistically, as it became politic to do so. Just in the way Grenville expected, the opposition launched two major attacks during the Commons' winter session: one based on discontentment with the cider tax, the other arising from unease at the way the government had employed a general warrant against John Wilkes without regard for parliamentary privilege. That the ministry expected these to be its great tests was evident from the start of the session. The king's opening speech, which Grenville wrote, emphasized the need for attending to "the heavy debts contracted in the course of the late war"; a royal message to the Commons, also Grenville's handiwork, asked the M.P.s to determine if Wilkes ought to be deprived of his seat in the House, and hence of parliamentary privilege. To set the agenda, however, was not to control the debates, and William Pitt determined to seize what seemed a glittering opportunity to bring down Grenville's ministry. Beside him stood Charles Townshend, whom some thought Pitt's peer in eloquence, and who many believed would inherit his political mantle.[1]

Despite Pitt's and Townshend's success in shifting the debate from Wilkes's rather nasty behavior to the abstract issues of liberty of the press and freedom from arbitrary arrest, the government retained comfortable margins in the early votes. Moreover, at Christmastime, Wilkes did Grenville the enormous favor of fleeing to France, and on January 19 the House, finding him in contempt, voted his expulsion. But the government's majority waned in late January and early February when Grenville defended the cider tax, beating down a critical resolution to modify it by just twenty votes. The opposition, scenting blood, mounted an all-out effort to overthrow the ministry in mid-February, on the grounds that it had abused its power in the use of general warrants. Such drastic measures, smacking as they did of despotism, worried many independent M.P.s who had little regard for Wilkes but harbored enormous affection for Pitt. Yet in the end not even the Great Commoner's speeches could carry the day, and a resolution that would have declared general warrants unconstitutional failed by ten votes. Having thus retained control despite an opposition challenge "beyond all example and belief," Grenville could propose his own legislative program—and indeed could do so with great confidence, for at the height of the debates the king had finally assured him that he would support the ministry, come what might. The independents who had been following Pitt's lead reassumed their accustomed posture of docility, and Grenville's majority swelled to comfortable dimensions at last.[2]

In February, Grenville showed, the hard way, that he could hold a majority in the House of Commons. He had squared off with William Pitt in debate; watched him take the constitutional high ground; ceded him the votes of the independents; and won. In March, Grenville therefore showed what he could do in another way when, at the zenith of self-confident strength, he introduced the colonial measures over which his subordinates had labored for months. On the ninth, Budget Day, he outlined the whole scope of his revenue program to a House of Commons that responded with applause and only a few insuppressible yawns. ("Brevity was not his failing," Horace Walpole quipped, but granted that Grenville's three-hour speech showed "art and ability too.") Sure of support from M.P.s and king alike, the prime minister now behaved like a man with a mission, submitting measures too detailed to be immediately comprehended in a tone that did not invite discussion. "This hour," he told the House, "is a very serious one. France is in great distress at present, greater even than ours. Happy circumstance for us, as we are little able to afford another war, we now have peace; let us make the best use of it."[3]

In the end Parliament passed every measure Grenville put before it, with small discussion and huge majorities. In part this was because the opposition had already failed to overthrow the government and its leading spokesmen had departed—Pitt in collapse retreated to his estate in Kent, while the mercurial Townshend went up to Cambridge for a brief sulk and some extended reflection on how he might most advantageously offer his services to the ministry. But the silence of the opposition also spoke a more resounding truth, which was that no significant segment of the Commons disagreed with anything Grenville proposed. As Israel Mauduit, one of the agents representing Massachusetts's interests to the House of Commons, reported,

> there did not seem to be a single man in Parliament, who thought that the conquered provinces ought to be left without Troops, or that England after having run so deeply in Debt for the conquering of these provinces, by which Stability & Security is given to all the American Governments, should now tax itself for the maintenance of them. The only Difference of opinion . . . was that Mr Grenville said he did not expect that America should bear more than a good part of this expense; whereas other leading Members not of the Ministry said it ought to bear the whole.[4]

The Commons consolidated all but one of Grenville's measures—a stamp tax that the prime minister proposed and then withdrew, in order to give the colonies' agents time to comment and officials in the Treasury a chance to collect needed information—into an omnibus measure, the American Duties Act of 1764, and passed it on March 22. The Lords concurred with even less debate and the king gave his approval on April 5. From the perspective of British politicians, the act's salient features were the speed of its passage (less than two weeks) and the size of the government's majority (nearly three to one) in the House of Commons. None of the M.P.s seemed especially concerned that it would radically revise the relationship between Britain and the colonies. But for the colonists, who first learned of it in May, nothing could have been more significant than the new law's contents.

Americans remember the American Duties Act of 1764 as the Sugar Act because it emphasized molasses and sugar duties, but this is as much a misnomer today as it was when the colonists coined it. In fact the bill contained a variety of provisions, all of which Grenville intended to work together to help resolve the problems of finance and control that plagued the postwar empire. While in form the act was a replacement for the expiring Molasses Act of 1733, it went well beyond any previous mercantilist statute. Its many sections included three kinds of measures: those intended to make customs enforcement more effective, those that placed new duties on items widely consumed in America, and those that adjusted old rates in such a way as to maximize revenues.

In the first category fell the act's most complicated provisions. Some sought to eliminate corruption in the customs service—for example, by requiring governors to take oaths promising to uphold the law, and by threatening dishonest customs officials with severe punishments, including dismissal, heavy fines, and disqualification from future appointments. Most of the act's new regulations, however, afforded protections to make the customsmen more secure in their jobs, or to give them tools to detect and suppress smuggling. From the customs officers' standpoint, the most important of these provisions limited the risks they ran when they made mistakes. Merchants or ship captains wrongfully accused of smuggling had always been able to sue the customs officers who had seized their property or ships, and colonial juries often subjected errant customsmen to heavy damage judgments and fines, even when they had acted in good faith on faulty information. The American Duties Act decreed that juries finding customs officers guilty of making illegal seizures could award damages not in excess of twopence and impose fines of no more than one shilling, and even forbade judges to charge court costs to customs officers who had lost suits. Accused officers had only to prove they had probable cause to suspect smuggling when they made illegal seizures. Neither the extent to which any customsman violated the law nor any losses his victim had suffered as a result were to be allowed as considerations.

As these protections tended to increase the self-confidence of colonial customs officers, provisions dealing with jurisdiction stacked the legal deck in the Crown's favor once the seizures came up for condemnation and sale. Since the end of the seventeenth century vice-admiralty courts had sat in the colonies to adjudicate customs cases. Defendants, however, could always petition to have their cases transferred from these prerogative courts, where judges alone heard evidence and delivered verdicts, to common-law courts where juries decided the outcome. The American Duties Act ended this indulgence by giving Crown prosecutors the authority to decide what court would conduct the trial—and then magnified their advantage by erecting a new court, the Vice-Admiralty Court for All America, with original jurisdiction over the colonies as a whole. If decisions in the eleven existing vice-admiralty courts were immune to the influence of juries, defendants might still appeal to mobs to intimidate their judges. But that was unlikely to be a successful defense strategy in the garrison town of Halifax, Nova Scotia, where the newly created court would sit.

Finally, the act tightened the lax procedures of the American customs service by requiring merchants and ship captains to post bonds (a thousand pounds for ships of less than a hundred tons, two thousand pounds for larger vessels) to insure their compliance with the law, and by creating an elaborate regimen of documentation to prevent frauds. Even in the coasting trade, which had never been closely regulated, customs officers were henceforth to certify the contents of ships' cargoes in advance of sailing and to list them on sealed "cockets." Upon arrival at his destination, the captain had to present the cocket to a customs inspector, who would unseal it and compare it to the cargo; any disparity between the contents of the hold and the cocket would be grounds for prosecution, fines, and the forfeiture of the bond posted at the port of embarkation. Such procedures had long been used in Britain, where swarms of customs officers, underofficers, and clerks searched cargoes and tracked the paperwork that sustained the system. This was, however, the first systematic extension of bonds and cocketing to the intercolonial trade, where the customs personnel had been few and documentation rudimentary. More officials would obviously be needed to staff the new system, but Grenville expected that the increased efficiency of collections and the prevention of smuggling would more than pay for increases in manpower.[5]

If these enforcement measures were sticks that the government could use to beat smugglers into submission, the provisions of the act that created new duties offered several carrots to induce British manufacturers and merchants to support the bill, as well as what Grenville believed was a very important sweetener to lure Americans into accepting it. The carrots included the act's elimination of "drawbacks," or customs rebates, previously given on certain fine Asian and European fabrics reexported to the colonies through Britain, and its addition of new duties of two or three shillings per pound on all foreign silks, calicoes, and linens to be reexported in the future. The intended effect was to raise the price in the colonies of textiles produced outside the British Isles, and therefore to encourage the colonists to consume even more British-made cloth. Similarly, the new charges of one pound two shillings per hundredweight on "foreign white or clayed sugars"—those grown and refined in the French West Indies—on top of the previous five-shilling duty, would give British sugar producers an even greater advantage in the mainland colonies. Grenville expected neither of these taxes to raise significant revenue, but rather to function as the duties collected under the Navigation Acts always had, keeping commerce within the empire and creating a privileged market for British produce and manufactures in the colonies. Thus, predictably, both M.P.s tied to the cloth manufacturers and those in the West Indian sugar interest enthusiastically supported the act. The case of a new tax on Madeira, however, was more complex and less conventional in its expected effects. Why Grenville believed that raising the price of the most popular wine in America would work to the colonies' advantage reveals his subtle conception of imperial trade—and suggests why colonists found it hard to discern in the American Duties Act the benefits he thought were obvious.

Along with an appetite for high-quality consumer goods, over the course of the eighteenth century Americans had developed a prodigious thirst for Madeira, which they imported, duty-free, from the Portuguese Wine Islands in exchange for wood products and fish. The American Duties Act imposed a new tax of seven pounds sterling on each tun—a cask holding about 252 gallons—brought to America directly from the Wine Islands. In contrast, wines imported from Britain (such as Madeira shipped to the colonies via the warehouses of British wine merchants) would bear a tax of only ten shillings per tun. The obvious results would be to diminish the direct trade between the colonies and Portugal, boost the incomes of British wine wholesalers, raise the price of wine in the colonies, and gain revenue for the Treasury.[6]

Significantly, Grenville also expected this measure to encourage the colonists to drink rum distilled in America, since alcohol in this form would now enjoy a greater comparative price advantage than ever. Paragraph 28 of the act made Grenville's motive clear to anyone who conceptualized the Atlantic trade system as he did, for this provision absolutely excluded French West Indian rum from America. Frenchmen in France drank little rum, and so long as grapes continued to grow, never would. Once the distilling planters of Martinique and Guadeloupe were denied access to the large American market, therefore, they would have little choice but to lay off rum-making and sell their molasses cheap to American distillers; lacking any other customers, they would have no alternative. In effect, market forces would compel French molasses producers to subsidize rum manufacture in the British colonies. Thus woven into the web of new duties was a boon to American rum manufacturers that—together with a final set of provisions—Grenville hoped would produce the most substantial customs revenues of all.[7]

For the third aspect of the American Duties Act was its adjustment *downward* of duties on molasses imported into the colonies from the French West Indies, and that formed the heart of Grenville's plan. This reduction recognized the ineffectuality of the old regulations on the molasses trade and sought to take advantage of changes the war had brought about. The Molasses Act of 1733 had sought to discourage the consumption of molasses from the French West Indies in British North America by laying a prohibitive tax of sixpence on each gallon imported. The intent had been to exclude French molasses from North America and encourage the consumption of molasses from the British West

Indies, but the law had never worked as it was intended. Unlike Frenchmen, Britons loved to drink rum, and British West Indian planters made handsome profits by distilling their own molasses into high-quality rum for sale in Britain; they therefore had little syrup to export to the mainland colonies, and what they did ship tended to be inferior in quality. American distillers had, as a result, come to rely on French suppliers. Because the sixpence duty on foreign molasses truly was prohibitive—molasses cost the equivalent of nearly fourteen and a half pence sterling per gallon and rum sold at wholesale for less than eighteen pence—the Americans had early resorted to smuggling. By the 1760s a remarkably open system of bribery was evident in every port with a rum distillery: customs officers pocketed "composition fines" of one and a half or tuppence per gallon on foreign molasses and made no effort to enforce the law.[8]

To a man with George Grenville's loathing of corrupt practices, this sort of behavior had been bad enough before 1763, but the war had changed conditions in ways that made it truly intolerable afterward. The American commanders in chief had never succeeded in slowing, let alone suppressing, trade with the enemy because the war had lowered the price and increased the value of French molasses. There had always been traffic between the French West Indies and New England, where most of the distilleries in North America stood, because the French planters needed wood products (especially staves for barrels in which to pack their sugar) and foodstuffs (particularly beef for themselves and cheap fish for their slaves). Before hostilities began, they had been able to supply part of these needs by trade with Canada and Louisbourg, but with the loss of access to those supplies they had sold their molasses at bargain-basement rates to whatever Yankee captains turned up with the cargoes of staves and cod they needed. Meanwhile, the market for New England rum grew fantastically during the war: in part because the army and navy used this rude anesthetic to dull the discomforts of American service, and in part because the conquest of France's trading posts in West Africa drove up the demand for rum there, where alcohol furnished the principal exchange commodity in the slave trade.

Thus the war had caused a boom in New England's consumption of French molasses: large before the conquests of Guadeloupe and Martinique made the trade legal; huge thereafter. With the end of the war and the return of the sugar islands to France, the molasses trade persisted—illicitly, once more—because the distillers had no other source capable of supplying their vastly expanded needs. The most authoritative estimate available to Grenville in 1763 held that the "Importation of foreign Molasses had increased greatly during the War to the Amount . . . of

Sixty thousand Hogsheads annually: five times the quantity" colonial distillers had consumed before the conflict began. That placed the total between 6,000,000 and 7,500,000 gallons—far too many gallons of any taxable commodity for Grenville to ignore. His only concern was how best to tap this great resource.[9]

In place of the sixpence duty, which supplied no money to the Treasury and occasioned so much corruption among customs officers, the American Duties Act therefore instituted a tax of threepence per gallon of foreign molasses. Grenville expected this new rate to bring in between seventy and eighty thousand pounds sterling annually. He knew that if he merely set the duty at the same level as the going bribe of twopence, and thereby made it as cheap to obey the law as to evade it, he might realize even larger sums for the Treasury. Nonetheless he believed that the higher rate was justified on policy, if not merely fiscal, grounds. The colonists needed to understand that Britain meant business, and the best way to convince them of that was to enforce a higher (if less remunerative) tax and flex a few of the muscles that the act gave the American customs service. Thus Grenville reduced the duty both to produce revenue and to prod the colonies toward submission. Yet he intended neither the exaction nor the enforcement to be harsh enough as to discourage colonial rum distilling, which—benefiting from the exclusion of French rum from North America—he wanted to grow into a goose that would lay egg after golden egg for the Treasury.

And there was one final benefit that Grenville expected to derive from these measures, perhaps the most ingenious of all: to weaken the French hold on the West Indies. With Canada now in British hands, French planters would rely more than ever on the mainland colonies for wood and provisions, and thus, in case of another war, would be more vulnerable than ever. If legitimating trade between the mainland colonies and the sugar islands of a foreign empire did not fit comfortably within the mercantilist conceptions that framed the rest of the act's provisions, it made excellent economic and strategic sense in the postwar world; particularly because Grenville trusted the Yankee consumers of molasses to pass along any increases in their own operating expenses to the French planters by charging higher prices for the staves, fish, and provisions the planters could get from no one else. Understood in this way, it was not British colonists who would ultimately foot the tax bill on molasses, but French planters on Martinique and Guadeloupe.[10]

Like an engineer constructing an intricate machine, Grenville designed the American Duties Act to perform many simultaneous complementary functions, all of which, he believed, would help create a workable empire. Better than most of his contemporaries, however, he understood that ingenious machinery alone would not suffice. Effective imperial reform required not only the erection of a militarily secure and financially sound institutional structure, but new habits on the part of the colonists and attitudes unlike the evidently self-interested ones they had shown during the war. Grenville thought of the American Duties Act, just as Halifax did the Proclamation of 1763, as a first step toward changing patterns of behavior long fixed, and attitudes deeply ingrained. The colonists needed to be taxed not only to provide the revenues necessary to defend and maintain order among them, but to habituate them to the duties and responsibilities that belonged to all British subjects.

Like the reform of the Indian trade and the prohibition of settlement beyond the Appalachian crest, the underlying issue in Grenville's package of fiscal measures was always control: sovereignty: dominion. By delaying the imposition of a stamp tax, he intended to ease the transition for colonists who were certain to resist their new, subordinated role in the empire. He expected colonial opposition, but he also expected to prevail. Nothing the colonists could do would deter George Grenville from pursuing the end of imperial control to which taxation was a means. No colonial protests would prevent him from exercising the parliamentary sovereignty of which taxation was both tool and symbol.

CHAPTER 61

The Currency Act

1764

Most members of Parliament, of course, agreed with the notions of sovereignty that Grenville's and Halifax's reforms embodied. Their lack of reservations about the American Duties Act indicated as much; and so, in an even more revealing way, did their nearly simultaneous passage of the Currency Act of 1764. This measure was not part of the ministry's program for the colonies, yet it was so deeply consistent with the ministerial measures that American colonists would assume that they formed part of the same design. They were not entirely wrong in that perception. While the pattern was not a conscious one, the Currency Act grew out of the same attitudes and perceptions that generated the Proclamation of 1763 and the American Duties Act, and which would soon produce the Stamp Act and the Quartering Act. Like all these measures, the Currency Act emerged directly from the experience of the war, the sense that certain practices that had benefited the colonies at Britain's expense needed to be changed, and the conviction that the House of Commons had both the right and the duty to make the necessary alterations.

When Anthony Bacon, the honorable member for Aylesbury and (as it happened) the man elected to replace John Wilkes, moved on April 4 to introduce a bill that would deprive the provinces south of New England of the authority to declare that the paper money they had issued was legal tender for the payment of private debts, he was responding in a public forum to the private concerns of merchants who traded to Virginia. He was himself such a merchant and thus knew how the war had occasioned big colonial currency issues and how those in turn had affected the value of debts the colonists owed their English creditors. What specifically worried him was a conjunction of factors unique to the

Virginia trade at the end of the war. These included the volume of paper money the province had issued to finance its military efforts, the House of Burgesses' stipulation that Virginia's treasury notes were to pass as legal tender for the payment of private debts, the long-term increase in the amount of money Virginia planters owed to merchants like himself, and the sudden rise in the rate of exchange between Virginia currency and British sterling at the end of the war.[1]

Like most of the colonies, from 1755 Virginia financed its war effort by issuing fiat paper money in amounts large enough to cover current expenditures. These notes were in effect IOUs printed by the colony government and given value by the colony's assurance that it would accept them in payment of taxes. A bit less than a quarter million pounds' worth of such notes remained in circulation by early 1764. Although Virginia's treasurer could not redeem notes presented to him in gold or silver, as the treasurers of Massachusetts or Connecticut could because their provincial currencies were backed by specie, the province's money had held its value reasonably well. In part this was because the House of Burgesses had been conservative in the amounts it had allowed to enter circulation, stipulating the future taxes that would be necessary to remove the notes as it issued each block of them, and then adhering more or less responsibly to the schedule of withdrawal-by-taxation. In part, too, Parliament's subsidies and the specie that the army and navy had spent in America had tended to support the value of all colonial currencies so long as hostilities had lasted. As the war wound down, however, military spending tapered off and British capital markets contracted. Sterling bills of exchange, with which Virginians settled their overseas debts, became more expensive.

In passing the legislation authorizing the province treasury to emit notes, the House of Burgesses had set the par of exchange at 125, meaning that £125 Virginia paper was in theory to be the equivalent of £100 sterling. Although £100 sterling bills of exchange actually had sold for £125 Virginia currency for a couple of months early in the war, from 1757 through 1761 the actual rate of exchange had hovered around 140. This was an inflated value, but so long as the rate remained relatively steady and so long as the Virginians paid their debts to British creditors in sterling bills of exchange rather than with Virginia treasury notes, the London merchants had little to fear: they knew that when their debts fell due the planters would be paying them in money worth roughly what it had been at the time the loans were made. Merchants like Bacon who traded heavily to Virginia became alarmed in 1762, however, when the exchange rate climbed from the 140s to about 160. They pressed the Board of Trade to protect their investments, and in February 1763 the board complied by trying to make the Virginia Assembly rescind the currency's legal tender status. In May, however, the Burgesses replied that the county courts were executing judgments against debtors at the actual rate of exchange, not at par, so there was no need to take action.

Their timing could hardly have been worse. Early that summer, a sudden crisis in international finance shook the City of London, threatening financiers and merchants, including those who traded to the colonies. Dutch bankers had lent a great deal of money in Britain during the war, so when an overextended Amsterdam house, Gebroeders Neufville, collapsed and precipitated a panic that soon spread to all the financial centers of northern Europe, British bankers and merchants found themselves scrambling to cover their obligations.[2] As the big London firms pressed their debtors—including, of course, traders to the colonies—for payment, men like Bacon worried about their outstanding debts. Solvency now depended on their ability to collect the money due them in Virginia at the market rate of 160, *not* at the official par of 125. Because its "legal tender" character made Virginia currency impossible to refuse when offered in payment of private debts, they worried that the planters would try to cheat them by tendering Virginia currency at the official rate, rather than what they desperately needed: sterling bills of exchange on London, reflecting full market value.

Interestingly enough, during the summer of 1763 Grenville had actually contemplated a currency bill for the colonies as part of his larger scheme of imperial reform: not to protect merchants like Bacon from inflation, but rather to create a common American currency that would facilitate payment of taxes to the British Treasury and ease the colonies' chronic money shortage. For reasons that remain unclear (possibly because he wanted to use revenue from his intended stamp tax to back the colonial currency, in effect offering a stable money supply as quid pro quo for accepting direct taxation) Grenville dropped the plan. Thus on April 16, 1764, Bacon's American currency bill, which the House had debated briefly and then passed on a voice vote, became law—not at the ministry's direction, but with its acquiescence. Unlike the currency measure that Grenville had pondered, which would have improved colonial finances and facilitated commerce within the empire, the Currency Act of 1764 served only the interests of London's jittery merchants. As the colonial agents who tried to argue against it pointed out, the net effect of a law forbidding colonial currencies from passing as legal tender within the colonies could only be to make business and exchange within America even more chaotic and uncertain than it was. Yet the debates on the bill suggest that the M.P.s passed it because they believed American debtors were manipulating exchange rates and inflating colonial currencies to defraud English merchants of their investments.

The Currency Act of 1764 aimed specifically at Virginia but was phrased broadly to include all of the mainland colonies south of New England, where the Currency Act of 1751 was to remain in force and hard-money regimes would operate as before. The act stipulated that all currencies in these colonies currently passing as legal tender had to be taxed out of circulation on an announced schedule, and might not be extended by act of any provincial assembly. It did not specifically prohibit future issuance of colonial currencies, but it strictly forbade colonial legislatures from ever again declaring paper money to be legal tender "in payment of any bargains, contracts, debts, dues, or demands whatsoever." This obviously applied to the private debts that Americans owed British creditors, but the language was broad enough to include debts held internally, between colonist and colonist within the individual provinces. From the perspective of the agents who tried to protest, this was bad enough; but in fact the wording was so inclusive as to suggest that the colony governments could no longer even make their currency legal tender for *public* debts—that is, for the payment of taxes.[3]

If this was indeed the case, the act would upend public finance in every colony south of New England, where the Currency Act of 1751 at least permitted province currencies as an acceptable legal medium for tax payments. There was no other way for colonies that lacked adequate supplies of currency to pay for wars and other government expenses except by issuing paper money—and no way to maintain that money's value except by taxing it out of circulation (and usually by paying a modest interest on the bills when their holders tendered them to the treasury) after the stipulated period. Unless province currency could at least be deemed legal tender for payment of taxes, it would rapidly, inevitably, depreciate to worthlessness. Since at that moment several of the colonies affected by the act were trying to defend their frontiers against Indian attack, this was scarcely a theoretical concern. The Commons had found a vastly inopportune time to diddle with colonial public finance.

And yet in the truncated debate on the bill only a few M.P.s quibbled with it. No one questioned the Commons' right to intervene in colonial affairs or suggested that it might be imprudent to do so, in that way, at that moment. And nobody paid much attention to the colonial agents who objected to the act's likely effects and sought to propose alternatives. Unlike the prewar Parliaments, which had been markedly reluctant to involve themselves in colonial affairs, this one had shown itself willing to take the bit of reform in its teeth and charge ahead, with or without a ministry's direction.

For George Grenville, whose job was to herd 558 unpredictable M.P.s in the general direction of the common good, the message in their passage of the Currency Act could scarcely have been clearer: he could take the lead in reforming relations with the colonies, or he could be trampled by temporary majorities acting according to their own notions and agendas. But the colonists, who lacked a clear sense of the internal workings of the House of Commons and did not understand its newfound activism, saw the emergence of American policy differently. In the sudden wave of reform rising from Westminster they perceived not the hasty and uncoordinated actions of ministers and M.P.s, each responding to short-run concerns on the basis of common assumptions and prejudices, but rather a degree of design and management that was not, in fact, there. The colonists did not understand how the war had raised awareness of American affairs in the House of Commons; nor did they see how unlikely the right honorable members were to interpret their objections in a favorable light.

Throughout the weeks in which the government proposed its reforms and the House of Commons adopted them, the two most striking features had been, as it were, absences: the absence of debate and opposition, which we have seen; and the complementary lack of any sense that there might be alternative means to achieve the ends of financial stability and military security in postwar North America. Why not request the colonists' financial support rather than try to compel it? Why not ask the colonial assemblies to raise provincial troops and garrison the necessary posts? The war's lessons, as understood in Whitehall and Westminster, answered those questions simply enough: there was no relying on Americans. The war had proven, to the satisfaction of everyone who had a voice in the formulation of policy, that American assemblies would only support the empire if they could profit from it; that American taxpayers were tightfisted and self-interested; and that American soldiers were too insubordinate and desertion-prone to be entrusted with colonial defense.

But had the war really proven those things so unequivocally? The last years of the conflict, in fact, could be understood to have shown exactly the opposite. From 1761 through 1763, over nine thousand provincials a year had volunteered for service, primarily in order to free regular troops for campaigns in the Caribbean. The armies in those years had been notably free of the mutinies and mass desertions that had cropped up so regularly in preceding autumns, merely because when the provincials enlisted they agreed to serve (and be paid for serving) *not* for eight-month campaigns, but for *annual* tours of duty. It should not have been inconceivable to carry on with such a system, enlisting (or reenlisting) nine or ten thousand provincials every year, to serve under the regular officers whom the king wished to keep in service, and to pay them by royal requisitions from the colonial treasuries. Yet men like Halifax and Grenville could not imagine it, for they remembered not the comparatively placid years at the end of the war when the colonial governments raised 80 or 90 percent of the men requested, but the difficult years of the war's beginnings. No one suggested that the Treasury might merely request support from the colonial legislatures, because the memory of American war finance centered on Braddock's and Loudoun's failure to make the colonies contribute to a general fund for the army's support. British politicians in general assumed that the million pounds sterling that Parliament had given the colonies as a reimbursement had paid for the colonial war effort, or most of it. No one noted that Parliament's transfer payments had covered only about two-fifths of the war's total cost to the colonies, and that the inhabitants of many provinces were presently struggling to pay off the public debts those wartime expenditures had occasioned.[4]

That British policy makers in 1763–64 reverted as if by instinct to measures that dated to 1748–54, then, comes as no surprise. Some of the most influential men engaged in formulating and approving policy proposals—including most significantly the earl of Halifax and Charles Townshend—had acquired their deepest familiarity with the colonies during the years after King George's War, when they had first responded to problems of control that seemed in retrospect to foreshadow the more intense problems that the Seven Years' War had spawned, and which they were now determined to solve. Others, particularly George Grenville, drew on attitudes formed when they applied themselves to meeting the fiscal challenges that grew out of Pitt's extravagantly expensive, and excessively successful, war leadership. None of them actually asked, because no one thought it worthwhile to ask, how much the colonial governments might be willing to continue contributing in order to maintain the empire they had helped to build. They grasped neither the real extent of colonial contributions nor the depth of the war's emotional impact in America.

Thus the hard experiences of defeat, lack of control, and financial stress—the predominant themes of the years from 1754 through 1757—dominated the understandings of the men who made policy for the postwar empire and encouraged them to adopt measures that would subordinate the colonies to Britain. But the war had other meanings—as a providential victory, secured by the cooperation of free men in a glorious cause—that shaped the understandings of the colonists, lifted their expectations of imperial partnership, and embittered their reactions to the seemingly high-handed, intrusive policies that Grenville, Halifax, and their colleagues sought to impose. The Seven Years' War had reshaped the world in more ways than anyone knew. But the lessons both Britons and Americans derived from the conflict would prove inadequate guides when men on opposite sides of the Atlantic tried to comprehend what those changes meant, and dangerous ones when each tried to understand the actions of the other.[5]

CHAPTER 62

Postwar Conditions and the Context of Colonial Response

1764

THE DISARRAYED condition of the colonies in 1764—economies and societies in flux with changes wrought by war, governments trying simultaneously to adjust to international peace and cope with the effects of Indian insurrection—helps explain how the colonists reacted to British efforts to reform imperial relations. Economic circumstances and political alignments shaped by the Seven Years' War initially governed the colonists' responses to Grenville's reforms; the army's efforts to suppress Pontiac's Rebellion complicated them. But the single most significant factor was the depression that by 1764 had fastened a clammy grip on trade in every colony, and which would not fully release it until the decade had ended.[1]

The sensitive antennae of the merchants in the northern ports had picked up the first signals of economic distress in late 1760, when their warehouses were crammed with the consumer goods they had acquired on credit, provided on easy terms by British correspondents. In the recent years of brisk business, large inventories had not seemed so much a problem as they suddenly became when British military spending began to taper off and the focus of operations shifted from Canada to the West Indies. But with fewer soldiers and sailors spending their pay on the mainland; with commissaries no longer buying vast volumes of American produce; and with the army no longer employing thousands of civilians to haul supplies and help build its roads, forts, and barracks, the colonists had less disposable income to spend on the cloth, Madeira, tea sets, wallpaper, furniture, and other imported goods they had come to love. At the same time, exchange rates of colonial currencies against sterling started edging upward, making it harder for the merchants to repay their British correspondents as debts fell due.[2]

Along with the decline in European demand for sugar and the rise in marine insurance rates that accompanied Spain's entry into the war, in 1761 and 1762 merchants had to face problems that grew out of drought and poor harvests throughout the colonies. Fortunately Parliament's subsidy payments continued to flow in, the army and navy still spent money to outfit Caribbean expeditions, and the conquests of Martinique and Havana furnished new markets for speculative trading: factors that moderated the recession's impact sufficiently that in 1761 and 1762 its victims remained the small, poorly capitalized traders who had entered business during the boom years. Better-established merchants—those with capital reserves or reputations sufficient to satisfy their creditors that they could be trusted—tended to experience the first two years of the downturn as a time of stagnation, not disaster. Most traders anticipated a return to prosperity when the war finally ended and "normal" trade could resume.[3]

As their inventories dwindled, the larger merchants' confidence revived; so that when their British correspondents once again began extending credit early in 1763, they unhesitatingly ordered new shipments and built up their stocks in anticipation of better times ahead. Their historical experience suggested the rationality of such optimism, for during previous wars, economic stagnation and recession had accompanied hostilities, and economic recovery came with peace. Although the last half of the present war had seen an unprecedented boom in British overseas trade, merchants had no reason to assume that the end of the war would bring anything but further prosperity. But sales did not meet their hopeful expectations, and when the Amsterdam-led panic of 1763 obstructed the flow of credit to the colonies many found themselves crushed between the rock of high exchange rates and the hard place of glutted markets.[4]

The bankrupts who appeared in the northern port cities late in 1763 and early in 1764 therefore included not only the scruffy upstarts who had been failing in the preceding years, but well-capitalized firms like Scott and McMichael of Philadelphia, which stopped payment on fifty thousand pounds in debts in December 1763. In New York during 1763 and 1764, the number of court-enforced sales of property in suits for debt trebled over previous levels; in Philadelphia, the number doubled. As the stress rose, merchants often tried to survive by gambling on ever-riskier ventures in the hope of making the great profit that would clear them of debt. Thus, for example, in 1764 Thomas Riche of Philadelphia formed a partnership with a New York merchant he barely knew in order to ship provisions to the French South American colony of Guiana—a flagrantly illegal enterprise, but one that promised fabulous returns. Riche, who had amassed a fortune as a wartime trader to the French West Indies only to suffer serious reversals in 1762 and 1763, hoped to make a killing and satisfy his creditors, but he only succeeded in delaying the day of reckoning. It would not be until 1770 that he could wipe the slate clean, and then it cost him nearly everything he had. He died raising sheep on a farm in New Jersey.[5]

Thomas Riche acted in accord with a principle that later businessmen would erect as a financial axiom: "If you owe your banker a thousand dollars and have five hundred to pay him, you've got a problem; if you owe your banker a million and you don't have a nickel, he's got a partner." The very size of Riche's debts helped keep him in business long after a smaller, more timid operator would have landed in debtor's prison. Many merchants, less big and bold than he, failed outright during the 1760s. Others reduced their operations. A few took Riche's kind of gamble and succeeded. What the depression meant was not universal bankruptcy, but rather that the ratio of failures to successes, always high in the colonies, rose higher than ever. So long as credit remained scarce, fewer prospective merchants could enter business to replace the unlucky or unskilled ones who failed. In the meantime large troubled firms like Riche's—those able to use their level of indebtedness to buy time or pry more loans out of their creditors—absorbed much of what credit remained available while they survived, and made bigger holes in their local economies when they fell.

For it was not only British merchants and financiers to whom American traders owed money. When a provision merchant like Thomas Riche went broke, his creditors included shipwrights, carpenters, coopers, sailmakers, cordwainers, block-makers, victuallers, tailors, shopkeepers, ship chandlers, and all the rest of the small businessmen and artisans with whom he kept accounts. When they in turn could collect only shillings on the pound, they were correspondingly less able to meet the demands of the people with whom *they* did business. Once they could no longer hire journeymen and laborers, or pay wages to their housemaids and cooks, urban unemployment rose. At the same time, military veterans, sailors, and ex-privateers tried to reenter the ports' labor markets, further depressing wages and increasing overall levels of poverty. Thus the failure of a bank in Amsterdam could cause a credit contraction in London that would in turn bankrupt scores of merchants in colonial port towns, threaten the livelihoods of hundreds of middling American artisans and petty entrepreneurs, throw thousands of colonial laborers and small craftsmen out of work, and render the lives of everyone who depended upon them miserable. These were cyclical, not structural, increases in business failure, unemployment, and poverty: an early, severe, prolonged version of the kinds of readjustments to peace that twentieth-century economists see as routine. But because the people who experienced them in Boston, New York, and Philadelphia did not necessarily understand that these were temporary conditions, and because they followed so closely on a period of high employment, high wages, and prosperity, they made life for everyone—from a merchant baron like Thomas Riche to the anonymous woman who washed his shirts—more stressful, more tenuous, than ever.

In varying degrees, all of the major northern ports were suffering in 1763 and 1764, and none of them had yet seen the worst of a depression that would deepen through 1766, moderate in 1767, and then plunge into even deeper distress.[6] Boston felt the pinch first, and worst. Already in 1760 its merchants had formed a Society for Encouraging Trade and Commerce in response to the downturn's beginnings. By 1763 the organization had dedicated itself to lobbying Parliament for special treatment in the hope of reviving their trade. The city's expenditures on poor relief, which had never exceeded the equivalent of eight hundred pounds sterling before the war, reached nearly two thousand pounds in 1764. In New York the presence of the army's headquarters, military contracting for the West Indies expeditions, and shipbuilding that remained strong even after the end of the conflict all delayed the onset of the recession, but by early 1764 New York merchants were complaining of cash scarcity, crushing exchange rates, and uncertainty. "Everything is tumbling down," one wealthy Manhattanite wrote, "even the merchants themselves." Philadelphia was fortunate in that the demand for flour in the West Indies remained strong well into 1763, so that the continuing vigor of the provision trade could offset the disastrous state of the market in dry goods, which collapsed in late 1760 and stayed flat for a decade. The disintegration of the West Indies trade in early 1764 inaugurated the greater collapse to which Thomas Riche responded with ultimately fatal ingenuity. Shipping clearances fell, the price of flour plummeted, currency vanished from circulation, merchants struggled to stave off creditors—and the Overseers of the Poor complained that the almshouse was so overcrowded that they were cramming as many as six beds into each tiny room.[7]

The northern countryside experienced less distress than Boston, New York, and Philadelphia, but the effects of recession extended at least to the limits of each city's commercial hinterland. The degree to which farmers suffered depended on the degree of their integration into the Atlantic market, but in general all those who had prospered during the war by selling the army their services (mainly in the middle colonies and New England), their grain (in the middle colonies), or their beef and pork (in New England) found that they were earning much less money. Rural storekeepers, pressed by the urban merchants who supplied consumer goods on credit and took produce in return, tried with new insistency to collect the debts their customers owed them. The less a farmer depended upon storekeepers, the lower his burden of indebtedness, the less the depression meant to him. Price movements in rural Massachusetts during the postwar years suggest that the droughts of 1761 and 1762 influenced most New England farm families' lives more than anything that happened in Boston, let alone London and Amsterdam. Even so, prices for agricultural commodities diminished enough during 1763 and 1764 to suggest that the postwar depression could be felt throughout a province that was by no means dominated by commercial agriculture. Where commercial farming dominated, as in the Delaware and Hudson Valleys, the effects of the depression were of course palpable. But even there farmers still had at least a limited option of "retreating into subsistence," or growing crops for consumption and local exchange rather than for sale, until prices recovered.[8]

In Virginia and Maryland, the tobacco provinces where commercial agriculture had been longest established in America, however, subsistence farming offered no safe haven of retreat. In the tidewater counties along the Chesapeake Bay, the effects of the postwar depression were as severe as in any northern city. Tobacco planters had been experiencing serious difficulties since about 1750. First, changes in international markets had destabilized the normal fluctuations in tobacco price levels, to which planters were accustomed; then, during the war, a series of poor crops had aggravated problems of selling in France's monopoly tobacco market. Despite these circumstances, however, the easy credit policies of London merchant houses encouraged the gentry to continue consuming high-quality English products. Planters whose detailed knowledge of tobacco production was more than matched by their ignorance of international markets, and even of the balances in their own accounts, mortgaged crops not yet planted to support extravagant tastes. Then came the escalation in exchange rates of 1762 and the planters' sudden discovery that their English merchant-creditors were no longer willing to let them defer payment by offering credit against the sale of future crops. Thus one planter, whose service against the French and Indians had scarcely prepared him to do battle with his London creditors, greeted the news of the Treaty of Paris only with expressions of hope for relief: "We are much pleased at the Assurances of Peace which 'tis to be hoped will be of long continuance, and that the Tobacco trade will fall into an easy and regular Channel again, to the Mutual advantage of all concerned."[9]

That Colonel George Washington reacted in such an evidently prosaic way to the most glorious peace in British history might seem surprising, but in fact his comment represented the views of his class as accurately as it reflected his own recent experiences and concerns. Since the heady moment when he married Martha Custis in 1759, combining their estates into one of the preeminent holdings in northern Virginia, everything Washington touched had turned to brass. He had failed repeatedly to grow profitable tobacco crops. In London his leaf had acquired an unshakable reputation for mediocrity. Meanwhile the expenses of maintaining a great planter's lifestyle, while keeping up a slave labor force and several plantations, had proved unrelenting. His own debtors—former comrades-in-arms who unhesitatingly touched him for loans, neighbors with whom he ran accounts, tenants who owed him rent—were slow to pay, and sometimes never did; yet he was too tightly bound by the expectations of gentlemanly behavior to refuse a loan when asked, or to press a debtor insistently when payment fell due. By 1763 Washington found himself deep in debt, doubting that he would ever extricate himself by growing tobacco, and casting about to find some way out of his predicament. In these ways he was absolutely typical of his fellow planters, and indeed differed only in that he had begun making efforts to economize. As a result Washington would never run into such spectacular trouble as his fellow colonel, William Byrd III of the 2nd Virginia Regiment. By the time Virginians first felt the bite of the Amsterdam panic in 1763, Washington was probably not far over two thousand pounds in debt, but Byrd was well on his way to racking up the twenty thousand pounds in obligations he would never pay off.[10]

The planters' responses to economic stress in some ways resembled those of the northern merchants. Like Thomas Riche, who preferred taking greater risks over liquidating assets to pay off his creditors, most planters tried to avoid selling land or slaves to reduce their debts, but instead looked for other ways to free themselves from their creditors' grasp. Some, frustrated with tobacco as a crop that seemed only to lead to greater debt, began looking for another staple to raise. Others experimented with plantation enterprises. Many plunged into land speculation, which had always provided Virginia gentlemen with a large part of their income, and never more so than when tobacco prices went slack.[11]

Washington tried all three methods. In 1764 he began experimenting with growing wheat, the crop that was fast displacing tobacco across the Chesapeake in Maryland—cautiously at first, then more confidently until he abandoned tobacco in its favor. He also began distilling brandy from peach cider: no longer just for home consumption, but for sale. But most of all he speculated in land. On the same day that Chippewa warriors seized Fort Michilimackinac (June 3, 1763), the master of Mount Vernon joined eighteen of his fellow gentlemen in a new company, limited in membership to fifty shareholders and formed to acquire the rights to lands on the Mississippi River. Many of these partners had previously been associates in the Ohio Company. But that venture, organized to claim a mere 200,000 acres, had been beggarly by comparison to this one. Each member of the new Mississippi Company expected to receive 50,000 acres of the nearly 4,000 square miles (2,500,000 acres) that the company proposed to acquire. To that end, each partner subscribed money to support an agent to represent the company in London until he could persuade the Privy Council to make the grant. Meanwhile, Washington was becoming even more deeply engaged in another, local speculative scheme. His purpose was to acquire the Great Dismal Swamp—perhaps 650 square miles of aptly named wetlands on the border between Virginia and North Carolina. He had convinced himself that this, the last large unoccupied tract near the coast, would yield tens of thousands of acres of salable land if it could be drained. Thus he spent much of the fall of 1763 looking over the territory, persuading others to become partners in the venture, and arranging for the preliminary surveys.[12]

Although Washington was unusually active as a land speculator, there was nothing atypical about speculation as a response to hard times in the early 1760s. Even before the Mississippi Company and the Great Dismal Swamp venture were getting under way, the Ohio Company had dispatched its agent to London in an effort to reanimate itself. Simultaneously its old rival, the Loyal Company, was trying to revive its prewar claim to 800,000 acres in the Kentucky Country, south of the Ohio River. And these were only the largest partnerships: individual gentlemen and informal associations of kin continually speculated in lands closer to home, if only because there was little else in which to invest that seemed to offer any prospect of return. Nor were Virginians the only colonists who saw speculative ventures as reasonable responses to a troubled postwar economy. Prominent and not-so-prominent colonists everywhere engaged just as eagerly in land speculation, with the same motives—as a gamble against adversity, a chance to regain ground lost or slipping away.

Examples of these efforts can be found in most colonies, but two of the most telling ones come from Pennsylvania and Connecticut.

In December 1763, before he left Philadelphia on the complex mission intended to serve the interests of Sir William Johnson as well as himself, George Croghan arranged to represent the interests of a dozen or so of Pennsylvania's biggest Indian traders—the "Suffering Traders," as they called themselves in light of the losses sustained in 1754 and again in 1763. Once in London, Croghan not only advised Halifax on his comprehensive plan for the reform of the Indian trade but tried to persuade the Board of Trade to grant him 200,000 acres in the Mohawk Valley in exchange for his tract at the Forks of the Ohio (now beyond the Proclamation Line). Because the board refused to approve his application for the compensatory New York grant and because it soon became clear that Parliament would never make a special appropriation to cover the Suffering Traders' losses, Croghan shifted his ground, advocating a new colony on the east bank of the Mississippi, between the Illinois and the Ohio Rivers. By the time he sailed for America in September 1764, he had evolved a plan that would transform the Suffering Traders' petition for compensation into a claim for western lands in the projected colony of Illinois, and he had made the necessary London contacts to sustain the project in his absence. One of these men was the agent of the Pennsylvania Assembly, Benjamin Franklin, who would become a leading proponent of the Illinois venture. Another was the Right Honorable Anthony Bacon, M.P. for Aylesbury, merchant, inveterate pursuer of American profits, and architect of the Currency Act of 1764. For the next four years Croghan would devote himself, tirelessly if without success, to promoting the Illinois enterprise. He would remain committed to it, in one form or another, for the rest of his life.[13]

While Croghan was using his relationship with Sir William Johnson to advance his and the Suffering Traders' case before the Board of Trade and Privy Council, a New Englander—less flamboyant but even more tenacious—was flogging his own contacts in pursuit of an equally ambitious speculative claim. Major General Phineas Lyman had commanded Connecticut's forces from 1755 through 1762 and at the end of the war was indisputably America's most experienced provincial officer. When the survivors of the Havana expedition, returning from a hellish campaign to face diminished prospects at home, met at Hartford in mid-June 1763 to form "a Company of Military Adventurers, for obtaining a Grant of Lands sufficient for a Government, in some of the conquer'd Lands in America," Lyman had been the consensus choice to represent them in

London. In typical New England manner, each man subscribed a small amount (two dollars initially, three dollars later) to support Lyman's efforts. Modest as it was, in the end this came to no insignificant sum, for by the middle of 1764 more than two thousand men—veterans, their heirs, and relatives—had taken shares in the company. By November 1763, the general was already in London, knocking on doors and making his case to anyone who would listen for a major grant to the New England veterans. The proclamation's promise to reward "the conduct and bravery of the officers and soldiers of our armies" with land bounties boosted Lyman's hopes, but he was still knocking and explaining when Croghan left in late 1764. Indeed he would continue to do so for almost a decade, plying as best he could his friendship with the British officers under whom he had served. Finally, in 1772, he would receive assurances that the grant he sought would be approved, and he returned to Connecticut. In 1773 he would head a major migration of New England veterans, their families, and others who had joined the venture as associates, to the lower Mississippi Valley, in the new colony of West Florida.[14]

Croghan's Suffering Traders were a handful of substantial Philadelphia merchants, and their venture would eventually spawn speculative companies with rich, influential shareholders on both sides of the Atlantic. Lyman's Military Adventurers were much more numerous, poorer, obscurer men, all from New England and many interested in actually settling on the lands they hoped to acquire, not just in selling them for profit. But these otherwise dissimilar groups were alike in that the members of both formed them during hard times, in the hope of improving their fortunes. As Riche had looked to Guiana as a place where risks, boldly undertaken, might produce fabulous rewards, both large and small speculators regarded the newly conquered lands as fields of opportunity that might deliver them from the constraints of a constricted postwar world.

Such perceptions and responses stretched not only from city to country and from region to region within the colonies, but across the sea as well. Great Britain was in economic straits of its own, in some ways worse ones than the colonies. In 1763 and 1764 streams of migrants were already flowing out of London, the depressed rural areas of the northern English counties, and Scotland, all in search of relief: the first freshets of what over the course of a decade would swell into a flood of British emigration. The willingness of migrants—the better-off families searching for farms to buy, the poorest individuals selling themselves as servants to escape pauperization—to move to North America intersected with the availability of land in the new colonies, making speculative ventures attractive to Britons with good connections and narrowing investment options.[15] The war, in effect, had radically contracted the Atlantic world by making America critical to Britain's welfare, stepping up the pace of interaction between colonies and metropolis, encouraging regularized communication, and stimulating transatlantic commerce. Recession contracted that world in another way as the promise of cheap land encouraged the flow of population westward in the direction of America, and hope.

The postwar speculative surge could, under the right circumstances, forge links between investors on opposite sides of the water, but the recession increased the likelihood that transatlantic relationships would be competitive, potentially antagonistic, ones. Within North America, hard times tended to make conflicts over contested lands—for example, those in the area between the upper Connecticut Valley and Lake Champlain that both New York and New Hampshire claimed, or those between the Berkshire Hills and the Hudson that New York and Massachusetts disputed—more anxious, and ultimately more ferocious, than ever. Thus if land speculation and frontier settlement were nothing new in British America, the context in which they now occurred altered their character and raised the stakes for the participants. Much more directly than before the war, changes in the metropolitan economy as well as shifts in imperial policy could influence even remote frontier regions in North America.

Influence, not control: a critical distinction. Vast stretches of the postwar backcountry were simply ungovernable, and as migration to the frontiers increased disorder would only grow worse. This was particularly true in the two Carolinas, although for different reasons in each. In North Carolina the problem grew from an impoverished economy and a chaotic land-distribution system that permitted British land speculators to dominate the real-estate market, inviting petty profiteering by their agents and local officials, and making it difficult for squatters to obtain clear titles to farms they had already improved. Migration into the piedmont during the last years of the war and in the early 1760s brought to the province families attempting to better their circumstances and hoping to escape Indian raids, and soon bred antagonism between the small, insecure, low-country elite and a growing population of backcountry farmers. Finally, while the war had brought high taxes to North Carolina, it had not created prosperity there, as in Pennsylvania, New York, and New England; and the postwar recession rendered this chronically disorderly, poor province less stable than ever.[16] In South Carolina, ironically, similar problems arose from the conjunction of much more favorable circumstances.

South Carolina experienced no significant Indian trouble after the conclusion of the Cherokee War and thus avoided heavy continuing taxation. When the southern European market for rice remained strong and British demand for indigo held steady through the 1760s, the colony became the single shining exception to the rule of depression in British America. In 1763 and 1764 the only significant problem the low-country merchants faced was the surplus of slaves on the local market, a legacy of the last years of the war when low prices had encouraged them to acquire the large inventories that they now had to clothe and feed until prices climbed to profitable levels. One reason for their sanguine outlook had been the "vast number of people setting down upon our frontier lands," who, the Charleston merchant (and former provincial officer) Henry Laurens believed, would "with a little management . . . take off insensibly a [slave] cargo by one or two in a lot." As it happened, Laurens and his fellows miscalculated the backcountry settlers' interest in acquiring slaves. They were right, however, about the boom in backcountry population, which South Carolina's liberal land-granting policies helped to promote.[17]

Laurens understood what was going on in the backcountry because he speculated in land there, a pursuit that set him apart from most other members of the low-country elite. Unlike their counterparts in Virginia, South Carolina's planter gentry did not promote the development of the frontier. The success of their staple crops of rice and indigo freed them from the necessity of looking sharp for supplementary sources of wealth, and their instinct was to minimize the political influence of the backcountry whenever possible. Virginia's speculating gentlemen readily created counties and fostered the power of new county leaders (who tended to be their own sons, sons-in-law, and nephews), but South Carolina planters feared that the burgeoning white population of the backwoods would dominate the colonial assembly, and so refused to establish new units of political representation. If this was a politically expedient practice, it was hardly a wise one. As frontier settlements mushroomed in the years following the Cherokee War, the absence of courts in the west became as much a grievance as the increasingly grotesque underrepresentation of the frontier districts in the assembly.

Already by the end of the war, and increasingly thereafter, the backcountry in both Carolinas was a magnet for all kinds of disorderly elements: debtors in flight from creditors, escaped convicts, military deserters, fugitive slaves, runaway servants, deerskin hunters, and outlaw gangs that settlers with property and families to protect called "banditti." The coincidence among a lack of county courts, a postwar recession spurring migration in search of opportunity, and the southward movement of refugees from the more dangerous frontiers of Pennsylvania and Virginia created serious problems of law and order along the whole length of the Carolina backcountry. At first, when the roving thugs whom most propertied, "respectable" frontier settlers would have preferred to see locked up or hanged could neither be arrested (because there was no sheriff) nor prosecuted (because there was no court), they formed posses, held kangaroo courts, and applied vigilante justice. Later, when the low-country elites persisted in ignoring their pleas for county governments, those same respectable backwoods farmers began to organize themselves politically.

The so-called Regulator movements that would emerge in the second half of the 1760s on the two Carolina frontiers would take different forms, depending on conditions in each province. South Carolina's Regulators would tend to concentrate on suppressing banditry and seek to develop ties with the low-country elite, while those in North Carolina would assume an antiauthoritarian tone and move toward armed resistance, leading the coastal gentry to identify the Regulators themselves as criminals. In both provinces, however, by 1763–64 pronounced divisions were developing between east and west, low country and backwoods: a pattern of sectional antagonism and mutual suspicion that would strongly mark the politics of the lower south for the next decade and color the response of those provinces to Grenville's reform program and all the British measures that would follow it.

The emerging sectional divisions in the Carolinas were new and unfamiliar, but in other colonies where sectional strains prevailed before the war had muted their expression, old patterns reemerged in the first years of peace, often in robust form. This was the case in Connecticut, where the political fault line split the colony's poorer, evangelical east from its richer, Old Light and Anglican west; in Rhode Island, where a mercantile faction centered in Newport competed for power with a mercantile-and-farming faction centered in Providence; and in New York, where Albany-based merchants and landed gentry joined farmers from the east end of Long Island (a group largely made up of Presbyterians and other dissenters, collectively called the Livingston Party) to oppose the faction of New York City–centered merchants (largely Anglicans, known as the De Lancey Party) that had controlled the provincial assembly during the war. Only New Jersey, long riven by internal tensions between proprietors and farmers and split between east and west, came out of the war with *less* sectional division and an elite more united and evidently in control.[18] Other colonies' political alignments were harder to plot on a map, but they generally reflected old patterns, often intensified after a long wartime lull.

In Maryland and Pennsylvania it was the familiar politics of deadlock. As proprietary colonies, both had developed polarized systems that opposed the interests of the proprietors, who controlled land grants, made executive appointments, and maintained blocs of votes in the assemblies, to those of antiproprietary parties that generally held legislative majorities and battled the proprietors for control. Maryland had virtually sat out the war because its governor could find no common ground with the antiproprietary party that controlled the lower house; now the colony remained locked in intractable conflict over the extent of proprietary powers. Pennsylvania's paralysis, by comparison, had been intermittent.

As we have seen, at the war's beginning the antiproprietary Quaker faction that controlled the assembly resisted the creation of military institutions until Indian and French raids had devastated the province's frontiers. In 1756 the Quaker grandees had withdrawn from politics, ceding leadership to Benjamin Franklin and others who lacked their pacifist scruples; those new leaders in turn had used the war to beat concessions out of the governor and the Penn family over taxation and related issues. With the return of peace and the outbreak of Indian insurrection, the proprietors moved to seize power in the assembly by allying themselves with westerners and Scotch-Irish Presbyterians against the antiproprietary party, which remained centered in Philadelphia and the eastern counties. This effectively revived Pennsylvania's furious prewar factionalism, lending it new sectional and religious hues. In 1763 and 1764, as the resurgent proprietary interest gained seats in the assembly, the antiproprietary party mounted an effort to turn Pennsylvania into a royal colony. As in 1755 and 1756, the defense of frontier settlements once more took second place to political infighting.[19]

Governors elsewhere retained more political control than in Maryland and Pennsylvania, albeit in different degrees and for different reasons. Georgia's royal governors ruled without effective opposition because the colony was young, militarily feeble, and unusually dependent on Britain. In New Hampshire, Benning Wentworth governed with a hard and grasping hand: his family had fixed its grip so tightly on the province's resources, trade, government posts, and land-distribution systems that no rival could mount a challenge without having his efforts repaid with political annihilation. Virginia and Massachusetts also had comparatively strong governors capable of evoking cooperation from their assemblies and limiting challenges to royal authority. In both cases, however, the potential for opposition existed in ways unknown in Georgia or New Hampshire.

Virginia's gentry, as we have seen, was experiencing significant strain as tobacco declined and debt mounted. Because the elite maintained substantial class solidarity and the House of Burgesses remained unfactionalized, certain kinds of challenges could turn the entire House against the governor. Thus while Governor Fauquier generally enjoyed an admirable record of success in dealing with the Burgesses from 1758 through 1763, their cooperation was never guaranteed. He discovered exactly how conditional his leadership was in January 1764, when he urged the House to appropriate money for frontier defense but refused to allow them to issue paper currency to fund it. With virtual unanimity the legislators refused to comply, forcing him to prorogue them without forts or troops to preserve the backcountry from Indian attack. In Massachusetts, by contrast, Governor Bernard had also enjoyed considerable success in controlling the General Court: not because he could summon the cooperation of a unified elite, but because the elite was factionalized in such a way as to make it more or less manageable. By the careful distribution of limited patronage resources Bernard and his lieutenant governor, Thomas Hutchinson, kept up an effective court party in the General Court: the firm (if not unassailable) majority that had withstood the assault of the country party and sustained the prerogative power in the writs of assistance controversy. In early 1764 signs of brittleness in the court party's majority appeared, but the fact remained that the opposition was far from breaking Hutchinson's and Bernard's hold.[20]

Throughout the colonies, then, a troubled transition to peace left political life and alignments in flux. Despite their complexity, most of the conditions that prevailed in early 1764—growing sectionalism in the lower south, reversion to prewar patterns of conflict and sharp revivals of factionalism in most other colonies, increasing instability or deadlock in the politics of all except the minor provinces of Georgia, New Jersey, and New Hampshire—derived from the war and its aftermath. The return of peace found the colonies as diverse as ever and, in the absence of a common enemy, diverging once more. Most were responding, according to local conditions and alignments, to what the war had done (increased public debts and raised taxes) and to what the recession was doing (making revenues scarce). In those colonies that had been most heavily engaged in the war effort, a hard-won political stability was vanishing. In New York, Connecticut, and Massachusetts, war governors had used large defense budgets, parliamentary subsidies, appeals to patriotism, and the expanded patronage resources that the war had provided to build effective court parties. In Pennsylvania the antiproprietary party, a country faction, had in effect used the war to co-opt the governor and dominate provincial politics. In Virginia the governor had employed patriotic arguments and parliamentary reimbursements to gain the cooperation of the entire provincial elite. Everywhere except Maryland, the appeals of governors to the colonists' instincts for patriotism had minimized public contentiousness from 1758 through 1762. But by 1763 and 1764, things were changing fast.

A half century earlier in England, Sir Robert Walpole had laid hold of the same elements that helped to stabilize colonial politics during the last half of the Seven Years' War—patriotism, patronage, and self-interest—and from them had fashioned an engine of "influence" to control Britain's unstable political system. He succeeded in creating a stable parliamentary regime largely because a funded national debt and standing armed forces allowed him to perpetuate levels of patronage previously possible only in time of war. Once Walpole had that indispensable resource in hand, everything else could be accomplished through the political management (in the language of his opponents, the corruption) at which he excelled. But the colonies in the 1760s offered no possibility of duplicating Walpole's feat. Colonial public debts could not be funded and made perpetual, but had to be paid off by the retirement of currency issues within stipulated numbers of years. Colonial governments, obligated to continue taxing their citizens at very high levels so long as war debts remained unretired, withdrew money from circulation and deflated colonial economies even as Parliament's subsidies ended and the worst recession in Anglo-American history strangled colonial commerce. Moreover, unlike Britain's regular army and Royal Navy, provincial armies were disbanded upon the return of peace, depriving governors of the commissions and supply contracts that had been the lifeblood of political influence during the war.

Thus the return of peace, the end of transfer payments from Britain, and the onset of the recession all weakened the ability of governors to suppress opposition and defend the prerogative, at the very moment that provincial tax burdens stood at their highest levels ever. Under these new circumstances, the arguments from patriotism that governors had used to good effect during the war lost resonance. Without an immediate and transcendent common cause to serve, local concerns loomed larger in the minds of colonial assemblymen, and local conditions cried out more loudly than the abstract needs of an empire that was, to all appearances, no longer at risk.

Given such losses of political capital, there was no way for governors like Francis Fauquier and Francis Bernard—men ambitious for the empire and earnest to manage colonial politics in Britain's best interest—to maintain the level of control they had achieved between 1758 and 1762. The reemergence of old obduracies, the reappearance of factionalism, the intensification of dissent as opposition groups maneuvered for public support and contended for scarce patronage: these could neither be stopped, nor long delayed.

And yet the meanings of the renewed conflicts and the appearance of new political configurations were obvious to no one. Like their masters in London, the governors did not understand that their influence was ebbing in the postwar colonies because in some realms it persisted, because the recent trend had been toward tighter integration between colonies and metropolis, and because the political leaders in their assemblies reacted uncertainly to the introduction of the imperial reforms. Indeed the ambiguous character of the colonies' responses to Grenville's program prevented imperial officials from understanding, for what would turn out to be a dangerously long time, what was really going on in America.

CHAPTER 63

An Ambiguous Response to Imperial Initiatives

1764

MERCHANTS AND OTHER well-informed colonists knew, at least from late 1763, that reforms in the empire's trade system were at hand. The arrival in America of dozens of previously absentee customs collectors and the accompanying flurry of orders directing the strict enforcement of the existing regulations had been a worrisome harbinger of change. "The publication of orders for the strict execution" of the customs laws, the governor of Massachusetts observed, "caused a greater alarm in this country than the taking of *Fort William Henry* did in 1757." The concern was at least as great elsewhere—indeed everywhere that merchants who had built careers within the casual framework of the old system began seeing cargoes subjected to minute scrutiny and ships seized for infractions of rules they barely understood. The mercantile community was already awash with anxiety when reports of Grenville's Budget Day speech arrived in May 1764 and gave colonists their first systematic sense of the character and scope of the reform program.[1]

Boston's merchants reacted first, convening their Society for Encouraging Trade and Commerce to consider what response to make, and then introducing their concerns at the spring town meeting, on May 24. Their voice spoke plainly in the instructions that the meeting issued to Boston's delegates to the General Court: "As you represent a town which lives by its trade, we expect in a very particular manner that you make it the object of your attention to support our commerce in all its just rights, to vindicate it from all unreasonable impositions and promote its prosperity. Our trade has for a long time laboured under great discouragements, and it is with the deepest concern that we see such further difficulties coming upon it as will reduce it to the lowest ebb, if not totally obstruct and ruin it." The representatives were to use their "utmost endeavours" to see that the assembly would make all necessary representations to Parliament and elicit all possible cooperation from the other colonial legislatures.

But the meeting's resolutions also made it clear that the representatives had more to protect than Boston's economy. Massachusetts's constitutional privileges, its inhabitants' very rights, were at stake. "What still heightens our apprehensions," the instructions continued,

> is that those unexpected proceedings may be preparatory to new taxations upon us; for if our trade may be taxed, why not our lands? Why not the produce of our lands and everything we possess or make use of? This we apprehend annihilates our charter right to govern and tax ourselves. It strikes at our British privileges which, as we have never forfeited them, we hold in common with our fellow subjects who are natives of Britain. If taxes are laid upon us in any shape without ever having a legal representation where they are laid, are we not reduced from the character of free subjects to the miserable state of tributary slaves?

Those more impassioned sentences articulated the concerns of the country party, quiescent since it had failed to prevent Chief Justice Thomas Hutchinson from issuing writs of assistance in 1761. But more specifically, the voice that spoke was that of Samuel Adams.[2]

At age forty-two Adams had not achieved the status that a Harvard education, a tidy inheritance, and a venerable Bay Colony name ought to have conferred. But this failed brewer, small-time political activist, and minor officeholder (currently in the middle of a term as a notably ineffectual tax collector) lacked ambition to amass either wealth or power. Unlike more practical, secular, and worldly men, he believed that politics ought to promote social cohesion and civic virtue—views that tended to align him with the highly moralistic stance of the country party. From the time of the writs of assistance controversy he, like James Otis and other members of the opposition, had come to see in Thomas Hutchinson all the qualities inimical to virtuous politics. As lieutenant governor, chief justice of the superior court, judge of probate for Suffolk County, and member of the council, Hutchinson was the province's leading plural officeholder, its ultimate political insider. Thus no one (least of all Hutchinson) would have been surprised when Adams as the town meeting's chosen penman devoted only half of the instructions to warning against Parliament's dangerous reforms. The other half denounced the corrupt practice of pluralism and instructed the representatives to seek legislation denying a salary to any judge who held more than one post, and prohibiting any member of the upper or lower house of the legislature from holding executive offices.[3]

The town meeting's denunciation of both imperial reform and the pluralist practices of Thomas Hutchinson and his political allies signaled a revival of the country party's campaign to gain control of the assembly. In the early summer it seemed as if this effort might bear fruit. Hutchinson had to leave Boston before the end of the legislative session to open the eastern circuit of the superior court, giving Boston's representatives—including his sworn enemy, James Otis Jr.—the opening they needed to act on their instructions. When, late in the session, the legislators named one committee to correspond with other assemblies and a second to rebuke the Massachusetts agent, Israel Mauduit, for failing to protest Parliament's measures, Otis secured himself places on both. When the committees sent out their appeals against the American Duties Act and the proposed Stamp Act, their reasoning echoed the arguments he had advanced in a recent pamphlet, *The Rights of the British Colonies Asserted and Proved.* Once again Otis was the country party's man of the hour. Even though he condemned the imperial reforms in terms obscure enough to daunt even determined readers, his pamphlet enjoyed immediate success and helped arouse public opposition to Grenville's measures.

Otis began with the conventional premise that the British constitution had no superior in human history, and that its beneficial, benign character flowed from the allocation of sovereign power to the king in Parliament. Great Britain's legislature, therefore, had the indisputable right to give law to the colonies. Yet absolute though its sovereignty was, Parliament's power could not extend to the destruction of the colonists' rights—either those that belonged to them as Englishmen or the natural rights that were theirs as creatures of God—because no power on earth could contravene the laws of nature. "The Parliament cannot," Otis wrote, "make 2 and 2, 5: omnipotency cannot do it." For the House of Commons to pass a law altering the principles of arithmetic would be plainly absurd; for it to abridge the British subject's right to consent to taxation would be tyrannical. Thus a body that could, if it chose, legitimately put a stop to the entire trade of the colonies, could not justly derive a penny's worth of revenue from taxes on colonial commerce (as in the American Duties Act) or extract a farthing from the pockets of the colonists directly (as in the proposed stamp tax): not until American

M.P.s sat in the House of Commons offering their constituents' consent. *The Rights of the Colonies* elaborated the natural-rights arguments Otis had first made in the writs of assistance controversy. As such they strongly appealed to people who revered the British constitution but wanted rational grounds to object to laws passed by a Parliament in which that constitution vested the ultimate state power to take property and life.[4]

Popular as they were in Boston and provocative as they were when read in the other legislatures to which the committee of correspondence sent them, however, Otis's arguments did not create a groundswell of opposition in the General Court. In the first place, they were ideologically inadequate to justify outright resistance. Otis himself admitted that Parliament's sovereignty could not legally be challenged, for only Parliament had the power to right any wrongs it might do. The colonists could only protest and wait for the constitutional system to correct itself. Second—and in the short term, most significant—the Bay Colony's country party still lacked the strength to break the grip on power of the governor and the court party.

When the representatives reconvened for the fall session and considered what formal petitions they might make against the American Duties Act and the proposed stamp tax, Thomas Hutchinson and his supporters were there to take control of the situation. The House of Representatives approved an ambitious country-party address to the king and Parliament that denounced the American Duties Act, the prospective stamp tax, and the erection of a new vice-admiralty court at Halifax as violations of colonial rights; but the Council, under Hutchinson's guidance, refused to concur. The upper house instead proposed a petition, written in Hutchinson's own neat hand, directed to the House of Commons: a chaste document that never once mentioned rights but rather argued against the new measures because they would inhibit Massachusetts's faltering trade.

The lieutenant governor, who kept his personal views to himself, disliked the idea of parliamentary taxation as much as Otis and Adams did, privately objecting on grounds quite similar to theirs. Yet he was, unlike either of them, a merchant, and he crafted the public petition to appeal to the province's traders. By avoiding arguments based on rights he hoped both to avoid offending Parliament and to co-opt the influential business interests that, he knew, valued political principles less highly than positive cash flows. The stratagem worked perfectly. As Bernard explained to Lord Halifax when he sent copies of the General Court's proceedings, all efforts "to inflame the people" by the country party "had no influence on the generality of the representatives; The proposers of Violent remonstrances were soon silenced; & the Business by degrees got into the hands of moderate men & friends to Govt.; & . . . was concluded with the utmost unanimity & good humour. The Council with the Lieut. Gov. at their head acted a most prudent & steady part thro' the whole."[5]

In Massachusetts, then, the merchants' howls of alarm at the American Duties Act were absorbed into the pattern of provincial politics as soon as the country party took up the cause of protest. The fusion of protest with conventional politics in turn allowed an adept lieutenant governor to minimize the stridency of the assembly's petition and preserve harmonious relations with London. In most other colonies, too, the prevailing political alignments and issues helped to create ambiguous responses and limit protests. Only the New York Assembly sent a petition to Parliament denouncing the act as a tax levied without the consent of the colonists and thus a violation of their rights.[6] This sole exception to the rule of reticence and moderation also arose from local political conditions, and when examined reveals the character and limits of colonial protest.

New York's war governor, James De Lancey, had built up the court party that bore his family name, and through it exercised reasonably consistent control in the assembly until his death in 1760. With the appointment of the nonresident General Robert Monckton as governor, the effective power of the governorship passed to the lieutenant governor, Cadwallader Colden. Meanwhile an assembly election gave new strength to the country party, the so-called Livingston faction. Colden, a crusty septuagenarian Scot, may have had a friend somewhere in the province, but if so that person did not belong to the assembly. Colden had sustained a four-decade-long career in New York politics by virtue of a Crown appointment as surveyor general and a reputation as a tireless defender of the prerogative. As acting governor he was determined to destroy both the De Lancey and the Livingston Parties as a first step toward rebuilding the depleted power of the prerogative in the province. He started by trying to make judicial appointments "at pleasure" rather than for life, as had been the practice: an effort that alienated the entire New York bar. The lawyers' enmity grew as Colden, who had been educated as a physician, began intervening in legal procedures. Late in 1764 he was engaged in a particularly intemperate effort to establish himself as supreme judiciary authority in the colony by agreeing to hear an appeal on a lawsuit that the supreme court had decided—and doing it in such a way as to suggest that he intended to destroy the right to jury trial in civil cases. Colden's position was one that even staunch royalists could not support without seeming to endorse the efforts of an "evil Genius" (or at best a "Petty T[yran]t") to make himself "superior to the whole Body of the Law."[7]

Without doing anything to subdue the most factious political system in North America, Cadwallader Colden had found a way to align both Livingston and De Lancey partisans against him and his defense of prerogative power. He had so abraded the nerves and sensibilities of the New York elite that by October 18, 1764, when the assembly petitioned the House of Commons against the American Duties Act and the prospective stamp tax, delegates who agreed on almost nothing else concurred in the most radical statement issued in America. "The People of this Colony," they wrote, "inspired by the Genius of their Mother Country, nobly disdain the thought of claiming the Exemption [from taxation] as a *Privilege.*—They found it on a Basis more honourable, solid and stable; they challenge it, and glory in it as their Right."

Like Otis in *The Rights of the Colonies,* the legislators granted that Parliament had "an incontestable Power, to give Laws for the Advancement of her own Commerce," but denied the legitimacy of involuntary taxation, including the raising of revenue by customs duties. Yet such Otis-like reasonings did not emerge solely from the legislators' "Regret, that the Laws of Trade in general, change the Current of Justice from the common Law"—where jury trials and procedural protections secured the rights of the accused—to vice-admiralty courts, which "proceed not according the old wholesom Laws of the Land, nor are always filled with Judges of approved Knowledge and Integrity." Those sentiments were equally the product of Colden's attacks on common-law procedure, and on the autonomy of the common-law courts. The sudden conjunction of threats that were general and imperial on one hand, with threats that were local and Coldenesque on the other, fueled the representatives' anxieties to a hyperbolic climax:

> The General Assembly of this Colony have no desire to derogate from the power of the Parliament of *Great-Britain;* but they cannot avoid deprecating the Loss of such Rights as they have hitherto enjoyed, rights established in the first Dawn of our Constitution, founded upon the most substantial Reasons, confirmed by invariable Usage, conducive to the best Ends; never abused to bad Purposes, and with the Loss of which Liberty, Property, and all the Benefits of Life, tumble into Insecurity and Ruin: Rights, the Deprivation of which, will dispirit the People, abate their Industry, discourage Trade, introduce Discord, Poverty and Slavery; or, by depopulating

> the Colonies, turn a vast, fertile, prosperous Region, into a dreary Wilderness; impoverish *Great-Britain,* and shake the Power and Independancy of the most opulent and flourishing Empire in the World.[8]

Thus the internal politics of New York made the legislature's petition as distorted a mirror of that province's reactions as the deceptively mild petition of Massachusetts was for those in the Bay Colony. Far from being stocked with radicals, New York's legislature was in fact as conservative as it was factious. Cadwallader Colden, however, did not hesitate to depict his personal enemies as the enemies of the Crown, Parliament, patriotism, and common sense itself. The old man's remarkable cussedness enabled him both to evoke opposition and to miscast it as the product of a republican spirit. Thomas Hutchinson's innate caution and deft parliamentary management, on the other hand, led him to smooth the surface of politics in a province where genuine radicalism was boiling up, making it seem as if those who opposed the American Duties Act cared less for principles than full pocketbooks. Ironically, by keeping his own deep reservations about the wisdom and justice of the imperial reforms a secret—something he did almost instinctively—Hutchinson was fast becoming as much a symbol of oppression as Colden, who entertained no personal qualms about the Grenville program.

Only Massachusetts and New York lodged official remonstrances against the American Duties Act with the British government. That none of the other colonial assemblies were sufficiently agitated to protest might be ascribed to confusion, since the act's purpose was not only to generate revenue but to regulate commerce within the empire, and the colonies had submitted to commercial regulation for a century. But something more significant than muddled thinking lay behind the colonies' quiescence. Because the provisions of the American Duties Act mainly affected rum distillers, merchants engaged in the coastwise trade, and consumers of expensive imports like Madeira, Grenville's reforms were simply of less than universal concern. It was not, in other words, that the colonists had trouble understanding the new duties as taxes: it was only that most Americans did not distill rum, trade in coasting vessels, or buy Madeira by the tun—and remained untroubled by taxes that they themselves would not have to pay.

Reasons arising from local self-interest and local politics led legislators in Rhode Island, Connecticut, Pennsylvania, and Virginia to protest against the prospect of a stamp tax while remaining silent on the reality of the American Duties Act. All four assemblies sent petitions or instructed their agents to oppose the stamp bill when Grenville introduced it, as he had promised he would, in 1765. Their petitions and instructions, like those of Massachusetts and New York, were strongly inflected by local circumstances and thereby clouded in argument. But all agreed that the House of Commons could not justly vote taxes out of the pockets of unrepresented Americans. The jumble in colonial thinking about the imperial reforms, therefore, did not originate in any lack of clarity about the acceptability of taxation by a sovereign Parliament. Rather, as the colonists' divided reactions showed, it came from the extreme difficulty Americans had in seeing themselves as a political community—a group with enough in common that a threat to any of them could actually be a threat to them all.

In Rhode Island the legislators mildly requested that the king confirm colonial rights, and they came no closer to asserting a universal principle than to state their belief that "colonists may not be taxed but by the consent of their own representatives, as your Majesty's other free subjects are." Connecticut's assemblymen contented themselves with commissioning a pamphlet that articulated their opposition to a stamp tax, entitled *Reasons Why the British Colonies, in America, should not be charged with Internal Taxes by Authority of Parliament,* and sending its author, Jared Ingersoll, to London as their agent. Elected officials in both colonies cared most about preserving their charters—perhaps the only issue that could unite all factions in either legislature—and out of their fear of offending Parliament, which possessed the power to annul the charters, chose to mute their protests. Anxiety over maintaining corporate privileges also produced Connecticut's unique effort to argue against "internal" taxation while accepting Parliament's authority to raise revenue by the "external" means of customs exactions. A stamp tax would operate directly on the population, effectively flattening the institutional barriers that had until now preserved the colonies' autonomy within the empire. Customs duties might be unpleasant but would not diminish local control. So long as the new duties were not so high as to put the local merchants out of business, Rhode Island and Connecticut could live with them.[9]

In Pennsylvania, circumstances tempered reactions to the impending Stamp Act in a different way. Pennsylvania's assemblymen learned of the imperial reforms in the midst of a battle between the antiproprietary party and the resurgent proprietary faction: a political dispute blown white-hot by a series of appalling incidents spawned by the Indian insurrection of the previous winter. On December 14, 1763, about fifty disguised frontiersmen had marched on the Indian town at Conestoga

Creek and murdered twenty Christian Indians. The vigilantes, calling themselves Paxton Boys after the Scotch-Irish settlement on Paxtang (Paxton) Creek, justified the massacre on grounds of self-defense. The Conestogas, they maintained, covertly aided Delaware war parties, while the assembly, dominated by the antiproprietary party, left frontier farmers exposed to attack. Two weeks later they renewed their protest by breaking open the Lancaster jail and butchering fourteen Conestogas whom the sheriff had placed in protective custody. As word spread that the vigilantes intended to kill all the Indians in Pennsylvania, their popularity and their numbers mounted fast. Soon they believed they could intimidate the province government directly. Thus early in February, some 500 Paxton Boys marched on Philadelphia, announcing that they would kill both the 140 or so Indian converts who had taken shelter there, and Israel Pemberton, whom they regarded as the province's leading Indian-lover. Benjamin Franklin and other government leaders intercepted them at Germantown, listened to their complaints, promised not to prosecute them for the previous murders if they went home, and thus defused the threat to Philadelphia.[10]

There was no further violence, but the incident alarmed everyone in eastern Pennsylvania, further polarized politics, and raised the stakes in the campaign for control of the legislature. In the fall elections both Franklin and his lieutenant, Joseph Galloway, lost their assembly seats: a stunning reversal for the antiproprietary faction, despite the fact that it retained a legislative majority. Under these circumstances, Grenville's reforms went unmentioned, if not unnoticed, until the fall. When the legislature finally acted, it directed Richard Jackson, its agent in London, to make a formal protest to the ministry and to lobby against the stamp tax in the House of Commons.

There was only a nod to the question of colonial rights in the assembly's instructions to Jackson because the antiproprietary politicians, now that the elections were over, were concentrating on a campaign to turn Pennsylvania into a royal province. It was with this goal in mind, not protesting the reforms in imperial relations, that the assembly voted to send a second agent to London to "assist" Jackson as Pennsylvania's representative. Over the objections of the proprietary minority, they named Benjamin Franklin, who had ambitions to become the province's first royal governor. He left quickly to take up his new job, unaware that imperial, not provincial, issues would consume his attention once he arrived in London. In this respect he was less than prescient but thoroughly representative. No politician in Pennsylvania thought that there could be any question more compelling than who would control the province. Thus in

Pennsylvania even more than in the New England colonies, domestic issues absorbed the attention of political leaders and moderated their response to imperial reforms.[11]

Virginia's local concerns surfaced in the House of Burgesses's three official protests—a petition to the king, an address to the House of Lords, and a remonstrance to the House of Commons. Through all three memorials ran mixed currents of principled and practical objection from planters who regarded themselves as put-upon and disadvantaged in relations with the metropolis. Provincial taxes, at the highest levels ever and committed to the retirement of the war debt, had lately been driven up further by the mobilization of militia units for frontier defense, but Lieutenant Governor Fauquier, and then the Currency Act, had prevented the Burgesses from easing the strain with paper money. Meanwhile tobacco prices continued to fall while exchange rates stayed stuck at the highest levels in their history. Planters' debts had climbed to frightening levels, but the prohibition against selling tobacco outside the empire doomed the planters to trade with British merchants who, many believed, were trying to turn them into permanent dependents.

Thus the Burgesses humbly prayed the king's protection, to preserve them "in their ancient and inestimable Right of being governed by such Laws respecting their internal Polity and Taxation as are derived from their own Consent . . . : A Right which as Men, and Descendents of *Britons,* they have ever quietly possessed. . . ." With almost equal humility and a hint of desperation they argued to those "fixed and hereditary Guardians of *British* Liberty," the House of Lords, that they were the descendants of men who "brought with them every Right and Privilege they could with Justice claim in their Mother Kingdom"; that to tax them without their consent would make them "the Slaves of *Britons,* from whom they are descended"; and that insofar as they had always taxed themselves, "they cannot now be deprived of a Right they have so long enjoyed, and which they have never forfeited."[12]

The remonstrance to the House of Commons concentrated on practical concerns more than rights, and perhaps for that reason sounded surlier. The Burgesses could not, they said, "discern by what Distinction they can be deprived of that sacred Birthright and most valuable Inheritance [of Englishmen's rights] by their Fellow Subjects, nor with what Propriety they can be taxed or affected in their Estates by the Parliament, wherein they are not, and indeed cannot, constitutionally be represented." Even "if it were proper for Parliament to impose Taxes on the Colonies," to do so "at this Time would be ruinous to *Virginia,* who exerted herself in the late War it is feared beyond her Strength," and whose people "are very greatly distressed already from the Scarcity of circulating Cash amongst them, and from the little Value of their Staple at the *British* Markets." Should Virginians be further burdened, the Burgesses observed, they would undoubtedly be forced to suspend importation and begin manufacturing substitutes for British consumer goods, to the great detriment of Bristol and London merchants. Thus no less because the stamp tax would "certainly be detrimental to [Britain's] commerce" than because "*British* Patriots will never consent to the Exercise of anticonstitutional Power," the House of Commons ought to be wise enough not to enact "a Measure . . . fitter for Exiles driven from their native Country . . . than for the Prosperity of *Britons* who have at all Times been forward to demonstrate all due Reverence to the Mother Kingdom, and are so instrumental in promoting her Glory and Felicity."[13]

What George Grenville and his ministerial colleagues inferred from this variety of American responses to the imperial reform program is easy enough to guess. All but two of the colonies had acquiesced uncomplainingly in the American Duties Act, and only one assembly objected that customs exactions were in fact taxes and therefore ought not to be levied on unrepresented subjects. The prospect of a stamp tax had elicited more widespread objections, but less than half of the colonial legislatures made even the minimal gestures of petitioning or instructing their agents to object. Compared to the resistance that the cider excise had evoked in England, the Americans' befuddled, erratic, and (in more than half the colonies) apathetic responses to taxation and a new regime of imperial administration were most encouraging. There was nothing in them to deter Grenville from proceeding to the next stage of reform and imposing a stamp tax.

With the benefit of two centuries' hindsight, of course, we can make inferences different from the ones Grenville and his colleagues could possibly have drawn. We can see that the political configurations of various American legislatures and the tendency of colonial leaders to be preoccupied with local concerns had inhibited the provinces from cooperating, even though the issues at stake were clear from the start and never, in fact, the subject of significant disagreement among colonists. Thomas Hutchinson himself detested the prospect of taxation without representation, and if not even James Otis could conclusively deny Parliament's sovereignty over the colonies, no one (except perhaps Cadwallader Colden) applauded its untrammeled exercise of power. The absence of coordinated resistance to imperial reform did not reflect internal division on the issues so much as the rudimentary state of intercolonial relations and the undeveloped sense of common interest within America.

During the previous half century, and particularly during the Seven Years' War, the most important bonds in colonial America had been those that extended across the Atlantic. The most significant trends in political and economic integration had not drawn colony closer to colony, but the colonies as a group closer to the metropolis. The American provinces had thus been able to demonstrate unprecedented coordination during the war, but only as a result of direction from above, not as a consequence of consultations among themselves.

The Seven Years' War had provided two unifying elements: a common enemy to animate agreement among colonies that were otherwise intensely localist; and a commander in chief to orchestrate colonial activities by issuing directives and transmitting requisitions through the governors to the legislatures. That only Maryland had sat out the war testified to the rude effectiveness of this system no less than to its limits, for only in Maryland did a governor and an opposition-dominated assembly fail to find enough common ground for the governor to become a conduit for the commander in chief's instructions and requests.

The end of the war left the other colonies free, once more, to behave like Maryland. There was no longer a common enemy to fear or a common cause to serve; the commander in chief no longer issued instructions to the governors; governors lacked the resources to control or even persuade assemblies; and the intercolonial cooperation of the war years faded into memory. Under these circumstances it is hardly surprising that opposition factions within various assemblies, responding to local concerns as much as to Grenville's reform initiatives, failed to coordinate their protests. Yet the memory of intercolonial cooperation clearly lingered on in the resolutions of assemblies like Massachusetts and Rhode Island to establish committees of correspondence, to communicate with other legislatures. Such committees reassured other assemblies that they were not alone in believing that Parliament had no right to tax unrepresented colonists. Given the fragmentation of postwar America, that was no insignificant accomplishment, but it could hardly have deterred George Grenville from proceeding with the Stamp Act.

Grenville and his fellow ministers also remembered the extent, and perceived the limits, of intercolonial coordination. They wanted to construct a system that would allow the colonies to respond to Whitehall's directives even more efficiently (and much more economically) than in the last years of the war. Until well into 1765 they did not understand that their efforts had begun to precipitate opposition out of Americans' inchoate, provincial disinclination to be governed from a distance and their widely held belief that taxes should not be levied without consent.

The various colonists who opposed Grenville's program, however, could not make common cause solely on the basis of localist biases and shared prejudices. In the first place, they could not agree that there was a common enemy: there was only the British state, which was much more the focus of patriotic devotion than a source of threat. Moreover, there was no agency with the backing of legitimate authority—no analog to a wartime commander in chief—capable of soliciting their cooperation. Thus local concerns, local interests, and local politics blocked the road to common action, even though most colonists feared and disliked the Grenville program.

There was, finally, one more factor that inhibited expressions of discontentment with an imperial program expressly designed to promote colonial defense: the Indian insurrection that was still in progress on frontiers from New York to North Carolina. It would have been hard enough for American politicians to question Parliament's authority if issues of sovereignty and representation could be debated at the level of abstraction. For them to question Parliament's authority when the issues at stake already had been stained by blood, and particularly when the blood was that of British soldiers spilled in defense of American colonists: *that* was another matter, entirely.

CHAPTER 64

Pontiac's Progress

1764–1765

ALTHOUGH NO ONE at army headquarters in New York quite grasped the fact, it was less Indian recalcitrance than British policy that sustained the insurrection beyond the end of 1763. Pontiac offered Major Gladwin peace when he suspended the siege oetroit in October. Gladwin accepted a truce but could not negotiate because he lacked the proper authority; all Indian diplomacy lay in the province of Sir William Johnson, whom Amherst in turn had instructed to make no treaty until the rebellious Indians had been properly "chastised." When the sieges of 1763 petered out in cease-fires, a commander without Amherst's visceral need to put the Indians in their place might well have seized the opportunity to make peace. Having not suffered Amherst's reversals and lacking his thirst for revenge, Major General Thomas Gage should have been able to put a prompt end to the bloodshed. But for reasons both technical and psychological Gage adhered to Amherst's plans for the campaigns of 1764, and that, together with the predictable array of unpredictable misfortunes, postponed the return of peace for more than a year.

Because Egremont had cloaked Amherst's dismissal in the pretext that the king needed his opinions on America, Gage became commander in chief ad interim only. Until the ministry decided to make his appointment a permanent one, Gage remained technically Amherst's subordinate, and bound by his orders. In practice, of course, Gage could alter campaign plans as he needed, and did indeed make a few changes. That he chose to adhere to the bulk of Amherst's instructions in 1764 had less to do with the requirements of military subordination than with a propensity for indecision. Gage had been in America since 1755 and in that time had shown a variety of admirable personal qualities, but not one of them outweighed a deep innate caution, born above all of a lack of imagination. He had proven his physical courage as the lieutenant colonel of the 44th Regiment at the Monongahela, and his capacities as a disciplinarian when he rebuilt the battalion in the months following the disaster. He had shown ambition in campaigning for a regiment of his own and perseverance in enduring repeated disappointments before receiving his colonelcy in 1758. And he had demonstrated initiative: his superiors finally decided to create his new regiment, the 80th Light Infantry, because he convinced them that it could replace the army's expensive, ill-disciplined ranger companies. But while soldiers from the 80th entered the abatis at Ticonderoga alongside the rangers and fought as bravely as they in that impossible situation, the regiment never did supplant them. Gage simply lacked the expertise and imagination to train his troops as anything but conventional infantrymen.

In 1759 Amherst took more account of Gage's seniority than his temperament and assigned him the command of a small expedition against the fort that guarded the upper St. Lawrence, La Galette. But instead of striking downriver from Lake Ontario to divert pressure from Wolfe at Québec, Gage fretted over the lack of intelligence concerning French troop strength, hesitated, and finally sat tight at Oswego. Amherst could not forgive this failure of nerve. Assigning Gage the ignominious station of rear guard commander in the invasion year of 1760, Amherst immured him at Montréal as governor thereafter. At Montréal, however, Gage finally found his forte, administering the region with patience, honesty, good humor, and careful attention to detail. By the time he inherited the office of commander in chief and the major generalship that went with it, he had demonstrated high competency as a bureaucrat and earned a reputation for personal decency. Yet as the pattern of his career suggested, he was always more lucky than insightful, more stolid than bold, more cautious than creative. At forty-three, Thomas Gage was too old to love risk. It probably never occurred to him to depart from the course his angry, confident predecessor had charted.[1]

Amherst planned to punish the western Indians as he had once punished the Cherokee nation. He had asked New York to raise 1,400 troops and New Jersey 600, while requesting 1,000 from Pennsylvania and 500 from Virginia: in all 3,500 provincials to be divided between two regular colonels and used to support the small number of available redcoats in a matched set of expeditions. In the north, Colonel John Bradstreet was to lead a bateau-borne force from Fort Niagara across Lake Erie to Detroit, chastising whatever Indians remained in arms and sending detachments to reopen posts as far west as Michilimackinac and Green Bay. In the

Ohio Country, Colonel Henry Bouquet had orders to march westward from Fort Pitt to the valleys of the Muskingum and the Scioto, subduing the Delaware, Mingo, and Shawnee villages there—the hard core of Indian resistance in the west. Bradstreet and Bouquet were to devastate all resisting settlements, liberate white captives, subject rebellious chiefs to British authority, and dispatch representatives from the defeated tribes to New York, where Sir William Johnson would dictate terms of peace. While all this was taking place, regulars from West Florida were to ascend the Mississippi and occupy Fort de Chartres and the trading posts in the Illinois Country, depriving the western Indians of French aid and encouragement. Gage altered the plan by adding 300 Canadian bateaumen and 1,600 New England provincials but otherwise did not tamper with Amherst's outline.[2]

Little worked out as intended. In the first place, Major Arthur Loftus and his detachment from the 22nd Regiment never left West Florida. Hostile Tunicas, not allied to the Illinois tribes but nonetheless unwilling to see the British replace the French upriver, blocked their advance on the lower Mississippi and sent them packing back to Mobile. Second, the colonies proved slow or unwilling to contribute provincials to the expeditions. Arguing that the Currency Act made it impossible to finance the necessary expenditures, the House of Burgesses refused to authorize a new Virginia Regiment. New Hampshire, Rhode Island, and Massachusetts all declined to raise men on the grounds that the Indians' peace overtures rendered all expeditions unnecessary. New York, New Jersey, and Connecticut came up with fewer than half the number asked. After a long dispute over the terms on which the expedition would be financed, Pennsylvania finally met its thousand-man quota, but the troops were slow to muster and quick to desert. Fewer than seven hundred Pennsylvanians, together with a couple hundred mounted Virginia volunteers (whom Bouquet enlisted on his own initiative and whom the Burgesses refused to pay), actually made it to Fort Pitt. They arrived only in mid-September, preventing Bouquet from opening his campaign until October 3. On that day he had just fifteen hundred men under his command—three-quarters of the number he had expected.[3]

The northern expedition fell even further shy of its planned strength. Gage had promised Bradstreet more than 4,000 regulars and provincials. By the time Bradstreet left Niagara in August, he had 1,400 men: 300 redcoats drafted from the 17th Regiment, still weak from the Havana campaign; 300 New Yorkers; 250 Connecticut provincials; 240 Jersey Blues; and 300 Canadian bateaumen. Bradstreet, however, started his campaign with one inestimable advantage over Bouquet. About five hundred Indian warriors, representing most of the nations that had been in arms against the British the previous year, accompanied him as auxiliaries.[4]

That Bradstreet's expedition included so many Indians resulted from the only significant departure Gage had been willing to make from Amherst's plans: he had allowed Sir William Johnson to convene a peace congress on July 11 at Fort Niagara. Amherst had instructed Johnson to agree to peace only "when the Indians, who have Committed the Hostilities, are Sufficiently Punished." Johnson barely waited for the *Weasel* to clear Paulus Hook before he began pressing the new commander in chief to let him dispatch emissaries announcing Britain's willingness to treat for peace. Gage hesitated, then assented. By spring, Johnson's messengers had fanned out across the *pays d'en haut,* spreading the word that the superintendent would kindle a council fire at Niagara. If the Indians who attended agreed to bury the hatchet, the British would "fill their canoes with presents; with blankets, kettles, guns, gunpowder and shot, and large barrels of rum, such as the stoutest [man] will not be able to lift."[5]

The response was enormous beyond expectation. Warriors from nineteen nations attended, numbering more than two thousand: in Johnson's estimation "the largest Number of Indians perhaps ever Assembled on any occasion," and a concourse equal to the great gathering at Fort Carillon in 1757. The Indians included representatives from every hostile tribe except the Potawatomies, Delawares, and Shawnees. A few notable warriors, including Pontiac, absented themselves, but this seemed only to suggest the extent to which their nations had repudiated them. The chiefs were eager to resume trade and welcomed the terms that Johnson proposed: returning white captives, severing relations with Indians who remained hostile, compensating traders whose stocks had been lost during the rebellion, guaranteeing the safety of the traders who would soon be coming among them, and submitting whatever disputes might arise to Johnson or to the commandant of Detroit for settlement. To prove that Amherst's policies were indeed dead, Johnson distributed a phenomenal quantity of presents—worth about £38,000 sterling—and, significantly, ended the prohibition on alcohol sales.[6]

When Bradstreet left on August 7 in the wake of the great peace congress, he believed that his task would consist not of carrying fire and sword from Niagara to Michilimackinac but rather of accepting the submission of a few remaining hostile bands. At least he hoped so. His force consisted of untrained provincials and sickly regulars, and his own health was hardly robust: an obscure debilitating ailment had felled him in May, and even in late July he could not walk unaided. When ten Indian chiefs approached his camp near Presque Isle on August 12 under a flag of truce, therefore, Bradstreet's spirits soared. Representing themselves as ambassadors from the Wyandots of Sandusky, Delawares, Shawnees, Mingos, and Munsees—the "Five Nations of Indians inhabiting the Plains in Scioto"—they asked for peace. Bradstreet replied with terms like those Johnson had offered at Niagara. The Indians were to cease all hostile activity immediately; to deliver all white prisoners to him in twenty-five days' time, at Sandusky Bay on Lake Erie; to send all Indians who subsequently killed or plundered whites to Fort Pitt for trial; and to leave hostages with his force pending fulfillment of the terms, while taking an officer and an Indian interpreter of his army along with them as they carried the peace terms back to their villages. In return the colonel promised to inform his superiors of the agreement and prevent Bouquet's expedition from devastating the villages in the Ohio Country.[7]

Sending Gage word of his negotiations, Bradstreet proceeded on what looked, with every passing day, more like a triumphal progress than a military expedition. As Indian bands met him and offered their submission he told them to meet him at Detroit in early September for a grand treaty conference. Confident that he was witnessing the last collapse of the rebellion, on August 26 he detached Captain Thomas Morris of the 17th Regiment and sent him up the Maumee River with a small escort and orders to proceed to the Illinois Country and assume command there. If he encountered Pontiac along the way, Morris was to tell him to meet Bradstreet at Sandusky, where the colonel would await the delivery of the Delaware, Shawnee, and other prisoners. Bradstreet assumed he was on the threshold of pacifying the entire American interior.[8]

When, in the last days of August, Bradstreet accomplished the formal relief of Major Gladwin's weary garrison and sent detachments on to reoccupy Michilimackinac and Fort Edward Augustus, he believed he had completed the mission that Gage had assigned. When he turned to the diplomatic task of confirming the peace with the assembled Indian representatives on September 5, however, he responded less to his orders than to the volatile combination of grandiosity and greed that had always defined his personality. The consequences would prove damaging to peace and deadly to Bradstreet's blossoming ambition to make himself overlord of the Great Lakes.

Long before leaving Fort Niagara, the colonel had seen his expedition as an opportunity to serve himself as well as his king, and therefore he had stowed a considerable quantity of trade goods belonging to himself and some business partners among the barrels of army stores destined for Detroit. But while in July he probably aspired only to make a tidy fortune in the revived Indian trade, the disintegration of Indian resistance reawakened an older dream. Since 1755, when Bradstreet had first seen Oswego and understood the *pays d'en haut* as a potential empire with himself at its center, he had promoted schemes to establish a "dominion of the lakes"—quietly at first, publicly after his triumph at Fort Frontenac in 1758. He had been frustrated then, but now it seemed that the dream lay within his grasp. To seize it he inserted an unprecedented article in the treaty he presented to the assembled chiefs of the Ottawas, Chippewas, Hurons, Miamis, Potawatomis, and Mississaugas. Calling the Indians not only the "Children" of George III, but his "Subjects," the treaty proclaimed His Majesty's "Sovereignty Over all and every part of this Coun[try, in as] full and as ample a manner as in any part of his Dominions whatever." The chiefs made their marks, but it is impossible to believe that they fully understood that Bradstreet intended to subordinate them to a degree that no Indian people had ever willingly accepted.[9]

The colonel's design at Detroit became unmistakable only later, when he reported to Whitehall on the peace conference and explained that by the terms of the treaty "His Majesty may in Justice and the ordinary Exertion of his Prerogative make what Grants of those Lands he pleases, & erect such Governments as in His Royal Wisdom he sees meet." That he had both grants and the erection of a government in mind subsequently became clear when he and "Sixty Officers Serving in the upper Lakes this Campaign" petitioned for a hundred thousand acres at Detroit, on which they promised to settle 639 families. This settlement, Bradstreet explained, would become the heart of an inland Crown colony that he himself was the man best suited to govern: a place to which the French from the Illinois Country could be relocated and kept under the vigilant eye of a regiment officered by Bradstreet's fellow applicants, and where the Indians of the Great Lakes might be taught the arts of husbandry that would give them a "Secure Subsistence." Detroit's geographical advantages, Bradstreet argued, conferred present strategic value and foretold future greatness. It was far enough west to dominate the fur trade of the interior, bypassing the scheming, unreliable Six Nations and insuring that the Indians of the lakes and the upper midwest would not take their peltry to the Spanish and French traders beyond the Mississippi. Once "properly settled," Detroit would be a "strong barrier" against future insurrections and a source of foodstuffs to ease the chronic "want of provisions" among the Indians. It would become the keystone of a stable American interior, a jewel in Britain's imperial crown.[10]

The vision that shimmered before his eyes blinded Bradstreet to the more immediate consequences of his actions at the conference—and nearly destroyed him. Mistaking momentary advantage for control, he behaved more like a conqueror than the mediating "father" whom the Indians had come to Detroit to find. While there is every reason to think that they did not understand the clause in the treaty that conferred on them the new status of subjects, they could not have mistaken the import of Bradstreet's response to the peace belt that Pontiac sent to Detroit in lieu of his own attendance. Professing outrage that the Ottawa had not come to make his submission in person, the colonel seized a hatchet, chopped the belt into pieces, and ordered the wampum cast into the river. Bradstreet intended to destroy Pontiac's dignity. By failing to understand that what he did was "roughly equivalent to a European ambassador's urinating on a proposed treaty," however, he chopped his own credibility to bits, restoring stature to an Indian leader whose own people had largely repudiated him.[11]

The man who unwittingly drowned the hope of peace in the Detroit River along with the shards of Pontiac's wampum began to see his dream fall apart soon after the conference ended. On September 12 the first of several letters arrived from Gage, informing him that he had exceeded his authority in concluding a peace treaty at Presque Isle and that he was now to abandon his agreement, move overland against the Shawnee and Delaware villages on the Scioto, and "use every means . . . to destroy them." Bradstreet, Gage had written, was to accept no offers of peace until the offending Indians had delivered up "Ten of the Chief promoters of the War, to be put to Death." Only then could he agree to a truce and send their delegates "in a proper manner to Sir William Johnson to sue for peace."[12]

Disconcerted as much by the unexpected rebuke as by the impossible orders, Bradstreet responded with a self-justifying letter (the first of a long series), then hastened to Sandusky Bay, where he expected the captives whom the Shawnee, Delaware, and other ambassadors had promised to deliver. The colonel was no stranger to tight spots or, for that matter, to his superiors' distrust. Always before, he had produced the successes that silenced his critics, transforming official censures into (at least grudging) approval. All he needed to improve Gage's temper was to return with the prisoners.

But no prisoners came to Sandusky. More letters did instead, and between them and the increasingly obvious fact that the Shawnees and Delawares would never bring in the captives, Bradstreet could see the looming outlines of disaster. The worst news came from Captain Morris, who never made it to Illinois. Before his party had paddled twenty miles up the Maumee River they met Pontiac. Although he had not yet abandoned his faith in the return of the French king, he listened to Morris's addresses and agreed to send a peace belt up to Bradstreet at Detroit. He also promised Morris safe passage to the Illinois Country, sending an escort with wampum to ease his way. But farther upriver Morris found that Pontiac's good offices mattered little. A band of Miami warriors that had lately accepted a war belt from the Ohio Indians seized him and tied him to a stake. They were at the point of torturing him to death when their chief, a kinsman of Pontiac's, dissuaded them and took Morris into his lodge. At the earliest opportunity the shaken captain fled overland to Detroit. There, describing his adventures to Bradstreet, Morris argued that while Pontiac might be useful, it seemed clear that the Indians' peace overtures at Presque Isle had been a ruse. "A mine is Laid, & the Match Lighted to blow us up. The Senecas, Shawnese, & Delawares, have sent their war belts to all the Nations; who only wait the signal for a General Attack."[13]

Bradstreet heard other fuses sizzle and hiss in the letters that arrived at Sandusky. From Gage and Bouquet, he learned that the Ohio Indians had not stopped attacking the Pennsylvania backcountry after the Presque Isle treaty; if anything, the pace of the raids had picked up. Gage, with increasing asperity, was ordering him to move his men up the Sandusky River, to cross to the Scioto Valley, and then descend on the Shawnee villages from the north, while Bouquet marched west from Pittsburgh against the Delawares. But this was not possible. The commander in chief, as heedless of western distances as of the water levels in the late-summer rivers, probably did not understand that he was in effect requiring Bradstreet's men to march two hundred miles overland, through a roadless forest, without even pack animals to haul supplies. The colonel, trapped between the knowledge of what happened to officers who disobeyed direct orders and the certainty that Gage had ordered a suicide mission, sat tight at Sandusky. He spent the remainder of the campaign ineffectually imploring his Indian allies to attack the Delawares and Shawnees and writing long defensive letters to Gage. Meanwhile his men gobbled up supplies and sickened with fevers, while the provincials among them anticipated the campaign's end with the usual loss of subordination. On October 18, dismayed and disillusioned, Bradstreet finally ordered a return to Niagara—and found disaster stretched across his path. On the first night out, a sudden storm destroyed half the expedition's boats. Bradstreet abandoned his artillery, sent a hundred or so Iroquois warriors back on foot, packed the remaining troops into what bateaux could still float, and limped onward. But the weather worsened and progress slowed to a crawl. Food ran short, and boat after leaky boat had to be abandoned; finally, he set hundreds of men ashore to march home "without a morsel of Provisions." It was November 3 before the surviving bateaux and their battered oarsmen reached Little Niagara. Those who had been forced to return on foot—the ones who did not starve to death or die of exposure—straggled in for weeks thereafter. When the Six Nations warriors whom Bradstreet had initially abandoned returned, they attacked the guards on the Niagara portage, nearly severing communications with Detroit once again.[14]

By the time Bradstreet's expedition crawled home, Colonel Henry Bouquet was concluding an altogether more successful campaign in the Ohio Country. After agonizing delays in assembling men, packhorses, supplies, cattle, and drovers, Bouquet finally marched from Fort Pitt on October 3, following the Ohio to the mouth of Big Beaver Creek and then striking cross-country for the Muskingum. Unlike the previous year, when he had blundered into a deadly trap at Bushy Run, Bouquet moved his force with great attention to security, making no mistakes. Mapping the country and clearing roadways as they went, Bouquet's men marched about eighty miles before word arrived that "the head men of the Delawares and Shawanese were coming as soon as possible to treat of peace."[15]

Bouquet ordered trenches dug and stockades thrown up near the Muskingum and awaited the arrival of the chiefs. From October 17 through October 20 he treated with them, offering essentially the same terms Bradstreet had offered and allowing them twelve days to bring in their white captives as a sign of goodwill. That interval gave him enough time to relocate his camp to a strong point in the very heart of the Delaware towns: "so that from this place the army had it in their power to awe all the enemy's settlements and destroy their towns, if they should not punctually fulfil the engagements they had entered into." There, a mile above the forks of the Muskingum, Bouquet's troops built a fortified camp like "a little town in which the greatest order and regularity were observed," stoutly defended by entrenchments and "four redoubts" with cannon. By November 9, the Mingos and Delawares had brought in over two hundred whites, while the Shawnees, whose main settlement lay on the Scioto eighty miles further west, promised to deliver their prisoners to Fort Pitt the following spring. After informing the chiefs that they would need to travel to Johnson Hall and confirm the peace by official treaty, Bouquet withdrew. By November 28, without firing a shot in anger, his little army was back at Fort Pitt, and peace in the Ohio Valley seemed secure.[16]

In his report on the year's campaigns, Gage credited Bouquet's "firm and steady Conduct . . . in all his Transactions with those Treacherous

Savages" with restoring order in the west. He admitted that Bradstreet had suffered more severe problems but nonetheless felt justified in observing that "the Country is restored to it's former Tranquility; and that a general, and it's to be hoped, lasting Peace is concluded, with all the Indian Nations, who have lately taken up Arms against His Majesty."[17] And yet the peace was neither so general nor so secure as Gage suggested, and it had less to do with firm and steady conduct than with the fact that the French commander in the Illinois Country had refused to provide the Indians with ammunition and arms. The French traders who had been supplying powder and shot had exhausted most of their stock and expected to be well paid for what they had left. Under these circumstances, most Indian groups north of the Ohio and east of the Wabash found it difficult to go on believing in the return of Onontio, who seemed so indifferent to their efforts. They simply found it more convenient to exchange their French father for a British one, and to trade their pelts and hides for British goods that were cheaper and more plentiful than those of the French anyway.

This willingness to bury the hatchet was far from universal. From the Scioto Valley to the Mississippi, significant leaders and their supporters remained unsubdued. Bradstreet's destruction of Pontiac's peace belt had only solidified the Ottawa chief's support among western Indians who still believed that the French king could be reawakened. In the Illinois Country, a half-German Catholic Shawnee named Charlot Kaské was rising to prominence as a war chief far more determined to resist the British than Pontiac. Thus the peace agreements of 1764 did not eliminate resistance so much as shift its center of gravity westward. Bringing Pontiac to terms and establishing control in Illinois therefore preoccupied Gage and Johnson in 1765, and neither task proved easy.

The expense of Bouquet's and Bradstreet's expeditions made it imperative to assert British authority over the far west by diplomatic means. Bouquet and Bradstreet both advised Gage that no fewer than three thousand men would be needed to pacify Illinois militarily, and that was simply too great a financial burden to bear for the commander in chief, whose budgets were already running 150 percent above authorized levels. The problems Major Loftus had encountered trying to ascend the Mississippi dictated, moreover, that the initial attempts to be made to reach the Illinois Country had best come by way of the Ohio. In January 1765, Gage accordingly sent a message to Pontiac, inviting him to help arrange a peaceful transfer of power from French to British occupation in the west, in effect asking a man who was still his enemy to become his partner. To follow up on this initiative, Gage authorized two separate diplomatic missions to the Illinois Country. The first party to make the attempt, led by Lieutenant John Ross of the 34th Regiment and an interpreter, Hugh Crawford, crossed overland from Mobile to the lower Ohio and reached Fort de Chartres in mid-February. They found the commandant, Captain Louis Groston Saint-Ange de Bellerive, to be most cooperative. The local Indians, by contrast, proved remarkably hostile. Ross and Crawford fled for their lives in April.[18]

While Ross and Crawford were paddling furiously down the Mississippi, the leader of the second mission, George Croghan, was still a month away from leaving Fort Pitt. Delay and misfortune had plagued him from the start. Upon his return from London, late in 1764, the tireless Irishman had pressed Gage to let him try to open the Illinois Country. Sir William Johnson strongly endorsed the scheme. Gage, of course, had no way of knowing that Croghan intended not only to make peace but to scout the region for his colonizing scheme and corner its fur trade for his business partners in the Philadelphia firm of Baynton, Wharton and Morgan. Gage was, however, well aware of Croghan's reputation as an Indian diplomat and late in 1764 allowed him two thousand pounds to purchase Indian presents. Croghan, as always, took the bottom line as his starting point. By late winter, when he left Philadelphia, he had spent nearly five thousand pounds on diplomatic gifts for the journey, virtually all of which he had bought either from Baynton, Wharton and Morgan, or from himself (after first setting up a penniless cousin as a merchant, to front the transaction). In addition to these supplies, which would be transported to Fort Pitt at Crown expense, Baynton, Wharton and Morgan shipped out an additional twenty thousand pounds' worth of goods to accompany the expedition and reprime the pump of the western trade. This occasioned the first disaster of the trip.

Before the firm's pack train had crossed Cumberland County on the Forbes Road, the local Scotch-Irish settlers learned that its panniers contained large numbers of skinning—in their view, scalping—knives. Following a Paxtonite policy of direct action, the frontiersmen organized themselves into a mob, blacked their faces, and destroyed or stole eighty horse loads of supplies; then they closed the road and besieged Fort Ligonier, to which the packhorse drivers had fled to save their lives. This left Croghan, already at Fort Pitt, in a particularly embarrassing position. Why, Gage angrily inquired, had massive quantities of Indian trade goods, including weapons and ammunition, been labeled as Crown property and directed for delivery to him—at a fort where the Indian trade was still under official embargo?[19]

Croghan brazened it out. In the face of massive evidence to the contrary, he denied that he had any private interest in Baynton, Wharton and Morgan's venture. He had, he maintained, merely permitted them to ship certain items to Fort Pitt to be stored until the embargo was lifted. With Johnson arguing vigorously in his defense, Gage finally let Croghan off with a reprimand, but it took all of March and April to convince him that the Irishman should be allowed to proceed. By then the expedition's military liaison, Lieutenant Alexander Fraser of the 78th Regiment, had lost patience and left for Illinois on his own. Croghan had advised Fraser to stay at Fort Pitt until he could confer with the Mingos, Delawares, and Shawnees downriver, and arrange safe passage through their country. The Shawnees, he explained, particularly had to be cultivated; as the nation located farthest west in the Ohio Country, they had the strongest ties with the peoples of the Wabash Valley and the Illinois, with whom the British had not yet made contact. Shawnee goodwill was thus crucial, but far from certain: the most incorrigible of the rebellious tribes, they still had not brought in the captives they had promised Bouquet the previous fall. But nothing could dissuade Fraser, who recruited a boatload of volunteers to row him down a thousand miles of dubious water and left Pittsburgh on March 22. Croghan stayed on at Pittsburgh, writing disingenuous letters, making preparations, and waiting for the chiefs of the Ohio nations to appear.

Unlike everything else that spring, George Croghan's Indian conference went remarkably well, once it finally convened on May 7. The Shawnee delegates not only brought in their prisoners and agreed to dispatch ambassadors to make a formal peace with Sir William Johnson, but assigned ten chiefs to accompany Croghan as a gesture of good faith. But Indian diplomacy remained, as ever, a ticklish and time-consuming business, and it was May 15 before Croghan and his two bateaux, laden with gifts, were afloat on the Ohio. By then Lieutenant Fraser was already in Illinois—with his neck on the chopping block.[20]

He had reached Fort de Chartres on April 17, not long after Ross and Crawford fled. Chances are good he would have been killed straightaway if Pontiac had not arrived at the fort just ahead of him. The Ottawa chief, notwithstanding the uncertainty Bradstreet had created at Detroit the previous year, was once again ready to make peace. Pontiac was not, in fact, the domineering civil leader that Gage and Johnson and the other British officials imagined him to be, but only one of many war chiefs. He was also a visionary whose views had long since been rejected by most of his own people in favor of peace and open trade. Bradstreet's rashness had enabled Pontiac to retain a following among western Indians who kept their faith in Onontio's return, or at least hoped to stall the British advance short of the Illinois Country. But in the months since Bradstreet's blunder, Pontiac's own faith in the French had faded. In contrast to the polite refusal of Captain Saint-Ange and other officials to deal with him, Gage's message of January had offered him the chance to become the most powerful Indian leader in America, for the letter promised him a kind of supreme chieftainship of the western Indians in return for his help in gaining control of the Illinois Country. Thus Pontiac listened closely to Fraser's unpracticed oratory, with its unmistakable offers of peace and partnership; heard Saint-Ange say, once again, that the French father wanted his Indian children to end their war; and replied that he was willing to bury the hatchet. That was all there was to it. Less than a week after Fraser's arrival, everything seemed settled. The delighted lieutenant, unaware of the tenuousness of his position, bought brandy and ordered a bullock slaughtered for a feast in Pontiac's honor. A delegation of chiefs set out to meet Croghan and escort him to the settlement of Kaskaskia, south of Fort de Chartres, where Pontiac and Fraser would await him, while wampum belts were prepared to confirm the peace.

But the politics of Indian resistance were more complex, and the peoples of the Illinois Country more divided, than a lieutenant infatuated with his own success could have dreamed. In early May it was not George Croghan but Charlot Kaské who came to Kaskaskia, and his coming set Alexander Fraser's scheme on its ear. He had been to New Orleans to seek aid from Charles Philippe Aubry, the French officer deputed to govern Louisiana until its permanent Spanish governor should appear. Aubry had discountenanced further hostilities and refused to make a gift of arms and ammunition, but he did permit a convoy of trade goods, which included a substantial supply of gunpowder, to accompany Charlot Kaské back up the Mississippi. Aubry intended to help the traders of the Illinois dodge the importation duties that the Spanish were sure to impose when Louisiana changed hands. In actuality, however, he helped Charlot Kaské, for the convoy gave the chief an opportunity to misrepresent his true position. Saying that the governor had encouraged resistance to the British, and pointing as evidence to the kegs of powder in the boats, Charlot Kaské instantly undercut Pontiac's agreement and put the lives of Fraser and his party in extreme peril. Fraser's—for that matter, Pontiac's—hopes now rested entirely on Croghan's arrival. But once more Croghan did not come. The chiefs who had gone to the mouth of the Wabash to await him returned, angry at being sent on a fool's errand. By the end of May, Pontiac could no longer protect Fraser and confessed that he and his few remaining followers would soon have to return to their villages. Fraser therefore wrote hasty letters to Croghan and the commandant of Fort Detroit, attesting to Pontiac's cooperation; handed them over to the Ottawa chief; and took to his canoe. He fled down the Mississippi on May 29.[21]

But Pontiac lingered at Kaskaskia, delayed by the unexpected arrival of yet another British emissary, Pierce Acton Sinnott. Sinnott, representing the southern Indian superintendent, John Stuart, had come from West Florida without any inkling of the state of affairs in Illinois. The ablest Indian diplomat would have found his prospects slim, but the inexperienced and "fractious" Sinnott—who a contemporary described as "a stranger to the art of pleasing"—fared even worse than Lieutenant Fraser. Within a few days he, too, ran for his life; but not before he had a chance to open a letter from George Croghan, which an Indian messenger brought on June 14. That letter, written at a camp near the mouth of the Wabash a week earlier, revealed that Croghan's party would soon reach Kaskaskia. News of Croghan's impending arrival could hardly have filled Pontiac with hope, but he decided to remain a few days longer anyway. The next news to arrive explained that Croghan would not be coming, after all. He had, Pontiac learned, encountered unexpected obstacles within a few hours of sending his letter of June 7. Perhaps only Pontiac could have seen that what befell Croghan on June 8 would give him one last chance to readjust the balance that had lately weighed so heavily against him.[22]

Croghan's trip down the Ohio had been a leisurely, calm one, lulling the agent and his companions into a false sense of ease. Even if they had been on their guard, however, they could scarcely have stood off a sudden, early morning assault by eighty Kickapoo and Mascouten warriors, followers of Charlot Kaské. The attack left three Shawnee chiefs and two of Croghan's servants dead. Only three men in the party escaped injury; Croghan himself sustained a dangerous hatchet wound in the head. The survivors expected to be tortured to death after the attack, and almost certainly would have been, had not one wounded Shawnee ambassador spoken up. Playing to the hilt his role as a doomed man, he taunted his captors with threats of his own. They were dead men, he said; his people, who had become friends with the British, would fall with fury on the Kickapoos and Mascoutens to avenge the killing of their chiefs. Unsettled, the warriors decided to spare the lives of their captives long enough to carry them up the Wabash to Vincennes and Ouiatenon, where they could consult with French traders and seek the counsel of their own leaders.

As they traveled, Croghan gradually recovered his strength, and as soon as he was able to talk, he too began playing on his captors' fears. So, for that matter, did the people in the villages they passed along the way, none of whom wanted a war with the Shawnees, especially when Croghan made it clear that they would come with British backing and illimitable supplies of arms and ammunition. By the time the party reached Ouiatenon, 250 miles upriver from the site of the attack, the warriors themselves were convinced that they had made a terrible mistake, and they did not demur when the civil chiefs of the village set Croghan and the other captives free. On July 1, the leaders of the five Wabash peoples (the Kickapoos, Mascoutens, Miamis, Piankashaws, and Weas) asked the Irishman to mediate a settlement that would avoid further bloodshed. Croghan, happily noting that "a thick Scull is of Service on some Occasions," agreed to write the necessary letters and sponsor the necessary talks.[23]

When news of the attack reached Kaskaskia, Charlot Kaské immediately sent word to have Croghan burned, but Pontiac—recognizing a chance to act as a mediator and recover lost influence—gathered up a delegation of Mingos, Delawares, and Shawnees, and set out for Ouiatenon. There, in July, the five nations of the Wabash renounced Charlot Kaské's leadership and asked Pontiac to represent them in meetings with Croghan. Irishman and Ottawa had no trouble in recognizing their opportunity and quickly made the most of it. In councils held at Ouiatenon in July and at Detroit in August, Pontiac and the chiefs of the Wabash Indians made their peace with the British. Pontiac's sole condition, which he knew would be necessary if the Illinois nations were to tolerate British garrisons on their lands, was that the British promise to occupy the Illinois posts as the French had, as tenants abjuring all claims to the surrounding territory, and even to the ground on which the forts stood. Croghan—disingenuously, since he had no intention of giving up his own scheme to colonize Illinois—raised no objections. Pontiac still had to travel to New York and formalize the treaty with Sir William Johnson. Croghan knew that the northern superintendent could disallow the article then, once the redcoats were in place, without risk.

As soon as the preliminaries had been completed, Croghan notified Gage that troops could safely be sent to take post in the Illinois Country. The first unit, a hundred Highlanders of the 42nd Regiment from Fort Pitt under Captain Thomas Stirling, reached Fort de Chartres on October 9, 1765. With no small relief Saint-Ange handed over the crumbling post and withdrew his troops to a more promising site across the river, the new village of St. Louis. Most of the habitants and traders went along, preferring life as Spanish subjects to military rule by the British. Charlot Kaské gathered his followers to waylay Stirling's detachment on the lower Ohio, in one last attempt to stop the invaders. But soon it became clear that the French traders would offer no more aid, while the Wabash tribes would take no action that might invite Shawnee and British retaliation. Thus Charlot Kaské followed the French across the river in the fall of 1765, the last leader of the great rebellion that the British always misunderstood as Pontiac's: a rebel unable to accept, as Pontiac finally did, a British father in the stead of Onontio, who would never wake again.[24]

CHAPTER 65

The Lessons of Pontiac's War

1764–1769

SO WHAT HAD IT proven, this seemingly endless protraction of the war? What did it portend? As usual, Indians and Britons and Anglo-Americans all found different lessons to learn, lessons that were by no means complementary or even mutually compatible. Pontiac himself drew a fatal conclusion. He thought that the war had earned him his enemy's respect, and that Gage's promise of support would establish him as a chief over all the peoples of the old *pays d'en haut*. He was right about the high opinion Gage and Johnson had of him, but wrong about its rewards. Seduced by the illusion that British support would enable him to lead many nations, he became only the focus of other leaders' resentments. When the British did not follow through with the stream of gifts that were necessary to affirm his status, by which he might maintain others as his supporters, the Ottawas themselves rejected his pretensions to chieftainship. By the spring of 1768 the young men of his own village were making such sport of him that to save himself from their casual beatings he withdrew to live among his wife's relatives in the Illinois Country. There, more isolated than ever, he lost even the ability to defend himself. On April 20, 1769, a Peoria warrior clubbed him senseless, then stabbed him to death in front of Baynton, Wharton and Morgan's trading post at Cahokia, on the Mississippi shore opposite St. Louis. No one—not even his own sons—felt obliged to avenge Pontiac's murder.[1]

Other Indian leaders learned the more reliable but equally dangerous lesson that the British could be coerced. Even if the rebel leaders had not been able to awaken and restore their French father, they could scarcely have failed to note that at the end of the war the British repealed every policy to which the Indians had objected. With the treaties of peace, diplomatic gift-giving resumed; limitations on the trade in powder, shot, and arms ended; the trade in alcohol opened once again. The Indians had forcibly instructed the newcomers in what residence in the *pays d'en haut* required of them and assumed that the British king and his representatives would take up the role of mediator that Onontio had abandoned.

Time would show that their faith in British goodwill was as mistaken, and ultimately as dangerous, as Pontiac's belief in British power. The British would never mediate disputes among the Indian nations as faithfully as the French had done, nor would they control the actions of their colonists so well as the French; but in 1765 and 1766, those uncomfortable truths lay shrouded in the future. In the meantime, the Indians who had participated in the rebellion knew only that their appeal to arms had earned them substantial dividends at the cost of very few lives.[2]

British imperial officials derived other lessons and applied them accordingly. The illusion of military success, fostered by the supposed relief of Detroit and Pittsburgh in 1763 and the lack of effective resistance to Bradstreet's and Bouquet's expeditions in 1764, prevented Gage and even Johnson from understanding the war's outcome as, in effect, a victory for the Indians. Yet neither of them was naive enough to mistake the formal acts of submission that ended the conflict for unconditional surrender. No responsible official, in America or at Whitehall, believed it possible to assert direct sovereignty as Bradstreet had tried to do, or even to reform trading practices to render the Indians docile and industrious, as Amherst had intended. Instead, despite the expenses it entailed, the British acquiesced in the resumption of diplomatic gift-giving because the Indians left them no alternative. They reopened the liquor trade both because the Indians demanded it and because alcohol seemingly offered the only means of making the Indians militarily manageable.

But most of all the war made the British authorities wonder, even before the final treaties had been concluded, whether in the future they could afford to maintain any significant military presence whatever in the west. The secretary at war, Lord Barrington, was the first to raise the question. On October 10, 1765, he wrote to Gage that, in his view, "if [the Proclamation of 1763] be right, the maintenance of forts to the westward of the line must be wrong. Why keep garrisons in a country professedly intended to be a desert?" Barrington hoped that "so old & good a friend" as Gage would advise him on what seemed to him the commonsense proposition that "difficulty of subsistance, expence of provisions, cost of fortifications etc . . . would no longer exist, if the forts were demolish'd, and the troops [withdrawn from] the west side of the line."[3]

On December 18 Gage penned a long and thoughtful reply that not only foretold British policy but explained its rationale. He agreed, for reasons that had as much to do with events in Boston and New York as conditions in Detroit or Kaskaskia, that forts erected "with immense labor, and at a most amazing expence" during the Seven Years' War, had become encumbrances in the postwar era.

> The forts were maintained at the peace for the purposes of keeping the Indians in awe and subjection, and protecting the trade. The Indian insurrection, shows the first purpose was not answered. The only use they may be said now to be really of, is that they are a protection to the traders, and prevent them from defrauding the Indians, making them drunk, and setting them one against another in the manner they used to do, which brought on quarrells with the provinces, and gave the Indians the worst opinion of all the English in general.

But if "the purposes of trade, gaining the Indians to our interest and preventing them, thro' French intrigues, from falling upon the provinces," were sufficient to justify "maintaining forts in the Indian country; [then] it may be asked, whether these ends . . . are equivalent to the expence of keeping up the forts? This is a difficult and nice point to be decided," and the decision depended entirely on the value of the Indian trade.

Questions of colonial defense, Gage thought, should not cloud the issue. In view of "the present temper of almost all the provinces, their scandalous behavior and ingratitude, their insolence to the whole Legislature of Great Britain, and unwillingness to contribute their quota towards the exigencies of the State," only direct benefits to the metropolis ought to be considered: "was it not that Great Britain is a gainer by the furr trade . . . there wou'd be no difficulty in deciding at once that the forts shou'd be abandoned, and the provinces left to manage their trade, counteract the French, and defend their frontiers as well as they could . . . at their own risque and expence." The colonists had shown themselves manifestly untrustworthy in such matters. Colonial traders had cheated the Indians, colonial speculators had chivied them out of their lands, colonial squatters had encroached on their hunting grounds. Indeed, it was to "avoid running into the same errors, [that] the present plan of forts, treating the Indians, and of circumscribing the limits of the provinces"—the Proclamation of 1763—had been adopted. So what, specifically, should be done?

Because the forts had been heavily stocked with cannon, small arms, ammunition, and other supplies, some military presence would have to be kept up, but Gage argued that it could be very modest. "If all is quiet" by spring, he believed, it would be possible to reduce the garrisons at the major forts to bare-bones levels: "Missilimakinak might be safely trusted with a garrison of 40 men, Detroit 70, Fort Erie 25, Niagara 40, Oswego 30." At Fort Pitt, 40 men would suffice, and some troops would have to be maintained in the Illinois Country to keep French traders from ascending the Ohio to interlope among the Indians there. All the "small posts of communication," way stations en route to these half-dozen "forts of trade," could be abandoned. Of the half-dozen posts on the Lake George–Lake Champlain–Richelieu River corridor, only one would need to be maintained, as an arsenal to store the cannon and munitions brought from the rest. In sum, no more than 350 regulars could support the commissaries of the Indian department and maintain royal authority in the forts where the traders would do business. The region north of the Ohio would truly become the Indian country that the Proclamation of 1763 intended.[4] The ceded lands south of the Ohio could be even more lightly garrisoned. Indeed they would have to be, for many of the old forts in the southwest were "tumbling down," while Governor Johnstone of West Florida had sited his new posts on the lower Mississippi so foolishly that they "may be said, in case of a quarrell, to be caught in a trap," and would have to be abandoned.[5]

To keep up a symbolic presence in the trans-Appalachian interior was all that Thomas Gage could hope to do after 1765. He was not so great a fool as to think that any of the big posts could actually be kept in repair by detachments as tiny as the ones he intended to station there. Nor was he such a naïf as to believe (as he officially maintained) that military officers and Indian department commissaries would be able to arrest or expel traders who carried their goods directly to Indian villages, as the Indians preferred, or who evaded trade regulations in other ways. Gage could only afford to keep up appearances and hope for the best. To avoid antagonizing Indian peoples whom he knew he could never subdue, he put his faith in the Proclamation of 1763 and its prohibition of white settlement beyond the Appalachian ridge. Yet he also knew that thousands of colonists already lived west of the Proclamation Line—five hundred families, as he would soon be informed, were squatting in the vicinity of Fort Pitt alone—and that his minuscule troop contingents could neither evict them nor keep the Indians from taking matters into their own hands.[6]

If anything was certain in the aftermath of the great insurrection, it was that the renewed surge of white settlers into Indian country would once more destabilize the west. For the lessons that backwoods settlers had extracted from the recent conflict and its predecessor, which they knew as the French and Indian War, were the clearest of all. Frontier farmers had suffered by far the heaviest casualties in both conflicts, losing two thousand or more men, women, and children killed or taken captive during the first year of the Indian war alone, and literally uncounted thousands in the greater war that had preceded it. The message of all these losses, for the colonists, could be reduced to the syllogism that lay behind the Paxton Boys' plan to exterminate every native person in Pennsylvania: if good Indians did not harm white people, then the best Indians must be those who could do no harm, for all eternity.

THUS A VAST, successful rebellion convinced the Indians that the British could be coerced into amiable relations and left the British army with neither the ability to control the west nor the disposition to try. These circumstances in turn married the ministry and its North American army to a proclamation unenforceable against white settlers who had no intention of honoring it, and convinced the backwoodsmen that the most prudent approach to Indian relations was with charges rammed home and hammers at the half cock. Gage, who hated uncertainty almost as much as he dreaded decisions, could do no more than take note of these impending tragedies because he was preoccupied with disorders that had erupted unexpectedly, literally outside his own front door. For in fact the most pressing problems that the commander in chief faced by late 1765 were no longer in the potentially explosive west, where so many of his troops were stationed. They were in actually exploding settlements up and down the whole Atlantic seaboard, where riots threatened to collapse the structure of imperial governance, and where Thomas Gage had scarcely any troops at all.

PART IX

Crisis Compounded

1765–1766

George Grenville completes his masterpiece, the Stamp Act, and dutifully attends to passing a Quartering Act for which he feels little enthusiasm; then loses the king's confidence and is forced to resign before he can complete his plan of imperial reform. The colonial assemblies react in a muddled way to the challenge of the Stamp Act, and mobs take the initiative in protesting an evidently tyrannical measure. Violence nullifies the law and paralyzes governments everywhere in America. Colonial elites struggle to moderate the protests and eventually reassert their leadership. The importance of nonviolent coercive methods in maintaining colonial solidarity. The issues at stake in the Stamp Act crisis.

CHAPTER 66

Stamp Act and Quartering Act

WINTER–SPRING 1765

THE SAME REPORT to the secretary of state for the South in which General Gage described Croghan's success in "taking Possession of the Ilinois by Treatys, Conferences, and Intrigues, with the Savages of that Country, and other Western Tribes," also carried his first account of "Clamor Tumults and Plots" against the Stamp Act. That letter, written on September 23, 1765, showed two sudden, significant shifts from his previous correspondence. The most obvious was a change in content. Before that date, virtually all of Gage's reports had focused on the west and the problems of imposing order there. After it, his letters thickened with news of riots in the cities and towns of the east—descriptions of what seemed a flood tide of anarchy. This change reflected Gage's amazement at the violence of colonial reactions against what he (like Grenville) saw as incremental additions to the imperial reform program. The other shift in Gage's letter was in the person addressed: a less dramatic change, perhaps, but an equally significant one. Gage had previously reported to Lord Halifax, but now he wrote to a new Southern secretary, General Henry Seymour Conway. This reflected a governmental upheaval that had taken place in July when, for reasons that had nothing to do with either America or imperial reform, the king sacked George Grenville and his associates in favor of a new set of ministers. The alterations in the temper of the colonists and in the composition of the ministry had both taken place with stunning swiftness, and together they added up to the gravest crisis yet to beset the postwar empire.

No one had foreseen crisis back on February 6, when George Grenville introduced legislation to impose a stamp tax on the North American colonists. Grenville, as always, had prepared the ground well. His most ingenious tactic had been to delay the introduction of the bill for nearly a year after the passage of the American Duties Act. That interval had given his subordinates at the Treasury the time necessary to draft a bill that would fit American circumstances as closely as possible, while Grenville used the time to meet with the agents of the colonies, soliciting their opinions and reassuring them that he sought only modest financial help in paying for colonial defense. The year had also enabled Grenville to gauge American reactions to the new duties and the tightened enforcement of customs regulations. Every sign had been encouraging. While it was clear that no one in America welcomed the prospect of taxation, the absence of organized protest suggested that the bridle of imperial subordination was one to which the colonies would soon grow accustomed. Colonial quiescence, indeed, lulled the House of Commons as much as the ministry into believing that the time was ripe for reform. Thus when the House resolved itself into a Committee of the Whole to discuss the Stamp Bill, only the most radical M.P.s questioned the measure or its timing. The titan of opposition, William Pitt, had not found the issue significant enough to stir from his retreat in Kent and attend the debates.[1]

Only a single exchange that Wednesday evening showed any passion, and that arose more from the personalities of politicians than from the clash of political principles. It took place not long after Grenville concluded a speech in which, with accustomed thoroughness, he had rehearsed and then dismissed every conceivable objection to a colonial stamp tax. A few opposition members spoke, granting Parliament's right to lay a tax on the colonists but questioning the "propriety" of doing so. Should not Parliament wisely avoid sowing "discord and confusion" by refraining from an open assertion of its sovereignty? Charles Townshend then replied, with his usual wit, in support of the ministry. He was glad, he said, to hear "the right of taxing America asserted and not disputed" by the honorable gentlemen, for if Parliament were ever to give up that right, then "he must give up the word 'colony'—for that implies subordination." The straitened "state of the mother country," he concluded, made it necessary and proper that colonies "planted with so much tenderness, governed with so much affection, and established with so much care and attention," should come to her aid. "If America looks to Great Britain for protection, she must enable [us] to protect her. If she expects our fleets, she must assist our revenue."[2]

With that, Lieutenant Colonel Isaac Barré, the scarred veteran of the Battle of Québec and inveterate opponent of the ministry, was on his feet. To him it seemed obvious that the sleek Townshend—Newcastle's protégé and erstwhile golden boy of the opposition, once celebrated as heir apparent to Pitt but now proving the truth of his sobriquet "Weathercock"—was ingratiating himself to Grenville, angling for some post of profit. Without premeditation Barré improvised the reply that would make him a hero in America. He began by quietly observing that he did not doubt the Americans' ability to pay a stamp tax, but only feared that making them do so would create "disgust. I had almost said hatred." Then, with growing vehemence, he heaped scorn on Townshend's peroration.

> They planted by your care? No! your oppressions planted them in America. They fled from your tyranny to a then uncultivated and unhospitable country. . . . And yet, actuated by principles of true English liberty, they met all these hardships with pleasure, compared with what they suffered in their own country, from the hands of those who should have been their friends.
>
> They nourished up by *your* indulgence? They grew by your neglect of them: as soon as you began to care about them, that care was exercised in sending persons to rule over them, . . . to spy out their liberty, to misrepresent their actions and to prey upon them; men whose behaviour on many occasions has caused the blood of those Sons of Liberty to recoil within them. . . .
>
> They protected by *your* arms? They have nobly taken up arms in your defence, have exerted a valour amidst their constant and laborious industry for the defence of a country, whose frontier, while drenched in blood, its interior parts have yielded all its little savings to your emolument. And believe me, remember I this day told you so, that same spirit of freedom which actuated that people at first, will accompany them still. . . . God knows I do not at this time speak from motives of party heat, what I deliver are the genuine sentiments of my heart; however superior to me in general knowledge and experience the reputable body of this House may be, yet I claim to know more of America than most of you, having seen and been conversant in that country. The people I believe are as truly loyal as any subjects the King has, but a people jealous of their liberties . . . will vindicate them, if ever they they should be violated[.] But the subject is too delicate and I will say no more.

According to Jared Ingersoll, the Connecticut agent watching from the gallery, "the whole House sat awhile as amazed, intently looking and without answering a word."[3]

Ingersoll—and those colonists who liked the old soldier's description of their virtues so well that they began calling themselves Sons of Liberty—wanted to believe that Barré had shamed his fellow M.P.s to silence. It is more likely, however, that most of the members present were simply not paying attention, for the House was half-empty and the hour was growing late. Those actually listening were as likely amazed by the one-eyed colonel's inconsistency as his eloquence. Earlier he had said, not once but twice, that he approved "that kind of [stamp] tax as being the most equal and producing" the most revenue. And at any rate Barré's passion spent itself to no effect. When William Beckford, Pitt's old ally and spokesman for the West Indian interest, moved to adjourn with the intent of delaying action on the measure, the M.P.s voted it down by nearly 5 to 1, 245 to 49. Then they sat, yawning and yearning for their Madeira, while the clerk read out the fifty-four resolutions that made up the bill. The clocks had struck ten before they adjourned. It was as if that long session had permanently sapped their interest in the measure, for thereafter it aroused no debate worth the name. In three weeks' time the Stamp Bill passed through the necessary committees and formal readings, and on February 27 received its final approval on a voice vote. On March 8 the House of Lords concurred without amendment or debate, and the king gave his assent on March 22. Once Barré resumed his seat on February 6, the Stamp Act stirred no emotion stronger than ennui.[4]

Yet if that was how George Grenville preferred it, he personally found nothing boring about this act, his masterpiece. For it was, in truth, a work of rare ingenuity: a tax that would be both unintrusive and virtually self-collecting. No excisemen would ever enter workplaces or homes to extract money from American purses, because revenues would arise from a benign Crown monopoly over the paper that the colonists used for legal purposes and the transmission of news. Before any sheet of paper could be used in a court proceeding or sold from a press, it would have to carry a small stamp to show that the duty set for its intended use had been paid. No overt enforcement would be needed because court clerks would not enter unstamped legal documents in court records, vendors could not sell unstamped newspapers or pamphlets without risking arrest, and customs officers would have yet another excuse to seize vessels if masters were so foolish as to use unstamped bills of lading or cockets. Colonists might try to counterfeit stamps—if they cared to risk prosecution for felony—but otherwise they could not evade the tax.

Finally, the revenues from the sale of stamps would grow as the colonies grew; legal actions, commercial transactions, and newspaper publication would all increase in close relation to the growth of America's population and prosperity. Grenville was particularly fond of the self-adjusting character of the tax, for it gave him the perfect argument to counter colonial protestations that the measure was unnecessary. When the colonial agents suggested that he could raise the same revenue by requisitioning it from the colonial assemblies, he replied that neither the colonies themselves nor the officers of the Treasury were capable of apportioning the various provinces' contributions equitably. The war had shown the difficulty of finding acceptable ratios; a stamp duty was the only way to parcel out the burden fairly, the only tax that would afflict neither poor colonists nor poor colonies unjustly. Moreover, as Grenville did not point out to the agents, the very modest cost of the stamps—on average only two-thirds the rates Britons paid under their stamp tax—could be increased once Americans became habituated to paying the levy.[5]

The Stamp Act thus promised to provide the Treasury with perhaps a hundred thousand pounds annually at the start, but much more later. It asserted the sovereign right of Parliament to tax American subjects—but did it so mildly, so reasonably, that the colonists would soon think nothing of contributing to the support of the army that defended them. If at first the Crown sent two or three pounds to the colonies for every pound that Americans contributed to the empire, the Stamp Act furnished the best possible means to inure colonists to their responsibilities, gently preparing them for the day they would bear a full share of the empire's burdens.

Like the American Duties Act, the new law was long, complex, and crafted with careful attention to producing the desired effects. Some provisions were explicitly intended to allay colonists' fears about the purposes of the tax. The preamble, for example, announced that this was only an extension of the legislation of 1764 and, like it, was intended to pay for America's defense; section 54 stipulated that all funds raised would be kept in a separate Exchequer account and spent solely within the colonies. Most of the provisions, however, listed those items that would require stamps and fixed their prices. A vast array of legal documents comprised the bulk of the list, ranging in value from threepence for common pleadings entered in civil courts upward through five shillings for each sheet of a will entered into probate. Deeds to land parcels of under 100 acres required one shilling sixpence stamps, while deeds to larger parcels cost more (five shillings for lots between 200 and 320 acres, for example, and an additional five shillings for each additional 320 acres).

The papers on which contracts were written required stamps costing two shillings sixpence per sheet. The modest sums required for shipping documents (fourpence per sheet for cockets and bills of lading) were more a means of preventing fraud than raising revenue, but rates on licenses for income-producing activities could be comparatively steep: four pounds to retail wine, ten pounds to practice law or act as a notary. Newspapers were to bear stamps at a rate of a penny per sheet, but advertisers would be required to pay two shillings for each advertisement. Each copy of a short pamphlet would carry a shilling stamp, but almanacs came cheaper, at twopence per year covered. Finally, each deck of playing cards sold in America would need a stamp costing a shilling, while each pair of dice would require the payment of a ten-shilling duty.[6]

In practice, then, the act would bear most frequently on lawyers and printers, who would presumably be scrupulous both about observing the law and about passing its costs along to their clients and customers. But with less frequency the law would touch almost every free subject in the colonies: or at least those who engaged in such quotidian activities as selling land, entering into contracts, buying newspapers, playing piquet or hazard, and dying with enough property to bequeath to their heirs. The near-universality of the law offered yet another testimony to the fiscal brilliance of the first lord of the Treasury and to the ingenuity of the functionaries who drew it up, and surely occasioned some quiet self-congratulation among them. Yet even that was not all. Grenville also took care to see that, once the law went into effect on November 1—an interval necessary to allow the stamps to be printed and shipped to America—it would be administered by the Americans themselves.

Grenville knew the colonists had complained, since his reforms in the customs service, that the officers and Admiralty judges who administered the American Duties Act were virtually all British placemen and cavalier in their regard for American sensibilities. He therefore took care, once the Stamp Act was passed, to ask the agents of the colonies to nominate prominent colonists to act as stamp-masters. Since each province was to have a distributor entitled to collect a fee equal to 7.5 percent of his gross sales, this was no trivial boon, and the agents jumped to take advantage of it. Jared Ingersoll, whose pamphlet explained why the colonies ought not to be charged with "internal" taxes and who had admired the spirit of Colonel Barré's speech, gave the matter careful consideration and then nominated himself. In May he took passage for New England, carrying his commission as Connecticut's distributor. The new agent for Pennsylvania, Benjamin Franklin, nominated John Hughes, his political ally at home and leader of the antiproprietary party in the assembly. The Virginia distributorship went to George Washington's colleague and friend Colonel George Mercer, who had been representing the interests of the Ohio Company in London. Mercer only narrowly beat out another prominent and politically powerful candidate from the Northern Neck, Richard Henry Lee. On advice from Massachusetts's agent, Grenville named Andrew Oliver—brother-in-law of Lieutenant Governor and Chief Justice Thomas Hutchinson, and secretary of the province in his own right—as the Bay Colony's distributor. These men, like their fellow stamp-masters, were socially prominent, propertied, and politically respectable figures. Their appointments, Grenville reasoned, would reassure colonial elites of his good intentions, and anchor his influence among the leaders of each colony. It was another stroke of organizational acumen. The first lord must have smiled to think how little he had left to chance.[7]

If Grenville had given the same scrupulous care to tending his relations with the king that he gave to reshaping the relationship between the colonies and the metropolis, his story might have played out more happily. Some unfavorable straws were blowing in the palace winds. Even as Parliament compliantly passed the Stamp Act, the king was showing an irritating reluctance to appoint Grenville's nominees for office; indeed, the king's appointees were so often friends of the earl of Bute that Grenville suspected the Northern Machiavel was once more whispering in his old tutee's ear. By late March the first lord, unable to hide his anger, had quarreled openly with the king over appointments. Had he known his master's mind better, Grenville might have held his tongue. But he was at that time preoccupied with another American measure, which had arisen unexpectedly at the beginning of March with a request from General Gage: a request he felt bound to honor, but one that entailed enough political risk to oblige him to proceed with caution. If the usual pattern in British politics was for domestic concerns to drive the formulation of American policies, here was a case in which an American issue distracted a prime minister's attention from the politics of the court, at the moment he could least afford it.[8]

The issues at stake were old ones, arising from the difficulty of quartering troops, impressing property, and maintaining discipline in America. Quartering had been on Gage's mind, in one way or another, since 1755, when in the aftermath of Braddock's defeat his regiment had found it difficult to secure winter accommodations. Colonists—particularly around Albany, where Colonel John Bradstreet managed the army's procurement and transportation requirements with exquisite attention to maximizing profits for himself and his Schuyler and van Rensselaer allies—had always been prickly about providing their horses, wagons, and fodder to the army. And the Indian war, coming on the heels of the debilitating Caribbean campaigns, had produced high levels of desertion, especially in regiments like the Royal Americans that had substantial numbers of colonists in the ranks. Early in 1765, Gage finally decided to attack these problems in the hope of preventing conditions from becoming worse. Thinking ahead to the day he would relocate troops from Indian country to the seaboard colonies, he wanted to be ready both to take care of their physical needs on the march, and to arm himself with authority to maintain order in the settled regions where they would be posted. Thus he asked for a set of amendments to the Mutiny Act. What resulted was a small debate over the place of the army in America and a badly muddled piece of legislation, the Quartering Act of 1765.[9]

Every year Parliament passed a complicated law known as the Mutiny Act to authorize the army's continued existence and govern its internal discipline. The Mutiny Act controlled recruitment practices, stipulated penalties for desertion, mutiny, and other military crimes, governed the rules by which the troops would be moved and housed, and touched on virtually every significant aspect of army administration. With a few exceptions, it applied only to the army in the British Isles, and so far as Gage was concerned, that was the problem. During the first phase of the Seven Years' War colonists and colonial assemblies had often refused to comply with the commander in chief's orders because the act made no mention of North America. Eventually the commander in chief and the provinces reached a modus vivendi when provincial assemblies agreed to pass their own annual Mutiny Acts; but everything still remained contingent on the colonies' willingness to cooperate. Gage worried that he lacked the legal power to compel the colonies to do their duty. As the provincial Mutiny Acts expired and the legislatures refused to reenact them, he anticipated a return to the conflicts and frustrations of a decade before; and when the mayor of New York refused to provide fuel to the troops quartered in his city in November 1764, Gage took action. Writing to the secretary at war, Welbore Ellis, he asked that Parliament extend the Mutiny Act to America, modifying it to allow commanders to quarter troops in private homes whenever barracks or public houses were inadequate to their needs.[10]

Since the freedom from having soldiers quartered in private homes was a precious English liberty guaranteed since 1628 by the Petition of Right, any bill drafted along the lines Gage asked would inevitably arouse a furor, in the House of Commons no less than in the radical press, and hand Pitt a weapon he would not even need to sharpen in order to skewer the ministry. Yet Secretary Ellis responded with the zeal of energetic ignorance, and within a week of receiving Gage's letter had drafted a new Mutiny Act that embodied the general's every wish. Ellis did not think to consult with Grenville, who was surprised on March 9 when the king, of all people, informed him of the bill just in time to avert disaster. Looking over Ellis's draft, however, Grenville thought that he could find language sufficient to enable Gage to quarter troops in private dwellings but vague enough to escape the notice of a keen-eyed opposition.[11]

Grenville suggested adding a clause to the Mutiny Act that would empower civil magistrates, wherever barracks or public-house rooms were unavailable, to order soldiers housed "in such manner as had hitherto been practiced to billet His Majesty's Troops in His Majesty's Dominions in America." That was better than Ellis's direct contravention of the Petition of Right, but not much. The practice in America during the war, and especially while Loudoun was commander in chief, had encompassed the forcible seizure of quarters in private dwellings, and enough opposition M.P.s knew it to raise the issue when Ellis introduced the bill in the House of Commons on April Fools' Day. The result, a much sharper debate than the one on the Stamp Act, showed that the ministry could not command even enough votes to direct that the bill be printed. Embarrassed, Grenville withdrew the measure until his subordinates could consult with the agents and other experts on colonial affairs.[12]

This tactic momentarily lessened the ministry's problems but in the longer run only complicated matters. Charles Jenkinson, Grenville's aide, asked Benjamin Franklin for advice on the provisions relating to quartering. Franklin had already contacted his old friend Thomas Pownall, the former governor of Massachusetts who now promoted himself as an all-purpose expert in colonial affairs. Together they suggested that the ministry adopt the formula that, Pownall maintained, he had used to defuse a Bay Colony quartering crisis in 1758. This forbade the billeting of troops in private houses but empowered colonial governors to take over vacant houses, barns, and outbuildings and turn them into temporary barracks; in which case the provinces were to furnish the troops with "firewood, bedding, candles, salt, vinegar, cooking utensils, and a daily ration of small beer, cider, or diluted rum"—items that would ordinarily be provided in a public house, or that a province would furnish to troops in permanent barracks. Other agents provided advice on other aspects of the bill, seeing to it that the measure would require only what colonial legislatures had previously granted in their own wartime statutes.

Thus in the end the Quartering Act authorized Gage to order the impressment of wagons at the customary rate of compensation; stipulated that commanders whose men were temporarily billeted in public houses would pay only for their food, not lodging; permitted troops to cross rivers on ferries at half the usual fare; and extended to the colonies all penalties current in Britain for harboring deserters. None of these provisions, Franklin and the other agents agreed, exceeded colonial understandings of reasonable support for the army. In view of their assurances and the absence of any other overtly objectionable provisions, opposition M.P.s would no longer be able to argue that the ministry intended to deprive colonists of their rights. Grenville therefore took the Commons once more in hand and on May 3 secured passage of the Quartering Act of 1765 on a voice vote. The Lords concurred, the king added his assent, and the bill became law on May 15.[13]

But the Quartering Act, while acceptable in London to the House of Commons and the American agents, was satisfactory nowhere else: least of all in America, where it would have to be applied. General Gage probably liked it less than anyone, for the law did not authorize him to quarter his troops in private homes. In fact, because it explicitly recognized only vacant buildings as suitable temporary barracks, it effectively *exempted* private dwellings from use, achieving the opposite of Gage's desire and depriving him of the ability to do even what Loudoun had once done—seize quarters according to the "Custom of Armies." Gage had asked for a freer hand, and the ministry had tied it behind his back.[14]

At the same time, the Quartering Act had nothing in it to please the colonists, despite the help that their agents and supposed friends had given the ministry in devising it. Thanks to Franklin, Pownall, and the rest, the new statute codified what had been the wartime practice of virtually all colonies. But in their eagerness to please they had overlooked a critical distinction that no colonist could miss. When the American legislatures passed their own versions of the Mutiny Act, they voluntarily committed their constituents to the support of the army. Insofar as firewood had a price, rooms in public houses cost money to rent, and ferrymen collected tolls, every locality that provided fuel to a garrison, every innkeeper who sheltered a file of soldiers, and every ferry owner who pocketed sixpence in place of his shilling fare paid a special tax. These were taxes in kind, but they were taxes nonetheless.

Towns or innkeepers or ferrymen no doubt resented being forced to contribute to the army's welfare in this way during the war, but their own representatives had granted this support, and they did so only after duly considering local circumstances. To have exactly the same burdens imposed by a distant Parliament, once the war was over, produced another sensation entirely. Colonial assemblymen would see in the Quartering Act as blatant a usurpation of their right to tax as the Stamp Act itself. Thoughtful colonists—no less conservatives than radicals—believed that the Quartering Act breathed "an air of both severity and contempt" toward all Americans.[15] In the end most colonists had no problem distinguishing between what their assemblies had once freely granted and identical contributions now levied by Parliament. It was, of course, more an emotional than an economic matter. However it might vanish, a dollar out of one's pocket will never be more than a dollar gone. But the feeling that comes from handing it to a friend will always differ from the sensation one gets from surrendering it to a mugger.

CHAPTER 67

Grenville's End

MAY–JULY 1765

WHILE GRENVILLE and his associates tried to minimize the damage that opposition members might do to them over the Quartering Act—and simultaneously fine-tuned the previous year's colonial legislation with a measure called the American Trade Act of 1765—the king was recovering from a mysterious illness. Fevers, chest pains, and a racking cough had confined him to bed from mid-January through March: symptoms his doctors could neither diagnose nor treat, and that put George in fear of his life. This may have marked the onset of a rare hereditary disease, intermittent porphyria, which would later manifest itself in even more alarming ways (delirium, the passing of bloodred urine, insomnia, hypersensitivity to touch, and mental derangement) and convince many, including the king himself, that he was going mad. In 1765 the disease had not impaired his reason, and the king indeed conducted business throughout much of his confinement. But he had plenty of time to contemplate his mortality and rose from his sickbed convinced that he had to make arrangements for a regent who could take over in case he died young (his son and heir, Prince George, having been born only in 1762).[1]

The king wanted to have the dowager princess of Wales designated as regent, in the event that a regency had to be declared, and to exclude his irresponsible younger brother, Edward, from the office. This was an understandable desire, since the king loved and trusted his mother, but given her continuing identification with the earl of Bute, it was hardly a wise one. Grenville, convinced that Bute had been manipulating the king in his illness, was furious; he lectured George on the inappropriateness of attempting to name his own regent, something no king had ever done before. The members of the cabinet quarreled bitterly among themselves, unable to choose between the desires of the king and the convictions of the prime minister. Finally, after much wrangling, the Commons declined to name a regent in advance and instead established a regency council from which one could, if necessary, be chosen. When the Regency Bill finally passed through Parliament on May 13, no one was happy with the result. The king, fed up to the back teeth with Grenville and his supporters in the cabinet, was ready to sack the lot of them.[2]

At that moment, to the amazement of a king and ministers preoccupied with court politics, mob violence erupted in London. No one in the cabinet had heretofore concerned himself with the silk weavers of the Spitalfields district, who were suffering severe unemployment as a result of the postwar depression and competition from Italian silk makers. Sympathetic M.P.s had tried to remedy the situation by passing a bill to raise import duties on silks, but the duke of Bedford had responded by opposing the measure in the House of Lords, persuading his fellow peers to kill it. Thousands of weavers responded by trying to kill Bedford. They stoned his carriage, attacked his house, and rioted outside the House of Lords—on the very afternoon that the king had gone there to give his assent to the Regency Bill. The army needed three days to ride down and saber enough rioters to restore order. George, still weak from his illness and frightened at the extent of the lawlessness, blamed his ministers for the breakdown of civil order. He therefore asked his uncle, the duke of Cumberland, to stand ready to take command of the army and, in the meantime, to approach William Pitt to see if he would consider forming a new government.[3]

The king took no pains to hide any of this from Grenville and his fellow ministers, but he would have been well advised to try. When Pitt spurned the offer and Newcastle declined to form a government in which Pitt would have no role, George found himself forced to retreat. Grenville, jubilant, thought that he had won a great victory. If (as he believed) Bute had been conspiring to destroy him but had made the error of setting his plot in motion prematurely, the king now had no alternative but to reject Bute and to announce his unconditional support for the present administration. As in August 1763, the last time the king had tried to eject him from office, Grenville had ridden out a political tempest only to emerge stronger than ever. Or so he thought.[4]

In fact, he could not have been more wrong. Bute's influence lived on more strongly in Grenville's mind (and in the radical prints) than it did in the royal closet. The king no longer sought advice, let alone took dictation, from his ex-tutor, and Bute had played no role in his decision to change ministers. Thus the humiliation George suffered at being forced to back down only redoubled his determination to rid himself of Grenville. In June he asked Cumberland to make another overture to Pitt. When the Great Commoner, who disdained to deal with a mere monarch through intermediaries, refused once more, George asked Cumberland himself to head a new ministry. In great secrecy the duke searched again among the Newcastle Whigs for men who would be willing to accept office. This time, for two reasons, he found them. First, while some still fretted about the absence of Pitt, Cumberland's willingness to act as prime minister—while he took no portfolio, he intended to chair all cabinet meetings and guide the formulation of policy—reassured Newcastle (and most others) that the new administration would enjoy the king's support. Second, Cumberland offered the leading offices to friends and clients, men unlikely to disoblige him. Two of them had no qualification for office beyond membership in the Jockey Club, Cumberland's racing circle: Charles Watson-Wentworth, second marquess of Rockingham, who agreed to become first lord of the Treasury; and Augustus Henry Fitzroy, third duke of Grafton, who accepted the secretaryship of state for the North. The man whom Cumberland asked to be secretary of state for the South and leader in the House of Commons, General Henry Seymour Conway, had once been his aide-de-camp. Most of the other offices were parceled out to aristocrats, including Newcastle, who accepted a ceremonial position as lord privy seal. Of those whom Cumberland approached, only Charles Townshend—miffed to be offered the chancellorship of the Exchequer but not the leadership of the House—refused him. But Townshend's scruples were not sufficient to drive him back into opposition, and he walked away with the lucrative, politically inconsequential office of paymaster general.

It was characteristic of this new ministry that Cumberland and Rockingham assigned the duke of Newcastle no role in the management of patronage, and thereby deprived themselves of the most useful service the old duke could still render. In general, the men chosen to hold the most powerful offices had the least political experience. Conway, at forty-eight, was the oldest of the administration's leaders, and he was the only one to have held prior office (as secretary to the lord lieutenant of Ireland). Rockingham was thirty-five years old, and Grafton just thirty; neither had occupied even minor posts. Only Cumberland had exercised major administrative responsibilities, but those had been exclusively military. Moreover, the duke was obese, paralytic, and pathetically frail. His close relationship with the king might sustain his administration, but without him it would be a ministry with no center, no strength, and no credibility. Insofar as the ministers had known views, they could be defined solely in terms of their disagreement with Grenville; otherwise they shared no sense of policy or direction. Even the king, at some level, understood what an unpromising cabinet they made. But he was desperate to be rid of Grenville, and therefore offered them his unconditional support.[5]

The king and his uncle did their best to hide the fact that they were constructing a new ministry, but nothing could stanch the flow of gossip out of the court. By the first week of July, Grenville knew he was finished, and he resolved to quit before he could be dismissed. On July 10, therefore, he attended the royal levee in order to hand over the seals of his office and to lecture the king, one last time, in the pompous style that had made George abhor the sight of him. He chose colonial policy as the text for this last sermon, telling the king that

> he understood that the plan of his new Administration was a total subversion of the former; that nothing having been undertaken as a measure without His Majesty's approbation, he knew not how he would let himself be persuaded to see it in so different a light, and most particularly on the regulations concerning the Colonies; that he besought His Majesty, as he valued his own safety, not to suffer any one to advise him to separate or draw the line between his British and American dominions; that his Colonies was the richest jewel of his Crown; that for his own part he must uniformly maintain his former opinions both in Parliament and out of it; that whatever was proposed in Parliament must abide the sentence passed upon it there, but that if any man ventured to defeat the regulations laid down for the Colonies, by a slackness in the execution, he should look upon him as a criminal and the betrayer of his country.[6]

Not to draw the line between his British and American dominions: there was the heart of it. All Grenville's efforts to construct a sound imperial relationship had centered on integrating the colonies into the British state system and subordinating the colonists to the sovereign power of the king in Parliament. Its ultimate logic would have welded the colonies and the realm together in a union like that of Scotland and England in 1707, extending the power of the metropolis over an even more distant periphery, forming a greater Great Britain. Grenville did not trust the men who would succeed him to see the issues so clearly and therefore devoted his last moments in office to impressing their importance on the king. George listened as politely as he habitually did—"imputing no blame," Grenville noted, but also "giving no word of approbation" and promising nothing.[7] The king obviously intended to stand behind his new servants. Whether they would adhere to their predecessor's policies, however, would depend entirely upon the circumstances they encountered, upon whatever unknowable developments lay ahead, upon—for all Grenville knew—sheer accident. As it happened, all of those would very soon put the new ministers, and the king's faith in their judgment, to the test.

CHAPTER 68

The Assemblies Vacillate

SUMMER 1765

THE NEWS THAT Parliament had passed a colonial Stamp Act arrived in America about mid-April, while Lieutenant Fraser was paddling up to Fort de Chartres and the king was telling Grenville that he wanted a regent to be ready to take over in the event of his death. Like Fraser's arrival and the king's request, both of which inaugurated weeks of confusion that only later resolved themselves into dramatic outcomes, the news of the Stamp Act opened a prolonged period of uncertainty. Although most provincial assemblies were sitting in spring sessions when word of the Stamp Act arrived, their members' responses spanned a range that extended no farther than the distance separating ambivalence from apathy. While the newspapers carried accounts of the act and dissected its implications during May and June, the halls of province houses rang with speeches on the necessity of maintaining public roads and protecting livestock from predators. Even in places where one might have expected to hear orators call for the defense of Englishmen's rights or the duty of resisting tyrants, all that echoed was a sort of embarrassed silence.

The assemblies of Rhode Island, Connecticut, New York, Pennsylvania, Massachusetts, and Virginia had previously petitioned against a colonial Stamp Act, but in all six provinces the news of the law's passage triggered only hesitation. Legislators in Rhode Island, Connecticut, and New York refrained from taking any action at all. In Pennsylvania, where the antiproprietary party was busy making up the ground it had lost in the last election, the agitation for royal government continued to absorb all political energies. Taking their cues from Franklin's letters, the party's leaders—John Hughes in the assembly and Joseph Galloway in the enforced leisure that followed his electoral defeat—did their best to promote compliance with the act. Hughes happily accepted the news of his appointment as stamp-master for the province, convinced that the proprietary party would mount no significant challenge in the legislature. The proprietary men were, after all, creatures of the governor, and the governor's job was to enforce the laws; Hughes's stamp distributorship would give him a certain amount of patronage, in the form of nominations to subordinate offices, that he could use to support his party's interest. Galloway contemplated writing newspaper articles to explain to a skeptical public, in the calm way Franklin might have done, "the reasonableness of our being Taxed." Neither Hughes nor Galloway liked the Stamp Act, but their need to ensure Pennsylvania's compliance swept away all qualms. The welfare of their party and its campaign for royal government demanded nothing less than perfect loyalty to the Crown. Similarly local considerations muted the response of Massachusetts politicians to the Stamp Act; but there the reluctance to criticize Parliament welled up from other sources.[1]

Boston's town meeting, the pit bull of Bay Colony politics, met on May 13 to instruct its delegation in the legislature to coordinate opposition to the act by making common cause with other colonies' assemblies. This directive reiterated the previous year's instructions, which had resulted in James Otis seizing the leadership of the assembly's committee of correspondence and using it to disseminate his views on colonial rights. Only Thomas Hutchinson's deft maneuvering had prevented the country party from retaining the initiative then. This time, however, the court party did not need to intervene to keep the opposition from orchestrating a vigorous protest against British policy, or to hobble the assembly's efforts to promote intercolonial cooperation. The country party reeled blindly through the spring legislative session not because Thomas Hutchinson had dealt it a heavy blow, but because James Otis had.

Following the publication of his *Rights of the Colonies Asserted and Proved* in 1764, Otis had entered a pamphlet debate with a Rhode Island royalist named Martin Howard Jr. Howard, a Newport lawyer, had helped organize a small group, the Newport Junto, dedicated to overturning the colony's charter in favor of royal government. When Governor Stephen Hopkins, a friend and legal client of Otis, published a pamphlet called *The Rights of the Colonies Examined* that echoed many of Otis's arguments, Howard responded with a pamphlet entitled *A Letter from a Gentleman at Halifax to His Friend in Rhode-Island,* ridiculing both Hopkins's and Otis's positions. Otis shot back with two pamphlets, intended both to refute Howard and to clarify his earlier positions, which he believed had been misunderstood. His essays, however, clarified nothing so much as his limitations as a controversialist. Chaotic, obscure, and violently abusive, the pamphlets seemed to contradict, not amplify, the arguments Otis had advanced in his first essay. In fewer than seventy pages of prose he sowed enough confusion to disable his political allies from protesting the Stamp Act.

In *The Rights of the Colonies Asserted and Proved,* Otis had not denied Parliament's sovereign power to tax the colonies, or indeed to do anything it chose; he only maintained that insofar as Parliament's right to rule rested on natural law, it could not exercise its power "wantonly" without calling its own legitimacy into question. In *A Vindication of the British Colonies, against the Aspersions of the Halifax Gentleman,* he reaffirmed this expansive definition of Parliament's powers but neglected to restate his insistence that Parliament must act with the self-restraint born of respect for natural law. *A Vindication* thus damaged his credibility, but his next pamphlet, published just a week before the May election, annihilated it.

In *Brief Remarks on the Defence of the Halifax Libel on the British-American-Colonies,* Otis chose to emphasize the duty of the colonists, as loyal subjects, to obey Parliament's enactments. Since Parliament embodied the supreme authority in the British state, true Britons could do no more than inquire into the members' reasonings and intentions: they could not rightfully resist. Otis went so far as to compliment Thomas Whately—the Treasury officer responsible for drafting most of the Stamp Act—for his exposition of the doctrine of "virtual representation," which dismissed the colonists' complaint that they could not be taxed by a House of Commons to which they elected no members. Whately's pamphlet, *The Regulations Lately Made Concerning the Colonies and the Taxes Imposed upon Them, Considered* (London, 1765), had tried to make a virtue of the irregular character of representation in the House of Commons by arguing that each member, once elected, represented the whole body politic and was thus freed from serving the narrow interests of any locality. Because legislative representation in the colonies tended to be much more regular—more reflective of the distribution of population and property and thus "actual"—most colonists instinctively dismissed such arguments as sophistry. When Otis endorsed them, writing that "the colonists are virtually, constitutionally, in law and in equity, to be considered as represented in the honorable House of Commons," he seemed to surrender the Englishman's fundamental right to be taxed only by consent.[2]

In Otis's own view he had merely elaborated what was implicit in *The Rights of the Colonies Asserted and Proved.* Practically everyone else, lost in the maze of his reasoning, concluded that he had recanted all. Governor

Bernard reported to the Board of Trade that "the author of the Rights of the Colonies now repents in Sackcloth and ashes for the hand he had in that book. . . . In a pamphlett lately published he has [begged pardon] in humblest Manner of the Ministry and of the Parliament for the liberties he took with them." Otis's Boston constituents demanded that he explain himself before they reelected him, by the narrowest of margins, to the General Court. Thereafter, however, he created further bewilderment by trying to explain himself in speeches and newspaper articles.[3]

Toward the end of the session, recalling the town's instruction to promote cooperation between the various colonial assemblies, Otis suggested that Massachusetts sponsor an intercolonial conference to discuss the Stamp Act. No one knew exactly what to make of that idea, but no one could find anything illegal about it; and in the end even the governor approved. Thus it was, on June 8, just before adjourning one of the most confused sessions in its history, that the House of Representatives voted to send a circular letter to invite the other colonial legislatures to send delegates to attend a congress at New York in October—a gathering "to consider of a general and united, dutiful, loyal and humble Representation of their Condition to His Majesty and the Parliament; and to implore Relief." Massachusetts's own delegation would reflect the extreme tentativeness of the General Court. Two of the delegates, Timothy Ruggles and Oliver Partridge, were members of the governor's council and had served as high-ranking provincial officers in the recent war; they were among the most conservative men in the colony. The third was James Otis. Not for nothing did Governor Bernard feel able to assure the Board of Trade that the Bay Colony's delegation would "never consent to any undutiful or improper application to the Government of Great Britain."[4]

Virginia's House of Burgesses would also hesitate before it took action, and then would act in a fundamentally ambiguous way. Down to the very end of May, no burgess said anything at all about the Stamp Act. Two-thirds of them, anticipating an uneventful end to the session, had already gone back to their plantations on May 20 when a new man, elected to replace a Louisa County representative who had retired, took his place on a back bench. The House's most junior member, Patrick Henry, was new to politics but not to public life. After six weeks of legal education and five years of practice, he had become one of the most successful attorneys in the province, a spellbinding advocate who flourished his reputation for oratory and his opposition to privilege like a sword.

Still a few days shy of his twenty-ninth birthday, Henry was shy of nothing else. New members ordinarily said nothing for a session or two, quietly deferring to their elders, and finally making a maiden speech on an issue carefully chosen for its lack of significance. Henry would have none of such becoming modesty and immediately took the floor to attack a bill, backed by the leadership of the House and the single most influential man in Virginia politics, John Robinson—a venerable figure who combined in his person the offices of secretary of the colony, treasurer, and speaker of the House. The bill that Robinson and his fellow grandees backed would have authorized the province to borrow £250,000 in London, secured by a tax that would run until 1795. Its ostensible purpose was to permit Virginia to retire its outstanding currency; but one provision quietly permitted indebted and cash-starved planters to borrow sterling from the public treasury, mortgaging their lands as security. Henry ridiculed the measure for its obvious self-interestedness, shocking the senior members of the House and contributing to its defeat.[5] Henry's next speech, however, would shock more than the few burgesses who lingered through the last, sweltering days of the session.

On May 29, its legislative business finished, the House resolved itself into a committee of the whole to discuss "steps necessary to be taken in consequence" of the Stamp Act. Henry immediately rose and introduced five resolutions, which he had written out, "alone, unadvised, and unassisted, on a blank leaf of an old law book." The first four recited historical commonplaces with which no burgess disagreed, for they paraphrased similar ones in the previous year's petitions. Virginia's founders, Henry began, had "brought with them" English liberties in the seventeenth century; royal charters (secondly) had confirmed those rights; taxation by the consent of elected representatives was (thirdly) central to the survival of all such liberties; and the right of Virginians to lay taxes on themselves had "never been forfeited or yielded up, but hath been constantly recognized by the Kings and People of Great Britain." The fifth resolution, however, struck another note. "Resolved Therefore that the General Assembly of this Colony have the *only and sole exclusive* Right and Power to lay Taxes and Impositions upon the Inhabitants of this Colony and that every Attempt to vest such Power in any Person or Persons whatsoever other than the General Assembly aforesaid has a manifest Tendency to destroy British as well as American Freedom."[6]

This resolve, which not only denied Parliament's right to tax Virginia but insisted that the attempt imperiled the liberty of all British subjects, sparked a debate so intense that even the preoccupied lieutenant governor, Francis Fauquier, took note. He had been attending to Indian diplomacy—he was hoping to prevent a war between the Overhill Cherokees and backwoodsmen beyond the Blue Ridge—and was as surprised as anyone in Williamsburg at the "rash heat" of the debates, in which "the Young, hot, and Giddy Members" had "overpowerd" the older, soberer burgesses. "Mr. Henry," Fauquier reported to the Board of Trade a few days later, "carryed all the young Members with him" and succeeded in passing all five resolutions, albeit by margins of five votes or fewer; the "virulent and inflammatory" final resolve carried "by a single Voice."[7]

Yet Fauquier, while momentarily taken aback, was not alarmed. As he explained to the Board, the debate would never have happened "if more . . . Representatives had done their Duty by attending to the end of the Session," and he had at any rate undone the damage merely by keeping the House in session until May 31. Once Henry left for home on the evening of the thirtieth, nothing could prevent the more conservative members from moving a reconsideration of the resolves. Then it had been a simple matter to have "the 5th which was thought the most offensive . . . struck off." With the regrettable business thus tidied up, Fauquier dissolved the House. His official report on the session made it clear that he thought the resolutions came to nothing more than grandstanding: a pettifogger's effort to pump up a political career.[8]

Not every witness would have agreed. Thomas Jefferson, a twenty-two-year-old student from the College of William and Mary who had listened to the debates from the hallway outside the chamber, would surely have taken exception. He thought he had heard something extraordinary—even though he was not quite sure what it was. As much swept away by the tide of Henry's oratory as were the hot and giddy burgesses who voted for the resolutions, Jefferson experienced the debate not as an exposition of colonial rights but as a kind of high moral theater. Later he would realize that he could recall little of what Henry had said; only that the debate had been "most bloody" and the speaker of the House furious. Just so: that was how Henry intended it. He had built his career not on abstract reasoning but on his ability to sway juries by appealing to them in the emotional, extemporaneous mode of evangelical preaching. When Henry inveighed against the Stamp Act as an infringement of the rights and liberties of Virginia Englishmen, therefore, he was *enacting* a moral position, not explicating a set of political principles.[9]

Patrick Henry had all the vehemence of Otis but employed it to better effect because he understood his task as persuasion, not exposition. Lacking the technical knowledge that drove Otis to take his stand amid impenetrable thickets of logic, Henry freely cast the debate as a contest between right and wrong. To tax an Englishman without his consent was to deprive him of his rights, to reduce him to slavery. Virginians were Englishmen, and only tyrants would seek to make them slaves. From principles so simple, anyone with common sense—anyone whose judgment had not been corrupted by his lust for power or taking of a placeman's filthy salary—could draw his own conclusions. If such ideas ceased to resonate in the House of Burgesses once Henry had departed and calmer colleagues repealed his final ringing resolve, they would reverberate long and loud outside the assembly hall. From the time that copies of the Virginia Resolves began to circulate outside Williamsburg, ordinary men would begin to draw conclusions from which sophisticated politicians shrank in fear.

CHAPTER 69

Mobs Respond

SUMMER 1765

THE *VIRGINIA GAZETTE* did not find the Burgesses' proceedings newsworthy, so the first newspaper to print the Virginia Resolves was the distant *Newport Mercury*, on June 24. Other newspapers followed suit, reprinting either the *Mercury*'s version or the slightly different one that ran in the July 4 issue of the *Maryland Gazette*. Neither account drew on the official journals of the House, and neither editor probably understood that the Burgesses had retained only the first four innocuous resolutions, repealing the fiery fifth. Certainly no reader of the *Mercury* or the *Gazette*, or of any newspaper that reprinted their stories, could have known that the sixth and seventh resolutions printed alongside the rest were utterly spurious and may not even have been debated. To this day no one knows who wrote them, or how they made their way into print alongside the other five. All that is really clear is that the newspaper accounts convinced readers everywhere that Virginia's legislators had taken a bold stand in defense of colonial rights.

> *Resolved*, That his Majesty's liege People, the Inhabitants of this Colony, are not bound to yield Obedience to any law or Ordinance whatever, designed to impose any Taxation whatsoever upon them, other than the Laws or Ordinances of the General Assembly aforesaid.
>
> *Resolved*, That any Person, who shall, by speaking or writing, assert or maintain, that any Person or Persons, other than the General Assembly of this Colony, have any Right or Power to impose or lay any Taxation on the People here, shall be deemed an Enemy to this his Majesty's Colony.[1]

Soon after this wildly inaccurate version of the resolves appeared, opposition to the Stamp Act began to overflow the channels of normal politics. Between the middle of August and the end of the year, the protests of ordinary colonists would astonish anyone who had thought (like Grenville or Franklin) that the Americans would knuckle under to parliamentary taxation, and perplex everyone (including Gage and the colonial governors) who had to respond, once it became clear that Americans would not submit.

The stimulus to resistance came from Williamsburg, but Boston was where talk first gave way to deeds. A handful of artisans and lesser merchants there had been meeting for some time past as a social club—long enough, at any rate, to invent a name for themselves, the "Loyal Nine." They were solid but far from eminent Bostonians. Among the club's two distillers, two brass-founders, merchant, jeweler, painter, ship captain, and printer, only two men were Harvard graduates. Three held town offices, but none had ever served in the General Court. Their politics aligned them with the country party, but after the Virginia Resolves became known in town, they seem to have soured on politicians generally. We get a hint of their mood from a column that Benjamin Edes, the printer among them, published in his newspaper, the *Boston Gazette,* on July 8.

> The People of Virginia have spoke very sensibly . . . : Their spirited Resolves do indeed serve as a perfect Contrast for a certain tame, pusillanimous, daub'd insipid Thing, delicately touch'd up and call'd an Address; which was lately sent from this Side the Water, to please the Taste of the Tools of Corruption on the other. . . . We have been told with an Insolence the more intolerable, because disguis'd with a Veil of public Care, that it is not prudence for us to assert our Rights in plain and manly Terms: Nay, we have been told that the word RIGHTS must not be once named among us! Curs'd Prudence of interested designing Politicians![2]

In this frame of mind, the Loyal Nine embarked on a course that would soon deprive prudent politicians of the ability to dilute Massachusetts's resistance to the Stamp Act. They decided to raise the biggest mob in the history of Boston and use it to force the designated stamp distributor, Andrew Oliver, to resign.

Boston had not one but two mobs in the 1760s: loose aggregations of laborers, apprentices, lesser artisans, sailors, blacks, and others of "the lower sort," who lived in the North and South Ends of the town. These groups enjoyed an annual day of exuberance and carnival each November 5, when Boston commemorated the defeat of the Gunpowder Plot of 1605. Bostonians knew this most English of holidays as Pope Day, not Guy Fawkes Day, because the local celebrations had come to focus on elaborate effigies of the pope and the devil, and the ritual brawl between the North Enders and the South Enders over which mob would have the honor of burning them. The Pope Day contests may have begun as manly scrimmages, but by the mid-1760s they had evolved into skull-cracking, limb-breaking affrays involving as many as four thousand men and boys.

Levels of Pope Day violence had escalated over time because members of mobs began using clubs and brickbats as well as their fists, and also because they created formalized command structures, with "captains" and subordinate leaders to direct each mob's actions. Thus when the Loyal Nine decided to take the Stamp Act protests into the streets, they were able to approach two men—Ebenezer Mackintosh, the twenty-eight-year-old shoemaker who captained the South End mob, and Henry Smith, the shipwright who headed the North Enders—with great experience in organizing crowd actions. The greatest challenge lay not in getting Mackintosh and Smith to bring their men out, but convincing them to forget their rivalry long enough to make Oliver resign. This was not easy to do, but the Loyal Nine finally persuaded the two leaders to take joint action on August 14.[3]

On that Wednesday morning nobody passing Deacon Elliot's Corner on High Street could have missed the pair of effigies dangling from a big elm tree's limb.[4] One was the figure of a man, with signs affixed identifying it as "A.O," the "Stamp-Man." The other inspired more curiosity, but members of the gathering crowd explained to one another that an old boot, bottomed with a new "green-vile" sole and topped with a figure of the devil, made a pointed comment on the earl of Bute, George Grenville's soul, and the motive force behind the Stamp Act. Before the day was out these images attracted as many as five thousand men, women, and children, a crowd that for the most part remained in a festive mood. In the afternoon, however, when the sheriff screwed up enough courage to try cutting the effigies down, he found himself so roundly threatened that he hustled off to warn the governor of an impending riot.

At evening three thousand men, taking directions from Ebenezer Mackintosh, made good on the sheriff's prediction. Cutting down the images, they paraded three-quarters of a mile to a small brick structure Andrew Oliver had recently built at his wharf. Calling it the Stamp Office, they tore it down in a matter of minutes; then, carrying its timbers as fuel for a bonfire, they marched on to Oliver's house. They paused long enough to behead his effigy and throw stones through his windows before ascending the nearby Fort Hill, where they "stamped" the figures to bits and burned them. Then they went looking for the Stamp-Man himself.

They did not find Oliver that night—he had taken refuge with friends—and so they demolished the interior of his house instead, drinking up the contents of his wine cellar while they turned his carriage, furniture, wainscoting, and privy to matchwood. The enthusiasm with which they destroyed Oliver's property suggests that as the evening wore on the members of the crowd acted less in response to direction from above than according to their own lights. Men who might work all year and earn less than fifty pounds—supposing they were fully employed, as in the midst of a depression few could have been—reacted furiously when they saw how luxuriously a wealthy merchant lived; and no one needed to explain that he would grow even richer on shillings to be extracted from their own thin purses, once the Stamp Act went into effect. Since by midnight whatever restrained the mob's behavior came entirely from within, the Loyal Nine may have felt as much relief as Oliver when the rioters dispersed.

The next day, several gentlemen visited Oliver and urged him to resign, pointing out that at least his house still stood—but would not long do so if he tried to execute his commission as tax collector. Oliver, who had not yet received the documents appointing him and could not resign what he did not have, agreed to refrain from collecting any duties once the stamps arrived and promised to write to London asking to be excused from the distributorship. That evening, when a second crowd gathered on Fort Hill and lit another bonfire, Oliver sent word renouncing his appointment. The crowd gave him three cheers before dispersing.

Andrew Oliver's surrender solved his own immediate problem but deepened Governor Bernard's perplexities. Bernard had been unable to maintain order on the fourteenth. When he ordered the colonel of Boston's militia regiment to raise his men and disperse the mob, the colonel only "answered, that it would signify nothing, for as soon as the drum was heard, the drummer would be knocked down, and the drum broke; [and] added, that probably all the drummers of the Regiment were in the Mob."[5] At that Bernard, never devoted to heroic gestures, ordered his servants to hide the silverware and row him out to Castle William. He spent that night and the next watching bonfires flare on Fort Hill, knowing that unless the city calmed down on its own, he dared not leave the safety of the fort.

To become a kind of prisoner in this way was humiliating enough, but Bernard worried even more about the fragility of civil order in the province. He was the king's direct representative, yet the riots had shown that he governed Massachusetts at the sufferance of Boston's mob. His lieutenant governor, Thomas Hutchinson, had actually been chased through the streets on the night of the fourteenth after he dragged the sheriff out to read the riot act to the mob. It was true that he and the sheriff had run fast enough to save everything but their dignity from harm; but as Bernard well understood, Hutchinson's boldness had served only to single him out for future harassment. Just how much danger the lieutenant governor was in, and just how tenuous the control of His Majesty's government had grown, would only become clear as the next week passed and the Loyal Nine—or perhaps, by now, Mackintosh and the mob independently—decided what steps to take next.

Rumors circulated in Boston and the surrounding towns as early as Saturday the twenty-fourth that the mob would come out again on the following Monday night, and that its targets would include leading customs officials, Hutchinson, and perhaps even Bernard. Since Oliver had already promised to resign, the Stamp Act alone could not account for this. Hutchinson, of course, had set himself squarely in the mob's sights on the night of the fourteenth, and the political gossip had it that he had actually advised Grenville on how best to tax America. But other animosities at work were personal and tinged more by economic than political factors. These can best be grasped when one understands that 1765 may well have been the worst year in Boston's commercial history, the grimmest time in the interminably grim postwar depression.

The city's economy had been no better than sluggish since 1761, but nothing prepared Bostonians for the financial disaster that had struck at the beginning of 1765. In mid-January, Nathaniel Wheelwright, a merchant who had grown rich during the war by simultaneously acting as a British military contractor and trading with the French, abruptly stopped payment on his debts and ran for Guadeloupe. There were as yet no banks in North America, but Wheelwright had been acting as a kind of banker for many of Boston's smaller merchants, shopkeepers, and artisans, taking their money on deposit and issuing interest-bearing personal notes in return. These notes had actually circulated as a kind of supplemental currency in Boston and the surrounding towns. Now he left £170,000 in unpaid obligations, a mountain of worthless paper, and a panic that flattened the town's economy as effectively as the earthquake of 1755 had devastated Lisbon.

In a panic of "pulling and hauling, attaching and summoning to secure themselves," those who had lent Wheelwright money as commercial creditors and depositors soon began following him into default and flight. The General Court passed an emergency Bankruptcy Act in March to regularize the processes of financial settlement and, the legislators hoped, to stabilize the economy. This stopped the wholesale flight, but desperate debtors continued to run from their creditors, and the lengthening list of warrants sworn out for the arrest of fugitive debtors bore witness to Boston's agonies: three warrants in March, four in April, four in May, nine in June, seven in July, eight in August. Ninety percent of them were authorized by Thomas Hutchinson, chief justice of the Superior Court—who (not coincidentally) collected generous fees on the administration of bankruptcies and seized estates. As Boston wallowed in the pit of depression, expressions of esteem for Hutchinson came as rarely to the lips of most merchants as they did to those of the artisans and laborers who made up its mobs.[6]

The few Bostonians who did not actively despise Thomas Hutchinson were mostly related to him by birth, marriage, or business partnership, and that was another part of his problem. Never content to be the Bay Colony's leading plural officeholder—he received salaries or fees as lieutenant governor, chief justice, probate judge for Suffolk County, and commander of Castle William—he had assiduously promoted members of the Hutchinson clan as candidates for government offices, along with the numerous Sanfords, Fosters, and Olivers to whom he was also related. In this critical respect the customs officers whose houses were said to be the mob's targets closely resembled the lieutenant governor. All of them were placemen who made their livings from fees. All were reputed to be greedy and corrupt. And all of them were quite visibly wealthy. Their mansion houses stood in imposing contrast to the homes of artisans, shopkeepers, and laborers that surrounded them.[7]

Thus did the personal and the political converge in the small world of Boston, where face-to-face relationships did little to dissipate resentment, and where memories ran long. In this respect too Boston's animosities pressed relentlessly against Thomas Hutchinson. Everyone in the cash-starved, debt-ridden colony knew that he had been responsible for creating its hard-money currency regime in 1749. If merchants thanked him for protecting their investments from inflation, Massachusetts's chronically indebted farmers, as well as Boston's tradesmen and laborers, had come to understand him as their foe. It was no accident that he held no significant elective office after 1749. The higher Governors Shirley, Pownall, and Bernard raised him in appointive offices, the lower he had sunk in public esteem.

All these anxious enmities blossomed with the bonfire's flames in King Street at dusk on August 26. Since morning people had been coming into Boston from the nearby towns, swelling the crowd of North and South End men who waited to hear Ebenezer Mackintosh's directions. Bernard, fearing the worst, had packed his plate off to Castle William and arranged to take shelter there himself when the trouble started. The town's customs officers similarly made themselves scarce. But beyond deciding to stay at home that evening rather than dining out, Hutchinson had made no effort to avoid the mob. He refused to believe they could hate him as thoroughly as, in fact, they did.[8]

The men who gathered in King Street chanted "Liberty and Property!"—which, as Bernard sourly observed, gave "the Usual Notice of their Intention to plunder and pull down a house"—and divided themselves into two groups.[9] The first set off for the house of Charles Paxton, surveyor of customs and marshal of the Boston Vice-Admiralty Court. Paxton rented; but the mob found his landlord at home and eager to exercise the better part of valor by offering them a barrel of punch. Thus refreshed, they moved on to the mansion of Benjamin Hallowell, comptroller of customs, where they drank a good deal more while they sacked the place, wrecking the interior and its contents. Meanwhile, at the house of the register of the vice-admiralty court, William Story, the other half of the mob was draining the wine cellar as they broke furniture, windows, and china, and committed the files of pending customs cases to a bonfire. Thus when the two halves of the mob reunited for the remaining business of the evening they had already consumed a good deal of alcohol; and that almost certainly contributed to their remarkably violent behavior when they reached the handsome Georgian house of Thomas Hutchinson.

The lieutenant governor had been at supper with his family when breathless messengers came to warn him that the mob was on its way. As Hutchinson later told the story to the province's agent, Richard Jackson, they fled

> to a neighboring house where I had been but a few minutes before the hellish crew fell upon my house with the Rage of devils and in a moment with axes split down the doors and entred[. M]y son being in the great entry heard them cry damn him he is upstairs we'll have him. Some ran immediately as high as the top of the house others filled the rooms below and cellars and others Remained without the house to be employed there. Messages soon came one after another to the house where I was to inform me the mob were coming in Pursuit of me and I was obliged to retire thro yards and gardens to a house

> more remote where I remained until 4 o'clock by which time one of the best finished houses in the Province had nothing remaining but the bare walls and floors. Not contented with tearing off all the wainscot and hangings and splitting the doors to pieces they beat down the Partition walls and altho that alone cost them near two hours they cut down the cupola or lanthern and they began to take the slate and boards from the roof and were prevented only by the approaching daylight from a total demolition of the building. The garden fence was laid flat and all my trees &c broke down to the ground. Such ruins were never seen in America. Besides my Plate and family Pictures houshold furniture of every kind my own children and servants apparel they carried off about £900 sterling in money and emptied the house of every thing whatsoever except a part of the kitchen furniture not leaving a single book or paper in it and have scattered or destroyed all the manuscripts and other papers I had been collecting for 30 years together besides a great number of Publick Papers in my custody.

The next morning proved a cool one, and Hutchinson—twelve hours earlier one of the wealthiest men in Massachusetts—found that he had no coat to ward off the chill but the one his host lent him. He had lost virtually all of his personal possessions. He told Jackson he guessed the damages could not amount to less than three thousand pounds sterling, concluding—because money alone could not measure what his family had lost—"You cannot conceive the wretched state we are in."[10]

Yet Hutchinson remained convinced that the Loyal Nine—"the encouragers of the first mob"—never intended the destruction to go so far. On the day after the riot the political leaders of the province and town did their belated best to restore order. Hutchinson said he hoped that their "detestation of this unparalleled outrage" would bring some good out of the evil he and his family had suffered, but he remained bewildered by the ferocious "resentment of the people against the stamp duty." He trembled to think of its consequences. The General Court, he thought, would not dare "enforce or rather advise the payment of it." But what could be done? The tax was so constructed that no business or legal proceedings could be conducted without stamped paper. If the province did not submit, then "all trade must cease all courts fall and all authority be at an end." If Parliament repealed the tax it would "endanger the loss of their authority over the colonies," yet if it chose to compel submission by "external force" it risked "a total lasting alienation of affection." Contemplating the ruin of his personal life, this master of the politic middle way found himself unable to imagine any alternative between anarchy on the one hand and brutal repression on the other. In the end he could only pray that the "infinitely wise God" might show Parliament a way out of the maze of violence in which he, and his colony, and the empire he loved, seemed hopelessly lost.[11]

Hutchinson did not yet know, when he wrote his plaintive letter to Richard Jackson, that riots were convulsing other towns beside Boston. The comparatively controlled crowd action of August 14, which so quickly produced Andrew Oliver's resignation as stamp distributor, seemed to demonstrate a practical means of preventing the act from taking effect. When word of it arrived in other colonies, counterparts to the Loyal Nine—groups that often called themselves Sons of Liberty after Colonel Barré's speech, which was now achieving a notoriety comparable to the Virginia Resolves—set about stuffing effigies, erecting mock gallows, and raising mobs to put the stamp-masters in a cooperative frame of mind. And they found, not infrequently, what the Loyal Nine had discovered on August 26: that mobs, once raised, could set their own agendas. Rhode Islanders first illustrated this principle on the day after the Boston mob destroyed Hutchinson's house.[12]

In Newport on August 20, the leaders of opposition to the Stamp Act began preparing to exhibit an effigy of the colony's designated distributor, Augustus Johnston. On August 26, the day before the hanging and demonstrations were to take place, Martin Howard, who had taken on James Otis earlier in the year, denounced the idea in the press. Unwisely so: on the twenty-seventh, his effigy and those of his political friends in the Newport Junto dangled alongside that of the stamp-master. That evening an orderly crowd burned the effigies. Johnston did not resign, however, and the next night, encouraged by fresh news from Boston, the Newporters raised the stakes. First they sacked Martin Howard's house as thoroughly as the Bostonians had demolished Hutchinson's; then they destroyed the house and goods of another member of the Junto and hunted through the town for the collector and the comptroller of customs (both of whom had taken refuge aboard H.M.S. *Cygnet,* a British man-of-war in the harbor); finally, lest he think they had forgotten him, they carried off as many of Augustus Johnston's household possessions as they could lay hands on.

The next morning Johnston publicly resigned his office, an act that saved his house, got much of his property returned, and allowed him to resume his place in the community. But the collector of customs, an English placeman named John Robinson who had dedicated himself to rooting out smugglers, remained so unpopular that he did not dare leave the *Cygnet* until September 2, when Governor Samuel Ward finally gave him a bodyguard. Like Bernard, Ward had been unable to intervene and stop the riots. Unlike Bernard, he had not wanted to do so—at least not so long as the victims were Howard and his Junto, the avowed enemies of Rhode Island's charter government. But Ward soon realized that the customhouse could not operate without its collector, ships could not enter and clear without an operating customhouse, and Newport could not live without its shipping.

The Newport riots thus showed that even an institutionally autonomous colony could ill afford to dispense with the empire. The significance of this paradox—that colonists unwilling to abide the direct application of parliamentary sovereignty could not long survive outside the legal and mercantile system that Parliament had created—would become fully clear only after virtually every other colony had followed the path of Newport and Boston, and riots had in effect nullified the Stamp Act before it could take effect. Meanwhile, colonial mobs savored power's sweet wine while stamp distributors choked down the dregs of humiliation.

The prudent resigned at the first sign of threat, if not before. In New York, James McEvers renounced his appointment on August 22 to save his warehouse; in New Jersey, William Coxe surrendered his commission before a single effigy had swung, merely because he had heard the news from New England. George Meserve of New Hampshire announced his resignation at Boston on September 10, even before he stepped off the ship that had brought him from England. He had not yet seen the effigies that the Sons of Liberty had prepared to greet him in Portsmouth. When he did, he resigned again. Colonel George Mercer returned to Virginia on October 31, aboard the ship that carried the stamps for Virginia, Maryland, and North Carolina. Finding a similar reception, he made a similar obeisance. "Surrounded by more than 2000 People," he wrote, "without a single Person, in the whole Colony, who dared openly to assist me, . . . I was obliged to submit . . . as the only possible Step, to secure his Majesty's Property and my Person and Effects." South Carolina's inspector of stamps arrived on October 26, discovered that a mob of two thousand men had been only narrowly dissuaded from leveling his house a week earlier, and resigned on the twenty-eighth. The North Carolina distributor, a physician who had not sought the office, renounced his commission as soon as it arrived, before a mob of several hundred men. None of these stamp-masters would have chosen to resign as they did, for such acts of submission robbed them of the personal dignity they cherished. But all of them at least managed to save the property that in the end they valued more.[13]

Others, less willing to defer to the mobs, found displays of personal courage repaid with economic or political ruin. For Maryland's designated distributor, the merchant Zachariah Hood, steadfastness meant bankruptcy. He withstood a hanging in effigy on August 29, then saw a mob demolish his warehouse on September 2. Fleeing to New York, he placed himself under General Gage's protection and vowed to execute his office, if necessary, from the deck of a man-of-war. But New York's Sons of Liberty made his life so miserable that he dared not leave Fort George. When he finally ventured out, on November 28, a hundred mounted men seized him, carried him five miles into the country, and forced him to resign. Thereafter he returned to Annapolis and tried to rebuild his fortune, only to find that no one would do business with him. A broken man, in 1771 he went to England to seek compensation from the Crown, and he never returned.[14]

Both Connecticut's distributor, Jared Ingersoll, and Governor Thomas Fitch paid heavy financial and political penalties for trying to enforce the Stamp Act. Fitch feared that Parliament would counter any resistance in Connecticut by revoking the colony's charter. During the war he had built a party of supporters among Old Light representatives from the colony's western half, and the charter was an object as sacred to the predominantly New Light eastern representatives as to the westerners, so Fitch thought it safe to call a special session of the assembly and ask it for what amounted to an endorsement of the stamp tax. He therefore urged Ingersoll to stand fast, and the stamp-master in turn defied newspaper denunciations and repeated hangings in effigy. But as Ingersoll was making his way to Hartford for the assembly session, five hundred Sons of Liberty from eastern Connecticut—primarily veterans, led by former provincial officers—marched out to intercept him at Wethersfield on September 18. There they held him hostage until he agreed not only to resign, but to toss his hat into the air and lead three cheers for "liberty and property." Forming an escort, they conveyed him to Hartford, installed him in a tavern, summoned his fellow representatives, and forced him to reenact his resignation.

Neither Ingersoll nor Fitch recovered his political standing thereafter, and the Old Light party to which they belonged soon lost its dominance in the assembly. Ingersoll's law practice declined so badly that he had to call on London friends to secure him a vice-admiralty judgeship; but the court sat in Philadelphia, and the price of retaining his livelihood was exile from his home colony. Fitch, who had been elected twelve successive times to the governorship and who was surely one of the ablest politicians in Connecticut's history, found that he had become unelectable. In the coming year he would publish a pamphlet explaining that he had been bound by his oath of office to uphold an act that he personally disapproved of, but no amount of explaining could restore his career. In the end he, too, solicited a position in the vice-admiralty court system—and, like Ingersoll, had to abandon his native colony to take it up.[15]

Pennsylvania's designated distributor, John Hughes, proved even braver than Ingersoll, while his partner Joseph Galloway remained as determined as Fitch to bring about a political solution. In the end, Hughes paid as dearly as any other stubborn stamp-master; and while by the quirks of Pennsylvania politics Galloway and the antiproprietary party maintained control in the assembly, they survived only to pay another day.[16] Accounts of the riots in New England reached Philadelphia at the beginning of September, and Hughes soon came under pressure to resign. When he refused, the proprietary faction began to dabble in mob organizing: an ironic move for a court party, perhaps, but a strategically canny one, given the prospects of tarring the assembly's dominant faction with the massive unpopularity of the Stamp Act. As rumors began to make it clear that Philadelphia houses could be demolished as easily as those in Boston, Galloway turned from writing newspaper pieces encouraging submission to organizing countermobs. On September 16 (a week after Hughes, as speaker of the House, failed to prevent the assembly from appointing delegates to the Stamp Act Congress), all that kept a mob from destroying Hughes's house—and Benjamin Franklin's—were the patrols of armed men whom Galloway sent into the streets. He and his property thus remained safe, but the strain of staying up all night under arms after weeks of enduring anonymous threats sent Hughes into physical collapse. When the stamped paper and his commission arrived from Britain on October 5, the fifty-three-year-old distributor seemed to be teetering on the edge of the grave. Nonetheless an antistamp crowd formed, thousands strong; and seven prominent Philadelphians called on him to urge his resignation. He tried to resist, and indeed managed to hold out for two more days before finally promising not to execute the act unless the neighboring colonies did so.

Hughes's quasi-resignation kept the mob from pulling the house down around his ears. Gradually, as tensions lessened, his health returned, but his career in politics was finished. During his absence the assembly passed a set of ten resolutions declaring the Stamp Act unconstitutional and subversive of the rights of Englishmen.[17] This shift in the temper of the House, among members of both parties, could not be reversed; nor could Hughes conform himself to it. The antiproprietary party soon capitalized on the fears of disorder that the riots had raised and—arguing that the proprietary faction was at fault—actually increased its majority in the assembly at the next election and strengthened its case for abolishing the proprietorship. Galloway engineered the party's revival and even regained his own seat, but only by making sure that Hughes's name stayed off the slate of antiproprietary candidates. Isolated and bitter, Hughes retired to a farm outside Philadelphia. In 1769 he accepted a Crown appointment as collector of customs for Portsmouth, New Hampshire, and left Pennsylvania for good. The Stamp Act, which transformed so many things in America and the empire, had changed him—like Ingersoll, like Fitch—from a powerful and popular politician into a placeman, and an exile.

CHAPTER 70

Nullification by Violence, and an Elite Effort to Reassert Control

OCTOBER–NOVEMBER 1765

BY THE DATE the Stamp Act formally took effect, November 1, only one royal governor in America had any hope of enforcing it, and that was the result of an administrative oversight. Governor James Wright of Georgia still had command of several troops of mounted men, the Georgia Rangers, raised during the war to defend the province. Because the colony was too small and poor to pay them, the Crown had placed the rangers on the regular establishment and somehow forgotten to demobilize them after the return of peace. Thus Wright alone had the military muscle to face down the local Sons of Liberty and execute the law.[1] Elsewhere governors could only command the militia (uselessly, since as the colonel of Boston's regiment had pointed out to Governor Bernard, the mobs were made up of militiamen) or request regulars from the commander in chief. But even though Gage offered a hundred men each to the governors of Massachusetts, New Jersey, and Maryland, none of them dared accept, for fear of inflaming the mobs to even greater destructiveness. Where the first unexpected riots had occurred—Boston, Newport, Annapolis—there had been no garrisons at all. Only New York had both redcoats on hand and a governor, fierce old Cadwallader Colden, willing to use force; but that made matters worse.

When the shipment of stamped paper arrived at Manhattan on October 23 the New York distributor had long since resigned. Colden intended to execute the law regardless, and two thousand men, determined that he would not, lined the Battery to prevent the stamps from being landed. That night the authorities sneaked them into Fort George for safekeeping, only to discover that in doing so they had placed the fort in peril. Major Thomas James, the commandant who had once boasted that he could subdue the city with two dozen troops, now feverishly prepared to stave off an attack. By November 1, James and his garrison of about 180 soldiers had sufficient cannon and grapeshot on hand to defend themselves and the governor, but the mob ruled everywhere else. That night two thousand "Rabble or rather Rebels" rioted in the city. By four the next morning, they had hanged Colden's effigy, then burned it on Bowling Green in a bonfire stoked with "his chariot & 2 sleighs & a chair"; seized the guards posted to protect Major James's house, then gutted the structure with extraordinary thoroughness; surrounded the fort, hammered on its gates, chucked rocks at the troops, and taunted them for lacking the courage to shoot.

That the redcoats in Fort George did not open fire owed less to the major's restraint or the governor's wisdom than to General Gage's fear of what would happen if so much as a pistol were discharged. Because there had been no time to remove ordnance stores from the army's warehouses on the East River, most of the muskets, field artillery, and ammunition in New York—a very large amount indeed—lay within easy reach of the demonstrators. Gage therefore refused to join Colden and James inside the fort, remaining at his residence in the city, maintaining outward calm, and quietly urging the governor to give up the God-damned stamps. Finally, on November 5, Guy Fawkes Day, facing highly plausible rumors that a mob would storm the fort that evening, Colden handed them over to the mayor, who removed them to City Hall under the escort of the Sons of Liberty and a crowd of perhaps five thousand people. Since the reports had credibly maintained that the mob leaders planned to take Gage hostage and use him as a shield, the commander in chief must have been relieved to discover that Colden possessed some small capacity for compromise, after all. But it had been a near-run thing, and a foot put wrong at the end might well have provoked civil war.[2]

War, of course, was something that no one wanted. That it came so close in New York can be attributed to local peculiarities: a garrison large enough to be provocative but too small to be effective; Major James's silly boast; Colden's ram-you-damn-you personality; and the socially fragmented, virtually ungovernable character of the New York mob. Unlike Boston, where the two standing crowds had internal structures that the Loyal Nine and other local leaders could use to gain control after August 26, New York's mob was largely made up of seamen, most of whom lacked deep community ties and felt little need to submit to the authority of the city's shorebound radical leaders. Moreover, New York's Sons of Liberty emerged latest of all in the colonies and did not succeed in becoming spokesmen for the opposition until after November 1.[3]

Everywhere outside New York, however, the late summer's riots had shocked local leaders into seeking leverage over the mobs, while provincial politicians had scrambled to stake out positions in opposition to the act. Thus it was in the interest of gaining control over a fluid, potentially anarchic situation that, from September through the end of the year, colonial assemblies outdid one another in passing resolutions denouncing taxation without consent. Ultimately nine provinces issued antistamp resolves, and nine sent delegates to the Stamp Act Congress, to articulate colonial objections, to petition for the act's repeal—and to try to demonstrate that they were willing to stand up for English liberties and Englishmen's rights.[4]

The twenty-seven delegates who had met at New York's city hall from October 7 through October 25 represented a range of opinions as well as colonies, but they agreed from the start on the necessity of moderation. Their caution could be seen when they chose as chairman the Massachusetts conservative Timothy Ruggles, rather than the less predictable James Otis. Thereafter this aggregation of fortyish lawyers, landowners, and merchants did their best to become invisible, meeting in secret, keeping a journal that recorded nothing anyone said, and refusing to publish the declaration and petitions upon which they finally agreed. There can be little doubt that they hurried to conclude their sessions and get out of town when it became clear that the mob and Colden were on a collision course. And—even though the public would not see them until the next spring, when a Boston newspaper finally got hold of copies—no one could have discovered any sentiment more bold than polite in either the congress's Declaration of Rights and Liberties or in the petitions it sent to king, Lords, and Commons.

In declaring their "humble Opinion, respecting the most essential Rights and Liberties of the Colonists and the Grievances under which they labour" the delegates tried to construct an argument not from abstract principles, but from what they hoped were indisputable historical facts. The colonists, they maintained, had never forfeited their liberties as Englishmen, including the rights to taxation by consent and trial by jury; their lack of representation in Parliament meant that they could give their consent only through their assemblies; therefore the Stamp Act was "inconsistent with the Principles and Spirit of the *British* Constitution," while Parliament's extensions of vice-admiralty jurisdiction under the American Duties Act "have a manifest Tendency to subvert the Rights and Liberties of the Colonies." As for other customs exactions, the congress remained cautious. These were "extremely Burthensome and Grievous," and insofar as they restricted commerce, unwise; but the delegates stopped short of calling them taxes, and therefore beyond the power of Parliament to grant. To send a petition to the House of Commons might be taken to imply submission to Parliament's authority, of course, and the delegates approached that touchiest of issues on tiptoes of circumspection.[5]

In their petition to the king and their memorial to the House of Lords the delegates ducked the issue of sovereignty, but in the petition to the House of Commons they could not avoid the question that lay at the heart of the dispute. Did the colonies' "due Subordination to the Parliament of *Great-Britain*" require their limitless submission to Parliament's will? Tentatively, delicately—in contrast to the torrent of practical objections they poured out elsewhere—the delegates responded only with a query: "It is also humbly submitted, Whether there be not a material Distinction in Reason and sound Policy, at least, between the necessary Exercise of Parliamentary Jurisdiction in general Acts, for the Amendment of the Common Law, and the Regulation of Trade and Commerce through the whole Empire, and the Exercise of that Jurisdiction, by imposing Taxes on the Colonies."[6] In other words, the Stamp Act Congress wanted the House of Commons to make a voluntary distinction between its legislative authority over the colonies and its authority to tax the colonists. Americans, the delegates implied, would submit to any laws Parliament might impose on their trade, or indeed on most other aspects of life, so long as it did not try to tax them directly, or meddle with such fundamental English rights as trial by jury. But how the delegates expected the House of Commons to draw a line separating acceptable legislation "in general Acts" from "the Exercise of Jurisdiction" in unacceptable acts, like tax laws, remained as foggy as their syntax.

That the Stamp Act Congress failed to achieve clarity on the central point of contention between the colonies and the British government is hardly surprising. Theoretical precision was never the delegates' goal. They were rather struggling to find a consensus that would embrace the conservatives as well as the radicals among them, and simultaneously convince the British authorities of their fundamental loyalty and reasonableness. That they produced only extremely moderate documents in doing these things should not obscure the fact that they actually acted together. Nor should their inability to articulate a coherent set of principles prevent us from understanding their desperate, shared need to find them.

The delegates to the Stamp Act Congress in effect acted out in microcosm a political drama taking place in every colony, as gentlemen accustomed to controlling public life confronted a loss of control that looked as if it might become total. That only New York City saw any serious violence on the day the act was to take effect testifies to their general, if imperfect, success. In Boston the Loyal Nine (who now called themselves Sons of Liberty) spared no effort, and the merchants of the town spared no expense, in bringing the rioting to an end. They must have heaved a collective sigh almost as big as Governor Bernard's when the united mobs of the North and South Ends paraded on November 1 and again on Pope Day in "the greatest order," carrying no weapons, throwing no stones, and burning their effigies in the afternoon to ensure "the Town might be perfectly quiet before Night." Most sizable towns in the colonies staged mock funerals for American liberty or enacted other protests on November 1. Whatever the rituals, however, everywhere an ostentatious decorum prevailed. The emergent leaders of opposition to the act were bent on proving their respectability, responsibility, and loyalty to the Crown. They wanted the Stamp Act repealed; and they knew that Parliament would never do that if the colonies remained the scene of licentiousness and violence.[7]

Most of the anti–Stamp Act activists' efforts in the autumn and early winter of 1765 thus came to center on finding means of resistance that would put pressure on the British government without provoking it to impose its authority by force. The single greatest factor in enabling the leaders to gain control over crowd actions was probably the news of Grenville's fall, which arrived in September and built up hope that a new administration would look favorably on the colonies' petitions. But what should be done in the meantime, and how could Parliament most effectively be induced to repeal the act? The intimidation of the stamp officers had made the tax uncollectible, but that did not settle the most significant issues that grew out of the act. Could colonists determined to prove their loyal and law-abiding character go on after November 1, carrying out the business that was supposed to require stamps, as if nothing had happened? Would courts and customhouses remain closed, or would they perform as usual? If the colonists allowed them to stay closed, they would in effect be recognizing the validity of the law even though they were not paying the tax. Yet as the governor of Rhode Island had discovered after the Newport riots, even a few days without trade could badly wound a seaport's economy. Could court officers and customsmen be forced to execute their duties if they chose not to join the majority of colonists in denying the law's validity?

These questions, aired in club rooms, coffeehouses, taverns, and the press, had no easy answers, but the very act of discussion helped colonists clarify their position to themselves. Courts and customhouses would have to operate or anarchy and economic stagnation would follow; everyone agreed on that. Everyone also agreed that the Sons of Liberty could not make judges decide cases or customsmen clear vessels by holding pistols to their heads. The debates thus pointed away from violence toward a subtler method of coercion: ostracism. Any judge who would not open his court, any customsman who refused to certify cockets on unstamped paper, could be shunned as an enemy of liberty. Even those with fortitude enough to hold out against their neighbors' hostile silence would eventually run out of food and clean clothes. Community solidarity, exerted in consistent and forceful boycotts, might be a slower means of gaining the officials' cooperation than threatening to pull down their houses, but in the long run it would be even more effective.[8]

So, too, colonial activists concluded that the most effective means of coercing Parliament to recognize their rights would simply be to refuse to trade with Britain until the offensive tax had been repealed. As early as August 1764 merchants in Boston had thought of protesting the American Duties Act by voluntarily restricting the importation of luxury items, and New England newspapers aired the suggestion to a wider audience in the fall of the year. In September 1765, Boston's merchants transformed suggestions into action by refusing to place orders for consumer goods from Britain until Parliament repealed the Stamp Act. "*Upwards of Two Hundred principal Merchants*" of New York followed suit at the end of October with an agreement to place no new orders with their correspondents in Britain "unless the STAMP ACT be repealed," and to allow no goods shipped from Britain after January 1, 1766, to be sold. In November more than four hundred of Philadelphia's merchants and traders entered a nonimportation covenant on similar terms.[9]

The architects of these boycotts intended to create so much distress in those sectors of the British economy dependent on colonial trade that English manufacturers and merchants would join Americans in demanding the repeal of the Stamp Act. If British workers, thrown out of employment, should be moved to riot, so much the better. With characteristic pith, a writer who signed himself Humphry Ploughjogger observed in the *Boston Gazette* that he would "rather the Spittlefield weavers should pull down all the houses in old England, and knock the brains out of all the wicked great men there, than [that Americans] should loose their liberty."[10]

Humphry Ploughjogger offered his opinions on "Pollyticks" as those of a humble countryman, one not "book larnt enuff, to rite so polytly, as the great gentlefolks, that rite in the News-Papers."[11] But there was nothing unlearned about Humphry's creator, John Adams, a thirty-year-old attorney with a Harvard degree and enough ambition for a dozen ordinary men. The son of a farmer from Braintree, he had spent a couple of rudderless years after graduation (in the class of 1754) before he found his calling in the law. Thereafter he suffered occasionally from self-doubt, but not from lack of success; yet while the growth of his practice and reputation pleased him, he was at heart not so much a barrister as a writer on politics, and the Stamp Act controversies whetted his appetite for publication. In 1765 he practically bombarded the *Gazette* with writings that ranged from Ploughjogger's dialect letters to a series of anonymous, scholarly essays on English liberties and natural rights that he misleadingly entitled "A Dissertation on Canon and Feudal Law."

Beyond composing the Braintree town meeting's instructions to its representative in the General Court, however, Adams still refrained from outright engagement in politics. Unlike his cousin Samuel, he was by temperament and preference more observer than organizer. His comparative detachment, however, sharpened his appreciation of the extraordinary character of recent events. In December a three-day northeaster gave him leisure to reflect on the Stamp Act crisis as he sat by the fire on his Braintree farm, together with Abigail, his wife of just over a year, and their infant daughter, Nabby. "The Year 1765," he mused,

> has been the most remarkable Year of my Life. That enormous Engine, fabricated by the british Parliament, for battering down all the Rights and Liberties of America, I mean the Stamp Act, has raised and spread thro the whole Continent, a Spirit that will be recorded to our Honour, with all future Generations. In every Colony . . . the Stamp Distributors and Inspectors have been compelled, by the unconquerable Rage of the People, to renounce their offices. Such and so universal has been the Resentment of the People, that every Man who has dared to speak in favour of the Stamps, . . . how great soever his Abilities and Virtues had been esteemed before, or whatever his fortune, Connections and Influence had been, has been seen to sink into universal Contempt and Ignominy.
>
> The People, even to the lowest Ranks, have become more atten-

> tive to their Liberties, more inquisitive about them, and more determined to defend them, than they were ever before known or had occasion to be. Innumerable have been the Monuments of Wit, Humour, Sense, Learning, Spirit, Patriotism, and Heroism, erected in the several Colonies and Provinces, in the Course of this Year. Our Presses have groaned, our Pulpits have thundered, our Legislatures have resolved, our Towns have voted[.] The Crown Officers have every where trembled, and all their little Tools and Creatures, been afraid to Speak and ashamed to be seen.[12]

Adams sensed, and over the next weeks frequently wrote, that a new kind of politics was emerging in the colonies. He found it astonishing that, "till the Stamp Act shall be repealed," Americans had "resolved unanimously to hold in Utter Contempt and Abhorrence every Stamp Officer, and every Favourer of the Stamp Act, and to have no Communication with any such Person, not even to speak to him, unless to upbraid him with his Baseness.—So tryumphant is the Spirit of Liberty, every where.—Such an Union was never before known in America. In the Wars that have been with the french and Indians, [such] a Union could never be effected." The kind of politics at which Adams marveled involved, as no politics before had, practically everybody: not just elite figures, but "the People, even to the Lowest Ranks."[13]

Abigail, at the very least John's intellectual equal, might well have added a category that did not occur to him: women. Women too had stood in the crowds that watched effigies being hanged, and if they did not join the men and boys who pulled down houses, it is inconceivable that they did not raise their voices in the chorus that demanded the stamp distributors' resignations. The Sons of Liberty implicitly recognized the importance of women as they devised their strategies of resistance. Ostracism of royal officials would never work unless it could be made universal, something it could never be unless the women who furnished essential domestic services and foodstuffs agreed to participate. Similarly, nonimportation had no hope of succeeding as a movement unless women, the main consumers of British textiles and other manufactures, were willing to forgo them, and increase their own burdens by producing homespun yarn and cloth to replace the boycotted items. If the implications of those facts still eluded men like Adams, who did not know how to think of women in political terms, they were none the less important and would not long elude the women themselves.[14]

Indeed, as 1765 shuddered to its end, practically everyone knew that amazing changes were taking place, but no one yet understood their significance. That so much turmoil between colonies and metropolis should have come about because of Britain's epochal victory in the recent war only made it more bewildering. American colonists had fought and sacrificed, as they understood it, for the good of *their* empire. How, they wondered, could any politician who was not a rogue deny that colonial contributions of men and money had enabled Britain to conquer Canada and the West Indies? How could anyone but a scoundrel demand that Americans pay for those conquests twice—once with their blood and sweat and treasure during the war, once more with their taxes, afterward?

Of course it was all a matter of perspective. A decade earlier, at the dismal beginning of the war, when British officers had tried to treat the colonists like subjects, they and their assemblies—fearing the loss of their prerogatives and the infringement of their constituents' rights as Englishmen—had balked. William Pitt had broken the impasse by treating the provinces as if they were tiny Prussias to be subsidized in proportion to their contributions to the war effort. The colonists—thinking of themselves not as mercenaries but as patriots, voluntarily participating in the winning of a great empire—had understood these subsidies as no more than just, for they believed that in contributing lives and labor to the cause they were performing all the duties that they as subjects were contractually bound to render to their king. But at the end of the conflict George Grenville had had other obligations on his mind and other conceptions of the contract between the British state and its subjects. His duty as first lord of the Treasury was to honor His Majesty's debt to the people and financial institutions that had lent the government the money it needed to carry on the war. Like Braddock and Loudoun, Grenville assumed that the colonists were neither more nor less than British subjects—and that the payment of taxes, not the bearing of arms, defined their responsibility to the state.

But colonists like John Adams failed to see how Americans could have been one kind of subject under Pitt's war effort and another kind in the reformed postwar empire of George Grenville. The only reasonable explanation seemed to be that the coercive policies of 1755–57 had been revived, and they were being deprived of their rights as Englishmen. But the truth was that Grenville and his fellow reformers really *were* treating the colonists like Englishmen: as subjects, not allies, of a sovereign state. The colonists liked that just as little as they understood it.

In 1765 as in 1755, most Americans saw the treatment they were receiving at the hands of the British as mere abuse and resolved to resist it. But the fact that the great war was over had changed everything. No longer would military necessity make ministers hesitate to demand the subordination that was a sovereign's due; nor would the colonists be able to stop short of articulating their reasons for resistance. But whereas in 1755–57 politicians in the assemblies had resisted by the traditional tactics of noncompliance and sullenness, in 1765 colonial politicians were no longer in effective control. Demonstrations and riots more fierce than any in living memory cracked open the shell of colonial politics, a carapace made brittle by war and depression and counterproductive efforts at imperial reform. The shape that stirred within—the inchoate form of a politics that called into question the colonies' relationship to Great Britain, and which in so doing required the participation of ordinary men, and even women—remained as yet half seen, unknowable, frightening. Whether it would emerge and destroy the empire itself, or whether the men who had heretofore controlled colonial governments would somehow subdue it, rested entirely with a new and untried British ministry. As the New Year 1766 dawned, no one—in Westminster any more than in Braintree, Massachusetts—knew whether Grenville's successors would resolve the crisis by repealing the Stamp Act, or try to preserve Parliament's supremacy by sending troops to America, to enforce it.

John adams spent the mild last day of 1765 walking the fields of Braintree, looking over the stand of young maples that grew in his hemlock swamp. He was thinking of "what wretched Blunders" the British "do make in attempting to regulate" the colonies because "they know not the Character of Americans." The next day the weather changed and he stayed home, defending himself against the sudden "Severe Cold" with tea, conversation, and reading. At evening he sat with his journal, contemplating the "Prospect of Snow," and a New Year "of greater Expectation than any, that has passed before it. This Year," he wrote, "brings Ruin or Salvation to the British Colonies. The Eyes of all America, are fixed on the B[ritish] Parliament. In short Britain and America are staring at each other.—And they will probably stare more and more for sometime."

With lawyerly precision he laid out the central issues on the page. "1st. Whether in Equity or Policy America ought to refund any Part of the Expence of driving away the French in the last War? 2d. Whether it is necessary for the Defence of the B[ritish] Plantations, to keep up an Army there? 3d. Whether, in Equity, the Parliament can tax Us?" Turning over the evidence and the authorities, including Thomas Hutchinson's *History of the Colony and Province of the Massachusetts-Bay,* he concluded that in fact "the Colonies were considered formerly both here and at Home, as Allies rather than Subjects. The first Settlement certainly was not a national Act, i.e., not an Act of the People nor the Parliament. Nor was it a national Expence. Neither the people of England, nor their Representatives contributed any thing towards it. Nor was the Settlement made on a Territory belonging to the People nor the Crown of England." Historically, he concluded, the colonies had a strong case. But Adams also understood that such matters would never be decided by legal pleadings and historical argument, and he ended his entry on a darker note. "It is said at N. York, that private Letters inform, the great Men are exceedingly irritated at the Tumults in America, and are determined to inforce the Act. This irritable Race, however, will have good Luck to inforce it. They will find it a more obstinate War, than the Conquest of Canada and Louisiana."[15]

PART X

Empire Preserved?

1766

The duke of Cumberland takes his last turn on the stage of British politics, leaving his followers to puzzle out a solution to the crisis in imperial governance. The Rockingham administration finds a way to retreat without sacrificing Parliament's claim to sovereignty: the Declaratory Act and the delicate politics of the Stamp Act's repeal. Americans respond without fully understanding the extent to which repeal has only crystallized divergent understandings of the imperial relationship. The hollowness of the empire in North America, and the insufficiency of the army as an instrument of power.

CHAPTER 71

The Repeal of the Stamp Act

JANUARY–MARCH 1766

THE LEADERS OF His Majesty's government reacted calmly enough when reports of the Virginia Resolves reached London in July 1765. The event that triggered such vast colonial opposition to the Stamp Act seemed, in Lieutenant Governor Fauquier's account, inconsequential: a momentary majority in the House of Burgesses had responded to a hot-head's eloquence, and the damage had soon been undone. Such matters required nothing beyond the Board of Trade's routine attention, and the cabinet merely took note of Fauquier's report at a meeting on August 30. When more sinister news began arriving from New England in early October, however—stories of royal officials resigning in fear for their lives, of houses pillaged, records destroyed, and towns in the hands of mobs—the ministers could not react so casually.

Nor could they agree on what to do. Some favored an immediate hard-line response, while others found fault less with the colonists than the Stamp Act, but most were simply confused. Those with the most powerful offices, the first lord of the Treasury and the two secretaries of state, either had no particular views on the colonies or actively hoped to shift Britain's imperial course into less confrontational channels. Only their patron, more sure of the issues at stake, entertained no doubts. The Victor of Culloden had never hesitated to apply military power in the service of the state and despised the thought that colonial hooliganism might be allowed to drive imperial policy. From the moment the first news of Boston's violent demonstrations arrived, he left his colleagues no room to doubt his resolve.

The cabinet meeting that the duke of Cumberland chaired on October 13 thus stiffened the spine of even the most publicly pro-American minister, Secretary of State for the South Henry Seymour Conway. Conway had been one of the few M.P.s to side with Colonel Barré in the debates on the Stamp Act, yet following the meeting of the thirteenth he drafted a circular letter to the governors that would have satisfied even the cabinet's most hawkish member, Lord Chancellor Robert Henley, first earl of Northington. The governors, Conway wrote, were to use all necessary means to enforce the laws; General Gage had orders to support them with whatever force they requested. When more distressing reports arrived from the colonies, Cumberland summoned the cabinet to meet at his house on the evening of October 31, to decide what further actions—presumably the dispatch of troops—would be necessary to uphold British authority in North America. He clearly intended to administer another dose of his bracing medicine to any minister who remained irresolute.[1]

But the stroke or heart attack that propelled the duke into eternity just after dinner on the thirty-first, before he could convene his meeting or even taste his port, changed everything. Suddenly a set of ministers whose sole previous distinction had been their attachment to Cumberland found themselves with no head, no direction, no credibility, and—worst of all—no assured support from the king. A death that would at any rate have required the cessation of policy-making until the relations of power and patronage could be sorted out therefore triggered a political crisis as the inexperienced ministers struggled to determine their own sense of precedence and define a plan of action that would restore peace in the colonies without simultaneously surrendering British sovereignty over them. Nothing about these processes would be easy or simple, and months would pass before they reached their fulfillment.

THE ASSEMBLAGE OF previously minor politicians whom Cumberland's demise turned into the Rockingham ministry faced a formidable array of problems on November 1, 1765, the day the Stamp Act should have taken effect. The worst of these arose as much from British political conditions as from the chaos in the colonies. Some of the most imposing difficulties, indeed, derived from the character and personality of the marquess of Rockingham, the first lord of the Treasury and by default the administration's leader. At thirty-five, Rockingham was an immensely wealthy and well-connected Yorkshire landlord whose riches, local prominence, and strong attachment to the Old Whig party had made him the man likeliest to inherit Newcastle's political mantle. Two personal qualities also augured well for that prospect. Rockingham had a singular capacity for making allies or dependents of men more talented than himself: just as he came to office, for example, he engaged Edmund Burke, the subtlest political thinker of the eighteenth century, to be his private secretary and his party's "man of business." He also enjoyed a reputation for integrity, an asset made valuable by its comparative rarity.

Yet Rockingham—perhaps because wealth and honesty and an amiable disposition inoculated him against the ruder dictates of ambition—was also lazy, absentminded, and perennially late. He lacked confidence in his political judgment and avoided public speaking at almost any cost, two frightful handicaps in a parliamentary leader. And he could not (or did not care to) hide the fact that he loved his estates, his racing stable, and popular acclaim infinitely more than the grubby business of managing Parliament, strengthening his party, and wielding power. Preferences and habits like these, which made him a political curiosity when in opposition, fitted him so poorly to head a government that no one who knew him expected his ministry to endure more than a few months.[2]

No one realized Rockingham's limitations more clearly than his secretaries of state. Both the duke of Grafton and Henry Conway worshiped the Great Commoner and longed to have him head the ministry; and Rockingham himself, at least at first, strongly agreed. But Pitt scorned their overtures—refusing, as always, to lead except on his own terms, which meant accepting office only at the direct request of the king, without obligation to any party. Weeks passed while the ministers waited for some sign that he had even heard their appeals. When he finally deigned to respond, in January, his terms were calculatedly outrageous: the duke of Newcastle, the only distinguished personage currently holding a portfolio, would have to be dismissed from his office so that Pitt could take over as lord privy seal, and Rockingham would have to resign as first lord of the Treasury in favor of Pitt's brother-in-law, the earl Temple.[3] Rockingham, affronted, broke off the negotiations, but Grafton and Conway went on hoping that Pitt could somehow be brought on board. Thus an administration that began weak soon became internally divided, as its principal executive officers took positions disloyal to the man who was supposed to be their leader.[4]

Significantly, while the ministers were trying to recruit the most idiosyncratic opposition politician in Britain, they neglected to make any overtures at all to the so-called King's Friends—the parliamentary group that routinely furnished ministries with their most reliable support. These pensioners, churchmen, military officers, Scots, and placeholders accounted for perhaps 120 votes in the House of Commons and about 60 in the House of Lords, and under ordinary circumstances would back any position a ministry cared to adopt. But because many of the King's

Friends were also friends of the earl of Bute, who had given them positions from which he had ejected adherents of the duke of Newcastle in the "massacre of Pelhamite innocents" late in 1762, the new ministers refused to have anything to do with them.[5]

In part this reflected a reluctance to rehabilitate Bute, whom many still regarded as the most dangerous man in Britain, but at bottom the Rockingham ministry's problem with the King's Friends was purely psychological. The men now responsible for His Majesty's government had known nothing but opposition before taking office, and once in office they found it impossible to think about influencing affairs of state *except* as opposition politicians. Instead of applying themselves to the levers of power and patronage, they sought support where they had always found it before: from middle-class popular opinion, the noisy press, the City of London, and the great merchants. In this way a weak, poorly led, internally divided ministry deprived itself of the single largest assured bloc of votes in Parliament and instead aligned its interests with forces antagonistic to the normal exercise of power; and it did so as it tried to resolve a crisis that seemed more likely with every passing week to drag the empire feetfirst into civil war. Small wonder, then, that virtually from the moment the feckless Rockingham inherited power, Charles Townshend and his fellow highfliers could be seen circling overhead, anticipating the feast.[6]

They had good reason. Reports that arrived from America in November and December made it clear that the disorders there were both nightmarishly complex and not susceptible to solution by military means. Less as a matter of principle than of necessity, therefore, the leading figures among the duke of Cumberland's ex-protégés abandoned their mentor's preferred response. Rockingham was probably the first to understand that Britain confronted not one crisis in America, but a set of interrelated problems that only conciliation could resolve. A series of conferences in November—in which, typically, Rockingham consulted neither members of the Board of Trade nor any other government officials with colonial expertise, but rather the richest of the London merchants who traded to North America—convinced him that these problems could be understood, in terms of descending urgency, as economic, political, and institutional; and that they could be addressed accordingly. In December and January—again, typically, not in cabinet meetings but at a series of dinners and informal gatherings to which he invited Grafton, Conway, and others from inside the cabinet and out—Rockingham began to discuss the policies and tactics that his administration might pursue in seeking first to resolve the crisis, and then to begin restructuring imperial relations along less antagonistic lines.

The first set of interrelated issues, of course, centered on the Stamp Act itself: a law that was not working and indeed could never be anything but a dagger in the empire's heart. With virtual unanimity, the colonists had nullified the act, and in doing so had disrupted trade so severely that the great London merchants on whom Rockingham relied for advice were growing extremely anxious. The trade depression that had plagued them since the end of the war had plummeted to its bottom, and their American correspondents still owed them vast sums. If colonial commerce, or at least the regular collection of colonial debts, was not soon restored, financial catastrophe would ensue. Unless the colonists began to consume British manufactures again, workers in the industries that fed colonial markets—and those prominently included cloth-makers in Rockingham's own Yorkshire—would be thrown out of work. Since the Spitalfields riots had lately demonstrated a close correlation between industrial unemployment and social disorder, the Americans' refusal to import British goods posed a threat to more than just the bank balances of a few great merchants. At this most fundamental level of analysis, therefore, Rockingham came to see that the economic dimension of the Stamp Act provided the most favorable grounds on which to seek repeal. In a memorandum to himself on November 28, he noted that in the coming session it would be necessary "to avoid the discussion on the Stamp Act" until "Consideration of N[orth] A[merica] in the Commercial [context could] . . . be brought on" and the members of Parliament had been shown "the high Importance of the Commerce [with] N[orth] A[merica] . . . to the Mother Country."[7]

And yet the Stamp Act was not merely a millstone around the empire's economic neck, but an urgent political issue as well. Whether they appreciated it or not, the Americans whose protests made the act unenforceable had in effect denied parliamentary sovereignty over the colonies. Parliament's authority therefore needed to be restored, and quickly. That much Cumberland had instinctively grasped, and the members of the Houses of Lords and Commons understood it no less viscerally. But Rockingham's consultations with Secretary at War Barrington and with Conway, both of whom were in touch with General Gage, convinced him that force could not restore Parliament's rule. The army was in the wrong place to impose order and lacked the strength to do so. Its gruesome losses to disease at the end of the war, casualties by the hundreds in Pontiac's War, chronic starvation for funds and replacements, and the difficulties of recruitment in America had hollowed out His Majesty's forces, leaving them capable of self-defense, but little more. Finally, weak as they were, most battalions were still dispersed across the conquered territories. In New England, where the riots had begun in late summer and where opposition to the Stamp Act blazed most fiercely, there were no troops at all. New York City had a modest garrison on hand at the time the act was to go into effect, but the reports that arrived in December demonstrated that, far from maintaining order, the redcoats' presence had stimulated the worst rioting in America.

As if all that were not enough, the Quartering Act had proven a grievous mistake. To the colonists it seemed yet another effort to tax and enslave them; to Gage it posed an insuperable obstacle to billeting troops in private homes, and thus to using them with maximum coercive effect. The necessary assertion of parliamentary sovereignty, Rockingham saw, would thus have to be *only* an assertion. He knew what risks he would run by relying on words, where Britain lacked swords to give them meaning. But his merchant tutors assured him that the Americans would reopen trade as soon as the Stamp Act was repealed, and Gage's reports persuaded him that any attempt to use force would create an insurrection that the army could not suppress. In the absence of any alternative, words would have to suffice.

Beyond these most pressing problems between America and the empire, Rockingham's consultations eventually convinced him that every postwar effort to reform imperial governance had served only to exacerbate tensions and reduce trade. The American Currency Act had alienated the Virginians, who had since become leading agitators against the Stamp Act, and it had disturbed the rest of the colonies to the south of New England as well, stoking the mobs' fury with economic anxiety and class antagonism. The American Duties Act, similarly, had failed to produce any substantial revenue but had very successfully created opposition to British authority within the colonial merchant community. The act's complex customs provisions enraged shipowners, coastal merchants, and their numerous artisan allies in all the important American ports, encouraging them to participate in the emerging nonimportation movement.[8]

These underlying problems flourished like weeds in the postwar depression and would not be rooted out by the repeal of the Stamp Act, but were virtually certain to grow large enough to choke off colonial goodwill once the repeal had been secured. To deal with them, Rockingham—again on the advice of his merchant friends, and in a typically chaotic way—began contemplating measures to abolish the Currency Act, reduce regulations on trade within the empire, modify the American Duties Act

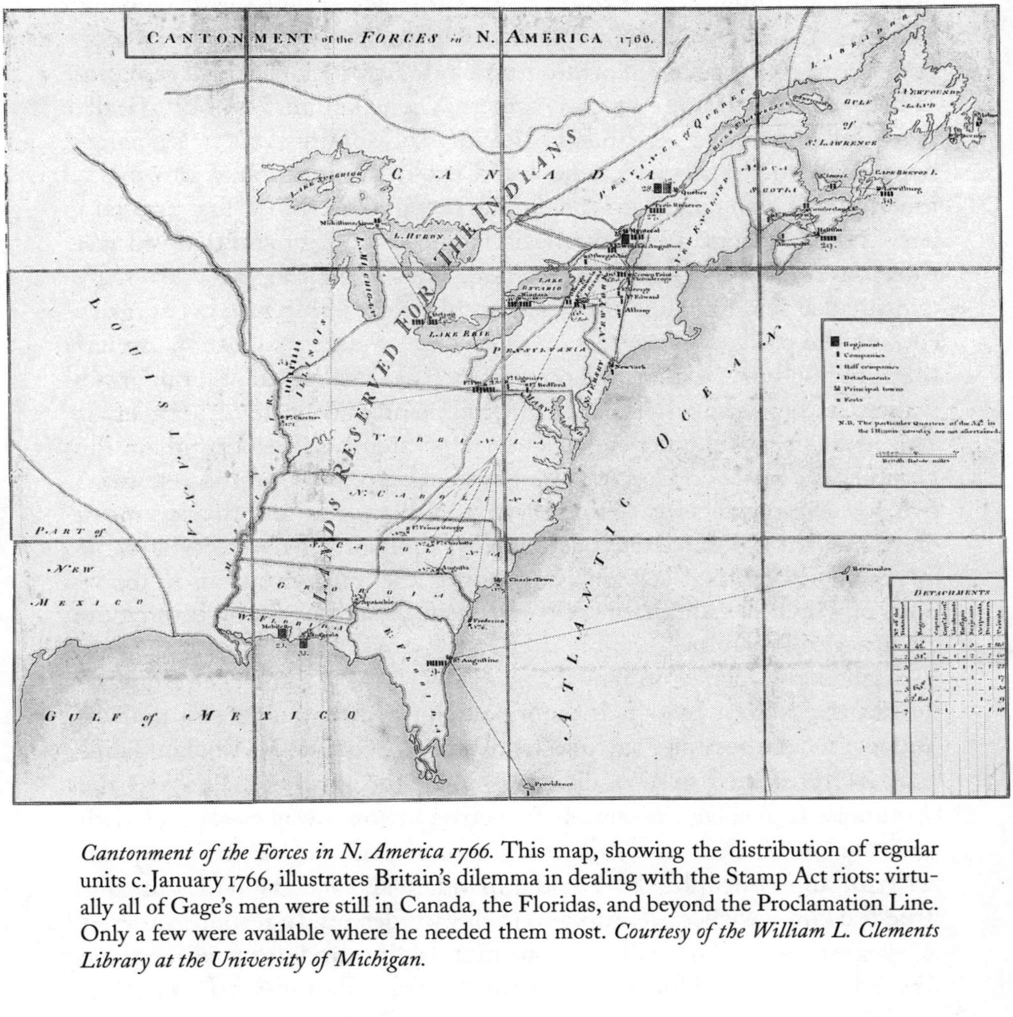

Cantonment of the Forces in N. America 1766. This map, showing the distribution of regular units c. January 1766, illustrates Britain's dilemma in dealing with the Stamp Act riots: virtually all of Gage's men were still in Canada, the Floridas, and beyond the Proclamation Line. Only a few were available where he needed them most. *Courtesy of the William L. Clements Library at the University of Michigan.*

to lower duties on foreign molasses, and increase the amount of silver coin available for circulation in America by opening avenues of legitimate trade with the Spanish and French Caribbean. He knew, however, that all such efforts would have to await the resolution of the economic and political aspects of the Stamp Act crisis. And even at the beginning of January, how the crisis could be resolved was far from obvious.[9]

In the first weeks of 1766, as Parliament prepared to reopen after its Christmas recess, Rockingham had finally concluded that repeal was imperative. Grafton and Conway agreed. But Rockingham still had not been able to bring himself to lay down his views as policy, and he knew that several of his colleagues—particularly the Crown's leading law officers, Lord Chancellor Northington and Attorney General Charles Yorke—strongly favored enforcement over conciliation. Until Pitt finally made his impossible demands for joining the administration, Rockingham clung to the hope that he could avoid making policy altogether, much less devising plans for the empire's long-term future. Only on January 11 did he decide to break off discussions with Pitt; and that was just three days before Parliament convened. Thus while the indecisive marquess had at length made the issues at stake clear to himself, his ministry entered the parliamentary session as much in the dark as ever, with neither a publicly articulated goal nor any internal consensus. The ministry's tactics, as they gradually surfaced in confusion and fluster during January's debates, would depend less on Rockingham's leadership in the House of Lords or on Conway's ability to manage the Commons than on two adventitious factors: the oratory of William Pitt and the actions of the merchant community. Together, Pitt's pursuit of notoriety and the merchants' pursuit of self-interest nudged the administration in directions of which Rockingham approved, even though he found it impossible to say so in public.[10]

Parliament opened on January 14, as always, with the speech from the throne, the address by which the monarch (in theory) and the ministry (in fact) set the session's agenda. In this case, because the Rockinghams had not yet agreed upon their own policy, the king merely asked the Commons to resolve the Stamp Act crisis in some way consistent with both the "authority of the British legislature" and "the welfare and prosperity of all my people." So broad a mandate allowed the M.P.s to construe the king's wishes according to their own desires. In response a series of speakers from Grenville's opposition faction and from among the King's Friends called for the enforcement of the Stamp Act. It was, they argued, no longer a matter of revenue, but of right. The colonists denied Parliament's lawful authority, which must now be asserted, regardless of expense: "a pepper-corn, in acknowledgment of the right," one speaker thundered, was "of more value, than millions without it." Against this chorus only a single speaker, one of Pitt's minor allies, called for repeal. On the Treasury bench, Conway and his colleagues fidgeted in silence. Then William Pitt stood and launched into a long speech in which he made his own views—until that moment mysterious—explicit.[11]

Announcing that he spoke only for himself, and not for a ministry he distrusted ("confidence is a plant of slow growth in an aged bosom"), Pitt affirmed that since "the Americans are the sons, not the bastards, of England," they deserved honorable treatment, not abuse, from their mother country. Parliament's sovereignty over the colonies was indeed complete, he continued, but it was absurd to think that sovereignty gave Parliament the right to levy an "internal" or direct tax on the colonists. Taxes were the free gift of the Commons, and American commoners "would have been slaves" if they had acquiesced in the late administration's fumbling tyrannies. "Virtual representation," by which Grenville had tried to justify the confiscation of the colonists' property, was the lamest of rationalizations, "the most contemptible idea that ever entered into the head of man." The Stamp Act, he concluded, "ought to be totally and absolutely repealed as an erroneous policy."[12]

Conway, relieved to find himself on the same side as his idol, piped up to thank Pitt on behalf of the ministry that Pitt had just said he could not trust. The Great Commoner doubtless valued Conway as the rhinoceros values the tick-bird, but whatever smile flickered as he acknowledged the secretary's tribute vanished as George Grenville rose to ridicule Pitt's effort to distinguish between internal and external taxation. The Stamp Act, Grenville declared, was wholly consistent with Parliament's sovereignty. As for the colonists, they

> border on open rebellion; and if the doctrine I have heard this day [Pitt's distinction between internal and external taxation] be confirmed, I fear they will lose that name to take that of revolution. The government over them being dissolved, a revolution will take place in America. I cannot understand the difference between external and internal taxes. . . . That this kingdom has the sovereign, the supreme legislative power over America, is granted. It cannot be denied; and taxation is a part of that sovereign power. . . . Protection and obedience are reciprocal. Great Britain protects America; America is bound to yield obedience. If not, tell me when Americans were emancipated? . . . The nation has run itself into an immense debt to give them their protection; and now [that] they are called upon to contribute a small share toward the public expence, an expence arising from themselves, they renounce your authority, insult your officers, and break out, I might almost say, into open rebellion.[13]

Pitt had already spoken, and under the rules of the House should not have been able to reply. But his brother-in-law had touched a nerve and, brushing aside the canons of debate ("I do not speak twice. I only finish") as the chamber "resounded with cries of Go on! Go on!" Pitt answered in the greatest extemporaneous speech of his career.

> The gentleman tells us, America is obstinate; America is almost in open rebellion. I rejoice that America has resisted. Three millions of people so dead to all the feelings of liberty, as voluntarily to submit to be slaves, would have been fit instruments to make slaves of the rest. I come not here armed at all points, with law cases and acts of parliament, with the statute-book doubled down in dog's ears, to defend the cause of liberty: if I had, . . . I would . . . have shown that, even under former arbitrary reigns, parliaments were ashamed of taxing a people without their consent, and allowed them representatives. . . .
>
> I am no courtier of America; I stand up for this kingdom. I maintain, that the parliament has a right to bind, to restrain America. Our legislative power over the colonies is sovereign and supreme. When it ceases to be sovereign and supreme, I would advise every gentleman to sell his lands, if he can, and embark for that country. When two countries are connected together, like England and her colonies, without being incorporated, the one must necessarily govern; the greater must rule the less; but so rule it, as not to contradict the fundamental principles that are common to both. If the gentleman does not understand the difference between external and internal taxes, I cannot help it; but there is a plain difference between taxes levied for the purpose of raising a revenue, and duties imposed for the regulation of trade, for the accommodation of the subject; although, in the consequences, some revenue might incidentally arise from the latter.
>
> The gentleman asks, when were the colonies emancipated? But I desire to know when they were made slaves. . . . I will be bold to affirm that the profit to Great Britain from the trade of the colonies, through all its branches, is two millions a year. This is the fund that carried you triumphantly through the last war. The estates that were rented at two thousand pounds a year, threescore years ago, are at three thousand pounds at present. Those estates sold then from fifteen to eighteen years' purchase; the same may now be sold for thirty. You owe this to America; this is the price America pays for her protection. And shall a miserable financier come with a boast that he can bring a pepper-corn into the exchequer, to the loss of millions to the nation? . . .
>
> A great deal has been said without doors of the power, of the strength, of America. It is a topic that ought to be cautiously meddled with. In a good cause, on a sound bottom, the force of this

> country can crush America to atoms. I know the valour of your troops. I know the skill of your officers. . . . But on this ground, on the Stamp act, when so many here will think it a crying injustice, I am one who will lift up my hands against it.
>
> In such a cause, your success would be hazardous. America, if she fell, would fall like the strong man. She would embrace the pillars of state, and pull down the constitution along with her. Is this your boasted peace? Not to sheathe the sword in the scabbard, but to sheathe it in the bowels of your countrymen? . . .
>
> The Americans have not acted in all things with prudence and temper. The Americans have been wronged. They have been driven to madness by injustice. Will you punish them for the madness you have occasioned? . . .
>
> Upon the whole, I will beg leave to tell the House what is really my opinion. It is, that the Stamp-act should be repealed absolutely, totally, and immediately; that the reason for the repeal should be assigned, because it was founded on an erroneous principle. At the same time let the sovereign authority of this country be asserted in as strong terms as can be devised, and be made to extend to every point of legislation whatsoever: that we may bind their trade, confine their manufactures, and exercise every power whatsoever—except that of taking their money out of their pockets without their consent.[14]

The debate boomed on, but Pitt's speech had already given the ministry its cue and its courage—and indeed virtually ratified the legislative strategy that Rockingham had decided upon but lacked the confidence to propose. As at the height of his influence a half-dozen years before, Pitt had captured the admiration of that largest and most refractory group in the Commons, the backbench independents. Now Grenville's party, Bedford's faction, and the Friends of the King and Bute could raise any hue and cry they wished; if Pitt could hold the support of the independents, the ministry would have its chance to repeal the Stamp Act. Thus in a series of informal meetings over the next ten days, Rockingham at last brought himself to advocate the course he had contemplated since November. His ministry would assert, as strenuously as possible, Parliament's sovereignty over America; then it would press the case for repealing the Stamp Act on the grounds of economic expediency.

In the last week of January, Rockingham therefore asked his hard-line attorney general, Charles Yorke, to devise a declaration of parliamentary supremacy that would leave no doubt about the legal subordination of the colonies, and he turned to his merchant friends to organize support for repeal as a measure of economic necessity. Both Yorke and the merchants were well ahead of him. Since late December the attorney general had argued that whether the ministry opted to pursue enforcement or repeal, it needed first to secure parliamentary approval for resolutions condemning the colonists' violence and unequivocally declaring Parliament's sovereignty; indeed, he had already identified the model for such a declaration in the Dependency of Ireland Act of 1719. Since December, too, the leading figure among the London merchants who traded to North America, an ex-Bostonian named Barlow Trecothick, had headed a great petition drive to testify to the distressed state of trade with America and to document the damage that the Stamp Act had done to the British economy. Before the end of January, the merchants of London and the outports, as well as manufacturers from the cities of the north, had sent no fewer than twenty-four petitions to the House of Commons, all blaming the Stamp Act for the hard times they were suffering, and all pleading for relief.[15]

Procedurally the ministry's strategy was to convene a Committee of the Whole House to discuss the measures to be taken on America. Tactically, this depended upon making no effort to harness Pitt (a futile enterprise at any rate), but otherwise to maintain the closest possible control over the debates. Rockingham intended to direct the discussions first toward an assertion of Parliament's sovereignty over the colonies, then to make an overwhelming case for the economic dysfunctions of the Stamp Act; only then would his administration move in favor of repeal, on purely pragmatic grounds. This solution in effect depended upon speaking the words that the M.P.s wanted to hear while taking the actions that the colonies demanded, and pretending that there was no contradiction between them. To achieve this end, the colonies' own protests had to be squelched. Thus amid all the petitions submitted to Parliament, the memorial of the Stamp Act Congress was conspicuously absent, buried by a ministry that knew any document—even a mild one—that originated in the proceedings of "an illegal congress, calling the right of Parliament into question," was too explosive to be read in open session.[16]

The House of Commons resolved itself into a Committee of the Whole on January 28, and for three long days sat listening to the clerk read aloud the official papers that detailed American reactions to the Stamp Act. On the thirty-first, with the readings complete, the House heard verbal testimony from four witnesses. These included Martin Howard of Newport, who described the riot that had destroyed his house and made him a refugee aboard H.M.S. *Cygnet,* and Major Thomas James, who testified that any effort to enforce the Stamp Act by military means in New York would have brought out twenty thousand rioters instead of the four thousand or so who had demolished his home, drained his wine cellar, and dared his troops to fire. The House of Lords, meeting separately, heard the same papers and testimony. In both Houses the ministry's spokesmen took exquisite care to orchestrate the evidence and the questions asked of the witnesses. With the ground thus prepared, and after Rockingham had made sure that the king would assent to repeal, the administration introduced resolutions affirming Parliament's supremacy over the colonies and denouncing colonial disorders.[17]

The first resolution, which Conway and Grafton moved simultaneously in the Commons and the Lords on February 3, would later become the Declaratory Act. It held that the king in Parliament "had, hath, and of a right ought to have, full power and authority to make laws and statutes of sufficient force and validity to bind the colonies and people of America in all cases whatsoever." The Lords debated the resolution all day and passed it, 125 to 5, by nine o'clock; the Commons stayed in session until nearly three the next morning, when they too approved the resolution, without a division. In both Houses, argument centered on whether the words "in all cases whatsoever," made explicit Parliament's right to tax the colonists directly. Although Pitt and Colonel Barré prolonged the Commons debate by denying that Parliament had any such right to grant American taxes without American representatives in the House, the distinguishing fact about the discussion was that almost no one shared their view. Indeed, the two finest legal minds of the age—in the House of Lords, the Lord Chief Justice William Murray, Baron Mansfield, and in the House of Commons the eminent constitutional commentator William Blackstone—agreed that Parliament's right to tax rested not on any principle of representation but on its sovereign power and denied that there was any distinction between tax laws and other kinds of legislation. If ever there had been doubts about the consensus of the Lords and the Commons on the unassailable, indivisible sovereignty of king in Parliament, the debates of February 3 should have extinguished them.[18]

With the declaratory resolution safely in hand, the ministry proposed its remaining resolves. After prolonged but generally less intense debate, these were passed in a form that condemned America's "Tumults and Insurrections," as well as the "Votes and Resolutions, passed in several of the Assemblies," which had "inflamed" the people; declared that those who had suffered as a result of the riots "ought to have full and ample Compensation made to them . . . by the respective Colonies"; assured His Majesty's "dutiful and loyal Subjects" in America that they would henceforth "have the Protection" of the British government; and shielded from prosecution all loyal colonists who had unwillingly broken the law when the "Tumults and Outrages in North America" prevented them from obtaining stamped paper. These resolutions were all reasonably innocuous and indeed milder than British public opinion would have supported. Grenville indeed succeeded in modifying many of the drafts that the ministry proposed to strengthen their language: small successes that emboldened him to introduce a final resolution on February 7, a forthright challenge to the ministry's plans. When Grenville moved "that an humble address be presented, in consequence of our [declaratory] resolution, expressing our indignation and concern at the proceedings in N[orth] America, and to assure the King that we will assist him in enforcing the laws of this Kingdom," he was doing nothing less than calling for a vote of confidence on the Rockingham ministry and seeking to reverse the direction of policy. It was his supreme gambit to regain power, and he thought that "in the present unsettled state of men and things" he stood a reasonable chance of winning.[19]

He guessed wrong. The debate that followed made it clear that however unimpressed many M.P.s were with the ministry, the depositions and oral testimony had convinced them that enforcement was impossible. Even Charles Townshend, watching as ever to see which way the winds blew, spoke in opposition to enforcement. Once Grenville's resolution failed, by a vote of 274 to 134, the ministry's way at last was clear. The opposition could no longer hope to see the act enforced, and that left only two options. It could try to delay the ministry's motion to repeal, hoping that some new outrage in America would alter the balance; or it might seek to modify the law, retaining some part of it—perhaps "a Stamp on cards and dice only"—as a symbolic gesture, "to keep up the claim of right." The administration thus was free to build its case for repeal on arguments from economic necessity, which meant convincing the majority of M.P.s that the Stamp Act was all that stood between Britain and prosperity. Beginning on February 11, that was what the ministry tried to do, by hearing the merchants' and manufacturers' petitions and carefully questioning expert witnesses on the content of each.[20]

Of the twenty-six witnesses examined before the House of Commons—the Lords opted to suspend their independent proceedings and resume deliberations after the Commons had finished taking testimony—the first, Barlow Trecothick, was by far the most important. Perhaps the richest merchant who traded to America and an important military contractor from the last war, Trecothick came armed with facts and figures that he laid before the House in a bravura four-hour performance.

Britain's trade with America, he affirmed, exceeded even the £2,000,000 annually that Pitt had named. Three million was nearer the mark, and its significance was all the greater because Britain's trade with the rest of the world was falling off, while its American commerce—until the Stamp Act—had continually grown. Now all trade with the colonies was at a standstill, and the interruption of court proceedings made it impossible for any merchant to recover a penny of what his American debtors owed. And the sums in question, Trecothick claimed, were immense. His computations showed that London merchants held American debts amounting to almost £3,000,000 sterling, and if one included the merchants of the outports the total would reach approximately £4,450,000.

Those figures added up to Trecothick's most significant testimony, but he also helped the M.P.s better understand the colonists' protests by explaining exactly how the Stamp Act would affect the colonial economies. It was true, he said, that no money collected was to leave America, since it would be paid out to maintain the troops stationed there; but America was a big place, and His Majesty's forces were not spread evenly throughout it. Much of the revenue collected would come from New England, a cash-starved region suffering severe depression, and would be disbursed among soldiers stationed in Canada and the Floridas, where infinitesimal sums could be collected. Of the colonies most inflamed against the Stamp Act, only New York and Pennsylvania were likely to recover, in army expenditures, the monies the stamp tax would remove from circulation. Colonial merchants thus were objecting to more than taxation without consent. They also feared the drain of precious metals from their specie-short economies, and they resented being forced in effect to promote the prosperity of territories mainly populated by former enemies.[21]

Trecothick's testimony, masterful and thoroughly rehearsed, forecast the arguments of the merchants and colonial agents who followed him. The thrust of their accounts confirmed his contention that the Stamp Act was aggravating Britain's depression by preventing the recovery of debts from the colonies and creating vast unemployment in Britain. From personal knowledge they told of thousands of workers already laid off and prophesied that as many as a hundred thousand might lose their jobs, with God knew what costs in poor relief and what risks of social unrest. The key to regaining British prosperity, they repeated in a kind of litany, was to resume American trade, and that was impossible without repeal. Only Benjamin Franklin, appearing as one of the ministry's final witnesses, refused to chant with this choir. Pennsylvania's agent went substantially beyond the earlier testimony to venture his judgments on a variety of topics—not all of which pleased the ministry.[22]

More than anyone else of his day, Franklin symbolized America; as a scientist and public figure he was the most famous colonist in London, and indeed in the world. He also had more to lose than any other witness, for he had severely miscalculated the colonials' reactions to the Stamp Act and damaged his political faction's position in Pennsylvania by securing a distributorship for John Hughes. Franklin therefore spoke not only as America's advocate, but as a man who desperately needed to repair his reputation at home. (In this light the presence of a stenographer in the gallery, and the immediate publication of his transcript in pamphlet form, can hardly have been coincidental.[23]) In choosing to depart from the ministry's carefully prepared line the Pennsylvanian took huge risks, for he exposed himself to a grilling by opposition M.P.s, including a hostile Grenville. Yet he also, clearly, relished matching wits with them. America's greatest celebrity may have come before Parliament as a sixty-year-old man with his political future on the line, but he danced through the interrogation like a cocky teenager waltzing down Philadelphia's Market Street with a Dutch dollar in his pocket and a great puffy roll tucked under each arm.

Why should Britain protect America, an opposition M.P. demanded, if America did not help pay the cost? Britain did not protect America, Franklin replied, Americans did: "The colonies raised, cloathed, and paid, during the last war, near 25000 men, and spent many millions." But Parliament had generously reimbursed America, had it not? Not particularly, Franklin said. The reimbursement had been necessary, but "it was a very small part of what we spent." Would the Americans accept a partial stamp tax? No. Another tax in its place? "They would not pay it." So they would contribute nothing? "Their opinion is, that when aids to the Crown are wanted, they are to be asked of the several assemblies, according to the old established usage, who will as they have always done, grant them freely." Suppose Parliament refused to repeal the Stamp Act and the dispute remained at impasse: how could Americans live without British manufactures? "I do not know a single article imported into the Northern Colonies, but what they can either do without, or make themselves." In the space of three years, the colonists could produce wool enough to make all the clothes they needed; in the meantime, they would patch their old ones. Suppose then that the Stamp Act were repealed, would the Americans acquiesce in a declaration of parliamentary sovereignty? Yes, said Franklin, so long as Parliament made no more effort to enforce the claim than they did in Ireland.

And so it went for perhaps four hours, as Franklin expanded upon the opportunities friendly questioners offered to explain the reasonableness of Americans, and parried the thrusts of the opposition. Always he stressed the Americans' ability to provide for their own needs—in effect, to manage independently of the empire to which they were bound only by a rapidly eroding tie of affection. Always he stopped short of affirming that Americans intended to make themselves independent. Only Parliament, he implied, would determine whether the Americans moved from resistance to reconciliation or from resistance to something more final. Franklin made his clinching argument in response to an opposition demand to know if "any thing less than a military force" could achieve the submission of the colonies: "I do not see how a military force can be applied to that purpose." When the interrogator, as convinced as Pitt that British force could crush America to atoms, shot back "Why may it not?" Franklin came coolly to the heart of the matter: "Suppose a military force sent into America, they will find nobody in arms; what are they then to do? They cannot force a man to take stamps who chooses to do without them. They will not find a rebellion; they may indeed make one."

If Franklin's testimony burnished his reputation at home, it also gave the opposition an opportunity to attack "the Ingratitude" of the Americans. "We have fought, bled, and Ruin'd ourselves, to conquer for them," complained the Bristol M.P. Robert Nugent, soon to become president of the Board of Trade; "and now they come and tell us to our Noses, even at the Bar of this House, that they are not obliged to us!" Yet neither Franklin's excessively clever performance nor Nugent's outcry against it, nor the witnesses whom the opposition called in to examine thereafter, could overturn the impression the ministry had created. When, with the petitions heard and the expert testimony concluded, the Commons formally debated repeal on the evening of February 21, the opposition could not hope to reverse what had become a decisive majority against the Stamp Act. As usual, the speeches were long. But at 1:45 a.m. when the House divided, 275 M.P.s voted in favor of repeal against 167 Grenvillites, Bedford Whigs, and King's Friends who still stood opposed.[24]

Thereafter the ministry needed only to couch the relevant resolutions in the form of a Declaratory Bill and a Bill to Repeal the Stamp Act and set in motion the machinery to enact them. There were more debates, notable chiefly for Pitt's insistence that the Stamp Act should be repealed on no grounds other than Grenville's stupidity, but the outcome was never in doubt. On March 4 the Commons passed the Declaratory Act by acclamation and approved the Repeal Act by a majority of 250 to 122. After several more days of debate in the upper house—debate of an unusually high quality, it was said, for there the sentiment favored repeal less than enforcement—the Lords formally concurred on March 17. The king attended the House of Lords on the following day to give his assent to both acts in person, and he returned to the palace from Westminster as bells pealed and crowds cheered to the echo his passing coach.[25]

CHAPTER 72

The Hollowness of Empire

1766

THE POPULAR demonstrations that greeted the repeal of the Stamp Act, both in America and in Britain, were scarcely less exuberant than those that had accompanied the Peace of Paris. In London fifty coaches, full of merchants, paraded to Westminster on March 18, to salute the king and the Lords. All day long church bells rang, and "houses at night were illuminated all over the city." Merchant vessels on the Thames broke out their colors and immediately prepared to sail for the colonies. When they reached America with the news two months later, colonists everywhere celebrated with memorial sermons and bonfires, banquets and loyal healths, draining "many Barrels of Beer" in a delirium of relief. Assemblies ordered broadsides printed and distributed free, announcing the news to anyone who might not have heard it by word of mouth; legislators made speeches and legislatures sent letters of gratitude to the ministry and the monarch. At Charleston the assemblymen were so transported with joy that they commissioned memorial portraits of several of themselves and ordered a marble statue of Pitt—in a toga—from England.[1]

The common folk who belched ale and approval by bonfire light, like the gentlemen who exhaled their more refined satisfaction in toasts to the king and Pitt and Rockingham, anticipated not only the restoration of harmony among true Britons but the revival of prosperity within the empire. Petitioners and experts by the dozen had assured the House of Commons that the Stamp Act had caused the depression, and the Rockingham ministry had deliberately fostered the belief that repeal would end it. That was, of course, nonsense. Both the depression and the Stamp Act grew from causes rooted in the Seven Years' War and the manner of its ending. But the truth that repeal could neither restore prosperity nor close the fissure that divided colonies from metropolis remained to be revealed only later, when events would undeceive Americans and Britons of the ministry's glib and hopeful assurances. For the time being everyone was content to rejoice in the faith that all would once again be well.

That what had passed in the Commons debates would for the most part prove poor prophecy should not surprise us; hope is, after all, the currency of popular politics, and a coin surprisingly hard to devalue. Most of all, however, the predictable disjunction between rhetoric and reality should not divert our attention (as it diverted the attention of the colonists themselves) from the much more interesting things that the rhetoric revealed about British assumptions concerning the colonies. Anyone who wanted to understand the grounds on which Great Britain's political elite reasoned about America needed to look no further than Pitt's great speech of January 14.

If the Great Commoner was no profound thinker, he possessed the rarer ability to articulate common beliefs in compelling terms. During the war he had come to embody the dreams and fears of his fellow M.P.s and indeed the political nation as a whole, and in the repeal debates he similarly captured their understanding of the imperial relationship. These notions were not strictly logical, and thus did not take the form of an argument. Rather they consisted of three assumptions that, taken together, laid the foundation for virtually every possible British policy toward the colonies. First among them came Identity.

"I rejoice," Pitt had said, "that America has resisted." *America* opposed Parliament, not *Americans,* much less the seamen and artisans and apprentices who had thronged the city streets, or the politicians who sat uneasily in the colonial assemblies, or the Sons of Liberty, or speculators and squatters hungry for new land, or any of the other segments of a diverse, fragmented populace. *America* had resisted: a place, a political and geographical abstraction that existed in the minds of British politicians but that had little to do with the social reality of the colonies, and even less to do with the self-understanding of colonists who resisted not because they thought of themselves as Americans, but as British subjects with Englishmen's rights.

Second was Sovereignty. "I maintain that the parliament has a right to bind, to restrain, America. Our legislative power over the colonies is sovereign and supreme. When it ceases to be sovereign and supreme, I would advise every gentleman to sell his lands, if he can, and embark for that country." That Parliament was sovereign, of course, was a truism; but in the curious advice that followed Pitt revealed what the cliché actually meant. Why gentlemen should sell their lands *in Britain* and flee to America if Parliament ceased to be sovereign *over the colonies* puzzles us today far more than it did M.P.s who assumed that sovereignty, the state's right to tax and take life, was also the source of political and social order. Sovereignty as an ultimate power could not be divided, for to fragment sovereignty was to destroy it: logically, by creating the absurdity of *imperium in imperio,* a state within a state; realistically, by inviting civil war. It was unthinkable for Parliament to resolve the crisis in America by recognizing the colonial assemblies as its equal in matters of taxation and legislation, and merely bound by common allegiance to the king. To abdicate authority in this way would be the same as recognizing the corporation of the most miserable borough in Wales as the equal of the House of Commons and would instantly end Parliament's supremacy in Britain. At best such an abdication would re-create the Dark Ages, when barons attacked each other at will under the gaze of an impotent king. At worst it would cast Britain into the state of nature itself, a Hobbesian war of every man against his neighbor. The only rational response to such nightmares would be, of course, to get the hell out: or, as Pitt wryly suggested, to sell one's lands and move to America, where the English were still men enough to hold their property and liberty sacred.

And last came Power itself. Pitt enunciated what was in effect an article of faith for the M.P.s when he said that "In a good cause, on a sound bottom, the force of this country can crush America to atoms." It was only to remind them of his own role in creating this circumstance that he had added "I know the valour of your troops. I know the skill of your officers." Every Englishman knew them. Great Britain led the world in naval and military power. A kingdom that could strip France of its empire and clip the wings of Spain as an afterthought could surely destroy America at will. The colonies posed no threat to such strength, except a moral one; which was why Pitt began by qualifying his assertion, "In a good cause." Only indirectly—by "pull[ing] down the constitution with her"—could America harm Britain. Parliament alone could destroy political order in Britain, and it would inevitably do so if it persisted in trying to eradicate the rights of the colonists. Moral factors aside, the equation of power stood irreducibly in favor of the metropolis.

A unitary America, a sovereign Parliament, an invincible British military: this trinity of beliefs defined what amounted to a consensus among the men who ordered political life and exercised power in Britain, regardless of their specific views on colonial policy. But *America* had not resisted; a great many *Americans* had. What they had resisted was Parliament's assertion of sovereignty over them—not because they denied Parliament's authority, but because they believed that sovereignty asserted in absolute terms deprived them of their birthright of English liberty. As for the invincibility of British arms, the colonists, who never understated their own contributions to Britain's victory over France, entertained other views. In truth America was more divided than Pitt and his contemporaries knew, Britain less omnipotent than they thought, and the rock of parliamentary sovereignty on which they assumed Britain's constitution was founded might easily become the rock on which Britain's empire would founder.

The Stamp Act crisis had shown that, given sufficient provocation, the colonists could overcome deep internal divisions to resist Britain's power—in the name of English liberty. The history of the crisis might reasonably have suggested that the empire's authority could be sustained, *not* by proclaiming parliamentary sovereignty and lending credence to the fears that had brought the colonists together, but rather by celebrating the colonists' British character and cultivating their emotional identification with the metropolis—and quietly letting America's intramural conflicts resume their natural course. But that message could not be read by anyone dazzled by the illusion of British military hegemony, and few Britons cared to blink away the brilliant vision of victories at Québec and Havana in order to contemplate the gloomier sight of Indian warriors annihilating redcoat garrisons at Michilimackinac and Venango while holding Detroit and Niagara hostage.

The simultaneous passage of the Declaratory Act and the Stamp Act Repeal resolved the crisis of empire without altering the trinity of beliefs on which British reasoning about America rested. Nor did the end of the crisis in any way reconcile colonial and British views of the imperial relationship—views the divergence of which had been made unmistakable by the combined pressures of war, depression, and George Grenville's effort to bring order to the empire. Grenville's program might lie in ruins, but all the problems he had tried to solve still stood, in forms reinforced by the passage of time, Indian rebellion, and the Stamp Act itself. The British government remained deep in debt and strapped for cash. Its army in the colonies was more expensive, and less effectual, than ever. The commercial depression had not ended, and public revenues, dependent on trade, would not increase until it did. The interior of North America remained ungoverned, and peace was sure to bring on a deluge of squatters that might well make it ungovernable. And finally, on top of everything else, the colonists' enthusiasm for the empire, so powerful a cohesive force during the last years of the war and so apparently limitless at the war's end, had been diminished by lingering, half-formed fears that in the highest circles of imperial power, men might yet plot to destroy the property and liberty of the colonists. Thus the Americans and their British kin had every reason to rejoice at the end of the Stamp Act crisis. But when at length they wiped the foam from their chins, their empire rang as hollow as the barrel that answered the last reveler's wishful rap.

CHAPTER 73

Acrimonious Postlude

THE COLONIES AFTER REPEAL

1766

Celebrations aside, the repeal of the Stamp Act brought little visible change to the colonies. During the winter and spring of 1766 the Sons of Liberty had served notice on judges and customsmen to

Open your Courts and let Justice prevail
Open your Offices and let not Trade fail

and had done their best to see that merchants observed the nonimportation agreements but otherwise carried on as usual. Since business had been so bad anyway, the ships swinging idly at anchor and the unemployed sailors hunting for work marked the period of boycott as one different in degree, not in kind, from the preceding months. Beyond brief increases in local demand for alcohol and firecrackers, then, the news of repeal impinged little on economic life, and nonimportation ended without creating a surge in business activity. While official letters from Secretary Conway nourished hopes for the future by explaining that the ministry intended to liberalize trade within the empire, the merchants' outlook remained dismal. The period of nonimportation had been too brief to clear shelves and warehouses glutted with British imports. With heavy debts to discharge and dull markets for their merchandise, most colonial traders continued to do what they had done before the crisis: dodge their creditors, press their debtors, and pray for better times.[1] The most significant alterations to follow repeal therefore came not in the form of improved economic conditions, but rather in the exaggeration of internal political tensions. The provinces that showed the trend toward rancor and internal division most dramatically were the three that had led the way in protests and violence: Massachusetts, New York, and Virginia.

IN MASSACHUSETTS, the signs that the crisis would leave a bitter legacy appeared before the word of repeal arrived and became unmistakable thereafter. The political balance in the Bay Colony had weighed in favor of the court party since William Shirley's administration, though ever more delicately so after the writs of assistance controversy. The Stamp Act changed that forever by giving the country party the leverage it needed to dislodge the court's majorities in the assembly and council. Rough as previous confrontations had been, none equaled the campaign that preceded the spring elections of 1766. Country politicians accused Thomas Hutchinson and Francis Bernard of conspiring with Grenville to destroy colonial rights and published a list of thirty-two members of the House of Representatives who had been "contrivers, promoters, and executioners of the Stamp Act." For the first time in the history of the Bay Colony, an attempt to organize a province-wide political campaign actually worked. Nineteen of the thirty-two targeted members lost to candidates aligned with the country party, which immediately used its majority in the House of Representatives to choose James Otis as speaker and Samuel Adams as clerk, and to purge the Governor's Council of Hutchinson and his allies, replacing them with country party stalwarts. "Thus the Triumph of Otis and his Party [is] compleat," observed John Adams, in Boston to attend the Election Day ceremonies. "But what changes are yet to come? Will not the other Party soon be uppermost?"[2]

Governor Bernard did his best to tip the balance back into his favor by vetoing Otis as speaker and refusing to assent to the election of six councillors (including Otis's father) whom he identified with the country party. But despite his vetoes and a "most nitrous, sulphureous Speech" to justify them, he would never make the court party uppermost again. The country party majority in the House of Representatives named one of Otis's most prominent followers, Thomas Cushing, as speaker and got on with the business of opposition. Thereafter the country party behaved with greater discipline than any political bloc in Massachusetts in a quarter century; and that in turn opened a new era of frustration for a governor who had been a reasonably effective, if fussy, servant of the Crown.[3]

Bernard's troubles began in earnest the very next day, when he received official notice of the repeal of the Stamp Act and with it Secretary Conway's directive to secure compensation for the victims of the previous year's riots—which was to say, principally, Thomas Hutchinson. The governor still had not regained control of his temper when he informed the House of Representatives that Parliament expected it to compensate "the late sufferers by the madness of the people," using language so intemperate as to accuse the legislators of treasonous intentions. The new leaders of the House, determined to teach Bernard a lesson in majoritarian politics, refused to cooperate. Only at the end of the year—after delaying the governor's salary grant to the last minute and including an amnesty for all rioters in the act that authorized compensation for Hutchinson—did the representatives conclude that Bernard had been sufficiently chastised.[4]

Christmas Eve found Bernard sunk in gloom, writing a letter to the Southern secretary and complaining that "the demagogues who have got the lead, are determined to bring all real power into the hands of the people." If they succeeded, he would be "reduced to the standard of a Rhode Island governor." He did not intend to let that happen, he wrote; but for all his resolute words, Bernard also knew that he could no longer influence Bay Colony politics as he had when Thomas Hutchinson had commanded a legislative majority in his service. He probably did not understand the extent to which his troubles were of his own making.[5]

Besides preventing the half-dozen most offensive new councillors from taking their seats, Bernard had stripped those members of the House of Representatives whom he identified with the country party of the offices in the militia that he controlled as commander in chief. By summarily depriving local notables of the commissions that symbolized their status, he made permanent enemies of dozens of moderates—men Hutchinson had been cultivating, in some cases, for years. In 1758, for example, Hutchinson had seen to it that Artemas Ward, a freshman representative from Shrewsbury with military ambitions, got the lieutenant colonelcy he wanted. As Hutchinson later recalled, "I thought I could bring [him] over [to the court party] by giving him a commission in the Provincial forces." For that same reason, he supported Ward's appointment as colonel of a Worcester County militia regiment the following year. During the Stamp Act crisis, Ward had tried to remain aloof; but his presence on a legislative committee with Otis and Adams made the governor jump to the conclusion that Ward had become a country party man. In fact, he was merely ambivalent, but Bernard soon cured him of it. On July 7, 1766, the governor dispatched a uniformed messenger to Shrewsbury with the curt notice that he had "thought fit to supersede [Ward's] commission of Colonel," thereby publicly humiliating a man whom he had no reason to alienate and negating eight years of Hutchinson's careful effort. Ward would henceforth, unsurprisingly, firmly support the country party. So, for that matter, would ex-Colonel Jerathmeel Bowers of Swansea, ex-Colonel Joseph Gerrish of Newbury, ex-Colonel Josiah Quincy of Braintree, and several other, similarly situated country gentlemen, whose loss of militia rank only confirmed their constituents' suspicion that the governor was a petty tyrant. Otis and Adams could have found no more able recruiter for their political machine than Francis Bernard.[6]

To make matters worse, events of the summer convinced Bernard that the mobs and certain smuggling merchants, having tasted power the year before, were now determined to defy the laws of trade. If the scale was less massive than in 1765, Bernard worried over reports arriving from Maine in August that a Falmouth mob had besieged two customs officers with stones and clubs while a second crowd hustled away the sheriff and a third liberated contraband goods lately seized from a smuggler. Bernard was, if anything, more alarmed to find that no one would come forward when he offered a fifty-pound reward for information. Yet whatever worries he experienced on Falmouth's account faded as Boston produced an even more outrageous incident.[7]

It began routinely on September 23 when an anonymous informer alerted customs officers that Daniel Malcolm, a sea captain, minor merchant, and smuggler, had stowed several casks of uncustomed wine in his cellar. The next day, armed with a writ, two customsmen and a deputy sheriff called on Captain Malcolm, who declined to grant them access to a locked storage room in his cellar. Since he declined with a pistol in each hand and a sword at his belt, the officers left to gather reinforcements. When they returned with the sheriff in tow, they found perhaps four hundred men and boys blocking the street in front of the captain's house. The sheriff called on the crowd to disperse; the crowd waited for the sheriff to go home; the sun set; the writ expired; and Malcolm hauled out wine by the gallon to thank his supporters for their help. Soon the crowd dispersed, sloshing with the evidence. Bernard thought that James Otis was behind it all and furiously collected depositions to forward to London. The Boston town meeting (James Otis, moderator) demanded copies on grounds that unspecified parties had "Designs" to represent Boston "in a disadvantageous Light to his Majesty's Ministers" as an excuse to ask for troops to enforce customs laws at bayonet-point.[8]

The confrontation collapsed almost immediately under the weight of its own absurdity. Bernard could not prove that Malcolm had ever hidden contraband wine, and the town meeting merely sent its own version of the episode to the colony's agent, to be used if the necessity arose. The

Malcolm affair was, in this sense, just one more squall in Boston's busy teapot. But in two other ways it was more significant. In the first place, Bernard's conviction that Otis and his supporters wanted to subvert the laws of trade and navigation was no fantasy. In the second, both the governor and his antagonists showed themselves capable of jumping to conclusions about each other's motives that stopped only inches short of paranoia.

Beginning in December 1765, Otis (writing as "Hampden" in the *Boston Gazette*) had published essays maintaining that British restrictions on colonial trade constituted an indirect but quite real tax on American commerce. Insofar as any regulation of trade restricted the merchant's ability to dispose of his property, he argued, it infringed on his rights; insofar as any exaction—including an excise charged to the manufacturer—added to the price of any import in American markets, it was a tax; and insofar as Americans had no representation in Parliament, all such taxes were illegitimate. Nor, Otis continued, were the sums in question inconsequential: by monopolizing colonial markets and imposing overgrown customs and excise establishments on the economy, the British added as much as 50 percent to the cost of manufactures. "What American peazant before the late regulations," Otis demanded, referring to the American Duties Act of 1764, "ever dreamt his dearly bo[ugh]t coarse coat . . . was taxed half its cost to those who live and die in the ease, luxury, and prodigality of Great Britain? Now they know."[9]

Moreover, as Bernard reported to the secretary of state, Otis now carried to new extremes his doctrine that "the distinction between inland taxes and port duties was without foundation." Asserting that the Declaratory Act had nothing to do with taxes because it did not mention them specifically, Otis maintained that when Parliament gave up its claim to levy a direct tax on the colonists by repealing the Stamp Act, it necessarily also renounced its claim to tax them through the customs. Therefore "the merchants were great fools if they submitted any longer to the laws restraining their trade which ought to be free." In Bernard's view, Otis had infected the mercantile community with principles that mocked Parliament, defied the king, and justified smuggling. The Malcolm episode proved the extent of his influence.[10]

Bernard analyzed events in ways simultaneously cogent, flawed, and deeply revealing. There *was* substantial opposition among Boston's merchants to parliamentary restrictions on trade, but Otis was by no means its author. Ever since the American Duties Act rigorized customs collections, merchants had complained that restrictions on commerce served only to hinder trade and prolong the depression; some had even justified smuggling as a reasonable response to severe and unwarranted regulation. Otis only articulated, in provocative ways, free-trading notions that merchants, not he, had originated.[11] And this, in turn, pointed to the second characteristic that the affair of Malcolm's wine cellar illuminated: the extraordinary mutual suspicions of the people involved.

By making Otis the author, not the reflector, of views widely shared among Boston's merchants, Bernard cast his nemesis as an archconspirator and the merchants of Boston as his dupes. In fact the merchants' views on trade and the counterproductive nature of mercantilism were becoming widespread—Adam Smith would put them, in a more sophisticated form, at the heart of *The Wealth of Nations*—and Boston merchants were by no means revolutionaries.[12] If Otis and the country party politicians found support among the smuggling part of the community, it was because they gave the smugglers' views a plausible political justification, not because they seduced honest merchants into smuggling by clever arguments. But Bernard believed that Otis was the author and contriver of the merchants' opposition, and thus could ascribe to Otis (and by extension to the entire country party) a diabolical influence that existed only in his imagination. By the same token, the country party's rhetoric ascribed to the governor, lieutenant governor, and their supporters a set of intentions and actions that made them sworn enemies to liberty, property, and colonial rights.

Thus what began as a routine customs search spiraled out of control because Bernard believed that Otis and his minions were conspiring to subvert the laws of trade and navigation, and because Otis and his supporters thought that Bernard, Hutchinson, and their lackeys were plotting to destroy the liberties of Bostonians and rule the town by military force. That neither side was engaged in these conspiracies did not matter. The internal dynamism of conspiratorial thinking absorbed the available evidence into patterns that seemed to prove the existence of plots, subterfuge, and malevolent design.[13]

A SIMILARLY DISORDERED situation materialized in New York almost before the rubble of the November riots had been cleared from the streets. Thanks largely to the personality of its lieutenant governor, New York early in the crisis had been a colony even more hagridden by conspiratorial reasoning than Massachusetts Bay, but the tensions that arose at the end of 1765 did not grow directly from Cadwallader Colden's clashes with the assembly. In fact, a new governor, Sir Henry Moore, arrived in November, blamed much of what he saw on Colden, and set out to restore peace by accommodation. It was neither Colden nor Moore, then, but General Gage, who started the trouble, and only because he was trying to do his duty.[14]

Before the Stamp Act crisis, Gage had mere handfuls of troops in and near the urban centers of the old colonies: a hundred redcoats in New York City, fifty at Albany, perhaps twenty at Charleston. When the riots started, he began to march men down from Canada—a sizable relocation that, by late spring 1766 would position more than a battalion in New York City, most of a second battalion in Philadelphia, a third between them in New Jersey, and augmented detachments in Albany and Charleston. Gage intended to bring these new troops south along Lake Champlain and the Hudson, which meant that they had to be billeted along the march in New York. At the beginning of December, therefore, he sent a copy of the Quartering Act to Governor Moore and asked that the assembly appropriate the funds that the law required.

Moore found the assembly in a balky mood. Instead of appropriating money (which, the representatives maintained, would have amounted to taxation without representation because Parliament had mandated it without New York's consent) the assembly passed resolutions. These pointed out that when troops were in barracks the Crown paid for their quartering; that barracks were available at Albany and New York; and that the assembly would consider reimbursing the army for marching expenses, but only "after the expense is incurred." Rummaging through the Treasury accounts, the representatives discovered funds appropriated in 1762—money from taxes voted before the Quartering Act went into effect—and directed that four hundred pounds be released to purchase firewood and other necessities for troops housed at New York. Otherwise, they simply refused to comply. As Gage reported to Conway, he and Moore did their best to explain the terms of the Quartering Act to the assemblymen, only to have them "Set the Demand aside by Evasions." Gage expected that the issue would come to a head the next spring, by which time there would be more troops in the colony than the existing barracks could accommodate.[15]

When spring came, however, Gage thought that the assembly might prove more tractable, for during the winter several of the great Hudson Valley landlords, who dominated the legislature, could no longer keep order on their estates. For fifteen years these "patroons," whose title to their "manors" dated to the period of Dutch control, had found the eastern edges of their lands increasingly infested with squatters: people from mountainous western New England who maintained they had freehold title to their farms on the basis of grants from Massachusetts and Connecticut. The Yankee claims were hard to refute, for land ownership east of the Hudson River was muddled by unextinguished Indian titles and the failure of New York and the New England provinces to fix a definitive line between themselves. With the end of the Seven Years' War, more New Englanders than ever descended on the inviting expanses of the Hudson Valley. By 1766 thousands of Yankees lived in a stretch of territory perhaps 150 miles long and 10 miles wide, from Long Island Sound to the Hoosic River, defending themselves against the manor lords' writs of trespass with countersuits in New England courts, but also organizing themselves into militia companies—just in case.[16]

The Yankees' resistance turned violent in the winter of 1765–66. Beginning in Dutchess County, and then with the spring spreading southward into Westchester and north into Albany Counties, armed bands of squatters and disaffected tenants broke out in open rebellion, intimidating landlords, harassing justices of the peace and sheriffs, and breaking open jails that held men imprisoned for rent debts. These disorders were similar in rhetoric to the Stamp Act riots but differed in that the rural "mobs" tended to be disciplined, quasi-military bodies made up of farmers who aimed to protect their land titles, rather than the comparatively unstable urban crowds of seamen, laborers, and artisans resisting imperial authority in the name of Englishmen's rights. Moreover, several of the patroons were among New York's most prominent Sons of Liberty and found it deeply unsettling to hear rioters on their estates claiming to be Sons of Liberty themselves. As Captain John Montrésor wryly observed in May, when five hundred Westchester County squatters threatened to march on New York and pull down the house of John Van Cortlandt (a leading Son of Liberty in the city) unless he recognized their titles, the "Sons of Liberty [are] great opposers of the Rioters as they are of opinion no one is entitled to Riot but themselves."[17]

Against this backdrop of social unrest and rising violence, the manor lords appealed to Governor Moore, who asked Gage to restore order. The commander in chief complied, ordering the 28th Regiment into Dutchess County's Philipse Patent in mid-June and later sending a detachment of the 46th Foot up to Albany County to be used against rioters on Livingston Manor. Gage did not sympathize with the manor lords. Far from it: "They certainly deserve any Losses they may sustain, for it is the work of their own Hands," he wrote to Conway. "Th[e]y first Sowed the Seeds of Sedition amongst the People and taught them to rise in Opposition to the Laws." Still, the law obliged Gage to provide troops when responsible civil authorities requested them, and he could also see potential benefits in offering military aid. First, he could show the army's strength as he had been unable to do during the Stamp Act disturbances. Second, by protecting the property of "the Rich[est] and most Powerfull People of the Province" he might win back their allegiance. Once the regulars had restored order, how could the assembly possibly deny them quarters? Thus the commander in chief could use his troops both to brandish the stick and to dangle the carrot, and he expected results. He got them—although hardly in the form he hoped to see.[18]

The redcoats of the 28th and the 46th did indeed suppress the rioting, but not with ease. Major Arthur Brown led the whole effective strength of the 28th Regiment, 330 men, into what amounted to battle with the squatters on the Philipse Patent. He succeeded in rounding up sixty "Miserable, harden'd Wretches," at a cost of three casualties, one of whom died of his wounds. When the 28th marched for New York City at the end of June, the situation was still unsettled enough that Brown left two companies behind to guard the Dutchess County jail. Captain John Clarke and his hundred men from the 46th Foot encountered even more frustration in operations against Robert Noble and his followers at "Nobletown," on the Livingston Manor. Noble's men confronted the regulars as guerrillas, and for nearly a month in July and August ducked in and out of refuges across the Massachusetts border, leading Clarke's troops on a wild chase around eastern Albany County. "They advance and retire at pleasure," the irritated captain reported, "playing a Game by no means Satisfactory." He pulled down their houses and stationed guards on their fields, hoping to provoke retaliation or at least to catch men returning to bring in their harvests. Nothing worked.[19]

Finally, in mid-August, Clarke positioned his men on the eastern slope of a mountain, a quarter mile west of the town line of Egremont, Massachusetts, hoping to catch Noble's raiders on their way into (or perhaps out of) New York. But misestimating one's position was easy enough in a place where no one agreed on boundaries, and Clarke soon found himself facing three Massachusetts justices of the peace and a battalion of militiamen who believed that he was about to attack Egremont. No one wanted a battle, however, and Clarke—after asserting his right to execute the king's commission—pulled his men back to what the Massachusetts men informed him was New York's side of the mountain.[20]

And there, uneasily, matters rested. Now that push had come to shove, the governments of Massachusetts and Connecticut proved unwilling to back the claims of their settlers with force, and the squatters had little choice but to abandon their farms or sign leases. The army, deployed on behalf of New York landlords, had effectively destroyed the New England claims. Yet this outcome, which went well beyond Gage's intention, also had adverse effects when the evicted Yankees published their side of the story in Boston. Within weeks, accounts of redcoats who "burnt and destroyed . . . houses, pillaged and plundered others, stove in their cyder barrels, turned their provisions out . . . into the open streets, [and] Ript open their feather beds" appeared in newspapers as far south as Virginia. That would perhaps have been bad enough; but the ministry first heard of the episode not from Gage, but from the Massachusetts agent, and reprimanded both commander in chief and governor for allowing the army to be used to settle a dispute between colonies. This "Affair," wrote the secretary of state, "has not been transacted with the Temper and Prudence requisite on such an Occasion. . . . It is to be hoped that the Right of the Parties were very well ascertained before the Military Power was called in to the aid of the Civil, for few Exigencies can justify such a kind of Decision." Thus Gage, making himself agreeable and his troops useful to the civil authorities of New York and hoping to make the assembly amenable to supporting the army, found himself blamed for exacerbating intercolonial tensions. But what must have astonished him most was that the New York Assembly responded to his gestures of goodwill by summarily rejecting the Quartering Act—and denying Parliament's authority.[21]

It was in June, when Major Brown and the 28th Regiment were collaring squatters and dodging bullets on the Philipse Patent, that the assembly passed a set of resolutions and a bill intended to sidestep the Quartering Act. The bill, called the Barracks Act, released £3,200 from the Treasury—once more, from funds appropriated in 1762—to purchase beds, bedding, firewood, candles, and kitchen utensils for two battalions, for one year. The measure made no mention of the small beer, salt, and vinegar stipulated in the Quartering Act, or indeed of the Quartering Act itself. Governor Moore, indignant, wanted to veto it—funds already in the Treasury were presumably at his disposal anyway, and the assembly was infringing his power by restricting their use—but Gage, who needed the money sooner rather than later, argued otherwise. A bad act was better than none at all; it was possible that the other colonies would interpret it as a submission to the Quartering Act; and he still hoped that the patroons in the assembly would appreciate the army's efforts enough to come around. So Moore unhappily assented to the Barracks Act, consoling himself with a letter to the secretary of state, warning him that the assembly would disregard every act of Parliament "not backed with a sufficient power to enforce it."[22]

Governor Moore tried one last time to extend his hand in conciliation, only to have it (as he thought) bitten again. In June he supported an assembly initiative to issue £260,000 in province currency by asking the Privy Council to make an exception to the Currency Act of 1764. Word arrived in November that the Privy Council would approve the currency issue, provided that the assembly include a suspending clause in the act. The same packet also brought the secretary of state's response to Moore's complaints about the assembly, and in it the secretary said, in no uncertain language, that the New York Assembly would have to accept the Quartering Act as passed and obey it to the letter, or face the consequences. The governor prudently made no mention of the secretary's instruction when he told the assembly that the Privy Council had approved the money bill, on the condition that they append a suspending clause. The legislators refused. Unless the governor agreed to sign the act without this "unusual clause," they replied, "we are prepared to bear our distresses as well as we are able."[23]

That did it. Moore—by now surely thinking the better of Cadwallader Colden—shot back with the secretary of state's directive ordering the assembly to submit unconditionally to the Quartering Act. The assemblymen took stock of their position and then, on December 15, stood fast. The result, of course, was deadlock. For six months the assembly would refuse to comply, and before the matter would finally be settled Parliament itself would intervene in New York's affairs.

OTHER WORRIES HAUNTED Virginia, and other tensions vexed its leaders; but here too they loomed larger in the aftermath of the Stamp Act. Before the war, the gentry of the Old Dominion had been more unified than perhaps any other ruling class in the Atlantic world, but in the aftermath of the Stamp Act crisis they split into factions that would quarrel for a decade. The source of this fissure was personal in the sense that the intemperate words and actions of a Northern Neck planter, Richard Henry Lee, first opened it. Yet Lee did no more than allege that a social fault line, long present beneath the smooth surface of the Virginia elite, originated in the moral failings of some of the province's greatest families. His accusations of self-interestedness—of conduct unbecoming to gentlemen—created irrevocable division because they exploded, within the public arena, a long-standing but previously private mixture of indebtedness, narrowing opportunities, and self-doubt.

No less than the rest of his class, Lee found it hard to support a family in the great planters' accustomed style. Whereas his neighbor George Washington sought to make up the difference between expenses and income by engaging in land speculation, wheat farming, and plantation manufacturing, Lee stuck with tobacco and tried to use his political clout to gain access to profitable employment. Thus while only Patrick Henry was said to excel Lee as an orator, no one in Virginia surpassed him as a seeker after public office. Lee had in fact applied for the colony's stamp distributorship, only to be disappointed when Grenville chose Colonel George Mercer, the agent of the Ohio Company who happened to be in London at the time. The proud, passionate Lee found the loss of income hard enough to bear, but the slight of being passed over was insupportable. In the Stamp Act agitation he led the attack on Mercer, organizing demonstrations in the Northern Neck and delivering a mock funeral oration at the burning of Mercer's effigy. The unsuspecting colonel, arriving to find that he had become the most hated man in Virginia, blamed Lee. He returned to London intent not only on pursuing the Ohio Company's land claims, but on finding his enemy's letter of application. In the meantime, Lee's political career prospered remarkably, for two reasons: he had violently opposed the Stamp Act, and he had been one of the few men ever to question the integrity of Virginia's greatest statesman, John Robinson.[24]

When Robinson died in May 1766 he was secretary of the province, treasurer, and speaker of the House of Burgesses, a combination that made him the most powerful politician, as well as one of the most beloved men, in Virginia. Beloved by many, that is, but not by Richard Henry Lee, whose ceaseless quest for profit and honor put him at odds with the speaker, who disliked him and thwarted his ambitions. In December 1764, Lee had insisted that the Burgesses audit Robinson's accounts as treasurer. The audit endorsed Robinson's stewardship—his friends saw to that—but Lee continued to question his practices. The following May he backed Patrick Henry's attack on Robinson's proposal to borrow £240,000 in London to finance a new currency and to erect a loan office from which needy gentlemen might borrow; and Lee was conspicuous by his absence among the eulogists when Robinson went to his reward. All this made him seem no more than the scapegrace that Robinson's friends said he was—until the administrators of Robinson's estate discovered two stunning facts. First, at the time Robinson died the Old Dominion's most prominent men owed him approximately £130,000. Second, most of this fabulous sum had accrued because, instead of burning the paper money collected in payment of taxes as the law required, Treasurer Robinson had lent it to his friends.

Affable old John Robinson had embezzled a fortune from the public accounts not principally for his own profit, but to save his fellow planters from financial embarrassment.[25] Unsurprisingly, Robinson's political allies had benefited most from his largesse, and his death exposed this group—which included Byrds, Burwells, Carters, Randolphs, and other tidewater grandees, but comparatively few from the Northern Neck and the new counties in the piedmont—not only to public censure, but to bankruptcy. The embezzled money had to be repaid to Robinson's estate because Robinson's estate owed it to the Treasury, which in turn was legally obligated to remove it (however belatedly) from circulation. But where were the improvident grandees in question going to find the tens of thousands of pounds that the law required as a burnt offering? And how could Virginia incinerate so much money without simultaneously lighting a funeral pyre for half of its First Families?

These questions did not particularly trouble Richard Henry Lee (who owed Robinson's estate twelve pounds) or Patrick Henry (who owed it eleven) as they demanded a full public accounting. In December the Burgesses' investigating committee reported not only that a hundred thousand pounds was still due the province (much in huge sums—Colonel William Byrd III alone owed fifteen thousand pounds), but that Robinson had also allowed certain sheriffs to run far into arrears in tax receipts. Robinson had served his friends at the expense of his province, and Lee and Henry seized the opportunity to show how private indebtedness and extravagance led to abuse of trust and corruption that had imperiled the solvency, the honor, of Virginia. In this direct, ungentlemanly way, Lee and Henry dealt the province's political establishment a staggering blow, making themselves the two most influential—and feared, and hated—younger politicians in the Old Dominion.

Indeed, a wholesale repudiation of Virginia's older leaders might have ensued, had not George Mercer's letters begun arriving from London. Mercer had found a copy of Lee's application for the post of stamp distributor, and now Mercer's family lost no time in publishing the proof that only bad luck had saved the self-appointed scourge of Virginia's corrupt elite from becoming a royally appointed scourge of every Virginian's rights. Confronted with the evidence, Lee maintained that he had soon thought the better of his application and would not have accepted appointment, had it come his way. This rang false—Lee had condemned the Stamp Act only after he knew of Mercer's appointment—but it gave Lee's friends enough cover to counterattack in the *Virginia Gazette,* where the controversy dragged on, at the pot-and-kettle level, into 1767. Lee's exposure also encouraged his supporters in the assembly to show restraint in settling the Robinson affair. The quality of mercy was such that in April the Burgesses voted to give the administrators of Robinson's estate three years to settle accounts with the province. (In the end it took twenty-five.)

What happened in Virginia after the repeal of the Stamp Act ran deeper than scandal and political realignment. The gentry of the province divided, for the first time since the seventeenth century, into openly hostile camps. Even planters like George Washington, who had not taken Robinson's money and who refused to join in the assault on those who had, could hardly avert their eyes from the fray or fail to see how it altered Virginia's political landscape. Nor indeed could they escape a public atmosphere that grew ever more rank with animosity and distrust. Great planters had always frowned on suits for debt among themselves, but such suits now became increasingly common not only out of necessity, but as political weapons. Few could miss the threat implicit in the announcement George Mercer's father placed in the December 25, 1766, *Virginia Gazette,* lecturing "his fellow planters . . . for their failure to behave like gentlemen" and serving notice that unless he received prompt payment he would "bring Suits, immediately after next April General Court, against all persons indebted" to him.[26]

Nor could anyone ignore the unedifying spectacle of great planters holding lotteries to raise the money they needed to pay off their debts. Several such desperate attempts to regain solvency followed the Stamp Act crisis, some directly stimulated by the need to settle the Robinson estate. Typically they involved the sale of drawing tickets, for five pounds each, entitling the lucky winners to take possession of hundreds or thousands of pounds' worth of slaves or land, and in some cases of whole functioning plantations. Perhaps the saddest of them all was the lottery William Byrd III held to raise (he hoped) fifty thousand pounds. In the end, he complained, "I disposed of a fine estate in order to settle my affairs . . . but to my very great disappointment, I have not received a third part of the money the tickets sold for."[27] Byrd had made the mistake of selling the tickets on credit.

These developments worried the gentlemen of Virginia because they drew a frightening but perfectly reasonable inference from them. Many of the greatest planters in the province, men who had advertised their status in magnificent houses, clothes, coaches, lands, and slaves, were in fact bankrupts. A once-unified social elite, overborne by debt, had fallen into public quarrels and divided into factions. Honor, the gentleman's most prized possession, seemed suddenly to have grown even scarcer than money. It was not clear that the lower social orders in Virginia were so deferential as to accept indefinitely the leadership of planters such as these. But what would restore the gentry's solvency, and its credibility? If ambitious men like Richard Henry Lee and Patrick Henry demanded their answers in a public forum, most planters could only look sharp for whatever opportunities appeared, tighten their belts, and dream of deliverance.

Meanwhile the colony's economic life stagnated, and politics and culture alike seemed to drift toward some unspecifiable disaster. At the end of 1766 a writer in the *Virginia Gazette* caught the character of the gentry's discontents when he asserted "That this colony is in a declining State, or, I may rather say on the Brink of Destruction, I fear is too evident to the most superficial Observer, to need any arguments to prove."[28] If the repeal of the Stamp Act removed an immediate threat to rights and property, the events that followed awakened in the minds of Virginia's leaders fears that gnawed all the more deeply because they had no tangible object, and indeed no definable form: no form, that is, except the nightmare image of a ruling class that, having lost control of its appetites, had pawned its sacred honor.

CHAPTER 74

The Future of Empire

1766–1767

In massachusetts, a seismic shift in the balance of political power; in New York, a standoff between governor and assembly; in Virginia, a divided elite. All of these followed the Stamp Act, and the controversies surrounding it intensified them all, yet the Stamp Act *caused* none of them. The country party's triumph in the Bay Colony culminated a campaign against Thomas Hutchinson's court party that had been in progress since before the end of the war and followed factional patterns that could be traced to Governor Shirley's day. New York's reactions against the Quartering Act emerged from encounters with the army that went back to 1756, when Lord Loudoun had seized quarters in Albany and threatened to station battalions in New York as if it were a conquered city. The Robinson scandal in Virginia arose from the interplay of planter indebtedness, depression, and the Currency Act's restriction on paper money issues. In every case, local competition, tensions, and anxieties defined the conflicts that the Stamp Act had aggravated and magnified. While factionalism, infighting, and deadlock had long been common features of the colonial political scene, there was something new in the ferocity of the post–Stamp Act disputes: something novel about the seeming ease with which the participants lost perspective on the issues that were in fact at stake. Far from restoring prosperity, peace, and harmony to the empire, the repeal of the Stamp Act seemed in some perverse way to have loosed devils into the colonial political arena, or perhaps into the colonists' minds.

Even areas untouched by the Stamp Act agitations seemed more unsettled than before in 1765–66. In West Florida, bizarre disputes over rank and precedence arose between Governor George Johnstone, a half-pay naval captain with a famously bad temper, and the colony's army officers. In the absence of a clear and consistent policy stipulating who was entitled to command the troops within a province, Johnstone had asserted his authority over the 21st and 31st Regiments. When the commanding officer of the 31st, at Pensacola, refused to obey Johnstone's orders, Johnstone ordered the 21st Regiment out from Mobile—to besiege the 31st! Eventually the governor arrested the regimental commandant and charged him with treason. Gage thought to resolve the mess by appointing a colonel from the St. Augustine garrison in East Florida as acting brigadier general and regional commander, and sending him to take command at Pensacola. When that unfortunate brigadier arrived, however, Johnstone refused to recognize his commission and challenged him to a duel. Had all this not taken place while the province was on the brink of war with the Creek nation, the governor's behavior might have seemed merely ludicrous; but under the circumstances it was no laughing matter. Johnstone tried summoning a popularly elected assembly to support his wish to declare war on the Creeks. This might have gained him the backers he needed, for many West Floridians lusted after Creek lands, but it came too late. Gage demanded Johnstone's recall; and on February 19, 1767, the Southern secretary summoned him home, disgraced, from a province verging on anarchy.[1]

Something oddly similar was happening in Canada at about the same time. Since becoming royal governor there in August 1764, James Murray—Wolfe's junior brigadier on the Plains of Abraham—had contrived to alienate not only the English-speaking merchants (mainly New Englanders) who had taken up residence after the war, but most of his colony's senior army officers. In petitions to the Board of Trade and appeals to their correspondents in London the merchants loudly demanded punishment for his high-handedness and partiality to the Canadians. Murray had refused to summon an assembly, they pointed out, and governed like a frog-eating tyrant, imposing taxes by decree and enforcing customs regulations without observing the forms of law. He had nullified the provisions of the Proclamation of 1763 that established English law in Québec by permitting inferior courts to continue using French law codes and allowing Catholics to serve on juries—even juries that decided suits to which Englishmen were party. Meanwhile, Murray had fallen out with the commandants of Canada's principal regiments over issues relating to quartering and troop discipline, but most of all because he, although now a half-pay officer, insisted on giving them orders. They resisted; public disputes erupted as Murray issued directives that the officers ignored; finally Gage had to intervene. In the spring of

1766 the ministry summoned Murray home to answer the complaints that had been leveled against him. Although he, unlike Johnstone, was never cashiered, he was never allowed to return to Québec. Even if Murray had broken no laws, he too had lost control of his province.[2]

In two new colonies out of the four carved from the North American conquests, then, government ground to a halt at the same time as in the older provinces, for reasons that had nothing to do with the Stamp Act. The cases of West Florida and Canada were superficially similar—headstrong governors, jealous of their authority, had meddled in military administration—but the roots of the conflicts in fact ran deep into the organization of the postwar empire. The problem was partly institutional, for civil and military authority overlapped so haphazardly as to make conflict almost inevitable wherever military units were stationed within the limits of colonial governments. Yet even outside the bounds of established colonies, in areas where their authority was undisputed, military officers were failing as colonial administrators in 1765–67. Events in trans-Appalachia showed that, at its heart, the problem was the army itself. However effective the redcoats had once been as conquerors, they were utterly unsuited to controlling the conquests. Nothing could have made this clearer than their inability to halt, or even diminish, migration beyond the Allegheny crest.

As the Indian war receded into the Illinois Country, illegal settlements began cropping up beyond the Proclamation Line. Hunters and farmers built cabins within sight of forts despite the protests of Indians and the formal prohibitions of post commanders. By June 1766 more than five hundred families, mainly from Virginia, were living in the valley of the Monongahela and its tributaries. In September, Gage ordered the commandant of Fort Pitt to warn them off, and to threaten them with force if they ignored his orders. Nothing happened. The following spring the squatters squatted in larger numbers than ever, and Gage was trying to excuse himself to the secretary of state. The settlements lay on land claimed by Virginia, he wrote, and the Virginians had lately been touchy about "the exertion of Military Power without their Authority." Only in May 1767, he explained, had he felt justified in ordering the commandant of Fort Pitt to burn out the illegals along Red Stone Creek and the Cheat River. Yet even that effort would prove futile. Within six months the squatters were back, in "double the Number . . . that ever was before."[3]

Gage knew that burning down a few accessible settlements was only a symbolic gesture, although he hoped it would scare off the other unauthorized inhabitants of the region. As he understood only too well, three regular companies at Fort Pitt could never locate all the squatters in the upper Ohio Valley, let alone chase them out of thousands of square miles of woods. But he also realized that if they did not evacuate the region, a new war would in all likelihood break out, and soon. For the backwoodsmen had not only been encroaching on the Indians' lands, poaching their game, and promiscuously selling them liquor; they had also been killing Indians in appalling numbers since late 1765.[4]

A decade of warfare had left frontier whites with innumerable scores to settle and a rage that eroded their willingness to make distinctions among potential victims. In the first half of 1766 alone British subjects in the old *pays d'en haut* murdered more than twenty Indians, mostly in the Ohio Country and especially around Pittsburgh. George Croghan, working to keep open the communication links between Fort Pitt and the Illinois Country, temporarily defused tensions with condolence ceremonies and gifts: a brilliant if expensive diplomatic feat that Croghan said "cost him more trouble than he had ever had in his life." But the pace of bloodletting did not slacken and tensions soon mounted higher than ever. By the middle of May 1767, the commander at Fort Pitt informed Gage, the settlers in the area were "under no Laws"; the Delawares and Shawnees were threatening to take revenge on the squatters and seemed likely to start a general war. Gage could only hope that the burning of the Red Stone and Cheat River settlements would reassure the Indians that the empire was on their side, for he was under no illusion that Fort Pitt's paltry garrison could maintain the peace. He privately advised the officer in charge to have his men keep their heads down: so long as the Indians retaliated only against "those who have injured them," His Majesty's troops were not to intervene in quarrels between squatters and natives.[5]

That a new Indian war did not erupt in the Ohio Country in 1767 had less to do with anything Gage or the garrison at Fort Pitt did than with three other factors: George Croghan's willingness to spend the king's money freely in practicing his own virtuoso diplomacy, the unprecedented quantities of alcohol flooding into trans-Appalachia, and the difficulty the Shawnees encountered in organizing a defensive coalition with the peoples of the lower valley. Croghan met with the Ohio chiefs at Pittsburgh in June, assuring them of British goodwill and asking them to control their young men until he and Sir William Johnson could set things right; then, in the fall, he traveled along the Ohio River, up the Muskingum through the Delaware towns, to Lake Erie and Detroit, condoling the Indians for their losses, covering the dead with presents, and promising punishments for white murderers. Croghan's ceremonial negotiations consumed huge quantities of time and money, but they helped preserve the peace. The Shawnees found that they had to postpone from the fall to the spring, and finally until 1769, a congress that would create an alliance between themselves, the Delawares, and other western nations, including their traditional enemies from the lands south of the Ohio River.[6]

If Croghan's diplomacy had something to do with forestalling this alliance, so did the essentially unlimited trade in rum at the western forts. Traders brought an estimated 13,000 gallons to Fort Pitt and 24,000 gallons to Detroit in 1767—quantities that Sir William Johnson himself sanctioned both for their utility in stimulating trade and for their debilitating effects. But Croghan's condolences and gifts could only cover past murders, and the binge drinking of young men, however it inhibited collective action in the short term, could also feed a rage that would make retaliation more devastating when it finally came. Meanwhile the western settlers went on murdering Indians and appropriating land. On the basis of Croghan's trip both he and Gage concluded that unless some more permanent solution to the problems of settlement could be found, a new Indian war would be inevitable.[7]

Whatever the solution to Britain's problems in North America might have been, by the end of 1767 it should have been evident that the army was not it. His Majesty's forces had been the starting point for British reasoning about the future of the empire at the end of the war. The Triumvirate's reforms and Grenville's revenue measures had aimed at paying for an American military establishment that was supposed to defend the colonies and control the conquered territories. But these efforts to solve problems of control and finance had strained relations between colonies and metropolis to the snapping point, and the army had proven incapable of projecting imperial authority beyond the gates of its forts. The preeminent agency of British sovereignty in America had proved itself a blunt instrument at best, but nonetheless one capable of striking sparks wherever it touched.[8] Whether anyone in London understood that the postwar colonies might grow more combustible with every administrative miscalculation—or for that matter if such an epiphany would enable the Rockingham ministry to shift British policy out of the course Halifax and Grenville had set at war's end—remained to be seen.

THUS A STORY that began with a blundering Anglo-American military force attempting to project British imperial power beyond the Appalachians, at the Forks of the Ohio, ends with British military detachments stationed not only at the Forks but at Michilimackinac on the upper Great Lakes, Fort de Chartres on the Mississippi, Pensacola on the Gulf of Mexico, St. Augustine in East Florida, and Louisbourg on Cape Breton Island. The distresses that followed the war, in the form of Indian rebellion and civil unrest in the colonies, had been resolved, and no immediate threat to the empire's future tranquillity loomed. Thus ministers and policy makers and members of Parliament might well have believed that, despite its unlikely beginnings and its anxious conclusion, the story had been a narrative of imperial triumph. But in truth the British army was fully in control at none of these far-flung posts. The vast empire survived not because of Britain's power, but despite its weakness, at the sufferance of the peoples whom the British believed they had conquered, and on the strength of the emotional ties between Britons and the Anglo-American colonists who had participated in the conquest. And the great Indian war had shown, as the Stamp Act crisis had demonstrated, that both the sufferance of the supposedly conquered and the allegiance of the colonists had limits that were all too easy to exceed.

EPILOGUE

Mount Vernon

JUNE 24, 1767

GEORGE WASHINGTON ordered his overseers to begin the 1767 wheat harvest on June 24, a hot, cloudy Saturday at the end of a dry week. Thus began twenty days of unrelenting exertion for Mount Vernon's slaves and no little anxiety for their master, who for the first time had given over his holdings almost entirely to the cultivation of grain. Much depended on the success of this experiment, which was a crucial element in Washington's scheme to free himself of the debts he had accumulated over the years of failing to produce tobacco that would sell on London's finicky market. Rich as he was in land, he feared that, like so many of his fellow planters, he too would become permanently dependent on his English merchant creditors. It was a fate he dreaded above all, for to suffer it meant that he would lose the essence of a gentleman's character, independence, and with it the capacity to behave in a truly virtuous way.

As a defense against dependency, Washington had made the hard decision to transform himself from tobacco planter into wheat farmer; and he had done much more, as well. When he built a new flour mill he took care to make it large enough to grind not only his grain but his neighbors', so that he could collect the miller's toll. He purchased a schooner to use for fishing and let it out as a charter vessel in the coastal trade. His orchards grew peaches for cider that his distillery made into brandy—not for consumption, but for sale. Since wheat farming required much less manual labor than tobacco growing did, he hired a master weaver who could teach otherwise underemployed slaves how to weave cotton, linen, and woolen cloth, and manage their output to insure that, once the plantation's clothing needs had been met, the surplus cloth

Colonel Washington. In the spring of 1772, when George Washington engaged Charles Willson Peale to paint his portrait, he chose to have himself represented in the uniform he had worn while colonel of the 1st Virginia Regiment. A paper inscribed "Order of March" protrudes from his waistcoat pocket, and in the background a pair of campaign tents appear in a mountainous setting beside a waterfall: details that suggest Washington wished to commemorate his regiment's participation in the march on Fort Duquesne in 1758. The background—so unlike the tidewater country around Mount Vernon, where Peale painted the portrait—also signified Washington's continuing interest in the western lands he had helped win for the British empire. He was even then pursuing that interest by pressing claims of the veterans of the 1754 campaign for a grant at the Forks of the Ohio, by speculating in other lands beyond the Proclamation Line, and by promoting a scheme to open navigation along the Potomac from Mount Vernon to Fort Cumberland. Everything in the portrait bespeaks Washington's commitment to making the ideal of British imperial dominion a reality in North America. *Courtesy of the Washington/Custis/Lee Collection, Washington and Lee University.*

would be of "merchantable" quality. Most of all, however, Mount Vernon's master had plunged more deeply than ever into land speculation, on projects that included (among others) draining the Great Dismal Swamp, acquiring rights to 2,500,000 acres of land in the Mississippi Valley, and seeking to revive the Ohio Company's claims.[1]

So many enterprises required constant supervision, and to sustain them Washington drove himself to ever-greater heights of self-discipline. He found his attention increasingly engrossed by the future, not only of his family and his plantations, but of his class and his colony. That preoccupation showed up clearly in the long letter he wrote from Mount Vernon on June 24, probably in the rainy evening that followed a day spent supervising the harvesters at Muddy Hole Farm. The letter was addressed to Captain John Posey, an old comrade from the Virginia Regiment who had recently asked for a £500 supplement to the £750 loan that was, in fact, two years overdue. Washington, whose sense of his worth as a gentleman depended upon openhanded generosity as much as independence, honor, and civic virtue, found it painful to tell Posey he would lend him no more. To soften the blow he promised not to press for repayment of the overdue amount, and then went on to offer "the same advice I w[oul]d give to my Bro[the]r were he und[e]r the same circumstan[ce]s."

If Posey could not meet his creditors' demands, Washington wrote, he should immediately sell everything, discharge his debts, and then move west, for

> there is a large Field before you—an opening prospect in the back Country for Adventurers—where numbers resort to—& where an enterprizing Man with very little Money may lay the foundation of a Noble Estate in the New Settlem[en]ts upon Monongahela for himself and posterity. [T]he Surplus money w[hi]ch yo[u] might save after discharg[in]g y[ou]r Debts, wou[l]d possibly secure yo[u] as much Land as in the course of 20 y[ea]rs w[oul]d sell for 5 times y[ou]r pres[en]t Estate—for proof of which only look to Frederick [County], & see what Fortunes were made by the . . . first takers up of those Lands: Nay how the greatest Estates we have in this Colony were made; Was it not by taking up & purchasing at very low rates the rich back Lands which were thought nothing of in those days, but are now the most valuable Lands we possess? Undoubtedly it was. . . .

Look at the newspapers, he continued, and you will see that "many good families" are selling out and "retiring into the Interior parts of the Country for the benefit of the[i]r Children." Indeed, Washington concluded, "Some of the best Gentlemen in the Country talk of doing so, who are not drove by necessity, but adopt the Scheme from principals of Gain."[2]

Washington's advice opens a window into the dreams of a Virginia gentleman struggling to retain status and honor in the face of narrowing opportunity. In counseling his old subordinate to seek a new life in the west, Washington was trying to offer a prescription for something more than an escape from the debt to which he himself remained in thrall. He was arguing in favor of a new life, the renewal of the virtue and independence he believed the gentry had once possessed.

This was explicitly an imperial solution, one that reflected Washington's faith that British ministers would soon lift the ban on western settlement. "I can never look upon that Proclamation," he wrote to another old army subordinate whom he was trying to persuade to become his confidential agent in acquiring lands beyond the Appalachian crest, "in any other light (but this I say between ourselves) than as a temporary expedient to quiet the Minds of the Indians & [one that] must fall of course in a few years especially when those Indians are consenting to our Occupying the Lands. [A]ny Person therefore who neglects the present oppertunity of hunting out good Lands & in some measure Marking & distinguishing them for their own (in order to keep others from settling them) will never regain it."[3]

There was nothing revolutionary in any of these aspirations and activities, any more than there was in the colonel himself—a man so Anglophile that he ordered his suits from London and left it up to the tailor to choose the fabric, color, and cut according to the latest fashion. Insofar as such plans required access to western lands, they depended upon policies decided in London, and thus upon factors that no American could control. Washington and his colleagues therefore had resolved to reserve places in the limited membership of the Mississippi Company for "nine [gentlemen in London] of such influence and fortune as may be likely to promote its success" in securing the millions of acres at stake in the venture. Such plans presumed—indeed required—as close an integration of London interests into the management of American land schemes as of American interests into the administration of the empire. On the basis of such cooperative relationships, Washington and most other colonial leaders agreed, the vast possessions that they had helped Britain win might indeed become the basis for the most glorious, enduring imperium since Rome itself. Whatever misunderstandings had caused the Stamp Act crisis lay in the past; whatever difficulties persisted in the economy would, with careful management, pass away. The prospects of empire glittered before them, just out of reach.[4]

REGARDLESS OF WHAT Britain's political leaders believed about their nation's capacity to crush America to atoms, it was not British power that could preserve the empire to which Washington and those like him were devoted. In truth the security of the empire depended on intangible qualities that the vigorous exercise of power could only destroy: faith in the justice and protection of the Crown, hope for a better future, and love of English liberty. Not all of these were equally important to the various peoples who inhabited the North American colonies and the conquests, but taken together they were indispensable to the survival of a transatlantic political community. For Indians on whose lands the Anglo-American settlers were pressing, as for the former subjects of Louis XV who now lived under British military rule, the first element was all-important: both needed a powerful patron to protect their communities from the vastly more numerous, aggressive Anglo-Americans. The Anglo-Americans themselves took the protection of the Crown for granted, as the basis of all political life. What mattered more immediately to them, in light of their rapidly expanding numbers, was the hope of improving their material circumstances. That in turn depended on access to the empire's new lands and to markets for their produce, both of which ranked with the preservation of their cherished Englishmen's rights and liberties as essential conditions of allegiance. Thus the aspirations and assumptions of the Anglo-American colonists were necessarily at odds with needs of the Indians and at least indirectly opposed to those of their new fellow subjects, the Canadians; yet George III was obligated to offer his protection and justice impartially, to them all.

In view of the difficulty of building any earthly kingdom on a foundation of faith, hope, and love, we may not find it surprising that even an earnest, conscientious king should have failed to find the formula that would harmonize such competing interests, fulfill so many conflicting expectations, and strengthen the emotional bonds that were the only durable cement of empire. The ministers who formed the Rockingham administration, and all those who followed them in the service of George III, conceived of the empire essentially as an institutional structure in which sovereign power, projected from the metropolitan core, brought order to its colonial periphery, organizing life within it to the mutual benefit of Britons and colonists. Given the mental constraints that their experiences, and the age itself, imposed—the memory of colonial refractoriness, the absence of any political theory that could justify the division of sovereign power within the state, the extraordinary difficulty of imagining a political community bound together by mere voluntary allegiance—the ministers' commitment to a strictly hierarchical conception of empire is utterly understandable. This is not to say that there was no alternative path to the creation of an enduring empire in North America; only that they could not see it. Or, more fairly, they *did* see that other path and rejected it out of hand. For the alternative approach to colonial governance had been there all along, and it had worked better than anyone at Whitehall in the mid-1760s realized.

In fact both the French and British empires in America had been most successful before the Seven Years' War when neither had tried to project metropolitan power in more than the most rudimentary ways. We have seen how the strength of the French empire depended on a tissue of assumptions about Onontio's fatherly regard for his Indian children, his willingness to use gifts, trade, and mediation rather than force in dealing with them. So long as the Indian alliances fostered by this forbearing approach endured, France maintained a surprisingly secure hold on Canada, Louisiana, and the Illinois Country. Only Montcalm's insistence on commanding Indians as auxiliaries, rather than using them as allies according to the norms that they understood, sufficed to destroy the Indians' faith in their French father. At the peak of its success, then, the Most Christian King's empire in North America had been less a French dominion than a multicultural confederation knit together by diplomacy, trade, and the necessity of defending against English aggression.

Britain's prewar empire had similarly rested on what looked like fragile foundations, for Whitehall too had allowed the colonists to choose their own course and refrained from intervening in colonial affairs beyond the settlement of disputes and the regulation of trade. The colonists wanted access to land and to the labor necessary to make that land productive, and they needed both commercial outlets for their produce and access to the manufactured goods they could not make for themselves. Imperial officials had responded either by not hindering the colonists in pursuing these, or by actually trying to help them satisfy their needs. Because British colonists focused their attention on acquiring land from native peoples rather than trading with them, Britain's empire had not developed into the kind of expansive multicultural community France's had; instead, English settlers explicitly predominated in the British colonies, exercising political, economic, and social hegemony with the backing of an otherwise detached king in Parliament.

Practically speaking, the Anglo-American colonists understood the imperial relationship as a combination of trade partnership and military alliance, superintended by a protector-king—an understanding that was not, in that sense, vastly different from the way the Indians conceived of their relationship with Onontio. On these minimalist terms, the British empire before the Seven Years' War had grown into an economically robust, if institutionally anemic, state system sustained by the cooperation and loyalty of the colonial elites, the members of which exercised local control. Any effort to tamper with the empire's equilibrium was liable to produce explosive results. Thus, like the Indians who reacted violently against Jeffery Amherst's efforts to place them in a newly subordinated relationship to the Crown, the Anglo-Americans had first resisted efforts by the commanders in chief to treat them as subjects, rather than as the allies they believed themselves to be; then, in the postwar era, they had rebelled against Parliament's efforts to project its sovereign power across the Atlantic. Thus the answer to the question, By what means could the British have created a durable empire after the Seven Years' War? is simply this: by refusing to exercise any new control, any new power, over the colonies.

But if Britain had allowed the colonists themselves to determine the shape of the postwar empire, what might the consequences have been? Surely not an early movement for independence, since colonists who had quite contentedly thought themselves Britons their whole lives and who had just shared in a glorious imperial victory would have had no reason to reject British authority. Rather, in the absence of a Franco-Indian cordon to the west, the colonies would almost inevitably have responded to their own vigorous demographic growth, and to the rising tide of immigration from the British Isles, by expanding settlement across the Appalachians into the heart of the continent. Such expansion would surely have occasioned friction between competing colonial governments and conflicts between speculative syndicates; but these kinds of disputes, if settled by the Board of Trade and Privy Council, would have tended only to strengthen imperial authority, for the overriding interest in acquiring lands would have made speculators and colonies seek the arbitration of Crown officials. The winners in this sort of decentralized, expansive empire would obviously have been the Anglo-American settlers. The losers, equally evidently, would have been the native peoples who stood in their way.

In the absence of a powerful European ally to trade with them, arm them, and coordinate their defense, Indian resistance might have lasted some decades into the nineteenth century, but it could not have endured indefinitely. The Spanish, preoccupied with reforming their own empire in the aftermath of defeat, could have offered little useful aid outside their footholds in Louisiana, Texas, and New Mexico. It is, therefore, possible to imagine a British North American empire that would have spread the English language, along with English-derived legal and governmental institutions, across the breadth of North America above the Rio Grande. Except for the absence of an international boundary at 49° north latitude, the result in two hundred years' time might not have been vastly different from the North America we know today. Or would it?

The kind of hell-for-leather expansion at the expense of native peoples just described, while desirable to colonial speculators and imperialists like Washington and Franklin, was precisely what the metropolitan authorities could not have tolerated—at least not indefinitely. The problem it posed for the Crown was fundamentally philosophical, but by no means merely academic, for Britain's monarchical political culture rested on the proposition that allegiance and protection were reciprocal obligations, imposing on the king the duty to defend his people from harm. The Peace of Paris obliged George III to extend his protection to his new subjects, Indian and French alike, and he and his ministers (as the Proclamation of 1763 attested) took this obligation quite seriously. Even if the king and his ministers had found it possible to look the other way while colonial populations surged into the interior, continued Anglo-American expansion would eventually have forced the Crown to intervene—or compelled it to acknowledge that the covenant of protection did not extend beyond the Anglo-American community.

The colonists would have found the latter course unproblematic, but insofar as it would have left the monarchy's claims to legitimacy in shreds, it could have had little appeal to George III or his successors. Metropolitan intervention, therefore, would have been the probable outcome at some point, and the ensuing confrontation would have centered on issues of imperial control, even as the American Revolution—the one that really occurred—did. But because the issues at stake would have concerned the exercise of power and the determination of policy within the empire, it is entirely possible to imagine an outcome that would have brought about American independence *without* an accompanying revolution—a result that would have paralleled the Mexican independence movement in 1821.

What actually happened, of course, brought matters to a head much earlier, in another way, with vastly different consequences. The ministers who served George III believed that the pressing postwar issues of public finance and imperial control did not allow them the luxury of delay, and therefore chose to exert sovereign authority over the colonists to achieve reform and avert chaos. Their actions put the colonists on the defensive, made them skeptical of the legitimacy of a power that evidently had no limits when applied to them. The long debate over the terms of empire that grew out of the Seven Years' War thus evolved on the colonial side into an effort to limit the exercise of state power by defining the natural and constitutional rights of individuals and groups within the body politic. In this way American leaders—men like Washington and Franklin, who otherwise would have liked nothing better than to pursue honor, wealth, and power within the British imperial framework—were compelled to confront issues of sovereignty in ways that imparted new, universalistic meaning to an inherited language of rights and liberties. Because the colonists' defense of local autonomy ultimately required them to fight a war of independence, Americans who would have been imperialists in any case became Revolutionaries first, and the concepts of equality, rights, and freedom on which they took their stand became the basis for the unconventional confederated polity that they liked to call "the empire of liberty."

But an empire of liberty was, of course, still an empire, and one might argue that the establishment of the United States merely resulted in the subjugation of a continent and its previous residents by the Anglo-Americans who would have dominated it anyhow. Surely the Delawares and Shawnees of the Ohio Country would have seen little difference in 1795, at the unsuccessful end of their own four-decade-long struggle for independence, between subjection to the United States and subjection to any other imperial power. And yet in the long run it *did* make a difference. However much the empire of liberty resembled its imperial predecessor in action, the founders of the United States had begun by grounding its institutions in statements of principle and fundamental law that defined rights so broadly that any man—or even woman—who aspired to become a member of the body politic might plausibly claim to be entitled to them, on the mere grounds of his or her humanity. That such claims would be automatically honored was not what mattered most, but rather that they would become the basis of repeated struggles for enfranchisement. Those struggles would become the distinguishing feature of American history, leading to a second revolutionary upheaval in the 1860s and reverberating in our public life down to this day.

Thus the Seven Years' War emerges not merely as the backdrop to the American Revolution, but as both its indispensable precursor and its counterpart influence in the formation of the early republic. In all its contingency, confusion, and cultural complexity, a conflict that extended

Britain's dominion over half of North America crystallized competing visions of empire, the contradictions and revolutionary potential of which only gradually became manifest. In shaping the world and the perceptions of both British and American leaders, the war became the necessary precondition for the development of an American nation-state that for most of its existence has been neither empire nor republic, but both. To see the Seven Years' War and the Revolution together as epochal events that yoked imperialism with republicanism in American political culture may therefore enable us to take another step toward understanding a national history in which war and freedom have often intertwined. For ours is, in the end, an inheritance shaped no less by the quest for power than by the pursuit of happiness.

Notes

INTRODUCTION:

The Seven Years' War and the Disruption of the Old British Empire

1. Eric Hinderaker, *Elusive Empires: Constructing Colonialism in the Ohio Valley,* 1673–1800 (New York, 1997), xi.

PROLOGUE: *Jumonville's Glen,* MAY 28, 1754

1. This account reflects inferences drawn from a variety of documents and described below, in notes for chapter 5. It derives from: W. W. Abbot et al., eds., *The Papers of George Washington, Colonial Series,* vol. 1, *1748–August 1755* (Charlottesville, Va., 1983), 107–25 (Washington to Dinwiddie, 29 May 1754 [two letters]; to Joshua Fry, 29 May 1754; to John Augustine Washington, 31 May 1754; to Dinwiddie, 3 June 1754); from "Journal de Joseph-Gaspard Chaussegros de Léry, Lieutenant des Troupes, 1754–1755," *Archives de Québec: Rapport de l'archiviste de la province de Québec, 1927–28,* esp. 372–3, 378–80; the deposition of John Shaw, 21 Aug. 1754, in William L. McDowell, ed., *Colonial Records of South Carolina: Documents Relating to Indian Affairs, 1754–1765* (Columbia, S.C., 1970), 3–7; evidence from the Dinwiddie papers quoted in L. K. Koontz, *Robert Dinwiddie: Servant of the Crown* (Glendale, Calif., 1941), 313–15. Also George F. G. Stanley, *New France: The Last Phase, 1744–1760* (Toronto, 1968), 54–5; Lawrence Henry Gipson, *The British Empire before the American Revolution,* vol. 6, *The Great War for the Empire: The Years of Defeat, 1754–1757* (New York, 1968), 30–2; Douglas Edward Leach, *Arms for Empire: A Military History of the British Colonies in North America, 1607–1763* (New York, 1973), 334–6; and Richard White, *The Middle Ground: Indians, Empires, and Republics in the Great Lakes Region, 1650–1815* (New York, 1991), 240–1.

PART I: *THE ORIGINS OF THE SEVEN YEARS' WAR,* 1450–1754

CHAPTER ONE: *Iroquoia and Empire*

1. The British colonists, having already named one war after the reigning monarch, tended to call this conflict the French and Indian War. Historians, equally stumped, have either followed the colonists' practice, invented other names (the Fourth Intercolonial War, the Great War for the Empire, the War of the Conquest), or used its European title, the Seven Years' War—despite the fact that it lasted seven years in Europe, where hostilities extended from 1756 to 1763, and slightly over six in North America. While a case can be made for referring to

the European and American phases of fighting by different names, I will use "the Seven Years' War" to describe the entire conflict.

2. Tanaghrisson's origins: Francis Jennings et al., eds., *The History and Culture of Iroquois Diplomacy* (Syracuse, N.Y., 1985), 250–1; *Dictionary of Canadian Biography*, vol. 3, s.v. "Tanaghrisson." On the Great League and the Confederacy see esp. Daniel K. Richter, *The Ordeal of the Longhouse: The Peoples of the Iroquois League in the Era of European Colonization* (Chapel Hill, N.C., 1992), 1–49; and id., "Ordeals of the Longhouse: The Five Nations in Early American History," in id. and James Merrell, eds., *Beyond the Covenant Chain: The Iroquois and Their Neighbors in Indian North America, 1600–1800* (Syracuse, N.Y., 1987), 11–27; also Anthony F. C. Wallace, *The Death and Rebirth of the Seneca* (New York, 1970), 21–107. The Iroquois were called the Five Nations until the 1720s, when they became the Six Nations by admitting the Tuscarora Indians to the Great League. On the defeat of the Tuscaroras by the Carolinian colonists, the Tuscarora migration to New York, and the adoption by the Iroquois, see Verner W. Crane, *The Southern Frontier, 1670–1732* (Durham, N.C., 1928), 158–61; Francis Jennings, *The Ambiguous Iroquois Empire: The Covenant Chain Federation of Indian Tribes with the English Colonies from Its Beginnings to the Lancaster Treaty of 1744* (New York, 1984), 297; and id. et al., *Iroquois Diplomacy*, 173.

3. On mourning war, ritual torture, and adoption practices, see Daniel K. Richter, "War and Culture: The Iroquois Experience," *William and Mary Quarterly*, 3rd ser., 40 (1983): 528–59. For the epic of Deganawidah and Hiawatha, see Paul A. W. Wallace, *The White Roots of Peace* (1946; reprint, Port Washington, N.Y., 1968). On the condolence ceremony as a basis for Iroquois diplomacy, see William N. Fenton, "Structure, Continuity, and Change in the Process of Iroquois Treaty Making," in Jennings et al., *Iroquois Diplomacy*, 3–36, esp. 18–21; also Richter, *Ordeal*, 30–49.

4. Dorothy V. Jones, *License for Empire: Colonialism by Treaty in Early America* (Chicago, 1982), 26; Wallace, *Death and Rebirth*, 42–3; Richter, "War and Culture," 528–59.

5. Francis Jennings, "Iroquois Alliances in American History," in id. et al., *Iroquois Diplomacy*, 39.

6. Richard White, *The Middle Ground: Indians, Republics, and Empires in the Great Lakes Region, 1650–1815* (New York, 1991); see esp. 1–185. I have adopted White's conceptual scheme and with it most of his terminology. Thus I speak of the refugee groups who gathered west of Lake Michigan (the heart of the geographical "middle ground") as Algonquians, even though, as White points out, the Algonquians were only the predominant linguistic grouping among peoples who included Iroquoians (the Huron-Petuns) and Siouans (Winnebagos). Although I have spoken of fatherhood in terms of Algonquian kinship systems, the cultural role of father as mediator was also common to the Iroquois, who like their enemies reckoned kinship matrilineally. (In both cases, the disciplinary parenting responsibilities belonged to mothers and maternal uncles.) The word "father" resonated very differently for Europeans—whose kinship structures were patrilineal and who thought in terms of patriarchal power—than for Indians in matrilineally organized cultures. As the French experience suggests, however, divergent meanings could open a path to fruitful intercultural relations, built creatively out of mutual misunderstanding; but this could happen only if the Europeans refrained from exercising power coercively.

7. Richter, *Ordeal*, 190–235.

8. For varying views of the character of Iroquois neutrality, see Jennings, "Iroquois Alliances," 39; Wallace, *Death and Rebirth*, 111–14; Richard Aquila, *The Iroquois Restoration: Iroquois Diplomacy on the Colonial Frontier, 1701–1754* (Detroit, 1983), 15–18 et passim; and Richter, *Ordeal*, 236–54.

9. For the French perspective on these aspects of the Iroquois policy, which served French interests but also, through the entente with the Far Indians, exacerbated the difficulties woven into the structure of the fur trade, see esp. W. J. Eccles, *The Canadian Frontier*,

1534–1760 (Albuquerque, N.M., 1983), 133–6. White tends to agree, although he argues for more complexity; see *Middle Ground,* 119–85. Jennings believes the French enjoyed more benefits; see "Iroquois Alliances," 39.

10. "Aggressive neutrality": Wallace, *Death and Rebirth,* 112. My account of the policy's operation follows Wallace's (111–14), Richter's (*Ordeal,* 236–54), and Aquila's versions (*Iroquois Restoration,* 15–18 ff.).

The Ohio Country included the territory between the Allegheny River and Lake Erie and stretched westward down the Ohio Valley as far as the French-controlled *pays des Illinois*—i.e., the area lying to the south of Lake Michigan, bounded roughly by the Wabash, the Mississippi, and the Illinois Rivers. See Jennings, *Ambiguous Empire,* 350–1; also Eccles, *Canadian Frontier,* 132–85, especially maps at 161, 169; and Eric Hinderaker, *Elusive Empires: Constructing Colonialism in the Ohio Valley, 1673–1800* (New York, 1997).

11. On the Illinois Country, see Winstanley Briggs, "*Le Pays des Illinois,*" *William and Mary Quarterly,* 3rd ser., 47 (1990): 30–56; and Hinderaker, *Elusive Empires,* 12–18, 53–64, 90–9. The importance of the Ohio Valley to France's strategic arc: "Memoir of the French Colonies in North America by the Marquis de la Galissonière" [Dec. 1750], in Sylvester K. Stevens and Donald H. Kent, eds., *Wilderness Chronicles of Northwestern Pennsylvania* (Harrisburg, Pa., 1941), 27–9; Eccles, *Canadian Frontier,* 154–6; and George F. G. Stanley, *New France: The Last Phase, 1744–1760* (Toronto, 1968), 35–6.

12. The depopulation of the Ohio Country: Richter, *Ordeal,* 15, 60–6. Shawnee migrations: Hinderaker, *Elusive Empires,* 18–22; James Howard, *Shawnee! The Ceremonialism of a Native Indian Tribe and Its Cultural Background* (Athens, Ohio, 1981), 1–8; and Michael N. McConnell, *A Country Between: The Upper Ohio Valley and Its Peoples, 1724–1774* (Lincoln, Nebr., 1992), 14–15. The Ohio Indians of the eighteenth century repopulation: id., "The Peoples 'In Between': The Iroquois and the Ohio Indians, 1720–1768," in Richter and Merrell, *Beyond the Covenant Chain,* 93–112; Jennings, *Ambiguous Empire,* 350–3; and id., *Empire of Fortune: Crowns, Colonies, and Tribes in the Seven Years War in America* (New York, 1988), 22–5. Tanaghrisson and Scarouady: Jennings et al., *Iroquois Diplomacy,* 250–2.

13. The operation of the system and the importance of the Ohio: Wallace, *Death and Rebirth,* 112–13. The numbers of Iroquois and Ohio warriors, for 1738 and 1748 respectively: Jennings, *Empire of Fortune,* 31–2. The Indian expert cited was Conrad Weiser, Pennsylvania's chief official interpreter, writing in late 1744 to Thomas Lee of Virginia; see Paul A. W. Wallace, *Conrad Weiser, 1696–1760: Friend of Colonist and Mohawk* (Philadelphia, 1945), 200–1. The populations that Weiser cited were reasonable enough; the claim that such vast numbers of warriors would join the Iroquois when summoned, utterly fanciful.

14. On wampum and diplomatic gifts, see Mary A. Druke, "Iroquois Treaties: Common Forms, Varying Interpretations," and Michael K. Foster, "Another Look at the Function of Wampum in Iroquois-White Councils," in Jennings et al., *Iroquois Diplomacy,* 85–114; also Wilbur Jacobs, *Wilderness Diplomacy and Indian Gifts: Anglo-French Rivalry along the Ohio and Northwest Frontiers, 1748–1763* (Stanford, Calif., 1950).

15. Aquila, *Iroquois Restoration,* 85–91; Jennings et al., *Iroquois Diplomacy,* 165–9.

CHAPTER TWO: *The Erosion of Iroquois Influence*

1. Ives Goddard, "Delaware," in William C. Sturtevant, gen. ed., *Handbook of North American Indians,* vol. 15, *Northeast,* ed. Bruce Trigger (Washington, D.C., 1978), 213–22; Michael N. McConnell, "The Peoples 'In Between': The Iroquois and the Ohio Indians, 1720–1768," in Daniel K. Richter and James Merrell, eds., *Beyond the Covenant Chain: The Iroquois and Their Neighbors in Indian North America, 1600–1800* (Syracuse, N.Y., 1987), 93–112; id., *A Country Between: The Upper Ohio Valley and Its Peoples, 1724–1774* (Lincoln, Nebr., 1992), 5–46; Francis Jennings, *Empire of Fortune: Crowns, Colonies, and Tribes in the Seven Years War in America* (New York, 1988), 31–5; id., *The Ambiguous Iroquois Empire: The Covenant Chain Confederation*

of Indian Tribes with the English Colonies from Its Beginnings to the Lancaster Treaty of 1744 (New York, 1984), 309–46; Eric Hinderaker, *Elusive Empires: Constructing Colonialism in the Ohio Valley, 1673–1800* (New York, 1997), 119–28.

2. Jennings, *Ambiguous Empire,* 356–60; Kenneth P. Bailey, *The Ohio Company of Virginia and the Westward Movement, 1748–1792: A Chapter in the History of the Colonial Frontier* (Glendale, Calif., 1939), 105–6.

3. Jennings, *Ambiguous Empire,* 360–2; quotation from Bailey, *Ohio Company,* 117.

4. On the Mohawk experience in King George's War and its effects on relations with New York, see Ian K. Steele, *Betrayals: Fort William Henry and the "Massacre"* (New York, 1990), 18–27. On New York's politics and the neutrality of Albany's merchants, see Stanley Nider Katz, *Newcastle's New York: Anglo-American Politics, 1732–1753* (Cambridge, Mass., 1968), 164–82.

5. Yoko Shirai, "The Indian Trade of Colonial Pennsylvania, 1730–1768: Traders and Land Speculation" (Ph.D. diss., University of Pennsylvania, 1985), 35–9.

6. Croghan quotation: Albert T. Volwiler, *George Croghan and the Westward Movement, 1741–1782* (Cleveland, 1926), 35. The rise of Pickawillany and Memeskia's activities: Richard White, *The Middle Ground: Indians, Republics, and Empires in the Great Lakes Region, 1650–1815* (New York, 1991), 215–22; and R. David Edmunds, "Pickawillany: French Military Power Versus British Economics," *Western Pennsylvania Historical Magazine* 58 (1975): 169–84. Croghan's enterprises: Nicholas Wainwright, *George Croghan, Wilderness Diplomat* (Chapel Hill, N.C., 1959), 5–37. The bounty on Croghan's head was $1,000, the equivalent of £225 sterling (Volwiler, *Croghan,* 78). In general it appears that Croghan could offer manufactures at about a fourth the price that French traders charged for comparable items: a testimony to the growing power of the British industrial economy that helps explain the anxiety of the French when confronted with the prospect of English competition in the Indian trade.

7. Inscription: Donald H. Kent, *The French Invasion of Western Pennsylvania, 1753* (Harrisburg, Pa., 1954), 8, my translation. Céloron quotation: George F. G. Stanley, *New France: The Last Phase, 1744–1760* (Toronto, 1968), 38. This encounter was at Scioto, and English traders as well as Indians were present.

8. Alarm at the numbers of traders: ibid. Céloron's report: ibid., 33–9; Gustave Lanctot, *A History of Canada,* vol. 3, *From the Treaty of Utrecht to the Treaty of Paris, 1763* (Cambridge, Mass., 1965), 75–6; Kent, *French Invasion,* 6–10. Both White, *Middle Ground,* 204–8, and Andrew R. L. Cayton, *Frontier Indiana* (Bloomington, Ind., 1996), 20–5, add significantly to these older accounts. Céloron's journals are translated in A. A. Lambing, ed., "Journals of Céloron de Blainville and Father Joseph Pierre de Bonnecamps," *Ohio Archaeological and Historical Society Quarterly* 29 (1920): 335–423.

9. Bailey, *Ohio Company,* 68–9.

10. Gist's surveys: Bailey, *Ohio Company,* 90, 94, 95. Croghan and Gist's cooperation: Wainwright, *Croghan,* 48–50. On the Logstown conference in general, see McConnell, *A Country Between,* 75–7; Hinderaker, *Elusive Empires,* 136–8; and White, *Middle Ground,* 236–7. The minutes of the conference appear in Lois Mulkearn, ed., *George Mercer Papers Relating to the Ohio Company of Virginia* (Pittsburgh, 1954), 127–38. Tanaghrisson was particularly dependent on the gifts the British had to offer; his ability to distribute these enabled him to create a following among locally powerful headmen. This made him more ardently pro-British than most of the Shawnees and Delawares, and for that matter more than the Great Council would have preferred (Jennings, *Empire of Fortune,* 37–45; McConnell, *A Country Between,* 75–6; Hinderaker, *Elusive Empires,* 138).

11. On Logstown's significance for the Ohio Indians, see McConnell, *A Country Between,* 77–82; and Jennings, *Empire of Fortune,* 21–45.

12. Quotations from Charles A. Hanna, *The Wilderness Trail, or The Ventures and Adventures of the Pennsylvania Traders on the Allegheny Path . . . ,* vol. 2 (New York, 1911), 292. The English document that describes Langlade's raid is Alfred T. Goodman, ed., *Journal of Captain*

William Trent from Logstown to Pickawillany (1871; reprint, New York, 1971). See also the versions in Volwiler, *Croghan,* 78–9; Stanley, *New France,* 45–6; White, *Middle Ground,* 228–31; Cayton, *Frontier Indiana,* 23–35; and the single most complete account, Edmunds, "Pickawillany." The predominance of Ottawas and Chippewas in the raiding party—peoples who practiced ritual cannibalism to transfer their enemies' spiritual power to themselves—explains the aftermath of the surrender. Langlade took no part but understood the importance of the feast and turned Memeskia over to the Indians ("some of [whom]," White notes, were "Langlade's own kinsmen") as a means of quite literally reincorporating him into the French alliance (White, *Middle Ground,* 231).

13. Bailey, *Ohio Company,* 154–5.

14. Pennsylvania-Virginia competition: ibid., 103–22. Gist's and Croghan's cooperation at Logstown: Jennings, *Empire of Fortune,* 44; Wainwright, *Croghan,* 48–50.

15. Bailey, *Ohio Company,* 64–9.

16. Duquesne's orders: Antoine-Louis Rouillé, comte de Jouy, Minister of Marine, to Duquesne, 15 May 1752, quoted in Stanley, *New France,* 45. Construction of French forts: ibid., 47–8; Lanctot, *History* 3: 85–6; and esp. Kent, *French Invasion,* 15–68.

CHAPTER THREE: *London Moves to Counter a Threat*

1. Except as noted, the following account derives from T. R. Clayton, "The Duke of Newcastle, the Earl of Halifax, and the American Origins of the Seven Years' War," *Historical Journal* 24 (1981): 573–84. On Newcastle, see Reed Browning, *The Duke of Newcastle* (New Haven, Conn., 1975), 82–8.

2. A few words about the curious institutional structure of the British empire and the conduct of foreign relations are in order. The king was responsible for all executive functions in the eighteenth-century British state but delegated authority to the members of his Privy Council, a body of dignitaries that varied in size from thirty to eighty members. Some of the councillors had purely advisory roles and ceremonial offices, while others were responsible for the actual administration of government. In 1696, King William III, worried that Parliament meddled too much in commercial and colonial affairs that were rightfully within his prerogative powers, created the Board of Trade and Plantations as a subcommittee of the Privy Council. Sixteen officials formally known as the "Lords Commissioners of Trade and Plantations" comprised the board: eight were Privy Council dignitaries; eight were salaried permanent members who did the board's real work.

The Board of Trade advised the Privy Council and the king on the appointment of officers in colonial governments, reviewed the legislation passed by the colonial assemblies to make sure that it was consistent with British law and the best interests of the realm (the Privy Council could "disallow," or veto, any repugnant colonial acts), and served as a clearinghouse for all official information on the colonies. Except for two problems, the Board of Trade might have become a genuinely effective agency for formulating and implementing colonial policy. The first difficulty was that the board had to concern itself not just with the colonies, but with literally all of England's trade and with many related issues. Thus among other duties it was charged with advising on all commercial treaties, supervising the state of domestic industries and the fisheries, and devising useful employments for the poor of the realm. But the second problem would ultimately prove worse: because the board could only advise on colonial matters, it had neither the authority to appoint officers in the colonial governments nor any executive power to compel the various government departments concerned in colonial affairs to follow its policies. All executive authority remained with the Privy Council, which in turn delegated power over the colonies to the secretary of state for the Southern Department.

The two secretaries of state, both privy councillors, together formulated "His Majesty's pleasure" in official papers and decrees and were therefore crucial intermediaries between the king and the rest of the British government. The division of responsibility between these "principal Secretaries" was traditional rather than legal—a circumstance that allowed them to meddle in each other's affairs more or less at will. The secretary of state for the Northern Department customarily exercised responsibility over the internal administration of England, Scotland, and Ireland, and over foreign relations with those states that lay north of a line bisecting Europe from Cape Gris-Nez on the north coast of France to Constantinople. The secretary of state for the Southern Department conducted foreign relations with all the world to the south of that line and administered colonial affairs. Colonial governors reported to the Southern secretary and received their instructions from him. From 1704 onward, he also exercised the undisputed right of patronage appointment within the colonial sphere. Needless to say, anyone charged with conducting foreign relations with France in an age of continual tension and hostility would have had his hands full; but to add to that burden the responsibility for relations with the rest of Catholic Europe, the Ottoman Empire, *and* the colonies meant that the secretary of state for the Southern Department was a very busy man indeed. Far too busy, in fact, to pay meticulous attention to the colonies—or even to inquire very closely about them. Most Southern secretaries simply ignored the colonies, using the patronage available within the colonial system to meet the pressing needs of domestic politics rather than seeking out capable officers to administer the colonial governments.

Thus the administration of the American colonies was not merely disorderly and confused but chaotic at its very heart. The Board of Trade knew everything there was to know about the colonies but had no power to translate its knowledge into policy. The secretary of state for the Southern Department had executive authority over the colonies but no real knowledge of them and little reason to inform himself on colonial affairs before he appointed officials or promulgated policies. This fundamental division between knowledge and power, together with the fragmentation and internal competitiveness of the bureaucracy, the absence of coherent direction given the colonial governments, and the paucity of effective political power available to the governors, hobbled the British government's ability to assert control over the colonies.

Even beyond these limits on the efficiency of the imperial system, however, the fact that most English administrators conceived of the empire in strictly commercial terms kept them from trying to make it into anything more than a structure for the control of trade. In a sense, the British empire in the 1750s was not and never had been a territorial entity, and it had never really *governed* much more than the produce and goods and credit that had traversed the Atlantic Ocean. The added fact that the Crown's colonial policy for most of the first half of the eighteenth century was to do nothing—showing, in Edmund Burke's famous phrase, a "wise and salutary neglect" of the colonies—only lent the weight of inertia to the institutional incapacity of English officials to influence American affairs. To intervene in the local government of the provinces themselves, as imperial administrators well understood, was to invite intense local opposition, which at the very least would be bad for business.

On the apparatus of imperial administration, see Charles McLean Andrews, *The Colonial Period of American History,* vol. 4, *England's Commercial and Colonial Policy* (New Haven, Conn., 1938), 272–425; Thomas Barrow, *Trade and Empire: The British Customs Service in Colonial America, 1760–1775* (Cambridge, Mass., 1967), 106–12; Arthur H. Basye, *The Lords Commissioners of Trade and Plantation, Commonly Known as the Board of Trade, 1748–1782* (New Haven, Conn., 1925); Oliver M. Dickerson, *American Colonial Government, 1696–1765: A Study of the British Board of Trade in Its Relations to the American Colonies* (Cleveland, 1912); and Leonard Woods Labaree, *Royal Government in America: A Study of the British Colonial System before 1783* (New Haven, Conn., 1930). Burke quotation: id., *Speech . . . on . . . Conciliation with the Colonies . . .* (London, 1775), par. 30.

3. On British balance-of-power politics before the Seven Years' War, see Eliga Gould, *The Persistence of Empire: British Political Culture in the Age of the American Revolution* (Chapel Hill, N.C., forthcoming), chap. 1; Jeremy Black, *British Foreign Policy in the Age of Walpole*

(Edinburgh, 1985); id., *A System of Ambition? British Foreign Policy 1660–1793* (London, 1991); H. M. Scott, " 'The True Principles of the Revolution': The Duke of Newcastle and the Idea of the Old System," in Jeremy Black, ed., *Knights Errant and True Englishmen: British Foreign Policy 1600–1800* (Edinburgh, 1989), 55–91.

4. Instructions to governors: cabinet minutes, 21 Aug. 1751. Circular letter: the earl of Holdernesse to the governors, 28 Aug. 1753. Both quoted in Clayton, "American Origins," 584.

5. Holdernesse to Dinwiddie, 28 Aug. 1753, in Kenneth P. Bailey, *The Ohio Company of Virginia and the Westward Movement, 1748–1792: A Chapter in the History of the Colonial Frontier* (Glendale, Calif., 1939), 202–3 n. 486.

6. Conference minutes quoted in Francis Jennings, *Empire of Fortune: Crowns, Colonies, and Tribes in the Seven Years War in America* (New York, 1988), 81.

7. Lords of Trade to Sir Danvers Osborne, 18 Sept. 1753, quoted in Jennings, *Empire of Fortune,* 82 n. 28.

8. Robert C. Newbold, *The Albany Congress and the Plan of Union of 1754* (New York, 1755), 17–37.

9. On Dinwiddie, see Bailey, *Ohio Company,* 57–8; Lawrence Henry Gipson, *The British Empire before the American Revolution,* vol. 2, *The Southern Plantations, 1748–1754* (New York, 1960), 16–17; L. K. Koontz, *Robert Dinwiddie* (Glendale, Calif., 1941), 33–49; and J. R. Alden, *Robert Dinwiddie: Servant of the Crown* (Charlottesville, Va., 1973), 18–19.

10. On the pistole fee controversy, see Alden, *Dinwiddie,* 26–37; Koontz, *Dinwiddie,* 201–35; and Jack P. Greene, *The Quest for Power: The Lower Houses of Assembly in the Southern Royal Colonies, 1689–1776* (Chapel Hill, N.C., 1963), 158–65.

11. Hayes Baker-Crothers, *Virginia and the French and Indian War* (Chicago, 1928), 18.

CHAPTER FOUR: *Washington Steps onto the Stage . . .*

1. Charles Moore, ed., *George Washington's Rules of Civility and Decent Behaviour in Company and Conversation* (Boston, 1926), rules 2, 9, and 13. On the formation of Washington's character, see Marcus Cunliffe, *George Washington, Man and Monument* (Boston, 1958), 35–60; James Thomas Flexner, *Washington: The Indispensable Man* (Boston, 1974), 5–18; John E. Ferling, *The First of Men: A Life of George Washington* (Knoxville, Tenn., 1988), 8–20; Douglas Southall Freeman, *George Washington: A Biography,* vol. 1, *Young Washington* (New York, 1948); Thomas A. Lewis, *For King and Country: The Maturing of George Washington, 1748–1760* (New York, 1993), 3–43; Paul Longmore, *The Invention of George Washington* (Berkeley, Calif., 1988), 1–24; Don Higginbotham, *George Washington and the American Military Tradition* (Athens, Ga., 1985), 1–38; Edmund Morgan, *The Genius of George Washington* (Washington, D.C., 1980); and id., *The Meaning of Independence: John Adams, George Washington, Thomas Jefferson* (Charlottesville, Va., 1975), 29–36.

2. This account follows Lawrence Henry Gipson, *The British Empire before the American Revolution,* vol. 4, *Zones of International Friction: North America, South of the Great Lakes Region, 1748–1754* (New York, 1967), 296–301; and Francis Jennings, *Empire of Fortune: Crowns, Colonies, and Tribes in the Seven Years War in America* (New York, 1988), 60–8. On Van Braam, see L. K. Koontz, *Robert Dinwiddie* (Glendale, Calif., 1941), 243 n. 299; and W. J. Eccles, *The Canadian Frontier, 1534–1760* (Albuquerque, N.M., 1983), 205 n. 15.

3. Legardeur's amusement: Jennings, *Empire of Fortune,* 63. Dinwiddie's warning: Dinwiddie to Legardeur de Saint-Pierre, in Sylvester K. Stevens and Donald H. Kent, eds., *Wilderness Chronicles of Northwestern Pennsylvania* (Harrisburg, Pa., 1941), 76–7. Washington's notes: "Washington's Description of Fort Le Boeuf," ibid., 79. The scope of Legardeur's career and achievements as an officer and diplomat can be fully appreciated in the excellent collection of documents edited with commentary by Joseph L. Peyser, *Jacques Legardeur de Saint-Pierre: Officer, Gentleman, Entrepreneur* (East Lansing, Mich., 1996); the documents dealing with his encounter with Washington are at 201–4.

4. Legardeur de Saint-Pierre to Dinwiddie, 15 Dec. 1753, in Stevens and Kent, *Wilderness Chronicles,* 78; cf. the more literal translation in Peyser, *Legardeur,* 205–6. Washington's return: Lewis, *For King and Country,* 114–19.
5. Dinwiddie to Trent, 26 Jan. 1754, quoted in Gipson, *North America,* 300.
6. Ibid., 299–302.
7. Ibid., 302–4. Croghan later wrote to Pennsylvania's governor: "The government may have what opinion they will of the Ohio Indians, and think they are oblig'd to do what the Onondago Counsel will bid them, butt I ashure your honour they will actt for themselves att this time without consulting the Onondago Councel" (to Gov. James Hamilton, 14 May 1754, quoted in Nicholas B. Wainwright, *George Croghan, Wilderness Diplomat* [Chapel Hill, N.C., 1959], 61).
8. Supply shortage: Ward testimony, 1765, quoted in Gipson, *North America,* 304. Approach of the French: Ens. Ward's deposition, 7 May 1754, ibid., 309–10 n. 113 (quotations from 309).
9. On the Virginia fort, see Gipson, *North America,* 307–10 n. 113; Jennings, *Empire of Fortune,* 64–5; and George F. G. Stanley, *New France: The Last Phase, 1744–1760* (Toronto, 1968), 51–3, 53. Fort Duquesne: Charles Morse Stotz, *Outposts of the War for Empire: The French and English in Western Pennsylvania: Their Armies, Their Forts, Their People, 1749–1764* (Pittsburgh, 1985), 81–7.

CHAPTER FIVE: . . . *And Stumbles*

1. For Washington's views on the undersupplied, underpaid quality of his troops, see Washington to Dinwiddie, 7 and 9 Mar. 1754, in W. W. Abbot et al., eds., *The Papers of George Washington, Colonial Series,* vol. 1, 1748–August 1755 (Charlottesville, Va., 1983), 75–87; on the poor pay of officers, same to same, 18 May 1754 (two letters), ibid., 96–100. For Dinwiddie's lack of sympathy for Washington's complaints, see Dinwiddie to Washington, 15 Mar. and 25 May 1754, ibid., 75–7, 102–14 (quotations from Dinwiddie at 102). See also Lawrence Henry Gipson, *The British Empire before the American Revolution,* vol. 6, *The Great War for the Empire: The Years of Defeat, 1754–1757* (New York, 1968), 22–30; James Titus, *The Old Dominion at War: Society, Politics, and Warfare in Late Colonial Virginia* (Columbia, S.C., 1991), 46–72; and Francis Jennings, *Empire of Fortune: Crowns, Colonies, and Tribes in the Seven Years War in America* (New York, 1988), 65–70.
2. "Instructs to Be Observ'd by Majr Geo. Washington on the Expeditn to the Ohio" [Jan. 1754], *Papers of Washington,* 1:65.
3. George F. G. Stanley, *New France: The Last Phase, 1744–1760* (Toronto, 1968), 54. My account follows Stanley's version, with additional information from Gipson, *Years of Defeat,* 30–2; Douglas Edward Leach, *Arms for Empire: A Military History of the British Colonies in North America, 1607–1763* (New York, 1973), 333–6; and Jennings, *Empire of Fortune,* 66–70.
4. On the topography of Great Meadows and vicinity, see Tom Thomas and Margaret DeLaura, *Fort Necessity National Battlefield, Pennsylvania* (Historic Resource Study, Sept. 1996: Denver Service Center, National Park Service, U.S. Department of the Interior), 91, 94–6, 99, et passim. Gist's plantation, established in 1753 on the divide between Red Stone Creek and the Youghiogheny River, was to be a way station for migrants to the Ohio Company's lands; twenty families had already settled there in 1754. See Thomas A. Lewis, *For King and Country: The Maturing of George Washington, 1748–1760* (New York, 1993), 68–70.
5. Donald Jackson, ed., *The Diaries of George Washington,* vol. 1, 1748–65 (Charlottesville, Va., 1976), 195 (27 May 1754 entry).
6. Cf. the phraseology in the diary and that in Washington to Dinwiddie, 29 May 1754, *Papers of Washington,* 1:110; same to same, 29 May 1754, ibid., 116; and Washington to John Augustine Washington, 31 May 1754, ibid., 118. In addition to Washington's record and the accounts analyzed below, a fifth (much later) witness's narrative also survives. Written by Captain Adam Stephen to prove that the Virginia troops had not been the aggressors but had behaved with discipline and observed the rules of civilized warfare, this embroidered version adds no verifiable facts to the other documents and distorts a good deal of what did occur (suggesting, for

example, that the Virginians "advanced as near [the French] as we could with fixt Bayonets, and received their Fire," before executing the kind of bayonet charge that European regulars might make, but of which the half-trained Virginians were incapable). Stephen's account appeared in the *Maryland Gazette,* 29 Aug. 1754, and the *Pennsylvania Gazette,* 19 Sept.

7. Contrecoeur's report was published in Europe. Translated into English in London, it appeared along with other documents on the beginning of the European phase of the war as *A Memorial Containing a Summary View of Facts, with Their Authorities. In Answer to the Observations Sent by the English Ministry to the Courts of Europe* (reprint, New York, 1757). The passage quoted appears in the reprinted version at 69; it is reproduced in *Papers of Washington,* 1:114. For the original, see Fernand Grenier, ed., *Papiers Contecoeur et autres documents concernant le conflit anglo-français sur l'Ohio de 1745 à 1756* (Québec, 1952). That members of the French party had been sleeping or had only recently awakened at the time of the attack—a detail mentioned by neither Washington nor Stephen—would seem clear from the fact that Monceau escaped without pausing to put on shoes. When an Indian messenger from the Forks joined Washington at Great Meadows on June 5, he reported having "met a *Frenchman* who had made his Escape in the Time of M. *de Jumonville's* Action, he was without either Shoes or Stockings, and scarce able to walk; however he let him pass, not knowing we had fallen upon them" (*Diaries of Washington,* 1:199).

8. "Affidavit of John Shaw," in William L. McDowell Jr., ed., *Colonial Records of South Carolina: Documents Relating to Indian Affairs, 1754–1765* (Columbia, S.C., 1970), 4–5.

9. Size and composition of Jumonville's party: *Summary View,* 67. I am much in debt to my colleague Dennis Van Gerven, professor of physical anthropology at the University of Colorado, Boulder, for explaining how skull bone would fragment under a blow from an edged weapon, the qualities of the meningeal sac, the volume of blood in the head, the consistency of brain tissue in a living (or recently killed) human being, and other aspects of violent trauma to the head.

10. Michael N. McConnell makes a parallel argument, though he stops short of describing Tanaghrisson as a refugee. See id., *A Country Between: The Upper Ohio Valley and Its Peoples, 1724–1774* (Lincoln, Nebr., 1992), 110.

11. "Journal de Joseph-Gaspard Chaussegros de Léry, lieutenant des troupes, 1754–1755," *Archives de Québec: Rapport de l'archiviste de la province de Québec* (1927–28), 372–3. My translation differs somewhat from that in the only other English version I have seen, a Works Progress Administration mimeograph publication in the Frontier Forts and Trails Survey series: Sylvester K. Stevens and Donald H. Kent, eds., *Journal of Chaussegros de Léry* (Harrisburg, Pa., 1940), 27–8. I am grateful to my colleague, Professor Martha Hanna, for help with the translation.

12. We may reasonably infer that the sight of Tanaghrisson's act would have temporarily rendered Washington incapable of acting. Even though he, like virtually all colonial Virginians, would have seen animals slaughtered and slaves whipped, it is extremely unlikely that he would ever have seen blood gush in such quantities as would have issued from the wound that Jumonville sustained: because at any given moment nearly a third of the human blood supply is in the brain, under great pressure, the discharge of fluid would have been prodigious. Such sights frequently induce physiological shock in observers; there is no reason to assume that Washington would have been immune to the reaction. (Again I thank Dennis Van Gerven for his careful explanation of the brain and its properties, and for his description of the effect on modern witnesses of seeing wounds similar to the one Jumonville sustained.)

13. Washington to Dinwiddie, 29 May (two letters), 3 June, and 10 June 1754, *Papers of Washington,* 1:110–12, 116–17, 124, 135. In the 3 June letter, Washington varied his story to come close to admitting what had happened, without suggesting that he bore any responsibility for it. In speaking of the encounter he noted that only seven of Tanaghrisson's warriors were armed, adding that "There were 5, or 6 other Indian[s], who servd to knock the poor unhappy wounded in the head and beriev'd them of their Scalps." This statement—an aside—was

ambiguous enough to allow Dinwiddie to infer that the killing occurred between the cessation of firing and Washington's acceptance of the French surrender. Lewis draws exactly that conclusion on the basis of Washington's letter in his able, careful account of Washington's youth: "Thoroughly panicked, the French turned and ran toward the Virginians again, waving their arms in the air. Before Washington could get down to the floor of the ravine to accept their surrender, the Iroquois began tomahawking the wounded and collecting scalps" (*For King and Country,* 143).

14. Washington to Dinwiddie, 29 May (physical stamina), and 10 June 1754 (ardent wish for direction of an experienced officer), *Papers of Washington,* 1:107, 129.

15. Entry of 2 June 1754, *Diaries of Washington,* 1:199.

16. "That little thing": Tanaghrisson's speech at Aughwick, 3 Sept. 1754, quoted in Jennings, *Empire of Fortune,* 67. "The attack of 500 men": Washington to Dinwiddie, 3 June 1754, *Papers of Washington,* 1:124.

17. Gipson, *Years of Defeat,* 32–3; Nicholas Wainwright, *George Croghan, Wilderness Diplomat* (Chapel Hill, N.C., 1959), 62–3.

18. Douglas Southall Freeman, *George Washington: A Biography,* vol. 1, *Young Washington* (New York, 1948), 391–3; *Diaries of Washington,* 1:202–7 (entries of 16–21 June 1754).

19. Tanaghrisson quoted by Conrad Weiser, "Journal of the Proceedings of Conrad Weiser in His Way to and at Auchwick . . . in the Year 1754," 3 Sept. 1754, in Paul A. W. Wallace, *Conrad Weiser, 1696–1760: Friend of Colonist and Mohawk* (Philadelphia, 1945), 367. Tanaghrisson's followers returned to the Forks and made their peace with the French. His successor as half-king, the Oneida chief Scarouady, had been with Tanaghrisson and Washington when Jumonville was killed. He remained as a refugee in Pennsylvania until 1756 (see Duquesne to the minister of marine, 3 Nov. 1754, in Sylvester K. Stevens and Donald H. Kent, eds., *Wilderness Chronicles of Western Pennsylvania* [Harrisburg, Pa., 1941], 84; Francis Jennings et al., eds., *The History and Culture of Iroquois Diplomacy* [Syracuse, N.Y., 1985], 250–2; and McConnell, *A Country Between,* 110–11).

20. Freeman, *Young Washington,* 395–7; "Minutes of a Council of War," 28 June 1754, *Papers of Washington,* 1:155–7.

21. Lewis, *King and Country,* 152.

22. Gipson, *Years of Defeat,* 35.

23. *Maryland Gazette,* 29 Aug. 1754, quoted in Gipson, *Years of Defeat,* 39; see also Harry M. Ward, *Major General Adam Stephen and the Cause of American Liberty* (Charlottesville, Va., 1989), 10–11.

24. "Account by George Washington and James Mackay of the Capitulation of Fort Necessity," 19 July 1754, and "George Washington's Account of the Capitulation of Fort Necessity," 1786, in *Papers of Washington,* 1:159–64, 172–3; affidavit of John Shaw, 21 Aug. 1754, *South Carolina Indian Affairs,* 5–7. The quotation on the composition of the Indian allies originated with Robert Callender (a business partner of Croghan's who was present at Fort Necessity), who reported it to a resident of Paxton, Pa., who in turn included it in a letter to Gov. James Hamilton, 16 July 1754; quoted in Gipson, *Years of Defeat,* 41, emphasis added. In general see ibid., 37–43; Lewis, *For King and Country,* 153–7; and Leach, *Arms for Empire,* 339–42.

25. English casualties: Gipson, *Years of Defeat,* 41 n. 60; French casualties: Varin to Bigot, 24 July 1754, in Stevens and Kent, *Wilderness Chronicles,* 81.

26. Physical condition and desertion: Titus, *Old Dominion,* 55–7; and Leach, *Arms for Empire,* 342. Quotation: Washington to William Fairfax, 11 Aug. 1754, *Papers of Washington,* 1:186–7.

27. Stanley, *New France,* 57; W. J. Eccles, *The Canadian Frontier, 1534–1760* (Albquerque, N.M., 1983), 164–7.

CHAPTER SIX: *Escalation*

1. Hayes Baker-Crothers, *Virginia in the Seven Years' War* (Chicago, 1928), 41–5; James Titus, *The Old Dominion at War: Society, Politics, and Warfare in Late Colonial Virginia* (Columbia,

S.C., 1991), 103–6; L. K. Koontz, *Robert Dinwiddie* (Glendale, Calif., 1941), 319–20; J. R. Alden, *Robert Dinwiddie: Servant of the Crown* (Charlottesville, Va., 1973), 47–8.

2. Newcastle to the earl of Albemarle, 5 Sept. 1754, quoted in T. R. Clayton, "The Duke of Newcastle, the Earl of Halifax, and the American Origins of the Seven Years' War," *Historical Journal* 24 (1981): 590–1.

3. On Braddock's career and character, see Lee McCardell, *Ill-Starred General: Braddock of the Coldstream Guards* (Pittsburgh, 1958); on the plan and Halifax's reaction, see Clayton, "American Origins," 593; and James Henretta, *"Salutary Neglect": Colonial Administration under the Duke of Newcastle* (Princeton, N.J., 1972), 333–40.

4. Stanley Pargellis, *Lord Loudoun in North America* (1933; reprint, New York, 1968), 31–3.

5. Francis Jennings, *Empire of Fortune: Crowns, Colonies, and Tribes in the Seven Years War in America* (New York, 1988), 124.

6. Clayton, "American Origins," 596–7, 603.

7. Newcastle seized on the French proposals as genuinely aimed at preserving the peace, but Halifax sabotaged the negotiations in Feb. 1755 by publishing a Board of Trade map of British claims in North America that precluded further compromise. Negotiations continued, fruitlessly, until June. Clayton, "American Origins," 597–601; Lawrence Henry Gipson, *The British Empire before the American Revolution,* vol. 5, *Zones of International Friction: The Great Lakes Frontier, Canada, the West Indies, India, 1748–1754* (New York, 1967), 298–338.

8. Lawrence Henry Gipson, *The British Empire before the American Revolution,* vol. 6, *The Great War for the Empire: The Years of Defeat, 1754–1757* (New York, 1968), 359–65.

9. Newcastle to Bentinck, 17 Dec. 1754, quoted in Clayton, "American Origins," 598; I have reversed the order of Newcastle's sentences ("the conduct . . ." and "the great System . . .") for the sake of clarity.

PART II: *DEFEAT,* 1754–1755

CHAPTER SEVEN: *The Albany Congress and Colonial Disunion*

1. See Thomas Pownall to My Lord [Halifax], 23 July 1754, in Beverly McAnear, ed., "Personal Accounts of the Albany Congress of 1754," *Mississippi Valley Historical Review* 39 (1953): 742, 744; and William Smith Jr., *The History of the Province of the State of New-York,* ed. Michael Kammen, vol. 2 (Cambridge, Mass., 1972), 161.

2. Lydius and the Wyoming scheme: Lawrence Henry Gipson, *The British Empire before the American Revolution,* vol. 5, *Zones of International Friction: The Great Lakes Frontier, Canada, the West Indies, India, 1748–1754* (New York, 1967), 90; Smith, *History of New-York,* 2:88–9; Francis Jennings, *Empire of Fortune: Crowns, Colonies, and Tribes in the Seven Years War in America* (New York, 1988), 106–7, 153; James Thomas Flexner, *Lord of the Mohawks: A Biography of Sir William Johnson* (Boston, 1979), 75–7, 128–30, et passim. The Susquehannah Company's scheme to acquire land within Pennsylvania rested on Connecticut's charter grant, which antedated Pennsylvania's and set the colony boundary at the Pacific Ocean. The Connecticut Assembly, whose members included many stockholders in the Susquehannah Company, refused to agree to the Plan of Union because it would have modified the charters of provinces with sea-to-sea patents. See Gipson, *Great Lakes Frontier,* 150; and Robert C. Newbold, *The Albany Congress and the Plan of Union of 1754* (New York, 1955), 137–40.

3. On Weiser's activities, see Gipson, *Great Lakes Frontier,* 121–2; Jennings, *Empire of Fortune,* 103–6; and Paul A. W. Wallace, *Conrad Weiser, 1696–1760: Friend of Colonist and Mohawk* (Philadelphia, 1945), 358–60.

4. On De Lancey, Johnson, Pownall, and the congress, see Patricia U. Bonomi, *A Factious People: Politics and Society in Colonial New York* (New York, 1971), 171–8; Stanley N. Katz, *Newcastle's New York: Anglo-American Politics, 1732–1753* (Cambridge, Mass., 1968), 200–13; and Jennings, *Empire of Fortune,* 71–108. De Lancey's formidable connections included his former Cambridge tutor who had gone on to become archbishop of Canterbury, and his brother-in-law,

Admiral Sir Peter Warren, a member of Parliament who had procured the lieutenant governorship for De Lancey. Warren was also the uncle of William Johnson, who had initially come to New York in 1737 to manage his interests in the Mohawk Valley. On the Warren-Johnson connection, see Flexner, *Lord of the Mohawks,* 13–27; Milton W. Hamilton, *Sir William Johnson, Colonial American, 1715–1763* (Port Washington, N.Y., 1976), 3–14; and Julian Gwyn, *The Enterprising Admiral: The Personal Fortune of Admiral Sir Peter Warren* (Montréal, 1974), 29–93.

5. Esmond Wright, *Franklin of Philadelphia* (Cambridge, Mass., 1986), 84–97; Pownall to My Lord [Halifax], 23 July 1754, in McAnear, "Personal Accounts," 744.

6. Hutchinson: Bernard Bailyn, *The Ordeal of Thomas Hutchinson* (Cambridge, Mass., 1974), esp. 1–34. During King George's War, Shirley had backed Gov. Clinton of New York, a fellow Newcastle client and thus an enemy of De Lancey's; Shirley thought De Lancey's faction "a factious, vain, upstart Crew" (Shirley to Clinton, 26 June 1749, quoted in Katz, *Newcastle's New York,* 206).

7. Reception of the Plan: Newbold, *Albany Congress,* 135–171. (Franklin to Peter Collinson, 29 Dec. 1754, expresses his views on compulsory union; summarized at 171.) See also Gipson, *Great Lakes Frontier,* 123–40.

CHAPTER EIGHT: *General Braddock Takes Command*

1. Braddock's appointment: Lee McCardell, *Ill-Starred General: Braddock of the Coldstream Guards* (Pittsburgh, 1958), 124–8; Paul E. Kopperman, *Braddock at the Monongahela* (Pittsburgh, 1977), 7–8, 277 n. 10; Lawrence Henry Gipson, *The British Empire before the American Revolution,* vol. 6, *The Great War for the Empire: The Years of Defeat, 1754–1757* (New York, 1968), 57–8. Braddock's rebukes: Alan Rogers, *Empire and Liberty: American Resistance to British Authority, 1755–1763* (Berkeley, Calif., 1974), 76. Quotation: Braddock to Robert Hunter Morris, 28 Feb. 1755, in Gipson, *Years of Defeat,* 69. Governors' conference: ibid., 64–70.

2. John Schutz, *William Shirley: King's Governor of Massachusetts* (Chapel Hill, N.C., 1961), 189–98; Douglas Edward Leach, *Arms for Empire: A Military History of the British Colonies in North America, 1607–1763* (New York, 1973), 355–6; Francis Jennings, *Empire of Fortune: Crowns, Colonies, and Tribes in the Seven Years War in America* (New York, 1988), 146–8; Gipson, *Years of Defeat,* 70–5.

3. Schutz, *Shirley,* 197.

4. Impossibility of establishing a fund: "Minutes of a Council Held at Alexandria," 14 Apr. 1755, quoted in Gipson, *Years of Defeat,* 71. Braddock bound by instructions: Leach, *Arms for Empire,* 355. Route: "Sketch for the Operations in North America," 16 Nov. 1754, in Stanley Pargellis, ed., *Military Affairs in North America, 1748–1765: Documents from the Cumberland Papers in Windsor Castle* (1936; reprint, New York, 1969), 45.

5. Schutz, *Shirley,* 198–9.

6. Jennings, *Empire of Fortune,* 153, 162 ff.; Gipson, *Years of Defeat,* 143 ff., 163; Milton W. Hamilton, *Sir William Johnson, Colonial American, 1715–1763* (Port Washington, N.Y., 1976), 125–39.

7. "Fine Cuntry": "The Journal of Captain Robert Cholmley's Batman," 21 Apr. 1755, in Charles Hamilton, ed., *Braddock's Defeat* (Norman, Okla., 1959), 11. Washington and Braddock: Robert Orme to Washington, 2 Mar. 1755, in W. W. Abbot et al., eds., *The Papers of George Washington, Colonial Series,* vol. 1, 1748–August 1755 (Charlottesville, Va., 1983), 241–2; Washington to Orme, 15 Mar. and 2 Apr. 1755, ibid., 242–8; Washington to William Fairfax, 5 May 1755, ibid., 262–4; Washington to Augustine Washington, 14 May 1755, ibid., 271–3. Washington had two motives in serving as a volunteer: to obtain a regular commission, which could come from serving with Braddock, and to avoid demotion. Virginia had restructured its provincial forces for 1755, abolishing the regiment in favor of independent companies commanded by captains, who would take orders from regular field officers. Had he accepted a demotion to captain, Washington would have lost more status and honor than a proud Virginia gentleman could afford, and he could never have attracted Braddock's attention.

8. Franklin makes himself useful: Benjamin Franklin, *The Autobiography and Other Writings,* ed. L. Jesse Lemisch (New York, 1961), 145–51 (quotations at 146 and 149); Jennings, *Empire of Fortune,* 149–51; Gipson, *Years of Defeat,* 75–6. Braddock's improved opinion of Pennsylvania: id. to Robert Napier, 8 June 1755, in Pargellis, *Military Affairs,* 85.

CHAPTER NINE: *Disaster on the Monongahela*

1. "The Journal of Captain Robert Cholmley's Batman," 20 and 23 May 1755, in Charles Hamilton, ed., *Braddock's Defeat* (Norman, Okla., 1959), 15–16.
2. Braddock's Indian diplomacy: Francis Jennings, *Empire of Fortune: Crowns, Colonies, and Tribes in the Seven Years War in America* (New York, 1988), 151–5 (quotation from Franklin's *Autobiography* is at 152; quotations from Shingas's account of the conference at 154–5); also Michael N. McConnell, *A Country Between: The Upper Ohio and Its Peoples, 1724–1774* (Lincoln, Nebr., 1992), 119–21; and Nicholas B. Wainwright, *George Croghan, Wilderness Diplomat* (Chapel Hill, N.C., 1959), 85–9. Numbers of Indians accompanying Braddock: "A Return of His Majesty's Troops," 8 June 1755, in Stanley M. Pargellis, ed., *Military Affairs in North America, 1748–1765: Documents from the Cumberland Papers in Windsor Castle* (1936; reprint, New York, 1969), 86–91.
3. John Rutherford to Richard Peters, recd. 13 Aug. 1755, quoted in Wainwright, *Croghan,* 90.
4. "An hundred and ten Miles": quoted ibid., 85. Artillery: Lawrence Henry Gipson, *The British Empire before the American Revolution,* vol. 6, *The Great War for the Empire: The Years of Defeat, 1754–1757* (New York, 1968), 79; Pargellis, *Military Affairs,* 91. (The siege train included four twelve-pound naval guns dismounted from H.M.S. *Norwich* and placed on wheeled carriages, six six-pound fieldpieces, four eight-inch howitzers, and fifteen Coehorn mortars. The twelve-pounders weighed more than a ton each.) Division of the column: "The Journal of a British Officer," 16 June 1755, in Hamilton, *Braddock's Defeat,* 42; also Cholmley's batman's diary, 29 May–19 June 1755, ibid., 17–22.
5. Order of march: Paul E. Kopperman, *Braddock at the Monongahela* (Pittsburgh, 1977), 31–49. There were only seven Mingo scouts because Scarouady's son had been shot dead, three days earlier, by a soldier who mistook him for a hostile Indian—a great blow to Scarouady, who "was hardly able to support his loss" ("Journal of a British Officer," 6 July 1755, in Hamilton, *Braddock's Defeat,* 48). Washington's malady: "Memorandum," 8–9 July 1755, in W. W. Abbot et al., eds., *The Papers of George Washington, Colonial Series,* vol. 1, 1748–August 1755 (Charlottesville, Va., 1983), 331. Use of flanking parties to provide security: Peter E. Russell, "Redcoats in the Wilderness: British Officers and Irregular Warfare in Europe and America, 1740 to 1760," *William and Mary Quarterly,* 3rd ser., 35 (1978): 629–52.
6. *Papers of Washington,* 1:332 n. 3; Kopperman, *Braddock at the Monongahela,* 19–30; Gipson, *Years of Defeat,* 90–2.
7. The Indians deployed in a half-moon attack formation; see Leroy V. Eid, " 'A Kind of Running Fight': Indian Battlefield Tactics in the Late Eighteenth Century," *Western Pennsylvania Historical Magazine* 71 (1988): 147–71.
8. Openness of woods: Sir John St. Clair to Robert Napier, 13 June and 22 July 1755, in Pargellis, *Military Affairs,* 94, 103. On Indian burning practices, see William Cronon, *Changes in the Land: Indians, Colonists, and the Ecology of New England* (New York, 1983), 49–52.
9. Disintegration of order: Robert Orme's account, in Kopperman, *Braddock at the Monongahela,* 214. (The eighteenth-century platoon was a firing echelon of a company, made up in theory of twenty-five to thirty-five men; given the company strengths in Braddock's force, these platoons probably had no more than twelve to fifteen men each.) Regular reactions, rear guard, and flight of teamsters: ibid., 79; Patrick Mackellar, "A Sketch of the Field of Battle . . . , No. 2," in Pargellis, *Military Affairs,* facing 115; quotation from Mackellar, "Explanation," ibid., 115; Don Higginbotham, *Daniel Morgan, Revolutionary Rifleman* (Chapel Hill, N.C., 1961), 4–6; John Mack Faragher, *Daniel Boone: The Life and Legend of an American Pioneer* (New York, 1992), 36–8. Fate of women: Kopperman, *Braddock at the Monongahela,* 31, 47,

137; Contrecoeur to Vaudreuil, 14 July 1755, in Pargellis, *Military Affairs,* 132 (twenty women made captive).

10. Quotation: "Relation sur l'action . . . par Mr. de Godefroy," in Kopperman, *Braddock at the Monongahela,* 259.

11. "Old Standers": "Journal of a British Officer," 16 June 1755, in Hamilton, *Braddock's Defeat,* 42. Quotations on difficulty of seeing Indians: extract of a letter from Fort Cumberland [Rev. Philip Hughes?], 23 July 1755, in Kopperman, *Braddock at the Monongahela,* 203; Cholmley's batman's diary, 9 July 1755, in Hamilton, *Braddock's Defeat,* 29. War cries: Duncan Cameron's account, in Kopperman, *Braddock at the Monongahela,* 178. Stories of Indian barbarity: account of "British A," ibid., 164. Memory of war cries: letter of Matthew Leslie, 30 July 1755, ibid., 204.

12. Firing by platoons: "Journal of a British Officer," in Hamilton, *Braddock's Defeat,* 50. Deaths by friendly fire: account of "British B," in Kopperman, *Braddock at the Monongahela,* 170. Washington believed that two-thirds of British casualties resulted from friendly fire; see id. to Dinwiddie, 18 July 1755, *Papers of Washington,* 1:340. Medical evidence supports his estimate: "that the men fired irregularly one behind another," Dr. Alexander Hamilton reported, "appeared afterwards by the Bullets which the surgeons Extracted from the wounded, They being distinguishable from those of the French & Indians by their Size, As they were considerably larger, For the bore of the Enemys Muskets . . . was very small. Among the wounded men there were two for one of these larger bullets extracted by the Surgeons, and the wounds were chiefly on the back parts of the Body, so we may reasonably conclude it must have also been among the killed" (to Gavin Hamilton, Aug. 1755, ibid., 341 n. 7).

13. Adam Stephen to John Hunter, 18 July 1755, in Kopperman, *Braddock at the Monongahela,* 226–7; also Harry M. Ward, *Major General Adam Stephen and the Cause of American Liberty* (Charlottesville, Va., 1989), 17–20.

14. Rum: Duncan Cameron, in Kopperman, *Braddock at the Monongahela,* 87, 179. Cameron hides in tree: ibid., 177–9 (quotation at 178). On Indian cultural values and their effects on warfare, see Ian K. Steele, *Betrayals: Fort William Henry and the "Massacre"* (New York, 1990), 10–18; and Daniel K. Richter, "War and Culture: The Iroquois Experience," *William and Mary Quarterly,* 3rd ser., 40 (1983): 528–59.

15. Washington quotation: Biographical Memorandum, c. 1786, *Papers of Washington* 1: 332–3 n. 4.

16. Cholmley's batman's diary, 12–17 July 1755, in Hamilton, *Braddock's Defeat,* 32–3.

17. Of 1,373 Anglo-American enlisted men "in the Field," 430 were killed or left for dead on the battlefield, while 484 were wounded; of the 96 officers, 26 were killed and 36 wounded. These figures, reported weeks after the battle, included only soldiers; no figures survive for the total of civilians (women, teamsters, and other camp followers) killed or wounded. Contrecoeur's report of the battle, however, mentioned "around 600 men killed, with many officers, and the wounded in proportion" but only "20 men or women made prisoner by the savages." This suggests an additional 150 killed from the camp followers. See the "Explanation" of Mackellar's map 1 and "Extrait de La Lettre part M^r^ De Contrecoeur . . . a Monsieur Le marquis De Vaudreuil . . . 14^e^ Juillet 1755," in Pargellis, *Military Affairs,* 114, 131, 132, my translation.

18. Maggots: Cholmley's batman's diary, 13 July 1755, in Hamilton, *Braddock's Defeat,* 32. (These may actually have had a beneficial effect in eating away putrescent tissue, and certainly they did less damage than the surgeons' attempts to clean and dress the wounds.) Dunbar requests winter quarters: Gipson, *Years of Defeat,* 128.

19. On contemporary opinions of Braddock's responsibility, see esp. Russell, "Redcoats in the Wilderness," 629–30.

20. "Dastardly behaviour": Washington to Dinwiddie, 18 July 1755, *Papers of Washington,* 1:339. "How little does the World": Washington to Warner Lewis, 14 Aug. 1755, ibid., 361. Later recollections (1783): Kopperman, *Braddock at the Monongahela,* 247–8. None of Wash-

ington's letters at the time of the battle criticized Braddock; see *Papers of Washington,* 1:331–54. Scarouady's address, 22 Aug. 1755: Jennings, *Empire of Fortune,* 152.

CHAPTER TEN:
After Braddock: William Shirley and the Northern Campaigns

1. Francis Jennings, *Empire of Fortune: Crowns, Colonies, and Tribes in the Seven Years War in America* (New York, 1988), 165–8; Lawrence Henry Gipson, *The British Empire before the American Revolution,* vol. 6, *The Great War for the Empire: The Years of Defeat, 1754–1757* (New York, 1968), 54; James Titus, *The Old Dominion at War: Society, Politics, and Warfare in Late Colonial Virginia* (Columbia, S.C., 1991) 102–3; Thomas Lewis, *For King and Country: The Maturing of George Washington, 1748–1760* (New York, 1993), 201–2.
2. Virginia casualties: Washington to Mary Ball Washington, 18 July 1755, and Washington to Robert Dinwiddie, 18 July 1755, in W. W. Abbot et al., eds., *The Papers of George Washington, Colonial Series,* vol. 1, 1748–August 1755 (Charlottesville, Va., 1983), 336, 339, 342 n. 10. Refugees and losses in autumn: Titus, *Old Dominion,* 71, 74. Quotation: Washington to Dinwiddie, 11 Oct. 1755, in W. W. Abbot et al., eds., *The Papers of George Washington, Colonial Series,* vol. 2, August 1755–April 1756 (Charlottesville, Va., 1983), 105.
3. Hayes Baker-Crothers, *Virginia in the French and Indian War* (Chicago, 1928), 82–5; Titus, *Old Dominion,* 73–7, 108–11. The ten-pound scalp bounty only served to encourage the murder of neutral, Christianized, and friendly Indians and was repealed as having not "answer[ed] the purposes . . . intended," in 1758 (W. Stitt Robinson, *The Southern Colonial Frontier, 1607–1763* [Albuquerque, N.M., 1979], 214). The Burgesses canceled the act only when parliamentary reimbursements enabled Virginia to offer cash enlistment bounties for the Virginia Regiment.
4. Acceptance of French alliance: Michael N. McConnell, "Peoples 'In Between': The Iroquois and the Ohio Indians, 1720–1768," in Daniel K. Richter and James Merrell, eds., *Beyond the Covenant Chain: The Iroquois and Their Neighbors in Indian North America, 1600–1800* (Syracuse, N.Y., 1987), 106. Scarouady's address to Morris and the council, 22 Aug. 1755, quoted in Jennings, *Empire of Fortune,* 165. Iroquois embassy to Vaudreuil: Louis Antoine de Bougainville, *Adventure in the Wilderness: The American Journals of Louis Antoine de Bougainville, 1756–1760,* ed. Edward Hamilton (Norman, Okla., 1964), 30. Captain Jacobs: Shingas's narrative, quoted in Jennings, *Empire of Fortune,* 166.
5. Cannon: Shirley to Robert Hunter Morris, n.d., quoted in John Schutz, *William Shirley: King's Governor of Massachusetts* (Chapel Hill, N.C., 1961), 201. Dispute with Johnson: memorandum, "Summary of Disputes Between Governor William Shirley and General William Johnson, 1755," in Stanley M. Pargellis, ed., *Military Affairs in North America, 1748–1765: Documents from the Cumberland Papers in Windsor Castle* (1936; reprint, New York, 1969), 153–4. Shirley's grief: Thomas Hutchinson, *History of the Colony and Province of Massachusetts-Bay,* ed. Lawrence Shaw Mayo, vol. 3 (1936; reprint, New York, 1970), 24.
6. Schutz, *Shirley,* 209; Gipson, *Years of Defeat,* 106–15, 132–3.
7. Schutz, *Shirley,* 212–16.
8. Lawrence Henry Gipson, *The British Empire before the American Revolution,* vol. 5, *Zones of International Friction: The Great Lakes Frontier, Canada, the West Indies, India, 1748–1754* (New York, 1967), 186–90, 193–206; *Dictionary of Canadian Biography,* vol. 4, s.v. "Le Loutre, Jean-Louis."
9. Enthusiasm for expedition: Hutchinson, *Massachusetts-Bay,* 3:20–1. Parallel progress of Braddock's and Nova Scotia expeditions: "The Journal of Captain Robert Cholmley's Batman," 2 June 1755, in Charles Hamilton, ed., *Braddock's Defeat* (Norman, Okla., 1959), 18; J. T. B., ed., "Diary of John Thomas," entries of 2–3 June 1755, Nova Scotia Historical Society, *Collections* 1 (1878): 122; John Frost diary, entries of 16 and 19 June 1755, ibid., 125, 126.
10. Carl Brasseaux, *The Founding of New Acadia: The Beginnings of Acadian Life in Louisiana, 1765–1803* (Baton Rouge, 1987), 22–34; Gipson, *Years of Defeat,* 212–344.

11. Brasseaux, *New Acadia,* 23; Schutz, *Shirley,* 204, finds the evidence of Shirley's involvement only compelling enough to merit a footnote. Gipson, *Years of Defeat,* 261, notes that Shirley planned to neutralize the Acadian "threat" as early as 1747 but stops short of suggesting that he planned the expedition as a final solution to the Acadian problem. George A. Rawlyk, *Nova Scotia's Massachusetts: A Study of Massachusetts–Nova Scotia Relations, 1630 to 1784* (Montréal, 1973), 145–64, does not assign Shirley a decisive role in the deportations. On the New England occupation, see ibid., 217–21.

12. Ian K. Steele, *Betrayals: Fort William Henry and the "Massacre"* (New York, 1990), 36.

13. Gipson, *Years of Defeat,* 139–40; Johnson to Pownall, 3 Sept. 1755, quoted ibid., 186.

14. Ibid., 165–8.

15. Steele, *Betrayals,* 43; unless otherwise noted, my account of French preparations follows his excellent second chapter, "To Battle for Lake George," 28–56.

16. Peter E. Russell, "Redcoats in the Wilderness: British Officers and Irregular Warfare in Europe and America, 1740 to 1760," *William and Mary Quarterly,* 3rd ser., 35 (1978): 633; Steele, *Betrayals,* 44–6; *Dictionary of Canadian Biography,* vol. 3, s.v. "Dieskau, Jean-Armand (Johan Herman?), Baron de Dieskau."

17. Steele, *Betrayals,* 47–8; Seth Pomeroy to Israel Williams, 9 Sept. 1755, in Louis Effingham DeForest, ed., *The Journals and Papers of Seth Pomeroy, Sometime General in the Colonial Service* (New Haven, Conn., 1926), 137. On the Mohawks' formation, see Leroy V. Eid, " 'National' War among Indians of Northeastern North America," *Canadian Review of American Studies* 16 (1985): 129.

18. Steele, *Betrayals,* 48–9; Seth Pomeroy to Israel Williams, 9 Sept. 1755, in DeForest, *Journals and Papers of Pomeroy,* 137; Peter Wraxall to Henry Fox, 27 Sept. 1755, in Pargellis, *Military Affairs,* 139; Milton W. Hamilton, *Sir William Johnson, Colonial American, 1715–1763* (Port Washington, N.Y., 1976), 157–60.

19. Wraxall to Fox, 27 Sept. 1755, in Pargellis, *Military Affairs,* 139; Wraxall was Johnson's private secretary.

20. Daniel Claus's narrative, quoted in Steele, *Betrayals,* 50. That Dieskau was facing what amounted to a mutiny is confirmed in Dieskau to d'Argenson, 17 Sept. 1755, quoted in Gipson, *Years of Defeat,* 172.

21. Pomeroy to Williams, 9 Sept. 1755, in DeForest, *Journals and Papers of Pomeroy,* 138 ("6 Deep & as I judg'd about 20 rods in Length Close Order ye Indians . . . hilter Scilter ye woods full of them—they Came with In about 20 rods & fir'd Regular Plattoons but we Soon brook there order ye Indians & Cannadians Directly took tree with In handy gun Shot"). Effects of artillery: anonymous gunner quoted in Steele, *Betrayals,* 50. Effects of Legardeur's death: Vaudreuil to the minister of marine, 30 Oct. 1755, in Joseph L. Peyser, ed., *Jacques Legardeur de Saint-Pierre: Officer, Gentleman, Entrepreneur* (East Lansing, Mich., 1996), 225–6.

22. Wraxall to Fox, 27 Sept. 1755, in Pargellis, *Military Affairs,* 139.

23. Quotation: Wraxall to Fox, ibid., 140. The taking of trophies: Steele, *Betrayals,* 53.

24. Aftermath of battle: Seth Pomeroy diary, entries for 9–11 Sept. 1755, in DeForest, *Journals and Papers of Pomeroy,* 115–16. Casualties: Steele, *Betrayals,* 47, 53; Wraxall to Fox, 27 Sept. 1755, in Pargellis, *Military Affairs,* 139. (The Anglo-Americans suffered 223 dead and 108 wounded; the official French tally was 149 dead, 103 wounded, and 27 taken prisoner, exclusive of Indian casualties. Including Indians, the total losses were almost identical, with 331 English casualties and 339 French; the French force, however, suffered the highest casualty rate, approximately 23 percent, as against 14 percent for the English.) Johnson, aware of the demands of mourning war, gave all the prisoners except Dieskau to the Mohawks after the battle; aware, too, of the expectations of European war-making, he hid the fact from Shirley (Ian K. Steele, *Warpaths: Invasions of North America* [New York, 1994], 193).

25. Gipson, *Years of Defeat,* 174–5; Steele, *Betrayals,* 55–6; Fred Anderson, *A People's Army: Massachusetts Soldiers and Society in the Seven Years' War* (Chapel Hill, N.C., 1984), 10.

CHAPTER ELEVEN:
British Politics, and a Revolution in European Diplomacy

1. See Reed Browning, *The Duke of Newcastle* (New Haven, Conn., 1975), 194–253 passim, esp. 222–3; and Richard Middleton, *The Bells of Victory: The Pitt-Newcastle Ministry and the Conduct of the Seven Years' War, 1757–1762* (Cambridge, U.K., 1985), 3–4.
2. W. A. Speck, *Stability and Strife: England, 1714–1760* (Cambridge, Mass., 1977), 260–1.
3. H. M. Scott, *British Foreign Policy in the Age of the American Revolution* (Oxford, 1990), 29–52; id., " 'The True Principles of the Revolution': The Duke of Newcastle and the Idea of the Old System," in Jeremy Black, ed., *Knights Errant and True Englishmen: British Foreign Policy 1600–1800* (Edinburgh, 1989), 55–91; also see, more generally, Eliga Gould, *The Persistence of Empire: British Political Culture in the Age of the American Revolution* (Chapel Hill, N.C., forthcoming), chaps. 1 and 2.
4. Browning, *Newcastle,* 219–21; Speck, *Stability and Strife,* 262–3.
5. Pitt's speech in the House of Commons, 13 Nov. 1755, quoted in Stanley Ayling, *The Elder Pitt, Earl of Chatham* (New York, 1976), 170; Lawrence Henry Gipson, *The British Empire before the American Revolution,* vol. 6, *The Great War for the Empire: The Years of Defeat, 1754–1757* (New York, 1968), 378–9.
6. Ibid., 386–91. On Frederick's fear of Russia, see Speck, *Stability and Strife,* 263; and Christopher Duffy, *The Military Life of Frederick the Great* (New York, 1986), 83–4.
7. Armies and populations: André Corvisier, *Armies and Societies in Europe, 1494–1789,* trans. Abigail Siddall (Bloomington, Ind., 1979), 113, table 1, "Effectives in the Regular Armies and Populations of the States."
8. On the demise of the Austrian alliance, see Gipson, *Years of Defeat,* 369, 379. On the ministry's newfound security, see Browning, *Newcastle,* 228–30.
9. Gipson, *Years of Defeat,* 187–8; Stanley M. Pargellis, *Lord Loudoun in North America* (1933; reprint, Hamden, Conn., 1968), 39–40.
10. Shirley's estrangement from Newcastle: John Schutz, *William Shirley: King's Governor of Massachusetts* (Chapel Hill, N.C., 1961), 153–4, 166–7, 226. Filius Gallicae: Nicholas B. Wainwright, *George Croghan, Wilderness Diplomat* (Chapel Hill, N.C., 1959), 106–9 (the letters are reprinted in American Historical Association, *Report* 1 [1896]: 660–703). Shirley's recall: Gipson, *Years of Defeat,* 188–9; Schutz, *Shirley,* 232–3; Pargellis, *Loudoun,* 76–7. Quotation: Fox to Shirley, 31 Mar. 1756, quoted in Gipson, *Years of Defeat,* 188.
11. Ibid., 188–91; Schutz, *Shirley,* 225–6, 232–4, 240–3, 245.
12. Ibid., 30–43.
13. On the effects of French efficiency vs. British slowness and commitment to introducing more conventional military order into American operations, see Ian K. Steele, *Warpaths: Invasions of North America* (New York, 1994), 195–6.

PART III: *NADIR,* 1756–1757

CHAPTER TWELVE: *Lord Loudoun Takes Command*

1. Francis Parkman's depiction of Montcalm as tragic hero continues to influence American historians; see David Levin, ed., *Francis Parkman: France and England in North America,* vol. 2, *Montcalm and Wolfe* (New York, 1983), 1088–92. W. J. Eccles's more judicious appraisal has greater value; see *Dictionary of Canadian Biography,* vol. 3, s.v. "Montcalm, Louis-Joseph de, Marquis de Montcalm." Ian K. Steele surveys the fluctuations in Montcalm's historical reputation in *Betrayals: Fort William Henry and the "Massacre"* (New York, 1990), 176–81; see also id., *Warpaths: Invasions of North America* (New York, 1994), 199–201, 205–6, 215–19.
2. Lawrence Henry Gipson, *The British Empire before the American Revolution,* vol. 6, *The Great War for the Empire: The Years of Defeat, 1754–1757* (New York, 1968), 183–4; Douglas Edward Leach, *Arms for Empire: A Military History of the British Colonies in North America,*

1607–1763 (New York, 1973), 381–2; "Information of Captain John Vicars of the 50th Regiment," 4 Jan. 1757, in Stanley M. Pargellis, ed., *Military Affairs in North America, 1748–1763* (1936; reprint, Hamden, Conn., 1968), 286–90.

3. Shirley's activities: John Schutz, *William Shirley: King's Governor of Massachusetts* (Chapel Hill, N.C., 1961), 224–30. Enlistments in 1755: Gipson, *Years of Defeat,* 181 n. 65; for means of estimating these as a proportion of the population in the prime military age range of sixteen to twenty-nine years, see Fred Anderson, *A People's Army: Massachusetts Soldiers and Society in the Seven Years' War* (Chapel Hill, N.C., 1984), 60 n. 83. (This evidently matched the rate of participation in Connecticut; see Harold E. Selesky, *War and Society in Colonial Connecticut* [New Haven, Conn., 1990], 166–70.)

4. Schutz, *Shirley,* 227–9; Thomas Hutchinson, *The History of the Colony and Province of Massachusetts-Bay,* ed. Lawrence Shaw Mayo, vol. 3 (1936; reprint, New York, 1970), 32–4.

5. Gipson, *Years of Defeat,* 177–81.

6. Anderson, *A People's Army,* 169; Douglas Edward Leach, *Roots of Conflict: British Armed Forces and Colonial Americans, 1677–1763* (Chapel Hill, N.C., 1986), 119–20.

7. Report of the Solicitor General to Sir Thomas Robinson, 3 Dec. 1754, quoted in Leach, *Roots of Conflict,* 111.

8. Anderson, *A People's Army,* 174.

9. Pargellis, *Military Affairs,* xviii, 187 n. 2; id., *Lord Loudoun in North America* (1933; reprint, Hamden, Conn., 1968), 155–7.

10. Gipson, *Years of Defeat,* 184–5, 193; Pargellis, *Loudoun,* 88; Schutz, *Shirley,* 231.

11. Pargellis, *Loudoun,* 83 ff.

12. Ibid., 89–90.

13. Anderson, *A People's Army,* 170; Pargellis, *Loudoun,* 88–9.

14. Ibid., 81–2; the description quoted is from Peter Wraxall, who had accompanied Sir William Johnson to wait on the new commander in chief.

15. Ibid., 47–9, 52–66, 81. Loudoun replaced the earl of Albemarle, who had recently died, as governor of Virginia; Dinwiddie remained as lieutenant governor.

16. Ibid., 132–66; Loudoun to Cumberland, 20 Aug. 1756, in id., *Military Affairs,* 223–30.

17. "A tree to a man": id., *Loudoun,* 44. Provincials ahead of regulars: Loudoun to Cumberland, 3 Oct. 1756, in id., *Military Affairs,* 240 ("It looks odd on the Map, to see the *Provincials* advanced before the Troops"). Contractualism and resistance to joint command: Anderson, *A People's Army,* 167–95, esp. 171–3; Alan Rogers, *Empire and Liberty: American Resistance to British Authority, 1755–1763* (Berkeley, Calif., 1974), 69–71; Pargellis, *Loudoun,* 83–93. "Dissolution": Winslow to Shirley, 2 Aug. 1756, in Charles H. Lincoln, ed., *Correspondence of William Shirley, Governor of Massachusetts and Military Commander in America, 1731–1760* (New York, 1912), 2:497–8.

18. "*First contriver*": Loudoun to Cumberland, 20 Aug. 1756, in Pargellis, *Military Affairs,* 226. Promulgation of the Rule of 1755: id., *Loudoun,* 92; Anderson, *A People's Army,* 169.

19. "Ready and willing": Winslow to Loudoun, 10 Aug. 1756, quoted in ibid., 174. "Terms and conditions": Joseph Dwight to Loudoun, 11 Aug. 1756, ibid. The terms were that Winslow was to be commander in chief of the provincials; that the men were to receive the wages, bounties, and subsistence stipulated by their respective provincial assemblies; that their service was to be confined to the Lake George–Lake Champlain region; and that they were to serve no longer than twelve months from the date of enlistment.

20. Ibid., 174–5.

21. Loudoun's outrage: id. to Fox, 19 Aug. 1756; to Cumberland, 20 and 29 Aug. 1756, in Pargellis, *Military Affairs,* 223–33. Provisioning: Anderson, *A People's Army,* 179–85; Pargellis, *Loudoun,* 184–5.

22. Ibid., 195–6; Rogers, *Empire and Liberty,* 82–3, 75–89, passim; Loudoun to Cumberland, 29 Aug. 1756, in Pargellis, *Military Affairs,* 231.

23. Albany quartering incident: id., *Loudoun,* 195–6; Rogers, *Empire and Liberty,* 83–4. Quotation: Loudoun to Cumberland, 29 Aug. 1756, in Pargellis, *Military Affairs,* 230.
24. "Opposition" and "*Cyphers* [who have] sold": Loudoun to Cumberland, 22 Nov.–26 Dec. 1756, in ibid., 272–3. "From whence": Loudoun to Halifax, 26 Dec. 1756, quoted in id., *Loudoun,* 185–6.

CHAPTER THIRTEEN: *Oswego*

1. Patrick Mackellar, "A Journal of the Transactions at Oswego from the 16th of May to the 14 of August 1756," in Stanley M. Pargellis, ed., *Military Affairs in North America, 1748–1765: Documents from the Cumberland Papers in Windsor Castle* (1936; reprint, New York, 1969), 207 (entry of Aug. 10); Louis Antoine de Bougainville, *Adventure in the Wilderness: The American Journals of Louis Antoine de Bougainville, 1756–1760,* ed. Edward P. Hamilton (Norman, Okla., 1964), 25 (entry of 10 Aug. 1756); Lawrence Henry Gipson, *The British Empire before the American Revolution,* vol. 6, *The Great War for the Empire: The Years of Defeat, 1754–1757* (New York, 1968), 199.
2. Vaudreuil quoted in Douglas Edward Leach, *Arms for Empire: A Military History of the British Colonies in North America, 1607–1763* (New York, 1973), 379. Ian K. Steele, *Warpaths: Invasions of North America* (New York, 1994), 197–200 and 205–6, masterfully explains the significance of Vaudreuil's commitment to *petite guerre* strategy and Montcalm's distaste for it—and for him.
3. Montcalm's strength: Leach, *Arms for Empire,* 385; George F. G. Stanley, *New France: The Last Phase, 1744–1760* (Toronto, 1968), 143. Indians: Bougainville, *Adventure,* 21, 24 (entries of 30 July and 6 Aug. 1756); Steele, *Warpaths,* 199–200.
4. Road: Mackellar's journal, 11 Aug. 1756, in Pargellis, *Military Affairs,* 208. Fortifications: Major W. H. Bertsch, "The Defenses of Oswego," New-York Historical Society, *Proceedings* 13 (1914): 108–27, esp. 114–20.
5. Mackellar's journal, 25 May 1756, and id., "Plan of Oswego with Its Forts," in Pargellis, *Military Affairs,* 189–90, 210 and facing page. Quotation from Sarah Mulliken, ed., "Journal of Stephen Cross of Newburyport, Entitled 'Up to Ontario,' the Activities of Newburyport Shipbuilders in Canada in 1756," *Essex Institute Historical Collections* 76 (1940): 14 (entry of 13 Aug.); see also 75 (1939): 356–7 (entries of 10–12 Aug.). Strength of the garrison: Leach, *Arms for Empire,* 385.
6. Stephen Cross journal, 13 Aug. 1756, 15.
7. Ibid.
8. Cf. Ian K. Steele, *Betrayals: Fort William Henry and the "Massacre"* (New York, 1990), 78–9.
9. Stephen Cross journal, 14 Aug. 1756, 16.
10. Montcalm to d'Argenson, 28 Aug. 1756, quoted in Francis Jennings, *Empire of Fortune: Crowns, Colonies, and Tribes in the Seven Years War in America* (New York, 1988), 296.
11. Bougainville to his brother, 17 Sept. 1757, in Bougainville, *Adventure,* 332.
12. Stanley M. Pargellis, *Lord Loudoun in North America* (1933; reprint, Hamden, Conn., 1968), 164–5.
13. Gipson, *Years of Defeat,* 208; Loudoun to Cumberland, 20 Aug., 3 Oct., and 22 Nov.–26 Dec. 1756, in Pargellis, *Military Affairs,* 223–33, 239–43, 263–80.

CHAPTER FOURTEEN: *The State of the Central Colonies*

1. "Troops in the Pay of the Province of Pennsylvania and Where Posted," 23 Feb. 1756, in Stanley M. Pargellis, ed., *Military Affairs in North America, 1748–1765: Documents from the Cumberland Papers in Windsor Castle* (1936; reprint, New York, 1969), 166–7; James Titus, *The Old Dominion at War: Society, Politics, and Warfare in Late Colonial Virginia* (Columbia, S.C., 1991), 94–5; Lawrence Henry Gipson, *The British Empire before the American Revolution,* vol. 7, *The Great War for the Empire: The Victorious Years, 1758–1760* (New York, 1967), 38. Mont-

calm quotation: Montcalm to d'Argenson, 12 June 1756, in Stephen F. Auth, *The Ten Years' War: Indian-White Relations in Pennsylvania, 1755–1765* (New York, 1989), 36. Washington quotation: Washington to ?, late 1756, in Titus, *Old Dominion,* 181 n. 54.

2. Gipson, *Victorious Years,* 35–6, 45–6. Washington actually traveled to Boston in Mar. 1756 to ask Shirley to decide the question of seniority; Shirley ruled in Washington's favor. See Thomas Lewis, *For King and Country: The Maturing of George Washington* (New York, 1993), 200–7.

3. Hayes Baker-Crothers, *Virginia in the French and Indian War* (Chicago, 1928), 102–3; Titus, *Old Dominion,* 77–100 passim; John Ferling, "Soldiers for Virginia: Who Served in the French and Indian War?" *Virginia Magazine of History and Biography* 94 (1986): 307–28. Quotation: Washington to Loudoun, 10 Jan. 1757, in W. W. Abbot et al., eds., *The Papers of George Washington, Colonial Series,* vol. 4, November 1756–October 1757 (Charlottesville, Va., 1984), 86.

4. Quotation: ibid., 88, 83. Appropriations: Baker-Crothers, *French and Indian War,* 102–3.

5. Virginia Regiment's record in 1756: Washington to Loudoun, 10 Jan. 1757, *Papers of Washington,* 4:83. Growth of discipline: Don Higginbotham, *George Washington and the American Military Tradition* (Athens, Ga., 1985), 7–38. Tenuousness of Virginia's frontier and Indian diplomacy: Titus, *Old Dominion,* 96–8.

6. Peter L. D. Davidson, *War Comes to Quaker Pennsylvania, 1682–1756* (New York, 1957), 163–4.

7. Gipson, *Victorious Years,* 48–9; Davidson, *Quaker Pennsylvania,* 163–5; Jack Marrietta, *The Reformation of American Quakerism, 1748–1783* (Philadelphia, 1984), 150–6; Benjamin Newcomb, *Franklin and Galloway: A Political Partnership* (New Haven, Conn., 1972), 21–32.

8. Ibid., 5–32; Marietta, *Reformation of American Quakerism,* 150–86, passim; Davidson, *Quaker Pennsylvania,* 166–96.

9. Prisoners and scalps: Report of Claude Godfrey Cocquard, c. Mar. 1757, in Auth, *Ten Years' War,* 37. Burning of Fort Granville: Loudoun to Robert Hunter Morris, 20 Aug. 1756, ibid., 36. "Deplorable situation": Denny to the council, 15 Oct. 1756, ibid., 37. Raid on Lebanon: Gipson, *Victorious Years,* 52–4.

10. Raid on Upper Kittanning: Davidson, *Quaker Pennsylvania,* 185–6; Gipson, *Victorious Years,* 53; Auth, *Ten Years' War,* 204 n. 5. "Without . . . Encouragement": Shingas's narrative, quoted in Francis Jennings, *Empire of Fortune: Crowns, Colonies, and Tribes in the Seven Years War in America* (New York, 1988), 166. "Seldom mist": Armstrong's report, quoted in Auth, *Ten Years' War,* 204 n. 5. "He could eat fire": "An Account of the Captivity of Hugh Gibson Among the Delaware Indians . . . ," Massachusetts Historical Society, *Collections,* 3rd ser., 6 (1837): 143. "Leg and Thigh": *Pennsylvania Gazette,* 23 Sept. 1756.

11. Auth, *Ten Years' War,* 37–9, 30–5, 62–5. Anthony F. C. Wallace's *King of the Delawares: Teedyuscung, 1700–1763* (Philadelphia, 1949) remains critical to understanding the ensuing diplomatic encounters at Easton.

12. Factions: Auth, *Ten Years' War,* 64. Effects of war: Wallace, *Teedyuscung,* 161–2. On the tenuousness of life at Shamokin and the significance of Fort Augusta, see esp. James Merrell, "Shamokin, 'the very seat of the Prince of darkness': Unsettling the Early American Frontier," in Andrew R. L. Cayton and Frederika Teute, eds., *Contact Points: American Frontiers from the Mohawk Valley to the Mississippi, 1750–1830* (Chapel Hill, N.C., 1998), 16–59.

13. Quotation from Easton treaty minutes, cited in Wallace, *Teedyuscung,* 76.

CHAPTER FIFTEEN: *The Strains of Empire: Causes of Anglo-American Friction*

1. Stanley M. Pargellis, *Lord Loudoun in North America* (1933; reprint, Hamden, Conn., 1968), 201–2, Denny quoted on 202.

2. Quartering disputes broke out in New York, Aug.–Dec. 1756; Pennsylvania, Oct.–Dec. 1756; Maryland, Nov. 1756; Massachusetts, Oct.–Dec. 1757; and South Carolina, June 1757–Feb. 1758. New Jersey and Connecticut towns quartered troops with less dislocation in

1757, but only after their assemblies (conscious of previous disputes) agreed to reimburse the towns in question. See ibid., 204–10; and Alan Rogers, *Empire and Liberty: American Resistance to British Authority, 1755–1763* (Berkeley, Calif., 1974), 84–7.

CHAPTER SIXTEEN: *Britain Drifts into a European War*

1. Pitt's speech in the House of Commons, quoted in Horace Walpole, *Memoirs of the Reign of King George the Second* (London, 1846), 2:189. For the collapse of the Fox-Newcastle ministry, see Reed Browning, *The Duke of Newcastle* (New Haven, Conn., 1975), 230–4; and Richard Middleton, *The Bells of Victory: The Pitt-Newcastle Ministry and the Conduct of the Seven Years' War, 1757–1762* (Cambridge, U.K., 1985), 22–46.
2. Lawrence Henry Gipson, *The British Empire before the American Revolution,* vol. 6, *The Great War for the Empire: The Years of Defeat, 1754–1757* (New York, 1968), 405–11.
3. George Bubb Dodington, *The Political Journal of George Bubb Dodington,* ed. John Carswell and Lewis Dralle (Oxford, 1965), 341–2.
4. On Byng's defeat, see Julian S. Corbett, *England in the Seven Years' War: A Study in Combined Strategy,* vol. 1 (London, 1918), 107–24; on the loss of the Minorca garrison, see Gipson, *Years of Defeat,* 413–14; and Corbett, *Seven Years' War,* 1:131–2. On disintegration of the ministry, see Middleton, *Bells,* 5. Fox quotation: Dodington, *Political Journal,* 342.
5. Encouraging admirals: *Voltaire: Candide, Zadig, and Selected Stories,* ed. Donald M. Frame (New York, 1961), 78–9. Frederick decides to invade Saxony: Christopher Duffy, *The Military Life of Frederick the Great* (New York, 1986), 86–8; Dennis Showalter, *The Wars of Frederick the Great* (London, 1996), 132–5.
6. Browning, *Newcastle,* 238–45; Middleton, *Bells,* 5–6; Gipson, *Years of Defeat,* 419–26.
7. Stanley Ayling, *The Elder Pitt, Earl of Chatham* (New York, 1976), 186–8; Middleton, *Bells,* 6–8; Browning, *Newcastle,* 254–6.
8. Rt. Hon. John, Lord Sheffield, ed., *Autobiography of Edward Gibbon* (London, 1907; reprint, 1972), 105. Gibbon valued his military service because "the habits of a sedentary life were usefully broken by the duties of an active profession" and because it made him "an Englishman, and a soldier. . . . In this peaceful service I imbibed the rudiments of the language, and science of tactics, which opened a new field of study and observation. I diligently read, and meditated, the *Mémoires Militaires* of Quintus Icilius (Mr. Guichardt), the only writer who has united the merits of a professor and a veteran. The discipline and evolutions of a modern battalion gave me a clearer notion of the phalanx and the legion; and the captain of the Hampshire grenadiers (the reader may smile) has not been useless to the historian of the Roman empire."
9. Ayling, *Elder Pitt,* 189–91 (policies), 200–3 (king's distrust). Marie Peters, in "The Myth of William Pitt, Earl of Chatham, Great Imperialist. Part 1: Pitt and Imperial Expansion," *Journal of Imperial and Commonwealth History* 23 (1993): 40–2, argues persuasively that at most Pitt can be credited with opportunism, and not with a consistent set of views on the colonies.
10. Fox and Cumberland: Browning, *Newcastle,* 257–8; Ayling, *Elder Pitt,* 202–3; Lewis M. Wiggin, *The Faction of Cousins: A Political Account of the Grenvilles, 1733–63* (New Haven, Conn., 1958), 193–202. "*Inter-ministerium*": Walpole, *Memoirs of George II,* 3:20.
11. Middleton, *Bells,* 16–17.
12. "Minister of measures" and "minister of money": Browning, *Newcastle,* 260–1. Allocation of offices: Ayling, *Elder Pitt,* 100–1, 205–6; Middleton, *Bells,* 17–18.
13. Relief and optimism: Middleton, *Bells,* 18; Ayling, *Elder Pitt,* 209. King's antagonism: Browning, *Newcastle,* 259. Newcastle on Pitt: Ayling, *Elder Pitt,* 206. "Bitter . . . cup": ibid., 208.

CHAPTER SEVENTEEN: *The Fortunes of War in Europe*

1. Frederick, quoted in W. F. Reddaway, *Frederick the Great and the Rise of Prussia* (New York, 1904), 225. "Dreadful auspices": the earl of Bute to Pitt, 1 July 1757, quoted in Stanley Ayling,

The Elder Pitt, Earl of Chatham (New York, 1976), 209. Deteriorating strategic position: Dennis E. Showalter, *The Wars of Frederick the Great* (London, 1996), 177–8; Reddaway, *Frederick and Prussia,* 214–18. For clear accounts of this campaign and astute (though differing) analyses of Frederick's generalship, see Russell F. Weigley, *The Age of Battles: The Quest for Decisive Warfare from Breitenfeld to Waterloo* (Bloomington, Ind., 1991), 167–95; Showalter, *Wars of Frederick,* 148–57; and Christopher Duffy, *The Military Life of Frederick the Great* (New York, 1986), 101–8.
2. Ayling, *Elder Pitt,* 211.
3. Showalter, *Wars of Frederick,* 176–7 (quotation at 176).
4. Lawrence Henry Gipson, *The British Empire before the American Revolution,* vol. 7, *The Great War for the Empire: The Victorious Years, 1758–1760* (New York, 1967), 120–2; Charles Chenevix Trench, *George II* (London, 1973), 283–4.
5. Ayling, *Elder Pitt,* 193; Lawrence Henry Gipson, *The British Empire before the American Revolution,* vol. 8, *The Great War for the Empire: The Culmination, 1760–1763* (New York, 1970), 113–21.
6. Clive in Bengal: Ibid., 127–36. "This cordial": Pitt to Bute, n.d., quoted in Peter Douglas Brown, *William Pitt, Earl of Chatham: The Great Commoner* (London, 1978), 152. "Infinitely happy": same to same, n.d., ibid., 154.

CHAPTER EIGHTEEN: *Loudoun's Offensive*

1. Pitt's plans vs. Loudoun's: Stanley M. Pargellis, *Lord Loudoun in North America* (1933; reprint, Hamden, Conn., 1968), 231–2; Lawrence Henry Gipson, *The British Empire before the American Revolution,* vol. 7, *The Great War for the Empire: The Victorious Years, 1758–1760* (New York, 1967), 90–5. "Refused nothing": Archibald Campbell, duke of Argyll, to Loudoun, Feb. 1757, quoted in Pargellis, *Loudoun,* 236.
2. On the supply system, see Daniel J. Beattie, "The Adaptation of the British Army to Wilderness Warfare, 1755–1763," in Maarten Ultee, ed., *Adapting to Conditions: War and Society in the Eighteenth Century* (University, Ala., 1986), 62–4; and Pargellis, *Loudoun,* 292–6. On the resistance of the New England assemblies to Loudoun's reforms, see Fred Anderson, *A People's Army: Massachusetts Soldiers and Society in the Seven Years' War* (Chapel Hill, N.C., 1984), 180–5.
3. Beattie, "Adaptation," 65–7; Pargellis, *Loudoun,* 296–9. In 1756 the cost of moving a barrel of beef to the lake was one pound nine shillings New York currency; in 1757 Bradstreet's estimate of the cost of transporting a barrel from Albany to Fort Edward (about fifty miles) was seven shillings (ibid., 296, 298).
4. In 1757 Loudoun requisitioned only four thousand men from the New England provinces; see ibid., 212–16. Plans to substitute light infantry for rangers: ibid., 301–4. Americans had used ranger companies as substitutes for Indians during previous wars; they probably grew out of earlier attempts to fight Indians by offering bounties and encouraging backwoodsmen to form private scalp-hunting companies. These units had seldom distinguished themselves in woodland warfare, although in King George's War a ranger company (largely composed of Christian Indians) under the command of John Gorham of New Hampshire performed useful service on the Louisbourg expedition (Douglas Edward Leach, *Arms for Empire: A Military History of the British Colonies in North America, 1607–1763* [New York, 1973], 183–5, 235). During the Seven Years' War, rangers first served on the Crown Point expedition in 1755—a New Hampshire company under Captain Robert Rogers and Lieutenant John Stark. In 1756 there were three such companies; in 1757, four. Shirley had, typically, handled the establishment of the ranging companies in an irregular manner, paying their officers on the same scale as regulars and their men as provincials. Ultimately he provided for them out of his own funds, in effect making them independent companies, paid by the Crown, on an establishment separate from both the regular army and the provinces. Loudoun systematized the arrangement, continuing to pay the rangers from his own contingency money, but enlisting them (unlike provincials) for the duration of the war. Both their notorious lack of discipline and the expense

of keeping them in service plagued him; in 1758, nine companies of rangers cost £35,000 sterling to maintain—twice as much as a regiment of regulars (Pargellis, *Loudoun,* 303).

The colonial rangers, while a subject of military legend and popular fascination, have not yet been adequately treated in historical scholarship. The best existing work is John R. Cuneo, *Robert Rogers of the Rangers* (1959; reprint, New York, 1987). An excellent doctoral dissertation, completed too late to influence this book, promises to fill this lacuna in the historiography: John Edward Grenier, "The Other American Way of War: Unlimited and Irregular Warfare in the Colonial Military Tradition" (Ph.D. diss., University of Colorado at Boulder, 1999); see esp. chaps. 2–4.

5. Quartering bill: Pargellis, *Loudoun,* 194. Submission of colonial governments: ibid., 198–201. Probably because of his insecurity in the Commons in early 1757, Pitt never introduced the promised quartering bill, and the measure lay dormant until it was revived at General Gage's request in 1765.

6. Loudoun to Henry Fox, 22 Nov.–26 December 1756, Loudoun Papers, Henry E. Huntington Library, San Marino, California.

7. Pargellis, *Loudoun,* 265; Alan Rogers, *Empire and Liberty: American Resistance to British Authority, 1755–1763* (Berkeley, Calif., 1974), 93–5.

8. Loudoun to Fox, 8 Oct. 1756, Loudoun Papers.

9. Pargellis, *Loudoun,* 266–7; Rogers, *Empire and Liberty,* 94–7.

10. Gipson, *Victorious Years,* 97–103; Pargellis, *Loudoun,* 214–27. The naval escort consisted only of one fifty-gun man-of-war, H.M.S. *Sutherland,* and two frigates (ibid., 238).

CHAPTER NINETEEN: *Fort William Henry*

1. On Webb, see Loudoun to Cumberland, 5 Jan. 1757, and Loudoun to Webb, 20 June 1757, in Stanley M. Pargellis, ed., *Military Affairs in North America, 1748–1765: Documents from the Cumberland Papers in Windsor Castle* (1936; reprint, New York, 1969), 293, 370–1; and *Dictionary of American Biography,* s.v. "Webb, Daniel." Quotation: Pargellis, *Lord Loudoun in North America* (1933; reprint, Hamden, Conn., 1968), 234.

2. Ian K. Steele, *Betrayals: Fort William Henry and the "Massacre"* (New York, 1990), 75–7; Lawrence Henry Gipson, *The British Empire before the American Revolution,* vol. 7, *The Great War for the Empire: The Victorious Years, 1758–1760* (New York, 1967), 67–9. Another sloop was damaged but not destroyed in the attack, and a third survived unhurt; several "Bay boats and Gondolas" also survived, probably because they had sunk offshore, the previous fall, to be raised after the thaw—a common means of protecting vessels from winter damage (Loudoun to Webb, 20 June 1757, in Pargellis, *Military Affairs,* 371).

3. Carillon scout and Rogers's wound: John R. Cuneo, *Robert Rogers of the Rangers* (1959; reprint, New York, 1987), 45–53. French and Indian activities: Steele, *Betrayals,* 84–5.

4. "Swimming": Louis Antoine de Bougainville, *Adventure in the Wilderness: The American Journals of Louis Antoine de Bougainville, 1756–1760,* ed. Edward P. Hamilton (Norman, Okla., 1964), 116 (entry of June 15). Ransom: Steele, *Betrayals,* 79.

5. French strength: Bougainville, *Adventure,* 152–3 (entry of 29 July 1757. The army included 6 battalions of "French Troops," or regulars, totalling 2,570; a battalion of "Colony Troops," or *troupes de la marine,* numbering 524, under Rigaud; 3,470 Canadian militia and volunteers, organized into 8 battalion-strength territorial "brigades"; and 180 artillerists). Indian participation: see ibid., 150–1 (entry of 28 July 1757); and the interpretation in Steele, *Betrayals,* 80–1, 111. "In the midst": Bougainville, *Adventure,* 149 (entry of 27 July 1757).

6. Garrison strength: Steele, *Betrayals,* 96. "An old Officer": Loudoun to Cumberland, 25 Apr.–3 June 1757, in Pargellis, *Military Affairs,* 344. "At daybreak": Bougainville, *Adventure,* 142–3 (entry of 24 July 1757); see also Steele, *Betrayals,* 91, 96–7, 217 nn. 46, 47.

7. Gipson, *Victorious Years,* 79–81; Steele, *Betrayals,* 229–30 n. 49.

8. Douglas Edward Leach, *Arms for Empire: A Military History of the British Colonies in North*

America, 1607–1763 (New York, 1973), 399–400; Bougainville, *Adventure,* 154–6 (entry of 31 July 1757). "We know": Monro to Webb, 3 Aug. 1757, quoted in Steele, *Betrayals,* 98.
9. Bougainville, *Adventure,* 157 (entry of 1 Aug. 1757).
10. Steele, *Betrayals,* 98–9; Bougainville, *Adventure,* 158–60 (entry of 3 Aug. 1757). Garden: "A Plan of Fort William Henry . . ." in Gipson, *Victorious Years,* facing 78.
11. Steele, *Betrayals,* 99.
12. Quotation: G. Bartman to Monro, 4 Aug. 1757, facsimile copy in ibid., 103 (fig. 9). Montcalm suggests surrender: Bougainville, *Adventure,* 163, 166–7 (entries of 5 and 7 Aug. 1757).
13. Ibid., 160–9 (entries of 4–8 Aug. 1757); Steele, *Betrayals,* 102–5.
14. Eleven of twenty-one guns had split or exploded by the end of 7 Aug., including both of the fort's thirty-two–pounders. Most of the fort's guns were iron and hence vulnerable to metal fatigue after prolonged firing. Brass guns stood up better under sustained use, but all ten of the brass cannon in the fort and the camp were small-bore fieldpieces, unable to damage the besiegers' fieldworks (ibid., 100–8).
15. Ibid., 105–6, 108.
16. Situation report: ibid., 107–8, 109. (The shortage of ammunition was far from absolute, for the French would later list 2,522 solid shot, 542 shells, and 35,835 pounds of powder in their "Return of Artillery Found in the Fort." Rather the problem was of a severe shortage of shot and shell for the five small-caliber cannon that remained functional. See Bougainville, *Adventure,* 177 [entry of 22 Aug. 1757].) "Quite worn out": Frye, quoted in Gipson, *Victorious Years,* 84.
17. Terms of surrender from Steele, *Betrayals,* 110; see also Gipson, *Victorious Years,* 84–5.
18. Steele, *Betrayals,* 110–11.
19. Ibid., 111–12. "More than usual malice": Joseph Frye, A Journal of the Attack of Fort William Henry by the French on the third day of August 1757 and the surrender of the 9th of the same month, Parkman Papers, vol. 42, Massachusetts Historical Society, Boston.
20. Steele, *Betrayals,* 115–19 (killing and taking of prisoners), 144 (maximum number killed; Steele's lower-bound estimate is 69), 134 (number of captives), 121 (number sheltered by French and early departure of Indians).
21. Refugees' arrival: Rufus Putnam, *Journal of Gen. Rufus Putnam, Kept in Northern New York during Four Campaigns of the Old French and Indian War, 1757–1760,* ed. E. C. Dawes (Albany, 1886), 42–3 (entries of 10–19 Aug. 1757). Montcalm's reassurances and efforts to recover captives: Steele, *Betrayals,* 129–31. Captive returns: ibid., 139 (table 2).
22. Ibid., 130.
23. Ibid., 132, 144–8, 154–6, 165–70; Kerry Trask, *In the Pursuit of Shadows: Massachusetts Millennialism and the Seven Years' War* (New York, 1989), 234–56.
24. Jean Elizabeth Lunn, "Agriculture and War in Canada, 1740–1760," *Canadian Historical Review* 16 (1935): 123 n. 3, 133–4, 136; Bougainville, *Adventure,* 171, 182, 185 (entries of 9 Aug., 10–22 and 27 Sept., 1–10 Oct. 1757).
25. Connecticut response: Harold E. Selesky, *War and Society in Colonial Connecticut* (New Haven, Conn., 1990), 110. Massachusetts response: Thomas Pownall to William Pitt, 16 Aug. 1757, in Gertrude Selwyn Kimball, ed., *The Correspondence of William Pitt* (1906; reprint, New York, 1969), 1:94–7. Militia at Fort Edward: Steele, *Betrayals,* 127. This conservative figure reflects Webb's desire to blame his failure to reinforce Monro on the laggard response of the American militia. Another witness estimated the number of militiamen who had reached Fort Edward by 15 Aug. at seven thousand (*Pennsylvania Gazette,* 25 Aug. 1757).
26. Expense: Selesky, *War and Society,* 110. Militia vs. provincial wages: Massachusetts House of Representatives resolve, 12 Jun. 1758, stipulated a two shillings eightpence daily wage for militia privates, plus subsistence and horse hire, or the equivalent of four pounds per month; provincial privates earned one pound sixteen shillings per month, exclusive of bounties and subsistence. (Massachusetts Archives, vol. 77, 623–3a; Fred Anderson, *A People's Army: Massachusetts Soldiers and Society in the Seven Years' War* [Chapel Hill, N.C., 1984], 225.) Comparison to England: The authorized strength of the English militia was 32,000, but the only time that

more than 16,000 men actually served was at the height of the French invasion threat of 1759. Even at its theoretical maximum, the English militia would have amounted to less than 3.3 percent of the male population in the sixteen to thirty age range. See Stanley Ayling, *The Elder Pitt, Earl of Chatham* (New York, 1976), 191; and Eliga Gould, *Persistence of Empire: British Political Culture in the Age of the American Revolution* (Chapel Hill, N.C., forthcoming), chap. 3.

CHAPTER TWENTY: *Other Disasters, and a Ray of Hope*

1. P. M. Hamer, "Anglo-French Rivalry in the Cherokee Country, 1754–1757," *North Carolina Historical Review* 2 (1925): 303–22; id., "Fort Loudoun in the Cherokee War, 1758–1761," *North Carolina Historical Review*, 422–58; Douglas Edward Leach, *Arms for Empire: A Military History of the British Colonies in North America, 1607–1763* (New York, 1973), 486–8; Tom Hatley, *The Dividing Paths: Cherokees and South Carolinians through the Era of Revolution* (New York, 1993), 96–9.
2. Lawrence Henry Gipson, *The British Empire before the American Revolution*, vol. 7, *The Great War for the Empire: The Victorious Years, 1758–1760* (New York, 1967), 45–6, 144; Hayes Baker-Crothers, *Virginia in the French and Indian War* (Chicago, 1928), 119–20.
3. "Want nothing but Commissions": Washington to Dinwiddie, 10 Mar. 1757, in W. W. Abbott et al., eds., *The Papers of George Washington, Colonial Series*, vol. 4, November 1756–October 1757 (Charlottesville, Va., 1984), 112–15; a fuller statement than the one he presented in the Memorial to John Campbell, Earl of Loudoun, 23 Mar. 1757, ibid., 120–1, and probably closer to the case as he stated it in person. Loudon's response: Stanwix to Washington, 23 May 1757, ibid., 159–60.
4. Difficulties of defending backcountry: Gipson, *Victorious Years*, 43–5; Baker-Crothers, *Virginia in the French and Indian War*, 111–26; James Titus, *The Old Dominion at War: Society, Politics, and Warfare in Late Colonial Virginia* (Columbia, S.C., 1991), 73–120 passim. Detachment to Charleston: Harry M. Ward, *Major General Adam Stephen and the Cause of American Liberty* (Charlottesville, Va., 1989), 42–6. Abandonment of forts: Gipson, *Victorious Years*, 41–2. Indians: Washington to Dinwiddie, 10 June 1757, *Papers of Washington*, 4:192–5 (quotation at 192).
5. "Another campaign": Washington to Dinwiddie, 24 Oct. 1757, in W. W. Abbot et al., eds., *The Papers of George Washington, Colonial Series*, vol. 5, October 1757–September 1758 (Charlottesville, Va., 1988), 25; cf. Washington to Stanwix, 8 Oct. 1757, ibid., 8–10. "Nothing very important . . . into the forest": Vaudreuil to the minister of marine, 13 Feb. 1758, in Sylvester K. Stevens and Donald H. Kent, eds., *Wilderness Chronicles of Northwestern Pennsylvania* (Harrisburg, Pa., 1941), 109–10. For a sense of the character of the war in western Virginia in 1757, see Samuel Kercheval, *A History of the Valley of Virginia* (1833; reprint, Strasburg, Va., 1973), 78–80, 95–6, 72–108 passim.
6. Francis Jennings, *Empire of Fortune: Crowns, Colonies, and Tribes in the Seven Years War in America* (New York, 1988), 281, 334–48; also, in general, Stephen F. Auth, *The Ten Years' War: Indian-White Relations in Pennsylvania, 1755–1765* (New York, 1989), 81–90; and Anthony F. C. Wallace, *King of the Delawares: Teedyuscung, 1700–1763* (Philadelphia, 1949), 155–60.
7. "In the morning": Richard Peters to Thomas Penn, 29 Jan. 1757, quoted in Nicholas Wainwright, *George Croghan, Wilderness Diplomat* (Chapel Hill, N.C., 1959), 123. Character of negotiations: Jennings, *Empire of Fortune*, 339–40.
8. Ibid., 346–7.

CHAPTER TWENTY-ONE: *Pitt Changes Course*

1. Julian S. Corbett, *England in the Seven Years' War: A Study in Combined Strategy*, vol. 1 (London, 1918), 168–9, 171.
2. Loudoun to Holburne and Holburne to Loudoun, 4 Aug. 1757, ibid., 171–2.
3. Ibid., 177–8.
4. Loudoun to Cumberland, 17 Oct. 1757, in Stanley M. Pargellis, ed., *Military Affairs in*

North America, 1748–1765: Documents from the Cumberland Papers in Windsor Castle (1936; reprint, New York, 1969), 399–403.

5. Loudoun's activities: id., *Lord Loudoun in North America* (1933; reprint, Hamden, Conn., 1968), 348. Resistance: ibid., 125–9.

6. Ibid., 268–76, 276 n. 45.

7. "My Sittuation": Loudoun to Argyll, 16 Feb. 1758, quoted ibid., 350. Wine: ibid., 167–8.

8. Ibid., 346.

9. For the strategic position of Cumberland and the provisions of the convention, see esp. Corbett, *Seven Years' War,* 1:223–7; also Stanley Ayling, *The Elder Pitt, Earl of Chatham* (New York, 1976), 210–12; and Peter Douglas Brown, *William Pitt, Earl of Chatham: The Great Commoner* (London, 1978), 155–6. For Frederick's position in the fall of 1757, see Dennis Showalter, *The Wars of Frederick the Great* (New York, 1996), 177–80; and W. F. Reddaway, *Frederick the Great and the Rise of Prussia* (New York, 1904), 232–3.

10. "A convention": king to Cumberland, 21 Sept. 1757, quoted in Charles Chenevix Trench, *George II* (London, 1973), 284. "His honour": Newcastle [memorandum?], quoted ibid., 284. "Here is my son": Horace Walpole, *Memoirs of the Reign of George II,* vol. 3 (London, 1846), 61. No regret: ibid., 62–5.

11. For Pitt's strategic plans and policies, see Corbett, *Seven Years' War,* 1:8–9, 28–9, 148, 150–2, 189–91, 374–6; and Richard Middleton, *The Bells of Victory: The Pitt-Newcastle Ministry and the Conduct of the Seven Years' War, 1757–1762* (Cambridge, U.K., 1985). For the character of his support among those who favored imperial growth, see Marie Peters, *Pitt and Popularity: The Patriot Minister and London Opinion during the Seven Years' War* (Oxford, 1980); and (for a skeptical view of his strategy, stressing pragmatism over any unifying vision) id., "The Myth of William Pitt, Earl of Chatham, Great Imperialist, Part 1: Pitt and Imperial Expansion, 1738–1763," *Journal of Imperial and Commonwealth History* 21 (1993): 31–74.

12. Pitt's speech on the army estimates for 1758, 14 Dec. 1757, quoted in Romney Sedgwick, ed., *Letters from George III to Lord Bute, 1756–66* (London, 1939), 19–20 n. 2.

13. Frederick to Newcastle, 26 July 1756, quoted in Corbett, *Seven Years' War,* 1:148.

14. Stanley M. Pargellis, *Lord Loudoun in North America* (1933; reprint, Hamden, Conn., 1968), 344–5; John Schutz, *Thomas Pownall, British Defender of American Liberty: A Study of Anglo-American Relations in the Eighteenth Century* (Glendale, Calif., 1951), 81.

15. Pargellis, *Loudoun,* 231, 342–5, 351, 358–9.

16. Anson: Horace Walpole, *Memoirs of the Reign of King George II,* (London, 1846), 3:32 (Pitt's nomination of Anson); Corbett, *Seven Years' War,* 1:180. Ligonier: ibid., 33–4, 230–2; Ayling, *Elder Pitt,* 191, 213.

17. Descents: Corbett, *Seven Years' War,* 1:192–6, 262–8, 287–9, 293–304. Ferdinand and Hanover: ibid., 227–30. Newcastle and Pitt: Reed Browning, *The Duke of Newcastle* (New Haven, Conn., 1975), 261 ff.; Middleton, *Bells,* 54, 60–1, 88–9, 113–18, 141, 148, 153–9, 193–4, 205–6, 213; Ayling, *The Elder Pitt,* 204–39 passim; Peters, "Myth of Pitt," 42–8; John Brewer, *The Sinews of Power: War, Money, and the English State, 1688–1783* (New York, 1989), 170–6.

18. Corbett, *Seven Years' War,* 1:232–4; Lawrence Henry Gipson, *The British Empire before the Revolution,* vol. 7, *The Great War for the British Empire: The Victorious Years, 1758–1760,* 125–6; Showalter, *Wars of Frederick,* 177–206.

PART IV: *TURNING POINT,* 1758

CHAPTER TWENTY-TWO: *Deadlock, and a New Beginning*

1. E. C. Dawes, ed., *Journal of Gen. Rufus Putnam, Kept in Northern New York during Four Campaigns of the Old French and Indian War, 1757–1760* (Albany, 1886), 49–50 (entry of 18 Nov. 1757); Rowena Buell, ed., *The Memoirs of Rufus Putnam* (Boston, 1903), 16.

2. Douglas Edward Leach, *Arms for Empire: A Military History of the British Colonies in North America, 1607–1763* (New York, 1973), 403; Lawrence Henry Gipson, *The British Empire before*

the American Revolution, vol. 7, *The Great War for the Empire: The Victorious Years, 1758–1760* (New York, 1967), 151–3. Stanley M. Pargellis, *Lord Loudoun in North America* (1933; reprint, New York, 1968), 275–6.

3. Learned: Buell *Memoirs of Putnam,* 16. Quotation: Dawes, *Journal of Putnam,* 50–2 (entry of 2 Feb. 1758).

4. Ibid., 54–6 (entries of 8–10 Feb. 1758); Buell, *Memoirs of Putnam,* 21.

5. "He is a good Soldier": ibid., 17.

6. "Concert measures": "Resolutions of the Massachusetts General Assembly," 24 Dec. 1757, in John Russell Bartlett, ed., *Records of the Colony of Rhode Island and Providence Plantations, in New England,* vol. 7, 1757 to 1769 (Providence, 1861), 115–16. Loudoun and Pownall: Pargellis, *Loudoun,* 268–73; Loudoun to Cumberland, 17 Oct. 1757, in id., ed., *Military Affairs in North America, 1748–1765: Documents from the Cumberland Papers in Windsor Castle* (New York, 1936), 404–5.

7. John Schutz, *Thomas Pownall, British Defender of American Liberty: A Study of Anglo-American Relations in the Eighteenth Century* (Glendale, Calif., 1951), 85.

8. Pownall's principles: ibid., 98. Breach with Loudoun: Schutz, *Pownall,* 110–18 (esp. Pownall to Loudoun, 15 Dec. 1757, quoted at 116–17); Pownall to Pitt, 1 and 28 Dec. 1757, 2 Jan., 15–19 Jan., and 20 Jan. 1758, in Gertrude Selwyn Kimball, ed., *Correspondence of William Pitt when Secretary of State with Colonial Governors and Military and Naval Commissioners in America,* vol. 1 (1906; reprint, New York, 1969), 128–9, 132–3, 155–6, 161–5, 166–7.

9. "There is a Spirit": Pownall to Pitt, 15 Jan. 1758, *Pitt Corr.,* 1:162–3. Schutz, *Pownall,* 119–22; Pargellis, *Loudoun,* 270–2.

10. Loudoun to Pitt, 14 Feb. 1758, *Pitt Corr.,* 1:188–9.

11. Pargellis, *Loudoun,* 356–8, 276–7, and n. 45.

12. Ibid., 277; Schutz, *Pownall,* 127; quotations: Pownall to Pitt, 14 Mar. 1758, *Pitt Corr.,* 1:203.

13. Pitt to governors in North America, 30 Dec. 1757, ibid., 135.

14. Pitt to the governors of Mass. Bay, N.H., Conn., R.I., N.Y., and N.J., 30 Dec. 1757, ibid., 136–8.

15. Ibid., 138–9.

16. Legislators' reaction: Pownall to Pitt, 14 Mar. 1757, ibid., 203; Schutz, *Pownall,* 128. Loudoun's departure: Loudoun to Pitt, 31 May 1758, *Pitt Corr.,* 1:263.

17. For the numbers of men voted, see the letters of various governors to Pitt in *Pitt Corr.,* 1:203, 209–11, 213, 216, 222, 227, 229, 230, 234, 235–6, 239, 240–1, 244, 311, 329–32. Maryland's assembly had fallen out with Loudoun in 1757 over the garrisoning of Fort Cumberland and had severed all ties with the commander in chief. At the time of Loudoun's recall the issue remained unresolved. Maryland's lack of participation after Loudoun returned to England had less to do with opposition to the war than with the dynamics of proprietary politics. In Apr. 1758 the House of Delegates voted to appropriate £45,000 and raise a thousand provincials, but the council refused its assent because the money would have been raised by a method of taxation repugnant to the proprietary family. See Horatio Sharpe to Pitt, 16 Mar., 18 May, and 27 Aug. 1758, ibid., 209–11, 242–5, 327–32; and Pargellis, *Loudoun,* 220–1.

18. This is not to say that no colonists enlisted in regular-army units; in fact, Thomas Purvis has estimated that eleven thousand Americans did so ("Colonial American Participation in the Seven Years' War, 1755–1763" [paper presented at the 10th Wilburt S. Brown Conference in History, University of Alabama, Feb. 11–12, 1983]; Don Higginbotham cites the number as authoritative in "The Early American Way of War: Reconnaissance and Appraisal," *William and Mary Quarterly,* 3rd ser., 45 [1987]: 235. I have not been able to determine whether the estimate includes slaves enlisted in British West Indian regiments). Most of these enlistments occurred in the ethnically diverse Middle Colonies, especially Pennsylvania, where regular recruiters attracted substantial numbers of German-speaking colonists to the four-battalion 60th Regiment—the Royal Americans—in the early years of the war.

While the social contexts of war and military service have yet to be studied in Pennsylvania as thoroughly as in Massachusetts, Connecticut, and Virginia, three factors (a high level of indentured servitude among men in the military age range, a large concentration of young tenant farmers in the eastern part of the province, and a socioeconomic makeup strongly shaped by poorer German and Scotch-Irish immigrants) would have tended to promote enlistment in the regular forces. It must be borne in mind, however, that these enlistments tended to come before 1758, when Parliament's subsidies began to enable the colonies to offer high bounties to attract men to their own provincial regiments; and that in order to enlist men, regular recruiters were compelled to offer term enlistments of three years or the duration of the war, rather than the life (twenty-year) enlistments typical of the British army as a whole.

Yet American enlistees never filled the ranks as Braddock and Loudoun assumed they should. Unlike provincial units, which tended after 1757 to recruit close to their full complements, regular units remained chronically and indeed increasingly understrength throughout the war. There were shortages of 1,710 men in America's 21 regular battalions in Jan. 1758; 3,280 in the equivalent of 24 battalions in Oct. 1758; 4,492 in 25 battalions in 1759; 4,750 in 25 battalions in Mar. 1760; and a shortfall of 7,000 the following Oct. (see Pargellis, *Loudoun*, 110–11). Such deficiencies in volunteers were compensated for by a variety of expedients, but for the most part replacements came in the form of drafts from Irish regiments. Thus, by Jan. 1759, only a quarter of the troops in the Royal American Regiment, whose soldiers were supposed to be recruited exclusively in the colonies, were in fact colonists (largely Germans). Apart from a few more Germans recruited directly from Europe, the bulk of the Royal Americans were "the 'refuse of the army in Ireland' " (ibid., 112).

More research needs to be done to clarify the social and economic contexts of colonial enlistment in regular regiments and to explore the wartime experiences of those soldiers. A Ph.D. dissertation in progress at the University of Western Ontario may answer many of these questions: Alexander V. Campbell, "Anvil of Empire: The Royal American Regiment, 1756–1775" (forthcoming). Campbell generously allowed me to read the thesis prospectus (April 1998), which contains a sketch of his argument.

19. New England enlistments: Abercromby to Pitt, 28 Apr. 1758, *Pitt Corr.*, 1:226. Virginia's lack of enthusiasm before 1758: John Ferling, "Soldiers for Virginia: Who Served in the French and Indian War?" *Virginia Magazine of History and Biography* 94 (1986): 308–9; James Titus, *The Old Dominion at War: Society, Politics, and Warfare in Late Colonial Virginia* (Columbia, S.C., 1991), 102–3, 138–9. (In 1755 the Virginia Regiment had come up to only 25 percent of its authorized strength; in 1756, 41 percent; in 1757, 55 percent. Less than 10 percent of the men in the army of 1756 reenlisted to serve in 1757.) Virginia's reversal of attitude, 1758: John Blair to Pitt, 29 June 1758, *Pitt Corr.*, 1:289. The Burgesses now revoked the statute placing bounties on enemy Indian scalps: the end of the fantasy that a war they were unwilling to finance as a public venture could somehow be carried on by private enterprise.

20. Quotation: Sir John St. Clair to Col. Henry Bouquet, 27 May 1758, quoted in Douglas Southall Freeman, *George Washington: A Biography*, vol. 2, *Young Washington* (New York, 1948), 309.

CHAPTER TWENTY-THREE: *Old Strategies, New Men, and a Shift in the Balance*

1. Stanley M. Pargellis, *Lord Loudoun in North America* (1933; reprint, Hamden, Conn., 1968), 356–8.

2. *Dictionary of National Biography*, s.v. "Abercromby, James," "Amherst, Jeffery," "Wolfe, James," "Forbes, John," and "Howe, Richard." Additionally, on Amherst, see J. C. Long, *Lord Jeffery Amherst* (New York, 1933); and Daniel John Beattie, "General Jeffery Amherst and the Conquest of Canada, 1758–1760" (Ph.D. diss., Duke University, 1976); on Wolfe, Beckles Willson, *The Life and Letters of James Wolfe* (New York, 1909); on Forbes, Lawrence Henry Gipson, *The British Empire before the American Revolution*, vol. 7, *The Great War for the Empire: The Victorious Years, 1758–1760* (New York, 1967), 247–8; on Abercromby, ibid., 211. On

their selection, see Rex Whitworth, *Field Marshal Lord Ligonier: A Story of the British Army, 1702–1770* (Oxford, 1958), 236–42. George II disapproved of irregular promotions and resisted Amherst's appointment so stoutly that the critical offensive of 1758 might be said to have been conducted not in the field but in the royal bedchamber, where Lady Yarmouth, his favorite mistress, lobbied on Amherst's behalf, at Ligonier's urgent request.

3. Gipson, *Victorious Years,* 177; Whitworth, *Ligonier,* 240–1; Beattie, "Amherst," 66.

4. Canadian defense forces: George F. G. Stanley, *New France: The Last Phase, 1744–1760* (Toronto, 1968), 165–6; W. J. Eccles, "The French Forces in North America during the Seven Years' War," in *Dictionary of Canadian Biography,* vol. 3, 1741 to 1770, xvii–xviii. (In practice the Canadian militia was much more effective than its counterpart in the British colonies and routinely detached men for service with expeditionary forces. Yet it was still a body mainly useful for home defense, for to remove any substantial number of men from availability for planting and harvest threatened the food supply of Canada, which was marginal at best.) Disaffection of Indians of the *pays d'en haut:* Louis Antoine de Bougainville, *Adventure in the Wilderness: The American Journals of Louis Antoine de Bougainville, 1756–1760,* ed. Edward P. Hamilton (Norman, Okla., 1964), 197, 204 (entries of 1–13 Mar. and 12–20 May 1758).

5. Failed harvests and high prices: Jean Elizabeth Lunn, "Agriculture and War in Canada, 1740–1760," *Canadian Historical Review* 16 (1935): 128, 130. (A *minot* was equivalent to about a third of a bushel.) Rationing and expedient substitutes: Bougainville, *Adventure,* 71–2 (22 Nov. 1756). Horse meat: Stanley, *New France,* 194. (Horse meat was available because animals were slaughtered to conserve fodder.) Protests: Bougainville, *Adventure,* 195 (12 Dec. 1757–12 Mar. 1758). Dwindling rations, 1758: ibid., 201–2 (entries of 15–25 Apr. and 3 May 1758). "Some of the inhabitants": ibid., 206 (21 May 1758). Four-ounce bread ration: ibid., 209 (30 May 1758).

6. Stanley, *New France,* 191–2.

7. Ibid., 201–6; Bougainville, *Adventure,* 196.

8. Inflation: ibid., 198 (8 Nov. 1757). Lack of circulating medium: Gustave Lanctot, *A History of Canada,* vol. 3, *From the Treaty of Utrecht to the Treaty of Paris, 1713–1763* (Cambridge, Mass., 1965), 162. Hoarding: Stanley, *New France,* 196–200.

9. Bougainville, *Adventure,* 213 (18–19 June 1758) and 215 (23 June 1758); Stanley, *New France,* 165; Ian K. Steele, *Warpaths: Invasions of North America* (Oxford, 1994), 205–6, 211–12; Stanley, *New France,* 211–12; Lanctot, *Utrecht to Paris,* 3:159, 162, 165.

CHAPTER TWENTY-FOUR: *Montcalm Raises a Cross: The Battle of Ticonderoga*

1. Abercromby's expedition: Lawrence Henry Gipson, *The British Empire before the American Revolution,* vol. 7, *The Great War for the Empire: The Victorious Years, 1758–1760* (New York, 1967), 217. "Every thing here": E. C. Dawes, ed., *Journal of Gen. Rufus Putnam, Kept in Northern New York during Four Campaigns of the Old French and Indian War, 1757–1760* (Albany, 1886), 63 (entry of 28 June 1758). "Covered the Lake": *Pennsylvania Gazette,* 27 July 1758. "Valuable Baggage": Dawes, *Journal of Putnam,* 67 (entry of 6 July 1758). Howe: Abercromby to Pitt, 12 July 1758, in Gertrude Selwyn Kimball, ed., *Correspondence of William Pitt when Secretary of State, with Colonial Governors and Military and Naval Commissioners in America,* vol. 1 (1906; reprint, New York, 1969), 297.

2. "His death" and "Granny": Rowena Buell, ed., *The Memoirs of Rufus Putnam* (Boston, 1903), 23. "I felt it" and dispatch of engineer: Abercromby to Pitt, 12 July 1758, *Pitt Corr.,* 1:298, 299. "A little Stagnant": Fabius Maximus Ray, ed., *The Journal of Dr. Caleb Rea, Written during the Expedition against Ticonderoga in 1758* (Salem, Mass., 1881), 25 (entry of 7 July 1758).

3. Louis Antoine de Bougainville, *Adventure in the Wilderness: The American Journals of Louis Antoine de Bougainville, 1756–1760,* ed. Edward P. Hamilton (Norman, Okla., 1964), 221 (30 June 1758), 231 ("List and Composition of the French Army, July 8, 1758"), 222 (1 July 1758), 229–30 (7 July 1758).

4. Gipson, *Victorious Years,* 226–9; William Eyre to Robert Napier, 10 July 1758, in Stanley M. Pargellis, ed., *Military Affairs in North America, 1748–1765: Documents from the Cumberland Papers in Windsor Castle* (1936; reprint, New York, 1969), 420–1; Bougainville, *Adventure,* 230 (7 July 1758). Although firing at extreme range, guns on Rattlesnake Hill would have enfiladed the French lines and quickly made them too risky to man. With too few provisions to withstand a siege, Montcalm would have been forced to withdraw; but the only escape was by boat, and even a few cannon atop the hill would have made a shambles of the embarkation.
5. Lt. Matthew Clark was, according to Capt. Charles Lee of the 44th Foot, Abercromby's "favourite Engineer," but "a stripling, who had never seen the least service" (Lee, "Narrative," enclosed in id. to Miss Sidney Lee, 16 Sept. 1758, New-York Historical Society, *Collections* 4 [1871]: 12).
6. "To march up": Abercromby to Pitt, 12 July 1758, *Pitt Corr.,* 1:300. The British attacked with 15 battalions, or about 13,000 men, organized in 3 brigades; the French opposed them with 7 understrength regular battalions reinforced by *troupes de la marine* and Canadian militia for a total of fewer than 3,500 men. For the Anglo-American order of battle, see William Eyre to Robert Napier, 10 July 1758, in Pargellis, *Military Affairs,* 420; and John Cleaveland, "Journal," *Bulletin of the Fort Ticonderoga Museum* 10 (1959): 199 ("Map Made July 8"). French order of battle: Bougainville, *Adventure,* 231–2 (8 July 1758).
7. "Trees were fell down": Eyre to Napier, 10 July 1758, in Pargellis, *Military Affairs,* 420, 421. "Cut . . . Down": Joseph Nichols diary, 8 July 1758, Huntington MS 89, Henry E. Huntington Library, San Marino, Calif. "The fier began": Archelaus Fuller, "Journal of Col. Archelaus Fuller of Middleton, Mass., in the Expedition against Ticonderoga in 1758," *Essex Institute Historical Collections* 46 (1910): 209–20 (entry of 8 July 1758).
8. David Perry, "Recollections of an Old Soldier . . . Written by Himself," *The Magazine of History* 137 (1928), 9–10 (reprinted from a pamphlet by the same title, pub. Windsor, Vt., 1822).
9. "Constant peele": Buell, *Memoirs of Putnam,* 24 (8 July 1758). "When I came": Dawes, *Journal of Putnam,* 70–1 (8 July 1758).
10. "It was therefore judged": Abercromby to Pitt, 12 July 1758, *Pitt Corr.,* 1:300. "News came": Joseph Nichols diary, 9 July 1758. Abercromby reported 1,610 regular casualties (464 dead, 1,117 wounded, 29 missing) and 334 among the provincials (87 killed, 239 wounded, 8 missing). The first battalion of the 42nd Foot (the Black Watch) lost 203 killed and 296 wounded, or half its strength.
11. "Shamefully retreated": Artemas Ward diary, 8 July 1758; reproduced in Frederick S. Allis, ed., *The Artemas Ward Papers* (Massachusetts Historical Society microfilm edition; Boston, 1967), reel 4. "This Day": John Cleaveland diary, 10 July 1758, 200. "Astonishing Disappointment": Joseph Nichols diary, 11 July 1758; providentialism, 12 July 1758. "The General [and] his Rehoboam-Counsellors": John Cleaveland diary, 12 July 1758 (orthography follows MS at Fort Ticonderoga Museum rather than printed version cited above). A closer look at the Bible illuminates what Cleaveland and similarly minded New Englanders made of the defeat: when the Israelites complained to King Rehoboam that their burdens were too heavy, he took counsel not with the wise elders, but only with his boon companions. They told him to say to the people, "whereas my father laid upon you a heavy yoke, I will add to your yoke. My father chastised you with whips, but I will chastise you with scorpions." This provoked an uprising, and "Israel has been in rebellion against the house of David to this day" (2 Chron. 10:6–19; quotations at vv. 11, 19). Rehoboam's reign destroyed Israel's unity: "He did evil, for he did not set his heart to seek the Lord" (2 Chron. 12:14).
12. Dawes, *Journal of Putnam,* 71 (retrospective entry preceding 20 July 1758).
13. Charles Lee, "Narrative," 12. A musket ball had broken two of Lee's ribs, and he was convalescing at Albany when he wrote.
14. Bougainville, *Adventure,* 235 (10 July 1758); 242 (12 July 1758); 264 (12 Aug. 1758). The Latin translates more literally as follows:

Who was the leader? Who was the soldier? What was the spread-out, immense wood?
Behold the sign! Behold the victor! This God, God himself triumphs.

My thanks to Professor Steven Epstein for providing this translation.

15. Ibid., 262 (10–12 Aug. 1758).

16. Ibid., 273–6 (6–12 Sept. 1758). Montcalm had asked to be recalled after the victory of July 8. The unlikelihood of this request being granted made him despair of his chances to stave off the British in the coming year. Something of his state of mind can be deduced from the chimerical plan he began to formulate in the fall of 1758. Thinking of the *Anabasis* of Xenophon, he resolved to resist the expected invasion of the St. Lawrence Valley, then to retreat westward at the head of as many regulars and *troupes de la marine* as he could save. After acquiring what support and provisions he could in the Illinois Country, he would descend the Mississippi and make his last stand in Louisiana. See Francis Parkman, *France and England in North America,* vol. 2, *Montcalm and Wolfe* (New York, 1983), 1313, 1317–18.

CHAPTER TWENTY-FIVE: *Amherst at Louisbourg*

1. "A rash . . . attempt": Wolfe to Maj. Walter Wolfe, 27 July 1758, in Beckles Willson, *The Life and Letters of James Wolfe* (New York, 1909), 384–5. As usual Wolfe was trying to minimize the credit due to his superior officer and to emphasize his own role. British prepare for siege: Amherst to Pitt, 11 June 1758, in Gertrude Selwyn Kimball, ed., *The Correspondence of William Pitt when Secretary of State with Colonial Governors and Military and Naval Commissioners in America* (1906; reprint, New York, 1969), 1:274; also map, "The Landing on Cape Breton Island . . . 1758," in Lawrence Henry Gipson, *The British Empire before the American Revolution,* vol. 7, *The Great War for the Empire: The Victorious Years, 1758–1760* (New York, 1967), facing 195. For a complete account, see J. Mackay Hitsman and C. C. J. Bond, "The Assault Landing at Louisbourg, 1758," *Canadian Historical Review* 35 (1954): 314–30. The British lost fifty dead (the majority drowned), sixty-two wounded, one missing; the French lost a hundred killed and seventy captured.

2. Louisbourg's defenses: Christopher Moore, *Louisbourg Portraits* (Toronto, 1982), 209–15. Disposition of defenders in 1758: Gipson, *Victorious Years,* 198–201. On Amherst's role in the siege, see Daniel John Beattie, "General Jeffery Amherst and the Conquest of Canada, 1758–1760" (Ph.D. diss., Duke University, 1976), 66–90. For the naval vessels in the harbor, a formidable force including six line-of-battle ships and five frigates, see Boscawen to Pitt, 28 July 1758, *Pitt Corr.,* 1:308.

3. Moore, *Louisbourg Portraits,* 215.

4. This account of the siege follows Gipson, *Victorious Years,* 197–207; Amherst to Pitt, 11 and 23 June, 6 July, 23 July, and 27 July 1758, in *Pitt Corr.*, 1:271–5, 281–4, 291–3, 303–7; and Boscawen to Pitt, 28 July 1758, ibid., 307–9.

5. Beattie, "Amherst," 83. Since the landings, the British had lost just 172 dead and 354 sick or wounded; naval casualties numbered approximately 50.

6. "Journal of the Proceedings of the Fleet," quoted in Gipson, *Victorious Years,* 196 n. 109.

7. Wolfe to Maj. Walter Wolfe, 27 July 1758, *Life and Letters of Wolfe,* 385.

8. Beattie, "Amherst," 85–6.

CHAPTER TWENTY-SIX: *Supply Holds the Key*

1. Boscawen's task force: Daniel John Beattie, "General Jeffery Amherst and the Conquest of Canada, 1758–1760" (Ph.D. diss., Duke University, 1976), 66; Lawrence Henry Gipson, *The British Empire before the American Revolution,* vol. 7, *The Great War for the Empire: The Victorious Years, 1758–1760* (New York, 1967), 180–5. Osborne and Hawke: ibid., 188–90; Julian S. Corbett, *England in the Seven Years' War: A Study in Combined Strategy,* vol. 1 (London, 1918), 258–62. Effectiveness of British naval interdiction: Ian K. Steele, *Warpaths: Invasions of North America* (New York, 1994), 210–11. Most of the British navy's achievement owed to its effec-

tiveness in breaking up convoys and blockading ports, but one of Osborne's captains fought the most spectacular single-ship action of the war in the Mediterranean off Cartagena. On 28 May 1758, H.M.S. *Monmouth,* a fast sixty-four–gun line-of-battle ship, chased and eventually closed to pistol-shot range with the far more powerful *Foudroyant,* an eighty-gun vessel. In a bloody four-hour engagement the *Monmouth* shot away two of its opponent's masts and forced her commander to surrender. This action fascinated contemporaries because the *Foudroyant* had been Admiral Galissonière's flagship in Byng's defeat off Minorca two years before; the *Monmouth*'s captain, Arthur Gardiner, Byng's flag captain in that action, engaged the heavily armed French vessel to wipe the stain of Minorca off his reputation; and the officer who surrendered the *Foudroyant* to Gardiner's lieutenant (Gardiner having been killed in the fight) was Admiral Ange de Menneville, marquis de Duquesne. The British repaired the *Foudroyant,* which became one of the Royal Navy's most celebrated vessels. Duquesne's defeat seriously damaged morale at Versailles even as it fanned British public enthusiasm for the war effort.

2. Gipson, *Victorious Years,* 247–60.

CHAPTER TWENTY-SEVEN: *Bradstreet at Fort Frontenac*

1. On Bradstreet generally, see William G. Godfrey, *Pursuit of Profit and Preferment in Colonial North America: John Bradstreet's Quest* (Waterloo, Ont., 1982); also the same author's entry in *Dictionary of Canadian Biography,* vol. 4, s.v. "Bradstreet, John." John Shy expresses similar views of Bradstreet's energy and a less favorable assessment of his character in *Toward Lexington: The Role of the British Army in the Coming of the American Revolution* (Princeton, N.J., 1965), 169–71. For his career before 1758, see Godfrey, *Pursuit,* 21–6, 50–1, 58–9; Stanley M. Pargellis, ed., *Military Affairs in North America, 1748–1765: Documents from the Cumberland Papers in Windsor Castle* (1966; reprint, New York, 1969), 187–8 ("bridel" quotation at n. 2); and Francis Jennings, *Empire of Fortune: Crowns, Colonies, and Tribes in the Seven Years War in America* (New York, 1988), 365–6. Bradstreet's advancement owed much to Shirley, whose plan to conquer Louisbourg depended on Bradstreet's unusually precise knowledge of the fortress. Bradstreet had come by that knowledge by supplying relatives on his mother's side of the family with English goods to sell in the city. For a regular officer to trade illegally with a foreign colony was of course frowned upon, and Bradstreet's English patron soon advised him to "Knock off" lest he ruin his career. Typically, Bradstreet did not knock off until war was imminent (Godfrey, *Pursuit,* 15–20; quotation from King Gould to Bradstreet, 15 Mar. 1742, at 17).

2. Bradstreet to Sir Richard Lyttleton, 15 Aug. and 5 Sept. 1757 in Stanley M. Pargellis, *Lord Loudoun in North America* (1933; reprint, Hamden, Conn., 1968), 342 n. 14; Godfrey, *Pursuit,* 99–110. Bradstreet could offer to fund the expedition privately because his post as quartermaster general had given him access to excellent lines of credit in the Albany merchant community, and he was never excessively scrupulous about separating private from public business; moreover, he did nothing to conceal the fact that Fort Frontenac's stocks of peltry and trade goods made it the richest prize in the interior.

3. Abercromby's orders, quoted in Lawrence Henry Gipson, *The British Empire before the American Revolution,* vol. 7, *The Great War for the Empire: The Victorious Years, 1758–1760* (New York, 1967), 238–9.

4. Ibid., 239.

5. Ibid., 240; Jennings, *Empire of Fortune,* 366; Godfrey, *Pursuit,* 126; George F. G. Stanley, *New France: The Last Phase, 1744–1760* (Toronto, 1968), 183. Quotation: [John Bradstreet], *An Impartial Account of Lieutenant Colonel Bradstreet's Expedition to Fort Frontenac, to which are added a few reflections on the conduct of that Enterprize,* ed. E. C. Kyte (Toronto, 1940), 15.

6. Stanley, *New France,* 185; Gipson, *Victorious Years,* 243.

7. *Dictionary of Canadian Biography,* vol. 4, s.v. "Payen de Noyan et de Chavoy, Pierre-

Jacques"; Godfrey, *Pursuit,* 129–30. (Because the flag of France under the Bourbons was white, French officers typically called for a truce with red.)

8. "Uncrediable": Capt. Thomas Sowers's account, quoted in Douglas Edward Leach, *Arms for Empire: A Military History of the British Colonies in North America, 1607–1763* (New York, 1973), 436–7. "The stores": Benjamin Bass, "Account of the Capture of Fort Frontenac by the Detachment under the Command of Col. Bradstreet," *New York History* 16 (1935): 450 (entry of 17 Aug. 1758). "The garrison made no scruple": Bradstreet to Abercromby, 31 Oct. 1758, "The Expedition to . . . Fort Frontenac in 1758," *Colonial Wars* 1 (1914): 210 n. Bradstreet estimated that the goods divided at Fort Bull amounted to less than "the one fourth part of what were burnt" in the destruction of the fort (*Impartial Account,* 25–6).

9. Expected reinforcements and demolition of fort: ibid., 22. Division of spoils: Godfrey, *Pursuit,* 130–1. Bradstreet was entitled to claim a quarter of the plunder, in which case an equal amount would have been divided among the officers, and the remaining half would have gone to the men. Thus he forwent about eight thousand pounds sterling, a remarkable act in a man not normally indifferent to money, but explicable by his own admission that he did it "to encourage the people" (id. to Charles Gould, 21 Sept. 1758, ibid.). Bradstreet had promised his soldiers equal shares at the outset and understood their contractualist views well enough to know that to stint their share would be to invite mutiny and tarnish an achievement from which he hoped his reputation—and his career—would benefit.

10. "To abandon their settlements": *Impartial Account,* 29. Abercromby demurs: Godfrey, *Pursuit,* 133.

11. "Had any one measure": *Impartial Account,* 29–30. "Blunders": Charles Lee to Miss Sidney Lee, 16 Sept. 1758, New-York Historical Society, *Collections* 4 (1871): 7–8.

CHAPTER TWENTY-EIGHT: *Indian Diplomacy and the Fall of Fort Duquesne*

1. On Johnson's lack of help and Forbes's intention to rely instead on Cherokee scouts, see Forbes to Abercromby, 22 Apr. 1758, in Alfred Procter James, ed., *Writings of General John Forbes Relating to His Service in North America* (Menasha, Wis., 1938), 69. Forbes's cousin, James Glen, governor of South Carolina from 1743 through 1756, had pursued diplomatic ties with the Cherokee; retiring as governor, he had stayed on as a merchant and used his contacts to obtain warriors for Forbes (see Tom Hatley, *The Dividing Paths: Cherokees and South Carolinians through the Era of Revolution* [New York, 1993], 69–79). Difficulties in coping with Indians: Forbes to Pitt, 19 May 1758, *Writings of Forbes,* 92; Forbes to Abercromby, 7 June 1758, ibid., 109. "A very great plague": Forbes to Henry Bouquet, 10 June 1758, ibid., 112. Alienation of Cherokees: Hatley, *Dividing Paths,* 102.

2. "He has the Publick Faith": Forbes to Denny, 3 May 1758, *Writings of Forbes,* 81–2. "A Treaty on foot": Francis Halkett to Washington, 4 May 1758, in W. W. Abbot et al., eds., *The Papers of George Washington, Colonial Series,* vol. 5, October 1757–September 1758 (Charlottesville, Va., 1988), 164. The Iroquois had not forwarded peace belts from the Pennsylvania government to the Ohio tribes, nor had Sir William Johnson pressed them to do so. This made perfect sense: the Confederacy had no interest in allowing the Ohio peoples to treat directly with the English, while Johnson's diplomatic position (like his future as a speculator in western lands) depended on preserving the Covenant Chain alliance system.

3. Francis Jennings, *Empire of Fortune: Crowns, Colonies, and Tribes in the Seven Years War in America* (New York, 1988), 384.

4. Forbes requests permission: id. to Abercromby, 27 June and 9 July 1758, *Writings of Forbes,* 126–8, 134–40 (Abercromby granted Forbes authority to conduct independent negotiations on 23 July; see endorsement, ibid., 140). Diplomatic success: Theodore Thayer, *Israel Pemberton, King of the Quakers* (Philadelphia, 1943), 155–7; Jennings, *Empire of Fortune,* 393–4; Anthony F. C. Wallace, *King of the Delawares: Teedyuscung, 1700–1763* (Philadelphia, 1949), 191; Richard

White, *The Middle Ground: Indians, Empires, and Republics in the Great Lakes Region, 1650–1815* (New York, 1991), 250; Michael N. McConnell, *A Country Between: The Upper Ohio Valley and Its Peoples, 1724–1774* (Lincoln, Nebr., 1992), 129–30. Pisquetomen's companion, Keekyuscung, was an important counselor.

5. On Post, see *Dictionary of American Biography*, s.v. "Post, Christian Frederick." He encountered two Frenchmen near Venango on 7 Aug.; see "The Journal of Christian Frederick Post, from Philadelphia to the Ohio, on a Message from the Government of Pennsylvania to the Delawares, Shawnese, and Mingo Indians, Settled There," in Reuben Gold Thwaites, ed., *Early Western Travels*, vol. 1 (Cleveland, 1904), 191.

6. "Journal of Post," 18–19 Aug. and 1 Sept. 1758, in Thwaites, *Travels*, 1:198–9, 213–17.

7. "It is plain": ibid., 214. "We long for that peace": 3 Sept. 1758, ibid., 218–20.

8. 8–22 Sept. 1758, ibid., 226–33; Jennings, *Empire of Fortune*, 396.

9. There is no detailed record of Post's encounter with Forbes. I have constructed this account from Forbes to Pitt, 6 Sept. 1758; to Denny, 9 Sept. 1758; to Washington, 16 Sept. 1758; to Horatio Sharpe, 16 Sept. 1758; to Bouquet, 17 Sept. 1758; to Abercromby, 21 Sept. 1758; to Bouquet, 23 Sept. 1758; and Francis Halkett to Sharpe, 30 Sept. 1758; all in *Writings of Forbes*, 210–22.

10. Forbes to Bouquet, 23 Sept. 1758, ibid., 218–19.

11. Forbes to Abercromby, 21 Sept. 1758, ibid., 215–16; Grant to Forbes, n.d. [c. 14 Sept. 1758], in Sylvester K. Stevens and Donald H. Kent, eds., *The Papers of Col. Henry Bouquet*, ser. 21652 (Harrisburg, Pa., 1940), 130–5.

12. Forbes to Bouquet, 23 Sept. 1758, *Writings of Forbes*, 218–19.

13. Forbes to Abercromby, 8 and 16 Oct. 1758, ibid., 227, 234.

14. Forbes to Richard Peters, 16 Oct. 1758, ibid., 234–7. I have interpolated the phrase "all the Waggoners . . . as brave as Lyons" from a letter Forbes wrote to Abercromby the same day; ibid., 234.

15. The following account of the Easton congress has been drawn from the versions in Thayer, *Pemberton*, 162–70; Stephen F. Auth, *Ten Years' War: Indian-White Relations in Pennsylvania, 1755–1765* (New York, 1989), 90–108; Jennings, *Empire of Fortune*, 396–404; Nicholas B. Wainwright, *George Croghan, Wilderness Diplomat* (Chapel Hill, N.C., 1959), 145–51; and Wallace, *Teedyuscung*, 192–207.

16. Teedyuscung's speech quoted in Wallace, *Teedyuscung*, 206; spelling of "Bough" altered for clarity, from original "Bow."

17. King quoted in Jennings, *Empire of Fortune*, 400.

18. Thayer, *Pemberton*, 168 n. 27.

19. Denny's message to the Ohio tribes, quoted in Jennings, *Empire of Fortune*, 403.

20. Wallace, *Teedyuscung*, 239–40; Thayer, *Pemberton*, 169.

21. "One of the worst": "Journal of Christian Frederick Post, on a Message from the Governor of Pennsylvania, to the Indians of the Ohio, in the Latter Part of the Same Year [1758]," in Thwaites, *Travels*, 1:241–2 (hereafter cited as "Second Journal of Post"), quotation from entry of 6 Nov. 1758. "I embrace this opportunity": Forbes to the Shawanese [*sic*] and Delawares on the Ohio, 9 Nov. 1758, *Writings of Forbes*, 251–2; see also id. to Kings Beaver [Tamaqua] and Shingas, 9 Nov. 1758, 252–3.

22. Hostile reception at Kuskuski: "Second Journal of Post," 253, 254, quoted from entries of 19 and 20 Nov. 1758. "The *Indians* concern themselves": 23 Nov. 1758, ibid., 258.

23. 29 Nov. 1758, "Second Journal of Post," 278. "Ketiushund" was Keekyuscung, Pisquetomen's companion in the Delawares' diplomatic mission of early July; when he spoke to Post, therefore, his words carried more than casual weight.

24. 3–4 Dec. 1758, "Second Journal of Post," 281–3; Charles Morse Stotz, *Outposts of the War for Empire* (Pittsburgh, 1985), 121–5.

25. *Dictionary of Canadian Biography*, vol. 3, s.v. "Le Marchand de Lignery, François-Marie." Reductions in Fort Duquesne's garrison: Vaudreuil to the minister of marine, 20 Jan. 1759, in

Sylvester K. Stevens and Donald H. Kent, eds., *Wilderness Chronicles of Western Pennsylvania* (Harrisburg, Pa., 1941), 126–31.

26. Account of raid and mistaken identity: Forbes to Abercromby, 17 Nov. 1758, *Writings of Forbes,* quotations at 255–6; also Lawrence Henry Gipson, *The British Empire before the American Revolution,* vol. 7, *The Great War for the Empire: The Victorious Years, 1758–1760* (New York, 1967), 282. Washington did not describe the episode in his contemporary correspondence but later recalled that he tried to stop the firing by "knocking up with his sword the presented pieces" (David Humphrey's notes toward a biography of Washington, quoted in W. W. Abbot et al., eds., *Papers of George Washington, Colonial Series,* vol. 6 [Charlottesville, Va., 1988], 122 n. 1). Another contemporary account, however, suggests that "Colonel Washington did not discover his usual activity and presence of mind upon this occasion," and that Capt. Thomas Bullitt stopped the firing by running "between the two parties, waving his hat and calling to them." "This censure . . . gave rise to a resentment in the mind of General Washington which never subsided" (Quoted from William Marshall Bullitt, *My Life at Oxmoor,* 3–4, in *Papers of Washington,* 6:123 n. 1).

27. General Orders and Brigade Orders, 14–15 Nov. 1758, *Papers of Washington* 6:125–9; Gipson, *Victorious Years,* 283.

28. 20 Nov. 1758, "Second Journal of Post," 255–6.

29. Vaudreuil to the minister of marine, 20 Jan. 1759, in Kent and Stevens, *Wilderness Chronicles,* 128–9.

30. Forbes to Abercromby and Amherst, 26–30 Nov. 1758, *Writings of Forbes,* 263.

31. Quotations from Forbes to Amherst, 26 Jan. and 7 Feb. 1759, *Writings of Forbes,* 283, 289. See also Forbes to Amherst, 18 Jan. 1759, 282–3.

32. James Grant to Bouquet, 20 Feb. 1759, ibid., 300. *Per tot discrimina:* Through so many dangers; *Ohio Britannica Consilio manuque:* By force and resolve, Britain [seized] the Ohio. (My thanks to Professor Steven Epstein for translating this inscription.)

33. Forbes's obituary, *Pennsylvania Gazette,* 15 Mar. 1759.

CHAPTER TWENTY-NINE: *Educations in Arms*

1. I have argued the following points at greater length in *A People's Army: Massachusetts Soldiers and Society in the Seven Years' War* (Chapel Hill, N.C., 1984), esp. 65–164 and 196–223. In the following paragraphs specific citations will be made only to direct quotations.

2. Rowena Buell, ed., *The Memoirs of Rufus Putnam* (Boston, 1903), 25 (entry of 9 July 1758).

3. Fabius Maximus Ray, ed., *The Journal of Dr. Caleb Rea, Written during the Expedition against Ticonderoga in 1758* (Salem, Mass., 1881), 36–7 (entry of 25 July 1758). Punishments other than flogging were commonplace and often applied at the company level without benefit of court-martial proceedings. In roughly escalating order of severity, the most common company punishments were the wheel, the mare, the gauntlet, the picket, and laying neck and heels. A man bound to the wheel would be spread-eagled across a wagon wheel for a day or longer: thirst, hunger, loss of sleep, and the humiliation of fouling himself publicly were the intended results. To ride the mare, or the wooden horse, was to be made to straddle the spine formed by boards nailed together in an inverted V. Muskets might be tied to the subject's ankles to increase his discomfort; the punishment might last from several minutes to more than an hour. A man subjected to the gauntlet would be forced to walk shirtless between parallel lines of men (usually the members of his company) armed with musket ramrods; each would give him a blow on the back as he passed. The victim's pace would be controlled by another man walking backward ahead of him and carrying a musket with bayonet fixed and pointed at his chest. To be picketed, a man would first have his shoes removed, then have his left wrist bound to his right ankle, and then be hoisted on a gallows by a rope tied around his right wrist. A sharpened stake, or picket, would be set beneath him. If the punishment was prolonged, the only way the victim could prevent his arm from being dislocated was to stand on the point of the picket with his bare foot. The most severe of the informal punishments

was to be laid (or tied) neck and heels: a man with hands tied would have a noose slipped around his neck, the other end of which would be tied about his ankles and tightened to arch his back, drawing neck and heels toward one another. A man might be left in this position of semistrangulation for an hour or more. Although laying neck and heels remained in the range of customary punishments through the whole of the eighteenth century, it was seldom practiced during the Seven Years' War because it too often resulted in the death of expensive, hard-to-replace soldiers.

4. "Extracts from Gibson Clough's Journal," *Essex Institute Historical Collections* 3 (1861): 104 (entry for 30 Sept. 1759).

5. "Obstinate and Ungovernable": Lieut. Alexander Johnson to Loudoun, 20 Dec. 1756, quoted in Douglas Edward Leach, *Roots of Conflict: British Armed Forces and Colonial Americans, 1677–1763* (Chapel Hill, N.C., 1986), 130–1. "Dirtiest most contemptible": James Wolfe to Lord George Sackville, 30 July 1758, in Beckles Willson, *The Life and Letters of James Wolfe* (New York, 1909), 392.

6. Anderson, *A People's Army,* 58–62; Harold Selesky, *War and Society in Colonial Connecticut* (New Haven, Conn., 1990), 166–70. Selesky, in the most complete study to date of a colonial military system, estimates that 60 percent of the eligible men served in the Connecticut forces during the war; my own earlier estimate that 40 percent of the eligible men in Massachusetts served was based on scrappier evidence and was intended to be as conservative as possible. In fact, participation in Massachusetts probably equaled that of Connecticut.

7. Washington to Francis Fauquier, 9 Dec. 1758, and Christopher Hardwick to Washington, 12 Dec. 1758, in W. W. Abbot et al., eds., *The Papers of George Washington, Colonial Series,* vol. 6, September 1758–December 1760 (Charlottesville, Va., 1988), 165–7.

8. Douglas Southall Freeman, *George Washington: A Biography,* vol. 2, *Young Washington* (New York, 1948), 301–2, 316–21.

9. Don Higginbotham, *George Washington and the American Military Tradition* (Athens, Ga., 1985), 15; Freeman, *Young Washington,* 368–99.

10. Washington to Bouquet, 6 Nov. 1758, *Papers of Washington,* 6:116.

PART V: *ANNUS MIRABILIS,* 1759

CHAPTER THIRTY:
Success, Anxiety, and Power: The Ascent of William Pitt

1. John C. Webster, ed., *Journal of William Amherst in America, 1758–1760* (London, 1927), 33–4.

2. Horace Walpole, *Memoirs of the Reign of King George II* (London, 1846), 3:134.

3. Quotation: Walpole to George Montagu, 21 Oct. 1759, in Paget Toynbee, ed., *The Letters of Horace Walpole, Fourth Earl of Orford,* vol. 4 (Oxford, 1903), 314. News of Ticonderoga: Stanley Ayling, *The Elder Pitt, Earl of Chatham* (New York, 1976), 233–4; Peter Douglas Brown, *William Pitt, Earl of Chatham: The Great Commoner* (London, 1978), 179. News of Forts Frontenac and Duquesne: see Pitt to Amherst, 23 Jan. 1759, in Gertrude Selwyn Kimball, ed., *Correspondence of William Pitt when Secretary of State with Colonial Governors and Military and Naval Commissioners in America* (1906; reprint, New York, 1969), 2:12. (Pitt learned of Duquesne's fall on 19 Jan.)

4. Richard Middleton, *The Bells of Victory: The Pitt-Newcastle Ministry and the Conduct of the Seven Years' War, 1757–1762* (Cambridge, U.K., 1986), 62–3; Lawrence Henry Gipson, *The British Empire before the American Revolution,* vol. 7, *The Great War for the Empire: The Victorious Years, 1758–1760* (New York, 1967), 129–30; Russell Weigley, *The Age of Battles: The Quest for Decisive Warfare from Breitenfeld to Waterloo* (Bloomington, Ind., 1991), 180–8; Dennis Showalter, *The Wars of Frederick the Great* (London, 1996), 207–8.

5. Julian S. Corbett, *England in the Seven Years' War: A Study in Combined Strategy,* vol. 2 (London, 1918), 233–53; Showalter, *Wars of Frederick,* 208.

6. Julian S. Corbett, *England in the Seven Years' War: A Study in Combined Strategy,* vol. 1 (London, 1918), 271–281, 286.
7. Reginald Savory, *His Britannic Majesty's Army in Germany during the Seven Years' War* (Oxford, 1966), 86, 460–1.
8. Annual expenses: Middleton, *Bells,* 92. Strategic situation at the end of 1758: Savory, *Army,* 112–15.
9. Weigley, *Age of Battles,* 188–90; Showalter, *Wars of Frederick,* 212–30.
10. Corbett, *Seven Years' War,* 1:286–304; Middleton, *Bells,* 81–2.
11. Newcastle's financial anxieties: Middleton, *Bells,* 88–90; Reed Browning, "The Duke of Newcastle and the Financing of the Seven Years' War," *Journal of Economic History* 31 (1971): 344–77. Newcastle's loyalty, and Pitt's growing regard: id., *The Duke of Newcastle* (New Haven, Conn., 1975), 261–2, 268.
12. Walpole, *Memoirs of George II,* 3:185.
13. Ayling, *Elder Pitt,* 232; on the king's blindness and loss of hearing, see Charles Chenevix Trench, *George II* (London, 1973), 292.
14. George, prince of Wales, to the earl of Bute, c. 8 Dec. 1758, in Romney Sedgwick, ed., *Letters from George III to Lord Bute, 1756–1766* (London, 1939), 18.
15. On the character of British military institutions, see Sylvia Frey, "British Armed Forces and the American Victory," in John Ferling, ed., *The World Turned Upside Down: The American Victory in the War of Independence* (New York, 1988), esp. 167–70.
16. On Barrington, see Lewis M. Wiggin, *The Faction of Cousins: A Political Account of the Grenvilles, 1733–1763* (New Haven, Conn., 1958), 299–300; and John Shy, *Toward Lexington: The Role of the British Army in the Coming of the American Revolution* (Princeton, N.J., 1965), 223–4, 231–50, 365–70. Pitt disliked Barrington for his connections to Halifax and thus to the Bedford Whigs; dealing directly with Anson and Ligonier offered a way to avoid dealing with him.
17. Savory (*Army,* 88–9) suggests that Ferdinand decided to go on the defensive between 14 and 24 July when it was clear that his opponents far outnumbered him and that his own strength was largely spent.
18. On Cumming and the expedition, see James L. A. Webb Jr., "The Mid-Eighteenth Century Gum Arabic Trade and the British Conquest of Saint-Louis du Sénégal, 1758," *Journal of Imperial and Commonwealth History* 25 (1997): 37–58, the most complete account; also Lawrence Henry Gipson, *The British Empire before the American Revolution,* vol. 8, *The Great War for the Empire: The Culmination, 1760–1763* (New York, 1970), 174–7; and Ayling, *Elder Pitt,* 193–4, 224, 238. On the economic impact of the venture, see John J. McCusker, *Rum and the American Revolution: The Rum Trade and the Balance of Payments of the Thirteen Continental Colonies* (New York, 1989), 2:1144–6 (table E-45); and id. and Russell Menard, *The Economy of Colonial British America* (Chapel Hill, N.C., 1985), 158, fig. 7.1.
19. Beckford to Pitt, 11 Sept. 1758, quoted in Gipson, *Culmination,* 84.
20. On Martinique's exports, see McCusker, *Rum and Revolution,* 1:143–4, 329 (tables 4-2 and 5-2). On Martinique's significance as a privateering base, see J. K. Eyre, "The Naval History of Martinique," U.S. Naval Institute, *Proceedings* 68 (1942): 1115–24. Most of the fourteen hundred Anglo-American ships taken in the West Indies during the war were lost to privateers operating out of Martinique.
21. On the strength and organization of the expedition, see Marshall Smelser, *The Campaign for the Sugar Islands: A Study in Amphibious Warfare* (Chapel Hill, N.C., 1955), 16–27. On Anson's fears, see Middleton, *Bells,* 87. Financial burdens: Ayling, *Elder Pitt,* 242; Gipson, *Victorious Years,* 289; Middleton, *Bells,* 113; John Brewer, *The Sinews of Power: War, Money, and the English State, 1688–1783* (New York, 1989), 117 (fig. 4.7). Quotation: Walpole to Horace Mann, 25 Dec. and 27 Nov. 1758, in W. S. Lewis, ed., *The Yale Edition of Horace Walpole's Correspondence,* vol. 21, *Horace Walpole's Correspondence with Sir Horace Mann* (New Haven, Conn., 1958), 261, 257.

22. Diplomatic and naval initiatives: Middleton, *Bells,* 96, 108–11. Army and militia: J. R. Western, *The English Militia in the Eighteenth Century: The Story of a Political Issue, 1660–1802* (London, 1965), 135–61; also see Eliga Gould, *Persistence of Empire: British Political Culture in the Age of the American Revolution* (Chapel Hill, N.C., forthcoming), chap. 3, for the riskiness of the decision to rely on the militia, which had provoked resistance and even riots in 1757 among men unwilling to be pressed into militia service.
23. Pitt to the governors of Mass. Bay, N.H., Conn., R.I., N.Y., N.J., 9 Dec. 1758, *Pitt Corr.,* 1:414–16; id. to the governors of Pa., Md., Va., N.C., S.C., 9 Dec. 1758, 417–20.
24. "A Memorandum of Orders Sent to General Amherst," 9 Dec. 1758–23 Jan. 1759, ibid., 426–7; quotation, Pitt to Amherst, 29 Dec. 1758, ibid., 433.
25. Daniel John Beattie, "General Jeffery Amherst and the Conquest of Canada, 1758–1760" (Ph.D. diss., Duke University, 1976), 135.
26. "No objection": Wolfe to Pitt, 22 Nov. 1758, in Beckles Willson, *The Life and Letters of James Wolfe* (New York, 1909), 400. The suggestion that Pitt found in Wolfe a kindred spirit is a virtual commonplace, although nowhere documented directly: see, e.g., J. H. Plumb, *Chatham* (New York, 1965), 75; Simon Schama, *Dead Certainties (Unwarranted Speculations)* (New York, 1991), 15.

CHAPTER THIRTY-ONE: *Ministerial Uncertainties*

1. Richard Middleton, *The Bells of Victory: The Pitt-Newcastle Ministry and the Conduct of the Seven Years' War, 1757–1762* (Cambridge, U.K., 1985), 115–16; J. R. Western, *The English Militia in the Eighteenth Century: The Story of a Political Issue, 1660–1802* (London, 1965), 154.
2. On Martinique, see Marshall Smelser, *The Campaign for the Sugar Islands: A Study in Amphibious Warfare* (Chapel Hill, N.C., 1955), 39–65; Lawrence Henry Gipson, *The British Empire before the American Revolution,* vol. 8, *The Great War for the Empire: The Culmination, 1760–1763* (New York, 1970), 88–94; and Julian S. Corbett, *England in the Seven Years' War: A Study in Combined Strategy,* vol. 1 (London, 1918), 378–80.
3. Hopson's frailty: Gipson, *Culmination,* 86–7; *Dictionary of Canadian Biography,* vol. 3, s.v. "Hopson, Peregrine Thomas." Expedition stalls at Basse-Terre: Smelser, *Campaign,* 75–102; Gipson, *Culmination,* 98–101; Corbett, *Seven Years' War,* 1:380–1. Hopson was evidently about seventy-five years old at the time of his appointment, which came at the direction of the king.
4. Smelser, *Campaign,* 113–20; Gipson, *Culmination,* 101–2; Corbett, *Seven Years' War,* 1:382–5.
5. Middleton, *Bells,* 115–20; Western, *Militia,* 154–6; Rex Whitworth, *Field Marshal Lord Ligonier: A Story of the British Army, 1702–1770* (Oxford, 1958), 297; Reginald Savory, *His Britannic Majesty's Army in Germany during the Seven Years' War* (Oxford, 1966), 118–50.
6. The earl of Holdernesse, 17 May 1759, cited in Western, *Militia,* 156.
7. Middleton, *Bells,* 120; Smelser, *Campaign,* 127–43; Gipson, *Culmination,* 102–3; Richard Pares, *War and Trade in the West Indies, 1739–1763* (Oxford, 1936), 186–95.
8. Smelser, *Campaign,* 113–15, 143–7.
9. Gipson, *Culmination,* 94–5; John J. McCusker, *Rum and the American Revolution: The Rum Trade and the Balance of Payments of the Thirteen Continental Colonies* (New York, 1989), 2:707 (table B-99).
10. Stanley Ayling, *The Elder Pitt, Earl of Chatham* (New York, 1976), 239; McCusker, *Rum and Revolution,* 2:924 (table D-20). On slave imports, see ibid., 673 (table B-70). Exports to the mainland: Pares, *War and Trade,* 488 n.

CHAPTER THIRTY-TWO: *Surfeit of Enthusiasm, Shortage of Resources*

1. Pitt to Barrington, 7 July 1759, in Gertrude Selwyn Kimball, ed., *Correspondence of William Pitt when Secretary of State with Colonial Governors and Military and Naval Commissioners in America* (1906; reprint, New York, 1969), 2:137.
2. Chests of coin arrive at Boston: Lawrence Henry Gipson, *The British Empire before the American Revolution,* vol. 7, *The Great War for the Empire: The Victorious Years, 1758–1760* (New

York, 1967), 312, 317–8. Default narrowly averted: Thomas Pownall to Pitt, 30 Sept.–2 Oct. 1758, *Pitt Corr.*, 1:358–64. Gipson, *Victorious Years*, 317–8. Military participation and a feared shortage of laborers: *Journals of the House of Representatives of Massachusetts, 1758*, vol. 34 (Boston, 1963), 340, 364, 372, 376 (hereafter cited as *JHRM*). Between a fourth and a third of all men in the prime military age range served in the Massachusetts provincial forces in 1758; a sufficiently concerning fact that on 14 Mar. 1758 a special legislative committee had been formed to determine what the likely impact of such participation would be. The committee felt strongly enough about the issue to set its conclusion in italics. *"[T]he great Scarcity of Labourers, which will be the natural Consequence of so large a Body of Forces as are rais'd and to be rais'd for his Majesty's Service within this Government the present Year,"* the committee found, *"makes it necessary that such as are left be not called off from their Labour"*; they therefore recommended that all men not serving as provincials be excused from militia training during planting and harvest to ensure an adequate labor supply. The House passed the resolution, in an apparently unanimous voice vote, on 23 Mar. 1758.

3. Report on governor's speech, 10 Mar. 1759, *JHRM 1759*, vol. 35 (Boston, 1964), 273; also Pownall to Pitt, 16 Mar. 1759, *Pitt Corr.*, 2:70–3.

4. Address to the governor, 17 Apr. 1759, *JHRM 1759*, 35:336–8.

5. Bounty: ibid., 335. With interest due, the net earnings for a Massachusetts private approximated thirty pounds in province currency, or twenty-two pounds ten shillings sterling—at least double an agricultural laborer's wages for the same period. On contemporary awareness of the consequences of such exceptional wages, see Thomas Hutchinson to Col. Israel Williams, 24 Apr. 1759: "I hope we shall not have occasion hereafter to go into the disagreeable measure of impressing men. The Bounty is extravagant & more than I would vote for on the Committee & will be a bad precedent, at least it appears to me who, I assure you, often think of the deplorable State we must be in if we have no reimbursement" (quoted in Gipson, *Victorious Years*, 321 n. 128). To ensure that the province's subsidy would not be held up, Hutchinson—now the lieutenant governor—personally screened all claims and prepared the paperwork for Parliament.

6. Gov. Thomas Fitch to Pitt, 14 July 1759, *Pitt Corr.*, 2:140; see also same to same, 16 Apr. 1759, ibid., 84–7; see also Harold Selesky, *War and Society in Colonial Connecticut* (New Haven, Conn., 1990), 149 (table 5.1), 150.

7. Gipson, *Victorious Years*, 308–10 (N.J.), 309–10 (N.Y.), 325–8 (N.H.), 313–15 (R.I.). Also see John Russell Bartlett, ed., *Records of the Colony of Rhode Island*, vol. 6 (Providence, 1861), 181, 194, 207, 213–14. Rhode Island's attempt to retain men over the winter reflected the unusual conditions within a colony where as much as a fifth of the male population in the military age range was engaged in privateering and where many merchants were trading heavily with the enemy's West Indies islands. The attractiveness of privateering necessitated paying men over the winter merely to have a claim on their services the following spring; meanwhile anxiety that the British government would punish the colony for its illicit trade made the assembly's merchants eager to avoid giving offense to the commander in chief in point of raising troops. On Rhode Island's trade with the enemy, see esp. Loudoun to Cumberland, 22 June 1757, in Stanley M. Pargellis, ed., *Military Affairs in North America, 1748–1765: Documents from the Cumberland Papers in Windsor Castle* (1936; reprint, New York, 1969), 376.

8. Gipson, *Victorious Years*, 317.

9. Amherst's financial problems: Daniel John Beattie, "General Jeffery Amherst and the Conquest of Canada, 1758–1760" (Ph.D. diss., Duke University, 1976), 133–5. Colonies' willingness to lend money: Gipson, *Victorious Years*, 310. Amherst quotation: id. to De Lancey, 8 July 1759, quoted ibid.

10. Ibid., 290–2, 296–8; Gov. Henry Ellis to Pitt, 12 Feb. and 1 Mar. 1759, *Pitt Corr.*, 2:38–40, 45; Gov. William Henry Lyttleton to Pitt, 26 Mar. and 15 Apr. 1759, ibid., 77, 84.

11. Gipson, *Victorious Years*, 293–6. The Burgesses renewed their offer of a ten-pound bounty and once more filled the ranks with volunteers, including the first substantial numbers of vet-

erans; see James Titus, *The Old Dominion at War: Society, Politics, and Warfare in Late Colonial Virginia* (Columbia, S.C., 1991), 197 n. 23.
12. Gipson, *Victorious Years,* 301–7. In 1760 the Board of Trade and the Privy Council condemned the legislature's action and ordered it to make restitution to the Penn family.
13. That there was real concern about this is clear from the panicky reaction of the Pennsylvania Assembly to the rumor that Byrd was about to be named commandant at Pittsburgh. The assembly hurriedly sent a delegation to Denny to discover whether there was any truth to the reports and to warn him that if there was, the assembly would deny all support for the coming campaign (ibid., 300–1).

CHAPTER THIRTY-THREE: *Emblem of Empire: Fort Pitt and the Indians*

1. Lawrence Henry Gipson, *The British Empire before the American Revolution,* vol. 7, *The Great War for the Empire: The Victorious Years, 1758–1760* (New York, 1967), 300; Nicholas B. Wainwright, *George Croghan, Wilderness Diplomat* (Chapel Hill, N.C., 1959), 160–1.
2. Francis Jennings, *Empire of Fortune: Crowns, Colonies, and Tribes in the Seven Years War in America* (New York, 1988), 411–12; Richard White, *The Middle Ground: Indians, Empires, and Republics in the Great Lakes Region, 1650–1815* (New York, 1991), 255. The raids continued and indeed intensified until May, when a French and Indian party from Venango killed thirty people near Fort Ligonier: one of the deadliest raids of the war in Pennsylvania (Wainwright, *Croghan,* 159).
3. Plan of trade: Eric Hinderaker, "The Creation of the American Frontier: Europeans and Indians in the Ohio River Valley, 1673–1800" (Ph.D. diss., Harvard University, 1991), 312–13, quotations from "An Act for Preventing Abuses in the Indian Trade" (1758). Pemberton and the Pittsburgh trade: John W. Jordan, ed., "James Kenny's 'Journal to ye Westward,' 1758–59," *Pennsylvania Magazine of History and Biography* 37 (1937): 440 (entry of 2 Sept. 1759); Theodore Thayer, *Israel Pemberton, King of the Quakers* (Philadelphia, 1943), 171–4.
4. Hinderaker, "Creation of the Frontier," 316–19; see also Wainwright, *Croghan,* 161–3.
5. Wainwright, *Croghan,* 159–63.
6. Construction of Fort Pitt: Gipson, *Victorious Years,* 340–1 (measurements based on "A Plan of the New Fort at Pitts-Burgh or Du Quesne," facing 340). Cannon and barracks: anonymous letter, 21 Mar. 1760, quoted in Charles Morse Stotz, *Outposts of the War for Empire: The French and English in Western Pennsylvania: Their Armies, Their Forts, Their People, 1749–1764* (Pittsburgh, 1985), 131.
7. "James Kenny's Journal," 433 (entry of 24 July 1759, recounting conversation of 9 July). Comparative sizes of Forts Pitt and Duquesne: Stotz, *Outposts,* 56, 81, 133, 137. All of Fort Duquesne could have been situated comfortably on the parade square in the middle of Fort Pitt, which encompassed 1.3 acres.

CHAPTER THIRTY-FOUR: *The Six Nations Join the Fight: The Siege of Niagara*

1. Amherst to Pitt, 19 June 1759, in Gertrude Selwyn Kimball, ed., *Correspondence of William Pitt when Secretary of State with Colonial Governors and Military and Naval Commissioners in America* (1906; reprint, New York, 1969), 2:124–5; "Prideaux and Johnson Orderly Book," James Sullivan, ed., *The Papers of Sir William Johnson,* vol. 3 (Albany, 1921), 55 (entry of 27 June 1759). Prideaux arrived at Oswego with about four thousand men, having detached about a thousand soldiers (mainly provincials) to garrison the forts at the Carrying Place. He left another thousand at Oswego to hold the river's mouth and to begin constructing a new post, Fort Ontario. Thus when he left for Niagara his force consisted of about two thousand regulars, a thousand provincials, and a thousand Iroquois warriors. For units and dispositions see Lawrence Henry Gipson, *The British Empire before the American Revolution,* vol. 7, *The Great War for the Empire: The Victorious Years, 1758–1760* (New York, 1967), 344; and Daniel John Beattie, "General Jeffery Amherst and the Conquest of Canada, 1758–1760" (Ph.D. diss.,

Duke University, 1976), 143 and app. 2. For the best overall account of the Anglo-American campaign and French defense, see Brian Leigh Dunnigan, *Siege—1759: The Campaign against Niagara* (Youngstown, N.Y., 1996).

2. Mercer to Forbes, 8 Jan. 1759, in Sylvester K. Stevens and Donald H. Kent, eds., *The Papers of Col. Henry Bouquet,* ser. 21655 (Harrisburg, Pa., 1943), 25–6.

3. Francis Jennings, *Empire of Fortune: Crowns, Colonies, and Tribes in the Seven Years War in America* (New York, 1988), 414–15. Quotation: Johnson to Amherst, 16 Feb. 1759, *Johnson Papers,* 3:19. That a delegation of Iroquois approached Johnson is a surmise on my part, based on the episode that Mercer reported from Pittsburgh.

4. See esp. Gregory Evans Dowd, *A Spirited Resistance: The North American Indian Struggle for Unity, 1745–1815* (Baltimore, 1992), 23–46; also Richard White, *The Middle Ground: Indians, Empires, and Republics in the Great Lakes Region, 1650–1815* (New York, 1991), 186–268. That the Iroquois regarded the threat as being of the utmost importance can be read in the number of Indians that accompanied Prideaux to Niagara: to field a thousand warriors was to make something like a total mobilization of the Confederacy's military manpower. In c. 1736 (the only year for which there is anything like a reliable estimate) the Iroquois could muster about eleven hundred warriors; given the slow growth of populations in Iroquoia it would seem unlikely that there were many more than that among the Six Nations in 1759. To send so many men with Prideaux was both an immense commitment and a great risk, since few warriors would have been left to defend the villages of Iroquoia. The Confederacy council could never have countenanced such extreme measures unless a powerful consensus justified it. (On Iroquois populations, see Jennings, *Empire of Fortune,* 31–2.)

5. Prideaux was only forty-one, and a colonel only since Oct. 1758, when he replaced Howe as commandant of the 55th Regiment of Foot; see *Dictionary of National Biography,* s.v. "Prideaux, John." On Niagara, see Charles Morse Stotz, *Outposts of the War for Empire: The French and English in Western Pennsylvania: Their Armies, Their Forts, Their People, 1749–1764* (Pittsburgh, 1985), 71, and esp. Dunnigan, *Siege,* 11–22, 34–44.

6. *Dictionary of Canadian Biography,* vol. 3, s.v. "Pouchot, Pierre." Unless otherwise noted, the account of the siege follows this excellent sketch and the account in Gipson, *Victorious Years,* 347–56.

7. "Bad business": Pouchot, *Memoir upon the Late War in North America, . . . 1755–60,* 11–14 July 1759, quoted in Jennings, *Empire of Fortune,* 417. Besides Gipson's account of the conferences of 11–14 July in *Victorious Years,* 349–51, see Ian K. Steele, *Warpaths: Invasions of North America* (New York, 1994), 216–17, and Dunnigan, *Siege,* 57–60.

8. *Ibid.,* 61–75; *Victorious Years,* 348–9.

9. Ibid., 351–2; Douglas Edward Leach, *Arms for Empire: A Military History of the British Colonies in North America, 1607–1763* (New York, 1973), 455–6; Dunnigan, *Siege,* 77–82.

10. Ibid., 88–93; "floating island": anonymous witness quoted in Gipson, *Victorious Years,* 352.

11. For the most comprehensive account of the engagement at La Belle Famille and the pursuit after the battle, see Dunnigan, *Siege,* 93–8. The *Pennsylvania Gazette,* 23 Aug. 1759, reported that the Iroquois hunted the retreating French through the woods to a "vast Slaughter." Captain Charles Lee of the 44th Foot reported to his sister that Lignery's men "were totally defeated . . . with the entire loss of officers and men, their Indians excepted," and remarked to his uncle that "almost their entire party [was] cut off" (id. to Miss Sidney Lee, 30 July [1759], *The Lee Papers,* vol. 1, New-York Historical Society, *Collections* 4 [1871]: 19; Lee to Sir William Bunbury, 9 Aug. 1759, ibid., 21). Captain James De Lancey, commander of a regular light infantry detachment at the abatis, reported that "Our Indians as soon as they saw the Enemy give way pursued them very briskly and took and killed great numbers of them . . ." (Capt. James De Lancey to Lt. Gov. James De Lancey, 25 July 1759, in E. B. O'Callaghan, ed., *Documents Relative to the Colonial History of the State of New-York,* 15 vols. [Albany, 1856–1887], 7:402). Lignery: see *Dictionary of Canadian Biography,* vol. 3, s.v. "Le Marchand de Lignery, François-Marie"; the author, C. J. Russ, suggests that Lignery died on

28 July. Johnson, however, did not leave Niagara until 4 Aug., at which time Lignery was still alive; see Johnson to Amherst, 9 Aug. 1759, *Johnson Papers,* 3:121.

Joseph Marin de La Malgue (called Marin *fils,* baptized 1719), son of the man to whom Duquesne had assigned the task of building the Ohio forts in 1752; his story is one of those small odysseys that illuminates the nature of eighteenth-century European colonialism. Marin *fils* had spent most of his life as a merchant, government administrator, and officer in the *troupes de la marine,* serving in posts over a huge geographical range, from Minnesota to Acadia. Imprisoned in New York after the battle, he was "repatriated" to France—a country he had never seen—in 1762. After failing to establish himself there he eventually participated in the attempt to establish a colony in Madagascar, where he died in 1774 (*Dictionary of Canadian Biography,* vol. 4, s.v. "Marin de la Malgue, Joseph").

12. Johnson to Amherst, 31 July 1759, *Johnson Papers,* 3:115.

13. "Settling an Alliance": ibid. Amherst sends Gage to take command: Amherst to Johnson, 6 Aug. 1759, ibid., 3:118–20.

CHAPTER THIRTY-FIVE: *General Amherst Hesitates: Ticonderoga and Crown Point*

1. News of Niagara's fall: see Amherst to Johnson, 6 Aug. 1759, in James Sullivan, ed., *The Papers of Sir William Johnson,* vol. 3 (New York, 1921), 118. The campaign to date: Daniel John Beattie, "Sir Jeffery Amherst and the Conquest of Canada, 1758–1760" (Ph.D. diss., Duke University, 1976), 137–63; on Bradstreet's role, see William G. Godfrey, *Pursuit of Profit and Preferment in Colonial North America: John Bradstreet's Quest* (Waterloo, Ont., 1982), 142–52.

2. Lawrence Henry Gipson, *The British Empire before the American Revolution,* vol. 7, *The Great War for the Empire: The Victorious Years, 1758–1760* (New York, 1967) 361–4; *Dictionary of Canadian Biography,* vol. 3, s.v. "Bourlamaque, François-Charles de"; Beattie, "Amherst," 153–9, 164.

3. "Great Post": Amherst's journal, quoted in Beattie, "Amherst," 164. Estimate of strategic situation: Amherst to Pitt, 22 Oct. 1759, a journal letter recounting developments from 6 Aug. onward; see esp. entries of 6–18 Aug. (Gertrude Selwyn Kimball, ed., *Correspondence of William Pitt when Secretary of State with Colonial Governors and Military and Naval Commissioners in America* [1906; reprint, New York, 1969], 2:186–90). On 1 Sept. Amherst ordered a third vessel built, the *Boscawen,* to counter a new sixteen-gun French sloop. This necessitated a new sawmill and further delays. Rufus Putnam supervised the mill's construction (Beattie, "Amherst," 161; E. C. Dawes, ed., *Journal of Gen. Rufus Putnam, Kept in Northern New York during Four Campaigns of the Old French and Indian War, 1757–1760* [Albany, 1886], 91 [entries of 26 July–4 Aug. 1759]; Rowena Buell, ed., *The Memoirs of Rufus Putnam* [Boston, 1903], 26–8).

4. Anticipations of Wolfe's failure: John Shy, *Toward Lexington: The Role of the British Army in the Coming of the American Revolution* (Princeton, N.J., 1965), 95. Preparations and roads: Amherst to Pitt, 22 Oct. 1759, entries of 6–31 Aug., *Pitt Corr.,* 2:186–92.

CHAPTER THIRTY-SIX: *Dubious Battle: Wolfe Meets Montcalm at Québec*

1. Course of the campaign: C. P. Stacey, *Quebec, 1759: The Siege and the Battle* (Toronto, 1959), 51, 75–80. "Reduced [his] Operations": Brig. George Townshend to Charlotte, Lady Ferrers [his wife], 6 Sept. 1759, ibid., 93. "Windmills, water-mills": Capt. John Knox, *An Historical Journal of the Campaigns in North America, for the Years 1757, 1758, 1759, and 1760,* ed. Arthur G. Doughty, 3 vols. (Toronto, 1914–16), 1:375. Atrocities: Stacey, *Quebec,* 91. Scalpings were common in the New England–raised ranger companies, but regulars also engaged in the practice, as when a detachment of the 43rd Regiment captured, killed, and scalped a priest and thirty of his parishioners at Ste. Anne on August 23. Wolfe himself sanctioned scalping, if not necessarily mass murder, by an order of 27 July, which sought to systematize what had already

become a general practice: "The Genl. strickly forbids the inhuman practice of scalping, except when the enemy are Indians, or Canads. dressed like Indians" (*General Orders in Wolfe's Army* [Quebec, 1875], 29).

2. Christopher Hibbert, *Wolfe at Quebec* (New York, 1959), 107–19.

3. Lawrence Henry Gipson, *The British Empire before the American Revolution,* vol. 7, *The Great War for the Empire: The Victorious Years, 1758–1760* (New York, 1967), 389.

4. Failed harvest: Jean Elizabeth Lunn, "Agriculture and War in Canada, 1740–1760," *Canadian Historical Review* 16 (1935): 2, 128–9. Severity of the winter: George F. G. Stanley, *New France: The Last Phase, 1744–1760* (Toronto, 1968), 221–2. Bougainville's arrival: Ian K. Steele, *Warpaths: Invasions of North America* (New York, 1994), 205–6; Gipson, *Victorious Years,* 389–90. Vaudreuil vs. Montcalm: Roger Michalon, "Vaudreuil et Montcalm—les hommes—leurs relations—influence de ces relations sur la conduite de la guerre 1756–1759," in *Conflits de sociétés au Canada français pendant la Guerre de Sept Ans et leur influence sur les operations,* ed. Jean Delmas (Ottawa: Colloque International d'Histoire Militaire, Ottawa, 19–27 Aug. 1978), 43–175, esp. 153–4.

5. Gipson, *Victorious Years,* 388–9.

6. Stacey, *Quebec,* 43–4; Stanley, *Last Phase,* 223–4; Steele, *Warpaths,* 219.

7. Knox, *Historical Journal,* 1:375.

8. Stacey, *Quebec,* 41–2.

9. "My antagonist": Wolfe to his mother, 31 Aug. 1759, in Beckles Willson, *The Life and Letters of James Wolfe* (New York, 1909), 469. Deadlock and council of war: Gipson, *Victorious Years,* 405–7, Willson, *Letters of Wolfe,* 466–8; Stacey, *Quebec,* 99–102 and app. ("Wolfe's Correspondence with the Brigadiers, August 1759"), 179–81.

10. Stacey, *Quebec,* 104–5.

11. Robert C. Alberts, *The Most Extraordinary Adventures of Major Robert Stobo* (Boston, 1965).

12. Stacey, *Quebec,* 106–8.

13. Wolfe to Brigadier [Robert] Monckton, 8½ o'clock, 12 Sept. 1759, in Willson, *Letters of Wolfe,* 485.

14. Ibid., 482–3, 493. Jervis, of course, would become a notable fighting admiral in the Napoleonic Wars, winning the Battle of Cape St. Vincent, 14 Feb. 1797, and earning the peerage, as Lord St. Vincent, that he would bear until he became admiral of the fleet and finally first lord of the Admiralty (a task at which, unlike battle, he did not distinguish himself).

15. Stacey, *Quebec,* 127–30; Hibbert, *Wolfe at Quebec,* 134–8.

16. There is obviously a substantial degree of speculation in this, for we cannot know Wolfe's state of mind or his plans for the assault. However, certain evidence does point in this direction. Brig. Gen. James Murray, the fourth-in-command on the expedition, never forgave Wolfe's "absurd, visionary" conduct and especially resented his abandonment of the brigadiers' advice to carry out the upriver landing at Pointe aux Trembles, where he could have cut off Québec's supplies as well as at L'Anse au Foulon, but with infinitely less risk to the army. In 1774 Murray was still angry enough to write: "It does not appear to me that it ever was Mr Wolfes intention to bring the Enemy to a general Action" on the Plains; the landing was "almost impossible," and "successful . . . thanks to Providence" (to George Townshend, 5 Nov. 1774, quoted in Stacey, *Quebec,* 176).

In the immediate aftermath of the battle, the Canadian intendant, Bigot, investigated Wolfe's plans. On 25 Oct. 1759 he wrote to Marshal Belle-Isle, "I know all the particulars of that landing from English officers of my acquaintance who have communicated them to me; adding, that Mr. Wolf did not expect to succeed; that he had not attempted to land above Quebec [at Pointe aux Trembles or Cap Rouge, the two strategically sound objectives], and that he was to sacrifice only his van-guard which consisted of 200 men; that were these fired on, they were all to reëmbark" (quoted in Gipson, *Victorious Years,* 416 n. 58).

Another French document, the anonymous *Journal tenu à l'armée que commandoit feu Mr. de Montcalm lieutenant general,* tells a similar tale. In a supposed council of war, Wolfe is said to have declared his intention to take 150 men ashore, "and the entire army will be prepared to follow. Should this first detachment encounter any resistance on the part of the enemy, I pledge you my word of honor that then, regarding our reputation protected against all sorts of reproach, I will no longer hesitate to reëmbark" (ibid).

Although the form in which it is reported (as a speech to a council of war) is an obvious fabrication, this sensitivity to reproach in fact rings true for Wolfe, who worried about his reputation for brilliance and who feared losing it rather more than he feared death. In 1755 he had written to his mother that "the consequence [of my reputation] will be very fatal to me in the end, for as I rise in rank people will expect some considerable performances, and I shall be induced, in support of an ill-got reputation, to be lavish of my life, and shall probably meet that fate which is the ordinary effect of such conduct" (letter of 8 Nov. 1755, Willson, *Letters of Wolfe,* 280).

17. Knox, *Historical Journal,* 2:94–102 (including quotation on the weather); Stacey, *Quebec,* 130–2; Gipson, *Victorious Years,* 414–16. For a masterful assessment of the British and French positions and their comparative advantages, see W. J. Eccles, "The Battle of Quebec: A Reappraisal," in id., *Essays on New France* (Toronto, 1987), 125–33, esp. 129 ff.

18. Stacey, *Quebec,* 121, 133–5; Gipson, *Victorious Years,* 416–17.

19. Stacey, *Quebec,* 137 (quotation: Major Malartic to Bourlamaque, 28 Sept. 1759).

20. Vaudreuil to Bougainville, 13 Sept. 1759 ("At a quarter to seven"), ibid., 135.

21. M. de Montbeillard, quoted ibid., 145–6.

22. Willson, *Letters of Wolfe,* 491–2; Knox, *Historical Journal,* 2:99. Eighteenth-century infantry commanders generally avoided ordering men to assume prone positions because it could be difficult to get them up from the relative safety of the ground to the much more dangerous standing position. In this case, however, Wolfe's men were thoroughly disciplined and separated from the enemy by a third of a mile; he had every reason to trust that they would rise to meet the French attack.

23. Knox, *Historical Journal,* 2:103, notes that entrenching tools were not brought to the heights until after the battle.

24. Even if Wolfe did not recite Thomas Gray's *Elegy Written in a Country Churchyard* on the night before the battle or exclaim that he would rather have written that poem than take Québec, as the legend maintains, he was clearly attached to it. His fiancée had given him a copy, which he annotated during the voyage from England. He underlined Gray's famous admonition that "The paths of glory lead but to the grave" but seems to have been more impressed by his observation on the adverse effects of "Chill penury," in response to which he penned an extended comment. See Beckles Willson, "General Wolfe and Gray's 'Elegy,' " *The Nineteenth Century and After* 434 (1913): 862–75.

25. Pessimism: Stacey, *Quebec,* 84. Topography and the battle: John Keegan, *Fields of Battle: The Wars for North America* (New York, 1996), 127–8.

26. Quotation: Malartic to Bourlamaque [28 Sept. 1759?], in Stacey, *Quebec,* 147.

27. Five other battalions were also on the field: the 2nd and 3rd Battalions of the 60th (Royal American) Regiment and the 15th Foot, deployed at a right angle to the line at the left, against a flanking maneuver; the 35th Foot, arrayed similarly on the right; and Howe's Light Infantry, in a line to the left and rear of the battlefield, to guard against Indian and Canadian skirmishers as well as to defend against Bougainville's column, should it make an appearance. See Stacey, *Quebec,* map 6; also Beattie, "Amherst," app. 2.

28. Stacey, *Quebec,* 147 ("one knee" is from Montbeillard, without citation); Gipson, *Victorious Years,* 420 n. 72 ("scattering shots" is from the journal of Major "Moncrief" [Mackellar]). "Musket-shot" range referred to the extreme limit of lethal musket fire, about three hundred yards, not to the much shorter maximum effective range of about eighty yards. Rounds fired at "half-musket-shot" range were only randomly effective. Major George Hanger, a British

cavalry officer, later wrote that "a soldier must be very unfortunate indeed who shall be wounded . . . at 150 yards, provided his antagonist aims at him . . ." (*General Hanger to All Sportsmen* . . . [London, 1814], quoted in Anthony D. Darling, *Red Coat and Brown Bess* [Bloomfield, Ont., 1971], 11).

29. "This false movement": Malartic to Bourlamaque, 28 Sept. 1759, quoted in Stacey, *Quebec*, 147. "Close and heavy discharge": Knox, *Historical Journal*, 2:101. This quotation combines one of Knox's footnotes (from "close and heavy discharge" to "*une coup de canon*") with the independent clause that follows the position of the asterisk in his text (from "Hereupon they gave way" to the end).

The loss of battalion integrity among Montcalm's forces did not indicate indiscipline so much as the coexistence within the same force of two different training regimes, only one of which was adapted to open-field battle. The regulars had been trained to do exactly what they did: fire, reload quickly, and advance. The militia, on the other hand, knew how to fight only in the bush and reloaded "according to their custom," either prone or under cover; thus they fell behind the regulars, breaking the line of battle. After Braddock's defeat the British had trained regulars in woodland as well as open-field tactics, taking care not to employ provincials in any role that required maneuver. The French regulars also knew how to fight both in the woods and in the open, but Montcalm had not been sufficiently alive to the dangers of diluting their ranks with militiamen trained only in woodland tactics.

30. Stanley, *New France*, 232; Stacey, *Quebec*, 149–50. Probably the most accurate version of Wolfe's death is Knox's, in *Historical Journal*, 2:114. There is little reason to doubt the general tenor, at least, of his last words as Knox reported them ("Now, God be praised, I will die in peace"). The captain interviewed eyewitnesses, and the quotation was quite in keeping with the tormented general's character. It also, at least in substance, squares with his last words as reported in a letter from Quebec, quoted in the *Pennsylvania Gazette* of 25 Oct. 1759: "I am satisfied, my Boys."

31. Gipson, *Victorious Years*, 422; Russell F. Weigley, *The Age of Battles: The Quest for Decisive Warfare from Breitenfeld to Waterloo* (Bloomington, Ind., 1991), 218; Stacey, *Quebec*, 152–5; Stanley, *New France*, 231–3; Willson, *Letters of Wolfe*, 494 n., 495–6; Knox, *Historical Journal*, 2:102–8.

32. Stacey, *Quebec*, 156–8.

33. Gipson, *Victorious Years*, 423–4.

34. Knox, *Historical Journal*, 2:121–32; Gipson, *Victorious Years*, 424–6; Stacey, *Quebec*, 159–61.

35. Gipson, *Victorious Years*, 424–6.

36. On Lévis, see esp. *Dictionary of Canadian Biography*, vol. 4, s.v. "Lévis, François (François-Gaston) de, Duc de Lévis."

37. On preparations for winter quarters at Quebec, see Gipson, *Victorious Years*, 429–30; Monckton to Pitt, 8 Oct. 1759, and Murray to Pitt (abstract), 12 Oct. 1759, in Gertrude Selwyn Kimball, ed., *Correspondence of William Pitt when Secretary of State with Colonial Governors and Military and Naval Commissioners in America* (1906; reprint, New York, 1969), 2:177–83.

CHAPTER THIRTY-SEVEN: *Fall's Frustrations*

1. Amherst journal, 9 Oct. 1759 [?], quoted in Daniel John Beattie, "General Jeffery Amherst and the Conquest of Canada, 1758–1760" (Ph.D. diss., Duke University, 1976), 180.

2. Amherst to Pitt, 22 Oct. 1759, entries dated 9–21 Oct., in Gertrude Selwyn Kimball, ed., *The Correspondence of William Pitt when Secretary of State with Colonial Governors and Military and Naval Commissioners in America* (1906; reprint, New York, 1969), 2:198–201.

3. "Robert Webster's Journal," *Bulletin of the Fort Ticonderoga Museum* 2 (1931): 146–8 (entries of 26 Oct.–18 Nov. 1759).

4. Rowena Buell, ed., *The Memoirs of Rufus Putnam* (Boston, 1903), 28–31 (reflections following entries of 26 July and 16 Dec. 1759); quotations at 31. After completing the mill, Putnam went to Crown Point to work as a master carpenter under "Major Skean" [Philip Skene], who

promised him the wage of a dollar a day for returning to Ticonderoga. Skene had commanded the post at Stillwater from which Putnam and the rest of Learned's company had deserted in Feb. 1758. If Skene recognized Putnam as a deserter, he may have intended to visit some small retribution on him, for a crime he could no longer punish.

5. B. F. Browne, comp., "Extracts from Gibson Clough's Journal," *Essex Institute Historical Collections* 3 (1861): 104–5 (entries of 26 Sept.–3 Nov. 1759; quotations from 26 and 30 Sept.).

6. "Made up [his] mind": Buell, *Memoirs of Putnam,* 31. "When I get out": "Extracts from Gibson Clough's Journal," 104 (entry of 3d [30] Sept. 1759). For troop disorders among New Englanders and their significance, see Fred Anderson, *A People's Army: Massachusetts Soldiers and Society in the Seven Years' War* (Chapel Hill, N.C., 1984), 167–95; and Harold Selesky, *War and Society in Colonial Connecticut* (New Haven, Conn., 1990), 187–9.

7. "The provincials have got home in their heads": Amherst's journal, entry of 3 Nov. 1759, quoted in Beattie, "Amherst," 192. "The Disregard of Orders": Amherst to Duncan, 6 Dec. 1761, quoted in Douglas Edward Leach, *Roots of Conflict: British Armed Forces and Colonial Americans, 1677–1763* (Chapel Hill, N.C., 1986), 132.

CHAPTER THIRTY-EIGHT: *Celebrations of Empire, Expectations of the Millennium*

1. Philadelphia: *Pennsylvania Gazette,* 24 Jan. 1760. New York: *Pennsylvania Gazette,* 15 Nov. 1759.

2. *Boston Evening Post,* 22 Oct. 1759; cf. the account in *Pennsylvania Gazette,* 25 Oct. 1759.

3. Samuel Langdon, *Joy and Gratitude to God for . . . the Conquest of Quebec* (Portsmouth, N.H., 1760), 37–8; see also quoted and explicated passages in James West Davidson, *The Logic of Millennial Thought: Eighteenth-Century New England* (New Haven, Conn., 1977), 211.

4. Samuel Cooper, *A Sermon Preached before His Excellency Thomas Pownall, Esq. . . . October 16, 1759. Upon Occasion of the Success of His Majesty's Arms in the Reduction of Quebec . . .* (Boston, 1759), 38–9; see also passage as quoted in Harry S. Stout, *The New England Soul: Preaching and Religious Culture in Colonial New England* (New York, 1986), 251.

5. Langdon, in *Joy and Gratitude,* spoke of Québec as "a token of assurance that God would 'continue his care of the reformed churches, till all the prophecies of the new testament against the mystical Babylon are accomplished,' " including Prussia as a leading partner in the " '*protestant interest*' " (Davidson, *Millennial Thought,* 210). Providentialists had no problem explaining the previous indecisive outcomes of the Anglo-French wars because in these the Protestant British had allied themselves with the Catholic Austrians.

6. "A mighty empire" and "Methinks I see": Jonathan Mayhew, *Two Discourses Delivered October 25th, 1759. . . .* (Boston, 1759), 60–1. On these sermons' millennialist content, see Davidson, *Millennial Thought,* 209–10.

7. Stout, *New England Soul,* 253; Kerry Trask, *In the Pursuit of Shadows: Massachusetts Millennialism and the Seven Years' War* (New York, 1989), 223–86.

CHAPTER THIRTY-NINE: *Day of Decision: Quiberon Bay*

1. Pitt's gloom and recovery: Stanley Ayling, *The Elder Pitt, Earl of Chatham* (New York, 1976), 261–2 ("with reason . . . gives it all over"—Newcastle to Hardwicke, 15 Oct. 1759, quoted 261). Wolfe's despair: Wolfe to Pitt, 2 Sept. 1759, in C. P. Stacey, *Quebec, 1759: The Siege and the Battle* (Toronto, 1959), 191 ("at a loss"); Wolfe to Holdernesse, 9 Sept. 1759, in Beckles Willson, *The Life and Letters of James Wolfe* (New York, 1909), 475 ("so far recovered").

2. "The incidents": Horace Walpole, *Memoirs of the Reign of King George the Second* (London, 1846), 3:219. "Pronounced a kind of funeral oration": ibid., 229–30.

3. On the Battle of Minden, 1 Aug. 1759, and its aftermath, see Reginald Savory, *His Britannic Majesty's Army in Germany during the Seven Years' War* (Oxford, 1966), 162–84; also, in gen-

eral, see Piers Mackesy's superb account, focusing on the actions of Lord George Sackville [later Germaine], *The Coward of Minden* (New York, 1979).

4. Battle of Lagos: Russell F. Weigley, *The Age of Battles: The Quest for Decisive Warfare from Breitenfeld to Waterloo* (Bloomington, Ind., 1991), 224; Julian S. Corbett, *England in the Seven Years' War: A Study in Combined Strategy,* vol. 2 (London, 1918), 31–40. French finances: Walpole, *Memoirs of George II,* 3:223–4. ("Even their future historians will not be able to parry" such a disgrace, Walpole chortled. "Defeated Armies frequently claim the victory, but no nation ever sung *Te Deum* upon becoming insolvent" [223].)

5. Dennis Showalter, *The Wars of Frederick the Great* (London, 1996), 243–52; Weigley, *Age of Battles,* 190–1, gives the number of Prussians engaged as 53,000 and their losses as 21,000. Christopher Duffy's estimate, in *The Military Life of Frederick the Great* (New York, 1986), 183–92, agrees with Showalter's.

6. Naval operations: Weigley, *Age of Battles,* 225–6; Corbett, *Seven Years' War,* 2:48–52; Richard Middleton, *The Bells of Victory: The Pitt-Newcastle Ministry and the Conduct of the Seven Years' War, 1757–1762* (Cambridge, U.K., 1985), 142–3. (The French used Le Havre to stage invasion preparations until a raid in July by Rear Admiral George Romney destroyed many of the invasion craft; thereafter they shifted preparations to other ports on the Brittany coast. By fall most were in the island-studded Quiberon Bay, a hundred miles to the southwest of Brest.) Vulnerability of Britain to invasion: J. R. Western, *The English Militia in the Eighteenth Century: The Story of a Political Issue, 1660–1802* (London, 1965), 162–8, 194 n., et passim. (Parliament, reluctant to arm large numbers of Scots and Irishmen, had created an *English*—not British—militia, leaving the defense of Scotland and Ireland to regulars, of whom there were too few both to guard against an attack and to suppress the uprising that would inevitably accompany it.)

7. Corbett, *Seven Years' War,* 2:57–60; Weigley, *Age of Battles,* 227.

8. On the dead hand of the Fighting Instructions of 1653, see Weigley, *Age of Battles,* esp. 145–7; Julian S. Corbett, *England in the Seven Years' War: A Study in Combined Strategy,* vol. 1 (London, 1918); 116 ff.

9. Character of the battle and its results: Weigley, *Age of Battles,* 228–9; Corbett, *Seven Years' War,* 2:60–70. Howe: *Dictionary of National Biography,* s.v. "Howe, Richard." "Had we had but two hours": Hawke's report to the Admiralty, 24 Nov. 1759, in Corbett, *Seven Years' War,* 2:69.

10. Threats to public credit: Middleton, *Bells,* 113–18, 136 (in Mar.–May, and again in July, there had been crises of confidence arising from the shortage of money available to meet current government obligations). Economic expansion and security of government finance: ibid., 153; Nancy F. Koehn, *The Power of Commerce: Economy and Governance in the First British Empire* (Ithaca, N.Y., 1994), 52–4. Perhaps as much as military victories, the highly atypical experience of prosperity in wartime—for British exports and reexports rose by a third during the war years, trade with the colonies increased to new levels with surges in demand for consumer goods, and the economy in general expanded as in no other military conflict—helped generate the sense of security that underlay this willingness to accept such increases in public indebtedness. No statistical series could testify more eloquently to this mood than the letter the earl of Pembroke wrote to Captain Charles Lee late in 1759. After expatiating on the victories of the year and relating army gossip, he concluded, "It don't often happen here, or any where else, I believe, but there is certainly at present amongst all here the greatest spirit and unanimity imaginable, and no appearance of want, much debauch and good living, so pray come amongst us soon" (26 Nov. 1759; New-York Historical Society, *Collections, Lee Papers* 1 [1871]: 23).

11. Pitt to the governors of Mass., N.H., Conn., R.I., N.Y., and N.J., 7 Jan. 1760; to the governors of Pa., Md., Va., N.C., and S.C., 7 Jan. 1760; to Amherst, 7 Jan. 1760; in Gertrude Selwyn Kimball, ed., *The Correspondence of William Pitt when Secretary of State with Colonial Governors and Military and Naval Commissioners in America* (1906; reprint, New York, 1969), 2:231–42.

PART VI: *CONQUEST COMPLETED,* 1760

CHAPTER FORTY: *War in Full Career*

1. Amherst to Pitt, 8 Mar. 1760, in Gertrude Selwyn Kimball, ed., *The Correspondence of William Pitt when Secretary of State with Colonial Governors and Military and Naval Commissioners in America* (1906; reprint, New York, 1969), 2:260–1; Daniel John Beattie, "General Jeffery Amherst and the Conquest of Canada, 1758–1760" (Ph.D. diss., Duke University, 1976), 200.

2. Lawrence Henry Gipson, *The British Empire before the American Revolution,* vol. 7, *The Great War for the Empire: The Victorious Years, 1758–1760* (New York, 1968), 446–7; Nicholas B. Wainwright, *George Croghan, Wilderness Diplomat* (Chapel Hill, N.C., 1959), 171.

3. The decision to retain men beyond the standard enlistment term caused great concern in both the House of Representatives and the Council, especially once the dissatisfaction of the men in "the Eastward service"—the Louisbourg garrison—became known. On 24 Apr. 1760, the members of both houses warned Pownall (and, by extension, Amherst) against further altering the enlistment terms of men unwilling to volunteer for further service. Their reasoning, identical to that of Winslow and his officers in 1756, indicates that even in the more cooperative atmosphere fostered by Pitt's policies, New Englanders had not changed their contractual notions concerning military service.

> What we have to Remark is, That the Time for which these Men inlisted into his Majesty's Service, is expired; they have a right therefore to a Discharge, and [a right to] Demand it. Their Detention hitherto is justifiable from the Necessity of it; but that Necessity no longer subsists. If they should be any longer detained, it will be not only unjust to them, but greatly lessen the Power of the Government to raise Men for his Majesty's Service in future. Men will never inlist, when they cannot depend upon the Promise of the Government for their Discharge: Justice therefore demand[s] and good Policy requires that these Men should be discharged. We have plighted our Faith, and your Excellency in your Proclamation, your Promise[,] that they should be discharged. The General's Acceptance of these Men, was an Acceptance of them with the Condition on which they were raised; namely, that they should be discharged at the Expiration of the Time for which they were inlisted. The General's Honour is therefore engaged as well as your Excellency's, and our own to procure the Liberation of these Men . . . (*Journals of the House of Representatives of Massachusetts, 1759–60* [Boston, 1964], 36:333 [Message to His Excellency the Governor, respecting the Detention of the Forces at Nova-Scotia, &c., 24 Apr. 1760]. Hereafter cited as *JHRM*).

4. Expenses of retaining and enlisting soldiers: *JHRM,* 36:113–14 (7 Nov. 1759), 191 (24 Jan. 1760); 37, part 1 (1760–61); 11 (30 May 1760). The men who remained at Louisbourg stood to make sizable sums, especially if they acted as artificers, which was the case with both Clough and Jonathan Procter (another private in the same regiment). Procter earned sixty-three pounds, five shillings lawful money in his twenty months at Louisbourg, including bounties, wages, and additional compensation for his work as a carpenter. During that time he spent about thirteen pounds, so Procter ended his service with fifty pounds in his pocket—a remarkable sum for a man who, even at the high wartime wages civilian artisans commanded in the Bay Colony, could have earned no more than forty-five pounds for the same period at home, and who would as well have had to purchase his own lodging, food, and clothing, items supplied as part of his ordinary compensation while on active duty. See "Diary Kept at Louisbourg, 1759–1760, by Jonathan Procter of Danvers," *Essex Institute Historical Collections* 70 (1934): 31–57.

5. Gipson, *Victorious Years,* 445–6. The figure of four thousand for Massachusetts is from

Thomas Hutchinson, *The History of the Colony and Province of Massachusetts-Bay,* ed. Lawrence Shaw Mayo, vol. 3 (1936; reprint, New York, 1970), 58. The evident shortfall in Massachusetts's contribution probably stems from the way Hutchinson counted them, as 3,300 having enlisted for general service and 700 having remained in service at Louisbourg. Unlike the other northern provinces, the Bay Colony also garrisoned forts on its own, including Castle William in Boston, a chain of forts along the western and northern frontiers of the province, and Forts Shirley, Western, and Pownall in Maine. Since these were manned and commanded entirely by provincials, they were not counted as part of the general service (i.e., as soldiers placed at the disposal of the commander in chief). This was, however, a distinction lost on the members of the General Court, who saw all the province's troops as equal in expense and importance, regardless of where and under whose command they had been placed. Thus by the reckoning of the General Court, if not that of Hutchinson or Amherst, the province met (indeed exceeded) the 5,000-man quota to which it initially agreed.

Finally, a word on the slowness of the provincials to arrive at their points of rendezvous for the campaigns, which was a matter of constant complaint for the commanders in chief from Braddock onward. At least in the later years of the war this was probably less a function of the reluctance of men to serve than of two other factors: the need to complete the spring planting, which afforded good wages to plowmen and rural laborers, and therefore delayed their enlistments; and the ability of men who intended to serve to wait until the government announced the impressment quotas of each militia regiment, and then to sell their services to the impressed men as substitutes. Because each of the provinces had statutes authorizing men to be drafted from the militia if enlistment quotas were not met voluntarily, impressment was routinely undertaken to fill out the last vacancies in the ranks. Because the decision on who would be drafted was left to local militia officers, however, the impressed men were not always, or even generally, the vagrants and unmarried men singled out by the statutes as the proper targets. Rather militia officers tended to impress men who had the money to hire substitutes to take their places. This in turn meant that men—and especially veterans like Rufus Putnam, who hired himself out as a substitute in 1759—would wait to strike a bargain with an impressed man (or men, since two or more draftees would sometimes pool their resources to hire a substitute), and then enlist on his behalf. Because the hired man was technically a volunteer, he was entitled to all the normal bounties as well as his wages.

Although it is difficult to know precisely what the going rate for substitutes was in the later years of the war, there would seem to be no doubt that a vigorous secondary market had arisen in military labor by 1758. As the war continued to demand more and more men and as bounties rose, so must the price needed to hire substitutes have risen; but as these were private transactions, we have no systematic evidence on the costs involved. The only documented case of which I have direct knowledge is that of Rufus Putnam, who in 1759 agreed to serve on behalf of Moses Leland of Sutton, in return for fourteen pounds thirteen shillings lawful money—a sum one shilling higher than the maximum bounty offered in that year (see Rowena Buell, ed., *The Memoirs of Rufus Putnam* [Boston, 1903], 25 n. 1). As a result of this bargain, Putnam in 1759 would have earned in excess of forty-four pounds lawful money for his service not counting the additional wages he received as an artificer and the increment he received when he was promoted to orderly sergeant. Thus unless Putnam's case represents an aberration—and there is no reason to suspect that it does—there were substantial economic incentives to delay enlisting, even in the years of high bounties: inducements that would have virtually guaranteed that the provincials would be slow to be raised and slow to appear in the field.

6. This highly conservative approximation is based upon figures in Jackson Turner Main, *Society and Economy in Colonial Connecticut* (Princeton, N.J., 1985), 118–19. Main shows that between 1756 and the end of 1759 the price of oxen on the hoof rose by 71 percent; of cows, by

33 percent; of pork, by 50 percent. The price of sheep during the same years doubled—a probable result not of demand for meat, but for wool, in high demand for the blankets that were issued as a part of the bounty in every province through every year of the war.

7. Hutchinson, *History,* 3:57. One good indicator of the prosperity that had overtaken the province was that one of the taxes laid to pay for the war was an excise on three prime consumer products, "Tea, Coffee and China-Ware." See *JHRM,* 36:111–12 (6 Nov. 1759).

CHAPTER FORTY-ONE: *The Insufficiency of Valor: Lévis and Vauquelin at Québec*

1. Lawrence Henry Gipson, *The British Empire before the American Revolution,* vol. 7, *The Great War for the Empire: The Victorious Years, 1758–1760* (New York, 1967), 434–5.

2. On Lévis's plans and the difficult but far from hopeless state of Canada's defenses, see esp. George F. G. Stanley, *New France: The Last Phase, 1744–1760* (Toronto, 1968), 242–4.

3. Ibid., 244–5 (quotation at 244).

4. Stanley, *New France,* 245–6; Gipson, *Victorious Years,* 438 n. 40. When the French landed at Pointe aux Trembles, a bateau had overturned, dumping a man into the frigid water; he scrambled onto an ice floe, floated downriver, and was fished out by the British, to whom he revealed the approach of Lévis's army.

5. Murray to Pitt, 25 May 1760, in Gertrude Selwyn Kimball, ed., *Correspondence of William Pitt when Secretary of State with Colonial Governors and Military and Naval Commissioners in America* (1906; reprint, New York, 1969), 2:292.

6. Gipson, *Victorious Years,* 432–4, 428.

7. Quotations: Murray to Pitt, 25 May 1760, *Pitt Corr.,* 2:292. Murray takes the field: Stanley, *New France,* 246–7; Gipson, *Victorious Years,* 438–9.

8. This account of the battle follows Stanley, *New France,* 246–8; Gipson, *Victorious Years,* 438–9; and Murray to Pitt, 25 May 1760, *Pitt Corr.,* 2:291–7.

9. Quotation: Lt. Malcolm Fraser, *Journal of the Operations before Quebec,* quoted in Stanley, *New France,* 297 n. 15. (Fraser concluded that Murray was "possessed of several virtues, and particularly the military ones, except prudence.") Artillery duel: ibid., 248–9.

10. On the destruction of the Bordeaux convoy, see Gipson, *Victorious Years,* 436–7; Stanley, *New France,* 259–61; Julian S. Corbett, *England in the Seven Years' War: A Study in Combined Strategy,* vol. 2 (London, 1918), 113; Ian K. Steele, *Warpaths: Invasions of North America* (New York, 1994), 220–1; and Alexander, Lord Colville, to Pitt, 12 Sept. 1760, *Pitt Corr.,* 2:333–4.

11. Desandrouins quotation: Stanley, *New France,* 259. Vauquelin: ibid., 172, 250; *Dictionary of Canadian Biography,* vol. 4, s.v. "Vauquelin, Jean." Before the *Atalante* ran out of ammunition her crew sank one of the two frigates that it had engaged, H.M.S. *Lowestoft.* Captain Vauquelin recovered from his wounds, was later released from British custody, and returned to French service. He participated in attempts to establish colonies in Guiana and on Madagascar until his death in 1772. A commoner, he never advanced beyond the rank of lieutenant commander. A better measure of his skills as a naval officer than his promotion record can be found in the comment of Admiral Boscawen, who declared at Louisbourg—after Vauquelin had given his own captains the slip—that if the Frenchman had been one of his officers, he would have put him in command of a ship of the line.

CHAPTER FORTY-TWO: *Murray Ascends the St. Lawrence*

1. Capt. John Knox, *The Siege of Quebec and the Campaigns in North America, 1757–1760,* ed. Brian Connell (Mississauga, Ont., 1980), 262–5; Lawrence Henry Gipson, *The British Empire before the American Revolution,* vol. 7, *The Great War for the Empire: The Victorious Years, 1758–1760* (New York, 1967), 458.

2. Knox, *Siege of Quebec,* 267–8.

3. Ibid., 268.
4. Gipson, *Victorious Years,* 457–61; George F. G. Stanley, *New France: The Last Phase, 1744–1760* (Toronto, 1968), 251–3.

CHAPTER FORTY-THREE: *Conquest Completed: Vaudreuil Surrenders at Montréal*

1. "Samuel Jenks, His Journall of the Campaign in 1760," Massachusetts Historical Society, *Proceedings* 25 (1890): 353–68 (entries of 22 May–16 Aug. 1760); Lawrence Henry Gipson, *The British Empire before the American Revolution,* vol. 7, *The Great War for the Empire: The Victorious Years, 1758–1760* (New York, 1967), 449–50.
2. George F. G. Stanley, *New France: The Last Phase, 1744–1760* (Toronto, 1968), 256.
3. Gipson, *Victorious Years,* 461–2.
4. Fortifications: Capt. John Knox, *The Siege of Quebec and the Campaigns in North America, 1757–1760,* ed. Brian Connell (Mississauga, Ont., 1980), 301; "Plan of the Town and Fortifications of Montreal or Ville Marie in Canada," in Gipson, *Victorious Years,* facing 463. Defenders' strength: Amherst to Pitt, 4 Oct. 1760, in Gertrude Selwyn Kimball, ed., *The Correspondence of William Pitt when Secretary of State with Colonial Governors and Military and Naval Commissioners in America* (1906; reprint, New York, 1969), 2:336.
5. Indians abandon French alliance: *Journal de Lévis,* quoted in Gipson, *Victorious Years,* 462.
6. Stanley, *New France,* 257.
7. Amherst never grasped this fact; in his official reports he mentioned the Indians only to compliment Johnson for having restrained them from the savagery he expected. See Amherst to Pitt, 8 Sept. 1760, *Pitt Corr.,* 2:332. It is also worth noting that while Amherst believed procuring Iroquois warriors was inordinately expensive—he had laid out gifts that came to a penny or two over twenty-four pounds New York currency for each warrior—they cost almost exactly as much, per man, as provincials from Connecticut (twenty-four pounds nineteen shillings) and Massachusetts (twenty-six pounds four shillings) who participated in the campaign (Harold Selesky, *War and Society in Colonial Connecticut* [New Haven, Conn., 1990], 151, 152; Fred Anderson, *A People's Army: Massachusetts Soldiers and Society in the Seven Years' War* [Chapel Hill, N.C., 1984], 226). Like his predecessors, Amherst never understood that the scarcity of labor in America meant that soldiers would necessarily be expensive. Since the Iroquois warriors represented a majority of the male population of the Six Nations, they were actually an infinitely bigger bargain than Amherst knew.
8. "Samuel Jenks, His Journall," 376–7 (entries of 6 and 7 Sept. 1760).
9. Amherst's journal, quoted in Daniel John Beattie, "General Jeffery Amherst and the Conquest of Canada, 1758–1760" (Ph.D. diss., Duke University, 1976), 216.
10. Proposed conditions: Gipson, *Victorious Years,* 464; Gustave Lanctot, *A History of Canada,* vol. 3, *From the Treaty of Utrecht to the Treaty of Paris, 1713–1763* (Cambridge, Mass., 1965), 181–2. Terms as finally agreed: ibid., 225–36.
11. "Must lay down their arms": "Articles of Capitulation of Montreal," article 1, ibid., 225. "The infamous part": Knox, *Siege of Quebec,* 289, quoting Amherst's reply to M. de la Pause, a French officer, who protested "the too rigorous article" that denied the honors of war. Money was also an important element in the officers' anger, for their inability to serve during the war would place them on half-pay for the duration—a huge personal loss, since an infantry captain received only ninety-five *livres* per month and typically parlayed that pittance into a respectable salary by collecting the wages of nonexistent men carried on his company roll. Article 1 thus doomed to poverty every officer who lacked independent means of support (Lee Kennett, *The French Armies in the Seven Years' War: A Study in Military Organization and Administration* [Durham, N.C., 1967], 70, 96 n. 39).
12. Amherst to Pitt, 4 Oct. 1760, *Pitt Corr.,* 2:335.
13. Amherst's journal, quoted in J. C. Long, *Lord Jeffery Amherst* (New York, 1933), 135.

CHAPTER FORTY-FOUR: *The Causes of Victory and the Experience of Empire*

1. Daniel John Beattie, "General Jeffery Amherst and the Conquest of Canada, 1758–1760" (Ph.D. diss., Duke University, 1976), 125–6 (quotation, from an anonymous officer's letter, 12 June 1758, at 125); and id., "The Adaptation of the British Army to Wilderness Warfare, 1755–1763," in Maarten Ultee, ed., *Adapting to Conditions: War and Society in the Eighteenth Century* (University, Ala., 1986), 71–4.
2. Ibid.
3. The significance of so many forts and the roads that connected them has been more often remarked upon than analyzed for its significance in American history. For a stimulating attempt to come to terms with the topic, see John Keegan, *Fields of Battle: The Wars for North America* (New York, 1996).
4. Amherst to Pitt, 4 Oct. 1760, in Gertrude Selwyn Kimball, ed., *The Correspondence of William Pitt when Secretary of State with Colonial Governors and Military and Naval Commissioners in America* (1906; reprint, New York, 1969), 2:335–8.
5. "Samuel Jenks, His Journall of the Campaign in 1760," Massachusetts Historical Society, *Proceedings* 24 (1889): 373 (entry of 28 Aug. 1760), 378 (9 Sept.), 382 ff. (e.g., 28 Sept.: two-thirds of the provincials sick, and smallpox spreading rapidly), 386 (27 Oct.), 387 (31 Oct.), 389 (16 Nov.: Haviland's broken leg).
6. "Extracts from Gibson Clough's Journal," *Essex Institute Historical Collections* 3 (1861): 201 (entry of 1 Jan. 1761).
7. "Deprived of the honour": Rowena Buell, ed., *The Memoirs of Rufus Putnam* (Boston, 1903), 34 (entry spanning 22 June–19 Nov. 1760). "And now": E. C. Dawes, ed., *Journal of Gen. Rufus Putnam, Kept in Northern New York during Four Campaigns of the Old French and Indian War, 1757–1760* (Albany, 1886), 103 (1 Dec. 1760).

CHAPTER FORTY-FIVE: *Pitt Confronts an Unexpected Challenge*

1. Pitt to Amherst, 24 Oct. 1760, in Gertrude Selwyn Kimball, ed., *The Correspondence of William Pitt when Secretary of State with Colonial Governors and Military and Naval Commissioners in America* (1906; reprint, New York, 1969), 2:344; Stanley Ayling, *The Elder Pitt, Earl of Chatham* (New York, 1976), 274–5.
2. Pitt to Amherst, 24 Oct. 1760, *Pitt Corr.*, 2:344–7. Amherst, whose wife had begun an irreversible descent into madness, longed to return to England and had begged to be relieved of command since Louisbourg. Pitt, to whom Amherst's personal troubles were meaningless, had always demurred.
3. Reginald Savory, *His Britannic Majesty's Army in Germany during the Seven Years' War* (Oxford, 1966), 201–82 and app. 13, 477–8.
4. Ludwig Reiners, *Frederick the Great: A Biography*, trans. Lawrence P. R. Wilson (New York, 1960), 208–11.
5. Lawrence Henry Gipson, *The British Empire before the American Revolution*, vol. 8, *The Great War for the Empire: The Culmination, 1760–1763* (New York, 1970), 144–56.
6. Gipson, *Culmination*, 159–62.
7. Ibid., 166–71.
8. On Pitt's views of the war in Europe, and his insistence on the Belleisle venture, see Richard Middleton, *The Bells of Victory: The Pitt-Newcastle Ministry and the Conduct of the Seven Years' War, 1757–1762* (Cambridge, U.K., 1985), 165–9.
9. Walpole to George Montague, 26 Oct. 1760, in Paget Toynbee, ed., *The Letters of Horace Walpole, Fourth Earl of Orford*, vol. 4 (Oxford, 1903), 439.
10. J. H. Plumb, *The First Four Georges* (Boston, 1975), 95.

PART VII: *VEXED VICTORY,* 1761–1763

CHAPTER FORTY-SEVEN: *The Cherokee War and Amherst's Reforms in Indian Policy*

1. Tom Hatley, *The Dividing Paths: Cherokees and South Carolinians through the Era of Revolution* (New York, 1993), 5–16; also David Corkran, *The Cherokee Frontier: Conflict and Survival, 1740–62* (Norman, Okla., 1962), 3–12. "As many as seven hundred warriors" reflects Forbes's estimate, based on provision requirements; Corkran estimates that about 450 served (ibid., 146), while Hatley places the number at "three hundred or more" (*Dividing Paths,* 100).
2. Corkran, *Cherokee Frontier,* 157–9. Thirty deaths must be regarded as a lower-bound estimate. John Richard Alden, in *John Stuart and the Southern Colonial Frontier* (1944; reprint, New York, 1966), suggests that thirty men were killed from the Lower Towns only (79 n. 15); Gov. William Henry Lyttelton reported in Oct. 1758 that thirty had been killed in the vicinity of Winchester, Virginia, alone (Hatley, *Dividing Paths,* 100, 268 n. 51).
3. P. M. Hamer, "Fort Loudoun in the Cherokee War, 1758–61," *North Carolina Historical Review* 2 (1925): 444; Corkran, *Cherokee Frontier,* 167–8, Hatley, *Dividing Paths,* 109–15.
4. Hatley, *Dividing Paths,* 111.
5. Lawrence Henry Gipson, *The British Empire before the American Revolution,* vol. 9, *The Triumphant Empire: New Responsibilities within the Enlarged Empire, 1763–1766* (New York, 1968), 61–5; Hatley, *Dividing Paths,* 113–15; Corkran, *Cherokee Frontier,* 170–83.
6. Hatley, *Dividing Paths,* 120–5; Corkran, *Cherokee Frontier,* 178–90.
7. Gipson, *New Responsibilities,* 67–8; Corkran, *Cherokee Frontier,* 196–8; Hatley, *Dividing Paths,* 125–9; Alden, *John Stuart,* 104–5.
8. Hatley, *Dividing Paths,* 124–5.
9. Corkran, *Cherokee Frontier,* 198–205.
10. Ibid., 208–11; Gipson, *New Responsibilities,* 70–2. Montgomery burned Keowee, Estatoe, Toxaway, Qualatchee, and Conasatche. "The neatness of those towns and their knowledge of agriculture would surprise you," wrote Lt. Col. James Grant, Montgomery's second-in-command; "they abounded in every comfort of life, and may curse the day we came upon them" (Grant to Lt. Gov. William Bull, in Hatley, *Dividing Paths,* 130).
11. Corkran, *Cherokee Frontier,* 212–13; Hatley, *Dividing Paths,* 131; Gipson, *New Responsibilities,* 73–4. Quotation: Amherst to Pitt, 26 Aug. 1760, quoted in Hatley, *Dividing Paths,* 132.
12. Corkran, *Cherokee Frontier,* 217–19; Gipson, *New Responsibilities,* 75–8; Alden, *John Stuart,* 116–17.
13. Quotation: *South Carolina Gazette,* 18 Oct. 1760, quoted in Corkran, *Cherokee Frontier,* 220. Killings and captives: Gipson, *New Responsibilities,* 78–9; Alden, *John Stuart,* 118–9; J. Russell Snapp, *John Stuart and the Struggle for Empire on the Southern Frontier* (Baton Rouge, 1996), 55–6. In a misdated letter from Fort Toulouse, a French naval officer described the torture of "Monsieur Dameri": "We have just learned that a war party of Cherokees, commanded by Wolf, has captured Fort Loudon, . . . and that the commanding officer, Mr. Dameri, was killed by the Indians. They stuffed earth into his mouth and said, 'Dog, since you are so hungry for land, eat your fill' " (Jean-Bernard Bossu to the marquis de l'Estrade, 10 Jan. 1760 [1761]; in Seymour Feiler, trans. and ed., *Jean-Bernard Bossu's Travels in the Interior of North America, 1751–1762* [Norman, Okla., 1962], 183–4).
14. Theda Perdue, "Cherokee Relations with the Iroquois in the Eighteenth Century," in Daniel Richter and James Merrell, eds., *Beyond the Covenant Chain: The Iroquois and Their Neighbors in Indian North America, 1600–1800* (Syracuse, N.Y., 1987), 144; Corkran, *Cherokee Frontier,* 236; William Bull to William Pitt, 18 Feb. 1761, in Gertrude Selwyn Kimball, ed., *The Correspondence of William Pitt when Secretary of State with Colonial Governors and Military and Naval Commissioners in America* (1906; reprint, New York, 1969), 2:394–6. Quotation: Amherst to Grant, 15 Dec. 1760, in Corkran, *Cherokee Frontier,* 245.

15. Ibid., 246, records eighty-one "Negroes" with the expedition; Gipson, *New Responsibilities,* 82, puts the pack train at seven hundred horses and the cattle herd at four hundred head.
16. Casualty figures and quotations from John Laurens to John Ettwein, 11 July 1761, in P. M. Hamer et al., eds., *The Papers of Henry Laurens,* vol. 3, Jan. 1, 1759–Aug. 31, 1763 (Columbia, S.C., 1972), 75. Executions: Hatley, *Dividing Paths,* 139.
17. Perdue, "Cherokee Relations," 144; Corkran, *Cherokee Frontier,* 255–6; Gipson, *New Responsibilities,* 84.
18. On Stuart's policies, aimed at reducing tensions by controlling white settlers, see Alden, *John Stuart,* 134–55; and esp. Snapp, *Stuart and the Struggle,* 54–67 et passim.
19. Amherst to Johnson, 22 Feb. 1761, in James Sullivan et al., eds., *The Papers of Sir William Johnson,* vol. 3 (Albany, 1921), 345. On the policy's significance in light of the propensity of Johnson and Croghan to bestow gifts freely, see Eric Hinderaker, *Elusive Empires: Constructing Colonialism in the Ohio Valley, 1673–1800* (New York, 1997), 146–50.
20. "Chastizement" and "Example": Amherst to Johnson, 11 Aug. 1761, *Johnson Papers,* 3:517. "Absolute necessity": Johnson to Amherst, 24 July 1761, ibid., 513. "You are sensible": Amherst to Johnson, 9 Aug. 1761, ibid., 515. Amherst previously concluded that, since the Indians could be no threat to a properly organized and supplied force of regulars, they could be dealt with forcibly, as a means of teaching them who was master within the empire. (See, e.g., Amherst to Johnson, 24 June 1761, ibid., 421.) On the Geneseo (or Chenussio) Senecas' scheme and western Indian relations, see Richard White, *The Middle Ground: Indians, Empires, and Republics in the Great Lakes Region, 1600–1815* (New York, 1991), 271–3.
21. John W. Jordan, ed., "Journal of James Kenny, 1761–1763," *Pennsylvania Magazine of History and Biography* 37 (1913): 28 (entry of 21 Nov. 1761); Hinderaker, *Elusive Empires,* 148–9.
22. Cf. Anthony F. C. Wallace, *King of the Delawares: Teedyuscung, 1700–1763* (Philadelphia, 1949), 232–7.

CHAPTER FORTY-EIGHT: *Amherst's Dilemma*

1. Eric Hinderaker, *Elusive Empires: Constructing Colonialism in the Ohio Valley, 1673–1800* (New York, 1997), 148–9; John Shy, *Toward Lexington: The Role of the British Army in the Coming of the American Revolution* (Princeton, N.J., 1965), 104–5.
2. Troop numbers, distribution, and replacements: ibid., 96–9, 112. Detachments: Pitt to Amherst, 7 Jan. 1761, in Gertrude Selwyn Kimball, ed., *The Correspondence of William Pitt when Secretary of State with Colonial Governors and Military and Naval Commissioners in America* (1906; reprint, New York, 1969), 2:384–7. (Amherst took action on these orders as soon as he received the letter, on 26 Feb.; see id. to Pitt, 27 Feb. 1761, ibid., 403.) Request for provincials: Jeffery Amherst, *The Journal of Jeffery Amherst,* ed. J. Clarence Webster (Chicago, 1931), 267 (entry of 8 June 1761), 332 ("Recapitulation").
3. Promotion of settlements near forts: Amherst to Pitt, 16 Dec. 1759, *Pitt Corr.,* 2:222–3; Doris Begor Morton, *Philip Skene of Skenesborough* (Glanville, N.Y., 1959), 17. New York settlements: on the ten thousand–acre tract at the Niagara portage, see Milo Milton Quaife, ed., *The Siege of Detroit in 1763* (Chicago, 1958), xxviii–xxix; on the authorization of the Fort Stanwix settlement and the accompanying grant of ten thousand acres to "Capt. Rutherford, Lieutenant Duncan and others," see Walter Rutherford to Amherst, 9 Apr. 1761, and Amherst to Rutherford, same date, in Louis des Cognets Jr., *Amherst and Canada* (Princeton, N.J. [privately printed], 1962), 310–11. Settlements along the Forbes Road: Solon J. Buck and Elizabeth Hawthorn Buck, *The Planting of Civilization in Western Pennsylvania* (Pittsburgh, 1939), 140–1. (Additional settlements, which Amherst did nothing to discourage, grew up in the vicinity of Fort Burd, near the site of Red Stone Old Fort, near the confluence of Red Stone Creek and the Monongahela River; and on two tracts that Croghan had acquired privately from the Iroquois—one on the Allegheny about four miles upriver from Pittsburgh, the other on the Youghiogheny about twenty-five miles south of the Forks.) Manorial ambitions: Col. William Haviland [at Crown Point] to Amherst, 5 Mar. 1760, quoted in Morton, *Skene,* 31 ("Major Skeen is . . . so full of the

Scheme that he writes once a week to his wife [who had remained in northern Ireland], and I dare say mostly on that subject, as I am sure very little that passes here would afford entertainment so frequent to any one on the other Side of the Water; Indeed he Owned last might that his wife was looking out for People to come and Settle here").

4. Settlers near Pittsburgh: Alfred P. James, *The Ohio Company: Its Inner History* (Pittsburgh, 1959), 113; Lawrence Henry Gipson, *The British Empire before the American Revolution,* vol. 9, *The Triumphant Empire: New Responsibilities within the Enlarged Empire, 1763–1766* (New York, 1968), 89–90. Development around Pittsburgh: Buck and Buck, *Planting of Civilization,* 140; also Anthony F. C. Wallace, *King of the Delawares: Teedyuscung, 1700–1763* (Philadelphia, 1949), 234; John W. Jordan, ed., "Journal of James Kenny, 1761–1763," *Pennsylvania Magazine of History and Biography* 37 (1913): 28–9. Kenny noted on 20 Oct. 1761 a report that there were perhaps 150 houses outside the walls of Fort Pitt, almost all of which had been built since the fall of 1759.

CHAPTER FORTY-NINE: *Pitt's Problems*

1. On Frederick, see Linda Colley, *Britons: Forging the Nation, 1707–1837* (New Haven, Conn., 1992), 204–6. On George's upbringing at Leicester House: John Brooke, *King George III* (New York, 1972), 23; cf. J. H. Plumb, *The First Four Georges* (London, 1956), 92.

2. Obsessive qualities and love of order: J. H. Plumb, *New Light on the Tyrant George III* (Washington, D.C., 1978), 5–17 et passim. Diet: Brooke, *George III,* 291–2.

3. "Horrid Electorate": George to Bute, 5 Aug. 1759, in Romney Sedgwick, ed., *Letters from George III to Lord Bute, 1756–1766* (London, 1939), 28. "Blackest of hearts": same to same, 4 May 1760, ibid., 45.

4. On the speech, see Bute's draft and Pitt's revisions as reprinted in Brooke, *George III,* 75; and Richard Middleton, *The Bells of Victory: The Pitt-Newcastle Ministry and the Conduct of the Seven Years' War, 1757–1762* (Cambridge, U.K., 1985), 170. George himself wrote the words, "Born and educated in this country, I glory in the name Briton," in order to distinguish himself from his predecessors, who had been born and educated in Hanover and who had put the interests of that "horrid Electorate" at least on a par with those of the realm. Critics—especially Newcastle—worried that the king's invocation of a political community that included Scotland signaled the influence that Lord Bute would exercise in the new reign. (See Stanley Ayling, *George the Third* [London, 1972], 70.)

5. "He must act": Gilbert Elliot, reporting a conversation between Pitt and Bute, 25 Oct. 1760, quoted in Lewis Namier, *England in the Age of the American Revolution* (London, 1930), 120–1. "Unknown": Horace Walpole, *Memoirs of the Reign of King George the Third,* ed. G. F. Russell Barker (New York, 1894), 2:9. Reed Browning, *The Duke of Newcastle* (New Haven, Conn., 1975), 275; Middleton, *Bells,* 170–9; Brooke, *George III,* 76.

6. Russell Weigley, *The Age of Battles: The Quest for Decisive Warfare from Breitenfeld to Waterloo* (Bloomington, Ind., 1991), 191; Julian S. Corbett, *England in the Seven Years' War: A Study in Combined Strategy,* vol. 2 (London, 1918), 104, 288; Dennis Showalter, *The Wars of Frederick the Great* (London, 1996), 285–96; Christopher Duffy, *The Military Life of Frederick the Great* (New York, 1986), 210–19. Casualty estimates for the Prussians vary from 40 percent to 60 percent. Either way, Torgau was a bloodbath that decided nothing.

7. Corbett, *Seven Years' War,* 2:104; Middleton, *Bells,* 178, 180–1; Reginald Savory, *His Britannic Majesty's Army in Germany during the Seven Years' War* (Oxford, 1966), 283–308.

8. Middleton, *Bells,* 182, 178; John Brewer, *The Sinews of Power: War, Money, and the English State, 1688–1783* (New York, 1989), 117; Browning, *Newcastle,* 276–8.

9. Browning, *Newcastle,* 275–6; Middleton, *Bells,* 179; Stanley Ayling, *The Elder Pitt, Earl of Chatham* (New York, 1976), 280–2.

10. Corbett, *Seven Years' War,* 2:160–70; Lawrence Henry Gipson, *The British Empire before the American Revolution,* vol. 8, *The Great War for the Empire: The Culmination, 1760–1763* (New York, 1970), 181–4.

11. Middleton, *Bells,* 188–9; Corbett, *Seven Years' War,* 2:141–70, esp. 150–4; Gipson, *Culmination,* 204–52 passim. A Franco-Spanish alliance became possible after the accession to the throne of Charles III, whose Saxon queen, Maria Amalia, loathed her homeland's conqueror. Pitt knew of the negotiations for this second Bourbon Family Compact in mid-March 1761, when British agents intercepted correspondence addressed to Madrid's ambassador in London. The deciphered letters suggested that Spain might soon abandon neutrality for an alliance—a plausible shift in light of the aggressive tone in recent negotiations over British logwood cutting in Honduras. The cabinet's peace party feared Spanish intervention as much as Pitt welcomed it, for exactly the same reasons.
12. Ayling, *Elder Pitt,* 284; Corbett, *Seven Years' War,* 2:172.
13. Quotation: Bedford to Newcastle, 9 May 1761, in Corbett, *Seven Years' War,* 2:172. Gipson, *Culmination,* 218–21; Browning, *Newcastle,* 278–80.
14. Gipson, *Culmination,* 248–51.
15. Middleton, *Bells,* 192–4; Ayling, *Elder Pitt,* 289–90; Browning, *Newcastle,* 280–1; Gipson, *Culmination,* 222–3.
16. George III to Bute, 19 Sept. 1761, *Letters from George III to Bute,* 63.
17. Middleton, *Bells,* 198; Ayling, *Elder Pitt,* 282, 290–2 (quotations at 291 and 292).

CHAPTER FIFTY: *The End of an Alliance*

1. Horace Walpole, *Memoirs of the Reign of King George the Third,* ed. G. F. Russell Barker (New York, 1894), 1:215.
2. Lewis M. Wiggin, *The Faction of Cousins: A Political Account of the Grenvilles, 1733–1763* (New Haven, Conn., 1958), 248–58; Philip Lawson, *George Grenville: A Political Life* (Oxford, 1984), esp. 121–5. Grenville was the brother of Hester, William Pitt's wife; Egremont was another of Grenville's brothers-in-law. Grenville's acceptance caused a deep, immediate breach within the family. Pitt severed all relations summarily; Earl Temple (George's older brother and custodian of the family fortune) cut George's sons out of his will.
3. Rex Whitworth, *Field Marshal Lord Ligonier: A Story of the British Army, 1702–1770* (Oxford, 1958), 358, 364.
4. On Townshend's rise, see Lewis Namier and John Brooke, *Charles Townshend* (New York, 1964); and Cornelius Forster, *The Uncontrolled Chancellor: Charles Townshend and His American Policy* (Providence, 1978). On manpower shortages and the need for surprise, see Richard Middleton, *The Bells of Victory: The Pitt-Newcastle Ministry and the Conduct of the Seven Years' War, 1757–1762* (Cambridge, U.K., 1985), 202.
5. Quotation: Egremont to the earl of Bristol, 19 Nov. 1761, in Lawrence Henry Gipson, *The British Empire before the American Revolution,* vol. 8, *The Great War for the Empire: The Culmination, 1760–1763* (New York, 1970), 252.
6. Ibid., 190–6; Julian S. Corbett, *England in the Seven Years' War: A Study in Combined Strategy,* vol. 2 (London, 1918), 218–26; Jeffery Amherst, *The Journal of Jeffery Amherst,* ed. J. Clarence Webster (Chicago, 1931), 280 (entry of 27 Mar. 1762). The British had 97 killed and 391 wounded; French casualties were probably comparable as a proportion of the smaller number of defenders (evidently fewer than 3,000, including militia). Amherst thought there was "surprisingly little loss" of life in the campaign.
7. Gipson, *Culmination,* 196.
8. Reginald Savory, *His Britannic Majesty's Army in Germany during the Seven Years' War* (Oxford, 1966), 309–59.
9. Frederick to the Gräfin Camas, n.d. [1761], quoted in Ludwig Reiners, *Frederick the Great: A Biography,* trans. Lawrence P. R. Wilson (New York, 1960), 215.
10. Reiners, *Frederick the Great,* 216; Gipson, *Culmination,* 61; Dennis Showalter, *The Wars of Frederick the Great* (London, 1996), 308–10; Christopher Duffy, *The Military Life of Frederick the Great* (New York, 1986), 226.
11. Reiners, *Frederick the Great,* 218 (quotation), 283. Frederick II had been married to

Princess Elizabeth Christine of Brunswick for nearly thirty years, but the couple remained childless, his homosexuality proving an insuperable obstacle to procreation. Thus his heir, Frederick William, was the son of his brother, Prince Augustus William, whom Frederick had disgraced in 1757 after he had failed to keep the Austrians from seizing a strategic junction and supply magazine. Augustus William died in 1758, a broken man (Duffy, *Military Life,* 17, 133).

12. Reiners, *Frederick the Great,* 219 (couplet, my translation); Duffy, *Military Life,* 233–4; Showalter, *Wars of Frederick,* 310–13.

13. Newcastle to Hardwick, 10 Jan. 1762, quoted in Middleton, *Bells,* 205.

14. Browning, *Newcastle,* 283–5; Middleton, *Bells,* 205–6. For the Treasury to issue two million pounds in Exchequer bills—short-term debt instruments usually emitted in smaller quantities, in anticipation of taxes—without the backing of the Bank of England, seemed to invite inflation, a fearsome prospect for an investing community that remembered the wartime devaluations of 1709–11. Any rift between the bank and the Treasury would have gravely shaken investor confidence, which had already endured a shock in 1761 when the bank's shares had fallen in value in anticipation of war with Spain. The buoyant state of trade, low bread prices in London, and military victories overcame this brief crisis, but Newcastle, an inveterate worrier, feared worse effects this time—as indeed did most of the "money'd men," for whom the fear of default transcended rational calculation. See Reed Browning, "The Duke of Newcastle and the Financing of the Seven Years' War," *Journal of Economic History* 31 (1971): 244–77; Julian Hoppit, "Financial Crises in Eighteenth-Century England," *Economic History Review,* 2nd ser., 39 (1986): 39–58, esp. 48; and John Brewer, *The Sinews of Power: War, Money, and the English State, 1688–1783* (New York, 1988), 193.

15. Lewis Namier, *England in the Age of the American Revolution* (London, 1930), 353–80; quotation is from Newcastle to the marquis of Rockingham, 14–15 May 1762, at 376.

16. George III to Bute, c. 19 May 1762, in Romney Sedgwick, ed., *Letters from George III to Lord Bute, 1756–1766* (London, 1939), 109.

17. Reiners, *Frederick the Great,* 219–20.

18. Ibid., 220–1; Duffy, *Military Life,* 236; H. M. Scott, *British Foreign Policy in the Age of the American Revolution* (Oxford, 1990), 30–1; Showalter, *Wars of Frederick,* 318–19.

19. Savory, *Army in Germany,* 360–434; Russell F. Weigley, *The Age of Battles: The Quest for Decisive Warfare from Breitenfeld to Waterloo* (Bloomington, Ind., 1991), 192.

CHAPTER FIFTY-ONE:
The Intersections of Empire, Trade, and War: Havana

1. Lawrence Henry Gipson, *The British Empire before the American Revolution,* vol. 8, *The Great War for the Empire: The Culmination, 1760–1763* (New York, 1970), 256–60.

2. Walter L. Dorn, *Competition for Empire, 1740–1763* (New York, 1940), 375; Gipson, *Culmination,* 270–2.

3. John Robert McNeill, *Atlantic Empires of France and Spain: Louisbourg and Havana, 1700–1763* (Chapel Hill, N.C., 1985), 26–45, 106–202.

4. Albemarle's appointment as general in charge of the expedition marked the completed rehabilitation of the duke of Cumberland, under way since the accession of George III. See Rex Whitworth, *Field Marshal Lord Ligonier: A Story of the British Army, 1702–1770* (Oxford, 1958), 349; J. C. Long, *Lord Jeffery Amherst: A Soldier of the King* (New York, 1933), 163; Julian S. Corbett, *England in the Seven Years' War: A Study in Combined Strategy,* vol. 2 (London, 1918), 283.

5. Allan J. Kuethe, *Cuba, 1753–1815: Crown, Military, and Society* (Knoxville, Tenn., 1986), 17; "An Account of the Taking of the Havannah," *Gentleman's Magazine* 32 (1762): 459–64.

6. "Memoir of an Invalid," quoted in Gipson, *Culmination,* 266 n. 39.

7. Jeffery Amherst, *The Journal of Jeffery Amherst,* ed. J. Clarence Webster (Chicago, 1931), 283 (9 June 1762), 287 (5 July 1762); Gipson, *Culmination,* 264–8; Corbett, *Seven Years' War,*

2:265–82. The Spanish navy had forty-eight ships of the line, only twenty of which were seaworthy; thus the naval toll at Havana was truly crippling for Spain. (See Richard Middleton, *The Bells of Victory: The Pitt-Newcastle Ministry and the Conduct of the Seven Years' War, 1757–1762* [Cambridge, U.K., 1985], 210.)

8. The most reliable figures available are only partial, ignoring the toll among provincials and evacuated regular soldiers. They are, nonetheless, horrifying: 5,366 dead in the land forces between 7 June and 18 Oct., 88 percent from disease; 1,300 seamen dead in the same period, 95 percent from disease, and another 3,300 still sick at the time of the report. Dr. Johnson's response—"May my country be never cursed with such another conquest"—aptly sums up the effects of a siege which was, day for day, Britain's costliest military operation of the Seven Years' War. See McNeill, *Atlantic Empires,* 104, 248–9 nn. 147 and 148. The one provincial unit for which accurate figures are available suggests that the mortality was actually worse than among the regulars: of the 1,050 men in the Connecticut Regiment, 625 (59.5 percent) died before returning home. See [Albert C. Bates, ed.], *The Two Putnams: Israel and Rufus in the Havana Expedition 1762 and in the Mississippi River Exploration 1772–73 with some account of The Company of Military Adventurers* (Hartford, 1931), 5.

9. Hides: McNeill, *Atlantic Empires,* 170–3. Tobacco and sugar backlogs and monopoly structure of Cuban-Spanish trade: Kuethe, *Cuba,* 53–4, 62–3. Demand for labor and transition to sugar: ibid., 66–7; McNeill, *Atlantic Empires,* 129–30, 166–70. Numbers of ships visiting Havana during the occupation, influx of cheap British goods and slaves: Peggy K. Liss, *Atlantic Empires: The Network of Trade and Revolution, 1713–1826* (Baltimore, 1983), 78–9.

CHAPTER FIFTY-TWO: *Peace*

1. Lewis M. Wiggin, *The Faction of Cousins: A Political Account of the Grenvilles, 1733–1763* (New Haven, Conn., 1958), 269–72; Lawrence Henry Gipson, *The British Empire before the American Revolution,* vol. 8, *The Great War for the Empire: The Culmination, 1760–1763* (New York, 1970), 300–4; Peter D. G. Thomas, *British Politics and the Stamp Act Crisis: The First Phase of the American Revolution, 1763–1767* (Oxford, 1975), 3.

2. Wiggin, *Faction of Cousins,* 272–6; Julian S. Corbett, *England in the Seven Years' War: A Study in Combined Strategy,* vol. 2 (London, 1918), 297–8, 318, 342, 361–4; Thomas, *British Politics,* 3–4.

3. Stanley Ayling, *The Elder Pitt, Earl of Chatham* (New York, 1976), 307–9.

4. Corbett, *Seven Years' War,* 2:377–90; Gipson, *Culmination,* 305–11; Walter F. Dorn, *Competition for Empire, 1740–1763* (New York, 1940), 378–83.

5. Ibid., 378, 384.

CHAPTER FIFTY-THREE: *The Rise of Wilkes, the Fall of Bute, and the Unheeded Lesson of Manila*

1. Horace Walpole, *Memoirs of the Reign of King George the Third,* ed. G. F. Russell Barker (New York, 1894), 1:184; and see Lewis B. Namier, *England in the Age of the American Revolution* (London, 1930), 469–70.

2. Ibid., 469.

3. J. H. Plumb, *The First Four Georges* (New York, 1957), 55, 83; Lewis B. Namier, *The Structure of Politics at the Accession of George III* (New York, 1957), 299–357; id., *England in the Age of the American Revolution,* 59–65.

4. On the political ideology of Georgian Britain and the colonies, see esp. Caroline Robbins, *The Eighteenth-Century Commonwealthman: Studies in the Transmission, Development and Circumstance of English Liberal Thought from the Restoration of Charles II until the War with the Thirteen Colonies* (Cambridge, Mass., 1959); Bernard Bailyn, *The Ideological Origins of the American Revolution* (Cambridge, Mass., 1967; rev. ed., 1992); and J. G. A. Pocock, *The Machiavellian Moment: Florentine Political Thought and the Atlantic Republican Tradition* (Princeton, N.J., 1975). On popular politics and the press, see John Brewer, *Party Ideology and Popular Pol-*

itics at the Accession of George III (Cambridge, U.K., 1976), 139–60. On the significance of the middle classes and professionals, see Linda Colley, *Britons: Forging the Nation, 1707–1837* (New Haven, Conn., 1992), 55–145.

5. On Wilkes generally, see George Rudé, *Wilkes and Liberty: A Social Study of 1763 to 1774* (Oxford, 1962); and R. W. Postgate, *That Devil Wilkes* (New York, 1929). On his context in political culture (and esp. the Scottophobia of his supporters), see Colley, *Britons*, 105–17 et passim; Brewer, *Party Ideology*, 163–200; and Ian R. Christie, *Wilkes, Wyvill, and Reform* (London, 1962), 1–24. On his ties with the earl Temple and the internal divisions in the Grenville-Pitt faction, see Lewis M. Wiggin, *The Faction of Cousins: A Political Account of the Grenvilles, 1733–1763* (New Haven, Conn., 1958), 204–5, 267–8, 294–5.

6. On Grenville's personality, see John Brooke, *King George III* (New York, 1972), 107–8; and, more charitably, Philip Lawson, *George Grenville: A Political Life* (Oxford, 1984). The king had a horror of Grenville's ability to bore: "When he has wearied me for two hours, he looks at his watch to see if he may not tire me for an hour more" (quoted in Brooke, 108).

7. Rudé, *Wilkes and Liberty*, 22–7.

8. Louis Kronenberger, *The Extraordinary Mr. Wilkes: His Life and Times* (New York, 1974), 54. Cf. the more favorable estimate of Sandwich's character and activities in N. A. M. Rodger, *The Insatiable Earl: A Life of John Montagu, Fourth Earl of Sandwich* (New York, 1993), 80–4.

9. Rudé, *Wilkes and Liberty*, 28–36; quotation is from Thomas Ramsden to Charles Jenkinson, 11 Dec. 1763, quoted at 35. On Martin's effort to kill Wilkes the best evidence is circumstantial; see Walpole, *Memoirs of George III*, 1:249–53.

10. Except as noted, the following account of the Manila campaign is based on Lawrence Henry Gipson, *The British Empire before the American Revolution*, vol. 8, *The Great War for the Empire: The Culmination, 1760–1763* (New York, 1970), 275–83.

11. Gregorio F. Zaide, *The Pageant of Philippine History: Political, Economic, and Socio-Cultural*, vol. 2, *From the British Invasion to the Present* (Manila, 1979), 10. The Manila galleon, taken as it arrived on 30 Oct., was worth about three million dollars in cargo and coin; Manila paid another half million in ransom; and soldiers, sailors, and irregulars seized at least a million dollars' worth of plunder in the sack of the city.

12. Zaide, *Pageant*, 2:17–24. On Anda's resistance, see Capt. Thomas Backhouse to the secretary at war, 31 Jan. and 10 Feb. 1764, and Backhouse to Draper, 10 Feb. 1764, in Nicholas P. Cushner, ed., *Documents Illustrating the British Conquest of Manila, 1762–1763* (London, 1971), 196–202. On the costs of administration (below), see "The East India Company's case with respect to booty," 2 Oct. 1764, and "Reimbursement requested by the East India Company for the Expedition to Manila," 28 June 1775, ibid., 208–11.

CHAPTER FIFTY-FOUR: *Anglo-America at War's End: The Fragility of Empire*

1. Quotation: Bernard's speech to the General Court, 14 Apr. 1762, *Journals of the House of Representatives of Massachusetts*, vol. 38, part 2, 1762 (Boston, 1968), 302 (hereafter cited as *JHRM*). Bernard (1711–79), allied by marriage with the family of Viscount Barrington, the secretary at war, had been governor of New Jersey from 1758; he moved to Massachusetts after Thomas Pownall was recalled, arriving on 2 Aug. 1760. (See *Dictionary of American Biography* and *Dictionary of National Biography*, s.v. "Bernard, Sir Francis.")

2. In 1759, the colonies as a whole fielded 81.4 percent of the men requested for the year (16,835 of 20,680); in 1760, 75.3 percent (15,942 of 21,180); in 1761, 9,296 of 11,607, or 80.1 percent; in 1762, 9,204 of 10,173, or 90.5 percent. Insofar as these were virtually all voluntary enlistments, it would seem that the northern colonies suffered little diminution in popular enthusiasm for the imperial enterprise once the French and Indian threat had been eliminated. The records of individual colonies bear this out in comparing the percentages of men raised to the number requested in each year from 1760 to 1762. Note the general consistency of Virginia, New York, New Jersey, and the New England provinces (with the exception of

Rhode Island, where the availability of berths on privateersmen cut heavily into the willingness of men to enlist in provincial regiments).

	% RAISED, 1759	% RAISED, 1760	% RAISED, 1761	% RAISED, 1762
N.H.	87.5	99.5	82.0	100.0
Mass.	88.5	90.3	81.9	92.9
R.I.	69.4	95.2	59.3	98.0
Conn.	72.8	67.9	86.9	100.0
N.Y.	83.9	92.0	86.6	82.5
N.J.	92.8	93.5	—	89.3
Pa.	76.7	50.0	0	0
Md.	0	0	0	0
Va.	80.0	100.0	100.0	65.7
N.C.	—	—	45.0	0
S.C.	—	80.0	50.0	—

Source: Jeffery Amherst, *The Journal of Jeffery Amherst,* ed. J. Clarence Webster (Chicago, 1931), App. A–D, 327–30. Blanks indicate missing or imperfect data.

The qualitative assessments of contemporaries tend to bear out the quantitative implications of this chart. See, for example, Bernard's comment to the Massachusetts General Court on the raising of provincials in 1762:

> Whatever shall be the Event of the War, it must be no small Satisfaction to us that this Province hath contributed its full Share to the Support of it. Every Thing that has been required of it hath been most readily complied with: And the Execution of the Powers committed to me for raising the Provincial Troops hath been as full and compleat as the Grant of them was. Never before were the Regiments so easily levied, so well composed, and so early in the Field as they have been this year. The common People seemed to be animated with the Spirit of the General Court, and to vie with them in their Readiness to serve their King (Bernard to the General Court, 27 May 1762, *JHRM,* vol. 39 *1762–63* [Boston, 1969], 10 May 1762).

Thomas Hutchinson observed that by the final years of the conflict the people of the Bay Colony had grown habituated to the demands of imperial warfare. (See *History of the Colony and Province of Massachusetts-Bay,* ed. Lawrence Shaw Mayo, vol. 3 [Cambridge, Mass., 1936], 70.)

Georgia did not appear in Amherst's calculations of colonial participation because it was too poor to raise and pay for provincials on its own; yet it contributed men to the war effort in proportions that may have approximated those of Massachusetts and Connecticut in the last years of the war, by raising several companies of "Georgia Rangers." These dragoons, or mounted infantry, patrolled the frontier against French (from Fort Toulouse), Spanish (from St. Augustine), and Indian enemies, and were American colonists. They were not *provincials,* however, because they received their pay and rations on the regular establishment, as did the rangers who served with the northern armies after 1756. On the Georgia Rangers, see Shy, *Toward Lexington,* 214–15; W. W. Abbot, *The Royal Governors of Georgia, 1754–1775* (Chapel Hill, N.C., 1959), 103–25; and esp. James M. Johnson, *Militiamen, Rangers, and Redcoats: The Military in Georgia, 1754–1776* (Macon, Ga., 1992).

3. For Amherst's views on the colonists, see id., *Journal,* 267 (8 June 1761), 279–80 (19 Feb. 1762), 286 (29 June 1762); Pitt to Amherst, 13 Aug. 1761, in Gertrude Selwyn Kimball, ed., *The Correspondence of William Pitt when Secretary of State with Colonial Governors and Military and Naval Commissioners in America* (1906; reprint, New York, 1969), 2:462–3; and (on fraudulent practices of various sorts) J. C. Long, *Lord Jeffery Amherst* (New York, 1933), 151–2. Quota-

tion: Egremont to Deputy Gov. James Hamilton, 27 Nov. 1762, in Lawrence Henry Gipson, *The British Empire before the American Revolution,* vol. 8, *The Great War for the Empire: The Culmination, 1760–1763* (New York, 1970), 261 n. 23.

4. Quotation: Pitt to Governors in North America and the West Indies, 23 Aug. 1760, *Pitt Corr.,* 2:320. On Hutchinson and the politics of Massachusetts during this crucial period, see Malcolm Freiberg, *Prelude to Purgatory: Thomas Hutchinson in Provincial Politics, 1760–1770* (New York, 1990), 1–54; Bernard Bailyn, *The Ordeal of Thomas Hutchinson* (Cambridge, Mass., 1974), 1–69; Clifford K. Shipton's sketch in id., ed., *Sibley's Harvard Graduates,* vol. 6 (Boston, 1949), 149–217; John Waters, *The Otis Family in Provincial and Revolutionary Massachusetts* (Chapel Hill, N.C., 1968), 76–161. The following account of the writs of assistance controversy is drawn principally from M. H. Smith, *The Writs of Assistance Case* (Berkeley, Calif., 1978); John W. Tyler, *Smugglers and Patriots: Boston Merchants and the Advent of the American Revolution* (Boston, 1986), 25–63; and Gipson, *The British Empire before the American Revolution,* vol. 10, *The Triumphant Empire: Thunder-Clouds Gather in the West, 1763–1766* (New York, 1967), 111–31. For general political context, see William Pencak, *War, Politics, and Revolution in Provincial Massachusetts* (Boston, 1981), 163–75. (Thomas Pownall appointed Hutchinson lieutenant governor in 1758, hoping to utilize his administrative and organizational talents in managing the Massachusetts war effort. Hutchinson served with distinction; but he fell out with Pownall, whose populist politics he abhorred. Bernard, recognizing Hutchinson's experience, capacity, and alienation from Pownall's political supporters, appointed him chief justice of the Massachusetts Superior Court of Judicature on 13 Nov. 1760. Two previous governors, Shirley and Pownall, had promised this post to James Otis Sr. This so alienated James Otis Jr. that he "swore revenge" on his father's behalf against both the governor and Hutchinson, and soon made himself a leading figure in the opposition, or country party, in the assembly [Waters, *Otis Family,* 119].)

5. "Carnival": Marcus Hansen, from *The Mingling of Canadian and American Peoples,* quoted in Bailyn, *Voyagers to the West: A Passage in the Peopling of America on the Eve of the Revolution* (New York, 1986), 364. On this phase in Nova Scotia history, see esp. Lawrence Henry Gipson, *The British Empire before the American Revolution,* vol. 9, *The Triumphant Empire: New Responsibilities within the Enlarged Empire, 1763–1766* (New York, 1968), 129–42; George Rawlyk, *Nova Scotia's Massachusetts: A Study of Massachusetts–Nova Scotia Relations, 1630 to 1784* (Montréal, 1973), 218–22; John Bartlett Brebner, *The Neutral Yankees of Nova Scotia: A Marginal Colony during the Revolutionary Years* (New York, 1937), 3–121; R. S. Longley, "The Coming of the New England Planters to the Annapolis Valley," in Margaret Conrad, ed., *They Planted Well: New England Planters in Maritime Canada* (Fredericton, N.B., 1988), 14–28; and Elizabeth Mancke, "Corporate Structure and Private Interest: The Mid-Eighteenth Century Expansion of New England," ibid., 161–77.

6. On the progress of Skene's settlement, see Doris Begor Morton, *Philip Skene of Skenesborough* (Glanville, N.Y., 1959), 31; on the rush to the Mohawk (presumably around Fort Stanwix), see Jack Sosin, *Whitehall and the Wilderness: The Middle West in British Colonial Policy, 1760–1775* (Lincoln, Nebr., 1961), 47–8.

7. Michael Bellesiles, *Revolutionary Outlaws: Ethan Allen and the Struggle for Independence on the Early American Frontier* (Charlottesville, Va., 1993), 28–32, 41–6; see also Matt Bushnell Jones, *Vermont in the Making, 1750–1777* (Cambridge, Mass., 1939), 22–3, 42–5, 76–7, 430–2.

8. Robert W. Ramsey, *Carolina Cradle: Settlement of the Northwest Carolina Frontier, 1747–1762* (Chapel Hill, N.C., 1964), especially 95–105, 152–70; 193–9; Rachel N. Klein, *Unification of a Slave State: The Rise of the Planter Class in the South Carolina Backcountry, 1760–1808* (Chapel Hill, N.C., 1990), 14, 54.

9. "Over run": Bouquet to Fauquier, n.d., quoted in Solon J. Buck and Elizabeth Hawthorn Buck, *The Planting of Civilization in Western Pennsylvania* (Pittsburgh, 1939), 141. On Bouquet's attempts to expel squatters, see Gipson, *New Responsibilities,* 89–90.

10. Buck and Buck, *Planting of Civilization,* 141.

11. Alfred P. James, *The Ohio Company: Its Inner History* (Pittsburgh, 1959), 113–26; Thomas Perkins Abernethy, *Western Lands and the American Revolution* (1937; reprint, New York, 1959), 10–11; Sosin, *Whitehall,* 42–6.

CHAPTER FIFTY-FIVE: *Yankees Invade Wyoming—and Pay the Price*

1. On Susquehannah Company operations and popularity in Connecticut, see Julian P. Boyd, ed., *The Susquehannah Company Papers,* vol. 2, 1756–1767 (Wilkes-Barre, Pa., 1930), xvii–xix; Thomas Penn to Lord Halifax, 10 Dec. 1760, ibid., 35; "Minutes of a Meeting of the Susquehannah Company," 9 Apr. 1761, ibid., 72–6; and Ezra Stiles to Pelatiah Webster, 21 May 1763, ibid., 221–33, 230–1. See also Lawrence Henry Gipson, *The British Empire before the American Revolution,* vol. 9, *The Triumphant Empire: New Responsibilities within the Enlarged Empire, 1763–1766* (New York, 1968), 387–8.
2. Quotation from the Opinion of Charles Yorke, Solicitor General, 30 Mar. 1761, *Susquehannah Papers,* 2:68; cf. Opinion of Charles Pratt [attorney general], 7 Mar. 1761, ibid., 64–6. On progress of settlements at Cushitunk, see Deposition of James Hyndshaw Regarding the Settlers at Cushietunk, 29 Apr. 1761, ibid., 81–4.
3. Narrative of Daniel Brodhead's Journey to Wyoming, 27 Sept. 1762, ibid., 166–9; conference with Teedyuscung, 19 Nov. 1762, ibid., 180.
4. Anthony F. C. Wallace, *King of the Delawares: Teedyuscung, 1700–1763* (Philadelphia, 1949), 253–4.
5. Quotation: Teedyuscung's speech, 28 June 1762, in Wallace, *Teedyuscung,* 249. On the conference generally, see ibid., 245–50; Stephen F. Auth, *The Ten Years' War: Indian-White Relations in Pennsylvania, 1755–1765* (New York, 1989), 163–72; and Francis Jennings, *Empire of Fortune: Crowns, Colonies, and Tribes in the Seven Years War in America* (New York, 1988), 434–6.
6. Auth, *Ten Years' War,* 183, 236–7 n. 59; Wallace, *Teedyuscung,* 252–4; Michael N. McConnell, *A Country Between: The Upper Ohio Valley and Its Peoples, 1724–1774* (Lincoln, Nebr., 1992), 179–80.
7. Wallace, *Teedyuscung,* 255–6.
8. Conference with Teedyuscung, 19 Nov. 1762, *Susquehannah Papers,* 2:180–1.
9. On the alienation of the Ohio delegation at Lancaster, see McConnell, *A Country Between,* 179–81; and Auth, *Ten Years' War,* 183–4. Croghan to Bouquet, 10 Dec. 1762: "Itt is Cartain that ye Dallaways [Delawares] have Received a Belt from ye Indians on Susquehanna and Sence that has ordered all thire Warrers to Stay Near there Towns to hunt this Winter and appears More Sulky than usual to the Treaders Residing Amungst them" (ibid., 237 n. 70).
10. Size of migrating population: Stiles to Webster, 21 May 1763, *Susquehannah Papers,* 2:230. Quotation: extract of a letter from Paxton, in Lancaster County, 23 Oct. 1763, ibid., 277. Battle and aftermath: Wallace, *Teedyuscung,* 264 et passim.

CHAPTER FIFTY-SIX: *Amherst's Reforms and Pontiac's War*

1. On Neolin and the other Delaware prophets, see Gregory Evans Dowd, *A Spirited Resistance: The North American Indian Struggle for Unity, 1745–1815* (Baltimore, 1992), 27–34; Richard White, *The Middle Ground: Indians, Empires, and Republics in the Great Lakes Region, 1650–1815* (New York, 1991), 279–83; Michael N. McConnell, *A Country Between: The Upper Ohio and Its Peoples, 1724–1774* (Lincoln, Nebr., 1992), 179, 220–1; and Peter C. Mancall, *Deadly Medicine: Indians and Alcohol in Early America* (Ithaca, N.Y., 1995), 116–17. For the best contemporary description of Neolin's ritual program, see John W. Jordan, ed., "Journal of James Kenny, 1761–1763," *Pennsylvania Magazine of History and Biography* 37 (1913): 188 (entry of 1 Mar. 1763).
2. On the epidemics, crop failure, and famine, all of which were prevalent in the Ohio Valley, see McConnell, *A Country Between,* 177–8, 181; and White, *Middle Ground,* 275.
3. War belts: ibid., 276–7. New leadership: McConnell, *A Country Between,* 183.
4. Apprehensiveness: Nicholas B. Wainwright, *George Croghan, Wilderness Diplomat* (Chapel

Hill, N.C., 1959), 194–5. "Pretended conspiracy": Bouquet [to Amherst?], Nov. 1762, quoted in McConnell, *A Country Between,* 181. "Meer Bugbears": Amherst to Sir William Johnson, 3 Apr. 1763, quoted in White, *Middle Ground,* 286. "This alarm": Amherst to Bouquet, 6 June 1763, quoted in Howard H. Peckham, *Pontiac and the Indian Uprising* (Princeton, N.J., 1947), 172.

5. Pontiac's council at the Ecorse River encampment and Indian strength: [Robert Navarre,] "Journal of Pontiac's Conspiracy," in Milton Milo Quaife, ed., *The Siege of Detroit in 1763* (Chicago, 1958), 5–18; strength of the Detroit garrison and early Indian successes: Peckham, *Pontiac,* 127–8 n. 12, 144, 156–8, 190, 200, 182–4.

6. Lawrence Henry Gipson, *The British Empire before the American Revolution,* vol. 9, *The Triumphant Empire: New Responsibilities within the Enlarged Empire, 1763–1766* (New York, 1968), 99–101; Peckham, *Pontiac,* 159–65; McConnell, *A Country Between,* 182.

7. Ecuyer to Bouquet, 31 May 1763, quoted in Gipson, *New Responsibilities,* 107.

8. On the Seneca, Delaware, and Shawnee operations between Lake Erie and the Ohio, see Peckham, *Pontiac,* 167–70; Gipson, *New Responsibilities,* 105–9; McConnell, *A Country Between,* 181–90 passim; and Solon J. Buck and Elizabeth Hawthorn Buck, *The Planting of Civilization in Western Pennsylvania* (Pittsburgh, 1939), 104–5.

9. McConnell, *A Country Between,* 190.

10. Lack of troops: J. C. Long, *Lord Jeffery Amherst* (New York, 1933), 182, 188–9; Lawrence Henry Gipson, *The British Empire before the American Revolution,* vol. 8, *The Great War for the Empire: The Culmination, 1760–1763* (New York, 1970), 261–2, 275. Response and quotations: Amherst to Egremont, 27 June 1763, quoted in Peckham, *Pontiac,* 177. Amherst responded to the reports about as quickly as anyone could have, given the limited information he had at hand; see the discussion in John W. Shy, *Toward Lexington: The Role of the British Army in the Coming of the American Revolution* (Princeton, N.J., 1965), 113–16.

11. "To extirpate that Vermine": Bouquet to Amherst, 25 June 1763; "We must Use Every Stratagem": Amherst to Bouquet, n.d. [probably 29 June 1763]; both quoted in Gipson, *New Responsibilities,* 108. "Immediately be put to death": Amherst to Gladwin, n.d., quoted in Peckham, *Pontiac,* 226. Amherst to Bouquet, 16 July 1763: "You will do well to try to inoculate the Indians by means of blankets, as well as to try every other method that can serve to extirpate this execrable race" (ibid., 227). In reply Bouquet wrote that he would "try to inoculate the bastards with some blankets that may fall into their hands, and take care not to get the disease myself. As it is a pity to expose good men against them [the Indians], I wish we could make use of the Spanish methods, to hunt them with English dogs" (Bouquet to Amherst, 13 July 1763, quoted in Long, *Amherst,* 187).

12. Ibid., 188–9.

13. Amherst to Johnson, 30 Sept. 1763, in E. B. O'Callaghan, ed., *Documents Relative to the Colonial History of the State of New-York,* vol. 7 (Albany, 1856), 568–9.

14. Shy, *Toward Lexington,* 116–17; Gipson, *New Responsibilities,* 115–17.

15. Gregory Evans Dowd, "The French King Wakes Up in Detroit: 'Pontiac's War' in Rumor and History," *Ethnohistory* 37 (1990): 254–78; White, *Middle Ground,* 277–88.

CHAPTER FIFTY-SEVEN: *Amherst's Recall*

1. Casualties: see Milton Milo Quaife, ed., *The Siege of Detroit in 1763* (Chicago, 1958), 211. Prisoners: Amherst to Maj. John Wilkins, 29 Oct. 1763, quoted in Howard H. Peckham, *Pontiac and the Indian Uprising* (Princeton, N.J., 1947), 239 n. 5.

2. Ibid., 201–10; Lawrence Henry Gipson, *The British Empire before the American Revolution,* vol. 9, *The Triumphant Empire: New Responsibilities within the Enlarged Empire, 1763–1766* (New York, 1968), 102–3. The *Michigan* ran aground and was wrecked near Niagara in August. The *Huron,* the only remaining link between Niagara and Detroit, was very nearly lost to Indian attack on 1 Sept. When the little ship arrived the following day at Detroit, its barrels of flour and pork intact, only six men of its crew had escaped being killed or wounded. The

weapons they had used to repel boarders reminded one witness of "axes in a slaughter house." "In short," wrote the trader James Sterling, "the attack was the bravest ever known to be made by Inds., and the Defense such as British subjects alone are capable of" (quoted in Quaife, *Siege of Detroit,* xx). Even after the *Huron* made a less eventful voyage in early October, the supply situation remained critical; on 3 Oct. Gladwin had only three weeks' supply of flour left. Four days later, nearly in despair, he wrote to Sir William Johnson, "I am brought into a scrape, and left in it; things are expected of me that cant be performed; I could wish I had quitted the service seven years ago, and that somebody else commanded here" (quoted in Peckham, *Pontiac,* 233). Even after Pontiac declared a truce, it was not the arrival of supplies from Niagara that enabled the fort's garrison to survive, but rather the belated willingness of the French community—hitherto neutral—to sell its surplus food to the British; within four days of the truce, they had sold Gladwin four tons of desperately needed flour (ibid., 237). It was well for Detroit that they did, for Seneca attacks at Niagara kept the *Huron* from adequately resupplying the fort before winter (ibid., 240–2). On the general state of Detroit and Gladwin's "want of flour, [so great] that he must either have abandoned his post, or listened to" Pontiac's proposals, see Gage to Halifax, 23 Dec. 1763, in Clarence Edwin Carter, ed., *The Correspondence of General Thomas Gage with the Secretaries of State, 1763–1775,* vol. 1 (New Haven, Conn., 1931), 5.

3. "I feel myself uterly abandoned": Bouquet to James Robertson, 26 July 1763, quoted in Gipson, *New Responsibilities,* 110.

4. On Bouquet's expedition to relieve Fort Pitt, the Battle of Edge Hill (or Bushy Run), and the end of the siege, see Michael N. McConnell, *A Country Between: The Upper Ohio Valley and Its Peoples* (Lincoln, Nebr., 1992), 191–4; Gipson, *New Responsibilities,* 109–13 and "Plan of the Battle near Bushy-Run," facing 124; Peckham, *Pontiac,* 211–13; Richard White, *The Middle Ground: Indians, Empires, and Republics in the Great Lakes Region, 1650–1815* (New York, 1991), 288–9; and John Shy, *Toward Lexington: The Role of the British Army in the Coming of the American Revolution* (Princeton, N.J., 1965), 119. Unlike the principally Scottish 42nd and 77th Regiments, the 60th Regiment included large numbers of colonists, especially Germans from Pennsylvania, who (after 1759) had been permitted to enlist for three years or the duration of the war. It was presumably these who demanded their discharges from Bouquet, and who threatened to mutiny when he refused.

5. Peckham, *Pontiac,* 224–5, 241–2.

6. Francis Jennings, *Empire of Fortune: Crowns, Colonies, and Tribes in the Seven Years War in America* (New York, 1988), 438, 451–2; James Thomas Flexner, *Lord of the Mohawks: A Biography of Sir William Johnson* (Boston, 1979), 258–60; Nicholas B. Wainwright, *George Croghan, Wilderness Diplomat* (Chapel Hill, N.C., 1959), 201–2.

7. Reactions of ministers: Shy, *Toward Lexington,* 121–5. Mutinies in regular units: ibid., 118–20; Paul E. Kopperman, "The Stoppages Mutiny of 1763," *Western Pennsylvania Historical Magazine* 69 (1986): 241–54. Reluctance of provincial legislatures to cooperate, Gipson, *New Responsibilities,* 115–17.

8. On Ligonier's demotion, see Rex Whitworth, *Field Marshal Lord Ligonier: A Story of the British Army, 1702–1770* (Oxford, 1958), 376–8; on Cumberland's physical decline, *Dictionary of National Biography,* s.v. "William Augustus, Duke of Cumberland"; on Gage's assumption of command, J. R. Alden, *General Gage in America: Being Principally a History of His Role in the American Revolution* (Baton Rouge, 1948), 61; on Amherst's belated understanding of the character of his recall, J. C. Long, *Lord Jeffery Amherst* (New York, 1933), 189–92.

PART VIII: *Crisis and Reform,* 1764

CHAPTER FIFTY-EIGHT: *Death Reshuffles a Ministry*

1. William James Smith, ed., *The Grenville Papers,* vol. 2 (1852; reprint, New York, 1970), 193–4.

2. On the arrival of news from America and the ministry's initial reactions, see John Shy, *Toward Lexington: The Role of the British Army in the Coming of the American Revolution* (Princeton, N.J., 1965), 121–4; on the death of Egremont and its impact on politics, see Philip Lawson, *George Grenville: A Political Life* (Oxford, 1984), 160–3; and Peter D. G. Thomas, *British Politics and the Stamp Act Crisis: The First Phase of the American Revolution, 1763–1767* (Oxford, 1975), 12–13; on Pitt, see Stanley Ayling, *The Elder Pitt, Earl of Chatham* (London, 1976), 315; on the king, see John Brooke, *King George III* (New York, 1972), 104–5.

CHAPTER FIFTY-NINE: *An Urgent Search for Order: Grenville and Halifax Confront the Need for Revenue and Control*

1. John Brewer, *The Sinews of Power: War, Money, and the English State, 1688–1783* (New York, 1989), 30; Angus Calder, *Revolutionary Empire* (London, 1981), 586–7.
2. John L. Bullion, " 'The Ten Thousand in America': More Light on the Decision on the American Army, 1762–1763," *William and Mary Quarterly*, 3rd ser., 43 (1986): 646–57; id., "Security and Economy: The Bute Administration's Plans for the American Army and Revenue, 1762–1763," *William and Mary Quarterly*, 3rd ser., 45 (1988): 499–509; John Shy, *Toward Lexington: The Role of the British Army in the Coming of the American Revolution* (Princeton, N.J., 1965), 69–83.
3. George III to Bute, 13 Sept. 1762, in Romney Sedgwick, ed., *Letters from George III to Lord Bute, 1756–1766* (London, 1939), 135. The king meant that the expense *to the British taxpayer* for maintaining the army would be "some hundred pounds cheaper," not that the *total expenditure* on the army would be less than in 1749. See below.
4. Bullion, "Security and Economy," 502–4; Shy, *Toward Lexington,* 73–4.
5. The national debt: Brewer, *Sinews,* 32. (Brewer's figure of £132,000,000 represents the most conservative estimate of the funded portion of the debt at war's end. Grenville himself believed that the funded portion of the debt amounted to £137,000,000, and the debt as a whole to £146,000,000; see Lawrence Henry Gipson, *The British Empire before the American Revolution,* vol. 10, *The Triumphant Empire: Thunder-Clouds Gather in the West, 1763–1766* [New York, 1967], 182.) For the winter session and its politics, see Peter D. G. Thomas, *British Politics and the Stamp Act Crisis: The First Phase of the American Revolution, 1763–1767* (Oxford, 1975), 17–20; and Philip Lawson, *George Grenville: A Political Life* (Oxford, 1984), 171–80. Annual expenses of twenty battalions: Peter D. G. Thomas, "The Cost of the British Army in North America, 1763–1775," *William and Mary Quarterly*, 3rd ser., 45 (1988): 510–16. (The sum with which Parliament was working, £224,906, excluded "extraordinaries"—operating expenses. The actual annual expense averaged £384,174 in 1763–73.) Budget inflexibility: John L. Bullion, *A Great and Necessary Measure: George Grenville and the Genesis of the Stamp Act, 1763–1765* (Columbia, Mo., 1982), 18; Brewer, *Sinews,* 117. (Grenville anticipated revenues of about £9,800,000 sterling annually, of which about 48 percent would be needed to pay interest on the funded debt. Virtually every farthing of its £5,000,000 in discretionary revenue was already committed to pay the costs of government administration and defense.)
6. Expenditures in the colonies: Julian Gwyn, "British Government Spending and the North American Colonies, 1740–1775," in Peter Marshall and Glyn Williams, ed., *The British Atlantic Empire before the American Revolution* (London, 1980), 77. Reimbursements: Jack P. Greene, "The Seven Years' War and the American Revolution: The Causal Relationship Reconsidered," ibid., 98. Contemporary understandings of British government spending and colonial prosperity: Bullion, *Measure,* 23–5. Rising colonial consumption: T. H. Breen, "An Empire of Goods: The Anglicization of Colonial America, 1690–1776," *Journal of British Studies* 25 (1986): 467–99; id., " 'Baubles of Britain': The American and Consumer Revolutions of the Eighteenth Century," *Past and Present* 119 (1988): 73–87; and id., "Narrative of Commercial Life: Consumption, Ideology, and Community on the Eve of the American Revolution," *William and Mary Quarterly*, 3rd ser., 50 (1993): 471–501. Impact of war on political

economy: Nancy F. Koehn, *The Power of Commerce: Economy and Governance in the First British Empire* (Ithaca, N.Y., 1994).

7. Bullion, *Measure,* 62–4; Gipson, *Thunder-Clouds Gather,* 203, 206–7.

8. Bullion, *Measure,* 73.

9. Ibid., 80–2; 106–8; Lawson, *Grenville,* 166–80, 187–94; Thomas, *Politics,* 45–7; Koehn, *Power,* 125–7.

10. Thomas, *Politics,* 41–3; Lawrence Henry Gipson, *The British Empire before the American Revolution,* vol. 9, *The Triumphant Empire: New Responsibilities within the Enlarged Empire, 1763–1766* (New York, 1968), 41–6; Jack Sosin, *Whitehall and the Wilderness: The Middle West in British Colonial Policy, 1760–1775* (Lincoln, Nebr., 1961), 52–65.

11. The proclamation also erected a fourth government, from the West Indian islands ceded to Britain in the Peace of Paris, in the colony of Grenada, or the British Windward Islands. See Gipson, *New Responsibilities,* 232–47. For the quotations in the following paragraphs, see David C. Douglas, ed., *English Historical Documents,* vol. 9, *American Colonial Documents to 1776,* ed. Merrill Jensen (New York, 1955), 640–3.

12. The same provisions for grants also extended to "such reduced officers of our navy . . . as served on board our ships of war in North America at the times of the reduction of Louisbourg and Quebec" (ibid., 641; sailors and petty officers were excluded, perhaps by oversight).

13. Indian plan draft: Halifax to Amherst, 19 Oct. 1763, in Clarence Edwin Carter, ed., *The Correspondence of General Thomas Gage with the Secretaries of State, and with the War Office and the Treasury, 1763–1775,* vol. 2 (New Haven, Conn., 1933), 4–5. (Cf. the complete proposal, reprinted as "Plan for the Future Management of Indian Affairs," 10 July 1764, in E. B. O'Callaghan, ed., *Documents Relative to the Colonial History of the State of New-York,* vol. 7 [Albany, 1856], 637–41.) Also see John Richard Alden, *John Stuart and the Southern Colonial Frontier* (1944; reprint, New York, 1966), 242–4; J. Russell Snapp, *John Stuart and the Struggle for Empire on the Southern Frontier* (Baton Rouge, 1996), 58–64; Nicholas B. Wainwright, *George Croghan, Wilderness Diplomat* (Chapel Hill, N.C., 1959), 207–8; and Gipson, *New Responsibilities,* 431–2. Parliament never implemented the plan formally (it was too expensive), but the superintendents organized the Indian trade after 1764 along the lines it laid down.

14. Sosin, *Whitehall,* 52–78.

CHAPTER SIXTY: *The American Duties Act (The Sugar Act)*

1. Lawrence Henry Gipson, *The British Empire before the American Revolution,* vol. 10, *The Triumphant Empire: Thunder-Clouds Gather in the West, 1763–1766* (New York, 1967), 180–1; Philip Lawson, *George Grenville: A Political Life* (Oxford, 1984), 171.

2. This account of the session follows Peter D. G. Thomas, *British Politics and the Stamp Act Crisis: The First Phase of the American Revolution, 1763–1767* (Oxford, 1975), 17–20; and Lawson, *Grenville,* 171–80. "Beyond all example": Grenville to Northumberland, 26 Feb. 1764, quoted in John L. Bullion, *A Great and Necessary Measure: George Grenville and the Genesis of the Stamp Act, 1763–1765* (Columbia, Mo., 1982), 90. King's support: William James Smith, ed., *The Grenville Papers,* vol. 2 (1852; reprint, New York, 1970), 491.

3. "Brevity": Horace Walpole, *Memoirs of the Reign of King George the Third,* ed. G. F. Russell Barker (New York, 1894), 1:309. "This hour": Grenville's speech to the Commons, 9 Mar. 1764, in Lawson, *Grenville,* 195.

4. Pitt and Townshend: Stanley Ayling, *The Elder Pitt, Earl of Chatham* (New York, 1976), 321; Cornelius P. Forster, *The Uncontrolled Chancellor: Charles Townshend and His American Policy* (Providence, 1978), 49–54. "There did not seem": Mauduit to the secretary of Massachusetts Bay, 7 Apr. 1764, in Gipson, *Thunder-Clouds Gather,* 231.

5. For the American Duties Act, see David C. Douglas, ed., *English Historical Documents,* vol. 9, *American Colonial Documents to 1776,* ed. Merrill Jensen (New York, 1955), 644–8. On the provisions relating to customs enforcement, see Edmund S. Morgan and Helen M. Mor-

gan, *The Stamp Act Crisis: Prologue to Revolution* (1953; rev. ed., New York, 1963), 40; Edmund S. Morgan, ed., *Prologue to Revolution: Sources and Documents on the Stamp Act Crisis, 1764–1766* (Chapel Hill, N.C., 1959), 4–8; Thomas, *Politics*, 45–8; and Gipson, *Thunder-Clouds Gather*, 227–31. On the operation of the more complex British system, see Elizabeth E. Hoon, *The Organization of the English Customs System, 1696–1786* (New York, 1938), esp. 143–8, 256–64; on the American customs, Thomas Barrow, *Trade and Empire: The British Customs Service in Colonial North America, 1660–1775* (Cambridge, Mass., 1967), 182–4 (on the provisions of the American Duties Act) and passim. For a discussion of the act that differs in emphasis from my own, by stressing the antismuggling intent of the Grenville administration as evidence of orthodox mercantilism, see John W. Tyler, *Smugglers and Patriots: Boston Merchants and the Advent of the American Revolution* (Boston, 1986), 75–83.

6. The tun was the unit from which most other English standard measures descended (the pipe, or butt, was a half tun; the puncheon, a third; the hogshead, a quarter; the tierce, a sixth; the barrel, an eighth); in 1700 Parliament defined a tun as holding 252 "wine gallons." The wine gallon, one of two official English gallons, measured 231 cu. in., eventually became the standard U.S. gallon. Cask volumes, of course, varied according to the bulge and height, the depth at which the head was set, and so on. For the most complete conceivable discussion of British measures and variations in usages from the late Middle Ages through the eighteenth century, see John J. McCusker, *Rum and the American Revolution: The Rum Trade and the Balance of Payments of the Thirteen Continental Colonies*, vol. 2 (New York, 1989), 768–878.

7. On the new duties, see Thomas, *Politics*, 47–8; Gipson, *Thunder-Clouds Gather*, 226; and Bullion, *Measure*, 100–4.

8. Molasses and rum prices are those at Boston in 1762, from McCusker, *Rum and Revolution*, 2:1078, 1080; adjusted to sterling according to the rates in id., *Money and Exchange in Europe and America, 1600–1775: A Handbook* (Chapel Hill, N.C., 1978), 142. On the openness of the trade, Thomas Hutchinson observed: "Such indulgence has been shewn . . . to that branch of illicit trade [in French molasses], that nobody considered it as such." As he went on to explain, the real cause of the smuggling was the poor compensation of customsmen, who were, generally speaking, the deputies of nonresident officials: "they are quartered upon for more than their legal fees [i.e., their employers charged them more than they could collect], &. . . without bribery & corruption, they must starve" (Hutchinson to Richard Jackson, 17 Sept. 1763, quoted in Gipson, *Thunder-Clouds Gather*, 208).

9. Quotation: Nathaniel Ware to Grenville, 22 Aug. 1763; reprinted in Bullion, *Measure*, 221. Ware noted that the Molasses Act's sixpence sterling duty could theoretically be collected, if provincial excise taxes levied on rum—wartime measures to finance the costs of raising provincial troops—could be eliminated. In Massachusetts, the leading rum distiller in the colonies, the provincial tax on rum was approximately sixpence per gallon and was indispensable to discharging the colony's war debt. Were rum to be subjected to an additional tax by the exaction of the full Molasses Act levy, Ware warned, "that Trade must Totally fail."

10. Morgan, *Crisis*, 41–2; Gipson, *Thunder-Clouds Gather*, 208–22; Bullion, *Measure*, 78–98, 220–3; Thomas, *Politics*, 47–50.

CHAPTER SIXTY-ONE: *The Currency Act*

1. Except where noted, the following discussion derives from Joseph Ernst, *Money and Politics in America, 1755–1775: A Study in the Currency Act of 1764 and the Political Economy of Revolution* (Chapel Hill, N.C., 1973), 43–88, 376; and Peter D. G. Thomas, *British Politics and the Stamp Act Crisis: The First Phase of the American Revolution, 1763–1767* (Oxford, 1975), 62–6. For information on exchange rates to supplement Ernst's graphs, see John J. McCusker, *Money and Exchange in Europe and America, 1600–1775: A Handbook* (Chapel Hill, N.C., 1978), 211.

2. Julian Hoppit, "Financial Crises in Eighteenth-Century England," *Economic History Review*, 2nd ser., 39 (1986): 49–50.

3. The Currency Act appears in David C. Douglas, ed., *English Historical Documents,* vol. 9, *American Colonial Documents to 1776,* ed. Merrill Jensen (New York, 1955), 649–50; quotation from 649.
4. On reimbursements in proportion to wartime expenditures, see Jack Greene, "The Seven Years' War and the American Revolution: The Causal Relationship Reconsidered," in Peter Marshall and Glyn Williams, eds., *The British Atlantic Empire before the American Revolution* (London, 1980), 98. The continental colonies as a whole expended £2,568,248 on the war and received £1,086,769 from Parliament as "free gifts"—42.3 percent of the total. The six colonies most heavily engaged in prosecuting the war—Massachusetts, Connecticut, New York, New Jersey, Pennsylvania, and Virginia—bore 88.5 percent of the expense, expending a total of £2,271,804. Parliament eventually reimbursed these provinces £949,023, or 41.8 percent. Connecticut, for reasons that probably had to do with its assembly's compliant attitude and its agent's speed in submitting accounts, received a disproportionate share of the reimbursement funds: £231,752, or 89.2 percent of its expenditures. If it is excluded from the calculation as an anomaly, parliamentary reimbursements to the remaining five colonies totaled £717,271, covering 35.7 percent of expenditures.

My point in arguing counterfactually that an alternative scheme of colonial defense might have averted problems that later arose is *not* to maintain that such a measure would have worked easily had it been proposed—there would inevitably have been problems with an army in which all officers were British and all enlisted men American—but merely to emphasize that nothing like it ever *was* proposed; and hence to point up the limitations in British thinking about the colonies' capacity to defend themselves.
5. On the backward-looking character of British policy, see esp. John Murrin, "The French and Indian War, the American Revolution, and the Counterfactual Hypothesis: Reflections on Lawrence Henry Gipson and John Shy," *Reviews in American History* 1 (1973): 307–18.

CHAPTER SIXTY-TWO: *Postwar Conditions and the Context of Colonial Response*

1. On the character and timing of the downturn, see William S. Sachs, "The Business Outlook in the Northern Colonies, 1750–1775" (Ph.D. diss., Columbia University, 1957), 107–13; Marc Egnal, *A Mighty Empire: The Origins of the American Revolution* (Ithaca, N.Y., 1988), 126–33; and Thomas Doerflinger, *A Vigorous Spirit of Enterprise: Merchants and Economic Development in Revolutionary Philadelphia* (Chapel Hill, N.C., 1986), 95–7, 168–80. On its British and macroeconomic context, see Nancy F. Koehn, *The Power of Commerce: Economy and Governance in the First British Empire* (Ithaca, N.Y., 1994), 52–3. Except as specified, the ensuing discussion follows these accounts.
2. In New York, the rate of exchange of province currency against sterling began to climb in late 1760. Starting in the mid-160s, it passed 180 in the spring of 1761, then hovered in the 182–190 range until late 1765. In Philadelphia, the rate rose from the mid-150s to 170 at the end of 1760, briefly touched 180 in mid-1762, and then oscillated between 178 and 170 until the fall of 1765. In Boston the rate jumped from 127 in May 1760 to 135 by the end of the year, bounced up to 145 in April 1761, and then gradually fell to 133 by late 1764—a level it maintained for the next five years. See the tables in John J. McCusker, *Money and Exchange in Europe and America, 1600–1775: A Handbook* (Chapel Hill, N.C., 1978), 186, 165, 142.
3. Sachs, "Business Outlook," 113–26.
4. Ibid., 126–30; Koehn, *Power,* 52–3.
5. Philadelphia and New York bankruptcies: Sachs, "Business Outlook," 131–3; Egnal, *Mighty Empire,* 131–2; Doerflinger, *Vigorous Spirit,* 56–7. The case of Thomas Riche: ibid., 49, 82, 133, 146–8.
6. Like all generalizations about the colonies, this one needs to be qualified. Not all regions suffered alike, or in precise synchrony. The recession barely touched the South Carolina low country in the 1760s. Virginia's tobacco economy would bottom out in 1764, begin to recover

in 1765, and improve significantly until suffering more reversals at the end of the decade. As we will see below, the Philadelphia dry goods sector would remain in serious trouble throughout the decade, but provision traders would suffer most severely only in 1764–68, thus providing some respite for Philadelphia business as other northern merchants were slipping into trouble, and brightening its outlook in 1769, when Philadelphia would lead the northern port towns in the recovery. Despite local exceptions and countertrends, however, most colonies and colonists (and particularly the northern ports and the most commercialized agricultural regions) experienced the 1760s as a decade of real and persistent economic dislocation. The resulting social strain carried significant consequences for colonial political life and helped impart an antagonistic character to colonial-metropolitan relations.

7. Boston: John Tyler, *Smugglers and Patriots: Boston Merchants and the Advent of the American Revolution* (Boston, 1986), 65–75, 285 n. 17; Gary Nash, *The Urban Crucible: Social Change, Political Consciousness, and the Origins of the American Revolution* (Cambridge, Mass., 1979), 254. New York: Sachs, "Outlook," 132–7 passim (quotation from John Watts to Scott, Pringle, Cheape and Co., 5 Feb. 1764, at 136); Nash, *Crucible,* 250, 497 n. 83. Philadelphia: Doerflinger, *Vigorous Spirit,* 173–7; Nash, *Crucible,* 255; Egnal, *Mighty Empire,* 132.

8. Winifed Barr Rothenberg, *From Market-Places to a Market Economy: The Transformation of Rural Massachusetts, 1750–1850* (Chicago, 1992), 109 (table 8, "Weighted Index of on-the-Farm Prices Received by Massachusetts Farmers, 1750–1855"); id., "A Price Index for Rural Massachusetts, 1750–1855," *Journal of Economic History* 39 (1979): 975–1001.

9. Disruptions in tobacco markets: Jacob Price, *France and the Chesapeake: A History of the French Tobacco Monopoly, 1674–1791, and of Its Relationship to the British and American Tobacco Trades,* vol. 1 (Ann Arbor, Mich., 1973), 588–677; T. H. Breen, *Tobacco Culture: The Mentality of the Great Tidewater Planters on the Eve of Revolution* (Princeton, N.J., 1985), esp. 125–32. Quotation: George Washington to James Gildart, 26 Apr. 1763, in W. W. Abbot et al., eds., *The Papers of George Washington, Colonial Series,* vol. 7, January 1761–June 1767 (Charlottesville, Va., 1990), 201. Most of the ordinary-quality tobacco grown by small and middling planters in the Chesapeake, unlike the sweet-scented premium leaf that the gentry grew for the London market, was bought by resident Scottish factors, or storekeepers, and shipped to correspondents in Glasgow, Whitehaven, and on the Clyde, who reexported it to France under contract with the state monopoly. The French crown needed the revenues it derived from the tobacco monopoly so badly that it allowed this trade to continue during the war; wartime conditions and restrictions, however—British tobacco ships had to return in ballast, insurance rates were extremely high, and so on—radically diminished the profits to be made by tobacco planters themselves.

10. On Washington as a representative planter responding to the recession of the 1760s, see Douglas Southall Freeman, *George Washington: A Biography,* vol. 3, *Planter and Patriot* (New York, 1951), 71–118; and Breen, *Tobacco Culture,* 147–50, 208–9.

11. The returns planter speculators realized on land sales to yeomen farmers have not yet been quantified, but the great planters clearly used their position as burgesses to make grants of land to syndicates that they themselves comprised (e.g., the Loyal Company and the Ohio Company), and from which they made speculative profits. Gentry surveyors like Peter Jefferson and George Washington aggressively pursued land acquisitions as individuals, while gentleman landholders sought to dominate the real-estate and rental markets wherever they could. The ability to control access to freehold land reinforced gentry social dominance, even in frontier counties where access to land was comparatively easier than in the tidewater. Thus any contraction in speculation carried social and cultural as well as economic consequences for the planter elite. See Turk McClesky, "Rich Land, Poor Prospects: Real Estate and the Formation of a Social Elite in Augusta County, Virginia, 1738–1770," *Virginia Magazine of History and Biography* 48 (1990): 449–86.

12. Distilling and the Great Dismal Swamp venture: Freeman, *Planter and Patriot,* 116–17, 100–3. Mississippi Company: Articles of Agreement, 3 June 1763, *Papers of Washington,* 7:219–25.

13. Croghan's mission: Nicholas B. Wainwright, *George Croghan, Wilderness Diplomat* (Chapel Hill, N.C., 1959), 203; Yoko Shirai, "The Indian Trade in Colonial Pennsylvania, 1730–1768: Traders and Land Speculation" (Ph.D. diss., University of Pennsylvania, 1985), 151–98. Croghan, Franklin, and the Illinois Company: Samuel Wharton to Franklin, 23 Nov. 1764, in Leonard W. Labaree et al., eds., *The Papers of Benjamin Franklin,* vol. 9, January 1 through December 31, 1764 (New Haven, Conn., 1967), 476–7. Croghan's persistence: Wainwright, 253–5, 305–10.
14. On Lyman and the Military Adventurers, see Harold Selesky, *War and Society in Colonial Connecticut* (New Haven, Conn., 1990), 204–5, 210–11; Bernard Bailyn, *Voyagers to the West: A Passage in the Peopling of America on the Eve of the Revolution* (New York, 1986), 484–8; and esp. [Albert C. Bates, ed.], *The Two Putnams: Israel and Rufus in the Havana Expedition of 1762 and in the Mississippi River Exploration of 1772–73 with Some Account of the Company of Military Adventurers* (Hartford, 1931), 1–20.
15. Bailyn, *Voyagers;* id., *The Peopling of British North America: An Introduction* (New York, 1986), 7–66.
16. A. Roger Ekirch, *"Poor Carolina": Politics and Society in Colonial North Carolina, 1729–1776* (Chapel Hill, N.C., 1981), esp. 168–83.
17. Quotation: Laurens to Richard Oswald and Co., 15 Feb. 1763, quoted in Egnal, *Mighty Empire,* 147–8. On the character of South Carolina's prosperity and the mild effects of the recession, see ibid., 147–9. In yet another instance of the smallness of the Anglo-American trading world and the powerful effects on it of the war, it is worth noting that Laurens's correspondent, Oswald, was part of a group of once-marginal, once-provincial British merchants that parlayed military contracts and government contacts into great wealth and postwar political clout. They had acquired formerly French slave-trading stations at bargain-basement rates, and at the end of the war they supplied Africans to the West Indies and the mainland. For a keen appreciation of how war and slavery offered matchless opportunities to those able to seize them, see David Hancock, *Citizens of the World: London Merchants and the Integration of the British Atlantic Community, 1735–1785* (New York, 1995).
18. On New Jersey, see Thomas L. Purvis, *Proprietors, Patronage, and Paper Money: Legislative Politics in New Jersey, 1703–1776* (New Brunswick, N.J., 1986), esp. 168–71, 229–45. On Connecticut, Rhode Island, and New York: Jackson Turner Main, *Political Parties before the Constitution* (Chapel Hill, N.C., 1973) 3–17; Patricia U. Bonomi, *A Factious People: Politics and Society in Colonial New York* (New York, 1971), 140–278; John M. Murrin, "Political Development," in Jack P. Greene and J. R. Pole, eds., *Colonial British North America: Essays in the New History of the Early Modern Era* (Baltimore, 1984), esp. 432–47.
19. Egnal, *Mighty Empire,* 191–8; Main, *Political Parties,* 8–9.
20. Virginia: Egnal, *Mighty Empire,* 217; Merrill Jensen, *The Founding of a Nation: A History of the American Revolution, 1763–1776* (New York, 1968), 95–7; Main, *Political Parties,* 11. Massachusetts: William Pencak, *War, Politics, and Revolution in Provincial Massachusetts* (Boston, 1981), 158–75.

CHAPTER SIXTY-THREE: *An Ambiguous Response to Imperial Initiatives*

1. Edmund S. Morgan and Helen M. Morgan, *The Stamp Act Crisis: Prologue to Revolution* (New York, 1963), 43 (quotation from Francis Bernard, *Select Letters on the Trade and Government of America* [1774]).
2. John Tyler, *Smugglers and Patriots: Boston Merchants and the Advent of the American Revolution* (Boston, 1986), 83–4. Quotations: "Boston instructions to its delegates in the Massachusetts Legislature," David C. Douglas, ed., *English Historical Documents,* vol. 9, *American Colonial Documents to 1776,* ed. Merrill Jensen (New York, 1955), 663–4 (hereafter cited as *Am. Col. Docs.*).
3. Merrill Jensen, *The Founding of a Nation: A History of the American Revolution, 1763–1776* (New York, 1968), 82–4; Pauline Maier, *The Old Revolutionaries: Political Lives in the Age of*

Samuel Adams (New York, 1980), 3–50. See also William M. Fowler, *Samuel Adams: Radical Puritan* (New York, 1997).

4. Jensen, *Founding,* 85–7; Morgan and Morgan, *Stamp Act Crisis,* 51–3. *The Rights of the Colonies Asserted and Proved* is reprinted with commentary in Bernard Bailyn, ed., *Pamphlets of the American Revolution, 1750–1775,* vol. 1 (Cambridge, Mass., 1965), 419–82, quotation at 454. For commentary on the pamphlet, see esp. Bailyn's introduction, ibid., 409–17; and id., *Ideological Origins of the American Revolution* (Cambridge, Mass., 1967), 176–81; also Gordon S. Wood, *Creation of the American Republic, 1776–1787* (Chapel Hill, N.C., 1969), 262–5.

5. Hutchinson objects, privately: Malcolm Freiberg, *Prelude to Purgatory: Thomas Hutchinson in Provincial Massachusetts Politics, 1760–1770* (New York, 1990), 71–7; Bernard Bailyn, *The Ordeal of Thomas Hutchinson* (Cambridge, Mass., 1974), 62–4. Quotation: Bernard to Halifax, 10 Nov. 1764, in Lawrence Henry Gipson, *The British Empire before the American Revolution,* vol. 10, *The Triumphant Empire: Thunder-Clouds Gather in the West, 1763–1766* (New York, 1967), 235 n. 30.

6. The North Carolina Assembly also registered a protest against the American Duties Act as a violation of colonial rights, but it did so only locally, in the form of a message to Governor Arthur Dobbs. It could have been known in Britain only if the governor transmitted it, which he seems not to have done. See Morgan and Morgan, *Stamp Act Crisis,* 57; A. Roger Ekirch, *"Poor Carolina": Politics and Society in Colonial North Carolina, 1729–1776* (Chapel Hill, N.C., 1981), 148–60; Jack P. Greene, *The Quest for Power: The Lower Houses of Assembly in the Southern Royal Colonies, 1689–1776* (Chapel Hill, N.C., 1963), 364.

7. On James De Lancey's political power, see Patricia U. Bonomi, *A Factious People: Politics and Society in Colonial New York* (New York, 1971), 171–8. On Colden, see ibid., 152–5; and Milton M. Klein, "Prelude to Revolution in New York: Jury Trials and Judicial Tenure," in id., ed., *The Politics of Diversity: Essays in the History of Colonial New York* (Port Washington, N.Y., 1974), 154–77. Quotations are from John Watts to Monckton, 10 Nov. 1764, Watts to Isaac Barré, 19 Jan. 1765, and Robert R. Livingston to Monckton, 23 Feb. 1765, ibid., 168.

8. Petition to the House of Commons, 18 Oct. 1764; in Edmund S. Morgan, ed., *Prologue to Revolution: Sources and Documents on the Stamp Act Crisis, 1764–1766* (Chapel Hill, N.C., 1959), 8–14.

9. "Colonists may not be taxed": Rhode Island petition, 29 Nov. 1764, quoted in Jensen, *Founding,* 87. Connecticut Assembly and Ingersoll: Gipson, *Thunder-Clouds Gather,* 236–7.

10. Gipson, *The British Empire before the American Revolution,* vol. 9, *The Triumphant Empire: New Responsibilities within the Enlarged Empire, 1763–1766* (New York, 1968), 114; Jensen, *Founding,* 27–8; "Remonstrance of the Pennsylvania frontiersmen," 13 Feb. 1764, *Am. Col. Docs.,* 614–17; Alden Vaughan, "Frontier Banditti and the Indians: The Paxton Boys' Legacy, 1763–1775," *Pennsylvania History* 51 (1984): 1–5.

11. Jensen, *Founding,* 88–90; Esmond Wright, *Franklin of Philadelphia* (Cambridge, Mass., 1986), 138–54.

12. Petition to the King, and Memorial to the House of Lords, both 18 Dec. 1764, in Morgan, *Prologue,* 14–15.

13. Remonstrance to the House of Commons, 18 Dec. 1764, ibid., 16–17.

CHAPTER SIXTY-FOUR: *Pontiac's Progress*

1. John Shy, *Toward Lexington: The Role of the British Army in the Coming of the American Revolution* (Princeton, N.J., 1965), 125–34; see also John Richard Alden, *General Gage in America* (Baton Rouge, 1948), 65–88.

2. Shy, *Toward Lexington,* 135–6; Alden, *Gage,* 93–4; Gage to Egremont, 17 Nov. 1763, in Clarence Edwin Carter, ed., *The Correspondence of General Thomas Gage with the Secretaries of State, 1763–1775,* vol. 1 (New Haven, Conn., 1931), 1–2; Gage to Halifax, 9 Dec. 1763, 2–4; Amherst to Gage, 17 Nov. 1763, *The Correspondence of General Thomas Gage with the Secretaries of State, 1763–1775,* vol. 2 (New Haven, Conn., 1933), 209–14.

3. Alden, *Gage,* 94–5; id., *John Stuart and the Southern Colonial Frontier* (1944; reprint, New York, 1966), 196; William Smith, *Historical Account of Henry Bouquet's Expedition against the Ohio Indians, in 1764* (Cincinnati, 1868), 29–44; Lawrence Henry Gipson, *The British Empire before the American Revolution,* vol. 9, *The Triumphant Empire: New Responsibilities within the Enlarged Empire, 1763–1766* (New York, 1968), 123–4. Pennsylvania's contribution was, as usual, delayed by the intractable dispute between the antiproprietary and proprietary factions in the assembly.

4. Gipson, *New Responsibilities,* 117–18; William G. Godfrey, *Pursuit of Profit and Preferment in Colonial North America: John Bradstreet's Quest* (Waterloo, Ont., 1982), 192–5, 197–8.

5. "When the Indians": Amherst to Gage, 17 Nov. 1763, *Gage Corr.,* 2:212. "Fill their canoes": James Thomas Flexner, *Lord of the Mohawks: A Biography of Sir William Johnson* (Boston, 1979), 268.

6. "The largest Number": Johnson to Cadwallader Colden, 23 Aug. 1764, quoted in Gipson, *New Responsibilities,* 118–19. Johnson negotiated treaties with each group present, evidently all on similar lines; see E. B. O'Callaghan et al., eds., *The Papers of Sir William Johnson,* vol. 4 (Albany, 1924), 511–14. Conference expenses: "Journals of Capt. John Montresor," ed. G. D. Scull, New-York Historical Society *Collections,* 14 (1881): 275.

The end of the alcohol ban has never been properly appreciated as a strategic move. On 1 Nov. 1763 Gladwin suggested to Amherst that "if your Excellency still intends to punish them [the Indians] further for their barbarities, it may be easily done without any expense to the Crown by permitting a free sale of rum, which will destroy them more effectually than fire and sword" (quoted in Howard H. Peckham, *Pontiac and the Indian Uprising* [Princeton, N.J., 1947], 238). Amherst ignored the suggestion, but Johnson embraced it. Like Gladwin, he knew that among the heaviest consumers of alcohol would be exactly those young men who, sober, had been such formidable opponents in 1763. With liquor to turn their aggressiveness against one another, disorder, murders, and suffering within Indian communities would doubtless increase, but with a few precautions (such as allowing the trade only at major posts and prohibiting consumption on the site) Britain's reestablished garrisons would have little to fear, and much to gain, by reopening the traffic in alcohol. In October 1764 he argued to the Board of Trade that the Indian trade "will never be so extensive without" the sale of rum, for four reasons:

> First, the extreme desire the Indians have for it, and the strong requests the several Nations made for the sale thereof, when lately at Niagara, which I was obliged to promise, should be complied with, and the same is approved by Genl Gage. Secondly, that as the Indians value it above any thing else, they will not stick at giving such price for it, as will make good addition to the fund for the purposes of the [Indian] Departm[en]t. Thirdly, that without it, the Indians can purchase their cloathing with half the quantity of Skins, which will make them indolent, and lessen the Fur Trade. And lastly, that from what I find, the Indians will be universally discontented without it (Johnson to the Lords of Trade, n.d. [8 Oct. 1764], in E. B. O'Callaghan, ed., *Documents Relative to the Colonial History of the State of New-York,* vol. 7 [Albany, 1856], 665 [hereafter, *DRCHSNY*]).

In short, Johnson argued that since the demand for rum was virtually unlimited, it might as well be taxed to support his department. This cynical view made enough sense to the Board of Trade that it sanctioned a resumption in the rum trade. In 1764, responding to what was presumably pent-up demand, Johnson's northern department sold approximately 50,000 gallons of rum to the Indians. This was high, but not too far from the amount ordinarily supplied in later years. By 1767, traders at Fort Pitt brought in an estimated 13,000 gallons of rum; in that same year at Detroit the quantity was approximately 24,000 gallons. Annual consumption among western Indians as a whole during the 1760s, exclusive of amounts obtained from Canadian traders, seems to have run between 80,000 and 170,000 gallons (Peter C. Mancall, *Deadly Medicine: Indians and Alcohol in Early America* [Ithaca, N.Y., 1995], 53–4, 163). Another work, published too late to inform the narrative here, generally supports this conclusion and suggests that with the Canadian trade reckoned in, the quantity may have been substantially larger—as much as 240,000 gallons annually, or a per capita consumption rate for adult males of 12 gallons annually. See Walter S. Dunn Jr., *Frontier Profit and Loss: The British Army and the Fur Traders, 1760–1764* (Westport, Conn., 1998), 178–9.

7. Godfrey, *Pursuit of Profit,* 193–5. Bradstreet's health never fully recovered after this episode, which may have marked the onset of the cirrhosis that would finally kill him, a decade later (ibid., 262–3).

8. Godfrey, *Pursuit of Profit,* 196–205; Gipson, *New Responsibilities,* 118–21; Peckham, *Pontiac,* 255–60; Richard White, *The Middle Ground: Indians, Empires, and Republics in the Great Lakes Region, 1650–1815* (New York, 1991), 291–6.

9. "Congress With The Western Nations," 7–10 Sept. 1764, quoted in Godfrey, *Pursuit of Profit,* 205.

10. "His Majesty": "A Short Abstract of the Proceedings at a Congress held at Detroit the 7th Septr. 1764 . . . ," quoted ibid., 206. Subsequent quotations: Bradstreet to Charles Gould, 4 Dec. 1764, and "Colonel Bradstreets opinion of Indians and their affairs," 4 Dec. 1764, ibid., 234–5. "Colonel Bradstreet's thoughts on Indian Affairs," 4 Dec. 1764, *DRCHSNY,* 7:690–4, makes clear the links between Indian culture, trade, military force, geography, and strategy central to his thinking:

> To insure a lasting peace, gain their affections, and wean them from the French, strict justice, moderation, fair Trade, with keeping them from frequent intercourse with each other, and a respectable force at Detroit, is the way to obtain it, unless their whole dependence for the necessaries of life depended upon the English, which will never be the case, as long as the French can come up the Mississippi in safety, land, and extend their Trade on our side with impunity. . . .
>
> It is absolutely necessary to make choice for the establishing posts, for . . . the Savages of each Lake to carry on their Trade with ease to themselves; . . . without this indulgence, they will never be contented, nor conspiracies warded off.

Thus a vigorous trade would have to be sustained at Detroit, along with enough force (two battalions) that the commandant would "have it in his power to detach from his Garrison Three Hundred good Men, besides Militia, to chastize any Nation or Band of Savages, the instant they deserve it; for, by taking immediate satisfaction, they will respect, and fear us, and thereby prevent a General War." Finally, Bradstreet stressed that establishing an emporium at Detroit was the only way to eliminate the Six Nations' malign influence over the interior Indian peoples. (That this would coincidentally cripple Sir William Johnson may also have crossed his mind.)

11. Godfrey, *Pursuit of Profit,* 228–9; Sir William Johnson, "Remarks on the Conduct of Colonel Bradstreet," 24 Nov. 1764, *Johnson Papers,* 4:601; "Journals of Montresor," 287 (entry of 31 Aug. 1764). "Roughly equivalent": White, *Middle Ground,* 297.

12. Gage to Bradstreet, 16 Aug. 1764, in Godfrey, *Pursuit of Profit,* 211.

13. Morris to Bradstreet, 18 Sept. 1764, ibid., 212. Also see "The Journal of Captain Thomas Morris of His Majesty's XVII Regiment of Infantry," in Reuben Gold Thwaites, ed., *Early Western Travels, 1748–1846,* vol. 1 (Cleveland, 1904), 301–28; and Peckham, *Pontiac,* 256–60. The failure of the chiefs to return with prisoners was probably not evidence that Bradstreet had been deceived, as his enemies argued, but an indication that the delegation had come to Presque Isle only on behalf of peace factions in their villages, hoping that news of British willingness to make peace would sway local majorities upon their return. Their nonappear-

ance, in that case, would prove only that they had not convinced their communities that peace was at hand (something that news of Bradstreet's behavior at Detroit would surely have argued against).

14. Godfrey, *Pursuit of Profit,* 218–21; Michael N. McConnell, *A Country Between: The Upper Ohio Valley and Its Peoples, 1724–1774* (Lincoln, Nebr., 1992), 206. Capt. Montrésor described the journey from Sandusky to Niagara (three hundred miles) in harrowing detail: "Journals of Montresor," 311–18.

15. Smith, ed., *Bouquet's Expedition,* 51.

16. Quotations: ibid., 60. Expedition: Gipson, *New Responsibilities,* 124–6.

17. Gage to Halifax, 13 Dec. 1764, *Gage Corr.,* 1:46.

18. Manpower and financial restraints: "Colonel Bradstreet's thoughts on Indian Affairs," *DRCHSNY,* 7:693; cf. Bouquet to Gage, 30 Nov. 1764, cited in Nicholas B. Wainwright, *George Croghan, Wilderness Diplomat* (Chapel Hill, N.C., 1959), 213. Gage's annual expenses were running between £335,000 and £411,000 as opposed to the £225,000 contemplated in 1763; see Peter D. G. Thomas, "The Cost of the British Army in North America, 1763–1775," *William and Mary Quarterly,* 3rd ser., 45 (1988): 514. (The Treasury restricted Gage's spending to funds appropriated by Parliament, allowing him to borrow only in emergencies, under stringent restraints. [Treasury Minutes, 28 Nov. 1764, *Gage Corr.,* 2:269.]) Diplomatic initiatives: White, *Middle Ground,* 304. Ross and Crawford: Gipson, *New Responsibilities,* 419–20; Gage to Halifax, 1 June and 10 Aug. 1765, *Gage Corr.,* 1:58–65; John Richard Alden, *Stuart,* 197, 204.

19. Wainwright, *Croghan,* 211–17; Thomas M. Doerflinger, *A Vigorous Spirit of Enterprise: Merchants and Economic Development in Revolutionary Philadelphia* (Chapel Hill, N.C., 1986), 148–9; Gage to Halifax, 23 Jan. and 27 Apr. 1765, *Gage Corr.,* 1:47–9, 55–8.

20. Wainwright, *Croghan,* 218–19; McConnell, *A Country Between,* 204–5; Peckham, *Pontiac,* 270.

21. Peckham, *Pontiac,* 270–7; White, *Middle Ground,* 301–3.

22. Alden, *Stuart,* 202–4; quotation is from Capt. James Campbell to Maj. Robert Farmar, 26 Mar. 1765, quoted at 203 n. 53.

23. Wainwright, *Croghan,* 220–1; Peckham, *Pontiac,* 280–1; White, *Middle Ground,* 302–5; quotation is from Croghan to William Murray, 12 July 1765, in C. W. Alvord and C. E. Carter, "The New Regime, 1765–1767," *Collections of the Illinois State Historical Library* 11 (1916): 58.

24. Peckham, *Pontiac,* 281–5; Gage to Henry Seymour Conway, 23 Sept. 1765, *Gage Corr.,* 1:66; White, *Middle Ground,* 303–5.

CHAPTER SIXTY-FIVE: *The Lessons of Pontiac's War*

1. Howard H. Peckham, *Pontiac and the Indian Uprising* (Princeton, N.J., 1947), 306–16; Richard White, *The Middle Ground: Indians, Empires, and Republics in the Great Lakes Region, 1650–1815* (New York, 1991), 312–13.

2. Ibid., 313–14. Walter S. Dunn Jr., *Frontier Profit and Loss: The British Army and the Fur Traders, 1760–1764* (Westport, Conn., 1988), 182–3, also treats the Indian rebellion as a success for the insurgents.

3. Barrington to Gage, 10 Oct. 1765, in John Shy, ed., "Confronting Rebellion: Private Correspondence of Lord Barrington with General Gage, 1765–1775," *Sources of American Independence: Selected Manuscripts from the Collections of the William L. Clements Library,* ed. Howard H. Peckham, vol. 1 (Chicago, 1978), 9–10.

4. All quotations are from Gage to Barrington, 18 Dec. 1765, ibid., 13–16.

5. Gage to Barrington, 8 Jan. 1766, ibid., 18–19.

6. John Shy, *Toward Lexington: The Role of the British Army in the Coming of the American Revolution* (Princeton, N.J., 1965), 229.

PART IX: *CRISIS COMPOUNDED*, 1765–1766

CHAPTER SIXTY-SIX: *Stamp Act and Quartering Act*

1. Stanley Ayling, *The Elder Pitt, Earl of Chatham* (New York, 1976), 322–4.
2. Quotations: Rose Fuller and Charles Townshend, in the diary of Nathaniel Ryder, in R. C. Simmons and Peter D. G. Thomas, eds., *Proceedings and Debates of the British Parliaments Respecting North America, 1754–1783*, vol. 2, 1765–1768 (Millwood, N.Y., 1983), 13 (punctuation altered to bring out sense of Townshend's speech).
3. "Disgust": Barré, in Ryder's diary, ibid (punctuation altered to bring out sense of passage). "They planted" to "a word": Jared Ingersoll's summary, id. to Thomas Fitch, 11 Feb. 1765, ibid., 16–17. (Barré's vehemence doubtless reflected his reverence for Wolfe's memory and his distaste for Townshend's older brother, Robert—the brigadier most bitterly antagonistic to Wolfe at Québec.)
4. Quotation: Ryder diary summary, ibid., 12. Defeat of adjournment motion and subsequent passage: Peter D. G. Thomas, *British Politics and the Stamp Act Crisis: The First Phase of the American Revolution, 1763–1767* (Oxford, 1975), 93–8.
5. John Bullion, *A Great and Necessary Measure: George Grenville and the Genesis of the Stamp Act* (Columbia, Mo., 1982), 147–9, 181–91.
6. Edmund S. Morgan, ed., *Prologue to Revolution: Sources and Documents on the Stamp Act Crisis, 1764–1766* (Chapel Hill, N.C., 1959), 35–43. The stamps were not, like modern postage stamps, gummed paper, but rather inch-tall impressions made on paper by a die, like a modern notary's seal. Newspapers and most legal documents would be printed on prestamped paper, which could be legally purchased only from stamp distributors or their designated agents. Because parchment (scraped animal skin) would not hold a stamped impression, legal documents customarily inscribed on parchment (diplomas and the like) would have a small piece of stamped paper affixed by glue and a staplelike metal fastener. Stamped paper would similarly be glued as seals on packs of playing cards or boxes of dice. For a description of the stamps and examples of the impressions, see C. A. Weslager, *The Stamp Act Congress* (Newark, Del., 1976), 35–9.
7. Lawrence Henry Gipson, *American Loyalist: Jared Ingersoll* (New Haven, Conn., 1971), 145–7; Edmund Morgan and Helen Morgan, *The Stamp Act Crisis: Prologue to Revolution* (New York, 1963), 301–11; Bullion, *Great and Necessary Measure*, 169–70, 173.
8. Philip Lawson, *George Grenville: A Political Life* (Oxford, 1984), 211–14; Thomas, *British Politics*, 115–16.
9. Gage and previous quartering difficulties: John R. Alden, *General Gage in America: Being Principally a History of His Role in the American Revolution* (Baton Rouge, 1948), 32, 34–5; Stanley Pargellis, *Lord Loudoun in North America* (1933, reprint, New York, 1968), 195–6; Alan Rogers, *Empire and Liberty: American Resistance to British Authority, 1755–1763* (Berkeley, Calif., 1974), 82–4. Postwar circumstances and quartering: John Shy, *Toward Lexington: The Role of the British Army in the Coming of the American Revolution* (Princeton, N.J., 1965), 169–71, 174–5.
10. Legal complexity of quartering: ibid., 163–76. Gage acts: Gage to Welbore Ellis, 22 Jan. 1765, with enclosures, in Clarence Edwin Carter, ed., *The Correspondence of General Thomas Gage with the Secretaries of State, 1763–1775*, vol. 2 (New Haven, Conn., 1931), 262–6.
11. Thomas, *British Politics*, 102–3; for an assessment of Ellis as a "genuinely incompetent" secretary at war, see Shy, *Toward Lexington*, 182.
12. "In such manner": draft bill, in Thomas, *British Politics*, 103. Opposition, and withdrawal of bill: Simmons and Thomas, *Proceedings and Debates*, 2:42.
13. Shy, *Toward Lexington*, 187; Thomas, *British Politics*, 108. The bill was approved as a separate act rather than an amendment to the Mutiny Act because the Mutiny Act of 1765 had expired and been reenacted before the Quartering Act debates concluded; thus the Quarter-

ing Act had to be reenacted annually as a kind of supplement directed specifically at America.

14. Quotation: Loudoun to the duke of Cumberland, 29 Aug. 1756, in Rogers, *Empire and Liberty,* 82.

15. John Watts to Gov. Robert Monckton, 1 June 1765, quoted in Shy, *Toward Lexington,* 188. Watts was no radical, Shy notes, but "an army contractor and future Tory."

CHAPTER SIXTY-SEVEN: *Grenville's End*

1. On the American Trade Act, which eased restrictions on small-scale coasting vessels, permitted colonial iron and lumber to be exported once more to Ireland, established bounties on colonial iron and lumber exported to Britain, relaxed restrictions on American trade to the Azores and southern Europe, and limited the fees customs collectors could charge, see Peter D. G. Thomas, *British Politics and the Stamp Act Crisis: The First Phase of the American Revolution, 1763–1767* (Oxford, 1975), 108–12; and Lawrence Henry Gipson, *The British Empire before the American Revolution,* vol. 10, *The Triumphant Empire: Thunder-Clouds Gather in the West,* 1763–1766 (New York, 1967), 280–1. On the king's illness, see John Brooke, *King George III* (New York, 1972), 109–10, 318–43; and esp. Ida Macalpine and Richard Hunter, *George III and the Mad-Business* (London, 1969).

2. Thomas, *British Politics,* 116–18; Philip Lawson, *George Grenville: A Political Life* (Oxford, 1984), 214–16; Brooke, *King George III,* 110–13; Stanley Ayling, *George the Third* (New York, 1972), 125–7.

3. Unemployment was symptomatic of the rapid shifts in technology and the relations of production then besetting silk weaving, the first branch of British textile manufacture to undergo industrialization. The London weavers, who possessed a long-standing intellectual tradition, achieved an early consciousness of class, understood the efficacy of collective action, and took the first steps in Britain toward industrial organization. By permitting combinations of masters and journeymen to set wages, the Spitalfields Acts of 1765 and 1773 in effect recognized trade-unionism among the weavers. See E. P. Thompson, *The Making of the English Working Class* (New York, 1966), passim; Charles Wilson, *England's Apprenticeship, 1603–1763* (London, 1965), 195, 351; and Harold Perkin, *The Origins of Modern English Society, 1780–1880* (London, 1969), 32–3. On the king's reaction to the riots, see Brooke, *King George III,* 113–16; and Ayling, *George the Third,* 127–9.

4. Lawson, *Grenville,* 217–18.

5. Brooke, *King George III,* 121–2.

6. William James Smith, ed., *The Grenville Papers,* vol. 3 (1853; reprint, New York, 1970), 215–16 (10 July 1765).

7. Ibid., 215.

CHAPTER SIXTY-EIGHT: *The Assemblies Vacillate*

1. On the responses of the various colonial assemblies, see Merrill Jensen, *The Founding of a Nation: A History of the American Revolution, 1763–1776* (New York, 1968), 111–19; also, esp., Edmund S. Morgan and Helen M. Morgan, *The Stamp Act Crisis: Prologue to Revolution* (New York, 1963): 132–4 (R.I.), 294–5 (Conn.), 121, 196 ff. (N.Y.). Similar inaction characterized N.H. (139), N.J. (139, 147, 198), Md. (100–8), N.C. (139), S.C. (201–2), and Ga. (202–3). On Pa., see ibid., 311–12; and Benjamin Newcomb, *Franklin and Galloway: A Political Partnership* (New Haven, Conn., 1972), 113–18; quotation from Galloway to Franklin, 18 July 1765, ibid., 116.

2. On the Hopkins-Howard-Otis controversy, see Bernard Bailyn, ed., *Pamphlets of the American Revolution, 1750–1775,* vol. 1 (Cambridge, Mass., 1965), 500–5, 524–30, 546–52; quotation from *Defence of the Halifax Libel* at 550 (original italics deleted here). On representation and the differing American and British understandings of this critical doctrine, see Gordon S. Wood, *The Creation of the American Republic, 1776–1787* (Chapel Hill, N.C., 1969), 25–8, 173–85, et passim.

3. Quotation: Bernard to John Pownall, May 1765, in Morgan and Morgan, *Stamp Act Crisis,* 140.
4. "To consider": Massachusetts circular letter, quoted in Morgan and Morgan, *Stamp Act Crisis,* 139. Delegation: ibid., 139–41. "Never consent": Bernard to the Board of Trade, 8 July 1765, quoted ibid., 140.
5. Douglas Southall Freeman, *George Washington: A Biography,* vol. 3, *Planter and Patriot* (New York, 1951), 129–30; Richard R. Beeman, *Patrick Henry: A Biography* (New York, 1974), 22–34.
6. Resolutions: Freeman, *Planter and Patriot,* 133; Beeman, *Henry,* 33–5 ("steps necessary" and "alone, unadvised": quoted from Henry's memoir on the resolves, at 35). The Virginia Resolves are reprinted in their variant forms in Edmund S. Morgan, ed., *Prologue to Revolution: Sources and Documents on the Stamp Act Crisis, 1764–1766* (Chapel Hill, N.C., 1959), 47–50; these quotations follow Henry's manuscript, 47.
7. On 8 May, a party of between twenty and thirty young men attacked ten Overhill Cherokee warriors passing through the Shenandoah Valley on their way to the Ohio Country, killing five. Fauquier issued a proclamation offering rewards for the perpetrators and tried urgently to reassure the Cherokee headmen that the killers would be brought to justice. He was clearly paying more attention to this affair than to the Burgesses until debates on Henry's resolves. See the series of letters from this period in George Reese, ed., *The Official Papers of Francis Fauquier, Lieutenant Governor of Virginia, 1758–1768,* vol. 3, *1764–1768* (Charlottesville, Va., 1983), 1235–48.
8. All quotations in this and the previous paragraph are from Fauquier to the Board of Trade, 5 June 1765, ibid., 1250–1.
9. Jefferson's reactions: Dumas Malone, *Jefferson and His Time,* vol. 1, *Jefferson the Virginian* (Boston, 1948), 88–94 (quotation is from Jefferson to William Wirt, 5 Aug. 1815, at 93). On Henry's rhetorical style, see Rhys Isaac, *The Transformation of Virginia, 1740–1790* (Chapel Hill, N.C., 1982), 266–9; and T. H. Breen, *Tobacco Culture: The Mentality of the Great Tidewater Planters on the Eve of the Revolution* (Princeton, N.J., 1985), 188–90.

CHAPTER SIXTY-NINE: *Mobs Respond*

1. On the resolves, see the variant versions in Edmund S. Morgan, ed., *Prologue to Revolution: Sources and Documents on the Stamp Act Crisis, 1764–1766* (Chapel Hill, N.C., 1959), 49–50; and the discussion in id. and Helen M. Morgan, *The Stamp Act Crisis: Prologue to Revolution* (New York, 1963), 127–30. The sixth and seventh resolves were probably written by John Fleming, who represented Cumberland County, and/or George Johnston, member for Fairfax; they were the only colleagues to whom Henry had shown his own five resolves (Richard R. Beeman, *Patrick Henry, A Biography* [New York, 1974], 39–40). The resolutions quoted here follow the version in the *Newport Mercury.*
2. On the composition of the Loyal Nine, see Morgan, *Stamp Act Crisis,* 160–1; G. B. Warden, *Boston, 1689–1776* (Boston, 1970), 163; Pauline Maier, *From Resistance to Revolution: Colonial Radicals and the Development of American Opposition to Britain, 1765–1776* (New York, 1972), 58, 85–6, 307; and the description of a meeting on 15 Jan. 1765 by John Adams, in Lyman H. Butterfield et al., eds., *Diary and Autobiography of John Adams,* vol. 1, *Diary, 1755–1770* (New York, 1964), 294. "The People of Virginia have spoke": Edes, quoted in Morgan and Morgan, *Stamp Act Crisis,* 135. (The "insipid Thing" was the polite protest against parliamentary taxation that Thomas Hutchinson had stage-managed through the Council and House of Representatives in late 1764.)
3. Maier, *From Resistance to Revolution,* 53–8, 69–70; Morgan and Morgan, *Stamp Act Crisis,* 161 ff; Peter Shaw, *American Patriots and the Rituals of Revolution* (Cambridge, Mass., 1981), 16–18, 180–97 passim; Dirk Hoerder, *Crowd Action in Revolutionary Massachusetts, 1765–1780* (New York, 1977), 91–7; George P. Anderson, "Ebenezer Mackintosh: Stamp Act Rioter and Patriot," Colonial Society of Massachusetts, *Publications* 26 (1927): 15–64.

4. There are many accounts of the events on August 14. This one follows Morgan and Morgan, *Stamp Act Crisis,* 161–5; Hoerder, *Crowd Action,* 97–101; Lawrence Henry Gipson, *The British Empire before the American Revolution,* vol. 10, *The Triumphant Empire: Thunder-Clouds Gather in the West, 1763–1766* (New York, 1967), 292–4; Bernard to Halifax, 15 Aug. 1765, in Morgan, *Prologue,* 106–8; and Diary of John Rowe, entry of 14 Aug. 1765, in Anne Rowe Cunningham, ed., *The Letters and Diary of John Rowe, Boston Merchant, 1759–1762, 1764–1779* (Boston, 1903; reprint, 1969), 88–9. Boston's High Street ran the length of the neck, connecting the town peninsula to the mainland; it was thus as close to a thoroughfare as the town could be said to possess in 1765. Later renamed Washington Street, in 1765 it had four separately named stretches from the neck to the Province House: Orange Street, Newbury Street, Marlborough Street, and Cornhill. Deacon Elliot's Corner was a small square where Frog Lane (today's Boylston Street) entered from the west, dividing Orange from Newbury. See Lester Cappon et al., eds., *Atlas of Early American History: The Revolutionary Period, 1760–1790* (Princeton, N.J., 1976), 9.

5. Bernard to Halifax, 15 Aug. 1765, in Morgan, *Prologue,* 108.

6. On the Wheelwright bankruptcy, see John Cary, *Joseph Warren: Physician, Politician, Patriot* (Urbana, Ill., 1961), 45–7, 120–1. Quotation and comparison of the panic and the Lisbon earthquake: James Otis to George Johnstone et al., 25 Jan. 1765, Massachusetts Historical Society, *Proceedings* 43 (1909–10): 204–7 (quotation at 205). See also the account in *Letters and Diary of Rowe,* 74–5 (diary entries of 15–21 Jan. 1765). Wheelwright complicated Boston's problems by making over his assets to a relative before he left, and then dying—intestate—soon after he arrived in the French West Indies; the probate proceedings on his estate lasted more than twenty-five years (Nathaniel Wheelwright Probate Records, docket 14148, Suffolk County Courthouse, Boston).

7. Bernard Bailyn, *The Ordeal of Thomas Hutchinson* (Cambridge, Mass., 1974), 29–32.

8. The following account derives from Hoerder, *Crowd Action,* 104–10; Morgan and Morgan, *Stamp Act Crisis,* 166–9; Bailyn, *Ordeal,* 70–155 passim; Gipson, *Thunder-Clouds Gather,* 295–7.

9. Bernard to the Board of Trade, 31 Aug. 1765, quoted in Lawrence Henry Gipson, *The Coming of the Revolution, 1763–1775* (New York, 1962), 93.

10. Hutchinson to Richard Jackson, 30 Aug. 1765, in Morgan, *Prologue,* 108–9.

11. Ibid., 109.

12. The following account is based on Morgan and Morgan, *Stamp Act Crisis,* 191–4; Thomas Moffat to Joseph Harrison, 16 Oct. 1765, in Morgan, *Prologue,* 109–13; and Jensen, *Founding,* 111–12.

13. Gipson, *Thunder-Clouds Gather,* 303–4 (McEvers), 306–7 (Coxe), 302–3 (Meserve), 316 (Mercer; quotation is from Mercer to Rockingham, 11 Apr. 1766, ibid.), 319–20 (South Carolina), 317–18 (North Carolina).

14. Ibid., 312–14.

15. Lawrence Henry Gipson, *American Loyalist: Jared Ingersoll* (New Haven, Conn., 1971), 177–85. On the participation of former provincials in the mob that compelled the resignation and on Fitch's loss of office, see Harold Selesky, *War and Society in Colonial Connecticut* (New Haven, Conn., 1990), 214–15, 222–4. On Fitch's effort to justify himself publicly by pamphlet, and on his later career, see *Dictionary of American Biography,* s.v. "Fitch, Thomas"; and Gipson, *Ingersoll,* 252–313, esp. 290–3, 296 n. On the transfer of assembly dominance from the Old Light, western, and conservative party to the New Light eastern insurgents, see Richard L. Bushman, *From Puritan to Yankee: Character and the Social Order in Connecticut, 1690–1765* (Cambridge, Mass., 1967), 261–6; on the cultural significance of Ingersoll's resignation, ibid., 284–8. See also Oscar Zeichner, *Connecticut's Years of Controversy, 1750–1776* (Williamsburg, Va., 1949), 44–77.

16. The following account derives from Morgan and Morgan, *Stamp Act Crisis,* 312–24; Gipson, *Thunder-Clouds Gather,* 307–11; and Benjamin Newcomb, *Franklin and Galloway: A Political Partnership* (New Haven, Conn., 1972), 115–25.

17. Morgan, *Prologue,* 51–2, reprints the resolves.

CHAPTER SEVENTY:
Nullification by Violence, and an Elite Effort to Reassert Control

1. James M. Johnson, *Militiamen, Rangers, and Redcoats: The Military in Georgia, 1754–1776* (Macon, Ga., 1992), 55–66. See also John Shy, *Toward Lexington: The Role of the British Army in the Coming of the American Revolution* (Princeton, N.J., 1965), 214–15; and W. W. Abbott, *The Royal Governors of Georgia, 1754–1775* (Chapel Hill, N.C., 1959), 105–16. Ironically, the British government disbanded the rangers in March 1767 as an economy measure (Johnson, *Militiamen*, 67).
2. "Journals of Capt. John Montresor," ed. G. D. Scull, New-York Historical Society, *Collections* 14 (1881): 336–9 (entries for 23 Oct.–5 Nov. 1765; quotations at 337); Shy, *Toward Lexington*, 211–14; Lawrence Henry Gipson, *The British Empire before the American Revolution*, vol. 10, *The Triumphant Empire: Thunder-Clouds Gather in the West, 1763–1766* (New York, 1967), 304–6. An excellent account of New York in the immediate postwar period and the Stamp Act crisis unfortunately came to hand too late to influence this narrative and the preceding account of the effects of the postwar depression on the northeastern port towns. It is, however, generally consistent with my own understanding, in that it stresses the significance of both the Seven Years' War and Cadwallader Colden as influences on New Yorkers' behavior in the years 1763–66. See Joseph S. Tiedemann, *Reluctant Revolutionaries: New York City and the Road to Independence, 1763–1776* (Ithaca, N.Y., 1997), 43–6 (impact of postwar depression), 49–55 (character of Colden), 55–61 (significance of the war), and 62–82 (riot and aftermath).
3. Pauline Maier, *From Resistance to Revolution: Colonial Radicals and the Development of American Opposition to Britain, 1765–1776* (New York, 1972), 68–9.
4. The nine colonial assemblies that passed resolves were Va. (31 May), R.I. (Sept.), Pa. (21 Sept.), Md. (28 Sept.), Conn. (25 Oct.), Mass. (29 Oct.), S.C. (29 Nov.), N.J. (30 Nov.), and N.Y. (18 Dec.); see Edmund S. Morgan, ed., *Prologue to Revolution: Sources and Documents on the Stamp Act Crisis, 1764–1766* (Chapel Hill, N.C., 1959), 47–62. Mass., R.I., Conn., N.Y., N.J., Pa., Del., Md., and S.C. sent delegations to the Stamp Act Congress. N.H.'s assembly, in the pocket of Gov. Benning Wentworth, declined to send a delegation, while the governors of Va., N.C., and Ga. refused to convene their assemblies and thus prevented the election of delegates (Edmund S. Morgan and Helen M. Morgan, *The Stamp Act Crisis: Prologue to Revolution* [New York, 1963], 139). Except where otherwise noted, the following account of the congress's proceedings derives from C. A. Weslager, *The Stamp Act Congress* (Newark, Del., 1976), 107–68.
5. Only Christopher Gadsden, delegate from South Carolina, protested against petitioning the House of Commons, on the grounds that the colonies derived none of their rights from it; he withdrew the motion when more conservative delegates objected (Morgan and Morgan, *Stamp Act Crisis*, 147–8).
6. Morgan, *Prologue*, 68.
7. Mob restraint: Maier, *From Resistance to Revolution*, 69–71. Quotation: Francis Bernard to John Pownall, 1 and 5 Nov. 1765, ibid. Boston's merchants made a large donation to the mobs and provided Ebenezer Mackintosh with a splendid uniform, a gold-laced hat, a cane, and a speaking trumpet. He marched, as "Captain-General of the Liberty Tree," at the head of the parade, arm-in-arm with a member of the Council. Later the merchants footed the bill for a magnificent "union" dinner at which two hundred men from the mobs and other antistamp constituencies celebrated the victory of liberty—and order (Peter Shaw, *American Patriots and the Rituals of Revolution* [Cambridge, Mass., 1981], 180, 188–90).
8. Maier, *From Resistance to Revolution*, 72–4.
9. Origins and spread of nonimportation: ibid., 74; Bernhard Knollenberg, *Origin of the American Revolution, 1759–1766* (New York, 1960), 192–3, cites articles from the *Providence Gazette* and the *Connecticut Courant* from Oct. 1764. Boston's association: Arthur Meier

Schlesinger, *The Colonial Merchants and the American Revolution, 1763–1776* (1918; reprint, New York, 1966), 78, 80. *"Upwards of Two Hundred"*: "The New York Agreement, October 31, 1765," in Morgan, *Prologue,* 106. Philadelphia: Schlesinger, *Colonial Merchants,* 79. Thomas M. Doerflinger, in *A Vigorous Spirit of Enterprise: Merchants and Economic Development in Revolutionary Philadelphia* (Chapel Hill, N.C., 1986), 189, notes that the Philadelphia merchants had been divided, generally, between antiproprietary Quakers who favored submission and proprietary Anglicans and Presbyterians who opposed it. Their evident unity on nonimportation may have reflected fears of violence, if they did not comply.

10. 14 Oct. 1765; reprinted in Robert J. Taylor et al., eds., *Papers of John Adams,* vol. 1, September 1755–October 1773 (Cambridge, Mass., 1977), 147.

11. Ploughjogger to the *Boston Evening-Post,* 20 June 1763, in *Papers of Adams,* 1:63. (Adams wrote three Ploughjogger letters in 1763, then no more until October 1765.)

12. Quotation: diary entry, 18 Dec. 1765, in L. H. Butterfield et al., eds., *Diary and Autobiography of John Adams,* vol. 1, *Diary 1755–1770* (Cambridge, Mass., 1962), 263; weather: entry of 19 Dec., ibid., 265 ("A fair Morning after a severe Storm of 3 days and 4 Nights. A vast Quantity of rain fell").

13. *Diary and Autobiography,* 1:285 (entry of 2 Jan. 1766).

14. On the significance of women in resistance, see esp. Mary Beth Norton, *Liberty's Daughters: The Revolutionary Experience of American Women, 1750–1800* (Boston, 1980), 155–94; and Linda K. Kerber, *Women of the Republic: Intellect and Ideology in Revolutionary America* (Chapel Hill, N.C., 1980), 35–42.

15. *Diary and Autobiography,* 1:282–4.

PART X: *EMPIRE PRESERVED?* 1766

CHAPTER SEVENTY-ONE: *The Repeal of the Stamp Act*

1. Paul Langford, *The First Rockingham Administration, 1765–1766* (Oxford, 1973), 77–83, and Peter D. G. Thomas, *British Politics and the Stamp Act Crisis* (Oxford, 1975), 132–8.

2. For an assessment of Rockingham's character, personality, and habits, see Langford, *Rockingham Administration,* esp. 16–21 and 244–8; also (less critically) Ross J. S. Hoffman, *The Marquis: A Study of Lord Rockingham, 1730–82* (New York, 1973), esp. ix–xii, 1–21, 79–80, 94, 333–4.

3. Since late May 1765, Temple had been reconciled with his younger brother, George Grenville, which meant that he had been estranged from his brother-in-law, William Pitt; thus Pitt's demand that Temple be offered the Treasury was either a ploy to detach him from Grenville (for Temple was notoriously covetous of both honors and office), or a nonnegotiable demand intended to make it clear that Pitt had assumed office on his own terms. Temple, it seems, hoped to restore the old family alliance, with himself as first lord of the Treasury and Pitt and Grenville as secretaries of state for the Southern and Northern Departments. See Stanley Ayling, *The Elder Pitt, Earl of Chatham* (New York, 1976), 330–1, 339–40.

4. Langford, *First Rockingham Administration,* 104–5, 135–8; Ayling, *Elder Pitt,* 335–7, 343–4; Thomas, *British Politics,* 175–6.

5. On the massacre, see Lewis Namier, *England in the Age of the American Revolution* (1930; reprint, New York, 1961), 403–15. The voting strength of the King's Friends was reckoned in Jan. 1766 at about 148; see Langford, *Rockingham Administration,* 156–8.

6. Edmund Burke would later make the alienation of the Rockinghams from the King's Friends a major theme of *Thoughts on the Cause of the Present Discontents* (1770), alleging that Bute's allies had deliberately undermined the Rockingham ministry. Paul Langford, in *A Polite and Commercial People: England, 1727–1783* (Oxford, 1989), 527–8, dismisses this view as "a sublime and beautiful form of sour grapes"; but cf. Conor Cruise O'Brien, *The Great Melody: A Thematic Biography and Commented Anthology of Edmund Burke* (Chicago, 1992), esp. i–lii.

7. "Plan of Business," 28 Nov. 1765 [misdated 27 Nov.], in Langford, *Rockingham Administration,* 111. I have reordered Rockingham's phrases for syntactical clarity.
8. Rockingham's analysis—which is to say, the analysis of the merchants whom he consulted—did not extend to the functioning of the Proclamation of 1763. This measure was failing to stabilize the backcountry and malfunctioning badly in Canada, where Yankee traders who had arrived after the war were in a state of virtual rebellion against a governor who, they claimed, favored Canadian papists in violation of the proclamation's terms (Hilda Neatby, *Quebec: The Revolutionary Age, 1760–1791* [Toronto, 1966], 36–55; and Lawrence Henry Gipson, *The British Empire before the American Revolution,* vol. 9, *The Triumphant Empire: New Responsibilities within the Enlarged Empire, 1763–1766* [New York, 1968], 172–6).
9. Langford, *Rockingham Administration,* 111–18, 200–12.
10. Thomas, *British Politics,* 168–70; Langford, *Rockingham Administration,* 135–6, 141–3.
11. "Authority" and "welfare": speech from the Throne, 14 Jan. 1765, in Thomas, *British Politics,* 170. "A pepper-corn": speech of Robert Nugent, Lord Clare, M.P. for Bristol, summarized in William Stanhope Taylor and John Henry Pringle, eds., *Correspondence of William Pitt, Earl of Chatham,* vol. 2 (London, 1838), 364. See also Edmund S. Morgan and Helen M. Morgan, *The Stamp Act Crisis: Prologue to Revolution* (New York, 1963), 267.
12. Quotations from "Confidence is a plant of slow growth" to "the head of man": *Chatham Corr.,* 2:365–7. "Ought to be . . . erroneous policy": summary of Pitt's position by James West, quoted in Thomas, *British Politics,* 172.
13. Quoted in Lawrence Henry Gipson, *The British Empire before the American Revolution,* vol. 10, *The Triumphant Empire: Thunder-Clouds Gather in the West, 1763–1766* (New York, 1961), 378.
14. Pitt's reply to Grenville, 14 Jan. 1766, in *Chatham Corr.,* 2:369–73.
15. Yorke and the Declaratory Act: Langford, *Rockingham Administration,* 151. Trecothick's petition drive: ibid., 119–24; and Thomas, *British Politics,* 187–8.
16. Langford, *A Polite and Commercial People,* 366; id., *Rockingham Administration,* 153–4; Thomas, *British Politics,* 189–90.
17. Ibid., 191–5; Langford, *Rockingham Administration,* 154–6. Rockingham's meeting with the king was only minimally reassuring. George preferred a modification of the Stamp Act to repeal and offered his support only if Rockingham refrained from making it public. He refused to countenance the dismissal of any minister—he was thinking of his friend Lord Northington, the lord chancellor—who broke with the administration's policy. He then sent an account of the meeting to Northington, implying that he expected the ministry to fall. See the king to the lord chancellor, 3 Feb. 1766, in John Fortescue, ed., *The Correspondence of King George the Third, from 1760 to December 1783,* vol. 1, 1760 to 1767 (1927; reprint, London, 1967), 252.
18. Thomas, *British Politics,* 195–9.
19. Resolutions: quoted in Gipson, *Thunder-Clouds Gather,* 390–1. Grenville's motion: Grenville to Hans Stanley, 6 Feb. 1766, in Thomas, *British Politics,* 206.
20. Langford, *Rockingham Administration,* 175–8; Gipson, *Thunder-Clouds Gather,* 392–3; Thomas, *British Politics,* 206–17 (quotation: Benjamin Franklin to Joseph Fox, 24 Feb. 1766, at 213).
21. Summary of Trecothick's testimony, ibid., 217–19.
22. On the risk of social disturbance arising from unemployment, see Langford, *Rockingham Administration,* 182–5. The following summary of Franklin's testimony derives from the version reprinted in Leonard W. Labaree et al., eds., *The Papers of Benjamin Franklin,* vol. 13, January 1 through December 31, 1766 (New Haven, Conn., 1969), 129–59.
23. *The Examination of Doctor Benjamin Franklin, before an August Assembly, relating to the Repeal of the Stamp Act, &c.* (Philadelphia, 1766).
24. Nugent quotation: Franklin's notes on the examination, quoted ibid., 159 n. 1. Vote: Thomas, *British Politics,* 233.

25. Ibid., 240–1, 246–7; Langford, *Rockingham Administration,* 190–5; Gipson, *Thunder-Clouds Gather,* 398–407. The House of Lords actually had a small majority in favor of using troops to enforce the Stamp Act, and its approval of the repeal bill looked doubtful because several powerful peers—notably the duke of Bedford and the earl of Sandwich—thought Rockingham too soft on the colonists. In the end a procedural issue determined the outcome. The Stamp Act had been a "supply bill"—a tax measure—which constitutionally could only be granted by the Commons; thus authority to repeal also lay solely with the Commons, and the Lords had only the duty of offering their advice (which they had done in debate) and consent (Langford, *Rockingham Administration,* 192–4).

CHAPTER SEVENTY-TWO: *The Hollowness of Empire*

1. "Houses at night": *Annual Register, 1766,* quoted in Lawrence Henry Gipson, *The British Empire before the American Revolution,* vol. 11, *The Triumphant Empire: The Rumbling of the Coming Storm, 1766–1770* (New York, 1967), 3. "Many Barrels": *Pennsylvania Gazette,* 22 May 1766. The Commons House of Assembly stipulated that Pitt should be depicted "in the Ciceronian character and habiliment" (Stanley Ayling, *The Elder Pitt, Earl of Chatham* [New York, 1976], 345).

CHAPTER SEVENTY-THREE: *Acrimonious Postlude: The Colonies after Repeal*

1. "Open your Courts": Placard posted before the Massachusetts Province House, Dec. 1765[?], quoted in John J. Waters Jr., *The Otis Family in Provincial and Revolutionary Massachusetts* (Chapel Hill, N.C., 1968), 157. Hopeful letters, dismal prospects: Conway to Francis Bernard, 31 Mar. 1766, quoted in John Tyler, *Smugglers and Patriots: Boston Merchants and the Advent of the American Revolution* (Boston, 1986), 94. Business went on as usual in all the major ports by the clearing of ships on unstamped paper, since it very soon became clear that without trade the economy would totally collapse. Virginia's surveyor general of customs was the first to allow coastal shipping to clear port without stamps, on 2 Nov. 1765; followed by Newport on 22 Nov.; Philadelphia, 2 Dec.; Boston, 17 Dec.; Annapolis (Maryland), 30 Jan. 1766; Savannah, sometime in Feb.; and Charleston, 4 Feb. Judges were more reluctant than customs officials to operate without stamps, and most merely granted continuances (which did not require stamps) from session to session through the spring term of 1766. Nonetheless, at least two court systems opened before news of the repeal reached the colonies, and operated with unstamped documents: the inferior courts in Massachusetts, on 13 Jan. 1766; and the entire court system of Maryland, on 8 Apr. 1766 (Lawrence Henry Gipson, *The British Empire before the American Revolution,* vol. 10, *The Triumphant Empire: Thunder-Clouds Gather in the West, 1763–1766* [New York, 1967], lxxiv–lxxv).
2. "Contrivers": quoted in Merrill Jensen, *The Founding of a Nation: A History of the American Revolution, 1763–1776* (New York, 1968), 193. "Thus the Triumph": entry of 28 May 1766, in L. H. Butterfield et al., eds., *Diary and Autobiography of John Adams,* vol. 1, *Diary 1755–1770* (Cambridge, Mass., 1962), 313. This account follows Jensen, *Founding,* 193–8; William Pencak, *War, Politics, and Revolution in Provincial Massachusetts* (Boston, 1981), 172–5; and Lawrence Henry Gipson, *The British Empire before the American Revolution,* vol. 11, *The Triumphant Empire: The Rumbling of the Coming Storm, 1766–1770* (New York, 1967), 13–38. The twenty-eight-member Governor's Council, which functioned as the upper house of the Massachusetts legislature, was elected by joint vote of the incoming representatives and the outgoing council members, with the consent of the governor. The governor could veto obnoxious appointments (and occasionally did), but the composition of the Council always remained in the control of the House of Representatives. Purges of the Council by the House were all but unknown: the election process (by secret ballot) was difficult to control, and coordination among the representatives highly uncommon. See Robert Zemsky, *Merchants, Farmers, and River Gods: An Essay on Eighteenth-Century Politics* (Boston, 1971), 221–9.

3. Quotation: *John Adams Diary,* 29 May 1766, 313. Bernard's power to affect appointments to leadership posts in the House was closely confined by the terms of the Massachusetts charter. Such executive weakness impressed contemporaries as one of the leading defects of the Bay Colony's constitution. See Zemsky, *Merchants, Farmers, and River Gods,* 221–9; and Bernard Bailyn, *The Origins of American Politics* (New York, 1967), 131–3.

4. Gipson, *Coming Storm,* 17–25; Jensen, *Founding,* 196–7. The grant of amnesty blatantly trespassed on the prerogative powers of the governor—and the Crown. Bernard understood the unconstitutional character of the act but assented to it on 9 Dec., because he knew the House would not otherwise make the grant. It was a shrewd move: the Privy Council later disallowed the act, thus solving the constitutional problem—after the "sufferers" had been compensated.

5. Bernard to the earl of Shelburne [secretary of state for the South], 24 Dec. 1766, ibid., 197.

6. James F. Smith, "The Rise of Artemas Ward, 1727–1777: Authority, Politics, and Military Life in Eighteenth-Century Massachusetts" (Ph.D. diss., University of Colorado at Boulder, 1990), 96, 120, 148–52, 166–7. "I thought I could": Hutchinson to Thomas Pownall, 7 June 1768, quoted at 167. "Thought fit to supersede": John Cotton, deputy province secretary, to Ward, 30 June 1766; quoted ibid., 153. The governor's messenger presented the notice to Ward while Ward was helping his fellow parishioners construct a new meeting house at Shrewsbury. Town tradition held that Ward read the message aloud to those present; then he told the messenger to tell the governor that he considered himself "twice honored, but more in being superseded, than in being commissioned" because in taking away his office Bernard had shown "that I am, what he is not, a friend to my country." Ward's response (if it was in fact so eloquent) could scarcely have been better calculated to shore up his status—so abruptly threatened—as Shrewsbury's leading citizen and public mediator. It also tied him permanently to the country party. As Smith observes of the incident, "From this moment on he would have no choice, if he hoped to maintain his local standing, but to oppose [Bernard,] the man whose peevishness had exposed him so unexpectedly on that summer's day" (ibid., 154). On Hutchinson's frustrations with Bernard, see esp. Bernard Bailyn, *The Ordeal of Thomas Hutchinson* (Cambridge, Mass., 1974), 45–7.

7. Gipson, *Coming Storm,* 34–5.

8. Ibid., 36–7; Jensen, *Founding,* 278; Hiller B. Zobel, *The Boston Massacre* (New York, 1970), 51–4. Writs of assistance operated only during daylight hours. The fear of military intervention was eminently rational: a principal duty of the army in the British Isles was to arrest smugglers and to break up coastal wrecking gangs. See Pauline Maier, *From Resistance to Revolution: Colonial Radicals and the Development of American Opposition to Britain, 1765–1776* (New York, 1991), 153–4; and Tony Hayter, *The Army and the Crowd in Mid-Georgian England* (Totowa, N.J., 1978), 23, 32, 35, 62, et passim.

9. *Boston Gazette,* 23 Dec. 1765; quoted in Tyler, *Smugglers and Patriots,* 92.

10. "The distinction" and "the merchants": Bernard to Shelburne, 22 Dec. 1766, quoted in Gipson, *Coming Storm,* 34.

11. Tyler, *Smugglers and Patriots,* 25–107.

12. Thomas Doerflinger's analysis of the divided and fundamentally apolitical character of the Philadelphia merchant community during most of the postwar era corrects the view that emphasizes radicalism among traders—a point also applicable to Boston, albeit with a few significant exceptions, especially John Hancock. See id., *A Vigorous Spirit of Enterprise: Merchants and Economic Development in Revolutionary Philadelphia* (Chapel Hill, N.C., 1986), esp. 180–96.

13. On conspiratorial thinking and its implications, see Bernard Bailyn, "A Note on Conspiracy," in *The Ideological Origins of the American Revolution* (Cambridge, Mass., 1968), 144–59; and Gordon S. Wood, "Conspiracy and the Paranoid Style: Causality and Deceit in the Eighteenth Century," *William and Mary Quarterly,* 3rd ser., 39 (1982): 401–41.

14. Except as otherwise noted, the following account derives from Jensen, *Founding,* 211–14;

Gipson, *Coming Storm,* 45–65; and John Shy, *Toward Lexington: The Role of the British Army in the Coming of the American Revolution* (Princeton, N.J., 1965), 250–8.

15. "After the expense": assembly resolve, in Gipson, *Coming Storm,* 46. "Set the Demand aside": Gage to Conway, 21 Dec. 1765, in Clarence Edwin Carter, ed., *The Correspondence of General Thomas Gage with the Secretaries of State, 1763–1775,* vol. 1 (New Haven, Conn., 1931), 77. Gage's expectations: same to same, 6 May 1766, ibid., 89.

16. Sung Bok Kim, *Landlord and Tenant in Colonial New York: Manorial Society, 1664–1775* (Chapel Hill, N.C., 1978), 298–347.

17. "The Montresor Journals," ed. E. D. Scull, New-York Historical Society, *Collections* 14 (1881): 363 (entry of 1 May 1766). On the rioting of winter and spring 1766, see Kim, *Landlord and Tenant,* 367–89, and the contrary interpretation of Edward Countryman, *A People in Revolution: The American Revolution and Political Society in New York, 1760–1790* (Baltimore, 1981), 36–71; also Dixon Ryan Fox, *Yankees and Yorkers* (New York, 1940), 147–51.

18. Quotations: Gage to Conway, 24 June 1766, *Gage Corr.,* 1:95. Gage's motives: ibid., and same to same, 15 July 1766, ibid., 99.

19. Quotations: Brown to Gage, 30 June 1766, and Clarke to Gage, 29 July 1766, in Shy, *Toward Lexington,* 219, 220.

20. Ibid., 219–21.

21. "Burnt and destroyed": "Geographical, Historical Narrative, or Summary. . . ." [Lansdowne MSS.], quoted ibid., 222. "Affair has not been transacted": earl of Shelburne to Moore, 11 Dec. 1766, quoted ibid., 223.

22. Jensen, *Founding,* 212–14; quotation, Moore to the secretary of state for the Southern Department, 20 June 1766, at 213.

23. Assembly to the governor, 13 Nov. 1766, ibid., 214.

24. Except as otherwise noted, the following account derives from Jensen, *Founding,* 198–205; Douglas Southall Freeman, *George Washington: A Biography,* vol. 3, *Planter and Patriot* (New York, 1951), 142–3, 146–50, 165–72; and Joseph Ernst, *Money and Politics in America, 1755–1775: A Study in the Currency Act of 1764 and the Political Economy of Revolution* (Chapel Hill, N.C., 1973), 175–96 (the only account that coherently estimates the scandal's economic impact). On Lee's character and finances, see Pauline Maier, *The Old Revolutionaries: Political Lives in the Age of Samuel Adams* (New York, 1980), 164–200, esp. 195–7.

25. There was one notable exception to this generalization, which illustrates another dimension of the scandal's disordering impact on gentry lives and relationships. Robinson had sunk ten thousand pounds into lead mines his father-in-law, John Chiswell, operated on the upper New River, a tributary of the Kanawha, west of the Allegheny height of land (and hence beyond the Proclamation Line). Robinson's death left Chiswell a de facto bankrupt; drunk and enraged, he murdered a creditor, Robert Routledge. He was arrested, but justices of the peace who were also his business partners released him—an abuse of power that disturbed many who feared for the honor of the gentry class. Chiswell died soon thereafter, a broken man. (See Carl Bridenbaugh, "Virtue and Violence in Virginia, 1766, or The Importance of the Trivial," Massachusetts Historical Society, *Proceedings* 76 (1964): 3–29; Ernst, *Money and Politics,* 187 n. 43.)

26. T. H. Breen, *Tobacco Culture* (Princeton, N.J., 1985), 168.

27. *Virginia Gazette* (Rind), 26 July 1770, quoted ibid., 170.

28. Quoted ibid., 176.

CHAPTER SEVENTY-FOUR: *The Future of Empire*

1. On Johnstone's career, see *Dictionary of National Biography,* s.v. "Johnstone, George"; on the tangled history of command and precedence of civilian and military authorities, see John Shy, *Toward Lexington: The Role of the British Army in the Coming of the American Revolution* (Princeton, N.J., 1965), 181–4; on the military dimensions of the dispute, ibid., 283–5; and on the larger context, Lawrence Henry Gipson, *The British Empire before the American Revolu-*

tion, vol. 9, *The Triumphant Empire: New Responsibilities within the Enlarged Empire, 1763–1766* (New York, 1968), 210–31.

2. Hilda Neatby, *Quebec: The Revolutionary Age, 1760–1791* (Toronto, 1966), 30–44. See also Gipson, *New Responsibilities,* 163–76; Shy, *Toward Lexington,* 287–8; and Walter S. Dunn Jr., *Frontier Profit and Loss: The British Army and the Fur Traders, 1760–1764* (Westport, Conn., 1998), 165–6. At least part of the antagonism between the American merchants and Murray was ethnic in origin. Dunn points out that Murray, a Scot, tended to treat Scots merchants most favorably, and particularly those Scottish officers who had remained in Canada and gone into the fur trade after the war.

3. "The exertion": Gage to Capt. James Murray, 5 May 1767, in Richard White, *The Middle Ground: Indians, Empires, and Republics in the Great Lakes Region, 1650–1815* (New York, 1991), 319. "Double the Number": George Croghan to Sir William Johnson, 18 Oct. 1767, ibid.

4. Shy, *Toward Lexington,* 229; Gage to Shelburne (Southern secretary), 13 June 1767, in Clarence Edwin Carter, ed., *The Correspondence of General Thomas Gage with the Secretaries of State, 1763–1775,* vol. 1 (New Haven, Conn., 1931), 142–3. Gage's reluctance to press the issue probably also reflected his reaction to being reprimanded for using regulars to kick Yankee intruders off New York estates; since Virginia and Pennsylvania both claimed the area, by expelling Virginia squatters he might be censured for putting the army at the service of the Penn family, as he had with the Hudson Valley patroons.

5. On Croghan's diplomacy, which kept open communications between Fort Pitt and Fort de Chartres, see White, *Middle Ground,* 436–47; and Nicholas B. Wainwright, *George Croghan, Wilderness Diplomat* (Chapel Hill, N.C., 1959), 238. (Croghan evidently bought the gifts he needed for this condolence diplomacy from Baynton, Wharton and Morgan, in which he was a silent partner; suggesting yet again that the wind never blew so ill as to waft George Croghan no good.) "Cost him more trouble": White's summary of Croghan to Gage, 15 June 1766, in *Middle Ground,* 347 n. 65. "Under no Laws": Capt. James Murray to Gage, 16 May 1767, ibid., 344. "Those who have injured them": Gage to Murray, 28 June 1767, ibid., 320 n. 9. On the alarming rise in frontier violence and retaliation, see Tom Hatley, *The Dividing Paths: Cherokees and South Carolinians through the Era of the Revolution* (New York, 1993), 183–6; and Michael N. McConnell, *A Country Between: The Upper Ohio Valley and Its Peoples, 1724–1774* (Lincoln, Nebr., 1992), 240.

6. Croghan's itinerary: Howard H. Peckham, ed., *George Croghan's Journal of His Trip to Detroit in 1767* (Ann Arbor, Mich., 1939), 31–47. Effects of diplomacy: McConnell, *A Country Between,* 241–2, 264–5.

7. For quantities of rum in the Ohio Country and elsewhere in the west, and for the role of Baynton, Wharton and Morgan in the trade, see Peter C. Mancall, *Deadly Medicine: Indians and Alcohol in Early America* (Ithaca, N.Y., 1995), 52–7, 181–2; and Dunn, *Frontier Profit,* 178–9. (Mancall estimates the per capita consumption of alcohol among western Indians under the British regime at between approximately .5 and 1.1 gallons annually, or between 2.1 and 4.5 gallons annually for "active drinkers," mainly young men; a notably higher rate of consumption than when the French were the principal traders in the region [211 n. 108]. Dunn makes the much higher per capita estimate of 12 gallons per annum "per warrior" [table 10.1, 178].) For Croghan's and Gage's anticipation of a new Indian war, see Wainwright, *Croghan,* 248.

8. Shy, *Toward Lexington,* 290: "the army, as an instrument of imperial control in time of peace, had a dull edge."

EPILOGUE: *MOUNT VERNON,* JUNE 24, 1767

1. Harvest and weather: Donald Jackson and Dorothy Twohig, eds., *The Diaries of George Washington,* vol. 2, 1766–1770 (Charlottesville, Va., 1976), 21, 23 (entries of 19–24 June and 14 July 1767). Wheat farming and plantation enterprises: Douglas Southall Freeman, *George Washington: A Biography,* vol. 3, *Planter and Patriot* (New York, 1951), 179–80. Weaving: W. W.

Abbot et al., eds., *The Papers of George Washington, Colonial Series,* vol. 7, January 1761–June 1767 (Charlottesville, Va., 1990), 508 n. 1. Speculative enterprises: ibid., 219–25, 268–75 et passim.

2. Washington to Capt. John Posey, 24 June 1767, in *Papers of Washington,* vol. 8, June 1767–December 1771 (Charlottesville, Va., 1993), 1–4.

3. Washington to Capt. William Crawford, 17 Sept. 1767, ibid., 28. Washington's mention of Indians' consent to white occupation beyond the Proclamation Line referred to the Six Nations' agreement, at the end of Pontiac's War, to cede lands west of the Alleghenies and south of the Ohio, as far as the Tennessee River. The Shawnees, Delawares, Mingos, Munsees, Miamis, and Wyandots who lived in the region, of course, were determined to resist white colonization.

4. Sartorial tastes: Washington to Charles Lawrence, 26 Apr. 1763, *Papers of Washington,* 7:201–2. "Nine of such influence": minutes of the Mississippi Land Company, 9 Sept. 1763, ibid., 223 n. 2.

Acknowledgments

The only thing that tempers the joy of thanking the many people and institutions that have helped me produce this book is the virtual certainty that the following list is incomplete. In that sense it seems fitting that a book that began with a confession should close with an apology: to those whose names deserve to appear below, but do not, I plead the poor defense of a faulty memory, and ask forgiveness. In the same spirit, I must also acknowledge my overwhelming debt to all the authors on whose work I have drawn, and without whose researches I could never have attempted to write a synthetic narrative—the kind of book that depends most of all on previous historians' creativity, industry, and insight. To anyone whose work I have misconstrued, let me say that I freely claim all shortcomings, misstatements, and errors as my own.

Many institutions have contributed expertise, goodwill, and (not least) money to support this project. The generous financial aid of the National Endowment for the Humanities, the Charles Warren Center of Harvard University, and the Council on Research and Creative Work at the University of Colorado, Boulder, supported me as I read and wrote my way through to the end. En route I benefited from the help of staff members at Norlin Library (especially the interlibrary loan office), Widener Library, the American Antiquarian Society, the Massachusetts Historical Society, and—particularly—the William L. Clements Library. A trip to Ann Arbor in late 1998 not only reminded me of the great generosity and kindness of Arlene and John Shy, but also revealed something that I had only dimly sensed before, the amazing richness of the Clements's collections of eighteenth-century maps and images. Thanks to the help, advice, and knowledge of Arlene, John Dann, and Brian Dunnigan, I found in that library's holdings nearly 90 percent of this volume's illustrations, including the *Scenographia Americana,* which appears complete (I believe for the first time) at its center.

In recognition of that extraordinary contribution, the Clements receives the special credit line that appears on the title page. This gesture must not, however, be understood to reflect any lack of gratitude to the other institutions that have contributed portraits and engravings from their collections. I am, therefore, most pleased to thank the John Carter Brown Library, the Albany Institute of History and Art, the Massachusetts Historical Society, the McCord Museum of Canadian History/Musée McCord d'histoire canadienne, the National Galleries of Scotland, and Washington and Lee University for copies of the images that each has furnished, along with the necessary permissions to reprint them here.

I doubt that any author has ever had better luck in the all-important endeavor of finding editors and others expert in the care and handling of manuscripts. Christopher Rogers initially encouraged me to undertake a book on the Revolutionary era and showed great forbearance when the project began to shift its shape. Chris's successor, Peter La Bella, saw the manuscript through its transition from a college-list to trade book. Jane Garrett read the unfinished manuscript, encouraged me to rethink the limits of my story, and ultimately enabled me to bring to light the book that lurked in what I had come to fear was an unpublishable heap of pages. I owe her more than I can easily say. I take pleasure, too, in acknowledging the patience and helpful good humor of Webb Younce and Megan Quigley, Jane's assistants; Hannah Borgeson's astonishing scrupulousness and skill as a copy editor; the discernment and care of Constance Areson Clark in creating the index; the professionalism of the production editor, Kathleen Fridella, and the production manager, Claire Bradley Ong; and the accomplished artistry of Robert Olsson and Archie Ferguson, who designed, respectively, the book and its jacket. Finally, Patricia Murphy's astuteness as a processor of words and ingenuity as a solver of computer problems—not to mention her willingness to work overtime—allowed me to submit the manuscript on time and in a usable electronic format. Without Pat, neither of those things would have been possible.

Friends and colleagues have helped out in numerous invaluable ways. At the University of Colorado I have benefited from the advice, support, and encouragement of colleagues in a history department well stocked with superb scholars. I am indebted to them all, but particularly to Professors Philip Deloria, Steven Epstein, Robert Ferry, Martha Hanna, James Jankowski, Gloria Main, Jackson Turner Main, Ralph Mann, and Mark Pittenger, all of whom have listened, offered advice, and helped me clarify my thinking over the long process of writing and revision. Others at the University of Colorado and other institutions have also contributed equally generously as readers, advisers, critics, and supporters: Gary Holthaus, John Stevenson, and Dennis Van Gerven; Robert Bakker, Michael Bellesiles, John Boles, Ira Gruber, and Timothy Breen (as well as the students in his graduate and honors seminars at Northwestern, who helped me improve a chapter from part 1, way back in the spring of 1990); Susan Hunt of the Charles Warren Center and Barbara DeWolfe of Widener J; and Barry Levy, David Sicilia, and the other participants in the 1992–93 seminars sponsored by the Warren Center and American Antiquarian Society.

As important as these, in another way, are the seven members of my "imagined audience." Knowing that the general readers whom I hoped to reach might have no more in common than a love of stories and a willingness to take ideas seriously, as I wrote I tried to keep in mind a group that shares those qualities: a biologist, a farmer, a teacher, a geologist, a lawyer, a college administrator, and a pillar of the RFLPOA. Dwight Anderson, Joseph Erickson, Donald Anderson, Scott Mefford, Christopher Jedrey, Micheline Jedrey, and Melva Anderson may all be surprised to see their names here. But in fact they have (as I imagined) looked over my shoulder for years, urging me to speak more directly, chiding me for my pomposities, helping me to decide what to write, what to keep, and what to throw away. I hope I have not disappointed them; they have been indispensable to me.

Whatever else it brings, arriving at midcareer allows one the gratifying opportunity to rely equally on former teachers and former students. I have continued to draw inspiration and encouragement, as well as a due measure of blunt criticism, from William Griswold, Arthur Worrall, and Bernard Bailyn: men who first taught me what historians do, and whose examples move me to admiration no less today than they did thirty years ago. Similarly, three former students, Ruth Helm (senior instructor in American Studies at the University of Colorado), Eric Hinderaker (associate professor of history at the University of Utah), and Brian DeLay (currently a doctoral candidate at Harvard), have reminded me of how much teachers stand to learn from those whom they have been privileged to teach. Ruth gave the manuscript a close reading when it was partially complete, in 1993; Eric and Brian read it all, when it was finished; and all three gave me criticism full of insight and helpful suggestions. Two old friends and graduate-school contemporaries of different disciplines also read the completed manuscript and offered their unique, and uniquely valuable, perspectives on it. Randy Fertel brought a literary critic's expertise to bear on the book's narrative structure and style, and for his generous commentary I am truly grateful. Andrew R. L. Cayton, on whose historical judgment and knowledge I have relied for two decades, performed the singularly heroic act of reading the book through *twice:* piece by piece as I wrote it, and again at the end, as a whole. In conversations touching not only on the Seven Years' War and its aftermath, but on a huge range of topics inside and outside of early American studies, Drew has helped me understand many things. Most of all, however, he has enabled me to see why it is a professor's duty at least to try reaching readers beyond the academy's bounds.

Two final obligations, the most important of all, remain to be declared. Samuel DeJohn Anderson is almost the exact contemporary in age of a project that has demonstrated a remarkable capacity for absorbing his father's time and attention, yet he has never shown anything less than tolerance toward the book and charity toward its too-often-preoccupied author. No son could reasonably have done more, nor could any have given a father more delight. Perhaps some of the camping and fishing trips that Sam has forgone can still, somehow, be repaid; the debt of happy memories that I owe him for the ones we've thus far managed to fit into our summers, however, can never be.

Similarly, what Virginia DeJohn Anderson has contributed to this project, and to my life, lies so far beyond reckoning that it seems fruitless even to try describing it. After twenty years together, she still listens patiently when I talk about my work; still helps me think though my interpretations; still reads my prose and prods me to write it more clearly. That I should have found such a partner in graduate school, of all places, fills me with gratitude, the smallest token of which appears at the front of this book. Though for years I thought that the only possible dedicatee would be Zeno's paradoxical frog, Virginia helped me kick the little wretch over the cliff's edge at last. And for that, as for so many other things, I owe her much, much more than she knows.

Index

Note: Page numbers in *italics* refer to illustrations.

abatis, 242–4, 337, 353, 393, 618
Abercromby, Maj. Gen. James, 141–2, 284, 286–8, appointed commander in chief, 226–7, 233–5; and assault on Ticonderoga (1758), 244–3, 246–9, 286; and Bradstreet, 260–6; authorizes Forbes to negotiate with Ohio Indians, 267, 269; opinion of Americans, 288, 371; recalled and promoted, 307
Acadia, *see* Nova Scotia
Acadians: deportation of, 75, 112–14, 255, 522, 526, 762n.11; at defense of Québec, 347; resistance by, 395; neutrality of, 407
Aché, Anne Antoine, comte d', 418
Act of Union (1707), 11
Adams, Abigail, 683–4
Adams John, 682–7, 715
Adams, Samuel, 605–7, 683, 715–16
Admiralty, British, 305, 309, 564, 646
Africa, *xxvii,* 213, 306, *307,* 504–6; *see also* empire; slave trade; trade
Aix-la-Chapelle, Treaty of (1748), *see* treaties: Aix-la-Chapelle
Alabama, 417, 460
Alabama River, 202, 462, 465
Albany, *xxviii,* xxxi, 38–9, 86–7, 110, 114–15, 117, 123, 137, 140, 142, 145, 147–8, 182, 194, 219, 264, 278, 388, 400, 599, 720, 729
Albany Congress (1754), 39–40, 77–85, 92, 183, 277
Albany County (N.Y.), 721
Albemarle, George Keppel, earl of, 441, 499, 501
alcohol: and British Indian policy, 471, 531–3, 620, 634, 732–3, 818–9n.6, 831n.7; Indian denunciations of, 535–6
Allegheny Mountains, *xxviii, xxx,* 27, 233, 258, 271, 278, colonial settlements beyond, 524–8, 550, 731; *see also* frontier; land speculation; Ohio Country; Proclamation Line; squatters
Allegheny River, *xxviii, xxx,* 7, 18, 26, 27, 29, 31, 47, 49, 87, *89,* 163, 328, 335, 474, 525
Aller River, 211, 216
Alexandria (Va.): conference at, 87, 90–2
Algonquian-speaking people, 14–15, 748n.6
Almeida (Portugal), *xxxviii,* 497
American Currency Act, 696
American Duties Act of 1764 (Sugar Act), xvii, 574–81, 642, 645–6, 680, 696; colonial responses to, 606, 608–10, 614, 646, 682, 696
American Revolution, xv–xvii, xx–xxiii, 745–6; *see also* intercultural relations; liberties; republicanism; rights; Seven Years' War
American Trade Act of 1765, 652
Amherst, Jeffery, *234,* 307–8, 310, 352, 369, 415, 461, 473–6; 490, 498, 535, 774–5n.2; and financing of war, 321, 387, 473; and Indians, 284, 404, 406, 455–6, 463, 466, 469–72, 518, 535–9, 541–7, 551–2, 617–20, 743, 797n.7, 800n.20, 809n.11, 818–19n.6; and Louisbourg, 233–5, 250–7, 297–8; and provincials, 314, 322–4, 371–2, 387, 389, 412–13, 473, 519,

Amherst, Jeffery (*cont.*):
521–2; and Ticonderoga and Crown Point, 340–3; conquers Canada, 387–8, 390, 397, 399, 400–10; recall of, 552–3, 557, 570, 617
Amherst, William, 297–8, 498
Amsterdam bank panic (1763), 583, 589–90, 593; *see also* economy; depression
Anda, Don Simon de, 517
Anderson, Samuel, 8, 22, 87
Ansbach, 127; *see also* diplomacy, European
Anson, George, Lord, 214–15, 305, 308–9, 381, 419, 483–4, 487–8, 490, 498
Appalachians, 17–18
Armstrong, Col. John, 163–4
army, British, 309, 410, 416, 487; cost of, 560–1, 563–4, 570–1, 645; in North America after war, 560, 570–1, 720–4, 730–2, 734; reorganization of, 557–64; *see also* regulars; military units
Army of Observation, 299–301; *see also* Cumberland, William Augustus, duke of; Ferdinand of Brunswick
Atkin, Edmund, 130, 268, 468
Attakullakulla (Little Carpenter), 268, 459–60, 463, 467–8
Aubry, Charles Philippe, 629
Aughwick, *xxxi*, 61, 94–5, 163
Augsburg, 380, 383
Augusta, Dowager Princess of Wales, 476
Austria, *xxxvi–xxxvii*; alliances of, 35–6, 67, 71–2, 126–9, 171; and Silesia, 35, 71, 127, 212, 216, 301; in Seven Years' War, 171–172, 176, 212, 215–216, 301, 380, 416, 480–1, 491–3, 495–6, 506; *see also* diplomacy; Diplomatic Revolution; Prussia; Seven Years' War; Silesia; War of the Austrian Succession
Austrian Netherlands, *xxxvi–xxxviii*, 299–300
authority, British imperial, and taxation, 605–11, 613–15, 711–2; colonial resistance to, 148–9, 219–31, 422, 512, 571, 616, 677–87, 692, 695–6, 698–702, 706–7, 712, 723, 743–6

Bacon, Anthony, M.P., 581–3, 595
Bagley, Col. Jonathan, 244
Baker and Kilby, London, 131; *see also* De Lancey, Oliver; patronage
Ball Play Creek, 464
Baltic, *xxxvi–xxxviii*, 492
bank panic (1763–64), 583, 589–90, 593
Bank of England, 312, 493
Bankruptcy Act (Mass., 1765), 669
Barracks Act, 723
Barré, Maj. Isaac, 354, 362, 408, 415, 643–4, 646, 672, 692, 703
Barrington, Maj. Gen. John, 313–5, 634, 695
Basse-Terre, *xxxv*, 314–15
Batiscan, *xxxi*, 348, 353, 355, 364
battle, nature of: effects of, on soldiers, 152–6, 286–9, 363, 498–501; sensory impressions of, 100, 362–3, 500; soldiers' descriptions of, 102–4, 240–1, 244–8, 254, 263, 361, 398, 500, 777n.8; *see also* battles; casualties; warfare
battles, Pontiac's Rebellion: Bloody Run, 539, 548–9; Fort Detroit (siege), *xxviii, xxx*, 538, *539*, 541–4, 547–8, 550; Fort Niagara (siege), *xxviii, xxx*, 540–1, 544, 547, 550, *551*, 809–10n.2; Fort Pitt (siege), *xxviii, xxx*, 540–1, 543–4, 547–50
battles, Seven Years' War: Bergen (1759), 314; Burkersdorf (1762), 496; Cassel (1762, siege), 496; Cherbourg (1758, raid), *xxxviii*, 302; Crefeld (1758); *xxxvi*, 299; Dresden (1758, siege), *xxxvii*, 301, 380; Fort Beauséjour, *xxix*, 112–15, 360; Fort Duquesne, *xxviii*, 49, 52, 54, 57, 60–2, 64–5, 87–8, 90–1, 94–108, 110, 115, 139, 162–3, 202, 204, 225, 227, 232–3, 236, 258, 268, 270–3, 278, 281–3, 289, 291, 298, 325–6, 328–9, 351, 738, 781n. 26; Fort Frontenac (1758), *xxviii, xxxi*, 258–66, *263*, 281, 298; Fort Lévis (1760, siege), *xxxi*, 401–2, *403*, 405; Fort Loudoun (1760, siege), *xxviii*, 463; Fort Louis (1758, siege), 306; Fort Necessity (1754), *xxviii, xxx*, 62–6, 72, 77–8, 351; Fort Niagara (1759, siege), *xxviii, xxx*, 330–9, *334*, 787 n.4; Fort Oswego (1756, siege), *xxviii, xxxi*, 150–7, 187, 346, 408; Fort Prince George (1760, siege), 459–61; Fort St. George (siege), 417; Fort William Henry (1757, siege), *xxviii, xxxi*, 185–201, *193*, 219, 346, 406; Freiburg (1762), 496; German Flats (1757, raid), *xxxi*, 219–20; Havana (1762, siege), *xxxiv*, 498–9, *500*, 501, 712; Hochkirch (1758), *xxxvii*, 301; Jumonville's Glen, 5–7, 53–8, 64, 77, 105, 453, 754–6n.6–7, n.12–13; Île-aux-Noix (1760, siege), *xxxi*, 400–1; Kittanning (1756, raid), *xxviii*, 163–4; Kloster Kamp (1760), 416, 481; Kolin (1757), *xxxvii*, 176; La Belle Famille (1759), *xxviii*, 337, 787–8n.11; Lagos (1759),

xxxviii, 395; Lake George (1755), *xxxi*, 119, *120*, 121, 131; Leuthen (1757), *xxxvii*, 298, 301; Liegnitz (1760), *xxxvii*, 416; Louisbourg (1758, siege), *xxix*, 207–8, 225, 250–1, *252*, 253–9, 297–8, 405, *422*; Loyalhanna (1758, raid), 274, 282, 474, 525; Madras (1758–59, siege), *xxxix*, 417; Manila (1762, siege), *xxvii*, 515–7; Minden (1757), *xxvii*, *xxxvi*, 378; Minorca, (1756, siege), *xxxviii*, 211; Monongahela, the (1755), *xxviii*, 94–107, *101*, 108, 114, 119; Pickawillany (1752, raid), *xxx*, 28, 750–1n.12; Plassey (1757), *xxxix*, 178, 417; Pondicherry (1760–61, siege), *xxxix*, 418; Prague, (1757, siege), *xxvii*, *xxxvii–xxxviii*, 176; Québec (1759) *xxxi*, *xxxiii*, 344–68, *358*, 393–4, 415, 790n.22, 290n.27; Second Battle of Québec (1760), *xxxi*, *xxxiii*, 391–6, 712; Quiberon Bay (1759), *xxxviii*, 381–3, 395, 416, 498; Rossbach (1757), *xxxvi*, 215–16, 298–9, 301; St.-Cas (1758, raid), *xxxviii*, 302–4, 477; St.-Malo (1758, raid), 299, 302; Ticonderoga (1758), *xxviii*, *xxxi*, 240–9, *245*, 247–8, 260, 286, 298, 618; Torgau (1760), *xxvii*, *xxxvi*, 480, 491; Wandiwash (1760), *xxvii*, *xxxix*, 418, 515; Wilhelmsthal (1762), 496; Zorndorf (1758), *xxvii*, *xxxvii*, 301
Bay of Biscay, *xxxviii*, 257, 309, 419
Bay of Fundy, *xxix*, 113–14, 223
Bay of Lagos, 378
Bay of St.-Cas, 302
Baynton, Wharton, and Morgan, 627–8, 633
Beauport, *xxxiii*, 348, 437
Beauport lines, 348–9, 355–6, 363–4
Beaver Creek, 270, 625
Beckford, William, 308, 644
Bedford, John Russell, duke of, 34–6, 83, 484, 487, 494, 503–4, 515, 526, 569, 653, 701, 707
Belle-Île-en-Mer (Belleisle), *xxxviii*, 419, 479, 483, 497, 506
Bengal, *xxxix*, 177–8, 417
Berlin, *xxxvii–xxxviii*, 128, 212, 301, 416, 481, 492
Bernard, Gov. Francis, 518, 520–1, 601, 603, 607, 659–60, 667–70, 681, 715–9, 829n.6
Bigot, François, 237, 239, 346
Bill of Rights, English, 148; *see also* Constitution, British; English law; liberties, English; rights, English
Bligh, Lt. Gen. Thomas, 302, 304, 477
blockades, 237, 381, 383, 395, 418
Board of Trade (Lords Commissioners of Trade and Plantation), *see* British government, Board of Trade
Bompar, Maximin de, 314–15, 381
Bordeaux, 395
Boscawen, Admiral Edward, 87, 110, 124, 250, 253, *255*, 257, 378, 395
Boston, *xxviii–xxxi*, 91, 182–3, 210, 223–5, 321, 373, 375, 421, *423*, 520–1, 591–2, 604–5, 607–9, 635, 658, 660, 677–9, 681–2, 691, 715, 717–8, 723; 824n.4, 825n.7; Stamp Act riots in, 665–72
Bougainville, Louis-Antoine de, *155*, 156, 189, 241, 248, 345, 347–8, 355, 357–9, 362–4, 401, 406
bounties, 319–20, 388–9, 785–6n.11, 794–5n.5; *see also* enlistment; volunteers
Bouquet, Col. Henry, 268, 272–4, 283, 290–2, 466, 524–5, 527, 537, 541–2, 544, 548–50
Bourbon dynasty, 484, 496, 498, 802n.11
Bourlamaque, Brig. Gen. François-Charles de, 342, 347, 369, 397, 401
boycotts, 682, 684, 695–6, 714
Braddock, Maj. Gen. Edward, 68–70, 72, 77, 85–6, *89*, *98*, *101*, 113–15, 119, 130, 139, 213, 233, 258, 271, 290–2, 321, 351, 454; aftermath of defeat of, 108–11, 647; and Battle of the Monongahela, 94–107, *98*, *101*, 360; and Indians, 94–6; defeat of, 108–10, 116–17, 124, 187, 216, 230, 240, 243, 272, 281; expedition of 1755, *xviii*, *xxx*, 86–107; killed, 104; opinion of American troops, 371, 519
Braddock's Road, *see* roads
Bradstreet, Col. John, 259–66, 298, 340, 647, 778n.1–2, 779n.9; and Pontiac's Rebellion, 618–20, 622–6, 628–9, 634, 819n.10, 819–20n.13
Brandenburg, *xxxvi-xxxviii*, 212, 506; House of, 492–3
Brest, *xxxviii*, 257, 378, 381, 498
British Empire: *see* Empire, British
British foreign policy, *see* British politics; diplomacy; Diplomatic Revolution; empire
British government, 38, 67, 71, 90, 124, 169–75, 305, 380; and defense, 169–70, 213, 239, 301, 308–9, 380–1; Board of Trade, *19*, 30, 34, 38–9, 66, 77–8, 182, 229, 279, 521, 525, 530, 552, 558, 565, 570, 582, 595, 660, 662, 691, 694, 730, 743, 751–2n.2; cabinet, 479, 484–5, 489, 493–4, 504, 653–5, 691–2;

British government (*cont.*):
Court of Common Pleas, 513; crisis of 1756 in, 169–75; Exchequer, 127–8, 493, 512, 642, 654; House of Commons, 125, 127–8, 169, 172–3, 213–15, 303, 308–9, 384, 477–8, 481, 485–7, 494–5, 504–5, 508–11, 513–4, 562–4, 572–4, 581, 583–5, 606–7, 609, 611–14, 643–4, 648–50, 653, 659, 679–80, 693, 695, 698–704, 707, 709–10; House of Lords, 511, 574, 613, 644, 650, 653, 679–80, 693, 695, 698–9, 703–4, 708–9; Parliament, 36, 131, 212–13, 215, 221, 226, 230, 305, 317–8, 320–2, 324, 351, 378, 389, 412, 478, 488, 495, 503–5, 570, 586, 591, 595, 602, 605–9, 615–16, 642, 645, 655, 657, 661, 686–7, 693–5, 710–12, 716, 718, 720, 723–4, 734; Privy Council, 33, 40, 175, 279, 474, 478, 526, 530, 558, 563, 565, 569, 594–5, 724, 743; Secretary of State, Northern Department, 503, 558, 570, 654; Secretary of State, Southern Department, 485, 487, 521, 557–8, 563, 565, 570, 641, 654, 691; Treasury, 479, 481, 495, 511–12, 558, 562–4, 571, 574, 583, 586, 642, 645–6, 654, 659, 685, 691–3; *see also* authority, imperial; British politics; diplomacy; empire, British; intercultural relations; George II; George III
British politics, 124–32, 169–75, 211–16, 265, 302–6, 383–4, 419–20, 476–86, 487–90, 493–5, 503–5, 507–18, 521, 552–3, 652–6, 826n.3, 826n.5; and class, 228, 507–15; and colonial administration, 507, 557–60, 572–4, 641, 647, 655–6, 691–708, 744; and economy, 560–4, 602, 695–7, 702; and growth of the middle classes, 509–10, 694; and radicalism, 510, 514–15; and patronage, 508–9, 511, 557, 602, 654, 692, 694; and political symbolism, 509–11, 513–14; and social unrest, 507–13, 516, 557, 653, 695, 705; and taxation, 510–12, 514, 641–6, 691–708; and the press, 510, 513, 552, 694; *see also individual politicians*
Brittany, *xxxviii*, 213, 381, 419, 483
Broglie, Victor-François, duc de, 314, 378
Brown, Maj. Arthur, 722
Brunswick, *xxxvi*, 211, 506
Bull, Lt. Gov. William, 465
Bunzelwitz, 491
Burgoyne, John, 497
Burke, Edmund, 693–4, 826n.5
Burton, Col. Ralph, 472
Bushy Run Creek, 549
Bute, John Stuart, earl of, 172, 178, 304, 420, 476–7, 479, *480*, 482–7, 490–1, 495, 503–4, 507–13, 557, 560, 562–3, 666, 694, 701, 826n.6
Buttes à Neveu, 355–6, *358*
Byng, Admiral John, 170–1, 173, 208
Byrd, Col. William III, 230, 272, 323, 467, 593, 726–7

Cádiz, *xxxviii*, 379, 502
Cahokia, 633
Calcutta, *xxxix*, 178
Canada, xix, xviii, xx, *xxvi–xxxiii*, 7, 14, 17, 20, 24–5, 30–1, 38, 139, 214, 395, 588, 742–3; campaigns against, 135, 179, 199, 232–6, 240, 310, 314, 317–24, 344–68, 384, 388, 453–5; and Indian relations, 135, 151, 260, 264, 330–9, 454–6, 742; conquest of, 387–409, 410–12, 422, *433–40*, 518, 685, 742; economy of, 237–8, 730; English administration of, 407, 472–3, 504–6, *697*, 720, 730–1, 741; food shortages and rationing in, 236–8, 345, 453–4, 775n.4; militia of, 31, 186–7, 192, 236, 337, 346–7, 356, 359–64, 366, 402, 404, 407, 775n.4
Canasatego, Onondaga diplomat, 23
Cape Breton Island, *xxix*, 24, 36, 208–9, 250, 255, 257, 371; *see also* Louisbourg; Nova Scotia
Cap Rouge (Carouge, Cape Rouge), *xxxiii*, 352, 357, 362, 393, 422, *438*
Captain Bull (Delaware war chief), 534–5
Captain Jacobs, 109–10, 162–4
Caribbean, *xxxiv–xxxv*, 309, 485, 498–502, 585, 589, 697
Carlisle (Pa.), *xxviii*, 204, 258, 268
Castle William, 667, 669–70
casualty rates, 105, 244–7, 258, 337, 344, 363, 378, 380, 383, 394, 401, 480, 499–501, 637, 760n.17, 762n.24, 776n.10, 777n.1
Cataraqui, *see* forts: Frontenac
Cataraqui River, *xxxi*, 261, 263
Catholicism, *see* religion
Catskills, *xxxi*, 421, *428*
Cavite, 515–17
Céloron de Blainville, Capt. Pierre-Joseph de, 25–6, 28–9, 35, 65, 171
Chaleur Bay, 395
Champlain corridor, 388, 523
Chandernagore, *xxxix*, 178, 417
Charles III, King of Spain, 504, 802n.11

Charleston (S.C.), *xxviii, xxx*, 204, 421, *423*, 458, 560–1, 463, 467, 709, 720
Charlot Kaské (Shawnee war chief), 626, 629–32
Chatham, *see* Pitt, William
Cheat River, 731–2
Cherokee: Lower Towns, *xxviii*, 202, 457–8, *459*, 462–3, 465, 467–8; Middle Towns, *xxviii*, 457, *459*, 462–3, 466–7; Rebellion, 457–71, 518–19, 524, 545, 598
Chignecto isthmus, 88, 112; *see also* battles, Fort Beauséjour
Choiseul, Étienne-François de Stainville, duc de, 482, 503–5, 515
cider tax, 510–11, 514–15, 562, 564, 573, 614; *see also* taxation
Clapham, Col. William, 540
Clarke, Capt. John, 722
class stratification: British and American compared, 228; in British politics, 507–15; reflected in military organization, 286–8
Cleaveland, Rev. John, 247–8, 776n.11
Clermont, Louis de Bourbon Condé, comte de, 299–300
Clinton, Gov. George, 24, 38
Clive, Robert, 178, 417
Clough, Pvt. Gibson, 370–1, 388–9, 413–14
Colden, Lt. Gov. Cadwallader, 608–10, 614, 677–9, 719–20, 724
colonial legislatures: and imperial authority, 148–9, 166–8, 201, 214, 221–5, 227–8, 229–31, 584, 605–8, 610–11, 613–15, 657–61, 664, 679, 684–6, 709; and Loudoun, 181–4, 209–11, 219–28, 317–24; and military organization, 140, 147, 221–31, 317–24; and Mutiny Acts, 648–50; and intercolonial union, 77, 84, 183; and Pitt, 214, 226–31, 384; and recruitment of troops, 384, 387–9, 518–9, 552; and republicanism, 223–4; and taxation, 228–9, 317, 645, 657–61, 664, 679, 684–6, 706; Connecticut, 222, 225, 227, 319, 320, 530, 610–11, 657; Maryland, 203, 322, 615; Massachusetts, 137, 220–5, 225–7, 318–20, 371, 374, 520–1, 601, 604, 606–8, 611, 657–60, 669, 671, 683, 715–16; New Jersey, 184, 219, 225, 227, 320; New York, 181, 219, 225, 227, 321, 387, 608–11, 657, 720, 722–4; Pennsylvania, 29, 84, 86, 92–3, 108–9, 160–3, 166, 181, 184, 207, 227, 269, 278, 322–4, 595, 610–12, 657–8, 675–6; Rhode Island, 222, 225, 227, 320, 610–1, 657; Virginia, 23, 40–1, 45–6, 51, 66, 84, 109, 159–60, 168, 183, 203, 230, 289, 323, 582–3, 598, 601, 610, 613–14, 619, 657, 660–4, 691, 725–6; *see also* Albany Congress; authority, imperial; colonial politics; economy, colonial
colonial governors, 275, 310, 563, 568–9, 600–3, 649, 665, 677, 681, 692; and Loudoun, 209, 214, 222, 225, 233; and Pitt, 213–14, 216, 229, 310, 384; *see also individual governors*
colonial politics: and class, 681, 684, 686, 724–8; and colonial charters, 605, 611, 658, 661, 673–4; and economy, 601–2, 613, 686, 729; and imperial authority, 148–9, 166–8, 201, 209–10, 214, 221–31, 317, 584, 603–15, 645, 648–51, 657–65, 679, 684–6, 706, 709, 729, 743; and intercolonial union, 77, 81–5, 183, 615, 658, 684; and Loudoun, 181–4, 209–11, 219–28, 317–24; and military organization, 140, 147, 221–31, 317–24; and Mutiny Act, 648–50; and Pitt, 214, 226–31, 384; and recruitment of troops, 384, 387–9, 518–19, 552; and patronage, 601–2, 658; and trade, 605–6, 610, 613; changing postwar alignments in, 599–602, 615, 724–8; factionalism of, 323–4, 599–602, 605–10, 612–15, 657–8, 674–5, 715–16, 724–8, 729; localism of, 168, 322, 324, 608, 613–16, 729, 743; role of elites in, 681, 684, 686, 724–9, 743; role of women in, 684, 686; *see also* Albany Congress; authority, imperial; economy
colonial union, 221–4; attempts to achieve, 77, 81, 84–5; difficulty of sustaining, 712; *see also* Albany Congress; intercolonial relations
Committees of Correspondence, 607, 615, 658
common law, English, 568, 609, 680, 730–1; *see also* rights, English
communications: corridors, 473; military, 186–7, 189, 194, 200, 232, 261–2, 264, 268, 282, 285, 292, 338, 346, 411, 461, 463; in postwar world, 597
Compagnie des Indies, 178, 417
condolence ceremony, 748n.3; *see also* diplomacy, Indian
Conestoga, 611–12
Conflans, Herbert de Brienne, comte de, 381–2
Connecticut, *xxviii–xxxi*, 139, 599; and imperial reforms, 610–11, 674; and expansion, 472–5, 523, 529–34, 569, 720–2;

Connecticut (*cont.*):
charter of, 529–30, 611; effect of war on, 288–9, 320; economy of, 582, 601; land speculators in, 78–9, 529–34, 569, 595–6; politics in, 599, 601, 611, 674; recruitment of troops from, 200, 210, 225, 320, 389; *see also* colonial politics; economy, colonial
Connecticut River, 474, 523
Connecticut Valley, *xxx–xxxi*, 343, 524, 597
conspiracy, rumors and accusations of, 36–8, 112, 472, 552–3, 561, 571, 715, 719
Constitution, British, 606–9, 614, 679, 701; *see also* common law; rights; liberties
consumer goods, 502, 577, 588, 592, 614, 682; *see also* trade
Contades, Marshal Louis, marquis de, 378
contingency: in conquest of Canada, 390, 392; influence of, in battle, 250–2; in history, xviii; *see also* warfare
contracts, military, 373, 455; *see also* patronage; provisioning; supplies
contractualism: and Seven Years' War experience, 145–7, 219–21, 370–2, 414, 685; and sovereignty, 147, 685
Contrecoeur, Capt. Claude-Pierre Pécaudy, seigneur de, 47, 49–57, 62, 65, 97, 105
Conway, Gen. Henry Seymour, 641, 654, 692–5, 697–9, 703, 714–5
Cooper, Rev. Samuel, 374
Coote, Lt. Col. Eyre, 418
Coromandel Coast, *xxxix*, 417–8
courts: British, 513, 564, 575; colonial, 583, 598–9, 608–9, 681, 730; common law, 609; vice admiralty, 609, 675, 681; *see also* Vice Admiralty Courts
Covenant Chain, 14–15, 38, 779n.2
Coxe, William, 673
Crawford, Hugh, 627–8
credit, 303, 308, 383, 479, 581, 588, 590, 592; *see also* British government, Board of Trade; currency; debt; economy; money shortage; subsidies
Croghan, George, 25, 27–30, 45–6, 60–1, 72, 94–5, 97, 99, 131, 206–7, 275–6, 283, 327, 524, 537, 545, 552, 595–6, 627–31, 641, 732–3
Crown Point, *xxviii, xxxi*; expedition of 1755, 68–9, 88, 91–2, 110–11, 114–16, *117*, 121, 123; expedition of 1758, 137, 140–3, 157, 310, 342, 369–71
Crown Point—Township Number 4 road, 343, 474, 524
Cross, Stephen, artificer, 153–4
Cuban campaign, *xxxiv*, *441–6*, 490, 498–502, 542; *see also* Havana; Spain, colonies of; trade; West Indies
Cuddalore (Fort St. David), *xxxix*, 417
culture, *see* intercultural relations
cultural intermediaries: missionaries as, 189, 199, 270; Quakers as, 205–7, 269; *see also* intercultural relations; missionaries; Quakers; Pemberton, Israel; Shirley, William
Cumberland County (Pa.), 627
Cumberland, Capt. Gen. William Augustus, duke of, 67–8, *69*, 70, 72, 86, 90, 123–5, 129–31, 144, 146, 148, 157, 172, 174–5, 177, 185, 209, 211–12, 214–15, 299–300, 401, 552, 653–4, 691–2, 694; *see also* Army of Observation; British politics
Cumming, Thomas, 306
currency: British, 312; colonial, 581–5, 589, 601, 668–9, 725, 729; *see also* Currency Act; economy; exchange, rate of; money
Currency Act of 1751, 584
Currency Act of 1764, 581, 584–5, 595, 613, 619, 724, 729
Cushing, Thomas, 715
Cushitunk, 530
customs (duties), 493, 520–1, 563–4, 574–80, 611, 614, 642, 668–70, 672–6, 680–2, 696–7, 717, 719; cockets, 576, 682; laws and regulations, 576, 604, 642, 696, 717, 730; *see also* British government; British politics; empire; smuggling; Stamp Act; taxation; trade

Dagworthy, Capt. John, 159
Dalyell, Capt. James, 539, 542, 544, 547–8
Daun, Leopold von, 176, 215–16, 301, 480, 496
debt: colonial, 228, 317–18, 389, 581–6, 598, 590, 592–3, 601–3, 613, 669, 695, 726–7; English, private, 583; English, public, 309, 481, 493, 562, 602, 811n.5
Declaration of Independence, xxi
Declaration of Rights and Liberties (Stamp Act Congress, 1765), 679
Declaratory Act, 703, 707, 712, 718
Deganawidah, 13
De Lancey family, 24, 91, 110, 131
De Lancey, Lt. Gov. James, 39, 79–80, 82–4, 91, 321, 608
De Lancey, Oliver, 131

De Lancey political faction, 91, 110, 599, 608–9, 757–8n.4
Delaware, *xxviii, xxx*, 210, 227
Delaware George (civil chief), 537
Delaware River, 530
Delaware Valley, 592
Demere, Capt. Paul, 463–5
Denny, Gov. William, 163, 165–7, 205–6, 267–71, 276, 278, 323, 529
Dependency of Ireland Act (1719), 702
depression, postwar, 588, 590–2, 597–9, 668–9, 695–8, 705, 709, 712, 718, 729; *see also* Amsterdam bank crisis; economy, British; economy, colonial
desertion: provincial, 204, 219–21, 371–2, 407, 463, 585, 650, 791–2n.4; in Bourbon armies, 497; of Wolfe's men, 345; *see also* discipline, military
Detroit, *xxviii–xxx*, 28–9, 338, 469–70, 472–3, 535–44, 547–8, 550, 634–5, 733; conference at, 518, 618, 620–4, 819–20n.13; *see also* battles, Pontiac's Rebellion; forts
Dieskau, Jean-Armand, baron de, 71, 111, 114–21, 132
Dinwiddie, Gov. Robert, 30, 37–8, 40–6, 50–3, 59–60, 65–8, 72, 84, 86, 92, 96, 109, 159–60, 183, 204
diplomacy: and intercultural relations, xv–xxii, 5–7, 11–21, 205–7, 457–71, 742–3; and war, 125–32, 308, 483–4, 503–7; European, 33, 65, 67, 70–2, 124–32, 169, 171, 211, 213, 215, 229, 308, 483–4, 487–96, 503–7, 751n.2; Indian, 11–18, 20–30, 38, 58, 72, 77–8, 81, 85, 92, 94–6, 106–7, 109, 162, 185–99, 205–7, 258, 267–71, 274–80, 284, 330–9, 405–6, 457–71, 470, 475, 518, 531–3, 548, 551–3, 618, 620–4, 627, 634, 641, 661, 732, 742, 749n.14; *see also* Albany Congress; Bradstreet, John; Covenant Chain; Croghan, George; diplomatic alliances; empire; Friendly Association; Johnson, Sir William; Pemberton, Israel; Pisquetomen; Six Nations of the Iroquois; Stuart, John; trade; Teedyuscung; *and individual conventions and treaties*
diplomatic alliances: European, 35–6, 67, 70–2, 125–9, 171, 213, 488, 493–6, French with Indians, 15, 16, 185–199, 258; Newcastle's system of, 35, 67, 70–1, 126–8, 169; Pitt's system of, 211, 490; *see also* Diplomatic Revolution
Diplomatic Revolution, 128–9, 169
discipline, provincial: absence of, 168, 273, 370–2, 519, 768–9n.4; and recruiting, 139–40, 228; *see also* desertion; discipline, regular; punishments
discipline, regular: and provincial discipline, 140, 221, 410–12; harshness of, 140, 220, 287, 781n.3; ironies of, 99–106, 243–8, 356–64, 760n.12, 791n.29; *see also* battles; punishment
disease, 13, 97, 136, 166, 199, 313, 320, 345, 393, 407, 413, 461, 465, 467–8, 499–501, 531, 536–7, 541–3, 549, 695; *see also* Amherst, Jeffery; smallpox
Dominica (Dominique), *xxxv*, 314, 422, *447*, 505
Draper, Lt. Col. William, 515–17
Dresden, *xxxvii*, 301, 380
Drucour, Augustin, chevalier de, 254–5
drought, 589, 592
Dutchess County (N.Y.), 721–2
Dunbar, Col. Thomas, 105, 108, 111. 292
Duquesne, Ange de Menneville, marquis de, 27, 31–2, 47, 53, 57, 65, 72, 777–8n.1

East India Company, British, 177–8, 309, 417, 506, 516–17
Easton conference (1756), 164–6; *see also* treaties: Easton
Echoe, 463, 466
economy, British, 383–4, 485, 493–4; and colonial trade, 682, 695–8, 702, 704–5; and financing of war, 214, 228–9, 303, 308–9, 312, 378–9, 387, 389, 453–5, 479, 481, 485, 493, 582, 803n.14; and postwar depression, 562, 572, 574, 583, 596–7, 602, 695–9, 702, 709, 712; and strains of empire, 472, 514, 557–71, 602, 695–8, 702; and taxation, 561–4, 572–80, 582–3, 682; and social unrest, 596–7, 653, 682, 695, 705, 822n.3; prosperity of, during war, 793n. 9
economy, colonial, 529; and currency 563, 581–5, 589, 591–2, 601, 668–9, 725, 729; and debts, 581–2, 584, 586, 589, 590, 592–3, 601–2, 668–9, 705, 714; and postwar recession, 588, 590–2, 598–9, 601, 668–9, 686, 705, 709, 728, 814–15n.6; and rates of exchange, 582–4, 589, 591–2, 613, 814n.2; and taxes, 601, 668–9, 695–8, 705, 707; and trade, 563, 577–9, 602, 682, 695–8, 705, 714; credit in, 228–9, 563, 590; effects of war on, 228–9, 317–24, 373, 389–90, 455, 563–4,

economy, colonial (*cont.*): 578, 582, 584, 586, 588, 601–3; shortage of money in, 228–9, 583–4, 591, 601–2, 668–9, 695, 697, 705
economy, French: and Compagnie des Indes, 178; effects of war on, 238, 378, 380, 417, 494, 498; shipping, 299, 412
Ecuyer, Capt. Simeon, 540–2
Edes, Benjamin, 665
Egremont, Charles Wyndham, earl of, 487, 489, 503, 512, 519, 552–3, 557, 565, 617
Egremont (Mass.), 722
Elbe River, *xxxvi*, 211–12, 416, 480
Ellis, Gov. Henry, 565
Ellis, Welbore, 649
embargo: 460; imposed by Loudoun (1757), 182–4; on Indian trade, 627–8
embezzlement, 204, 519, 725–6
Emden, 299
empire: allegory, symbols and emblems of, 329, *365*, 421–2, *423–50*, 517; and war, xxii, 213–16, 503–6, 418, 453–4; as site for intercultural relations, xix–xx, 20–1, 219–31, 412–13, 453–6, 744–6; British contrasted with French, in North America, 453–5, 503–6, 741–4; colonial autonomy within, 745–6; concepts of, xix, 222, 741–6; French, xvi, xviii, xix, xx, 7, 12–21, 36–8, 67, 72, 213, 265, 298, 306–7, 378–84, 408, 418, 422; frontiers of, 518–28; historiography of, xix, xxii; Indian alliances as critical to, 13–21, 151, 742–5; ironies and paradoxes of, 501–2, 685; lessons of, 516–17; relations of metropolis and periphery of, xvi, xix–xxi, xxiii, 84, 138, 239, 265, 317–24, 455, 501–2, 512, 521, 527, 559, 563, 570, 597, 603, 613, 635, 647, 655, 685, 710–11, 733, 741–4, 815n.6; strains of, 166–9, 238–9, 379, 411–12, 456, 472–5, 507–17, 557–9, 560–71; 741–6; Spanish, 503–6; trade as cement of, 306, 315–16, 454, 501–2, 576–80; wars of (1689–1815), 11; *see also* diplomacy; empire, British; intercultural relations; trade
empire, British, xvi–xxiii, 7, 12–21, 166–9, 222–31; 240; administration of, 557–9, 560–71, 572–80, 583, 585, 588, 603–4, 634, 641, 655, 677–87, 696, 712, 731, 733–4, 740–4, 751n.2; American enthusiasm for, 518–9, 712, 805–6n.2; and the British populace, 507–15; and sovereignty, 579–80, 634, 655, 710–12, 741–3, 745–6; character, of, xix, xxi, 222, 741–6; colonial autonomy within, 611, 707, 743–4; colonial resistance to imperial authority in, 512, 519–22, 571, 579–80, 635, 637, 641–2, 664–76, 677–87, 695–7, 707, 711–12, 717–19, 743–6; commerce within, 519–22, 576–80, 583, 597, 604, 610, 641–6, 682, 695–8, 714, 718–19; control of alien populations in, 561, 634, 712, 732–4, 741–4; financial strains of, 214, 228–9, 303, 308–9, 312, 387, 389, 453–5, 472, 479, 481, 493, 557–9, 560–71, 582; global reach of, 503–6, 516–17; military power of, 711–12, 733; paradoxes of, 673; prosperity of, 501–2, 793n.9; Seven Years' War and, 570–1, 685, 711–12, 742, 745–6; taxation in 563–4, 572–80, 641–6, 650, 664–76, 677–87, 718–19; *see also* diplomacy; British politics; colonial politics, economy; liberties, English; rebellion; rights, English; riots; Stamp Act; taxation; Proclamation Line; sovereignty
England, defense of, 169, 213, 378–83
English Channel; *xxxviii*, 169–70, 237, 239, 309, 312, 379, 381
English law, 730, 751–2n.2
enlistment, provincial: and bounties, 230, 388–9, 773–4n.18; of volunteers, 388, 585–6, 805–6n.2; quotas for, 519; terms of, 219–21, 228, 794n.3, 794–5n.5; *see also* provincial armies; recruiting
Estremadura (Portugal), *xxxviii*, 497
Eyre, Maj. William, 119, 120, *121*, 123, 186, 189, 243, 244

Fairfax, Thomas, Lord, 42
famine, 165, 237–8, 467–8, 537; *see also* diet; food shortages; provisions; supplies
Falmouth, 717
Family Compact, 484, 488, 802n.11
Fauquier, Gov. Francis, 461, 525, 527, 601, 603, 613, 661–2, 691, 823n.7
Ferdinand of Brunswick-Wolfenbüttel, 215–16, 299, *300*, 301–2, 304, 307, 309, 314, 378–80, 383–4, 416, 419, 453, 481–3, 490–1, 495
Fighting Instructions, Royal Navy, 381, 418
Filius Gallicae, 130
fisheries, 483–4, 488, 503, 506
Fitch, Thomas, 530, 674
Five Nations of the Iroquois, *see* Six Nations of the Iroquois

food shortages, 236–39, 241–42, 391, 624–5; *see also* diet; drought; famine; harvests; provisions; rations; siege; supplies
Forbes, Brig. Gen. John, 233–6, 258, 267–9, 271–5, 279–81, 283–5, 290–2, 298, 325–6, 405, 457–8, 466
Forbes Road, *see* roads
Forks of the Ohio, 27–30, 40, 43, 45–7, 50–2, 56, 60, 62, 65, 87, 258, 270, 272–3, 277, 281–4, 310, 322–4, 325–30, 333, 335, 347, 474, 525, 541, 549–50, 595, 733, 738; *see also* forts: Duquesne *and* Pitt; frontier; Ohio Country; Pittsburgh
forts: Allen, *xxviii, xxxi*, 326; Augusta (Shamokin), *xxviii, xxxi,* 158, 164–5; Beauséjour, *xxix*, 112–15; Bedford, *xxviii,* 258, 271, *273*, 474, 525, 540; Bull, *xxviii, xxxi*, 137, *138*, 157, 261; Burd, 800n.3; Carillon, *see* Ticonderoga; Cavite, 515–7; Chambly, *xxxi*, 401, 406; Chiswell's, *xxviii,* 467; Cuddalore, *see* St. David; Cumberland (Md.), xxviii, *89*, 94, 96, 104–5, 108, 158–9, 202–3, 209, 526; Cumberland (N.S.), 113; de Chartres, 619, 627–9, 631, 657, 733; Crown Point, *xxviii, xxxi*, 68–9, 114, 116–17, *117*, 118, 121, 137, 210, 259–61, 264, 286, 340–3, *343*, 369–72, 388, 400, 474, 524; d'Orléans (Chandernagore), *xxxix,* 178; Detroit, *xxviii*, 538, *539* , 541–4, 547–8, 550, 618, 620–2, 625, 628–9, 712, 733; Duquesne, *xxviii*, 49, 52, 54, 57, 60–2, 64–5, 87–8, 90–1, 94–108, 110, 115, 139, 162–3, 202, 204, 225, 227, 232–3, 236, 258, 268, 270–3, 278; 281–3, 289, 291, 298, 325–6, 328–9, 351, 738, 781n. 26; Edward, *xxxi*, 115, *116*, 117–19, 121, 123, 142, 187, 190–1, 193–4, 196–201, 209, 340, *341*; Edward Augustus, 539, 621; Frederick, *xxviii*, 158–9, 203; Frontenac (Cataraqui), *xxviii, xxxi*, 139–42, 225, 232–3, 249, 258–66, 281, 298, 333, 338, 622; George, *xxxi,* 340, 342, 674, 678; Granville, 162; Île-aux-Noix, *xxxi*, 400–1, *402*; Johnson, *332*; La Galette (later Ft. Lévis; later Ft. William Augustus), *xxxi*, 139, 400–1, *403*, 405, 618; Lawrence, 112–13; LeBoeuf, *xxviii*, 43–4, 47, 118, 338, 540, 544; Lévis, *see* La Galette; Ligonier, *xxviii*, 272–3, 279, 282–3, 325–6, 474, 525, 540, 548, 550, 627; Loudoun, *xxviii*, 158, 202, 459, 461–5, 468; Louis, 306, *307*; Machault (Venango), *xxviii,* 31, 45, 283, 326, 335–6, 338, 540, 544, 712; Massachusetts, 523; Miami, 538; Michilimackinac, 473, 538–9, *540*, 594, 618, 620–1, 712, 733; Morro Castle, 498–9, *500*, 501; Necessity, *xxviii,* 59, 60, 62–5, 78, 105, 351, 390; Niagara, *xxix–xxx*, 69, 87–8, 90–1, 110, 112, 115–16, 232, 262, 264, 310, 330–9, *334*, 340, 342, 347, 387, 390, 392, 470, 474, 537, 540–1, 544, 547, 550, *551*, 618–21, 624, 712, 809–10n.2; Number 4, *xxix–xxxi*, 343, 474, 524; Oswego, *xxix–xxxi*, 110, 112, 136–7, 140–3, 150–7, 164, 167, 169, 172, 210, 259–61, 264, 310, 330–1, 333, 335, 338, 388, 400, 405, 618, 622; Ontario, 150, 152; Ouiatenon, *xxx*, 538, 630–1; Pelham, 523; Pitt, *xxviii,* 323, 325–7, *328*, 329, 343, 387, 390, 472–4, 424–5, 540–1, 543–4, 547–50, 619, 621, 625, 627–8, 636, 731–3; Presque Isle, *xxviii,* 338, 540, 544; Prince George, *xxviii*, 202, 459–63, 465–8; Punta, 498–9, *500*, 501; Rascal, *see* Oswego; Red Stone, 29, 525; Royale, 313; St. David (Cuddalore), *xxxix*, 417; St. Frédéric, *see* Crown Point; St. George, 417; Saint-Jean, 401; St. Joseph, 538; St. Michaels, 306; Sandusky, 538; Shirley, 163, 523; Stanwix (Great Carrying Place), *xxviii, xxxi*, 260, 474; Ticonderoga (Ft. Carillon), *xxxi*, 117–18, 123, 142, 146, 185–7, 189–90, 196, 200, 209, 225, 232–3, 240–4, *245*, 246–8, 260, 262, 265, 286, 298, 341–2, 618, 620; Toronto, *xxviii,* 338; Toulouse, 202, 460, 462, 465; William (Calcutta), *xxxix,* 178; William Augustus, *see* La Galette; William Henry, *xxviii, xxxi*, *122*, 123, 142, 146, 157, 185–200, 208–10, 219, 222, 240, 245–56, 454; Wills Creek, 27; *see also* battles
fortifications: fort building, 27, 29, 31, 36–7, 41, 45–7, 49, 59–60, 79, 109, 112, 117, 123, 158, 161, 258, 272, 281, 323, 328, 333, 340, 343, 390, 411; as magnets for settlement, 525–7, 800–1n.3; cost of maintaining, 635–6; design of, *122*, 123, 152, 158, 250–1, *252*, 253, 262, *328*, 333–4, *334*, *343*, 351–2, 404, 464; *see also* Eyre, William; Louisbourg; Vauban architecture; forts, *listed individually*
Fox, Henry, 68, 70, 125, 127, 131, 137, 144, 148, 169–75, 212, 504, 508, 511
France: and Indian relations, 14–21, 31, 61, 135–6, 151, 155–6, 185–200, 238–9, 254 258, 301, 346, 453–6, 742; European alliances of, 35–6, 71, 124–30, 169–71, 213, 483–4, 503–4; empire of, 213, 239, 306–8, 408, 422,

France (*cont.*):
423–50, 453–5, 490, 498, 501, 503–6, 521, 590; government of, 71, 128, 169, 345, 347, 395, 417; in North America, 31–8, 67, 406–10, 503–6; in war, 127, 169–171, 176, 211–16, 232, 239, 240, 261, 263–4, 298, 301, 308, 312, 314, 378–84, 416, 419, 483, 503, 793n.6, 769n.5; 797n. 11; population of, 129; *see also* Africa; Bourbon dynasty; economy, French; Canada; diplomacy; empire; Family Compact; Louis XV; Seven Years' War; West Indies; trade
franchise, British, 508–9
Frankfurt an der Oder, *xxxvi,* 301, 380
Franklin, Benjamin, *82*, 166, 612, 706–7; and Albany Congress, 80–5; and Braddock expedition (1755), 92–3; and quartering, 646, 649–50; and Stamp Act crisis, 675, 705–7; and western expansion, 595, 744–5; in Pennsylvania politics, 161–2, 600, 706
Fraser, Lt. Alexander, 628–30, 657
Fraser, John, 31, 43, 45, 47
Frederick II, king of Prussia, 127–9, 171, 176–7, 212–13, 215–16, 298–302, 307, 380, 384, 416, 480, 482, 490–3, 495–6, 506, 802–3n.11; *see also* diplomacy; Prussia; Seven Years' War
Frederick William (Prussia), 492
French and Indian War, 747n.1; *see also* Seven Years' War
French Revolution, xvi
French West Indies, 182, 213, 239, 306, 308, 415, 490, 501, 521, 576–9, 590
Friendly Association for Regaining and Preserving Peace with the Indians by Pacific Means, 205–7, 269, 278–9, 326, 531; *see also* cultural intermediaries; diplomacy; intercultural relations; pacifism; Pemberton, Israel; Quakers; Treaty of Easton
Friendly Society, *see* Friendly Association
Friesland, 176, 299
frontier, American: *xxviii–xxx*; 40, 81, 117, 158–60, 166–7, 205, 227, 289, 290, 322–4, 457–71, 518, 598–9, 611–13; British curtailment of settlement on, 566–71; clash of empires on, 11–21, 30–41, 46–7, 72, 77, 325–9; expansion of settlement into, 17, 23, 323–4, 327–9, 473–5, 518, 522–8, 568, 595, 597–9, 636–7, 731–4, 738–41, 743–4; defense of, 108, 158–65, 179, 184, 202–7, 227, 320–4, 335, 454–5, 457–9, 548, 584, 597–9, 601, 635–7; violent conflict on, 72, 108–9, 124, 151, 160–1, 202–7, 454–71, 527, 541, 611–12, 624, 627–37, 823n.7; *see also* Albany Congress; Cherokee War; empire; land speculation; Ohio Country; Pontiac's Rebellion; Proclamation Line; Frye, Lt. Col. Joseph, 190, 194, 197

Gabarus Bay, 250, 257
Gage, Maj. Gen. Thomas, 97, 99, 100, 243, 338, 341, 472, 553, 641, *697*, 720–3, 830n.4; and Pontiac's War, 617–21, 623–9, 631, 633–7, 730–3; and Stamp Act crisis, 641, 665, 677–8, 692, 295; and quartering, 647–9, 696, 720, 723
Galloway, Joseph, 161–2, 612, 657–8, 675–6
Gates, Capt. Horatio, 97
Gaspé Bay, 422, *434*, 435–6
Gebroeders Neufville, 583; *see also* Amsterdam bank panic
general warrants, 573
George I, 126
George II, 38, 41, 67, *69*, 113, 126, 129, 172–6, 212, 214–15, 297, 304, 306, 368, 415, 419, 481, 509; death of, 419–20
George III, 125, 420, 476–7, *478*, 479, 482, 485, 487–8, 494–5, 503–4, 507–10, 518, 557–8, 561–2, 572–4, 622, 641, 649–50, 652–6, 741, 744, 801n.4; illness of, 652
Georgia, 322, 461, 468, 565, 600–1, 677
German Flats, *xxxi*, 157, 219–20
Germany, *xxxvi–xxxviii*, 35, 127–8, 173, 213, 215, 505–6; British subsidies of, 67, 127, 481–2; war in, 299, 314, 380, 482, 491–6; *see also* diplomacy; Hanover, Prussia
Gibbon, Edward, 173
Gibraltar, *xxxviii*, 170–1, 237, 257, 378
Gist, Christopher, 27–8, 30, 43, 52, 61, 65
Gladwin, Maj. Henry, 538, 542, 544, 547–8, 550, 617, 621
Good News of Peace and Power, 13
Goree, 306, *307*, 309, 506
Gnadenhutten (Pa.), 160
Grafton, Augustus Henry Fitzroy, duke of, 654, 693–4, 697, 703
Grand Council (Iroquois), 12–16, 18, 20–3, 28, 65, 78–9, 91, 109, 165, 260, 275–7, 279, 330–3, 531; *see also* diplomacy, Indian; Six Nations of the Iroquois
Grand Dérangement, 112–14; *see also* Acadians, deportation of

Grant, Maj. James, 272–3, 281, 466–7, 470
Great Britain, *see* British government; British politics; empire, British
Great Carrying Place (Hudson–Lake George), 115, *341*
Great Carrying Place (Mohawk–Wood Creek), 137, *156*, 157, 260, 261, 264, 474
Great Dismal Swamp, *xxviii*, 594, 739; *see also* Washington, George
Great Lakes, 13–14, 20, 141, 150–2, 187, 264–5, 338, 473, 622, 733
Great League of Peace and Power, *see* Six Nations of the Iroquois
Great Meadows, 52–3, 56, 59–61, 390
Grenada (West Indies), 490, 505
Grenadines (West Indies), *xxxv*, 505
Grenville, George, 487–8, *489*, 494, 503–4, 511, 513–15, 552, 652–6, 704; postwar imperial reforms of, 557–9, 562–5, 570–5, 577–81, 583, 585–8, 599, 603, 606, 611, 614–6, 641–2, 644–7, 650, 668, 685, 712, 715, 733
Grenville, Richard, Earl Temple, 173
Grenvilles (political faction), 172, 175, 707
Guadeloupe, *xxxv*, 239, 313–5, 317, 380, 422, *448–50*, 503, 506, 577–9
Guiana, 590, 596
Gulf of St. Lawrence, *xxix*, 87, 110, 209, 237, 345, *434–6*,
Guy Fawkes Day, 666, 678

Half King, *see* Tanaghrisson
half-kings, 18
Half-way Brook, 198, 340
Halifax, George Montagu Dunk, earl of, 34–6, 38, 68, 70, 77, 79, 85, 112, 115, 130, 148, 175, 229, 504, 512–14, 552, 557–9, 565–6, 568–71, 580–1, 586–7, 595, 607, 641, 733, 757n.7
Halifax (Nova Scotia), 36, 112, 208, 369, 473, 498, 575, 607
Hallowell, Benjamin, 670
Hamilton, Gov. James, 530, 532–3
Hanover, 126–7, 129, 169, 171, 173–7, 211–2, 215–16, 229, 239, 299, 304, 314, 378, 416, 419, 476–7, 491, 493–6, 506–7
Hanover, House of, 125–6, 212, 509
Hartford (Ct.), 225, 233, 595, 674
harvests, 236–37, 249, 368, 391, 465, 492, 589, 775n.4
Havana, 422, *441–6*, 490, 498–9, *500*, 501, 503–6, 54, 549, 589, 595
Haviland, Brigadier Gen. William, 388, 397, 399–402, 404, 406
Hawke, Adm. Edward, 257, 258, 381–3, 419
Hawks's Fort (Charlemont, Mass.), 221
hegemony: English, in North America, xvi, 742–3, British illusion of, in North American empire, 711–12; Iroquois claims to, in Ohio, 22, 106–7, 269, 276–8, 330–9, 529–35, 551–2; *see also* empire
Hendrick, Chief (Theyanoguin), 38, *39*, 79, 92, 107, 115, 118–19, 331
Henry, Patrick, 660–3, 725–6, 728
Hesse, 173, 211, 309, 314, 378, 481, 506
Hessian troops, 169, 173
Highland Uprising (1745), 67
Hinderaker, Eric, xix
Hochkirch, *xxxvii*, 301
Hogg, Capt. Peter, 52, 55–6
Holburne, Adm. Francis, 208–9
Holdernesse, Robert D'Arcy, earl of, 37–8, 40, 45, 175, 481–2
Holland, 126, *see also* bank panic; Low Countries
Holmes, Rear Adm. Charles, 351–2, 367
Holstein-Gottorp, duke of (Peter III), 492–6
honors of war, 195–6, 254, 367, 407–8, 501
Hood, Zachariah, 674
Hopkins, Gov. Stephen, 658
Hopson, Maj. Gen. Peregrine Thomas, 312–13
hostages, 351, 460–1, 621, 678; *see also* prisoners
Howard, Martin, Jr., 658, 672–3, 702
Howe, George Augustus, Viscount, 233–4, 241
Howe, Richard, Viscount, 353–4, 357, 499
Howe, William, 353–4, 357, 499
Hudson Valley, 185, *427–8*, 592; land disputes in, 597, 720–3
Hughes, John, 162, 646, 657–8, 675–6, 706
Hutchinson, Thomas, 80–2, *83*, 84, 91, 224–5, 389, 520–1, 601, 605–7, 610, 614, 647, 658, 686, 715–16, 719, 729; and Stamp Act crisis, 668–72, 715–16, 719, 807n.4

Île-aux-Noix, *xxxi*, 342–3, 369, 388, 392, 400–1, *402*
Île d'Orléans, *xxxiii*, 344, 352
Île Perrot, 402, 404, 406
Île Ste.-Hélène, 408

Île-St.-Jean (Prince Edward Island), *xxix*, 114
Illinois Country, 17, 31, 72, 232, 283, 338, 473, 548, 561, 595, 619, 621–2, 624, 626–31, 633, 636, 731–2, 742
impressment, provincial, 319–20; *see also* enlistment, provincial; recruiting
Imperium in imperio, 711
independence, American, xv–xxiii, 705–7, 745–6
India, *xxxix*, 177–8, 417–18, 490, 506, 516
Indian Ocean, 309, 417–18
Indian peoples, *xxx*; Abenaki, 112, 114, 117–21, 186–8, 192, 254; Algonquian speaking, 15–16, 748n.6; Catawba, 12, 16, 23, 96, 160, 204, 462, 466–7, 469; Caughnawaga, 14, 117–21, 186–9, 405–6, 551; Cayuga, 12; Cherokee, 16, 23, 96, 160, 202, 267–9, 387, 415, 457–71, 823n.7; Chickasaw, 466–9; Chippewa, 28, 187, 338, 537, 539–40, 550, 594, 622; Creek, 460–9, 730; Delaware, 16–31, 46–7, 56, 60–1, 65, 79, 94–5, 99, 109, 162–5, 188, 205–8, 268–78, 281–2, 325–6, 330–1, 406, 529–37, 540–1, 549, 551–2, 612, 619, 623–31, 732, 745; "Far Indians," 16, 20, 99, 281; Huron, 13, 189, 538–9, 622; Iroquois, *see* Six Nations of the Iroquois; Kickapoo, 538, 630–1; Mascouten, 538, 630–1; Menominee, 151, 187, 189, 236; Miami, 25–6, 28–9, 188, 330, 537–8, 547, 622, 624, 631; Micmac, 112, 114, 189, 254; Mingo (western Seneca), 18, 21, 25, 27–8, 30, 44–6, 52, 56, 60–1, 65, 94–9, 109, 270, 281, 325–6, 533, 540–1, 547, 551, 619, 621, 628, 631; Mohawk, 12, 14, 24, 38, 79, 91–2, 107, 110, 115–20, 123, 276, 331, *364*, *365*, 405, 466; Mississauga, 99, 118, 187, 622; Nipissing, 187–9; Ojibwa, 187–9, 326; Oneida, 12, 18, 94, 150, 276–7, 532; Onondaga, 537; Ottawa, 28, 99, 109, 186, 189, 236, 281, 326, 535, 537–40, 547, 550, 633; Piankashaw, 631; Potawatomi, 99, 186–7, 189, 236, 326, 537–9, 622; Seneca, 12, 16, 18, 275–6, 331, 334–5, 470, 533, 537, 540, 544, 550–1, 624; Shawnee, 13–4, 16, 18, 20–5, 27, 30, 46, 56, 60–1, 65, 94, 99, 109, 202, 270, 281, 325–6, 330–1, 406, 532, 537, 540–1, 547, 551–2, 619–32, 732, 745; Tuscarora, 21, 467; Wea, 538, 631; Wyandot, 25–6, 99, 109, 281, 283, 537–8, 547, 621
Indian peoples: Anglo-American attitudes toward, 94–6, 199–201, 470–1; and Amherst, 284, 404–6, 408, 455–6, 463, 466, 469–72, 518, 535–7, 542–6, 551–2, 617–8, 743; and colonial expansion, 474–5, 525, 529–34, 536–7, 566–71, 732–3, 741; and Montcalm, 135–6, 151, 155, 187–90, 196–200, 346, 454, 456, 742; and traffic in alcohol, 471, 535–6, 732–3; contested land claims of, 22–4, 84, 106–7, 269, 276–8, 327–33, 529–34, 551–2, 721, 732; crucial role of, in British-French rivalry; 11–24, 72, 90–1, 94–107, 109, 151–2, 154–5, 167, 186–201, 232, 236, 258, 267–8, 270, 278, 330–9, 346, 392, 404, 453–5, 467, 742–3; effects of European war on, 164, 470–1, 536; geographic ranges of, *xxx*, 16; gift-giving in diplomacy of, 13–15, 18, 20–1, 23, 25–6, 28–9, 58, 92, 205, 278, 331, 405, 459–61, 465, 468, 470, 475, 551–3, 620, 634, 732, 742, 749n.14; murders of, on frontier, 466, 732–3, 823n.7; politics of resistance by, 629, 732–3; relations among Indian nations, xviii, 12–16, 21–4, 96, 330–9, 346, 404–6, 412, 454–6, 470, 535–46, 547–53, 732–3, 742; religion of, 332, 535–7, 546; style of warfare of, 12–13, 102–4, 123, 151, 154–5, 196–8; trade relations of, 453–5, 566, 570–1, 580; *see also* diplomacy, Indian; intercultural relations
Indian rebellions, 512, 515; Cherokee War, 457–71, 598; Pontiac's Rebellion, 535–46, 547–53, 557, 565, 571, 588, 611, 616–31, 633–7, 647, 712, 734
Indian superintendents, *see* Atkin, Edmund; Johnson, William; Stuart, John
Ingersoll, Jared, 611, 644, 646, 676
insubordination, 219–21, 624; *see also* desertion; intercultural relations
intercolonial relations: competition, 30, 284, 323–4, 327, 597, 720–4, 743; cooperation, 77, 81, 84–5, 221–4, 615, 658, 660, 684, 712; *see also* Albany Plan; frontier; land speculation; New England; New York; Ohio Company; Pennsylvania; Plan of Union; Virginia
intercultural relations: and administration of empire, xviii–xxiii, 566, 568, 686–7; and American social conditions, 227–31, 286–9, 742–6; and Amherst's Indian policy, 284, 404–6, 408, 455–6, 463, 466, 469–72, 518, 535–7, 542–6, 551–2, 617–18, 743; and attitudes toward warfare, 5–7, 12–15, 94, 102–4, 135–6, 151, 155, 187–90, 196–200; 346, 454, 456, 742; and Easton conferences, 205–7, 455; British and

American relations, xix–xx, 136–49, 166–9, 146–9, 219–31, 286–9, 370–2, 412–14, 454–6, 519–28, 581, 585–8, 635–7, 683–7, 696, 706–7, 710–12, 741–6; Canadians and French, 345–6; Catholic and Protestant; 566, 568; cultural intermediaries and, 189, 205–7, 269, 270; English contrasted with French relations with Indians, 545–6; European, colonial, and Indian relations, xix–xx, 11–20, 62, 94–6, 102–4, 106–7, 135–6, 151, 155, 187–90, 192, 196–200, 268, 346, 404–6, 454–6, 469–71, 545–6, 551–2, 568, 635–7, 742
Ireland, 381, 497, 562, 706
Irish Parliament, 562
Iroquois: *see* Six Nations of the Iroquois

Jacques-Cartier, 363–4, 366, 395
Jackson, Richard, 612, 670–2
Jamaica, 308, 315, 461
James, Maj. Thomas, 678, 702
Jefferson, Thomas, 662
Jenkinson, Charles, 649
Jenks, Capt. Samuel, 413–14
Jervis, Lt. John, 353, 789n.14
Johnson, William, 79–80, *81*, 84–5, 115, 138, 205–07, 269, 327, 332, 543–4, 552, 617; and Battle of Lake George, 110, 116–19, 121, 131; and Crown Point expedition (1755), 87–8, 90, 110–11, 114, 117, 123; and Indian diplomacy, 87, 91–2, 94, 96, 107, 130–1, 267, 387, 406, 469–70, 472, 518, 531, 544, 551–2, 732–3, 779n.2; and Niagara expedition (1759), 330–1, 333, 335–8; and Pontiac's Rebellion, 617, 619–21, 623, 626–8, 631, 633–4; and land speculation, 284, 595; and Treaty of Easton (1757), 205–7, 275, 279, 531; *see also* Amherst, Indian policy of; diplomacy, Indian; Indian rebellions; Six Nations of the Iroquois
Johnson Hall (Ft. Johnson), 332, 551, 625
Johnston, Augustus, 672
Johnstone, Gov. George, 636, 729–30
joint military operations, regular and provincial, 144–7, 149, 179–80
Jumonville, Ens. Joseph Coulon de Villiers de, 6, 12, 5–54, 56–9, 62, 64, 72, 78
Jumonville's Glen, 5–7, 53–8, 64, 77, 105, 453, 754–6n.6–7, n.12–13
juries: Catholics precluded from serving on 730; right to trial by, 608, 679–80

Kaendaé (Seneca chief), 335–6
Kaninguen, Denis, 57–8
Kaskaskia, 17, 629–31, 635
Kaunitz, Wenzel von, Count, 71, 506
Kayaderosseras partners, 38, *see also* land speculation
Keekyuscung (Ketiushund), 280, 780n.23
Kenny, James, 328–9
Kentucky, 25, 30, 525, 594
King George's War, 11, *19*, 24, 87, 112, 142, 237–8, 586
King, Thomas, 276–7, 532
King William's War, 11, 14
King's Friends, 693–4, 698, 701, 707
Kloster-Zeven, Convention of, 211–12, 215–16, 299; *see also* diplomacy
Knox, Capt. John, 398
Kolberg, 492
Kunersdorf, 380
Kuskuski, 270, 280–2

La Belle Famille, 335–7
labor: shortage of, 141, 227–9, 318, 372, 797n.7; *see also* economy
La Galissionière, Michel Barin, comte de, 25, 31, 171
Lagos, 395
La Jonquière, Pierre Jacques de Taffanel, marquis de, 26
Lake Champlain, 24, 68, 88, 116–18, 187, 232, 245, 310, 341–2, 347, 369, 377, 400, 402, 474, 524, 597
Lake Erie, 25–6, 31, 264, 333, 473, 538, 550
Lake George (Lac St. Sacrement), 24, 115, 118, 123, 142, 145–6, 185–6, 209, 241, 245, 248, 261, 265, 310, 340
Lake Huron, 265, 473, 538
Lake Michigan, 15, 473, 538–9
Lake Ontario, 26, 69, 87, 110, 139, 141, 225, 232, 258, 260–1, 310, 331–3, 338; naval command of, 232, 261, 263–4
Lally, Thomas-Arthur, comte de, 417
Lancaster, 24, 524
Lancaster Council (1763), 532
land claims, contested, *see* Forks of the Ohio; frontier; Indian rebellions; Hudson Valley land disputes; land speculation; Ohio Country; Royal Proclamation of 1763; Teedyuscung; Treaty of Easton; Walking Purchase; Wyoming Valley

land grants, 92, 206–7, 594–5; and Proclamation Line, 566, 568; as pay for military service, 50, 473–4; sought by Americans 596, 622; and colonial politics, 600; *see also* frontier; land speculation; New Hampshire grants; Treaty of Easton; Walking Purchase
land speculation, 7, 23–4, 27, 38, 40, 72, 78–9, 206, 255, 284–5, 327, 474, 523–8, 568–9, 593–8, 635, 724–5, 739–41, 743, 815n.11; *see also* Albany Congress; Croghan, George; Forks of the Ohio; Great Dismal Swamp; Illinois Country; Johnson, William; Loyal Company; William; Ohio Company; Ohio Country; Pennsylvania; Susquehannah Company; Virginia; Washington, George
Langdon, Rev. Samuel, 374
Langlade, Ens. Charles-Michel Mouet de, 28–30, 99, 187
L'Anse au Foulon (Fuller's Cove), 352–4, *358*
La Prairie, 404
La Présentation, 109, 405
La Rochelle, 257, 419
Laurel Ridge, 52, 258, 272
Laurens, Henry, 466, 598, 816n.17
Lawrence, Gov. Charles, 522–3, 526
League Council (Iroquois), *see* Grand Council; Six Nations of the Iroquois
Learned, Capt. Ebenezer, 219–21
Lechawanock (Lackawanna) Creek, 530, 532
Lee, Lt. Col. Charles, 247, 265, 497
Lee, Richard Henry, 647, 724–6, 728
Legardeur de Saint-Pierre, Capt. Jacques, 44–5, 47, 118–19, 121
Le Havre, 314
Leicester House, 125, 172, 174, 302, 304, 420, 476–7; *see also* British politics
Le Loutre, Abbe Jean Louis de, 112
Léry, Lt. Joseph-Gaspard Chaussegros de, 57, 138
Lévis, François-Gaston, chevalier de, 191, 194, 338, 364, 367, 391–7, 404, 407–8, 454
Leuthen, 215, 298, 301
liberties, English, 167, 509–11, 513, 520, 572, 643, 648, 661, 679, 683, 711–13, 741; as birthright, 712; of conscience, 523; of the press, 572; rhetoric of, 223, 509–13, 520, 643, 661, 670, 674, 681–2, 684, 700, 711; symbolism of, 511, 513–4; *see also* Constitution, British; Petition of Right; republicanism; rights
Liegnitz, 416
Ligonier, Gen. John, Lord, 215–16, 233, 235, 297, 305, 313, 483–4, 487–8, 490, 497–9, 552
Lignery, Capt. François-Marie Le Marchand de, 281–3, 326, 335–7, 347
Lisbon, 497
Littlehales, Lt. Col. John, 153
Livingston Manor, 721
Livingston-Morris political faction, 91, 131
Livingston Party, 599, 608–9
Livingston, Peter Van Burgh, 91
Loftus, Maj. Arthur, 619, 626
Logstown (now Ambridge, Pa.), 18, 27–30
London, xxiii, 30, 33, 124, 167, 215, 377, 476, 490, 505, 583–4, 596, 653; financiers of, 303, 308, 479, 583, 590; mob, 507–15; growth of middle class in, 509–10; *see also* British government; British politics; merchants, British
Lords Commissioners of Trade and Plantations, *see* British government, Board of Trade
Loudoun, John Campbell, earl of, 130, 132, 135, 142–3, *144*, 155–8, 162, 173, 178–85, 202–4, 206–14, 216, 233, 259–260, 497; campaign against Louisbourg (1757), 179–84, 208–9; and embargo on trade, 182–4; and Louisbourg, 207–8, 214; and military discipline, 144–9, 371; and North American style of warfare, 155; and provincial relations, 77, 136, 144–9, 166–9, 179–83, 203, 209–10, 214, 219–31, 259, 288, 454, 456, 519; and quartering, 147–9, 166–7, 181, 209, 223, 321, 648–9, 729; and recruitment, 180–1, 219–24, 227–8; recall of, 211, 225–7
Louis XV, 6, 26, 33, 128, 239, 347, 384, 407, 482, 504
Louis, Prince of Brunswick, 380
Louisbourg, *see* battles; contingency; fortifications, architecture; Treaty of Aix-la-Chapelle; warfare, conventions of
Louisiana, 17, 335, 505, 561, 629, 742, 744
Low Countries, British and French competition in, 35–6, 67, 126–7, 301
Loyal Company, 30, 525, 594; *see also* land speculation
Loyalhanna, 272–3, 279–82, 474, 525
Loyal Nine, 665–8, 671, 678, 681
Lydius, John Henry, 78, 92, 110, 131, 277
Lyman, Maj. Gen. Phineas, 595–6
Lyttelton, Gov. William Henry, 458, 460–1, 464–5, 467

Mackay, Capt. James, 60
Mackinac, Straits of, 539
Mackintosh, Ebenezer, 666–8, 670, 825n.7
Madeira, 576–7, 610
Madras, *xxxix*, 178, 417, 516
Maine (York County, Mass.), 717
Malcolm, Capt. Daniel, 717–19
Malgue, Capt. Joseph Marin de La, 337, 787–8n.11
Manila, 490, 512, 515–17
manufactures, British, 501–2, 684, 695, 706, 718, 742; in Indian trade, 468–9
Maria Amalia, 802n.11
Maria Theresa, Empress Queen, 71–2, 128–9, 171, 506
Marie-Galante, *xxxv*, 315
Martin, Samuel, M.P., 514
Martinique, 239, 308–9, 312–15, 473, 479, 490, 499, 503, 506, 521, 577–9, 589
Maryland, 202, 209, 230, 322, 524, 615, 773n.17; defense of, 108, 158–9; and trade, 182–4; and recruitment, 322, 519; and Stamp Act crisis, 674, 677
Massachusetts, 82, 190, 195, 288, 388; and westward migration, 474–5, 523–4, 597, 720, 722; economy and society of, 317–20, 582, 607, 668–9; impact of war on, 288–9, 317–20, 390; militia of, 223, 230, 716; politics of, 131, 520–1, 601, 604–8, 658–60, 715–19, 729, 828n.2, 829n.3–4, 829n.6; troop recruitment by, 137–9, 200, 209–10, 219, 221, 225, 317–20, 388–90; responses of, to imperial reforms, 604–8, 658–60, 665–72, 677, 679; troops of, 219–21, 288–9, 370–2; *see also* Bernard, Gov. Francis; colonial legislatures; economy, colonial; Hutchinson, Thomas; Pownall, Gov. Thomas; provincial troops; Shirley, Gov. William
Massacre of Fort William Henry (1757), 196–9
Massey, Lt. Col. Eyre, 337
Mauduit, Israel, 574, 606
Maumee River, 621, 623
Mayhew, Rev. Jonathan, 375
McEvers, James, 673
McGinnis, Capt. William, 121
McNutt, Alexander, 523
Mediterranean, *xxxviii*, 309, 485, 493
Memeskia (La Demoiselle; also Old-Briton), 25, 29
Mercer, Lt. Col. George, 230, 282, 526, 647, 673, 725–7
Mercer, Lt. Col. Hugh, 283, 327, 331, 333
Mercer, Lt. Col. James, 137, 150, 152–3
merchants: British, 581–4, 590, 614, 682, 696, 701–2, 704, 709; colonial, 86, 501, 588–9, 590–2, 596, 599, 604, 607–8, 610, 681–2, 696, 714, 717–9, 730, 829n.12
Meserve, George, 673
Mexico, 501, 516
Miami River, 25–6
Michigan, 25
Michilimackinac, 232, 338, 407, 473
middle ground, 748n.6
Mifflin, John, 162
migration: and deportation of Acadians, 112, 522–3, 526; by New Englanders, 112–14, 529–34, 596, 720–4; and expansion into conquered territories, 473–5, 522–8, 597–9, 731; *see also* land grants; frontier; land speculation; Ohio Country; Royal Proclamation of 1763
Military Adventurers, 596
military justice, 286–7, 781–2n.3; *see also* punishments
military units, British provincial (by commander's name and province): Col. Jonathan Bagley's Mass. regiment, 244; Col. William Byrd III's Virginia regiment (2nd Virginia), 230, 282, 289, 467–8, 593; Col. Joseph Frye's Mass. regiment, 190, 194, 197; Capt. Ebenezer Learned's Mass. company, 219–21; Capt. William McGinnis's N.H. company, 121; Col. John Parker's N.J. regiment ("Jersey Blues"), 189, 190; Capt. Adam Stephen's Virginia company, 97, 102; Col. George Washington's Virginia regiment (1st Virginia), 50, 51, 62, 106, 109, 159–60, 203, 230–1, 282, 289, 738–9; Col. John Winslow's Mass. regiment, 113
military units, British regular (by regiment number): *1st*, 462, 466; *17th*, 466, 541, 619, 621; *21st*, 730; *22nd*, 466, 619; *27th*, 474; *28th*, 360, 362, 721–3; *31st*, 730; *34th*, 627; *35th*, 143, 189, 433; *40th*, 259; *42nd*, 143, 541, 548, 631; *43rd*, 360–1, 398; *44th*, 86–8, 93, 100, 103–4, 156, 243, 247, 265, 618; *46th*, 337, 501, 721–2; *47th*, 360–1; *48th*, 86–8, 93, 100, 360; *50th*, 87–8, 137, 141, 408; *51st*, 87–8, 137, 140–1, 259, 408; *55th*, 234, 547; *58th*, 353, 360, 501; *60th* (originally numbered *62nd*, "Royal Americans"), 143, 166, 181, 190, 203–4, 547–9; *77th*, 462, 541, 548; *78th*, 360–2, 392–3, 628; *79th*, 515–6; *80th*, 243, 547, 550, 618; *84th*, 418

military units, British regular, other: Louisbourg Grenadiers, 360, 362, 366; Rangers, 186, 188, 243, 547, 768–9n.4; New York Independent Companies, 189, 501; South Carolina Independent Companies, 69, 62, 63
military units, French, colony regulars (*troupes de la marine*): 150–1, 187, 191, 236–7, 241, 251, 262, 281, 337, 347, 392, 404
military units, French, regular army (*troupes de la terre*): *Régiments Béarn*, 151, 347, 359; *Guyenne*, 151, 347, 359; *La Sarre*, 151, 347, 359; *Languedoc*, 120, 347, 359; *Royal-Roussillon*, 347, 359; *La Reine*, 120
militia and other colonial military organizations, British: Connecticut militia, 200–1; Georgia Rangers, 677; Massachusetts militia, 200–1, 223, 230, 667, 716, 770n.26; South Carolina Rangers, 462
militia and other colonial military organizations, French: Canadian militia, 119, 185–7, 191, 337, 345–7, 356, 359–61, 366–7, 392–3, 404; *Compagnie Royal-Syntaxe*, 347
millennialism, 373–6; *see also* providentialism; religion
military strategy, eighteenth century, 381–2, 483; *see also* Seven Years' War; warfare
Minden, 314, 378, *379*, 380
Minorca, 170–1, 194, 308, 483, 506
Miquelon, 506
Mirepoix, Charles de Levis, duc de, 124, 130
Missaguash River, 112
missionaries, 14–15, 18, 326, 347; as cultural intermediaries, 189, 198–9, 270
missions: and Indians, 392, 404, 406; and war, 392, 404
Mississippi Company, 594, 740
Mississippi River, 417, 473, 505, 594–5, 619, 626, 630, 633, 733
Mississippi Valley, 14, 16–17, 415, 596, 739
Missouri River, 17
mobs, 415, 507–15, 520, 619, 664–79, 717
Mohawk River, 157, 259, 330, 332, 335, 400, *429*, 474
Mohawk Valley, 87, 91, 232, 260, 523, 595
molasses, 315, 521, 564, 574, 577–9, 697, 813n.8–9; *see also* rum; sugar; trade
Molasses Act of 1733, 574, 577, 813n.9
Monceau, Canadian militiaman, 53–4, 56
Monckton, Brig. Gen. Robert, 349, *350*, 351–4, 362, *365*, 368, 387, 490, 499, 608
money: paper, 581–2, 584; shortage of, 583, 591, 614, 705; *see also* currency; economy, colonial
Monongahela, 7, 27, 29, 43, 47, 49, *89*, 97, 99, 108, 114, 283, 328, 525, 541
Monro, George, 189, 190–5, 198, 208
Montcalm-Gozon de Saint-Véran, Louis-Joseph, marquis de, 135, *136*, 149, 158, 236, 346–9, 369, 777n.8; and American style of warfare, 136, 151, 155–6, 196–200, 345–7, 742; and concept of military honor, 347; and defense of Montréal, 338, 342, 346–9; and defense of Québec, 346–9, 354, 355–63, 367, 391, 393–4; and expedition against Oswego, 150–7, 346; and Indians, 135–6, 151, 155–6, 187–90, 196–200, 238–9, 346, 454–6, 742; and siege of Fort William Henry, 191–200, 208, 248, 253, 256, 346; and Ticonderoga, 240–9; disdain of, for Canadians, 135, 151, 238, 345–6, 454; death of, 363, *364*, 408; interpretation of, by scholars, 135; ransom of English prisoners, 187, 198–9; relations of, with Vaudreuil, 238–9, 249, 345–6
Montgomery, Col. Archibald, 462–3, 465–6
Montmorency River, 348, 356
Montréal, *xxvii, xxx, xxxi*, 20, 24, 26, 116, 139, 187, 198, 232, 234, 236, 249, 338, 342, 346–7, 368, 384, 412, *422, 440*, 539; conquest of, 388–410, 453, 472, 618; geography of, 404, *405*
Montrésor, Lt. John, 539, 721
Moore, Gov. Sir Henry, 719–21, 723–4
Moore, Commodore John, 312–13, 315
Moravia, 301
Morris, Lewis, 91
Morris, Gov. Robert Hunter, 86, 91, 109, 131, 161–3
Morris, Capt. Thomas, 621, 623–4
Morro Castle (Havana), 499, *500*, 501
mortality levels, *see* casualty rates
Mount Vernon, 737
mourning war, 12–13, *see also* Indian peoples; intercultural relations
Mount Defiance (Rattlesnake Hill), 242
Mount Johnson, 91
Muddy Hole Farm, 739
Murray, Brig. Gen. James, 349–53, 362, 367–8, 388, 391–5, 397–9, 400–2, 404–6, 435, 472, 730–1, 789–90n.16
Muskingum, 619, 625
mutinies: British, 552; French, 418; provincial, 370–2
Mutiny Act, British (1754), 648–50, 821–2n.6

natural law, laws of nature, 606, 659
Navigation Acts, 576
Navy, Royal, 208, 212, 237, 257, 309, 381–3, 412, 417–8, 454, 487–8, 498–9, 563, 777–8n.1
Neolin, 536–8
neo-Progressive historians, xvii
neo-Whig historians, xvii
Netherlands, 35–6, 299–300; *see also* diplomacy; Low Countries
neutrals, importance of, 13, 15–18, 20–1, 24, 72, 258, 309, 333–9, 367, 407, 455, 467–8, 551; *see also* diplomacy, Seven Years' War; Six Nations of the Iroquois
Newcastle, Thomas Pelham-Holles, duke of, 33, *34*, 85; and British politics, 124–5, 129, 169–75, 212, 214–15, 482, 484, 487, 494, 505, 508, 511, 653–4, 692–4; and cost of war, 303–4, 308, 384, 479, 481, 485, 493–4, 803n.14; and patronage, 215, 303–4, 508; and Pitt, 303, 308, 477, 479, 482; and Seven Years' War, 38, 66–8, 70, 72, 169–72, 176, 277–83, 314, 491; dismissal of, 494–5; system of alliances, 35–6, 67, 70–1, 126–9, 169, 172, 493; *see also* diplomacy; British politics; economy, British
Newcomer, 533
New England, *xxviii–xxxi*, 14, 24, 35, 596; economy and society of, 146–7, 227–31, 286–89, 389; 595–6; land grants to settlers from, 523–4, 720; migration from, 112–14, 522–8, 529–34, 720–4; population growth of, 113, 526; recruitment of troops in, 137, 139, 140, 200, 229–30, 317–24, 387–9, 473, 519, 782n.6; religion in, 374–6; *see also* Acadians, deportation of; battles; Crown Point expedition; economy, colonial; provincial armies; religion; riots; Stamp Act crisis; *and individual states*
Newfoundland, 473; expedition of 1762, 498; fishery of, 483–4, 488, 503, 506
New France, *see* Canada
New Jersey, 184, 225, 320–1, 430; politics in, 601; recruitment of troops from, 389, 473, 519; response of, to Stamp Act, 673, 677
New Hampshire: and frontier settlement, 523, 526; land claims of, 597; politics in, 600–1; providentialism in, 374; responses of, to Stamp Act, 673, 676; troops of, 210, 225
New Hampshire grants, 523–4, 529
New Orleans, 505
Newport Junto, 658, 672–3
Newport (R.I.), 599, 672–3, 677, 681, 702
newspapers, 679, 682, 723; *Boston Gazette*, 665, 682–3, 718; *Maryland Gazette*, 664; *Newport Mercury*, 664; *North Briton*, 510–14; *Pennsylvania Gazette*, 490; *Virginia Gazette*, 664, 726–8
New York, 12, 14, *19*, 21, 24, 36, 38–9, 79, 181–2, 184–6, 194, 208–9, 236, 321, 373, 473, 601, 677; and expansion of settlement, 524, 720–3; and imperial authority, 322, 657, 660, 673–4, 703, 720–1, 723–4; and patronage, 110, 131, 601; and troop recruitment, 225, 320–1, 473, 519; politics in, 91, 110, 599, 608–10, 715, 719, 729, 757–8n.4
New York City, 79, 91, 112, 143, 181, 421, *425–6*, 589, 591, 635, 648, 677–9, 681–2, 696, 720, 722
Niagara, 115, 232, 264, 330–9, 340, 470, 474, 809–10n.2; *see also* battles; forts: Niagara
Niagara portage, 333–4, 337–9, 550, *551*, 625
Niagara River, 333, 336
Nichas, Mohawk chief, 276
Nichols, Pvt. Joseph, 244, 247
Ninety-six (stockade), 461–2, 466
Noble, Robert, 722
Norris, Isaac, 162
Northampton County (Pa.), 530
North Carolina, 322, 467–8, 524, 597–9, 673
North End (Boston), 665–6, 670, 681
Northern campaigns (1755), 108–23
Northern Neck (Va.), 724–5
Northington, Lord Chancellor, Robert Henley, earl of, 692, 698
North Sea, 35, 299, 309
Nova Scotia, *xxix*, 35–6, 68–9, 88, 111–14, 178, 207, 233, 473, 498, 522–3, 526
Noyan, Maj. Pierre-Jacques Payen de, 262, 264, 265
Nugent, Robert, M.P., 707

Ohio Company of Virginia, 23, 27, 29, 30–1, 37, 40, 42–3, 45, 51, 62, 106, 569, 594, 725, 739; *see also* land speculation
Ohio Country, *xxviii, xxx*, as scene of imperial competition, xviii, xx, 7, 24, 26, 33, 36–8, 65, 67–8, 72, 164, 202, 207, 232–3, 264, 267–85, 325–9; competition for land in, 17–18, 24–9, 276, 284, 323–4, 475, 525–8; defined, 749n.11; expansion of colonial settlement into, 61, 270–1, 278–9, 281, 327–9, 473–5, 524–34, 732; French loss, of,

Ohio Country (*cont.*):
31–2, 337–9; Indian rebellion in, 540, 619, 621, 625, 628, 632; Iroquois claims to, 13, 20–2, 50, 106–7, 269, 276–8, 330–3, 529–34, 551–2; land grants in, 473–4; land speculation in, 40–2, 45–6, 80, 106, 285, 524–8; *see also* land speculation; Forks of the Ohio; Fort Duquesne; Fort Pitt; Ohio Company of Virginia; Ohio Indians; Pittsburgh; Six Nations of the Iroquois; Treaty of Easton; Walking Purchase
Ohio Indians, *xxviii–xxx,* 94–6, 106–7, 109, 164, 207, 232–3, 258, 282, 406, 462, 529–34; and colonial expansion, 270–1, 278–9, 327–9, 474–5, 524–34, 732–3; as factor in military campaigns, xix, 267–8, 330–9; competition among, for hegemony, 106–7, 269, 276–8, 330–3, 529–35, 551–2; importance of alliances with, 267–70, 274–5, 279, 325–9, 330–9, 454–5, 462, 732–3l; *see also* diplomacy, Indian; frontier; Indian peoples; Six Nations of the Iroquois; Proclamation Line; Treaty of Easton
Ohio River, 17–18, 25–7, 30–1, 44–5, 57, 61, 90, 732
Oliver, Andrew, 647, 665–7
Oneida Lake, *156*, 261
Onondaga, *see* diplomacy, Indian; Grand Council (Iroquois); Six Nations of the Iroquois; Treaty of Easton
Onondaga River, 260
Onontio, 15, 26, 58, 65, 124, 545–6, 626, 628, 632, 634, 742–3
Orangeburg, 461
Order in Council of 1 June 1763, 563
Osborne, Adm. Henry, 257–8
Oswegatchie, *see* forts: La Galette
Otis, James, Jr., 520–1, 605–7, 609, 614, 658–60, 679–80, 715–19, 807n.4
Ottawa River, 402
Ouiatenon, *xxx,* 538, 630–1
Overhill Cherokee country, Overhill Towns, *xxviii*, 202, 457–9, *459*, 461

Pacific war, 515–17
pacifism, *see* Friendly Association for Regaining and Preserving Peace with the Indians by Pacific Means; Pemberton, Israel; Pennsylvania politics; Quakers
Palais, suburb of Québec, 348
Pampanga (Philippines), 517
pamphleteers, 486, 510
pamphlets, 606–7, 609, 611, 646, 659–60, 675, 706, *see also* Hopkins, Stephen; Howard, Martin; Franklin, Benjamin; Otis, James; Whately, Thomas; Wilkes, John
Parker, Col. John, 189–90
Partridge, Lt. Col. Oliver, 660
patriotism, of provincials, 389, 519, 601–3
patroons, 720–1, 723, 830n.4
patronage: colonial, 91, 110, 112, 131, 223, 229, 601–3; in British politics, 125, 131, 173, 215, 508–9, 511, 602
Paulus Hook, 620
Paxtang Creek, 612
Paxton Boys, 612, 637
Paxton, Charles, 670
pay, of colonial troops, 50, 88, 319–20, 417–18, 455, 768–9n.4, 794n.4; *see also* economy, colonial; wages
pays d'en haut, *xxx*, 15–16, 187–8, 198–9, 232, 236, 261, 264, 281, 326, 338–9, 346, 404, 406, 454–5, 470, 537–8, 545, 561, 620, 622, 633–4, 732
peace: agreements of 1764, 626; conferences, 498, 503–6; *see also* Detroit; Lancaster Council; treaties
Peale, Charles Willson, portrait of Washington, *738*
Pelhamites, 508, 694; *see also* British politics
Pemberton, Israel, 205–7, 269, 275–6, 279, 326, 329, 531, 612; *see also* Friendly Association for Regaining and Preserving Peace with the Indians by Pacific Means; Pennsylvania politics; Quakers; Treaty of Easton
Penn family, 22, 161, 206–7, 269, 277–8, 285, 323, 519, 530–1, 535, 600
Penn, William, 278, 535
Pennsylvania, *xxviii, xxx*, 11, 36, 40, 57, 80, 108, 131, 166, 183–4, 204–7, 233, 258, 285, 326–9, 373, *432*; and competition for western land, 78–9, 165, 204–7, 277, 284, 323–4, 327–9, 524–34, 541, 548, 600, 611–12, 624, 637; and Indian relations, 16, 18, 20–2, 24–30, 78, 165, 268–74, 326–30, 530–4, 534, 595–6; politics of, 160–2, 181, 323–4, 519, 600, 602, 611–12, 657–8, 675–6, 706; recruitment of troops from, 322–3, 519, 548; Quakers' role in, 160–2, 205–7; responses of, to imperial reforms, 611–13, 657–8, 675–6; *see also* colonial legislatures; Franklin, Benjamin; frontier; land speculation; Ohio Country; Paxton Boys; Penn

family; Philadelphia; Pittsburgh, Six Nations of the Iroquois; Treaty of Easton
Penobscot, 223, 318
Pensacola (Fl.), 730, 733
Peter III, Tsar, 492–6
Petition of Right (1628), 648–9
petitions, 679–80, 702, 704
Philadelphia, 30, 91, 108–11, 162–3, 166, 181, 184, 270, 278, 281, 284–5, 327, 373, 531, 589, 591, 596, 600, 612, 627, 675, 720; *see also* colonial politics; economy, colonial; Pennsylvania
Philippines, war in, *xxvii*, 515–17
Philipse Patent, 721–3
Pickawillany, *xxx*, 25, 28, 750–1n.12
Pisquetomen, 270–1, 277–80, 327–9, 537
Pitt, William, later earl of Chatham, 125, *126*, 224–31, 245, 312, 314–5, 408, 439, 468, 520; American enthusiasm for, 227–31, 322, 324, 709; and Amherst, 307, 384, 373, 474, 552; and expense of war, 301, 303–4, 308–9, 312, 384, 479, 481; and George III, 419–21, 477–9; and Newcastle, 127–9, 169–70, 172, 477, 482; and recall of Loudoun, 211, 225–7, 305; attitudes of, toward provincials, 214, 225–31, 454–5, 685; character of, 303–5, 477, 485–7; and subsidies, 213–5, 226–9, 298, 302, 304–5, 309, 317, 384, 389, 454–5, 495, 685; descent of, from power, 482–6, 488–9; diplomatic system of, 211–13; directs war effort, 176–9, 181, 208, 211–16, 232–6, 260, 266, 297–311, 344, 377–8, 380, 383–4, 387, 383–4, 389, 408, 415–20, 476–86, 503–5, 586; historians' interpretations of, 303; in British politics, 172–4, 303–5, 308, 351, 383–4, 419–20, 476–89, 495, 503–5, 508, 511, 557–8, 572–3, 648, 653–4, 693, 698–703; war strategy of, 211–16, 225–31, 240, 288, 298–304, 307, 310–11, 317, 322, 324, 412, 418–9, 454–5, 477, 482–3, 490; oratory of, in Stamp Act crisis, 698–701, 710–12; *see also* British government; British politics
Pitt-Newcastle ministry, 175, 177, 303
Pittsburgh, 281, 286, 323, 325, 327, 329–31, 474, 524, 541–4, 547–50, 628, 634, 732
Plains of Abraham, 348, 352, 355–6, 362, 375, 393; *see also* battles; Montcalm; Québec; warfare; Wolfe, James
Plan of the Union, 78–81, 84–5, 183; *see also* Albany Congress
platoons, eighteenth century, 759n.9
Ploughjogger, Humphry, *see* Adams, John
Pocock, Adm. George, 418
Pointe aux Trembles, 352, 392, 395
Poland, 492
Pomerania, 176
Pondicherry, *xxxix*, 417–18
Pontiac, 538–9, 545, 548, 550, 560, 617, 620–1, 623–4, 626, 629–34; death of, 633
Pontiac's Rebellion, xx–xxi, 535–53, 557, 565, 571, 588, 611, 616–32, 695; 731, 809–10n.2; lessons of, 633–37; *see also* Amherst; intercultural relations
poor relief, 591, 705
Pope Day, 666, 681
population, 14, 16–18; and expansion of settlement, 523, 526–8; and war, 317, 319; colonial British, 17, 113, 318, 523, 526; Indian, 14, 15, 468; *see also* Acadians, deportation of; disease; frontier; migration
porphyria, 652
portages, *see* Niagara portage; transportation
Portsmouth, 499, 673, 676
Portugal, *xxxviii*, 375, 488, 494, 497–8, 577; invaded by Spain, 497–8
Posey, Capt. John, 739
Post, Christian Frederick, 270–5, 279–81
Potomac, 27, *89*
Pouchot, Capt. Pierre, 333–7, 392, 400–3
Pownall, John, 565
Pownall, Gov. Thomas, 79–80, 82, 85, 115, 130, 143, 200, 209, 214, 374, 669; drawings by, *423*, *427–32*; and Loudoun, 222–7, 305; and recruitment, 318–20; and republicanism, 223–4; and quartering, 649–50; and Shirley, 130–1, 223
Presque Isle, *31*, 620, 623–4
press: and Stamp Act, 664–5, 672, 679, 684, 694; English popular, 510, 513, 552, 557; liberty of, 572; radical, 648; *see also* newspapers; Wilkes, John
prices, in response to war, 183, 238, 592, 795–6n.6; *see also* economy
Prideaux, Brig. Gen. John, 330–1, 333, 336, 340, 787n.5
Prince Rupert Bay, 314
prisoners, 351–2, 499, 620–1, 623, 625, 628, 630, 637; exchange of, 262, 264, 265; killing of, 542–3
privateers, 237, 306, 308, 315, 369, 785n.7
Privy Council, *see* British government
Proclamation Line, *xxx*, 569, 595, *696*, 731, 738; *see also* empire, British; Royal Proclamation of 1763

professionalism, military, 166–9, 179–84, 222, 254–6, 292, 359, 408–9, 410, 412–13, 488; *see also* discipline
profiteering, 175, 238
Progressive historians, xvii
Protestantism, *see* providentialism; religion
Providence (R.I.), 599
providentialism, 247–8, 298, 374–6, 414, 587, 776n.11
provincial armies: and effects of military service on soldiers, 286–9, 370–2, 411–14; and military discipline, 142–3, 146, 203, 228, 286–8, 370–2, 410, 585, 624, 768–9n.4; composition of, 225–6, 230, 286–8; contractualism of, 145–7, 180, 219–21, 286, 288, 370–2, 414; desertions and mutinies by, 286–7, 370–2; enlistment agreements of, 146, 180, 219–21, 226, 286–8, 370–1, 414; in conquest of Canada, 388–90, 412, 498, 685; in conquest of West Indies, 501, 685; land grants to, 473–4; marksmanship of, 411; morale of, 317–24; patriotism of, 685; payment of, 203, 228–9, 310, 317–20, 370–1, 388–9, 473, 768–9n.4, 785n.5; rank in, 214, 225–6, 229–30; serving under regular officers, 142, 286–9, 370–2, 773–4n.18; role in Pitt's strategy of war, 213–14, 216, 310; training of, 102, 119, 142, 144–6; versus British regular army, 286–8, 412–14; uniforms of, 410–11; voluntarism of, 200–1, 286, 288, 585, 685, 774n.18, 785–6n.11; weapons of, 410–11; *see also* battle; bounties; discipline; intercultural relations; professionalism; providentialism; recruiting; warfare
provisioning, 131, 136–7, 143, 159–60, 168, 179–80, 182–4, 200, 203, 235, 238, 325–6, 344–5, 356, 368, 370, 391, 400, 547–50; *see also* diet, provincial; rations; Seven Years' War; siege; supply system
Prussia: and relations with Britain, 35, 71, 126, 128–9, 298–9, 480–3, 495; and relations with France, 128–9, 213; British subsidies of, 215, 229, 298, 309, 481; diplomatic alliances of, 35, 71, 128–9, 171, 495; in war, 171, 176–7, 298–302, 380, 416, 480, 482–3, 491–6, 506; *see also* diplomacy, European; Frederick II; Seven Years' War
punishments, military, 220, 287, 781n.3, 781–2n.3
Putnam, Ens. Rufus, 220, 240–1, 245, 247, 370, 371, 414, 794–5n.5
Quakers: as intermediaries, 205–7, 269, 329; in Pennsylvania politics, 160–2, 165, 269, 600; *see also* Friendly Association; Pemberton, Israel
quartering, 147–9, 166–7, 181, 209, 223, 321, 647–51, 720–4, 730
Quartering Act of 1765, 581, 648–52, 696, 720, 723–4, 729, 821–2n.13
Québec, *xxxiii*, 25–6, 31, 111, 115, 173, 179, 232, 236–7, 317, 342, 369, 373–8, 380, 388, 391–96, 422, *439*, 434, 438, 542; battalion integrity at, 791n. 29; Battle of (1759), 348, 352–62, 394; British administration of 472, 565–6, 568, 730–1; capitulation of (1759), 363, 366–8; defense of 344–9; fortifications of, 356–7; Second Battle of (1760), 391–6; topography of, 348–9, 358–9, 404; Wolfe's attack on, 344–62, 618; *see also* Canada; Lévis; Montcalm; Seven Years' War, warfare; Wolfe, James
Queen Anne's War (1701–13), 11, 20, 21
Quiberon Bay, 381–3, 395, 419, 479; as key to outcome at Québec, 395; *see also* Fighting Instructions; Royal Navy; Québec; warfare
Quincy, Col. Josiah, 717
quitrents, 522–3

Ramezay, Maj. Jean-Baptiste-Nicholas-Roch de, 364–7
ranger companies 181, 188, 209, 219, 254, 411, 461, 466, 547–8, 768–9n.4, 788–9n.1; *see also* Rogers's Rangers; Seven Years' War; military units; warfare
rations, 236–8, 370, 418, 463, 548; *see also* food shortages; provincial armies; Seven Years' War; supply
Rea, Dr. Caleb, 241, 287
rebellions: Cherokee, 387, 415; Pontiac's, 538–53; Stamp Act Crisis, 664–87, 699, 716; squatters', 721–4
recruiting, and demands of war in Europe, 473, 488; and provincial discipline, 142; and terms of enlistment, 219–21, 228–9, 519; by provincials, 137–9, 143, 159, 167–8, 200–1, 209–10, 214, 225–30, 317–24, 387–8, 412, 461, 566, 473, 518–19, 552, 618–19, 696, 706, 784–5n.2, 794–5n.5; by regulars, 200–1, 209–10, 309, 473, 805–6n.2; cost of, 200–1, 317–21, 552, 706; in New France, 187; *see also* enlistment; provincial armies
Red Stone Creek, 29, 51, 62, 731–2

Red Stone Fort, 29, 52, 61, 65
refugees, 114, 391, 395, 407, 467, 541, 599, 748n.6; *see also* Acadians, deportation
Regency Bill, 653
regiments, *see* military units
regulars, British: and provincial relations, 286–9; mutinies of, 552; professionalism of, 99–107, 147, 244, 357–63, 408–9, 412–14, 488, 760n.12, 791n.29; social composition of, 228, 286, 288; versus provincials, 140, 221, 286–8, 410–14
regulars, French, 346–7; contrasted with Canadian militia, 357–63
regulator movements, 599
Rehoboam, king of Israel, 247–8, 776n.11
reimbursements to colonies, 305, 317–20, 322, 454–5; *see also* subsidies
religion: and legacies of Puritanism, 146, 376; and anti-Catholicism, 113, 199, 374–5, 407, 566, 568, 730, 827n.8; and Protestantism, 374–5, 599, 674; and politics, 407, 566, 568, 599, 674, 730; as an inducement to migration, 523; freedom of, 566–7; Indian, and warfare, 13, 26, 104, 123, 535; *see also* diplomacy; Indian peoples; intercultural relations; Pontiac's Rebellion; providentialism
republicanism, xvii, xxii, 148, 167, 221, 223–34, 610, 746
resistance to imperial authority: colonial, xx, 148–9, 219–31, 422, 512, 521–2, 571, 616, 637, 641–2, 658–87, 692, 695–6, 698–702, 706–7, 712, 716, 721–4, 743–6; Indian, xx, 387, 415, 538–53, 743–6
Restigouche River, 395, 407
Revenue Act of 1762, 563
Revolution, American: xv–xxiii, 745–6; *see also* intercultural relations; republicanism; resistance to imperial authority
Reynolds, Joshua, 234
rhetoric of liberty, 520, 710–12, 719, 721; *see also* liberty; resistance; rights; republicanism; Stamp Act
Rhine, 378, 481
Rhineland, 483, 491–2, 506
Rhode Island: and expansion of settlement, 523; and recruitment, 225, 320, 389; response of, to imperial reforms, 610–11, 658, 672–3; politics in 599, 611; *see also* colonial politics; economy, colonial
Riche, Thomas, 589–90, 593, 596
Richelieu, Louis-François-Armand de Plessis, duc de, 211–12, 216
Richelieu River, 24, 232, 388, 392, 397–8, 400–1
Rigaud de Vaudreuil, François-Pierre de, 150–1, 155, 185, 186, 209
rights: British, 147, 221, 223, 605–6, 613, 659, 661–2, 675, 679, 683, 685, 710, 721, 741, 745–6; by charter, 605; colonial, 605–6, 611–12, 661–2, 665, 679, 685, 710, 711, 719; common law, 520, 609; constitutional 605, 614, 675, 745; customary, 455; language of, 520, 710–12, 719, 721, 745; natural, 520, 606–7, 683, 745; of accused, 609; to representation, 605–6, 608–9, 611, 614, 661; to trial by jury, 608, 679–80; *see also* Constitution, British; liberties; republicanism; Stamp Act crisis
Rights of the British Colonies Asserted and Proved, see Otis, James, Jr.
Rio Grande, 744
riots: 637, 641, 665–79, 681, 686, 691, 696, 702–3, 716, 721–4; anti-recruitment, 210; *see also* mobs; resistance; Stamp Act
Rivière aux Boeufs (French Creek), 31, 283
Rivière Parent, 539
roads: Braddock's Road, *xxviii*, 108, 139, 524; construction of, 51, 96, 115, 180, 233, 258, 268, 272–3, 340, 343, 411, 467, 474, 523, 530; Forbes Road, *xxviii*, 268, 272–3, 279, 285, 323, 325, 524, 540, 548, 627; Fort Number 4 to Crown Point, 343
Robinson, John, 661, 672, 725–7, 729, 830n.25
Rockingham, Charles Watson-Wentworth, marquess of, 654, 692–8, 701–4, 709, 733, 741, 826n.6
Rocque, Mary Ann, *A Set of Plans and Forts in America, Reduced from Actual Surveys*, maps from, *116, 122, 252, 263, 334, 343*
Rogers's Rangers, 186, 188–9, 243, 547, 768–9n.4; *see also* ranger companies; military units, regular; warfare
Rogers, Major Robert, 186, *188*, 547, 768–9n.4; *see also* Rogers's Rangers
Rollo, Lord, 447
Ross, Lt. John, 627–8
Rossbach, 298–9, 301
Royal Artillery, 366, 516
Royal Navy, 208, 212, 237, 257, 309, 381–3, 412, 417–8, 454, 487–8, 498–9, 563, 777–8n.1
Royal Proclamation of November 12, 1754, 139–40
Royal Proclamation of 1763, 565, *567*, 568–71, 580–1, 596, 634–7, 730, 740, 827n.8
Ruggles, Brig. Gen. Timothy, 240, 660, 679

Rule of 1755, 145
rum: use of, in Indian diplomacy, 78, 471, 542, 818–9n.6; trade, 315, 471, 577–9, 813n.6–9; *see also* alcohol
rumors: of French expansion in North America, 36–8, 552–3, 561, 571; concerning Indians, 458, 472; of slave revolts, 159–60, 304, 461, 490; of peace, 503; role of, in Stamp Act riots, 668, 675; *see also* conspiracies
Russia: and war in Europe, 176, 128, 212, 301, 380, 416, 491–6; European alliances of, 71, 127–8, 171

Sabbath-Day Point, 189
Sackets Harbor, 261
Saint-Ange de Bellerive, Capt. Louis Groston, 627, 629, 631
St. Augustin (Que.), 367
St. Augustine (Fl.), 734
St.-Cas, 302–3, 477
St. Charles River, 348, 355, *358*, 359, 362
St. Clair, Sir John, 92–3, 96–7, 99, 230
Ste. Foy, 392–3
St.-Jean, 255
St. John's (Newfoundland), 473
St. Lawrence missions, 392, 404
St. Lawrence, *xxviii–xxxiii*; Gulf of, 17, 24, 87, 110, 209, 237, 345, *434–6*; River, 14, *19*, 25–6, 71, 135, 139, 232, 261, 310, 338, 342, 347–8, 352, 354, 359, 363, 368, 388, 391–2, 394–5, 398, 400–1, *438*, 618; Valley, 346, 473
St. Lucia (West Indies), *xxxv*, 490, 503, 506
St. Louis, 631, 633
St.-Malo, 299, 302
St. Philip's Castle, Minorca, 170
St. Vincent (West Indies), 490, 505
Sandwich, John Montagu, earl of, 514, 558
Sandusky, 621, 623–4
Saratoga, *xxxi*, 115, 123
Saunders, Rear Adm. Charles, 351, 355, 366–8
Saxe, Arminius Maurice, comte de, 118
Saxony, 171, 176, 215, 301, 380, 416, 492, 496, 506
scalping, 788–9n.1
Scarouady (Half King; Oneida civil chief), 18, 94, 96, 99, 106–7, 109, 759n.5
Scenographia Americana, Or, a Collection of Views in North America and the West Indies From Drawings taken on the Spot, by several Officers of the British Navy and Army, 421–2, *423–50*
Schenectady (N.Y.), 137, 140–1, 261, 330
Scioto River, *xxviii*, 550, 619, 621, 623–5
Senegal 306, *307*, 505; *see also* Africa; empire; trade
sermons, 373–6; *see also* providentialism
Seven Years' War: American colonists' interpretation of victory in, 587, 685, 712; and American frontier settlement, 11, 518–28; and American resistance to British authority, 148–9, 166–9, 219–31, 422; and American social and economic conditions, 227–31, 286–9, 317–24, 370–2, 588, 615, 709–10; and attitudes toward warfare, 12–16, 94, 102–4, 136, 151, 155–6, 189–90, 195–200, 254–6, 345–7, 742; and ironies of empire, 685; 709–12, 741–6; and trade, 182–3, 422, 454–5, 457, 483, 490, 498–502, 506, 519–22, 577–80, 588–9, 591; and transition to peace, 588–616, 641–51, 709–12; as formative experience, 370–2, 411–14; as precursor to American Revolution, xv–xxiii, 745–6; as struggle for control of territory, 11, 106–7, 114, 318, 323–4, 329, 479; character of, in America, 100–7, 119, 135–6, 147, 151, 155, 166–9, 179–84, 187–90, 196–200, 222, 244, 254–6, 262, 292, 357–63, 408–9, 410, 412–13, 488, 498–502, 254–6, 760n.12, 791n.29; civilians in, 255–6, 344–6, 367–8, 407, 412, 552; contingency in, 209, 219, 236, 250–2, 390, 392; costs and financing of, 17, 51, 66, 70, 88, 90, 93, 95, 138, 167–8, 180, 214, 228–9, 298, 301, 303, 308–9, 312, 317–21, 324, 378–9, 388–90, 411–12, 453–5, 473, 479, 481, 485, 493–4, 498, 582, 602, 709–10; crucial battles of, *see* battles, Ft. Duquesne, Ft. Necessity, Ft. William Henry, Louisbourg, Québec; cultural dimensions of, xix–xx, 12–20, 62, 94–6, 102–7, 135–49, 148, 151, 155, 166–9, 187–90, 192, 196–200, 205–7, 219–31, 254–6, 268–9, 270, 286–9, 370–2, 453–6, 520–1, 685, 709–10, 754–6n.6–7, n.12–13; disease as a factor in, 499–501; effects of, on colonial economies, 582, 586–8, 589, 601–3, 709–10; end of, 482–3, 484, 488, 497–506; geographical factors in, xix, 88, 90, 96, 100, 232–3, 250, 348–9, 358–9, 404, *405*, 490, 498, 549–50; in Europe, 169–72, 176–7, 211–13, 215–16, 298–302, 377–84, 416, 419, 453, 473, 476–98; in India and Bengal, 177–8, 417–18; in the Caribbean, 312–16, 422, *441–50*, 498–502; in the Mediter-

ranean, 170–1, 237, 257, 309, 378, 485, 493; Indian allies as factors in, xviii–xx, 94–107, 109–10, 118–21, 151, 167, 199, 236, 258, 267, 330–9, 404–6, 412, 453–6; lessons of, 559, 570–1, 581, 585–7, 711–12; morale of soldiers in, 123, 370–1; naval role in, 208, 212, 237, 257, 309, 351, 356, 369–70, 378–83; 395, 412, 417–18, 453–4, 483, 487–8, 490, 498–9, 563, 777–8n.1; other names for, 747n.1; Pacific war, 515–17; payment of troops in, 50, 88, 109, 113, 167–8, 317–22, 370–1, 387–9, 417–8, 454–5, 473, 768–9n.4, 794n.4; tactics and strategies in 102–7, 211–16, 120–1, 169–71, 232–3, 239, 378–84, 388; terrorism during, 344–5, 368; *see also* British politics; casualty rates; diplomacy; empire; empire, British; military units; patronage; recruitment; regular armies; provincial armies; prisoners; providentialism; provisioning; supply; transportation; treaties; warfare
Shamokin, 164, 205, 271, 277
Sharpe, Gov. Horatio, 203, 209
Shaw, Pvt. John, 55–8
Shenandoah Valley, 108, 524
Shingas (Delaware war chief), 28, *48*, 94–6, 162–3, 270, 279–80, 327, 351, 536–7
shipbuilding, 309, 591
ship design and construction, 309
ships, *see* vessels
Shirley, Gov. William, 110, *111*, 143–7, 259, 669; and Acadians, 762n.11; and Albany Congress, 81–4; and command, 87–8, 90–1, 108, 110–12, 115, 136, 143, 144; and Newcastle, 83, 130–1; and Niagara campaign (1755), 87, 91, 110–12, 115; and Northern campaigns (1755), 108, 110–12, 136, 143–44; and patronage, 91, 112, 115; and plans for 1756, 132, 139, 140; and politics, 715, 729; and Pownall, 82–3, 115, 130; as mediator, 143, 137–40, 143–4, 147; recall of, 130–2, 137, 141, 167
siège en forme, 349, 355, 363, 366, 499
siege lines, 394
Silesia, 35, 71, 127, 212, 215, 301, 380, 416, 491–2, 495–6, 506
Silesian War (1740–42), 35
Sillery Woods, 362
Sillery (village), 394
Sinnott, Pierce Acton, 630
Six Nations of the Iroquois, xviii, xix, 7, 9, 72, 79, 85, 91–2, 96, 109, 165, 205–7, 260–1, 267–9, 275–9, 327, 410, 467, 469, 529–34, 544, 551, 622, 748n.2, 779n.2; and balance of power, 11–32, 72, 333, 336; in alliances with British, 330–9, 387, 404–6, 455, 787n.4; Great League of Peace and Power, 9, 12–13, 22, 24, 28; *see also* diplomacy, Indian; empire; frontier; Grand Council; intercultural relations; Ohio Country; Tanaghrisson; Treaty of Easton; warfare
Skene, Maj. Philip, 220, 221, 474, 523
slaves: and rumors of rebellion, 159–60, 204, 461, 490; and slavery, in rhetoric, 662, 696, 699–700; trade in, 306–8, 315, 380, 422, 501–2, 578, 598, 816n.17
smallpox, 166, 199, 236, 461, 465, 541–3; *see also* Amherst; disease
Smith, Adam, 719
smuggling, 182–3, 520–2, 563–4, 575–6, 578, 672, 727–9, 813n.8
Society for Encouraging Trade and Commerce, Boston, 591, 604
Sons of Liberty, 643–4, 673–4, 677–9, 681–2, 684, 710, 714, 721; *see also* Barre
South Carolina, 16, 36, 202, 322, 462, 468–9, 524, 597–9, 673; *see also* Cherokee War
South End, (Boston), 665–6, 670, 681
sovereignty: and nature of empire, 741–6; British claim to, over Indians, 622, 634, 733; British, in Canada, 407; defined, 711; Indian, 468; of king in Parliament, 580–1, 606–7, 611, 614, 616, 642, 645, 655, 659, 680, 685–6, 692, 695–6, 698–703, 706, 710–12, 733, 741–2, 745–6
Spain: alliances of, 36, 67, 484–5, 802n.11; American attitudes toward, 375; and terms of peace; 503–6; empire of, 483–4, 498–506, 515–17, 744; influence of, on trade, 589; invasion of Portugal by, 488, 494, 497–8; navy of, 501, 506; war with Britain, 487–90, 493–5, 515–17; *see also* Bourbon dynasty; Charles III; Family Compact
spies, 352; *see also* Stobo, Robert
Spitalfields riots, 653, 682, 695, 822n.3
squatters, 525, 597, 635, 720–4, 731–2
Stamp Act, xvii, xx–xxi, 581, 606, 611, 614–5, 642–7, 649–50, 657–62, 664–76, 677, 705, 729, 821n.6, 825n.7, 828n.1; crisis, 664–5, 677–87, 691–2, 712–13, 715, 720, 725, 729, 734, 740–1; repeal of, 692–5, 697–702, 705–8, 709–12, 714, 718, 727–8, 827n.17, 828n.25
Stamp Act Congress, 675, 679–81, 702
Stanwix, Brig. Gen. John, 203–4, 206, 233, 260–1, 323, 325–6, 329, 390

Stephen, Lt. Col. Adam, 63, 97, 102–3, 159, 204, 230, 323
Stillwater (N.Y.), 219, 221
Stirling, Capt. Thomas, 631
Stobo, Capt. Robert, *48*, 64, 95, 351–2, 369
Story, William, 670
Stuart, Capt. John, 465, 468
subsidies: British, of European allies, 213, 215, 229, 298, 302, 416, 492–6; of colonies, 214, 226–9, 384, 563, 570–1, 589, 601, 685, 706, 814n.4
Suffering Traders, 595–6
sugar: duties on, 574, 576; trade in, 182, 239, 306, 308, 315, 501–2, 589; *see also* empire; Havana; rum; trade; West Indies
Sugar Act, *see* American Duties Act of 1764
Sugar Islands, 578–9
supply system, 258, 292, 404, 407, 454–5, 458, 260–6, 464–5, 467–9; and navies, 397, 550, 777–8n.1; and Québec, 345, 348–9, 351, 364, 366–8, 391, 395, 397; and shortages, 325–6, 338, 356, 391, 465, 481, 491, 497, 547–50; as key to outcome of North American war, 453–5; as key to outcome of siege warfare, 257–8, 367, 547–50, 801–10n.2
Susquehanna River, 22, 25, 78, 108, 158, 163–4, 205, 271, 277, 533
Susquehanna Valley, 16–18, 164, 530, 535–6
Susquehannah Company, 78, 84, 92, 277, 528–34, 537, 757n.2
Sweden, 176, 212, 493
symbols, 329, *365*, 421–2, 498, 511, 513–14, 537, 545, 580, 610, 706, 731

Tagashata (Seneca chief), 275
Tamaqua (Beaver; Delaware civil chief), 270, 279–80, 327, 532–3, 536–7, 540
Tanaghrisson (Half King; Seneca civil chief), 5, 6, 12, 16, 18, 27, 28, 30, 44–6, 49, 52–8, 60–1, 63, 65, 72, 94, 750n. 10, 755–6n. 13, 756n. 19
taxation, xx, 40, 66, 137, 161, 228–9, 309, 312, 384, 412, 481, 510–12, 558, 562–4, 568, 570, 573–80, 582–4, 602, 605–16, 610, 613, 641–6, 657–87, 699–700; and representation, 605–9, 611, 614–15, 650, 659, 679, 686, 699–700, 703, 718, 720, 730; and sovereignty, 579–80, 642, 645; *see also* American Duties Act of 1764; cider tax; Molasses Act of 1733; Navigation Acts; Quartering Act; Stamp Act
Tea Act, xxi
Teedyuscung (Delaware chief), 164–5, 205–7, 258, 267–71, 275–9, 529–34, 535, 537; *see also* diplomacy, Indian; Indian peoples, Delaware; Treaty of Easton
Temple, Richard, Earl, 485, 487, 510–11, 558, 693
Tennessee, 202, *457*, *459*
Texas, 744
Titcomb's Mount, 190–4
tobacco trade, 498, 502, 592–4, 601, 613, 815n.9
Tobago, *xxxv*, 505
Torgau, 416, 480, 491
Toulon, 378
Townshend Acts, xxi
Townshend brothers, 175
Townshend, Charles, 175, 488, 572–3, 586, 642–3, 654, 694, 704
Townshend, Brig. George, 175, 349–53, 362–3, 366–8, 377, 394
trade, 24–31, 35, 38, 237, 493, 501–2, 506; 695–7, 705; Amherst's reforms in, 537, 544, and intercultural relations, 25, 454–5, 742–3; Indian, 13–17, 20, 24–6, 29, 38, 65, 72, 79, 232, 260, 264–5, 285, 326–9, 390, 405, 454–5, 457–8, 467–70, 472, 475, 518, 536, 544, 552–3, 561, 595, 620–2, 626–7, 629–30, 632, 635–6, 742; with the enemy, 182–3, 519–22, 578; and empire, 306–7, 312, 315–16, 326, 454–5, 483, 490, 501–2, 515, 517, 521, 566, 570–1, 577–9, 588–9, 591, 680, 695–8, 700, 717–9, 742–3; and war, 422, 454–5, 457, 483, 490, 519–22, 588–9, 591; *see also* American Duties Act; customs; economy; empire; Stamp Act
transportation: costs of, 180; difficulties of, 90, 96–7, 168, 186, 189–90, 281, 325–6, 411, 474, 523; roads and road-building, 51, 96, 115, 180, 233, 258, 268, 272, 411, 474, 523; portages, 25, 90, 115, 180, 333–4, 337–8; *see also* roads
treaties: Aix-la-Chapelle (1748), 11, 24, 35–6, 71, 126; Convention of Versailles (1756), 71, 129, 171; Convention of Westminster (1756), 128–9; Grand Settlement of 1701, 15; Hubertusburg, 506–7; Lancaster (Pennsylvania, 1744), 23–4; Logstown (1752), 18, 27–8, 30; San Idlefonso (1762), 505; Easton (1742), 22–3; Easton (1757), 205–7, 268–70, 275–6, 455, 525–6, 529, 531; Easton (1758), 274–80, 326–7, 330, 529, 531, 570; Paris

(Peace of Paris, 1763), xvii, 505–6, 508, 510, 566, 593, 744; Utrecht (1713), 113, 407
Trecothick, Barlow, 702, 704–5
Trent, Captain William, 45–7
Triumvirate, 512, 557, 733
Trois-Rivières, 346, 348, 391, 398, 472
Turtle Creek, 282

Upper Kittanning, 163

Van Braam, Jacob, 43, 64, 351–2
Van Cortlandt, John, 721
Varenne, 398, 401
Vauban, fortifications, xvi, 251–3; *see also* fortifications, fort design; Louisbourg
Vauban, Sebastin Le Prestre de, 251, 253
Vaudreuil de Cavagnial, Pierre de Rigaud, marquis de, 109, 115–16, 204, 236, 262, 335, 366, 395, 453, 472, 537; and Battle of Oswego, 150–9; and Montcalm, 238–9, 249, 345–7; and ransom of prisoners, 198–9; and use of Indian and Canadian troops, 151, 187, 199, 238–9, 346; and defense of Québec, 345–7, 356, 363, 366; and surrender of Canada, 406–8
Vauquelin, Capt. Jean, 395–6, 408, 796n.11
Vellinghausen, 491
Venango, *see* forts: Machault
Vergor, Capt. Louis Du Pont Du Chambon de, 354, 356
Versailles, 128, 239; *see also* France, government; treaties
Versailles, Convention of, *see* treaties
vessels: *Atalante*, 392, 395–6, 796n.11; *Bienfaisant*, 254; *Boscawen*, 369–70; *Duke of Cumberland*, 369–70; *Cygnet*, 672–3, 702; *Formidable*, 382; *Foudroyant*, 777–8n. 1; *Gosport*, 208; *Huron*, 548, 809–10n.2; *Ligonier*, 369–70, 401; *Lowestoft*, 796n.11; *Machault*, 395; *Magnanime*, 382; Manila galleon, 516, 805n.11; *Michigan*, 548, 809–10n.2; *Mohawk*, 400; *Monmouth*, 777–8n.1; *Morro Castle*, 422, *446; Nightingale*, 142; *Onondaga*, 400; *Pomone*, 392, 395; *Punta*, 422, *446; Soleil Royale*, 382; *Sutherland*, 353; *Thésée*, 382; *Vanguard*, 395, 439; *Weasel*, 553, 620
Vice-Admiralty Court for All America, 575, 607
Vice-Admiralty Court, Boston, 670
vigilantes, 599, 611–12; *see also* frontier; Paxton Boys
Vilaine River and estuary, 382–3
Villiers, Capt. Louis Coulon de, 62–5
Vincennes, 630
Virginia, *xxviii, xxx*, 7, 14, 16–17, *19*, 22, 28–30, 36–38, 40–1, 45–6, 51, 57, 66, 167–8, 202, 230, 468; and land speculation, 593–4, 598, 724–5; and Loudoun, 143, 183–4; and frontier, 108–9, 158–60, 203–4, 227, 284, 289, 322, 323–4, 461, 468, 524–8, 569, 613, 731; economy of, 582–4, 592–4, 613–14, 724–9; politics of, 598–602, 613, 660–3, 715, 724–8; recruitment of troops from, 322–4, 519, 613; responses of, to imperial reforms, 660–5, 696; ruling class of, 724–9, 815n.11, 830n.25; trade of, 468, 581–2, 592–4; *see also* land speculation; Ohio Country; Treaty of Easton; Washington, George
Virginia Resolves, 663–5, 691, 823n.1
Voltaire, 171

Wabash River, 630
Wabash Valley, 628
Wales, Prince of: as office, 508–9, 652; Frederick Lewis as, 476; George III as, 172, 178, 297, 302, 304, 420; *see also* British politics; Leicester House
wages, American, 17, 228, 319, 388–9, 590–1, 760n.26; *see also* economy, colonial
Walking Purchase of 1737, 22, 165, 205–7, 269, 276, 279, 531, 535; *see also* Treaty of Easton; Wyoming Valley
Walpole, Horace, 174, 298, 309, 377–8, 419, 479, 508, 573
Walpole, Robert, 304, 602
Wandiwash, 418, 515
Ward, Lt. Col. Artemas, 247, 716–17
Ward, Ens. Edward, 45, 47, 49–50, 56
Ward, Gov. Samuel, 672
War of the Austrian Succession, 24, 35, 71, 118, 126
War of the Spanish Succession, 126
warfare: American versus European styles of, 12–16, 99–107, 135–6, 189–90, 196–9, 254–6, 345–7, 410–12; amphibious expeditions in, 299, 308, 313–14, 352, 422, *447–8*, 499; and empire, xxii, 453–6; as site of intercultural interactions, 94, 99–107, 136, 254–6, 453–6, 754–6n. 6–7, n.12–13; captives taken in, 187, 196–200, 351–2, 458,

warfare (*cont.*):
460, 465, 499, 534, 538, 542–3, 620–1, 623, 625, 628, 630, 637; civilians involved in, 255–6, 344–6, 367–8, 407, 412, 552; contingency in, 209, 219, 236, 250, 390; conventions of European, 245–56, 262, 349, 406–8, 501; costs and funding of, 17, 51, 66, 70, 88, 90, 95, 138, 167–8, 180, 167–8; economic impact, 453–4; forest, 188–9, 290, 292, 346, 361, 372, 411, 768–9n.4, 791n. 29; geographic influences, 88, 90, 96, 100, 232–3, 250, 348–9, 358–9, 404; open field, 349, 359–60, 379, 394, 791n. 29; naval, 257, 351, 356, 369–70, 395, 453–4, 490; paradoxes of, 99–107, 381–2, 468–9, 483, 488–9; siege operations in, 251–3, 157–8, 394, 498–501, 547–50, 776n.4; supply problems as a factor in, 60–2, 64, 88, 90, 92–3, 110, 257–8, 344–5, 351, 453–4, 547–50; transportation difficulties in, 90, 96–7, 180, 257–8, 550; weapons and ammunition, 63, 770n.14, 770n.16, 776n.6, 790–1n.28, 809–10n.2; weather as a factor in, 209, 219, 236, 250, 302, 352, 369, 380–3, 550; winter as a factor in, 345, 351, 368–71, 392–4, 398, 548, 550; *see also* battle, nature of; battles, discipline; intercultural relations; professionalism; Seven Years' War
warrants, 321
Washington, George, xxi, 72, 88, 90, 118, 158, 168, 323, 351, 390, 646, 727; *738*; and empire, 737–41, 744–5; as commander of Virginia Regiment, 109, 159–60, 168, 203–4, 230, 282, 738, 754n.1; as land speculator, 106–7, 272, 593–4, 738–41, 815n.11; as volunteer in Braddock expedition (1755), 92, 97, 104, 758n. 7; at Ft. Duquesne, 282, 738, 781n.26; at Jumonville's Glen, 5–7, 53–58, 77–8, 293, 435, 754-n.6–7, n.12–13; at Loyalhanna, 282; attitudes of, toward Indians, 62, 106–7; defeat at Ft. Necessity, 52–66, 78; economic situation of, 593–4, 724, 727, 737–41; expedition of 1753, *xxviii–xxx*, 41–66; military education of, 289–93; professionalism of, 290
Washington, Martha Dandridge Custis, 289, 593
Wealth of Nations, The, 719
Webb, Maj. Gen. Daniel, 156–7, 185, 187, 190–5, 198, 200, 260
Weiser, Conrad, 78, 92, 275, 277–8
Wentworth, Benning, 523–4, 526, 529, 600
Weser River, 177, 314, 378, 491
West Africa, 213, 306, 309, 380, 505–6, 578
West, Benjamin, *Death of General Wolfe*, *364*, *365*
West Indies, 182, 213, 306, 308, 312–16, 417, 422, *441–50*, 473, 490, 498–502, 505–6, 519, 521, 564, 576–9, 590–1, 685
Westchester County (N.Y.), 721
Westover, 230
Whately, Thomas, 659
Wheelwright, Nathaniel, 668–9, 824n.6
Whigs, 476–7, 562, 654, 692, 707
Wilkes, John, 510, 512–16, 557–8, 564, 572–3, 581
Williams, Ephraim, 118–9
William Henry, battle at Ft., *122*, 123, 142, 146, 157, 185–200, 208–9, 240, 246–54, 340–1, 454; as critical juncture, 199–201; 210, 219, 222, 254–6, 454
Wills Creek, 27, 50–1, 64–6, 90, 93–4, 113
Winchester (Va.), *xxviii*, 109, 158
Winslow, Maj. Gen. John: and Crown Point expedition (1756), 139, 142, 146, 157; and joint service with regulars, 142, 144–6, 149
Wolfe, Maj. Gen. James, 233–4, *235*, 257, 314, *365*, 369, 421–2, 434–5, 437, 439, 788–9n.1, 790n.24; and expedition against Québec, 310–11, 317, 342–63, 368, 391, 618, 789–90n.16; and Louisbourg, 250–4; illness and death of, 345, 349, 351, 362, *365*, 375, 377–8, 791n.30
Woodbridge, Rev. Timothy, 78, 92, 529
Wood Creek, *156*, 157, 260, 341, 474
writs of assistance, 520–1, 601, 605, 607, 829n.8
Wright, Gov. James, 677
Wurzburg, 127
Wyalusing, *xxxi*, 534
Wyoming Valley, *xxviii*, *xxxi*, 22, 78–9, 84, 165, 206–7, 268, 270, 276–7, 279

York (Pa.), 524
Yorke, Charles, 698, 701–2
Youghiogheny River, *xxviii*, 27, *89*, 474, 525

Zinzendorf, Count Nikolaus Ludwig von, 421
Zorndorf, 301